CALENDAR

OF

STATE PAPERS,

DOMESTIC SERIES,

EDWARD VI., MARY, ELIZABETH,

1547—1580.

Printed by G. E. Eyre and W. Spottiswoode,
Her Majesty's Printers.

CALENDAR

OF

STATE PAPERS,

DOMESTIC SERIES,

[*A*] OF THE REIGNS OF

EDWARD VI., MARY, ELIZABETH

[1.] 1547—1580,

PRESERVED IN THE

STATE PAPER DEPARTMENT

OF

HER MAJESTY'S PUBLIC RECORD OFFICE.

EDITED BY ROBERT LEMON, ESQ. F.S.A.
UNDER THE DIRECTION OF THE MASTER OF THE ROLLS, AND WITH THE SANCTION OF
HER MAJESTY'S SECRETARY OF STATE FOR THE HOME DEPARTMENT.

LONDON:
LONGMAN, BROWN, GREEN, LONGMANS, & ROBERTS.
1856.

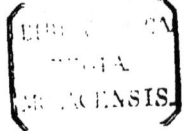

CONTENTS OF THIS VOLUME.

		PAGE
PREFACE	- - - - - - - -	vii
CALENDAR, EDWARD VI., 1547—1553	- - - -	1
" MARY, 1553—1558	- - - -	54
" ELIZABETH, 1558—1580	- - - -	115
GENERAL INDEX	- - - - - -	705
ERRATA	- - - - - - -	799

PREFACE.

In the Preface to the First Volume of STATE PAPERS, published in the year 1830, under the authority of a Royal Commission, the public were informed of the nature of the collection of papers arising in the Secretarial Department of the State, of its growth under various Secretaries, and of its arrival at comparative maturity by the establishment of an office for its reception in 1578. The office thus instituted was popularly known by the name of the STATE PAPER OFFICE, which name it retained until a recent period, when by the operation of the Record Act of 1 & 2 Vict. cap. 94., and by an Order in Council dated 5th March 1852, the custody of the State Papers became vested in the Master of the Rolls, as Keeper of the Public Records, and the State Paper Office now forms a branch of the Record Department.

As the Preface above alluded to shews the collection of State Papers to commence principally in the reign of King Henry VIII., it is necessary, in this Preface, briefly to explain the reasons why the volume now laid before the public commences at a period subsequent to that Monarch's reign.

The Commissioners for Printing and Publishing State Papers, in order to facilitate the execution of their work, directed descriptive catalogues to be made of numerous documents, of the nature of State Papers, deposited in various public collections, so as to enable them to determine, without examining the originals, what letters or other historical papers should, or should not, be admitted into their volumes. For this purpose, and without any view of ultimate publication, such catalogues were prepared, giving at considerable length an abstract of each particular paper; and from those catalogues selections were made for the work subsequently published, with the sanction of Government, under the title of STATE PAPERS, of the reign of King Henry VIII. The papers in that work are printed *in extenso*, and the selections from the catalogues were made with reference only to that particular subject, leaving many of an extremely interesting character, which, either from their length, or from being irrelevant as State Papers, were inadmissible in that work, and yet were of such general importance that it appeared desirable the public should, by some more eligible channel, be made fully acquainted with their existence. A new commission was therefore issued for that purpose, under Her Majesty's sign manual, dated 25th of January 1840, containing the following additional power:—

" And We do also hereby further authorize and empower
" you, or any three or more of you, to print and publish
" Calendars of the principal contents of the papers deposited
" in the said office."

Under this authority the Commissioners commenced an extensive system of Calendars, embracing the principal series of the State Papers as then arranged and settled by the late Right Hon. Henry Hobhouse, the Keeper of State Papers: —the word CALENDAR having been adopted to express the arrangement and description of papers and documents in the order of time; as any other form, without chronological arrangement, would be merely a CATALOGUE.

At the time when the above additional power was given to the Commissioners, a large portion of the STATE PAPERS of the reign of Henry VIII. had been already published, and the remaining volumes were in the press for immediate publication; but as it was impossible to tell, until the whole were completed, what papers might be required for insertion in the text of that work, it was deemed expedient not to disturb that publication by the simultaneous issue of Calendars of the same period, as the two works would unavoidably clash with each other. But in order not to delay the progress of so important a work as the Calendars, it was resolved to commence with the reign of King Edward VI. as the fairest point for starting; none of the papers of that reign having been printed by the Commissioners, nor was it in contemplation so to do.

The State Papers spring from three great and original sources; namely, the offices of the Secretaries of State for the Foreign, the Colonial, and the Home Departments. In the State Paper Office they are classified under those several denominations; the papers emanating from the Home Department being technically denominated the DOMESTIC PAPERS, as representing the correspondence of the Domestic or Home Affairs of the nation, in contradistinction to those of the Foreign and Colonial interests. Of these three it was thought that the Domestic Papers would be more interesting to the student, and more available to the advancement of English history, than either of the other branches; and, therefore, that Series was selected for the commencement of the work of the Calendars of State Papers.

The preparation of the Calendars, concurrently with the important operations of classifying and arranging the State Papers, was the labour of several years. It was not until January 1853 that the present volume was sent to press; and when upwards of 350 pages had been printed, the proceedings of the Commissioners were interrupted by the death of the Keeper of State Papers, which took place in April 1854.

PREFACE.

It having been determined by Her Majesty's Government that on the occurrence of that event the consolidation of the State Papers with the Public Records should be effected, the Master of the Rolls accordingly took formal possession of the State Papers on the 11th of August in that year; and after some delay, unavoidably consequent upon the change of custody, the printing of the Calendars was resumed under the superintendence of the Master of the Rolls. Under that superintendence the present volume, extending from the 1st of Edward VI. to the 23rd of Queen Elizabeth, or rather to the close of the year 1580, has been completed, and is now published with the sanction of Her Majesty's Secretary of State for the Home Department. Other succeeding portions of the same work are also in various stages of progress.

The circumstance that this publication commences with the reign of Edward VI. will not be productive of any practical inconvenience. The chronological arrangement of the State Papers admits of any portion of the Calendar being taken up at any period, and, without difficulty, added to the parts preceding or following the period first published: the separate books not being distinguished, numerically, as volumes, but ranging only in their order of time. Thus, the remaining portion of the reign of Queen Elizabeth, from 1581 to 1603, although it is in hand, may not appear until after the Calendar of a portion of the reign of James I. shall have been published; and again, the first volume of Charles I. may be in print before the reign of James I. is fully completed. The whole, when finished, will make one consecutive series, in complete chronological order; and the Calendar of the Papers of the reign of Henry VIII. will in fact, when published, form the *First* volume of the Series.

The principle of the plan and arrangement of the present

publication will, in the main, be acted upon in the subsequent volumes. It affords the easiest reference possible to the originals described, in whatever shape such references may be made, either by the page, the date, or the number of any article, or by all combined together. Each separate paper or document is briefly abstracted, the leading facts stated, and the persons and places to which it relates are mentioned, sufficiently to indicate to what particular subject it belongs. The student, whether of history, biography, genealogy, or general literature, at however remote a distance he may be placed, can thus ascertain precisely the amount of information existing among the State Papers on whatever may be the subject of his inquiry. Every one acquainted with, or in the habit of consulting original documents, will know that it is impossible to compress within descriptions, necessarily so brief, all the information that may be required. Such slight entries rather point out where information may be found, than supply the information itself; but for the fully satisfying the purposes of study recourse must be had to the originals.

For the general reader, papers of great interest will appear in the reign of Edward VI., elucidatory of the intrigues of Seymour, of Somerset, and of Northumberland; and in that of Mary, the obscure plots of Dudley and Throgmorton and the rebellion of Wyatt will be more fully opened. Immediately upon the accession of Queen Elizabeth a strongly marked change in the character of the papers will not fail to be observed. Rich as they are in the particular departments of biography, genealogy, and local history, it is in the details of the social condition of the Empire under her reign, that the greatest amount of information will be found: the insight into curious and minute points of domestic habits, the intermixture of the utmost simplicity with regal magnificence, the germs of thought then dimly conceived but lying dormant for three centuries before ripening into perfection, the projects and inventions of mechanical genius still in the nineteenth century remaining uncompleted, are all traceable in the present volume.

The intimate connexion of Lord Burghley with the University of Cambridge has been the means of exhibiting in these pages details of a highly interesting character, relating to some of the most celebrated men of the age, connected as well with that University as with the sister one of Oxford: nor will the instances of the cultivation of the useful arts, the rise and progress of mining operations, and the general spread of commercial enterprise, be found scarcely less attractive.

The proposition of Gawen Smith [p. 700] "*for the erec-*
"*tion of a beacon on the Goodwin Sands, twenty or thirty*
"*feet above high-water mark, and able to receive and*
"*preserve thirty or forty persons at least,*" notwithstanding our amazing advance in all the mechanical arts, remains yet unaccomplished; while in the application to Walsyngham by one called John the Almain [p. 696] on behalf of one of his countrymen,—"*who had invented an harquebuse that shall*
"*contain ten balls or pellets of lead, all the which shall goe*
"*off one after an other, havinge once given fire, so that with*
"*'one harquebuse one man may kill ten theaves or other ene-*
"*mies,*"—will be seen the prototype of an idea, successfully carried into execution only in the present generation.

In the department of biography, perhaps no letters will excite greater interest than those of Sir Christopher Hatton to Queen Elizabeth. Through what channel they found their way into the collection of State Papers has been a matter of speculation. Strong presumptive evidence exists that they must have been in the keeping of Thomas Windebank, the Queen's confidential Private Secretary, and so, passing from him to his son Sir Francis Windebank, Secretary of State to Charles I., became mixed up with his official papers. When he fled to France in December 1640, these private and confidential letters remained, with others of the ordinary official character, in the office of the Secretary of State.

The wisdom and energy of Elizabeth's government will be conspicuous in the care taken to put the defences of the realm, both by sea and land, in a complete state of efficiency. The Navy was greatly enlarged, and a vast impetus given to maritime adventure by the efforts to suppress piracy on the one hand, and by the voyages of Hawkyns, of Furbisher, of Gilberte, and of Drake on the other. The details of these adventures will be found full of interest. The reception given to Drake, on his return from circumnavigating the globe, and the immediate reward he received, no less a sum than 10,000*l.* being paid into his hand "without account," [pp. 682, 686,] at once dispel the imputation that Elizabeth delayed the recognition of his services until the amount of his booty was ascertained. That that amount was actually enormous, the extremely interesting particulars given in p. 691, art. 60, afford sufficient evidence.

The internal defences were promoted by the systematic organization of the militia, by the holding of general musters periodically at intervals of about three years, by surveys of all the creeks and landing places, and by attention to the increase and breed of horses in gentlemen's parks throughout the kingdom. These operations were carried on through the medium of commissions addressed to the nobility and gentry in every county; and the returns to those commissions, and the certificates of the Commissioners transmitted by them to the Privy Council, will be found of the greatest value in their statistic and local details. The certificates from Warwickshire may be pointed out by way of specimen as the most complete of their kind, and the occurrence in them of the name of Shakespeare and of several members of his family connexions will be read with peculiar interest. All the certificates of Commissioners, whether of musters, or inquiry into piracy, or for the breed and increase of horses, are very numerously signed; and added to these, the returns from the Justices of Peace of the several counties in relation to the due execution of the laws against rogues and vagabonds, the certificates of inns and alehouses, the quantities and exportation of corn, and other subjects of magisterial jurisdiction, all bearing the signatures of persons of the greatest distinction, present an amount of contributions to the studies of history, of biography, and of genealogy, the value of which will not fail to be highly appreciated.

It is scarcely too much to say that these details, taken together, lay open to historical students the actual condition of England under Queen Elizabeth, to a degree which has never yet been approached in the historical materials of this or perhaps of any other country.

With regard to the orthography of proper names, the principle adopted by the Editor of the State Papers in giving the name of the individual, as he himself spelt it, has been followed in this volume, and will be continued to the end of the sixteenth century. It is also necessary to state that in all cases, and throughout the general arrangement of the State Papers, the commencement of the historical year on the 1st of January has been followed, and the dates of all papers having the civil or legal year, commencing on the 25th of March, have been reduced to that mode of computation.

Dates have been assigned to every paper, either of the month or year, according to the best judgment of the Editor. It is highly probable many of these papers will be found capable of better location through the acquirement of subsequent information, and even the index to the volume itself affords the means of correction not existing at its commencement. Had all undated papers been placed at the end of the several reigns, they would have presented, in the case of the long reign of Elizabeth especially, so formidable a mass of almost useless matter, as very materially to impair the chronological character of the arrangement; and it has been found by experience that approximate dates, assigned upon well-considered principles, have led in numerous instances to the true ones; and thus due importance has been restored to many papers, of which, by adventitious circumstances, such for instance as the separation of inclosures from the letters transmitting them, they had been deprived.

ROBERT LEMON.

State Paper Office,
   Dec. 1856.

DOMESTIC PAPERS.

EDWARD VI.

Vol. I. January—June, 1547.

1547.
Jan. 29.
Hertford.
1. Edw. Earl of Hertford to Sir Wm. Paget (Sec. of State). Directions as to publication of the will of Henry VIII. Sends the key of the will.

Jan. 30.
Envil.
[Enfield.]
2. Same and Sir Anth. Browne (Master of the Horse) to the Council. Are of opinion it would be best to issue a pardon at the Coronation; the late King being in Heaven, has no need of the merit of it. King Edward to be at the Tower next day.

Feb. 3 (?)
3. Heads of business to be considered preparatory to the King's coronation.

Feb. 4.
4. Proclamation for all persons claiming to do service at the Coronation, to give attendance at the Court of Claims.

Feb. 5.
Southwark.
5. Stephen Gardyner, Bp. of Winchester, to Paget. Intends to have a solemn dirge and mass for the late King. At the same time the players in Southwark are to have "a solemne playe to trye who shal have most " resorte, they in game, or I in ernest." Requests the Lord Protector will interfere.

[Feb. 7.]
6. Abstract of cases before the Court of Claims, for the Coronation of King Edward VI.

[Feb. 7.]
7. Detailed Statement of the claims of several Noblemen, &c. to do service at the Coronation of Edw. VI. [*Imperfect.*]

Feb. 8.
Portsmouth.
8. Edw. Vaughan (Captain of Portsmouth) to Paget. Recommends the bearers, two poor men. The mayor is gone to London on affairs of the town. Desires to be made a Justice of Peace.

Feb. 13.
9. Order prescribed by the Privy Council for the ceremonies to be observed at the Coronation of King Edward VI., to take place upon Shrove Sunday (which was the 20th of February). [*Hall, in his Chronicle, states that Edward VI. was crowned on the 19th of February.*]

Feb. 14.
Westminster.
10. Commencement and ending of Inrollment of the will of Henry VIII. Lat.

Feb. 15.
11. Names of certain lords and gentlemen to be promoted to dignities, &c., and the value of lands to be granted to them.

	Vol. I.
1547.	
Feb. 15.	12. Draft preamble of grant by King Edw. VI. to Edward Duke of Somerset, of manors, lands, &c., in conformity with the will of Henry VIII. Lat.
Feb. 15.	13. Translation of the above.
Feb. 15.	14. Minute of the style and titles of Edw. Duke of Somerset, Lord Protector.
Feb. 15.	15. Orders and regulations for the despatch of public business, and for matters to be brought before the King and Privy Council. In Sir Wm. Petre's hand.
Feb. 15.	16. Copy of the above.
[Feb. 15.]	17. Order for "the buriall of Kinge Henrye the Eight of Most "Famous Memorye," by Gilbert Dethicke Garter King at Arms, detailing the regulations for conveying the body from Westminster to Windsor, and the ceremonial of the Interment at the latter place.
Feb. 15.	18. Account of the quantities of Cloth of Gold, Satins, Velvets, and other materials, issued for the funeral of King Henry VIII.
Feb. 16. Portsmouth.	19. Edw. Vaughan to the Council. Has received Commission for levying 200 men in Surrey, Wilts, and Berks. The fortifications of Portsmouth are out of repair. Gunners are wanted.
Feb. 16.	20. List of ordnance mounted on the fortifications at Portsmouth.
Feb. (?)	21. Memorial of matters necessary for defence of Portsmouth, Southampton, and the Isle of Wight.
Feb. (?)	22. Note of the charge of the block houses in the County of Essex.
Feb. 27.	23. Instructions by the Council to Andrew Duddeley, Esq., appointed to be Admiral of the Fleet, to command the Pauncy, and to cruize in the North Seas off the coasts of England and Scotland.
March 1.	24. Grant by the King to the Dean and Chapter of St. Paul's, London, of faculty and licence to exercise ecclesiastical jurisdiction within the places to them appertaining. Lat.
March 1. Southwark.	25. Ste. Bp. of Winchester to Sir Wm. Paget. Requests he will expedite the commissions for the Bishops, as favourably as he promised. Gives his opinion on various points thereof.
March 2. Westminster.	26. Sir Wm. Paget to the Bp. of Winchester. Defends himself from the charge of over assumption of power. Has no ill will towards Bishops, nor to his Lordship in particular.
March 4.	27. Commission to the Lord Chancellor to issue free pardons, in conformity with the general free pardon openly proclaimed at the Coronation.
March 5. Durham Place.	28. Sir Francis Knollys to Paget. Declares his long services, which had impaired his estate : states the amount of his debts.
March 12. Harwich.	29. Andrew Duddeley to Thos. Lord Seymour (Lord High Admiral). Sends letters taken in the late action, and desires to know what to do with the prisoners. Repairs necessary for the Pauncy.

1547.
March [24.] 30. John Earl of Warwick to Sir Wm. Paget. Applies for a grant of Warwick Castle, park, &c., or of Tonbridge and Penshurst, together with Hawlden and Canonbury. Writes in favour of Mr. Denney for Waltham Tower. The Master of the Horse desires to have Lord Lawarre's lordship in Sussex.

March 31. 31. Indenture of all gold and silver bullion, coined monthly into moneys by Sir Wm. Sharington, Under Treasurer of the Mint at Bristol, from the 3ᵈ of May 1546.

March 31. 32. Account of Sir Wm. Sharington, of the bullion coined according to the foregoing indenture, and of the expenses thereof.

April 6. 33. Indenture between Sir Wm. Sharington and Roger Wigmore, (Comptroller and Surveyor of the Mint at Bristol,) of money delivered to Wigmore for necessaries for the Mint there.

April 8. 34. Acknowledgment by Tho. Shipman of having received from Sir Wm. Sharington 300 fodder of lead, to be put into the joint stock of the heirs of Nicholas Thorne & Co.

April 8. 35. Similar receipt, by Shipman, for 500*l*. from Sir Wm. Sharington, to be invested as above.

April 16. 36. The King to the Commrs of Musters in all the shires. To survey the quantity of weapons and military stores in each county, and to warn all persons, obliged by statute to maintain great horses, demilances, &c. for the wars, to have them in readiness after the 20th of May next.

April 20. The Mount. (Cornwall.) 37. Tho. Lord Seymour to the D. of Somerset. Will go to Scilly, and take order for the shipping there to return to Portsmouth.

April 24. St. John's. 38. Princess Mary to the Duchess of Somerset. In favour of Richd. Wood and George Bryckhouse: the latter desires to be one of the Knights of Windsor.

April 24. St. John's. 39. Copy of the above.

April 30. 40. Account of fees and pensions paid out of the Exchequer to foreigners.

May 17. St. James. 41. Lord Seymour to Queen Catharine Parr. Informs her their meetings at Chelsea were known to his sister. Declares his affection, and begs one of her pictures.

May 17. 42. Copy of the above, not very correct, but supplying some words mutilated in the original.

May (?) St. James. 43. Same to same. Directs her as to Mr. Long's suit. Mentions a conversation with the Duchess of Suffolk about their being married, Signs himself "Yoʳ lovynge and faythfull hosbonde."

June 20. 44. Particulars of Fees paid to the Heralds at the obsequies of Mary the French Queen, 1533; the Empress Isabella, 1539; and the French King, 1547.

June 27. Hedingham Castle. 45. Sir Tho. Darcy to [Wm. Cecill?] has enquired into the love affair between the Earl of Oxford and Mrs. Dorothy. Begs to know if it is Somerset's pleasure the match should be stayed. Suggests a marriage between the Earl and one of Lord Wentworth's daughters.

VOL. II. JULY—DECEMBER, 1547.

1547.
July 14. Grant of Arms to Robert Knyght of Bromley, Kent, by Tho. Hawley, Clarencieux. [*Grant of Arms*, No. 5.]

July 15. 1. Copy of the book of the names of such as furnish forth great horses in various counties.

July 18.
Hampton Court.
2. The King to Sir Ralph Vane; directions to be at Newcastle on the 24th of Aug., with as many of his servants and others as he could raise, to serve against the Scots. [Signed by a stamp.]

July 22. 3. Sir Edw. North (Chancellor of the Augmentations) to Wm. Cecill. Mr. Fitzwilliams is to have a lease of the lands of Chertsey Abbey, the same as Sir Anth. Browne lately had.

July 25.
Horsley.
4. Elizabeth Lady Browne to same. Requests that her brother may be amongst those appointed to go into Scotland.

July 25.
Offington.
5. Tho. Lord Lawarre to same. Has received letters to furnish certain horses and demilances to meet at Newcastle, against the Scots. Requests further instructions.

July (?) 6. Prayer for general peace and prosperity, and for success of the proposed marriage between Edw. VI. and Mary Queen of Scots. [*Probably in July, before commencement of the war with Scotland.*]

Aug. 30.
Westminster.
7. Grant to John Lyon and Alice his wife, of the tenement called Buckhurst alias Monkhill, in the parishes of Woodford and Chigwel, co. Essex, late belonging to the monastery of Stratford Langthorne.

Sept. 30. 8. Bond of Wm. Lanway, in 40*l.*, not to take excessive toll of such as should resort to his mill for grinding corn.

Sept. 30. 9. Commission to Wm. Lord St. John (of Basing), Sir Wm. Petre (Sec. of State), Sir Walter Mildmay, and Robt. Keyllewey, to examine and report upon the state of the Crown revenues.

Sept. 30. 10. Indenture of all gold and silver bullion, coined into moneys in the office of Sir Wm. Sharington, from the 1st April to 30th of Sept., in the mint at Bristol.

Sept. 30. 11. Duplicate of the above.

Sept. 30. 12. Account of Sir Wm. Sharington, of gold and silver bullion coined into moneys from April 1, and of the expenses thereof.

Oct. (?) 13. Book of Remembrance for the Lord Protector, touching the rate of subsidy to be granted to the King on wools, woolfells, &c., with reference to the state of the staple in the reigns of Edw. III. and Hen. VIII.

Oct. (?) 14. Note of the weight, qualities, and charges of wools in England.

Oct. (?) 15. Memorandum of wools brought to Calais, the charges of packing, &c., and the quantities exported.

Oct. (?) 16. Statement of Calais weights of wool, in ounces, pounds, nails, &c., according to the manner of the staple.

DOMESTIC—EDWARD VI.   5

1547.   VOL. II.
Oct. (?)   17. Similar statement of English weights of wool.
Oct. (?)   18. Tabular synopsis of the Statute Laws of England concerning the royal, military, ecclesiastical, and other orders of the Commonwealth, drawn up apparently about the accession of Edw. VI.
Oct. (?)   19. Proviso in the Act 1 Edw. VI. relative to a limitation on the exportation of horses, by the Wardens of the Cinque Ports.
Nov. 3.   20. Letters Patent appointing the place of honour in the High Court of Parliament for the Duke of Somerset, as Lord Protector, &c.
Westminster.
Nov. (?)   21. Draft of Bill in Parliament for increase of tillage, and for preventing dearth and scarcity of provisions by the overbreeding of cattle.
Dec. 12.   22. George Revelay to Somerset. Waste of the King's beer by leakage. Distress of the fleet in the north by foul weather. Wants money.
Newcastle.
Dec. 14.   23. Robt. Heylord (Captain of the Lewis) to the same. The King's ships are detained at Shields, and all their victuals and money expended.
Newcastle.
Dec. 28.   24. Princess Mary to the same. Thanks for his attention to her requests as to pensions for some of her servants.
Beaulieu.
Dec. (?)   25. Princess Elizabeth to the Queen [Dowager]. Thanks her for her kindness. Is grateful to God for providing her such friends.
Cheston.
1547 (?)   26. Petition of Hen. Pony to Somerset; to be restored to his brewhouse called the Pye in Smithfield, detained from him by Alice Dacres.
(?)   27. Dorothy Wyngfeld to the Duchess of Somerset; requests her to move the Lord Protector that no sale or grant be made, under the new Commission, of the lands of the late Priory of Woodbridge, Suffolk.
(?)   28. Petition of Vincent Bellacio to Somerset. Prays to serve with his company, &c., against Scotland.
(?)   29. Names of such persons certified by the sheriffs of several cities and counties, as have not compounded for their fines for Knighthood.
(?)   30. Names of Commissioners, and directions for their proceeding, in the sale and exchange of Crown Lands.
(?)   31. Names of Commissioners, and directions for their proceeding, in the receipt and expenditure of the public revenues.
(?)   32. William Parr, Marq. of Northampton, to the King. Prays for a commission of learned men to determine whether he may lawfully marry again, his first wife Lady Anne Bourchier, from whom he was divorced, being still alive.
(?)   33. Extract from a compotus of the value of the rectory of Stowe, with the chapel of Burthropp, part of the possessions of the late Priory of Sempringham, co. Lincoln.
(?)   34. The names of certain persons who have had license to preach under the ecclesiastical seal, since July 1547. [Among other celebrated names occur those of Hugh Latimer, Dr. Coxe, Robt. Horne, Edwyn Sandys, James Pilkyngton, Mathewe Parker, John Knoxe, Edmunde Gryndall, &c.]

Vol. III.   January—February, 1548.

1548.
Jan. 8.
Ely Place.
1. John Earl of Warwick to Somerset. Requests him to further an exchange of lands between Nicholas Heath, Bishop of Worcester, and himself.

Jan. 9.
Hampton Court.
2. Somerset to the town of Cambridge. Desires to know their reasons against the requests and privileges claimed by the University.

Jan. ( ).
3. Answers of the Mayor, &c. of Cambridge, as to the privileges claimed by the University; and the further answers of the same to the new requests of the University. Privileges of Sturbridge fair.

Jan. 12.
4. Account by John Bird, Bishop of Chester, of the sale of church ornaments, plate, jewels, bells, &c., within the diocese of Chester, and of the appropriation thereof.

Jan. 19.
Pensance.
5. Examinations of John Ladweke and Thos. Werdon, as to seven French ships arrived at Dumbritton, in Scotland, having on board young Gerald, Earl of Kildare, who purposed to marry the Scottish Queen, and thus to raise all Ireland, in alliance with Scotland, against England.

Feb. 1.
Ely Place.
6. Warwick to Wm. Cecill. To credit the bearer, who will explain the suit of certain of the Earl's neighbours, relative to founding a free school.

Feb. 12.
7. Account of gold, jewels, and precious stones, taken out of the King's secret jewel house, by command of the Duke of Somerset, principally for making the King's crown.

Feb. 20.
8. Muster-roll for the three Hundreds of Aylesbury, co. Bucks, taken by Sir Anth. Lee, Ric. Greneway, John Babam, and Wm. Dormer.

Feb. 27.
9. Muster-roll of the inhabitants of the hundred of Northwich, co. Chester, taken by Sir Wm. Brereton, Sir Thos. Venables, and Wm. Moreton.

Feb. 28.
10. Certificate of musters of the city of York, with the Wapentake of the Aynsty and liberties of the same; taken before Robt. Paycok, mayor, Sir Wm. Fairfax, Sir Robt. Stapleton, and others.

Feb. 29.
11. Certificate of the Commissioners names appointed to take the musters within the whole county of Cambridge, specifying the several hundreds allotted to each.

Feb. (?)
12. Certificate of musters for the hundreds of Radfield, Cheveley, Chillford, and Wittlesford, within the county of Cambridge.

Feb. (?)
13. Similar certificate for the hundreds of Arnyngford, Stowe, Wetherley, and Tryplow, co. Cambridge.

Feb. (?)
14. Similar certificate for the hundreds of Stane, Staplehoo, and Flendyche, co. Cambridge.

Feb. (?)
15. Similar certificate for the Isle of Ely, co. Cambridge.

VOL. III.

1548.	
Feb. (?)	16. Similar certificate for the whole county of Surrey.
Feb. (?)	17. Similar certificate for the rape of Bramber, co. Sussex.
Feb. (?)	18. Similar certificate for the rape of Chichester, co. Sussex.
Feb. (?)	19. Similar certificate taken upon Portsdown, for the hundreds of Portsdown, Bosmer, Tychefeld, Fareham, Hamyldon, and the town of Havant, co. Hants.
Feb. (?)	20. Certificate of the ships of the town of Whitby, with the master's names, able to serve the King.
Feb. (?)	21. Similar certificate of ships at Scarborough.
Feb. (?)	22. Comparative estimates of the charge of an army for the invasion of Scotland, by sea or by land, showing the difference of expence; together with estimates for victualling, carriages, &c.

VOL. IV. MARCH—AUGUST, 1548.

March 11. Glamorgan.	1. Muster-roll of able men in the hundred of Lantrissent, co. Glamorgan, taken before George Mathew, Esq.
March 15.	2. The Council to the Bishops. To give directions to the whole clergy to administer the holy Sacrament to the laity, in both kinds.
Mar. 24 (?)	3. Indenture of all bullion of gold and silver coined and made into moneys within the office of Sir Wm. Sharington, in the Mint at Bristol.
March 26. Newcastle.	4. Thomas Wyndam to Somerset. Arrival of the navy at Newcastle. Sickness and weakness of the fleet. Desires a reinforcement of 200 men.
April (11?)	5. Obligation given to Lazarus Toucher, securing the repayment of the sum of 167218 florins, lent by him to the King. Lat.
April 14. London.	6. R. Goche (or Gough) to Wm. Cecill. Has received an application for the bailiwick of Weston. Complains of the conduct of one Troughton, a servant of Cecill.
April 19.	7. Certificate of the Dean and Chapter of St. Pauls, London, specifying the chantries, rents, &c., belonging to them.
May 10. Westminster.	8. Thos. Lord Seymour to Mayors, Sheriffs, &c; to make search for goods taken out of certain French ships plundered at sea.
May (?)	9. Instructions to Edw. Lord Clynton, appointed Admiral of the Fleet, sent into the North; to act against the Scots and French, to proceed to the Frith of Forth to intercept the enemy's ships there, and to fortify Inchkeith and other places.
May (?)	10. The King to the Sheriffs and Justices of Peace; to see the beacons duly set up and watched, and to repress unlawful assemblies.
June 4. Ely Place.	11. Warwick to Cecill. Thanks for remembrance of his suit to the Lord Protector.

1548.
June 5.

VOL. IV.

12. The Council to the Justices of Peace, &c., in various counties directions to provide for the watching of beacons and for guarding the sea coasts. *Inclosing,*

  12. I. *Names of gentlemen appointed to remain at home on the advance of the whole shire in case of invasion.* June 5.

June [5]. 13. Earl of Warwick to Cecill. Sends information of a design of certain Scots and Frenchmen in Dieppe to surprize the Castle of Pevensey.

June 9.
Westminster.
 14. Thos. Lord Seymour to the Queen Dowager. Relates his proceedings with the Protector as to her affairs. Hopes "his little man," if God should give him life, may live to revenge his and her wrongs. Desires her to keep him lean and gaunt.

[June 11.] 15. Warwick to Cecill. Is pleased Somerset accepts the offer of his services. Trusts the Frenchmen (their enterprize northward being known) will not much like their journey.

[June 12.] 16. Same to same. Solicits the Protector's favor on behalf of one Browne.

June 14.
Ely Place.
 17. Same to same. Requests to know how "the arrogant Bishop" [Stephen Gardyner] has been proceeded with. Wished to take Mr. Gosnall with him into the Marches, but hears Mr. Townshend holds his office for life. [*Gardyner, Bishop of Winchester, was examined several times before the Council, between the 25th September 1547 and the 30th June 1548, and on the latter day was committed to the Tower.* Co. Reg.]

June 14. 18. Licence from the King to the Bishop of Exeter to grant to Sir Thos. Darcy the town, manor, and mansion of Crediton, co. Devon, the manor of Morchard Episcopi, with all the natives and villains and their followers thereto belonging; together with the advowsons and patronage of the church of Morchard Epi., and of the vicarage, alias the rural deanery, of Crediton. Lat. [*With a pen and ink portrait of King Edw. VI. in the initial letter.*]

June 18.
Sudeley.
 19. Seymour to Cecill; in favour of one Busshe, to be maintained in the manor of Yanworthe, co. Gloucester, to which Thos. Culpeper laid claim.

July 1. 20. The Council to the Ambassadors; detailing the reasons for committing Bishop Gardyner to the Tower.

July 2.
Barnet.
 21. Warwick to Cecill; in favor of the bearer, who was in much distress, and had suffered wrong by the Duke of Norfolk.

July 2.
Canonbury.
 22. Same to same. Desires resolution as to the Commission for the Marches.

July 2. 23. Indenture between Sir Edmund Pekham, treasurer of all the Mints, and Sir Wm. Sharington, of the receipt of certain sums arising from the profits of the mint at Bristol, to the King's use.

July 4.
The Court.
 24. John Cheke to Cecill; relative to a suit to the Protector for some benefice. [*Much mutilated.*]

VOL. IV.

1548.
July 6.
25. Sir Edw. North to Wm. Cecill. Sends draft of a lease in reversion of the manor of Hothome, co. York. *Incloses*,

25. I. *Sir Michael Stanhope to Sir Ed. North. Prays him to expedite the lease of the manor of Hothome to Ric. Maunsell. St. James, 27 June.*

July 7.
Penley.
26. Earl of Warwick to same. Complains of the irresolution in placing and displacing certain persons in the government committed to him, whereby his honour had been smally considered.

July 13.
Southwark.
27. Sir Anth. St. Leger to same (Master of Requests). Will send to his brother to answer certain charges. Desires to exchange with the Archbp. of Dublin, the Dean of Christchurch, or the Bp. of Meath, certain benefices for temporal lands.

July 13.
London.
28. Sir Edw. North, and others of the Court of Augmentations, to same (Secretary to the Protector); to procure the appointment of commissaries and registers to certain exempt jurisdictions in the dioceses of York, Lincoln, London, and Westminster.

July 15.
Eton.
29. Thos. Smith (Secretary of State) to same. Solicits the deanery of Peterborough for Mr. Gascoigne, if the present dean should die, who was in great danger.

July 16.
Penley.
30. Warwick to same. Begs that the Surgeon of Boulogne may remain with his lady, who was in great danger by the ill-treatment of the London surgeons, and "*lokyd owerly to have her legge to be sawed of.*"

July 19.
Hampton Court.
31. John Fowller to Seymour. Sends two small notes written with the King's own hand, His Ma'y not having time to write more. The Duchess of Somerset brought to bed of a fine boy: hopes the Queen will have another. One of the King's notes relates to Latimer; the other desires to be remembered to the Queen.

July 21.
Penley.
32. Warwick to Cecill. In favour of the suit of Cuthbert Musgrave. Complaint by Sir Anth. Lee of the ill-conduct of a priest belonging to Lord Windsor.

July 22.
Windsor.
33. John Hales to Somerset. Describes the good disposition of the people in the circuit they had just passed. Thinks them well-disposed to the new order of things. Care to be taken that jurors be not corrupted, nor sheriffs ill-chosen.

July 26.
Penley.
34. Warwick to Cecill. Solicits for a chaplain of his, a prebend in Canterbury, held by Dr Ridley, now Bp. of Rochester.

July 27.
Waltham.
35. Tho. Fisher to same. Delay in getting out of London, not being able to procure horses.

July 27.
Stamford.
36. Same to same. Details his journey in post to Stamford. Ill-conduct of the postmaster at Royston. Dreadful weather. Found Cecill's relations well in health.

August 3.
37. Lord Lawarre to same. Requests his brother Sir Anth. Sayntmond, may deliver his letter to the L. Protector.

1548.   VOL. IV.

August 6.   38. Somerset to Seymour. The last evil chance in Scotland is not so
Hampton   bad as at first thought. None of note, except Mr. Bowes and Mr. Pal-
Court.   mer, are taken. Proceedings of the French at Boulogne.

[August 7.] 39. The Council to same. Details the spoils and wrongs done by
the French at Boulogne and elsewhere. Directs him to commission
privateers to take French ships and goods, extending only to Devon
and Cornwall. With a memorial of the course to be pursued.

August 9.   40. Lord Seymour to Sir Peter Carew, Sir T. Denys, and Sir Ric.
Sudeley Castle. Grenfelde, for Devonshire, and John Grenfelde, Sir Hugh Trevanyon,
and Sir Wm. Godolphin, for Cornwall. Instructions according to the
effect of the preceding letter and memorial.

August 11.   41. Same to the Council. Has given ample directions to the gentle-
Sudeley Castle. men of Cornwall and Devonshire.

August 11.   42. Same to Somerset, in answer to his of the 6th, as to the loss in
Sudeley Castle. Scotland, and to the Council's letters relating to Devon and Cornwall.

August 13.   43. Somerset to Seymour. Decision in a cause between Tho. Agard
Oatlands.   and one Leche, for lands. Sends a note of the northern news. Loss
sustained by the French and Scots at Haddington.

August 13.   44. John Lord Russell to same; thanks for two bucks. Success
Oatlands.   against the Scots at Haddington and the French at Boulogne. Requests a lease of two messuages for his secretary John Gale. *Incloses,*

44. I. *Particulars of two messuages called Poterelles and Boltons,
within the parish of Mymms co. Hertford, belonging to
Lord Seymour.*

August 16.   45. Somerset to same. In favour of Matt. Hulle, who had been
Shene.   troubled in the Admiralty Court, wherein Hussey, the Judge of the
Admiralty, had not behaved uprightly.

August 19.   46. Seymour to Somerset. Explains as to Agard and Leche.
Sudeley Castle. Had apprehended two fellows, Walter ap John and John ap Thomas
Lewes, for counterfeiting coin; and they had impeached one Joyne
Goughe, a smith.

August 23.   47. Same to same. Answer as to Matthew Hull, who was guilty of
Lacock.   piracy, and ought to have sued for pardon rather than for compensation.

August 24.   48. Abstract of the rights and privileges granted to Sir Ric. Sakevyle,
in his commission as Chancellor of the Augmentations; among other,
to "take order for the manumyssion of villeyns." [*Sakevyle's commission is dated* 24 *Aug.* 2 *Edw. VI.*]

VOL. V.   SEPTEMBER—DECEMBER, 1548.

Sept 1.   1. Somerset to the Lord H. Admiral Seymour. Remonstrates with
Sion.   him on his arbitrary course of conduct. In the case of Matt. Hull,
the goods to be put in safe custody, for further trial. Insurrection in
Brittany.

DOMESTIC—EDWARD VI. 11

VOL. V.

1548.
Sept. 1.
Sion.
2. Somerset to Seymour. Congratulates him on the safe delivery of the Queen of so pretty a daughter.

Sept. 7.
Faye.
3. John Graynfyld to same. Action with the French, off the coast of Brittany; many of their ships driven on shore, and ten sail captured. Reported landing of the Scotch Queen in France. *Incloses*,

3. I. II. III. *Three papers of lading, &c, taken in the French ships.*

Sept. (?)
Cheshunt.
4. Princess Elizabeth to Somerset. Thanks for his care in sending Dr. Bill to her in her sickness. Is also thankful for the expediting of her patent.

Oct. 1.
5. Lady Jane Gray to Seymour. Thanks for his kindness to her. Shall be always ready to obey his monitions and good instructions

Oct. 2.
Brodgate.
6. Frances, Marchioness of Dorset, to same. Thanks for his kindness to her daughter Jane in desiring to have her continue with him.

Oct. 17.
Hackney.
7. The King to Thomas Hayberne and Stephen Andrewes, both of London. Demise of messuages and tenements in the parish of St. Mary at Hill. Lat.

Oct. 22.
Geneva.
8. John Calvin to Somerset. Advises him steadfastly to prosecute the Reformation of Religion begun in England, and to promote the diffusion of the true doctrine of the Gospel. [*Contemporary translation.*]

Oct. 26.
9. John Yonge to Mr. Throckmorton. States the opinion of the Protector as to letters, &c., from Card. Pole. If the Cardinal thinks fit to write private letters to the Protector, for the good of the nation, they would be received.

Oct. (?)
10. Names of the prisoners in the Tower, with the causes of their imprisonment there, as far as the Lieutenant knows.

Nov. 2.
11. Wm. Lord St. John (Lord Great Master) to Somerset. Gives his opinion that the holders of counterfeit coin were answerable for the loss, and that the King should not be charged.

Nov. 8.
Oxford.
12. President and Fellows of Magdalen Coll. Oxford to the same. Are willing to adopt and to further the measures taken for the Reformation of Religion. Have administered the Communion as set forth.

Nov. 12.
Westminster.
13. Commission from the King to Thomas [Goodrich] Bishop of Ely, Nicholas [Ridley] Bp. of Rochester, Sir Wm. Paget, Thos. Smith, John Cheke, Dr. Wm. Maye, and Dr. Tho. Hendy, for the visitation of the Universities of Cambridge and Oxford, and the College of Eton.

Nov. (?)
14. Sir Richard Ozeir (Hosier) to   ; solicits to be set at liberty. Details the good services performed by him to Englishmen in Scotland. *Incloses*,

14 I. *Names of persons willing to become sureties for Sir R. Ozier.*

Dec. (?)
15. Monthly accounts of ingots, &c., received for the coinage, from April 1547.

DOMESTIC—EDWARD VI.

Vol. V.

1548.

(?)   16. Petition of Sir Wm. Drury, Sir John Constable, and others, for restoration to them of the fee intail of the Manor of Wrenthorp, co. York, devolved to the Crown under the Act concerning colleges and chantries.

(?)   17. Abstract of the light horses and demilances to be furnished by assessment throughout the realm.

(?)   18. Book of assessment of the city of London, for finding light horses and demilances.

(?)   19. Certificate of the churchwardens of the parishes within the city of London and the several deaneries in Essex and Hertfordshire within the diocese of London, of the sale of all the church plate, ornaments, jewels, bells, vestments, &c., lately belonging to their respective churches, and of the appropriation of the proceeds.

(?)   20. Statement of the causes of the universal dearth of provisions. Remedies proposed. Exactions of purveyors to be suppressed, &c.

(?)   21. Copy of the above, with some omissions and alterations.

(?)   22. Draft of Bill in Parliament against the monopoly of farms; converting arable into pasture, &c.

(?)   23. Land sold and bought by Sir Richard Lee, knight, since the death of King Henry VIII.

(?)   24. Memoranda, in the hand writing of Cecill, relative to various matters of public business, &c., to be transacted.

(?)   25. Memorandum of things worthy examination, for the King's Majesty.

Vol. VI. January—April, 1549.

1549.

Jan. 11.
"My howse"
Friday.
   1. Thos. Lord Seymour to the Duke of Somerset. Excuses himself from coming to speak with him till to-morrow at the Parliament House, or at Westminster in the afternoon. [*Lord Seymour was committed to the Tower on Thursday the 17th of January 1549, and not on the 19th, as stated by Burnet, and after him by all subsequent historians. This Holograph letter of Seymour's being dated on Friday "from my howse," cannot therefore be later than Friday the 11th of January.*]

Jan. 18.   2. Instructions to Sir Hugh Pawlett, Sir Thomas Chaloner, and John Yernley, to search the Lord Admiral's house at Bromham, in Wiltshire.

Jan. [21].   3. Inventory of the goods, chattels, &c. in and about the manor of Cheseworth, co. Sussex, belonging to the Lord Admiral, taken by Sir Thos. Cawerden and Sir Wm. Goryng.

Jan. 21.   4. Similar inventory of goods, &c. belonging to the Lord Admiral, at the Manor Place of Sheffield and Forest of Worthe, co. Sussex, taken by the same parties.

1549.		Vol. VI.
Jan. 28. London.	5.	Wm. Gyffard to Laurence Lee. Has received commission to make sale of woods in the manor of Colleweston, and 30 acres in Tomlyn's Wood, in the manor of Apthorpe.
Jan. 31. Hatfield.	6.	Sir Robt. Tyrwhit to Somerset. His endeavours to ascertain what had passed about a marriage between Lord Seymour and the Princess Elizabeth. Her statements. Supposes Mrs. Ashley knows all.
Jan. (?)	7.	Deposition by Henry, Marquis of Dorset, relative to matters at sundry times imparted to him by Seymour. His promise to get Lady Jane Grey married to the King, &c.
Jan. (?)	8.	Deposition by Edw. Rouse. Orders given by Seymour for keeping his house at Bewdley, in Shropshire.
Jan. (?)	9.	Deposition by Sir Ric. Cotton, as to speeches of the Lord Admiral after the death of his wife.
Jan. (?)	10.	Confessions of John Fowler, as to his being urged by the Lord Admiral to procure the King's opinion as to his marriage. To incite the King with money given by Seymour, &c. With a note of sums received by Fowler.
Jan. (?)	11.	Depositions by Edw. Lord Clynton, relative to certain speeches of the Lord Admiral.
Jan. (?)	12.	Deposition by Henry, Earl of Rutland, of conversations with the Lord Admiral.
Jan. (?)	13.	Depositions by Sir Wm. Sharington, as to speeches of the Lord Admiral. Money lent by him to Seymour. His designs on Lady Jane Grey and the Princess Elizabeth.
Jan. (?)	14.	Deposition by Wm. Marquis of Northampton, relative to the tenour of certain discourses held with the Lord Admiral, previous to his committal.
Jan. (?)	15.	Deposition by Thos. Earl of Southampton. Conversation between him and Seymour on their way to dine at Sir John Gresham's. His advice to Seymour not to make a party or breed a faction.
Jan. (?)	16.	Deposition relative to certain communications between John Lord Russell (Lord Privy Seal) and the Lord Admiral, principally about a marriage with either Princess Mary or Princess Elizabeth, and Sharington's affairs.
Jan. (?)	17.	Depositions of Sir George Blagge and the Earl of Warwick, relative to certain speeches of Seymour, who threatened to stab any that should attempt to arrest him.
(?)	18.	Memorandum of certain points, by which the subject may be liable to forfeit his lands to the Crown.
Feb. 2.	19.	Examination of Mrs. Katherine Aschyly as to her communications with the Princess Elizabeth, touching marriage with the Lord Admiral.
Feb. 4.	20.	Further examination of the same, as to the Princess Elizabeth and Seymour. Conversation with Thos. Parry.

1549.

Vol. VI.

Feb. 4. 21. Deposition of Mrs. Katherine Aschyly relative to familiarities between Seymour and the Princess Elizabeth.

Feb. 4. 22. Final confession of the same. Conversations with Seymour about Princess Elizabeth, and with Parry, on the same subject. Prays for change of her prison and for mercy to be shown to her.

Feb. 11.
Ely Place.
23. Warwick to Cecill; in favour of Harry Makerel the King's surgeon to be joined in the patent with old Vicars. Also asks for a farm for his servant Turpin. Sends Cecill the half-year's fee of his patent.

Feb. 14. 24. Indenture between the King and the Mayor, &c., of Plymouth, for erecting and maintaining the fort on St. Nicholas Island.

Feb. 15. 25. The Council to Commissioners in every shire. Instructions to make a true inventory of all church ornaments, plate, jewels, bells, vestments, &c., and to forbid the sale and embezzlement of any part of the same.

Feb. 20. 26. Declaration by Mr. John Cheke of the effect of the message the Lord Admiral requested him to procure the King to make to the House of Lords.

Feb. 24. 27. Answer of the Lord Admiral to the articles objected against him by the Privy Council.

Feb. (?) 28. Note of certain silks, plate, jewels, &c., taken out of the King's secret houses at Westminster by the Duke and Duchess of Somerset and others.

Feb. (?) 29. Specification of the plate, money, jewels, &c., belonging to Sir Wm. Sharington at the time of his arrest in January.

March (?) 30. Extract of a confirmation by the King of a lease of certain lands and tenements in Chancery Lane, abutting on the Rolls estate, from Ric. Sampson Bp. of Chichester to the Guild and Fraternity of St. Mary and St. Dunstans, Fleet Street.

April 6.
Thropp
Mountvell.
31. Wm. Gyffard to Cecill. A claim has been made on the part of the Princess Elizabeth to the woods sold by him in Colleweston and Apthorpe. Will pay the proceeds to Laurence Lee.

April 6.
Rome.
32. Cardinal Pole to Warwick. Has written to Protector Somerset, and offers to give further information for the benefit of the realm.

April 9.
Sion.
33. Somerset to the Vice Chancellor, &c., of the University of Cambridge. Concerning the Commission for visiting the University. *Lat.*

April 10.
Westminster.
34. The King to the same, urging them to forward the Commission for visiting the University. Attested by the Commissioners. *Lat.* [*Much uncertainty exists as to the exact day on which Sec. Smith received his Knighthood. In this letter he is styled a Knight, which he certainly was not on the 17th of Jan. 1549, as appears by the Minute of Council on that day, where he is called " Thomas Smith esquier."*]

1549.
April 11 (?)
Derby Place.

VOL. VI.

35. Ric. Whalley to Wm. Cecill. Sees no likelihood of obtaining Wimbledon for him. Thinks he may get for him the park, with the tythe of Mortlake, and Ambrose Wolley's house.

April 12.
Leyghtone.

36. Sir Robt. Tyrwhyt to same; concerning the lodge and park of Mortlake and parsonage of Wimbledon; the latter being promised to Whalley.

VOL. VII. MAY—JUNE, 1549.

May 4.
Stepney.

1. Mary, Duchess of Richmond, to Sir Thos. Smith. Requests licences for certain persons to preach; also for one Huntingdon and Dr. King of Norwich. Thanks for his favours shewn to Sir Wm. Farmer.

„

2. Copy of the above.

May 5.
Stepney.

3. Same to same. Prays him to withdraw his evil opinion of Huntingdon, for whom, and Dr. King of Norwich, she could answer.

May 5.
Eton College.

4. Wm. Goldwyn, Vice Provost of Eton, to Sir Tho. Smith as Provost of Eton. Mr. Cross and Mr. Dobson have been chosen Bursars. The report that the master of the school is a dice-player, &c. is untrue.

May 8.
The Court.

5. W. P. [Wm. Paget] to Somerset. Remonstrates with him on his angry and snappish conduct towards those of the Council who differ in opinion from him, or who venture to express their own sentiments. Gives excellent advice.

May 8.
Westminster.

6. Commission to John Earl of Warwick and others, to visit the Royal Free Chapel of Windsor, the College of Winchester, and the Universities of Oxford and Cambridge. Lat.

May 8.

7. Another copy of the above. Lat.

May 10.
London.

8. W. Wightman to Cecill. Gives a statement of his connexion and dealings with Lord Seymour. Protests his entire innocence.

May 12.

9. Benjamin Gonson to Sir Wm. Petre. Sends list of ships nearly ready to sail under [Thos.] Cotton.

May 14.
Cambridge.

10. Wm. Rogers to Sir Thos. Smith. Detail of the daily proceedings of the Commissioners for visiting the University.

May 15.
Cambridge.

11. Same to same. Further account of the visitation. The Fellows of Trinity Hall are willing that their College should be united with Clare Hall. Destitute condition of the latter.

May 16.

12. Instructions to Thos. Cotton, appointed Vice Admiral, to cruize in the Narrow Seas, to clear the coast of French and Scotch ships, and to carry a supply of munition to Alderney.

May 16.
Greenwich.

Warrant to pay Thos. Matson, captain of 100 men, certain sums for their coats, passage money, and arms. [*Docquet*, 21 *May.*]

May 16.
Greenwich.

Warrant to pay 73*l*. in prest to Captain Petro Zanzy, Albanois. [*Docquet* 30 *May.*]

1549.   Vol. VII.

May 17. Greenwich. — Warrant to pay 8l. 10s. to Owter Van Brunswick and 16 other lanceknights, for their expenses northwards. [*Docquet* 21 *May.*]

May 17. Greenwich. — Warrant to pay 26l. 13s. 4d. to Oliver Dawbney, for conveying treasure from Bristol to Ireland. [*ib.*]

May 17. Greenwich. — Warrant to repay 3l. to S. Smith, for riding post during the commotion in Somersetshire. [*ib.*]

May 17. Greenwich. — Warrant to pay 5000l. to be conveyed to the Treasurer of the wars in the North. [*ib.*]

May 18. Greenwich. — Warrant to pay 7l. in prest to Edm. Berwick, man at arms. [*ib.*]

May 18. Greenwich. — Warrant to pay 60l. to Sr Thos. Woodlock, for bringing pirates taken in Ireland. [*ib.*]

May 18. Windsor. — 13. Wm. Fytzwilliam to Cecill and Mr. Kellwaye. On the matter in variance between Mr. Hawtrye and his brother-in-law John Danyell.

May 18. Cambridge. — 14. The Bishops of Ely and Rochester, and others, to Sir Tho. Smith. Refer to Mr. Rogers for relation of their proceedings in their visitation.

May 18. Cambridge. — 15. Same to Somerset. They have visited Clare Hall, and state their objections to unite that college with Trinity Hall.

May 18. — 16. Bp. Ridley to Somerset. Remonstrates against uniting Clare Hall with Trinity. Commends Latimer, who had been educated at Clare. [*Fuller, and succeeding biographers, state Latimer to have been educated at Christ's College.*]

May 18. — 17. Copy of the above.

May 20. — Warrant to Sir Edm. Pekham, to send 5000l. to the Treasurer in the North. [*Docquet* 21 *May.*]

May 20. — Warrant to Sr John Williams, to send 3000l. to the North. [*ib.*]

May 22. — 18. Proclamation for stay of the people's attempts at breaking up enclosures, &c.

May 22. — 19. Draft of the above.

May 25. Rye. — 20. Mayor, &c., of Rye to Somerset,. Scarcity of timber occasioned by the iron mills. Requests permission to use the mortar and stone of Camber Castle for their fortifications.

May 26. Greenwich. — Warrant to pay 20l. to Robert Wy, for conducting 200 Italians, and 10l. in prest to Jasparo Como and nine other Italians sent into the North. [*Docquet* 30 *May.*]

May 26. — Warrant to pay 8l. 10s. to Sec. Sir Tho. Smith, for money advanced by him to 17 lanceknights sent into the North. [*ib.*]

May 27. — Warrant to repay to Jacob Schult 1000 crowns (talers), lent to Dymok for the King's use. [*ib.*]

1549.
May 27.   Warrant to pay 135*l*. 10*s*. in prest for payment of the Irishmen's wages. [*Docquet, May* 30.]

May 27.
Hemingford Abbot.
21. Simon Kent to the Bishop of Lincoln [Henry Holbeach], complaining of a young man named Robt. Jaye, who had nailed up a dead cat, as on a cross, in St. Ives' Market. [1549 ?]

May (28?)   22. The Council to the Commissioners at Cambridge. Instructions relative to Clare Hall; to pronounce it dissolved, and then to unite it to Trinity.

May 29.
Cambridge.
23. Wm. Rogers to Sir T. Smith. Has sent him by the bearer, Mr. Holinshed, six pair of double gloves. Dr. Redman has been before the Visitors and made a protestation as to certain passages in the Homilies. The Commissioners purpose to proceed with Clare Hall.

May 29.   Warrant to Thos. Chamberlayn (Under-Treasurer of Bristol) to deliver 60*l*. to Rice A. Morgan, Ph. Lower, and N. Buckingham, of the King's reward for the taking of Cole the pirate. [*Docquet,* 30 *May.*]

May 29.   Further warrant to pay 40*l*. to Morgan and Buckingham for the same affair. [*ib.*]

May 30.   Warrant to repay 2*l*. 10*s*. to Sec. Smith, advanced by him to 5 lanceknights sent to the North. [*Docquet.*]

May.   24. Proposal for erecting a college of civil law in the University of Cambridge, to be called Edward's College; and a college of civilians, to attend on the Council, &c.

May.   25. Duplicate of the above.

May.   26. Assignment of money for the charges of the King's household.

June 1.
Pembroke Hall, Cambridge.
27. Bishop Ridley to Somerset; exculpates himself from blame as a Visitor at Cambridge, particularly as to the proposed union of Clare Hall with Trinity. Prays that in matters relating to that office his scruples of conscience may be received with favourable allowance.

June 2.   Warrant to repay 5*l*. to Mr. Sec. Smith, advanced by him for the King's service. [*Docquet,* 7 *June.*]

June 2.   Warrant to deliver 15*l*. in prest to Carlo Dado, the Italian, sent into the North. [*ib.*]

June 2.   Warrant to pay 20*l*. in prest to Vincent Bellachy, and others in his company, for service in the North. [*ib.*]

June 3.   Warrant to deliver 10,000*l*. to the bearer, to be conveyed into the North. [*ib.*]

June 3.   Warrant to pay 3,000*l*. to the bearer, to be conveyed to the Treasurer in the North. [*ib.*]

June 5.   Warrant to pay 40*l*. to Mathew de Mantua for service done. [*ib.*]

June 4.
Greenwich.
28. Somerset to Cardinal Pole, in answer to his letters of 6th May; hopes that he at last perceives the abuses of the Church of Rome. Exhorts him to take advantage of the King's mercy and to return. Sends him a copy of the Book of Common Prayer.

1549

June 6. Warrant to pay 39*l*. 5*s*. to Edward Walshe for the pay and conduct of 200 Irish kern. [*Docquet, 7 June.*]

June 6. Warrant to repay to Mr. Sec. Smith 8*l*. advanced by him to Joachim Camerhurst and others, for their expenses northwards. [*ib.*]

June 7. Warrant to repay to the same 5*l*., advanced by him to 5 Almain gentlemen, for their expenses in the North.

June 9. Cambridge. 29. Wm. Rogers to Sir T. Smith. Bishop Ridley is loth to proceed against Clare Hall. The Master of that college is very stout in his opposition to the Visitors. Detail of proceedings.

June 10. Richmond. 30. Somerset to Bishop Ridley. Thinks his scruples of conscience as a Visitor groundless. Shews precedents for the proposed union of Clare Hall with Trinity.

June 11. Syon. 31. Same to Henry Marq. of Dorset, and Francis Earl of Huntingdon; to publish the proclamation against the assembling of lewd persons to throw down enclosures; and to keep themselves in readiness to suppress any insurrection.

June 11. Kew. 32. Wm. Turner to Wm. Cecill. The Archbp. of York (Robt. Holgate) has sent for him to go into Yorkshire. Has heard that Somerset wishes him to go to Winchester. Is willing, if he can have a living there.

June 15. Cambridge. 33. Wm. Rogers to Sir T. Smith. Bishop Ridley is now willing to deprive the master and fellows of Clare Hall.

June 15. Cambridge. 34. Visitors at Cambridge to the same. Are sorry Bishop Ridley has been recalled. Pray that he may remain till the visitation be concluded.

June 17. Richmond. Warrant to repay 5*l*. to Sir T. Smith, for money advanced to Cecase Dattylo, an Italian, and 4 servants, sent to the North, and 1*l*. to the keeper of Colchester jail. [*Docquet, 3 July.*]

June 18. Warrant to pay 5*l*. in prest to Capt. Spinola, serving in the North. [*ib.*]

June 18. 35. Warwick to Cecill. Complains of trespasses committed on his lands, and of the boasts of Mr. Skynner.

June 19. London. 36. Olyver Leder to same. Sends his reply in the matter at variance between himself and one Edm. Hatley.

June 20. Richmond. 37. The King to the Justices, &c. of Devon; offering pardon to all persons who have refused to receive the Book of Common Prayer, if they will return to their duty and allegiance.

June 22. Richmond. 38. Sir Tho. Smith to Somerset. Progress of the coinage. Mints must be established at York, Canterbury, and Bristol. Bullion comes in slowly. Details sources of revenue. *Incloses,*

  38. I. *Sir Edm. Pekham to Sec. Smith; details of mint affairs. Bullion is much wanted to carry on the coinage. June 22.*

  38. II. *Certificate of money paid on warrants out of the Mint from 1st June 1549 to the above date; and of testons received as bullion and re-issued as current money. June 22.*

DOMESTIC—EDWARD VI.

VOL. VII.

1549.
June 22. 39. Sir Edm. Pekham to Sir T. Smith. Further details of mint affairs. Will obtain the Moneyer's account of the quantity of the King's plate melted and converted into coin.

[June 24.] 40. Instructions to Lord Russell (Lord Privy Seal) for the government of the Western counties of Devon, Cornwall, Somerset, and Dorset, and for suppressing the disaffection and commotions there.

[June 24.] 41. Observations by Mr. Dudley and Mr. Travers on the defensive nature of the country about Sherburn in Dorsetshire, for the purpose of opposing the rising in the West. Signed by Lord Russell.

[June 26.]
Syon. 42. [The Council] to Sir Thos. Denys, Peter Courtenay, and Anthony Harvy, and the Justices of Devon; directions for the course to be pursued towards the rebels in Devonshire, to induce them to retire peaceably.

June 27.
Pinchebeck. 43. Ric. Ogle to Cecill. Recommends him to purchase the demesne lands of Spalding. Neglected state of the fens in the Holland division of Lincolnshire. *Incloses*,

43. I. *Particular of the lands and demesne of Spalding.*

June 29.
Guildford. 44. Henry Earl of Arundel to Sir Wm. Petre. The country remains "in a quavering quiet." The people have an unfavourable opinion of Sir Wm. Goring.

June 30.
Gray's Inn. 45. Wm. Dalyson to Cecill. Requests the wardship of Wm. Dalyson, son and heir of George Dalyson, deceased.

June (?) 46. Petition of the Inhabitants of Staines to the Council, praying not to be compelled to break down Staines bridge for the purpose of impeding the approach of the rebels.

June (?) 47. Articles upon the doctrine of the Holy Eucharist, by Martin Bucer; slightly mutilated.

June (?) 48. Copy of the above, before the mutilations.

VOL. VIII.   JULY—SEPTEMBER, 1549.

July (1).
Richmond. 1. Circular Letter to various Noblemen and Gentlemen. Orders to attend the King at Windsor with as many horsemen and footmen as could be raised.

July 1. 2. "The names of suche as had letters to come or send to Windsour, primo Julÿ 1549."

July 3. Warrant to repay 3*l.* 10*s.* to Sec. Smith, advanced by him to seven Almains, sent to serve in the North. [*Docquet.*]

July 4.
Aldingborne. 3. George Day, Bishop of Chichester, to Cecill. Offers the use of his house at Chichester to Somerset, if he should come into those parts.

July 7. 4. W. P. [Wm. Paget] to Somerset. Expostulates at great length with him on his system of government, pointing out the ill effects of it, and the consequences that would ensue; gives advice what course he ought to pursue. On the back of the last leaf of this letter are some verses in praise of women, concluding "Finis q^d Gilpin."

Vol. VIII.

1549.
ily 8.   5. Answer of King Edw. VI. to the rebels of Devon and Cornwall, in reply to their supplication and demand for redress of grievances. [*A contemporary copy; supposed to be drawn up by Archbp. Cranmer*]

July 8.   6. Another copy of the above.

July 8.   7. A fragment of the above document.

July 8.   8. Copy of the above fragment, with alterations.

July (8?)   9. "Ordre to be taken for repressing of commotions and uproures, if any suche shall happen, in the counties of Oxforde, Berkes, and Bucks."

July (8?)   10. Instructions given to the Commissioners appointed for execution of the Statutes of 4 Hen. VII. and 7 & 27 Hen. VIII. relative to inclosures, decay of husbandry, &c. [*Printed in black letter by Ric. Grafton.*]

July (8?) Richmond.   11. Protector Somerset to the Commissioners for redress of unlawful enclosures, decay of houses, &c. Directions to proceed as soon as possible in execution of their Commission according to the articles annexed [No. 9 ?], and to begin with reforming themselves.

July (8?)   12—15. Four copies of the above circular, with the date, "From Richemount the   of July 1549."

July (8?)   16—23. Eight copies of same, without the date.

July 10. London.   24. Sir Tho. Darcy and Sir John Gates to Cecill. Insufficiency of the Commission concerning decay of houses of husbandry, enclosures, &c.; require further powers in several specified points.

July 13. Syon.   25. Somerset to the Commissioners for reformation of enclosures, &c.; directions to act jointly together in each place, without division of their body.

July 13.   26—29. Four copies of the above, all signed.

July 18.   30. The Council to Princess Mary; complain of certain of her retainers attending seditious assemblies, particularly a Chaplain at Sandford Courtenay in Devon, and one Pooley, a leader of the worst sort of the rebels in Suffolk.

July 18.   31. Copy of the above.

July 19.   32. Order prescribed by Lord Gray for the execution of rebels in Oxford and other counties; some of the priests to be hanged on their own steeples. Names of the rebels to be executed.

July 19. Eton.   33. Sir T. Smith to Cecill; deplores the evil state of the realm; suggests the appointment of one or two responsible gentlemen in each shire to inforce the King's proclamations. The watchmen are the great promoters of the rebellion. Lord Gray's doings are worth 10,000 proclamations. Thanks for his favor to Mr. Gascoyne.

July 23.   34. The Council to Sir Wm. Herbert; directions as to raising troops, and furnishing them with coats, weapons, &c., to serve against the rebels.

Vol. VIII.

1549. July 24. Grimsthorpe.	35. Katharine Duchess of Suffolk to Wm. Cecill; cannot without an annual pension continue to maintain the late Queen's child and her attendants; would transfer that burthen to the Marq. of Northampton, but he is ill able to bear it.
Aug. 2.	36. The King to the Bishop of London [Edm. Bonner]. Through his evil examples the people absent themselves from prayer and the Holy Communion; he is peremptorily commanded to reform that neglect. The heads prescribed for his first sermon at St. Paul's, particularly against the sin of rebellion.
Aug. (10?)	37. Another copy of the heads of Bp. Bonner's sermon to be preached at St. Paul's; with further directions in consequence of the defeat of the rebels.
Aug. 10. Warwick.	38. Warwick to Cecill: State of affairs with France. Has received Commission to lead the shires of Cambridge, Bedford, Huntingdon, Northampton, and Norfolk; advises the employment of the Marq. of Northampton.
Aug. (11?) Westminster.	39. The Council to _____ ; directions not to come to London on the 14th instant as appointed, but to continue in readiness at an hour's warning.
Aug. 10.	40. Another copy.
Aug. 12.	41. Deposition of Andrew Blakman and Ric. Sylver, relative to the treasonable speeches of John Garnham of Winchester, inciting them to rebellion.
Aug. 15.	42. Robert Broke and Ric. Goodrick to Somerset; have examined Roger Lansdale, and report his deposition relative to John Gyle and Ric. Gyle, a priest, on certain matters concerning the Princess Mary.
Aug. 16.	43. The Council to the Bishops; directions to preach the true word of God, and to teach the people their duty towards God and the King.
Aug. 17. Westminster.	44. Fair copy of the above.
Aug. 19.	45. [Dr.] Glynn, of the Arches, to Sir T. Smith; solicits the Advocateship of the Admiralty. Mr. Clapham has obtained his purpose.
Aug. 19.	46. The Council to Hen. Marq. Dorset; thanks for the quietness of the shires of Leicester and Rutland. Object to the return of his brother, the Lord Tho. Grey, and have sent him with troops to Lord John Grey at Newhaven.
Aug. 21.	47. Same to Lord Russell. Rejoice in his success over the rebels. To search for Sir Tho. Pomery, and to send up Sir Humfrey Arondell, Maunder, and the Mayor of Bodmin, and two or three others of the rankest traitors. To delay a short time issuing the general pardon.
Aug. 29.	48. Henry Polsted to Cecill. Weakness of the co. of Surrey for want of more Justices. Death of Sir Chr. More. Recommends the appointment of Wm. More his son, John Vaughan, John Agmondesham, and John Byrche. Money is wanted for a county gaol.

1549.

Aug. 31.
Norborough.
49. Alys Browne to Wm. Cecill. Prays him to expedite the pardon and return of her husband John Browne.

Aug. 31.
Ledes Castle.
50. Sir Anth. St. Leger to same. Progress of raising men in Kent. Solicits the Bishoprick of Kildare for a chaplain of his, named Lewes Tedder.

Aug. (?)
51. The King to Princess Mary; marvels at her refusing to conform to the order of Common Prayer lately set forth. Gives dispensation to her and her household to have private service in her own chamber. [*Much mutilated.*]

Aug.
52. Draft of the above.

Aug.
53. Copy of the above, made before the mutilation.

Aug.
54. Lord Russell, William, Lord Grey (of Wilton), and Sir Wm. Herbert to the Council; send up Pomery, Arundell, and other prisoners. Castell, Arundell's secretary, comes as an accuser, not as a prisoner.

Sept. 6.
Babrame.
55. Sir Wm. Woodhows to Cecill; sets forth the claims of his brother. *Incloses,*

> 55. I. *Sir Tho. Wodhous to his brother; Warwick has executed many at Norwich, and bestowed their goods. Complains of being unremunerated for his services and losses during the rebellion, and of being left out of the Commission of Oyer and Terminer. Waxham, Sept. 3.*
>
> 55. II. *Same to same; desires to have a Commission for the Admiralty, being appointed Vice Admiral of Norfolk and Suffolk. Norwich, Sept. 5.*

Sept. 10.
56. Sir Anth. Auchar to Cecill. Sends information of words spoken by George Flecchar. Is apprehensive of the new party called Commonwealths men, thought to be favored by the Protector.

Sept. (12?)
57. Commission to Archbp. Cranmer, Bp. Ridley and others, commanding them to call Bishop Bonner before them for not having complied with certain injunctions in the sermon preached by him at St. Paul's.

Sept. 13.
58. Interrogatories administered to the Bishop of London.

Sept. 14.
Ely Place.
59. Warwick to Cecill. Recommends the payment of Thos. Drury and his troop, for their services against the rebels.

Sept. 15.
Lynn.
60. Sir Nicholas Le Strange to the same. Exonerates himself from participation in any commotion in Norfolk.

Sept. 18.
Lees.
61. Richard Lord Rich (Lord Chancellor) to same. Directs that Essex and Nich. More, two prisoners, be sent to Brentwood for trial; and to know where each should be executed.

Sept. 18.
Warwick Lane.
62. Sir Edw. Wotton to same. In favor of Hugh Darrel for the office of Bailiff of certain lands in Kent, void by the death of Deryng, late Bailiff there.

DOMESTIC—EDWARD VI. 23

Vol. VIII.

1549.
Sept. (28?) Hatfield.
63. Tho. Parry to Wm. Cecill. Transmits a letter from Princess Elizabeth to Somerset. Her commendations to Cecill. Parry assures Cecill of his friendship. The Princess will not yet remove to Ashridge.

Sept. 25.
64. Same to same. Interview of the Venetian Amb. with the Princess Elizabeth. She requests the Lord Protector may be informed of it.

Sept. 28.
65. Sir Fr. Dawtrey to same. Prays for a licence for a thousand tons of wine.

Sept. ?
66. The King "to certen speciall men in the Shires where tumultes and rysinges have byn." Directs the proclamation against idle vagabonds to be strictly enforced, and all stirrers up of tumults to be hanged without delay.

Sept.
67. Sir Harry Hussey to Cecill; in behalf of Ric. Cooke and John Francis for certain goods taken from them in France.

Sept. (?)
68. Edw. Morley to Sir T. Smith. Solicits payment of the annuity of 10*l*. per ann., granted to his wife out of Sherburn House, with all arrears. Dr. Bellasis has become possessor of the said House since the death of Dr. Legh.

Vol. IX. October—December, 1549.

Oct. 1. Hampton Court.
1. Proclamation, signed by the King, commanding all his loving subjects to repair to Hampton Court to defend him and the Lord Protector.

Oct. 5.
2. The same, to all Justices of Peace, Mayors, Sheriffs, &c. Certified copy of the above.

Oct. 5. Hampton Court.
3. The King to Sir Hen. Seymour. Warrant to raise men and to bring them to the Court without delay, to suppress a conspiracy. Signed by the King's stamp

Oct. 5. Hampton Court.
4. Somerset to his servant Golding. Orders to assemble the Earl of Oxford's servants for the King's service.

Oct. 5. Hampton Court.
5. Same to Lord Russell and Sir Wm. Herbert. Desires their presence, with their servants.

Oct. 6. Hampton Court.
6. Same to same. Describes the conspiracy which has arisen against the King. Desires them to hasten to Court.

Oct. 6. Hampton Court.
7. Same to same. Sends his son, Sir Edw. [Seymour], to inform them of the state the King is in.

Oct. 6. Hampton Court.
8. The King to the same. To attend with all the force they can raise, to defend him and Somerset.

Oct. 6. Hampton Court.
9. Same to same. Urges them to hasten to his defence. The conspirators report that Somerset has sold Boulogne.

Oct. 6. London.
10. The Council in London to . Directions to declare to the people the treasons of Somerset, and to be ready to repair to London.

1549.	Vol. IX.
Oct. (7?)	11. Address, signed Henry A., to the people of England, exhorting them not to be carried away by the crafty policy of traitors who have conspired to depose the Lord Protector. Indorsed "A seditious bill found in London," addressed, " Rede it and gyve it furth."
Oct. (7?)	12. Another address to the people, calling on them to defend the King and the Lord Protector.
Oct. (7?)	13. "A device for letters to be sent from the King to the Nobilitie " in favour of the Duke of Somerset."
Oct. (7?)	14. Minutes of various transactions, in the same hand as the preceding. Lord St. John (Lord Great Master) takes possession of the Tower; Sir Thos. Darcy committed, &c.
Oct. 7. Windsor Castle.	15. The King to the Bailiffs and Constables of Uxbridge, &c.; to levy all the force in their power, especially archers, and to bring them well victualled to Windsor Castle.
Oct. 7. Windsor Castle.	16. Somerset to the Council. Marvels that they have stayed Sir Wm. Petre, and have returned no answer to the message sent by him. Every reasonable condition will be granted by the King.
Oct. 7.	17. The Council to the King. Have heard his message sent by Petre. They are grieved his Majesty should doubt their fidelity to him. The only cause of their consulting together is to get rid of Somerset. [Draft, partly in Petre's, partly in Wriothesley's hand.]
Oct. 7.	18. 19. Two copies of the above.
Oct. 7. London.	20. Same to the Sheriff of . Declaring the treasons of Somerset, who endeavoured to levy great numbers of men for the purpose of compassing his treasons. Directs the Sheriff not to suffer any of the King's subjects to be raised, but by their order.
Oct. 7. London.	21. Same to the Justices of Peace. To the same effect.
Oct. 7. London.	22. Same to Archbp. Cranmer and Lord Paget, at Windsor. Protest their loyalty; are willing to treat with Somerset, if he will absent himself from the King, disperse his forces, and submit.
Oct. 8. Andover.	23. Lord Russell and Sir Wm. Herbert to Somerset. Are sorry for the dissensions between him and the Nobility. Have received advertisement from the Lords in London that they intend no displeasure against the King. They mislike Somerset's proclamations for raising the Commons, &c.
Oct. 8. Windsor Castle.	24. The King to the Council in London. Laments the present state of affairs. Somerset means no hurt to his royal person, therefore thinks it not wise to proceed to extremity against him. *Incloses,*
	24. I. *Articles offered by the Lord Protector to the King, in presence of the Council and others, at Windsor, to be declared to the Lords, &c. remaining in London. Oct. 8. Signed by the King.*
Oct. 8. Windsor Castle.	25. 25. I. Copy of the King's letter to the Lords, and Somerset' articles.

1549.

VOL. IX.

Oct. 8.
Windsor Castle.
26. Cranmer, Paget, and Sir T. Smith to the Council, in answer to their letter of the 7th. Explain the state of both parties; and assert their own loyalty. Somerset is willing to resign the office of Protector.

Oct. 8.
Windsor Castle.
27. Sir T. Smith to Secretary Petre. Urges him to moderation: the Protector is willing to resign his office. Entreats that the realm should not be in one year made the scene of a double tragedy.

Oct. 8.
London.
28. The Council to the Sheriff, Justices, &c. of Counties. Directions not to levy any forces, under authority of the King's hand, stamp, and signet, the same having been abused by the D. of Somerset, unless signed by the Privy Council.

Oct. 8.
29. Duplicate of the above.

Oct. 8.
Mark-hall.
30. Harry Lord Morley to the Council. Will hold himself ready to defend the King at an hour's warning.

Oct. 9.
Wilton.
31. Lord Russell and Sir Wm. Herbert to the same. The country in great uncertainty and confusion. Have stayed all the forces of the Western parts from going to the Protector's assistance. Request directions. *Inclosing,*

Oct. 9.
Wilton.
31. I. *Russell and Herbert to the Sheriff of Gloucester and other Sheriffs; to suppress the publication of any idle rumours within that county; and to forbid all persons from assembling without due authority.*

Oct. 9.
Wilton.
32. Copy of the above.

Oct. 9.
33. The Council to the Princesses Mary and Elizabeth. Set forth the alleged malpractices of the Lord Protector, and express their trust that their Graces will adhere to their party against him.

Oct. 9.
34. Copy of the above.

Oct. 9.
35. The same to the King, in answer to his letter of the 8th. The present troubles arise entirely from Somerset. Profess their loyal attachment, and require that the forces assembled by the Protector be sent away, and they, the Lords, be recalled to his Majesty's presence.

Oct. 9.
36. Copy of the above.

Oct. 9.
Westminster.
37. Same to Cranmer and Paget. Desire them to be careful not to suffer the King to be removed from Windsor. They marvel that he should remain under Somerset's protection. Exhort them to join in measures for the King's protection.

Oct. 9.
38. Copy of the above.

Oct. (9?)
Windsor Castle.
39. Smith to Petre. Begs him to appease the present disturbances. Expresses the difficult position he is in.

Oct. 10.
40. Proclamation, by the Council in London, against the putting forth seditious bills and papers for aiding the traitorous acts of the Duke of Somerset.

1549.

Oct. 11.	41. Minute of the whole discourse of the Duke of Somerset's doings; addressed to the Ambassadors. [*A Proclamation by the Council in London, dated on the 8th of October, (which is not preserved among the State Papers,) declaring the whole of the treasonable acts of the Duke of Somerset, is extant in the Library of the Society of Antiquaries, London.*]
Oct. 11. Windsor.	42. Cranmer, Paget, and Sir Anth. Wyngfeld (Vice-Chamberlain) to the Council. Arrest of Somerset, and removal of his family. Particulars of the King's health and deportment.
Oct. 11.	43. Copy of the above.
Oct. 11. London.	44. The Council to . Directions to stay their forces. The King is in health and safety, and Somerset in custody.
Oct. 14.	45. Same to the Lieut. of the Tower. To suffer no one to speak with Somerset, or the other prisoners. Their servants not to be suffered to go abroad.
Oct. 16.	46. Same to the Lords Lieuts. of certain Counties, to levy men for the service at Boulogne, and to select those who had been ringleaders in the late commotions.
Oct. 16.	47. List of Counties and of the numbers to be raised therein for Boulogne. With minute for the Lord Warden (Sir Thos. Cheyne) and Dr. Wotton to be sent to the Emperor, to declare the causes of Somerset's removal. [*By a Minute of Council, it appears that Sir Ph. Hoby was sent instead of Wotton.*]
Oct. 22.	48. Report of prisoners in the Tower, with the causes of their commitment, and directions in the margin for their disposal, with a list of those lately committed.
Oct. 31. Westminster.	49. The Council to the Captain of the Isle of Scilly (Mr. Godolphin), to inform Sir Ric. Southwell and Sir Edw. North of the state of his charge there, and to follow their directions.
Oct. (31).	50. List of different Governments and Commanders, to which letters similar to the above were addressed, and of the Councillors with whom they are to correspond.
Oct.	51. Remembrance of certain duties pertaining to the Earl of Warwick, as Constable of Dover, Lord Warden, and Admiral of the Cinque Ports.
Oct. (?)	52. Information given to the Council, of the conveying away of goods, &c. belonging to Protector Somerset, from his houses at Sion and Shene.
Oct. (?)	53. Information given by Sir Walter Mildmay of certain stuff, money and plate of the King's, which the Duke of Somerset appropriated to his own use.
Nov. (5).	54. A memorial for William Tirrell, sent to the Scilly Isles for survey of the same.
Nov. 20. Westminster.	55. The Council to the Justices of the Shires. Directions to search all barns, &c. for corn, and to compel a sufficient supply to be brought to market, and to apprehend all regrators and forestallers.

VOL. IX.

1549.
Nov. 27. 56. The Council to the Justices of Peace of certain Shires; to arrest such of the new levies for Boulogne as have returned without passport.

Dec. 25.
Westminster. 57. The King and Council to the Bishops. Reports, since the apprehension of Somerset, that the old Latin service and Popish superstitions are to be restored. The Bishops to command the clergy to bring in all the books of the old Church services, and to enforce obedience to the King's ordinances.

Dec. 28.
Kingston. 58. Duchess of Suffolk to Cecill. Received his letters on horseback, as she was going to Mr. Bucer's. Friendly conversation. Promises poor [Dr.] Cornelius shall have his money. On the back of this letter is copy of one addressed by Cecill to Cornelius, advising him to take heed of his diet; their hope comes slowly forward; sends him the Duchess's letter.

1549 (?) 59. The names of all the almsmen of Christ's Church, Oxford, what they be, and their abiding places.

VOL X. JANUARY—OCTOBER, 1550.

1550.
Feb. 21. 1. Indenture of assignment from Dr. John Storye to Sir Wm. Herbert (Master of the Horse), of the lease of the Prebend of Tottenhall or Tottenham Court, within the Church of St. Paul's, London.

March 6. Grant of Arms to Richard Elken, of London, by Sir Gilbert Dethick, Garter King-at-Arms. [*Grant of Arms*, No. 6.]

March 25.
Cottage of Kingston. 2. Duchess of Suffolk to Cecill. He has set her greatest fear at rest, relative to Somerset's matter with the Council. Has heard that there is hope of his being called shortly to the Council, &c. [*Somerset was restored to the Council on the 10th of April 1550.*]

March 25.
Salisbury. 3. John [Salcott or Capon] Bishop of Salisbury to same; cannot grant his request in favour of Mr. Brown for the next vacant prebend. Has already granted two advocations, one to Sir Wm. Herbert, the other to Dr. Oking, his Chancellor.

April 23.
London. 4. Sir John Thynne to same; in favour of Mr. Lok, for a benefice in Somersetshire.

April 27.
Kingston. 5. Duchess of Suffolk to same. Thanks are due to Somerset for appointing a hearing of the matter between Fulmerton and Nawnton. The right is with her friend, whose cause she recommends.

May 9.
Kingston. 6. Same to same. Much desires a match between Somerset's daughter and her son, but wishes to let the parties have their free choice.

May 12. 7. Particular of the rental of the manor of Cheatham (Chatham?), co. Kent, for one whole year.

May 18.
Kingston. 8. Duchess of Suffolk to Cecill. Desires his opinion touching the purchase of Spilsby Chantry, according to Lord Paget's advice.

June 26.
Ware. 9. Ric. Whalley to same. Details particulars of an interview with Warwick, relative to the proceedings of the D. of Somerset. Blames Somerset's endeavours to procure the enlargement of Bishop Gardyner and Lord Arundel, and his efforts to regain his former power.

DOMESTIC—EDWARD VI.

VOL. X.

1550.

June 30.
Baston.
10. Randoll Lynne to Wm. Cecill. The inhabitants of Baston, co. Lincoln, are willing to contribute towards the erection of a chapel, and hope he will make it their parish church.

July 1.
11. Ric. Whalley to same. Begs to know when Somerset begins his journey to Reading, and his circuit westward.

July 8.
12. Sir Tho. Parry to same. The Princess Elizabeth thanks Somerset for his remembrance of her. Parry would not have solicited the office of the Princesses Keeper at Hatfield, if she had not freely given it to him. She will pass Mr. Cecill's patent of Surveyor under her hand and seal.

July (19?)
13. Case for legal opinion as to a lease of the rectory of Dale, during the sequestration of the Bishop.

July 19.
14. Sentence of sequestration of Stephen Gardyner from his Bishoprick of Winchester.

July 24.
Leighs.
15. Attested copy of Letters Patent, granted by Edward VI., for founding a Dutch Church in London, for the pure interpretation of the Scriptures and administration of the Holy Sacraments. Lat.

July 24.
16. Translation of the above, in French.

July 24.
Leighes.
17. Grant to Sir Thomas Wrothe, Gent. of the Privy Chamber, of the manor of Bardfield, with the Great and Little Park thereof, and the manors of Chigwell and Westhatche, co. Essex. [*On the back of the second leaf is a draft (temp. Ch. I.?) of the bond of Hughe Justyce, plumber, to keep in repair the waterworks at Oxford and Carfoxe, made at the charge of Otho Nicholson.*]

July 24.
Lee.
18. John Eason to Cecill. Details and explains his transactions connected with the disgrace of Somerset. Examinations before the Council. Ill feeling of the Chalenors towards Cecill and himself. Desires to be restored to his friendship.

Aug. 2.
Wells.
19. John Goodman (Dean of Wells) to Mr Barwyke. Desires him speedily to inform Somerset of the conduct of Wm. Barlow, Bishop of Bath. *Incloses,*

19. I. *Brief notes of the unseemly reports of the Bishop of Bath declared by him to sundry persons against the Duke of Somerset.*

Aug. 5.
Wells.
20. Same to same. Further charges against Bishop Barlow, who is determined to retain the Lordship of Wells.

Aug. 8.
Ersbye.
21. Duchess of Suffolk to Cecill. Has received his letters and heard his ill news with regret.

Aug. 9.
Venice.
22. Sir Rob. Stafford to same. Congratulates him on the favourable termination of his late adversity, which he has just heard of by Yaxley.

Aug. 16.
Reading.
23. Thos. Fisher to same. Has been at Banbury to superintend Somerset's works there. Is detained at Reading by the illness of his wife.

Sept. 3.
Stamford.
24. Duchess of Suffolk to same. Thanks him for his gentle deportment towards her cousin Nawnton. Has resolved to allow 40*l.* per annum to Fulmerston.

1550.

Sept. 8
Ersbye.

25. Duchess of Suffolk to Wm. Cecill. Thanks for his letter and the news communicated. Has received and answered Lady Somerset's letter.

Sept. 9.
London.

26. Thos. Birkhed (Vicar of Christ Church) to same. Prays him to intercede with Somerset for some other living near London, either at Westminster or Windsor.

Sept. 10.
London.

27. Charles Lord Stourton to Wm. Cecill, Secretary of State. The bearer, Robert Eton, has served at Newhaven and at Boulogne. Prays Cecill to procure his wages to be paid.

Sept. (14?)

28. Sir Edw. North to same. Begs him to forward Sir Arthur Darcy's lease in reversion. Congratulates him on his new office.

Sept. 14.
Reading.

29. Sir John Thynne to same. Congratulations on his appointment. Desires to resign his Stewardship.

Sept. (15?)

30. Warwick to same. Wonders that the matter of the Proclamation had not been despatched on the coming of the Lord Chancellor. Purposes to take a bath for his health. Will sign anything relating to the proclamation that Somerset, Cecill, and the others resolve upon. [*This letter has no date, but by a Minute in the Council Register of the 14th September 1550, it appears that a letter was sent to Warwick with the draft of the proclamation for bringing in of grain, for him to " amende it as he shall see cause."*]

Sept. 16.
Ely Place.

31. Same to same. Sends the abstract of the writings which came from the B. of D. [Bishop of Durham] and M. [Ninian Menvile] to be submitted to Somerset. Has had conference with the Bishop.

Sept. 18.
Grimsthorp.

32. Duchess of Suffolk to same. Fears that Naunton may have fallen under Somerset's displeasure; prays Cecil will deliver him from that position.

Sept. 22.
Asheridge.

33. Thos. Parry to same. Writes by command of Princess Elizabeth in favour of John Ronyon (yeoman of her robes) for the parsonage of East Harptree, Somerset. Her Grace has been indisposed.

Sept. 27.
London.

34. Wm. Turner to same. Prays to be preferred to the Presidentship of Mag. Coll. Oxford, if the Archdeaconry of the East Riding of York, vacant by the death of Thos. Magnus, should be given to Dr. Oglethorpe. *Lat.*

Sept. 28.
Tykyncote.

35. Harry Digby to same. Solicits him to admit his son Jasper to be at his commandment.

Sept. 30.

36. Ric. Goodrick to same. Difficulty in getting assurance of Mr. Grey's lands. Offers to be Cecill's agent for the purchase of two houses that Lord Paget has in Chanon Row.

Oct. 1.
Tatershall Castle.

37. Duchess of Suffolk to same. Desires a commission to determine a controversy between her and the inhabitants of East Deeping, for a marsh and common in her Lordship of Pinchbeck.

Oct. 2.
Tatershall.

38. Same to same. In favour of the bearer, for expedition of a suit in Jersey; until the bearer returns to his garden she can have neither salads nor sweet herbs.

DOMESTIC—EDWARD VI.

Vol. X.

1550.

Oct. 2.
Tatershall.
39. Duchess of Suffolk to Wm. Cecill. Congratulates him on the success of his exchanges, and having come to a good market (alluding to his office of Secretary). Is fitting out a ship at Boston.

Oct. 2.
Oatlands.
40. The Council to special persons in every County, directing them to enforce execution of the proclamation for reducing the high price of corn and other commodities.

Oct. 2.
Oatlands.
41. Minute of the above.

Oct. 2.
Oatlands.
42. Same to the Justices of Peace, to the same effect.

Oct. 3.
Oatlands.
43. Same to the Lords Lieutenants of Counties, informing them of the two preceding letters; with similar directions.

Oct. 5.
44. Ric. Goodrick to Cecill. Beseeches him to discharge Mr. Grey. Sends draft of the indenture between Cecill and Mr. Pope, for a house of Lord Paget's.

Oct. 8.
Richmond.
45. Warrant to Sir Edm. Pekham to deliver to Sir John York (Treasurer of the Mint in Southwark) all such coin as shall be made of bullion brought by him into the Mint.

Oct. 8.
Tatershall.
46. Duchess of Suffolk to Cecill. Is grieved by Somerset's dealing in the matter between her cousin Naunton and Fulmerston. Blames his Grace's Lady for it.

Oct. 12.
Grantham.
47. William Rede, minister of God's word at Grantham, to same. Is disturbed by Mr. Armstrong in some chantry land attached to his residence, there being no mansion-house belonging to the vicarage of Grantham.

Oct. 23.
Sydmanton.
48. John Kyngysmyll to same. In favour of the bearer, who is ill-used by the Parson of Broughton, at the instigation of John Coke and John Richards, for giving certain information to the Council.

Oct. 26.
49. Tho. Lord Lawarre to same. Begs him to forward certain letters to the Duke of Somerset and the Council.

Vol. XI. November—December, 1550.

Nov. 2.
Pinchbeck.
1. Ric. Ogle to Cecill. Has sent him four marks for the fees of Toft and Gosberkyrke. Thanks for kindness to his daughter.

Nov. 5.
2. John Beamont to same. Desires to occupy a piece of land under him. Certain slanders have been reported of him, Beamont.

Nov. 14.
3. Tho. Lord Lawarre to same. Proceedings in executing the orders for taking up grain for victualling Calais and other places in France, for six months.

Nov. 15.
Stamford.
4. Duchess of Suffolk to same. Desires an amended warrant for Spilsby Chantry.

Nov. 17.
Westminster.
5. The Council to special persons in each County, appointing them Commissioners to enforce the execution of the King's proclamation for bringing grain, butter, cheese, &c. to the markets.

	VOL. XI.
1550.	
Nov. 17. Westminster.	6. The Council to the Lords Lieuts. of Counties. Concerning the execution of the proclamation for grain.
Nov. 18.	7. List of the messengers that carried the letters concerning grain.
Nov. 19. Westminster.	8. Demise to Ralph Sherman, Yeoman of the Ewry, of the rectories of Braifelde (late of the Monastery of St. Andrew's, in Northampton), Wenlingburghe (late of the Monastery of Croyland), Woolaston and Barton Yerles (late of the Monastery of De la Prey), in co. Northampton, for 21 years, after the expiration of the interest therein granted to William Lord Parr of Horton. Lat.
Nov. 19 Stamford.	9. Duchess of Suffolk to Cecill. Thanks for what he has done in her cousin Naunton's cause.
Nov. 19. Offington.	10. Lord Lawarre and Edw. Shelley to same. Delay in executing the proclamation for grain, &c., owing to the number of Justices of Peace now absent in London. Have begun a survey of the contents of the barns. Deficiency both of barley and malt.
Nov. 19 Boston.	11. Mayor. &c. of Boston to same. In great distress for want of wheat and other grain. Pray for licence to buy grain in other shires.
Nov. 23. Beaulieu.	12. Princess Mary to Lord . States her reasons for not wishing to change her present residence. Was driven from Wansted by one dying of the plague there. Thanks him for the offer of one of the King's houses. [1550 ?]
Nov. 28 Newark-on-Trent.	13. Wm. Rygges to Cecill. Exculpates himself from any intention of giving offence. Cecill would not be displeased relative to the quit rents, if he knew the circumstances.
Nov. 28	14. Wm. Turner to same. Remarks on his non-appointment to either Magdalen or Oriel Colleges. The Papists will live their time in the College benefices. Begs Cecill will sue for no more benefices for him. Proposes to go into Germany, and offers to correct the whole New Testament, and finish other works.
Dec. 6. Westminster.	15. The King and Council to the Justices of Peace. The former proclamation relative to grain, butter, and cheese is revoked, and the matter left to the discretion of buyers and sellers.
Dec. 20. Boston.	16. Mayor, &c. of Boston to Cecill. Thanks for his forbearance towards them in not entering their lands, pending the suit between the King and themselves.
Dec. (20?)	17. Draft of a Bill in Parliament for the better administration of justice by Sheriffs and Bailiffs.

VOL. XII.

1550.	MS. intituled "A discussion of Mr. Hoper's oversight, where he entreeteth amonge his other Sermons the matter of the Sacrament of the Bodye and Bloode of Christe, 1550." These answers to Hoper's arguments are by Gardyner, Bp. of Winchester.

Vol. XIII:—1551.

1551.
Jan. 5.
Somerset Place.
1. Wm. Turner to Wm. Cecill. Opinion of Archbp. Cranmer that the Bishop of Bath had no authority to depose the Dean. The lawyers of the Arches Court will obstruct him in succeeding to the Deanery.

Jan. 16.
Westminster.
2. Licence by the King for John Earl of Warwick to sell the manor of Lydney, co. Gloucester, to Sir Wm. Herbert.

Jan. 18.
London.
3. Wm. Lane, merchant of London, to Cecill. Concerning several matters affecting the interests of the realm. Project for debasing the coin, exchanges, commerce, &c.

Jan. 20.
4. Walter Bower to Wm. Turner, doctor of physic. The President of their College has desired to know their mind if they will be content to retain him for their head. Solicits Turner to use all his influence to obtain it. Objections to Mr. Harley.

Feb. 8.
Blankeney.
5. Thos. Husey to Cecill. Has received by his nephew Thorold his pleasure touching the lease of Caythropp Park. Desires an impartial hearing in the difference between him and Nicholas Bayly.

Feb. 17.
Cambridge.
6 Duchess of Suffolk to same. Begs his aid in forwarding a letter of Martin Bucer's, who is sick. [*Bucer died on the 27th of February 1551. There is a Minute of Council of the 31st of March, directing Mrs. Bucer to be paid her husband's half year's pension due to him at Lady Day last, " although he died before."*]

March 4.
Ingatestone.
7. Sir Wm. Petre to same. Is sorry for the news contained in his letters. Thanks him for a book. His little ones, when they are able, shall send him some proof of their progress.

March 4.
8. Memoranda relating to various matters of business.

March 23.
9. Patent by the King, constituting John Poynet, Bishop of Rochester, Bishop of Winchester, in place of Stephen Gardyner, deprived. Lat.

March (?)
10. Two papers of Memoranda of matters for the Privy Council.

March (?)
11. Remembrances for the Council; of the same period as the preceding.

March (?)
12. Another paper of Memoranda of matters for the consideration of the Council; fuller than the last.

April 17.
13. John Hoper, Bishop of Gloucester, to Cecill. Urges him to oppose the grant of any licence for one man to hold two livings. Laments the dearth and scarcity of provisions. Requests license to eat flesh upon fish days, for himself and John Samford.

May 2.
Pinchbeck.
14. Ric. Ogle to same. Sends him the deed for the Recordership of Boston, and also his fees as Steward of the manors of Toft and Gosberkyrk. Lady Suffolk was never so well served therein as now.

May 14.
Ratcliff.
15. Edw. Lord Clynton (Lord Admiral) to same. Beseeches him to forward a certain matter for Mr. Wynbeshe, and also that the parsonage of Oldkirk near Calais may be reserved during his absence.

Vol. XIII.

1551.
May 14. East Thorndon. 16. Sir Wm. Petre to Wm. Cecill. Thanks for his letters, especially for the news that his health is recovered.

May 15. Westminster. 17. Wm. Earl of Wiltshire (Lord Treasurer) to same. Has written to Bishop Tunstall and the Dean of Durham to be at the Court on Monday. Other points of business. Sir Robt. Brandling to attend.

May 20. Sempringham. 18. Lord Clynton to same. Requests dispatch in Wynbeshe's matter. Wishes to be informed what personage is coming from France.

May 22. Wells. 19. Wm. Turner (Dean of Wells) to same. Will help "Acanthinus," the person recommended to be schoolmaster at Wells. Mr. Cardmaker will favor him. Describes the opposition he has met with in taking possession of the Deanery. The canons annoy him and favor Goodman.

May 22. Bourne. 20. Sir Anth. Auchar to same. Illness has prevented him from coming to the Court. Advises him to go through with Ballerd as to some purchase.

May 24. Bourne. 21. Same to same. Particulars of the rental of Horton; Ballerd has some land adjoining; advises Cecill to take both.

May 24. Lees. 22. Lord Chancellor Rich to Lord Trev. Wiltshire. Has despatched the Commission and Instructions for the Lord Marquis (Dorset) and the Commission of Lieutenancy for Kent to the Lord Warden (Sir Thos. Cheyne) only.

May 25. Bourne. 23. Sir A. Auchar to same. Intends to be at the Court on Thursday. Wishes to know how he proceeds with his purchase.

May 25. Gloucester. 24. Bishop Hoper to same. Pernicious doctrines set forth by one Thomas Penne. Commends the bearer, Mr. Restell, alderman of Gloucester. *Incloses,*

24. I. *Articles of Religion set forth and upheld by Thos. Penne particularly as to the human nature of the Saviour.* May 25.

May 28. Sempringham. 25. Lord Clynton to same. Thanks for despatch of Mr. Wynbeshe. Wishes to know when the French Ambassador will arrive.

May (?) 26. Sir Ric. Rede and others to same. Certificates in favor of John Gunwyne, as a person of learning, having diligently studied at Oxford and Cambridge.

June 17. 27. Form of Oath subscribed by John Scorey, Bishop Elect of Rochester, taken before the King.

June 17. 28. Copy of the above.

July 1. Lenwich. 29. The King to the Sheriffs of Counties, commanding them not to break the seal of the writ then sent them until the morning of the 8th instant. Indorsed, "M. to the Shryves for the pclaiming of the pclamacōn for coyne." [*This was a proclamation dated in June, but without a day of the month, for reducing immediately the value of the teston or shilling to 9d., and the groat to 3d.*]

July 18. Hampton Court. 30. The King and Council to the Bishops. Desiring them to exhort the people to a diligent attendance at Common Prayer, and so to avert the displeasure of Almighty God, He having visited the realm with the "extreme plague of sudden death."

1551.		VOL. XIII.
July 20. Hampton Court.		31. The King and Council to Sheriffs of Counties. To put the laws in force against Regrators, Forestallers, &c., according to the Proclamation..
July 31. Bonham.		32. Roger Basyng and others to the Council. Proceedings of the Sheriff of Wilts. Mrs. Ryse keeps forcible possession of the manor place of Stourton against Mr. Fauntleroy. Taunting speeches of Wm. Hartgill.
Aug. (11 ?)		33. Proclamation for still further reducing the teston or shilling to 6d. sterling, the groat to 2d., the 2d. to one penny, &c.
Aug. 12. Hampton Court.		34. The King and Council to the Sheriff of commanding him not to break open the writ to him addressed until 16th Aug. instant. ·Indorsed, "For proclayming the coyne downe."
Aug. 29.		35. Report of the Lord Chancellor Rich, Sir Anth. Wingfield, Comptroller, and Sir Wm. Petre, of the execution of their charge to visit the Princess Mary at her house at Copthall, Essex, and to forbid that Mass should be performed in her house, &c. [*Injured by damp. The above Report, and the letters between the King and Princess Mary on the subject, are entered at length in the Council Register, Edw. VI., Vol. 3., pp. 360, 364, 381.*]
Aug. 29.		36. Copy of the above.
Sept. 3. Sempringham.		37. Lord Clynton to Cecill. Arrest of seditious persons in Stamford. Recommends him to send for and examine them.
Sept. 7. Lincoln.		38. Sir Francis Ayscough and others to same. As arbitrators with Sir Edw. Dymoke in the matter between Mr. Dyon and the Vicar of Taithwell, co. Lincoln, have not yet been able to determine the case.
Sept. 9. Putney.		39. Ric. Goodrick to same. Is left sole solicitor in Mr. Morrisyn's affair; desires a warrant for 600l. for his diet.
Sept. 9. London.		40. Sir Wm. Petre to same. Recommends the bearer, who desires to succeed to the Mastership of the Savoy. [*Sir Robt. Bowes was nominated on the 24th of October following. Co. Reg.*]
Sept. 10. Scilly Isles.		41. John Kyllygrew, junr., to same. Requests more money for payment of the works at Scilly. Begs to know if he is to keep any men at work during winter.
Sept. 13. Lincoln.		42. J. Dyon to same. Transmits the letter of the arbitrators in the matter between him and the Vicar of Taithwell, by whom he has been maliciously slandered.
Sept. 14. London.		43. Sir Wm. Petre to same. Thanks for his pains in the matter of the Savoy. Sends draft of a commission for visitation of that house. Begs him to take charge of some papers relative to the Bishop of Durham's cause.
Sept. 16. Fulham.		44. Nich. Ridley, Bp. of London, to same. Playfully promises to spare him half a dozen trees. Complains of spoil made in the woods belonging to his See.

DOMESTIC—EDWARD VI. 35

1551. VOL. XIII.

Sept. 21.
Denton.
45. Geo. Williams to Wm. Cecill. Has taken order for repair of the Chancel of Ewrby. Rigges, the auditor, has felled some ash trees in the King's lordship of Cathrop.

Sept. 19.
Guildford.
46. Bartholomew Traheron to same. Solicits the King's letter to the Prebendaries of Chichester in his favor. [*On the 2d of October the Council wrote to the Prebendaries directing them to elect Mr. Traheron as their Dean. Co. Reg.*]

Sept. 25.
47. The Council to Sir Edm. Pekham. The matter of the coinage has been submitted to the King. Directions thereon relative to the standard and impressions of the coin.

Sept. (25?)
Oatlands.
48. Council with the King to the Council in London. Sending up Tho. Troughton to be put in the pillory for sedition on the next market day in London. [*The Council only held two sittings at Oatlands, in Sept. 1551, viz., on the 24th and 25th.*]

Sept. 26.
London.
49. Sir Ric. Rede and Ric. Lyell to Cecill. Have sent the commission (for trial of the matters of the Bishops Heath of Worcester and Day of Chichester), and request directions.

Sept. (26?)
50. Names of Commissioners for examination of the Bishops of Chichester and Worcester, and names of those eligible for the two Archbishopricks in Ireland. [*Some names selected by the King himself.*]

Sept. 27.
51. Ric. Goodrick to Cecill. Confides in his friendship. Knows not what suit Mr. Cheke has made, but he himself had made suit for the same matter. Mr. Cheke's unkindness has thrown him into a fit of illness.

Sept. 28.
[4 Kal. Oct.]
52. Ric. Alan to same. Has been incarcerated for four months, and deprived of the use of ink and paper. Prays for his liberation. Lat.

Sept. 30.
Ingatestone.
53. Sir Wm. Petre to same. Is not able to travel towards the Court. Recommends Lady Southampton's suit. *Incloses,*

53 I. *Jane Countess of Southampton to Petre. Complains that Hierom Colas, French teacher to her children, has left her service; begs he may be compelled to return. Subbarton, Sept. 23.*

Sept. (?)
Grimsthorp.
Monday.
54. Duchess of Suffolk to same. Is thankful to God for all his benefits. Her resignation under this last sharp and bitter trial (the death of her two sons, ob. 14 July). Thanks Cecill for his friendship.

Oct. 1.
55. The King to Lord Chanc. Rich. Desires to know why execution of the commission for trial of the causes of the Bishops of Worcester and Chichester has been so long delayed. What the King directs, by advice of his Council, though less than eight in number, is of sufficient authority.

Oct. 1.
56. Copy of the above.

Oct. 11.
Hampton Court.
Ceremonies on the creation of Henry Grey Duke of Suffolk, John Sutton (Duddeley) Duke of Northumberland, William Paulett Marq. of Winchester, and Sir William Herbert Earl of Pembroke; and the making of Sir Wm. Cecill, Sir John Cheke, Sir Henry Sidney, and Sir Henry Nevil, Knights. [*See 2 Sept. 1554.*]

VOL. XIII.

1551.
Oct. (16?) Westminster.
57. The Council to Justices of Peace. Declaration of the detestable attempts of the Duke of Somerset against the State. Committal of him to the Tower; as also Lord Grey, Sir Ralph Fane, and others.

Oct. 19. Northampton.
58. John Hanbie to Sir William Cecill. Particulars of the demise of Pyckeworth Outfield and Pyckeworth Infield, co. Rutland, parcel of the late Lord Hussey's lands, and other lands, parcel of the monastery of Oulveston, co. Leicester, claimed by Sir John Harrington and Edm. Hall. *Has no survey of the manor of Barrodon, granted to the ¡Princess Elizabeth.*

Oct. 20
59. Certificate, by inhabitants of Thorpe and Achurch, attested by Geo. Williams, of the amount of tithes claimed and paid for the close called the Great Coneynger, appertaining to the manor place of Thorpe-waterfelde, Northampton.

[Oct. 20.]
60. Note of timber required to mend the barn and mill at Thorpe Achurch.

[Oct. 20.]
61. Estimate of timber and carpenters wages for the above work.

Oct. (?)
62. [   ] to Cecill. Detail of his proceedings with Edward Marsh, parson of Swafield, relative to the apportionment of the tithes of Belton. *Incloses,*

> 62 I. *Declaration of Harry Laughton and Nich. Topper of the proportion of tithes of Belton, in the fields of Swafield, due to the parsonage of Corby, co. Lincoln. May 27.*

Oct. (?)
63. List of the new Commissioners for visitation of Oxford.

Nov. 24.
64. The King to Lord Chancr Rich. Directions to make out a commission under the Great Seal, for trial of the Duke of Somerset and others for high treason.

Nov. (?)
65. Deposition of   Crane relative to the alledged treasonable proceedings of the Duke of Somerset, the Earl of Arundel, &c.

Nov. (?)
66. Report by divers Lords of the Council of the deposition of the Earl of Arundel, prisoner in the Tower, relative to certain conferences between him and the Duke of Somerset.

Nov. (?)
67. Further report of the depositions of the Earl of Arundel, relative to the plot devised by the Duke of Somerset for seizing Northumberland and Northampton at the Council.

Nov. (?)
68. Charges against Mr. Kymball, mayor of Cambridge, of factious conduct towards the University, disclosing the Council's letters, making untrue reports to the Duke of Northumberland (Chancellor of Cambridge), and following the seditious courses of Roger Slegge, a common disturber. [*On the 9th of Nov.* 1551, *the Privy Council wrote lette to the townsmen of Cambridge to observe the privileges granted to the students. Co. Reg.*]

Dec. 1. Wotton.
69. Roger Lees (Bailiff of Wotton under Wyver, co. Stafford) to Sir W. Cecill. Rejoices that the King has given him the manor of Wotton.

Dec. 11.
70. Valerand Pollan (Superintendant of the Community of Flemish weavers settled at Glastonbury in Somersetshire) to the Council. Prays that the promises and articles entered into with them by the Duke of Somerset, may be carried into effect. Lat.

DOMESTIC—EDWARD VI. 37

1551.   VOL. XIII.

     71. Copy of the Covenants entered into by the Duke of Somerset at the instance of Valerand Pollan, for settlement of the Flemish weavers at Glastonbury. Lat. [*Probably the document referred to in the preceding article.*]

Dec. (18?) 72. Valerand Pollan to the Council. Prays for a grant of 131*l.* and 9*d.* to pay their debts contracted in England. Lat.

Dec. (18?) 73. Same to Sir W. Petre. Prays that he will forward their petition. Lat.

Dec. 18. 74. The Council to Wm. Barlow, Bishop of Bath, Sir Hugh Poulet,
Westminster. Sir John Seyntlow, Sir Tho. Dyer, and Alex. Popham. To supply the foreigners at Glastonbury with fit habitations in Orwell Park. Money advanced to them for the purchase of Wools, &c.

Dec. 18. 75. Minute of the above, *in Petre's hand.*

Dec. 18. 76. Same to Wm. Crouch, (receiver of the D. of Somerset's revenues)
Westminster. to pay the superintendent of the Strangers at Glastonbury certain sums to the amount of 340*l.*, for provision of wool, &c.

Dec. 18. 77. Minute of the above.

Dec. (?) 78. Depositions of Gregory Shard and Eliz. Tracy, relative to a plot to destroy the King.

Dec. (?) 79. Memoranda of business for the Privy Council.

1551 ? 80. Petition of the Merchants of the Staple to the King for renewal of their Charter for thirty years on payment of 1,000*l.* in three years.

(?) 81. Statement of the causes of the great decay of the Fellowship of the Staple, by reason of the burthens imposed upon them, and by the importation of Spanish wools.

(?) 82. Statement of "Dyvars good consyderations why wollen clothes "hathe been excepted from subsydews in all Parliaments."

1552.   VOL. XIV.—JANUARY—AUGUST 1552.

Jan. 8. 1. John Duke of Northumberland to Sir Wm. Cecill. Directions to
Ely Place. send letters to Lord Conyers to attend the Parliament; Sir Ingram Clifford to be Captain of Carlisle, and Dep. Warden in his absence. Dispute between the Lord Dep. of Calais and the Duke's brother, Sir And. Duddeley.

Jan. 12. 2. Abstract of Articles touching the Strangers of Glastonbury; addressed to the Council by Bishop Barlow, Sir John Seyntlow, and Alex^r Popham. With a schedule of other requests of the said Strangers.

Jan. 15. 3. Bishop Barlow, Sir John Seyntlow, and Alex^r Popham to the Council. Report on the state of the Strangers at Glastonbury. *Inclosing,*

   3 I. *Articles drawn up as the answer of the Bishop of Bath, Seyntlow, and Popham, relative to the foreigners settled at Glastonbury, describing their present condition, and various things necessary to be done for them.* Jan. 12.

1552.   Vol. XIV.

Jan. 23.	4. Memorandum in the King's handwriting of "Actes for this "Parliemente."
Jan. 27.	5. Northumberland to Sir Wm. Cecill. The Ambassador of France has appointed a meeting that afternoon; the Lords must meet him, or else his coming must be deferred.
Jan. (?)	6. Names of the Lords and others of the Privy Council in 1552.
Feb. (10?)	7. "Memoryall of diverse thinges for the Counsell."
Feb. (?)	8. Another paper of memoranda of matters for the Council. *Nearly duplicate of the above.*
Feb. (?)	9. Similar papers of memoranda.
Feb. 24.	10. Informations exhibited to the Council by the Merchants of England against the Merchants styling themselves of the Hanse or Stillyards.
Feb. (24?)	11. Statement of the causes declared to the King why the Merchants of the Stillyard, called the Merchants of the Hanse, ought not to have any such pretended privileges or liberties as they claim within the realm of England.
March 1.	12. Indenture of Lease between the Dean and Chapter of St. Paul's and Dr. John Denman and others, Churchwardens of St. Faith's, demising to them a certain vault under the Cathedral of St. Paul's, called the *Crowdes* or *Jesus Chapel*, together with the *Chapel of our Lady and St. Nicholas*.
March 3.	13. Orders taken for the Strangers at Glastonbury, Co. Somerset.
March 3.	14. Minutes relating to the same.
March 4.	15. Memorandum of matters to be considered in the Privy Council.
March (?)	16. Names of the Commissioners for execution of Penal Laws and Proclamations; and abstract of their Instructions.
March (?)	17. Instructions to the Commissioners for the consideration and execution of Penal Laws.
April 7. Chelsea.	18. Northumberland to Cecill. To remember the Dean of Worcester's licence. Desires a grant to himself of the Palatine Jurisdiction of Durham. Lady Margaret Douglas wishes to return home, being pregnant.
April 8.	19. Clause of an Act for restraint of the sale of offices.
April 12.	20. Draft of a Bill in Parliament for limitation of the late Duke of Somerset's lands.
April 25. St. James's.	21. Northumberland to Sir W. Petre or Cecill. To deliver to Lord Huntingdon's servant the warrant for the wages of his band of 50 demilances.
April (?)	22. Memorial of certain matters to be considered by the Council.
May 3. Witham.	23. Geo. Williams to Cecill. Has spoken with Mr. Browne for purchase of the land at Barholm. Has held Courts at Barroden and Casterton and endeavoured to hold a Court at St. Leonards.

DOMESTIC—EDWARD VI.

Vol. XIV.

1552.

May 10. 24. Lease from the Dean and Chapter of St. Paul's, London, to the 12 Peticanons of the same, of the churchyard called Pardon Churchyard, for 98 years at 2s. per year, the said Peticanons covenanting to keep in repair the Cloisters standing between the Library and the Church.

May (11?) 25. Memorial of the affairs of the Council. Answer to the Orators of the Hanse Towns, &c.

May (13?) 26. Remembrances of matters for the Privy Council.

May 13. Grimsthorp. 27. Duchess of Suffolk to Sir Wm. Cecill. Acknowledges his good will to her. Monson troubles her with complaints to the Lord Chancellor. (Tho. Goodrich, Bp. of Ely.)

May 20. 28. Sign Manual of the Patent of Translation of John Hoper, Bishop of Gloucester, to the see of Worcester, and annexing the Bishopric of Gloucester to that of Worcester. Lat.

May (28?) 29. Petition of Wm. Winter to Northumberland; relative to the ship and goods taken from him and George, his brother, by the French.

May 28. Otford. 30. Northumberland to Cecill. Winter's ship was wilfully spoiled by the French, and he desires letters to Baron de la Garde for reparation.

May 28. Otford. 31. Same to same. In favor of an Italian gentleman named Peche for a passport for two geldings. Mr. Young has applied for the release of one Cornish.

May 28. Otford. 32. Same to same. Desires licence for a son of John Harford to travel abroad for his education. Sends a letter from Sir And. Duddeley at Guisnes. The French King must dissemble, and the Scots make the fight.

May 30. Otford. 33. Same to the Lord Chamberlain (Thos. Lord Darcy of Chiche). Has received Lord Paget's several submissions; finds great difference between them. Thinks the proposed liberation of the Countess of Sussex should be well considered.

May 31. Otford. 34. Same to Cecill. Submissions of Paget and the late Master of the Rolls (John Beaumont). Will visit Cecill's Father in his way northward, and take a cup of wine at the door.

May 31. Otford. 35. Same to same. Approves of the letter written to Lord Conyers. Has written to the Greymes. Lord Cobham is in danger of his life.

May 31. 36. Memorandum of matters for the Council.

June 1. 37. Northumberland to the Lord Chamberlain and Vice Chamberlain (Sir John Gates). John Fisher appointed Receiver of Yorkshire, which Mr. Whalley had. Death of the wife of his son, Lord Ambrose Duddeley. Her next heir is the son of one Horwood. [Whorwood ?]

June 2. Otford. 38. Same to Lord Darcy and Cecill. Describes the symptoms of the disorder of which his daughter (-in-law) died, and awaits the King's pleasure.

June 4. Otford. 39. Same to the Council. Has received their letters for staying himself and his sons till the full of the moon, for fear of infection. Purposes to be at the Court on Tuesday with his sons, and the Lords Huntingdon and Hastings, and his son [Henry] Sydney.

Vol. XIV.

1552.
June 4. — Licence to Bishop Scorey to preach himself, and to license or forbid others to preach, within the Diocese of Chichester. [*Docquet.*]

June 6. Otford. — 40. Nortumberland to Sir Wm. Cecill. Thanks for the expedition of his warrants. Hopes on the morrow to return thanks in person.

June 7. — Lease to Sir Tho. Wrothe for 21 years of the demesne lands of the late monastery of Syon and the mill of Istelworth [Isleworth], parcel of Somerset's lands. [*Docquet.*]

June 7. — Grant to the same for life, of the keeping of the capital house of Syon, with the stewardship of the lordship of Istleworth, and the keeping of various woods in co. Middlesex. [*Docquet.*]

June 7. — Grant, to Robert Cock, of the office of Chief Mason of the Castle of Killingworth, co. Warwick, for life. [*Docquet.*]

June 7. — Grant to Dr Bellowsesse of a prebend in the Cathedral Church of Carlisle, on the death of one Pyrrie. [*Docquet.*]

June 9. — Grant to Sr Robt Bowes of the office of Master of the Rolls for life. [*Docquet.*]

June 9. — Warrant to pay to Elizabeth Smythe, the King's Laundress, 6*l.* 13*s.* 4*d.* per annum, for augmentation of her wages. [*Docquet.*]

June 9. — Grant to Gyles Forrest, groom of the Chamber, of an allowance of 12*d.* per diem. [*Docquet.*]

June 9. — Lease for 21 years to Sr W. Cecill of the farm of Combe Nevell, alias Combe park, co. Surrey, parcel of Somerset's lands. [*Docquet.*]

June 9. — Presentation to Mathew Parker of the prebend of Corringham in the church of Lincoln. [*Docquet.*]

June 9. — Letter to the President and Chapter of Lincoln to elect Mathew Parker, D.D. to the Deanery of Lincoln. [*Docquet.*]

June 9. — Warrant to deliver to Tho. Mayneman certain parcels of stuff for the King's Wardrobe at Greenwich. [*Docquet.*]

June 9. — Warrant to pay to John Browne, one of the King's players of Interludes, five marks yearly for his wages and 1*l.* 3*s.* 4*d.* a year for his livery. [*Docquet.*]

June 9. — Lease for 21 years to Wm. Aylmer, of the manor of Evercriche, co. Somerset, at the yearly rent of 49*l.* 17*s.* 4½*d.*, parcel of Somerset's lands. [*Docquet.*]

June 9. — Grant to Abraham Longwel, Roger Shakespere, and Tho. Best (Yeoman of the Chamber) of a forfeit of 36*l.* 10*s.* [*Docquet.*]

June 9. — Restraint of the killing of game for three years in the Parks of Eye and West-thorpe in the county of Suffolk. [*Docquet.*]

June 9. — Restraint of the killing of game in the Park of Morlewood, Co. Gloucester. [*Docquet.*] *This is marked in the margin by the King* UNSIGNED.

1552.
June 10.   Grant to Hugh Ellys of a lease in reversion for 21 years, of the Manor, &c. called Parkers, in the County of Warwick, lying in Shustoke, parcel of Sir James Fitzgarret's lands. [*Docquet.*]

June 10.   Licence for John Tailour, Bishop of Lincoln, to preach, and to forbid any not having the King's licence to preach, within his diocese. [*Docquet.*]

June 18.   41. Northumberland to the Lord Privy Seal (Bedford) and Marq. of
Royston.   Northampton. Recommends the suit of Sir Ralph Bagnal for the Monastery of Delecrest, Stafford, and Sir John Copwold for a Bishopric vacant in Ireland.

June 19.   42. Lord Clynton to Cecill. Begs to be informed at what time
Sempringham. Northumberland will be at the house of Cecill's Father. Purposes to meet him.

June 26.   43. Conveyance by Sir John Williams (Treasurer of the Augmentations) to Richard Warde, of the lands called Wood's Grove, in the parish of Hurst, Co. Wilts.

June (29?)   44. Petition of Sir Nicholas le Strange to the Council. Praying that 200*l.*, the ransom for James Steward, may be paid to him, or a grant of land to the value of 10*l.* yearly in lieu thereof.

June 29.   45. List of Suits to be made to the King, moved on Sunday 29th June, viz:—For the children of the Earl of Surrey. Relief for Sir Anth. Cooke. For Norroy King at Arms to hold a visitation. For Mr. Cofferer (John Ryther) to have either the Manor of West Pemered [Pennard?] or of Baltonsborough, Co. Somerset. For Chittewood for two Parks in Sussex. For Dr. Leyson for lands in Carmarthen and the farm of Manerbery, Co. Pembroke. For Sir Tho. Dacres, for the Priory of Lanercost. For Sir Nich. le Strange, for 200*l.* in money or 10*l.* a year in land. For Sir Ralph Bagnal, for the Monastery of Delecrest, Co. Stafford For deliverance of Sir John Arundel. For my Lord of Worcester's debts. And pardon to John Smallwell for slaughter of Geo. Johnson.

June 29 ?   46. Another list of suits to be made; all contained in the foregoing.

June.   47. Duchess of Suffolk to Cecill. Sends him a buck: wished to
Grimsthorp. have sent one to Mr. Latimer for the churching of his wife, but she must be churched without it. Invites Cecill to hunt in her parks. Mr. Bertie is in London.

June.   Grant to the Duke of Northumberland of the wardship and marriage of Wm. Flamock. [*Docquet.*]

June.   Grant to the Duke of Northumberland of the wardship and marriage of Margaret Whorwood. [*Docquet.*]

June.   Grant to Tho. Welden of the wardship and marriage of Tho. Welden, son and heir of Edw. Welden. [*Docquet.*]

June.   Grant to Sir Ric. Lister of the wardship and marriage of Richard Lyster. [*Docquet.*]

June.   Grant to John Payne of the wardship and marriage of Henry Chamber. [*Docquet.*]

1552.
Vol. XIV.

June. Grant to Michael Wentworth of the wardship and marriage of Gervays Storthes. [*Docquet.*]

June. Grant to William Hellard of the wardship and marriage of John Rokeby. [*Docquet.*]

June. Grant to Robert Carr of the wardship and marriage of Augustyne Smythe. [*Docquet.*]

June. Grant to John Holte of the wardship and marriage of Richard Seyman. [*Docquet.*]

June. Warrant for the allowance and discharge of 118*l.* 8*s.* 2¾*d.*, owing by Gregory Raylton late Treasurer of the wars against Scotland, on settling his accompt. [*Docquet.*]

June. Warrant for the delivery of certain stuff to the Master of the Horse and the Clerk of the Stable. [*Docquet.*]

June. Grant to Sir Anthony St Leger in fee farm, of the Castle, Manor, and Park of Ledes, Co. Kent, at the yearly rent of 10*l.* [*Docquet.*]

July 1. 48. Particular of the grant by the King to John Ryther (Cofferer of the Household) of the Manor of Balstonbury, Co. Somerset.

July 26. Tower. 49. Sir Ph. Hoby (Master of the Ordnance) to Cecill. Thanks him for his letter of the 24th. Transmits a statement of the Venetian Ambassador's to be delivered to the King.

July 27. Carlisle. 50. Northumberland to same. Is glad of his return to Court. Has received a letter from Mr. Vannes (from Venice) and likes his advice that Mr. Pickering should gently entertain the Duke of Ferrara's son, who would be a good match for one of the King's sisters.

July 28. The Tower. 51. Sir Phil. Hoby to same. Can only send a very small proportion of munition to Calais and Guisnes.

July 28. Pinchbeck. 52. Ric. Ogle to same. Thanks him for the matter of the Sewers in those parts. Does not know if Hall's lease were granted by the Duke of Suffolk or Bishop of Durham. Is competent to discharge the office of a Baron of the Exchequer. *Incloses,*

 52 I. *Names of the Commissioners proposed for the new Commission of Sewers within the five Shires, &c.*

July. 53. Note-book of Sir Wm. Cecill of various matters of public and private affairs in the months of June and July, with an Intinerary during an excursion in the country from 12 June to 20 July 1552.

Aug. 1. Tower. 54. Sir P. Hoby to Cecill. Sends foreign news of Germany, Flanders, and France. Mr. Damsell requires money for the King's gunpowder at Antwerp. *Incloses,*

 54 I. *Note of certain intelligence relative to the Emperor's army. Arrival of the Duke at Alva.*

Aug. 1. Tower. 55. Same to same. Proceedings of the Commissioners at Windsor. They of the College are very untoward. [*On the 8th of Aug. the Council directed the Commissioners for the survey of Windsor to examine the Prebendaries there, " and to get as much as they can of that hath byn embeselyd, or the valu thereof." Co. Reg.*]

VOL. XIV.

1552.

Aug. 3.
Tower.
56. Sir Ph. Hoby to Sir Wm. Cecill. Miseries in the office of Ordnance for want of money, particularly in the case of Ch. Wolman, the gunpowder maker.

Aug. 4.
Wilton.
57. Wm. Earl of Pembroke to same. In behalf of James Stumpe to be under-steward of Malmsbury, and also for Mr. Sharington to have the wardship of Mr. Hall's heir.

Aug. 6.
58. Indenture between Owen Oglethorpe, President of Magdalen Coll., Oxford, and Walter Haddon, in consideration of the King's letters for preferment of the said Haddon to be President thereof.

Aug. 14.
Wilton.
59. Wm. Thomas (Clerk of the Council) to Cecill. The Earl of Pembroke is well contented with the wardship (Hall's heir) procured for Cecill's sister. Would like to spend a year or two at Venice, if sent.

Aug. 18.
London.
60. Gregory Raylton to same. Prays for licence for himself and those in his company to eat flesh, on account of his own ill-health.

Aug. 11.
Giddy Hall.
61. Sir Anth. Cooke to same. Thanks for the relief he found by the good air at Wimbledon. Wishes him well through the progress. His and Cecill's son, Thomas Cecill, is merry.

Aug. (21?)
62. Sir Ric. Sakevyle (Chancellor of the Augmentations) to the Council. Reports on the matter in dispute between Lord Lawarre and Francis Sherley, relative to the lands called Estcourt lands, said to be parcel of the manor of Knappe, but really in West Grinstead. *Incloses,*

 62 I. *Articles exhibited by Lord Lawarre against Francis Sherley.*

 62 II. *The confession or answer of Francis Sherley to these Articles.*

Aug. 22.
London.
63. Ric. Goodrick to Cecill. Hears he is going to Bath; cannot accompany him on account of public business. Advises him for sundry reasons not to go to Bath.

Aug. 22.
Cobham Hall.
64. Geo. Lord Cobham to same. Thanks him for furthering the suit of John Knight, of Calais, and for despatch of his servant Normanton.

Aug. 22.
Cobham Hall.
65. Same to same. Transmits letters from the Treasurer of Calais requesting licence to repair to England.

Aug. 26.
Salisbury.
66. Memorandum of matters to be brought before the Council, with names of candidates for the offices of Comptroller and Marshal at Calais.

Aug. 26.
67. Sir John Godsalve to Cecill. Has obtained Mr. Cheke's consent to be joined with him in the office of one of the Chamberlains of the Exchequer.

Aug. 26.
Richmond.
68. Henry Duke of Suffolk to same. Describes the extreme illness of his wife.

44   DOMESTIC—EDWARD VI.

Vol. XIV.

1552.

Aug. 27.
Salisbury.
69. Wm. Thomas to the Lord Chancellor. Applies for a commission for trial of pirates within the Cinque Ports, for piracy about Dover.

Aug. 28.
Putney.
70. Ric. Goodrick to Sir Wm. Cecill. Sends particulars of divers manors in Somerset and Devon. [*Probably to be bestowed upon Sir Anth. Cooke who on the 27th of Oct. following had a grant of lands "in consideration of service."*—See Vol. xix. fol. 42.]

Aug. 28.
Wimbledon.
71. Francis Armstrong to same. With an inventory made by Rich. Norwood of the goods of D. Clement remaining in the house of Marshfoot, in the parish of Hornchurch, co. Essex, with a particular of the house of Marshfoot.

Aug. 30.
Andover.
72. Northumberland to same. Communicates particulars of various suits which he made to the King. Border affairs.

Vol. XV.—September—December 1552:

Sept. 3.
Knoll.
1. Northumberland to Cecill. Is glad to hear the King's progress is to be abridged, &c. Laments the cruel dealings of the French against English merchants.

Sept. 4.
Knoll.
2. Same to same. A suit is to be made to the King by the merchants for licence to ship cloths to Flanders; secret reasons exist for its being granted.

Sept. 7.
Knoll.
3. Same to same. Bishop Poynet has set forth a catechism in Latin and English; begs that the bearer may have licence for the sole printing thereof.

Sept. 8?)
4. Memorandum of various matters to be transacted.

Sept. 15.
Wilton.
5. Pembroke to Cecill. In favour of Thomas Gresham's suit for some reward for his service.

Sept. 17.
Windsor.
6. Northumberland to same. Important matter has transpired on questioning Stukley as to his first departing.

Sept. 17.
Richmond.
7. Henry Earl of Westmorland to same. Sends up John Burge, whom he has examined as to slanders against Northumberland.

Sept. 21.
Bisham.
8. Sir Ph. Hoby to same. In reply to inquiries as to one Harbert; has a servant named Harbert Clarvys, who keeps his hawks.

Sept. 28.
9. Book of the Annuities appointed for the officers of the bulwarks in Essex.

Sept. 29.
Hampton Court.
10. Memorandum of matters to be brought before the Council.

Sept. (?)
11. A brief declaration of the whole military and naval expenses incurred by King Henry VIII. and Edward VI., during their wars with France and Scotland; the Insurrection in England; the charges of Calais and Boulogne, and the charges of Castles, Garrisons, &c., from Sept. 1542 to Sept. 1552; amounting in the whole to the sum of 3,491,471*l*. 19*s*. 5¾*d*.

VOL. XV.

1552.
Sept. (?)   12. Northumberland to Sir Wm. Cecill. Wishes to know what answer should be sent to Lord Willoughby's request to tarry at Calais. Censures his conduct.

Oct. 3.   13. Minute of the King's debts, and of a plan for the discharge of the same, &c; and agreement made by the Privy Council with the Merchant Adventurers.

Oct. 4.   14. Memorandum of certain suits to be preferred to the King.

Oct. 7.
Lambeth.   15. Archbp. Cranmer to the Council. Has received their directions that the Book of Common Prayer should be diligently pursued, and the printer's errors therein amended. Arguments defending the practice of kneeling at the Sacrament.

Oct. 7.
Sandwich.   16. Sir Tho. Cheyne (Lord Warden of the Cinque Ports) to Cecill. Has sent his letters to the Customers, Searchers, &c. Words will be all that can be got of the Commissioners in compensation to the Merchants.

Oct. 7.   17. Sir Walter Bucler and Thos. Parry to same. The Princess Elizabeth has applied to the Dean, &c., of Worcester, for a little farm. They request the King's letters to further it.

Oct. 8.
Byland.   18. Earl of Westmorland to same. Will send the lease of Cranmore and other evidences relating to Stow and Deeping.

Oct. 9.
Lowth.   19. Lawrence Eresbye to same. Has provided for Cecill's horses out of his own store of beans, and will send 20 sheep for his housekeeping.

Oct. 11.   20. Memoranda for the Council. Mr. Wayneman's business; one Dyrrick, a goldsmith, to be examined.

Oct. 12.   21. Geo. Williams to Cecill. Proceedings of the Escheator at Grantham as to Hall's lands. Claim to the Guild Lands in Baston. Details the proceedings and verdict of the Jury.

Oct. 13.   22. Northumberland to same. To move the Council concerning Princess Elizabeth's application in favour of Penn; and also for an answer as to West Tilbury. Is unwell.

Oct. 14.
Stamford.   23. Aldermen, &c., of Stamford, to same. Desire a commission to call John Allen and Wm. Campanet to account for money received from the sale of Church property.

Oct. 15.
Saint James's.   24. Northumberland to same. Desires to know what answer he must make to Princess Elizabeth's letter; and for payment of Morysine's half year's diet. His illness continues.

Oct. 16.
Ashridge.   25. Tho. Parry to same. Desires him to take Digby's summons in good part. Arrangement for payment of Rents, &c.

Oct. (18.)   26. Northumberland to same. To hear the bearer's statement as to the letter he brings. *Incloses*,

       26 I. *Henry Cornyshe to Northumberland. Offers to renew a correspondence for the delivering up of the Castle and Town of Cherburg to the English. Oct. 18.*

Oct. 20.   27. Memoranda of matters to be brought before the Council.

Vol. XV.

1552.
Oct. 20. 28. "Articles concerning an Uniformite in Relligion." [*These contain 45 Articles, and are the basis of the 39 Articles of the Anglican Church. They were submitted to the Privy Council, and by the Council returned to the six Royal Chaplains, on the 21st of October 1552.*]

Oct. 21.
Higham Park. 29. Sir Ro. Tyrwhyt to Sir Wm. Cecill. Has a right to two acres of wood yearly within the Lordship of Wimbledon. Makes him a present of it.

Oct. 23.
Burleigh. 30. Geo. Williams to same. Has written to the escheator for some document. By the death of John Hall, of Grantham, more land has descended to Arthur Hall, Cecill's ward. Particulars of rents paid in.

Oct. 25.
Launde. 31. Eliz. Lady Crumwell to same. Regrets that he did not visit her poor house of Launde. Is willing to take on her the charge of her four nieces, Somerset's daughters.

Oct. 26.
Gedney. 32. Adlard Welby to same. Repairs and erection of bars on a bank called Gouxland. Wishes to do the same at Baston Dyke. Works at Pinchbeck and Spalding. *Incloses,*

    32 I. *Indenture of lease between the King and Adlard Welby, of certain Lands in the Lordship of Sutton, co. Lincoln, parcel of the Duchy of Lancaster. Westminster, June 1.*

Oct. 27.
Pinchbeck. 33. Ric. Ogle to same. Good works of the Commission of Sewers, under the direction of John Burton. Has sent to the Council a forged licence taken from the players; a matter worthy of correction.

Oct. 27.
St. James's. 34. Northumberland to same. Confessions of one Hawkins that he has circulated seditious libels and counterfeited the Archbishop of Canterbury's handwriting; thinks, by fair means or foul, he should be made to discover his accomplices.

Oct. 28. 35. Same to same. Wishes the King would appoint Mr. Knox to the bishopric of Rochester, he would be a whetstone to the Archbishop of Canterbury and a confounder of the Anabaptists lately sprung up in Kent. Proposes the Dean of Durham to be bishop there, and other changes.

Oct. 30. 36. Same to same. Offences of Mr. York, in packing up groats and bullion for Ireland. Requests certain benefices and gifts for his friends. Advises one Litster in York, who uses a book of prophecy, to be apprehended.

Oct. 37. Same to same. Evil consequences throughout the realm of the restraint laid upon lead.

Oct. 38. Same to same. Private conference with the French Ambassador's Secretary, relative to Stukley's false dealings.

Oct. 39. Same to same. Slanderous words spoken by one Ford against the Duke and his brother.

Oct. (?). 40. Memoranda of matters to be brought before the Council.

Oct. (?) 41. A brief of all the King's debts, external, and within the realm.

Oct. (?) 42. "The note of ye K^s Ma^{ts} dettes, w^t some meane towarde ye discharge thereof," in Cecill's hand.

VOL. XV.

1552.

Nov. 4.
Pinchbeck.
43. Ric. Ogle to Sir Wm. Cecill; in behalf of Wm. Middleton, who had purchased lands in Swaton in the parts of Kesteven, Lincoln, which were claimed by one Horseley.

Nov. 8.
Shene.
44. Duke of Suffolk to same. Requests licence for J. Walgrave, his servant, the bearer, to pass into Flanders.

Nov. 9.
Bisham.
45. Sir Ph. Hoby to same. Is sorry he is unwell. Begs his aid to get certain documents signed relative to the manor of Bisham. The Lady Ann of Cleves is dissatisfied.

Nov. 9.
Wilton.
46. Earl of Pembroke to same. In favour of the bearer.

Nov. 13.
Wilton.
47. Same to same. Recommends the suit of Mr. Kaylewey, who desires to be released from the Commission of the Peace.

Nov. 14.
Denton.
48. Geo. Williams to same. Cecill's father does not like his appointment for the lands of Manthorp and Sempringham. He rather wished for lands about Barholm and Deeping.

Nov. 16.
Rownore.
49. John Brune to same. Cannot find his own pedigree; sends a book of conveyances of his heritable lands.

Nov. 17.
50. Northumberland to same. Solicits that one John Borroghe [Burgh] may not be put to the public punishment of the pillory. [*On the 13th of Nov. John Burgh and several others were ordered to be put in the Pillory at Westminster on the following Friday 18 Nov. Co. Reg.*]

Nov. 24.
51. Memorandum in Cecill's hand of matters to be transacted.

Nov. 27.
Boston.
52. Mayor, &c., of Boston to Cecill. Thanks for his great services in checking the pulling down of fair buildings in their town. Complains of the conduct of John Brown therein.

Nov. 27.
Uffnam.
53. Sir Ph. Hoby to same. Thanks for his bill for Bisham, and for other manifold favours.

Nov. 27.
London.
54. John Heron (Head Master of the King's School at Rochester) to same. Applies for the appointment of a Prebendary in Rochester cathedral. Lat.

Nov. 29.
55. The Council to Bishop Barlow and others. Directions as to the Strangers at Glastonbury. Henry Cornish, Keeper of the House there, claims a right to the park of Worrall.

Nov. 30.
Stamford.
56. The Aldermen, &c., of Stamford to Cecill. Particulars of a trespass by cutting down certain willows in the stream near the Blackfriars wall. [*This paper is signed by Richd Cecill, father of Sir Wm.*]

Nov.
57. Northumberland to same. The Auditor of the late Bishop of Durham's possessions must be sent for, in order to gain a true knowledge for the proceedings with the newly elected Bishop.

Nov. (?)
58. Offers of Lord Paget to the King. Proposes to deliver for the King's use certain parcels of land specified, in lieu of the fine of 8,000*l.* imposed upon him.

VOL. XV.

1552.
Nov.
59. Note of certain causes to be moved to the King's Majesty. Declaration of the Earl of Arundel's and Lord Paget's causes. Lord Eure to be Dep. Warden of the Middle Marches, and Thos. Graye, of Chillingham, of the East Marches, &c.

Dec. 2.
Chelsea.
60. Northumberland to Sir Wm. Cecill. Sends certain papers to be signed; one is for the Prebend in Worcester for Arthur Duddeley; another the presentation to Kidderminster to Mr. Kreek (both which Mr. Harley had); the third is Somerset's pardon for "pykyng."

Dec. 3.
Chelsea.
61. Same to same. The Merchants of the Staple are dissatisfied with the late licence. Regrets he had caused that matter to be moved. Is sorry for his cousin Nevill's mishap. His health daily grows worse.

Dec. 3.
Chelsea.
62. Same to same. It is necessary a Bishop of Durham should be appointed without delay. Does not think it expedient "this pevishe Dean" [*Horne*] should have the appointment.

Dec. (4 ?)
63. Same to same. Concerning the election of two fit personages, on Bruno's advice. Regrets the delay in filling up the two vacant Bishopricks. Poor Harley (afterwards Worcester) is still in attendance. One of the Schets is arrived on his way to Spain. [*On the 3d of Dec. Mr. Pickering was directed to obtain a French passport for Balthazar Schets, for Spain.—Co. Reg.*]

Dec. 3.
Beaulieu.
64. Princess Mary to the King. Thanks for his care of her health. Is willing to exchange her manors of St. Osyth, Little and Great Clafton and Willeigh, for other lands.

Dec. 4.
Bulieu.
65. Same to the Council. Thanks to the King for reimbursing her for the sums she had expended in certain reparations, and also for giving her intelligence of foreign occurrences. [*On the 7th of Dec. Sir John Williams had warrant "to pay to Mr. Rochester, the Lady Maries "servaunt, the sume of 557l. to be by him bestowed about the repara- "tions of certaine of the said Lady Maries lands, decayed by the rage "of the water this last yere." Co. Reg.*]

Dec. 7.
Chelsea.
66. Northumberland to Cecill. Returns Master Knox, because he loves not to have to do with men neither grateful nor pleasable. Character of him and Dean Horne. Sends the letter he purposes to address to the Constable of France. Reminds Cecill of the matter revealed by the Dean of Durham. Professions of loyalty.

Dec. 8.
Wilton.
67. Pembroke to same. Thanks for his good will on many occasions.

Dec. 9.
Chelsea.
68. Northumberland to same. Forwards letters from Berwick, from Dr. Smith out of Scotland, Bruno, and the French Ambassador. Observations on the contents of Dr. Smith's letters. Treasons to be guarded against.

Dec. (9 ?)
Friday.
69. Winchester to Sec. [Cecill?]. Desires a warrant for 150l. for payment of the works at the Mews, done since Michaelmas.

Dec. 11.
Chelsea.
70. Northumberland to Cecill. Recommends his chaplain for the King's presentation to the Vicarage of Kidderminster, which Mr.

Vol. XV.

1552. Mr. Harley, now Bishop of Hereford, had. Affairs of Lady Lennox and her husband.

Dec. 14. Stamford.
71. The Aldermen &c. of Stamford to Cecill. Resignation of their Recorder Mr. Hunt. They solicit Cecill to accept of that office.

Dec. 20. (?) 72. Notes of public business. Suits to be moved to the King. Discharge of Lord Paget's fine, &c.

Dec. 28. 73. Northumberland to the Council. Has received from Lord Shrewsbury a note of such things as are necessary to be preferred in the next Parliament. Pressure of the King's debts; observations thereon, and on the maladministration of Somerset during his Protectorate.

Dec. 28. 74. Same to Cecill. Wonders at the blind deportment of the Chamberlain. Finds the King purposes to employ some ministers abroad. Suggests that his brother (Sir Andrew Duddeley) should be sent to the French King, and his son Sydney (his son-in-law Sir Henry Sydney) to the Emperor. Opinions on various points.

Dec. 75. Barth. Traheron to same. Mr. Warner deals harshly with good Mr. Cornelius. Is determined to resign the Deanery of Chichester. Recommends Tho. Samson to succeed him.

Dec. 76. Names of Commissioners to inquire how the King is answered of the lead and bell metal of abbeys, and of the plate, jewels, &c., of monasteries, colleges, chantries, &c.

[Dec. 77. Treatise, in Latin, showing the unlawfulness of transferring Church property to secular uses.

1552. 78. Statement of " The yerely vallue of all spirituall promotions " within the Realme of Englande, being of the yerely vallue of 50l. " and above."

(?) 79. ———— to Lady Jane Grey. Presents to her a copy of the works of Basil the Great, which may be more profitable to her than gold and precious stones. Greek. [Indorsed " *To my Lady Jane, in Grek, in a boke.*"]

Vol. XVI. 1552.

1552. Original account of the Treasurer of the First Fruits and Tenths (Sir William Petre), stating the arrears due on 1st Feb. 1552; the names of the various benefices, and of the parties holding them, with the sums due by way of composition or otherwise; containing upwards of 1,100 entries; with memoranda of subsequent payments.

Vol. XVII. 1552.

1552. A manuscript on vellum (probably drawn up by Sir Wm. Cecill), containing the Statutes of the Order of the Garter, as ordained by King Edward VI. At the conclusion is the following memorandum:—" *Rudimenta sunt hæc ordinis quæ potius colliguntur quam com-*" *ponuntur. Gulielmus Cæcilius Ord. Gart. Cancellari⁹, 29 Deceb.* " 1552. *Sexto* ℞. *Edw. Sexti.*"

Vol. XVIII. January—June, 1553.

1553.
Jan. 2.
Chelsea.

1. Northumberland to Cecill. Hopes the new year will receive a new Bishop for Durham. He has been much deceived by Dean Horne.

Jan. 3.
Chelsea.

2. Same to same. Has never absented himself from the King's service, but through bad health. The Italian proverb is true: *A faithful servant will become a perpetual ass.* Wishes to retire and end his days in tranquillity.

Jan. 6.
Chelsea.

3. Same to same. Wishes to confer with him. Has not been told if there is to be a Bishop of Durham or not. Hears nothing of the prebend Mr. Harley had in Worcester.

Jan. 6.
Chelsea.

4. Same to Lord Chamb. Darcy. Thanks for the King's letter for Ambrose (Duddeley). Returns the King's book of the Order of the Garter: offers his opinion on certain portions of it.

Jan. 9.
Chelsea.

5. Same to Cecill. Sends letters from Lord Wharton, and one from poor Knox, whose perplexity will be thereby perceived. Thinks letters should be sent down to the North in his favour.

Jan. 14.
Chelsea.

6. Same to Darcy. Returns the arguments and collections of Sec. Cecill, on which he has scribbled some of his own observations. The King's necessity and debts are the points to be insisted on, and not to account to the Commons for his liberality. Princess Elizabeth's communication as to Durham Place. She purposes to pay a visit to the King. Suggestions for Divine Service at the opening of the Parliament.

Jan. 15.
Kelsay.

7. Sir Fr. Ayscough to Cecill. Desires the resumption of the manor and lands of Bishop's Burton, now come to the Crown by the death of Elizabeth Horsman.

Jan. 19.
Chelsea.

8. Northumberland to same. Question as to calling heirs apparent to Parliament by writ. Specifies various instances. Placing of Peers' sons. Hopes a learned man will be appointed to the See of Durham.

Jan. 23.
Chelsea.

9. Same to same. Professes his solicitude for the welfare of the State, equally in the South as in the North.

Jan. (?)

10. Same to Darcy and Cecill. Suggests that the Countess of Oxford should be written to, to deliver up Lady Arundel's jointure. [*On the 13th of Feb. 1553, the Chancellor of the Augmentations was directed to appoint to Lady Arundel a third of the lands forfeited by the attainder of Sir Thos. Arundel. Co. Reg.*]

VOL. XVIII.

1553.
Jan. (?)   11. Northumberland to Petre, or Cecill. Desires dispatch of Gresham's and Stukley's affairs [1553?]. Fears he is about to be very ill.

Jan. (?)   12. List of persons to be appointed for hearing all such private suits as are customably brought to the King or his Council, and delivered to the Masters of Requests.

March 1.   13. List of Acts to be proposed in the Parliament then sitting.

March 20.   14. Declaration of all such sums of money as the Receivers of the Court of Augmentations have paid into the treasury of the said Court.

March (?)   15. Grant by Princess Elizabeth to Sir William Cecill, of Ladybrigg close, and other lands, co. Northampton, formerly held by Richard Cecill his father, deceased. Lat.

March.   16. Memoranda of matters to be moved to the King's Majesty.

April 11. (?) London.   17. Winchester to Cecill. Hopes to hear of his recovery. Desires him to remember the King's letter, for Sir John Bowes to be absent from St. George's Feast.

April 30.   18. Declaration of the sums received by Sir Edmund Pekham since the 23d of April, upon sale of the King's lands.

May 6. Dartington.   19. Nicholas Adams to Cecil. Concerning the concealment of collegiate, chantry, and obit lands, in Devon and Cornwall.

May 7.   20. Information given by Mr. Griffin against Valentine, a Benedictine priest, apprehended in Clerkenwell, and one Roper, suspected to be a Jesuit.

May 9. Greenwich.   21. John Lord Audley to Cecill. Comforts him in his illness. Prescribes several remedies, particularly a stewed "sowe pygge of ix " dayes olde."

May 10. Greenwich.   22. Winchester to same. Rejoices at his recovery; sends him a bill for his fee; and will make out his book for the wardship of young Mr. Hall.

May 15.   23. Particulars of a grant to Sir John Gates of Dylay Wood, co. Southampton, parcel of the late Duke of Somerset's lands.

May 17. London.   24. Tho. Gresham to Northumberland. Has spoken with his uncle, Sir John Gresham, who stormed not a little at his settling the course of Exchange at so low a rate. Sends copy of their privileges granted in 1296, whereby the falsity of the new Hanse Company will appear. Desires that 1,200*l.*, owing to him by Martin Pirry, may be retained.

May.   25. The King to the Bishops. Requiring them to subscribe and observe the Articles of Religion newly set forth, and to cause the catechism to be taught by all schoolmasters within their respective dioceses. [*In Bishop Ridley's Register, this letter appears with the date of 9 June* 1553.—See Strype, M. II. 2. p. 104.]

VOL. XVIII.

1553.	
May.	26. Copy of the preceding.
June 3.	27. Memorial of various public matters to be transacted.
June 11.	28. Memorandum of various official matters to be transacted; among other things, a list of persons to be constituted Bishops.
June 27. Westminster.	29. Grant to Lord Robert Duddeley (Gentleman of the Privy Chamber), and Willm. Glaseour, of certain tenements and lands in Rolingham (indorsed Rockingham), co. Northampton, and in Eston, co. Leicester, parcel of the possession of the late William Lord Parr, and late in the occupation of Edw. Watson.
June.	30. Account of stipends paid the Clerks in the Office of the Signet, from 38 Hen. VIII. to the last year of Edw. VI.

[The following Papers without date, are probably in the reign of Edw. VI.]

31. Notes of evidence to prove that the land called Dover Down, lying near St. Dunstan's, in the Woldes of Canterbury, belonged to the Priory of Dover.

32. Memorandum of certain suits to be made to the King.

33, 34. Two other papers of memoranda of certain suits to be made to the King.

35. "Sir William Stanley's Cheques," being a list of names and wages for days.

36. List of the principal gentlemen in the county of Kent.

37. Memorandum of the duties and antiquity of the office of Warden of the Mint, the amount of his fee, and of other Officers of the Mint.

38. Note of the fees and emoluments of a Groom of the Privy Chamber extraordinary.

39. Account of the yearly profits of the manor and parsonage of Boxgrave, and of certain lands in Halfnaked, demised to the late Sir John Jenyns, and now in the tenure of Lord John Gray.

40. Names of Officers in the Exchequer, the Courts of Augmentations, First Fruits, and Wards, the Duchies of Cornwall and Lancaster, the Mint, &c.

Vol. XVIII.

41. Certificate of horsemen, armour, &c., sent into the North last Easter, from Yarborough, Welshcrofte, Braidley, and Havershow, co. Lincoln; under the hands of Sir Robert Tyrwhit and Wm. Maneby.

42. Injunctions relative to the government of a College in Oxford. Lat.

43. Ground plan of several Law Courts, probably at Westminster Indorsed, "The Plattes of Harfurd, bye G. Ganthorn."

44. Names of certain gentlemen who tarry at home in every shire.

45. Collection of Precedents and Statutes, in proof that all Ecclesiastical Jurisdiction in England is properly derived from the King, and not from the Pope.

Vol. XIX. 1547—1553.

A register of all gifts, exchanges, and purchases of Crown lands in every year of King Edward's reign; specifying the names of the Purchasers or Recipients, the consideration of the gift and amount of purchase money, the yearly value of the lands, the rents reserved, and the dates of the respective patents in each case. With a copious personal index.

QUEEN MARY.

Vol. I. July—December, 1553.

1553.

July 10.
The Tower.
1. Proclamation of Lady Jane Grey as Queen of England, &c. Setting forth that the Lady Mary and the Lady Elizabeth are illegitimate, and calling upon persons of all estates and degrees to be obedient to her, their lawful sovereign. [*This is a modern and not very accurate copy. An original printed Proclamation is in the collection of the Society of Antiquaries, printed by Richard Grafton; and it is a remarkably fine specimen of his workmanship. In the imprint he styles himself Queen's Printer.*]

July 20.
2. Account of arrears of the tenths and subsidies of the Clergy, due by divers Bishops at and before Christmas last.

July.
3. Memoranda of things to be done for government of the State on the accession of Queen Mary.

July.
4. Certain articles, wherein the Queen's pleasure is to be known for her Highness's affairs. Given in charge to Sir William Cecill to be declared. Signed by Archbp. Cranmer, Bp. Goodrich, and the Marq. of Winchester.

August 4.
5. "A memoriall, what is to be don after y̆e death of K. Edwd. the Sixt," *in Sec. Petre's hand.*

August 8.
6. Account of cloth, velvet, and other materials, to be used at the funeral of King Edward VI., with the quantities and price of the same.

August 18.
7. Proclamation by the Queen for avoiding the inconvenience and dangers that have arisen in times past through the diversity of opinions in questions of religion.

August 18.
8. Questions moved by the D. of Northumberland on his trial, as to his own justification, and as to the legality of some of his Judges.

August 19.
London.
9. The Council to the Council with the Queen. Arrangements for welcoming the French Ambassadors. Affair between the Earl of Pembroke's and Lord Sturton's servants. Four gentlemen condemned that morning.

August 20.
Richmond.
10. The Queen to Bishop Gardyner, Chancellor of the University of Cambridge, and others. Commands that the ancient statutes, foundations, and ordinances of the University be inviolably kept and observed.

August 20.
Richmond.
11. Same to Sir John Masone, as Chancellor, and others of the University of Oxford. Of the same tenor as the above.

1553. VOL. I.

August 25. London.
12. Bishop Gardyner to the Vice-Chancellor, &c., of Cambridge. Is prevented from going to them in person. Sends his Chaplain, who will give them, in his name, the information they require. Lat.

August 28.
13. Declaration of all such sums of money as have been paid into the hands of Sir John Williams, Treasurer of the Court of Augmentations, for the half year ending 25th March last.

August (?)
14. Statement of debts due by the Crown incurred in the late King's reign.

Oct. 1.
15. The manner of the ceremony of the Coronation of Queen Mary. Names of those created Knights of the Bath; and order of the procession of the Queen with her train, from the Tower through London to Westminster. [*Imperfect.*]

Oct. 1.
16. The oath of a Knight of the Bath, as it was given to those made at Queen Mary's Coronation; with the names of the Knights then made, and of their Esquires.

Oct. 23.
17. Henry Lord Stafford to the Queen. His distressed condition. Enumerates the services done by his father, the D. of Buckingham, to the noble Queen her mother. Anecdotes of Wolsey and Buckingham.

Nov. 4. Westminster.
18. Grant to Sir Edw. Waldegrave and John Coseworth, of the Office of Receivers General of the Duchy of Cornwall. Lat.

Nov. 13. Westminster.
19. Grant to Stephen Hadnoll (one of the Grooms of the Chamber) of the office of Keeper of the Mansion of Stansted in Essex, and Bailiff of the Manors of Stansted and Halsted. Lat.

Dec. (?)
20. Articles, and secret articles, devised as the basis of a treaty of marriage between the Queen and Prince Philip of Spain. Signed by the whole of the Privy Council. [*The Emperor's Commissioners for the marriage arrived at Canterbury on the 28th December* 1553.]

1553. (?)
21. Warrant by the Queen (*her first signature*) to the Chancellor, &c., of the Court of First Fruits and Tenths to accept from John Payne the Manor of Cryston and all his other lands in Uphill, Culstocke, and Worell, co. Somerset, in discharge of his debt to the Crown.

(?)
22. "A remembraunce of thinges worthie examination for the " Quene's Majestie." Principally relating to the sale, exchange, &c., of Crown lands.

(?)
23. "List of shippes decayed since the 36 yere of Kinge Henrye " the VIII. untyll the death of Kinge Edwarde," and from his death to the present time.

(?)
24. Tabular account by Sir Wm. Cecill of his profits and expenses for Wimbledon benefice from 1550 to 1553, anno Reg. 1 Mary.

(?)
25. Account of rents received by H. Whythed, *in Cecill's hand.*

VOL. II. JANUARY 1554.

1554.
Jan. 1.
Westminster.
1. The Queen to Sir John Masone (Treasurer of the Chamber), warrant to deliver 3s. 5d. daily to Dr. Bill, Chief Almoner, to be by him distributed every day at the Court gate.

Jan. 13.
Cornwall.
2. Sir John Arundel of Trerice to the Earl of Arundel (Lord Steward). Sends information of disrespectful words spoken by S. Jackson and John Cowlyn, against the Queen and the Catholic religion.

Jan. 19.
Monse Awtrey.
3. Sir Peter and Sir Gawen Carew to Sir Thos. Denys. Profess their loyalty. Will resist being arrested, if he acts without due authority.

Jan. 22.
Lees.
4. Ric. Lord Rich to Sir Wm. Petre. Hears that certain of the pensioners are to be removed, and others appointed; recommends Charles Tyrell, brother to Sir Henry Tyrell, to one of the vacancies.

Jan. 22.
St. James's.
5. The Queen to Sir Hugh Pollard and others of Devon. Efforts of evil disposed persons to hinder the Catholic religion and divine service, now restored. Directions to suppress false and seditious rumours about the Prince of Spain's coming into the Kingdom. Sends the effect of the articles of the Treaty with Spain, to be declared to the people.

Jan. 22.
6. Same to the L. President and Council of Wales, and to the Bishops of Exeter and Salisbury, *to the same effect as the above, to be declared to the people of Devon and Cornwall, in sermons, &c.*

7. Same to Lords Justices of Counties, to the same effect. To suppress the rebellion raised by the Duke of Suffolk, &c.

Jan. 22 (?)
St. James's.
8 Same to the Justices, &c., of Counties. Directions to declare to the people the articles of her marriage with Philip of Spain, and to suppress all attempts at rebellion.

Jan. 22 (?)
9. Same to Sir Edw. Hastings and Sir Thos. Cornwallys. Instructions to repair to Wiat, and to declare to him the motives of her marriage with Prince Philip. Offers to appoint persons to confer with him hereon.

Jan. 23.
Mereworth
10. Sir Robt. Southwell (Sheriff of Kent) to the Council. Sends deposition against one Isley. Desires instructions how to proceed. *Incloses,*

10. I. *Deposition by Wm. Cotman of Ightham concerning words spoken by Wm. Isley, son of Sir Harry Isley, inciting to rebellion, on the coming of the Spaniards into the realm. Jan. 23.*

Jan. 23.
Mohun's-Ottery.
11. Sir P. Carew to Sir Tho. Denys (Sheriff of Devon). Is going to the Court. Doubts not to be able to answer any charge brought against him.

Jan. 24.
Tiverton.
12. Sir Gawen Carew to same. Wonders at the preparations within the city of Exeter, which were the sole cause of his repairing to Sir Peter Carew, thinking Sir T. Denys purposed to apprehend them both.

1554.

Vol. II.

Jan. 24.
Torr.
13. John Ridgewaye to Sir Tho. Denys. Sir Arthur Champernown has conferred with Sir Peter Carew, and they could not agree concerning the enterprise to resist the landing of the Prince of Spain.

Jan. 24.
14. Articles concerning the causes of shutting the gates, and watch and ward done in the city of Exeter, on the report that certain gentlemen of Devon would enter the city.

Jan. 24.
15. Declaration of John Predyaux concerning rumours of things lately done in the county of Devon to oppose the landing of the Prince of Spain.

Jan. 25.
16. Sir Tho. Denys to the Council. Reports his proceedings against Sir Peter Carew, whose house was too strong to be taken by assault.

Jan. 25.
17. Sir Ro. Southwell to Petre. Suggests that Mr. Covert should join him in Kent. Arrangements for opposing Wiat, and recommends he should be intercepted either at Rochester or Dartford.

Jan. 26.
Andover.
18. Sir John St. Leger to the Earl of Arundel. Intelligence of P. Carew. The commons of Devon and Exeter are faithful to the Queen.

Jan. 26. (?)
19. The Queen to the Lieuts. of Counties; to proclaim as traitors Henry Duke of Suffolk, the Carews, Wiat, and others, who threatened her destruction and to advance Lady Jane Grey and her husband.

Jan. 27.
Southwark.
20. Bp. Gardyner (Lord Chancellor) to Petre. Has arrested Harrington, who confesses that he and Wroth had a conference with Lord John Grey. Has found a copy of Princess Elizabeth's letter to the Queen in the French Ambassador's packet.

Jan. 28.
Gravesend.
21. Thos. Duke of Norfolk to the Council. Found Lord Cobham, the Vice-Chamberlain, and Sir John Fogg, at Gravesend, with a force not exceeding 300 men. Sir George Harper has come over from the rebels. Beseeches their indulgence for having promised him pardon

Jan. 28.
Gravesend.
22. Geo. Lord Cobham and Sir Hen. Jernegan to the Council. Intelligence from Abergavenny. A French post intercepted. *Incloses,*

 22. I. *Abergavenny, Sir Ro. Southwell, and others, to Jernegan. Intention of the rebels to sack and spoil Mr. Clerk's house. Detail of proceedings against them, &c. Malling, Jan. 28.*

Jan. 29.
Gravesend.
23. Norfolk to the Council. Being furnished with 700 or 800 men, intends to march towards Rochester. Wiat has fortified Rochester bridge. Recommends that Abergavenny and others should fall on the rear of Wiat's forces. *Incloses,*

 23. I. *Cobham to Norfolk. Informs him of Wiat's intentions to fight it out. Advises the Duke not to advance too far. Cowling Castle, Jan. 29.*

Jan. 29.
Cowling Castle.
24. Lord Cobham to the Queen. Consultations as to the best mode of proceeding against the rebels. Norfolk's retreat. *Incloses,*

 24. I. *Cobham to Norfolk.* (Copy of 23. I.)

 24. II. *Wiat to Cobham. Invites him to join with him and proceed to London. Begs Cobham to take means to arrest Norfolk. Rochester, Jan. 29.*

1554. VOL. II.

Jan. 29. Lees.
25. Ric. Lord Rich, the Earl of Oxford, and others, justices of Essex, to the Council. Measures for the safeguard and quiet of those parts and stay of the passages. Lord Thomas and Lord John Grey had been at Enfield and were going to follow the Duke of Suffolk into Leicestershire.

Jan. 29. Exeter.
26. Sir John St. Leger to same. Particulars of his apprehending Sir Gawen Carew at his nephew's John Carew's of Bickley, Devon. State of Devon.

Jan. 30. Sherborne.
27. Sir John Rogers and others to Sec. Petre. Have proclaimed the Duke of Suffolk, the Carews, and Sir Thomas Wiat as traitors, at Sherborne market; and also published the articles of the Queen's marriage. They vouch for Sir John Horsey's fidelity.

Jan. 30. Cowling Castle.
28. Cobham to the Queen. Describes Wiat's attack on Cowling Castle. Cobham obliged at last to surrender.

Jan. 31.
29. Marquis of Winchester to Petre. His regret for Lord Cobham, but hopes the news is untrue. Has equipped 500 foot and 100 horse towards the defence of the city of London. Recommends other measures.

Jan. 31. Mereworth.
30. Henry Lord Abergavenny to the Council. Called upon the Lord Warden for his aid to fall upon the rear of Wiat's forces. Has marched from Maidstone towards Rochester, but on hearing the Duke of Norfolk's band had deserted, many of his own men had gone off. Blames Norfolk for his rash attack on the rebels.

Jan. 28. Wrotham.
31. John Dodge to same. Skirmish with the rebels under Sir Harry Isley, his son, and the two Knyvetts, near Wrotham. Defeat of the rebels, and 60 taken prisoners.

Jan. 31. Winchester Palace.
32. Bishop Gardyner to Petre. Count D'Egmont and the rest of the Ambassadors have required his advice as to the safest mode for their return. Proposes to convey them down the river.

Jan. (?)
33. Deposition of Chr. Mompesson relative to words spoken by Sir Ralph Hopton concerning the coming in of the Prince of Spain and the Spaniards.

VOL. III. FEBRUARY 1554.

Feb. 1.
1. Indenture between Edmond Downynge, and Roger and Robert Taverner of London, for purchase of the Manor of Boyton and the Barton of Bradridge, co. Cornwall, and also the Manor of Stoke and Bradley, co. Worcester, &c.

Feb. 1. Sheerlands.
2. Sir Tho. Cheyne to the Council. Thinks his letters have been intercepted by the rebels; doubts the loyalty of his own people; the treason of those with the Duke of Norfolk having much discouraged all parties, serving-men and others. Advises that Lord Pembroke should not be too hasty to advance against Wiat.

Vol. III.

1553.
Feb. 2.
Mereworth.
3. Lord Abergavenny and others to the Council. The Lord Warden will join them to oppose Wiat. Mr. Moyle and other gentlemen of East Kent are coming with him. *Inclosing,*

> 3. I. *Cheyne to Abergavenny. Is determined to join him, and to spend his heart's blood in the quarrel. Will be at Rochester on Sunday. Shurland, Feb. 1.*

Feb. 3.
Chelmsford.
4. Lord Rich and others to the Queen. Offers of Charles Tyrrel and Robert Cornwall to serve Her Majesty. Rich has furnished them with some of his own armour.

Feb. 4.
Exeter.
5. Sir John St. Leger to the Council. Has arrested Sir Arthur Champernon, although he tendered his service as a loyal subject. The county of Devon is well affected. The proclamation against the Duke of Suffolk, &c., has been published. Reported escape of Sir Peter Carew. *Incloses,*

> 5. I. *John Graynfeld to Sir John St. Leger, Sir Tho. Denys, and Sir Roger Blewet. Intelligence of the three gentlemen who took shipping at Weymouth, endorsed, "Touching the escape of Sir Peter Carew." Dartmouth, Feb. 3.*

Feb. 4.
Exeter.
6. Sir John St. Leger to Sec. Petre. *Same effect as to the Council.* Escape of William Thomas into Wales.

Feb. 4.
Sittingbourne.
7. Sir Tho. Cheyne to the Council. Has sent the proclamation to Canterbury, Dover, and other towns along the coast. Causes of his delay in quitting the Isle of Sheppy. Is going forward to Rochester.

Feb. 4.
8. Grant of the office of one of the Tellers of the Exchequer to Richard Stonley, for life. Lat.

Feb. 4.
9. Grant to Thomas Danyell of the office of Surveyor of the Melting House in the Mint, within the Tower of London. Lat.

Feb. 5.
10. Sir Tho. Denys to the Lord Chancellor. Rumour of the landing of the Prince of Spain in Devon. The report is untrue that an obligation had been signed by the inhabitants to oppose the Prince's coming. States his own service in saving Exeter. *Incloses,*

> 10. I. *Inventory of the goods and chattels of Sir Gawen Carew at Tiverton, of William Gibbs at Heysell, and of Sir Peter Carew at Mohuns Ottery, with bill of chattels delivered for payment of Sir P. Carew's debts. Feb. 2.*

> 10. II. *Depositions and statements made by Sir Gawen Carew, that he scaled the walls of Exeter, repaired to Sir Peter Carew, and put himself in armour. Of John Portington relative to the said Sir Gawen Carew. Also that Sir Peter Carew had persuaded Walter Ralegh, Esq., to convey him away in his bark, and that Willm. Gibbs armed himself on an absurd pretence, &c. &c. Jan. 28.*

Feb. 7.
Rochester.
11. Sir Tho. Cheyne to the Council. Intention of Wiat to cross the Thames at Kingston. Has appointed to meet Sir Thos. Moyle, Lord Abergavenny, and Sir R. Southwell at Dartford.

1554.

Feb. 9.
Hadlow.
12. Deposition by John a Barton and others, that the alarum was rung in the parish of Hadlow, in Kent, by order of Sir Henry Isley and Sir Thomas Culpeper.

Feb. 9.
Dounapney.
13. Sir Anth. Hungerford (Sheriff of Gloucester) to the Council. Statement of words spoken by Sir Nicholas Arnold relative to the coming of the King of Spain. Measures taken for preserving the peace of the Shire.

Feb. 9.
Westminster.
14. Grant to Sir Edmund Pekham of the office of Treasurer of the Mint within the Tower of London, together with all houses, mansions, buildings, &c., thereunto belonging. Lat.

Feb. 9.
Westminster.
15. Grant to William Hopkin of the office of blacksmith to the Mint, within the Tower of London. Lat.

Feb. 9.
Westminster.
16. Grant to Margaret Bevell, widow of William Bevell, Esq., deceased, of an annuity of thirty pounds nine shillings and threepence; together with the wardship and marriage of Robt. Bevell, his son and heir.

Feb. 10.
Westminster.
17. Grant of pardon to John Flatcher of Combe, co. Hereford, for having feloniously slain Hugh Flatcher. Lat.

Feb. 10.
Allington Castle.
18. Sir Robt. Southwell (Sheriff of Kent) to the Council. Arrest and committal of various traitors, some to Allington Castle, others to Maidstone Gaol. Specifies to whom he has given the custody of rebels' houses in Kent. Proposes to occupy Allington Castle (Wiat's residence) himself. *Incloses,*

    18. I. *Deposition by Sir Anth. Norton, of Trocheley, relative to a conversation he had with Wiat at Allington Castle. Feb.* 10.

Feb. 11.
19. Deposition by John Bowyer relative to treasonable transactions of the Duke of Suffolk, and Lord Thomas and Lord John Grey.

Feb. 11.
20. Confession by Tho. Rampton of his practice at Coventry for gaining that town to the Duke of Suffolk's purposes, and proposals for taking the castles of Warwick and Killingworth.

Feb. 11.
Ashridge.
21. Wm. Lord Howard, Sir Edw. Hastings, and Sir T. Cornwaleys, to the Queen. Interview with the Princess Elizabeth at Ashridge, who professed her willingness to repair to the Queen, but desires to be lodged further from the water than at her last being at Court. *Incloses,*

    21. I. *Memorandum of the stages of the Princess Elizabeth's journey to the Court. Feb.* 11.

Feb. 11.
Winchester House.
22. Bishop Gardyner to Sec. Petre. Sends letters and confessions received from Sir Robt. Southwell. Recommends one "little Wyatt, a bastard of no substance," to be examined in the Tower. Sends a confession of one Parker.

Feb. 13.
Ludlow.
23. Examination of Sir James Croft relative to his connexion with Lord Thomas Grey. Denies any familiar intelligence with him or with one John Davies, a soothsayer.

Vol. III.

1554.

Feb. 13.	Westminster.	24. Grant to William Dallison of the office of one of the Justices of Common Pleas, within the County Palatine of Lancaster. Lat.
Feb. 13.	Westminster.	25. Grant of like office to Edward Saunders, within the same County Palatine. Lat.
Feb. 16.	Westminster.	26. Warrant for the Treasurer and Barons of the Exchequer to give exonerations and discharges to Escheators of counties, or their lawful attorneys.
Feb. 19.	Westminster.	27. Grant to Sir John Parratt, of lands of the value of 100l. per ann. from concealed Abbey or Chantry lands.
Feb. 19.	Tunbridge.	28. Declaration of Martin Drew, Bailiff, and others, of Tunbridge, Kent, that Sir Henry Isley was the sole cause of the alarum being rung in that town.
Feb. 20.		29. Letters Patent for the naturalization of Peter Wolffe, native of the Emperor's dominions. Lat.
Feb 22.		30. Examinations of John a Mynde, Parson of Bagendon, Willm. Tawney Parson of Barnesley, co. Gloucester, Tho. Fowler, and Alice Henlowe, touching the conduct of William Thomas, in connexion with Wiat's insurrection.
Feb. 23.		31. Minute of Council, appointing Committees for conducting several parts of public business, as for Debts, Calais, the Borders, Ireland, and the Navy.
Feb. 24.	Merewood. [Mereworth.]	32. Sir Robt. Southwell to the Council. Proceedings of the rebels. Proclamation issued at Tunbridge by Sir Henry Isley, Anthony Knevet, and another gentleman, servant to the Lady Elizabeth. Arrival of Tho. Culpepper from London, and report that all England was in insurrection to oppose the coming of the Spaniards. Execution of some of the rebel prisoners ; desires directions as to disposal of others. *Incloses,*

    32. 1. *Proclamation by Sir Thos. Wiat, Sir Geo. Harper, Sir Henry Isley, and Anthony Knevett, declaring Harry Lord Abergavenny, Sir Robt. Southwell, and Geo. Clarke, traitors to God, the Crown, and the Commonwealth.*

    33. Copy of the above proclamation.

Feb. 25.	The Tower.	34. Sir John Bourne and others to the L. Chancellor and Sec. Petre. Have laboured to make Sir Thomas Wiat confess concerning the Lady Elizabeth and her servant, Sir Wm. St. Loo. Wiat declares that Sir James Croft knows more of the matter.
Feb. 26.	Westminster.	35. Grant to Stephen Hadnoll, of the Privy Chamber, of certain lands in the county of Essex. Lat.
Feb.		36. The names of certain lords and gentlemen that were with the Queen's power against the rebels ; with notes against several of their names, of the rewards to be given them.
Feb. (?)		37. Note of the armour issued to divers persons out of the armoury of the Tower, during Wiat's rebellion ; with the value of the same.

VOL. IV. MARCH—DECEMBER, 1554.

1554.
March 5.
Westminster.
1 Grant to Stephen Hadnoll, Groom of the Privy Chamber, of certain lands in Stansted, co. Essex. Lat.

March 16.
2. Princess Elizabeth to the Queen, on being commanded to go to the Tower. Protests her innocence, and demands to answer any charge against her. Disavows holding any correspondence with the traitor Wiat, and energetically denies that she ever sent any letter or message to the French King. [*Holograph.*]

3. Modern copy of the above.

March 24.
At the Court.
4. The Council to Lord Cobham. The Queen is pleased, at the intercession of Count D'Egmont, to order his release from the Tower, and also to extend her clemency to his eldest son (Willm. Brooke) at the intercession of his wife.

March (?)
5. Statement of what prejudice the tinners of Devon and Cornwall shall sustain, by reason of the exclusive grant of the sale of tin to one Brokehowse.

April (?)
6. An estimate made by the Lord Chancellor, for payment of the debts due by the Crown.

April (?)
7. Reasons in favour of a stricter observance of the Act of Apparel.

May 1.
8. Receipt by George Williams for money received of Thomas Armstrong for Sir William Cecill.

May 9.
9. The Queen to the Lord Privy Seal (Earl of Bedford) to aid Lord Howard of Effingham (Lord Admiral), in victualling the Fleet now going to Spain to bring over the Prince, her husband.

May.
10. Articles devised for a joint commission to the Alcalde Mayor, and an Englishman, for the trial of all offences within the households of the Queen and Prince Philip.

June 9.
Plymouth.
11. Wm. Lord Howard to the Council. Arrival of the Marquis de Les Naves at Plymouth from Spain. The Prince is not expected for a fortnight.

June 16.
12. Warrant to the Exchequer to pay the Marchioness of Northampton for a glass of crystal garnished with jasper, procured by her for the Queen. [*Much defaced.*]

June 19.
Basing.
13. Edwd. (Sutton) Lord Duddeley to the Council. Honourable reception of the Marquis de Les Naves, at Wilton House, by the Earl of Pembroke. Praises the little Lord Herbert.

June 21.
Guildford.
14. Grant to Thomas Reve and George Cotton of certain pasture grounds in Pewisham Forest, Wilts, parcel of the lands of the late Thomas Lord Seymour. Lat.

June 28.
Oxford.
15. The Chancellor and University of Oxford to the Queen. Testify their gratitude for the benefits conferred on the University by the restoration of ancient discipline. Have entrusted this address to be delivered by Dr. Tresham. Lat.

DOMESTIC—MARY. 63

1554.   Vol. IV.

July 10.   16. Receipt by Geo. Williams for money received of Tho. Armstrong for the use of Sir W. Cecill.

July 19.   17. A breviate of the most material facts of a packet remaining in the Office of State Papers relative to the reception of the Prince of Spain, at his first landing in England.

August 4. Hever.   18. Princess Anna of Cleves to the Queen. Thanks for favour shown to her last suit. Is desirous to wait upon Her Majesty and the King.

August 4. Hever.   19. Copy of the above.

August 14. Stamford.   20. William Campynete, Alderman of Stamford, to Sir Wm. Cecill; complains of the conduct of Mr. Fenton in spoiling of the churches lately united, contrary to the order of Sir John Harrington and the other Commissioners.

Sept. 1. The Court.   Lord Chancellor Gardyner, Bishop of Winchester, to the students of Christ Church, Oxford. Commands them to obey the honest and lawful injunctions of their Dean. [*See* 1556, June 20.]

Sept. 2.   21. Ceremonies at Hampton Court on the creation of Sir Anthony Browne as Viscount Montague.

Oct. 5. Westminster.   22. Grant to Sir John Parrot [Perrot] in fee farm, of the lordship and castle of Carew, Mill Park, and Williamson Park, for past services.

Oct. 5. Westminster.   23. Grant to the same, of the castle of Carew, the said two parks, together with other lands and tenements in New Carew, in fee simple.

Oct. 9. Westminster.   24. Grant of pardon to Edward Randoll, late of Baddilsmere, Kent, of all treasons, rebellions, &c. Lat.

Oct. 20. Witham.   25. Robt. Haryngton to Cecill. Desires instructions how to act in the matter between Obbyns and Wymberley. Wymberley has got a supersedeas out of the Court of Chancery, &c.

Oct. 20. Westminster.   26. Grant of exemption to persons deprived of promotions, dignities, and offices ecclesiastical, from payment of first fruits due to the Crown.

Oct. Grantham.   27. Thos. Sklater, alias Tomson, to Cecill. Reports the charges alledged against Mr. Troughton, Bailiff of South Witham, by one Wymberley.

Oct.   28. Thomas Wymberley to same. Complains of vexatious and tyrannical proceedings in the Manor Court of Witham.

Nov. 1. Denton.   29. Geo. Williams to same. Has been with Mr. Goche of Newark relative to receipt of arrears and rents for Stamford and Deeping.

Nov. 25. Stamford.   30. Same to same. Particulars of receipts of rents, &c. Sends accompt of the Bailiff of Deeping.

Nov. 28. Stamford.   31. Henry Lacy and Geo. Williams to same. Concerning a grant made by Cecill to Thomas Hunter of a farm in the occupation of one Brickett. Sir Wm. Hussey's men misuse the woods of Pickworth.

1554.

Dec. 16.
Ketton.
32. John Markham to Sir Wm. Cecill. Has been applied to, on behalf of Lord Clynton, to produce his lease of the pasture at West Cote.

Dec. 16.
Clyff.
33. Nich. Smyth to same. Prays that the order for delivery of does for the Queen's household may be delayed. Has made certain payments for felling trees, &c.

Dec. 18.
Stamford.
34. Aldermen and Co-burgesses of Stamford to same. Thanks for setting forward their charter, and for obtaining certain decayed cottages and other lands in the town and fields of Stamford, for the support of their school.

Dec. 18.
Stamford.
35. Geo. Williams to same. Gives sundry particulars relative to tenants. Hears of a great sale at Grimsthorp, which he will attend and purchase according as he shall be directed.

Dec.
36. Statement of the injury to the Realm, and the prejudice of English merchants, &c., arising from the usurped commerce which the Easterlings have for many years carried on.

(?)
37. Grant of pardon to Anthony Baldes, a Spaniard; remitting the penalty of branding and of the loss of an ear, for wounding another in a church. Lat.

(?)
38. The Queen to   , relative to appointment of a Clerk of the Signet in the place of Gregory Raileton, absent more than a year beyond sea.

(?)
39. Declaration of Thomas Wheyton, servant to Henry Peckham, Esq., relative to Henry the Eighth's will.

(?)
40. Account of the lands, &c., of the Ladies Katharine and Mary Grey, daughters of Henry late Duke of Suffolk and of Lady Frances his wife.

(?)
41. Grant to John Austen of all the herbage of Sedgeley Park, co. Stafford, part of the possessions of the late John Duke of Northumberland. Lat.

(?)
42. Legal opinions in the case of a Venetian ship being taken by the French during a war between France and England, and re-captured by Dutchmen.

(?)
43. Accompt of what the Queen's Majesty owes to Florence de Diaceto. His losses sustained in Wiat's commotion, &c. Fr.

(?)
44. Duplicate of the above. Fr.

(?)
45. Suit of Florence de Diaceto to the Queen. For licence to import 4,000 tuns of French wines.

(?)
46. Another suit of the same. For licence to import 1,000 tuns of French wines, free of impost; or 4,000 tuns, paying the impost in 4 years.

(?)
47. Grant from the King and Queen to John Christopherson, Master, and 8 Fellows of Trinity College, Cambridge, empowering them to make laws for the government of the College. Lat.

DOMESTIC—MARY.

VOL. V. JANUARY—JULY, 1555.

1555.
Jan. 15 (?) 1. Ordinance of Parliament relative to the tutelage and government of any children born of the marriage of Philip and Mary, in case of the Queen's death. Lat.

Jan. 15 (?) 2. Address to the King and Queen on the above resolution of Parliament, and also against the employment of foreigners, in case of the King's Government, after the Queen's death. (*In Petre's hand.*)

3. John Carrow, Clerk of the Peace, to Sir Wm. Petre. Lady Norwich has surrendered to him all her lands of the Manor of Dodinghurst. Complaint of the corrupt conduct of Mr. Benlowes. *Incloses*,

3 I. *Account of fines assessed at the Quarter Sessions at Chelmsford, by Mr. Benlowes and other Justices of Essex.*

Feb. 26.
Westminster. 4. Letters patent constituting William Marquis of Winchester and others, a body corporate, by the name of Merchant Adventurers of England for the discovery of lands, territories, &c., unknown, and not before frequented, &c. S[ebastian] C[abot] to be the first Governor.

Feb. (?) 5. Memorial of the Merchant Adventurers to the Privy Council, setting ·forth the cause of the obstruction and disorder of their affairs in the Emperor's Low Countries, and of the misdemeanours of the Merchants of the Hanse Towns.

Feb. (?) 6. Book of Justices of the Peace in the several counties of England and Wales.

April 3.
London. 7. King Philip to his Treasurer Dominico d'Orbea. Order to pay an annual pension of two hundred crowns, English, to Edward Randolph, Colonel of Infantry, for services performed.

April 29.
The Court. 8. Tho. Martyn to Edw. Courteney Earl of Devonshire. Has delivered his Lordship's message to the Cardinal, the Chancellor, and Sec. Petre. Sends him the commission for taking up carts and post horses. Has also sent a letter of commendation to Tho. Aldersey, which may be useful in his transactions with the merchants.

May 3.
London. 9. James Basset to same, at Calais. Thanks him for his gift of a great horse. Sends him a new patent and several letters. King Philip has requested the Duke of Alva to present him to the Emperor. Advice as to his journey. The Queen is thought to be pregnant.

May 4. 10. Same to same. Commends Mr. Cordell the Solicitor-General, and advises he should be joined in the same trust with himself and the rest.

May 6.
Westminster. 11. Sir Francis Englefyld to same. Recommends Mr. Cordell should be joined with him, and others, in trust for the Earl's affairs.

May 8.
Calais. 12. Earl of Devonshire to his mother (Gertrude Marchioness of Exeter). Notifies his arrival at Calais; sets out on the morrow for Flanders.

1555.

May 8. Calais.	13. Earl of Devonshire to Lady Barkley. Thanks for her letters. Has been very sorry whenever he has thought of her broken bow.
May 8. Calais.	14. Same to Jas. Basset. Desires him to procure for his uncle John Blount a licence to travel.
May 16. Malsanger.	15. Gertrude Marchioness of Exeter to the Earl of Devonshire, at Brussels. Examination of his household stuff at Kew and in London, with the inventories he had left.
May 16. Malsanger.	16. Same to same. In answer to his letter of the 8th; hopes to see him safe back again in England, and prays for the preservation of his soul and body.
May 21.	17. Devonshire to Jas. Basset. Has written letters to the King and Queen, and Sec. Petre will deliver them. The Duke of Alva has introduced him to the Emperor.
May 21. Bruxelles.	18. Same to Queen Mary. Has been presented to the Emperor, and describes his interview.
May 21. Bruxelles.	19. Draft of the above.
May 21. Bruxelles.	20. Same to King Philip. The same in effect as to the Queen. Italian.
May 21. Bruxelles.	21. Same to Bernard de Fresneda, the King's Confessor. Describes his gracious reception by the Emperor, to which he considers that he has been greatly instrumental. Lat.
May 25. Bruxelles.	22. Same to Lord Chancellor Gardyner. His audience with the Emperor. Has delivered his letters to Mr. Gresham and Mr. Mason. The former will furnish him with money.
May 27 Westminster.	23. Jas. Basset to Devonshire. Congratulates him on his good reception by the Emperor. Advises that he should continue to send his letters to the King and Queen through Sec. Petre. P.S. by Sir Fr. Englefyld, assuring the Earl of his good will.
May 27. London.	24. Wm. Cordell to same. Particulars of the sale and alienation in trust for his Lordship of the burgh of Stoke-gursey, containing the two manors of Weke-Fitzpayne and Wyndeyatts. Advises caution in the disposal of his property.
May 27. Westminster.	25. Grant to Stephen Hadnoll, of the manor of Clavering Lucas Pitchards, parcel of the lands lately belonging to Wm. Marquis of Northampton, attainted.
May 29. Bruxelles.	26. Devonshire to James Basset. Desires his friendly assistance in certain affairs. The King promised him licence to go into Italy; begs Basset to prosecute that suit. Has disease in his hip from cold.
May 31. Staple Inn, at Calais.	27. Tho. Martyn to Devonshire. Has moved the Lord Chancellor for licence for him to go to Milan or Naples. Differences between the Commissioners and other great personages. Arrival of the Bishop of Orleans and Monsr. Viglius. There are four named for the popedom; Card. Pole is likely to be chosen.

1555.

VOL. V.

May (?)
Hampton Court.
28. K. Philip and Q. Mary to Cardinal Pole, notifying that the Queen has been delivered of a Prince. [*Several copies of similar letters were prepared about the end of May, but are otherwise without date.*]

May (?)
Hampton Court.
29. Passport, signed by the King and Queen, for Sir Henry Sydney to go over to the King of the Romans, and the King of Bohemia, to announce the Queen's happy delivery of a Prince. [*Not dated.*]

May (?)
30. Warrant, signed by the same, for a sum of money to be delivered to some person going over to the Emperor, for the same purpose.

May (?)
31. Similar warrant for a person sent to the King of the Romans.

May (?)
32. Similar warrant for a person sent to the King of France.

June 6.
Bruxelles.
33. Earl of Devonshire to Jas. Basset. Is going to pass a little time in Lorraine, and visit Mr. Bonvise, who has promised to advance him money on Basset's credit.

June 8.
Calais.
34. Tho. Martyn to Devonshire. Lord Chancellor Gardyner is returning to England. All is quiet in England. Dee, Cary, and Butler, who calculated the nativities of the King, Queen, and Princess Elizabeth, are apprehended on the accusation of one Ferys, whose children thereupon had been struck, one with death, the other with blindness.

June 8.
Malsanger.
35. Gertrude Marchioness of Exeter to same. Upbraids him for not writing to her with his own hand.

June 11.
Hampton Court.
36. Sir Fr. Englefyld to the same. Supposes he has heard that the sale of the land in Dorset cannot take effect. Desires further directions.

June 14.
Hampton Court.
37. Bernard de Fresneda to same. Was overjoyed to hear of his good reception at the Emperor's Court. If he desires to go to Aix la Chapelle to take the baths, the King and Queen have given permission. Lat.

June 14.
Mantua.
38. Michael Throkmarton to Henry [Edward?] Earl of Devonshire; congratulates him on recovering the Queen's favour, and that he is on his travels, and intends to visit Italy. Invites him to Mantua.

June 16.
Lincoln's Inn.
39. John Haydon to same. Has paid over to John Walker the half year's rents due at Lady Day last. Sends him particulars of all the manors, boroughs, &c., which he holds in fee simple in the counties of Devon and Somerset. Suggests his expenditure should be limited to 1,200*l.* a year.

June 17.
40. Account of the charges of the obsequies of the Queen of Spain celebrated in the Cathedral Church of St. Paul, London, amounting to 1,068*l.* 11*s.*

June 21.
Namur.
41. John Strowd to Devonshire. News from the camp; 600 pioneers, clothed in red, had been sent into Marienburgh by the French King.

June 30.
Bruxelles.
42. Devonshire to Lord Abergavenny. Requests him to procure for him some bucks and does that graze. Wishes for his company abroad, but hopes one day to see him again in England with his broad dagger at his back.

E 2

1555.

July 1. Bruxelles.	43. Earl of Devonshire to Mr. Tho. Gresham. Thanks for his good cheer. Begs him to advance money to purchase him "a scytheraine" [*Gittern ?*], and to provide for him as much good black velvet as will make "a long straight night gowne."
July 1. Bruxelles.	44. Same to the Marchioness of Exeter. Likes his residence abroad, but his purse begins to get light. Is resident at Brussels, where the Emperor, the French Queen, and the Duchess of Lorraine continually reside. Sometimes visits the most notable towns of the country. Complains of the neglect of Wm. Dabeney.
July 1. Bruxelles.	45. Same to Tho. Smith. Is glad to hear that Sir Tho. Tresham's health has amended. Wishes that he could have been practising with Mr. Smith, with their crossbows among Tresham's deer.
July 1. Bruxelles.	46. Same to Dr. Martyn. Thanks for his letters. Sends him a plan of the fortifications at Bruxelles.
July 10. Windsor Castle.	47. Sir Fr. Englefyld to Devonshire. Has conferred with his servant [Walter] Prune, and also written to Mr. Basset on his affairs.
July 12. Hampton Court.	48. Sir Wm. Petre to same. Assures him of his friendship. The Queen's delivery is now daily expected.
July 14. Hampton Court.	Warrant to permit seven score of white cloths to be exported duty free for livery of the gentlemen of the Archbishop of Cologne. [*See* 1558, *undated*, No. 52.]
July 20. Bruxelles.	49. Devonshire to Mr. Bonvise. Has need of a thousand crowns, which he desires him to pay into the hands of Tho. Gresham. Has received a letter from Sir W. Petre, informing him the Queen's hour was daily expected.
July 22. Bruxelles.	50. Same to Lord Cobham. Thanks him for the offer of one of his great horses: would prefer the loan of a jennet or bastard jennet.
July 23. Bruxelles.	51. Same to Sir Robert Rochester (Comptroller of the Household), Sir Fr. Englefyld, Sir Edward Walgrave, Mr. Basset, and Mr. Cordell. Approves of the proposed survey of his estates, and requests it may be expedited. Thinks the idle reports that he is a prisoner should be refuted. Is in want of money.
July 24. Bruxelles.	52. Same to same. Warrant to pay certain wages to John Walker and Thos. Browne for their services at Kew.
July 25. Bruxelles.	53. Same to Gresham. Directions to purchase plate for him, not to exceed 1,000 crowns.
July 25. Bruxelles.	54. Same to Bonvise. Thanks for the order he has taken for payment of the 1,000 crowns. Sends his bill for the same.
July 26. Bruxelles.	55. Same to Sir Tho. Tresham. Has received his letter by Stephen Harrington. Is glad of his good health.

Vol. VI. August—December, 1555.

1555. Aug. 3. Bruxelles.	1. Earl of Devonshire to Gresham. Had arrived at Malines on his way to Antwerp, but was obliged to return. Begs the plate may be expedited.
Aug. 6. Bruxelles.	2. Same to the Marchioness of Exeter. Rejoices to hear of her good health, and that the Queen has called her again to her Privy Chamber. Thanks for the token she has sent him.
Aug. 14. Bruxelles.	3. Same to Sir Arthur Darcy. Begs he will command him in any friendly offices.
Aug. 20. Malsanger.	4. G. Marchioness of Exeter to the Earl of Devonshire. Received his letter of the 6th. The messenger was much impeded on his passage, as there was a great fight between the French and Spaniards at sea. Is going to Canford; Serjeant Tymwell, George Gattys, and Mr. Warham's daughter accompany her. Trusts he will avoid all sinful company.
Aug. 25. Bruxelles.	5. Devonshire to Lord Paget. Thanks for the assurance of his friendship. Troubles him with a request, the particulars of which will be found in the Lord Ambassador's letters.
Aug. 26. Bruxelles.	6. Same to the Lord Chancellor Gardyner. Letter of compliment by the bearer, who was the Lord Cardinal's Chaplain.
Aug. 26. Bruxelles.	7. Same to Mr. Basset. Excuses his slackness in writing, and sends by the bearer a discourse of his estate, and the particulars of his affairs.
Aug. 29. Greenwich.	8. Tho. Harvey to Devonshire. Begs to be employed in his service.
Sept. 2.	9. Receipt of George Williams for the sum of 3*l*. 13*s*. 4*d*. of Francis Armstrong, due to Sir Wm. Cecill.
Sept. 7. Greenwich.	10. Tho. Harvey to Devonshire. Has sent his letter to my Lord of Worcester, and returns his answer. The Queen is well and merry.
Sept. 9.	11. Jas. Basset to same. The King and Queen displeased that he has been molested and troubled by unworthy persons. The King will see him on his going over to Flanders, who will not be long there, as the writs for a new Parliament are issued. Gives him advice.
Sept. 12. Bruxelles.	12. Devonshire to Sir Tho. Tresham. Thanks him for his letters. His son still remains with him, and is worthy of his father.
Sept. 17. Greenwich.	13. Sir Wm. Petre to Devonshire. Has received his letter, and is willing to do him any service at Court.
Sept. 17. Greenwich.	14. Sir Fr. Englefyld to same. The bearer will inform him of the progress made in his affairs, and of Englefyld's opinion as to his proposed journey into Italy.

Vol. VI.

1555.

Sept. 30.
Bruxelles.
15. Earl of Devonshire to (Anthony Browne) Lord Montague. Thanks for his good offices, and professes friendship.

Sept. (?)
16—21. Six papers of memoranda, of sundry important matters transacted in Council from the last of August, and in the month of September, during the absence of King Philip in Flanders. With marginal annotations, by the King's authority.

Sept. 30.
22. Articles relative to the Crown lands, customs, revenues, &c., preparatory to the meeting of Parliament. Lat.

Sept. (?)
23. Account of the rents and revenues of the lands of Richard, late Earl of Warwick, called Warwick's lands and Spencer's lands, temp. 21 Hen. VII., 31 Hen. VIII., and 1 & 2 Phil. and Mary, in the counties of Wilts and Berks. Lat.

Oct. 11.
Bruxelles.
24. Devonshire to Mr. Basset. The Emperor's departure is stayed till the 14th of the ensuing month, and it is hoped King Philip will return to England soon after. Rumour that the Lord Ch. Gardyner is grievously sick.

Oct. 12.
London.
25. G. Marchioness of Exeter to Devonshire. Prays that he may have grace to avoid bad company. Has been at Canford, and is now in London to see the Queen.

Oct. 12.
26. Orders given by the King and Queen's Majesties Philip and Mary, touching the Tower of London, the officers and ministers thereof. Declaring the number of officers, soldiers, &c., their wages, allowances, &c., and the prerogatives, duties, and privileges of the Constable and other officers; with the bounds and limits of the said Tower.

Oct. 12.
27. Selection from the foregoing, of the orders relating to the wages of the Constable, and the fees payable by prisoners of various grades.

Oct. 15.
Bruxelles.
28. King Philip to the whole Parliament of England. Cannot be present at the meeting of the Parliament, but hopes to return to England shortly. Exhorts them to continue in their accustomed obedience to the Queen, and faithfully to discharge their duties. Lat. [*This letter is not entered on the Minutes of either House of Parliament.*]

Oct. 15.
29. Minute of the above. Lat.

Oct. 15.
Bruxelles.
30. Same to the Privy Council. Exhorts them to a diligent discharge of their public duties. (*Nearly illegible.*)

Oct. 17.
Westminster.
31. Englefyld to Devonshire. Survey of his lands by Mr. Hummerston; who has brought to light divers obsolete and concealed rents. No wood sales have been made.

Oct. 22.
32. Devonshire to Sir Wm. Petre. Has obtained King Philip's licence to travel: desires the Queen's concurrence.

Oct. 22.
33. Same to the Queen on the same subject. Proffers his humble service abroad.

Oct. 22.
34. Same to Lord Ch. Gardyner, to the same effect.

DOMESTIC—MARY.

VOL. VI.

1555.

Oct. 22. — 35. Earl of Devonshire to Card. Pole, to the same effect as No. 32.

Oct. 22. — 36. Draft of the copy to Petre. (No. 32.)

Oct. 29.
St. James's. — 37. T. Harvey to Devonshire. Desires to accompany him in his travels, and if he does not, to know how he may communicate with him.

Oct. 30.
At the Court. — 38. Jas. Basset to same. The Queen's affection for him continually increases, and she would be pleased to see him in England before going further abroad.

Nov. 2.
Bruxelles. — 39. Devonshire to Sir Wm. Petre. Is willing to dispose of the Manor of Whitford to him.

Nov. 2. — 40. Same to Walgrave, and others, his trustees. Authorizes them to part with the manor of Whitford in Devon to Sir Wm. Petre.

Nov. 2.
Bruxelles. — 41. Same to Mr. Basset. Has complied with his request for Sir Wm. Petre. Wants money.

Nov. 2.
Bruxelles. — 42. Same to same. Directions for the sale of the manor of Whitford to Petre. Has taken leave of the Emperor, and also of the King, who has given him letters of introduction to various States and Ambassadors. His want of money to prosecute his journey is urgent. His application for leave to return to England was not well taken.

Nov. 3. (?) — 43. Same to Englefyld. Urges him to be diligent in the sale of his lands, mortgages, &c.

Nov. 5.
Bruxelles. — 44. Same to Mr. Basset. Has received his letters of the 18th and 30th October. The King has promised to make his excuse to the Queen for his not visiting her in England before his setting out to travel. Commends his affairs to Basset's care.

Nov. 7.
Bruxelles. — 45. Same to Sir Tho. Tresham. Complains of his son, whom he has dismissed from attendance on him. Has taken leave of the Emperor, King Philip, &c., and sets out that day, through Germany, for Italy.

Nov. 7.
Bruxelles. — 46. Same to Mr. John Trelawny. Being able to retain only a small number of attendants, he sends home his son, who has the heart of a gentleman.

Nov. 8.
Malsanger. — 47. G. Marchioness of Exeter to Devonshire. Is sorry he is going to travel so far from home, but trusts he will come first to England to see the Queen and his poor mother. Is ill, and writes with difficulty.

Nov. 12.
Louvaine. — 48. Devonshire to Sir Tho. Kemys. Has received his letter with the things enclosed : hopes to hear from him frequently.

Nov. 12.
Louvaine. — 49. Same to Mr. Rise. Thanks him for his good report of him to the Queen. Has taken leave, and sets out without visiting England.

Nov. 13.
Louvaine. — 50. Same to Mr. Fowler. Was prevented from visiting England ; has therefore taken leave, and begun his journey.

1555.

Nov. 13.
Bruxelles.

51. King Philip to the Council. Has written to the Queen in favour of Chr. Bloncquet for restoration to certain lands in Ireland. Lat.

Nov. 14.
Louvaine.

52. Earl of Devonshire to Sir Robt. Rochester and others. Complains that the Sheriff of Somersetshire withholds from him certain goods, &c., escheated to him on account of a murder done by one Wikes within his manor of Crockhorne.

Nov. 16.
Louvaine.

53. Same to Humphrey Mitchell, Bailiff of his Manor of Crockhorne, Somerset. Commends his diligence in recovering the goods of the felon Wikes.

Nov. 16.
Louvaine.

54. Ri. Tremayne to Sir Nich. Arnold. Concerning the rate of allowance to be made to the son of Sir Nicholas and himself while residing abroad. Payment of debts already incurred. [Indorsed "Found in John Walker's chamber."]

Nov. 16.
Louvaine.

55. Devonshire to Rochester and others. Represents his urgent necessity for money. Directions as to raising it, and appeasing his creditors.

Nov. 16.
Louvaine.

56. Same to Sir Fr. Englefyld. Thanks him for the conduct of himself and Mr. Hummerston in his affairs. Explains his not coming into England. Directions as to raising money, &c.

Nov. 16.
Louvaine.

57. Same to Sir W. Petre, on the same topics as the preceding. Desires him to acquaint the Queen with his state and condition.

Nov. 17.
Louvaine.

58. Same to same. Directions as to sending over forty tuns of beer for the use of his household.

Nov. 18.
Louvaine.

59. Same to the Marchioness of Exeter. The bearer can state the particulars which prevented his coming to England. Is sorry he cannot confer a certain prebend on Willm. Dawbeny.

Nov. 18.
Louvaine.

60. Same to Basset. Details of arrangements on dismissing his household.

Nov. 18

61. Charges of victualling 2,800 men, appointed in 15 ships to transport the Emperor, beginning Oct. 14, 1555.

Nov. 20.
Louvaine.

62. Devonshire to Sir John Masone. Regrets the death of the Lord Chancellor Gardyner, but was glad he died reconciled to Lord Paget. Means shortly to go forward on his journey.

Nov. 20.
Louvaine.

63. Same to Sir Tho. Chamberlaine. Thanks for his friendship. Authorizes him to make certain sales of property.

Nov. 20.

64. Same to Mr. Peto. Excuses himself for not fully answering his first letter.

Nov. 23.
St. James's.

65. Sir Wm. Petre to Devonshire. Takes leave of him by letter : offers him service, and advises him to avoid all cause of any ill-report.

Nov. 23.
Louvaine.

66. Devonshire to Sir W. Petre (?). Commends Sir Peter Carew, whom he met at Antwerp, and finds him well disposed towards the service of the King and Queen. His conscience is still, however, influenced by his religion.

VOL. VI.

1555. Nov. 23.	67. Earl of Devonshire to Lady Berkeley. Is sorry that he cannot take leave of her before he goes into Italy. Will write, but if he should extend his travels to Constantinople, she may not expect letters from him. Desires her prayers.
Nov. 23 (?)	68. Same to Sir Gawen Carew. Desires him to forward a suit of his servant Humphrey Michell.
Nov. 23 (?) Louvaine.	69. Same to same. Remonstrates with him for signing a certain restraint at the instigation of Haidon [Haydon].
Nov. 23. Louvaine.	70. Same to Englefyld and Basset. Complains of the conduct of Haidon, and the general neglect of his affairs. Will not be influenced through the Earl of Bedford. Hopes to receive some account of his affairs at Cologne, and either money or credit, or he must shift as he can.
Nov. 24. Louvaine.	71. Same to the Commissioners for his estates. Finds none of his instructions are complied with. Regrets that credit should have been given to the statements of Haidon, whom he is resolved to discharge of all his employments.
Nov. 28. St. Tron.	72. Same to Lord Hastings. Thanks him for his letter : will often write to him from Italy.
Nov. 29. Louvaine.	73. Same to the Commissioners. Approves of the arrangements they have made for his supply on his travels. Has executed the instrument of sale, &c.
Nov. 29. Louvaine.	74. Same to Basset. His business is at length happily effected. Desires him to return thanks in his name to the Commissioners, particularly to Mr. Comptroller. Further directions as to money affairs.
Dec. 9.	75. Inquisition in the Court of Admiralty of the Cinque Ports relative to a ship wrecked on the Goodwin Sands.
Dec. 10. Colaine. [Cologne.]	76. Devonshire to Sir Tho. Chamberlaine. Thanks for his letter to Herman Ringe, who has been of service to him. Desires to be remembered to several friends.
Dec. 10. Cologne.	77. Same to Mr. Aldersay. Has received the bill of exchange for 400 Italian crowns, and returns him thanks.
Dec. 18. St. James's Palace.	78. The Select Council to King Philip. Object to any licence being granted to Anthony Guarras. Recommend that Mr. Williams, his Chamberlain, should be allowed his table during His Majesty's absence. Lat.
Dec. 21. Rhinehouse.	79. Devonshire to Masone. Arrived at Spires, but finding the plague there, had crossed the Rhine to the little village of Rhinehouse. Could write much of the barbarous character of the people, but dare not for fear of his life.
Dec. 27 (?)	80. John Bedell to Chr. Ashton. Has been in London and left a nag at the Checkers without Temple Bar. Understands Mr. Dudley is gone, and that Sir Anth. Kingston is at liberty.

VOL. VI.

1555.	
Dec. 30. Augusta. (Augsburg.)	81. Earl of Devonshire to Sir Philip Hoby. Has arrived at Augusta, and delivered his letter to the Shorers. Desires to be remembered to various friends.
Dec. 31.	82. Memorandum of matters transacted in the Select Council. Despatch of merchants for the journey of Mina. Commissions for collecting the subsidy, and for enclosures on the Scottish borders, &c. Lat.
Dec. 31.	83. English minute of the preceding, in Sec. Petre's hand.
Dec. (?)	84. Articles addressed to Sir Richard Southwell, by Robert [Holgate] late Archbishop of York, relative to his marriage with Mrs. Barbara Wentworth, by the advice of the late Duke of Somerset, and for fear of the late Duke of Northumberland, for which he had been deprived. Prays for restoration to liberty, and to the celebration of divine service, for which he offers to Her Majesty one thousand pounds.
(?)	85. List of the names of parks, forests, and chaces in the Queen's hands, and of the officers belonging to them.
(?)	86. Statement of the revenue of the Crown in England and Wales, anno 1555.

VOL. VII. JANUARY—MARCH, 1556.

1556. Jan. 13. London.	1. Henry Lord Hastings to the Earl of Devonshire. Thanks for his letters, and wishes he were in his company. The King's return to England has been long looked for.
Jan. 15. Venice.	2. Peter Vannes to same. Has heard of his arrival at Padua. Invites him to come to Venice on the next day, when there was to be a grand public ceremony.
Jan. 25. Brooke.	3. John Blount to same. Commends the bearer, who brings news from his Lordship's mother and Lady Bartley [Berkeley]. The weather has been exceedingly severe.
Jan. 29. Westminster.	4. Grant to William Lord Paget of the office of Keeper of the Privy Seal, vacant by the death of John, late Earl of Bedford. Lat.
Feb. 11. Antwerp.	5. King Philip to the Select Council. Has received the account of their proceedings with much satisfaction. Recommends the affairs of the Realm to their diligent care. Accredits John de Figueroa to confer with them on the subject of the Royal Titles. Lat.
Feb. 15. Antwerp.	6. Sir John Masone to Devonshire. A truce has been concluded. The Estates to assemble at Brussells. King Philip will shortly go to England. Great part of the Priests of England wish the Cardinal back again in Rome. Robbery and murders on London Bridge.
Feb. 23.	7. Account of monies received by Walter Prune, for the use of the Earl of Devonshire, from 1 Nov. 1554 to 23 Feb. 1555.

VOL. VII.

1556.	
Feb. 23. St. Mary Overy's.	8. Anth. Visct. Montague to the Earl of Devonshire. Is very desirous to hear of his safe arrival in Italy. Hopes he will be able to avoid the numerous evils which will be daily before his sight.
Feb. 23. London.	9. John Storie to same. Prays for his prosperity, so useful in future to the Christian religion and his native land. The Queen and the Cardinal (Pole) have the spiritual and civil matters of the realm in contemplation. Justice is reduced to order by the activity of the present Lord Chancellor (Nich. Heath, Archbishop of York).
Feb. 23 (?)	10. The Select Council to the King. Have conferred with Signor Figueroa concerning the matter of Their Majesties' titles, and cannot, as faithful Counsellors, accede to the proposition. The Lord Privy Seal and Bishop of Ely, are coming over to his Majesty.
Feb. 25. Greenwich.	11. Anth. Kemp to Devonshire. Makes excuse for not writing, being so engaged in posting between Greenwich and Brussells. The King not yet returned to England, whose absence makes the Queen melancholy.
Feb. (?)	12. Wm. Bygott to the Council. Details the circumstances of his receiving a letter from Andrew Ryvett: confesses his error, and throws himself upon the Queen's mercy. [*On the 16th of Feb. 1555-6 Wm. Bygott was committed to the Tower for receiving a seditious letter from Andrew Ryvett. Co. Reg.*]
Feb. (?)	13. Draft of the above. [*In a P.S. (which is not added to the above) he asks leave to go to chapel, and receive the Sacrament.*]
March 8. Bruxelles.	14. Masone to Devonshire. Will deliver his letter to Ruiz Gomez. The truce everywhere proclaimed in France. Mr. Prune is about to proceed towards his Lordship, and Mr. Bouchier has been sent for by my Lord of Huntingdon.
March 9. Bruxelles.	15. John Butcher to same. Begs to enter in his service, though it were but to serve him as one in his stable.
March 10. Southampton.	16. Richard Vuedall (or Uvedale) to his servant Dominick. Directions to repair to Master Cranwell for eleven bars of silver, and to send him a letter in answer.
March 11.	17. Confession of William Draper of Heth, co. Southampton, concerning certain persons in his house, some of whom went on board ship; and one Davy, a servant of Ric. Vuedall's, was there, and one Ric. Flud a butcher.
March 13. Venice.	18. Devonshire to Michael Throkmarton. Acknowledges several letters on money affairs. Will come to Mantua about Easter, and wishes some horses to be brought for him. Has visited and been entertained by the Doge and Senate of Venice.
March 15. Bruxelles.	19. Masone to Devonshire. Ruiz Gomez thanks him for his letter, and would communicate it to the King. His servant is coming towards him with a fine gelding from the Earl of Pembroke.
March 16. Bruxelles.	20. King Philip (signed *Yo el Rey*) to the Queen. He has received the two pardons for Peter Carew. Spanish.
March 16.	21. Copy of the above. Spanish.

DOMESTIC—MARY.

Vol. VII.

1556.

March 16.
Bruxelles.
22. The King to the Select Council. Cannot at present reply to their letters of the 23d, but will consider of the matter submitted to him by the Bishop of Ely and Privy Seal. Refers them to John de Figueroa. Lat.

Mar. 16 (?)
23. Notes relative to the conspiracy, and names of the conspirators, for robbing the Exchequer, and levying war in the realm.

Mar. 16 (?)
24. Names of noblemen and gentlemen vehemently suspected to be participators in the above conspiracy.

(?)
25. Another list of suspected persons.

March 16.
26. Confession of John Peers, concerning the transporting certain men out of the realm into France; conversation with Ric. Vuedall.

March 16.
27. Confession of Stephen Rike, a mariner belonging to John Peers, that nine persons were embarked at Heath (on 1st March) and landed at Newhaven, in France.

March 17.
Mantua.
28. M. Throkmarton to the Earl of Devonshire. Regrets not hearing from him. Introduces the merchant Geronimo Peveraro to him. News from England; confirmation of the archbishoprick to Card. Pole, who thereupon intends to take upon him the order of priesthood. The matters of religion proceed coldly enough, albeit seven heretics have of late been burnt.

March 20.
Venice.
29. Devonshire to M. Throkmarton. Has received his letters. Departs to-morrow towards Ferrara, and will afterwards visit him at Mantua.

March 20.
30. Deposition of Catharine Butteler, alias Throgmorton, wife of Anthony Throgmorton, taken before Sir John Bourne, as to her knowledge of persons suspected of the conspiracy.

March 23
31. Confession of Richard Vuedall that Henry Dudley, one of the conspirators, took shipping at his house at Chillinge in Hampshire; that John Bedell and Christopher Ashton were also there.

March 24, 25.
32. Full confession and detail by Richard Vuedall concerning Henry Dudley's measures for privately going beyond sea. Disclosure of a plot in which Dudley, Throckmerton, Ashton, and Bedell were concerned, for transporting men from England into France, landing with them again on the coast near Portsmouth, driving out the Spaniards, &c.

March 24.
33. Statement of Wm. Coulynge relative to the purchase of a crayer by Bedell and John Throgmerton.

March 25.
34. Statement of Robert Gyre, of Yarmouth (I. of Wight), before the Mayor and two others, as to hire of his crayer, by Ric. Vuedall, to convey two strangers to Cherbourg, in Normandy.

March 26.
35. Interrogatories to be put to Bedell.

March 26.
36. Notes from the deposition of Bedell, relative to Dudley, Sir A. Kingston, Vuedall, Throkmerton, Sir Francis Dawtry, &c.

DOMESTIC—MARY.

VOL. VII.

1556.	
March 26.	37. Confession of Thomas White, detailing the progress of the conspiracy. The Queen, on hearing that the King would not return to England for a long time, was in a rage, and caused his picture to be carried out of the Privy Chamber. Conversation between the Queen and Lady Dudley. Headed, "my seconde writing." (*Imperfect, beginning at folio* v.)
March 27.	38. Confession of William Hennewes (Hinnes). Relates conversation with Bedell, who endeavoured to persuade him to go to sea fishing with him, &c.
March 28.	39. Examination of Willm. Hinnes. Deposes that Bowes stated he had a letter of licence from the French King, to use a mint in France for coining testons, to be employed to aid the English in driving out the Spaniards. Conversation with Dethicke as to sale of the Earl of Devon's lands for the purposes of the conspiracy.
March 29. Bruxelles.	40. Masone to Devonshire. Foreign news. The King's journey to England deferred, by reason of a visit from the King of Bohemia. Cranmer burnt, standing obstinately in his opinions, and Card. Pole made Archbishop. Other English news.
March 29.	41. Devonshire to Masone. Thanks for his letters and kindness, and particularly for forwarding his journey to Italy. Arrival and grand reception of the Queen of Poland at Padua. Has been to Ferrara, and was honourably received by the Duke and entertained in his palace there.
March 30.	42. Confession of William Hinnes, relating to the conversation he had with Bedell at Green wichand Fleet Bridge; with other particulars.
Mar. 30 (?)	43. Report of a conversation of Wm. Hinnes with Chidle's man, as to conveyance of a letter.
March (?)	44. Notes out of Hinnes's confession, to charge John Benbow, of the Chapel Royal, as to his delivering shovels, spades, and poles to Bedell, to be shipped; and procuring a ship of 80 tons burthen for Bedell's use.
March (?)	45. Notes out of Hinnes's confession, to charge Bethell with, as to meeting him at Fleet Bridge, &c. Reported landing of certain English gentlemen in the West of England.
Mar. 30 (?)	46. Statement by Hinnes that John Dethicke applied to him, as having skill in alchymy, to make experiments on a foreign coin called *ealdergylders*, to convert them into gold.
Mar. 30 (?)	47. Confession by Tho. White: proposal by Dethicke to acquaint Hinnes with the plot for seizing the treasure in custody of Brigham, a Teller of the Exchequer, and for killing the Queen and King.
March (?)	48. Deposition by the same, implicating Sir Tho. Carden [Cawarden] and Sir Nicholas Arnold.
Mar. 30 (?)	49. A paper of notes, indorsed "Hinnes's last confession;" and notes from other confessions.
Mar. 30 (?)	50. Notes from Rosey's confession, to charge Bedell with, who was brought to him by Dethicke.

Vol. VII.

1556.	
March (?)	51. Interrogatories put to Bedell.
Mar. 30 (?)	52. Deposition by Bedell relative to the first conference between himself, Ashton, and Dudley, at Fifield, in Berkshire. Inculpates Vuedall. [Indorsed, Bedell's first Book.]
Mar. 30 (?)	53. Another confession, by Bedell, of what passed between himself, White, Ashton, and Vuedall, on board a passage-boat in Southampton Water.
March 30.	54. Deposition by Bedell concerning a conversation with Stanton, relative to Dudley and Ashton.
March (?)	55. Declaration by Bedell of a conversation between himself and Mr. Henry Pekham as to Ashton and Dudley. Desires to be confronted with Pekham.
March (?)	56. Notes out of the depositions of White and Bedell.
(?)	57. John Bedell to his wife Bessy. Recommends her to take the adversity which has happened to him with patience. Hopes to obtain mercy. Desires she will apply to Mr. Alderman White to intercede for him.
(?)	58. Confession of Bawcriff concerning measures taken by Bedell and Ashton for procuring one Castell and Andrew Pomeraye, two engravers, to make dies for coining.
(?)	59. Examination of Martin Dare, relative to the occasion of his going to France. His communications with Chr. Aston, Horsey, Tremaynes, Dudley, Vuedall. General detail of the conspiracy, robbery of the Exchequer, &c.
(?)	60. Interrogatories put to Rosey relative to his participation in the conspiracy, and to his knowledge as to Sir Anth. Kingston, Sir Nich. Arnold, Sir Tho. Carden, Sir Tho. Throkmerton, Sir Nich. Throkmerton, Henry Dudley, Aston, or any of them.
(?)	61. Replies made by William Rosey to the above interrogatories.
March (?)	62. Draft of the above.
(?)	63. Notes from Rosey's deposition to charge Throkmerton with Conversation between Rosey and him, &c.
March.	64. Deposition of William Stanton as to Henry Dudley staying several days at his house, and his conversation with Chr. Ashton. Dudley on his departure promised him a horse.
March.	65. Copy of the above.
March 31.	66. Examination of John Throgmerton. Deposes that there was no oath of secrecy taken by himself or others. He never said the Queen took down King Philip's picture, and kicked it out of the Privy Chamber. Stanton's deposition as to conversation between Dudley and Ashton.

VOL. VIII. APRIL—MAY, 1556.

1556.
April 5.
Wimbledon.

1. The Easter Book of the parish of Wimbledon, containing the names of many parishioners, and of those who were confessed and received the sacrament, beginning with Sir William Cecill and the Lady Mildred his wife.

April 8.
Coberley.

2. Examination of Sir Anthony Kingston relative to a conversation which he had with Ashton and Dudley. Ashton broke a piece of coin, and delivered it to Sir Anthony Kingston as a token, &c.

April 9.
Coberley.

3. Examination of Sir A. Kingston as to his connection with John Throgmerton, Vuedall, or Aston, and his fitting out a pinnace.

April 10.

4. Confession of Willm. Stanton, relative to Henry Dudley's taking up his abode at his house; that Bedell visited Dudley there. Neither Throgmerton, Bedell, Dudley, or Ashton ever communicated to him their intention of going beyond sea. Conversation between Dudley and Ashton.

April 10.

5. Memorandum of conversations of Stanton with John Danyell and Ferdinando Lygons, relative to Henry Dudley.

April 11.

6. Full confession of John Danyell. Transactions of Dudley and others charged with the conspiracy. Offer made to Danyell by Dudley to engage him in the service of the King of France. Danyell fractures his leg.

April 13.

7. Statement by John Danyell relative to conversations with John Throgmerton. Report of dissentions between Dudley and Francis and Edw. Horsey in France.

April 13.

8. Examination of Roger Horton, taken before John Throkmerton, Esq., at Greenwich, relative to the attempt of Mr Prestall, his master, to go abroad.

April 14.

9. Deposition by John Peerse, ship-master of Southampton, as to his conveyance of Ashton and his company, over seas to Newhaven, of their landing in their way in the Isle of Wight, calling at Vuedall's house.

April 15.

10. Interrogatories to be put to Richard Vuedall, as to his transactions with John Peerse.

April 15.

11. Answer by Vuedall to the above. Denies all knowledge of John Peerse.

April 16, 17.

12. Examinations of William Bury, servant of Christopher Chudleigh, now in France. He conveyed letters from France to various persons in England. Conversations with John Danyell, who expressed his desire to join the Horseys and Dudley.

April 18.

13. Examination of Dethicke. Had been informed by Carter of the design of Sir Thos. Carden, and others, to stay any treasure going over to King Philip. The plot communicated to one Captain Powell.

1556.
Vol. VIII.

April 18. 14. John Throgmerton's confession, that he heard White, Bedell, and Dethicke talk of obtaining the treasure. Knew not of Dudley's going over to France ; never was acquainted with Ashton, nor had any intercourse with the French ambassador.

April 18. 15. Receipt, by John Abraham, to William Tymyng, for 13*l.* for rent of St. Leonard's and Stamford, due to Sir W. Cecill.

April 18.
Venice. 16. Earl of Devonshire to Sir John Masone. Thanks for his letters and news. Unfavourable opinion of England by reason of the late frequent arrests. Fears he is not in good favour with the Queen, as his servant, Walker, has been imprisoned. Conversion of a hundred courtezans at Rome during Lent, and their relapse at Easter.

April 18.
Bruxelles. 17. Masone to Devonshire. Contradicts the report of the number of arrests in England ; only three or four men taken for an attempt to rob the Treasury. His servant Walker was implicated therein.

April 21. 18. Summary of a woodsale made for Sir W. Cecill at Wootton-under-Wyver.

April 22. 19. Henry Wasse to Sir Edw. Hastings. Gives information of the Englishmen he met with in France, among others, Sir Robt. Stafford, Sir Ralph Bagnall, Hen. Dudley, and two of the Horseys.

April 23.
Bruxelles. 20. King Philip to the Select Council. Letter of credence for John de Figueroa. Lat.

April 24. 21. Memorandum of the conversation which the Dean of St. Paul's had with John Throgmerton, warning him to prepare for death. Throgmerton refuses to betray any of the conspirators, but solicits a month's respite.

April 23. 22. Memoranda of statements made by Throgmerton, Stanton, and Rosey relative to Ferdinando Lygyns.

April 23. 23. Confession of Ric. Vuedall, that Dudley delivered up two geldings to Bedell. Cyphers between Throgmerton and Dudley. Inculpates the two Horseys, Danyell, and the French ambassador. Attested by Hugh Weston and Thomas Aysshe.

April 23. 24. Further deposition of Ric. Vuedall as to Dudley, Throgmerton, and the French ambassador. Attested by Hugh Weston and Wm. Cordell.

April 23 (?) 25. Extract from White's confession that Vuedall provided a boat to convey Ashton away into France.

April 23 (?) 26. Notes to put the Council in remembrance of concerning Danyell, Lygons, Turner, and Stanton.

April 23. 27. Declaration by Farnando Lygyns that he has not conferred with John Throgmerton, John Danyell, Wm. Stanton, nor Edw. Turner, as to any treason, conspiracy, or rebellion, intended by Henry Dudley, Chr. Ashton, Francis Horsey, Edw. Horsey, nor Cornewayle, nor any of them.

1556.

	Vol. VIII.
April 23 (?)	28. "Notes for the Quenes Maties Counsell for Stanton." His talk in prison with Rosey. Hints for his conduct when on the rack. His signs to Lygyns, Turner, and Ashton.
April 23 (?)	29. Replies of Ferdinando Lygyns to questions put to him on examination. Explains his dealings with John Throgmerton, and his reasons for proposing to go beyond sea. His conversation at dinner at Lady Butler's house.
April 23 (?)	30. Statement by same, of the times he had been in company with the two Horseys (Francis and Edward). Was with them in the Emperor's wars.
April 23 (?)	31. Minute of communications made by Lygyns to Rosey, respecting the lodging of one of the Tremaynes in London.
April 23.	32. Examination of William Bury. Conversations with Danyell as to Dudley, the Horseys, and Cornewayle.
April 24.	33. Deposition of William Rosey, that he had often talked with John Danyell in prison concerning Dudley and Ashton. Relates their conversation.
April 24 (?)	34. Deposition by Wm. Bygott, as to conversations between Danyell and Lygyns.
April 24 (?)	35. Interrogatories to John Danyell as to his dealings with the conspirators, with his answers thereto. Names of the parties who met at Arundel's house.
April 24 (?)	36. John Danyell to the Council. Conversation and violent language of Edw. Horsey. The breaking of his leg was a feigned stratagem between himself and Mr. Blacklock, the bone-setter, to avoid continuing in company with the conspirators. Is ill, and confined in a dark and filthy dungeon.
April 24 (?)	37. Same to same. Begs them to discredit Rosey's sayings against him. Details the conversation between Rosey and himself, that the French King would not permit such large sums to be carried out of his dominions.
April 24 (?)	38. Confession of John Danyell. Further detail of conversation with Edwd Horsey. Implores to be released from his horrible dungeon, where he lies among newts and spiders : is afflicted with the stone, and has no convenience for nature.
April (?)	39. Memorandum of conversation between Lewknor and Danyell.
April (?)	40. Statement by Danyell, as to remarks by Stanton relative to a shirt of mail and 2 daggs hanging against the wall.
April (?)	41 Extract from the confession of White, that he had often seen Danyell with Ashton at Mr. Pekham's house at Blackfriars.
April (?)	42. Interrogations to be put to Nutt, a poor man, relative to Danyell and Rosey.

1556.

April 28.	43. The Select Council to the King. Further conference with Figueroa, and their resolution as to the Royal Titles in England and foreign parts. (*Minute in Petre's hand.*)
April 28.	44. Translation of the above into Latin.
April (?)	45. Examination of Launcelot Stooker relative to his intercourse with certain individuals. He never had conversation with John Stumpe and others, but has dined and supped with the three Tremaynes at Lady Butler's house; never carried any letter or message from them or Lady B.
April 30.	46. Statement of Sir Robt. Pekham, detailing the conversations between him and Henry Pekham, his brother, touching Dudley and Ashton, and the objects of the conspiracy.
May 2. Venice.	47. Devonshire to Masone. Thanks him for the information about his servant Walker. Is sorry for Tremayne's foolish departure. Reception of the Queen of Poland at Venice. A hundred of the fairest gentlewomen of Venice appointed to wait upon her.
May 3. Bruxelles.	48. Masone to Devonshire. He had forwarded his letter for release of his man Walker, who would probably be at large in a few days.
May 6.	49. Deposition of Sir Nich. Arnold relative to his conferences with Ashton and Dudley.
May 7.	50. The Select Council to King Philip. The Kingdom is tranquil, and justice duly administered. Measures taken for defence of Portsmouth and the Isle of Wight. Orders against players and pipers strolling through the Kingdom, disseminating seditions and heresies. Employment of workmen before discharged, on account of the deficient harvest. Lat.
May 7.	51. English translation of the above.
May 9 (?)	52. Declaration by Henry Pekham of the particulars of the conspiracy in which Sir Anth. Kingston and a great many of the western gentlemen were concerned, for deposing Queen Mary, and making the Lady Elizabeth Queen, and for her to marry the Earl of Devonshire. Communications between Pekham and Chr. Ashton.
May 9 (?)	53. Further declaration by H. Pekham concerning words spoken by John Frokmarten, Hunnys, [Hinnes] and Walpull, prisoners in the Tower at the same time with himself.
May 9 (?)	54. Declaration by Mrs. Ashley that she had no knowledge of the conspiracy, but by common report of Throkmorton's plot to seize the Queen's treasure, and to kill the Queen. Entreats to be released from confinement.
May 9 (?)	55. Deposition of Henry Wasse, as to his knowledge of Henry Dudley. Heard Sir Robert Stafford had denounced Sir Ralph Bagnold to the French Government as a spy. Prays to be released from his wretched dungeon. (Two papers.)

DOMESTIC—MARY.

VOL. VIII.

1556.

May 9 (?)   56. Interrogatories put to John Vaughan, with his replies thereto. Denies all communication with Dudley and other conspirators.

May 9 (?)   57, 58. Two papers containing memoranda by one of the conspirators, of questions to be put to Bygott, as to words uttered by Rosey and Danyell touching the seizure of the Tower.

May 9 (?)   59. Notes from the deposition of Rosey, to charge Dethicke with, as to the conspiracy and seizure of treasure.

May 9 (?)   60. Other notes from Rosey's confession to charge Dethicke with, as to seizure of treasure.

May 9.   61. Statements of conversations between Rosey, Dethicke, Stawnton, and Bedell, as to conveyance of treasure to Henry Pekham's house.

May 9 (?)   62. Interrogations drawn by White, to be put to Dethicke, Bedell, and others.

May 9 (?)   63. Directions to Dethicke to put in writing all he knows concerning the embarkation of Ashton and Dudley, and what he knows concerning John Throgmerton, the Earl of Devonshire, and others.

May 9 (?)   64. Questions to be put to Dethicke as to raising a rebellion for establishing the Lady Elizabeth as Queen, and driving out the Spaniards and Popery, and to confer with the Earl of Devonshire.

May 9 (?)   65. First confession of Dethicke concerning his knowledge of the conspiracy, &c.

May 9 (?)   66. Second confession of Dethicke concerning seizure of treasure. Meetings between himself, Throgmerton, Bedell, White, Hinnes, and Rosey.

May 9 (?)   67. Declaration by Dethicke, relating the events of his life, from the time he was 10 years of age. His connexion with the conspiracy.

May 9 (?)   68. T. Sawtrey to John Dethicke. Privately desires to make a discovery to him, provided he will prevail on Mr. Locton to set him at liberty.

May 10. Stamford.   69. Geoffrey Vyllers and other parishoners of St. Michael to Sir Wm. Cecill. Thanks for procuring the union of St. Stephen's Church with St. Michael's, Stamford. Desires Mr. Gouch may be discharged of a year's rent.

May 11.   70. Examination of Wm. Crowe, bricklayer, before Sir Wm. Garrard, Lord Mayor of London, and Mr. Sheriff Legh. Conversation with a man at midnight near Fynesbury Fields, who said the Earl of Pembroke was about to fetch the Crown from the Earl of Shrewsbury to crown Philip King with.

May 13. Bruxelles.   71. King Philip to the Select Council. Answers their letters of 28 April and 7 May, particularly as to the Royal Titles, and the defence of Portsmouth and Isle of Wight. Lat. *Incloses,*

     71 I. *Statement of matters lately transacted by the Council, and of the present state of the Kingdom, with annotations in the margin.* Apr. 29. Lat.

1556.

VOL. VIII.

May 13 (?)   72. A paper headed "The Effect of this dayes Travayll," being statements by Dethicke and White as to Walker, and proceedings with Rosey and Danyell.

May 13 (?)   73. Statement by Roger Cartar that John Dethycke told him the King would not return to England until two hundred thousand pounds were sent over to him: conversation with one Alday proposing to intercept it. Cartar's refusal to join the conspiracy

May 13 (?)   74. Declaration by William Dedycke (Dethicke?) as to a conversation with Cartar in the garden of the Master of the Horse.

May 22.   75. Declaration by John Palmer as to his communications with Ric. Vuedall.

May 24.   76. Account of money received for the use of Sir Wm. Cecill, for hi rents at Osterwyck, to March 1556.

May 28.   77. Deposition by John Danyell, that Edmd. Verney never asked him if Sir Wm. Courteney or Sir John Pollard were privy to the conspiracy. Denies that he ever knew Lord Braye or Francis Verney were privy to it.

May 29.   78. Receipt by J. Abraham to Mr. Thomas Dudley for half a year's rent of Thorpe Achurche, due to Sir W. Cecill at Lady day.

May 30.
Venice.   79. Earl of Devonshire to Sir John Masone. Thanks for all his services. The arrest of his servant was excusable.

May 31.   80. Answers by Baptist to interrogatories as to correspondence with any persons abroad, or communications with the French or Venetian Ambassadors since Christmas last.

May 31.   81. Declaration by Sir John Seyntlowe. Denies ever having had conference with Henry Dudley, Christopher Assheton, Henry Pekham, John Danyell, Edmund Verney, Lord Braye, or any of the conspirators.

VOL. IX.   JUNE—DECEMBER, 1556.

June 1.   1. Grant to Ralph Donne, Ric. Gerrard, Edw. Frodsham, and Robt. Littlar, of the office of collectors, within the Hundred of Eddesbury, of the Mize granted by the county of Chester.

June 9.   2. Orders of Court of Chancery for staying the cause Tho. Bouger v. Jerome Souger, in the King's Bench, in order to preserve to the Crown a fine of 300*l*.

June 12.
Gedney.   3. Tho. Ogle to Sir Wm. Cecill. Sends the writ and process for holding a Court of Swanymote. Has been at Croyland to take order for marking the swans, &c.

June 13.
Burleigh.   4. Roger Warde, mason, to same. Desires instructions as to the building of three "*lucan*" windows for the inner court, and for the stairs from the base court to the terrace, and for the gate at the end of the terrace. The best stone for stairs is to be had at Clypsham. [*The "lucan" windows are the projecting windows in the roof; dormer or garret windows.*]

VOL. IX.

1556.

June 13.
Burleigh.
5. J. Abraham to Sir Wm. Cecill. Report on the progress of his buildings and other works ; materials requisite for completion.

June 14.
Bruxelles.
6. Sir John Masone to the Earl of Devonshire. Mr. Kemp has received his letter. Recommends him to write more frequently to his friends, as it was not well known in England where he was nor what had become of him.

June 14.
Bruxelles.
7. Anthony Kemp to same. Is sorry to hear the Plague has visited his house. The Queen is in good health. Some of the traitors in the late conspiracy have been executed. The King is still detained in Bruxelles.

June 15.
St. James's.
8. Warrant for a grant to re-establish the Hospital of the Savoy, dissolved 7 Edw. VI., and constituting Ralph Jackson, clerk, first master of the same.

June 15.
St. James's.
9. The Select Council to the King. Detail their proceedings in the suits recommended by His Majesty. Permission for certain individuals to have a large number of oaks, and for remission of duty on merchandize they have thought fit not to grant. Lat.

June 15. 10. Minute of the above, in English.

June 16.
Venice.
11. Humfrey Michell to the Earl of Devonshire. Thought it his duty to attend him at Padua, and did not intend to offend by so doing. Offers his devoted service, and prays for remission of his most grievous displeasure.

June 19.
Bruxelles.
12. The King to the Queen. Recommends the petition of Sir William Wallerthum's to her favourable attention. Lat. *Incloses,*

12 I. *Sir Wm. Wallerthum to the King. Petitions for payment of the arrears of a pension granted to him by the late King Edw. VI. for service in the French and Scottish wars, for which the King also made him a Knight. June 21, Bruxelles. Lat.*

June 19 (?) 13. The Select Council to the King. Are glad he approves of their proceedings. Depredations by English pirates upon French vessels. Advices from Calais. Claim of the French to St. Englebert alias Sandingfeld. Lat.

June 20.
London.
14. Lord Chancellor Heath to the students of Christ Church. Enforces obedience to the late Lord Chancellor's letter to them, of 1st Sept. 1554, *which see.*

June (?) 15. The Select Council to the King. Apparent objects of the conspirators. Measures taken for defence of the western counties. The Earl of Bath and Sir H. Pawlet to take the command, and the Earl of Sussex to repair to Norfolk.

July 4.
Venice.
16. Devonshire to Masone. Is sorry to hear suspicions have been raised about him ; assures him they are unfounded, and would soon be disproved. Complains that a packet of his had been opened in Flanders.

1556.

Vol. IX.

July 6.
17. Declaration of the receipt and defraying of Sir Wm. Cecill's money, since the 5th of May.

July 6.
18. Sir Wm. Cecill's saddler's bill, received by Ralph Wallis (?).

July.
19. Account of Wm. Cayworth of money received and paid, for Sir Wm. Cecill.

July.
20. Bill of Mathew the tailor for making clothes for Sir Wm. Cecill, Tho. Cecill, and others.

July 11.
Venice.
21. Earl of Devonshire to Lady Masone. Thanks for the token she has sent him by Mr. Prune. Has sent her other token to her son-in-law, Mr. Cheke. Severity of the plague. His doings at Venice. [*This is the last letter from the Earl of Devonshire. Dugdale in his Baronage and Collins in his Peerage both state that he died at Padua on the 4th of October 1556. But by a despatch from Peter Vannes, the English Ambassador at Venice (then at Padua), it is placed beyond a doubt that he died on the 18th of September, on the very day and hour that despatch was written.*]

July 19.
Brussells.
22. Sir John Masone to Devonshire. Was glad to hear from him, as the death of his kitchen boy was reported more dangerous than has since proved. The Queen retains her good opinion of him. Particulars of his man Worth, who was now employed in France. Walker is still detained in prison. His packet had not been opened at Antwerp. *Incloses,*

22 I. *Extract from a letter relative to the Earl of Devonshire, affirming that nothing was intended or believed against him or the Lady Elizabeth; for everybody thought them both to be of too much wisdom, honour, and truth to be parties to any such matter.*

August 18.
Southwyke.
23. John White (Sheriff of Hampshire) to the Council. He has received 13 Privy Seals, and delivered all except to Ri. Pexall, who was away. Others were imperfectly directed. Has examined William Morys, Peter Kyllygrew's man. Has no jurisdiction in the town of Southampton.

Aug. 21 (?)
24. Interrogatories for the examination of Peter Kyllygrew, relative to an intended invasion of England, and aid promised from France.

Aug. 21 (?)
25. Answers of Peter Kyllygrew to the above. His dealings with Dudley, Ashton, the Tremaynes, and Horseys. Ships taken by Kyllygrew and his companions at sea.

August 21.
26. Further confession of Peter Kyllygrew relative to the fitting out and arming two ships and plundering of a Spanish vessel and others at sea, at which young Ashton was present. Henry Dudley complains of poverty.

August 27.
27. Deed of sale from Thos. Clayton to Margaret Levezam, of a house and shop at St. Mary-at-Hill, in the occupation of Thomas Fyshe. Lat.

1556.		Vol. IX.
Sept. 10. Croydon.	28.	The Select Council to the King. The six ships waiting to convoy the Emperor to Ushant, must be revictualled before they can proceed. Measures for putting away one Brockhusen and others, servants of Lady Anne of Cleves. Claims of Captain Godfrey de Buckholt. The suit of Francis Peyto for a yearly pension. Don Cesar de Gonzaga's matter.
Sept. 10. Croydon.	29.	Translation of the above into Latin. They will take care that Don Cæsar de Gonzaga's suit shall be attended to.
Sept. 13. Ghent.	30.	The King to the Select Council. Thanks them for their care as to the six ships to convoy the Emperor. Approves of the measures relative to the Lady Anne of Cleves, and also of Cæsar Gonzaga's affair. Is likely yet to be absent from England for some time. Lat.
Sept. 16. Croydon.	31.	The Select Council to the King. Recal of Peter Vannes, Ambassador at Venice. Permission granted to Anth. Hussye, Governor of the English merchants at Antwerp and Agent in Flanders, to return to London for six weeks. All the members of that Society are Catholic, only four hold out : the Queen desires they should be proceeded against. Claim for restitution of a French ship taken with the Pirate Kyllygrew. Dr. Wotton to be recalled from the French Court, and Dr. Tho. Martin to succeed him. P.S. The six ships shall be victualled. Lat.
Sept. 16.	32.	English minute of the above.
Sept. 23. Ghent.	33.	King Philip to Queen Mary. Suit of the Burgesses &c. of Enchuysen, for restoration of their ship St. Pierre du Port, captured and afterwards retaken and carried into Portsmouth. Fr.
Sept. 30. Ghent.	34.	The King to the Select Council. Answers their letter as to the recal of Peter Vannes. Leave for Anth. Hussey to go to London, and return quickly to Antwerp. Has referred the matter of the four persons who obstinately maintain their absurd opinions, to the Inquisitor of Flanders. Thinks Wotton's recal should be delayed until he, the King, returns to England. Lat.
September.	35.	Note of matters lately transacted in the Select Council relative to Ireland. Descent of the Scots in Ireland. Communications thereon to the Queen of Scots and the Court of France. Lord Fitzwater recommended as Lord Deputy. Lat.
September.	36.	Account of rents due to Sir Wm. Cecill in the collection of Andrew Scare, at Michaelmas 1556.
September.	37.	Brief declaration of Andrew Scarre's account with Sir W. Cecill, at Michaelmas.
September.	38.	Note of arrears of lands in St. Martin's parish, Stamford, due to Sir W. Cecill, by Emly, Boocher, Sir John Abraham, Rowland Milling, and John Goodlad.
Oct. 1. Ghent.	39.	King Philip to the Queen. Recommends the continuance of a pension granted to Angelo Mariano by King Henry VIII. Sp.
Oct. 12.	40.	Receipt by Sir Wm. Cecill for rents collected for him in Stamford by Wm. Tymyng, and Tymyng's particulars of the same, for one year.

Vol. IX.

1556. Oct. 19. St. James's.	41. The Select Council to the King. The French King urges the restoration of the ship "Sacrett." Intelligence of the affairs of Italy. Towns taken by M. Antony de Colonna. The Pope has applied to Venice, to the Duke of Mantua, and other Italian States, for assistance. Match between the Constable's son and the Duchess de Castro. Lat.
Oct. 19.	42. English minute of the above.
Oct. 20.	43. Memoranda, by Sir W. Cecill, of matters to be inquired of; to write to Edmund Atkynson of Lincoln for the feoffment of Leonard Brown and Anthony Trappes. The feoffment of Crowland, &c.
Oct. 25.	44. Translation of a case concerning accusers and witnesses in trials of treason, &c.
Oct. 28. Old Bailey.	45. Sir Roger Cholmeley to Sir Wm. Cecill; to be favourable to the bearer in a suit concerning a house in St. Paul's Churchyard.
October.	46. Memorandum of the orders given by the Select Council to the Lord Warden of the Cinque Ports respecting the Castle of Dover, &c. copy of a letter from the Queen to the Constable of Dover Castle, giving directions for his vigilant care thereof. Lat.
Nov. 2. Ghent.	47. The King to the Select Council. Thanks for their letters. Approves of their doings in the matter of the ship Sacret. Observations on the affairs of Italy. The report of peace is without foundation. Refers them to Don Juan de Figueroa for further information. Lat.
Nov. 13.	48. Receipt of John Abraham for 15*l*. half a year's rent due from Thos. Dudley to Sir Wm. Cecill, for Thorpe and Achurch, to Michaelmas.
Nov. 22.	49. Receipt of the same for money collected in Stamford by Wm. Tymyng, for Sir Wm. Cecill, to the same day.
Nov. [22.]	50. The Select Council to the King. Information from Dr. Wotton that the profligate traitor Dudley had been tampering with the soldiers at Guisnes and Hammes. Detail of French affairs. The Queen of Scots is ill of a quartain ague. Measures taken for the security of Calais, of which the Earl of Pembroke is appointed Governor. Beg to be instructed if the Sacrett shall be restored to the French. Lat.
Nov. [22.]	51. English minute of the above.
Nov. (?)	52. Memorial of Sir Robt. Southwell to the Council, praying relief from certain grievances and prosecutions against him, particularly by Sir Geo. Harper and Tho. Culpeper, for acts done in execution of his office of Sheriff of Kent, in Wiat's rebellion.
Dec. 1. Bruxelles.	53. The King to the Select Council. Approves of their precautions against the designs of the French, and of sending Pembroke to Calais. Opinion on foreign affairs. Directions as to the ship Sacret. Desires to hear of the proceedings of the Commissioners at St. Englebert. Lat.

VOL. IX.

1556.
Dec. 8.   54. Receipt by John Abraham from Mr. Dudley for rent of Thorpe and Achurch, due to Sir Wm. Cecill at Michaelmas.

Dec. 30.   55. Account of receipts and payments by Wm. Cayworth, servant of Sir W. Cecill, from 8th Nov. to 30th of Dec.

1556.   56. Rental of lands belonging to the House of the Nuns in Stamford, co. Lincoln, now belonging to Sir W. Cecill, with a note of the decays thereof.

57. Sir W. Cecill's book of the charges of the quarry in Clyff Park, anno 1556.

58. Note of money laid out by Andrew Skarre for the service of Sir W. Cecill.

59. Accounts, receipt, and expenditure of Thomas Cooper, with additions by Sir Wm. Cecill.

60. Account of rents, &c., of Stamforde cum Cranmore.

61. Account of Tho. Dudley of divers rents for Thorpe Achurch.

62. Brief of such money as Sir W. Cecill owes, for rents of manors, lands, &c. (amongst which is due in the Court of Wards for livery 23l.). With an estimate of money due to him.

63. Memorandum of money paid to Ric. Cayewood, John Glassyor, and others, for work done.

64. Rental of Bereholm and other estates of Sir W. Cecill.

65. Account of monies due to and by Sir W. Cecill.

66. Sir W. Cecill's accounts of various rents in Lincoln, Northampton, Rutland, and Surrey.

67. Note of lands let by Sir W. Cecill to John Milner, Emlin, and Bocher, with the sale of fruit that was in Hethcote's house.

68. Account in Sir Wm. Cecill's hand, and indorsed by him "Y^e Booke of Wȳbletō p̄snage."

69. Wm. Haddon's account of sheep bought and sold for Sir W. Cecill.

70. Rental of Bereholm, Stowe, and Deping, parcel of the possessions of Sir W. Cecill, in the collection of H. Stephenson, bailiff.

71. Account of Rents of Bereholm and Deping, for Sir W. Cecill.

72. List of kerseys, cloths, &c. of English manufacture carried into the town of Antwerp within one year, for which it is suspected due customs have not been paid.

73. A Treatise in Italian, on the means by which the Church of Rome has arrived at her present grandeur.

DOMESTIC—MARY.

VOL. X. JANUARY—MAY, 1557.

1557.
Jan. 8.
Greenwich.
1. Conditions upon which the Lord Treasurer (Winchester) is willing to undertake the responsibility of signing warrants for the Navy, instead of the Queen.

Jan. 10.
Greenwich.
2. Warrant by the King and Queen to the Exchequer to pay 7,000*l*. every six months to Benj. Gonson, Treasurer of the Admiralty, for reparation and maintenance of the Navy, during pleasure.

Feb. 12.
3—5. Three accounts of receipts and payments by Wm. Cayworth on behalf of Sir Wm. Cecill, from the 8th of Nov. 1556 to 12th Feb. following.

Feb. 13.
Greenwich.
6. The Queen to Wm. Tirrell. Directions to send all merchant ships, bound for Spain, to Plymouth, to go from thence, under conduct of Signor Ruy Gomez, to that coast.

March 16.
7. Articles of agreement between Willm. Honnyng, Nycasius Yetsweirt, John Clyff, and Francis Yaxley, Clerks of the Signet, as to conducting the business and sharing the fees of that office.

March (?)
8. An account (in Italian) of the expenses of Card. Pole, from January 1556 to March 1557 inclusive.

A number of bonds given by certain Merchants to the following effect.

March 27.
9—13. Five bonds to the King and Queen, by Gabriel Galvanus, Merchant of Ragusa, restricting him from unpacking at Antwerp more than a third part of certain kerseys shipped, and from uttering or selling any part thereof in the Emperor's Low Countries, under certain penalties.

March 27.
14—18. Five bonds of John de Rest, Merchant of Ragusa, to the same effect.

March 27.
19—27. Nine bonds of James Ragason, Merchant of Venice, to the same effect.

March 27.
28—30. Three bonds of Augustine de Sexto, Merchant of Lucca, to the same effect.

March 27.
31, 32. Two bonds of Bastian Wrytza, Merchant of Venice, to the same effect.

March 27.
33—35. Three bonds of Stiatta Cavalcante, Merchant of Florence, to the same effect.

March 27.
36—39. Four bonds of Francis Marotzo, Merchant of Venice, to the same effect.

March 27.
40, 41. Two bonds of Nicholas de Gottzo, Merchant of Ragusa, to the same effect.

March 27.
42. Bond of Antony Donat, Merchant of Venice, to the same effect.

March 27.
43. Bond of Albert de Marare, Merchant of Venice, to the same effect.

Mar. 27, 29.
44—46. Three bonds of Vincent Guichardin, Merchant of Florence, to the same effect.

March 29.
47. Bond of Balthazar de Mafio, Merchant of Venice, to the same effect.

VOL. X.

1557.		
March 29.	48, 49.	Two bonds of James Ragason, Merchant of Venice, to the same effect.
March 29.	50, 51.	Two bonds of Bastian Wrytza, to the same effect.
March 29.	52.	Bond of Francis Marotzo, to the same effect.
April 3.	53.	Bond of Stiatta Cavalcante, to the same effect.
April 22.	54.	Bond of James Ragason, to the same effect.
April (?)	55.	Articles to be considered of in Council, that the Queen be no more defrauded of the duties on cloths exported from London.
May 3.	56.	Names of the noblemen and gentlemen of several counties on the English coast, to whom instructions relative to beacons were sent.
May 3.	57.	Duplicate of the above.
May 4.	58.	Commission to Sir Robert Rochester, K.G., Comptroller of the Household, Sir Edw. Hastynges, K.G., Master of the Horse, Sir Francis Englefield, Knt., Master of the Court of Wards, Sir Edw. Waldegrave, Knt., Master of the Great Wardrobe, and Sir John Baker, Knt., Chancellor of the Exchequer, to take surrender of indentures, patents, grants, &c., for lands and profits of the Crown, and to grant renewal of the same for adequate fines.
May 4.	59.	Articles for the execution of the above Commission.
May 22. Westminster.	60.	The King and Queen to the Lord Admiral (Wm. Lord Howard). Desire him to have a diligent care of Hampton and the Isle of Wight, and the coast as far as Portland.
May 22. Westminster.	61.	The same to Lord St. John. Instructions for the safeguard and government of the county of Dorset, particularly for the defence of Poole, Weymouth, and Portland, in conjunction with Sir Hugh Paulet.
May 23. Westminster.	62.	Fair copy of the above, with further corrections. [John] Lewson to be restored to the office of Capt. of Portland. [*By the Orders in Council of the 29th and 31st of May* 1557, *John Lewson is appointed Captain of the Isle and Castle of Portland, in the place of Geo Strangwishe.*]
May 29. (4 Kal. Junij.) Croydon.	63.	Grant by Card. Pole to Dr. Tho. Watson, Bp. Elect of Lincoln, to hold the deanery of Durham pro tempore in commendam with the bishoprick of Lincoln. Lat.
May 29.	64.	Instructions given by the King and Queen to the Lord High Admiral, preparatory to the declaration of war against France.
May 29.	65.	The Queen to Lord Admiral Howard. Sends him instructions for the important service assigned to him.
May 29.	66.	Secretary of State to the same. Directions to furnish a list of the ships under his command. The French are preparing ships and vessels of all kinds for sea.
May 29.	67.	List of ships appointed to serve under the Lord Admiral.

VOL. XI. JUNE—DECEMBER, 1557.

1557. June 2. The Court.	1. Sec. (Bourne ?) to the Lord Admiral. The King and Queen do not wish him to put to sea without sufficient force. Directions have been given to Benj. Gonson to prepare a number of ships to reinforce him.
June 6.	2. List of ships, their names, and tonnage, including the fleet called "the Flanders fleet."
June 6.	3. Duplicate of the above list of shipping.
June 6.	4. Triplicate of the same.
June 6. Raby.	5. Henry Earl of Westmorland to the Queen. Solicits the office of Steward of Richmondshire and Keeper of the forest of Galtres, vacant by the death of John Lord Conyers.
June 8. Royston.	6. Wm. Lord Dacre to the same. Has heard of the death of Lord Conyers: solicits the office of Steward of Richmondshire and Middleham.
June 10.	7. List of noblemen and gentlemen who went over to serve the King.
June 12. From the Great Bark.	8. Lord Adm. Howard to the Queen. Has sailed as far as Falmouth, and hears no news of the Spanish fleet; details of his cruize. Awaits the first fair wind to haul over to the French coast.
June 12.	9. Cayworth's account of receipts and payments for Sir W. Cecill.
[June 15.]	10. The Queen to Francis Earl of Shrewsbury. To deliver up Lord Latimer's daughter to her mother Lady Latimer.
June 15.	Grant of arms to David Poole, Bishop of Peterborough, by Tho. Hawley, Clarencieux. [See *Grant of Arms*, No. 7.]
June 18.	11. Draft Decree of Lord Chancellor Heath in the matter of Ambrose Saunders, John Johnson, and Richd. Johnson, bankrupts.
June 20.	12. Lord Adm. Howard to the Queen. Detail of services on the French coast. No French ships are at sea between Britanny and Boulogne. Begs to know what ships are to reinforce him.
June 20.	13. Names of gentlemen appointed to levy the pioneers, and in what shires.
June 22.	14. Answer of the Lord Adm. Howard, in reply to certain articles sent to him by the Lord Treasurer touching the ships in the Narrow Seas. The Lord Admiral has spoken with Signor Don Lewys, who, after landing the treasure at Calais, intends to repair to Portsmouth.
June 25. Sheffield.	15. Fr. Earl of Shrewsbury to the Queen. Cannot deliver Lord Latimer's daughter to her mother at present, as she is in bad health and not able to travel. Will gladly do it hereafter.
June 27. The Great Bark.	16. Lord Adm. Howard to the Council. Don Lewys safely landed at Calais with the treasure. Preparations to convoy the merchants' ships. Difficulty of victualling.

Vol. XI.

1557.
June 28.
Westminster.
17. The Queen to Lord Adm. Howard. Directions to prepare sufficient vessels to convey the Earl of Pembroke and others over to Calais, with forces for the service of the King.

June 29.
18. The King and Queen to Same. The King will be ready to pass over to Calais by the following Monday.

June.
19. Abstracts of the musters in twenty English counties.

July 5.
20. The Queen to the Lord Treasurer. Proceedings on the various points of his letter about the Admiralty and victualling. The Lord Admiral is willing to be revoked. Directions.

July 5.
21. Council with the King and Queen to the Council in London. Send copy of the letter to the Lord Treasurer about victualling the ships.

July 7.
22. The Queen to the Council. Approves of their measures for defence of the Borders against Scotland. Sir Hugh Paulet and Sir Leonard Chamberlayn, Captains of Jersey and Guernsey, to repair with all speed to their respective charges.

July 8.
Canterbury
23. Same to the Lord Adm. Howard to deliver up to John Fox his ship Mary Fortune, of Alborough, recaptured from the French.

July 8 (?)
24. Proclamation giving licence to all English subjects to set forth ships to sea, to act against the public enemies the French and Scots.

July 8.
Canterbury.
25. The Council to the Mayor and Jurats of Rye. Directions to aid all persons freely to fit out vessels for the annoyance of the enemy in pursuance of the above proclamation.

July 8.
Canterbury.
26. The King and Queen to the Treasurer and Comptroller of the Admiralty. Directions for setting forth to sea, the Pawncys, the Sacret, and the Falcon Grey.

July 9.
27. Same to the Masters of the Ordnance. To furnish the necessary munitions, &c. for fitting out the Pawncys, the Sacret, and the Falcon Grey.

July 16.
Snape.
28. John Lord Latymer to the Queen. Prays that Catherine Nevyle, his daughter, may remain with the Earl of Shrewsbury. His wife, Lady Latimer, has already three of his daughters, with his consent.

July 26.
Richmond.
29. The King and Queen to   Order to repair to Mr. Wynter at Dover, and to serve as Captain in the fleet in the Narrow Seas. (Circular.)

July 26 (?)
30. List of noblemen and others to be employed in defence of the Kingdom, specifying the proportions of men to be furnished by various cities, counties, noblemen, and gentry.

July 26.
31. Duplicate or fair copy of the above.

July 26.
32. The Queen to the Lord Steward (Henry Lord Arundel). Appoints him Lieutenant General and Captain of the forces for defence of the Kingdom. Directs him to muster and arm all the Queen's servants and tenants.

1557.

Vol. XI.

July 31. Richmond.
33. The Queen to Sir John Arundel, Sir Richard Edgcomb, and others in Cornwall. Appoints them Commissioners of musters in Cornwall. War having commenced with France, and King Philip having passed the seas in person, she commands them to call out and arm 300 able soldiers from the whole manred of that county, for defence of the realm.

July.
34. Same to the gentlemen and others appointed to attend her; to attend with their servants and tenants, armed, according to proportions specified.

July (?)
35. The number and names of the shippes and capitains servinge at the seas, viz, nine under the command of Sir John Clere, and 15 in the Narrow Seas.

July (?)
36. Duplicate of the above.

July (?)
37. Number of soldiers, mariners, and gunners serving with the Lord Admiral, Sir Wm. Woodhouse, and other naval commanders. (Imperfect.)

July
38. The Council to several seaports; commanding them to fit out certain ships to reinforce the Queen's fleet of nine ships under Sir John Clere, for the protection of the homeward bound Iceland fleet : with a P.S. to confer with Vice-Admiral Sir Wm. Woodhouse.

[July.]
39. The Queen to the Earl of Derby. Has restored the incorporation of the College of Manchester. Thanks him for the favor he has shown them. Minute. [*The Charter of Manchester College is dated 13 July.*]

August 10.
40. Particulars of the amount and deductions of the subsidy granted by the Temporalty and Spiritualty, 4 & 5 Phil. and Mary, indorsed " Sir Thomas Sanders, 10 August."

August 16. Hartlebury.
41. Bishop of Worcester [Richard Pate] to the Queen. Rumour that the Lord Legate (Cardinal Pole) is to be recalled to Rome. Beseeches her not to suffer him to depart the realm.

Sept 3. Camp at St. Quentin's.
42. Francis Earl of Bedford to Sir Wm. Cecill. Account of the storming of St. Quentin's by the army under King Philip.

Sept. 19. Wimbledon.
43. Sir W. Cecill to Mr. Rede ; relative to the affairs of Johnson and Saunders, bankrupts. Explains that no claim can attach to him, Sir W. Cecill, in favour of the above parties. (*Written in Cecill's own hand on the blank spaces of the above letter of Bedford's to him.*)

September.
44. Instructions by the Queen for the Commissioners appointed to raise a loan for Her Majesty's use, from all persons whom they shall find competent, priests or laymen. (Minute signed.)

September.
45. The Queen to the Collectors of the loan in various counties. Directions to receive and collect money from those to whom letters of Privy Seal had been sent.

September.
46. Same to the Council of Wales. Directions to appoint Commissioners and a Collector in every county for raising a loan.

VOL. XI.

1557.

September. 47. The Queen to the Collectors for Wales. Instructions to collect the loans in Wales.

September. 48. The Council to the Commissioners for the loan for the County of . Directions and instructions for their proceedings in raising the loan.

September. 49. The Queen to the Commissioners for the loan in Kent. Necessity for raising money to carry on the wars with France and the Scots. Sends lists of parties to whom applications for money are to be made, to be repaid at Christmas 1558.

September. 50. Same to Mr. Wilbram. Authority to receive the money from the Collectors of the loan; with list of the Collectors in various counties.

September. 51. List of the Commissioners for the loan in various counties, distinguishing the names of the Collectors.

Sept. (?) 52. Godefrey de Bocholt to the Queen. Having served her husband against the French, offers now to serve with 10 ensigns of foot and 1,000 horse against the Scots. Fr.

Oct. 1. 53. Account of the moneys paid by the Bishops towards the subsidy of the Clergy.

Oct. 9. 54. An account of sums disbursed for Cardinal Pole's household from Oct. 1, 1556, to October 9, 1557.

Oct. 22.
Dover. 55. Order from Sir Tho. Cheyne, Lord Warden of the Cinque Ports, to the Mayor, &c. of Rye, to cause certain mariners of that town to appear in the Admiralty Court at Dover, to answer the complaint of Adrian Cornelisson and others, Flemings.

Oct. (?) 56. The Queen to Sir Edw. Saunders, Sir Robt. Throkmerton, Sir Fulke Greville, Sir Edw. Grevill, Sir Ambrose Cave, and Ric. Newport; joining with them Sir Wm. Wigston, Clement Throkmerton, John Digby, and John Fisher, as Commissioners for more speedily collecting the loan within the county of Warwick.

Nov. 19 57. Account of all such money as Henry Pynynges has received and expended for the use of Cardinal Pole from Dec. 25, 1556 to the 19th November 1557.

Nov. 22.
Blackfriars. 58. Sir Philip Hoby to Sir W. Cecill. Invites him and his lady to come and spend Christmas at Bisham. Mr. Mildmay and his wife will be there.

Nov. 30.
Bisham. 59. Same to same. Has heard that he will not come to Bisham, which he thinks is owing to Lady Cecill not being willing to leave little Tannikyn her daughter. Begs Lady Cecill will come and bring Tannikyn with her.

November. 60. Another account by Henry Pynynges of all monies received and expended by him, for Card. Pole, for 23 months, from Jan. 1, 1556, to 30 Nov. 1557, including several items of the former account of 19 Nov.

VOL. XI.

1557.
Dec. 10.
St. James's.
61. The Queen to the Sheriffs of counties and the Mayors and Burgesses of corporate towns, urging them to see that discreet and good Catholic members be chosen to serve in the Parliament to be holden on the 20th of Jan. (*Minute, signed, but the signature cut off.*)

Dec. 12.
St. James's.
62. Copy of the above; made before the loss of the signature.

Dec. 12.
St. James's.
63. The same to the Collectors of the loan in every shire; to use all possible diligence in getting in all arrears, to be paid to Richard Wilbram, the Master of the Jewel House, by the 8th of Jan.

Dec. 19.
Stamford.
64. Ralph Harroppe, Alderman of Stamford, and Henry Lacy to Sir W. Cecill. The burgesses of Stamford do not intend to burthen the inhabitants of St. Martin's parish with the finding of post horses. Resort of foreigners to Cecill's mills for grain.

Dec. 29.
65. List of ships and barks already in the Narrow Seas; also of ships to be equipped to serve there.

Dec. 29.
66. Memorandum of works to be done to the Phenix and four other ships, to be sent to sea forthwith.

1557 (?)
67. Note of wages and charges of victualling the Ayde and Barke of Bulleyn.

68. Tho. Langdon to Mrs. Brydeman. Thanks her for some Popish relics. Promises to transcribe St. Austin's Psalter. Requests the loan of a little book on the Sacrament and the Mass.

69. Memorandum for grant of a lease of the Manors of Kilmington and Norton Ferris, co. Somerset, parcel of the late Lord Stourton's estate.

70. Note of the assessment of certain Venetian merchants residing within the City of London, towards the subsidy.

71. Statement of the establishment and wages, for garrisoning certain forts, castles, and bulwarks in various counties.

72. Account of the Queen's castles and forts, with the expenses of the same.

VOL. XII. JANUARY—APRIL, 1558.

1558.
Jan. 1.
1. The Lord Almoner to Lord   . Sends a crucifix of gold to be presented to the Queen, as a new year's gift.

Jan. 2 (?)
2. The Queen to the Sheriffs of counties, to use their best means to procure the election of men of knowledge and experience, to serve in the new Parliament, specially such as the Council shall recommend.

Jan. 2.
Greenwich.
3. Same to certain noblemen and gentlemen, urging them to levy and arm their servants to the number of 50 each, for the relief of Calais; to be sent to Dover, to be received there by Thos. Keyes, the Serjeant Porter.

Jan. 4.
Greenwich.
4. Warrant of King and Queen to the Exchequer, to pay 6d. per diem to James Welder and others, gunners of the Tower of London from last Christmas, for their lives.

VOL. XII.

1558.

Jan. 6.   5. Instructions by the Queen to Valentine Browne, for paying and disbursing 3,000*l.*, under the direction of Sir Thos. Cheyne, K.G., Lord Warden, to the captains and soldiers assembled at Dover, for succour of the town of Calais, for which service Browne is to receive 10*s.* per day, and to be allowed two Clerks at 12*d.* per day.

Jan. 7.   6. The Queen to the special gentlemen in every shire, urging them immediately to raise men for the succour of Calais, "the Chief Jewell of the Realme;" not to spare any liberties or franchises, nor any lord, gentleman, nor other man's tenants: the men to be clothed in white coats, with red crosses on them.

Jan. 7.   7. Names of the special persons who have charge to levy men in twenty-nine counties.

Jan. 9.   8. The Queen to the Lieutenants of certain neighbouring counties, to levy and send to Dover the whole number of soldiers appointed for the protection of Calais.

Jan. [9].   9. Memoranda of the numbers of men to be immediately raised in thirty counties, for defence of the Kingdom, and relief of Calais.

Jan. 9.   10. Names of ten counties, with number of men raised in each.

Jan. 9.   11. Fair copy of the above, as to counties and numbers.

Jan. 9.   12. Instructions by the Queen to Sir Willm. Woodhouse, Vice Admiral, to repair to the Narrow Seas with as many ships as possible, the French King having besieged the town of Calais.

Jan. 9.   13. The Queen to same. Authorizes him to promise compensation to the owners of such ships as may be lost in the service for relief of the town of Calais.

Jan. 9.   14. Same to Sir Walter Mildmay. Appoints him Treasurer for the Wars in the present service beyond sea.

Jan. 9.   15. Same to the Treasurer and Comptroller of the Mint. To deliver to Sir Walter Mildmay the sum of 5,000*l.*, in new-coined silver, to be defrayed according to his instructions.

Jan. 10.   16. Same to Sir Tho. Cheyne, the Earl of Rutland, and others. Loss of Calais. Directions to select all the able men at Dover raised for its succour, and to convey them over to Dunkirk to join the army of the Duke of Savoy. Howlet, Officer of Ordnance, appointed instead of Brook, who is sick. P.S. Unserviceable men to be discharged.

Jan. 12.   17. Same to Sir Tho. Chaloner. Appoints him to the charge of providing carriages for the troops at Dunkirk, under the command of the Earl of Pembroke.

Jan. 12.   18. Same to Vice-Ad. Sir Wm. Woodhouse. Directions to return with the greatest part of his fleet, for repairs, the principal cause of their sailing having now ceased; the smaller ships to remain in the Narrow Seas.

Jan. 12.   19. James Hurst, curate of Essenden, to Sir Wm. Cecill. Gives him particulars of the tithes of Reall and Essenden. Has sent grafts of pear and apple trees to Burleigh.

VOL. XII.

1558.

Jan. 13. 20. The Queen to the Lieutenants of certain counties; to stay the men appointed for Calais, a storm having dispersed and damaged the fleet.

Jan. 15. 21. The Council to the collectors of the loan. To collect forthwith all arrears of the loan still unpaid, and to bind defaulters.

Jan. 17. 22. The Queen to the Duke of Norfolk; for levy of 1,000 men in Norfolk and 1,000 in Suffolk; to the Earl of Oxford for 1,000 men in Essex; to the Lord Warden of the Cinque Ports for 1,000 men in Kent; to London for 500; to Hertford for 300; Middlesex 100, and Surrey 100, to co-operate with King Philip in preserving Guisnes and recovery of Calais.

Jan. 19. 23. Same to the Lord Ad. Howard. Commands him to put the navy into an effective state; all ships and vessels to be stayed in all the ports, and as many of them equipped for her service as shall be necessary.

Jan. 19. 24. Same to the Duke of Norfolk. Directs him to levy only 1,000 men in the counties of Norfolk and Suffolk, instead of the numbers at first appointed; to remain in the county, and to take proper order for defence of the coasts of those counties.

Jan. 19. 25. Note of the reduced numbers of men to be raised in Norfolk, Suffolk, Middlesex, and Hertford.

Jan. 19. 26. Special directions for raising 500 picked men within the City of London, to serve under the Earl of Rutland.

Jan. 19. 27. Note of the messengers that went with the letters sent out the 17th, 18th, and 19th January, for levying men in various counties.

Jan. 23. 28. Sir Edward Dymok to   , relative to a suit in the Star Chamber, concerning a convent seal plucked off from a lease. An arbitrement desirable. (*Damaged*).

Jan. 23. 29. The Queen to Sir Tho. Cheyne. Accepts his offer to go over and join the King's forces under the Duke of Savoy, for the relief of Guisnes. Directions as to the forces in Kent. Wishes the white coats for the soldiers had been ready.

Jan. 23.
Dover Castle. 30. Sir Tho. Cheyne to the Queen. The men furnished by Sir Anthony St. Leger are found deficient in numbers. Supplies of arms and ammunition required. Difficulty of clothing the forces.

Jan. 24. 31. Statement of the order used in granting the subsidy to the King and Queen, by the Parliament then assembled.

Jan. 26. 32. The Queen to Sir Thos. Cheyne. To proceed against Robert Cockerell by martial law, and to put Francis Borton in the pillory at Canterbury, for seditious words.

Jan. 26.
Dover. 33. Sir Tho. Cheyne, the Earl of Rutland, and Sir Antony Sentleger to the Queen. Muster of the Kentish men hindered by the bad weather. Report on the condition and equipment of the forces there assembled.

Jan. 27.
Dover. 34. Rutland and others to the same. Further report of musters of the Kentishmen and others. St. Leger's men will be shipped on the morrow. Lord Aburgavenny's cannot before Saturday.

DOMESTIC—MARY.

Vol. XII.

1558.

Jan. 27. 35. The Queen to the Earl of Rutland. To stay the forces intended for Dunkirk from going over; but to keep them in readiness at an hour's warning.

Jan. 27. 36. Same to the Duke of Norfolk. To stay the forces levied in Norfolk and Suffolk for Dunkirk; but to have them remain in readiness in those counties and in Essex.

Jan. 27. 37. The Council to the Lord Mayor of London, directing him, on the next market-day, to cause all Frenchmen, not being denizens, to leave the realm.

Jan. 28 (?) 38. The Queen to [Sir Tho. Cheyne ?]. Calais being lost, directs him to select a sufficient number of picked men to remain for defence of Dover, and to discharge and send home the rest. Sir Walter Myldemay, Val. Browne, and the Earl of Pembroke to return.

Jan. 29. 39. Same to the Collectors of the loan in Norfolk and Essex. To issue money to the Duke of Norfolk to pay the wages of the forces raised in Norfolk and Suffolk, on their discharge.

Jan. 30. 40. Same to Duke of Norfolk, Lord Rich, and others. Directions to dismiss the forces assembled at the sea side. Rich. Fulmerston, collector of the loan in Norfolk, has been appointed to pay the said forces. The levies from Essex are to return home.

Jan. 30. 41. Same to Lord St. John. Appoints him to have charge of the Isle of Wight, and to raise and arm 300 of his own tenants, part of the 2,600 able men levied for defence of that Isle.

Jan. 31. 42. Same to the Earl of Rutland. Commands him to dismiss the forces under his command at Dunkirk, leaving only 100 men at Dover with Sir Thos. Cheyne, Lord Lieutenant of Kent.

Jan. 31. 43. Same to Sir Thos. Cheyne. Notifies the recal of the Earl of Rutland and forces under his command. Only 100 men to be left at Dover under charge of the Lord Lieutenant.

Jan. 31. 44. Same to [the Commissioners of Musters] in various shires, to levy and arm certain numbers of men, and to send them to the Isle of Wight by the 10th of Feby. under the leading of gentlemen of skill and experience, being inheritors.

Jan. ? 45. Clauses in the Act of Parliament relative to furnishing horses, armour, and weapons, and for taking musters.

Feb. 3. Dover Castle. 46. Sir Tho. Cheyne to the Queen. Has received her letters for the recall of Rutland. Represents the exposed position of the county of Kent, and that it is now weaker in "*manred*" and military equipment than ever. Begs to resign his office of Lieutenant of the county, and to retire to his estate in the Isle of Sheppy and protect Queenborough. *Incloses,*

    46. I. *William Oxenden to Cheyne. Execution of Robert Cockrell at Canterbury, who died blasphemously. Fr. Borton has been put in the pillory there, and cautioned the people as to what they say of the King and Queen. Canterbury. Jan.* 29

1558.

March 5. Westminster.	47. The Queen to Sir E. Waldegrave and others. Directions to compound with Elizabeth Cobham for lands held by her, parcel of the estate of the late Marq. of Northampton.
March 8. Haseley.	48. T. Tresham (Prior of St. John of Jerusalem) to the Queen. He has surveyed the Isle of Wight; the gentry and commons are well disposed for its defence. Sends Sir Edw. Warner to London for further directions.
March 8.	49. Warrant (to Thos. Gresham?) to pay to Sir W. Pickering 200l. in advance, and 4 marks per diem during his service abroad.
March 14.	50. The Queen to the Lord Privy Seal, (Lord Paget) the Bishop of Ely, and others, Commissioners for Finances and Revenues, to devise means for the supply of treasure for the service now in hand.
March 15.	51. Same to Lord Adm. Howard, to cause all prizes taken to be sold, as also those that shall hereafter be taken.
March 17.	52. Same to the Lord Mayor and Aldermen of London. Is desirous to borrow 100,000 marks in the city, on the security of the crown lands, and will dispense with the act of usury in favour of those who lend to her.
March 17.	53. Instructions by the King and Queen to the Earl of Bedford, Lieutenant of the counties of Dorset, Devon, Cornwall, and the city of Exeter, as to raising and watching of beacons, mustering forces, &c., for defence of those parts.
March 17. Greenwich.	54. The King and Queen to Thomas Wilson. Command him to return to England and appear in person before the Council.
March 18.	The Queen to . Appoints them Commissioners to assess the whole county for the subsidy granted by the late Parliament. [See 19 May 1559.]
March 18.	The same to . Appoints him a Special Commissioner to superintend his colleagues in levying the subsidy. [See 19 May 1559.]
March 27.	55. Inquisition against Michael Powle of Berkhamstead, Herts, for burglariously entering and robbing the house of John West at Chesham, Bucks. Lat.
March 28.	56. Memorial by Sir W. Cecill of various works to be done at several of his houses and estates, survey of woods, hangings at Grimsthorpe, &c.
March 30.	57. Memorial for Thomas Harvey, knight marshal. Instructions for taking musters of the forces at Portsmouth and the Ise of Wight.
March 30.	58. Duplicate of the above.
March 31. Greenwich.	59. The Queen to Prior Sir Thomas Tresham. Directions to discharge a portion of the garrison of the Isle of Wight, as a fleet will arrive for protection of the Island.

VOL. XII.

1558.

March 31. 60. Minute of a letter to Prior Sir Tho. Tresham, to assist Thomas Harvey in taking musters of the forces in the Isle of Wight; and similar directions to Lord Chidiock Paulet, Captain of Portsmouth.

March. 61. The Queen to the Lord Mayor, &c., of London. Authorizes Nicholas Brigham to receive the money lent to her by the city.

April 2. 62. List of gunners and soldiers appointed to serve in Deal, Walmer, and Sandown Castles, co. Kent.

April 6.
Bruxelles. 63. The King to the Select Council. Directs them to inquire into the matter concerning the Hanse Towns. Lat.

April 8.
Canterbury. 64. Sir Henry Jernegan to the Queen. Sends intelligence out of France from the Lord Grey, that the Scots had returned to Scotland, with the Duke of Guise in their company. Has committed the care of the coasts to Sir Henry Cryps, Mr. Kempe, and Mr. Fynche.

April 9.
Senate House. 65. The Vice Chancellor and Senate of Cambridge, to the Queen. Acknowledge Her gracious favour to the University. Pray to be exempted from contributing to the subsidy. Lat.

April 15.
Greenwich. 66. The Queen to the Company of Merchant Adventurers. Thanks for their forbearing to claim payment of their loan to her. Will be punctual in the next payment.

April 18. 67. Instructions and orders given at Exeter by Francis Earl of Bedford, Lieut.-General of Devon, Cornwall, Dorset, and Exeter, and the Justices of the Peace, to be used for the quiet estate of the said shires and city; with names of the gentlemen appointed for the defence of Devon.

April 21.
Grafton. 68. Survey of the parks of Grafton, Stoake, Potterspury, Haselborough, Norton, and Hartwell, co. Northampton; taken before John Mershe, Giles Isham, and William Gent, Esquires. Lat. and Engl.

April 26. 69. The Queen to certain gentlemen appointed captains of ships, to take charge of the said ships, and to be at Portsmouth, under the orders of Lord Clynton, Lord High Admiral.

April 26. 70. Names of the gentlemen appointed captains of ships to be at Portsmouth by the 10th of May.

April 26. Answer of the Lady Elizabeth given at Hatfield, to Sir Thomas Pope, as to the proposal of marriage made by the King Elect of Sweden. [*Imperfect MSS., James I.*]

April 30.
Worcester. 71. Bishop Pate to the Queen. Was a suitor about twelvemonths past that Cardinal Pole should not depart the realm. Again entreats that she will not part with him.

VOL. XIII. MAY—SEPTEMBER, 1558.

May 1. 1. Table of rates for lands, goods, annuities, fees, and copyholds chargeable with horses and armour, according to the Act 4 & 5 Phil. and Mary.

Vol. XIII.

1558.
May 4.
2. Accompt of John Thetcher, Esq., Collector of the loan in the county of Sussex.

May 4.
Greenwich.
Warrant dormant to pay the wages and entertainments of Sir Robt. Oxenbridge, Constable of the Tower, and of the Guard and Warders of the same ; amounting in the whole to 580*l.* 4*s.* 2*d.* per annum. [*See* 25 *March* 1559.]

May 11.
, 3. The Queen to Lord Admiral (Edwd. Lord Clynton ?) to be in readiness to receive the King on his return to England.

May 12.
4. The King and Queen to Nich. Brigham. Appoint him to be receiver of all money due or payable on any subsidy, fifteenth, loan, or other benevolence.

May 16.
5. Note of the dates of certain commissions of sales, and of the persons to whom they were addressed.

May 17.
Greenwich.
6. The Queen to Lord Ad. Clynton. The King being unable to return to England, the Lord Admiral is directed to go over and visit His Majesty, to know and obey his pleasure.

May 17.
James Gage's House.
7. Anth. Visct. Montague to the Queen. Survey of the coasts of Sussex : the people are willing to serve for its defence. Has caused Dr. Langdale to preach in places not well-affected in religion. Has appointed all the west end of the shire for the aid of Portsmouth Mr. Hungatt, who has accompanied him, can state the particulars.

May 17.
Brussels.
8. The King to the Count de Feria, concerning the memorial of Pedro Ortiz de Brivarri. Span.

May 18.
Lion, in the Downs.
9. Lord Adm. Clynton to the Queen. Is about to sail for Dunkirk to wait on the King, leaving the fleet in the Narrow Seas in charge of Mr. Wynter, and captains of good experience.

May 20.
10. The Queen to Fr. Earl of Huntingdon. The Marq. of Winchester being Lieut. of the forces of London and the adjacent shires raised for defence of her person, she appoints him to command the vanguard of the same.

May 22.
Dover.
11. Wm. Wynter to Secry. Boxall. The Lord Adm. Clynton landed at Dunkirk. Proceedings of the fleet in the Narrow Seas. Mr. Gresham applied for convoy from Flanders. Engagement between the French and certain Burgundians. *Incloses,*

11. I. *List of ships (Queen's and Merchant's) appointed to repair to Portsmouth, remaining at present in the Narrow Seas. May* 22.

May 29.
St. James's.
12. The Queen to the Earl of Arundel, K.G. (Lieut. of the co. of Surrey). Commands him to be present at a council of the Knights Companions of the Garter.

May 29 (?)
13. List of the Knights of the Garter in the 4th & 5th of Phil. and Mary.

May 30.
St. James's.
14. The Queen to the Dean and Chapter of Winchester. Has appointed Dr. Harding, a Prebendary of Winchester, to preach in the diocese of Sarum. Desires that he may receive the revenue of his prebend while absent on that duty.

1558.

May 30 (?)   15. The Queen to John Fezard, Parson of Donhedmary, Dr. Harding, and Dr. Hosskyns; directs them, during the vacancy of the see to preach throughout the diocese of Salisbury.

May 30 (?)   16. Same to same. Rough draft of letter to the same purport.

May.   17. Articles proposed by Col. William de Wallerthum on entering the English service. Ital.

May. Westminster.   18. Articles and conditions for regulation of the foreign German infantry in the service of Philip and Mary, under command of Colonel William de Wallerdumb. Fr.

May. Westminster.   19. English translation of the above.

May.   20. Note of the proportion of soldiers assigned to each standard, their officers, and pay. Fr.

June 2. Antwerp.   21. Order by King Philip to Tho. Gresham to advance to Sir Wm. Pickering 40,000 Rhenish florins, for pay of the 3,000 German infantry under Sir William de Wallerthum. Sp.

June 2. Antwerp.   22. Similar order to Tho. Gresham to advance 6,000 crowns to Herman Piper to provide arms for the said troops. Sp. (See *Borders*, *June* 16.)

June 3. St. James's.   23. The Queen to Sir Tho. Cheyne, to give directions for the seafaring men within the Cinque Ports, to hold themselves in readiness to serve under the Lord Admiral at an hour's warning.

June 8. Rye.   24. The Mayor and Jurats of Rye to the Council. Have sent up in custody Tho. Wait and John Pope, supposed owners of a vessel that had committed some offence. Recommend the case of Jas. Pottyn and Wm. Firrar.

June 14.   25. Interrogatories to be put, on the part of the Crown, to John Bowyer, prisoner in the Fleet, as to his connexion with the late Duke of Suffolk.

June 14   26. Examination and answers of John Bowyer, on the above interrogatories, taken before Sir Tho. Whyte and John Throkmarton, Masters of Requests.

June 15.   27. The Queen to   . Appoints him Lord Marshal of the forces for defence of the realm.

June 18.   28. Estimate of the charge of the wars for five months, to end the last of October; with an estimate of money to be provided for the same.

June 21. Bruxelles.   29. The King to Sir Wm. Pickering. He has directed Walderthum to take his route with his troops through Antwerp to Dunkirk. Fr.

June 26. St. James's.   30. The Council to Sir Ric. Reade and John Vaughan, to examine the claim of Laurence Johnson (from Denmark) to a ship taken from him last year.

June 26.   31. The Queen to Lord St. John. Directions to embark the 500 men, in pay in the Isle of Wight, on board the fleet under the command of Lord Adm. Clynton.

VOL. XIII.

1558.
June 26. 32. The Queen to Lord Adm. Clynton; authorizes him to take up 500 men in the Isle of Wight, for manning his fleet.

June 23. 33. Same to John Bourchier Earl of Bath, and others, Commissioners, to hear and determine a suit, in the Exchequer, between the Crown and Sir Oliver Wallop, as to the manor of Upton, co. Somerset.

June 28.
St. James's. 34. Same to Benj. Gonson, Treasurer of the Admiralty, to pay the land-wages of such as shall serve in the expedition under the Lord Admiral.

June (?) 35. Note of the number of pensioners and men-at-arms attending on the Queen's person. Lat.

July 2. 36. Accompt of Ric. Wilbraham, Master of the Jewel House and Receiver-General of the Loan, of the whole amount received by him of the same loan, viz. 109,269*l*. 0*s*. 4*d*., Signed by Thomas Mathewe, auditor.

July 8.
The Lyon. 37. Lord Adm. Clynton to the Queen. Informs her of the best points in Flanders to convey letters to the King, Dunkirk being stopped by the French. Has sent 10 ships into the Narrow Seas.

July 8.
Rochford. 38. Ric. Lord Rich to same. Prays for expedition of his patent for the grant of the manor of Hockley, in Essex, the price of which he has paid. Will never trouble or quarrel with Edmund Tirell, to whom it is leased.

July 9.
Pomfret. 39. George Lord Talbot to same. Has received her commands to prepare himself as General of 400 demilances, and to receive them at Newcastle. Is perfectly destitute of equipments for that service.

July 15. 40. The Queen to Sir Clement Higham and Sir John Sulyarde. Directions for them to take inventories, &c. of the goods, &c. of Lord Wentworth, and to make account of his revenues since the loss of Calais. The same proceedings to be taken with the goods, &c. of Sir Ralph Chamberlain, Edwd. Grymeston, John Harleston, and Nich. Alexander.

July 27. 41. Same to the Mayor and Aldermen of London. To exempt Simon Lowe, merchant, from the offices of Sheriff and Alderman during the time he is in her service.

July 27. 42. Same to Dr. Robinson, Dean of Durham. To repair to the Earl of Lenox, being visited with some sickness, and to comfort him by godly and learned counsel.

July 27. 43. Same to Sir Tho. Cheyne. Commends him for receiving his wife again, and continuing in house with her, lovingly.

July 27. 44. Same to Sir Edw. Waldegrave and others. Authority to keep a Justice Court at Ilford, in the absence of the Earl of Sussex, Chief Justice of all forests south of Trent, for redress of disorders in Waltham Forest, while he is Lord Deputy of Ireland.

July 30. 45. Lord Treasurer Winchester to the Queen. Difficulty felt by the subjects to raise money for military service, owing to the restraint on sale of corn. Has sent her warrant for finishing the works at Windsor.

VOL. XIII.

1558.
July 30. 46. Lord Treasurer Winchester to the Queen. Will forward the building of the new Custom House and Wharfs. Thinks Mr. Coke, Captain of Sandown Castle, I. of Wight, will die.

July (?) 47. William Dalyson, John Predyaux, Edw. Gryffyn (Att. Gen.), and Ric. Weston (Sol. Gen.), to the Queen. Report on the case of Dionysius Thymblebie, lately attainted for highway robbery. Recommend that witnesses be not heard against the verdict.

July. 48. Memoranda of fees on passing certain grants, licences, pardons, and other public instruments in the months of June and July.

July (?) 49. Declaration of loss sustained by the Queen, by lack of diligent circumspection of the weight of wools exported, and of the sums saved by the Staplers from 1550 to 1555.

July (?) 50. Declaration of the Customs the Kings and Queens have of their wools, and of the loss in their Customs in the same.

August 5. 51. The Queen to [John] Malyn, Vice-Admiral on the Narrow Seas. Thanks for his services: makes him a present of wines he had taken from the enemy.

August 5.
Richmond. 52. Same to Wm. Basset, Sheriff of Glamorgan. To apprehend William Herbert, Esq., of Cogan Pill, and send him up in custody to the Privy Council.

August 8. 53. Winchester to the Queen. Has sent by Mr. Basshe warrants for venison, to be presented to the city, as customary. The disease of his nose is better. He will set forward the 1,000 pioneers for King Philip.

August 9.
Richmond. 54. The Queen to Tho. Lodge, Alderman of London. Thanks for his willingness to become surety for redeeming Sir Henry Palmer, prisoner in France.

August 12.
Richmond. 55. Same to the Fellows of Magd. Coll., Oxford. Recommends them to elect either [Tho.] Marshall, Archdeacon of Lincoln; John Somer, Preb. of Windsor; or [Tho.] Slythehurst, Master of Trinity Coll., to be President of their College, in place of their late President, Arthur Cole, deceased. [*Tho. Coveney, A.M., was elected.*]

August 14. 56. List of payments of the subsidy granted by the temporalty in the 4th & 5th of Phil. and Mary, made before the 14 of Aug. in each County, City, Division, and Town.

August 16.
Auckland. 57. Cuthbert Tunstal, Bishop of Durham, to Card. Pole. Thanks him for procuring the grant to him of the reversion of Durham Place. Expects daily that Pole will send for the arrears of the farm of benefices, about 700*l.* His Chancellor is dead; prays for another as good.

August 19. 58. Minute of articles between James Harryngton and Robt. Lyvesey for lease of certain lands. Corrected by Sir Wm. Cecill.

August 27. 59. The Queen to Lord Chidiock Paulet, Capt. of Portsmouth. Directs him to deliver 200 men of that garrison, to Lord Adm. Clynton, to serve on board the fleet.

Vol. XIII.

1558.
August 27.
60. Abstract of several letters in July and August from Lord Adm. Clynton to the Council. Weather, and operations on the coast of France. Cannot find matter sufficient to charge Stukeley with, &c.

August 29.
61. List of persons committed to various prisons between the 15th of Aug. 1553 and the 29th of Aug. 1558, including Latimer and Cranmer.

August 31.
Eltham.
62. Sir Henry Jernegan, Master of the Horse, to the Queen. Gives a report, by Mr. Colsell, of the proceedings in the Narrow Seas of Vice-Admiral Malyn, who offers to recover Newhaven.

August.
Wilton.
63. Earl of Pembroke to same. Has received her letters, stating that the Marches of Wales are in disorder for want of a President residing there. Is willing to resign, but declines recommending a successor.

Sept. 1.
Portsmouth.
64. William Wynter to . Statement of services performed by the fleet, from the time of the burning of Conquet, till their return to Portsmouth.

Sept. 6.
Letley.
65. John Lord St. John to the Queen. Death of Ric. Cooke [or Coke], Captain of the Fort in Sandown Bay, I. of Wight. Sickness affects more than half the people in Southampton, Portsmouth, and the Island.

Sept. 9.
66. The Queen to Sir Henry Jernegan. To consider of the offer of Malyn to make a descent on the coast of France, and to give directions accordingly; and, if he approves, to supply Malyn with the 100 soldiers at Dover.

Sept. 29.
67. Declaration of the value of the lands and possessions of Reginald Pole, Cardinal and Archbishop of Canterbury. Lat.

Sept. 30.
68. The Queen to the Master of the Wards (Sir Fr. Englefield). Has granted the wardship, and marriage of the son and heir of Sergeant Prideaux, to Thomas Stukeley, Esq.

Vol. XIV. October—November, 1558.

Oct. 4.
Lambeth.
1. Copy of the will of Cardinal Pole. Lat.

Oct. 16.
2. The Queen to the Duke of Norfolk, the Earls of Derby, Pembroke, Shrewsbury, Westmorland, Huntingdon, and Rutland, and Visct. Mountague; directions to leave their respective charges, and to repair to the Queen immediately.

Oct. 22.
Ad arcem Flerij.
3. The King to the Select Council. Has despatched the Count de Feria to England, on hearing of the illness of the Queen. Lat.

Oct. 22.
St. James's.
Grant to the Lord Chamberlain of a tenement in Westminster, late belonging to Sir John Gate. [*Docquet, Nov.* 10.]

Oct. 22.
St. James's.
Grant to Mr. Allen (Clerk of the Council), of the office of Queen's Remembrancer in the Exchequer. [*Doc., Nov.* 10.]

Oct. 22.
St. James's.
Grant to Robt. Moulton, of the office of Auditor of the Exchequer. [*Doc., Nov.* 10.]

1558.

VOL. XIV.

Oct. 25.
St. James's.
Warrant to pass a lease in reversion to Christopher Skevington, Esq., of certain parcels of ground nigh Reading. [*Doc., Nov.* 10.]

Oct. 25.
Lease of the said parcels of ground according to the above warrant. [*Doc., Nov.* 10.]

Oct. 25.
St. James's.
Warrant for Robert Catlen, to be one of the Justices of the Common Pleas. [*Doc., Nov.* 10.]

Oct. 25.
St. James's.
Warrant for William Rastall, to be one of the Justices of the King's Bench. [*Doc., Nov.* 10.]

Oct. 25.
St. James's.
Warrant for making new Sergeants at Law. [*Doc., Nov.* 10.]

Oct. 25.
St. James's.
Warrant to Mr. Walgrave to pay the Queen's Bedmaker and her Embroiderer for certain materials used. [*Doc., Nov.* 10.]

Oct. 25.
St. James's.
Warrant to same, to deliver to Mr. Norrys, Mr. Lyggons, and Mr. Hungate of the Privy Chamber, each 8 yards of black velvet for a coat. [*Doc., Nov.* 10.]

Oct. 25.
St. James's.
Warrant for "watchinge lyveryes" for the guard. [*Doc., Nov.* 10.]

Oct. 25.
St. James's.
Warrant for the discharge of the subsidy out of the Exchequer, for the wages of the guard. [*Doc., Nov.* 10.]

Oct. 25.
St. James's.
Grant to Ric. Drewe of the office of Master of the Queen's Barges. [*Doc., Nov.* 10.]

Oct. 25.
St. James's.
Grant to John Lloyde for life of the keeping of the Park of Mallwycke, co. Denbigh. [*Doc., Nov.* 10.]

Oct. 25.
St. James's.
Warrant for payment of the guard, for the months of August and September. [*Doc., Nov.* 10.]

Oct. 25.
St. James's.
Grant to Sir Tho. Cornewallys, his wife, and heirs male, of the Manor of Wilton in Cleveland, on the payment of 50*l.* per annum. [*Doc., Nov.* 10.]

Oct. 25.
St. James's.
Warrant to Mr. Walgrave, for saye and other things, for furniture of the Parliament Chamber. [*Doc., Nov.* 10.]

Oct. 25.
St. James's.
Grant to Wm. Rawson of three messuages in Springfield, Essex, for the term of 40 years, free of rent. [*Doc., Nov.* 10.]

Oct. 25.
St. James's.
Grant to Sir Wm. Brereton of the office of Escheator of Cheshire. [*Doc., Nov.* 10.]

Oct. 25.
St. James's.
Grant to Justice Greyme of the office of Gaoler of St. Albans. [*Doc., Nov.* 10.]

Oct. 25.
St. James's.
Warrant for a lease to John Powell of certain lands in Denbigh, for the term of 50 years. [*Doc., Nov.* 10.]

Oct. 25.
St. James's.
Warrant to pay 20*l.* to Wm. Stephin, shipwright, for making the Queen's new barge. [*Doc., Nov.* 10.]

Oct. 25.
St. James's.
Grant to Ralph Bossevyle of the office of Clerk of the Wards. [*Doc., Nov.* 10.]

1558.

Vol. XIV.

Oct. 25.	St. James's.	Grant to Card. Pole and his successors, Archbishops of Canterbury, of the patronage of certain livings within that diocese. [*Doc.*, *Nov.* 10.]
Oct. 25.	St. James's.	Grant to John Pigeon of the Bailiwick of Hemmyngford Graye. [*Doc.*, *Nov.* 10.]
Oct. 25.	St. James's.	Licence for Sir Ric. Sowthewell to assign certain lands to the house of Shene. [*Docquet, Nov.* 10.]
Oct. 25.	St. James's.	Commission to the Lord Chief Justice and others, to consider the title of Tho. Husseye, Esq., to certain lands claimed by him. [*Doc.*, *Nov.* 10.]
Oct. 25.	St. James's.	Licence to Lord Ogle to be absent from Parliament, in respect of his sickness. [*Doc.*, *Nov.* 10.]
Oct. 25.	St. James's.	A purchase for William Rolfe and John Marsshe, of Barnet, signed by the Commrs. of Sales. [*Doc.*, *Nov.* 10.]
Oct. 25.	St. James's.	Warrant to Mr. Walgrave for a livery for the Lord Chamberlain. [*Doc.*, *Nov.* 10.]
Oct. 27.	St. James's.	4. The Select Council to the King. Send a copy of the statement made by the Portuguese Ambassador relative to the trade of the Merchants of London, and declare their opinion on that matter. Lat.
Oct. 27.		5. Copy of the above.
Oct. 28.		6. Certificate of assessment for arms and armour for the City of Lincoln.
Oct. 28.		7. Certificate of musters in the Division of Lindsey, co. Lincoln.
Oct. (?)		8. The certificate of the Wapentake of Corringham, co. Lincoln, to the articles ministered by the Privy Council, respecting the supply of arms, armour, and conduct money, at the charge of the respective towns.
Oct. 29.	St. James's.	Letter to the Bishop of Bath, signifying that the Queen had appointed him President of the Council of Wales. [*Docquet, Nov.* 10.]
Oct. 29.	St. James's.	Ten Letters to the Lord Treasurer, the Duke of Norfolk, the Earls of Arundel, Oxford, Pembroke, and Bedford, the Visc. Montague, the Lords Willoughby and St. John, and the Master of the Horse (Jernegan), signifying the determination of their several Commissions of Lieutenancy. [*Doc., Nov.* 10.]
Oct. 29.	St. James's.	Licence for Lord St. John to be absent from Parliament. [*Doc.*, *Nov.* 10.]
Oct. 29.	St. James's.	Letter to the Lord Mayor and Aldermen of London to admit Tho. Cawston into the freedom of the City. [*Doc., Nov.* 10.]
Oct. 29.	St. James's.	A Release for 1,362*l.* 8*s.* 4*d.* due by the Lord Admiral to the Queen. [*Doc., Nov.* 10.]

1558.
Oct. 29. St. James's. Licence for five years to the Lord Privy Seal and Sir Hen. Pagett, to import yearly 10,000 tuns of French wine at a custom duty of 4 marks per tun. [*Doc, Nov.* 10.]

Oct. 29. St. James's. Grant to Sir John Masone, of the Offices of Treasurer of the Chamber and Master of the Posts at 240*l.* a year, and 12*d.* a day. [*Doc., Nov.* 10.]

Oct. 29. St. James's. Warrant for a lease for 21 years to Ric. Lewes, of two mills and certain lands, parcel of the possessions of the late Monastery of Reading, at the accustomed rent. [*Doc., Nov.* 10.]

Oct. 29. St. James's. Warrant for a lease for 60 years to Sir Robert Chester, of certain lands in Cambridgeshire at the accustomed rent. [*Docquet, Nov.* 10.]

Oct. 29. St. James's. Grant to the Archbishop of York, and his successors, of the patronage of certain livings within that Diocese. [*Doc., Nov.* 10.]

Oct. 29. St. James's. Grant to Edw. Cole, of a lease for 21 years, of certain lands at Colchester, in Essex. [*Doc., Nov.* 10.]

Oct. 29. St. James's. Warrant for a grant in fee simple, to Mr. Kempe of the Privy Chamber, of the house at Kew, Surrey. [*Doc., Nov.* 10.]

Oct. 29. St. James's. Grant of pardon for Ric. Knightley, Esq., for felony. [*Doc., Nov.* 10.]

Oct. 29. St. James's. Warrant for 100*l.* to be given by way of reward to the Grooms and Pages of the Queen's Chamber. [*Doc., Nov.* 10.]

Oct. 29. St. James's. Grant of the custody of the temporalities of the Bishoprick of St. Asaph, to Mr. Wood, one of the Queen's Chaplains, nominated to the see. [*Doc., Nov.* 10.]

Oct. 29. St. James's. Grant to Mr. Raynolds of the custody of the temporalities of the Bishoprick of Hereford. [*Doc., Nov.* 10.]

Oct. 31. St. James's. Grant to Awdrey Beckensall, to be denizen of the realm. [*Doc., Nov.* 10.]

Oct. 31. St. James's. Warrant to the Receiver of the Wards and Liveries, to pay to the Cofferer of the Household 12,000*l.* per annum, quarterly, towards the Household charges. [*Doc., Nov.* 10.]

Oct. 31. St. James's. Warrant to the Exchequer to pay to the same 8,000*l.* per annum, quarterly, for the same purpose. [*Doc., Nov.* 10.]

Oct. 31. St. James's. Warrant to the Receiver of the Duchy of Lancaster to pay to the same 10,000*l.* per annum, in quarterly payments, for the same purpose. [*Doc., Nov.* 10.]

Oct. 31. St. James's. Warrant to deliver to Benjamin Gonson, Treasurer of the Admiralty, 758*l.* 7*s.* for the discharge of the ships. [*Doc., Nov.* 10.]

Oct. 31. St. James's. Instructions for the Lord President and Council in the Marches of Wales. [*Doc., Nov.* 10.]

Oct. 31. St. James's. Grant in reversion to Anthony Rone of the office of Auditor of the Exchequer, now in the occupation of Fr. Southewell. [*Doc., Nov.* 10.]

Oct. 31. St. James's. Presentation for Christopher Kytchen to the parsonage of Walkerne, in the diocese of Lincoln. [*Doc., Nov.* 10.]

VOL. XIV.

1558.

Oct. 31.
St. James's.
Warrant to deliver to Wm. Holstocke 500*l*., for payment of the garrison at Portsmouth. [*Doc., Nov.* 10.]

Oct. 31.
St. James's.
Warrant to Jas. Harman to deliver certain church stuff to the Lord Chamberlain. [*Doc., Nov.* 10.]

Oct. 31.
St. James's.
Grant to Wm. Cade for life of the office of General Receiver of the Duchy of Lancaster, with the usual fees, &c. [*Doc., Nov.* 10.]

Oct. 31.
St. James's.
Grant to Mrs. Susan Clarentieux [Harvey?] of the wardship and marriage of Henry Morgan, and of the right heir of Wm. Sandon. [*Doc., Nov.* 10.]

Oct. 31.
St. James's.
Grant of lease for 30 years to Edmund Clerke, upon surrender of an old lease, of the manor of Hoke and Worthy-Mortimer, co. Southampton, at 20*l*. rent. [*Docquet, Nov.* 10.]

Oct. 31.
St. James's.
Grant of pardon for Robert Phillipps, for felony. [*Doc., Nov.* 10.]

Oct. 31.
St. James's.
Warrant for Humfrey Holte to deliver to the officers of the Mint, 200 lb. weight of silver bullion, to be coined and re-delivered to him. [*Doc., Nov.* 10.]

Oct. 31.
St. James's.
Warrant to deliver to Mr. Harvye, 30*l*. for his charges, being sent to the Commissioners abroad. [*Doc., Nov.* 10.]

Oct. 31.
St. James's.
Warrant to pay to Sir Gyles Poole 52*l*. 15*s*. expended by him for coat and conduct money for 200 soldiers sent into Ireland. [*Doc., Nov.* 10.]

Oct. 31.
St. James's.
Presentation for Ruben Stynton to the prebend of Alveley, dioc. of Lichfield and Coventry. [*Doc., Nov.* 10.]

Oct. 31.
St. James's.
Warrant to Mr. Walgrave, for velvet, satin, and other things, for the livery of Robert Cotton and Anthony Stoughton, Grooms of the Privy Chamber. [*Doc., Nov.* 10.]

Nov. 5.
St. James's.
Letters to the Lord Privy Seal, the Bishop of Norwich, the Earl of Bath, and the Lords Stafford, Berkeley, and Dudley, licensing them to be absent from Parliament. [*Doc., Nov.* 10.]

Nov. 5
St. James's.
Warrant for a grant to Sir Thos. Wharton of certain woods, coppices, &c., intended to have been included in the patent to Sir John Gage. [*Doc., Nov.* 10.]

Nov. 5.
St. James's.
Presentation for Mr. Marshall to a prebend in Windsor, void by the death of Mr. Bowthe. [*Doc., Nov.* 10.]

Nov. 5.
St. James's.
Presentation for Robert Hyll, B.D., to a prebend in Windsor, void by the death of Arthur Cole. [*Doc., Nov.* 10.]

Nov. 5.
St. James's.
Presentation for John Norryce to the parsonage of St. Olyve's, dioc. Winchester. [*Doc., Nov.* 10.]

Nov. 5.
St. James's.
Grant to Simon, Katharine, Jone, and Eleanor Dyer, of an annuity of 20 nobles per annum, to each of them for life. [*Doc., Nov.* 10.]

Nov. 5.
St. James's.
Presentation of William Baynes to the vicarage of Lancaster [*Doc., Nov.* 10.]

VOL. XIV.

1558.

Nov. 5. St. James's. — Grant of lease to Mr. Comptroller [Sir Robt. Rochester], for the term of 30 years, of the manor of Walsham, co. Suffolk. [*Doc., Nov.* 10.]

Nov. 5. St. James's. — Grant of pardon for William Hatchett. [*Doc., Nov.* 10.]

Nov. 5. St. James's. — Licence to Sir Thos. White, John White, and Roger Marten, Aldermen of London, and to Wm. Blackwell, to take 12 per cent. interest on the money lent by them to the Queen. [*Doc., Nov.* 10.]

Nov. 5. St. James's. — Assurance to the said Sir Thos. White and the others, of lands and tenements of the yearly value of 1,007*l.* 10*s.* 7¼*d.*, in consideration of the sum of 20,150*l.* 12*s.* 1*d.* lent to the Queen, redeemable, by re-payment of the money, at Easter, 1560. [*Doc., Nov.* 10.]

Nov. 5. St. James's. — Grant of lease for 60 years to Sir Robt. Chester, of the manor of Denny and other lands and tenements in Cambridgeshire. [*Docquet, Nov.* 10.]

Nov. 5. St. James's. — Release of the 15th and 10th due by the town of Yarmouth, in Norfolk, in consideration of the decay of the said town. [*Doc., Nov.* 10.]

Nov. 5. St. James's. — Grant of pardon for John Conway for felony. [*Doc., Nov.* 10.].

Nov. 5. St. James's. — Presentation for Robt. Iseham to a prebend in Windsor, void by the death of Mr. Robynson. [*Doc., Nov.* 10.]

Nov. 5. St. James's. — Grant to Mr. Goldwell, now Bp. of St. Asaph, and nominated to Oxford, of the custody of the Temporalities of the Bishoprick of Oxford. [*Doc., Nov.* 10.]

Nov. 5. St. James's. — Grant to the Bishops of Chichester, of the patronage of certain livings within that diocese. [*Doc., Nov.* 10.]

Nov. 5. St. James's. — Grant to the Bishops of Lincoln, of the patronage of certain livings within that diocese. [*Doc., Nov.* 10.]

Nov. 5. St. James's. — Grant to Viscount Hereford, of the stewardships of Tomworth, Buelth, and other places. [*Doc., Nov.* 10.]

Nov. 5. St. James's. — Grant of pardon for Robt. Mallory for felony. [*Doc., Nov.* 10.]

Nov. 5. St. James's. — Grant to John Hutchenson, of the office of Bailiff of Hatfield and Thorneton, co. York, with a lease, for 21 years, of the agistments of Hatfield Park, and a fishing called Brathmere. [*Doc., Nov.* 10.]

Nov. 5. St. James's. — Grant to the Master of the Rolls [Sir Wm. Cordell] and Ric. Allington of the wardship and marriage of the heir of Matthew Kniveton. [*Doc., Nov.* 10.]

Nov. 5. St. James's. — Grant to Robt. Raynes, in tail male, of the Manor and Lordship of Staunford and other lands in the county of Nottingham. [*Doc., Nov.* 10.]

Nov. 5. St. James's. — Warrant for a conveyance to Anthony Manxwell of certain manors, &c., lately belonging to Rice Gruffyth, after the rate of 20 years purchase. [*Doc., Nov.* 10.]

Nov. 5. St. James's. — Warrant to pay 50*l.* to the Master of the Rolls, for the making of presses to keep the records in the Rolls. [*Doc., Nov.* 10.]

Vol. XIV.

1558.
Nov. 5.
St. James's.
Grant to John Malyn of an annuity of 20*l.* a year, in consideration of his services. [*Doc., Nov.* 10.]

Nov. 5.
St. James's.
Warrant to the Exchequer to deliver to Benjn. Gonson 807*l.* 19*s.* for wages, &c., of the captains and mariners in the Narrow and North Seas. [*Doc., Nov.* 10.]

Nov. 5.
St. James's.
Like warrant to deliver to same 275*l.* 16*s.* 8*d.* for a captain and 100 soldiers at Guernsey. [*Doc., Nov.* 10.]

Nov. 5.
St. James's.
Warrant to the Woodward of Cranbourne Chace in Windsor Forest to deliver to Robt. Plumbe 20 beech trees and 4 oaks. [*Doc., Nov.* 10.]

Nov. 5.
St. James's.
Warrant to the Exchequer to deliver to Ric. Woodward, Clerk of the Castle of Windsor, 362*l.* for the new works there. [*Doc., Nov.* 10.]

Nov. 5.
St. James's.
Like warrant to deliver to the same 422*l.* 4*s.* 10*d.* for lead, &c. for the works at Windsor Castle. [*Doc., Nov.* 10.]

Nov. 5.
St. James's.
Warrant for allowance to Lord Williams, upon his account, for certain quantities of lead delivered by him out of the store at Grafton to the Serjeant Plumber, for the repairs at Windsor Castle. [*Docquet, Nov.* 10.]

Nov. 5.
St. James's.
Like warrant to Sir Fr. Knowlles for lead delivered by him out of the store at Wallingford Castle for the same repairs. [*Doc., Nov.* 10.]

Nov. 10.
St. James's.
Release to Lord Montague of 849*l.* 15*s.* 10*d.*, claimed to be due by him for lands, &c. bought by his father. [*Docquet.*]

Nov. 10.
St. James's.
Grant of lease for 40 years to John Heywood, of the manor of Bolmer and other lands in Yorkshire, at the rent of 30*l.* for his life, and 51*l.* 10*s.* for the rest of the term. [*Docquet.*]

Nov. 10.
St. James's.
Roll of the sheriffs for the year, pricked by the Queen. [*Docquet.*]

Nov. 10.
St. James's.
Grant to the Bishops of Worcester, of the patronage of certain livings in that diocese. [*Docquet.*]

Nov. 10.
St. James's.
Grant to the Bishops of Winchester of certain spiritual promotions within that diocese. [*Docquet.*]

Nov. 10.
St. James's.
Grant to the Bishops of Carlisle, of similar patronage within that diocese. [*Docquet.*]

Nov. 10.
St. James's.
Grant to the Bishops of London, of similar patronage within that diocese. [*Docquet.*]

Nov. 10.
St. James's.
Grant to the Archbishops of York, of similar patronage, before omitted. [*Docquet.*]

Nov. 10.
St. James's.
Release to the executors of Sir Robt. Rochester, late Comptroller of the Household, from all debts due to the Crown. [*Docquet.*]

Nov. 10.
St. James's.
Presentation for Mr. Secretary Boxoll to the Prebend of Graham in the Cathedral of Salisbury. [*Docquet.*]

VOL. XIV.

1558.
Nov. 10. St. James's. Grant to Mr. Tomewe of the office of Master of the Jewel House, for life. [*Docquet.*]

Nov. 10. St. James's. Grant to Sir Thos. Wharton of certain woods and coppices, left unnamed in a former grant to Sir John Gage. [*Docquet.*]

Nov. 10. St. James's. Commission to Mr. Walgrave and the Auditor of the Duchy of Lancaster, to take the accompt of Dr. Owen, late Receiver-General of the Duchy. [*Docquet.*]

Nov. 10. St. James's. Grant to Sir Edward Walgrave, exempting him from payment of fines, &c., on purchase of the manor of Hever-Cobham. [*Docquet.*]

Nov. 10. St. James's. Grant to Lord St. John, of the offices of Lieutenant and Keeper of the forests of Alisholte and Wolmer, with the manor of Wardelham, co. Southampton, lately held by the Lord Treasurer. [*Docquet.*]

Nov. 10. St. James's. Grant to Wm. Holstocke, of the office of Keeper of the Storehouses and Docks at Portsmouth, with the fee of 20*l.* for life. [*Docquet.*]

Nov. 10 St. James's. Grant to the Lord Admiral [Clynton] for life, of the office of Bailiff of Hatfield and Thorne, co. York, with a lease of the agistments of Hatfield Park, and a fishing called Brathemere. [*Docquet.*]

[Papers without date, temp. Mary.]

9. Warrant to deliver 300*l.* to Reginald Holingworthe, Surveyor of the County of Essex, towards repairing the breaches of the embankments in Barking Marsh; and 100*l.* to Wm. Hanington, towards repairs of Dover Castle.

10. Notes concerning the Manors of Wridefyn, Brimicham, Berkeswell, Melton Fauconbridge, and Barnstaple.

11. Ordinances devised by the King and Queen for regulation of posts and hackney men between London and Dover.

12. Mameranus to the King and Queen. Statement of certain regulations which would be useful to the welfare of the Kingdom. Lat.

13. A list of books furnished by Mameranus for the Queen; of some of these Mameranus appears to be the author. Lat.

14. List of powder and other munitions bought abroad, for transportation whereof license is to be demanded of the King of Spain.

15. Demands of Sir William Godolphin touching the farming of the Isles of Scilly.

16. Account of the total receipts of the revenue of the Court of Wards and Liveries, and of the allowances and payments out of the same.

17. Statement relative to the expenses of the Queen's wardrobe, of the garrisons of Calais, Guisnes, and other forts, the North Marches, the Ordnance, and the Armoury.

18. Statement of the old Mint Establishment, the salaries of the officers, &c. Proposal for a new order of the Mint Establishment, if approved; specifying the names of existing officers.

19. Statement laid before the Council, of the reckoning of fine silver; also the variableness in standard of the current moneys; and a proposal for a re-coinage.

20. Accompt of charges bestowed upon Bowes's ship; by Martin Cunstable.

21. Accompt of charges done and bestowed upon the Mary Bowes, signed by John Upton.

22. Memorandum of Mr. D. Aubrey's case and request, in the matter between him and D. Clerk for some office.

23. Note of the amount raised by several subsidies granted by the laity in Queen Mary's reign.

24. Notes made in the margin of the Act " to repress the oppression of common promoters."

Directions of Queen Mary to her Council, touching the reformation of the Romish Religion. [*Imperfect MSS., Jac.* 1.]

Questions propounded by Queen Mary, touching the treaty made by Henry VIII. with the Emperor and King of France, for maintenance of a quarrel between the King of France and Philip of Spain. [*Imperfect MSS., Jac.* 1.]

25. A brief declaration of the contents of the proclamation made and set forth for the true winding of wools. [*A copy of this proclamation is extant in MS. in the Collection of the Society of Antiquaries, London, attested by Hum. Dyson, and is placed by him among the undated of the reign of Philip and Mary.*]

26. Petition of Edmund Jenney to   , soliciting him to procure his pardon from the Queen, he having officiously presented a supplication on behalf of some poor people   Will never do so again.

QUEEN ELIZABETH.

Vol. I. November—December, 1558.

1558.
Nov. 17. 1. Proclamation of Queen Elizabeth on her accession.

Nov. 17. 2. Memorandum of matters necessary to be done on the accession of Queen Elizabeth, with form of the oath of a Privy Councillor. *In Sir Wm. Cecill's hand.*

Nov. 18. 3. Another memorandum, in Cecill's hand, of matters necessary to be immediately performed.

Nov. 18.
London. 4. Sir Nich. Throkmorton to the Queen. Has executed her commission to the Duke of Norfolk, Earl of Bedford, and Lord Cobham. Measures taken for staying the passage at the ports. Has conferred with Sir Wm. Cecill concerning a proper order for Her Majesty's entry into London. Order taken for securing Card. Pole's house and goods.

Nov. 19.
St. James's. 5. Dr. John Boxoll to Cecill, Sec. of State. Sends the commission and instructions for the Lords now beyond sea; also papers, &c. relating to Gresham's money transactions.

Nov. 19.
Lambeth. 6. Aloisius Priuli to the Queen. Thanks her for attention to the memory of the Cardinal his late master. Wishes her a quiet, happy, and long reign. *Ital.*

Nov. 20. 7. Words spoken by the Queen to Sir Wm. Cecill and the Lords of the Council, at her accession.

Nov. 20. 8. Modern copy of the above.

Nov. 20. 9. Sir John Masone, Treasurer of the Chamber, to Cecill. The peace is the first and principal object now to be considered, and the instructions for that purpose. Great suits will be made to the Queen. Policy of Henry VIII. in such cases.

Nov. 21.
Lambeth. 10. Earl of Rutland, Sir Gawen Carew, and Sir Nich. Throkmorton to the Queen. Proceedings at Lambeth. They have conversed with Signor Priuli, and caused a copy to be taken of Card. Pole's will. Priuli's requests. *Inclosing,*

    10. I. *List of horses remaining in the stables and pastures at Lambeth, Canterbury Park, and Ford, belonging to Card. Pole. Nov.* 19.

    10. II. *Inventory of all the bedding and other moveables belonging to Card. Pole, in divers chambers and offices. Nov.* 20.

    10. III. *An inventory of the wardrobe of Card. Pole. Nov.* 20.

Nov. 30.
St. James's. 11. Edw. Lord Hastings of Loughborough and Sir Thos. Cornwaleys to Sec. Cecill. Soliciting a reward for Lodovicus Nonnius, a physician, sent over from Spain to attend the late Queen.

1558.
Nov. 30. 12. Names of the Captain, officers, &c. serving at the blockhouse at East Mersey, Essex, whose wages are unpaid: signed by the Earl of Oxford.

Nov. 13. Declaration of the account of Thomas Parry, Esq., Cofferer to the Lady Elizabeth, of money paid and disbursed for one year, from 1st October, 3 & 4 Philip and Mary, to the 30th of September following.

Nov. 14. Similar declaration of the account of Thomas Parry, Esq., from 1st October, 4 & 5 Philip and Mary, to November following.

Nov. (?) 15. Names of certain persons of the county and city of Worcester, who lent money on Privy Seals to the late Queen Mary; received by William Sheldon, collector.

Nov. (?) 16. Names of certain persons who received Privy Seals for money lent to the late Queen Mary.

Nov. (?) 17. Prayer by Queen Elizabeth; probably soon after her accession.

Dec. 1. Lease from the Dean (Hen. Cole) and Chapter of St. Paul's, London, to John Cawood, citizen and stationer, of a vault under the quire of St. Paul's, and two sheds adjoining to the Church. [*Case* A., *Eliz.*, No. 1.]

Dec. 2.
Whitefriars. 18. Sir Francis Englefyld to Sec. Cecill. States the effect of the laws respecting the possessions and custody of lunatics.

Dec. 4.
Norwich. 19. John Eyer to same. Has been desired by Mr. Tho. Bacon to repair to Sir W. Cecill, in London, but excuses himself on the score of ill health.

Dec. 4. 20. Form of warrant for issuing writs for calling a Parliament during the vacancy of the office of Lord Keeper.

Dec. 5.
Whitefriars. 21. Sir Fr. Englefyld to Cecill. Advises caution in the removal of officers of the Customs, and placing others in their room.

Dec. 8.
London Stone. 22. John Earl of Oxford to same. Urges his right to the Lieutenancy of Waltham forest.

Dec. 8.
Exeter. 23. John Buller, Mayor, and others, of Exeter, to same. Solicit him to favour the incorporation of a Company of Merchant Adventurers of Exeter.

Dec. 9.
Lambeth. 24. Aloisius Priuli to same. Sends him a silver inkstand, left for him by the late Cardinal Pole some days before his death. Lat.

Dec. 9.
Lambeth. 25. Same to same. Requests an order from the Council to Sir Tho. Finch, to permit the officers of the late Cardinal to dispose of the oxen, hay, wood, deer, &c., in St. Augustine's Park, Canterbury. Lat.

Dec. 11. 26. Captain Edward Turnour to same. Requests that coats may be allowed for the soldiers, and wages to himself and officers from the 2d instant.

Dec. 12. 27. Charges of Sir Tho. Cawarden, for himself and 100 men, serving in the Tower of London, from 19th Nov. to 12th Dec. 1558.

	Vol. I.
1558.	
Dec. 12.	28. Charges of Sir Robert Oxenbridge, for himself and 40 men serving in the Tower, for the same period.
Dec. 12.	29. Charges of Sir Edward Warner, for himself and 60 men serving in the Tower, for the same period.
Dec. 12. The Tower.	30. Sir Ric. Southwell to Sir Wm. Cecill. Is busy with the offers of serving the Queen with saltpetre: will make his report next day.
Dec. 12.	31. Memorial of the supply of saltpetre, powder, &c. remaining in store, and of the quantities required from abroad. Provisions necessary for supply of the armoury.
Dec. 14.	32. Account of the ceremonial of interment "of the Most Highe, " Most Puysant, and Most Excellente Princes, Mary, the first of that " name, late Qwene of England," &c. With the names of her executors, the attendants at the ceremonial, the ceremonies of embalming, lying in state, &c.
Dec. 14.	33. Account of charges in the office of the Great Wardrobe, for the interment of the late Queen Mary, solemnized at Westminster on the 14th of December, and of the sum still remaining unpaid.
Dec. 15.	34. Warrant to pay Lord Chidiock Poulet 220l. 14s. 8d., for discharge of the soldiers at Portsmouth to the 15th of December, of Captain Turnour's band.
Dec. 17. Winchester.	35. Mayor, &c. of Winchester to Cecill. Suit for a grant to them of the custody of Winchester Castle.
Dec. 17. London.	36. Henry Earl of Westmoreland to same. Requests him to further the suit of Geo. Neville, Archdeacon of Carlisle, to be appointed Queen's chaplain.
Dec. 19.	37. The Queen to Bishop Tunstall. Dispenses with his attendance in Parliament and at the Coronation. Three meet persons will be appointed to perform his duties in the latter ceremony.
Dec. 19. Westminster.	38. Marq. of Winchester to Cecill. The performance of the obsequies of the late Emperor at Westminster, instead of St. Paul's, will be a great saving of expense.
Dec. 20. Canon Row.	39. Dr. John Boxoll to same. The valuation of the loan made by Mr. Wilbram is in the packet of loan and subsidy, which his clerk will point out.
Dec. 20. Dover Pier.	40. Wm. Southaick to same. Complains of the practice of bringing merchandize into the realm without reporting the same to the officers of customs.
Dec. 21.	41. Winchester to same. Sends him a statement of what is necessary for the obsequies of the late Emperor.
Dec. 22. Westminster.	Grant to Sir Ambrose Cave of the office of Chancellor of the Duchy of Lancaster, in the same manner as Sir Edw. Waldegrave enjoyed the same. [*Docquet.*]

1558.
Dec. 23.

Vol. I.

42. Marq. of Winchester to Sir Wm. Cecill. Begs him to remember the 100*l*. required for the Emperor's obsequies. Death of Sir John Baker: recommends Sir Walter Mildmay to succeed him in his office [of Chanc. of the Exchequer]. John Abingdon's licence to come home.

Dec. 26.
Overton in Wilts.

43. Ric. Kyngesmyll to same. Solicits to be appointed an attorney or solicitor in the Court of Wards, in the room of Mr. Bacon or Mr. Kalowaye.

Dec. 26.

44. Account of armour remaining within the Tower of London, and of the expenditure of the same in the past year.

Dec. 26.

45. Note of the prices of divers munitions, and of the quantities still remaining for the Queen at Antwerp.

Dec. 27.
Lincoln.

46. Sir Francis Ayscough to Cecill. In favour of Nicholas Bullingham, who had been deprived of the Archdeaconry of Lincoln on account of his marriage. [*Much obliterated.*]

Dec. 27.
Westminster.

47. Warrant to Sir Edw. Walgrave (Master of the Great Wardrobe,) to deliver to John Roynon, and other Officers of the Robes, to each a gown of satin, guarded with black Lucca velvet, and other habiliments.

Dec. 28.
Peterborough.

48. David [Pole] Bishop of Peterborough to Cecill. Thanks for the gift of a buck and doe. Sends to the Queen a poor gift of 20 marks, and begs that she will excuse his attendance at the Parliament.

Dec. 29.
Ippesley.

49. John Throckmarton to same. Has heard of his kindness towards him from his brother Sir Nicholas Throkmorton. Craves leave to attend the Parliament.

Dec. 30.
London.

50. Winchester to same. Thanks for a Privy Seal for 100*l*. Rates on Spanish wines. Payment to be made by the Duke of Florence.

Dec.

51. Notes of matters to be observed concerning the Queen's coronation. Commissioners of claims. Sir Ric. Sakevyle to take charge of the whole ceremony. Certified by Wm. Le Neve, Clarencieux.

Dec.

52. Tho. [Goldwell] Bishop of St. Asaph to Cecill. Desires to be absent from the Parliament, but thinks it strange the Queen's writ has not been sent to him, as he considers himself still Bishop of St. Asaph.

53. Account of arms, armour, and weapons issued from the armouries of the Tower and Westminster, and the Office of Ordnance, at the time of Sir Tho. Wiat's rebellion; specifying the names of all the parties receiving the same, the several pieces delivered to each, and the quantities lost or embezzled at the time of the battle, February 1554. [*On the 5th of Dec. 1558 Sir Ric. Southwell, Master of the Ordnance, was directed by the Council "to make his repayre to the "Lordes, and to bringe with him a perfecte declaraĉon of the state "of his offyce;" and on the 17th a Committee was appointed to hear his declaration, and make report thereof accordingly. Co. Reg.*]

54. Note of allowances for the garrisons at Queenborough and Sheerness, in the Isle of Sheppy.

VOL. I.

1558.

55. The Queen to the Dean and Chapter of Canterbury. Presents John Howseman to the Prebend in that Church, vacant by the decease of Hugh Glasier. Lat.

56. Petition of Geo. Cobham, Tomazo Chanata, and others, to the Queen, for the sole use of an engine to cleanse and carry away all shelves of sand, banks, &c. out of all rivers, creeks, or havens; and for licence to export 3,000 tons of beer, free of duty.

57. Names of several Committees appointed to inquire into the business of various departments of government, revenues and debts of the Crown, the Admiralty, Household, Wardrobe, Ordnance, Mint, &c.

58. Ph. Cockeram to Sir Wm. Cecill. Informs him of the quantity of cloths exported for the Archbp. of Cologne, under authority of a warrant granted by the late King and Queen, and of the loss of customs sustained thereby.

59. Particular of part of the possessions of the late Monastery of Meux, in the East Riding of Yorkshire, leased to Lancelot Alford in the year 1540.

60. Minutes of the pleadings in the cause of Sir Robert Chester against Lord Hastings of Loughborough, for the Receivership of Middlesex, &c.

61. Pleadings in a suit of intrusion versus Wm. Lord Dacre and Leonard Dacre in the manors of Ekington, West Harilsey, Assulby, Upsall, Whawton, and Heyton, claimed by James Strangways.

62. Form of the oath of a Privy Councillor.

63. Note of fees of the Under Clerks of Parliament, temp. Hen. VIII., with a note for those in Queen Mary's time to be added.

64. Names of noblemen and others attainted in the reigns of Henry VIII. and Edward VI., and restored in the time of Queen Mary; of religious houses erected by Mary; of lands given to Card. Pole, and abbey lands to various parties, and grants from the possessions of attainted persons.

65. Brief note of such wines as appear in the Queen's Exchequer, imported from France, from anno 26 Hen. VIII.

66. An elaborate paper headed "The Distresses of the Common-"welth, with ye meanes to remedy them." Indorsed, "A. Wade," probably Armigill Waad.

67. Offers touching the reparations of the harbours of Rye and of the Camber, on the redemption of Mr. Vaughan's lease. *In the same hand as the preceding.*

68. Notes respecting the form of public prayer to be established. Arguments against the power of the Church of Rome. The Queen and her subjects may lawfully use the English Litany of the time of Henry VIII.

69. Copy of the above.

VOL. II. JANUARY—FEBRUARY, 1559.

1559.
Jan. 1. 1. Verses presented to [Sir Wm. Cecill?] as a new year's gift, signed, Art. Hall, and indorsed by Cecill "*Arth. Hall.*"

Jan. 2. 2. Wm. Sneyde, Sheriff of Stafford, to the Council. Has apprehended Tho. Leveson and John Alsop, collectors of the 15ths and 10ths, and bound them over to make payment of such sums as they shall collect.

Jan. 7. 3. Bishop Boner to same. Acknowledges the receipt of letters for payment of the first fruits of benefices appropriate within his diocese.

Jan. 15. 4. Claim of the Earl of Sussex for fees for the office of Sewership, which his father had at the last Coronation.

Jan. 16. London. 5. Robt. Warmyngton to the Council. Has received orders to pay over such sums as have been levied by the Commissioners for inquiring into heresies and misdemeanours. Has none remaining in his hands.

Jan. 17. Westminster. 6. The Queen (signed) to   . Warrant to issue money for payment of 200 labourers, to be levied in Gloucester and Worcester, for service at Berwick.

Jan. 17. Westminster. 7. Similar warrant for payment of 100 labourers to be levied in Nottingham and Derby.

Jan. 20. Westminster. 8. Similar warrant for payment of 200 labourers to be levied in Suffolk and Norfolk.

Jan. 21. 9. Commission of the Queen, proroguing the meeting of Parliament from the 23d to the 25th of January. Lat.

Jan. 25. Crossen. 10. Katharine Duchess of Suffolk to the Queen. Congratulates her on her accession, and for the relief it brings to her afflicted subjects. Hopes for a prosperous journey to repair to her native land.

Jan. 25. 11. Allotment of Justices of Herefordshire, for the purpose of taking musters of the whole county.

Jan. 26. Portsmouth. 12. Edw. Turnour to the Council. Urges the necessity of completing the fortifications at Portsmouth. Refers to the opinion of Mr. Worsley.

Jan. 26. Southsea Castle. 13. John Basing to same. The late Queen gave him the keeping of Southsea Castle, near Portsmouth. Begs that the same number of men may be allowed for that service as were ordained in the time of Henry VIII.

Jan. 30. 14. Certificate of Commissioners of musters, of the men, armour, horse, and weapons within the town of Newcastle.

Jan. (?) 15. List of noblemen in various counties in England.

Jan. (?) 16. List of noblemen and gentlemen in various counties in England.

Jan. (?) 17. Lists of Justices of the Peace in various English counties; on 25 separate leaves of paper.

Vol. II.

1559.
Jan. 18. Lists of the Peers of Parliament in the Parliaments of 6 Hen. VIII., 33 Hen. VIII., 3 Edward VI., 1 & 2 Phil. and Mary, and 1 Elizabeth.

Jan. 19. Minute for a warrant, rehearsing that the Marquis of Northampton is restored to his estate, and for certain lands to be allotted to him : with list of manors annexed, of which the Marquis may take his choice.

Feb. 5. 20. Certificate by Wm. Bromfield of provisions made towards the furniture of the Office of Ordnance, over and above such as are to be made by Thomas Gresham.

Feb. 9.
Cambridge. 21. The Vice-Chancellor and Senate of Cambridge to Sir Wm. Cecill. Soliciting him to accept of the office of Chancellor of the University. Lat.

Feb. 10. 22. The Queen to the Houses of Parliament, in answer to their address urging her to marry. Declares her determination to remain single.

Feb. 12.
Dover Castle. 23. Wm. Cryspe, Lieutenant of Dover Castle, to the Council. Sends a note of things necessary for that fortress. His applications to Sir Henry Jernegam, and to the late Sir Tho. Cheyné, Lord Warden of the Cinque Ports, have been without success. Arrears of wages due to the garrison.

Feb. 12.
Charing Cross. 24. Sir Robt. Stafford to Cecill. Has arrived in London, and requested Sir Nich. Throkmorton to inform him thereof. Solicits a personal interview.

Feb. 18. 25. Certificate of Commissioners of musters for the town of Kingston-upon-Hull, and county thereof.

Feb. 18. 26. Certificate of Commissioners of musters for the city of New Sarum, of all able men meet to serve on horseback or on foot in the said city.

Feb. 19. 27. Sir Wm. Cecill to the University of Cambridge. Thanks them for the distinguished honour they had conferred on him by electing him to be their Chancellor. Lat.

Feb. 19. 28. Translation of the above.

Feb. 20. 29. The Queen to Sir Ric. Southwell. Orders to recover all munition, artillery, or weapons taken out of the Office of Ordnance in the late Queen's time : according to his late declaration.

Feb. 20. 30. Names of all the Queen's ships, and where at present they do remain, with the amount of tonnage and number of men.

Feb. 30.
Lostwithiell. 31. Commissioners of musters for the county of Cornwall to the Council. Report their proceedings in that service. *Inclosing,*

31. I. *Certificate of musters for the whole County of Cornwall.*

Feb. 21.
Salop
(Shewsbury). 32. Commrs. of musters for Shropshire to same. Certify the number of able men fit to bear arms in the said county.

DOMESTIC—ELIZABETH.

1559.

VOL. II.

Feb. 23.
Chester.
33. Commrs. of musters for the city and liberties of Chester to the Council. Report their proceedings in that service.

Feb. 23.
Westminster.
34. The Queen to Wm. Rastell, Justice of the King's Bench, Nich. Powtrell, Rob. Meynell, Gerard Salwayn, and Mich. Wandisford. Appoints them Justices Itinerant and of Assize in the counties of Durham and Sadberg, during the vacancy of the See of Durham. Lat.

Feb. 23.
Westminster.
35. Same to the same, and to Sir Tho. Hilton, Sir Geo. Conyers, Sir Ralph Hedworth, Robert Tempest, Ric. Hebborne, and Ralph Dalton, appointing them Justices for gaol delivery in the same counties.

Feb. 24.
Lowther.
36. Commrs. of musters for the county of Westmoreland to the Queen and Council. Report their proceedings in taking the musters. *Inclosing,*

36. I. *Certificate of musters for the county of Westmoreland. Feb. 20.*

Feb. 24.
37. Certificate of musters, by Commrs. for the city and county of the city of Gloucester.

Feb. 25.
Northwiche.
38. Justices of Cheshire to the Council. Proceedings in taking the musters. The county weakened by the prevalence of the plague. *Inclosing,*

38. I. *Certificates of musters within the hundreds of Buclowe, Macclesfield, Namptwyche, Northwyche, Broxton, Eddesburye, and Werrall. Feb. 20.*

38. II. *Summary of musters of light horse for the county of Chester.*

Feb. 25.
39. Certificate of Commrs. of musters for the county of Norfolk.

Feb. 25.
40. Certificate of Commrs. of musters for the West Riding of York.

Feb. 26.
41. Certificate of Commrs. of musters for the North Riding of York.

Feb. 27.
Stafford.
42. Commrs. of musters for co. Stafford to the Council. The county weakened by sickness. Certify the number of men, armour, &c., mustered.

Feb. 27.
Leicester.
43. Commrs. of musters for the county of Leicester to same. Report their proceedings. *Inclosing,*

43. I. *Certificate of musters within the county of Leicester, with a summary of the whole. Feb. 20.*

Feb. 28.
Northampton.
44. Commrs. of musters for the county of Northampton to same. Report their proceedings, and certify the numbers mustered.

Feb. 28.
Mansfield in Shirwood.
45. Justices of Nottinghamshire to the Council. Proceedings in taking musters of the county. Much distress in the county by the plague and sickness. *Inclosing,*

45. I. *Certificate of general musters for the county of Nottingham. Jan. and Feb.*

Feb.
46. Certificate of musters for the hundreds of Ossulston, Edelmeton (Edmonton), and Gore, in the county of Middlesex.

VOL. II.

1559.
Feb.   47. Certificate of musters for the hundreds of Elthorpe, Spelthorne, and Isleworth, in the same county.

Feb.   48. Licence by the Queen to Francis Bertie, merchant of London, to import and export all kinds of goods and merchandize to the amount of 10,000 tons in the whole.

Feb. (?)   49. The Queen to the Bishop of [Bath and Wells]; revoking him from the office of Lord President of Wales, having appointed Lord Williams of Thame to be President, and Sir Hugh Poulet Vice President.

VOL. III. MARCH 1559.

March 1. Hereford.   1. Commrs. of musters for Herefordshire to the Council. Forwarding the books of musters taken in certain hundreds of Hereford. *Inclosing*,

       1. I. *Certificates of musters within the hundreds Radlowe, Wormelowe, Greytree, and Broxashe, the city of Hereford, and the hundreds of Webtre and Ewyaslacy.*

March 1. Havering at Bower.   2. Sir Edw. Waldegrave to Sir Wm. Cecill. Has a grant for life by patent of Henold [Hainault] Walk in Waltham Forest, in the same manner as Sir John Gates had it.

March 1.   3. M[atthew] P[arker] to same. Disordered state of some of the Colleges at Cambridge as to their possessions and other matters. Bishop Gardyner, their late Chancellor, had been authorized by Queen Mary to visit every College. [*The inclosures referred to in this letter will be found in pp.* 54, 55; *the Queen to Gardyner,* 20 *Aug.; and Gardyner to the Vice Chancellor,* 25 *Aug.* 1553.

March 1. Lincoln.   4. Sir Fr. Ayscough to same. Recommends the suit of his friend, Mr. Boolles.

March 1.   5. Certificate of the general musters for the whole county of Wiltshire.

March 1.   6. Certificate by Sir Wm. Wroughton and others, of the musters in certain hundreds in Wiltshire.

March 1.   7. Account of money passed by warrant from the beginning of Queen Elizabeth's reign to the 1st of March following.

March 4.   8. Sir Wm. Petre to Cecill. Will attend him at the Court if necessary, but wishes to be excused on account of the disease in his leg.

March 4. Crossen.   9. Kath. Duchess of Suffolk to same. On the changes in the services of the Church. Laments the halting between two opinions. Report that the Queen tarried only while the Gospel was read, and then departed, which she hopes is not true. Exhorts Cecill to forward the true faith.

March 5. Arundel Place.   10. Henry Earl of Arundel to same. Has given to Sir Ric. Sakevyle the office of Steward of the Duchy lands in Sussex.

March 5.   11, Wm. Lord Paget to same. Recommends certain words for free commerce to be inserted in the treaties.

Vol. III.

1559.
March 5.
Paulscray.
12. Tho. Wotton to Sir Wm. Cecill. Sends a letter of importance received from Sir Henry Crispe, touching the tranquillity of the realm. Will send the books of musters when completed.

March 5.
Rockborne.
13. Wm. Keyllwey to John Foster. Has agreed with Mr. Seymour that the return of the certificates respecting armour should pass through his hands, as the Bishop [of Winchester?] has denied having any corslets.

March 5.
Westminster.
14. The Queen to the Receivers, &c. of North Wales. Warrant for payment of the diets, &c. of Lord Williams of Thame, President, and the Council, in the Marches of Wales.

March 6.
Portsmouth.
15. Capt. Edwd. Turnour to Cecill. Is unwilling to speak of the faults of others, but "the sacred profession of perfect men of war is " now by ill-training grown to misorder and mischief." Lives like a conjuror among devils.

March 7.
Carmarthen.
16. Commrs. of musters for Carmarthenshire to the Council. Report their proceedings, &c. Return of the musters.

March 8.
17. Sir Robt. Stafford to Cecill. Has the same claim to the Queen's mercy, which he entreats, as the Lord Ferrys made to Queen Mary.

March 8.
Cambridge.
18. Justices of Cambridge to the Council. Have taken the musters for the whole county, the town of Cambridge excepted. Great lack of able men in the county. *Inclosing,*

18. I. *Certificate of musters for the county of Cambridge. Feb. 6.*

March 8.
Gretford.
19. Edmond Hall to Cecill. Concerning musters taken in the wapentake of Nes and Belteslow, co. Lincoln. *Incloses,*

19. I. *John Stoyte, Parson of Offington, to Mr. Hall and Mr. Sherwod. Has been charged to find certain soldiers for the Queen's service. Has none but his own hired servants, and begs they may not be otherwise charged. March 2.*

March 9.
Hereford.
20. Commrs. of musters for Herefordshire to the Council. Have taken the musters of certain hundreds. *Inclosing,*

20. I. *Certificates of musters within the hundreds of Wolsey, Stretford, Wygmor, Grymsworth, and Huntyngton. 1559, Feb. 3–6.*

March 9.
Derby.
21. Commrs. of musters for Derbyshire, to same. Report proceedings, and certify the result of the musters for the whole county. *Inclosing,*

21. I. *Certificate of musters for the hundred of Morleston, co. Derby.*

21. II. *Certificate for the hundreds of Repyngdon, Greysley, and Melburneholme.*

21. III. *Certificate for the hundreds of Skarresdale and Appletree.*

21. IV. *Certificate for the wapentakes of Wyrksworth and High Peak.*

VOL. III.

1559.
March 9.
Exeter.

22. Commrs. of musters for Devonshire to the Council. Delay in receiving the letters and instructions for taking musters, the parties being at the coronation. *Inclosing,*

    22. I. *Certificate of musters for the county of Devon.*

March 9.

23. Sir Wm. Godolphyn to Sir Wm. Cecill. Detention of a vessel and cargo which lately robbed and spoiled, in a piratical manner, a Flemish vessel at Scilly. *Incloses,*

    23. I. *Particular of such goods as John Courteny hath brought from the Isles of Scilly to Mountsbay.*

March 10.
From Prison.

24. John Morren to same. Thanks him for consolation afforded, which has greatly renewed his spirit. Lat. [*On the 22d of Feb. John Murren, Chaplain to the Bp. of London, was committed to the Fleet for preaching contrary to the Queen's proclamation. He was released on the 16th of March following. Co. Reg.*]

March 12.

25. Austen Styward to same. In behalf of his poor daughter the bearer, wife to John Pyckrell, who was cofferer and paymaster of the Duke of Somerset's household.

March 12.

26. Certificate of musters for the county of Buckingham.

March 13.

27. John Hales to Cecill. Controversy between the Chief Justice of the Common Pleas (Sir Jas. Dyer) and the Clerk of the Hanaper, for appointing to the office of Keeper of the Seal of the Common Pleas. [*Strype, A. I. 1. p. 74, calls John Hales himself Clerk of the Hanaper.*]

March 16.
Cambridge.

28. Mayor, &c. of Cambridge to the Council. Report their proceedings as to the musters for that town.

March 16.
Queen's College.

29. Tho. Pecocke, President, and part of the Fellows of Queen's College, Cambridge, to Cecill. Relative to the forms of admission of students to that college. Lat.

March 17.
Cambridge.

30. Part of the Fellows of Queen's College, Cambridge, to same. Complaining of the irregular conduct of their President. Lat.

Mar. 17 (?)

31. Sir Wm. Cecill to the President and Fellows of Queen's College. Desires further information from them with respect to their statutes. Lat.

March 17.

32. William Tailer (Master of Christ's College, Cambridge,) to Cecill. Sends him a copy of the statutes of that College. Lat. *Incloses,*

    32. I. *Statutes of Christ's College, Cambridge. Lat.*

March 17.

33. Sir Edw. Saunders (Ch. Jus. of the King's Bench) to same. Reports on two cases tried by him on the circuit; one of Mr. Hearle for killing Paul Penye, servant to Sir Leonard Chamberlain; the other of John Osland of Aymour, accused of the death of one Fr. Lawlye. *Incloses,*

1559.

VOL. III.

33. I. *The Queen to Sir Ed. Saunders and Sir John Whiddon. To examine the case of John Oseland of Aymour, co. Worcester, a keeper of the forest of Wyre, imprisoned for slaying Fr. Lawley. Westminster, Feb. 21.*

March 17. 34. Lord Paget to Sir Wm. Cecill. Lord Williams of Thame is very sick and not likely to recover. Solicits his office of Lord President of Wales.

March 18. 35. Mat. Coltehirste to same. Has been appointed auditor of the
Old Bailey. First Fruits and Tenths; prays him to forward the signing the grant.

Mar. 18 (?) 36. Sir Wm. Cecill to [the President and Fellows of Queen's College?]. Laments the dissensions that have arisen in the college. Necessity that the statutes should be observed. Has referred the matter in dispute to the decision of Dr. Porye the Vice-Chancellor, Dr. Parkar, and Edward Leedes. Lat.

Mar. 18 (?) 37. Same to [the Fellows of Queen's Coll.?]. Has read the letter of the 17th, and disapproves of the violent part taken against the Principal and certain Fellows of the College. Has appointed Dr. Porye, Dr. Parkar, and Edward Leedes, to be arbiters. Lat.

Mar. 18 (?) 38. Same to [Dr. Porye, Dr. Parkar, and Edward Leedes?]. His unavoidable absence from the University prevents his personal attendance in its affairs; refers to their arbitration the dispute that has arisen between the Principal and certain of the Fellows of Queen's College. Lat.

March 19. 39. Wm. West (afterwards Baron de la Warr) to Sir Wm. Cecill. Makes a statement relative to lands he has claim to, and of his income since his attainder, and shows who are his heirs.

March 20. 40. John Hales to same. The merchants of London complain of the new imposition on cloths. States his opinions on the policy of heavy duties on merchandize.

March 22. 41. John Lord Williams of Thame to same. Has appointed him one of the supervisors of his will, and left him his interest in Grafton Pastures. Solicits his favour in a controversy between Mr. Harcourte, Mr. Wentworth, and Anth. Docwray.

March 22. 42. Ann Lady Fytzwylliams to same. Return of her banished son; solicits favour in his behalf. Expresses her grateful sense of the Queen's goodness.

March 22. 43. Extract of several clauses of the statute against unlawful assemblies.

March 24. 44. A book for sea causes, made by the officers of the Queen's Majesty's navy. Specifying the names of all the ships, their tonnage, and number of men.

March 24. 45. Declaration by William Wynter, Master of the Queen's Ordnance for the seas, of all the ordnance, munitions, &c., which remain at this present as well in Her Highness's ships as in her storehouses.

VOL. III.

1559.
March 25.   46. Articles of a commission under the Queen's signature, delivered to Sir Wm. Seyntlo, Captain of the Guard, and Sir Peter Carew, for survey of the Tower of London, and the officers and ministers of the same; with the answers to the said articles, shewing the state of the Tower, &c.

March 27.   47. Sir Roger North to Sir Wm. Cecill. Requests to know the issue of his suit, as the first day of the ensuing month is near at hand.

March 27.   48. Lord John Grey to same. Begs him to acquaint the Queen with his embarrassed circumstances, as they affect her former grant.

March 28. Cheynis.   49. Fr. Earl of Bedford to same. Desires leave of absence until the next session of Parliament.

March 29. Corpus Christi Coll.   50. Dr. John Porye, Vice-Chancellor of Cambridge, to same. On behalf of one Clybburne, accused of having uttered unseemly words of the Queen, calling her a rascal. Incloses,

> 50. I. *Depositions of Geo. Wythers and Geo. Bonde, as to words spoken by Clybburn, calling the Queen a rascal; exhibited by Geo. Bullock, Master of St. John's. March 28.*

March.   51. Proposition of the Bishops of Winchester, Lichfield, Chester, and Carlisle, and Drs. Cole, Harpsfeld, Landgale, and Chedsey, on the part of the Catholics, to conduct the conference at Westminster in writing.

March 31.   52. Declaration of the proceedings of a Conference begun at Westminster, concerning certain Articles of Religion; and the breaking up of the said conference by default and contempt of certain Bishops, parties of the said conference. Signed by the Privy Council.

March 31.   53. Draft of the above declaration. Corrected by Cecill.

March 31.   54. Copy of the above proceedings.

March 31. Greenwich.   55. The Queen to Lord Chidiock Pawlet. Has sent Thos. Hardy, Knt. Marshal, to take the musters at Portsmouth previous to the discharge of the garrison there.

March (?)   56. Account of various forts and blockhouses in Essex and Kent, with the number of men in each, and the pay due to them.

VOL. IV. APRIL—JUNE, 1559.

April 8.   1. Notes of the rate of wages due to the captains, with their sub-officers and soldiers, from the 20th of June 1558.

April 17.   2. Bill for giving authority to the Queen upon avoidance of any archbishoprick or bishoprick, to take into her hands certain temporal possessions of the same, and to make recompence by parsonages impropriate or tenths.

April 17.   3. Copy of the above.

1559.
April 17.
Hereford.
4. Commrs. of Musters for the City of Hereford to the Council. Have taken the musters within their city. *Inclosing,*

April 17.
4. I. *Certificate of musters for the city of Hereford, and liberties of the same.*

April 19.
St. Alban's.
5. Frances Duchess of Suffolk to Sir Wm. Cecill. Gives him notice that she has a right to the wardship and marriage of Ann Odell, now wife to Mr. Chetwood. Desires warrant to traverse the pretended title of Margaret Blackbourne to the said office.

April 21.
6. Licence for Benedict Spinola, a free denizen, to import and export certain kinds of cloth and merchandize, wines, &c., to a certain amount.

April 24.
7. Grant by the Queen to Lord John Grey (son of the late Marquis of Dorset), of the manors of Evercriche Hame, or Higham, and Stoke Dennys, co. of Somerset; and of the house and lands of Pirgo, in the co. of Essex, &c. Lat.

April 26.
Westminster.
8. Grant of the Office of Master of the Court of Wards and Liveries to Sir Thos. Parry, Comptroller of the Household.

April 28.
9. Proclamation releasing the restraint of merchant ships; all vessels not exceeding 80 tons burthen may proceed to sea.

April.
10. Note of all such passports for arms and munitions as Sir Thos. Gresham has remaining in his hands for behoof of the Queen.

April.
11. Accompt of sums received by Sir Ric. Sakevyle, for divers provisions and necessaries for the Coronation.

April.
12. Similar accompt; together with an accompt of sums to sundry persons for articles supplied.

April.
13. Accompt of money due to various persons for provisions and necessaries for the Coronation, the amount paid, and the sums remaining unpaid.

May 3.
Westminster.
14. Warrant to pay 3*l.* 6*s.* 8*d.* per diem to Sir Nich. Throkmorton, appointed Ambr. Resident at the Court of France.

May 3.
15. Warrant for a loan of 1,000*l.* to Sir Nich. Throkmorton, for the purposes of his embassy.

May 6.
16. The Queen to William Lord Cobham (Lord Warden of the Cinque Ports). Instructions to give honourable reception to the French ambassadors, whom he is to escort as far as Canterbury.

May 6.
17. Same to Thomas Wotton, Esq. (Sheriff of Kent). To confer with Lord Cobham as to reception and entertainment of the French ambassadors.

May 8.
18. Account of rents, annuities, &c, to be paid out of the revenues of the lands of Dame Katherine   , wife of   , during his absence, by Mr. Stafford and Mr. Yate his attorneys.

May 12.
Westminster.
19. The Queen to the Mayor of Exeter. Revokes her grant of incorporation for the Merchant Adventurers of that city, until the same has been further considered.

1559.

[May 19.] 20. The Queen to . Appoints them Commrs. to assess the whole county for the subsidy granted by the late Parliament.

[May 19.] 21. The same to . Appoints him a special Commissioner to superintend his colleagues in levying the subsidy. [*This and the preceding paper are drafts, indorsed 18 March 1557, which date is clearly inapplicable to the reign of Elizabeth, as her* LATE *Parliament was not dissolved till the 8th May 1559. They are evidently drafts prepared in the reign of Q. Mary, and subsequently made use of by Elizabeth.*]

May 19. 22. The same to Sir John Masone, &c., Commrs. for the subsidy in Middlesex; to use all diligence and discretion in assessing the same for the said county.

May 19. 23. The same to Viscount Montague, &c., Commrs. for the subsidy in the county of Surrey. Similar to the above.

May 19. 24. Fair copy of the above. Circular.

May 19. 25. Draft of the above.

May 21. (12 Cal. Junij). Sherborn. 26. John Cock to Sir Wm. Cecill. Urges a strict course to be held in religion. Complains of the Popish practices of the Vicar of Sherburn. Lat.

May 21. 27. List of jewels taken out of the Jewel House and delivered to the Queen.

May 26. Cobham Hall. 28. Wm. Lord Cobham to Cecill. Has received the Queen's letters by his brother Henry Cobham. Has appointed 7 gentlemen, well acquainted with languages, to attend the Fr. ambassadors.

May 26. 29. Names of the Lords Lieutenants in several counties.

May 26 (?) 30. Names of Lieutenants of various shires. Lord Williams Lord President of Wales. Aid to go from each county to particular parts, for their defence.

May 26. 31. Instructions by the Queen to Lord Robert Duddeley, Master of the Horse, and Sir Ambrose Cave, Chancellor of the Duchy of Lancaster, Lieutenants of the county of Warwick, for governance of the same in good order and quiet.

May 29. Hanesworth. 32. George Lord Talbot to Cecill. Has met with Sir Tho. Gargrave for the purpose of taking order relative to the matter of Saville's lands. Harry Saville, the heir male, and Robert Saville, the bastard son, attended. Detail of proceedings. *Incloses,*

32. I. *Notes of questions, communications, and answers moved to Edward Saville, son and heir apparent of Sir Henry Saville, decd. Names of all the Savilles present. Tankersley, May 27.*

1559.

Vol. IV.

May 29.
Westminster.
33. Sir Wm. Cecill to Dr. Porye, Vice-Ch. of Cambridge. To give notice to all the Heads of Colleges of an intended royal visitation. *Incloses,*

> 33. I. *The Queen to Sir Wm. Cecill, Chancellor of Cambridge.* Intimates her intention to have a visitation of the University. *Westminster, May 27.*

34. Schedule of names of great officers of state, noblemen, gentlemen, and divines, classed under separate dioceses, and the Universities of Oxford and Cambridge, probably Commissioners for a general visitation.

May 29.
35. The Queen to . To receive and admit certain persons as Alms Knights at Windsor, specifying their names. Will cause statutes to be made for governing the College.

May 31.
36. Certificate of sums of money due within the Offices of Ordnance and the Armoury at the last of May 1559, and to be due at Midsummer next.

May 31.
37. Certificate of sums of money now owing to the Great Wardrobe, for debts incurred in the time of the late Queen, and to the last of May 1559.

May (?)
38. Names of the spiritual men without promotion at this present; and also list of bishopricks and other spiritual promotions presently in the Queen's disposition, with the value of the livings.

May (?)
39. List of bishopricks in England and Wales, and their values; with names of various divines.

May (?)
40. Memorial, drawn up by Sir Wm. Cecill, of things to be reported to the Queen : of dangers to Her Majesty's Government, both within the realm and from foreign parts. Recommends reformation in Ecclesiastical affairs, &c.

June 2
41. A tract on controversial points of divinity. Conditions without which the Protestants will not consent to the Council proposed in the Diet at Augsbourg. Lat.

June 3.
42. Sir Ric. Southwell to Sir Wm. Cecill. Reminds him that 315*l.* 2*s.* 8*d.* is due in the Office of Armoury at Greenwich. State of the Offices of Armoury and Ordnance.

June 4.
43. Account of money paid by the Receiver-General of the Court of Wards and Liveries, by virtue of the Queen's special warrants.

June 5.
44. Account of money received by Sir John Masone, Treasurer of the Chamber, by warrants from several Courts.

June 6.
45. Account of the whole receipts of Thomas Weldon, Esq., Cofferer of the Household, by virtue of Her Majesty's warrants.

June 7.
46. Sir Ric. Southwell to Cecill. Further detail of the state of the Offices of the Ordnance and Armoury. Proposes a sale of corslets to gentlemen who are suitors for the same. Answer of the gentlemen who had armour and weapons delivered to them in Wyatt's rebellion.

DOMESTIC—ELIZABETH.

VOL. IV.

1559.

June 8. 47. Account of debts owing in the office of the Revels and Tents.

June 8. 48. Sir Tho. Cornwaleys to Francis Yaxley. His Uncle Alyff is de-
Copthall. sirous Mr. Darcy of Tolson should see his cousin, Margaret Sylyard, and is willing to bestow her on him in marriage. Begs Mr. Yaxley will bring the matter about.

June 9. 49. Marq. of Winchester to Sir Wm. Cecill. Money affairs; payment might presently be made, and the garrisons in Ireland and at Berwick discharged.

June 9. 50. Declaration made by William Wynter, Master of the Ordnance for the Seas, of the debts due in the said office. Also estimates for works for fitting out the great ship now making at Woolwich.

June 10. 51. Dr. D. Lewis to Cecill. States his opinion on the sentence
Arches Court. passed on certain Frenchmen for robbing and spoiling a Flemish vessel within the Queen's dominions.

June 12. Grant of arms to Tho. Whyte of Fytleforde, Dorset, by Wm. Harvey, Clarencieux. [See *Grant of Arms*, No. 8.]

June 14. 52. Order for Henry Duke of Buckingham to bear the arms of Thomas of Woodstock alone, temp. Edw. IV., and declaration of the officers of arms of the manner in which a foreign prince may bear or quarter the arms of England.

June 20. 53. Commission from the Queen to Sir Wm. Cecill, Chancellor, and others, to hold a visitation of the University of Cambridge.

June 22. 54. Winchester to Cecill. The Duke of Florence and the Signory bound for Signor Guidodi's debt. Payment for Ireland must be considered. Has sent two warrants for payment of the Queen's debt in the Isle of Wight.

June 22 (?) 55. Same to same. Has made a survey of Hampton Court. Points out many alterations and improvements to be made for the Queen's comfort. The grounds will be laid out with as many pleasures as can be imagined.

June 23. 56. Same to same. Survey of the Queen's houses. Desires a copy of the gestes, to know what works are necessary to be done. Works at Greenwich, and repairs necessary to be done at Windsor.

June 23 (?) 57. Report on the state of the Queen's Majesty's houses, and of the repairs necessary to be done, all being greatly out of repair.

June 23. 58. Winchester to Cecill. Lady Sussex, that [Andrew?] Wyse married, has applied to him and others for order to be taken with her husband for clearing his accounts and discharging him from imprisonment.

June 24. 59. Citation from the Commissioners and from the Vice-Chancellor for visiting the University of Cambridge, appointing the 7th July for appearance before the Commissioners.

June 24. 60. Account of fees and wages due to the Lieut. of the Tower, the Gentlemen Porter, and Yeoman Warders there, to Midsummer 1559.

1559.
June 25.   61. Marq. of Winchester to Sir Wm. Cecill. Will see Thos. Cokerell paid 60l., and the rest to Sir Henry Crips. Has taken order for the Wood Beam.

June 25.
Westminster.   62. Commission from the Queen to the Earl of Shrewsbury, President of the North, and others, and to Dr. Edwyn Sandys, Dr. Henry Harvey, and others, to hold a visitation of the province of York.

June 25.
Shrewsbury.   63. Sir Hugh Poulet to Cecill. Has received letters from the Lord President of Wales to meet him at Worcester. Resigns that charge cheerfully, and is anxious to go to his charge in Jersey. Want of books of Common Prayer. *Incloses,*

> 63. I. *John Lord Williams of Thame to Sir Hugh Poulet. Has received his Commission and Instructions (as Lord President of Wales), and will meet him and the Council at Worcester. June* 18.

June 25.   64. James Aldaye to same. Details a conversation with Champneys, and covertly promised to join him in a plot to encounter the Queen's ships sent against Harry Strangwyshe. Proposes a scheme for the arrest of himself and the hoy at Gravesend.

June 25.   65. Same to same. Has inquired into the matter on foot. Has not had much conference with Francis Lambart. Further conversation with Champneys on his coming from the Court. Some of the Queen's ships to be sent forth against Strangwyshe. Danger of his own position.

June 27.
Cambridge.   66. Dr. John Porye to same. Informs him that the mastership of Christ's College is vacant, the late master (Wm. Tailer) having absconded. Recommends Mr. Hawford to succeed him.

June 27.   67. Chancellor Cecill to the Fellows of Christ's College. Regrets the manner of the departure of the late master. Recommends them to elect Mr. Hawford, B.D.

June 27.   68. Winchester to Cecill. Gives him the heads of certain documents transmitted.

June 28.   69. Account of sums due by the office of the Great Wardrobe, for stuff and workmanship for the use of the Queen's stable.

June 29.
London.   70. Sir Ric. Sakevyle to Cecill. Has agreed, with others, on the award between George Heron and John Carr. Proposes application to be made to Giles Heron's wife to release the appeal now depending.

June 29.
London.   71. Sir Nicholas Bacon (Lord Keeper) to same. Particulars of the sudden departure of the Bishop of St. Asaph. The ports have been instructed not to suffer him to pass.

June 26.
St. Alban's.   71. I. *Bishop Goldwell to his brother Stephen Goldwell. Has determined to leave his Bishoprick, being in debt to the Queen above* 300l. *for the subsidy. Requests him to go into Wales to sell his goods there.*

June 27.
Goldwell.   71. II. *John Goldwell to Lord Keeper Bacon. Five of the servants of his brother the Bishop of St. Asaph came to Mr. Ste. Goldwell's house, not knowing what had become of their master.*

Vol. IV.

1559.

June 30. — 72. Marq. of Winchester to Sir Wm. Cecill. The Dean and Canons of the Cathedral Church, the Warden and Fellows of New College, and the Master of St. Crosse, Winchester, have left their services, and will enter no new service, being against their consciences; wherein order must be taken.

June 30. — 73. Certificate by Ric. Ward of the monies received by the Cofferer of the Household for the expenses of the Household, and what remains to be received.

June. — 74. Note of debts due at Midsummer in various offices of the State.

June 30. — 75. Andrew Scare to Cecill. Particular of the sale of goods at the George in Stamford, under distress for rent.

June. — 76. The Queen to the Customers, &c. of the port of London. To release the restraint on merchant ships above the burthen of 80 tons.

Vol. V. July, 1559.

July 1. — 1. Charges of the Queen's household to 1st July 1559, and the amount remaining unpaid.

July 6. Tower. — 2. Sir Edw. Warner (Lieut. of the Tower) and Thos. Stanley (Comptroller of the Mint) to Cecill. Report on the fittest place in the Tower to erect a convenient armoury. No place so fit as the great mill erected by Mr. Brocke.

July 12. — 3. Statement of wages payable monthly to the Almain Armourers at Greenwich.

July 14. — 4. Certificate of musters of the Hamlets belonging to the Tower of London, taken before Sir Edw. Warner, Lieutenant of the Tower.

July 15. — 5. The Queen to the Dean and Chapter of Windsor. Is desirous to give effect to the will of King Henry VIII. that certain poor Knights should be continually maintained at the College within the Castle of Windsor. Has therefore transmitted certain rules signed by her own hand for the government of the said poor Knights.

July 15. — 6. Establishment, under the Queen's signature, for the erection and governance of thirteen Poor Knights at Windsor, attached to the institution of the Noble Order of the Garter, in pursuance of the will of King Henry VIII.

7. Draft of the above, prepared temp. Philip and Mary, Queen Elizabeth's name substituted, and other alterations made; with the apportionment of the revenue of 600l. per annum, as settled by Philip and Mary.

1559.

Vol. V.

8. List of the lands and livings granted in various counties for the maintenance of the College of Poor Knight's at Windsor; stating the value of each; amounting in the whole to 665l. 6s. 8d. per annum.

July 15. 9. The yearly limitation and distribution of the revenue of 600l. per annum, appointed for the maintenance of 13 Poor Knights at Windsor, and for further performance of the testament of King Henry VIII.; under the Queen's signature.

July 15. 10. Draft of the above, corrected by Sir Wm. Cecill.

July 15. 11. An order for Obits at Windsor four times a year, or at the end of every term there shall be commendations of the most noble Kings Henries the VII. and VIII., and of their Royal succession, founders and benefactors of so worthy a college. Probably the order drawn up for the service under Philip and Mary.

July 15. 12. "The ordre for ye 4 quarter Obites in ye Chappell at Wyndsore "for ye memorye and cōmēdatiō. of y^c Q. Ma^{ten} progenitors, foundors "of ye Ord^r of ye Gart^r.'" Originally drawn up by Sir John Masone, and corrected by Sir W. Cecill.

July 15. 13. The order for the 4 quarter Obits in the Chapel at Windsor for the memory and commendation of the Queen's Majesty's progenitors, Founders of the Order of the Garter. Copy of the above, with slight additions, by Cecill.

July 15. 14. Fair copy of the above.

July 15. Leighton. 15. Sir Robert Tyrwhyt to the Council No letter nor instructions had formerly been received for taking musters in Huntingdonshire. Incloses,

15. I. *Certificate of musters for the county of Huntingdon.* Huntingdon, *July* 15.

July 15. 16. Dean and Chapter of Hereford to the Queen. Have elected John Scorye to the Bishopric of Hereford, vacant by the demise of Robert Warton. Lat.

July 18. 17. Heads of urgent affairs consequent on the death of the French King, Henry II. Maintenance of the faction in Scotland; to send to King Philip to renew the League. Letters to various parties in France.

July 19. Westminster. 18. Commission by the Queen, constituting Matthew Parker Archbishop elect of Canterbury, Edmund Grindall Bishop elect of London, and others, Commissioners for carrying into execution the Acts for the uniformity of Common Prayer, and for restoring to the Crown the ancient jurisdiction of the State Ecclesiastical.

July 19. 19. Another copy of the above.

July 19. 20. Abstract of the several clauses of the above commission.

July 23. 21. Declaration of the elections of Proctors in the University of Cambridge, in order of colleges; confirmed at the visitation of the University, July 23d. Lat.

VOL. V.

1559.

July 28.
Guildhall.
22. Sir Nich. Bacon and others, Commissioners of Sales, to Sir Wm. Cecill. So few suitors attend the Commission, that very little money will be raised thereby. *Inclosing*,

  22. I. *Certificate of the clear yearly value of all lands sold by the Commissioners of Sales since the 14th of July 1558. July 28.*

July 31.
23. Declaration by Sir Ric. Southwell, of his resignation of the office of Master of the Armoury and Ordnance, on certain conditions specified.

July (?)
24. The Queen to Thomas Thirlby, late Bp. of Ely. Commands him to pay over forthwith to the present Bishop (Cox) the sum of 706l. 13s. 4d., given by King Edwd. VI., to be paid over to each new Bishop by his predecessor; and also to pay a reasonable sum for dilapidations.

July.
25. Order for consecration of an Archbishop of Canterbury; the mode to be pursued; with marginal notes by Cecill.

July.
26. Notes of debts in various offices of the Crown.

July.
27. Certificates of musters of the hundreds of Brixton, Wallington, Woking, Godalming, Godley, Farnham, Blackheath and Wotton, Kingston and Elmbridge, Copthorne and Effingham, and Tandridge and Reygate, in the county of Surrey.

July.
28. Certificate of musters of the wapentakes of Flaxwell, Langoo, Boothby Graffoo, Aswardhurne, and Aveland, &c. in Kesteven division, co. Lincoln.

VOL. VI. AUGUST—SEPTEMBER, 1559.

Aug. 1 (?)
1. Dispensations reserved to the Archbishop of Canterbury, probably at the consecration of Archbp. Parker.

Aug. 2 (?)
2. The Queen to the Lord Treasurer and Barons of the Exchequer. Warrant to release Katharine Duchess of Suffolk, and Ric. Bertie, her husband, from all payments or accounts of lands, &c. seized by the Crown, and restoring to them all their said lands, goods, and other possessions. [*Letters of naturalization for their son, Peregrine Bertie were passed on the 2d of August 1559; and it is probable this document may have had the same date.*]

August 7.
3. Marq. of Winchester and Sir Tho. Leigh, Lord Mayor of London, to the Council. Details of an affray between the Marquis de Neale's servants and Mr. Watson's servants.

August 9.
4. The Queen to Winchester. To give directions to the officers of the Cinque Ports, for the honourable reception of the King of Spain, if he should land in England.

August 9.
5. The same to the Earls of Arundel and Bedford, and Lords Cobham and Mountjoy. Directions to receive the King of Spain with honour, if he should touch at any English port.

1559.

VOL. VI.

August 10. 6. Lease by Thomas Norton and Eleanor Norton to John Norton, of certain lands called the Chese lands at Milton, near Sittingbourne, Kent.

August 10. 7. Account of charges of the Queen's house for 6 days at Nonsuch, defrayed by the Earl of Arundel, Lord Steward.

August 10. 8, 9. Certificates of musters for the Rapes of Bramber and Chichester, Sussex.

August 11. London. 10. Marq. of Winchester and Sir John Masone to Sir Wm. Cecill. Report particulars of their conference with the Marquis de Nesle, the French Ambassador, relative to the murder committed by the Frenchmen in Mr. Watson's house.

August 11. London. 11. Sir John Masone to same. Unreasonableness of the Frenchmen. The Book of Common Service in Latin is ready to print; also the little book of Private Prayer for children and servants.

August 14. 12. The Queen to Mr. Browne and Mr. Estofte. Has put them in the Commission for visitation of the clergy in the northern circuit.

August 14. 13. Winchester to Cecill. Has sent him the Bishops' books. Dealings with the Bishops. Death of Dr. Stuard. The matter between the French hostages and Watson's folks remains quiet. Ceremonies to be observed at the obsequies of the French King.

August 15. 14. Same to same. Sends letters out of Yorkshire. Thinks Signor Priuli might have leave to go, who hopes to be discharged of the 700*l*. demanded of the house of Canterbury. The book of the Bishops' lands shall be immediately brought forth. Henry Matthewe, Vicar of Hoo in Kent, is prisoner in the Marshalsea for contempt.

August 16. 15. Submission of Robt. Raynolds, clerk, to the laws and ordinances provided by Parliament for the service of the Church.

August 16. 16. Note of all sums of money taken up by exchange, in Antwerp, for the use of the Queen.

August 17. Yollyston. 17. Sir John Chichester to the Earl of Bedford. Sends him his commission of Lieutenancy, &c. The subsidy is well received. Has punished several for bruiting the death of the Queen. Thanks for a goshawk.

August 18. London. 18. Sir Ric. Sakevyle to Cecill. The Lord Treasurer has promised that Mr. Osborne should that day receive 1,000*l*. Several parties have been with him to buy lands and parsonages in Kent and Sussex. Many warrants to be paid.

August 18. Hampton Court. 19. Dr. Nich. Wotton to same. Opinion of jurists as to ownership of property taken by pirates. They who have captured the pirates (Strangwishe) have had the greater part of their prizes.

August 19. London. 20. Same to same. Further opinion on the subject. Goods taken by pirates can be lawfully claimed by the owners.

Vol. VI.

1559.
August 19. 21. Vice-Chancellor and Scholars of Cambridge to their Patron and Chancellor, Sir William Cecill. Solicit his protection of their privileges and immunities. *Lat.*

August 19. 22. Bishop Tunstall to Cecill. The Queen has left Hampton Court, and he was unable to see her. Cannot consent to the visitation of his diocese, if it is to extend to the pulling down altars, defacing churches, and taking away crucifixes.
London.

August 19. 23. The same to Sir Thos. Parry, to the same effect. Gestes of the Queen's progress.
London.

August 20. 24. Elizabeth Lady Chandos to Cecill. To favour her daughter (Lady Frances) Throgmorton, whose innocence will be apparent if she has impartial judges. Violent conduct of Geo. Throgmorton, her husband, towards the witnesses.

August 20. 25. Winchester to same. Progress of works at Windsor. The Castle is ready for the Queen's reception. Domestic articles wanting. The College at Windsor (the poor Knights) are desirous to have their statutes.

August 23. 26. The Queen to Marq. Winchester. Licence for the merchants of the Stillyard to ship 356 woollen cloths by the 30th January next: with schedule of cloths annexed.
Hampton Court.

August 24. 27. The Council to divers Ports, requiring a return of all horses and geldings exported since Christmas last.

August 28. 28. Winchester to Cecill. Further repairs necessary at Windsor Castle. New materials required.

August 28. 29. John Earl of Oxford to same. Has administered to the Justices in the last sessions at Chelmsford, the oath concerning the abolishing of all foreign power and superiority. *Incloses,*

    29 .i. *Names of such Justices of Peace as were sworn to renounce and abolish all foreign power and superiority. August* 21.

August 31. 30. Tho. Duke of Norfolk to same. Expresses his sorrow for the sickness under which the Queen has lately been suffering.
Kenninghall.

August 31. 31. The Queen to James Lord Mountjoy. Thanks for having stayed and arrested a great number of vagabonds using the manner of Egyptians (Gypsies).

August 31. 32. Edmund Gest to Cecill. Mr. Seth Holland, Dean of Worcester, will not renounce the Pope: solicits to succeed him in his Deanery.

August 31. 33. Certificate of such sums of money as are owing in the office of the Great Wardrobe for debts incurred in the time of Queen Mary, and to the 31st of August.

August. 34. Brief notes to prove the evil meaning of the French towards England, with measures necessary to make England strong against invasion: by Sir Wm. Cecill.

DOMESTIC—ELIZABETH.

VOL. VI.

1559.
August.
(Saturday.)
Croydon.
35. Lord Robert Duddeley to Francis Yaxley. Thanks him for his letter and a present, both of which he takes in good part, and will be glad to see him.

August.
36. Estimate of the wages of 146 yeomen of the guard for 4 months, ended August, and for the next month to come.

Sept. 2.
37. Estimate of debts due, 30th June, and to be due on the last day of September, within the charge of Benj. Gonson, Treasurer of the Navy.

Sept. 4.
Hampton Court.
38. The Queen to Lord Cobham, Lord Warden. To discharge all persons within the Cinque Ports exceeding the peace establishment, except the gunners returned from Guisnes.

Sept. 5.
Dorchester.
39. Ric. Weston and Ric. Harper to the Council. Proceeding against the "Egyptians" at the assizes at Dorchester. Find that they came out of Scotland into England.

Sept. 9.
40. Note of the charges of the obsequies of Henry II. King of France, the officers present as mourners, &c.

Sept. 9.
41. The Queen to Bishop Tunstall and others. Commands them to consecrate Matthew Parker, as Archbishop of Canterbury. Lat.

Sept. 13.
42. The same to the Marq. Winchester, Sir Ric. Sakevyle, Sir Walter Mildmay, and Mr. Kelleway, appointing them Commissioners to examine certificates of Bishops lands, made under the act granting to the Crown a year's revenue of Archbishopricks and Bishopricks on vacancy of the sees.

Sept. 13.
43. Account of all sorts and kinds of ordnance, artillery, &c., remaining at the present day within the Tower of London, with an estimate of the supply necessary for the next year.

Sept. 16.
44. Certificate of musters for the hundreds of Dorchester, Bollyngton, and Thame in Oxfordshire.

Sept. 16 (?)
45. Certificate of the muster of 200 footmen of the county of Oxford, to be kept in readiness, upon one hour's warning.

Sept. 17.
46. Account of charges due to the Captains and soldiers serving in the castles and bulwarks of Kent from September 2, 1558.

Sept. 20.
47. The Queen to   commanding them to attend Her Majesty on occasion of receiving the Ambassador of Sweden. *Attached to the above,*

47. I. *A list of noblemen commanded to attend the coming of the Swedish Ambassador.*

Sept. 20.
48. Same to (Edw.) Lord Hastings of Loughborough. Commands him to repair to the Court to attend the coming of the embassy from Sweden.

Sept. 20.
(12 Cal. Oct.)
49. The Vice-Ch. and University of Cambridge to the Queen. Complaining of the conduct of the townspeople of Cambridge, in resisting the collection of tolls claimed by the University. Lat.

Vol. VI.

1559.

Sept. 20. — Rent roll of the manor of Founthill Gyfford, co. Wilts, belonging to Sir John Mervyn. (*Case* A. *Eliz.* No. 2.)

Sept. 23. Canford. — 50. Jas. Lord Montjoy to the Queen. Proposed indictment of the vagabonds called Egyptians. The lawyers are of opinion they are not chargeable with felony, because they did not come from beyond seas.

Sept. 25. — 51. The Queen to Henry Lord Stafford, Lord Robt. Duddeley, and Sir Ambrose Cave, and Lord Williams. Directions to raise 300 men in Staffordshire, 200 in Warwickshire, and 200 in Shropshire, for the service at Berwick.

Sept. 26. — 52. Account of cloths shipped at the port of London, with names of the merchants.

Sept. 27. — 53. Winchester to Cecill. Forwards account of cloths shipped at the port of London by the Merchant Adventurers. Offers of the Staplers for payment of duties by their Company.

Sept. 29. — 54. Account of wages, &c. due to the Lieut. of the Tower, the Gentleman Porter and Yeomen Warders there, to Michaelmas 1559.

Sept. 29. — 55. Note of such sums of money as will be owing within the office of the Treasurer of the Chamber at Michaelmas.

Sept. 29. — 56. Another account of debts due in the same office, to the same period.

Sept. 29. — 57. Note of debts presently due or shortly to be due.

Sept. 29. — 58. Note of debts due by the Crown at Michaelmas, to be paid at subsequent periods.

Sept. 30. — 59. Note of debts due within the office of Armoury, to the last of September.

Sept. — 60. Names of the captains and petty captains appointed to have the leading of 1,000 footmen levied in the county of Somerset.

Sept. — 61. Summary of the general musters taken within the county of Somerset by Sir Maurice Berkeley, and others, amounting to 4,326 able men.

Sept. — 62. Certificate of musters of 100 able men within the rapes of Chichester and Arundel, appointed for Portsmouth and the Isle of Wight to be ready at an hour's warning. (*See October* 15.)

Sept. — 63. Similar certificate for the rapes of Bramber, Lewes, Chichester, and Arundel.

Sept. — 64. General certificate of all the able men, weapon, and armour in the county of Sussex.

Sept. — 65. General certificates of musters of all the able men, armour, and weapon, within the co. of Surrey.

Sept. — 66. Certificate (brief declaration or summary) of the musters of all the able men, horses, armour, &c., for the whole co. of Essex.

Vol. VI.

1559.
Sept. 67. Names of captains and petty captains appointed for leading 500 footmen within the county of Wilts.

Sept. 68. Certificate of musters for the whole county of Wilts, taken by George Penruddock, Esq., Provost Marshal, and others, Justices of Peace for the same county.

Vol. VII. October—December, 1559.

Oct.
Colchester. 1. Earl of Oxford to the Council. Conversation with the Duke [Eric of Sweden] about the uttering and exchange of the Swedish coin. His arrival at Colchester.

Oct. 1.
Colchester. 2. Sir Tho. Smith to Cecill. Reception of the Duke [Eric of Sweden] in England. He likes the country, and nothing is omitted needful for him. Popularity of the Earl of Oxford. The dollars are made bullion.

Oct. 1. 3. Memorial by Sir Hugh Poulet to the Privy Council, of certain things seeming meet and expedient for the good order of Wales. *Annexing,*

    3. I. *Order of Council of the Marches of Wales, in cases of misdemeanor; form of conviction, &c. Sept.*

Oct. 4. 4. Account of powder delivered and expended since the beginning of the Queen's reign.

Oct. 4. 5. Note of provisions of powder and other stores to be made in parts beyond seas; necessary defence of the realm.

Oct. 5. 6. Certificate of musters of all the able men within the counties of Nottingham and Rutland.

Oct. 5. 7. Confessions of Ric. Sweet, servant to Ric. Prestwood, Humphrey Parris, and John Hockley, concerning the behaviour of Parson Smart and Parson Yendall, who went to Morlaix in order to enjoy liberty of conscience: attested by Sir John Chichester.

Oct. 13. 8. Account of the store of armour within the Tower of London, with memorial of such armour as is needful to be provided.

Oct. 15. 9. The Queen to the Earl of Arundel. The musters having been taken for the county of Sussex, his commission of lieutenancy ceases. The force of the county is to be kept in readiness for defence of Portsmouth and the Isle of Wight, if need require.

Oct. 16. 10. The same to Mr. Wynter. To re-deliver certain artillery, armour, &c., taken out of the offices of Ordnance in Queen Mary's time.

Oct. 17. 11. The same to Marq. Winchester. To give directions to all officers having charge of the woods, to use henceforth as much husbandry as ossible for the preservation of the timber.

DOMESTIC—ELIZABETH.

Vol. VII.

1559.

Oct. 20. — 12. Proclamation (signed by the Queen) against excess in apparel.

Oct. 20 (?) — 13. Articles agreed upon by the Lords of the Privy Council for reformation of their servants in abuses of apparel. [*Mutilated at the edge.*]

Oct. 20. — 14. Copy of the above, made before the mutilations.

Oct. 20. — 15. Obligation of the Privy Council to observe and enforce the above articles and clauses.

Oct. 20. Westminster. — 16. The Queen to the Dean of Windsor and Registrar of the Garter. Warrant to provide the poor men lately established at the College of Windsor, under the name of "Alms Knights," with things necessary for their houses and utensils.

Oct. 23. — 17. Account of money received by and due to Sir Thomas Gresham, for payment of the Queen's debts beyond sea.

Oct. 26. Westminster. — 18. The Queen to Sir George Haward. To call upon all persons (except of the Privy Council) to deliver up all weapons and munition received by them in the time of Queen Mary.

Oct. 26. — 19. The same to ——. The Archbishop elect of Canterbury, and the Bishops elect of London, Ely, Hereford, and Chichester remain unconsecrated, by reason that the exchange between the Crown and them for certain temporalities has not been effected. Directs the same to be executed. Remission of the first fruits, to a certain extent.

Oct. 26. — 20. Certificate of Geo. Jones, Escheator of the county of Gloucester, that he has apprehended certain persons called Egyptians, specifying their names.

Oct. 28. — 21. The Queen to Lord Trer. Winchester. Directions to preserve the timber in Westwood, near Lewisham, Kent, for the purpose of ship building.

Oct. 28. — 22. The same to Sir Thos. Woodhouse. To confer with the Mayor of Yarmouth, Norf., as to what is necessary to be done for the security of that important haven.

Oct. 28. — 23. The same to Lord Cobham. To provide measures for the security of the town of Sandwich.

Oct. — 24. Note of the sittings of the Commissioners in the Visitation of the Province of York.

Oct. (?) — 25. Petition of Geoffrey Pynchebek to Sir Wm. Cecill. Has renewed the commission for certain lands depending in variance between him and Mr. Colvylle. Requests his favour therein.

Oct. — 26. Certificate of musters for the whole county of Dorset, by order of James Lord Mountjoy, Lord Lieutenant of the county.

Oct. — 27. Summary of the above musters.

Nov. 1. Westminster. — 28. The Queen to Winchester. Has lately restored the Marq. of Northampton to his former estate. Desires a grant of certain lands of 500*l.* annual value to be prepared, to be settled upon him.

1559.   Vol. VII.

Nov. 1.
Magdalen Coll.
Cambridge.
29. Roger Kelk (Master of Mag. Coll. Camb.) to Sir Wm. Cecill. Requests him to procure the Queen's presentation in his favour for an Archdeaconry.

Nov. 3.
Charter House.
30. Frances, Duchess of Suffolk to same. Thanks him for furthering her suit for licence to sell one of the manors of her jointure. Incloses,

30. I. *Particular of the lands held by Lady Frances Duchess of Suffolk, as well by jointure as by inheritance.*

Nov. 6 (?)
31. Certificate of the value of certain lands, parcel of the possession of Lady Frances Duchess of Suffolk, as one of the co-heirs of Charles late Duke of Suffolk.

Nov. 6.
32. Matthew Parker, Archbishop elect of Canterbury, to Cecill. Is to speak with the Queen again in the principal matter in hand. "God keep us from such a visitation as Knox has attempted in Scotland."

Nov. 6.
Brome.
33. Sir Thos. Cornwaleys to same. Thanks him for his late letters, and sends him 22 partridges; part to be presented to Lord Robert [Duddeley].

Nov. 7.
34. Decree of the Court of Wards, declaring Gregory Fynes Lord Dacre of the South to have attained his full age of 21 years, contingent on the birthday of King Edward VI. [*It is extraordinary that in this decree the birth of Edward VI. is antedated by a whole year.*]

Nov. 9.
Melles.
35. Mrs. Margaret Yaxlee to Francis Yaxley. Desires to see the titles of certain copyhold lands bought of his father by her late husband. Project for uniting the rectories of Little Thornham and Melles, co. Suffolk.

Nov. 11.
Wortham.
36. Geo. Waller to same. Gives particulars of the manor and perquisites of Mildenhall. Has heard the D. of Norfolk desires them for Sir John Tyrrell.

Nov. 16 (?)
37. A paper indorsed "Ex Rotulis Parliament," from 3 Henry VI. to 1 Eliz., containing the names of Peers in each Parliament.

Nov. 17.
38. Account of armour remaining in the Tower of London and other places, to 17th November.

Nov. 18.
39. Archbp. Parker to Cecill. Death of Bishop Tunstall. The will of King Henry VIII. found among the few effects left by him.

Nov. 18.
40. Copy of the above.

Nov. 25.
41. Account of brass ordnance and powder received into the Tower for the Queen's use from Anth. Hickman and Edw. Castelyn.

Nov. 26.
Westminster.
42. Sir Ric. Sakevyle, Sir John Warner, and others, to the Queen. Report particulars of examinations taken by them of certain persons accused of sorcery, witchcraft, poisoning, enchantment, &c.; particularly in the case of George Throgmorton and Lady Frances Throgmorton, his wife, who was accused of poisoning her husband.

Nov. 28.
43. Note of armour delivered to Adrian Poynings, Esq., for service to be done at Portsmouth.

Vol. VII.

1559.
Nov. 30.   44. Account of debt due and payable to the Queen for fustians. The principal debtors being Anth. Hickman and Edw. Castelyn.

Nov.   45. General account of subsidy paid by the Laity in England and Wales in the first year of the Queen's reign.

Nov.   46. List of Bishops who returned into England on Queen Elizabeth's accession, and of the Bishops present in her first Parliament. Progress of the Convocation in framing the book of Common Prayer.

47. Another copy of the above.

Nov. (?)   48. Petition of George Glover to Sir Wm. Cecill. Prays him to request the Lord Keeper to call before him Mr. Stambridge and his other creditors, and to compound with them.

Nov. (?)   49. Memorandum of the quantities of bow staves received into the Ordnance stores.

Nov. (?)   50. Estimates of charges and materials of the masks and other pastimes to be shewn in presence of the Queen at Whitehall at Christmas and Shrovetide.

Dec. 3.   51. The Queen to Sir Gilbert Dethicke, Garter, and Wm. Harvey, Clarencieux. Directs that the arms of the Lady Frances Duchess of Suffolk shall be augmented by quartering the Royal arms with them, to be placed on the escutcheon at her funeral.

Dec. 3.   52. Order of the personages to attend the funeral of the Lady Frances Duchess of Suffolk.

Dec. 3.   53. Another order for the above funerals, the personages differing in several particulars.

Dec. 3 (?)   54. Sir John Masone to "Mr. Secretary" [Cecill ?]. Solicits an assignation to be made of payment to the Office of Treasurer of the Chamber. Indorsed by Masone.

Dec. 3.   55. Abstract of all arrerages due in King Edward's and Queen Mary's times, paid within the office of the Treasurer of the Chamber, to the 3d of December. Indorsed by Masone.

Dec. 6.   56. The Queen to Anthony Kitchen, Bishop of Landaff, and others. Commission to consecrate Matthew Parker, Archbishop elect of Canterbury. Attestation of Dr. Wm. Mey and others that the above was of sufficient force for the purpose.

Dec. 6.   57. Royal assent for the consecration of Matthew Parker as Archbishop of Canterbury.

Dec. 6.   58. Survey of the centon of Arreton in the Isle of Wight, viz., of the number of parish churches and their condition, names of villages within the centon, and the holders of property therein; of the number of able men, archers, billmen, &c., woods, shipping, &c.

Dec. 6.   59. Similar survey of the centon of Motston, including the town and port of Yarmouth, and several other districts in the Isle of Wight. Value of the Queen's lands therein, &c. Sworn to by Thomas Cheke, Centoner, and others.

1559.

Vol. VII.

Dec. 6. 60. Presentment by Geo. Oglander, Centoner, and others, of St. Elyns [St. Helens], I. of Wight. The church of St. Elyns hath been evil served and worse repaired ever since Dr. Cole has been Provost of Eton. Particulars of several adjacent manors, villages, &c.

Dec. 10. 61. Presentment by William Burrell and Humphry Frost, Bailiffs, and others Burgesses of Newport in the Isle of Wight, containing answers to all particulars as in the preceding. No parish church within the borough of Newport. Give their opinion how the old town Medine, now called Newport, may be restored and replenished.

Dec. 10. 62. Supplication of the Ministers, Elders, and Deacons of the Strangers' Church in London, to the Queen, for confirmation of the privileges granted to them by Edw. VI., at the instigation of John à Lasco. Lat.

Dec. 11.
London.
63. Johannes Utenhovius to the Queen. Was expelled from his country 15 years ago by the Emperor, for maintaining the truths of the Gospel. Details private affairs and desires aid to recover 700*l.* Flemish, owing to him. Lat.

Dec. 16 (?) 64. Warrant to pay 6,760*l.* to Benjamin Gonson, Treasurer of the Admiralty, for provisions of victuals for the navy.

Dec. 16 (?) 65. Instructions by the Queen to William Wynter, appointed Admiral of a fleet of 14 ships of war to convey stores to Tynemouth, Holy Island, and Berwick; to intercept any succours coming from France to Scotland; and to pick a quarrel with the French fleet, if he can.

Dec. 16. 66. Another set of instructions to the same, nearly to the same purpose as the preceding. *Both drawn up by Cecill.*

Dec. 17. 67. Memorandum of the consecration of Archbp. Parker. Lat.

Dec. 17. 68. Relation of the rites and ceremonies observed at the consecration and installation of Matthew Parker, Archbishop of Canterbury. Lat.

Dec. 17. 69. Copy of the above.

Dec. 17. 70. Lease from Tho. Norton, of Allyngton Castle, Kent, to Edw. Norton, of a piece of land called Courteleese, parcel of the manor of Mylton, for ten years.

Dec. 20. 71. Note of armour remaining within the Tower, the 20th of Dec.

Dec. 27.
Harwich.
72. Henry Knolles to Cecill. Details his interview with the Duke [of Sweden]. Congratulated him, in Her Majesty's name, on his safe arrival in her dominions. The Earl of Oxford took him out hawking. He wished to go to London by sea.

Dec. 27. 73. The Council to the Queen. Address on the proceedings of the French King and Queen [Mary Queen of Scots] on their assumption of the arms and style of England, being in many points derogatory to the Queen's undoubted right. State of the nation; suggest measures to be pursued to counteract the evident designs of the French in Scotland. *In Cecill's hand.*

DOMESTIC—ELIZABETH.

VOL. VII.

1559.
Dec. 29.   74. Marq. Winchester to Sir Wm. Cecill. Declaration of what has been received by Edw. Hughes and Thomas Wentworth. Much of the subsidy remains unpaid. Requests some discreet person may be appointed to take that charge. Statement of the receipts of the treasurer of Berwick.

Dec. 29.   75. The Queen to Lord Cobham. Warrant for allowing certain Frenchmen to pass over into France, and to release the French ships stayed at Dover.

Dec. (?)   76. Arthur Poole to [Cecill ?]. Declares his good will and desire to obey him in all things. His uncle, the late Cardinal Pole, would never see him, and left him nothing in his will. Has been informed he could be of service to Her Majesty, which would give him much satisfaction.

Dec. (?)   77. Dr. Francis Mallett, Master of St. Katharine's Hospital. Report on the foundation, history, and present state of St. Katharine's Hospital. Offers to resign the Mastership.

Dec. (?)   78. Note of the clear yearly value of all the lands, &c. of St. Katharine's Hospital, and of the annual charges of the Tower of London; with a proposition to make the Lieut. of the Tower Master of St. Katharine's. [*See post, Feb.* 1560.]

Dec.   79. The Queen to the Commissioners of Visitation in the Provinces of Canterbury and York. To suspend their proceedings, and to determine such matters only as have been already commenced. With a list of Commrs. in each diocese.

Dec.   80. Andrew Perne, Vice Chancellor of Cambridge, to Sir Wm. Cecill. Acknowledges the Queen's letters, declaring her desire to encourage the study of Divinity, and what she is willing to do for that purpose. Lat.

VOL. VIII.   1559.   Undated Papers.

1. Notes relative to the number of horsemen, lances, and corsletts in divers counties.

2. The Breviate of an intended Act made for the maintenance of armour and armourers.

3. Account of the monthly charge of the Almain Armourers at Greenwich.

4. List of prices of arms and armour of various descriptions.

5. Device for the preparation of armour to be deposited in Yorkshire, to be ready for service on any sudden emergency.

6. Note of prices demanded by Edmund Nicholson for armour, muskets, &c., with the prices at which the Queen can be served with the same, and equally good.

1559.

Vol. VIII.

7. Memorandum of the quantity of certain military stores.

8. Another memorandum of stores, with the prices.

9. Statement of the revenue of the Bishoprick of Durham, with the charges incident to the same.

10. Account by Ric. Stonley, Teller of the Exchequer, of the names of officers of the Queen's Household being deficient in payment of the late subsidy. The musicians of all classes being defaulters.

11. Note of matters to be moved by Sir John Masone to the Privy Council, relative to the supply of stores, artillery, &c. to the office of Ordnance.

12. The Powder-makers to the Privy Council. State the prices at which they can undertake to supply Her Majesty with gunpowder.

13. Note of a tender for the supply of gunpowder, by a manufacturer.

14. Statement of the advantages of using latten metal for great ordnance rather than copper.

15. List of gunners of the Tower, serving also in the Queen's ships, with note of their patents, and the time they have been unpaid.

16. Lady Arundel's bill of charges incurred by Sir John Arundel, of Lanherne in Cornwall, on the Castle of Pendennis, near Falmouth, in the first year of Queen Mary.

17. Names of Captains, with numbers of men under their command, distinguishing those who were sick and those returnable by passport.

18. Grant to Geoffrey Samways of the Office of Receiver-General of Crown rents in the county of Dorset.

19. Warrant dormant to pay 12,000$l.$ yearly, and other sums to Thomas Weldon, Esq., as Cofferer of the Household and Keeper of the Great Wardrobe, for the annual expenses of those offices.

20. Warrant to the Receiver of the Court of Wards and Liveries, to pay 10,000$l.$ yearly to Thomas Weldon, Cofferer, for expenses of the Household.

21. Warrant to the Receiver General of the Duchy of Lancaster, to pay 8,000$l.$ yearly to Tho. Weldon, Cofferer, for expenses of the Household.

22. Estimate of the debt owing in the Queen's Household.

23. Names of officers in the Queen's Household.

24. Account of the deficiency in the jewels lately in charge of the Lady Jane Countess de Feria, on their delivery into the custody of Lady Knollys, Mrs. Norris, and Mrs. Blanch Parry.

Vol. VIII.

1559.

25. Account of the overplus of jewels delivered to the Queen by the Lady Jane Countess de Feria, she being not charged with the same by her book of account.

26. Note of the Earl of Northumberland's suits to the Queen, viz., for the Manor of Holme in Spaldingmore, the tythes of Tynemouth, &c.

27. Suit of the executors of Lord Williams of Thame, for the cancellation of recognizances entered into by him as Treasurer of Augmentations.

28. Statement of debts due by the Crown in various departments of public service, amounting to 226,910l. 19s. 8d.

29. Legal opinion on the claim of the Duchess of Somerset as to arrears of payment of either dower or jointure.

30. Marq. Winchester to Robt. Hare. Requests that Sir Robt. Brandling's man be speedily paid.

31. Account of the value of certain necessary and unnecessary wares brought into the port of London, the excess of which is prejudicial to the realm. Some of the articles are curious, viz., babies (dolls), value 178l. 3s. 4d. Tennis balls, 1,699l. Cabages and turnops, 157l. 16s. 8d. Cardes, 2,837l. 10s. Eles, fresh and salt, 1,580l. 13s. 4d. Iron, 19,559l. 10s.

32. Proposals of Richard Springham and Michael Loke, for the manufacture of silks in England.

33. Details of a proposition for manufacturing silks in England. Indorsed by Cecill, "1599, Italians demandes for silkes."

34. Requisitions of persons offering to establish a manufactory of silk in England.

35. Answer to the above demands of the persons proposing to make silks, and such things as are farther to be considered ; with Cecills resolutions thereon.

36. Reasons to move the Queen to discharge her town of Great Yarmouth from payment of the fifteenth.

37. Plan of Lothyngland, near Yarmouth ; being the land between Yarmouth and Lowestoft, Suffolk.

38. Note of articles regulating the grant of leases, advowsons, &c., by the Bishops.

39. Extracts from the Charter of Queen Elizabeth, granting certain privileges and immunities to the Dean and Chapter of the Collegiate Church of St. Peter's, Westminster. Lat.

40. Attestation of John Incent, Notary Public, to the assent to the election of Dr. Pilkington as Bishop of Winchester. [*The assent or body of the document has been cancelled and cut off : Pilkington was not promoted to that see.*]

DOMESTIC—ELIZABETH.

1559.

Vol. VIII.

41. Pedigree of Edmund Boner, *alias* Savage, Parson of Dunham, Dean of Leicester, and twice Bishop of London, bastard son of Geo. Savage, Parson of Dunham, who was bastard son of Sir John Savage of Cheshire.

Vol. IX. 1559.

Accounts of the first payment of the subsidy of the laity, 1° Elizabeth, within the following counties, viz., Berks, Bucks, Cambridge, Derby, Dorset, Hereford, Herts, Huntingdon, Lancaster, Leicester, Middlesex, Monmouth, Norfolk, Northampton, Notts, Shropshire, Somerset, Southampton and the I. of Wight, Suffolk, Surrey, Sussex, Wilts, and Worcester.

Vol. X. 1559.

A book of the Visitation of the Province of York, comprehending the Dioceses of York, Durham, Carlisle, and Chester, taken before Dr. Edwyn Sandes and Dr. Henry Harvye, and others, the Queen's Commissioners for the visitation of that Province. *Also containing*,

Certificate of recognizances taken before Drs. Sandes and Harvye, Commissioners General, for offences detected in the visitation of the Province of York.

Vol. XI. JANUARY—MARCH, 1560.

Jan. 8.
Eton.

1. M. Constable to Sir Ambrose Cave. Cannot suffer certain enormities and abuses to exist without notice. *Incloses*,

    1. I. *Statement of the doings and orders of the Commissioners of Musters within the county of Warwick*, detailing many abuses.

Jan. 14.

2. Account of sums of money received by Sir John Masone by several warrants, from 1st Nov. 1558, with details of the expenditure thereof.

Jan. 14.

3. Marq. of Winchester to Sir Wm. Cecill. The Lord Admiral has delivered to Mr. Bashe the great book of provisions for the navy. The store-house at Crossed Friars must be had; the brew-house and fresh water must be supplied for Portsmouth.

Jan. 15.
Bletshoe.

4. Oliver Lord St. John of Bletshoe to the Council. Has received the Queen's letters for sending demi-lances and other horsemen to Newcastle.

Jan. 16.

5. Note of armour thought meet to be continually reserved in the Tower, for preservation of the Queen's royal person.

VOL. XI.

1560.
Jan. 20 (?) 6. Proposal by the Queen for reducing her coin to the state it was in before her father's wars at Boulogne; with the reasons moving her thereunto.

Jan. (?) 7. Estimate of a proportion of moneys of two ounces fine, to be made out of the base moneys now current, into small moneys.

Jan. 21.
Lathom House.
8. Edw. Earl of Derby to Cecill. Has appointed the gentlemen of the county of Lancaster to muster with their horses, armour, &c. before him on the 29th of January. It is not possible they can be at Newcastle by the 1st of February.

Jan. 22.
Warwick.
9. Robert Throkemorton and Tho. Lucy to the Council. Did not receive the Queen's letters till the 21st, for sending demi-lances and other horsemen to Newcastle.

Jan. 22
Ferrybridge.
10. Fr. Earl of Shrewsbury to Cecill. Concerning the raising demi-lances, &c. to be sent to Newcastle. Has appointed Sir Tho. Gargrave to be his Vice-President during his absence.

Jan. 28. Grant of arms to John Weld, gentleman, haberdasher of London, son of John Weld, of Eton, Chester, by Sir G. Dethick, Garter. [*See Grant of Arms, No. 9.*]

Jan. 11. Note of the yearly value of the Manor of Stansted, Essex.

Jan. (?) 12. List of Bishops elect; containing some who were not Bishops as here assigned, as Dr. Pilkington for Winchester.

Feb. 1.
Ashby-de-la-Zouche.
13. Fr. Earl of Huntingdon to the Council. Has dispatched 14 horsemen to the Duke of Norfolk. Particulars of parties who have failed to send any. *Incloses,*

13. I. *Names of horsemen with their furniture sent from Ashby-de-la-Zouch towards Berwick, furnished by gentlemen of the county of Leicester.* 31 *Jan.*

Feb. 4.
Batehall (?)
14. Sir John Bourne to Francis Yaxley. Gives an account of his rural occupations. Invites him to come and enliven them, and promises all manner of rural delights.

Feb. 16.
Brome.
15. Sir Thomas Cornwaleys to same. Solicits him to favour the suit of the Vicar of Yaxley. Has given leave to Yaxley's man to take some partridges, though out of season.

Feb. 18.
Durham.
16. Robert Horn, Dean of Durham, to Sir Wm. Cecill. Prevalence of licentious manners. Good influence of the Duke of Norfolk being in those parts. Robt. Dalton, Nic. Merley, and John Tutting, three Prebendaries of Durham, refuse the oath. Thinks Mr. Ebden, Mr. Carvill, and Mr. Horton proper men to succeed them. Urges a suit of his own.

Feb. 23. 17. Winchester to same. Desires to be discharged of the custody of Carisbrooke Castle, I. of Wight. Charges at Berwick, &c. *Incloses,*

17. I. *Estimate of the charges of maintaining the garrisons in the North.*

1560.

VOL. XI.

Feb. 28.
Settrington
18. Matthew Earl of Lennox to Cecill. Marvels at his servant Nesbet's crime, knowing his own uprightness. Explains his own dealings with the French Ambassador. Is determined to support his claims in Scotland against Arran's bastardy. Asserts his innocence in all his transactions.

Feb.
19. Account of the yearly charges of the Tower of London in the time of Queen Mary, and as set forth in Feb. 2° Eliz.

20. Another copy of the above, with an additional memorandum.

Feb.
21. Account of the yearly revenue and expenditure of the Hospital of St. Katharine's; and of the yearly charges of the Tower of London, in the time of Q. Mary, and now lately set forth by authority. [*See ante, Dec.* 1559.]

Feb. (?)
22. Warrant for a grant to Sir Edw. Warner, Lieut. of the Tower, of the Mastership of St. Katharine's, on surrender of Dr. Mallett; together with the Stewardship of the Manor of East Smithfield.

Feb.
23. Declaration by Matthew Parker, Archbishop of Canterbury elect, acknowledging the Queen's supremacy, and taking the oaths of homage and allegiance to Her Majesty, with subscription to the same by the Bishops of the realm.

Feb.
Westminster.
24. The Queen to the Marq. of Winchester. Empowering him to deliver over the church of the late Augustine Friars to the Bishop of London, for the celebration of divine service by the strangers in London.

Feb. (?)
25. Wm. Barlow, Bishop of Chichester, to Cecill? Complains of Tho. Stapleton and Edw. Goddeshalffe, Papist Prebendaries of Chichester. Intends to deprive the latter of his prebend.

March 4.
Gedney.
26. Tho. Ogle to same. Informs him that John Eccles has selected 14 horses at Spalding, and 16 more at Boston. *Incloses,*

26. I. *Provision of* 14 *cart horses made by John Eccles, on the last of Feb., with the names of their owners.*

March 5.
27. List of ships and vessels of 100 tons and upwards, specifying the ports to which they belong, and the number of mariners there.

March 15.
Indenture of sale from Tho. Levizam and others to Tho. Allen and Tho. Ellyott, of a messuage or tenement in the parish of St. Mary at Hill, near Belingesgate, London, now in the occupation of Tho. Fisshe, Barber Surgeon. [*Case A. Eliz. No.* 3.]

March 15.
28. Deed of conveyance of the above premises by Tho. Shotsham, Tho. Sotham, and William Thurston, Trustees, by advice of Tho. Levizam, to the said Tho. Allen and Tho. Ellyott. Lat.

March 18.
29. Estimate for a further supply of stores of all kinds necessary for the Office of Ordnance.

Vol. XI.

1560.
March 19.
Westminster.
30. Warrant dormant for Sir Ric. Sakevyle, Under Treasurer of the Exchequer, to pay and discharge the diet, wages, &c. of the Privy Council, of the Officers, &c. of the Exchequer, the Judges' salaries, and other offices.

March 19.
Remission by Tho. Levizam of all his interest in the house and premises leased by his mother Margaret Levizam to Tho. Alleyn. [*Case A. Eliz. No. 4.*]

March 23.
31. Address of the Privy Council to the Queen. Declaring their opinion touching the unjust attempts and pretensions of France, and shewing that the Queen of Scots and her husband, with the House of Guise, are her mortal enemies. Advise that it is just and honourable for her to aid the Scots to expel the French forces from that kingdom.

March 25.
32. Account of wages payable to the Earl of Sussex, captain, and to the band of gentlemen pensioners and gentlemen-at-arms, for the quarter ending at Lady Day.

March 25.
33. Account of board wages due to the Earl of Sussex, captain, and to the band of gentlemen pensioners and gentleman-at-arms, for the same period.

March 25.
34. Note of the revenue of the manors of Loundonthorpe and Towthorpe, in occupation of Thomas Tailour, and of the manor of Hareby, in the county of Lincoln, of late belonging to Francis Hall.

March 25.
35. Memorandum of matters to be considered by the Queen for the safety and welfare of the kingdom : *by Sir Wm. Cecill.*

March 25.
36. Memoranda relative to several persons and matters, in Cecill's hand.

March 25.
37. Account of sums of money due to the Lieutenant of the Tower, the Gentleman Porter, and others, to Lady Day.

March.
38. Thomas Young, Bishop of St. David's to Cecill. Used the mediation of Lord Robert Duddeley in his suit for restoration of his temporalities.

Vol. XII. April—June, 1560.

April 1.
Pirgo.
1. Lord John Grey of Pirgo to Sir Wm. Cecill. Praises his Protestant principles. Expresses his wish that the devices of Paget and Masone may be defeated.

April 6.
2. Memoranda in Cecill's hand relative to several points of public business.

April 8.
Bughfourthe.
3. George Lord Talbot to Cecill. Edward Savile being divorced from his wife, has proposed a marriage between one of Lord Talbot's daughters and the son of Henry Savile, who is his next heir male. Asks his advice thereon.

1560.

VOL. XII.

April 10.
Settrington.
4. Mrs. Mabell Forteskue to "her governor," Francis Yaxley. Thanks him for her gloves and other articles. Mary Silles also returns her thanks.

April 10.
Ferrara.
5. John Battista Pigna to the Prince of Ferrara. Touching duels or single combats; arising upon the question that a gentleman, being called "a knave," answered simply that "he was an honest man." Translated for the Right Hon. Lord Carew.

April 12.
6. Memoranda, in Cecill's hand, of things necessary for the preservation and good order of the realm. Meetings of Council; appointment of Bishops; Earl of Sussex to be sent into Ireland, &c.

April 18.
7. Names of Lieutenants and muster masters in several English counties. Sir Henry Sydney, Lord President of Wales.

April 18.
8. Another list of Lord Lieutenants and muster masters.

April 18 (?)
9. List of Lieutenants of counties; with order for aid to and from various points, for defence in case of attack.

April 20.
10. Instructions, by the Queen, to the Earl of Arundel (Steward of the Household), Lieutenant of the counties of Surrey and Sussex, to have the forces of those counties in readiness.

April 20.
11. Similar instructions, mutatis mutandis, to Sir Tho. Parry, Treasurer of the Household, and Sir Henry Nevill, as Lieutenants of Berkshire.

April 24.
12. Warrant to the Exchequer to pay the allowances of persons named, appointed to repair as muster masters into divers counties.

April (?)
13. Thos. Lardge to the Council. Prays to be relieved from penalties he has incurred by having heard mass in the house of Sir Thos. Warton at Boreham, Essex.

May 1.
14. Memoranda by Cecill, of business for consideration by the Queen and the Council.

May 1.
15. The Lieutenants of Berkshire (Sir Tho. Parry and Sir H. Nevell) to the Justices of Peace. To assemble forthwith the force of the county, with weapons, furniture, and horses necessary for military service.

May 1.
Westminster.
16. Warrant to Sir John Salisbury and Wm. Wightman, Receivers of Wales, to pay the diets of Sir Henry Sydney, President, and the rest of the Council of Wales, at the rate of 20l. a week.

May 5.
17. Memorial from the Council ? to the Queen, on the proceedings of the French Queen, i.e. Mary Queen of Scots, derogatory to the state and title of Elizabeth as Queen of England.

May 8.
18. Lieutenants of the county of Berks to Tho. Warde and Wm. Barker. Appointing them captains to have the leading of the forces levied in the county.

May 8.
19. Remembrances for calling out 2,000 mariners from divers counties for the furnishing of the ships with seamen.

DOMESTIC—ELIZABETH.

Vol. XII.

1560.
May 11. 20. Marq. of Winchester to Sir Wm. Cecill. Is sorry that the Queen sustains any uneasiness. Has 25,000*l.* for Mr. Gresham and 12,000*l.* for Berwick. Is providing 15,000*l.* more for Berwick.

May 12.
Windsor. 21. Lord Admiral Clynton to same. Desires supply of powder. The Duke of Norfolk should be apprised what may be spared at Berwick. Necessity for opposing the French in Scotland.

May 13. 22. Orders taken at Winchester by the Lord St. John and the rest of the Justices of Peace in the county of Hampshire for the firing of beacons, as signals for assembling the forces of the adjoining counties.

May 13. 23. "Memoryall of thynges to be doone with spede," touching the war in the North : by Sir Wm. Cecil.

May 18. 24. Henry Earl of Arundel to Sir Tho. Parry. Has received his letter touching Warde and Barker, whom he intends to employ himself. Tho. Stoughton will shortly come to him.

May 15.
Songehyll.
(Sunning hill?) 25. Sir Henry Nevell to same. Will forward the musters in Berkshire as much as possible. Does not know what to do without the Earl of Arundell's men, (Warde and Barker).

May 20.
Windsor. 26. Same to same. Details his proceedings in the musters ; hopes to have 1,000 men before them to-morrow.

May 20.
Windsor. 27. Tho. Stucley to same. Regrets they cannot have the services of Warde and Barker. The Lieutenant (Sir H. Nevell) has taken musters that day at Windsor without the help of any Justice or gentleman of rank, except the Mayor.

May 21. 28. Certificate of general musters for the county of Hertford, taken before Harry Lord Morley, Lieutenant, and others.

May 22. 29. Memoranda by Sir Wm. Cecill of various points of business.

May 24.
Newbury. 30. Sir Henry Nevell to Sir Tho. Parry. Mustered 1,000 good men at Reading, " besides other rascall," and 1,500 at Newbury. Great want of armour.

May 25.
Newbury. 31. Tho. Stucley to same. Musters have been taken by Sir Henry Nevell at Reading and Newbury.

May 25. 32. Memoranda by Cecill, relative to divers points of public affairs.

May 28.
Sunninghill. 33. Sir Henry Nevell to Sir Tho. Parry. Musters at Abingdon and Wallingford. Great willingness of the county. Appointment of captains.

May 30.
Arundel. 34. Henry Earl of Arundel to Cecill. Thanks for his friendly letters ; is sorry to hear of his indisposition.

May (?) 35. The Queen to the Lord High Admiral. Bestows upon him one-third part of all ships or vessels taken as prizes from the enemy.

May. 36. Certificate of general musters for the county of Wilts.

May (?) 37. "Articles of diverse thinges given by the Quenes Matie in charge to Richard Worsleye, Esq., Captain of the Isle of Wight," for the welfare and security of the same.

VOL. XII.

1560.
May (?)
38. Particular of the manor of Ashridge, Bucks, assigned to Her Majesty before her accession to the throne. Expense of repairs, &c.

June 2.
On board the "Elizabeth Jonas."
39. Lord Adm. Clynton to Sir Wm. Cecill. Has been detained where he at present is by bad weather. The fleet is in good order. Report that the French forces have proceeded towards Scotland.

June 3.
40. Lord Robert Duddeley and Sir Tho. Parry to same. Assure him of their good wishes for his prosperity. Desire to be informed of his welfare.

June 6.
41. Sir Tho. Parry to same. The Abbate de Salute is despatched from Rome, and a licence will be requested for him to come into England. The Queen desires to hear often of his health. Treasure sent to him.

June 6.
Greenwich.
42. Sir W. Petre to same. The Queen is glad to hear of his being in health. Dr. May has been proposed for election to York. None are willing to go as Bishops to Ireland. His advice is desired as to the licence for the Abbot of St. Salute's coming into England.

June 6.
Sunninghill.
43. Sir Hen. Nevell to Sir Tho. Parry. Has promised armour to the people. 2s. is charged at the Tower instead of 1s. 10d. for a sheaf of arrows, contrary to the Queen's regulated price.

June 7.
Greenwich.
44. Wm. Marq. of Northampton to Cecill. Has nominated Mr. Vyllars for leading the appointed number of men of Northamptonshire. A letter sent to the Queen out of Spain.

June 8.
45. Account of armour received from Sir Tho. Gresham, from Christmas 1558 to 8th of June 1560.

June 8.
46. Account of arms, munition, and military stores for the office of the Ordnance, received from Sir Tho. Gresham, from 8th September 1559 to 8th June 1560.

June 8.
47. Account of munitions, warlike stores, and corslets brought into the port of London by way of merchandize, from Christmas 1559.

June 11.
48. Sir Hen. Nevell to Sir Tho. Parry. Alarm of the beacons on fire in the Isle of Wight and on Portsdown. Purchase of armour in London. Requests orders may be sent to the keepers of the beacons, so that the country be not troubled with false alarms.

June 12.
Sunninghill.
49. Same to same. Blames the conduct of those in charge of the beacons. Complains of one come down in the county to take up men by commission.

June 12.
50. Account of sales by   Alford, and of moneys paid therefrom under Privy Seal warrants.

June 15.
Hedingham Castle.
51. Earl of Oxford to the Council. Charge against Tho. Holland, Parson of Little Bursted, of uttering malicious words against the Queen. He only confesses that he heard the Vicar of Storford, Herts, say that one was sent to the Tower for reporting the Queen was with child.

VOL. XII.

1560.
June 16. 52. Note of the number of men to be levied in certain shires for furniture of the navy.

June 19. 53. Marq. of Winchester to Sir Wm. Cecill. Will do his best endeavour in the Queen's service. Has sent 22,000*l*. to Mr. Brown, Treasurer of the army, out of which the ships must be paid; and also 3,000*l*. to Berwick.

June 21.
Kirkby-Moorside. 54. Henry Earl of Westmorland to same. Thanks for his letters. His venison or any other thing is at his command. Justifies his late marriage, as conformable with God's law; and for which under the Romish jurisdiction he could have obtained a licence, for money.

June 22.
Greenwich. 55. B. Hampton to same. The Queen is in good health, and desires to hear from him. News of preparation of ships, &c. in France. The Queen's fleet is in good order at Portsmouth.

June 23.
Sunninghill. 56. Sir Hen. Nevell to Sir Tho. Parry. Has received the certificate of musters of Oxfordshire, on which he cannot act for want of captains. Has no instructions about the beacons. Desires to have the timber work of an old house at East Hampstead, to repair his stables.

June 24. 57. Sir Rich. Sakevyle to Cecill. Desires to be remembered to Mr. Wotton. Wishes Sir William good success and speedy return.

June 25. 58. Summary of particulars given by Mr. Gresham relative to the Fulkers undertaking to refine the base moneys now current in England.

June 26. Lease from Tho. Wattz to Henry Earl of Arundel (Lord Steward), Lord Robt. Duddeley (Master of the Horse), Sir Tho. Parry (Treasurer), Sir Edw. Rogers (Comptroller), and Tho. Weldon (Cofferer), of the prebend, manor, and lordship of Tattenhall, or Tottenham Court, in trust for the Crown, for 99 years, at the rent of 46*l*. per annum. [*Case A. Eliz. No.* 4.]

June 27. 59. Sir Henry Nevell to Sir Tho. Parry. Thanks for his good news. Has returned the certificate of musters by Mr. Stucley. Further particulars of musters to inspect the armour, &c. Wishes for a quiet day to go a wooing in. Complains of the person taking up labourers by commission, and selling them at fairs for 10 groats and 2*s*. each.

June 29. 60. Memoranda of four grants of concealed lands to Sir Geo. Howard and his heirs.

June (?) 61. Certificate of the musters of men, armour, and weapons of the whole county of Sussex.

June (?) 62. Similar certificate for the whole county of Surrey.

June (?) 63. Certificate of the able men, gunners, archers, horses, armour, weapons, &c., for the county of Somerset.

June (?) 64. Account of money received from Sir Tho. Gresham by Alford, and of further sums to be received of the merchants.

June. 65. Account of arms, armour, and munitions to be provided by Sir Thomas Gresham, and of the quantities received.

1560.
June (?)

Vol. XII.

66. Account of munitions already in the Tower, and of other quantities ready to be shipped. With request of Ric. Candeler for a warrant.

June (?)

67. Commission to examine the present state of the Mint, the standard value of the moneys now current, in order that they may hereafter be made of such standard as shall be to the Queen's honour and the common weal.

Vol. XIII. July—September, 1560.

July 2.
Sunninghill.

1. Sir Henry Nevell to Sir Tho. Parry. Observations relative to the musters in Berkshire. *Incloses,*

    1. I. *Certificate of musters of the selected soldiers furnished with weapons of the seven hundreds of Cookham and Bray, and the town of New Windsor, co. Berks.*

    1. II. *Similar certificate for the hundreds of Morton, Ocke, and Hormer, with the townships of Wallingford and Abingdon, co. Berks.*

    1. III. *Similar certificate for the hundreds of Shrivenham, Wantinge, Farrington, Lamborne, and Ganfilde, co. Berks.*

    1. IV. *Similar certificate for the hundreds of Reading and Theale, co. Berks.*

    1. V. *Summary of musters of men, horsemen, and armour for the whole county of Berks. June 28.*

July 11.
The Court.

2. Lord Adm. Clynton to Cecill. The peace gives him great satisfaction. The ships under Winter's command are to go to Portsmouth, where the rest of the fleet is, and not to the Thames.

July 12.
Wadley.

3. Sir Edward Unton to Sir Tho. Parry. Is sorry the certificate for assessing the armour is not satisfactory. Gives particulars of the musters. *Incloses,*

    3. I. *Certificate of the armour and weapons assessed upon particular persons within the division of Sir Edw. Unton and others, with the augmentation above the assessment.*

    3. II. *Certificate of the armour and weapons assessed upon the inhabitants holding lands above 5l. per annum in the hundreds of Wanting, Ganfilde, Shrivenham, and Farrington, co. Berks. June 17.*

    3. III. *Another certificate for the same hundreds, on owners of lands under 5l. per annum. June 18.*

    3. IV. *Another certificate for the same hundreds, showing the augmentation above the rate assessed.*

July 14.
Belvoir.

4. Henry Earl of Rutland to Sir Francis Knollys. Has seen the muster taken by the muster master Anthony Digby in Rutlandshire. Reports their numbers and appointments.

Vol. XIII.

1560. July 15.	5. Certificate of musters for the whole county of Dorset, specifying the numbers of able men, their arms and weapons, and the captains commanding them.
July 17. Sunninghill.	6. Sir Henry Nevell to Sir Tho. Parry. Has received his orders for stay of the musters. Will take order for preservation of the game in the neighbourhood; but the gates of the great park must be repaired.
July 20.	7. Certificate of musters for the county of Northampton.
July 20.	8. Certificate of musters for the county of Essex.
July 22. Brome.	9. Sir Tho. Cornwaleys to Francis Yaxley. Wishes to be excused from attendance on the Prince of Swevia (Sweden). Urges him to prevent his being appointed.
July 22 (?)	10. Certificate of the horsemen sent out of Oxfordshire.
July 22.	11. Certificate of musters for the county of Oxford.
July 23. Melford Hall.	12. Sir Wm. Cordell, Master of the Rolls, to Francis Yaxley; his dear friend Sir Ambrose Jermyn desires to be relieved from giving attendance on the Prince of Sweden; requests Yaxley to procure his release from that service.
July 29. Newcastle.	13. Mayor, &c. of Newcastle-on-Tyne to Cecill. Complaining of the infringement of their ancient privileges by the inhabitants of Hartlepool. *Inclosing*,
	13. I. *Particulars of injuries that the inhabitants of Newcastle sustain by those of Hartlepool.*
July 31. Long Melford.	14. Sir Wm. Cordell to Fr. Yaxley. Thanks for soliciting Sir Ambrose Jermyn's suit. Sir Tho. Cornwaleys, the Countess of Bath, and Lord Windsor and his wife, have been with him making merry.
July 30. Brome.	15. Sir Tho. Cornwaleys to same. Thanks him for good offices performed. Intentions of the King of Denmark to intercept the Prince of Sweden.
July 31.	16. Certificate of musters for the county of Kent.
July.	17. The Queen to divers Lords and Ladies, commanding them to attend the Court on the coming of the King elect of Sweden.
July.	18. Certificate of musters for the county of Devon.
July.	19. Certificate of musters of able men, armour, &c., for the county of Cornwall.
August 1.	20. Certificate of musters for the city and county of Norwich, and the names of the captains appointed to have charge of them.
August 13.	21. Ric. Lord Rich and Thos. Mildmay, Esq., to Cecill. Incloses examinations of certain persons of the shire of Essex, touching slanderous reports raised against the Queen. Have committed Anne Dowe, the principal offender, to gaol. *Inclosing*,
	21. I. *Examinations of persons stating that Mother Dowe of Brentwood openly asserted that the Queen was with child by Robt. Duddeley.*

Vol. XIII.

1560.
August 18. — 22. Certificate of able men mustered by Lord St. John in the county of Bedford.

August 22.
Zurich. — 23. Peter Martyr to Ric. Cox, Bp. of Ely, about his prebend at Oxford. His opinion of the proposed Free General Council. His wife is again pregnant. Mentions his commentaries on the Book of Judges. Lat.

August 22. — 24. The Queen to the Lieutenants of Counties. To give directions that no soldiers be suffered to live out of employment, idly or suspiciously, nor to carry arms about with them.

August 30.
Dunstable. — 25. Mrs. Eliz. Leeche to Fr. Yaxley. Their hasty departure was occasioned by the coming of a King [of Sweden] to the Court. Hopes soon to be at her journey's end.

Aug. ? — 26. Articles to be considered touching the trade of the Easterlings and of the Italians.

August (?) — 27. Valuation of the base moneys now current in England, with proposition to convert them into sterling money, and the expense attending the same. "Mr. Stonley's opinion."

Sept. 6. — 28. The Queen to the Lord Keeper Bacon. To appoint certain persons to examine a matter in controversy between Henry Fawkener and Martha his wife, and the executors of John Browne, her late husband, concerning administration of his estate.

On the back of the above is the unfinished draft of a warrant for return of munitions lent to the town of Newcastle for the furnishing of certain ships set forth by that town to serve in the fleet under Sir John Clere in the late Queen's time.

Sept. 8. — 29. The Queen to the Earl of Oxford and Tho. Lord Wentworth. Directions to receive the young King elect of Sweden, who has for some time been ready to make a journey from Sweden to England.

Sept. 9.
Theydon Mount. — 30. Sir Tho. Smith to Cecill. Asserts his undoubted right to the Deanery of Carlisle, which he intends to maintain now Launcelot Salkeld is dead.

Sept. 10.
Belvoir. — 31. Earl of Rutland to same. Requests him to procure for the bearer, John Barker, a licence to transport a gelding beyond sea.

Sept. 19.
Windsor. — 32. Proclamation against breaking or defacing monuments of antiquity set up in churches, or converting church bells to private uses.

Sept. 19. — 33. Draft of the above, corrected by Cecill.

Sept. 22.
London. — 34. Wm. Burd to Cecill. Concerning a report of a fall in the price of gold and silver. Gives his opinion of all moneys now current.

Sept. 22. — 35. Proclamation against Anabaptists and others of dangerous and pernicious opinions, coming into England from abroad.

Sept. 22. — 36. Copy of the above.

Vol. XIII.

1560.

Sept. 23. — 37. The Queen to Marq. Winchester. Warrant to make a grant to Sir Francis Knollys, and the Lady Catherine his wife, and to Robt. Knollys one of their sons, of the manor of Taunton and Tandene, Somerset, parcel of the possessions of the Bishoprick of Winchester; for term of their lives.

Sept. 23. — 38. Same to same. To deliver a mass of base money into the Mint, to be recoined into standard silver of 5s. per ounce.

Sept. 26. — Lease from Tho. Norton to Tho. Busbredge of a barn called Court Lodge Barn, in the parish of Myddelton or Mylton next Sittingbourne, co. Kent, and certain pieces of land adjoining. [*Case A. Eliz. No. 5.*]

Sept. 28 (?) — 39. Proclamation for calling in all base money from circulation.

Sept. 28 (?) — 40. Same, forbidding all persons from buying up base moneys, called in from circulation.

Sept. 28 (?) — 41. Same, regulating the current value of pieces of gold in circulation, called pistolets.

Sept. 28. — 42. Summary of certain reasons which have moved the Queen to proceed in the reformation of her base and coarse moneys, and to reduce them to their values, as declared by proclamation.

Sept. 28. — 43. Printed copy of the above summary, with types of the various coins.

Sept. 29. — 44. The Queen to the officers of the Mint. Directions to refine and recoin a certain mass of base money into fine sterling silver of 5s. the ounce.

Sept. 29. — 45. Account by John Marwood of the customs of London, from Michaelmas, 4 & 5 Phil. & Mary.

Sept. 29. — 46. Account by the same, of the customs of Bristol, from the same period.

Sept. 29. — 47. Account of debts depending on the Receivers of the Court of Exchequer, for the year ending Michaelmas 1560.

Sept. 29. — Account of John Yonge, Bailiff of the Barony of Lewes, co. Sussex, of all the receips and income of the Barony for one whole year, ending Michaelmas 1560. [*Case A. Eliz. No. 6.*]

Sept. 30.
Exeter. — 48. Earl of Bedford to Sir Wm. Cecill. Effect of the proclamations for calling in the base coin. Proceedings in promulgating that proclamation, and also the one against defacing monuments.

Sept. — 49. Declaration of debts due by Lord Grey of Wilton, amounting to 10,330*l*., including 8,000*l*. for his ransom. [*Lord Grey became a prisoner of war on surrender of Culais to the French, Jan.* 1558.]

Sept. — 50. Brief estimate of the revenue of the Cathedral Church of the Holy Trinity in Norwich, with the charges thereof, according to a valuation made temp. Edward VI.

160   DOMESTIC—ELIZABETH.

Vol. XIII.

1560.
Sept. 51. Remembrances for the Cofferer of the Household, for release of Alex. Horden, and payment of the Household charges.

Sept. 52. Notes in the handwriting of Sir Wm. Petre, of business to be dispatched in London.

Sept. 53. Certificate of musters for the county of Lincoln.

Sept. (?) 54. Certificate of musters for the county of Worcester.

Sept. (?) 55. Certificate of musters for Gloucestershire, and the cities of Gloucester and Bristol.

Sept. (?) 56, 57. Abstracts of the first and second general musters for the county of Suffolk.

Sept. 58. Certificate of musters for the whole county of Somerset.

Sept. 59. Abstracts of the certificates of all the musters throughout England.

Sept. (?) 60. Observations on the effect which the crying down certain moneys will have upon the exchange.

Vol. XIV. October—December, 1560.

Oct. 1. 1. Memoranda by Cecill of business to be performed.

Oct. 3. 2. Declaration of receipts and payments by Sir Ric. Sakevyle.

Oct. 4. 3. Particulars of sundry parcels of powder, saltpetre, and match received into the Office of Ordnance within the Tower, for the Queen's service, from 24 July.

Oct. 4. Sir Wm. Cecill to Lord Ambrose Duddeley. To furnish certain strangers, at the request of Sir T. Gresham, with a quantity of sulphur, at an advanced price, to finish a certain amount of gunpowder. [*See back of* 10 *Sept.* 1560.]

Oct. 4. 4. Warrant to the Lord Treasurer to deliver certain old plate, gilt and parcel gilt, to the Treasurer of the Mint, to be converted into coin.

Oct. 4. 5. The Queen to Sir Wm. Hewet, Lord Mayor of London. Directions
Hampton Court. to affix the marks of a greyhound and portcullis on the testons in currency, to distinguish the base from the better sort.

Oct. 4. 6. Draft of the above.

Oct. 4. 7. Tho. Stanley to Cecill. Has sent 8 testons stamped, 4 with the
Tower. portcullis, and 4 with the greyhound. The Goldsmith's company request licence to melt sterling silver at their houses under 2 lbs. weight, and to supply the Mint with base moneys to be recoined.

Oct. 5. 8. Same to same. Has not yet received his commission. Particulars of refining bullion for coining. Is sorry the Queen mislikes the die of the fine moneys.

1560.

Vol. XIV.

Oct. 5. — 9. The Queen to the Master of the Jewel House. To deliver to Sir Edmund Pekham, High Treasurer of the Mint, all unserviceable and broken plate in his custody, to be made into coin.

Oct. 5. London. — 10. Sir John Yorke to Sir Wm. Cecill. Concerning the recoinage and the exchanges. Scarcity of the new money. Recommends the establishing of two Mints.

Oct. 5. — 11. Winchester and others, Commissioners for the Coinage, to Sir Tho. Parry and Cecill. Detail of proceedings relative to the new coinage.

Oct. 6. — 12. The Queen to Winchester. Warrant to deliver into the Mint all unserviceable old plate of gold and other utensils of gold, remaining in his custody, to be coined.

Oct. 6. — 13. Winchester and Sakevyle to Parry and Cecill. Thanks for removing from the Queen's mind that they had deceived her in the coinage. Offers of the Merchant Adventurers. Transactions with the Staplers. *Inclosing,*

13. I. *Account of wools and woolfells shipped by the Merchant Staplers from the Port of London for Bruges.*

Oct. 6. — 14. Same to the Council. Have sent such irons, proclamations, &c. to Berwick as were necessary. Directions to various officials there. Marks by which the good and the base testons may be distinguished.

Oct. 7. — 15. Winchester to Cecill. Proceedings in forwarding the coinage. Warrant, &c. received.

Oct. 10. — 16. Same to same. The Alderman of the Stillyard has been with him to return thanks for the licence granted to his Company for shipping cloths.

Oct. 10. — 17. The Queen to Mayors, &c. of corporate towns. Directions for publicly causing certain stamps to be placed on testons in circulation, so as to distinguish their relative values.

Oct. 10. — 18. List of towns having the order for stamping the testons with the portcullis and greyhound.

Oct. 10. — 19. Winchester to Cecill. The Merchant Adventurers are content to lend the Queen 30,000*l.* They request deliverance of their ships, the better to make money for the Queen's service.

Oct. 13. Sudeley. — 20. Edmund Lord Chandos to same. Quiet state of the county of Gloucester. Great rise in price of all commodities, owing to the decreased value of money.

Oct. 15. — 21. The Queen to Affabell Partridge and Robt. Brandon. Authority to collect and receive base moneys and bring the same to the Mint.

Oct. 16. Lambeth. — 22. Archbp. Parker to Cecill. Requests some Bishops to be appointed for the North. Recommends Dr. Young, Bishop of St. David's, should be translated to York, the Bishop of Rochester to Durham, and Mr. Skynner to be Dean of Durham.

VOL. XIV.

1560.
Oct. 15. 23. The Queen to the Lord Treasurer and Lord Keeper. Directing them secretly to admonish the Merchants of London to abstain from sending ships to France, until the designs of France shall more plainly appear.

Oct. 19. 24. Inquisition post mortem, taken at Peterborough, Northamptonshire, as to the estate of John Browne, Esq., decd., certifying that he died on the 12th of March, and that his son Charles Browne, aged 15 years, was his heir.

Oct. 19. 25. Note of the yearly value of the manor of Northborowe, &c., Northampton, accruing to Her Majesty by the wardship of Charles Browne.

Oct. 22. 26. Lord Keeper Bacon to Cecill. Sends him the proclamation which is now fit to be passed, and also Mr. Wootton's letter. Gives his opinion as to the degree of fineness necessary for the standard coin.

Oct. 23. Mounthall. 27. Sir Tho. Smith to same. Still urges his claims and right to the Deanery of Carlisle. Ill characters of Sewell and Barnaby Kirkbride.

Oct. 24. 28. Wm. Lord Cobham to same. Is solicitous in the due execution of his charge. Sends him advertisements received from Calais. *Incloses,*

 28. I. *Advertisements received from Calais, relative to great preparations made by the French at Brest, in Bretagne, &c. Preparations for the French Queen (Mary) to go into Scotland.*

Oct. 25. 29. The Council to the Lord Warden. To have good regard to his charge in the Cinque Ports and county of Kent, till the Spaniards are past that are going from Flanders into Spain.

Oct. 25. 30. Same to the Captains of the Isle of Wight and Portsmouth. To the same purport as the preceding; to have aid from Hampshire and other counties in case of emergency.

Oct. 28. Exeter. 31. Sir Peter Carew and Tho. Williams to the Earl of Bedford. Have not yet received any stamps for marking the testons. The people are perplexed about taking the testons as current money.

Oct. 28. Cowdrey. 32. Anth. Viscount Montague to Fr. Yaxley. Thanks him for his letters. The barren country where he resides affords no news.

Oct. 29. 33. The Queen to the Marq. Winchester, Sir Tho. Parry, Sir Wm. Cecill, Sir Ric. Sakevyle, and Sir Walter Mildmay. Commission to direct the proceedings of the Mint, to expedite the issue of the new coinage, &c.

Oct. 30. 34. Lord Keeper Bacon to Cecill. Is grieved the Queen thinks him to blame for what he has done concerning the commission for passing leases. Enters into explanations. *Incloses,*

 34. I. *Notes by Sir N. Bacon of the points contained in the Bill concerning Leases, which he would not have allowed if his advice had been asked. Oct.*

VOL. XIV.

1560.

Oct. 30. 35. Winchester and Sakevyle to Sir Wm. Cecill. Requests warrant for the Treasurer of the Chamber to receive his ordinary fees on the money returned into the Mint.

Oct. (?) 36. Answers of George Chambrelayne to interrogatories touching his intercourse with Papists beyond the sea. Letters received by him from Lady Dormer, the Countess Feria, &c.

Nov. 1. 37. Winchester to Cecill. Desires commissions to be sent to Durham for execution of justice.

Nov. 1. 38. Petition of Sir Henry Sydney (Lord President of Wales) to the Queen, for levying money in various shires for expenses of the musters; for water to be conducted to the President's house of Tikinhill by Beaudeley; allowance for diet, and for wines consumed in Her Majesty's household, in the Marches of Wales, &c.

Nov. 2. 39. The Queen to Winchester. Survey to be made of lead to convey water to the house of Tikinhill near Beaudley, the residence of the President and Council of Wales.

Nov. 5. 40. Winchester to the Council. Refers to their letters sent to his cousin Poynings at Portsmouth, and the Governor of the Isle of Wight, warning them to be upon their guard for security of their respective charges. Has taken measures to have the force of the county of Hampshire in readiness.

Nov. 6.
Shrewsbury. 41. Orders and regulations for conducting public business in the Civil and Criminal Courts in the Principality and Marches of Wales, by order of the Lord President and Council.

Nov. 7.
Hampton Court. 42. The Queen to the Earls of Arundel and Sussex. Warrant to deliver timber for repair of all the castles in the Isle of Wight and Hampshire, and the works at Portsmouth, under the superintendence of Lord St. John.

Nov. 11. 43. Winchester to Cecill. Sureties for Chr. Hansel and his Company, the refiners. Affairs of the Mint. *Incloses,*

43. I. *List of sureties for Chr. Hansel and his Company to the extent of* 30,000*l*.

Nov. 12. 44. The Queen to the Commissioners for demising lands. Instructions for their proceedings.

Nov. 13. 45. Dr. Robert Horn to Cecill. Approves of the order for divine service at Berwick. Stipends of the ministers. Recommends one Sanderson to be curate and Cuthbert Diconson clerk there, and Adam Halydaye to be a prebendary in Durham.

Nov. 17. 46. Memoranda by Cecill, briefly referring to various names and matters.

Nov. 24. 47. The Queen to the Dean and Chapter of Winchester. To elect Dr. Robt. Horn to the bishoprick of Winchester in the place of Dr. Pilkington, who has been nominated to the see of Durham.

DOMESTIC—ELIZABETH.

1560.   VOL. XIV.

Nov. 25.   48. The Queen to Winchester. Licence to the Merchant Adventurers to export five brewings of beer, each brewing to consist of six tons, as a present to the town of Antwerp.

Nov. 29.   49. Henry Earl of Huntingdon to Sir Wm. Cecill. Inconvenience in
Lubsthorpe.   the county of Leicester relative to the currency of the testons. Having the new money quickly is the only remedy.

Nov. 29.   50. Warrant to pay Sir Andrew Corbet certain allowances for the coat and conduct money of 200 men to Berwick.

Nov. 30.   51. Mabel Foteskew (Forteskue) to Francis Yaxley. Thanks him
Settrington.   for having placed her with "my Lady's Grace" (Margaret Countess of Lennox), who as yet is very gentle and gracious. Was obliged to leave London without seeing him. Mary Silles sends her remembrances.

Nov.   52. Memoranda of business by Sir Wm. Cecill.

Dec. 1.   53. ———— to Tho. Wybarne. Gives his opinion on the tenure of Abbey lands, held in capite by knights tenure. Desires to know if Mr. Stokes has put in another answer in Chancery.

Dec. 3.   54. The Queen to Winchester. Directions to send down parcels of the new moneys to sundry places of the realm for circulation

Dec. 5.   55. The Queen to Mr. Stanley and Mr. Fleetwood. Warrant to deliver all the base moneys brought into the Mint to Jasper Seeler, Alderman Lodge, and others, to be refined by them and delivered back as bullion for coinage.

Dec. 5.   56. John Lyttelton to Fr. Yaxley. Apologises for his sudden
Frankelye.   departure. Has no news to communicate.

Dec. 11.   57. The Queen to Winchester. To deliver 18 cwt. of base moneys to Peter Osborne, who has undertaken to refine the same at a less charge than the Almayn refiners in the Tower.

Dec. 11.   58. Decree of Dr. Lewis, Judge of the Admiralty Court, in the cause between Archibald Graham and Richard Thomson versus Thomas Clavering, for restitution of a ship and cargo by him taken. Lat.

Dec. 12.   59. Winchester, Sakevyle, and Mildmay to Cecill. Have taken measures to prevent the transportation of the base testons into Ireland.

Dec. 17.   60. The Queen to the Lord Admiral or the Judge of the Admiralty.
Westminster. Warrant to release Henry Strangwiche the pirate, in order to judge of his conduct before his pardon is finally given to him.

Dec. 18.   61. Same to Winchester. Warrant to permit a hulk arrived in the Thames, laden with malmseys, currants, and other wares, to be unloaded.

Dec. 21.   62. Process by the Dean and Chapter of Peterborough of the
Peterborough. election of Edmund Schambler, B.D., to be Bishop of that see, vacant by the deprivation of David Pole, the last Bishop.

Dec. 24.   63. Memoranda of divers matters in Cecill's hand.

Dec. 25.   64. Brief estimate of the account of William Bromefeld, Lieutenant of the Ordnance, for two years ending Christmas

VOL. XIV.

1560.
Dec. (?)   65. Petition of Fulk Onslowe to the Queen for the offices of Paymaster and Clerk of the Works.

Dec.   66. The Queen to Lord Keeper Bacon. Relative to purchases and privileges granted by her progenitors to Queen's College, Cambridge; and to issue a writ for assurance to the said College of the lands, manors, &c. of Hockington, purchased of Anthony Pope and his wife.

Dec.   67. Brief of the matter depending in the Court of Exchequer between the Queen and Sir Edward Lyttleton, for the herbage, pannage, &c. of the haye of Teddesley, co. Huntingdon.

Dec.   68. Another brief statement of the above.

Dec.   69. Copies of letters between Lord Stafford (as Justice and Ranger of the forest of Cannock) and Sir Edward Lyttleton, relative to the claim of two fee does within Teddesley.

Dec.   70. A short declaration of the matters in variance between Lord Stafford and Sir Edward Lyttleton; Lord Stafford claiming the herbage, &c. of Teddesley.

VOL. XV.

[Undated Papers, but all probably in the year 1560.]

1560?   1. Notes in proof that the authority of a General Council is greater than that of the Pope. Lat.

2. Allowance, wages, &c. for a ship of 80 tons burthen and a crew of 31 men, appointed for the service of the Queen, for one month.

3. List of ships and barques belonging to the Cinque Ports in the service of the Crown, from the 37th of Henry VIII. to the 2d of Elizabeth.

4. Ordinances and decrees made by the Queen for the regulation and government of the office of Admiralty and Marine affairs, the Navy being the chief defence of the realm.

5. List of the names of Treasurers of the several mints in England and Ireland, from the time of Henry VIII.

6. Note of the proportion of alloy contained in certain coinages from 1st Edward VI. to the 3d Eliz.

7. Petition of the clerks of the Petty Bag in the Court of Chancery, complaining of the attempts of the Six Clerks to obtain the sole privilege of enrolling all manner of indentures, deeds, and recognizances.

8. Particulars relating to the manor of Nettlested, Kent, parcel of the inheritance of the Lady Rainsford, which, during her lunacy, was granted to Sir Geo. Howard, Knt.

9. Question if Henry Tutchet, Lord Audley, should sue for livery of the manors of Audley, Holeycastle, and others, co. Stafford, as of lands descended to him in reversion.

1560 ?

Vol. XV.

10. Statement of lands entailed to James Lord Audley and to Lady Joan, his second wife, and the heirs of their two bodies.

11. Rough plan of the course of the river Lee from Lock Bridge to Bow Bridge.

12. Warrant to the Exchequer to issue 115*l.* 16*s.* 5½*d.* to the Comptroller and Carpenter of the works for repairs at Windsor and Hertford Castle.

13. Extract from the Book of Process of the Court of Wards and Liveries, relative to an obligation taken of Sir Humphrey Ratcliffe, Knight, to answer a debt for the executor of Edmund Harvey of Elviston, Bedford. Indorsed "Lady Ratcliffe."

14. Offers of [the Duke of Norfolk?] to surrender and convey to the Queen the lands of Chesworth, Segwyck, Beybush, Shelley, and the forest of St. Leonard's, &c., in discharge of the debts due by him to the Crown.

15. Statement of the manner in which the Queen is defrauded of the custom of cloths exported from London.

16. Warrant to the Exchequer to dispose of the residue of the sum issued for coat and conduct money of the men raised in various counties for service in the North.

17. Particular of lands delivered in exchange between the Lord Adm. (Clynton) and the Queen, in the county of Lincoln.

18. Certificate of Sir Gilbert Gerrard of the sealing of the indenture of exchange of lands between the Queen and Lord Clynton.

19. Account of allowances to William Bramfeld, Feodary of the county of Bedford, for a whole year ending Michaelmas.

20. Henry Smith to the Queen. Has made discovery of certain abuses in the Mint and the Custom-house, by which the Crown sustains loss. Prays to be employed in superintending the Customs.

21. Names of gunners belonging the Tower of London, with their wages and fees payable out of the Exchequer.

22. Warrant for a licence to John Bodleigh to print the English Bible, with annotations, faithfully translated in the year 1560.

23. Lists of names of noblemen and gentlemen fit to be appointed generals, counsellors, leaders of horse and foot, and other officers in an army.

24. Testimony in favour of William Marshal, Fellow of Merton College and Principal of Alborne (Alban) Hall, Oxford, who was persecuted by Dr. Gervase, Warden of Merton College.

25. Articles showing how the Queen is defrauded of her customs at Plymouth.

26. State of the borough of Boston. Suit for a licence to the corporation to purchase lands to the value of 100 marks per annum.

Vol. XV.

1560 ?

27. Letter of admonition, by the Queen, touching the sinister construction put by certain evil disposed persons on the form of the oath of allegiance.

28. Suit of the Earl of Cumberland to the Queen, to take into her possession his manors of Hart and Hartlepool, and to grant to him certain lands in exchange.

29. Petition of the Earl of Cumberland to the Queen, for grant of the assignment of the office of Registrar of Customs on certain merchandize, under Stat. 14 Ric. II.

30. Reasons shewing that no prejudice will arise to any English subject or foreigner by granting the prayer of the above petition.

31. Suit of Sir Henry Knevit, for confirmation of the grant by Edward VI. of the manors of Escrick, Hawghton, and Ellerton.

32. Particulars of such manors and lands as have had warrants to pass, but are stayed until the Queen's pleasure be further known.

33. Lady Strange to Sir Wm. Cecill. Sends particulars of articles on which she desires Morrys Freeman and William Hatley may be examined, as to dissentions between her and Lord Strange.

34. Notes and memoranda by Sir Wm. Cecill, relative to the above business.

35. Wm. Lord Paget to Sir Thos. Parry. Begs of him to obtain the stallment of his debts. *Incloses,*

35. I. *Note of Lord Paget's debts due to the Queen.*

36. Form of licence for using a cross-bow or hand-gun, for sporting and other purposes.

37. Articles contained in a book for the Stationers Company, drawn out in form of law, by Mr. Richard Faulsete; probably for a charter for the Company.

38. Petition of the Company of Stationers to the Privy Council. Complain of John Wolfe and others unlawfully printing books, and thereby infringing the patents of the Queen's Printers.

39. Articles of the insolent and contemptuous behaviour of John Wolfe, printer, and his confederates.

40. State of the case between Christopher Barker and John Wolfe, the latter having infringed the patent of Queen's Printer. Barker's persuasion to Wolfe to quit the Fishmongers' and to join the Stationers' Company.

41. Thomas Barnes to [Cecill ?] Desires him to forward his supplication to the Queen.

42. Supplication of John Barnes to the Queen, pointing out the abuses in the Customs, and offering to farm them and to increase the revenue

44. Wm. Hayworthe to the Council. Requests to be allowed to disclose certain disloyal practices and dealings of some of Her Majesty's undutiful subjects.

1560?

44. Licence by the Queen to Sir Wm. Cecill, to keep during his life certain retainers in his household, each of them to wear a livery badge or cognizance.

45. Proposition by the writer, for easing of suits to the Queen, to bring her out of debt, and to enrich the realm by converting the base coin now current into fine silver.

46. Suggestions by the same writer to [Cecill?] on the same subjects. Private affairs.

47. Grant by the Queen to Cuthbert Vaughan of certain saltmarshes known as the Washpits, Stoneridge, Kedle grounds, William Fynche's salts, and the Prior of Christchurch salts, within the parishes of Lydd and Bromhill, in the counties of Kent and Sussex, late in the occupation of John Phillips.

48. Petition of Wm. Travers to the Council. Prays to be released from the Marshalsea.

49. Submission of William Travers, acknowledging that the Lady Elizabeth is the only true and lawful Queen of England.

50. Petition of the Company of Merchant Staplers to the Queen. Setting forth the great injury they have sustained since the loss of Calais, and praying that certain new regulations be made for them, according to articles subjoined.

51. Report on the above petition, by the Marq. of Northampton, Earl of Pembroke, Sir Wm. Cecill, and Sir Wm. Petre, to whom it was referred.

52. Certain articles relative to the above, in answer to the article touching wools and fells, proposed by the Merchant Staplers.

53. Observations in support of the answer to the articles proposed by the Merchant Staplers.

54. Statement of the loss which the revenue has suffered owing to the decay of the staple.

55. A reckoning of good and middle Cotteswold wool, with the charges and profits arising on sale of three serplers of the same.

56. Account of the charges of a serpler of wool.

57. Notes of various statutes made for regulation of the staple of wool.

58. Reckoning of good and middle Cotteswold wools, with observations on the charges and duties payable on wool shipped by the Merchants of the Staple.

59. Things to be observed on the part of the Staplers. Notes of various statutes.

60. Certain things collected, to prove where and in what places the staple hath been kept.

1560.

Vol. XV.

61. Inconveniences which arise to the Queen's realm and subjects by reason that the Company of the Merchant Staplers is not established.

62. Account of the sale of Cotswold wool, with the prices of the same, and observations thereon.

63. The same account truly made in such order as it is at this day used.

64. Notes relative to the provisions of the new patent for the Merchants of the Staple.

65. Replication to the articles demanded by the Merchants of the Staple.

66. Table of the weights of wools, and notes relative to customs payable on the exportation of wool.

67. Notes relative to the vent and sale of English cloths, &c. on various parts of the continent.

68. Particulars of the manor of Escrope, in the parish of Highworth, co. Wilts, late in the tenure of Tho. Lord Seymour, on payment of a certain rent; 2 lbs. of wax, a pair of gilt spurs, 1 rason ginger, and a pair of gloves. Thos. Weldon's suit.

69. Suit of   to the Queen, for a grant of the keeping of Berkhampstead Park and the parsonage of North-church, for a term of years.

70. Mr. Hart ? to Sir. Wm. Cecill ?. His efforts to procure Lord Grey's deliverance. Affray with a thief: has no money to carry on his suit for the killing of him. Desires a licence for Richard Collsonsack to keep a tavern at Yarmouth ; or the Queen's Majesty's pardon for Mr. Krigdote, in exile for piracy.

71. Orders and regulations for the better direction of the office of the Ordnance, within the Tower of London and the Minories.

72. Petition of Chas. Spencer and Robt. Randall, constables, and others, to the Council. Being opposed by Mr. Ryvet, in what they were appointed to do by the Council and Mr. Roger Colte, deceased.

73. Dr. Awbrey's answer to certain complaints against his re-letting of the lands granted to him in reversion by the Queen.

74. Table showing the estimated rate of beef and mutton for any number of men between 20 and 400,000, for the space of 40 days.

75. Appointment of Alex. Jones to be Inspector of the Port of Bridgewater, in the room of John Mors, deceased. Lat.

76. "Orders, taken within the City of London, to repress the "inordinate gain of certain drapers, clothiers, and other artificers, that "make any kind of apparel."

1560?

VOL. XV.

77. Grant to Wm. Herbert of London, of the offices of Keeper of the Forest of Radnor and Constable of Cardigan Castle, on surrender of Wm. Abbott. Lat.

78. Rent roll of the manors of Brameley and Armeley, in the West Riding of Yorkshire, formerly belonging to the Monastery of Kirkstall, co. York. Lat.

79. Portenary (to the Council), relative to the plans for the fortifications at Berwick and Portsmouth. Abstraction and loss of his plans for Berwick. Has made plans, and desires a commission for the works at Portsmouth. Has brought with him a new invention "of an artilyrye portative."

1561.

VOL. XVI. JANUARY—APRIL, 1561.

Jan. 1. 1. Memoranda in Cecill's hand of business to be performed.

Jan. 2. 2. Similar paper of memoranda.

Jan. 7. 3. Winchester, Sakevyle, and Mildmay, to Sir Wm. Cecill. New money will be sent into Wales. The English refiners will refine as much as the Almayns, and at a cheaper rate. Great want of lead.

Jan. 13. 4. Submission of Dru Drury, acknowledging that he has offended the Queen, and imploring her pardon.

Jan. 16. 5. Memoranda of business, by Sir W. Cecill.

Jan. 20. Kirby. 6. H., Earl of Huntingdon to Francis Yaxley. Thanks him for his letters.

Jan. 22. Westminster. 7. The Queen to Archbps. Parker and others, Commrs. for Ecclesiastical Causes. Directs certain lessons in the Book of Common Prayer to be altered, and others substituted in their place. Latin copies of the Book of Common Prayer to be used in Collegiate Churches: with additional clauses to be inserted, as to setting up Tables of the Commandments in Chancels, &c.

Jan. 25. Bielsano (Belsys, Mr. Waad's House.) 8. Paul Cypræus to Cecill. Is encouraged by Mr. Waad to address him. Assures him of his great respect for him, and his devotion to his service. Lat.

Jan. 26. 9. Winchester to same. Has received letters from Lazarus Coboz, and also from Sir T. Gresham, on debts owing to merchants abroad. Rate of the exchange.

Jan. 30. Bristol. 10. Wm. Carr, Mayor of Bristol, to the Council. Proceedings of the goldsmiths at Bristol in exchanging new moneys for base. *Incloses,*

10. I. *Note of base moneys exchanged into new moneys at Bristol, by Francis Eton and Robt. Wells.*

Feb. 3. 11. The Queen to the Lord Treasurer. Directions to deposit the surplus money in the hands of the four Tellers of the Exchequer in the Tower, without delay.

DOMESTIC—ELIZABETH.

1561.

VOL. XVI.

Feb. 5.
Cowdrey.
12. Viscount Montague to Fr. Yaxley. Excuses himself for his long silence.

Feb. 6.
13. Thomas Parkar to Sir Edward Waldegrave. Private affairs. Informs him that the wine will cost him 10*l*. per tun. Forster, the fishmonger, is gone to Lynn mart. Gives an ill character of Goldney, a serving-man.

Feb. 6.
14. Notes by Cecill, concerning examinations of various persons; particularly of Tho. Parkar, as to fraud in wines, in his letter to Waldegrave; also of Ramridge, Bonar, and Etheridge.

Feb. 6.
15. The Queen to Winchester. Restriction of the licence granted to the Merchants of the Stillyard to export only 600 cloths, and those not to be sold in the Low Countries.

Feb. 12.
16. Lease from Tho. Norton to Tho. Heyward, the elder, of certain salt marshes lying within the manor of Mylton Court, Kent, for 10 years.

Feb. 13.
17. Recognizance of Wm. Bullyn to render account of the rents and profits of the possessions of the late Matthew Baxter, co. Northumberland.

Feb. 14.
Newhall.
18. Sir Thomas Wharton to Mr. Yaxley. Begs that he will obtain for himself and his wife, from Lord Robert [Duddeley], a lease of the parks and house at Newhall, on reasonable composition.

Feb. 14.
Newhall.
19. Same to same (?) Further urging him to procure the lease of the house at Newhall.

Feb. 21.
Westminster.
20. The Queen to Lord Keeper Bacon. To hear the cause between Thomas Wilkes and Edward Leveson and John Skevington, concerning the inheritance of the manors of Hadnall and Radbourne, co. Warwick; and for the rectory of Middleton Cheyney, co. Northampton.

Feb. 22.
Newhall.
21. Sir Tho. Wharton to Fr. Yaxley. Thanks for his letter, &c. Forwards an answer to the Master of the Rolls. Offers to compound, by giving up his rule and offices of Beverley, to be at peace.

Feb. 25.
Setrington.
22. Mabell Forteskew to same (whom she addresses as "Good Governor"). Urges him to ascertain the cause of her mother's anger. Mrs. Mary Silles, and all his other charges, are well. Requests some gloves.

Feb. 26.
St. Faith's,
beside Norwich.
23. Sir Ric. Southwell to Fr. Yaxley. He may forward any letter to him, through John Appleyard, Esq.

March 1.
24. Memoranda by Cecill, of public business.

March 1.
Belsys.
25. Arnigill Waad to Cecill. Describes Mr. Vaughan's house. Has given orders to Cecill's gardeners as directed. Recommends a person for the works at Dover or Sandwich, who has a new method of excavating.

March 7.
26. Same to same. The gardener at Greenwich will provide Cecill with all that he can. Recommends that lavender, spike, hissop, thyme, rosemary, and sage be sent for. If more is necessary, then to send to Hampton Court or Richmond.

1561.
March 7.
Wells.

VOL. XVI.

27. Gilbert Barckley, Bp. of Bath and Wells, to same. Impoverished state of the bishoprick, by the ill management of his predecessor Bp. Borne. Seeks for amendment at the Queen's hands. *Incloses,*

> 27. I. *Supplication of Bishop Barckley to the Queen. Shows that Gilbert Borne, the late Bishop, had sought means to alienate the revenues of the see to his own use. Prays a commission to examine and redress the above matter. March.*

> 27. II. *Note of manors, lands, tenements, annuities, and advowsons granted and given away from the see of Bath and Wells, by Gilbert Borne, late Bishop there. March.*

March 8.

28. The Queen to the Lord Admiral. The bulwark at Upnor to be completed. Number of ship-keepers to be reduced. *Incloses,*

> 28. I. *List of vessels in Gillingham Water, and statement of the number to which their keepers may be reduced.*

March 13 (?)

29. Statement of the true and perfect art of making saltpetre grow in cellars, barns, &c., or in lime and stone quarries.

March 13.

30. Articles of agreement between the Queen and Gerard Honrick, a German captain, who undertakes the making of saltpetre. Fr.

March 13.

31. Duplicate of the above.

March.

32. Tender by [Marco Antonio?] for supplying the Queen with 20,000 bow-staves, 2,000 cwt. of brimstone, and saltpetre of Naples, and to put into the same bargain an excellent jewel worth not less than 2,500*l.*

March.

33. Abstract of the above tender.

March.

34. Request of Marco Antonio for a speedy answer as to his tender for a supply of bow-staves, brimstone, and saltpetre of Naples.

March.

35. Remarks by Wm. Bromefield, on the above tender for bow-staves, brimstone, and saltpetre of Naples, and on the prices demanded for the same.

March 15.
The Tower.

36. Wm. Bromefeld to Cecill. Advises him to conclude a bargain with Mark Antonio, for a certain quantity of saltpetre and bow-staves, at reduced prices.

March.

37. Particulars of prices at which Mark Antonio has finally agreed to deliver certain quantities of bow-staves, brimstone, and saltpetre.

March 16.

38–40. Certified copies of proceedings against Thomas Dewy, goldsmith, dwelling in Foster Lane, London, before John Hardyman, Archdeacon of Westminster, in the Church of St. Leonard within the precinct of the exempt jurisdiction of St. Martin le Grand; with articles against the said Dewy. Three papers.

1561.

VOL. XVI.

March 21. 41. Dr. Anth. Draycot to Dr. Ramrydg. Is sorry he is troubled with the headache. Wishes for a General Council.

March 23. 42. Note of armour to be returned to Mr. Gresham, being old and unserviceable.

March 25. 43. Account of the remain of armour within sundry of the Queen's armouries.

March 26. 44. Account of the clear annual value of all the manors, lands, &c., of the late Sir Thomas Parry, deceased, descended to his son and heir, Thos. Parry, Esq.

March 29.
Ingatestone.
45. Sir Wm. Petre to Lord Clynton and Sir Wm. Cecill. Gives his opinion on the articles exhibited by the King of Portugal's Ambassador, for restraining the traffic of English merchants to the Indies.

April 5. 46. Nicholas N., an Englishman, to John N., a Frenchman, his old friend, residing at Paris. MS. treatise on ecclesiastical matters. Lat.

April 10. Lease from the Peticanons of St. Paul's, London, to Richard Jugge, citizen and stationer, "of all that their shop with a chymney in it," now in the occupation of the said Richard, and other premises, for 31 years. [*Case A., Eliz.*, No. 8.]

April 15.
The Rolls.
47. Sir William Cordell to Cecill. Can find no record of any grant of the nature which he mentions made to the subjects of the King of Portugal. Regulations to which the trade of foreigners was always subject. Complaint of poor prisoners in the Fleet.

April 16. 48. Articles of remembrance for the Duke of Norfolk, touching the repair and maintenance of the haven of Great Yarmouth, sore decayed.

April 17. 49. Edmond Grindall, Bishop of London, to Cecill. Examination of Coxe, alias Devon, the priest, taken that day. The Council surely will punish him for his magic and conjuration. *Incloses,*

    49. I. *Examination of John Devon, before Hugh Darell, Esq., a Justice of Peace for Kent, touching mass being celebrated in the house of Sir Thos. Wharton of Newhall, Essex. He afterwards was received at the house of Sir Edward Waldegrave, at Burley, in Essex; and at other places, where he saw various Popish books and superstitious ornaments. April* 14.

    49. II. *Further examination of John Coxe, alias Devon, before the Bishop of London, touching mass being celebrated at Sir Edw. Waldegrave's, Sir Thomas Wharton's, and in Stubbes' house at Westminster. April* 17.

April 19.
Hedingham.
50. Earl of Oxford to the Council. Arrest of divers persons for unlawful practices in religion. Has searched Sir Thos. Wharton's house at Newhall, who humbly submits himself to the Queen. Search

1561.

	made at Sir Edward Waldegrave's house. Sends letters found there. Intercedes for Wharton. *Incloses,*
	50. I. *An inventory of all such implements of superstition as were found in the chamber near Lady Wharton's bed-chamber at Newhall, Essex. April 17.*
	50. II. *Confession of Emms Barnes as to celebration of mass by John Coxe in the house of one Stubbes at Westminster; also confession of Anne Pallady, as to Coxe's resort to Lady Waldegrave.*
	50. III. *Chr. Stubbes to his wife. Desires her to send him part of the money given to her by Lady Waldegrave.*
April 19 (?)	51. Chr. Stubbes to Sir Wm. Cecill. Denies having received money of Lady Waldegrave. Had only requested his wife to send him part of what she had received.
April 19.	52. Anne, Duchess of Somerset, to same. Is contented to submit to her son's (the Earl of Hertford) going abroad; but wishes him matched at home in some noble house to the Queen's liking. Is sorry for his wilfulness, and begs Cecill not to spare, but to over-rule him.
April 20 (?)	53. Examination of Roger Bell, and others, before Hugh Darell, Esq., as to the passage of Ric. Baker over the ferry at Gravesend, and of Mr. Webbe to London.
April 20 (?)	54. Examination of Wm. Morrys, as to passage of Ric. Baker over into Essex.
April 20.	55. Note of the prisoners committed to the Tower, the Fleet, Marshalsea, King's Bench, or otherwise placed in custody.
April 20.	56. Robert Catlyn, Lord Chief Justice, to Cecill. On the law for punishment of witchcraft and sorcery. Allusions to the opinions of Henry de Bracton, and an extract from Brytton.
April 20.	57. Grant by the Corporation of New Romney, Kent, to Wm. Lord Cobham, Constable of Dover Castle and Lord Warden of the Cinque Ports, of one half of their right in all wrecks and "fyndells," by sea or land.
April 22.	58. Winchester to Cecill. Coat and conduct money to be sent. Prest of 500*l.* required. Affairs of the Merchants of the Staple, and Merchants of the Stillyard. The Frenchman's money at Hampton is clearly forfeit.
April 22.	59. Examination of Tho. Wood. Has not said nor heard mass since Midsummer, 1559. Has written to Lady Waldegrave and Dr. Scott. Deposes as to intelligence from various quarters.
April 23.	60. Examination of Thomas How, organ-maker, and servant to Dr. Freer, before Sir William Chester, Lord Mayor of London. Visit of his master to Dr. Martyn at Buntingford. Neither himself nor his master, to his knowledge, have received the Communion since the Queen's accession.

Vol. XVI.

1561.
April 25. 61. The Queen to Sir Edw. Warner, Sir William Garret, and others. Commission to further examine the case of Richard Puttenham, Esq., found guilty of rape.

April 25.
Westminster. 62. The Queen to the Mayors of Bristol and Chester. To aid the embarkation of troops for Ireland, under the charge of Geo. Delves and Robt. Audeley.

April 25.
Westminster. 63. Duplicate of the above letter to Chester.

April 25. 64. The Queen to Sir Henry Sydney, Lord President of Wales. To levy 200 men in North and South Wales for service in Ireland.

April (?) 65. List of prisoners in the Tower, the Fleet, the Marshalsea, and at Westminster; with the names of persons appointed to examine them.

April (?) 66–68. Three papers of interrogatories to be administered to the persons imprisoned, as to the design of calling a General Council; of a former design to deprive Queen Elizabeth of the succession; and for marriage of the Queen of Scots.

Vol. XVII. May—June, 1561.

May 1. 1. Consultation at Greenwich, held by the Queen's command, relative to a request by the Spanish Ambassador that Abbot Martinengo, Nuncio from the Pope, who had arrived at Brussels, might come into the realm with letters from the Pope, and other Princes, to the Queen.

May 5. 2. Answer to the Spanish Ambassador, refusing to admit the Abbot Martinengo, the Pope's Nuncio, into the realm.

May 5. 3. The above rendered into Latin.

May 6. 4. Winchester to Cecill. Sends notes of 3 indentures for assigning certain land to the Bishop of Durham. The Bishop is about to return home.

May 6.
Cambridge. 5. The Vice Chancellor and University of Cambridge to the Queen. Praying for her protection, in regard to their rights and privileges. Lat.

May 7.
Westminster. 6. Grant of pardon to Henry Wilcocks of Shitlington, Bedford, for having feloniously harboured and entertained William Snagg and Henry Finch, the murderers of William Colman. Lat.

May 11.
Oxford. 7. Dr. Tho. Francis, Jas. Calfhill, and others, scholars of Oxford, to Cecill. On the serious disturbances at the inauguration of Doctor Francis, as Provost of Queen's College. Lat.

May 16. 8. Decree of the Admiralty Court in the cause Wm. Kerr and others v. Clavering. Condemning Clavering to pay 2,080*l*. 3*s*., for damages and spoil committed on a ship stranded at Saterburn-mouth. Lat.

VOL. XVII.

1561.

May 22. 9. James Pilkington, Bishop of Durham, to Cecill. Is about to repair homeward. Losses which he has sustained in the revenue of his see. Desires a warrant to receive 30 barrels of salmon from the Farmer of Norham Castle. Beseeches his favour that good heads of houses may be appointed in Cambridge, particularly for St. John's.

May 24. Greenwich. 10. Warrant to deliver 18 yards of crimson velvet to the Earl of Sussex, due to him as Chief Sewer of England, by inheritance, at the Coronation.

May 24. Greenwich. 11. Warrant to deliver to the same, one horse and foot cloth, or 10l. in lieu thereof, for executing his office of bearing the Queen's cloak-bag through London, the day before her Coronation.

May 24. Greenwich. 12. Warrant to deliver to the same the surnapp wherewith the Queen was served on the day of the Coronation.

May 26. 13. Names of prisoners in the Tower, and of the causes of their commitment, briefly set forth by Sir Edw. Warner, Lieut. of the Tower.

May 28. 14. Examination of Tho. Burman, servant to Thomas Annot of Leistoff, as to landing certain quantities of canvas and poldavies, robbed from a Spanish ship.

May 28. 15. Statement of wrongs done to certain merchants, subjects of the King of Spain, by English pirates. Goods landed at Leistoff by Annot and Burman.

May 30. 16. Receipt by Tho. W[indebank] for 300 crowns, to be laid out for the necessary expenses of Tho. Cecill, being sent into France by Sir Wm. Cecill.

May. 17. Note of base money delivered out of the Receipt of the Exchequer to Thomas Stanley, Under Treasurer of the Mint in the Tower.

June 3. 18. Names of offenders indicted and convicted at the Commission of Oyer, held at Brentwood, Essex, before the Earl of Oxford; amongst others, Sir Tho. and Lady Wharton, Sir Edw. and Lady Waldegrave, Lady Hubblethorne, Lord Hastings of Loughborough, Sir Tho. Stradlyng, &c. &c.

June 5 (?) 19. Petition of Sir Thos. Stradlyng to the Queen. Prays to be released from the Tower; committed for having caused four pictures to be made of the likeness of the Cross, which appeared in the grain of a tree blown down on his estate in Glamorganshire.

June 5. Cowbridge. 20. Sir Roger Vaughan and Edward Lewis to the Council. Have repaired to the park of Sir Thomas Stradling, at St. Donat's, Glamorgan, and examined the supposed picture of a cross, discovered in a tree broken by a tempest there. *Inclosing,*

> 20. I. *Depositions taken at St. Donat's, touching the figure of a small cross seen in an ash tree, split by a tempest in the park of Sir Thomas Stradling, of that place. June 5.*

1561.   Vol. XVII.

June 5.   21. Fellows of Merton College, Camb., to Sir Wm. Cecill. In favour
Merton College. of Dr. Chambers to be head of their college. Lat.

June 7.   22. Fellows of Queen's College, Oxford, to same. Desiring their
Oxford. privileges in the nomination to prebends may be preserved. Lat.

June 8.   23. Robert Horn, Bishop of Winchester, to same. Has proceeded
Wulvesey. on his visitation throughout Surrey and Hants. Is going to the Isle
of Wight. Reports his observations.

June 8.   24. Certificate by Wm. Cook and Wm. Gerrard, of the survey of
certain tenements in Bread Street, London, part of the inheritance of
Robt. Losse, the Queen's ward.

June 8.   25. Anthony Kyme to Cecill. Search in the Records for proofs of
Brough. the tenure of the late Mr. Fulstow's land at Ingoldmelles and Toynton,
in question between the Queen and the Duchess of Suffolk. Mr. Bertie
has been misinformed.

June 9.   26. John Arundell of Lanherne, and others, to same. Report their
Lanherne. proceedings as Commissioners for inquiry into the possessions of Sir
John Arundel of Trerice, deceased.

June 12.   27. Sir Henry Sydney to same. Has apprehended two more of the
Bridgenorth. coiners. Phillip Tynker, one of them, is an old knave. John Gammage is indicted for rape, and fled to London.

June 12.   28. Discourse concerning the true cause of the burning of the spire
and church of St. Paul, London. Printed at London, by John Day.

June 17.   29. Sir Walter Mildmay to Cecill. Sends an account of the Mint
London. fees. Observations on Mr. Stanley's bill of fees due to him.

June 19.   30. Mabell Forteskue to Fr. Yaxley. Requests him to apply to her
mother for money for her support, her wages being but 4 marks a year.

June 19.   31. Thos. Windebank to Cecill. Arrival of Mr. Thos. Cecill and
Dieppe. himself at Dieppe. Have been visited by M. de Veulles, the Lieutenant-Governor. Intelligence from the French Court.

June 21.   32. John Scory, Bishop of Hereford, to same. Requests to have
Whiteburne. power to nominate impartial persons as Commissioners to survey his
bishoprick. Great disorders in the Cathedral Church of his diocese:
it is "a very nurserye of blasphemy, whoredom, pryde, superstition,
" and ignorance."

June 22.   33. Names of all the German or Dutch strangers of the German
Church in London, arranged alphabetically according to their Christian
names, and specifying their various trades and occupations. Signed by
John Utenhovius and others, elders and pastors of the German
congregation.

[June 24.]   34. Commission for repairing the Cathedral Church of St. Paul's,
London, lately damaged by tempest. Commissioners to examine concerning the best means of re-edifying the cathedral, and procuring
funds for that purpose.

M

Vol. XVII.

1561.
June 24.   35. The Queen to the Lord Mayor of London. Has deputed certain of her Council to confer with him as to the best means of raising contributions for the repair of St. Paul's.

June 24.   36. Copy of the above, by Sir Tho. Wilson, Keeper of State Papers.

June 24.
Greenwich.   37. The Queen to Archbishop Parker; recommending a collection amongst the clergy of his province, for rebuilding St. Paul's.

June 24.   38. Copy of the above, by Sir Tho. Wilson.

June 24.   39. Another copy of the above; with copies of subsequent letters on the subject.

40. Note by Sir Thomas Wilson of such documents as are in the Office of State Papers, relative to the burning and rebuilding of St. Paul's, London.

June 26.   41. Winchester to Cecill. Mr. Kingsmell is desirous of farming part of the forest of Chute, near Andover. Days appointed for payments to be made beyond sea.

June 28.   42. The Queen to the Lord Treasurer. Injurious reports that armour is conveyed from England to Muscovy. Strict orders to be given that no manner of armour or artillery be transported out of the realm.

June 28.
Greenwich.   43. The same to the Lord Admiral. To deliver four ships to Sir Wm. Chester, Sir Wm. Garret, and others, to make a voyage to the coasts of Africa.

June 28.
Paris.   44. Tho. Windebank to Cecill. Arrival with Mr. Thos. Cecill in Paris; they are lodged in a house provided for them by the Queen's Ambassador, who advises them to repair to the Court with the Lord Hertford, as long as it remains at Paris. Propose to sell their horses.

June 28.   45. Draft of the above.

June (?)   46. Questions to be proposed to the Council, touching the sums to be paid to the Lord Lieutenant by prisoners in the Tower, for diet, fees, and other charges.

June   47. The Queen to the Justices of Assize. Proposed restriction in the appointment of Justices of the Peace. None to be appointed who are retainers or servants of any other person.

[June.]   48. Thos. Trollope to Cecill. Details of his plan for erecting mills for beating hemp, and for manufacture of canvas and linen cloths in England.

[June.]   49. "The briefe contentes of a lyttle booke, entituled A profitable "Newyeres Gyfte to all Englande," being a small printed tract, of a device by "Thos. Trollope," for the setting up "of a mille to knocke "hempe for the makinge of canvas and other linnen clothes."

VOL. XVIII. JULY, 1561.

1561.

July 1.
Croydon.
Archbishop Parker to Bishop Grindall. Directions to set on foot a contribution among the clergy of his diocese, for rebuilding St. Paul's; and to communicate his letters to all the other bishops in the Province of Canterbury. [See June 24.]

July 1.
1. List of prisoners of the High Bar, commonly called the King's Bench, from 1553; with the causes of their commitment.

July 2.
2. Calendars of the names of prisoners remaining in the Marshalsea.

July 3.
3. Names of all the prisoners in the Tower, with the dates and causes of their committal.

July 3.
4. List of prisoners in Newgate, men and women, cast and judged for felony.

[July 3.]
5. Certificate of prisoners remaining in the Fleet Prison, with the causes of their committal.

July 3.
6. Particular of the rents, lands, and possessions of the Deanery of St. Bees, in Cumberland.

July 4.
7. Answers of Sir Tho. Wharton, Sir Edw. Waldegrave, John Gaywood, Allen Chynery, and others, being prisoners in the Tower, and other prisons, touching certain questions propounded to them.

July 5.
Mr. Sackvyle's House.
8. Edw. Lord Hastings, of Loughborough, to the Council. Solicits pardon for the offence which he committed at Newhall, in hearing mass.

July 6.
Greenwich.
9. Warrant for a grant to the Mayor, &c. of Sandwich, authorizing them to allow a limited number of foreigners to inhabit the town and port of Sandwich, and to pursue the art of making says, bay, and other cloths there.

July 8.
10. Proclamation prohibiting the transportation of armour into Russia, or to any other place in war with any nation in Christendom.

July 9.
11. Account of the remain of armour and arms, &c., within the Tower of London; also at Greenwich, Westminster, Hampton Court, and other places.

July 10.
Paris.
12. Tho. Windebank to Cecill. Still at Paris. The King of Navarre has excused himself from receiving Mr. T. Cecill at present. Cannot send an estimate of their monthly expenses. Mr. Thomas has no great taste for the lute, but likes the cistern [gittern?]. He has been presented to the Queen of Scots.

July 12.
London.
Bishop Grindall to Bishop . Directions to raise a contribution for repair of St. Paul's. [See June 24.]

July 12.
13. Thomas Browne, Feodary of Cornwall, to Cecill. Proceedings of the Commission for inquiring into the possessions of Sir John Arundel of Trerice. Deaths of Ric. Power of Foy, and Michael Vivian.

1561.

July 14.
London.
14. Sir Wm. Cecill to his son Thomas. Desires he will remember his duty, and the instructions which were given to him. Gives further advice.

July 14.
London.
15. Same to Windebank. Relies on his discretion. Desires him to see that his son serves God with fear and reverence.

July 14.
16. Grant of pardon to John Pellowe of Modbury, convicted of felony for stealing cattle from various parties at Dartmoor, in the parish of Lydforde, Devon.

July 15.
17 Winchester to Cecill. Has spoken with Sir Thomas Gresham as to the double usance required by merchants. Particulars thereof.

July 16.
18. Dr. Nich. Wotton and Peter Osborne to same. Have conferred with Steynbergh, and the Master of the Savoy, upon articles for the incorporation of a company for working mines in England. *Inclosing,*

18 I. *Indenture between the Queen and John Steynbergh and Thos. Thurland (Master of the Savoy), for erecting a corporation for working mines in England. Lat.* [July 16.]

18. II. *Draft of the above, in English.*

July 16.
London.
19. Sir John Masone and others to the Council. Detail their proceedings with the prisoners in the Tower. Sir Thos. Wharton submits. Ryce behaved very reverently, but demurs to take the oath. Lord Hastings, of Loughborough, willingly took the oath, but prays to be excused from giving bond for good behaviour.

July 18.
Stafford Castle.
20. Henry Lord Stafford to Cecill. Contempt shewn to him by Mr. Lyttleton's keepers. Has committed one of them to prison. [*See ante, Dec.* 1560.] *Incloses,*

20. I. *Information given by Henry Lord Stafford of the spoils committed by Sir Edw. Lyttleton in the Chace of Teddesley Haye, in the Forest of Cannock, co. Stafford. Dec. ?*

July 19.
Rose Castle.
21. John Best, Bishop of Carlisle, to same. Reports the state of his diocese. "The priestes are wicked impes of Antichrist;" for the most part very ignorant and stubborn; past measure false and subtle.

July 22.
Stamford.
22. The Aldermen of Stamford to same. Have conferred with Thomas Trollop touching the manufacture of canvas. The mill for beating of hemp will cost 50*l.* They purpose to begin on a small scale first.

July 22.
Beaulieu.
23. Articles (signed by the Queen) for the instruction of all the Vice-Admirals of the realm how to proceed for preservation of the quiet trade of all merchants and fishermen, as well strangers as English.

July 22.
24. List of Vice-Admirals in some English counties.

Vol. XVIII.

1561.

July 22. 25. A Book of Survey, made by John Gwynne, containing therein particulars of all the lands granted by the Queen to the Right Honble. Walter Visct. Hereford.

July 22. 26. Abstract of the Book of Survey of lands granted by the Queen to Visct. Hereford, made by John Gwynne.

July 24. Stafford. 27. Lord Stafford to Knollys and Cecill. Reasons for having committed one of Mr. Lyttleton's keepers to custody.

July 24. 28. Winchester and Sakevyle to Cecill. Concerning certain sales; list of persons who have passed the Queen's signet for purchases. Money affairs.

July 25. 29. Same to same. They have dined with the Lord Mayor, and conferred with the Aldermen of the Stillyard on matters depending between them and the City.

July 25. Paris. 30. Thomas Cecill to his father, Sir William. Confesses he has been more occupied in sight seeing than in his studies. Has accompanied Throckmorton to the Court, and been present at a fight between a lion and three dogs. The dogs were victorious. Lat.

July 25. Paris. 31. Windebank to Cecill. Has been unable to send an account of their charges. The Ambassador recommends them to remain at Paris the ensuing winter. Mr. Thomas Cecill must have his horse and foot cloth. Course of his studies.

July 25. Paris. 32. Draft of the above.

July 27. London. 33. Sir Wm. Chester (Lord Mayor) to same. Proceedings with the Merchants of the Stillyard. The Corporation of London desire to proceed against that Company according to law. Requests that the Queen may be moved to bring St. Martin's le Grand within the jurisdiction of the City of London.

July 30. London. 34. Same to same. Thanks for moving the Queen in the matter between the City and the Stillyard. Desires that a commission, if necessary, be issued to examine the controversy. *Incloses,*

34. I. *Articles agreed on to be granted to the Merchants of the Hanse Towns or Stillyard. August.*

July 30. London. 35. Wm. Bowyer to same. Reminds him that the High Stewards of Westminster have always bestowed on the people of Westminster two bucks and forty shillings annually.

July ? 36. The Queen to the Sheriffs and Justices of Peace of Counties. Signifies her intention not to issue any Commission of Lieutenancy this summer; but to leave the government of the counties to their charge. List of Lieutenants of Counties attached.

July ? 37. Copy of the above.

1561.

VOL. XIX. AUGUST—SEPTEMBER, 1561.

August 1.
London.
1. John Shers to Sir Wm. Cecill. Has purchased for him at Venice the statues of 12 of the Emperors. Will be happy to procure any thing else for him from Venice.

August 2.
Westminster.
2. Licence by the Queen to Sir William Garrard, Sir William Chester, and others, of London, to receive 10 per cent. upon their loan of 30,000l. to the Crown, without incurring the penalties of the statute against usury.

August 3.
London.
3. Tho. Wood to Cecill. Requests the wardship of the daughter of the late Bartholomew Pala, a leather-seller in Holborn, who had purchased certain tenements of Lord Mountjoy.

August 4.
4. Winchester and Sakevyle to same. Warrants forwarded. Order with Sir Tho. Gresham for payments beyond sea. Money affairs.

Aug. 4 (?)
5. The Council to the Lord Mayor of London. Send five obligations for money advanced by Merchant Strangers abroad, to be sealed with the common seal of the City, and delivered to Sir Tho. Gresham.

August 4.
Paris.
6. Tho. Windebank to Cecill. Have taken a house. Thinks it better Mr. Cecill should not travel in company with Lord Hertford, as well for the sake of avoiding the English tongue, as for other considerations.

August 5.
Cawood.
7. Tho. Young, Archbp. of York, to same. Great want of current coin in his diocese. Begs to have a lease of the Queen's coining houses, for the purpose of setting forward his mint in York.

August 6.
8. Winchester to same. The Merchant Adventurers must be directed to pay the 30,000l. to Sir Tho. Gresham, for the Queen's use in Flanders.

August 8.
9. Same to same. Manner in which the Queen is deprived of her customs on wine and cloth. Mr. Russell's lease of woods in the Forest of Wyre. Desires to have the wardship of young Waldegrave, if Sir Edward dies.

August 9.
Ipswich.
10. The Queen to Cecill, as Chancellor of the University of Cambridge. Sends an injunction to be observed for removing families of women and children from residence in the Colleges. *Incloses,*

    10. I. *Injunction, by the Queen, that the wives and children of all governors, prebendaries, or students of cathedral churches or colleges, residing within houses belonging to the same, shall not be permitted to remain or abide therein. Aug. 9.*

August 9.
Ipswich.
11–13. Three contemporary copies of the above injunction.

August 9.
Paris.
14. Thos. Windebank to Cecill. Gives information concerning Theophilus (an assumed name for Mr. Thos. Cecill). Philoponus (an assumed name for Windebank) can only express hope of the future progress of Theophilus in his studies. Thinks they had better travel

1561.   VOL. XIX.

in company with Frenchmen ; Lord Hertford has been an impediment to Mr. Cecill's progress in the language. Prevalence of the plague at Paris. *Incloses*,

14. I. *Note of the Articles on which the Bishops at Poissy have assembled.* Aug. 5.

August 9.   15. Draft of the above letter and inclosure.

August 11.   16. Lady Elizabeth Seyntlo to Fr. Yaxley. Is sorry she cannot have
Ipswich.   his company when the Queen comes to Hatfield. Hopes he will join them in Derbyshire. Mr. Seyntlo is in London.

August 11.   17. Archbp. Parker to Cecill. Reasons for wishing Mr. Martyr
Lambeth.   or Calvin could attend the conference of learned men in France. Thinks Lady Lincoln ought to be chastised in Bridewell.

August 11.   18. Bp. Grindall to same. The French Minister, Mons. Saul, has been
Fulham.   with him. Thinks no one is more fit for the conference of divines in France than Peter Martyr, with Dr. Francis Baldwyn to assist him. Reminds Cecill of Eton and the hedge priests there.

August 11.   19. Sir John Masone to same. Thanks for his answers respecting
London.   Mr. Byng. The Queen's injunction shews how careful she is for the Church. Some heads of the Colleges of Oxford have taken wives, and occasioned much irregularity.

August 11.   20. Copy of the above.

August 14.   21. Sir Wm. Chester, Sir Wm. Garrard, and Thomas Lodge, to
London.   same. Have conferred with the Portuguese touching the new voyage he offered to discover to the coast of Barbary ; have traded there for some years past. As the Portuguese is recommended by the Queen's Ambassador, they purpose to defray his charges and present him with 100 crowns.

August 15.   22. Declaration of all the revenues and possessions lately belonging to Guy Fairfax, Esq., a lunatic, being in the custody of Geo. Earl of Shrewsbury.

August 15.   23. Declaration of the charges expended by the Earl of Shrewsbury in the custody and maintenance of the said Guy Fairfax.

August 17.   24. Bishop Scory to Cecill. Impediments to religion by Popish
Whitborne.   Justices, particularly by Mr. Havard and Mr. John Scudamore. Compulsory observance of Popish fasts. Messrs. Mug, Blaxton, Arden, Gregory, and others, Popish priests, driven out of Exeter and elsewhere, received and feasted in the streets with torch lights.

August 17.   25. The Queen to Archbp. Young. Directions to institute proceedings against the Earl of Westmorland, for keeping the sister of his former wife as his wife.

August 17.   26. Cecill to Windebank. Is sorry for the sickness at Paris, and
Hemingham.   for Kendall's illness. Has heard that his son spends his time in idleness, for which he shall hold Windebank accountable.

1561.

August 18. Rochester.	27. Sir Ric. Sakevylle and others, Commissioners for Rochester Bridge, to Sir Wm. Cecill. Have assembled and viewed the state of the bridge. Mode proposed of levying money for its repair.
August 20.	28. Will of Sir James Boleyn of Blickling, Norfolk.
August 20.	29. Account of charges at the Earl of Oxford's, and rewards to various officers of the household, anno 3 Eliz.
August 22.	30. The Queen to Archbp. Parker. To hold a visitation of Eton College, and examine the proceedings in the late election of a Provost, done without her assent or knowledge.
Aug. 22 (?)	31. Anne Duchess of Somerset to Cecill. Report of Lady Catherine Grey's marriage with her son, the Earl of Hertford. Denies all knowledge of it, and hopes the willfulness of her unruly child will not diminish the Queen's favour.
August 22.	32. Sir Edw. Warner to the Queen. Has questioned Lady Catharine Grey as to the love practices between her and the Earl of Hertford. She will confess nothing.
August 24. Paris.	33. Thos. Windebank to Cecill. Account of their expenses. Now Lord Hertford has left, the Ambassador has advised them to remain at Paris. Thinks Mr. Cecill should keep a horse.
August 24.	34. Draft of the above.
August 27. Hallingbury Morley.	35. Sir William Cecill to his son Thomas. Desires to have letters from him either in Latin or French, and to know how he spends his money. Requests him to send anything meet for his garden.
August 29. Waltham.	36. Bishop Horn to Cecill. Being entrusted both with the ecclesiastical and civil jurisdiction in Hampshire, details his proceedings in that charge. State of religion in his visitations.
August 29.	37. List of Heads of Colleges at Cambridge. Lat.
August 30. (3 Kal. Sept.) Cambridge.	38. The Vice Chancellor and Senate of the University of Cambridge to Cecill. Solicits the protection of the Queen and himself against the town of Cambridge. Lat.
August (?)	39. Account of the clear yearly value of all manors, lands, &c., appointed by Sir Edw. Waldegrave for the jointure of Dame Frances, his wife, and for performance of his last will and testament.
August (?)	40. Grant to John James Scaramuzar of an allowance of one and a half per cent. on all sums repaid without cost to the Queen, of money borrowed of English and foreign merchants. Lat.
	41. Draft of the above. Lat.
Sept. 1. Lambeth.	42. Archbp. Parker to Bishop Grindall. Is of opinion the clergy of London should contribute in a higher proportion than the rest of the clergy towards re-edifying St. Paul's.
Sept 1.	Copy of the above. [See June 24.]

DOMESTIC—ELIZABETH.

1561.

Vol. XIX.

Sept. 3.
Burnham.
43. William Tyldsley to Sir Wm. Cecill. Gives numerous statistical particulars relative to the county of Buckingham; penal statutes, alehouses, archery, forestallers and regrators, provisions, wines, woods, rates of wages, rules to be observed by husbandmen and labourers, &c., &c.

Sept. 6.
Fulham.
Bishop Grindall to the Dean of St. Paul's [Alexr. Nowell]. To urge the Clergy of the Peculiar and Exempt Churches within the Diocese of London to contribute towards the repair of St. Paul's. [*See* 1 *Sept.*]

Sept. 9.
Baconsthorpe.
44. Sir Chr. Heydon to the Queen. Certifies her of his proceedings in taking an account of the estate of Sir James Boleyn, Knt., deceased, of Blickling.

Sept. 9.
Paris.
45. Thos. Windebank to Cecill. Mr. Thomas has been ill of an ague. Sir Nich. Throgmorton, the Ambassador, has been as kind as a father to him. Sir Nicholas is very anxious to be recalled home.

Sept. 10.
46. Cecill to Windebank. Has received his letters by the Earl of Hertford. Question of expences. Knows his son's faults, and if they continue or increase, he were better at home than abroad. Wants a man apt for his garden.

Sept. 12.
Chatsworth.
47. Sir William and Lady Seyntlo to Fr. Yaxley. Are sorry they cannot have his company in Derbyshire.

Sept. 13.
Enfield.
Bond of indemnity by the Queen to the City of London, for repayment of various sums of money borrowed of certain Flemish merchants. Lat. [*Case* A., *Eliz.*, No. 9.]

Sept. 17.
London.
48. David Whithed to Cecill. Acknowledges his obligations to him, but laments the necessity he is under of refusing the living which he offers him.

Sept. 18.
49. Proclamation against vending new wines by retail.

Sept. 19.
50. Tho. Cecill to Sir Wm. Cecill. Has recovered from his sickness, and been with the Ambassador at Court. Will write again about a man for the garden. Thinks of sending Tho. Kendall back to England. Draft in French.

Sept. 19 (?)
51. Windebank to same. Mr. Thomas promises to be more diligent in his studies. Refers to the letter written by him in French.

Sept. 19.
Paris.
52. Same to same. Mr. Thomas has recovered from his sickness. Hopes he will now diligently apply himself to recover the time lost. Lord Hertford being at Paris was an impediment to his studies, &c. Requests his commands that Mr. Thomas should not keep a horse: his promises of amendment.

Sept. 20.
Brancepeth.
53. Earl of Westmorland to same. Is called by the Archbishop of York into the Spiritual Court. Justifies his marriage. Regrets the Queen is incensed against him for it.

1561.

Vol. XIX.

Sept. 24.
Cambridge.
54. Robt. Beaumont, Master of Trin. Coll., Cambridge, to Sir Wm. Cecill. Sends him a Minister fit to read prayers in his family. Begs him to continue his care towards King's College. Wishes Mr. Daye to be appointed to King's College, Mr. Leonard Pilkington to St. John's, Mr. Newton to Jesus, and Mr. Robinson or Mr. Hutton to Pembroke. College grounds. Election of alms men.

Sept. 25.
Woburne.
55. Fr. Earl of Bedford to same. Has assisted the well-affected townsmen of Oxford in the election of an honest and religious person for their Mayor. *Incloses,*

55. I. *Ric. Chambers to the Earl of Bedford. Deprivation of Coveney, President of Mag. Coll., Oxford, who has appealed. Has proposed Dr. Laurence Humfrey for his successor. Dr. Butcher, President of Corpus Christi, is also put out.*

Sept. 26.
Oxford.
56. Bishop Horn to same. Visitation of the Colleges at Oxford. Three of the Colleges have demurred to acknowledge the Queen's supremacy, &c. Has deprived Dr. Coveney, and the President of Corpus Christi has resigned. Causes for which New College refused to subscribe.

Sept. 29.
57. Account of Tho. Edmunds, Collector of the Customs at Plymouth and Fowey and ports adjacent.

Sept. 29.
58. Account of Wm. Rickthorne, Collector of Customs in the port of London.

Sept. 29.
59. Account of Wm. Knight and Peter Smith, Collectors of Custom for Southampton and ports adjacent.

Sept. 29.
60. Account of Tho. Blunt, Collector of the subsidy of Tonnage and Poundage in the port of London.

Sept. 29.
61. Declaration of the total charges of the Queen's Great Wardrobe, from Michaelmas 1560 to Michaelmas 1561.

Sept. 29.
62. Account of the value of lands and possessions of the Bishoprick of Gloucester, ending Michaelmas 1561.

Sept. 30.
63. Warrant to pay an allowance of 5 marks a day to Sir Tho. Chaloner, as Ambassador Resident in Spain, and other sums for his incidental charges.

Sept. (?)
64. Estimate of the cost of various materials for repair of St. Paul's Church.

September.
65. Names of all those who have bargained for wards, and of the wards themselves, &c., with the faults found in Mr. Bosvyle's books.

Vol. XX. October—December, 1561.

Oct. 1.
Indenture of sale from Trystram Holcam of Aston and Gryzegon his wife, to John Arres and Elizabeth his wife, of their great house in Chepynge Campden, co. Gloucester, and a close and orchard in the same town. [*Case A., Eliz.,* No. 10.]

VOL. XX.

1561. Oct. 13. St. James's.	1. Sir Wm. Cecill to Tho. Windebank. Thanks for his attention to his son. Has returned his French letter, corrected. Proposed return of Sir Nich. Throckmorton.
Oct. 3 (?)	2. Same to Mr. Cecill, or Tho. Windebank. Specifies certain books of which he desires to know the prices. Wishes to know what bibles and charts can be procured.
Oct. 8. Paris.	3. Windebank to Cecill. Gives particulars of his son's being seized with an ague. Expense of horse-keeping.
Oct. 11.	4. Account of timber received for re-edifying St. Paul's Church, London.
Oct. 13.	5. Bp. Pilkington to Cecill. Disordered state of his diocese: like St. Paul he has to fight with beasts at Ephesus. Has a double jurisdiction, and would be glad of such a helper as Mr. Fleetwood. Has had private conference with the Earl of Westmorland as to his marriage.
Oct. 14. Paris.	6. Windebank to same. Sends him by Kendal an account of their expenses. Mr. Cecill's health is restored. Sends prices of the books he required; charts can be better had at Antwerp. *Incloses,*
	6. I-IV. *Four papers of accounts, in Windebank's hand, of expenses to the time of Kendal's departure.*
Oct. 15. (Id. October.) Cambridge.	7. Bartholomew Dodington to same. Requests his influence to be elected Public Orator. Lat.
Oct. 18. Burleigh.	8. Peter Kemp to same. Sends him a plan of the brewhouse. Progress of other works at Burleigh. *Incloses,*
	8. I. *Ground Plan of a brewhouse, &c., at Burleigh.*
Oct. 18.	9. The Queen to the Dean of Westminster. To give order to all Prebendaries and others, ministers of that Cathedral Church, to observe the late injunction relative to the exclusion of women and children therefrom.
Oct. 18.	10. Certificate of debts due by the Queen within the Office of the Armoury.
Oct. 29.	11. Winchester to Cecill. Sends a list of noblemen and others desiring the privilege of having wine delivered for their use, free of impost.
Oct. (?)	12. Richard Cox, Bishop of Ely, to the Queen. Shews, by the example of the Patriarchs and the primitive Church, that marriage is an honourable state, and not forbidden to Priests.
October.	13. Statement of the matter in question between the College of St. John's, Cambridge, and Thomas Snagge the elder, referred to the decision of Sir William Cecill, relative to 16 acres of arable land in Shetlington, Bedford.
Oct. (?)	14. Declaration of the misdemeanors which various Italian merchants daily use, to the great detriment of the Queen, by evading her customs.

DOMESTIC—ELIZABETH.

VOL. XX.

1561.
Oct. (?)

15. Account of clothes, kerseys, &c., shipped from the port of London, and received in Antwerp and Brabant by the merchants of Italy and their factors.

October.

16. Survey of the Assart lands in Windsor Forest.

Nov. 2.
Ely.

17. Bishop Cox to Sir Wm. Cecill. Begs him to forward his requests. Is troubled with Dr. Thirlby, who is fast in the Tower. *Incloses,*

17. I. *Requests of the Bishop of Ely to the Queen. Nov. 2.*

Nov. 3.
Mag. Coll.
Cambridge.

18. Roger Kelk to same. Applies to be promoted to the Archdeaconry of Lincoln, which will shortly be vacant. Lat.

Nov. 3.
Burleigh.

19. Peter Kemp to same. Progress of works at Burleigh House, and in the gardens. *Incloses,*

19. I. *Plan of a conduit to be erected at Burleigh.*

Nov. 4.
Westminster.

20. Cecill to Windebank. Has received his letters, &c., by Kendal. Decides for his son not to keep a horse. Fears his son will return home like a spending sot, meet only to keep a tennis court.

Nov. 10.

21. Account of travelling expenses, of Sir Tho. Challoner, (?) from Gravesend to Dover.

Nov. 10.
Cawood.

22. Archbp. Young to Cecill. Complains of favour shewn to Ellis Markham, against whom he has brought an action. Has conferred with the Earl of Westmorland, who is strangely in love with his pretended wife. Suit of Wm. Strickland for lands.

Nov. 12.
Paris.

23. Windebank to same. Mr. Thos. Cecill is well in health, as Kellegrew can tell. Describes his studies and accomplishments.

Nov. 14.
St. James's.

24. Cecill to Windebank. The note of the books sent was imperfect. Wishes to have proclamations and edicts as they are published. Sir Wm. Cecill's sister Margaret is to be married to Mr. Roger Cave.

Nov. 14.

25. Bp. Pilkington to Cecill. Suit of Sir Francis Jopson. Disaffected and insubordinate state of his diocese. Bad character of Serjeant Meynell. Great want of good officers.

Nov. 17.

26. Citation for Mr. James Dugdale to appear before the Commissioners for the Visitation of the University of Oxford. Lat.

Nov. 19.
Mag. Coll.

27. Roger Kelk to Cecill. Requests his support against his competitors for the Archdeaconry of Lincoln. Lat.

Nov. 19.

28. Edw. Williams to same. As to the suit between the Queen and Mr. Harcourt for the wardship of Elizabeth Harcourt.

Nov. 25.
(? Cal. Dec.)
Oxford.

29. The Vice Chancellor, &c., of Oxford to same. Thanking him for his favors conferred on the University. Lat.

Nov. 26.
Paris.

30. Windebank to same. Has received his letters by Sir Tho. Challoner. Hopes he has recovered from his sickness. Progress of Tho. Cecill's studies. Reasons for not sending the proclamations, &c. Course for sending remittances.

Vol. XX.

1561.
November. 31. The Queen to the Lord Treasurer. The persons named in the schedule attached are to be exempt from payment of duty on certain quantities of wine, for use in their own households.

November. 32. A device for the discharge of certain principal persons from the new impost set upon wines.

November. 33. Copy of the above.

Dec. 9. 34. Confession of John Powell before Sir Edw. Warner, Lieutenant of the Tower, William Wynter, and Benj. Gonson, relative to a highway robbery committed at Tyburn, upon Mr. Harcourt and two of his servants.

Dec. 9. 35. Confession of Roger Ratcliff, servant of Mr. Robert Hopton, the Knight Marshal, concerned in the above robbery.

Dec. 9. 36. Confession of Robt. Durrant, concerned in the same robbery.

Dec. 13. 37. Peter Kemp to Cecill. Concerning plantations in the park at
Burleigh. Burleigh, felling of timber, &c. Device for reducing the household, and letting off part of the land. Mr. and Mrs. Cave (Cecill's sister) have returned home.

Dec. 13. 38. Charges of wages and materials provided for the Queen's works at various places, from the 13th April 1560.

Dec. 23. 39. Windebank to Cecill. Progress of Mr. Thomas in French. Gives
Paris. particulars of various books sent; difficulty of procuring the printer's names to them. Desires to know if they shall travel to see the country.

Dec. 27. 40. Cecill to Windebank. Money affairs. Has himself been so
Westminster. embarrassed that he has been obliged to sell his office in the Common Pleas. Is not certain of Mr. Dannet's coming.

Dec. 27. 41. Same to his son Thomas. Is wearied with hearing of his dis-
Westminster. solute conduct and waste of time. Children, as gifts of God, ought to be a comfort to their parents, but he is the contrary.

December. 42. Account of cloths, kerseys, and cottons shipped by the Merchants of the Hanse Towns, from Michaelmas 1560 to Christmas 1561.

43. Account of money owing by Sir William Cecill to Mr. Gresham; with the sums expended for purchase of marbles, chairs, &c., &c.

[Papers without date, probably in 1561.]

44. Account of gross amount of charges for works at Dover, Somerset Place, Windsor, Westminster, and Hampton Court.

45. Notes relative to certain arrangements to be made for the public service on various heads; the safety of the Tower; three ships to lie in Gillingham Water.

1561?

Vol. XX.

46. Bill of the surveyor, for building materials supplied to John Mounte, for Sir Wm. Cecill's house at Burleigh.

47. Bill of charges for carpentry and other materials, supplied by Mr. Smith, for the same.

48. Account by John Mounte of charges incurred by him on account of Sir William Cecill's buildings.

49. Note of benefits derived by the city of Norwich, by the residence of the strangers therein, for the space of ten years.

50. Account of ordnance and warlike stores delivered to various persons therein named, from April 1557; and a proposal for a general survey of all the ordnance in the kingdom.

51. Note of sundry leases of the lordship of Raskell, in the county of York, parcel of Sheriff Hutton.

52. Account of damages done at Richmond, Eltham, Greenwich, and Hampton Court, by the late tempest.

53. Considerations for the placing of a Bishop in the See of Gloucester, now vacant.

54. Notes concerning the Bishoprick of Gloucester during the incumbency of the first three Bishops.

55. Account of dispensations and licences granted in the Court of Faculties, by Barth. Kempe, Deputy to James Marburye.

56. Memorial by Chr. Bumpstede to the Queen. Shewing the necessity of coining small moneys, and the precedents which there are for the same.

57. Brief abstract of privileges granted by charter to the University of Cambridge; particularly as to the trial of certain cases before the Chancellor. Indorsed "Mr. Aldrich of Bennet Coll. his case." Lat.

58. Attested copy of a clause from the charter granted by Queen Elizabeth to the University of Cambridge. Lat.

59. Note of variations in the old and new grants of privileges to the University of Cambridge. Signed by the Attorney and Solicitor General, Sir G. Gerrard and Wm. Rosewell.

60. Note of additional privileges desired to be inserted in the charter of the University of Cambridge.

61. Account of arrears due to the Queen by Henry Earl of Westmorland, in the office of Anthony Reve, Auditor of the Exchequer. Lat.

62. Account of charges of the Queen's stable.

63. List of names of merchants of divers Companies of the City of London trading and occupying in silks.

1561 ?

VOL. XX.

64. Particulars of lands within the manors of St. Bees, Cumberland, and Gisburgh, Yorkshire, assured to the Queen by Sir Thomas Chaloner, for repayment of the sum of 320*l*.

65. Petition of merchants trafficking in Spain to the Council, to have authority to choose a Council and Assistants in the City of London.

66. Certain other considerations why the merchants trading into Spain require further privileges.

67. Substance of the above petition.

68. John Cutlerd to [Cecill?]. Is desirous to be admitted a student of Trinity College under Dr. Beaumont, the Master. Lat.

69. Account of expenses for hay and oats for the deer at Greenwich, for the year 1561; and for reparations in the Park.

70. Gascoigne (son of Adam Gascoigne) to Cecill? Shews his right to the chantry of Brampton, purchased of John Browne and William Twisden, but now claimed by the present Earl of Shrewsbury.

71. Declaration of the issues and revenues of the manors of Nunnyngton and Stangrave, Berwick on Tees, and Estanfelde in the county of York, from anno 1 Mary to anno 3 Eliz.

72. Account of the issues of the manors, &c., in Troutbeck, Hamelesett, &c., in the counties of Lancaster and Westmorland, for the same period.

73. Nich. Franckleyne to [Cecill?]. Survey and rental of the manor of Chetham [Chatham?], in the county of Kent; with a note of the difference between the particular and the actual survey.

VOL. XXI. JANUARY—FEBRUARY, 1562.

1562.
Jan. 1.

1. Peter Kemp to Sir Wm. Cecill. Sends some papers relating to Pickworth parsonage. Cecill's mother and Mrs. Cave and her husband are well. *Incloses*,

> 1. I. *Writ of summons to Gilbert Holme, Rector of Pickworth, to appear in the Court of Exchequer, to answer to certain contempts by him committed. Nov. 30, 1561.*

Jan. 1.
Burleigh.

2. Same to same. Requests directions relative to works in progress at Burleigh. *Incloses*,

> 2. I. *List of parish churches in Stamford, with the names of the patrons and incumbents of the same. Jan. 1.*

1562. VOL. XXI.

Jan. 3. 3. Articles ministered to John Hille, parson of St. Olave's, Silver Street, relative to John Apleforth, curate of Newington. In Bishop Grindall's hand.

Jan. 3. 4. Answers of John Hille to the above.

Jan. 8. Oxford. 5. Laurence Humfrey, President of Mag. Coll., Oxford, to Sir Wm. Cecill. States his reasons for applying for Mr. Kent's prebend. Instances in which others have held several livings together.

Jan. 10. 6. Account of charges of the Queen's works, from April 13, 1560.

Jan. 12. South Waltham. 7. Bishop Horn to Cecill. Has laboured to bring the inhabitants of Winchester to uniformity in religion. Great want of able ministers.

Jan. 12. Prid. Id. Jan. 8. The Prebendaries of Christ Church, Oxford, to the Queen. Recommending Thomas Dunn, Harbart Westfaling, and John Hill, all of one standing, that one of them may be selected for a prebend there. Lat.

Jan. 12. Westminster. 9. Cecill to Windebank. Will send him a bill for 200 crowns. Desires his son should know the estates and families of the nobility of France, and to get that information from some herald.

Jan. 13. 10. Bond of Stephen Tucker of Westminster, yeoman, and three others his sureties, in a sum of 80l., that he will not play at dice, cards, nor any other unlawful game, for the rest of his life.

Jan. 13. 11. Certificate by Benjamin Gonson, Treasurer for Marine Causes, of sums due by the Queen within his office.

Jan. 13. 12. Account of the yearly value of all the manors, lands, &c. of the late Francis Gayle of Acame, in the city of York, now in possession of Robt. Gayle, his son and heir, a minor.

Jan. 14. Rose Castle. 13. John Best, Bishop of Carlisle, to Cecill. Great prevalence of Popery in his diocese. Articles of religion in French circulated among the disaffected Papists in the north. *Incloses,*

    13. I. *A paper intituled, " La conclusion des articles de la religion." Jan.*

Jan. 14. 14. Account of debts due by the Queen within the Office of Armoury at Greenwich and the Tower.

Jan. 15. 15. Note of the sum owing by the Queen in the Office of Ordnance.

Jan. 15. 16. Declaration of such sums of money as Thomas Weldon, Esq., Cofferer of the Household, has received from the 1st of January 1559.

Jan. 19. 17. Observations on the relative values of Scottish money. Indorsed by Cecill, "Wm. Humfrey's opinion concerning Scottish moneys."

Jan. 19. Downham. 18. Bishop Cox to Cecill. Has perused a little treatise, called "Apologia Ecclesiæ Anglicanæ," and approves of it. Proposes a new translation of the Bible.

Vol. XXI.

1562.	
Jan. 19. Paris.	19. Tho. Windebank to Sir Wm. Cecill. Speaks in extenuation of Mr. Thos. Cecill's conduct. In his own mind he wishes Mr. Thomas were safe returned. Desires to know if he is to return.
Jan. 19. Paris.	20. Draft of the above.
Jan. 20. Winfield.	21. Geo., Earl of Shrewsbury, to same. Shews that the application of Thos. Fairfax to be put into full possession of the manor of Nun-Apleton is not founded on facts.
Jan. 20.	22. Account of expenses due and owing within the office of the Queen's Tents and Pavilions.
Jan. 20.	23. Account of receipts and charges of the revels, estimated for one year.
Jan. 21.	24. Winchester to Cecill. Thanks of the Aldermen of the Stillyard for the licence for cloths, paying English custom.
Jan. 23.	25. Advertisement for a mare, stolen or strayed out of a pasture near Hull. Notice to be given to Mr. Lister. (q. date.)
Jan. 25. Tynemouth Castle.	26. Sir Henry Percy to Cecill. Having married a daughter of Lord Latimer, recommends the second, 15 years of age, as an eligible wife for Cecill's son.
Jan. 25. Cawood.	27. Archbp. Young to same. Has given effect to the suit of the bearer. Desires a commission to administer the oaths of the Act of Uniformity.
Jan. 25. Oxford.	28. Laurence Humfrey to same. Desires he may be confirmed in the Prebend of Christ's Church, Oxford ; the Presidentship of Magdalen College was a post of honor, but of small profit. Lat.
Jan. 26. Paris.	29. Windebank to same. Names the places in France which it is desirable Mr. Thos. Cecill should visit. Estimate of charges for the journey.
Jan. 26.	30. Draft of the above.
Jan. 27. Paris.	31. Same to same. The bearer, Hugh Bannister, has offered to raise money for them from a Mr. Wingate. *Incloses,*
	31. I. *Thos. Windebank to Mr. Wingate. Requests that he will accommodate him with the loan of 150 or 200 crowns. Jan. 27.*
Jan. 27. Paris.	32, 33. Drafts of the above to Cecill and Wingate.
Jan. 27.	34. Peter Kemp to Cecill. Concerning sales of cattle, payments to be made, and other business at Burleigh. Solicits to be appointed Bailiff of Stamford.
Jan. 28.	35. Same to same. Offer of Sir Wm. Gresley to sell the manors of Brasborough and Carlby to Sir William Cecill.
Jan. 29.	36. The Council to the Presientd of the North and President of Wales, stating that the report of the fall in the value of money is without foundation.

VOL. XXI.

1562.
Jan. 30.
Westminster.
37. Proclamation enjoining all persons to cease from circulating false reports as to a decry of the moneys.

Jan. 30.
38. Draft of the above.

Jan. 31.
39. Commission to Archbp. Parker, Bishop Grindall, and others, to examine the circumstances of the intercourse between Edw. Seymour, Earl of Hertford, and the Lady Catherine Grey, who is with child by him. Lat.

Jan.
40. Note of the amount and the several kinds of moneys received in the Queen's Jewel House, at Christmas 1561.

Feb. 1.
Burleigh.
41. Peter Kemp to Sir Wm. Cecill. Mr. More wishes to know his terms for lease of a pasture near Burne. The rent of Castleton is paid to Mr. Kyrlington.

Feb. 3.
42. Winchester to same. Requests all the Tellers money may be brought to the Tower.

Feb. 4.
Ipswich.
43. Fr. Yaxley to Lord Robert Duddeley. Beseeches him to extend his protection towards him, having been sent for to appear before the Council.

Feb. 5.
44. Mr. Gascoigne to Tho. Windebank. Apologises for delay in correspondence. Begs to be remembered to Mr. Cecill. Mr. Yaxley is sent to the Tower.

Feb. 5.
Westminster.
45. H. Alington to same. Windebank's father, Coxe, and Mr. Tuydall, are thankful for his commendations. Notices other acquaintances. Mr. Daye is translated to the Provostship of Eton.

Feb. 5.
Paris.
46. Windebank to Cecill. Concerning a remittance to be made by a bill of exchange. [*Imperfect.*]

Feb. 6.
47. Peter Kemp to same. Has sold the thorns at Cliffe Park; works in the garden, &c. of the Park. *Incloses,*

47. I. *Articles of agreement for lease of the capital messuage of Tetforth (Thetford) Hall, in Baston, co. Lincoln, by Sir Wm. Cecill to John Hynde. Feb. 3.*

Feb. 6.
48. Winchester to same. Suit of the town of Beaumaris for repair of their walls, which they will undertake on condition of having their charter renewed. *Incloses,*

48. I. *A brief declaration of the cause and effect why the inhabitants of Beaumaris, in the Isle of Anglesey, sue to have a fee farm of the said borough.*

48. II. *A brief note of such articles as are to be considered for safeguard and defence of Beaumaris from the sea.*

Feb. 10.
Westminster.
49. H. Alington to Windebank. Has been blamed for letting him have 300 French crowns at his going to France. Desires an acknowledgement for it, to be dated on the 30th of May (*see that date*). Death of Mr. Eresby.

1562.

Vol. XXI.

Feb. 12.
Whitehall.
50. Edm. Molyneux to Thos. Windebank. Professes friendship. Desires remembrance to Mr. Thos. Cecill.

Feb. 12.
51. The Queen to the Treasurer, &c. of the Exchequer. Order to cause 25,000*l.* in gold to be brought from the Tower, or the Exchequer, to be delivered into the Queen's Palace at Westminster.

Feb. 14.
Paris.
52. Windebank to Sir Wm. Cecill. The merchant who was to lend them 200 crowns, will only advance 40 crowns; which he has declined. Recommends one Rogers, the Ambassador's servant.

Feb. 14.
53. Draft of the above.

Feb. 22.
54. Peter Kemp to same. Has surveyed the house and ground at Lalam. Particulars thereof.

Feb. 22.
Ivy Lane.
55. Peter Osborne to Sir Tho. Chaloner. Commission of inquiry as to validity of the marriage between Lady Catharine Grey and the Earl of Hertford. Yaxley sent to the Tower. Design to marry the young Lord Darnley with the Queen of Scots.

Feb. 26.
56. Winchester to Cecill. A scheme has been presented to himself and the Lieutenant of the Ordnance for making gunpowder. *Incloses*,

56. I. *Tender by Bryan Hogge, Robert Thomas, and Francis à Lee, for supply of gunpowder for the Queen's service.*

Feb. 28.
Prid. Kal. Mar.
Merton Coll.
57. The Sub-warden and Fellows of Merton Coll., Oxford, to Cecill In favour of Dr. Huick to be elected Warden. Lat.

Feb. 28.
58. Indenture of assignment of certain tenements within the precinct of the dissolved monastery of the Minories, without Aldgate, by Lord John Grey to George Medley, Esq.

Feb.
Westminster.
59. Warrant by the Queen for respite of the debt of 500*l.* due to her by John Ayleworth, because Sir Tho. Benger owed him 400*l.* and had mortgaged the keepership of Berkhampstead Park to him.

Feb.
60. Series of accounts by Sir Tho. Gresham of sums taken up by him at various times in London and Antwerp, with the rate of interest, &c., extending generally from March 1561 to February 1562.

Vol. XXII. March—April, 1562.

March 3.
Quint. non. Mar.
Oxford.
1. Herbert Westfaling to Sir Wm. Cecill. Thanks for his patronage in obtaining for him the prebend of Christchurch, Oxford. Lat.

March 4.
2. Winchester to same. Suit of the town of Beaumaris, as to repair of their sea walls, &c. The town of Radnor also makes suit for a charter of incorporation.

Vol. XXII.

1562.
March 4. 3. Tho. Windebank to Sir Wm. Cecill. Has received 100 crowns by
Paris.   Mr. Sommer. Understands that he and Thos. Cecill are to travel. Requests funds for that purpose. Particulars of their proposed route. Their expenses.

March 4. 4. Draft of the above.
Paris.

March 5. 5. Abstract of the matter depending before the Queen's Commissioners between John Green and Michel Wingham, alias Green, his wife.

March 5. 6. Brief rehersal of the matter which gave occasion of the words that were between Lady Ratcliffe and the Bishop of London, relative to Green's wife.

March 5. 7. Report by Bp. Grindall of the conversation between him and Lady Radcliffe, on the terrace at the Court, relative to Green's wife.

March 7. 8. Mayor, &c. of Bristol to Cecill. Praying that Bristol may be
Bristol. continued as an independent Bishoprick, without being united to any other.

March 8. 9. Windebank to same. State of expenses. Has bought and sent
Paris.   over the two treatises on the civil and canon law. Desires a supply of money for their journey; and Mr. Thomas is in need of some apparel.

March 8. 10. Draft of the above.

March 13. 11. Tho. Gardiner to same. Desires his assistance in his suit,
Sexto Id. Mar. being engaged in the public service. Lat.

March 12. 12. Archbishop Parker and Bishop Grindall to same. Think it
Lambeth.   necessary the Dean, Prebendaries, and Ministers of the Church at Hereford were under the control of the Bishop of that see.

Mar. 13 (?) 13. Walter Haddon ("oculis affectis et lippinctibus") to Sir Tho. Chaloner. Wishes his assent to a marriage between Chaloner's sister, the widow Farnham, and Francis Saunders, Haddon's brother.

March 14. 14. Adam Halliday to Cecill. Gives him particulars of the studies he is pursuing. Lat.

March 15. 15. Winchester to same. Sends warrants for money. Part of the Ordnance House in the Tower given way, being overladen; has therefore purchased the Minories as a storehouse.

March 20. 16. Petition of   to same. Solicits employment. Is well skilled in the Latin tongue; and gives specimens of handwriting.

March 23. 17. Windebank to same. Mr. Thos. Cecill has been borrowing
Paris.   money. The disturbances in France, make it unsafe to travel into the provinces. Sends some books. Requests him in his next letter to remind his son to observe the custom of prayer.

March 23. 18. Draft of the above.

VOL. XXII.

1562.
March 24. 19. Marq. Winchester to Sir Wm. Cecill. Has received the writings relative to the Almain refiners. Mint matters.

March 24. 20. Sir Wm. Cecill to his son. Reproves him for his dissolute and idle courses. Desires he will transmit a copy of his diary in French.

March 24. 21. Same to Windebank. Is grieved at the misconduct of his son, and blames Windebank for concealing it. P.S. stating that the severe terms of the letter is only for the purpose of producing an effect on Tho. Cecill.

March 25. Westminster. 22. Same to same. Desires him to send over a lemon, a pomegranite, and a myrtle tree, with directions for their culture, which may be brought to London with Mr. Carew's trees.

March 26. London. 23. Earl of Westmorland to Sir Tho. Chaloner. Desires to purchase or rent his house in London, during his absence.

March 31. 24. Ric. Alington to Cecill. Complimentary Latin letter: the writer signs himself Cecill's nephew.

March. 25. Proclamation by the Queen for fixing the current value of gold and silver moneys.

March. 26, 27. Two copies of the above.

March. 28. The Queen to the Earl of Derby. Desires him to order the Sheriff of Lancashire to publish the proclamation sent. *Incloses*,

28. I. *Proclamation for fixing the value of gold and silver moneys throughout the realm.*

March. 29. The Queen to the Sheriff of   . Order to publish the proclamation for fixing the value of gold and silver coins.

March. 30–44. Fifteen copies of the above.

March. 45. Account of money due for fees and wages to the Lieut. of the Tower, the Gentleman Porter, and Yeomen Warders there, from Michaelmas 1561 to Lady-day 1562.

March. 46. Demands of Sir Edward Warner, Lieut. of the Tower, for diet of certain prisoners under his custody, to Lady-day 1562.

March (?) 47. Tho. Bischop to Cecill. Offers all service in peace or war against Scotland. Henry VIII. having granted to him the manor of Pocklington, York, he now solicits the reversion, to entail on his heirs, or to have the lands of Belthorp and Kilwick in exchange for Pocklington.

March (?) 48. Note of gifts made to Lady Margaret Lennox and her husband, in the days of Queen Mary, and of her ill treatment of Queen Elizabeth, when Princess: probably by Tho. Bischop. [See vol. xxiii. No. 6.]

April 2. Westminster. 49. Cecill to Windebank. Is still grieved at his son's dissolute conduct. Had rather have lost him by an honourable death than be troubled with him in this way. Begs him to consult with Sir Nich. Throkmorton what is to be done with him.

Vol. XXII.

1562.
April 2.
Paris.
50. Tho. Windebank to Sir Thos. Gresham. Thanks for sending them 300 crowns. Apologizes for apparent neglect. *Incloses*,

    50. I. *Acknowledgment of the receipt of 300 French crowns from Sir Thos. Gresham, by the hands of Mr. John Fitzwilliams, Governor of the Company of Merchant Adventurers.*

April 3.
Stamford.
51. Wm. Cayworthe to Cecill. Concerning the deer to be provided for stocking Sir William's new park

April 8.
52. Windebank to same. Sends him a lemon tree, which cost 15 crowns, and two myrtle trees, price 1 crown each, which is very cheap. Gives directions for their culture.

April 8.
Paris.
53. Same to same. Is greatly grieved at his displeasure. Beseeches him to suspend his judgment until he can return home. Travelling in France is dangerous.

April 8.
54. Draft of the above.

April 10.
Cobham.
55. Lord Cobham to same. Requests him to further a design by Edw. Durant for constructing a harbour at Hastings.

April 13.
Boston.
56. Mayor, &c. of Boston to same. Pray that effect may be given to the wills of such persons as are desirous to make bequests in favour of the town of Boston.

April 13.
Westminster.
57. The Council to Winchester. Desire to be informed of what has taken place under the Order in Council of 11th Mar. 1556, for permitting the Italian and Arragonese merchants to ship certain kerseys and broad cloths for exportation.

April 15.
58. Note of kerseys, broad cloths, &c. shipped by merchants, Italians and Arragonese; by Ric. Tomyow, late collector of the subsidy, &c. in the port of London.

April 15.
Westminster.
59. The Queen to Winchester, Sakevyle, and Mildmay. To take order for the safer custody of treasure in the receipt of the Exchequer; loss having occurred by the deficiencies of Darkenall and Shelton, late Tellers.

April 17.
Paris.
60. Windebank to Cecill. Troubles in France. If the Prince of Condé should come to Paris they could not tarry there, on account of the fury of his soldiers and the populace.

April 17.
61. Draft of the above.

April 21.
Medlow.
62. Agatha Bawdwen to same. The Marq. of Winchester has the wardship of her son John Bawdwen. She is unable to come to London, being sick.

April 23.
Burleigh.
63. Peter Kemp to same. The deer have been brought to the park. Charges of the buildings in progress there.

April 25.
Burleigh.
64. Same to same. Has receieved a precept from the Queen's Receiver for payment of the rents of Casterton and Pickworth.

VOL. XXII.

1562.
April 26.   65. Tho. Windebank to Sir Wm. Cecill. Mr. Thomas has no disposi-
Paris.   tion to apply himself to learning, and is drawn away by other affections, which rule him entirely. Recommends he should be recalled to England: but that the letters of recal should not be too sharp or bitter.

April 26.   66. Draft of the above.

April 30.   67. The effect of the new licence desired by Lord Robert [Duddeley] on surrender of his old licence for exportation of wool.

April 30.   68. Note of wool shipped by licence granted to Lord Robert [Duddeley].

April 30.   69. Brief account of all the money received towards the re-edifying St. Paul's Church, from the 30th of June 1561 to 30th April 1562.

April 30.   70. John Mounstevynge to Cecill. Transactions with Peter Kemp, at Burleigh.

VOL. XXIII. MAY—JULY, 1562.

May 1.   1. Sir John Savage to Cecill. Applies for lease of the lands of Lady Brereton when she dies, and during the minority of her son.

May 2.   2. Declaration of homage of Richard Cheney, Bp. elect. of Gloucester. [*Bishop Cheney had the temporalities of Gloucester restored to him on the 2d of May. Rymer, xv., p. 624.*]

May 7.   3. Windebank to Cecill. Cannot refrain from acquainting him with
Paris.   the increase of the evil propensities of his son.

May 7.   4. Draft of the above.

May 7.   5. Same to same. Continued ill behaviour of Mr. Thomas, in spite
Paris.   of all severe letters, all counsels, and all shame of the world. He boasts Sir William cannot disinherit him, and attempted to flee away.

May 7.   6. Articles against Lady Margaret, Countess of Lennox, by Thomas Bischop. Consisting of 14 articles, particularly as to overtures for marriage of Lord Darnley with the Queen of Scots; and objections to her unjust pretensions in England.

May 7.   7. Memoranda for answering the Earl of Lennox and Lady Margaret, his wife, in case they allege unthankfulness or brag of their covenants with Henry VIII.: in Bischop's hand-writing.

May 7.   8. "The brief contents of certain Actes of Parliament against "thinordinate use of apparel," corrected by Cecill. [*These are nearly the same as those of* 20 *Oct.* 1559].

May 7.   9. Copy of the above.

May 8.   10. Peter Kemp to Cecill. Works in progress at Burleigh.

DOMESTIC—ELIZABETH.

Vol. XXIII.

1562.
May 8.
Westminster.
11. The Queen to Sir George Howard, Master of the Armoury. Warrant to convert certain old armour into plates for the manufacture of 1,500 jacks for the use of the Navy.

May 9.
12. Bond of Nicholas Revell and 8 others, Tailors, of St. Martin-le-Grand, not to put more than one yard and three quarters of kersey into any one pair of hosen; and to cut the same so as " to lye close to " the legges and not loose or bolstred as in auncyent tyme."

May 9.
13. Similar bonds by William Vaughan, and 49 others, hosiers, in Westminster, to the same effect.

May 9.
14. Deposition of William Forbes, concerning the Countess of Lennox; founded on the articles by Tho. Bischop.

May 10.
Westminster.
15. Cecill to Windebank. Has written to that naughty boy of his, and commanded him " to putt away his servant and to banish his " wanton lustes." Is indifferent where he travels to, so that he amends.

May 12.
Westminster.
16. Exemplification of the Act 31 Hen. VIII., for annexing certain manors and lands to the Castle at Windsor; at the requisition of Robert Lord Duddeley, Constable of the same.

May 14.
Shene.
17. Margaret, Countess of Lennox and Angus, to Cecill. Begs he will obtain her husband's release from the Tower, or that his imprisonment may be less strict.

May 16.
Canon Row.
18. Tho., Earl of Sussex, to same. Has endeavovred to bring about marriages between two of his men and two of the daughters of one Averly, a yeoman, who is since dead. Requests the wardship of the daughters.

May 16.
Burleigh.
19. Peter Kemp to same. Progress of works. Has sent a note of the extent of Worthorp. Recommends Mr. Anth. Burton for the parsonage of Leffnam (Luffenham ?).

May 17.
20. The Queen to William Gerard. Appointing him Vice-President of the Council of Wales, in the absence of Sir Hen. Sydney, sent Ambassador into France.

May 17.
21. Ch. Justice Catlyn to   . Gives his opinion as to the pardon of a foreigner convicted of manslaughter.

May 17.
Paris.
22. Windebank to Cecill. Understands that he wishes Mr. Thos. Cecill to continue at Paris rather than go to Flanders. The Ambassador advises they should remove to a house 7 leagues from Paris.

May 17.
23. Draft of the above.

May 17.
Paris.
24. Thos. Cecill to same. Finds he is very angry with him for spending his time in the vanities of love. Entreats him to bestow his blessing on him, and promises better obedience for the future. Fr.

May 21.
Shene.
25. Countess of Lennox to same. Has received his answer, by which she finds new matter is alledged against herself and husband. Doubts not they shall be able to clear themselves.

VOL. XXIII.

1562.

May 23. 26. Peter Kemp to Sir Wm. Cecill. Unruly proceedings of Henry Tampion, in reading a bill in the Common Hall, at Stamford.

May 23. 27. Same to same. In favour of Anth. Burton, for the living of Leffnam. The parson of Barroden is dead.

May 25. 28. Notes by Sir Wm. Cecill, for the examination of the Countess of Lennox.

May 26. Heston. 29. Wm. Amondesham to William Tildesley. Requests him to favor the suit of John Fernam, of Isleworth, fletcher. Will send Adams shortly.

May 27. 30. Sir Ric. Sakevyle to Cecill. Himself and others, Commissioners of Sewers, have arrived at Rye. Reports a quarrel at Dieppe between the Protestants and Papists; 150 of the former slain.

May 28. 31. Notes of proceedings in Merton College, Oxford. Lat.

May 29. Dammart. 32. Windebank to Cecill. Have removed from Paris; and Mr. Cecill has no opportunity of frequenting his customary places of resort. Advises his removal altogether out of France.

May 30. 33. Declaration and confession of Arthur Lallart, Lord Darnley's schoolmaster, sent into Scotland relative to the affairs of the Earl and Countess of Lennox.

May 30 Shene. 34. Countess of Lennox to Cecill. Desires to meet those who urge new and strange matters against her. The Queen bears her little love and affection.

June 3. Bocton Malherbe. 35. Tho. Wotton to same. Reasons which induced the Commissioners of Sewers to bring part of the water of Chestelet Valley through Sandwich Haven. *Incloses*,

35. I. *Considerations touching the Commission for bringing the water of Chestelet Valley into Sandwich Haven.*

June 8. 36. Warrant to pay 1,000*l*. to J. Ravile, Surveyor of Works, to be employed about necessary repairs.

June 12. Shene. 37. Countess of Lennox to Cecill. Complains of the Queen's determination not to grant her husband more liberty; he is suffering from ill health.

June 12. 38. Statement of the causes of the high prices of all commodities, owing to the inordinate trafficking and overgreat number of merchants; with remedies to be applied.

June 12. 39. Confession of Elizeus Halle, calling himself Ely the Carpenter's son, a pretended messenger from heaven; taken before the Bishop of London.

June 14. 40. Representations made to the Council by the Lieut. of the Tower, relative to prisoners in his custody. The late Bishops, Mr. Fecknam, and Mr. Boxoll, 8 in number, together with Francis Yaxley, Lallart, and other prisoners, desire more liberty within the Tower.

Vol. XXIII.

1562.

June 18. [Rye.] 41. Armigill Waad to the Lord Admiral. Details his proceedings in surveying the watercourses between Newenden and Rye, with the view of improving Rye Harbour.

June 16. Upnor. 42. Humphrey Lock to Sir William Cecill. Recommends using the stone of Rochester Castle for the purpose of completing a block-house at Upnor.

June 19. Shene. 43. Countess of Lennox to same. Requests permission to be admitted to the society of her husband in the Tower, and that he may have more liberty there

June 20. 44. Walter Haddon to [Cecill ?]. Respecting the watercourses in Cambridge ? Lat. [*Mutilated and obscure.*]

June 20. Tower. 45. Matt., Earl of Lennox, to the Council. Has answered to many matters untruly charged against him. Declares his innocence, and complains of the course allowed to his accusers.

June 21. 46. Deposition of Thomas Lower, of St. Winnowe, in Cornwall, relative to outrages committed by certain French at Conquet, in Brittany, on himself, John Trester, and others.

June 22. 47. Memoranda of public business, by Sir Wm. Cecill.

June 27. Tower. 48. Earl of Lennox to the Council. Hoped to have received some comfort from the Queen. Explains the two points in his letters which their Lordships dislike.

June. 49. Names of noble persons belonging to the Society of Gray's Inn, from 11 Hen. VIII.

June (?) 50. Names of all the Dukes, Marquises, Earls, Viscounts, and Barons of the realm.

July 5. Newcastle. 51. Ric. Hodsham to Cecill. Concerning 400 paving stones to be shipped for Sir Wm., and delivered in London, free of all charges.

July 10. Shene. 52. Countess of Lennox to same. Still solicits to have access to her husband, or that he may be permitted to come to Shene, to be placed under the same custody as herself.

July 12. London. 53. Henry Kyllygrew to Lord [Robt. Duddeley]. Preparations made for the meeting at Nottingham, between Queen Eliz. and the Queen of Scots. Tilts set, and warning given to all lusty young knights, to shew feats of arms. Verses in French and Latin sent to the Queen by Queen Mary, with a token of a heart of diamonds.

July 15. Greenwich. Declaration and accord by Queen Elizabeth, postponing the proposed meeting with the Queen of Scots, until the next year, and then to meet at York, between the 30th of May and the last day of Aug. [*See under 4 Aug.* 1563.]

July 16. 54. Cecill to Windebank. Directs him and his son to return to England, if they cannot pass safely to Strasburg or Antwerp.

July 17. 55. Mem. of public business, by Sir W. Cecill, with reference to the disturbances in France.

DOMESTIC—ELIZABETH.

Vol. XXIII.

1562.
July 20.
Westminster.
56. The Queen to the Earl of Derby, the Bishop of Chester, and others. Appointing them Commissioners for Ecclesiastical Causes, within the diocese of Chester; to enforce the Acts for the Uniformity of Common Prayer, and for restoring to the Crown the ancient jurisdiction over the estate ecclesiastical and spiritual.

July 20.
57. The Queen to Lord Admiral Clynton. To prepare 2 ships, for conveying munitions, &c. to Ireland.

June 24.
Shene.
58. Countess of Lennox to Cecill. Severity of her husband's imprisonment. Prays that the Queen will appease her anger against them.

July 24.
Shene.
59. Same to same. Has received intimation by her servant, Fowler, that her husband must acknowledge his offences. The only offence she could think of was his sending the schoolmaster (Lallart) into Scotland.

July 24.
London.
60. Anonymous letter to the Queen. Has conveyed letters to Sir Fr. Englefield, and held treasonable conversation with his servant, John Payne, concerning the restoration of Heath, Thyrlby, Boner, and the old religion.

July 24.
London.
61. John Payne to [Sir Fr. Englefield ?]. Has delivered the letters. Remembrances from the Lady Abbess and Nuns of Sion, the Prior of Shene, Boner, Fecknam, &c.

July 24.
Monthall.
62. Sir Tho. Smith to Cecill. Does not understand whether he is to go into France or not; but is indifferent where he shall be commanded to go.

July 29.
Portsmouth.
63. Sir Fr. Knollys to the Council. Has received intelligence from the Earl of Warwick and Mr. Basing. Arrival of Mr. Winter with 1,200 men off New Haven. Provisions of victuals. Intends to ship off 800 more men.

July 30.
Greenwich.
64. The Queen to Lord Adm. Clynton. To fit out 4 ships, under the charge of Sir Wm. Woodhouse, to clear the Narrow Seas of pirates.

July 30.
65. Inventory of the goods of Richard Beare, taken by the Bretons out of the ship Anne, of London.

July 30.
66. Inventory of the goods of Tho. Wilson, taken out of the Elizabeth, of London, by the Bretons.

July 31.
67. Articles of recantation, proposed by the Bishop of London, to be made by Hadrian Hamsted, Minister of the German Church in London, of certain doctrines propounded by him, contrary to the Scriptures. Lat.

July.
58. Note for the ordering of eight hoys, to be taken up to convey soldiers, &c. to Dieppe.

VOL. XXIV. AUGUST—SEPTEMBER, 1652.

1562.
August 1. 1. Account of the collection made in the parish of St. Margaret's, Westminster, for the setting forth 12 soldiers; giving the names of the contributors.

August 5.
Shene. 2. Countess of Lennox to Sir Wm. Cecill. Has received the message of the Queen's desire that her husband's submission should come from himself, and not by her teaching.

August 6. 3. Bishop Grindall to same. Johannes Utenhovius has recommended to him a certain Count of Germany, who is willing to serve the Queen in the contest for religion. *Incloses*,

3. I. *Note by John Utenhovius, recommending Christopher, Count of Oldenburg. Lat.*

August 9.
Antwerp. 4. Tho. Windebank to Cecill. Have left France secretly, and arrived safely at Antwerp. Requests directions for their future course. Message from Sir N. Throkmorton, the Ambassador. Are staying in Sir Tho. Gresham's house. Improvement in Mr. Cecill's conduct.

August 9. 5. Draft of the above.

August 10. 6. The Queen to the Master and Fellows of Trinity College, Cambridge. Concerning the Statute which forbids the granting of any parsonages in reversion.

August 10.
Greenwich. 7. Same to Thomas Stanley, Under Treasurer of the Mint, and others. Warrant to pay into the Exchequer 2,276*l*. 11*s*. arising from parcel gilt and white plate, delivered to them to be coined into money.

August 12.
La Tower. 8. ———— to ————. Note, in French, as to delivery of two pipes of white wine of Orleans, for which the writer will not forget to supply the "Karasei." (sic).

August 12. 9. Countess of Lennox to Cecill. Has heard that the Earl, her husband, has made his submission, and that the Queen thinks it a very slight amends.

August 12. 10. Note of the exchange of lands between the Queen and the Duke of Norfolk. Also note of money owing by the Duke to the Queen.

August 14. 11. Cecill to Windebank. Thanks him for the care of his careless son. Thinks they may visit Brussels, Ghent, &c. Requests him to teach his son to spell his French more correctly.

August 15. 12. Account of the monthly charges of the new block-house at Upnor; conveyance of materials, &c.; by Ric. Watts, paymaster.

August 16.
Antwerp. 13. Windebank to Cecill. Are going into Germany in company with Mr. Henry Knolles, and have taken 200 dollars of Sir Tho. Gresham, for their expenses. Further message from Throkmorton. Civilities paid them in Antwerp.

Vol. XXIV.

1562.
August 17.   14. Mr. Thos. Cecill to Sir Wm. Cecill. Arrived with Mr. Knolles
Antwerp.   at Antwerp, and has learnt, by letters to Sir Thos. Gresham, his pleasure
              for their going into Germany. Fr.

August 18.   15. Winchester to same. Returns Browne's letter to him, and a bill
              concerning the payments at Easter and Midsummer. Money affairs.

August 19.   16. Mayor, &c. of Exeter to same. Complain of the rough treat-
Exeter.   ment which certain merchants have received in returning from Morlaix.
              Inclosing,

August 19.   16. I. *Complaint made to the Privy Council by the Mayor and
              others, merchants of the city of Exeter, as to the treatment
              they received at Morlaix, in Brittany.* Fr.

August 22.   17. Countess of Lennox to same. Ruinous effect of her lord's long
Shene.   imprisonment. Prays Cecill to intercede for his release.

August 27.   18. Windebank to Cecill. Arrived with Mr. Knolles at Spires, who
Spires.   would not allow them to pay anything. Has been in fear of an ague.

August 27.   19. Tho. Cecill to his father. Has awaited the coming of Dr. Mont
Spires.   two days. He intends to visit the Palsgrave. Kindness of Mr. Knolles,
              Fr.

August (?)   20. Grant to Wm. Holstock of the office of Comptroller of the
              Navy; the office of General Surveyor of Victuals for the Navy, formerly
              granted to him and Edw. Baesh, to cease. [*Much obliterated.*]

August (?)   21. Note, in Sir W. Cecill's hand, of things to be considered for
              transporting an army from Portsmouth, procuring money, provisions,
              &c. with reference to Newhaven and Dieppe.

Sept. 2.   22. Windebank to Cecill. Continue their journey, and have been
Heidelberg.   well entertained by the Count Palatine. Will be obliged to buy
              horses, waggons being scarce. Requests to know if they are to return
              with Mr. Knolles or remain at Strasburg.

Sept. 6.   23. Note of amount of wages for the crews of the Hope, the Lion,
              the Hart, the Swallow, and the Hare.

Sept. 8.   24. Bishop Grindall to Cecill. Graciousness of the Queen towards
Fulham.   the persecuted strangers. Has required the French and Dutch ministers
              to give him a catalogue of their communicants.

Sept. 9.   25. Note of armour sent to Portsmouth and Rye, from the office of
              Armoury.

Sept. 9.   26. The Queen to Lord Adm. Clynton. To send the New Bark and
Greenwich.   the Saker to keep the Narrow Seas, under Capt. Geo. Beston.

Sept. 10.   27. Note of coat and conduct money for 1,600 men to be sent to
              Portsmouth.

Sept. 10.   28. Note of ships now at sea.

Sept. 10.   29. Statement of the proposals of marriage made by Sir Thomas
              Benger to the Lady Essex; not to be told to Tom Fool, her son.

Vol. XXIV.

1562.

Sept. 11. 30. The Queen to the Mayor of Rye. To prepare vessels to transport certain numbers of soldiers.

Sept. 11. 31. Estimate of ordnance stores, and of the cost of transporting them from the Tower of London to Newhaven.

Sept. 12. 32. Account of augmentation of allowance to Capt. Reade, for such soldiers as were in his band, and had served as officers.

Sept. 12. 33. Winchester to Sir Wm. Cecill. Has spoken with Mr. Abingdon as to rate of pay, &c. for certain soldiers for Newhaven.

Sept. 15. 34. Sir Thos. Gargrave to same. Concerning the wardship and marriage of Edward Saville, under the charge of the Earl of Shrewsbury.

Sept. 16. Greenwich. 35. The Queen to the Earl of Arundel. To muster 400 soldiers of Sussex, to be equipped and sent to sea.

Sept. 16. Greenwich. 36. Same to Lord St. John. To muster and send 400 soldiers of Hampshire to Portsmouth.

Sept. 17. Peterborough. 37. John Mounstevinge to Cecill. Sessions of gaol delivery at Peterborough. The church of Artleborough or Irtlingborough is in a ruinous state. Has bargained for the lead thereof for Cecill's use.

Sept. 18. 38. The Queen to Armigill Waad. Instructions to take the musters of 600 soldiers at Rye, to be transported under command of Edward Ormesby, for service beyond sea.

Sept. 19. The Tower. 39. Sir Edw. Warner, Lieut. of the Tower, to Cecill. Requests as to a yeoman warder, and for the pardon of Rob. Goddard. Fr. Saunders is not worthy to be a prisoner, not for his offence, but for his poverty. *Incloses,*

39. I. *A list of prisoners in the Tower, 5 Sept. 1562, including Lady Katharine Grey, Earl of Hertford, &c.*

Sept. 20. The Tower. 40. Same to same. Is annoyed by the extreme passions of the Earl of Lennox, who has been more unquiet since the Earl of Hertford was allowed his small liberty.

Sept. 20. 41. The Queen to the Sheriffs of London. Reprieve for Tho. Borough and Nicholas Malby, who are to be delivered over to the Earl of Warwick, for service abroad.

Sept. 22. 42. Same to Lord Cobham. To take care that no annoyance be offered to French fishermen within his jurisdiction.

Sept. 22. 43. Same to Sir Maurys Denys Directions to issue money for four days pay to the soldiers at Portsmouth.

Sept. 23. 44. Same to same. Warrant to issue several sums of money for payment to Wm. Bromfield for ordnance stores, coat and conduct money, and other expenses of troops going abroad, under the Earl of Warwick, Sir Adrian Ponynges, and others.

Sept. 23. 45. Draft of the above.

Vol. XXIV.

1562.		
Sept. 23.	46.	The Queen to Armigill Waad. Similar instructions to those of the 18th Sept., for service at Dieppe; with additional corrections by Cecill.
Sept. 24. Rye.	47.	Richd. Wyndebanck to Sir Wm. Cecill. Has received and mustered the soldiers at Rye. Certain portions of armor deficient.
Sept. 24. Rye.	48.	Tho. Kemys to same. Arrival of the Canterbury men at Rye, altogether unfurnished. The Sussex and Kentish men are still wanting.
Sept. 25. Rokeburne.	49.	Sir Wm. Keyllwey to same. Will proceed with all diligence to Portsmouth to execute the Queen's instructions.
Sept. 26.	50.	The Queen to Sir Maurys Denys. To make certain payments for a Provost Marshal, and for officers under him; and also to Armigill Waad, paymaster at Rye, and 2s. per diem for his clerk.
Sept. 26. Portsmouth.	51.	Tho. Morley to . Progress in victualling the ships for 14 days, to carry troops over to Newhaven. *Incloses,*
Sept. 25. Portsmouth.	51. I.	*Order for transporting 1,600 soldiers, under the captains named.*
Sept. 27.	52.	The Queen to Lord Keeper Bacon. To take order in the case of Edward Saville, ward to the Earl of Shrewsbury, conveyed away by his base brother, Ro. Saville, and married to a simple poor woman.
Sept. 27.	53.	Same to Winchester. Has appointed Sir Wm. Keyllwey to take charge of Portsmouth, in place of Lord Chidiock Paulet.
Sept. 28. Hampton Court.	54.	Sir Wm. Cecill to Robt. Loughter, Archdeacon of Totness. Urges him to perform his promise made to Mr. Gibbs.
Sept. 28.	55.	Orders to be observed by the English soldiers serving the Queen at Newhaven, set forth by Sir Adrian Ponynges.
Sept. 28. Rye.	56.	Indenture of the armour, weapons, and munitions left in the charge of the Mayor, &c. of Rye, by Armigill Waad, for the Queen's service.
Sept. 29. Portsmouth.	57.	Sir Wm. Keyllwey to Cecill. Complains of the way in which Sir Adrian Ponynges has stripped the house at Portsmouth, which is unfit to receive the Earl of Warwick. Account of arms and stores now at Portsmouth.
Sept.	58.	Note of the particular wages of the crew sent to Portsmouth and Rye, to be paid by Sir Maurys Denys.
Sept. 29.	59.	Statement of allowances claimed by Martin Almayne for dressing the Queen's coursers, from Christmas 1559 to March 1562; specifying the names of the horses, and signed by Lord Robt. Duddeley, G. Howard, and Henry Norreys.
Sept. (?)	60.	Note of officers, soldiers, and artificers, to be transported to Newhaven and Dieppe.

VOL. XXV. OCTOBER—NOVEMBER, 1562.

1562.
Oct. 1.
Portsmouth.
1. Sir Wm. Keyllwey to Sir Wm. Cecill. Sends letters from Newhaven. Conference between the Vidame de Chartres and Sir Adrian Ponynges. Delivery of armour. Departure of the fleet.

Oct.
South Waltham.
2 Bp. Horn to same. Recommends Mr. Laybourne, a preacher of God's word. Burgasio [Venturini], the Italian, is yet very pensive. Has persuaded him to communicate his griefs to Cecill in writing.

Oct. 4.
Portsmouth.
3. Sir Wm. Keyllwey to same. Departure of the fleet, with a fair wind. The soldiers from Berkshire have not yet arrived.

Oct. 4.
4. Sir. Anth. Cooke to his son-in-law, Sir Wm. Cecill. Thanks for his favour towards his son, William Cooke, and for Cecill's favours towards himself. Is thankful God has provided him such a staff to rest upon in his old years.

Oct. 6.
5. Robert Rolles, schoolmaster of Westminster, to same. Concerning a prebend. Lat. [*Much obliterated.*]

Oct. 6.
6. Note of Almsmen absent on the 6th October from Christ Church, Oxford. Suit in favour of John Norris. Ordinances to be observed by the Almsmen.

Oct. 6.
Portsmouth.
7. Sir Wm. Keyllwey to Cecill. There is no other place in which the armour may be stowed but the church. Thinks it had better be returned. Muster of soldiers from Wilts and Berks.

Oct. 9.
8. Winchester to same. The Merchant Adventurers have made application respecting 31,800*l.* payable to them on the 1st Nov.

Oct. 10.
Hampton Court.
9. Cecill to Windebank. It is long since he heard from him. Asks his advice whether he shall let his son, Thomas Cecill, pass into Italy this winter or not.

Oct. 11.
Hampton Court.
10. H. Alington to Tho. Cecill and Tho. Windebank. Intelligence of the expedition to Newhaven. The Queen of Scots has made a progress, and got into trouble with the Earl of Huntley. All friends are well.

Oct. 13.
3 Id. Oct.
11. Fellows and Students of Christ Church, Oxford, to Cecill. Lat. [*Much obliterated.*]

Oct. 14.
12. Cecill to the Commissioners for the Queen's debts. Not to press Mr. John Fisher for a debt of 600*l.* due to the Crown, he having been appointed Gentleman Porter of the town of Newhaven.

Nov.
13. Estimate of charges of 3 of the Queen's ships, for wages and conduct money, they having on board 460 men.

Oct. 15.
Rye.
14. Ar. Waad to Cecill. Muster of soldiers arrived under charge of Mr. Walgrave. Has ordered an account to be made of the armour remaining in Rye; which has given offence, as interfering with the privileges of the Lord Warden.

Oct. 16.
Rye.
15. Same to same. Mr. Walgrave has sent one to London to make provision of armour, &c. Some of the band of Sir Maurys Denys have arrived. Mr. Winter's return from Dieppe expected. Gives his opinion on the expedition to Newhaven.

Vol. XXV.

1562.

Oct. 19.
Rye.
16. Wilfrid Entwyssell to Sir Wm. Cecill. Reports his arrival at Rye, with his men. Dilatory proceedings of the Justices of Newport and Buckingham. Praises Cecill's godly and virtuous conduct.

Oct. 20.
17. Note of the rate of wages of the force sent to Portsmouth and Rye, to be paid by Sir M. Denys.

Oct. 21.
12 Kal. Nov.
King's College
18. Provost and Fellows of King's College, Cambridge, to Cecill, Relative to a suit concerning a wood of which they have been in free possession for one hundred years. Lat.

Oct. 22.
Frankford.
19. Tho. Windebank to same. Has not written, having been travelling about the country. Have returned to Frankford to be there during the Diet. Thinks Mr. Cecill will profit little by remaining in Germany. Money affairs. The Queen is highly esteemed.

Oct. 22.
20. Draft of the above.

Oct. 23.
Franckfort.
21. Thomas Cecill to his father. His joy at reconciliation. Has visited the Landgrave of Hesse, the Duke Augustus, and the Duke John Frederick, in company with Mr. Knolles. Fr.

Oct. 25.
Shene.
22. Countess of Lennox and Angus to Cecill. Hopes the Queen will consider her husband's long imprisonment, and suffer them to be together during the approaching winter.

Oct. 28.
23. Bishop Grindall to same. Begs to know if that second Julian, the King of Navarre, is killed; as he intends to preach at St. Paul's Cross on Sunday next, and might taken occasion to mention God's judgments on him.

Oct. 28.
24. Archbishop Parker to same. Desires to know the Queen's pleasure as to certain guests sent to him, and who had been living upon him with a free table, for nearly 5 weeks. Mons. de la Haye was a gentleman, but his associates were otherwise.

Oct. 30.
Portsmouth.
25. Edw. Baesh to same. Small stock of provision at Portsmouth. Reminds him of the arrangements made when he had the victualling of Calais.

Oct. 30.
26. Lord Robert Duddeley to same. Deplores the loss which God has suffered his people to sustain by the overthrow at Rouen. The Queen is much grieved at it. Bespeaks Kyllygrew's office for John Duddeley, if he be dead.

Oct. 31.
Portsmouth.
27. Sr. Wm. Keyllwey to same. Has discharged the two ships at Portsmouth, from St. Martin's, near Rochelle. Arrival of the Saker and Hare from Newhaven. The Earl of Warwick and all the rest safely arrived there.

Oct. 31.
Portsmouth.
28. Edw. Baesh to same. Arrival of the Saker and Hare from Newhaven. Quantity of stores, provisions, &c. delivered to Mr. Abington.

Oct. 31.
Rye.
29. John Young, Mayor of Rye, to same. Mr. Waad has departed for London. News from Dieppe, that all the captains and their forces were shipped for Newhaven. Great loss of English and Scots at Rouen.

DOMESTIC—ELIZABETH.

Vol. XXV.

1562. Oct. [31].
30. John Young to Sir Wm. Cecill. Intelligence from Newhaven. Great slaughter at Rouen. The fate of Capt. Leyton and his men is unknown.

Oct.
31. Note of such provisions of which a speedy supply is required at Newhaven.

Oct.
32. The Queen to the Sheriffs of various counties. Directions to raise a certain number of soldiers for immediate service in Normandy.

Nov. 1. Portsmouth.
33. John Abington to Cecill. Measures for supplying Newhaven with provisions. Scarcity of bread there.

Nov. 1. Portsmouth.
34. Sir Wm. Keyllwey to same. Arrival of the Phœnix from Newhaven, and return of Sir Maurys Denys.

Nov. 2. Rye.
35. John Young to same. Arrival of M. de Velles, Lieut. of M. de Force. Monsr. Montmorency is about to make his entry into Dieppe. Particulars of the capture of Rouen and slaughter of the English and Scots. Kyllygrew taken prisoner. Great resort of French fugitives to Rye. Persons condemned to death at Rouen.

Nov. 2. Portsmouth.
36. Edw. Baesh and John Abington to the Council. Report proceedings in victualling men and ships. Want of mills at Newhaven.

Nov. 3.
37. The Queen to the Sheriff and Justices of Essex. To raise and send 600 soldiers to the sea coast, to be embarked for Newhaven.

Nov. 4. Rye.
38. John Young to Cecill. Arrival of French fugitives from Dieppe. Montmorency with 400 soldiers has entered Dieppe, and determined to intercept the English victuallers from entering Newhaven. Arrival of a Flemish hoy, with armour and other military stores.

Nov. 5. Portsmouth.
39. Sir Wm. Keyllwey to same. Arrival of three hulks in Southampton Water, with wheat and rye, bound for Rochelle; but they will discharge their cargoes at Portsmouth. Return of Sir M. Denys to Newhaven.

Nov. 6. Portsmouth.
40. Same to same. Complains of evil disposed persons unlawfully hunting in his park and warren. Desires to know if he shall detain a Rochelle ship laden with wine.

Nov. 6. Rye.
41. John Young to same. Order taken with the French refugees. Communication with the Earl of Warwick. Monsr. de Fors, Mr. Rybande, and Monsr. de Veles are going to London. Rye and meal shipped for Newhaven.

Nov. 6.
42. Estimate of the cost of sundry ship stores necessary for the new bark lately built at Deptford.

Nov. 9. Rye.
43. John Young to Cecill. Conference between the Rhingrave and the Earl of Warwick, on the sands at Newhaven. The King and the Guises still remain at Rouen.

Nov. 9. Portsmouth.
44. John Abington and Edwd. Darell to same. Victualling of Newhaven. Victuals for 3 months must be supplied, and mills must be sent from London to grind wheat, &c.

VOL. XXV.

1562.

Nov. 1.
Rye.
45. John Young to Sir Wm. Cecill. News that the King of France is at Rouen, with his mother and the King of Navarre, who is sore wounded, the bullet remaining in his body. The Guises, with their forces, are on their way to Paris.

Nov. 10.
4 Id. Nov.
Cambridge.
46. The Vice-Chancellor and Senate of Cambridge to same. Solicit his protection for the University, Lat.

Nov. 11.
Rye.
47. John Young to same. Arrival of Monsr. St. Marie, with news from France. The King of Navarre remains dangerously ill at Rouen.

Nov. 11.
48. Note of Edward Baesh for victualling certain vessels for sea.

Nov. 11.
Strand.
49. Warrant to Sir Wm. Damsell, Receiver General of the Court of Wards, to pay 300*l.* quarterly to the Vidame of Chartres; and 40*l.* to one Capt. Mazines, an Italian, and 15*l.* to him quarterly.

Nov. 12.
Shene.
50. Countess of Lennox and Angus to Cecill. Complains of the long imprisonment of her husband. Beseeches him to intercede with the Queen to set them both at liberty.

Nov. 12.
Portsmouth.
51. Sir Wm. Keyllwey to Winchester. Requests allowance to be made to Nich. Williamson for certain hops and powder brought by him from Antwerp. *Incloses,*

51. I. *Note of powder imported by N. Williamson.*

Nov. 14.
Portsmouth.
52. Same to Cecill. Explains the circumstances of the detention of a French ship, named the Charlotte of Maraines, laden with wine for the French Ambassador.

Nov. 14.
●
53. Peter Kemp to same. Charges of the works in progress at Burleigh. Desires directions as to taking of deer, &c.

Nov. 16.
My house next the Savoy.
54. Cecill to Tho. Windebank. Wishes his son Thomas to leave Germany, and to visit, incognito, Italy, Switzerland, and Geneva. Intends on his return to induce him to marry.

Nov. 16.
Rye.
55. John Young to Cecill. Fugitives from Dieppe. The King and his mother have left Rouen for Paris. Executions at Rouen. Reported death of the King of Navarre.

Nov. 17.
56. Winchester to the Queen. Decayed state of the piers of Bridlington and Robin Hood's Bay, in Yorkshire. Requests that certain lordships of the Crown may be let for defraying the necessary repairs.

Nov. 18.
57. Estimate of the charge of lining 1,000 morions and 300 burgonets, to be sent to Newhaven.

Nov. 18.
Frankford.
58. Windebank to Cecill. Thinks it advisable Mr. Cecill should not go to Italy, "by reason of the inticements to pleasure and wantonness "there," and the expense. If he is to go, recommends his being placed under the charge of Mr. Nowell. Sends account of expenses. State of parties in Germany. *Incloses,*

58. I. *Account of expenses, travelling in Germany, from 10th Sept. to 18th Nov. 1562.*

Nov. 18. 59. Draft of the above.

DOMESTIC—ELIZABETH.

Vol. XXV.

1562.

Nov. 20.
Portsmouth.
60. Sir Wm. Keyllwey to Sir Wm. Cecill. Report of Sir Adrian Ponynges return. Has sustained loss by the provision and furniture he has already made. Transmits a letter for the Vidame.

Nov. 23.
61. Receipts by Thos. Windebank and Thos. Cecill, for money advanced by the heirs of George Wolfe, on the credit of Sir Tho. Gresham.

Nov. 24.
62. Similar receipt by Tho. Windebank for 100 dollars.

Nov. 24.
Shene.
63. Countess of Lennox and Angus to Cecill. Thanks him for exertions in behalf of her husband, and for the liberty which he now enjoys.

Nov. 27.
64. The Council to Lord Rich. Remonstrating with him for seeking to procure his son to be elected a Knight of the shire, in preference to Sir Wm. Petre, whom they had recommended.

Nov. 29.
Burleigh.
65. Peter Kemp to Cecill. Concerning works in progress at Burleigh. Sources of various rents; planting of trees, &c. [*Much obliterated.*]

Nov. 30.
66. Estimate of the diet and wages of Captains, Mariners, and Gunners in some of the Queen's ships.

Nov.
67. Account of receipts and disbursements by Armigill Waad, sent to Rye by virtue of the Queen's letters, made to Sir M. Denys, Treasurer of the Garrisons in Normandy.

Vol. XXVI. December, 1562.

Dec. 1.
Burleigh.
1. Peter Kemp to Sir Wm. Cecill. Mrs. Haryngton recommends her son, John, to be elected a member [for Stamford?] although Sir William has preferred Mr. Robt. Wyngfield. Cecill's priest is given to daily intoxication. [*Much obliterated.*]

Dec. 1.
2. Marq. of Winchester to same. In favour of Sir Thos. Benger; recommends him to have a licence for 1,000 tons of beer. [*Much obliterated.*]

Dec. 5.
3. Estimate of the charges of victualling certain vessels for the sea.

Dec. 6.
Portsmouth.
4. Sir Wm. Keyllwey to Cecill. Has despatched Mr. Clayton and the carpenters to Newhaven. Asks leave to appoint a deputy.

Dec. 8.
Portsmouth.
5. Same to same. Has mustered part of Tremayne's band, 26 in number, able men and well mounted.

Dec. 9.
6. Extent or annual valuation of the lands of Edward Ludloe and Matilda his wife, deceased, now in the hands of the Queen, by reason of the minority of Robert Ludloe, their son and heir.

Vol. XXVI.

1562. Dec. 10. Rye.	7. John Young to Sir Wm. Cecill. Arrival of a number of French refugees from Dieppe and Rouen. Intelligence brought by them from France.
Dec. 13. Rynehousen, near Spires.	8. Tho. Windebank to same. Mr. Knolles is of opinion that Mr. Cecill should pass the winter at Strasburg. Windebank advises he should return to England, and not go to Italy; and that some other person should have charge of him.
Dec. 12.	9. Draft of the above.
Dec. 13. Rienhowsen, near Spires.	10. Thomas Cecill to his father. Met the Count Palatine at Heidelberg. Desires permission to return and see the war. His anxiety to leave Germany. Fr.
Dec. 13. Lambeth.	11. Guido Cavalcante to Cecill. Thinks the matter which he wishes him to transact will be best performed by his going in person. He will act with zeal and secrecy.
Dec. 14. Strond.	12. H. Alington to Tho. Windebank. Recommends him to return home with young Mr. Cecill.
Dec. 15.	13. Cecill to same. Leaves his son's going to Italy, or to return, to the discretion of Mr. Knolles and himself. His young son is dead.
Dec. 15. Portsmouth.	14. Sir Wm. Keyllwey to Cecill. Causes of delay of Mr. Worsley's passage; he departed on Tuesday. Arrival of Sir Hugh Poulet with the treasure in his charge, who with the French will embark on the morrow.
Dec. 15 (?)	15. Account, by Sir Wm. Keyllwey, of treasure received of Sir Hugh Poulet, for the service of Newhaven.
Dec. 17. Portsmouth.	16. Sir Wm. Keyllwey to Cecill. Embarkation of Sir Hugh Poulet, in the Aid, with the Frenchmen, to the number of 300. Order for transporting Mr. Tremayne's cavalry.
Dec. 18.	17. List of the Gentlemen Pensioners and Gentlemen at Arms.
Dec. 19.	18. Account of the charges of a new block-house erected at Upnor, upon Gillingham Water, but not yet completed.
Dec. 20. Strasbourg.	19. Windebank to Cecill. Urges the selection of Mr. Nowell to have charge of Mr. Cecill, and for his own recal.
Dec. 20. Burleigh.	20. Peter Kemp to same. Transactions at Burleigh. Has delayed the election of the Burgesses of Stamford. The parson of Thorpe Achurch is dead.
Dec. 23. Portsmouth.	21. Sir Wm. Keyllwey to same. The Phœnix has been obliged by contrary winds to put back. Arrangements necessary for victualling the ships.
Dec. 23. Rye.	22. John Young to same. Execution of a plot laid by Mons. Gaskin, to surprise the Castle of Dieppe. Ricarvele, the Governor, slain; and Gaskin now keeps the Castle for the King.

VOL. XXVI.

1562.
Dec. 24. 23. The Queen to Lord Wentworth and the Sheriff of Norfolk. Directions to send 600 soldiers by sea to Newhaven. 100 pioneers to be also provided for that place.

Dec. 25. 24. List of stores to be provided and bought for supply of Newhaven.

Dec. 25. 25. John Young to Sir Wm. Cecill. News from Dieppe. Particulars
Rye. of an action between the forces of the Prince and 500 Spaniards, at a place called Chartres. M. Montgomeri has not yet come to Dieppe.

Dec. 28. 26. Windebank to Cecill. Both Mr. Cecill and himself wish they were in England. Germany is not the place to acquire the accomplishments of a gentleman.

Dec. 30. 27. List of the Queen's ships now serving on the seas.

Dec. 31. 28. Sir William Keyllwey to Cecill. Francis Clarke has brought
Portsmouth. with him into Falmouth a Spanish vessel laden with wool, and other vessels with fruit and wine.

Dec. 29. Estimate of a proportion of provender for 300 horses, for four months.

1562 ? 30. Statement of the prices of bay and white salt, from the year 1544 to 1562, with names of the Lord Mayors of London for those years.

31. Resolution made at a Chapter holden by the Office of Arms, at the Embroiderers Hall, in London, as to crests and cognizances to be borne by heiresses, either maids, wives, or widows.

32. Account of the rental of the manor of Farsett, co. Huntingdon, with summary of the customs and privileges of the manor. Lat.

33. Extract from the Court roll of the manor of Farsett, of the lease granted to Rose Henson, and Richard Henson and Agnes his wife. Lat.

34. Mr. Tamworth's declaration of the names of such persons as have not paid their farms and tenths due at Michaelmas, in the county of Lincoln. Lat.

35. Note of armour and ammunition wanting in certain counties, required to be supplied from the Queen's store.

36. Note to the same effect, with similar requisitions for other counties.

37. Estimate of prices of corslets, harquebuses, and pistolets.

38. A note of the prices of armour, signed by Cecill.

39. Duplicate of the above.

40. Account of debts due upon specialties in the Court of Wards and Liveries ; arranged alphabetically.

Vol. XXVI.

1562 ?

41. Brief abstract of the heads of the Commission for Ecclesiastical Causes.

42. Copy of the above.

43. Indenture and Charter-party between the Queen and Thomas Lodge, Lord Mayor, and others, citizens of London, for setting forth two ships, the Mynyon and Prymrose, to pass, sail, and traffic in the parts of Africa and Ethiopia.

44. Points of difference between the covenants last made for the voyage to Africa and the present voyage, there being now only two ships, the Mynyon and the Prymrose.

45. Note of the covenants between the Queen and the Merchants Adventurers, trading to the coast of Africa.

46. Brief declaration of the value of the manors and possessions of the honour of Leicester, in the Duchy of Lancaster. Lat.

47. Memoranda, in Cecill's hand, of expenses of an army of 8,000 horse and 13,000 foot.

48. Brief declaration of the estate of inheritance of John de Vere, late Earl of Oxford, with limitations to various branches of his family.

49. Extent of Knight's Fees belonging to John de Vere, late Earl of Oxford, in various counties.

50. An order, by Sir Wm. Cecill, for the exercises and studies of Edward de Vere, the young Earl of Oxford, a minor.

51. Rental of divers manors and tenements in the counties of Essex, Cambridge, Chester, Northampton, and Warwick, the jointure of the late Countess of Oxford.

Vol. XXVII. January—February, 1563.

1563.
Jan. 1.
Portsmouth.

1. Sir Wm. Keyllwey to Sir Wm. Cecill. Arrival of a Breton vessel from Morlaix, laden with wines. Other vessels with similar lading expected. News from Dieppe.

Jan. 2.

2. Sir Wm. Cecill to the Sheriff of Lincoln. Thanks for being elected to represent them in Parliament. Declines the honour ; but is willing to aid and assist whoever they may elect instead of him. [*Much defaced.*]

Jan. 5.
Portsmouth.

3. Sir Wm. Keyllwey to Cecill. Complaint against Francis Clarke, for taking two Portuguese ships. The packet of letters detained above 20 days.

Jan. 7.
Portsmouth.

4. Geoffrey Vaughan to Lord Adm. Clynton. The bands of Mr. Tremayne were shipped with all their horses and furniture the preceding day.

Jan. 7.
Portsmouth.

5. Sir Wm. Keyllwey to Cecill. Tremayne's band of soldiers embarked ; are under sail on their way to Newhaven.

Vol. XXVII.

1563.
Jan. 8.
Portsmouth.
6. Sir Wm. Keyllwey to Sir Wm. Cecill. Departure of the Queen's ships for Newhaven. Has bargained with the Breton vessel for her cargo of sack; but the merchant will not discharge it at Newhaven.

Jan. 8.
Shene.
7. Countess of Lennox and Angus to Cecill. Complains of the hard usage she and her husband sustain after their submission to the Queen. Requests leave to retire to the country whence they derive their support.

Jan. 8.
8. The Queen to the Sheriffs of various counties. To levy and raise 100 labouring men in each, to serve as pioneers at Newhaven.

Jan. 9.
Portsmouth.
9. Sir Wm. Keyllwey to Cecill. Mr. Casselin is very desirous to have a portion of the sack bought of the Breton merchant.

Jan. 10.
Portsmouth.
10. Same to same. The ships for Newhaven put back by reason of contrary winds; also the Portuguese ship laden with oranges, one of Francis Clarke's prizes.

Jan. 10
Burleigh.
11. Peter Kemp to same. Payment of rents. Progress of works at Burleigh.

Jan. 11.
12. List of Knights of Shires and Burgesses returned to serve in the Parliament, at Westminster.

Jan. 11.
13. Tho. Windebank to Cecill. Gives his opinion that Mr. Tho. Cecill should return, as it hath pleased God to take away Cecill's younger son. Conversation with Otto Franciscus Ottomanus, on French affairs.

Jan. 11.
14. Same to Lady Cecill. Condoles with her on the death of her youngest son.

Jan. 12.
Portsmouth.
15. Sir Wm. Keyllwey to Cecill. Complains of the dilatory conduct of the Admiral in sailing for Newhaven. Suggests that a light boat should be dispatched weekly from Newhaven, with letters,

Jan. 16.
Portsmouth.
16. Same to same. The Admiral has not yet set sail for Newhaven. This delay proceeds from some wilfulness or bad advice.

Jan. 17.
17. Countess of Lennox and Angus to same. She does not blame him for the slow progress of her suits to the Queen, on the contrary, she has just cause to thank him for his advocacy.

Jan. 19.
Burleigh.
18. Peter Kemp to same. Transactions at Burleigh. [*Much defaced.*]

Jan. 20.
19. Certificate of the number of strangers, of all nations, remaining within the City of London, the Borough of Southwark, and the suburbs.

Jan. 20.
20. Duplicate of the above.

Jan. 20.
21. Notes in the handwriting of Sir Wm. Cecill, briefly referring to various persons and matters.

Jan. 21.
Burleigh.
22. Peter Kemp to Cecill. Particulars of receipts and disbursements on his account at Burleigh.

Vol. XXVII.

1563.
Jan. 22.
23. Resolution of the House of Commons, that the Burgesses for Tregony, St. Germain's, and St. Mawe's, Cornwall, Tamworth, in Staffordshire, and Stockbridge, Hants, shall repair to the House and shew Letters Patents why they are returned to serve in the present Parliament.

Jan. 22.
24. Notes of proceedings in Parliament (temp. Jac. I.) relative to the boroughs above named.

Jan. 23.
25. Sir Owen Hopton to the Council. Sends the depositions of Robert Garrerde as to slanderous words spoken by one Ed. [Baxter?] against the Queen. Baxter sent to Melton gaol. [*Much defaced.*]

Jan. 26.
26. Memorandum, in the hand-writing of Sir Wm. Cecill, of the charges of the force at Newhaven.

Jan. 27.
Portsmouth.
27. Sir Wm. Keyllwey to Cecill. Measures for victualling the pioneers. Francis Clarke has removed from St. Helen's, and is offended at the detention of his prize. Report of a defeat of the Guises.

Jan. 28.
28–30. Probates of the wills of William Lambe of Buttisbury, 1474; Alan Lambe of Finchley, 1549; and of James Lambe, clerk, Vicar of Henham, Essex, 1563.

Jan. 28.
31. Charter of Incorporation of the Merchant Venturers [Adventurers] of the city of Exeter. John Peter, the elder, to be the first Master; and Wm. Hurst, John Mydwinter, Gilbert Saywell, and Simon Knyght, to be the first four Wardens of the same.

Jan. 28.
Portsmouth.
32. Sir Wm. Keyllwey to Cecill. Certificate of victuals at Newhaven. Movement of the nobility, particularly of the two Dukes of Medina, against the Inquisitors of Spain. Arrival of Fr. Clarke at Newhaven.

Jan. 28 (?)
33. Speech in Parliament, setting forth the claims of the issue of Lady Frances Grey, daughter of Mary the French Queen, to the succession of the Crown of England; and excluding the claim of Mary Queen of Scots.

34. Another copy of the above.

Jan. 28.
35. Addresses of both Houses of Parliament to the Queen, that she would dispose herself to marry; and that she would settle the succession of the Crown in case she should die without issue.

36. Answer of the Queen to the above; delivered to Mr. Speaker Williams.

37. Copies of the above.

Jan. 29.
Antwerp.
38. Tho. Cecill to his father. His arrival at Antwerp. Desires to hear from him, as he was in doubt what to do. Is more desirous to return and see him than to re-visit Germany. Fr.

Jan. 30.
Portsmouth.
39. Sir Wm. Keyllwey to Cecill. Muster of labourers for Newhaven, who will be embarked forthwith. Slanderous reports circulated by persons returned from Newhaven, concerning wages due to them

Vol. XXVII.

1563.

Jan. 31. 40. Articles of Religion agreed on by the Archbishops, Bishops, and Clergy of the Realm, in Convocation at London, for avoiding of diversity of opinions, and establishing of consent touching true religion.

Jan. 31. 41. Another copy of the above, differing in the enumeration of the Canonical books.

Jan. 31. 42. Articles of Religion (as above) agreed upon by the Archbishops and Bishops of both Provinces, and the whole Clergy, in the Convocation holden at London, in the year 1562. Reprinted by command of King Charles II., with his royal declaration prefixed thereunto.

Jan. (?) 43. Minutes from divers Statutes touching the breeding, keeping, and exporting of horses.

Jan. (?) 44. Bill for regulating the importation and exportation of merchandize at the sea-ports of the realm.

Jan. 45. Message from the Queen to the House of Commons. Explaining her former message in the matter of the succession.

Jan. (?) 46. Bill for repealing part of the Act 25 Hen. VIII., touching the office of Faculties and Dispensations, and limiting the granting of the same.

Jan. (?) 47. Bill for reformation of "the abuse that cometh by impropria-"tions."

Feb. 1. Portsmouth. 48. Sir Wm. Keyllwey to Cecill. Begs to be informed of the time fixed for the return of Sir Adrian Ponynges to his charge at Portsmouth. Has given directions for the daily muster of the pioneers. The 200 from Hertford and Essex are left in charge of the conductors. Skirmish near Newhaven.

Feb. 1. Portsmouth. 49. Same to the Council. Stores of various sorts, delivered to John Vaughan, have been brought into the Armoury at Portsmouth. Arrival of labourers from Herts and Essex.

Feb. 3. Sackville Place. 50. Countess of Lennox and Angus to Cecill. Herself and her Lord cannot reckon themselves fully restored to the Queen's favor, unless they be admitted to her presence. Requests him to intercede with the Queen to that effect.

Feb. 8. Portsmouth. 51. Sir Wm. Keyllwey to same. The victuallers have sailed for Newhaven. The Earl of Warwick has requested him to discharge Francis Clarke's prize; desires directions therein. Has given orders for merchant ships in Southampton Water and off the Isle of Wight not to be molested.

Feb. 8. Portsmouth. 52. Same to same. The labourers were shipped and out of sight before he received the Council's letters. Will execute their orders on the next opportunity.

Feb. 10. 53. The Queen to Sir Wm. Keyllwey. Warrant to deliver 14,000*l.* to Sir N. Throkmorton.

VOL. XXVII.

1563.

Feb. 10.
Portsmouth.
54. Sir Wm Keyllwey to Sir Wm. Cecill. The proclamation, dated Westminster, Feb. 8, has been solemnly proclaimed by sound of trumpet; and forwarded to other post towns. The shipping of Merchant Strangers have been favourably dealt with. The ships with the labourers being driven back by stress of weather, he will now execute his former orders. [*The proclamation here alluded to was " against " suche as did helpe the Frenchmen to rob and take divers ships and " merchandise of the King of Spaine, and of divers other Merchants " Strangers."*]

Feb. 10.
55. Information by Cuthbert Berwicke against Sir Robert Brandling concerning the fraudulent conveying away of one Matthew Ellison.

Feb. 11.
Rye.
56. John Young to Cecill. Return of the ships with the 200 pioneers, except 26 of them who had been left on shore at Dieppe, where they remain.

Feb. 11.
Burleigh.
57. Peter Kemp to same. Receipts and disbursements on his account. Planting of young trees. Deer brought to the park at Burleigh. Cecill's mother is in good health.

Feb. 13.
Rye.
58. Ric. Overton to same. Has mustered the labourers, and found only 108 out of the 200. Payment which he has made after taking the muster. More money required.

Feb. 13.
Portsmouth.
59. Sir Wm. Keyllwey to same. Has discharged 100 of the labourers; the others are paid and re-embarked. Has also paid for the sack purchased by order. The Queen's ships stayed at Portsmouth.

Feb. 14.
60. Estimate of the value of the hulls, tackle, equipments, stores, &c. of the Queen's ships called the Brigandine and Flower de Luce, at their departure for Rouen.

Feb. 15.
61. Sir Ric. Sakevyle to Cecill. The Comptroller is content to be bound with the others. On the same paper:

Draft in Cecill's hand. The Queen to Mr. Comptroller (Sir Edw. Rogers), requiring him to enter into a joint bond with the Lord Treasurer and Under Treasurer, for repayment of 10,000*l.* borrowed of the City of London for the service at Newhaven.

Feb. 15.
Portsmouth.
62. Sir Wm. Keyllwey to Cecill. Has made the payments mentioned in his letter, without express warrant. The victuallers are daily demanding money.

Feb. 16.
Antwerp.
63. Dr. John Dee (the mathematician) to same. Has studied certain occult sciences, and repaired to Antwerp to put his labours to press. Solicits Cecill's advice as to his return. Has purchased a book, for which 1,000 crowns have been offered in vain, called the STEGANO-GRAPHIA, JOANNIS TRITEMII, meet and commodious for a Prince. Trusts Cecill will procure for him that learned leisure of which his country and the republic of letters shall reap the fruit.

Feb. 16.
Rye.
64. Ric. Overton to same. Has returned to Rye, after encountering a violent tempest. Hopes the labourers have reached Newhaven. 30 of the fleet set sail; hopes to hear good news of them.

Vol. XXVII.

1563.

Feb. 16.
Rye.
65. John Young to Sir Wm. Cecill. Arrival of Overton at Rye, and muster of the labourers. Report that the Admiral of France has taken Humflete.

Feb. 18.
Portsmouth.
66. Sir Wm. Keyllwey to same. Dispersion of the Newhaven fleet, and return of the greater part to Rye. Allowance must be provided for the returned labourers.

Feb. 20.
Portsmouth.
67. Same to same. Perceives that letters of the 18th have not been received. Departure of Sir N. Throkmorton. The labourers still remain at Rye.

Feb. 21.
Portsmouth.
68. Same to same. News from Newhaven. Monsr. Chastillon has put 2,000 men into Caen. Arrival of Throkmorton at Newhaven.

Feb. 24.
Portsmouth.
69. Same to same. Will provide a ship for Hugh Cownsell. Has received the Queen's letters for discharge of his accounts.

Feb. 27.
Portsmouth.
70. Same to same. Sends a packet from Sir N. Throkmorton. Sends also certificate of soldiers and labourers landed at Portsmouth. Their distress.

Feb.
71. Arguments, by Cecill, for increasing the navigation of England by encouraging the fisheries, and making every Wednesday a fish day. [*This is evidently the basis of the Act 5 Eliz. c. 5.*]

Feb.
72. Notes, in Cecill's hand, of clauses in a Bill for observance of fast days. Providing for three dishes of fish to one dish of flesh, on every Wednesday.

Vol. XXVIII. March—May, 1563.

March 2.
Portsmouth.
1. Sir Wm. Keyllwey to Sir Wm. Cecill. Exaction on the poor returned soldiers and labourers. The treasure is shipped for Newhaven. Is preparing to leave Portsmouth, to return home.

March 8
2. Warrant for delivery of the ship Jesus, of Lubeck, lent by the Queen to the Earl of Pembroke, Lord Robert Duddeley, and others, for a voyage.

March 8.
3. Certificate of all manner of shipping in the Cinque Ports, as it was 30 years ago, and at this day.

March 10.
4. Draft of a Bill (largely corrected by Sir Wm. Cecill), for the augmentation of small livings.

March 13.
Westminster.
5. Cecill to Gaspar Seler. Has obtained for him the Queen's licence to manufacture common salt in England. Advises him to come over directly. Lat.

Vol. XXVIII.

1563.
March 20.
6. Bp. Grindall to Sir Wm. Cecill. Will send to Velsius' lodgings, to bring him to Cecill, if he can be found. His turbulent disposition; whatever church he comes to, he stirs up dissension in it. Advises he should be ordered to depart. *Incloses,*

> 6. I. *Justus Velsius to the French Ambassador. Denouncing the vengeance of God on all who refused to receive his propositions. With notes thereon by Bp. Grindall. Lat. March 7.*
>
> 6. II. *Same to Calvin. With certain propositions laid down by Velsius contrary to Calvin's doctrines. Lat.*
>
> 6. III. *Summary of Religion by Justus Velsius, under the title " Christiani Hominis Norma," &c. Lat.*
>
> 6. IV. *Duplicate of the above, signed by Velsius.*
>
> 6. V. *Animadversions, by Bishop Grindall, on the propositions of Velsius' " Christiani Hominis Norma," &c.*

March 20.
7. Justus Velsius to the Queen. Expositions of his theological opinions, supported by numerous references to Scripture. Lat.

March 20.
8. Same to Cecill. Professes his zeal for the establishment of true religion. His dispute with the ministers of the Dutch Church in London, and his challenge to them. Lat.

March 21.
9. Declaration, by William Barlo, Bishop of Chichester, formerly Ambassador in Scotland, of his knowledge in the case of the Countess of Lennox, relative to the marriage of her father, the Earl of Angus, with Margaret Queen Dowager of Scotland.

March 21.
10. Similar declaration, on the same affair, by Wm. Lord Howard, Lord Chamberlain. Interview at Greenwich between Henry VIII., the Earl of Angus, Geo. Douglas his brother, and Lord Howard.

March 22.
11. Bill for the better observance of Fast Days, and regulating how many dishes of flesh shall be at table.

March 24.
12. Bill for the better maintenance of the Navy and mariners of England.

March 26.
Portsmouth.
13. Sir Wm. Keyllwey to the Council. Estimate for repair of a decayed wharf. Sir Adrian Ponynges has landed at Portsmouth.

March 29.
Hanworth.
14. Earl of Hertford to Lord Robert Duddeley. Grief which he endures by lying under the Queen's displeasure. Desires a reconciliation, and begs he will present the Queen, on his behalf, with a poor token of gloves.

March 30.
Portsmouth.
15. Sir Wm. Keyllwey to Cecill. Thanks him for his letters of " enlargement." The Frenchman of whom he wrote is not at Portsmouth.

VOL. XXVIII.

1563.

March 30. Portsmouth. 16. Sir Wm. Keyllwey to Marq. Winchester. Excuses himself fo having permitted the Frenchman to pass with the wines. Desires payment for his service at Portsmouth.

March. 17. Bill for the better increase of tillage; and for maintenance and increase of the Navy and mariners of the realm.

March. 18. Notes of amendments proposed in the above act, corrected by Cecill.

March. 19. Notes of the prices of wheat and other grain in several counties specified; relating to the above.

March. 20. Draft (in Cecill's hand-writing) of a clause to be inserted in an Act providing for the constitution of a Council of State in case of Her Majesty's demise. Noted as "not passed."

March. 21. Copy of the above.

March (?) 22. Bill for restraining all persons from "attempts or hopes to the "Queen's Majesties peril," forbidding them to assume a right to the succession of the Crown during her lifetime.

April 2. 23. Marq. of Winchester to Cecill. Report on the state of Her Majesty's causes in the Court of Exchequer. Answered Mr. Russell's and the Lady Kempe's case, yesterday. Plan for a wharf at Portsmouth. Advises Cecill to consult thereon with Sir Ric. Lee.

April 3. 24. Proportion for victualling 1,400 men for land service, 14 days; viz., 10 flesh days and 4 fish days.

April 10. 25. Act of Parliament granting to the Queen another subsidy on all manner of wools, wool-fells, and cloths, which after the last day of the present Parliament, shall be exported from the realm. [*Parl. prorogued, April* 10.]

April 10. 26. Note of the subsidy payable by the clergy and the laity, anno v. Eliz.

April 10. 27. Act of Parliament touching the account of the Sheriff of Northumberland.

April 10. 28. Bill for repealing the Act, 7 Edw. VI., regulating the prices of wines.

April 10. 29. Notes of the titles of various Acts of Parliament, from 1 & 2 of Philip and Mary to the 5th of Elizabeth.

April 14. 30. Cecill to Mr. Herd. Understands he has preserved certain collections and common place notes made by the late Archbishop Cranmer. The Queen thinks such a rare and precious treasure should not be hid in secret, and desires him to send up without delay the precious documents for perusal.

April 14. 31. Copy of the above.

VOL. XXVIII.

1563.

April 15. Westminster.
32. Warrant to Sir Edw. Rogers (Comptroller) to issue to Hugh Counsell certain sums, to discharge certain soldiers and workmen at Newhaven; also to receive monies on old Privy Seals, issued in Q. Mary's time.

April.
33. Particulars of Edward Dacre's leases of the parsonages of Plumpton, Bolton, and Langothbye, and of the rectories of Kyrkeland and Camberton.

April.
34. Answer of the Searchers of the Customs, to the articles alleged against them, in searching stranger's ships.

April (?)
35. Articles entitled "the doings of the Dean and Chapter of Worcester;" shewing in what manner they have violated the ordinances of King Henry VIII., the founder of their corporation

April (?)
36. Charges by Sir John Bourne against the Bishop of Worcester (Edwin Sandys), for abuses in the administration of the affairs of that See.

April (?)
37. The Bishop's answer to Sir John Bourne's book of information or accusation, which he entitleth "The doinges of the Busshop of "Worcetour."

April (?)
38. Declaration of the matters wherewith the Bishop of Worcester has charged Sir John Bourne in the Bishop's answer to the articles alleged against him by Bourne: with Bourne's answer in detail, charging the Bishop with much new matter.

April.
39. The Bishop of Worcester to the Council, in reply to the preceding declaration of Sir John Bourne, answering in great detail to the heinous crimes imputed to him by Bourne. Prays that the whole matter between him and Bourne may be heard at the Council Board.

April (?)
40. Summary of above answer of the Bishop of Worcester.

April (?)
41. A note of some of the apparent slanders, uttered by Sir John Bourne, Knt., against the Bishop of Worcester.

April (?)
42. Bishop of Worcester to the Council. Sir John Bourne has falsely charged him with misbehaviour in his episcopal office, and sought to blemish his parentage, his mode of living, preaching, and doctrine. Charges Sir John Bourne, in articles annexed, with various flagrant misdemeanors.

April.
43. Statement, by Francis Alen, touching his knowledge of the matters depending between the Bishop of Worcester and Sir John Bourne.

May 4.
44. Sir John Bourne to the Privy Council. Confesses his great offence, and that he has greatly misbehaved himself towards the Bishop of Worcester. [*Slightly mutilated.*]

May 4.
45. Copy of the above, before the mutilation.

May 4.
46. Notes and observations on the submission made by Sir John Bourne, respecting the Bishop of Worcester.

Vol. XXVIII.

1563.
May 7.
Portsmouth.
47. John Abington and Edw. Darell to the Council. Difficulty in procuring provisions for Newhaven. Delay for want of money, without which nothing could be done.

May 8.
Portsmouth.
48. Same to same. Scarcity of provisions in Newhaven. Negligence of the Commissioners. Nothing can be done without an immediate supply of money. Statement of provisions, &c. sent to Newhaven.

May 10.
Portsmouth.
49. John Abington to same. Is sorry for the untrue report of scarcity at Newhaven. On hearing the rumour he and Mr. Darell agreed to go to Arundel and ship such provisions as could be obtained there.

May 20 (?)
50. Note by Cecill, of several matters relating to supply of men, stores, &c. for Newhaven. To think of a Marshal there.

May 20.
Westminster.
51. Minute of the Privy Council, that certain Officers and Jurats of the Cinque Ports had produced a copy of their charter, by which it appears that they are exempt from any charge by Privy Seals.

May 21.
Westminster.
52. The Queen to the Lord Treasurer. Warrant for the Merchants of the Stillyard to transport yearly out of the realm 5,000 cloths unwrought.

May 21.
53. Draft of the above, corrected by Cecill.

May 21.
Westminster.
54. The Queen to Edward Randolph, appointing him High Marshal of the Garrison at Newhaven.

May 21.
55. List of the Captains and Lieutenants serving in Kent.

May 22.
56. Receipt by Arthur Goldyng, for a half year's rents, collected by John Dawe, Bailiff of the manor of Colbrooke, Devon, due to the Earl of Oxford.

May 22.
57. Memorandum of money received by Arthur Goldyng for the use of the Earl of Oxford.

May 24.
58. Certificate of John Purevey, Feodary of the county of Herts, in return to the Commission for survey of the manors, lands, &c. of John, late Earl of Oxford.

May 24.
Westminster.
59. The Queen to Lord Cobham, Warden of the Cinque Ports. To fit out such vessels as shall be needful to make reprisals on French vessels, not to plunder them, but to take a perfect inventory of the goods they may contain.

May 24.
60. Draft of the above, in Cecill's hand.

May 26.
61. The Queen to the Lord Mayor of London. Commanding him to allow Captain John Shute and others to levy 600 men within the City of London, to be employed on service at Newhaven.

May 26.
62. Receipt by Arthur Goldyng, for 20*l.* of Jerom Balborowe, Bailiff of the manor of Christen Malford, co. Wilts, due to the Earl of Oxford.

May 27.
63. Names of as many prisoners as be in Newgate fit to be pardoned, and that be able to serve.

Vol. XXVIII.

1563.
May 29.
Portsmouth.
64. Sir Henry Sydney to the Council. Has conferred with Mr. Darell and other officers as to provisions at Newhaven. Materials to make gabions provided by Sir Adrian Ponynges. Deficiency of money. News from Newhaven. Capt. Tremayne killed there.

May 30.
Court.
65. The Queen to the Sheriff of ⸺. Commands him to pay into the Exchequer, all sums due on account of his Sheriffwick.

May.
66. Same to the Marq. of Winchester, Sir William Petre, Sir Richard Sakevyle, Sir Walter Mildmay, Robert Kelwey, and Gilbert Gerrard, Att. Gen., appointing them Commissioners for the sale of Crown lands.

Vol. XXIX. June—August, 1563.

June 7.
1. Wm. Wynter, *not signed*, to Lord Adm. Clynton. Forwards a letter from the Earl of Warwick, and denies having made the Earl any promise to send him six-score mariners to Newhaven for manning two pinnaces.

June 10.
2. List of gunners to be sent from Berwick, Harwich, and Carlisle, to Newhaven.

June 23.
Greenwich.
3. The Queen to the Lord Lieutenant of Berks. To raise a certain number of men in the county forthwith, provided with corslets, at the least charge to the county.

June 24.
4. Another list of gunners to be sent from Carlisle and Berwick to Newhaven.

June 25.
5. Statement of the numbers of men appointed to be levied in several counties of England, for service at Newhaven.

June 26.
Dover.
6. Philip Strelley, Arthur Higham, and others, Captains of the Norfolk and Suffolk levies, to the Council. Arrived off Dover, and the fleet scattered in a great tempest. Want provisions.

June 26.
Dover.
7. E. Dryver to Lord Robert Duddeley. Embarked with the Norfolk levies, and met at Harwich the soldiers from Suffolk. A great tempest has dispersed the fleet.

June 28.
8. Petition of Arthur Golding, uncle of Edw. Earl of Oxford and Lady Mary his sister, for staying a suit begun against the said Earl and Lady Mary by Catherine, wife of Sir Edward Windsor; the said Earl being a minor, and the Queen's ward. Lat.

June 29.
9. Return, by Lord Mordaunt and Justices of Essex, of the rates and assessments of 1,000 men, to be levied within that county; and stating the principle on which the same had been made.

June 30.
10. The Council to Lord Rich. Directing him to carry into effect the principle laid down by Lord Mordaunt and other Justices of Essex, in the levying 1,000 soldiers in that county.

P

Vol. XXIX.

1563.
June 30. Portsmouth.
11. Sir Adrian Ponynges to Sir Wm. Cecill. Has sent to Rye to Mr. Darell to gain intelligence of the ships dispersed in the late storm. A ship of London, laden with beer, run ashore near the Camber.

June 30.
12. Anthony Anthony to same. Two ships have been laden with the Queen's stores for Newhaven. Requests an advance of 200*l*.

June. Greenwich.
13. The Queen to John Newdigate. Directs him, as trustee of the late Thomas Wilks, to convey two houses and gardens to William Wilks, brother of the deceased.

June (?)
14. Note of reparations necessary at Colne House and Hedingham Castle and Park, belonging to the Earl of Oxford.

July 3. Portsmouth.
15. Sir Adrian Ponynges to Cecill. News brought from Newhaven : batteries erected commanding all the outlets from the town.

July 3.
16. Memorandum in Cecill's hand-writing, of stores to be provided for Newhaven.

July 5.
17. Another memorandum in Cecill's hand, relating to Newhaven.

July 6. Portsmouth.
18. Sir A. Ponynges to Cecill. Measures for transporting soldiers to Newhaven, which is surrounded on all sides. Skirmish in which Captain Saunders was shot. The plague continues there.

July 6. Portsmouth.
19. Same to same. The plague rages at Newhaven. The 1,200 men lately sent will scarcely supply the deficiency. The enemy increasing ; trenches and batteries opened against the place. Great want of pioneers.

[July 7.]
20. The Aldermen and Society of the Stillyard to same. Requests renewal of their licence for exporting 5,000 cloths.

July 7. Greenwich.
21. The Queen to the Marquis of Winchester. Warrant for the Company of Merchants of the Stillyard to export 5,000 cloths.

July 8.
22. Same to Sir Fr. Knollys, Vice-Chamberlain. Directions to proceed to Portsmouth to superintend the supply of victuals, soldiers, and pioneers for service at Newhaven. On the back is a cancelled draft of a letter, dated 23d June 1563, to the Sheriff, &c. of Wilts, as to provision of armour for the levies raised in that county.

July 8.
23. Same to Sir Arthur Champernowne, Vice-Admiral of Devon. To deliver up to the bearer certain persons arrested on suspicion of offences at sea, in order to be employed in the Queen's service.

July 9. Portsmouth.
24. Sir A. Ponynges to Cecill. Report from Newhaven that the plague has abated. Signior Melurine landed at Portsmouth from thence.

July 10. Portsmouth.
25. Sir Fr. Knollys to same. Has written to the Earl of Warwick, at Newhaven. Armour for that place will be shipped that night. Victualling of soldiers. Arrival of 600 men from Gloucester.

1563.

VOL. XXIX.

July 12.
Portsmouth.
26. Sir A. Ponynges to Sir Wm. Cecill. Concerning delivery of armour and weapons to such soldiers as are sent out of Somersetshire. They have not yet arrived.

July 12.
27. Marq. Winchester to same. Victualling of Newhaven. Sends letter from Sir Maurys Denys. Money wanted to pay the army there. *Incloses,*

> 27. I. *Instructions to Lord St. John, concerning victualling Newhaven. 12 July.*

July 13.
Berks.
28. Brief declaration of all the manors, lands, &c. in the counties of Berks and Wilts, whereof Sir Francis Englefyld is seised in his own or his wife's right, &c.

July 13.
29. List of the manors, lordships, and hundreds held by Sir Francis Englefyld in right of Lady Katherine, his wife.

July 14.
London.
30. Pieter de Reulx to Cecill. Has attended Court to explain why 500 crowns demanded of him by Sir Thomas Gresham for the woode [woad ?] partly restored at Newhaven, have not been paid.

July 15.
31. Marq. Winchester to same. Desires him to procure safe convoy for a purveyor of butter and cheese to Newhaven. *Incloses,*

> 31. I. *Wm. Foster to Marq. Winchester. Gives particulars of certain quantities of butter and cheese, which he has procured for Newhaven. Ipswich, 14 July.*

July 15.
32. Same to same. Is glad he has applied for the victualling money for Newhaven. Arrival at Dover of wheat and malt out of Norfolk. Butter shipped. Orders given for brewing beer.

July 16.
Greenwich.
33. The Queen to the Sheriff and Justices of Huntingdon. To levy and arm 200 soldiers; and to send them to Portsmouth for embarkation.

July 16.
Portsmouth.
34. Sir Fr. Knollys to the Council. Need of reinforcements at Newhaven. Has taken measures for levying men. Victualling of the place to be effected with all diligence. Has sent to the Isle of Wight for armour and weapons.

July 16.
Portsmouth.
35. Same to Cecill. Is glad to hear of 9,000*l.* being advanced for provisions for Newhaven. Explains as to Admiralty stores. Wood required for fires at Newhaven. Gabions to be supplied, &c.

July 17.
Portsmouth.
36. Same to same. Has sent into Hampshire and Sussex for a supply of 2,000 men. Prevalence of the plague at Newhaven; and vigorous proceedings of the enemy. Has shipped 700 men for that place.

July 18.
Portsmouth.
37. Same to same. The convoy has sailed for Newhaven; and other supplies will be sent to the Earl of Warwick with all possible speed. The Lord Admiral is at sea. Has caused woolpacks to be placed in three hoys to protect the soldiers from the enemy's shot.

Vol. XXIX.

1563.
July 18. 38. Note of the number of men appointed to go to Newhaven.

July 22.
Portsmouth.
39. Sir Fr. Knollys to the Council. Forwards letters from the Earl of Warwick. The supply for Newhaven seems to be too late. He has therefore, by Mr. Wynter's advice, stayed the 1,319 men, turned back by contrary winds. Advises to conclude a peace, or to abandon the town.

July 23.
Portsmouth.
40. Same to Sir Wm. Cecill. Complains of Mr. Wynter having stayed the troops intended for Newhaven. To conclude a peace would be the best measure, especially if the French perceive that the town cannot hold out. Arrival of fresh levies. Loss of services of the Marshal (Randolph) and the Comptroller (Vaughan).

July 24.
South Foreland.
41. Lord Adm. Clynton to the Council. Stormy weather. The galliots have taken refuge at Harwich. Intends immediately to ascertain the state of Newhaven.

July 25.
Portsmouth,
42. Sir Fr. Knollys to Cecill. Sends copies of letters from the Earl of Warwick, and note of the number of men and provisions sent to Newhaven. *Inclosing,*

    42. I. *Note of the number of soldiers sent to Newhaven from several counties. July 25.*

    42. II. *Note of provisions remaining in Newhaven: with note on the back, by Mr. Abington, as to remains of wines there. July 22.*

July 26.
Portsmouth,
43. Same to same. The convoy of men and victuallers driven back by stress of weather. Great want of victuals at Newhaven. Desires to know whether on that consideration he shall stay the sending over of more men. Has conferred with Mr. Wynter as to the best means of bringing away the Earl of Warwick and the troops.

July 26.
The Downs.
44. Lord Adm. Clynton to same. Henshawe, Captain of the Aid, has proceeded with letters from the Earl of Warwick to the Court. The French have approached Newhaven so near that none can enter or come out.

July 27.
Portsmouth.
45. Sir Fr. Knollys to same. Mr. Wynter, with the Phœnix and the Falcon, has sailed for Newhaven, with 1,200 men and victuals. Wishes the Earl of Warwick and his force were well returned. Trusts that a convenient peace will end the present troubles.

July 27. 46. Account of emptions made for supply of Newhaven; and charges for transporting the same thither, &c. since 22d May.

July 28. 47. Account of military stores sent over for the furniture of Newhaven, between the 22d of May and the 26th July; with the supply to be sent to Portsmouth on the 28th.

July 28.
Portsmouth.
48. Sir Fr. Knollys to Cecill. Doubts if he can send over the letter for the Earl of Warwick. Proclamation making Frenchman's goods prizes. Has stayed Hugh Counsell and the treasure; but has sent 3,000*l.* over to Newhaven. Hopes for a speedy peace.

VOL. XXIX.

1563.
July 31.
Portsmouth.

49. Sir Fr. Knollys to Lord Clynton. Is glad to hear of his arrival off Newhaven to assist the Earl of Warwick. Difficulty of entering the harbour. Wishes to know if the men sent by Mr. Wynter have been able to disembark. [*This letter was probably not sent in consequence of Warwick's arrival at Portsmouth.*]

July 31.
Portsmouth.

50. Lord Adm. Clynton to Sir Wm. Cecill. Ships left at Newhaven under charge of Mr. Wynter to bring off the garrison. Embarkation of the Earl of Warwick. Has been visited by M. de Lynerols, sent with a message from the French Court. Told him the plague had done more for the success of the French than their arms.

July 31.
Portsmouth.

51. Sir Fr. Knollys to same. Return of the Captains sent for Newhaven under Mr. Wynter. The Earl of Warwick had given up Newhaven to the French, under certain conditions. Will send shipping to bring off all the troops.

July 31.
Portsmouth.

52. Same to the Queen. Notifies the arrival of the Earl of Warwick at Portsmouth; who after a little rest will wait on Her Majesty.

July 31.
Portsmouth.

53. Warwick to the Council. Has advertised the Queen of the order and manner of his departure from Newhaven. Intends on the morrow to go to Mr. White's at Southwick, until he be better able to travel.

July 31.
Portsmouth.

54. Thos. Wood to Lord Robert Duddeley. Passage of his brother, the Earl of Warwick, by sea; so sick, that the pain of the wound in his leg was forgotten. His preservation has been miraculous.

July.

55. Note of charges of coat and conduct money for soldiers sent from Huntingdon to Portsmouth.

August 1.

56. The Queen to the Archbishops of Canterbury and York. To give orders for a day of general prayer and fasting throughout the realm, on account of the plague.

August 1.

57. Proclamation, signed by the Queen, declaring the true causes of the delivering up of Newhaven, and return of the Earl of Warwick. Recommending the captains and soldiers to the charitable succour of their fellow subjects, on their return to their habitations.

August 2.

58. Sir Fr. Knollys to Cecill. Great numbers of men arrive from Newhaven, without captains or officers; and there is no money for their discharge. Fears some disorder will fall out among them.

August 4.
Windsor.

59. Commission by the Queen to Lord Scrope, Sir John Forster, and others, to treat with Scotland for matters of the Borders.

August 4.

60. Instructions to the said Commissioners.

[August 7.]
Bagshot.

61. Lord Robert Duddeley to the Queen. Thanks her for the gracious advertisement, in her own hand-writing. Regrets having so soon visited his brother (Warwick), lately returned from Newhaven. Will refrain from her presence, till commanded, for fear of introducing the plague at Court. Has stayed his brother's coming till Wednesday.

DOMESTIC—ELIZABETH.

Vol. XXIX.

1563.

August 21. 62. The Queen to the Lieutenant of the Tower. Directions to remove Lady Catherine Grey and the Earl of Hertford from the Tower, on account of the plague; the former to Sir John Grey's house in Essex, the latter to that of his mother's in Middlesex.

August 27. 62. Sir Wm. Cecill to Sir Wm. Petre. Congratulates him on some recent preservation of himself and lady. Reminds him of Mr. Stafferton's matter, for a copyhold of the manor of Burfield, parcel of Mr. Talbot's estate.

Vol. XXX. September, 1563.

Sept. 21. 1. Lord Keeper Bacon and Sec. Cecill to the Countess of Rutland. Directions for the burial of the late Earl to take place as soon as convenient, on account of the plague now prevailing.

Sept. 22. 2. Note of armour from Newhaven, belonging to various counties, delivered to Davy Savior, Master Gunner of Portsmouth.

Sept. 22. 3. Indenture of bargain and sale of the site of the capital messuage and mansion house, commonly called the Minories, without Aldgate, by William Marquis of Winchester, to the Queen, her heirs and successors, for ever.

Sept. 22. 4. Note of the evidences of the conveyance of the dissolved Monastery of the Minories, without Aldgate, from the 30th Hen. VIII. to Queen Elizabeth; to be used by her as a magazine or store-house.

Sept. 29. 5. Account of fees and wages due to the Lieut. and others of the Tower, to Michaelmas 1563.

Sept. 29. 6. Account of the rents of the manors of Thorncombe and Colbrook, of the estate of the Earl of Oxford, to Michaelmas 1563.

Sept. 29. 7. Account of Thomas Lee, Deputy of Jerome Balborowe, Bailiff of the manor of Cristen Malford, co. Wilts, belonging to the late Earl of Oxford.

Sept. 29. 8. Account of customs and subsidy paid on woollen cloths and wines, for four years ending Michaelmas, anno reg. Eliz. v°.

Vol. XXXI. October—December, 1563.

Oct. 1. 1. Sir Wm. Cecill to Mr. Lenard. In favour of an offer of marriage made by Mr. Googe for the daughter of Mr. Thomas Darell, opposed by Mr. Lenard.

Vol. XXXI.

1563.	
Oct. 1.	2. Sir Wm. Cecill to Mr. Tho. Darell. On the same subject, in favor of Googe.
Oct. 1.	3. Warrant by way of assignment for the charges of the Queen's household, payable out of various offices.
Oct. 15.	4. Balthazar Raynestorp, "the Styliarde Secretary," to Cecill. Has received from Mouritz Ranzew and Pawell Brookdorp, a letter from the Duke of Holstein to the Queen's Highness, with which, by reason of the infection, they have been unable to attend the Court.
Oct.	5. George Lord Zouch, and others, Justices of Northampton, to same. Thanks for relieving the county of purveyors. Offer to furnish certain provisions of sheep, oxen, &c. for the Queen's household.
Oct.	6. Note of the assessment on the Lord Mayor and Aldermen of London, for the first payment of subsidy, in anno 5 Eliz.
Oct.	7. Account of disbursements for repairs done at Colne House in Essex; signed by John Glascock, Feodary, and delivered to the Earl of Oxford.
Nov. 2. Kimbolton.	8. Justices of Huntingdonshire to the Council. Request payment of coat and conduct money for the 200 soldiers levied in the county, and sent to Portsmouth in July last.
Nov. 6.	9. The Queen to Marq. Winchester. Licence for the Merchant Adventurers to transport a certain quantity of broad cloths. Allowance for a debt due to them to be made on the customs payable thereon.
Nov. 17.	10. The Council to the Earl of Worcester. The Queen has heard of the disagreement between him and his wife. He is commanded immediately to repair to the Court, and in the meantime to take no further steps in the affair.
Nov. 18.	11. The same to Marq. Winchester. Declining to set apart any sum of money to make up the deficiency in the customs occasioned by the small quantity of cloths shipped by the Merchant Adventurers. Other items of expenditure to be first provided for.
Nov. 29.	12. The Queen to same. To license George Lundy and Robert Monbury, Scotchmen, to depart for Scotland, with their ship laden with wines.
Nov. 30.	13. John Prestall to Cecill. Eulogizes his great qualities. Requests letters of protection that he may safely come to make answer to certain charges preferred against him.
Nov. 30.	14. The Queen to the Officers of Customs. Prohibits the exportation of woollen cloths by any natural subject or stranger until further notice.
Nov. 30. Norwich.	15. Duke of Norfolk to Sir Wm. Cecill. Denies being the originator of certain reports. Reminds him of what the Queen said when she made him one of her Council.

Vol. XXXI.

1563.
Nov. (?) 16. Abstract of the several numbers of footmen divided out of several shires into small companies : total 300.

Dec. 1.
Apthorp. 17. Sir Walter Mildmay to same. Understands, by Lawrence Mayedwell, that he was desirous to have the articles of composition for supply of provisions for the Queen's household. *Incloses,*

> 17. I. *Articles for making a composition with the Queen's officers for provision of beefs, muttons, and lambs to be delivered yearly for the service of Her Majesty's household, for the county of Leicester.*

Dec. 7.
Exeter. 18. John Chidley to Tho. Williams, Feodary of Devon. Has paid in the rents received from the manor of Thorncombe, due to the Queen, during the minority of the Earl of Oxford.

Dec. 11. 19. Account of the prices of white salt in the City of London from the time of the mayoralty of Sir George Barne, 1552.

Dec. 13.
Herefelde. 20. Robert Newdegate, Feodary of Bucks, to Sir Wm. Cecill. Sends up by the bearer, John Newdegate, three-score pounds, which is all he has received of the Michaelmas revenue of the Earl of Oxford.

Dec. 20. 21. Account of silver and gold bullion delivered by John Bull, Comptroller of the Mint, to Richard Candeler, Factor for Sir Thos. Gresham.

Dec. 20. 22. Estimate of the value of bullion when made into certain denominations of foreign coin.

Dec. 20. 23. The Queen to John Bull, Comptroller of the Mint. Warrant to convert 12,000*l.* sterling money into bullion, and to deliver the same to Sir Thomas Gresham.

Dec. 21. 24. Account of the weight and number of certain silver bullion received into the Tower by Mr. Bull, Comptroller of the Mint, and by Ric. Candeler.

1563 ? 25. Proclamation prohibiting all " payntors, pryntors, and gravors " from drawing Queen Elizabeth's picture, until " some conning person " mete therefor shall make a naturall representation of Her Ma$^{ty's}$ " person, favour, or grace," as a pattern for other persons to copy. [*Draft in Cecill's hand. As this curious proclamation is not given in Humfrey Dyson's list of Queen Elizabeth's proclamations, it probably was never published.*]

26. Declaration of the account of William Bromefield, Lieut. of the Ordnance, for carriage of munitions to West Chester.

27. Warrant for expediting payments to be made by Sheriffs into the receipt of Exchequer.

28. Notes concerning the plurality of ecclesiastical benefices. Lat.

VOL. XXXI.

1563.

29. Account of the possessions and hereditaments of John de Vere, late Earl of Oxford, with statement of the assignment of the same to the Queen, the present Earl, and other parties.

30. Statement of all manors, lands, tenements, &c. belonging to Edward, Earl of Oxford, in the county of Cornwall, demised by lease or by copy of court roll.

31. Note of the rents of such of the Earl of Oxford's tenements as are void in Cornwall, and of the fines offered for the same.

32. Notes of the Earl of Oxford's rents in various counties: in Cecill's hand.

33. Another note of the Earl of Oxford's rents.

34. Application, by Thomas Browne, Feodary of Cornwall, to Sir Wm. Cecill, for lease of certain parcels of the Earl of Oxford's lands ,in Cornwall.

35. Directions for preventing the infection of the plague, for dressing and fumigating chambers, with a description of the symptoms which occur on a person's falling sick, and the remedies to be immediately applied.

36. Gilbert Gerrard, Att. Gen., to Sir W. Cecill. His opinion as to the punishment to be inflicted on one Compton, for forging a warrant from Lord Duddeley for transporting horses.

37. Copy of the above.

38. Note by Wm. Rosewell, Sol. Gen., of the grant of the advowson of the parsonage of Northchurch, the closes of Longstable-mead and Castle-mead, to be contained in Sir Tho. Benger's bill.

39. Names of certain doctors and scholars, graduates of Christ's College, Oxford, and in other colleges.

40. Names of students of Christ Church, Oxford, who entered that college before King Henry VIII. died, and proceeded in learning and degrees ; also names of forward young men still remaining there.

41. Notes of the days of the year appropriated for fish days, on certain fasts and festivals of the Church, and for every Wednesday.

42. Calculation of the number of holidays and fast days in the year ; probably for fish days.

43. Petition of John Awger to Lord Robert Duddeley. Requests him to move the Lord Admiral to let him have a hoy, called the George, in compensation for his hoy lost in the Queen's service.

44. Answer of William Bowyer, touching the claim of Mr. Newdigate, to the Bailiffwick of Westminster.

45. Grant to John Glynne of so much as he can recover and receive of the goods, chattels, and money, devised by Dr. Francklyn, late Archdeacon of Durham, for superstitious uses.

Vol. XXXI.

1563 ?

46. Proportion of victuals for 1,000 men for one month, with the charge thereof.

47. Account of the number of communicants, the value of livings, and deficiency of preachers, in several deaneries in Lancashire.

Vol. XXXII.

1563 ?

MSS. bound in vellum, stamped on the covers, "Elizabetha Regina," describing the founders and benefactors of various Colleges in Cambridge; and the names of all those at present in the University.

Vol. XXXIII. January—April, 1564.

1564.
Jan. 4.
Windsor.

1. Geo. Carew to Sir Wm. Cecill. With respect to two Privy Seals, directed to Mr. Somers and Mr. Bruerne, Canons of Windsor College.

Jan. 8.
Stafford Castle.

2. Edw. Lord Stafford to same. Complains of an outrage committed by one Bowyer, who claims to be Keeper of the Records in the Tower, on a servant of Lord Stafford's deputy, and depriving him of Stafford's key of the Records, which he prays may be restored. *Incloses,*

    2. I. *Considerations why the Queen's Highness' Records ought not to be kept under one man's key; detailing Lord Stafford's labours in arranging the Public Records in the Tower. Jan. 8.*

Jan. 10.

3. Proclamation prohibiting the importation of French wines, by reason of the enmity between England and France.

Jan. 14.
Exeter.

4. John Dawe to Cecill. Has paid the money due at Allhallowtide into the hands of Ric. Sherlonde, who could not repair to the Court on account of the sickness in London.

Jan. 15.

5. Indenture between the Queen and Caspar Seeler, for the sole manufacture and sale of white salt in England, for the term of 20 years.

Jan. [ ]

5 *a.* Heads of articles of licence and indenture with Caspar Seeler and Peter de Ruse, for the making and sale of white salt in England. [*No date, but probably near in date with the preceding.*]

Jan. 16.

6. The Council to Lord Tfer. Winchester and another Lord. Summoning them, by command of the Queen, to attend a conference concerning certain matters relating to the King of Spain.

Jan. 17.

7. Ceremonial of the interment of "the noble and puissant Princesse "Margaret Duchesse of Norfolk," at Norwich.

Vol. XXXIII.

1564.

Jan. 20. 8. Indenture between Wm. Clopton and Wm. Porter, indorsed " This is the copy of the false deede which Grivel and Porter caused a " suborned personne to acknolege afore a M^r. of the Chauncery, in the " name of Clopton, wherby Porter conveyed to himself all Clopton's " lands."

Jan. 22. 9. " A short fourme of thankesgevyng to God for ceassing of the " contagious sickness of the plague, to be used in Common Prayer ; " set forth by the Byshop of London, to be used in the Citie of London, " and the rest of his diocesse." " Printed by Richard Jugge and " John Cawood, printers to the Quene's Majestie."

Jan. 23. 10. Receipt by John Wood, Steward of Lord John Gray, of Pirgo, for fourteen weeks diet of Lady Hertford and her train.

Jan. 24. 11. Note of charges incurred by Lord Grey of Pirgo, for Lady Hertford, her son, and servants, since her enlargement from the Tower and her coming to Pirgo.

Jan. 28. 12. Tho. Browne to Cecill. Has taken a survey of the Earl of Oxford's lands within the county of Cornwall, and certified the same to the Court of Wards and Liveries. *Incloses*,

    12. I. *Breviate of the rents of the Earl of Oxford's lands in Cornwall, shewing the annual value of the same.*

Feb. 3. 13. Receipt by Wm. Seres, of certain rents in Cornwall, from Tho. Browne, on accompt of Sir Wm. Cecill.

Feb. 12. 14. Receipt, by Sir John Tyrell, for the sum of 15*l*. for a year and a half's annuity, out of the manor of Christen Malford.

Feb. 14. 15. John Mershe to Sir Wm. Cecill. Forwards a letter. The plague having ceased, he requests the prohibition of exportation of cloth may be annulled.

Feb. 20.
London. 16. Same to same. Request of certain merchants trading with France to export cottons, kerseys, &c., and import canvas, thread, lockrams, &c. Hopes the prohibition of trade with Flanders will soon be removed.

Feb. 21.
Hertford. 17. Sir Nich. Bacon to Lord Robert Duddeley. Complains of the answer made to a former letter, which he thinks it did not deserve ; is certain his intention did not.

Feb. 24.
Lambeth. 18. David Lewes, Judge, and others of the Admiralty Court, to the Council. Concerning a ship of Dundee, stayed at Lowestoft, by Wm. Smith, of Woodbridge, for which certain Scottish merchants claim redress.

March 1. 19. Warrant to the Chamberlain of the Exchequer, to repay the amount due to each particular person on producing their Privy Seals for money lent to the Queen.

March 3. 20. The Council to Sir Adrian Ponynges. Concerning a complaint made of his having taken some wine out of a Spanish ship, at Portsmouth, and committed two of the crew to custody.

Vol. XXXIII.

1564.
March 8. — 21. The Council to certain Vice-Admirals. The Queen's proclamation for restraining piratical depredations on the seas to be observed. Daily complaints are made of spoil committed on the subjects of Spain.

March 8.
London. — 22. John Mershe to Lord Robert Duddeley. The Company of Merchant Adventurers are earnest suitors that the Easterlings should be restrained from shipping cloths.

March 8.
London. — 23. Sir Wm. Chester and others, Merchant Adventurers, to same. Praying that the suit of the Easterlings for licence to ship and transport from England to their own country sundry sorts of cloths, may not be granted.

March 8.
London. — 24. Same to Sir Wm. Cecill. Urging the same request as the preceding.

March 8.
London. — 25. John Mershe to same. Thanks for his care for the Company of Merchant Adventurers, who will be ruined if the Easterlings succeed in their suit.

March 15. — 26. Same to same. The Merchant Adventurers are preparing their fleet. Sends draft of a licence to export 30,000 cloths, which the Queen reserved to the Merchant Adventurers in her licence to Lord Robert Duddeley.

March 18.
Hanworth. — 27. Edw. Earl of Hertford to Lord Robert Duddeley. Thanks for the honourable reception his mother has had at Court. Prays for restoration to the Queen's favour, which would turn their mourning, as captives, into comfort.

March 22. — 28. Duddeley to Hertford. Has moved the Queen on their behalf for their further liberty, which was not disliked. Lord Hertford's mother also has done her part. He must wait the event with patience.

March 23. — 29. Proclamation remitting the distribution of the Maundy by the Queen in person, in the present time of contagious sickness; but alms will be given to the poor of Windsor and Eton.

March 23. — 30. Another copy of the above, with corrections by Cecill.

March 23. — 31. Proclamation licensing English merchants to export cloths into any foreign parts except the Low Countries, and prohibiting the importation of any merchandize from thence.

March 25. — 32. Declaration of the accounts of all the officers of the lands and possessions of Edward, now Earl of Oxford, for two years ended at Lady Day, anno vi. Eliz. Lat. and Eng.

March 25. — Account of the rents and profits of lands and manors in various counties in England and Wales, of the annual value of 403*l*. 13*s*. 8*d*., to be granted to Ambrose, Earl of Warwick, and the heirs males of his body. Lat. [*Case* A., *Eliz.* No. 11.]

March 30.
Windsor Castle. — 33. The Queen to the Lord Treasurer. Order that no cloths should or a time be exported to the Low Countries or imported therefrom. Charge to be given to the officers of the ports to give effect thereto.

March 30. — 34. Draft of the above, in Cecill's hand.

VOL. XXXIII.

1564. March 30.	35. John Mershe to Sir Wm. Cecill. Complains of one Lawrence Coxsoon illegally shipping cloths at Colchester, for Flanders. Asks for a passport for the Commissaries of Emden.
March 30.	36. Sir Wm. Cecill to Bishop Grindall. Signifies that the Queen has granted a pension of 2,000 crowns per annum to John of Emden, Count of Friesland. Utenhovius to be made acquainted with it.
April 1.	37. Lord Robert Duddeley to the Earl of Hertford. Has delivered his handy work as required. Will further the greater matter as opportunity may occur. The Queen's clemency should inspire good hope.
April 1. Windsor.	38. The Queen to Winchester. Licence to be given to certain persons to export coloured cloths to Dantzic.
April 1. Westminster.	39. Bond of Wm. Porter, of Aston Underedge, co. Gloucester, to Lodovic Grevile, of Milcote, Warwickshire, in the sum of 2,000*l*. Lat.
April 3.	40. Edw. Randolph, Lieut. of the Ordnance, to Cecill. Concerning a contract for gunpowder for the Queen's service. *Incloses*,
	40. I *Estimate of the rate of a last of corn powder, made within the realm.*
April 5.	41. Marq. Winchester to same. Desires to know what is to be done with the merchant and his goods who clipped the money. Order with the Merchant Adventures. Desires to know if vessels laden in Flanders before the proclamation are to be permitted to come in.
April 5. Hertford Castle.	42. Sir Nich. Bacon to Duddeley. Gives his opinion concerning the traffic to the Narve, which if discontinued he thinks the best traffic for the realm would be lost. Desires to know if he may come to the Court.
April 6.	43. Articles devised for the reformation of sundry disorders in the forests, chaces, and parks belonging to Her Majesty, north of Trent, committed to the charge of George Earl of Shrewsbury.
April 6. The Court.	44. Earl of Warwick to the Earl of Hertford. Has received his letter by Ireland, his servant. Is willing to do him any possible service.
April 6.	45. Marq. Winchester to Cecill. Desires to be spared attendance at St. George's feast. Requests a licence from the Queen for the two children to pass the seas, and directions what is to be done with the prisoner who clipped the gold.
April 6. Mapledurham.	46. Sir Ric. Blount to same. Perceives that the Queen has granted the Provost of Paris leave to come from Oxford to London. Cannot take upon him to leave the Provost at any place in London but the Tower.
April 7 (?)	47. The Queen to Winchester. Order to be taken for admission of vessels arrived from the Low Countries laden before the late proclamation. Cannot dispense with his attendance at St. George's feast. The clipper of coin to be prosecuted.

1564.
VOL. XXXIII.

April 8.
Antwerp.
48. Sir Fr. Englefyld to Sir Wm. Cecill. Complains of malicious insinuations against him to the prejudice of his suit to Her Majesty. Professes great loyalty and reverence. Sends copy of the assignment of his wife's revenues, which he intreats may be faithfully performed. *Incloses,*

> 48. I. *Account of rents, annuities, &c. to be paid out of the revenues of the lands of Dame Katherine Englefyld, by Mr. Stafford and Mr. Yate, during the absence of Sir Fr. Englefyld. May 8,* 1559.

April 8.
Antwerp.
49. Same to the Council. Prays them to intercede with the Queen in his favour. States at great length his circumstances, the causes that have induced him to remain abroad, confutes the slanderous imputations against him, and supplicates the Queen's forgiveness.

April 9.
50. John Mershe to Cecill. Sends him a letter received from the City of Hamburgh. Effects of the late proclamation relative to the trade of the Merchant Adventurers with the Low Countries.

April 11.
Barrow.
[Berghem op Zoom.]
51. Francis Berty to Mr. Thomas [Heneage ?]. Shipment of pans and other implements for making salt, to be set up in England.

April 12.
52. Merchant Adventurers to Cecill. Request that the late proclamation by the Queen may be explained, for the Netherlanders bring the commodities of the Low Countries through France. Frauds used to deprive the Queen of her customs.

April 13.
Windsor.
53. The Council to Marq. Winchester. To permit Lewis Scape and others, merchants, subjects of the King of Spain, to export, duty-free, certain goods taken out of the ship Tiger, by one Corbett, and reclaimed by them.

April 14.
54. Marq. Winchester to the Customers, &c. of the Port of London. To permit the above goods to be exported duty-free.

April 14.
55. The Queen to Winchester. To give orders to prevent the importation of commodities from the Low Countries through France.

April 14.
Canterbury.
56. Archbp. Parker to Cecill. Requests his advice as to certain letters sent to him by Mr. Knox and other ministers, concerning a question of divorce in Scotland. [*This refers to the case of Anne Goodacre, wife of John Baron, a minister of the Kirk, summoned to appear before the Consistory Court in Scotland, to answer the charges brought against her by her husband. See Scotland,* 1563, *Dec.* 29, *and* 1564, *Feb.* 10.]

April 15.
London.
57. John Mershe to same. Sends him a map of East Friesland. Has received from Ric. Ellice a copy of the Queen's letters explanatory of the proclamation.

April 16.
Hanworth.
58. Earl of Hertford to same. Is about to send the bearer, his [younger] brother, Edward Seymour, to the University. Recommends him to Cecill's favour.

April 16.
Hanworth.
59. Same to Lord Robert Duddeley, by the same bearer, and to the same effect.

Vol. XXXIII.

1564.
April 16. 60. **The Queen to Winchester.** Directions for the great Venetian ship lying off Margate, to repair to Southampton, and take in her cargo there, to prevent fraud on the customs; also to prevent the exportation of rams and sheep to Spain.

April 16.
Newport (in Flanders). 61. **Lord Cobham to Sir Wm. Cecill.** Arrival of the Lady Marques (Elizabeth Brooke, daughter of Lord Cobham, and wife of Wm. Parr, Marq. of Northampton), himself and his wife, on their way to Antwerp. Stay of shipping in Flanders.

April 20. 62. Account of the rate of provisions for the Office of Ordnance, to be made yearly in time of peace for furnishing the said office; and the supply necessary for various ports and garrisons specified.

April 20. 63. Estimate of the charges of erecting new platforms for the ordnance at the Tower of London.

April 20.
Windsor. 64. Proclamation declaring the conclusion of peace between England and France.

April 20 65. Copy of the above.

April 21. 66. **Sir Wm. Cecill to Winchester.** To permit Arnold Birkman and Conrad Mullar, of Cologne, to unlade certain books shipped at Frankfort before the proclamation. Also for four boxes of green ginger to be landed by the said parties.

April 23.
Antwerp. 67. **Lord Cobham to Cecill.** Effects of the stay of shipping. Arrived with the Lady Marques at Antwerp. She has consulted the physicians and surgeons, " and as yet they agre not of the curyng of her " breste."

April 23. 68. Narrative of the ceremonies observed in celebrating St. George's feast, by the Sovereign and Knights of the Garter at several periods, from 1561 to 1564, with the installation of various Knights during those periods.

Vol. XXXIV. May—September, 1564.

May 2. 1. **Bishop Grindall to Sir Wm. Cecill.** Sends copy of a commission for a collection to be made in Essex for repair of St. Paul's. His opinion about Dr. Boner's oath.

May 3. 2. **Bishop Cox to same.** Proposes a revision of the Bible, in order that one uniform translation may be used. Has been strangely used by Dr. Thirlby. Requests the Queen's letter therein.

May 3.
London. 3. **Tho. Aldarsey to same.** Is ready to undertake the voyage to Emden, and endeavour to the utmost of his power for the success of the same. Objects to Italians being allowed to export kersies. Observations on establishing a commercial intercourse with Emden.

Vol. XXXIV.

1564.
May 4.
Hanworth.
4. Earl of Hertford to Lord Rob. Duddeley, by his brother Henry Seymour. Hopes through his mediation to be restored wholly to the Queen's favour.

May 5.
Richmond.
5. The Council to Marq. Winchester. Licence to be given to the Merchants of the Stillyard to export the residue of 5,000 unwrought cloths to such places only as lie beyond Emden eastward.

May 7.
Hanworth.
6. Earl of Hertford to Lord Rob. Duddeley. Thanks for being permitted again to write to him. Still hopes by his means to be restored to the Queen's favour.

May 13.
The Arches.
7. Dr. Lewes to Sir Wm. Cecill. State of the case of three Frenchmen committed to the Marshalsea, taken prisoners by Wm. Rogers, and who were detained in prison by Mr. Appleyarde.

May 14.
8. The Queen to Archbp. Parker. Directions to receive and entertain M. de Gonnor, at Canterbury, coming over as Ambassador from the French Court.

May 14.
9. Same to the Earl of Abergavenny. Similar directions to meet the French Ambassador at Dover, and to escort him through Kent to Greenwich.

May 14.
10. Same to the Lieutenant of Dover Castle. To join with the Sheriff of Kent in honourably receiving the French Ambassador.

May 14.
11. Same to the Sheriff of Kent. To prepare for the honourable reception of the French Ambassador at Dover, and to escort him to Rochester.

May 15.
Hanworth.
12. Earl of Hertford to Duddeley. The Queen's continued displeasure overwhelms him. Begs he will intercede in his behalf.

May 19.
Hampton Court.
13. Wm. Huggon to Cecill. Mr. Appleyard's name affixed to the bill sent by Cecill, is not his signature. Liberation of some Englishmen detained in France, is required, for certain Frenchmen detained in England.

May 20.
Court.
14. Lord Robert Duddeley and Sir Wm. Cecill to the Earl of Hertford. Desiring him to send 114*l*. to Pirgo, to defray the charges of Lady Catherine Grey (his wife) while in the custody of Lord John Grey her uncle.

May 21.
Paris.
15. Nicholas de Lemborch (called Ost) to Cecill. Concerning the expense which he has incurred in the matter of coinage.

May 21.
Paris.
16. Same to the Queen. Great profit will arise to her from the mode of coinage which he has communicated to her through her Ambassador.

May 22.
17. List of the gentlemen of Kent appointed to meet M. de Gonnor, the French Ambassador, at Dover.

Vol. XXXIV.

1564.

May 25. Dover.
18. Wm. Crispe to the Council. Inquiry respecting the ill usage received by Angier de la Strille, a French merchant, prisoner at Dover.

May 25.
19. Marq. of Winchester to Sir Wm. Cecill. Suit of Mr. Vice-Chamberlain (Sir F. Knollys) and his lady, touching the exchange of Taundeane [Taunton Dean?] and its members, for other lands belonging to the Queen, near Reading, in Berkshire.

May 25.
20. Copy of the above.

May 25.
21. Sir Wm. Cecill to Sir Tho. Offeley, Mayor of the Staple. Sends for his consideration copy of clause in the confirmation of privileges about to be granted to the Merchant Adventurers.

May 26.
22. Marq. of Winchester to the Council. Details particulars of his late communication with the Merchant Adventurers and Merchants of the Stillyard.

May 26.
[Privy Council] to [the Lieutenant of the Tower?]. Committing the Earl of Hertford to his custody, and discharging him of Fr. Newdegate, who is to confine himself to his own house. [*See Borders, 26th May.*]

May 30. London.
23. John Mershe to Cecill. News received from Emden of the arrival there of the cloth fleet. Sends a proviso for the Company of the Staple.

May (?)
24. Fr. Newdegate to same. Contradicts Sir Thos. Smith's report of his speech touching the Duke of Bedford, and the proposed marriage of the " Swecian " with one of my lady's daughters.

June 1.
25. Copy of survey of the manor of Chakendon, Oxford, by John Cupper, Feodary there.

June 3. Bekesbourn.
26. Archbp. Parker to Cecill. Particulars of a conversation which he has had with M. de Gonnor, the French Ambassador, on the subject of religion, and state of the Church in England.

June 7.
27. Marq. of Winchester to same. Sends minutes of letters for the North. Survey of the castles of Norham, Wark, and Harbottle necessary. Has sent a book of the certificates of five bishops relative to void benefices within their dioceses. Has written to the Bishop of Durham.

June 10.
28. The Council to the Sheriff of Kent. Complaints of the non-attendance of the gentlemen of Kent on the entry of the French Ambassador. Commands the Sheriff to see that better attendance be given on his return. Lord Abergavenny is appointed specially to attend him.

June 21.
29. Account of various sums of money received by Wm. Cooke, for the use of the young Earl of Oxford.

June 22.
30. The Queen to Marq. Winchester. To permit subjects of the French King to import wines and woad in their own vessels, notwithstanding the statute to the contrary.

VOL. XXXIV.

1564.
June 24.   31. Note of the charges of felling and preparing timber for the flooring of the church in God's House; the Hospital at Portsmouth.

June 27.   32. Order in Council permitting French subjects to import wine or woad into the realm; to export cottons, friezes, and north country cloths, &c.

June 30. Richmond.   33. The Queen to Sir Geo. Howard, Master of the Armoury. Warrant to make a complete suit of armour for Christopher Hatton, Gentleman Pensioner; to be delivered to him on his paying the just value thereof.

June.   34. Treatise on a French decree relative to the coinage, and regulating the exchanges. Proposing a re-issue of coinage, with offers on the part of Capt. Oste [Lemborch?] to give the fullest explanations. Translated from the French.

July 1.   35. The Queen to the Mayor, &c. of Cambridge. Prohibiting them from licensing any victuallers or tiplers in the town, against the privileges of the University. *Incloses*,

     35. I. *Extract from the Queen's grant of additional privileges to the University, relating to the licensing of alehouses and victuallers. 26 April 1561.*

July 11.   36. Marq. Winchester to Sir Wm. Cecill. Sends Mr. Lamplugh's bill of reparations for the city of Carlisle, the castle and town wall being in great decay. Is prevented from attending the Queen at Greenwich.

July 16.   37. Estimate of the charges of a ship at the rate of 2s. per ton the month, and of the monthly wages to the officers and company.

July 17. London.   38. John Utenhovius to Cecill. Concerning a pension of 2,000 French crowns promised to the Count of Emden. Lat.

July 24.   39. List of divers grants and incorporations made to the Merchant Adventurers of England from the time of King Henry IV.

July 24.   Lease in reversion from James Calfhill, Prebendary of St. Pancras, to Henry Spence, of meadows and pastures in Kentish Town, in the parish of St. Pancras in the Fields, for 31 years. [*Case A. Eliz.* No. 12.]

July 27.   40. Grant by the Queen to the Mayor, &c. of Gloucester, of the House or Hospital of St. Bartholomew, and the lands, &c. thereto belonging, for the purpose of maintaining 40 poor people, a minister, a physician, and a surgeon.

July 27. London.   41. John Utenhovius to Cecill. As Michaelmas Day is approaching, it will be necessary to make some answer to John Count of Emden, concerning his promised pension. Lat.

July 31.   42 Proclamation for observance of peace with foreign Princes, and to repress piracies and depredations on the seas.

VOL. XXXIV.

1564.
August 1. 43. The Council to Sir Henry Nevill and Robert Keyllwey. To exhort the clothiers of Reading and Newbury not to give over the exercise of their trade, and thereby throw many out of employment.

August 3.
Westminster. 44. Grant of the capital messuage and park of Copthall, in Essex, in reversion, to Thomas Heneage and Ann his wife, as held of the Duchy of Lancaster, by the service of the 40th part of a knight's fee.

August 9. 45. Theological disputations held at the University of Cambridge, in presence of Her Majesty. Quest. 1. "Major est Scripturæ quam Ecclesiæ auctoritas." Quest. 2. "Civilis Magistratus habet auctoritatem in rebus Ecclesiasticis."

August 12.
London. 46. John Shers to Sir Wm. Cecill. With the substance of all his week's advices. *Incloses*,

46. I. *Substance of the advertisements from Venice, Genoa, and Poland. The Pope's speeches in the Consistory, touching the advantages of granting permission for the administration of the Sacrament in both kinds. Council of Trent. Affairs of Corsica. San Pietro Corso. Affairs of Sweden. 40,000 Tartar horsemen had entered Moscovy.*

August 20. 47. The Queen to Sir Francis Jobson. Appoints him Lieutenant of the Tower, in the room of Sir Ric. Blount, deceased.

August 22. 48. Acknowledgement, by Henry Howard, that he is indebted to Edward Randolph, Esq., in the sum of five pounds.

August 26.
London. 49. John Shers to Sir Wm. Cecill. Is glad he approves of his communicating the foreign advices.

August 29. 50. Marq. of Winchester to the Council. Has received the French Ambassador's letter for delivery of the fustians to a French merchant. The Merchant Adventurers object to the importation of wares from the Low Countries, through France.

August 30.
Greatford. 51. Edmund Hall to Cecill. Has been at Burleigh, and conferred with Kemp and Norris. Progress of buildings there. Calls to his remembrance the poor Merchants of the Staple. The state of trade between Flanders and England must be well considered.

August 31.
London. 52. John Shers to same. Sends foreign advices. *Incloses*,

52. I. *Advices from Venice. Death of the Emperor Ferdinand, and accession of Maximilian. Reduction in the Pope's household. The Genoese had determined to enter Corsica against San Pietro Corso, who threatens to roast alive all the Genoese that fall into his hands. 6 August.*

August (?) 53. Manuscript treatise in Italian, on the use and study of history, dedicated to Sir Robert Duddeley, afterwards Earl of Leicester, by Giacopo Acontio.

DOMESTIC—ELIZABETH.

Vol. XXXIV.

1564.
Sept. 2. 54. Depositions of certain persons, made upon oath before Dr. Hawford, Vice-Chancellor of Cambridge, and others, relative to a tumult at that place, in which Mr. Slegge and Mr. Serle were concerned.

Sept. 3.
London. 55. Dr. Valentine Dale to Sir Wm. Cecill. Desires instructions how to act on the application of the French Ambassador for release of a Frenchman, in custody at the suit of a Fleming.

Sept. 3. 56. Marq. of Winchester to same. On the coming of the French gentlemen to Windsor and Hampton Court, has sent orders to have the houses put in order. Proceedings between the Merchant Adventurers and Merchants of the Stillyard. The Ambassador of France daily applies for free intercourse between France and England.

Sept. 5. 57. Same to same. Details as to shipment of cloths by the Merchants of the Stillyard.

Sept. 10. 58. Articles proposed for amendment of the new drawn charter of incorporation of the Company for the working of Minerals.

Sept. 10. 59. Memorial of Thomas Thurland, Master of the Savoy, and Sebastian Spydell, and their Company, desiring their grant for working of mines and minerals in certain counties in England and Wales may be transferred and assigned to Daniel Hechstetter.

Sept. 10. 60. Statement of the articles contained in the book of privilege to be granted to Thomas Thurland and Daniel Hechstetter, for working mines and minerals in certain parts of the realm.

Sept. 14. 61. Articles describing the outrageous conduct of Mr. Serle, on his being brought before the Vice-Chancellor of Cambridge, and of his rescue by Mr. Slegge.

Sept. 14. 62. Information of Thos. Errant and John Ludham, as to words spoken by Mr. Serle, in contempt of the Proctor's authority.

Sept. 23. 63. Estimate of the wages and victuals for 280 mariners and gunners to serve in the Swallow and Aid, for two months.

Sept. 29. 64. Ceremonial of the creation of Sir Robert Sutton, *alias* Dudley, to be Baron of Denbigh and Earl of Leicester. On the same paper, the creation of William Lord Berkeley as Viscount Berkeley.

Sept. 29. 65. The Queen to Sir Peter Carew. Commands him immediately to fit out two vessels to clear the coasts of Devonshire and Cornwall from pirates which have lately infested there.

Sept. 66. William Herlle to [Cecill?] Concerning Monsr. de la Strille, whom the French Ambassador maintains is not lawfully a prisoner. Urges his own interest in the prisoner.

Sept. 67. Brief account of sums due by the Receivers of various counties on declaration of their accounts.

[Sept.] 68. Mem. by Sir Wm. Cecill of matters of most weight to be considered in the treaty of the Entercourse.

Vol. XXXIV.

1564.
Sept. (?) 69. Account of charges for celebrating the obsequies of the late Emperor Ferdinand, in London, with the names of the creditors, and sums due to each.

Vol. XXXV. October—December, 1564.

1564.
Oct. 2. 1. Account of wares exported and imported without paying customs, contrary to the proclamation; principally wools and cloths.

Oct. 3. 2. Account of charges of making great ordnance, specifying the weight of each piece, with the cost for the whole.

Oct. 10. 3. Extract of an indenture made by the Queen on one part, and Thomas Thurland and Daniel Hechstetter on the other, for the discovery and working of minerals.

Oct. 11. 4. Articles for the establishment of good order, very necessary to be executed amongst the victuallers of the city of Westminster, by Henry Williams, Dep. Clerk of the Market.

Oct. 12. 5. The Queen to Sir Peter Carew. Approves of his readiness in suppressing pirates. Allowances to the parties employed.

Oct. 12. 6. Note of charges for victuals for 246 persons serving in the ships which Sir Peter Carew was commanded to send to sea to capture the pirates.

Oct. 19.
St. Paul's. 7. Alexr. Nowell, Dean of St. Paul's, to Sir Wm. Cecill. Claim of the officers of the Great Wardrobe to certain pieces of coarse cotton with which the walls of the choir of St. Paul's were hanged at the exequies performed for the late Emperor. Prays such claim may not be allowed, as they are the perquisites of the inferior officers of the church.

Oct. 20. 8. Marq. Winchester to the Council. Sends them a paper from the records of the Wardrobe, touching the disposal of all things decorating the hearse of Princes. Claim of the Earl of Arundel.

Oct. 24. 9. Articles sent down by the Council for examination of divers persons, concerning Henry Serle and Roger Slegge, late Mayors of Cambridge.

Oct. 24. 10. Examinations of divers persons on the above articles concerning Serle and Slege, taken before Dr. Hamford, Dr. Perne, and others.

Oct. 26. 11. Note of the sale of certain parcels of cast iron ordnance, by Mr. Randolph, Lieut. of the Ordnance.

Oct. 12. Account of the annual value of the lands, parcel of the manor of Kenilworth, given to Lord Robert Duddeley, on his being created Earl of Leicester.

Vol. XXXV.

1564.
Oct. (?) 13. Note of lands which the Earl of Leicester doth offer to part with by exchange to the Queen.

14. Copy of the above, with slight variations.

Oct. 15. Memorandum of sums received by Sir Peter Carew for service against the pirates, and his suit for a warrant for an advance of 400*l*. more.

Nov. 8.
London. 16. Bishop Grindall to [the Master of the Savoy]. Order is to be taken with the inhabitants of the Strand to unite them to certain parishes, and desiring him to give notice to that effect on Sunday next in the Savoy Church.

Nov. 8.
St. James's. 17. The Queen to Dr. David Lewis, Judge of the Admiralty Court, Dr. Robert Weston, Dean of the Arches, and others. Constituting them Commissioners to enquire into complaints of piratical depredations committed at sea on the subjects of the King of Spain. Lat.

Nov. 10. 18. Account of the remain of armour in the Queen's several armouries.

Nov. 20. 19. Note of the charges that Her Majesty is at in the castles and bulwarks within the Cinque Ports.

Nov. 20. 20. Memorial of the Merchant Adventurers to the Council. Have at great expense provided ships for the newly established route to Medea and Persia. Request that William Bond and his partners be restrained from trading to the Narve.

Nov. 25. 21. Answer of William Bond and John Foxall, merchants, to the bill of complaint exhibited against them and others, to the Privy Council, by the Company of Merchant Adventurers.

Nov. 25. 22. Answer of Bond and Foxall to articles exhibited against them by the Governors, &c. of the Merchant Adventurers. Showing that the traffic of the said Bond and Foxall to the Narve is in no way prejudicial to that Company.

Nov. 25. 23. Replication of the Governors, &c. of the Merchant Adventurers to the above answer of Bond, Foxall, and others, trading to the Narve.

Nov. 24. Notes concerning the exportation of cloths by English and foreigners by the Merchants of the Stillyard, and the importation of goods from the Low Countries.

Nov. 25. Account of the yearly value of all the manors, lands, and hereditaments in the counties of Wilts and Berks, being the possessions of Sir Francis Englefyld, now seized into the Queen's hands, with the annuities and pensions payable out of the same.

Dec. 3. 26. Tabular account of the lands and revenues of Edw. Earl of Oxford, by Mr. Wiseman, the Auditor. Lat.

Vol. XXXV.

1564.
Dec. 9.
Westminster.
27. The Queen to the Lord Chief Justice and Solicitor General. Directing them to assist and advise the Earl of Sussex, in holding a Court for redressing disorders within the forest of Windsor, and for preservation of the vert and venison there.

Dec. 10.
28. Company of the Merchant Adventurers to the Council. Memorial concerning the course of trade and commerce to various countries in Europe and other parts of the world.

Dec. 12.
29. Marq. Winchester to Sir Wm. Cecill. Concerning the application of the Merchants of the Stillyard and the Merchant Strangers to ship cloths.

1564?
30. An estimate of the charges for the Office of the Armoury within the Tower of London, and in divers other places.

31. Duplicate of part of the above, with an additional article, and an account of decayed armour.

32. Account of all such armour as was received by the Master Gunner of Portsmouth, of divers captains that came from Newhaven.

33. Reasons for withholding the restitution of commercial intercourse with Antwerp, and for restraint of foreign traffic.

34. Note of the customs levied in France on wines.

35. List of names of all persons to whom William Flower, Norroy King at Arms, has granted arms since he was created Norroy.

36. Licence to John Dunning and Wm. Haynes the Queen's Purveyor of Sea Fish, to bring into the realm all manner of cod-fish and lings, and other fish commonly called green fish or green cod, in barrels or casks.

37. Note of the several commodities brought into the realm from divers foreign parts.

38. Bond of the late Dr. Cuthbert Scott, of Finchingfield, Essex, to remain within twenty miles distant of that place, and to make his personal appearance before the Commissioners Ecclesiastical when duly summoned.

39. Regulations for the customers and collectors and their deputies, in every creek and port, as to entries and subsidy to be taken of all cloths, wares, and merchandise exported from the realm.

40. Request of the Merchant Adventurers to Guinea to have two of the Queen's good ships, the Minion and the Primrose, placed at their disposal. Her Majesty to receive a third part clear of the gains of their voyage.

41. Account of divers parcels of silver and gold plate given by the Queen to several Ambassadors, and at various christenings.

DOMESTIC—ELIZABETH.

Vol. XXXV.

1564 ?

42. William Carre to Sir Wm. Cecill. Thanking him for his patronage. Lat.

43. Latin verses, addressed to Sir Wm. Cecill, by John Studley.

44. Notes concerning the tenure of Her Majesty's manors of Newbury and Cosham.

45. Bartholomew Dodington to Sir Wm. Cecill. Complimentary, and thanking him for favours shown whilst at the University. The whole academy deeply indebted to him for procuring the exemption of the University from public burdens and securing to them the favour of the Queen. Gr.

46. Tho. Richmond, John Olam, Wm. Olyfe, and others, to Tho. Sackford, Master of Requests, on behalf of themselves and others, prisoners at Feccamp, to aid the suit of John Redman in raising money for their ransom.

47. Names of Justices of Assize, with their shires: probably in 1564.

Vol. XXXVI. January—July, 1565.

1565.
Jan. 15.

1. Survey of the manor of Ernewood, co. Salop, taken by Roger Taverner, by warrant from the Marq. of Winchester, Sir Ric. Sakevyle, and Sir Walter Mildmay.

Jan. 20.

2. Complaint of English merchants trading to Iceland, that one Symonde Surback holds the Island of Westmonege of the King of Denmark, and prevents their trade there.

Jan. 24.

3. Note of a memorial to be presented to Sir Wm. Cecill, concerning the English merchants at Emden.

Jan. 25.

4. Articles declaring the commodity or discommodity that the Queen may have in using or forbidding the traffic at Emden.

Jan. 25.

5. Another copy of the above.

Jan. 28.
Whaddon.

6 Arthur Lord Grey of Wilton to Cecill. The debt claimed by the Marquis de Nesle, as due to him by Lord Grey's late father, was paid to Nichs. Tremayne, as will appear by his acquittance.

Jan. 30.
Salisbury.

7. Bishop Jewell to same. Reasons which prevented him from making a shorter answer to Harding's book. Desires not to be called to preach before the Queen in the ensuing Lent.

Vol. XXXVI.

1565. Jan.	8. Note of all such sums as remain unpaid in the Exchequer, upon warrants.
Feb. 1.	9. Names of persons to whom arms have been granted by Garter King at Arms, in the first year of the Queen's reign; also of persons and corporate bodies to whom arms have been given by consent of the Duke of Norfolk.
Feb. 1.	10. Note of arms granted by Clarencieux King at Arms, since the Duke of Norfolk's order to the contrary.
	11. List of persons to whom patents for armorial bearings have been issued by Clarencieux King at Arms, from the 1st to the 7th of Elizabeth.
Feb. 7.	12. Memorial of Cornelius de Alneto, *alias* Lannoy, to the Queen. Offering to produce for Her Highness' use 50,000 marks of pure gold yearly, on certain conditions. Lat.
Feb. 9. London.	13. Cornelius de Lannoy, *alias* de Alneto, to the Queen. Shows that he has acquired great skill in the transmutation of metals, and repeats the offers made in the preceding. Lat.
Feb. 10.	14. Stephen Bagat to Sir Wm. Cecill. Particulars of the receipts from the Earl of Oxford's lands at the manor of Acton Trussel, Staffordshire.
Feb. 13. Westminster.	15. Special Commission by the Queen, appointing Sir Francis Knollys, Sir Ambrose Cave, Sir John Mason, and others, Commissioners for examination of persons committing murders, burglaries, and other felonious offences.
Feb. 13.	16. Account of the whole remain of the Queen's armour within her several armouries at the Tower, Greenwich, Westminster, and Hampton Court.
Feb. 17.	17. The Queen to the Attorney General. Order for suspending certain ordinances lately made in Parliament for opening the intercourse of merchandise with the Low Countries.
Feb. 20.	18. Account of ordnance wanted within the Office of Ordnance, for supply of the Queen's ships.
Feb. 23.	19. Note of broken ordnance of brass remaining in the hands of the Queen's gun-founders; also of the copper and bell metal in the Ordnance Office.
Feb. 24.	20. The Queen to Mr. Justice Brown. Directs him to hold the next Justice Court of the Forest of Waltham, in place of the Earl of Sussex, who cannot attend at that time; and minute of same letter to Mr. Attorney, for Windsor Forest.
Feb.	21. Dr. Lewes to Cecill. Desires directions as to cancelling the recognizances of John Vaughan.

1565.

Feb. 22. Estimate of charges for the representation of various plays and masques before the Court, at Windsor Castle and Richmond, in several years from 1563; amounting in the whole to 444*l*. 11*s*. 5¾*d*. Indorsed "for the revels."

March 14. The Tower. 23. John Fecknam, Priest, to Sir Wm. Cecill. Forwards the correspondence between himself and the Bishop of Winchester touching the Queen's supremacy, in which he requested to be instructed on that point by authority of the Scriptures, Doctors, and General Councils.

March 14. Northampton. 24. Justices of Northampton to Sir Wm. Cecill and Sir Walter Mildmay. The inhabitants of the hundred of Neasabrough refuse to supply provisions for the Queen's household. Request to have some special warrant to compel them.

March 20. Keswick. 25. Tho. Thurland, Master of the Savoy, to Cecill. Has received his letters, with the report and assay of the copper ore. The report made by those who assayed it is incorrect.

March 20. 26. Proclamation against forcibly resisting process issued out of sundry Courts of Record.

27. Fair copy of the above, with further corrections.

March 25. 28. Sir Ric. Malorye, Lord Mayor of London, to Cecill. Informs him of the regulations made for the sale of butter, eggs, and butchers meat in the city. *Incloses*,

28. I. *Recognizance for keeping a victualling house in the city of London.*

March 26. 29. Account of ordnance and munitions to be provided for supply of the Office of Ordnance.

March 31.] 30. "Estimate for the funeralles of ye Lady Marques" of [Northampton]. Containing particulars of many curious items incidental to the funeral of a personage of high rank.

March 31. 31. Account of the debts of the Lady Marques, amounting to 1,879*l*. 6*s*. 8*d*.

March 31. 32. Memorandum of instructions, by Humphry Marbury, addressed to his cousin, Marbury, for purchasing certain quantities of grain in France.

April 7. 33. Sir Walter Mildmay to Cecill. Has forwarded the indentures between the Queen and Mr. Bashe, drawn according to agreement. Recommends sending Parkinson, the butcher, to Berwick.

April 9. 34. Alexander Fitz Jeffrey to same. Assures him of his devotion to his service, and of his desire to fulfil the charge with which he has been entrusted. Lat.

April 15. Cambridge. 35. Lord Edward Seymaur to same. Thanks him for his patronage and for recommending him to the Master of Trinity College, Cambridge. Lat.

Vol. XXXVI.

1565.
April 14.
Farnham Castle.
36. Bishop Horn to Sir Wm. Cecill. Has written to the Earl of Leicester a reply to Mr. Fecknam's book. Sends Cecill a copy of the letter. *Incloses*,

    36. I. *Bp. Horn to the Earl of Leicester. Observations on the conference between himself and Mr. Fecknam, the Priest, and on the misrepresentations which the latter has published of that matter. Farnham, 14th April 1565.*

April 17. 37. Ric. Tracy to same. The Holy Scriptures command the people to root out and destroy images. Recommends that the Queen should forbid any graven image to be placed, or tapers to be lighted, on any altar.

April 17.
Mohuns Ottery.
38. Sir Peter Carew to the Council. Services of his ships against pirates. Arrest of a hulk of Stukeley's in Cork Haven. Unsuccessful attack on the pirates Haydon, Lysyngham, Corbet, and others, who had withdrawn into a castle belonging to O'Sullivan Beer, at Beer Haven, in Ireland. Disbursements he has made from his own purse. The sale of the hulk, as ordered, would not produce half the amount of wages due.

April 17.
Mohuns Ottery.
39. Same to Cecill. States the circumstances of service performed by the ships which he fitted out for sea for the apprehension of pirates. Has received command to deliver the hulk to one John Peterson, a Fleming. *Incloses*,

    39. I. *Account of charges of three ships sent out of the west parts by Sir Peter Carew, furnished, with 246 men, for apprehending pirates. 2 May (sic).*

April 20. 40. Certificate, by Sir Ric. Malorye, Lord Mayor, Sir Wm. Garrard, and Lionell Duckett, of depositions by John Bradbury and Tho. Wilson., beer brewers, in favour of the furnaces invented and set up for them by one Sebastian Brydigonne, a German.

April 28. 41. Instructions by Tho. Bentham, Bishop of Lincoln, to Mr. Sale, for his better proceeding in visitation of the diocese of Coventry and Lichfield; with articles addressed to the churchwardens and clergy of that diocese, for regulating ecclesiastical matters. At the end is a list of ministers and deacons admitted in 1567 and 1569.

April 28. 42. Copy of the above, except the list of ministers and deacons.

April. 43. Grant of discharge to Thomas Thurland, Master of the Savoy, Daniel Hechstetter, and others, from all fifteenths, tenths, and other impositions during the first beginning of their operations in mineral matters, according to indenture of the 10th of October last.

April. 44. Remembrance, by George Gilpin, to Mr. John Sheres, to forward the proposal of certain persons to make salt of salt by a new and unusual process, without prejudice to a former grant to Francis Barty. In a P.S. States the name of the party requiring the placaart to be Mr. Buckholt. Will carry his own grant for erecting furnaces into execution.

Vol. XXXVI.

1565.
May 2.   45. Tho. Duke of Norfolk to Sir Wm. Cecill. Forwards a letter received from the Earl of Arundel. *Incloses,*

> 45. I. *Earl of Arundel to the Duke of Norfolk. Returns a certain writing with his reasons for not subscribing it.* Nonsuch, 2d *May* 1565.

May 2.
Bodmyn.   46. P. Edgecomb to same. Detail of measures adopted by the Lord Warden of the Stannaries of Devon and Cornwall, as to the Queen's prerogative of the pre-emption of tin.

May 7.   47. Margaret Countess Dowager of Oxford to same (as Master of the Wards). Desires that part of the inheritance of her son, the present Earl of Oxford, may be set apart for his maintenance during his minority.

May 8.   48. Winchester to same. Forwards a letter from the Earl of Bedford as to the Queen's commissions. Mr. Sakevyle has the commissions for Northumberland and Cumberland.

May 12.   49. Wm. Humfrey to same. Finds the Almains complain of his report of the stone and "marquesyte;" particulars of the assay made by him. Importation of Flemish angels to all quarters of the realm continues.

May 12.   50. Statement of allegations made by the Mayor, &c. of Chichester, for pulling down certain wears for the preservation of the haven there; with the answer of the Bishop of Chichester.

May 12.   51. A brief declaration concerning the matter of the wears in Chichester Haven, on behalf of the Bishop of Chichester.

[May 12 ?]   52. Report by Sir Wm. Strickland to Cecill, of the condition of some of the piers and havens in Yorkshire.

May 20.   53–55. Statements of the Queen's debts, and of sums owing to her, under various heads.

May 22.
Cambridge.   56. Dr. Robt. Beaumont to Cecill. Forcet is too young for admission, and Cutlerd is not forward enough. Mr. Barrowgh's licence to practise physic was against the statutes of the University. High price of grain in Cambridge market, "to the pinching of poore scholers' bellies."

May 22 (?)   57. Extract from the statutes of the University relative to practising physic, with reference to the case of Mr. Barrowgh.

May 23.   58. Wm. Humfrey to Cecill. Explains his former report, relative to the copper ore. Reports on some Scotch ore. Lead land to let in Northumberland.

May 26.   59. Thos. Thurland, and Daniel Hechstetter to same. Have found copper ore containing silver, in certain places in Cumberland. Request to have warrant from the Queen to bring in 300 or 400 foreign workmen to work it.

Vol. XXXVI.

1565.
May 30. 60. Memorial addressed by Anthony Jenckynson to the Queen, on the navigation of the Northern seas. Urges the probability of the existence of a north-west passage, from the fact of a unicorn's head having been discovered on the island of Vagatts, near the mouth of the river Obbe.

May 31. 61. Proclamation against the currency of certain foreign pieces of gold, stamped like to English angels, or to pass only as bullion.

July. 62. Grant by the Queen to Tho. Thurland and Daniel Hechstetter (Houghsetter), to fell and appropriate, within Her Majesty's woods, timber sufficient to construct the buildings necessary for smelting all ores of gold, silver, copper, quicksilver, &c. within certain counties.

May (?) 63. Account of jewels sent by Baptist Spinola to his brother Pasqual Spinola, in Flanders, to be sold there. Items of disbursements for Lord Cobham, and for the funerals of "my Lady Marques" [of Northampton] at Blackfriars.

May (?) 64. Dr. Lawrence Humfrey, President Mag. Coll., Oxford, to the Bishops. Against the apparel now ordered to be adopted: the mass will follow, &c. Condemns the evil tendency of introducing Popish practices into the English Church.

June 4. 65. "A summarie of the consultation and advice given by the "Lordes and others of the Privye Counsell, collected out of the sundrye "and severall speaches of the said Counsellors," on the questions as to what peril might arise to the Queen, on the marriage of the Queen of Scots with the Lord Darnley.

June 17 (?) 66. [Earl of Sussex] to the Queen. Complains of the conduct of the Earl of Leicester, who, notwithstanding Her Majesty's injunction that neither should molest each other, has assembled great bands of armed men to waylay him.

June 18. Cambridge. 67. Dr. Rob. Beaumont to Cecill. Complains of the excessive exportation of corn from the neighbourhood of Cambridge, especially from Lynn. Requests that authority may be given for stay of all corn within five miles of the University.

June 24. 68. Wm. Lord Cobham to same. Touching head money demanded by the officers of Dover and Sandwich. Dover can only contribute 100*l.* towards repair of their haven.

June 25. 69. Earl of Leicester and Sir Wm. Cecill to Dr. Beaumont. In reply to his letter relative to the exportation of grain from Cambridge, which shall be stayed until further order can be taken.

June. 70. A note of silver and gold monies coined since January 1563-4.

June. 71. Copy of the above, in other numerals.

June. 72. Indenture between Cornelius de Vos on the one part, and others on the part of the Queen, for the working of all manner of mines or ores of alum, copperas, or the "lycours" of them, specially within the Isle of Wight.

Vol. XXXVI.

1565.

July 2. 73. Wm. Humfrey to Sir Wm. Cecill. Concerning the working of copper mines; and recommends an Almain engineer, who can raise water one hundred fathoms high, by a newly invented engine.

July 5. 74. Estimate of the charges of one hundred men to serve the Queen, in the ship Ayde, and stores for the same.

July 10. 75. Note of money received at various dates by Willm. Cocke, for the Earl of Oxford's use.

July 13. 76. Indictment of G. Berye, of New Romney, and others, for piracy committed off the North Foreland, in Kent, within the jurisdiction of the Cinque Ports.

July [14.] Greenwich. 77. Proclamation for all persons bound to maintain horses and geldings for light horsemen, to have the same in readiness for the musters.

July 15. 78. Memorandum of persons chargeable under the statute of Queen Mary, with keeping horses and armour.

July 15. 79. Copy of the above.

July 15. Canterbury. 80. Sir Roger Manwood to Cecill. Has examined the charter of the Cinque Ports, and finds that they are discharged, among other exemptions, *"de prestacionibus,"* which he considers to mean "of loans;" also of aids, contributions, talliages, &c.

July 16. 81. Wm. Humfrey to same. Observations on the supposition that Ireland is rich in minerals. Solicits the privilege of introducing battery works in England.

July 18. 82. Same to same. New suitors have arisen for a grant of the mines in Ireland, as Mr. Spendelo, Sir Thos. Chaloner and Cornelius De Vos. Hopes they may not prejudice his suit for the same. Could make the grant thereof worth some thousands of pounds to Cecill and to the Earl of Leicester.

July 22. 83. Same to same. Reasons for his having mentioned the islands of Lambay on the coast of Ireland, in the articles of grant of mines which he solicited. Objects to the introduction of Mr. John Challenor, in his grant.

July 22. Cologne. 84. Charles Utenhovius to same. Professes his admiration of his virtues. Describes the studies in which he is engaged. Lat.

July 23. 85. Note of monies paid to Sir Thomas Chaloner.

July 24. 86. Declaration of sale of the advowsons of certain rectories, vicarages, and other spiritual promotions by virtue of commission directed to Wm. Marq. of Winchester, Sir Willm. Petre, Sir Richard Sakevyle, and Sir Walter Mildmay.

July 27. 87. Commission for Thos. Thurland and Daniel Hechstetter to apprehend disorderly persons employed by them in the mines.

Vol. XXXVI.

1565.
July 28.   88. Commission to certain noblemen and gentlemen to take view and muster of all manner of horses and geldings which any person within the shire, liberty, franchise, corporate town, or other place, is bound to maintain ; and to make certificate thereof accordingly.

July 28.   89. List of noblemen and gentlemen Commissioners for mustering horses in various counties.

July 29.
Richmond.   90. The Queen to Lord Wentworth, Sir Francis Jobson, Sir Tho. Gresham, Ric. Onslow, and Edward Randolph, Esquires. Authorizes them to take muster and view of horses and geldings in the county of Middlesex.

July 30.   91. Tho. Thurland to Sir Wm. Cecill. Sends him a piece of ore from Borrowdale, which he is glad to say is to be procured plentifully. Has been arrested for debt. He is impoverished by the prosecution of his search for minerals.

July 31
Richmond   92. The Queen to the Lord Mayor of London and others. To take view and muster of all manner of horses and geldings within the city and liberties of London.

July.   93. Grant by the Queen to Francis Bertie, a stranger born, of the exclusive privilege of making white salt, for 20 years.

July.   94. Indenture between the Queen and Francis Bertie, of Antwerp, for the granting him exclusive privilege of manufacturing white salt, for the term of 20 years.

July.   95. Offers of Mr. Daniel Hechstetter, touching his suit and petition for privilege of waterworks for draining mines, &c., to form a company for the same, and to give certain shares to the Earls of Pembroke and Leicester, Sir Wm. Cecill, Mr. Tamworth, and Mr. Alderman Duckett

Vol. XXXVII. August—November, 1565.

1565.
August 7.   1. Francis Chaloner to Mr. Ferres. The suit of his brother, Sir Tho. Chaloner, to the Bp. of London, for Sir Tho. Fitzherbert, was without success. His brother has been ill of a burning fever, and made a new will, under evil influence, excluding his relations, and leaving all his lands to the bastard only.

August 7.
Chesterton.   2. Thos. Wakefield to Cecill. Concerning the quantity of grain transported by water from water from Cambridge, by way of Lynn. Lat.

1565.
                              Vol. XXXVII.

August 7. Belsize.   3. Ar[migill] Waade to same. Progress of the manufacture of glass and pottery, under Cornelius de Lannoy. Clumsiness of the English glass-makers. Recommends the suits of Henric Literhows, Mr. Prestoll, and William Herle. *Incloses,*

        3. I. *Note of payments made by Arm. Waad to Cornelius de Lannoy on account of the glass works.*

August 15. Lyes.   4. Lord Rich to the Queen. One of his servants being at Braintree, received from one Geoffrey Cawdwell a certain pedigree, the intention of which he does not comprehend. *Incloses,*

        4. I. *A pedigree tracing the descent of Mary Queen of Scotland, now married to Lord Darnly, from Richard Plantagenet, Duke of York, and placing her in close proximity to the crown of England.*

August 16.   5. Wm. Humfrey to Sir Wm. Cecill. States the reason of his delay in the business of the Mint, having been engaged with the Almain, Christopher Shuts, who is bound in 10,000*l.* to communicate his art in working metals. Desires to have a joint patent with him.

August 18. London.   6. John Shers to same. Sends news from Venice. Loss of St. Elmo, in Malta.

August 19. Lyes.   7. Lord Rich to the Queen. Has caused the writer of the pedigree to write another copy from memory, and to state his intentions upon it. *Incloses,*

        7. I. *Copy of the pedigree of descent from Richard Duke of York, made from memory.*

        7. II. *Deposition of (Geoffrey Cawdwell) why he made the above pedigree and genealogy, and to what intent he directed the same to the Lord Rich : asserting it was to advance the house of the Capels of Essex.*

        7. III. *Duplicate of the above deposition.*

August 19.   8. Articles for examination of Lady Mary Grey, with reference to her marriage with [Thomas Keyes], the Serjeant Porter.

August 19.   9. Answers of Lady Mary Grey to the above interrogatories.

August 19.   10. Examination of Tho. Keyes, the Serjeant Porter, respecting his marriage with Lady Mary Grey.

August 19.   11. Examination of Mrs. Frances Goldwell, relative to the above marriage.

August 19.   12. A slip of paper found with the above depositions, on which certain names are noted. [*Qy. of witnesses.*]

August 20. Reigate.   13. Wm. Lord Howard (Lord Chamberlain) to Cecill. Has received his letter respecting the marriage of Lady Mary Grey with the Serjeant Porter on the evening his cousin Knollys was married. *Incloses,*

Vol. XXXVII.

1565.

13. I. *Confession of Frances Goldwell before Lord Howard denying that any marriage had taken place between Lady Mary Grey and the Serjeant Porter.* 20 *Aug.*

August 22.   14. Lord Adm. Clynton and Mr. Secretary to Lord Burgh and Justices of the county of Lincoln. Touching supply of provisions for the Queen's Household.

August 22. London.   15. Monsr. Cousin, Preacher of the French Church in London, to Cecill. The Queen being at Richmond, intimated to him she would communicate her answer, through her Secretary, to Theodore Beza. Fr.

August 22.   16. Bartholomew Clercke to same. Compliments him as the Mecœnas of the University of Cambridge. Lat.

August 23.   17. The Council to the Commissioners of Musters of Essex. To give order to Sir Anth. Cooke, Steward of the liberty of Havering, to muster the horses, &c. there.

August 24.   18. The Queen to William Acliff, Sheriff of Essex. To attend Lady Cecilia, daughter of the King of Sweden and married to the Marquis of Baden, if she lands in Suffolk or Essex, and to conduct her to London.

August 26.   19. The same to Lord Cobham. To attend the Lady Cecilia if she lands at Dover, and to conduct her on her way to London. Similar directions having been given to the Lord of Burgavenny.

August 27.   20. Marq. of Winchester to Cecill. Sends him a remembrance of accommodation to be afforded to the Merchant Strangers.

August 28.   21. Wm. Humfrey to same. Explains the cause why Hans Louver has refused to bring the art of battery into the realm. In case of his own death, he has prepared many young Englishmen to work in various branches of goldsmith's work.

August 29. London.   22. Tho. Thurland to Sir Edw. Rogers Comptroller of the Household, Sir Fr. Knollys Vice-Chamberlain, and Sir Wm. Cecill. Has proposed a composition with his creditors and the executors of one Warde.

August 29.   23. Winchester to same. Has had great calls for money, and with difficulty obtained 4,000*l.* of Sir Tho. Gresham.

Sept. 1.   24. The Council to Mr. Hawtrey. The Queen being much offended with the Lady Mary Grey, has committed her to his custody. Directions for her treatment.

Sept. 1.   25. The Queen to Mr. John Vaughan. Directions to go to Setrington, and to take into his charge Charles Stuart, whose father, the Earl of Lennox, is at present in Scotland, and his mother in the Tower of London.

DOMESTIC—ELIZABETH.

Vol. XXXVII.

1565.

Sept. 1.
Hall, the house of Mr. Scott.
26. Lord Cobham to Sir Wm. Cecill. Lady Cobham, although she is with child, will attend the Lady Cecilia when she arrives at Dover. Requests to know where she is to be lodged at Canterbury, his own house there being altogether unfurnished.

Sept. 2.
Sir Thomas Kempe's house.
27. Same to same. Has heard of the arrival of the Lady Cecilia, at Calais, and therefore purposes to repair to Dover to receive her. Fears his wife will be unable to meet her.

Sept 3,
Windsor.
28. The Queen to Sir Henry Crispes, Sir Chr. Allen, Tho. Walsingham, Lady Hart, Lady Finch, Lady Norton ? Lord Cobham, Sir Tho. Kemp, Sir Tho. Kempe, Tho. Wotton, Warham St. Leger, Richard Baker, Tho. Scott, and N ? St. Leger. Commanding them to attend the Lady Cecilia on her arrival in England.

Sept. 14.
At my pore Croft.
29. Sir James Croft to Thomas Lovell. Desires him to speak with Mr. Sakevyle concerning the parsonage of Kynsland ?

Sept. 15.
30. Wm. Humfrey to Cecill. Desires the commission for working mines, &c. may be in the name of himself, Christopher Shutz, Thomas Smyth, Wm. Williams, and Humfrey Cole, and that the privilege for the battery works may be kept secret for eight months.

Sept. 16.
Wyntney.
31. Sir John Masone to same. Has received sundry letters from Sir Edward Warner since he went beyond sea. *Incloses,*

    31. I. *Sir Edwd. Warner to Sir John Masone. Vast quantities of corn are exported from England to those parts, especially from Norfolk. If it be without licence, the Queen must be greatly defrauded of her customs. Middleburgh, 5 Sept. 1565.*

Sept. 17.
32. Answer of Mr. Offley, on the part of the Company of the Staple, whether the Staple should be established at Calais, Emden, or within the realm of England.

Sept. 18.
33. Copy of Court Roll of the manor of Heveningham Castle, of which the Earl of Leicester is lord, for a cottage and garden in the tenure of William Ayleston. Lat.

Sept. 20.
Keyswyke.
34. Daniel Hechstetter, Johan Louver, and Ludwig Hans, to Cecill. The progress of their works in the mines impeded for want of wood. Begs that Needham may be dispatched into Ireland to procure it.

Sept. 21.
The Arches.
35. Dr. Lewes, Judge of the Admiralty, to same. To give order for restoration of the ship belonging to Agas Zibrandson, of Amsterdam.

Sept. 23.
36. Marq. of Winchester to same. Transmits form of letters to be written to Sir Tho. Gargrave and other Commissioners for seizure and management of the Earl of Lennox's lands. Measures for repressing the exportation of corn. Jeffrey Vaughan has been sent into Flanders for that purpose.

Vol. XXXVII.

1565.

Sept. 28.	37. Sir James Croft to Thos. Lovell. Thanks him for his friendly advertisements.
Sept. 29. Leighton.	38. Sir Robert Tyrwhyt to the Council. Certificate of the persons who have passed through Stilton during the last week, by post; specifies their names.
Sept.	39. A note of such things as Lady Margaret Lennox has for her apparel and furniture in the Tower, and of the wages of her attendants.
Sept.	40. Grant to William Humfrey, a Paymaster of the Mint, and Christopher Shutz, an Almain born, authorizing them to search for mines and smelt minerals within England and Ireland, with certain limitations.
Sept.	41. Notes of certain clauses to be inserted in the above grant.
Sept.	42. Indenture between Queen Elizabeth, William Humfrey, and Christopher Shutz, for working of mines and minerals.
Sept.	43. Grant to Wm. Humfrey and Chr. Shutz of the sole privilege of searching mines, &c. for discovery of the stone called lapis calaminaris or calamine, and for erecting and setting up in England the manufacture of mineral and battery works.
Sept.	44. Licence to Wm. Humfrey, Chr. Shutz, Tho. Smyth, Wm. Williams, and Humfrey Cole, to dig for minerals and ores in England, with power to impress workmen, waggons, and horses.
Sept. (?)	45–46. Two papers of accounts of the issues and annual income of the manors and lands belonging to the late Marchioness of Northampton; particularly those of West and East Tansfield, co. York, and Halsted and Stansted, in co. Essex.
Oct. 6.	47. Warrant for commissions under the Great Seal, for superintendence and care of the ports and havens of the realm, for the suppression of piracy, &c.
[Oct. 6.]	48. Articles of instructions for suppressing pirates and other disorders on the coast of Norfolk, and upon other sea coasts.
[Oct. 6 ?]	49. List of persons in several counties of England and Wales fit to act as Commissioners for care of the ports and havens thereof.
[Oct. 6 ?]	50. List of ports and havens in certain counties of the realm: probably connected with the above.
Oct. 6.	51. The Queen to the Duke of Norfolk. To repress the ingrossing of grain within the county of Norfolk, by certain Merchant Strangers.
Oct. 8.	52. Wm. Humfrey to Cecill. Requests that the commission to Mr. Shutz and himself may pass as it is now drawn. Desires Mr. Stanley may be called upon for some explanations.
Oct. 8.	53. Estimate of the charge of the ship, the Saker, for a month's service at sea.

Vol. XXXVII.

1565.
Oct. 12.
St. Paul's.
54. Bishop Grindall to Sir Wm. Cecill. Has received from the Archbishop of Canterbury certain advertisements relative to Malta. Thinks the offering up of public thanks should be deferred for eight days, till the news be confirmed.

Oct. 13.
[3 Id. Oct.]
King's College.
55. Bartholomew Clercke to same. Assures him of the respect and devotion which he entertains for him. Lat.

Oct. 17.
56. Confessions and circumstantial presumptions charging William Humfrey with a robbery committed at the Treasury of the Mint; and statement of the misdemeanor of Humfrey towards Tho. Stanley.

Oct. 20
57. Declaration, by Wm. Humfrey, of the manner in which he passed his time, from the 15th August to 24th September 1565, and of his several visits to the Tower within that period; in answer to Mr. Stanley's charge.

Oct. 20 (?)
58. Confession of John Bull, concerning the robbery at the Mint, committed by Bull and Mr. Humfrey, in order to do Mr. Stanley a shrewd turn.

Oct. 20.
59. Letters of safe conduct for the Princess of Portugal, in case of her landing in England, being on her way from Spain to the Low Countries.

Oct. 20.
60. Marq. Winchester to Cecill. Sends him a piece of gold of the size and weight of 10s., but worth no more than 3s. 6d., of which kind much will be imported if its real value be not declared by proclamation.

Oct. 23.
61. Certificate by Wm. Wynter, Benj. Gonson, and others, Officers of the Admiralty, for allowing the acceptance of 500l. for use of the ship Jesus, now returned; which had been granted to the Earls of Pembroke and Leicester, for a voyage to the coast of Africa and America.

Oct. 28.
62. George Lamplughe to Cecill. Progress of the Almain miners in their search for ores. Their want of wood for smelting. Recommends that some restraint be made for preservation of the Queen's woods.

Nov. 1.
Westminster.
63. Commission to Sir Edward Rogers and others, authorizing them to examine the accounts of David Vincent, deceased, late Keeper of the Wardrobe at Hampton Court.

Nov. 5.
Cobham Hall.
64. Lord Cobham, Thos. Wotton, and others, to the Council. Detail their proceedings as Commissioners for Ports and Havens for the co. of Kent. Quantities of bread and grain clandestinely exported.

Nov. 7.
Chekers.
65. Lady Mary Grey (signed "Graye") to Cecill. Thanks for his endeavours to restore her to the Queen's favour. Begs him to continue his efforts.

Vol. XXXVII.

1565.
Nov. 9.
Exeter.
66. Sir Peter Carew to Sir Wm. Cecill. Cause of the decay of shipping in the port of Dartmouth, owing to the impost on wines. *Incloses,*

> 66. I. *A remembrance of such ships and barks of the port of Dartmouth, co. Devon, as have been lost, sold, or decayed since the beginning of the impost on wines.*

Nov. 10. 67. Marq. of Winchester to same. Sends him a letter from the Archbishop of York as to a sale of the Earl of Lennox's lands. Requests his opinion on it.

Nov. 10. 68. Note of the places where the Earl of Oxford's evidences are deposited.

Nov. 10. 69. Tho. Smyth to Wm. Humfrey. Wishes he could deliver him from his unexpected thraldom. Good prospect arising from the survey of mines in the North. Bargain with the Earl of Westmoreland.

Nov. 10.
Baconsthorpe.
70. Sir Christopher Heydon and others to the Council. Have received the commission for creeks and havens. Sir Edward Warner has since deceased. Report their proceedings. *Inclosing,*

> 70. I. *A list of the several havens, creeks, and landing places in the county of Norfolk, and of the deputies appointed for the*

Nov. 10. 71. Sir Owen Hopton and others to same. Have received their commission for ports and havens, and appointed deputies. *Inclosing,*

> 71. I. *List of ports and havens in the co. of Suffolk, and of the deputies appointed to superintend them.*

Nov. 21.
Westminster.
72. Sir Wm. Cecill to Mr. Ascham, Secretary for the Latin tongue. Requests him to turn into Latin a patent for allowance of an annual pension of 1,000 crowns, of the Lady Cecilia, daughter of the King of Sweden.

Nov. 27. 73. Wm. Humfrey to Cecill. The search for calamine stone has proved a failure; but he can procure it from abroad to carry on the battery and latten works in England. Suspects that Dan. Hechstetter and Hans Louver wish to keep that art a secret.

Nov. 29. 74. Copy of Court Roll of Anthony Daston and Anne his wife (late wife of Francis Savage, deceased,) of the manor of Aston sub Edge. Lat.

Vol. XXXVIII. December, 1565.

Dec. 1 (?) 1. Petitions requested of Mr. Sec. Cecill, by Mr. President, that the Master of St. John's Coll. may be examined by the Vice-Chancellor, and Mr. Fulke by Cecill himself. [*Indorsed by Cecill* " *Mr. Bohun, Mr. Smith.*"]

Dec. 1 (?) 2. Articles, touching the Master of St. John's (Longeworth), and Mr. Fulke; charging the Master with receiving bribes, and Mr. Fulke with improper conduct.

Vol. XXXVIII.

1565.
Dec. 1 (?) — 3. Copy of the statute of St. John's College, for the election of a Master.

Dec. 1 (?) — 4. Extracts from the statutes of several colleges in the University of Cambridge, on the election of Fellows, &c.

Dec. 4. Westminster. — 5. Warrant to the Exchequer to pay 1,200*l*. a year to the Surveyor, &c. of the works, for repair of the Royal houses.

Dec. 4. — Certificate of the Bishop of Ely, Edmund Beaupre, and others, Commissioners for the ports and havens in the Isle of Ely, of particulars of their survey. [*Case* A. *Eliz.* No. 13.]

Dec. 6. — 6. The Queen to the Commissioners for Ports and Havens. Directions to restrain the exportation of corn and grain in certain counties.

Dec. 8 (?) — 7. Articles showing that the disorders in regard to apparel and surplices in St. John's College, Cambridge, have arisen by the disorderly acting and preaching of Mr. Fulke and others, making Robin Hoodes penny-worthes of their copes, and other vestments.

Dec. 9. Baconsthorpe. — 8. Sir Chr. Heydon and others, Commissioners for Ports, to the Council. Have surveyed all the ports, creeks, and landing places in co. Norfolk, and state the results. *Inclosing*,

    8. I. *Abstract of all the schedules of surveys of ports and havens in co. Norfolk.*

    8. II.–XIII. *Twelve schedules of returns of shipping, mariners, &c. in all the ports and havens in Norfolk.*

Dec. 12. Hook. — 9. Sir Wm. Poulett and others to same. Forward certificate of their proceedings in survey of ports and havens in co. Dorset. *Inclosing*,

    9. I. *Certificate, by the above Commissioners, of survey of ports and havens throughout the county of Dorset.*

Dec. 12. Cambridge. — 10. Dr. Ro. Beaumont to Sir Wm. Cecill. Has answered several of his letters, and sends copy of one of them. *Incloses*,

    10. I. *Dr. Beaumont to Cecill. Has laboured to get a couple of preachers into Ireland, without success. Particulars of the unhappy quarrel about ministers' apparel. Dr. Hutton and Mr. Fulke's preaching thereon. Cambridge, 6 Dec.*

Dec. 12. St. John's Coll. Cambridge. — 11. Ric. Coortesse to same. His proceedings as to St. John's College and Mr. Fulke. Has had conference with the Vice-Chancellor [Dr. Stokes] and the heads of houses thereon. Mr. Whitgift is scarce indifferent. *Incloses*,

    11. I. *Articles against Mr. Richard Longeworth, President, and now Master of St. John's College, of undue election and mal-practices.*

    11. II. *Articles against William Fulke, of St. John's College, of disorderly conduct, particularly in the article of apparel.*

VOL. XXXVIII.

1565.
Dec. 12.
Feltwell.
12. Osbert Moundeford to Sir Wm. Cecill. Acknowledges the receipt of the Queen's letter to the Commissioners for the survey of Ports, &c. in the county of Norfolk; will follow the instructions.

Dec. 13.
13. Sir Wm. Cecill to the Vice-Ch. of Cambridge [Dr. Stokes], Mr. Coortesse President of St. John's, and the Bp. of Ely. On the gross irregularities committed in St. John's College. [*Drafts of three separate letters sent by Mr. Bohun and Mr. Smith.*]

Dec. 13.
Southwick.
14. John Whyte, a Commissioner for the Ports, &c. in Southampton, to Cecill. Sends up certain commissions and letters. Doubts raised by the Custom-house officers as to the powers of the deputies of the Commissioners. *Incloses*,

14. I. *Certificate of John Lord St. John and other Commissioners, of the survey of all ports and havens in the county of Southampton, the Isle of Wight excepted.*

Dec. 16.
Chekers.
15. Lady Mary Grey to same. Thanks him for being so earnest a suitor to obtain Her Majesty's pardon, which she is so unhappy a creature to be without.

Dec. 17.
St. John's Coll.
16. Ric. Coortesse to same. Good conformity of the college in the matter of apparel. Sends lists of those who conform and wear surplices, &c. *Incloses*,

16. I. " *Nomina oñm Studentium tam Tutorum quam Pupil-*
" *lorum in Collegio Sci Johis Evangeliste.* 15 *Dec.* 1565."

Dec. 17.
Gedney.
17. Adlard Welby to same. Has sent his servants into all the towns of Holland (Lincolnshire) to inquire the price of grain. States the result of their inquiry. *Incloses*,

17. I. *John Manne to Mr. Adlard Welby. Informs him of the high prices of grain in his neighbourhood. Bolingbroke Castle.* 14 *Dec.*

Dec. 17 (?)
18. Note of certain persons upon Humber side who buy up great quantities of corn, two of whom are authorized badgers.

Dec. 18.
19. Ric. Longeworth, Master of St. John's Coll., to same. Has prevailed on the members of the College to follow the Queen's injunctions for wearing surplices. Desires to know if common bread may be used in administration of the Sacrament, and whether as often as he preaches "by the hour" in the chapel, to the house only, he may do so without the surplice.

Dec. 20.
20. Same to same. Has endeavoured to reform all things in his College. Nearly all have now appeared at chapel in their surplices.

Dec. 22.
King's Coll.
21. Roger Broune to same. Intreats his assistance in a cause in which the University was interested. Lat.

Vol. XXXVIII.

1565.
Dec. 22. 22. The Queen to Lord Trer: Winchester. To give instructions not to suffer any grain to be shipped for exportation, without special licence.

Dec. 28. 23. Sir Edw. Dymock and others to the Council. Report their proceedings in survey of ports and havens, and have given order for restricting the exportation of grain. *Inclosing,*

    23. I. *Certificate of Commissioners for survey of ports and havens, for the county of Lincoln.*

Dec. 28. Rye. 24. Dep. Commissioners for the port of Rye to Mr. John Theaher. The Custom officers at Rye dispute their powers. Desire instructions as to searching vessels.

Dec. 29. Rye. 25. John Donnynge, Customer of Rye, to Sir Wm. Cecill. Complains that the eight persons appointed to search under the orders for restricting the exportation of grain have exceeded their instructions.

Dec. 29. 26. Archbishop Parker to same. Detail of dissensions in Gonvill Hall, about the differences between the Master, Dr. Caius, and two Fellows, Dethicke and Clarke, recently expulsed.

Dec. 30. Southampton. 27. Edw. Horsey, Geo. Mylle, and John Worsley, Commissioners for the Isle of Wight, to same. Have laboured in execution of their commission, and forward a certificate.

Dec. 30. 28. Certificate of John Thetcher [or Theaher] and others, Commissioners of Ports for the rapes of Pevensey and Hastings, co. Sussex.

Dec. 31. 29. Articles (probably by Ric. Coortesse) exhibited against Ric. Longeworth, Master of St. John's, describing his arbitrary dealings with the Fellows and Scholars, since his return from London.

Dec. Bala. 30. Commissioners for Ports in Merioneth to the Council. Have surveyed all the creeks, havens, and landing places in the county, and report particulars.

Dec. 31. Certificate of Robert Elyot of the quantities of grain bought within the rapes of Chichester, Arundel, and Bramber, co. Sussex, for the use of the Queen's ships.

1565? 32. Note of regulations for weighing wool, lead, packing leather, &c.

33. Memorandum of repairs necessary to be done at the Castle of St. Andrew's, co. Southampton, of which the Marq. of Winchester hath charge.

34 Note of annual pensions and allowances paid to sundry persons; probably the Council in Wales.

35. Warrant to pay to Garter King at Arms, and to his brethren the Heralds and Pursuivants, 145*l.* for fees at the Queen's coronation, and for the justs royal and tourney then holden; "*vizt. for the " clouage and hynder partes of the trappers behynde the saddle,*" as of ancient custom; and for the Queen's largess at Christmas.

Vol. XXXVIII.

1565?

36. List of wares and commodities of the realm which may be transported over the sea, and not restrained at this day.

37. Observations on the Queen's grant to the Merchants trading to Barbary, in pursuance of the Earl of Leicester's contract with them and others, against the claim of Eustace Travacie and other Frenchmen.

38. Note of sundry kinds and quantities of grain to be purchased in various counties, with names of persons to superintend the same.

39. Another note of certain quantities; indorsed by Cecill, "for " grain to be carried into Flanders."

40. Notes of the prices of grain " to be delivered at the ports in " England," and the prices.

41. Observations on the enactment of penal statutes.

42. A note of what the Farmer of the Mint is to gain yearly, paying the Queen 12d. upon every pound weight of silver coined; indorsed by Cecill, " first offer."

43. An offer for farming the Mint, to be granted by the Queen, on the same principle as in 32d of Henry VIII.; indorsed by Cecill, " the " offer of 9d.; Lannison's last offer."

44. Proposal that the Queen should for one or two years make trial of the offer for farming the Mint; indorsed by Cecill, " the laste offer, " Lannyson's; 2s. uppon gold, 9d. uppon silver."

45. Account of the remain of military stores in the Office of Ordnance in the Tower, and the supply for the same, to the end of the year 1565.

46. Advantages to be gained by prohibiting the exportation of barley and malt, and by the brewing of beer for exportation instead.

47. Statement of particulars relating to the town and castle of Scarborough, showing the importance of maintaining the pier at that port.

48. Another copy of the above statement, with some slight variation.

49. Particulars of things desired in a commission for defence of the fort and island at Plymouth.

50. Estimate of the charge for new making two quays at Portsmouth; by Robert Welles, the Queen's Majesty's Carpenter there.

51. Estimate of the number of labourers necessary for speedily making up the quay at Portsmouth, and of the monthly amount of their wages.

52. Plan of the old quay at Portsmouth, with the plan of the cranes.

1565?

Vol. XXXVIII.

53. Plan of the quay that is to be new made of stone, at Portsmouth.

54. Statement of the title of Gabriel More, D.D., to the patronage and advowson of the rectory of Ingoldsby, co. Lincoln.

55. Petition of Richard More, of Bristol, grocer, to the Council. Complaint against John Roberts and others, who had fraudulently deprived him of his lands and goods and imprisoned him, under colour of a suit at law.

56. Account of armour and munition provided by Sir Tho. Gresham, the Queen's Agent in Flanders, and delivered into the Tower.

57. Notes on the petitions of Mr. Throckmorton and Mr. Fisher, at the suit of Joan Wilkes, for sums due on respite of homage, &c.

58. Certificate touching the fines of copyholders, payable to the Queen, within the manors of Hampton in Arden, and Rowington, co. Warwick; Kingsnorton, co. Worcester; Marden, and Kingsland, co. Hereford; Muchland and Torvor, co. Lancaster; and Penrith, co. Cumberland; by Fr. Phelips, Auditor.

59. Note of certain sums of money received and paid by the Lord Treasurer's order, since the Queen's going in progress.

60. Account of the rents of certain lands in the manor of St. Alban's, Herts, in the occupation of Walter Morgan.

61. Petition of Elizabeth Shelton to Sir Wm. Cecill. Shews that Sir James Bulleyn, by his last will, gave petitioner a legacy of 400*l.* to be paid by the Queen, in consideration whereof, an annuity of 30*l.* per ann. has been granted her; prays that the same may be augmented.

62. Note of inconveniences likely to follow if the privileges of the Intercourse should cease between England and the Low Countries.

63. Petition of John Wynnington to Sir Wm. Cecill. Touching certain abuses committed by Thomas Green, in his office of Feodary of Chester.

64. Petition of Sir John Perrot to the Queen. For a grant in fee of certain impropriate parsonages in Wales, belonging to the College of Leicester, the Commandery of Slebidge, and the Abbey of Tawley, which he now holds upon lease.

65. Petition of Ste. Barrowe, citizen of London, to Cecill. Desires privilege of the Sanctuary at Westminster, being at present unable to satisfy his creditors.

66. The answer of Sir Ric. Sakevyle to the complaint of Sir Edw. Gage, for taking mine in his ground.

VOL. XXXIX. JANUARY—MAY, 1566.

1566.
Jan. 2.
Cardigan.
1. Commissioners for Ports, &c. in Cardiganshire, to the Council. Report proceedings under their commission. *Inclosing,*

 1. I. *Description of the nature of the haven of Cardigan, and of other creeks and landing places in the county.*

Jan. 2.
2. The Queen to Marq. Winchester. To give licence for certain cloths to be exported to Sweden, at the request of the Lady Cecilia.

Jan. 4.
3. Same to same. In favour of Wm. Allyn and others of the Merchant Adventurers Company, for money due for customs.

Jan. 4.
4. Order taken by Sir Wm. Cecill, relative to certain contentions between Dr. Caius, Master and Founder of Gonville and Caius College, and Mr. Stephen Warner and other Fellows of the said College.

Jan. 7.
5. Petition of Stephen Warner and Robert Spencer, Fellows of Gonville and Caius College, Cambridge, to Cecill, praying for mitigation of the above order.

Jan. 8.
6. Commissioners for Ports, &c. in Radnorshire, to the Council. Report their proceedings, and make return of all ports, havens, shipping, &c. in the county. Complain of the presence and acts of one Fytiplace, a pirate, in Milford Haven.

Jan. 10.
7. Further order taken by Cecill, in the controversy between Dr. Caius and the Fellows of Gonville and Caius College; pronounced on the 10th of January.

Jan. 10.
Norwich.
8. Sir Chr. Heydon and others to the Council. Find the chief dealers in corn conformable and willing to supply the quantity required.

Jan. 11.
Westminster.
9. The Queen to Winchester. Warrant for Benedict Krugh, goldsmith, of Antwerp, to import certain jewels specified, duty-free.

Jan. 13.
10. John Cutlerd to Cecill. Sends him some Latin verses, as annexed, in different metres. Lat.

Jan. 15.
11. Commissioners for Ports in the rapes of Lewes and Bramber, Sussex. Report their proceedings, and desire directions as to transporting herrings from port to port. Schedule annexed, describing the ports, creeks, and landing places in the above rapes.

Jan. [15.]
12. Certificate of Commissioners for Ports and Havens in the rapes of Chichester and Arundel, co. Sussex.

Jan. 16.
13. Declaration of debts due in the Office of First Fruits, by obligation; with names of parties and places specified.

Jan. 20.
Cambridge.
14. John Welles to Cecill. Order taken in Cambridge. The Bishop of Ely sends him a doe. The Bishop of Lincoln has visited King's College. Mr. Beaumont wishes to know if he can deprive a man for not wearing a surplice.

1566.

Jan. 20.
Westminster.
15. Proclamation against the exportation of corn, and for preventing the forestalling and regrating of grain and other victuals. Special commissions will be issued in sundry counties. "Imprinted at London, "in Powles Churchyarde, by Rycharde Jugge and John Cawood, "printers to the Queenes Majestie."

Jan. 20 (?)
16. The Queen to Lord Keeper Bacon. Warrant to issue Commissions to gentlemen in certain shires to prevent the importation of grain, and to enforce the acts against engrossers, forestallers, an' regrators.

Jan. 21.
17. Sir Owen Hopton and others, Commissioners for Ports, &c. in Suffolk, to the Council. Report their proceedings in that service. *Inclosing,*

17. I. *Certificate of the said Commissioners of particulars relating to the ports, havens, and landing places in Suffolk.*

Jan. 24.
18. The Queen to Winchester. To appoint persons of credit and honesty to export out of the port of London, beyond sea, 1,000 tuns of beer, on which the duty, 20s. per tun, is to be paid. Also that all books imported, of a seditious nature, be subjected to the view of the Bishop of London.

Jan. 28.
St. John's Coll.,
Cambridge.
19. Ric. Coortesse to Sir Wm. Cecill. Has been discouraged by the strange dealings at Cambridge. Sir Henry Cheyney advised him to leave. Mr Longeworth will much deceive him if he alters his purpose.

Jan. 30.
Bishopsgate
Street.
20. Certificate by Tho. Wytton, Public Notary, that Sir Tho. Gresham hath appointed Mr. William Fayre to be his lawful procurator, agent, and factor.

Jan. 31.
21. Lord Mayor, &c. of London to the Council. Pray that the wheat bought and provided for the Queen may be sold to the city at the full rate of its cost to the Queen.

Jan.
22. Certificate by the Commissioners of Ports, &c. for the county of Essex; signed by John Lord Darcy.

Jan. (?)
23. Certificate by the Commissioners of Ports, &c. for the county of Carnarvon.

Jan.
24. Names of the deputy Commissioners appointed to superintend the ports, havens, and creeks in the Isle of Anglesea.

Jan. (?)
25. Warrant to the Exchequer to pay 165l. 2s. per month to Edw. Baeshe and John Ellyott, victuallers of the Navy, out of the allowance of 500l. a month to Benj. Gonson, Treasurer of the Admiralty.

Jan. (?)
26. Grant to Tho. Hennage of the office of Receiver and Treasurer of the tenths of the profits of the salt manufacture, under the patent granted to Francis Bertie, of Antwerp.

Feb. 1.
Abergwylly.
27. Certificate of Commissioners for survey of Ports and Havens in the county of Carmarthen.

Vol. XXXIX.

1566.

Feb. 8.	28. Licence for the exportation of certain quantities of barley and malt to the Low Countries; and for sale of grain to London and other parts of the realm.
Feb. 8.	29. Commissioners for the Ports in Flintshire to the Council. Certify particulars of the Welsh Lake, the only creek for ships, and of three other creeks for boats and barges, within the said county.
Feb. 12. Greenwich.	30. Proclamation against excess in apparel, and for restraining the use and length of arms and weapons.
Feb. 20. At Sir Harry Lee's house.	31. Earl of Leicester to Sir Wm. Cecill. Thanks for his gentle and friendly letter, by which he perceives how far Her Majesty has resolved. There is nothing which would settle her in good estate better than marriage. Nothing has been done in the matter of enclosures for Buckinghamshire.
Feb 20. Greenwich.	32. The Queen to Winchester. Limiting what persons of the Household, Noblemen, Bishops, Privy Councillors, Judges, &c. shall be exempt from the impost on French wines.
Feb. 20.	33. Licence by the Queen for her servants to wear such apparel as they shall have of her gift, out of the Great Wardrobe.
Feb.	34. Copy of the above.
Feb. 21. Greenwich.	35. List of persons licensed by the Queen, being officers and servants of Her Household, to wear certain apparel according to the degree of rank allowed by the proclamation.
Feb. 24.	36. The Queen to Winchester. Licence to allow the exportation of certain cloths to Sweden, at the request of the Lady Cecilia.
Feb. Cambridge.	37. Henry Cheke to Cecill. Expresses his desire to gratify him, and returns him thanks. Greek.
March 2. London.	38. Notarial instrument, by Thomas Wytton, of the depositions of Guido Cavalcanti, as to the last will and testament of M. G. Tarlink.
March 7 Somerset Place.	39. Armigill Waad to Cecill. A certain person has arranged the plan of his departure. First to speak with the Lady Cec[ilia?]. The medicine or elixir he carries with him. Proposes his arrest. The irons for casting ingots, and other things for projection, he takes with him.
March	40. A table of moneys formerly current at Calais, used in the Staple.
March 20. Mrs. Onley's.	41. Earl of Leicester to Cecill. Is glad to hear of the Queen's intention to reform the affairs of Ireland. Discusses Irish affairs. Confederacy of Scotland with O'Neil. Would have been glad of an extension of his leave of absence.
March 20.	42. Winchester to same. Sends the book of debts in Mr. Fanshaw's office. Other pecuniary matters noticed. Sends also the declaration of Mr. Neale, on the Earl of Lennox's account.

Vol. XXXIX.

1566.
March 22.
Lyes.
43. Lord Rich to the Queen. Has received the letters of the Council concerning the lack of wool among the clothiers of Essex, and has proceeded to the speedy execution of their instructions.

March 28.
Rochford.
44. Robert Stafford to Sir Wm. Cecill. Thanks him for good will shown towards him, and for benefits conferred. Lat.

March 29.
45. Roger Lord North to Leicester. Requests him to continue his friendship towards his sister, and that by his means her writings may be sealed.

April 3.
46. Edward Browne, Mayor of Rochester, to the Council. Christopher Marquis of Bawdwyn [Baden] is now prisoner under arrest in the said city. His outrageous behaviour. Prays that the said Marquis may be made to obey the laws, or that he may be discharged of keeping him.

April 4.
47. Petition of Ric. Bramley butcher, Robert Audrey poulterer, and other tradesmen, to the same, praying for payment for goods supplied the household of the Lady Cecilia [Marchioness of Baden].

April 4.
48. Complaint, addressed to Cecill, of the disrespectful and slanderous allegations preferred by certain tradesmen to the Privy Council, against the Lady Cecilia. Lat.

April 4.
49. Statement, by Tho. Sympson, of sums due to him for articles of plate and jewellery, supplied to the Lady Cecilia.

April 4.
50. Statement of a debt due to Ludovico Barbaro by the Lady Cecilia, for a kirtle wrought with gold, a Venice lute, &c.

April 4.
51. Note of money received by Bradford for the Lady Cecilia, being part of a sum of 3,300*l.* appointed to be paid to her.

April 4.
52. Account of debts due by the Lady Cecilia.

April 4.
53. A view of the debts of the Princess Cecilia's Grace, collected the 4th of April 1566.

April 6.
London.
54. Francis Pope and others to the Council. Have made suit in vain to the Lady Cecilia for sums due to them. Pray their just claims may not be defeated.

April 20.
55. Certificate, by Gillot Pullaim and others, goldsmiths, of the value of a certain jewel belonging to the Lady Cecilia.

April 22.
56. Note of sums received by George North and Walter Bradford towards payment of the debts of the Lady Cecilia.

April 23.
Augsburgh.
57. Daniel Hechstetter and Hans Louver to Alderman Duckett. Progress of the works for melting copper and silver. It is joyful news to hear that Mr. Secretary has shewn himself so favourable; they had hoped Leicester would have been the same. Complain of Mr. Humfrey. Are sorry the Marquis of Baden has quitted England in debt. German news.

April 23.
58. Lady Cecilia to Cecill. Complains of the conduct of her groom, John Sturtenn, who detains certain silver mountings made for her saddles. Lat.

Vol. XXXIX.

1566.
April 23. 59. Marq. of Winchester to Sir Wm. Cecill. Has dispatched the Irish Lords' bonds. Has endeavoured to ascertain the fees, &c. granted by the Crown to Mr. Masone and Mr. Sakevyle. Disposal of their offices. *Incloses,*

> 59. I. *Note of fees payable at the receipt of the Exchequer, now determined by the death of Sir John Masone.*
>
> 59. II. *Account of fees and annuities granted to the late Sir Ric. Sakevyle, deceased, in the counties of Kent and Sussex, in the office of Auditor Thompson.*
>
> 59. III. *Another account of fees and annuities paid to the late Sir Ric. Sakevyle as Sub-Treasurer of the Exchequer and Chancellor of the Court of Augmentations, and from various manors.*
>
> 59. IV. *Account of fees paid to same, in the Exchequer; and to Sir John Masone for various offices.*

April 25. 60. Declaration by Alderman Lionel Duckett, that the Lady Cecilia hath deposited in his hands a certain jewel of the value of 600*l.* by way of security for payment of her creditors, under certain conditions.

April 26. 61 The Queen to all Mayors and other officers. Authorizing them to allow, at any time hereafter, any person or persons to pass out of the realm with any jewel, &c. of the Lady Cecilia's, on producing a certificate signed by Ald. Duckett.

April 29. 62. Declaration by the Mayor, &c. of Dover, that one George Northe, gentleman, has applied for a precept to attach the Lady Cecilia or her goods for the sum of 330*l.*, but that it had been stayed by the Lord Abergavenny.

April (?) 63. [Dr. Humfrey ?] to Cecill. Prays that the articles of the Archbishop may be some ways mitigated, and that pastors may be relieved from observing certain ceremonies, &c.

May 3. 64. Winchester to same. Thanks for obtaining the Queen's licence for the exchange with the Parson of Chelsea. Alterations in the garden at Hampton Court. Will take care that the Collar and George shall be furnished for the Emperor. Sakevyle's and Masone's offices.

May 3.
Chekers.
65. Lady Mary Grey to same. Reminds him of her suit to the Queen for pardon. If admitted to the Queen's favour, she will never again forfeit it.

May 4.
St. Paul's.
66. Bishop Grindall to same. Suspension of one Barthlett, a Divinity Lecturer of St. Giles, Cripplegate (Mr. Crowley's parish). Sixty women came to the Bishop to make suit for him; who would not depart, but at the request of Mr. Philpot, another suspended reader.

May 6.
Cambridge.
67. John Stokes to same. Wishes to know his pleasure as to Mr. Fulke's remaining in Cambridge.

VOL. XXXIX.

1566.
May 7. 68. Winchester to Sir Wm. Cecill. Desires to know if the attendants Lady Lennox has with her in the Tower, are to be maintained at the Queen's charge.

May 11. 69. Declaration of homage and allegiance to Queen Elizabeth, by Hugh Jones, Bishop of Landaff.

May 14. 70. Sir John Wentworth to the Council. Has received a letter from the Queen commanding him to take charge of the Lady Catherine Grey. Prays to be excused from that service.

May 20.
London. 71. Gilbert Gerrard, Attorney General, to Cecill. One Spencer. being condemned for treason, cannot be set at liberty without the Queen's pardon.

May 18.
Whitb[orn.] 72. Bishop Scorey to same. Concerning confirmation of the reversion of the lease of Ewithington prebend for Richard Gibbes; the present farmer thereof being one John Bromme.

May 20. 73. John Burton to same. Thanks him for letters in favour of his son. Solicits in behalf of Mr. Tho. Ogle, for his two pastures of Goodram Toft and Stonecote. Proceedings relating to sewers in the fens of Lincolnshire.

May 21.
Basingstoke. 74. Earl of Pembroke to Leicester and Cecill. His own ill health. Intercedes for the pardon of one Prestcott, an offender.

May 21.
" My poore howse." 75. Sir Wm. Petre to Cecill. Is too ill to go abroad; is well recovered of his fever, but wishes to retire to Ingatestone, where he thinks the open air will do him good.

May 21.
London. 76. Bishop Grindall to the Dean and Chapter of St. Paul's, Enjoining them to use such mode of apparel as is ordained by the Queen's authority in the treatise intituled "the Advertisements."

May 22
Poole. 77. James Lord Mountjoy to Cecill. Thanks for sending Dr. Julio to him. Progress of the mineral, copperas, and alum works.

May 23. 78. Bishop Pilkington to same. Requests the warrant for his restitution may be completed. Is now at liberty to walk, and dares go abroad into gardens.

May 23.
Whorwelle. 79. Sir Adrian Ponynges to same. Concerning compensation for his service at Portsmouth. *Incloses,*

79. I. *Note of the annual value of the manor of Loder, co. Dorset, parcel of the possessions of the late Monastery of Sion.*

May 24. Indenture of assignment from Tho Norton, of Norwood, Kent, to William Burde, of all his right and interest in the manors and hundreds of Myddleton and Merden, co. Kent. [*Case* A. *Eliz.* No. 14.]

May 25.
Keswick. 80. Thos. Thurland to Cecill. Understands that there are certain ores of gold and silver to be found in the mines there, a secret which the strangers keep to themselves. Wishes for a skilful man out of Flanders. If Cecill will not answer his letters, he will write no more, though he be the Queen's Chief Secretary of England.

Vol. XXXIX.

1566.

May 26.
London.
81. Winchester and Sir Walter Mildmay to same. Approve of the Queen's consent and agreement to the restoration of the Bishop of Durham's lands. He is to pay 1,000*l.* a year to the Queen during the time he continues Bishop.

May 27.
Chancery Lane.
82. Tho. Fitzwilliam to Hugh Fitzwilliam. Rejoices to hear of Sir Thomas Hoby's good acceptance. The Queen supped at Durham Place with the Earl of Leicester, and Mr. Sec. Cecill has sumptuously banquetted M. de la Foret, the new French Ambassador. Scottish news. Proceedings against ministers for refusing to wear crossed caps. Progress into Northamptonshire purposed by the Queen.

May 27.
Bruges.
83. Walter Haddon to Archbp. Parker. Our Saviour had a Judas Iscariot and a Simon Magus among his Apostles; the devil creates divisions among Christians. Lat.

May 29.
84. Rich. Longeworth, Master of St. John's College, to Sir Wm. Cecill. Complains of the contumacy of some of the Fellows of that College.

May 29
85. George Whetle to same. Thanks him for remembering their old friendship. Would be glad to do Mr. Danet any pleasure. Trusts the marriage will proceed prosperously. Is sorry to hear of Cecill's illness.

May 29.
The Compter in the Poultry.
86. Examination of Walter Darby, taken before Dr. Lewes, concerning his entering into an undertaking with Martin Frobiser for a voyage to the coast of Guinea.

May 30.
London.
87. Oliver Lloyd to Sir T. Hoby. Desires his recommendation to Mr. Sec. Cecill, to be appointed Sheriff for Cardiganshire: with note thereon, by Sir T. Hoby, to Cecill.

May.
88. A receipt for transmutation of metals into gold. Lat.

May (?)
89. Declaration of all such sums of money as have been received by the Treasurer and Surveyor of the works for rebuilding St. Paul's; with the expenditure thereof.

Vol. XL. June—October, 1566.

1566.

June 4.
1. Bishop Grindall to Sir Wm. Cecill. The bearer will inform him of "a womannyshe brabble" in a church in London. Requests a warrant for a buck. Regulations respecting payment of first fruits.

June 5.
Saltash.
2. Mayor, &c. of Saltash to the Council. Have received instructions for seizing a ship owned by Martin Frobiser: no such vessel has arrived at that port.

June 5.
Croydon.
3. Archbp. Parker to Cecill. The Earl of Sussex has recommended his chaplain, Mr. Rushe, for a prebend in Canterbury; thinks he will honestly deserve that appointment.

1566.

June 6.
Fleet Prison.
4. Tho. Keys to Sir Wm. Cecill. Begs him to intercede with the Queen for his release.

June 8.
5. Memoranda relative to various points of business; in Cecill's hand.

June 8.
6. Remembrances sent by Mr. Thurland, Master of the Savoy, touching the mining operations at Keswick.

June 11.
7. Examinations of Martin Frobiser, of Normanton, co. York, on 30th May and 11th June, taken before Dr. Lewes, on suspicion of his having fitted out a vessel to go to sea as a pirate; in which one Tho. Yonger was implicated.

June 11.
Cambridge.
8. John Welles to Cecill. Has thought it his duty to acquaint him with the controversy in St. John's College, between the Master and certain of the senior Fellows.

June 14.
9. Wm. Humfrey to same. Sends him a statement of such rivers as have been surveyed for the purpose of erecting thereon works for iron wire.

June 20.
Lease from the Dean (Alex. Nowell) and Chapter of St. Paul's, to Simon Bland, of a tenement in Knight Ryder Street, near the Bakehouse of St. Paul's, for 31 years. [*Case* A. *Eliz.* No. 15.]

June 20.
[12 Cal. Quintiles.]
10. Adam Waughendoorpe, Alderman of the Stillyard, to Cecill. Concerning a licence to the Merchants of the Stillyard for exportation of a quantity of cloths. Lat.

June 22.
Sluys.
11. Francis Berty to same. Recommends Chr. Shutz, who is coming to England to establish battery and wire works. New invention for making salt.

June 22.
Southampton.
12. John Mount to same. Sends a plan of the furnaces and pans for manufacturing salt. *Incloses*,

12. I. *Plans of furnaces and pans for making salt.*

June 24.
The Lady Mason's, London.
13. Edw. Earl of Hertford to same. Complains of the continuance of the Queen's heavy displeasure towards him; and that his brother, Henry Seymour, bears part of the penalty.

June 25.
Augsburgh.
14. Daniel Hechstetter and Johan Louver to same. Report progress of mining works at Keswick. Necessity for discharging some of the workmen there. The ores tested in Germany have produced good copper. Are coming to England. *Inclosing*,

14. I. *Account of the charges of mining operations at Keswick.*

June 28.
St. James's.
15. The Queen to Winchester. Warrant to permit the Company of the Stillyard to export 5,000 pieces of unwrought cloths.

June 29.
London.
16. Antonio Bruschetto to Cecill. Concerning a debt of 300*l.* due to him by the late Captain Tiberio Perroni. Ital.

VOL. XL.

1566.	
June 30.	17. Wm. Humfrey to Sir Wm. Cecill. Has succeeded by the aid of the German miners in finding calamine in Somersetshire. The Forest of Dean contains plenty of good iron, and there is a mine of sea coal within a mile of Bristol.
June (?)	18. Account of assessments of subsidy in the different wards of the city of Bristol.
June.	19. Regulations for reform of divers disorders in the publication of books.
June.	20. Note of fees in the Offices of the Treasurer of the Chamber and Master of the Posts, held by the late Sir John Masone.
July 4.	21. Wm. Humfrey to Cecill. Mr. Alderman Hayward has consented to become Treasurer of the mineral works. A meeting of proprietors is requisite. Requests that his application relative to Bristol Castle may be granted.
July 4.	22. The Queen to the Sheriff and Justices of Devon, Somerset, Monmouth, Hereford, and Gloucester. Warrant to levy and arm certain forces for service in Ireland.
July 4.	23. Draft of the above, corrected throughout by Cecill.
July 5. Cobham.	24. Wm. Lord Cobham to Cecill. Wishes for a final resolution as to his burden. Sends copy of letter of marque granted to Menard Frize; also a letter from Mr. Kell. *Incloses,*
	24. I. *Eric XIV. King of Sweden to Menard Frize. Letter of marque for him to exercise hostilities against the subjects of the King of Denmark and his allies. Stockholm, 30 March. Lat.*
July 6.	25. Articles of composition for regulation and government of the Company of the art and mystery of Shermen, of the town of Shrewsbury. [See the Act 8 *Eliz.* cap. 7. " touching drapers, cottoners, and " freesers in the towne of Shrewisburye."]
July 7.	26. James Hawys, Sheriff of London, to Cecill. Has delivered the articles to Chr. Lascelles, and returns his answers to the same.
July 8. Westminster.	27. Grant to Edward Randolph of the office of Lieutenant General of the Ordnance in England and Berwick-on-Tweed, for life. Lat.
July 15. Belsize.	28. Arm. Waad to Leicester and Cecill. Has repaired to the Tower and examined Mr. Cornelius [Lannoy ?] as to delay in assays of metals, &c. Particulars of the conversation which took place.
July 16. Fleet Prison.	29. Thomas Keys to Cecill. Begs that he will give him instructions how to act, as to his going into Ireland.
July 16.	30. Wm. Humfrey to same. Opinion of the Earl of Leicester that the calamine is not worth having, being at so low a price.
July 17. London.	31. Mayor, &c. of the Merchants of the Staple to same. Have entrusted two of their Company to receive the determination of the Council on their application for licence to export in the accustomed manner.

1566.

July 19.
London.
32. Arm. Waad to the Earl of Leicester and Sir Wm. Cecill. The Lieutenant of the Tower has shewn him the letter enclosed. Explains the meaning of a passage. Cornelius has greatly abused the Queen. Incloses,

 32. I. *Cornelius de Lannoy to Leicester and Cecill. Long explanation of his proceedings. Begs for mercy from the Queen, and acknowledges his delinquency. Lat.*

July 21.
Kimbolton.
33. The Queen to Winchester. Warrant for a licence to the Merchants of the Staple to ship and export wool in the accustomed manner.

July 22.
Croydon.
34. Archbp. Parker to Cecill. Sends a form of prayer for the Queen, for his approval. Wishes for her safe return home.

July 23.
35. Letter of Attorney by Edw. Randolph, Esq., Lieut. General of the Ordnance, constituting Sir James Shelley, of Michelgrove, Sussex, and Robt. Giles, his true and lawful attorneys.

July 24.
36. Assignment, by Edw. Randolph, Esq., to Wm. Painter, Clerk of the Ordnance, Richard Webb, Master Gunner of England, and Edw. Partridge, Keeper of the Queen's Harquebutts, Dagges, and Curriers, of certain annuities or yearly pensions, for a term of years.

July 25.
Fleet Prison.
37. Thomas Keys to Cecill. Prays that he would intercede with the Queen, that if he is not employed he may be permitted to remain as a prisoner with some of his friends.

July 25.
London.
38. J. Asteley, Master of the Jewel House, to same. Sends a note of the gift which Edward VI. sent to the christening of the French King's child; as a precedent for the christening now at hand in Scotland.

July 26.
London.
39. John Shers to same. Forwards some letters received from Venice.

July 28.
London.
40. Winchester to same. Sends an estimate of charges for Berwick. Is glad he takes in good part the Lady St. John's answer respecting Luddington. Sir Martin Bowes is in ill health. Watch and ward will be kept in the city till the Queen returns.

August 1.
Keswick.
41. Thos. Thurland to same. Progress of works. A copper mine has been discovered at Newlands, the best in England.

August 2.
42. Deposition of Thomas Meidlar, of Wexford, taken before John Leweston, Esq., Capt. of Portland, touching his ship being boarded and plundered off the Land's End by a vessel of Normandy, in which were an English captain and several Irish kernes.

August 2.
43. Deposition, by Edward Gellye of Plymouth, taken as above, relating to the same transaction.

August 3.
Tower of London.
44. Declaration, by Cornelius de Lannoy, that if it shall please the Queen to release him from confinement, he will without delay put in operation that wonderful elixir for making gold for Her Majesty's service. Lat.

DOMESTIC—ELIZABETH.

Vol. XL.

1566.

August 5.
Fulham.
45. Bishop Grindall to Sir Wm. Cecill. States what he has done in the Sergeant Porter's matter. If the marriage contract be dissolved it must be done judicially. Is sorry he has no fruit to offer him but some grapes.

August 5.
Fulham.
46. Same to the Council. Particulars of the examination of Thomas Keys, late Sergeant Porter, touching his marriage with the Lady Mary Grey.

August 10.
47. John Shers to Cecill. Letters received from Vienna. Particulars of German and Italian intelligence. *Incloses,*

    47. I. *Form of prayer in Latin to be said daily by every one in the Emperor's Court, for protection against the Turks.*

August 13.
48. The Queen to Winchester. Is about to take measures to remedy defaults committed in payment of customs and subsidies, and will require his counsel therein.

August 13.
Tower of London.
49. Cornelius de Lannoy to Leicester and Cecill. Implores the Queen's mercy. Shews the impediments which he has encountered in the operations he undertook for the making of gold. Lat.

August 19.
London.
50. Jas. Lord Mountjoy to Cecill. Begs that the Queen will advance him 6,000*l.*, and undertakes at the end of two years to deliver 150 tons of alum, and 150 tons of copperas, as good as the Danish sort.

August 20.
51. Winchester to the Queen. Has received her letters from Collyweston. Gives his opinion on the frauds committed in the customs on woollen cloths and wines.

August 22.
52. Same to Cecill. Sends a declaration of five accounts, shewing the Queen's profit on woollen cloths and wines for the years therein specified.

August 26.
Tower of London.
53. Sir Francis Jobson and Armigill Waad to same. Have conferred with Cornelius on the subject of his letter. Requisitions made by Cornelius for carrying on his alchemical operations, for which a small sum of money will be required.

August.
54. Note of the number of days William Dyx has been in attendance on the Privy Council at Collyweston and Woodstock.

Sept. 1.
55. Presentments by a Jury at Folkestone, of the value of certain articles taken up at sea, being droits of Admiralty. [*The Jury were fifteen in number, and every one makes his mark.*]

Sept. 2.
56. Return of the Jury of Inquisition held at Dover Castle, to certain articles relating to the jurisdiction of the Cinque Ports.

Sept. 2.
57. Congratulatory verses on the arrival and reception at Oxford, of the Earl of Leicester and Sir Wm. Cecill, Chancellors of the two Universities, by George Coryat. Lat.

VOL. XL.

1566.

Sept. 2 (?) — 58. Similar verses, by James Calfhill, addressed to Sir Wm. Cecill, on the same occasion. Lat.

Sept. 3 (?) Lincoln Coll. — 59. Anthony Marcham to Sir Wm. Cecill. Apologizes for troubling him with his rude letter. His poverty. Desires Cecill's assistance, for without his aid he shall be compelled to leave Oxford. Lat.

Sept. 3. London. — 60. H. Kyllygrew to Mr. Hugh Fitzwilliams. Gives particulars of his visit to the Scottish Court. Description of Queen Elizabeth's progress to Kenilworth, where she was magnificently entertained by the Earl of Leicester.

Sept. 6. Chekers. — 61. Lady Mary Grey to Cecill. Begs he will continue his good offices towards her, and solicits to have an interview with the Queen, at Lord Windsor's.

Sept. 12. — 62. Winchester to same. Specifies the charges of the Marches of Berwick, Carlisle, and the Borders, from time of King Henry VIII. Exposition of finance affairs

Sept. 19. Tintern Abbey. — 63. Wm. Humfrey to same. The Earl of Pembroke has befriended them, allowing them the use of Bristol Castle. Details their proceedings there, and in the adjacent country.

Sept. 20. Rose Castle. — 64. Tho. Thurland to same. The smelting house and other mineral operations are in progress, but are more chargeable than he imagined. There is plenty of copper ore in the country.

Sept. 24 Cambridge — 65. Mayor, &c. of Cambridge to same. As to the return of two Burgesses to serve in Parliament; Roger Slegg and Henry Serle being disqualified.

Sept. 30. Chekers. — 66. Lady Mary Grey to same. Entreats him to intercede with the Queen for pardon, and that she may be received again into Her Grace's favour.

Sept. 30 — 67. Matthew Maperley, Schoolmaster of Grantham, to same. Complains of the obtrusion of certain little children into the school of Grantham, contrary to the regulations, and of other innovations attempted. Lat.

Sept. — 68. A memorial of things fit to be considered by the Parliament. Mr. Walsyngham to be of the House.

Sept. — 69. Account of the second payment of the subsidy granted to the Queen.

Sept. — 70. Account of the customs and subsidies payable on wines in the ports of England and Wales, commonly called the Butlerage.

Sept. — 71. The offer of James Morley and Henry Smythe for the custom of woollen cloths and wines payable to the Queen.

Sept. — 72. Ordinances and decrees established at Sempringham, co. Lincoln, by the Right Hon. Edward Lord Clynton and others, Commissioners of Sewers, for works in the fens there.

Vol. XL.

1566.
Sept. 73. Bond of Sir Thos. Gresham in the sum of 500 crowns, to John Fuggar, as security for payment to John Steinberg, for sending 20 German miners into England. Indorsed by Cecill, "Parson Thurland." Lat.

Sept. 74. Conditions for John Steinberg (Hans Stainbarge) to come over into England with 20 or 30 Germans, skilled in minerals, to try some newly discovered mines. Sureties for repayment of the 500 crowns.

Oct. 1. 75. Tho. Warcope to Sir Wm. Cecill. Recommends the bearer, his brother, to his favour.

Oct. 1.
Liverpool. 76. Sir Ric. Molyneux and the Mayor of Liverpool to the Council. Have delivered to Wm. Aldersey certain leather and calf skins, for the use of Henry Sackforthe.

Oct. 2. 77. Winchester to Cecill. Requests to know what answer he is to give to the merchants of the Venetian ships, as to importation of wines.

Oct. 3. 78. Objections made by the town of Southampton, against the merchants of Venice, that they ought to unlade their malvesies and sweet wines at Hampton, and not elsewhere.

Oct. 7.
Keswick. 79. Tho. Thurland, Provost of the Mines, to Cecill. Great progress of the mining works. Smelting houses and furnaces erected. Gold found on Crawford Muir.

Oct. 7. 80. Same to the Queen. Proof of gold found on Crawford Muir, in Scotland. Recommends her to compound with the Scottish Queen for lease of those lands, to prevent them getting into the hands of foreigners.

Oct. 10.
Keswick. 81. Daniel Hechstetter to Johan Louver. Reports on the state of the mining works at Keswick. Shall discharge some of the workmen. The Germans ill treated by the English workmen. Murder of Leonard Stoultz, by one Fisher and his accomplices, who were protected by Lady Ratcliffe.

Oct. 12.
Hallrennys. 82. William Cicill to Cecill. Recommends the bearer for employment in his service.

Oct. 13.
London. 83. Lionel Duckett to same. Is about to despatch a messenger to Keswick. The inhabitants of Keswick ought to be friendly to the foreigners there.

Oct. 13.
The Arches. 84. Dr. Lewes to same. Has received his letters, to prevent certain persons, namely, John Chichester, Hawkyns at Plymouth, William Cooke, and Geo. Fenner, from repairing armed, for the purpose of traffic to places privileged by the King of Spain.

Oct. 14. 85. A brief note of what the subsidy and two fifteens granted by the laity, anno 5 Eliz., amounts to.

1566.

Oct. 14. 86. Declaration of the opinions and resolutions of Sir William Cordall, Master of the Rolls, and others, to the Duke of Norfolk, Committee of the body of George now Lord Dacre, of Gillesland, touching the supposed deed of entail made by William, late Lord Dacre.

Oct. 16. 87. The Queen to Lord Scrope and the Justices of the Peace in Westmoreland and Cumberland. To repress the assaults, murders, and outrages on the Almain miners lately come there for the purpose of searching for and working minerals.

Oct. 17. 88. Committee of the Privy Council, the Master of the Rolls, and forty members of the House of Commons, to consider of the aid or subsidy necessary, and in what manner it shall be paid.

Oct. 18.
Witham. 89. Sir Henry Norreys to Sir Wm. Cecill. Requests he will allow him a reasonable time for despatch of his own affairs.

Oct. 18 (?) 90. Notes concerning the grant of a subsidy to the Queen; Her purpose to marry. Renewal of suit for establishing the succession. Prayers for safety of the realm.

Oct. 19 (?) 91. Heads of a proposed address to the Queen, relative to her marriage and the succession. *In Cecill's hand.*

Oct. 20.
Borley.
[Burleigh?] 92. Lady Lucy Harryngton to Cecill. Begs him to prevent the match between her son and Mistress Wynser; and to intercede that the Queen and the Earl of Leicester should not take offence at breaking it off.

Oct. 20. 93. Notes concerning a bill to be exhibited in the Parliament House for traffic of the Company of Merchant Adventurers into Russia.

Oct. 27.
[6 Kal. Nov.]
Cambridge. 94. Thomas Bing to Cecill. Acknowledges his great goodness towards him. Lat.

Oct. 28.
London. 95. Dr. Lewes to same. Has taken bonds of George Fenner not to spoil any of the Queen's subjects, nor to traffic into India or any other places privileged by the King of Spain. Will take order with Mr. Hawkyns.

Oct. 28. 96. Note of the days appointed for payment of the subsidy.

Oct. 29.
Layton. 97. Walter Morgan to Cecill. Complains of being charged with arrears of tythes juxta Smalford, to which he was not liable.

Oct. 30. 98. Notes relative to the tythes of St. Peter's Grange, in the tenure of Wm. Sleape, of St. Alban's, and of St. Michael's in the tenure of Sir Ric. Lee and Wm. Hudson; with directions that Walter Morgan should not be charged with arrears of tythes juxta Smalford.

VOL. XL.

1566.
Oct. 31.
Arches.
99. Dr. Lewes to the Council. Has taken the recognizances of John Hawkyns of Plymouth, who does not go in the voyage himself. *Incloses,*

> 99. I. *Bond of John Hawkyns of Plymouth, in* 500l. *to forbear sending his ship, the Swallow, about to make a voyage to the coast of Guinea, to any place in the Indies privileged by the King of Spain.* 31 *Oct.*

Oct. 100. Abstract of the book of survey and examination taken before the Bishop of Carlisle and others, Commissioners appointed by the Queen to examine the state of the revenues of the College of Carlisle, and other abuses and evil doings of the prebendaries there.

Oct. 101. Rent roll of certain Bailiffwicks within the Duchy of Lancaster.

Oct. 102. Notes, in Cecill's hand, of business to be moved in Parliament concerning the expediency of declaring the Queen's successor, of her entertaining the subject of marriage, &c.

VOL. XLI. NOVEMBER—DECEMBER, 1566.

1566.
Nov. 2.
1. L. V. to   . Explanation of Dr. Sanders' letter. Authority to him and Dr. Harding from the Pope. Exposition of various points of doctrine as taught and enforced by the Romish Church. Urges his good example towards reviving the Catholic religion in England. Wishes his letter to be communicated to Sir Ric. Mollineux, and other his friends. [*See post*, 1568, *July* 31, *and Nov.* 1.]

Nov. 3.
Naples.
2. Thomas Champneys to Sir Wm. Cecill. Recommends one Jenkinson to be employed on a voyage of discovery to Cathaia.

Nov. 3. 3. Oath, by Nich. Robynson, D.D., now Bishop of Bangor, acknowledging the Queen's supremacy in all matters temporal or ecclesiastical.

[Nov. 5.] 4. Answer of Queen Elizabeth to the Parliament on the subject of marriage being proposed by them to her. Thinks the single life she leads most acceptable to God. She approves however the manner of their petition.

Nov. 5. 5. Note, in the Queen's own hand, concerning the proposal of marriage made to her by the Parliament.

Nov. 5. 6. Copy of the above.

Nov. 5. 7. Note of a conversation with the Queen, in which she expressed her opinion relative to the petition, by the Parliament, on the subject of her marrying, and settlement of the succession to the Crown. [*In Cecill's hand, who has indorsed it "this was not reported."*]

VOL. XLI.

1566.
Nov. 5. 8. Brief note of sundry things contained in the Queen's reply to the Parliament. *In Cecill's hand.*

Nov. 5. 9. Report of the Queen's answer, by Sec. Cecill, to the address of the House of Commons, on the subject of their petition, for marriage and succession.

Nov. 5. 10. Bill for maintaining the havens in the Narrow Seas, between the Thames mouth and Portsmouth.

Nov. 5.
Arches Court.
11. Dr. Lewes to Sir Wm. Cecill. Concerning a Bill which he introduced into the Lower House for regulating appeals in civil and maritime causes.

Nov. 7. 12. Wm. Humfrey to same. The house for manufacturing wire is in a state of forwardness. Sends a sample of the calamine to him.

Nov. 7.
Combe.
13. John Mount to same. Has been in Northumberland at a village called Blythe, near Newcastle, and set up certain salt works there. Is about to take a coal pit on lease.

Nov. 7.
[? Idus Nov.]
Gray's Inn.
14. Thomas Hatcher to same. Solicits his patronage in collecting into one body the works of the eloquent and learned Dr. Haddon. Lat.

Nov. 9. 15. Message from the Queen, to be declared to the Speaker of the House of Commons, not to treat any more about the succession.

[Nov. 11.] 16. Question whether the Queen's commandment, forbidding the Lower House to speak or treat relative to the succession, be not a breach of the privileges of the House.

Nov. 11. 17. Copy of the above.

Nov. 11. 18. Bill against tailors using the trade of skinners, and against exporting lamb skins.

Nov. 11. 19. Cecill to Dr. Beaumont, Vice-Chancellor, and the Heads of Houses in Cambridge. Desires that the irregularities of the students respecting apparel may be suppressed.

Nov. 15. 20. Address to the Queen by the House of Commons, stating their intentions in recommending to Her Majesty the settlement of the succession and for her marriage; and of their entire submission to Her Majesty's pleasure. *Draft, corrected by Cecil.*

Nov. 15. 21. Copy of the above, with corrections by the same.

Nov. 16. 22. Another copy, with further corrections by the same.

Nov. 16 (?) 23. Bill for the establishing of the Company of Curriers of London.

Nov. 18. 24. Heads of the Bill against pluralities of benefices, and non-residence.

Nov. 21, 25. Act to restrain the printing, selling, and uttering of unprofitable and hurtful English books.

Vol. XLI.

1566.

Nov. 22. 26. Wm. Humfrey to Sir Wm. Cecill. Requests to be informed of his pleasure respecting the Bill concerning battery and mineral works.

Nov. 23. 27. Note relative to the debt of Christopher Lascelles, in the Court of Wards.

Nov. 24. 28. Note of words spoken in the Parliament House by Jas. Dalton : upon Mr. Melvyn's information.

Nov. 24 (?) 29. Explanation by James Dalton, of the speech made by him in the House, relative to seditious books, and a slanderous libel calling the Prince of Scotland, Prince of Scotland, England, and Ireland.

Nov. 24. 30. Minute of a message to the House of Commons from the Queen, releasing the House from her former commands as to discussion on the succession. [*Corrected by the Queen herself.*]

[Nov. 25.] 31. Substance of the message by the Queen to the House of Commons, in conformity with the above.

Nov. 25. Cliff Park. 32. Wm. Cayworthe to Cecill. Has sent by John Clement, a servant of Sir Walter Mildmay, the rent of the assarts, due at Michaelmas.

Nov. 26. 33. Archbishop Parker to same. Is glad the deanery of Chichester has been given to Mr. Curtis. Has distributed the Bible in parts to divers persons for translation. Wishes Cecill had leisure to undertake one of the Epistles.

Nov. 30 (?) 34. Bill repealing the Act of 7 Edw. VI., and granting full liberty to the Company of Vintners of London to buy and sell wines wherever they pleased.

Nov. 35. Titles of various Bills passed in the House of Commons relative to matters ecclesiastical, temp. Edw. VI., Mary, Eliz.

Nov. 36. Heads for an address proposed to be delivered to the Queen, at the end of the Parliament. *In Cecill's hand.*

Dec. 2. Chekers. 37. Lady Mary Gray to Cecill. Entreats him to continue her friend, and to obtain for her the Queen's mercy.

Dec. 5. Keswick. 38. Tho. Thurland to same. Has received his letters, and conferred with experienced persons concerning the earth brought out of Scotland from Crawford Muir, which they assert is very rich in gold.

Dec. 11. 39. Winchester to the Council. Transactions relative to grain in the North. Seven ships have been laden with corn in Norfolk. Has commanded that no corn be shipped, except for Berwick.

Dec. 12. 40. Preamble to the Bill for the subsidy. *Corrected by Cecill.*

Dec. 12. 41. Another copy, with further corrections, by the same.

Dec. 13. 42. Wm. Humfrey to Cecill. Diversity of opinion among the Lords, touching the privilege for mines. Has caused the Bill to be divided, and has placed the battery and calamine works separately.

1566;

[Dec. 14.] 43. Petition of the Archbishops and Bishops to the Queen, praying that the Bill for Uniformity in Religion, which had passed the Lower House, and been read once in the Upper House, and there stopped by Her Majesty's order, might be allowed to pass, and that she would give her Royal assent thereto. [*This is signed by the two Archbishops and thirteen Bishops. The Bill was read a first time in the House of Lords on the 14th December 1566 : which date has been assigned to this petition.*]

Dec. 19. 44. Bill extending the privileges of the Fellowship of Merchant Adventurers of England, and re-enacting the Act 12 Hen. VII.

Dec. 20. 45. Wm. Humfrey to Cecill. The Bill for the manufacture of latten has been again disapproved. Reasons why it is disagreeable to some of the Lords.

Dec. 21. 46. Archbp. Parker to same. Requests the loan of the Book of Articles. The Queen is displeased with the Bishops, and laments much the neglect of prayer and fasting in her Court.

Dec. 21. 47. Tho. Keys to same. Complains of ill usage by the Warden of the Fleet, who keeps him close prisoner, under severe restrictions. *Incloses*,

    47. I. *Statement, by Thomas Keys, respecting his having been supplied with a rib of roast beef for his dinner which had been immersed in a liquid wash prepared for mangy dogs. His illness thereon, &c.*

Dec. 21.
Dover Castle. 48. Wm. Lord Cobham, Constable of Dover Castle, and Admiral of the Cinque Ports, to the Mayor, &c. of Folkstone. Precept to levy the assessment made on the inhabitants of Folkstone, according to the schedule. Lat.

Dec. 21. 49. Observations on the Clothworkers' Bill, with objections thereto, and answers to the said objections.

Dec. 21 (?) 50. Answer, by Sir Wm. Garrard and others, to the bill of complaint made by the Clothworkers, with respect to exportation of Kentish cloths.

Dec. 22. 51. Edmond Gheast, Bishop of Rochester, to Cecill. Is sorry for his ill health. Supposes he has heard of the Bishop of Gloucester's objection to the adverb " only " being placed in the article respecting the Holy Sacrament.

Dec. 25. 52. Account of the tenths due by the clergy at Christmas.

Dec. 28. 53. Wm. Humfrey to Cecill. The Earl of Worcester insists on having the lease of the ground for the erection of wire works drawn by his own officers in Wales. Objects to certain clauses.

54. Questions in theology, natural and moral philosophy, law, &c. to be argued at Oxford.

55. Another paper of questions propounded at Oxford. *In Cecill's hand.*

VOL. XLI.

1566?

56. List of questions, arranged after the manner of Bellarmin; to be discussed at Oxford.

57. Observations whether or not it be convenient for the Company of Merchant Adventurers, at their first return into the Low Countries, to repair to Antwerp.

58. Notes, in the hand-writing of Sir Wm. Cecill, of the inconvenience of extending the power of bringing more wines into the realm.

59. Answer on behalf of the town of Shrewsbury to the petition on the part of West Chester to have a staple of the cottons and friezes made in North Wales, to be settled at that city.

60. Certificate of Sir Christopher Draper, Lord Mayor of London, of the assessment of certain foreigners to the first payment of the subsidy granted to the Queen. With attestation of John Mershe, Gov. of the Merchant Adventurers, as to exemption of the Company in Flanders.

61. Extract from an old book in the Exchequer, containing certain notes relative to customs, scavage, and other duties, payable by strangers.

62. Abel Sylvius to Cecill. Compliments him on his virtues, and solicits his patronage. Lat.

63. List of the Judges and principal officers in several Courts of Law.

64. Note of the rents of Thomas Robinson, son and heir of William Robinson, deceased, at Alvecote, in the county of Warwick.

65. Orders to be observed in the Office of Ordnance, as appointed by the Earl of Warwick.

66. Warrant for releasing such persons as have been deprived for non-conformity, from payment of first fruits of promotions to dignities and offices ecclesiastical.

67. A treatise on the well government of a Commonwealth, under the head of Faith, Concord, Order, and Discipline; showing chiefly that encouragement of husbandry and education of the lower orders, were the principal elements of prosperity.

68. Account of the Bailiff and Collector of the manor of Howton, in the county of York, late parcel of the possessions of the Monastery of St. Oswald.

69. Grant to Hugh Councell and Ambrose Earl of Warwick, of certain revenues from concealed lands, which have been forfeited to the Crown under attainder, or as having been appropriated to superstitious uses.

70. Commission by the Queen to   , for taking up money for her service.

1566?

VOL. XLI.

71. Reasons to move the Queen that orders may be appointed for the redress of many things concerning the Posts.

72. Ordinances for the order of the Posts and hackneymen, between London and Dover.

73. Table of the wages of the Posts northwards, as they have continued from the beginning of the Queen's Majesty's reign to the present, 1566. Indorsed by Randolph.

74. Wages of the Posts from the Court to Berwick.

75. Petition of artificers and labourers to the Parliament, praying that the exportation of leather and raw hides be restrained.

76. Notes in Cecill's hand. Definition of the term "vagabond;" and draft of clauses against exporting grain; and for preservation of woods.

77. Effect of the Act prohibiting any one to use any trade or art unless he has been apprenticed to the same.

78. Re-grant to Robert Earl of Leicester (the original grant being 9th June 1563) of the manor and lands of Cleobury Mortimer, as well in the county of Salop as of Worcester, parcel of the possessions of the late Earl of March.

79. " Allegations in the behalf of the high and mighty Princess, the " Lady Mary, now Queen of Scots, against the opinions and books set " forth in the part and favour of the Lady Katharine [Grey] and the " rest of the issues of the French Queen, touching the succession of " the Crown."

80. Petition of the inhabitants of St. Katherines, near the Tower, to Sir Wm. Cecill, for his aid and assistance in resisting the attempts of Doctor Willson, Master of the Hospital, to sell the liberties and royalties of the same to the Lord Mayor of London.

81. Petition of Leonard Bates, of Welbury, York, to Cecill; showing that he held the manor of Welbury from the late Wm. Lord Dacre, on condition of marrying Margery, the widow of James Kyrton, and bringing up his son, an infant, which he had done; but was now troubled by one Bennet Chomelly for the possession thereof. Prays that he may have undisturbed possession during the minority of George Lord Dacre.

1567.
Jan. 10.
The Temple.

VOL. XLII. JANUARY—JULY, 1567.

1. Robert Keyllwey, Surveyor of the Court of Wards, to Cecill. Observations on the cause of Sherman and Brereton. *Incloses,*

    1. I. *Case to be submitted to the Master, &c. of the Court of Wards, between the Queen and Thos. Brereton, relative to the manor of Whetnal, Chester.* 20 *Nov.* 1566.

Vol. XLII.

1567.
Jan. 10 (?) 2. Commission by the Queen to Lord Chidiock Powlett, Sir Robt. Oxenbridge, and others, touching inquiry into concealed lands belonging to suppressed religious houses, within the counties of Southampton and Berks.

Jan. 11. 3. The Queen to Lord Keeper Bacon. Desires he will put the Great Seal of England to a proclamation for apprehending certain Frenchmen who have attacked and spoiled the island of Madeira.

Jan. 11. 4. Proclamation for staying young Montluc, who, under pretence of trafficking by sea, has invaded the island of Madeira, belonging to the King of Portugal.

Jan. 24.
London.
5. Sir Wm. Garrard and Rowland Hawarde to Cecill. Sends answer to Mr. Gylbarte's articles. *Inclosing,*

    5. I. *Answer of the Company of Merchant Adventurers to the requests made by Mr. Gylbarte to be allowed two of the Queen's ships to be employed in the voyage he proposes to undertake.*

Jan. 24. 6. Account of sums of money for which the Queen's warrants are to be procured for various public works and services, principally for the Navy.

Jan. 25. 7. Bishop Horn to Cecill. Recommends one Mr. Whitgift "a "man honest and verye well learned" to be promoted to the deanery of Canterbury, or some other preferment of the late Dr. Wootton's; and for Dr. White to be made a Bishop.

Jan. 25.
Cambridge.
8. John Wells to same. Regrets extremely to hear of his illness. Expresses great attachment. Lat.

Jan. 29.
Lerpool.
[Liverpool.]
9. John Bland to Wm. Wynter and Edw. Baeshe. Gives an account of his proceedings in procuring a store of provisions at Liverpool. News by a passenger from Ireland.

Feb. 2.
London.
10. Lord Cobham to Cecill. The mariners of the vessel lately wrecked on the Goodwin Sands are suspected of keeping back and concealing a quantity of goods with which she was freighted.

Feb. 4. 11. Richard Beseley, an old Chaplain of Henry VIII., to same. Refers to some past event which has become matter of history, and observes that it is necessary to take warning for the future. [*Imperfect.*]

Feb. 12. 12. Wm. Humfrey to Cecill. Money due from Bristol, for which a warrant is necessary. The lease for the calamine will soon be perfected. Sends an account by which Mr. Stanley's debt to the Queen will appear.

Feb. 13.
[Idib. Feb.]
Keswick.
13. Daniel Hechstetter to Sir Wm. Cecill. Thomas Thurland, who is going to London, will acquaint him with all things necessary for furthering their mineral operations. Lat.

Vol. XLII.

567.

Feb. 16. 14. Wm. Humfrey to same. By the assays made at the Star Chamber he will find how much the silver of the moneys is bettered between the assay of the pot and that of the Pyx. The trial of the Pyx at the Star Chamber shews only that the moneys have been truly made.

Feb. 17. 15. The Queen to the Mayor and Customer of Chester. Order to provide transports for conveyance of 250 soldiers to Ireland, also for shipping twelve cart-loads of ammunition and other warlike stores.

Feb. 18. 16. Same to the Sheriff and Justices of Lancaster (and to other counties). Order for levy of certain footmen to be transported out of England for service in Ireland. Draft.

Feb. 18. 17. Same to the Earls of Derby and Shropshire. Directions to aid in the levy of a certain number of able men in the counties of Lancaster and Derby for service in Ireland.

And on the same paper. Minute of letter to Sir John Savage, Sir Hugh Cholmley, and Sir Lawrence Smith, to view and muster all the levies at the port of Chester.

Feb. 19. **Westminster.** 18. Earls of Pembroke and Leicester, and Sir Wm. Cecill, to the Earl of Northumberland. Require him to obey the Queen's injunction to suffer Thomas Thurland and Daniel Hechstetter, or their assigns, to carry away the ore dug up at Newland, in Cumberland.

Feb. 19. 19. Note of certain works of art of marble jasper, brought into England for Sir Wm. Cecill and the Earl of Pembroke, by Dominicque Troisrieux, a Frenchman. Further description of the same, and note of such as the Queen has licensed to be brought into the realm, and to return duty-free if unsold ; three papers, two French.

Feb. 20. Petition of the Aldermen and Company of Easterlings of the Dutch House at the Stillyard, London, to the Queen. Soliciting licence to transport certain Suffolk cloths beyond sea.

Feb. 21. Copy of the above.

Feb. 22. Offers made for carrying on a trade with Barbary, with certain allowances to the Queen.

Feb. (?) 23. Humfrey Gilberte to the Queen. Proposals for undertaking the discovery of a passage to Cataia ; to be performed in four voyages, under certain privileges, to endure for ten years commencing March come twelvemonth 1568.

March 4. 24. Indenture of lease from Sir Wm. Cecill to James Blunt Lord Mountjoy, of the tenth part of the profits of the patent for manufacturing alum, formerly assigned to Sir Wm. Cecill.

March 7. 25. The Queen to the Earl of Northumberland. Commands him to offer no further obstruction to the workers of the mines and minerals at a place called Newlands, co. Cumberland. Any lawful claim he may have in the said minerals shall be reserved to him.

VOL. XLII.

1567.
March 7. 26. Earls of Pembroke and Leicester and Sec. Cecill to the Earl of Northumberland. Refer to the preceding letter ; and have given instructions thereon to George Nedham.

March 7. 27. Tho. Thurland to Sir William Cecill. Sends him a plan of Keswick, the smelting house, Newlands, and the other mines. Denton, sent last year into Ireland for wood, has returned.

March 8. London. 28. Lord Cobham to same. Recommends the bearer, John de la Bersona, employed to assist in collecting the goods saved from the ship of Middleborough, wrecked on the Goodwin sands.

March 12. 29. Marq. Winchester to same. The Lady Lennox is now by the the Queen's order in the custody of Lady Dacre and Lady Sackvile. He cannot help her with money.

March 13. 30. Cornelius Alnetanus [Lannoy] to same. Promises to perform the things mentioned in his offers to the Queen. Lat. *Incloses,*

> 30. I. *Cornelius Alnetanus to the Queen. Solemnly engages to produce gold and gems by a chemical process.* 13 *March* 1567.

[In Cecill's diary, under the date 10 Feb. 1567, is the following entry: " Cornelius de la Noye, an alchymist, wrought in Somerset " House, and abused many in promising to convert any metall into " gold."]

March 14. York. 31. Earl of Northumberland to the Earls of Pembroke and Leicester and Sir Wm. Cecill. Has ascertained beyond doubt that the minerals dug up at Newlands belong to him only, and that the workers thereof are trespassers on his land.

March 14. York. 32. Same to same. Another copy of the above, with copies of letters to the Queen, the Lord Treasurer and Sir Walter Mildmay, the Lord Chief Baron and other Barons of the Exchequer, praying that the injunction respecting the ore dug up on his lands at Newlands may be dissolved.

March 16. 33. Tho. Thurland to the Earl of Leicester and Sir Wm. Cecill. Explains the grounds on which he has always commended the richness of the mines of gold, silver, and copper in England. Obstacles which he has encountered by the Earl of Northumberland.

March 16. Westminster. 34. The Queen to the Earl of Arundel. Thanks for the things he has sent her, and hopes he will enjoy his health on his return. Has visited his house at Nonesuch.

March 20. 13 Cal. Aprilis. Keswick. 35. Daniel Hechstetter to the Queen. Complains that the Earl of Northumberland has obstructed the mining operations at Newlands. Lat.

March 20. 36. Suit to be made to the Queen for a grant of the survey of all the customs inward and outward.

March 22. Mint. 37. Tho. Thurland to Cecill. Requests his advice, according to Her Majesty's permission, in mining operations, particulars of which he details.

T

Vol. XLII.

1567.

March 22. 38. A summary of the charges for apparel with rapier and daggers, for the Earl of Oxford, from 3 Sept. 1563 to the quarter ending 22 March 1567.

March 24.
Topcliff. 39. George Nedham to Sir Wm. Cecill. Reports his proceedings with Northumberland about the ores dug up at Newlands. The Earl claims as ample right to the said ores as to any of his possessions.

March 25.
Topcliff. 40. Northumberland to the Earls of Pembroke and Leicester and Sir Wm. Cecill. Has conferred with Mr. Nedham respecting the ores dug up on his land at Newlands, and has consented that he shall take away 200 buckets of the same.

March 29. 41. Certificate of proportions of the subsidy payable within certain hundreds of the county of Surrey.

March. 42. Names of merchants of Holland who are exempt from contribution to the subsidy within the City of London. Lat.

April 11. 43. Marq. Winchester to Cecill. In favour of Mr. Bowyer, Keeper of the Records in the Tower. Proposes that the Records of the Chancery and of the Parliament be transferred to his custody Has compiled a book of his own pedigree and armorial bearings.

April 12. 44. Articles brought into Berkshire by WilliamHuggon, of Hampton Court, gentleman, for examination of the clergy and laity, relative to concealed lands.

April 12. 45. Certificate of the clergy of Berkshire in reply to the Commission for inquiry into concealed lands.

April 13. 46. Names of the ordinaries and priests attesting the above, annexed.

April 13. 47. Account of the provisions and payments contained in six books of the Revels, with the book of the progress, from Christmas, anno 2do. Eliz. to 13 April 1567.

April 17.
Chekers. 48. Lady Mary Grey to Cecill. Entreats him to continue his good offices in procuring her restoration to the Queen's favour.

April 25. 49. Suit of merchants trading to Barbary, that the Queen would be pleased to incorporate them as a Company, for the better regulation of trade, and to prohibit all unskilful persons from intermeddling therewith.

April. 50. Petitions humbly exhibited by the Company of Goldsmiths to the Marq. of Winchester, Sir Wm. Cecill, and Sir Walter Mildmay as Commissioners appointed for the affairs of the Mint; and among other things for Ric. Rogers to be restored to his office of Assay Master for the Company. [*See post* 7 *Feb.* 1568.]

April. 51. Answer by Wm. Stanley to the six petitions exhibited by the Company of Goldsmiths to the Commissioners appointed for affairs of the Mint.

VOL. XLII.

1567.
April. 52. Copy of the petitions of the Company of Goldsmiths; with orders of the Commissioners for the Mint thereon. Wm. Humfrey to be restored to his office of Assay Master of the Mint.

April. 53. Copy of the above petitions and orders.

April (?) 54. Answer of Thos. Stanley to the bill of complaint exhibited by certain Goldsmiths against him to Sir Wm. Cecill.

May 4.
Chester. 55. Sir Laurence Smyth and Sir Hugh Cholmondeley to the Council. Have taken order for the transportation of 250 soldiers to Ireland. Have borrowed money of the city of Chester for their expenses. *Inclosing,*

55. I. *Note of all the charges defrayed within the county of Chester for transportation of 250 men into Ireland.*

May 5. 56. Account of arrears due to the Duchess of Somerset on her jointure, since the death of the Duke of Somerset; and suit of the Duchess for recompence for the same.

May 7.
Norwich. 57. Orders established by the Earl Marshal for regulation of the College of Arms, in which are recited the proceedings of several chapters of the Heralds and Officers at Arms previously held.

May 8. 58. Notes of the contents of Geo. Nedham's letters from Keswick to Mr. Alderman Duckett, about minerals and mining affairs.

May 9.
Westminster. 59. Sir Nich. Throkmorton to the Earl of Leicester. Mr. Colville has delivered his letter to the Queen. She much commended the manner of his writing, and desired to see what he had written to Throkmorton himself. Her observations. Proceedings with Applierd and Trendell. The Earl of Sussex going to the Emperor.

May 9. 60. Same to same. Intelligence from Scotland. Confederacy of the nobles to annul the Queen of Scots marriage with Earl Bothwell. Conciliation between the Lutherans and Calvinists. Marriage of Lord Paget to be solemnized at Drayton.

May 10.
Keswick. 61. Geo. Nedham to the Queen. Reports his proceedings on conveying her letters to the Earl of Northumberland, requiring the delivery of certain ores stayed by him at the mines in Cumberland.

May 11.
Westminster. 62. Grant to the Burgesses of Great Yarmouth of the remission of the sum of 100*l.* payable by them on account of the fifteenths and tenths granted by the Parliament.

May 11.
Westminster. 63. The Queen to Thomas Stanley and others. Warrant to attend the assays of gold and silver at the Mint, within the Tower of London, and the pixing of the moneys according to the Mint indenture.

May 12.
[4° Idus Maii.]
Cambridge. 64. Bartholomew Clerke to Cecill. Expresses his gratitude for benefits conferred. Lat.

May 13.
[3° Id. Maii.] 65. William Lewin to same. Extols his patronage of learning. Lat.

VOL. XLII.

1567.
May 23.
Cobham.
66. Wm. Lord Cobham to Sir Wm. Cecill. Intelligence received of warlike preparations making by the French and King of Spain in Flanders and Holland. Money may be had in Bremen.

May 25.
[8 Cal. Junii.]
67. Bartholomew Dodington to same. Acknowledges the paternal friendship which he has shown to the University of Cambridge. Lat.

May 25.
Keswick.
68. Geo. Nedham to same. Describes the haven and castle of Pillafowdre, in Lancashire: an extraordinary fish lately taken there. Mineral operations in Cumberland. Recommends an exchange of certain lands between the Queen and the Earl of Northumberland.

May 27.
The Prison in Wood Street.
69. Eliseus Bomelius, M.D., to same. Exposes the ignorance of Dr. [Thomas] Francis, in Latin and astronomy. Solicits to be released from prison.

May 28.
Somerset House.
70. Ar. Waad to same. Has taken order for keeping back all boats on the Thames, and for bringing Cor. [Cornelius Alnetanus?] to Court to-morrow. His personal manner.

May 29.
Southampton.
71. Mayor, &c. of Southampton, to same. Are willing to admit certain foreigners, to the number of one hundred or more, to reside in the town, as they are disposed to communicate certain arts of manufacture.

May 29.
Chester.
72. Sir John Savage, Sir Lau. Smyth, and Sir Hugh Cholmondeley to the Council. Have borrowed certain sums of money for the purpose of sending the soldiers into Ireland; for repayment of which they request a sufficient remittance. *Inclosing,*

72. I. *Account of money borrowed of certain merchants and others of Chester, for the purpose of transporting soldiers to Ireland.*

May 30.
73. Bishop Grindall to Cecill. Has examined the book (a Greek MS.) brought by the stranger; it contains 30 homilies of Chrysostom. Thinks the MS is undoubtedly written by Chrysostom, and worthy to be presented to the Queen.

May.
74. The Queen to the Master of the Rolls. Warrant to deliver the Rolls of Parliament, Patent Rolls, and other Records belonging to the Court of Chancery, into the custody of William Bowyer, Keeper of the Records in the Tower.

May.
75. Petitions by the tenants and inhabitants of the Soke of Bolingbroke, Lincolnshire, to the Chancellor of the Duchy of Lancaster. Complain of being unduly assessed by the Duchy Court with the whole charge of diking Wainfleet Haven, &c.; and question as to Mr. Bertie's manor of Spilsby.

May.
76. Note of matters to be transacted by the Commissioners of Sewers relative to Wainfleet Haven and the Soke of Bolingbroke.

May.
77. Chancellor of the Duchy of Lancaster to Lord Willoughby, Sir Edw. Dymock, and Sir Wm. Skipwith Commissioners of Sewers for Lincolnshire. Directions for assessing certain foreigners who ought to be charged with the diking of Wainfleet Haven, &c.

VOL. XLIII. JUNE—AUGUST.

1567.
June 1.
Ipswich.
1. Edw. Gooddinge to Sir Wm. Cecill. Gives an account of his proceedings in salt works established in Essex and Suffolk.

June 7.
Southampton.
2. Earl of Lennox to same. Has made humble submission to the Queen in writing; begs him to use his good offices that he may be restored to her favour again.

June 7.
London.
3. Peter Back to the Queen. Solicits to be allowed to carry on certain experiments in the manufacture of salt, and preparation of madder as a dye. Lat.

June 15.
London.
4. Wm. Bowyer to Cecill. Touching the removal of records into his custody in the Tower. The Master of the Rolls objects to their being wholly transferred thither. [*Mutilated.*] Incloses,

  4. I. *Collection by Mr. Bowyer of documents showing that it was customary from the time of the Conquest to deposit all records of the Crown in the Tower. Also that the Record Office there is a distinct office by itself, and does not appertain to the Master of the Rolls.*

June 15. 5–6. Copy of Bowyer's letter, before the mutilation, and of the inclosure.

June 16. 7. Earl of Leicester to Cecill. Upon the affairs of Scotland. The Scottish Lords have agreed their Prince should ever remain under Her Majesty's protection. They are opposed to Earl Bothwell. The Queen of Scots is said to be with child. Queen Elizabeth's conversation with Leicester thereon. Suit of Mr. Power for a farm at Windsor.

June 17.
Cambridge.
8. John Whitgyfte to same. Acknowledges his singular goodness in placing him in Trinity College. Repels a charge of encouraging nonconformity; but it grieveth him that any man should cease from preaching on account of things indifferent. Smallness of his income and extreme necessity have brought him into debt.

June 21.
Westminster
College.
9. Gabriel Goodman, Dean of Westminster, to same. Conference between Sir Tho. Cornwaleys, Mr. Provost, and Mr. Harpsfield on matters of religion. The opinions of Cornwaleys respecting the Church of Rome. Thinks when his conscience is further enlightened he will yield to the truth.

June 21.
Westminster.
10. Sir Thomas Cornwaleys to same. His humble submission to the Queen, shewing that he is willing to conform himself in matters of religion. *Incloses,*

  10. I. *Submission of Sir Thomas Cornwaleys to the Queen. Entreats pardon for his offence in having withstood her laws for establishing true religion.*

June 22. 11. Petition of certain foreign artists in various branches of weaving to Cecill, that he would permit them to settle at Stamford, in Lincolnshire, and to occupy his house and 200 or 300 acres of ground there.

Vol. XLIII.

1567.

June 24. 12. Proportion of ordnance, powder, &c. for the fort at Genoia [Guinea] if there shall be need of any fortification: signed John Hawkyns.

June 25. 13. Remembrances touching the mines collected out of Geo. Nedham's letters from Keswick to Mr. Alderman Duckett.

June 27. 14. Wm. Mount to Sir Wm. Cecill. Acknowledges the favourable mention which he has made of him in letters to his patron Smyth. Lat.

June 28. 15. Memorandum of arrears due by collectors of subsidy granted anno 8° Eliz.

June 30. Farnham. 16. Bishop Horn to Cecill. The township of Southampton is willing to admit the Netherlanders who have been driven from their country on account of their religion. Recommends their case.

June 30. 17. Note of assignments and payments in the Exchequer.

June. 18. Account of the charges for transporting 250 soldiers from Chester to Ireland, by order of Sir J. Savage, Sir L. Smyth, and Sir H. Cholmondeley, and of sums advanced for payment of the same.

June. 19. Mayor, &c. of Maidstone to the Queen. Pray for licence under her Letters Patent to receive certain families of foreigners, artificers in the various branches of manufacture detailed.

June. 20. Petition of John de Beaulieu, for himself and other foreigners resident at Southampton, to Cecill, praying to be discharged of the customs for such wares and merchandizes as they shall manufacture there.

June. Richmond. 21. The Queen to the Master and Council of the Court of Wards and Liveries. Warrant to permit Lady Catharine and Lady Mary Grey, daughters and co-heiresses of Henry Duke of Suffolk and Frances his wife, to receive the rents and profits of certain lands late parcel of the possessions of the College of Astley, co. Warwick.

June. Grant of lease in reversion to Richard Procter of tythes in Panswyke, co. Gloucester, for 21 years. *Docquet.* [*See Borders,* 21 *June* 1567.]

June. Grant of lease to Lady Parry of lands in Chelveley, for 21 years. *Docquet.* [*See Borders, ib.*]

June. Grant of lease to Doctor Lewes of the parsonage of Llandona and others, for 21 years. *Docquet.* [*See Borders, ib.*]

June. Grant of lease to Mr. Roger Mauers of the parsonage of Barton-upon-Humber and manor of Wiscote, for 31 years. *Docquet.* [*See Borders, ib.*]

June. Warrant to discharge the Merchant Strangers of the Low Countries and other Strangers, of the two payments of subsidy granted by the last Act of Parliament. *Docquet.* [*See Borders, ib.*]

Vol. XLIII.

1567.
June. Grant of lease in reversion to Wm. Sekes of the scite of the manor of Enbroke, for 21 years. *Docquet.* [*See Borders, ib.*]

June. Grant of lease to Michael Hawtry of the parsonage of Wendover, for 21 years. *Docquet.* [*See Borders, ib.*]

June. Grant of pardon to John Ap Thomas Ap Richard, for a rape. *Docquet.* [*See Borders, ib.*]

June. Warrant to allow Garter King at Arms 20s. a day, whereof 10s. in reward attending on the Earl of Sussex, to the Emperor. *Docquet.* [*See Borders, ib.*]

June. Discharge for a collector of subsidy of 105l. issued for service of Newhaven. *Docquet.* [*See Borders, ib.*]

June. Warrant for " scochens of Armes set up in Chapell of Court, at " St. George's day." *Docquet.* [*See Borders, ib.*]

June. Grant to Walter Jones of a prebend in Westminster, void by resignation of Dr. Hutton *Docquet.* [*See Borders, ib.*]

June. Grant to Ed. Marten for life of the office of Surveyor of Berkshire, void by resignation of Roger Amyce. *Docquet.* [*See Borders, ib.*]

June. Grant of pardon to Richard Cave for killing Christopher Hall. *Docquet.* [*See Borders, ib.*]

July 1.
London.
22. Earl of Lennox to Sir Wm. Cecill. The Queen has restored him and his wife to favour, but has not made restitution to them of their estate. They are upwards of 3,000l. in debt. Solicits a loan of 1,000l. from the Queen.

July 7.
Fleet Prison.
23. Tho. Keys to Leicester and Cecill. Prays that they will bear in mind his long imprisonment, and intercede with the Queen for his pardon.

July 13.
Fulham.
24. Bishop Grindall to Cecill. Begs him to further the suit of the bearer for a licence to make a collection for ransom of certain Englishmen, captives in Algiers.

July 18.
Westminster.
25. Bond of Sir Roger Vaughan, of Talgarth, co. Brecon, and others, to Thomas Earl of Northumberland and others; condition not specified. Indorsed " for the Lady Eleanor Vaughan."

July 20.
Althorp.
26. Examination of Morris Freman upon certain interrogatories administered to him at Richmond, as to transactions which took place while he was in the service of Lord and Lady Strange.

July 18.
27. Sir Walter Mildmay to Cecill. Does not understand the object of Throkmorton's legation. The Scottish affairs are in a doubtful position. The French should not be suffered to gain influence there. The Irish affairs go on prosperously.

July 21.
Maidstone.
28. Serjeant Nich. Barham and Tho. Wotton to same. Have sent a form of licence, for the residence of certain foreigners in Maidstone, nearly similar to one granted to Sandwich.

Vol. XLIII.

1567.
July 22.
Fulham.
29. Bishop Grindall to Sir Wm. Cecill. In favour of certain articles required by the foreigners for their establishment and carrying on of trades and manufactures in various towns. *Incloses,*

> 29. I. *Supplication to the Queen by the foreigners driven from the Low Countries on account of their religion, to be allowed to settle and carry on their occupations in various towns in England.* 16 *May* 1567.

July 22.
30. Foreigners from the Low Countries to the Earl of Pembroke and Sir Wm. Cecill. Have represented to the Queen and Council the extremity to which they are reduced. Particulars of their request as to the persons to be brought with them, and the manufactures to be carried on.

July 23.
31. Wm. Humfrey to Cecill. The house for manufacturing wire is in readiness for use. The experiments already made shew that 25 cwt. may be produced weekly.

July 27.
Chelsea.
32. Marq. of Winchester to same. Sends him for consideration the plans for the tomb of Henry VIII. to be put up at Windsor.

July 31.
33. Anthony Smetheley, Foedary of the East Riding of Yorkshire, to same. Concerning the repair of the sluice called the Gallow Clowe, by order of the Commissioners of Sewers of Kingston-upon-Hull. *Incloses,*

> 33. I. *Mayor, &c. of Hull to Anth. Smetheley. Applying for the amount assessed on Mr. Stapleton's lands for repair of the Gallow Clowe on the Humber.* Kingston-on-Hull. 27 *June* 1567.

> 33. II. *Copy of the verdict of the Jury, finding Robert Stapleton and Francis Hawldenbye liable to the repair of the Gallow Clowe.* 21 *June* 1567.

> 33. III. *Estimate for repairs of the Gallow Clowe, within the county of Kingston-on-Hull, parcel of the inheritance of Mr. Stapleton, the Queen's ward.*

July.
34. Statement of sums due by collectors of the subsidy from the laity, for which they had not accounted on the 5th July.

July.
35. Note of the first payment of the subsidy by the clergy, due 24th May and to be paid before the last of October.

August 4.
Althorp.
36. Sir Walter Mildmay to Cecill. Affairs of Scotland. The marvellous tragedy which has occurred there shews the end of those who do not live in the fear of God. Thinks the government of Murray will be favourable to the establishment of religion.

August 6.
37. Earl of Leicester to same. The Queen has ordered the Lord Treasurer to pay over to the Earl and Countess of Lennox the yearly rents of their estates. His opinion on the affairs of Scotland.

August 6.
38. Articles delivered to John Van Trere for the Lord of Buckholte and others co-partners of the salt works in England and Ireland, touching their privilege of making salt.

VOL. XLIII.

1567.
August 8.
The Minories.
39. Richard Bertie to Sir Wm. Cecill. Thanks him for intelligence. Thinks the Scottish Queen has resigned her crown. Great concourse of people at Boston in consequence of the suit between Pinchbeck and Burne concerning sewers.

August 9.
Greenwich.
40. K. Duchess of Suffolk to same. The Lady Mary Grey has been brought to her and placed under her charge. Insufficiency of her means for her accommodation. Describes the miserable condition of Lady Mary's furniture.

August 9.
41. Estimate of the charges of transferring eight of the Queen's ships from Chatham to Portsmouth; and their charges for one month afterwards.

Aug. [9].
42. Pierre Briet and Jean Carre to Cecill. Desiring permission to erect glass works, similar to those of Venice. Recommended by the Vidame de Chartres. Fr.

[August 9.]
43. Petition of certain foreigners to same. Pray that he will procure a licence from the Queen for them to establish a manufactory of glass. Fr.

August 9.
Windsor.
44. John Quarre to same. Repeats the assurance that the persons above mentioned are willing to pay to the Queen the duty proposed on the glass which may be manufactured by them. Fr.

August 9.
45. Proposals of Anthony Becku, alias Dolin, and John Quarre, natives of the Low Countries, for establishing a manufactory for table glass, such as is used in France. Fr.

August 12.
46. Articles touching the making of glass for glazing, within the realm, such as is made in France and Lorrain; agreed on by the Queen with Anthony Becku, alias Dolin, and John Carre [Quarre].

August 12.
47. Archbishop Parker to Cecill. The produce of the broken plate and bullion found in the Cathedral at Canterbury, has been applied to church uses only. Not a tenth of the plate and ornaments was left which was there at the time of Dr. Wotton's coming.

August 12.
48. The Queen to the Sheriffs of various counties specified in the indorsement. In consequence of preparations made on the opposite coasts they are to cause the whole of each shire to be mustered, with all suitable array of armour and weapons.

August 12.
49. Same to the Lords, Lieutenants, &c. of the southern and western counties, to aid in the musters and appointment of captains in their respective counties.

August 12.
Althorp.
50. Sir Walter Mildmay to Cecill. Arrival of the King of Spain in Flanders. Recal of Sir Nich. Throkmorton out of Scotland. Hopes religion and amity with the latter country will stand fast.

August 19.
Winchester.
51. William Overton to same. His letters have been received with great respect. Communication made by the Earl of Southampton. Rents paid to him. Lat.

Vol. XLIII.

1567.
August 27. 52. The Queen to Lord Trer. Winchester. Has taken order for musters to be made on the sea coast in divers shires, the King of Spain being expected to pass through the Narrow Seas. Directions if he should chance to land at Portsmouth. Repairs at Calshot Castle.

August 27. 53. The Queen to Viscount Montague. Directions to pay every attention to the King of Spain if he should touch at any port in Hampshire, in his passage to the Low Countries. To consult with the Earl of Arundel thereon.

August 27.
London. 54. Valentine Dale to Sir Wm. Cecill. Has discharged Mr. Wynter's brother and examined Corbet, and sends copy of his examination. Will examine Wrench as to his doings with Coke. [*The draft of the preceding letter is written by Cecill, on the blank space of this letter, which is original.*]

August 28. 55. Marq. of Winchester to same. Returns the indenture between the Queen and Henry Smith and James Morley of London, with note of the years to be reserved to the Queen. *Incloses,*

> 55. I. *Indenture between the Queen and Henry Smith and James Morley for farming the customs and duties payable on all woollen cloths and wines imported and exported. Corrected by Cecill, in conformity with Winchester's letter.*

August 29.
Keswick. 56. Geo. Nedham to same. Progress of the mining operations. The Earl of Northumberland's officers have objected to their working a mine called "the Copper Plate" as not within the compass of Newland. With P.S. of the quantity of copper which the six furnaces will smelt daily.

August 29.
London. 57. William Bowyer to same. Sends the middle part of his device relating to the Parliament. Has in hand another respecting decrees, orders, and powers of the King, Council, and Lords of the Star Chamber, which will show how happy it is for England to have nothing to do with the Pope.

August 29. 58. John Best, Bishop of Carlisle, to same. Thanks him for his commendam of Romalde Church, and requests him to further the suits relative to the Church of Carlisle.

August.
Windsor Castle. 59. Earl of Warwick, Master-General of the Ordnance, to all Officers of Ordnance, &c. Has appointed William Pelham, Lieut.-General of the Ordnance, to take account of the remain and survey of all the Queen's ordnance, stores, &c. Directions for all Officers of Ordnance to render yearly account of stores, &c. under their charge.

August.
Cambridge. 60. Andrew Pearne to Cecill. Solicits him to write to Dr. Young, Master of Pembroke College, in favour of a youth named Coxe. Lat.

August. 61. Notes in Bishop Grindall's hand relative to the mode of electing a Bishop of Oxford. Doubts if the Archbishop may grant his commission for confirmation to be done in Ireland. [*Hugh Curwen Archbishop of Dublin, was elected Bishop of Oxford in Sept.* 1567.]

VOL. XLIV. SEPTEMBER—DECEMBER, 1567.

1567.
Sept. 1.
London.
1. Marq. Winchester to Sir Wm. Cecill. Explains the grounds of his answers respecting the bargain for the Queen relative to the duties on cloth and wine. The house of Groby is almost down, and Broadgate will follow, if not repaired.

[Sept. 9.]
2. Grant to Henry Smith and Jas. Morley of the office of Surveyors of the customs on woollen cloths and wines. Draft, corrected by Cecill.

Sept. 9.
Gorhambury.
3. Fair copy of the above.

Sept. 10.
From the Court.
4. Alfonso Ferrabosco to Cecill. Understands he has instructions that the patent should be made out for his life: begs that the words " de heredibus et successoribus nostris " may be inserted therein. Ital.

Sept. 12.
[Prid. Id. Sept.]
5. William Hughes to same. Desires permission to preach the funeral sermon of the late Duchess of Norfolk. Lat.

Sept. 15.
Monthall.
6. Sir Tho. Smith to same. Mr. Scott, prebendary of Carlisle, is about to sue for a remedy of certain unreasonable leases at Carlisle. Desires the Council at York may be directed to take the matter in hand.

Sept. 16.
Plymouth.
7. John Hawkyns to the Queen. The Portuguese who were to have directed them in their enterprize, have fled. Will undertake it himself. The voyage which he contemplates is " to lade negroes in Genoya " [Guinea], and sell them in the West Indyes, in truck of golde, perles, " and esmeraldes." [*The origin of the slave trade.*]

Sept. 19.
Winchester.
8. Bishop Horn to Cecill. The Mayor, &c. of Southampton are willing to admit the Merchant Strangers to reside there. The Strangers have undertaken no corrupt religious sects or opinions shall be encouraged among them.

Sept. 19
9. Winchester to Cecill. Waste of corn in Norfolk and Suffolk. They cannot keep the plough going unless order is taken therein. Proposes a general restraint of exportation.

Sept. 22.
10. Same to same. The Prior of St. John of Jerusalem desires a licence to transport certain kerseys; and the Treasurer of the Duke of Alva another to export two or three horses. *Incloses,*

> 10. I. *The Prior of Jerusalem (son of the Duke of Alva) to Winchester. Solicits permission to transport 2,000 pieces of kerseys and 200 pieces of cloth for clothing the King of Spain's troops. Brussells, 5 Sept.* 1567. *Lat.*
>
> 10. II. *Francis de Lixalde to same. Requests licence to export two or three horses from England for his own use. Brussells,* 13 *Sept.* 1567. *Lat.*

Sept. 26.
St. Bartholomew's.
11. Notes of difference between the old and new privileges granted to the Merchants trading to Muscovia, by the Emperor there.

VOL. XLIV.

1567.
Sept. 27.   12. John Jewell, Bp. of Salisbury, to Sir Wm. Cecill. Is about to print his answer to Harding. Desires leave to address it to her Majesty as Harding already, in a bad cause, has done.

Sept. 28.
Plymouth.   13. John Hawkyns to same. Exculpates himself from three serious charges which have been reported against him to the Queen. Knows the Spaniards and Flemings hate him. Hopes to depart with the next fair wind.

Sept. 29.   14. Tho. Thurland to the Queen. They have at length attained to the making of fine and perfect copper: sends her a specimen. The mines promise well; nothing is wanting but workmen, &c.

Sept. 29.
Keswick.   15. Daniel Hechstetter and Hans Lover to same. Can now make copper and have sent some to London. Will make trial if the copper ores contain silver and gold. Recommend that some conclusion be made between the Queen and the Earl of Northumberland.

Sept. 29.
Keswick.   16. Same to the Earls of Pembroke and Leicester and Sir Wm. Cecill. Describe their success in making copper from ores at Boroughdale; Mr. Alderman Duckett was present. Recommend Geo. Nedham, who has laboured diligently.

Sept. 30.   17. Account of debts due to the office of the Armoury from the 1st of May, and estimate of charges to 31st Dec. 1567.

Sept. 30.   18. The Queen to Winchester. Warrant for easing the amount of customs payable on commodities imported by certain Russian traders.

Sept.   19. Declaration of the account of the receipt and revenues of the lands and possessions of the Earl of Oxford in various counties, to Michaelmas 1567. Lat.

Sept. (?)   20. "The talke" between the Bishop [of London] and Master Pattenson, who had been suspended for preaching without a cure, and had in his sermons called the Bishop a traitor and antichrist.

Oct. 2.   21. The Queen to Sir Owen Hopton. Directs him, in consequence of the demise of Sir John Wentworth, to take into his charge the Lady Catharine Grey, but to keep her from the access of all strangers.

Oct 2.
Windsor.   22. Same to Mr. Roke Grene. Warrant to deliver Lady Catharine Grey into the charge of Sir Owen Hopton.

Oct. 3.
London.   23. Sir Nich. Throkmorton to Cecill. Doubts not he is acquainted with the state of France by means of Sir Henry Norris. If the Protestants get the upper hand, it were well the Queen should make some favourable declaration towards them.

Oct. 3.
Gosfield Hall.   24. Mr. Roke Grene to same. Represents the inconvenience it will be for him to take charge of Lady Catharine Grey.

Oct. 5.   25. Archbishop Parker to same. The Bishop of Oxford elect must be sent to him for confirmation, as he is not exempt from the jurisdiction of the see of Canterbury.

Vol. XLIV.

1567.
Oct. 5.
London.

26. Lionel Duckett to Sir Wm. Cecill. Does not doubt the mineral works will be profitable to the realm. Provision of wood and coal necessary. Requests he will cause some persons to be set at liberty, imprisoned for making certain cloth.

Oct. 7.
Bangor.

27. Nicolas Robinson, Bp. of Bangor, to same. The three shires of Carnarvon, Anglesey, and Merioneth are in great order and tranquillity. Ignorance of the Welsh. The use of images, altars, pilgrimages, and vigils very prevalent among them.

Oct. 11.

28. Sir Owen Hopton to same. Has made arrangements to take charge of the Lady Catharine Grey.

Oct. 19.

29. Dr. Wm. Hughes to same? Notes made on the authority of Scripture and the Fathers of the Church, relative to the descent of Christ into Hell. Lat.

Oct. 20.
[13 Cal. Nov.]
King's College.

30. Wm. Mount to same. Professes his great satisfaction in being placed at the University under his patronage, his most honoured Mecænas. Lat.

Oct. 25.
Cambridge.

31. Lord Edward Seymour to same. Thinks it his duty to entertain a grateful recollection of the benefits received at his hands. Lat.

Oct. 27.
London.

32. Bishop Grindall to same. Works at St. Paul's. The south aisle is to be covered with lead. Solicits contributions from the officers of the Court of Wards.

October.

33. Joseph Josephe to same. In praise of virtue and charity. Solicits his assistance. Lat.

October.

34. Account of the first payment of subsidy by the clergy due 24th May, and payable before the last of October.

Nov. 3.

35. Note touching the raising of 4,000 Harquebusiers to be taken from the artificers in certain towns specified; with regulations for their equipment and train.

Nov. 4.

36. Lease by the Dean and Chapter of St. Paul's to Ric. Pickering, demising for 24 years certain tenements in Carter Lane, London, to the said Pickering, with his bond for performance of the same.

Nov. 7.

Assignment by Robert Constable to Tho. Randolph, Esq., of Milton, Kent, of the office of Constable or Keeper of the Castle of Queenborough, and Steward of the lordship or manor of Middleton and Merden, co. Kent. [*Case B. Eliz.* No. 1.]

Nov. 8.
Bisham.

37. Lady Elizabeth Hoby to Cecill. Mr. John Burlace has requested her to solicit that the shrievalty of Buckinghamshire should be bestowed on Mr. Edmund Ashfield, or some other person more able to bear the charge thereof than himself.

Nov. 9.
London.

38. Lady Margaret Lennox to same. Touching the great loss which she and her lord have sustained in their estate. Begs he will acquaint the Queen therewith.

VOL. XLIV.

1567.
Nov. 10. 39. Wm. Humfrey to Sir Wm. Cecill. Has been employed in making certain instruments for the copper and latten works. Proceedings in mineral operations.

[Nov. 12.] 40. Nich Stere to same. Professes his attachment to the doctrines of the Gospel, and solicits his favourable opinion and assistance against Jones. Lat.

Nov. 12.
[Prid. Id. Nov.]
Cambridge.
41. The heads of various houses and the Public Orator of Cambridge to same, in favour of Mr. Stere. Lat.

Nov. 15
Norwich.
42. The Duke of Norfolk to Cecill. The Earl of Sussex has imparted to him the subject of his negociation. The Duke is in favour of the match: the only obstacle is the Archduke's religion. Denies himself to be papist.

Nov. 19. 43. Bishop Grindall to same. Thinks the appointment of Mr. Dorrell to be Primate of Armagh will hinder the cause of religion in Ireland.

Nov. 21. 44. Thurland, Hechstetter, and Lover to Pembroke, Leicester, and Cecill. In favour of the bearer, Geo. Lamplugh. The great flood has much damaged the works. Ores are plentiful.

Nov. 22. 45. Wm. Humfrey to Cecill. Reasons for the low rate of his tender for farming the copper mines. Years may pass before any profit can arise to the workers of them.

Nov. 24.
Norwich.
46. Norfolk to same. Fears he will think him long in answering his most gentle letter. Has lately been greatly vexed by the devices which now begin to be sown abroad. Can justify any thing he has written.

Nov. 24.
[8° Cal. Dec.]
47. Master and Fellows of Queen's College, Camb. to same, relative to the Queen's letter in favour of Mr. Worthington. Lat.

Nov 27. 48. Earl of Leicester to Cecill. Has sent him a letter with French intelligence. The Prince there is very strong and has double the force of the other party. Purport of the Prince's letter to the Queen.

Nov. 28.
[4° Cal. Dec.]
Cambridge.
49. The Vice-Chancellor and Senate of Cambridge to same. Acknowledges his care of the interests and privileges of the University. Lat.

Nov. 28.
[4° Cal. Dec.]
Cambridge.
50. William Lewin to same. Gratefully acknowledges the facility of access to him which he permits the members of the University to enjoy. Lat.

Nov. 28. 51. Wm. Humfrey to same. Proofs have been taken of the different weights of latten and copper, especially for great ordnance, of which he communicates the result.

Nov. 28. 52. Speech of the Lord Keeper in the Star Chamber before the Council and others, touching the rumors circulated by the bringing in of seditious books, to the derogation and dishonour of Almighty God, and the established religion. Is no advocate for bloody laws; but " it is " better for a man to be twice whipped than once hanged."

Nov. 28. Another copy of the above. [*See Vol.* 45, *p.* 4.]

Vol. XLIV.

1567.
Nov. 29. 53. Sir Geo. Stanley to the Earl of Derby. Letter sent by the Countess of Derby to Lady Strange, which was so blotted and powdered with tears as it could not well be read. The subject has come under the notice of the Queen. Foreign news. Proceedings of the Earl of Sussex, &c.

Nov. (?) 54. Petition of Hugh Alyn to Sir Wm. Cecill. His poverty. Desires to be released from prison as he has no means of maintaining himself.

Dec. 2. 55. Account of money paid in Michaelmas Term on debts remaining in the office of the Queen's Remembrancer of the Exchequer.

Dec. 20.
Chester. 56. Ric. Hurleston to the Earl of Pembroke. Gives intelligence, by good information, of great preparations making by the King of Spain for the invasion of England. Certain gentlemen in Lancashire have taken a solemn oath not to come to the communion, and they rejoice greatly at the report of a Spanish invasion.

Dec. 57. Petition of Geo. Lamplugh to the Council, to be authorized to superintend the mineral works, in the place of Mr. Thurland, and to have a grant of certain tythes, &c. in Great and Little Broughton, co. Cumberland.

1567 ? 58. Account of the revenue in the Court of Wards and Liveries for the possessions of the following noblemen, deceased, Thomas Earl of Southampton, John de Vere Earl of Oxford, Henry Earl of Rutland, and Edward Duke of Somerset.

59. Petition of Wm. Peterson and others, merchants, trading to the eastern ports, to the Queen, complaining of injuries done to them by the King of Denmark and his subjects.

60. Instructions for the training of Harquebusiers throughout the realm of England, and for their incorporation with certain privileges. Indorsed by Cecill, " Mr. Pelham's devise for Harquebusyers."

61. Names of Dukes, Marquises, Earls, Bishops, creeks, ports, and havens, and the shires of England.

62. Abel Sylvius to Cecill. Has endeavoured to conduct himself conformably to the profession of Christ's religion. Lat. [*Defaced by damp.*]

63. Petition of Edward Jackman, Francis Bowier, Barnard Field, and many others, merchants, to the Queen. Complaining of the seizure of their cloths, under an edict of the King of Barbary.

64. Memorandum, in Cecill's hand, relative to measures of defence to be adopted. The Navy to be put in readiness; musters taken; beacons to be prepared, &c.

65. John Brantar, a mariner of Brittany, to the Queen. Prays for the restoration of his vessel, which has been captured, and is detained by Capt. Wm. Piers.

66. Petition of the Dean and Chapter of Norwich to the Queen, praying to be released from the payment of arrears of a certain rent-charge from the 1st Edw. VI.

Vol. XLIV.

1567 ?

67. Notes of various public occurrences from the year 1564 to 1567; by whom does not appear. Lat.

68. Statement of the sources and amount of income of Wm. Lord Howard of Effingham, shewing the excess of his expenditure, and soliciting a grant from the Queen of 300*l*. a year in land.

69. Paper of intelligence, indorsed by Cecill, " Jho. Spencer's wrytyg." Giving information principally against Papists and Recusants in England and abroad. A letter to be sent as from Dean Goodman, to bring Mr. Allatt from Venice. Book of complaint of the Queen of Scots to her son, &c.

70. Grant to John and James Conyers of the Office of Auditors of the Duchy of Cornwall.

71. Note of divers disorders needful to be reformed in the University of Cambridge [*by a Vice-Chancellor; probably Ric. Longeworthe*]. Refusal of Mr. Hammond, Mr. Bille, and Mr. Swale to read their lectures. Disorder in keeping the University chests, and of the fund for loan of money to poor scholars.

72. Letters Patents of incorporation, granted at the suit of the Earl of Leicester, to the Earls of Huntingdon and Warwick, Sir Ambrose Cave, Sir Nich. Throkmorton, Sir Thos. Lucye, Sir Ric. Knightley, and Clement Throgmorton, Esq. Constituting them Governors of the possessions and revenues of the Preachers of the Gospel in the county of Warwick.

73. Dr. Eliseus Bomelius to Sir Wm. Cecill. Complains of his treatment by the College of Physicians. Has always treated Dr. Francis, the President, with respect. Refers the matter to Sir Tho. Smith. Prays to be liberated from prison. Lat.

1567.

Vol. XLV. 1567.

An entry book of letters and papers of very miscellaneous character, from 1567 to the end of Q. Elizabeth's reign. The separate articles are described in their respective dates as near as can be ascertained.

Vol. XLVI. January—June, 1568.

1568.
Jan. 11. 1. Sir Owen Hopton to Sir Wm. Cecill. Illness of Lady Catharine Grey. She has kept her bed three days. Requests permission for Dr. Symonds to visit her again.

Jan. 22. 2. Resolutions to move a proposition for the indraping of the cloths termed ulterfyne and cromplystes, and to procure a licence for the same.

Jan. 22 3. Another copy of the above

[Jan. 22.] 4. Articles against the licence required for making of cloths with cromplists and ulterfynes, and such like.

Jan. 5. Copy of the above.

VOL. XLVI.

1568.
Jan. 6. Answer unto certain articles devised against the making of the cloths called ulterfynes and cromplists.

Jan. 7. Copy of the above.

Jan. 8. Reply of the Merchants of the Staple to certain articles devised against the making of cloths called crumplystes and oultrefynes.

Jan. 23. Chichester. 9. Dr. William Overton to Sir Wm. Cecill. Concerning certain proceedings of the Dean of Chichester. Lat.

Jan. 24. Cambridge. 10. The Vice-Chancellor (Ric. Longeworth) and Heads of Houses of the University and principal inhabitants of Cambridge, to same. On the differences existing between the Town and University. A perpetual concord and agreement might have been settled, but for the factious conduct of Mr. Kymball, the Mayor, and his adviser Roger Slegge.

Jan. 27. 11. Countess of Lennox to same. Regrets not meeting with him when she was last at Court. Great loss they have sustained by the sale of their goods.

Jan. 27. 12. Memorandum by Sir Owen Hopton of receiving the Lady Catharine Grey into his custody, and of her death on the 27th January, anno x. Eliz.

Jan. 13. The Queen to Lord Adm. Clynton. Commission authorizing him to arrest the ships and goods of the subjects of Poland, to recover a debt due to Willm. Martin, son of Tho. Martin, deceased. Lat.

Jan. 14. Tho. Gardenar, Robert Wygges, and others, goldsmiths of London, to Cecill. Complain that certain laws and ordinances established for government of the Mint have been broken by Mr. Stanley, Treasurer of the Mint.

Jan. 15. The Provost and Fellows of King's College, Cambridge, to same. Complain of the great diminution in the revenues of their college, and pray for protection and redress. Lat.

Jan. 16. Same to same. Soliciting his influence in favour of their college. Lat.

Feb. 1. 17. Wm. Humfrey to same. Progress of the works at the foundry for calamine and copper. Parties present at the first melting.

Feb. 3. 18. Same to same. Sends him a piece of new made latten. The calamine continues as good as the first proof.

Feb. 3. 19. The Queen to the Earl of Derby, the Bishop of Chester, the Sheriff of Lancaster, and others. Directs them to attach such persons who, under pretence of religion, draw sundry gentlemen and other persons from their duty and allegiance. [*Drafts of three letters on one sheet.*]

Feb. 3. 20. Copy of the above.

1568.
Feb. 3.
Chapter House, Wells.

VOL. XLVI.

21. The President and Prebendaries of Wells to Sir Wm. Cecill. Complain of the non-residence of Dr. Turner, their Dean, which was against the statutes of their Cathedral Church. *Inclosing,*

 21. I. *Oath of the Dean of Wells, for observance of the statutes of that church.*

 21. II. *Oath of the Dean of Wells for observation of the statute that none while absent should share in that which is due only to those present.*

 21. III. *Agreement between the Chapter and the Dean of Wells, as to the terms on which a lengthened absence should be granted to him.* 21 *May* 1565.

Feb. 4.
22. The Queen to Tho. Randolph, Master of the Posts. He is to discharge all the posts unless they will serve for half their wages, except the posts of the Court.

Feb. 6.
23. The Queen to the Exchequer. Warrant to pay to Sir Owen Hopton 76l. towards the charges of the funeral of Lady Catharine Grey.

[Feb. 6.]
24. Particular account of the expenditure of 76l. received by Sir Owen Hopton at the Exchequer, for the funeral of Lady Catharine Grey. Sums paid to the Heralds, &c.

Feb. 7.
Ingatestone.
25. Sir Wm. Petre to Cecill. The non-residence of Dr. Turner, Dean of Wells, is contrary to the statutes of that church. Recommends that he should accede to some reasonable composition with the Chapter.

Feb. 7.
26. Articles by the Goldsmith's Company against Mr. Stanley, Treasurer of the Mint, complaining of his neglect of former promises made by him to the Marq. of Winchester and Sir Walter Mildmay. [*See ante April* 1567.]

Feb. 7.
27. Answer to the above articles exhibited against Thomas Stanley by certain goldsmiths.

Feb. 7.
28. Information given by Mr. Thos. Stanley, Treasurer of the Mint, relative to the misdemeanor of certain goldsmiths towards him; particularly Ric. Martyn, Tho. Gardenar, Robt. Wygges, &c.

Feb. 7.
29. Thos. Stanley to Cecill. Prays that the standard of the Goldsmith's Hall and the weights of the Mint at the Tower, and the Queen's standard for the coin at the Exchequer, might be tried and compared.

Feb. 7.
30. John Hales to same. Has been subpœned to appear in the Court of Chancery, which he cannot do unless carried in a waggon or horse litter. Is under bond not to quit his house without the Queen's licence.

Feb. 16.
Westminster.
31. The Queen to the Marquis of Winchester. Order, at the intercession of the Spanish Ambassador, to restore to the owners certain pearls and rubies, seized by John Martyn, John Wood, and Peter Killigrew; with proceedings thereon.

VOL. XLVI.

1568.
Feb. 21. 32. The Queen to Edw. Holland, Sheriff of Lancaster. To cause certain deprived ministers to be apprehended and committed. On the back the following names are indorsed: " Alen, who wrote the late booke of " Purgatory ; Vause, ones Warden of Winchester ; Murrey, Chaplen " to Boner, late Bushop of London ; Marshall, ones Deane of Christ- " church, in Oxford ; Hargrave, late Vicar of Blackbourne ; and one " Norreys, tearming himself a Physician." [*In the names above written, Winchester is an error for Manchester, and Murrey for Murren : but they are printed exactly from the MS.*].

Feb. 21. 33. Same to William Downman, Bishop of Chester. Urges him to take especial care for maintaining uniformity of religious worship within his diocese.

Feb. 21. 34. Marq. of Winchester to Sir Wm. Cecill. Gives his opinion of the tender made to the Queen for farming the duty on beer for exportation. *Incloses*,

    34. I. *Articles proposed for farming the duty on beer to be exported ; at a rent of 500l. a year.*

Feb. 25. 35. Wm. Humfrey to same. Opinions of the Solicitor-General, Serjeants Wray and Manwood, and Mr. Ployden, touching the state of the privileges for battery and the use of the calamine stone.

Feb. 28. 36. B[aptist] S[pinola] to same. Observations on the course of foreign exchange. Italian.

Feb. 28.
Nedham.
37. Nicholas Bullingham, Bishop of Lincoln, and others, to same. Have issued letters for collections for relief of those persons who have fled out of France and Flanders to avoid persecution for religion. *Inclosing*,

    37. I. *Circular letter addressed to the clergy of the diocese of Lincoln, requiring them to cause collections to be made on Sundays and Festival days, in their respective parishes.*

Feb. 29. 38. Marq. Winchester to the Queen. Many years experience have shewn him how necessary the possession of Calais is to England, for defence of the coast between Dover and Portsmouth. Wishes it were again in the hands of the English.

Feb.
Bamptom.
39. Hugh Curwen, Bp. of Oxford, to Cecill. The value of his Bishopric is but 500 marks per ann. from which various outgoings specified are to be deducted. Solicits a remission of the present subsidy.

Feb. 40. Answer of John Tremayne to the Commissioners for Stannary matters in Cornwall.

Feb. 41. Reply made by the Merchants of the Staple to certain articles devised against the making of cloths, called " crumplysts and oulterfynes."

Feb. 42. Answer to the reply made by the Merchants of the Staple against the making of ulterfynes and cromlysts.

Vol. XLVI.

1568.
Feb.
43. Dr. Eliseus Bomelius to Sir Wm Cecill. His care and attendanc on Robert Wyngfeld. Has expended while residing in London more than 100*l*., and only received 12*l*. Desires Cecill to use some good means for his better remuneration. Lat.

March 1.
44. The Council to Bishop Grindall. To repress conventicles, and to confer with Alderman Bond, one of the Sheriffs of London, and devise proper measures for enforcing uniformity of religious worship.

March 2.
Canterbury.
45. Lord Cobham to Cecill. Intelligence brought by English merchants from France. Application of the Secretary of the French Ambassador to pass with his old passport. Detention of goods brought from Calais.

March 4.
46. List of names of 72 persons found together within the parish of St. Martin's in the Fields, at the House of James Tynne, goldsmith, the fourth day of March.

March 4.
47. Articles devised by the Merchants of the Staple to be observed by the makers of the cloths called owtrefynes and cromplysts.

March 10.
48. Charges for the household expences for diet of mourners, and cering the corps of the Lady Catharine, and other expences, for which Sir Owen Hopton craveth allowance.

March 10.
49. Charge of diet, &c. for the funerals; included in the above.

March 10.
The Queen to the Exchequer. Warrant to pay 140*l*. to Sir Owen Hopton for household expences and funeral charges of Lady Catharine Grey.

March 12.
Westminster.
50. The Council to Peter Killigrew. Ordering him to restore certain rubies seized by him belonging to a foreigner.

March 14.
51. Sir Wm. Cecill to Sir Ralph Sadleyr. Sends him news out of France, and other foreign intelligence. Return of the Earl of Sussex, in good health. Is going with the Earl of Leicester to St. Alban's to assist the Lord Keeper. *Incloses*,

51. I. *Abstract of letters containing intelligence from France and Spain.* 1 *March* 1567-8.

March 14.
52. Articles to be observed by the Mayor, &c. of Coventry for the true making of the cloths called owtrefines and cromplysts. Delivered by Mr. Mershe.

March 14.
53. Articles which the Mayor, Bailiff, &c. of Coventry, must be bound by indenture to perform, in making the cloths called ulterfines and cromplysts.

March 17.
54. Notes relative to the coinage of tin at the Stannary towns in Cornwall. Allowed by Edward Lord Hastings, of Loughborough, Warden of the Stannaries, and by John Cosowarthe, the Queen's Receiver.

March 17.
55. Copy of the above, with observations thereon, signed by G. Gerrard.

VOL. XLVI.

1568.

March 20. 56. Wm. Burd to Sir Wm. Cecill. Has perused the indenture for cloths to be made at Coventry. States the rate of duty to be paid on such as are shipped by English merchants.

March 28. 57. Sir Wm. Cecill to Sir Ralph Sadleyr. The French Ambassador has stated that peace is concluded. Has intelligence from Scotland, that the Queen of Scots is to marry the Lord of Meffyn, a Stuart.

March 29. Cobham. 58. Lord Cobham to Cecill. Concerning the cargo of a vessel lost on the Goodwin Sands, on the 22d of March.

March. 59. The Queen to the Lord Warden of the Stannaries in Devon and Cornwall. The coinage of the tin is in future to be kept at certain periods specified, at the towns of Liskeard, Helston, Truro, and Lestwithiel.

March. 60. Licence to Lucas de Hallye and Cornelius de Hooghe to exercise certain occult sciences, from which great advantage will arise to the Queen and her Dominions. Lat.

April 12. 61. Latin acrostic verses, by Hadrianus Junius, in honour of Cecill. Prays him to present his suit to Her Majesty.

April 27. Greenwich. 62. Sir Wm. Cecill to Sir Ralph Sadleyr. Cannot say the Queen entertains any dislike towards him, because of his being recommended for the place of Chancellor of the Duchy of Lancaster. She will sometimes say that he likes to live at home. He knows that " as fishees are " gotten with baytes so ar officees caught with sekyng."

April (?) 63. Considerations to be had in the choice of a Chancellor of the Duchy of Lancaster, stating the arduous nature of his duties and the qualifications necessary for the discharge of them. [*Probably on the death of Sir Ambrose Cave.*]

May 3. 64. Offer of John Powell, prisoner in the King's Bench for counterfeiting coin, that he will make certain implements for coining which will prevent the possibility of forgery.

May 10. Treasury Chamber. 65. Sir Walter Mildmay to Sir Ralph Sadleyr. The Earl of Leicester has informed him the Queen has nominated Sir Ralph to the office of Chancellor of the Duchy.

May 20. Presentments by a Jury held at the manors of Myddelton, of encroachments made by Tho. Haywarde and James Newlande upon the watercourses of a mill, called Pyrryncle Mill, in the occupation of one Geo. Dylett. [*Case B. Eliz.* No. 2.]

May 22. 66. Marq. Winchester to Cecill. Knows Oliver Dawbeny to be an honest man. Recommends that his suit concerning the impost on beer should be granted. *Incloses,*

66. I. *Suit of Oliver Dawbeny for grant of the office of Surveyor of all such beer as shall be exported; commonly called strong beer.*

May 28. Indenture of sale and release by William Clopton and others to William Porter, Esq., of the manor of Aston Underedge, co. Gloucester. [*Case B. Eliz.* No. 3.]

Vol. XLVI.

1568.
May 31. 67. Names of such persons as are thought meet to be Ecclesiastical Commissioners for the diocese of Coventry and Lichfield.

May 30. 68. Grant by Thomas Randolph, Master of the Queen's Posts and Couriers, constituting Robt. Parmenter of London, his Deputy for executing the said office.

May 69. Abstract of the contents of the patent to be granted to Daniel Hechstetter for draining mines, and recovery of surrounded lands.

May. 70. Articles devised by Hugh Smith and John Morley as Surveyors of the customs on cloths and wines.

June 4. 71. Edmond Mathew to Sir Wm. Cecill. The Lord Treasurer is favourable to Mr. Dawbeny's suit for the exportation of beer.

June 6. 72. Edw. Lord Windsor to same. Peter, his trumpeter, has requested
Louvain. him to write in his favour that he may be entertained in Cecill's service until Lord Windsor's return.

June 6. 73. Lord Cobham to same. Has been desired by the Earl of
Cobham. Leicester to report what ships had passed and were passing northward. Sends intelligence.

June 7. 74. Edw. Earl of Hertford to Leicester, Mildmay, and Cecill. Is
Sir John most bound to the Queen for her favourable acceptation of his
Spencer's. mother's suit, and for her intention to take 700*l.* a year till the 10,000*l.* be paid.

June 11. 75. Archbp. Parker to Cecill. In favour of Mr. Colby, his steward,
Croydon. for a farm adjacent to a piece of his land in Suffolk.

June 13. 76. Lord Cobham to same. Report of there being ten sail of ships
Cobham. at Rochelle, under command of M. Montluc. Arrival of troops at Calais. Offer of 1,000 crowns for arrest of La Planché.

June 14. 77. Survey, taken by Sir Henry Crisp and others, of the decays and wants in all the Queen's castles and forts within charge of the Lord Warden of the Cinque Ports.

June 19. 78. Sir Hugh Poulet to Cecill. Ten loads of stone have been
Tytenhanger. conveyed from Langley to Cecill's house at Theobald's. Matter in hand touching the traffic of Jersey and Guernsey. His nephew Tho. Stewkely fears that Cecill has conceived an ill opinion of him.

June 21. 79. William Cryspe to Lord Cobham. No truth in the report of
Dover. foreigners passing over to the Low Countries. Muster of Strangers, Flemings, or Walloons near Sandwich.

June 25. 80. Daniel Ulstatt [Hechstetter?] to Cecill. Is surprised at the
Keswick. mineral riches of the kingdom. Progress of their works; which are opposed by Lady Radcliffe. A preacher in their own language is much wanted among his workmen.

June 30. 81. Geo. Lamplugh to same. Has sent him two cwt. of stones, glistering like gold and silver, but which have however no value. There is a kind impregnated with copper.

Vol. XLVI.

1568.
June 30. Spa.
82. Lord Windsor to Sir Wm. Cecill. Has received great benefit from the waters at the Spa.

June ?
83. Note of the valuation of the Archbishopric of York.

1568. Vol. XLVII. July—September, 1568.

July 1.
1. Estimate of repairs to be executed at the glazing mill and Mr. Kelke's house, certified by T. Stockett, surveyor.

July 3.
2. Marq. of Winchester to Sir Wm. Cecill. The Company of the Stillyard have shipped 5,000 cloths, and are now suitors for shipping the other 5,000. Speaks in commendation of the Company.

July 4. Croydon.
3. Archbishop Parker to same. Requests him to peruse certain letters concerning the right of England to the superiority of Scotland. The King is not Dominus Hiberniæ but Rex Hiberniæ. Such records should be preserved.

July 4. Loseley.
4. William More to the Council. Forwards a book brought to him by one William Children, dropped by a stranger in a place near Guildford Park, containing an allegation on behalf of the Queen of Scots touching the succession.

July 4.
5. John Dymocke to same. Sends intelligence by a Dutchman arrived in a ship from Biscay with letters from merchants in Spain, which were sent to the Spanish Ambassador and opened by him. Desires a renewal of his protection.

July 8. Portsmouth.
6. Ric. Popynjay, Surveyor of the Works at Portsmouth, to the Marq. Winchester. Want of money for carrying on the works there; plan of which is sent.

July 8.
7. Submission of William Roper before the Lords of the Privy Council, for having relieved with money certain persons who have departed out of the realm, and who, with others, have printed books against the Queen's supremacy and government.

July 9. 7° Id. Julii.]
8. Petition of Hadrianus Junius to the Queen. For licence to transport sixty dickers of leather in recompence for his publication of the Greek author Eunapius. Lat. [*Probably Eunapius de Vitis Philosophorum et Sophistorum. Antv:* 1568.]

July 9.
9. Latin verses by Hadrianus Junius, in honour of Cecill. Desires his assistance in the furtherance of his suit to the Queen. Praise of Lady Cecill, &c. [*Five pieces.*]

July 10.
10. Wm. Humfrey to Cecill. Has delivered up his books and accounts to Mr. Auditor Coddenham, by which all charges will appear relative to the calamine works.

July 11.
11. Same to same. Impediments which the mineral works sustain for want of funds. Proposes an assessment of 40*l.* each.

1568.

Vol. XLVII.

July 13.
Croydon.
12. Archbishop Parker to the Council. Sir John Southworth has been with him, but refuses to subscribe to the form of submission tendered to him. *Incloses,*

    12. I. *The submission tendered to Sir John Southworth, expressing his contrition for having disobeyed the Ecclesiastical Laws of the realm, and relieved certain priests who have refused the ministry and spoken against the present state of religion. July* 1568.

July 14.
London.
13. Sir Wm. Garrard and Sir Thomas Offley to Sir Wm. Cecill. Measures necessary to promote the lottery. The matter should be recommended to the Justices of Assize, &c. and be published to the commonalty at large. [*The great lottery was for raising a sum of money for reparation of the havens of the realm. Five proclamations upon the subject were issued.*]

July 15.
14. Tho. Thurland to same. Has received his letter complaining of his having departed from London without taking leave. Explains the circumstances of that omission. Transactions in mining operations detailed.

July 16.
London.
15. Dr. Walter Haddon to same. Has examined the matter between Wilson and Bent. Bent made an untrue report of his case. The Spanish Ambassador is greatly incensed and utters great threats. Reminds him of the venison.

July 19.
Cobham.
16. Lord Cobham to same. Reports intelligence received from places on the French coast, Boulogne, Calais, &c. Two French spies are in London.

July 19.
17. Marq. of Winchester to same. Repairs necessary at the Exchequer and the Great Tower in the Tower of London for preservation of the records. Estimate of the cost.

July 20.
18. A MS. intituled " Tractatus Noni Anni Cicli Solaris Bissextilis,' attested by Mathew de Questor, Notary Publick. Lat.

July 21.
19. Sir Wm. Cecill to the Lord Mayor of London. To return a true certificate of the names and profession of all such foreigners as have arrived in London since the last inquisition.

July 21.
Gorhambury.
20. The Queen to the Earl of Leicester, Robt. Bishop of Winchester, Sir Wm. Cecill, and others. Commission for visitation of Corpus Christi College, Oxford. Lat.

July 22.
London.
21. Hieronymus Jerlitus, Minister of the Italian Church, to Cecill. Recommends Raphael Vanden Putte to be appointed Post Master for the foreigners. Lat.

July 22.
22. Jean Cousen, Minister of the French Church, to same. Testimonial in favour of Raphael du Puitz [*Van den Putte*] for the same office. Fr.

Vol. XLVII.

1568.
July 23.   23.   — to Sir Wm. Cecill. Narrates the fearful judgments of God upon Kings and Rulers who contemn his word; particularly in the cases of Scotland and Flanders. Indorsed by Cecill, "a lre of "an unknown psō of zeale."

July 25.
London.   24. Merchant Strangers to same. Have elected and recommend Godfrey Marshall to be their Post Master instead of Raphael Vanden Putte.

July 25.
[Oct. Calend. Aug.]   25. Latin verses, by Thos. Wilson, addressed to Sir Wm. Cecill, on his recent sickness.

July 26.   26. List of certain ships of Newcastle-upon-Tyne stayed at Dantzic.

July 30.
Hatfield.   27. F. Alen (Clerk of the Council) to Cecill. Informs him the nobleman's name who comes as Ambassador from Spain, is Don Guerau de Spes. The Queen will not remove from Hatfield till next Friday.

July 30.   28. Sir Roger Martyn, Lord Mayor, to same. Relative to the Strangers. *Incloses,*

         28. I. *Certificate of all strangers that had arrived in London and suburbs, either for religion or any other cause, since the 20th March last.*

August 1.
[Cal. Aug.]   29. Nicholas Stere to same. Complains of the conduct of one Jones. Lat.

August 1.
Exeter.   30. Sir Peter Carew, Sir Gawen Carew, and Sir John Chichester to same. Complaints by merchants of the West of England of captures made in the Queen's waters, under colour of commissions by the King of Sweden.

August 3.
Cobham.   31. Lord Cobham to same. Has received letters from Scotland. The Prince of Orange will take the field, and he has borrowed money of the Landgrave and the young Duke of Brunswick.

August 6.
Cobham.   32. Same to same. Arrival of the post at Dover. Overthrow of Count Lewis of Nassau. God have mercy on his poor folks.

August 7.
Cobham.   33. Same to same. Confirmation of Count Lodovick's (Lewis of Nassau) defeat.

August 7.
[7° Id. Aug.]
St. Catharine's.   34. Tho. Wilson to same. Has been at Hatfield, but not finding him could not finish his business. Has left the letters with the Earl of Leicester. Desires Cecill to hasten the signing of them.

August 7.
London.   35. Hieronymus Jerlitus to same. Sends him a confection of the Saccarum Rosaceum, with directions how it is to be taken. Recommends the bearer. Lat.

August 8.
St. Alban's.   36. Notes in Cecill's hand concerning various matters of public business of the Borders, Scotland, Musters, &c. Terms for a treaty with Scotland.

1568.

Vol. XLVII.

August 9.
London.
37. Sylvester Bride? to Mr. Oswald Wilkenson. News of the overthrow of the Protestants in Flanders. The Spanish Ambassador has made great rejoicings to celebrate the event.

August 13.
Rye.
38. Mayor of Rye to Sir Wm. Cecill. Arrival from France of one Mr. Stewart, a gentleman of Scotland, and also of a passenger who pretends he was sent over to give notice of the coming of an ambassador.

August 14.
Cobham.
39. Lord Cobham to same. Is grieved to hear he expects some new vexation on coming to Court. News from Flanders.

August 14.
Chichester.
40. Wm. Overton to same. Death of William Barlow, Bishop of Chichester. Recommends William Day, provost of Eton, to succeed him. Lat?

August 18.
41. Francis Walsyngham to same. Has been desired by Sir Nichs. Throckmorton to say that the Queen is displeased at the choice made by the Prince (of Condé) and the Admiral in sending Mr. Stewart over to her. Stewart desires favourable audience of the Queen. The lady that came over with him is Madame de Muye.

August 18.
Fulham.
42. Bishop Grindall to same. Is glad to hear of his improved health. Thanks him for favour shown to Raphael. Desires to know his opinion concerning the benevolence. Death of the Bishop of Chichester.

August 19.
Lambeth.
43. Archbishop Parker to same. Death of the Bishop of Chichester. Recommends Mr. Courtes, the Queen's Chaplain, as a fit successor.

August 19
London.
44. Dr. Valentyne Dale to same. The letters received from Lubeck are respecting the ships which were brought in by the company of Mr. Keyle and North. Arrest of English ships and goods at Dantzic.

August 25.
Towcester.
45. The Earl of Ormond and Ossory to the Marq. of Winchester. Recommends the suit of the bearers, Alkynton and others.

August 28.
London.
46. Lionel Duckett to same. Has sent him such protests as the English merchants have made against the Danskers for staying English ships. Cause of the trouble.

August 29.
47. Owen O'Connor to same. His silence has been occasioned by diffidence, not disrespect. Thanks him for great and singular benefits conferred on him. Lat.

August 30.
48. Earls of Pembroke and Leicester and Sir Wm. Cecill to the Merchant Adventurers. Request they will promote the lottery established in London by the Queen's proclamation, by adventuring for their Company in general, and themselves individually.

August.
49. Henry Ravenscroft, George Alkynton, and Robert Wiltshier, Citizens of London, to the Queen. Offer to increase Her Majesty's customs by 1,000*l.* per ann., if they have a grant of the survey of silks, Venice gold and silver, and divers other costly commodities brought from beyond sea.

Vol. XLVII.

1568.
August. 50. Declaration by William Wade of the sinister dealing of Mr. Cockerham towards him, before and after the death of Mr. Wade's father.

August. 51. A note of the things wanting to finish the platform for the great ordnance at Portsmouth.

Sept. 2.
Keswick. 52. Note of the contents of Mr. Nedham's letter touching his negociation with Mr. Curwen for a piece of ground at Workington, on which to erect a wharf; and of the progress of the mining affairs.

Sept. 2.
Fulham. 53. Sir Nich. Throckmorton to Sir Wm. Cecill. Thanks for attentions during his illness. Approves of the course taken with the French. The Regent of Scotland has received a great overthrow. Proposes to kill a buck of Cecill's, at Mortlake.

Sept. 4. 54. Stephen Fulwell (of the Jewel House) to same. A proportion of plate has been set out for the Spanish Ambassador, of greater value than that which M. de Foies had.

Sept. 6.
Cobham. 55. Lord Cobham to same. Dispensation for the exportation of Kentish cloths: state of that trade. French news. The new Spanish Ambassador landed at Dover. *Incloses,*

> 55. I. *Je. Jourdain to Nicolas Jourdain his brother. The new Assembly will end all controversies by fire and sword. Warlike movements daily take place in France. Dieppe, 31 Aug. 1568.*

Sept. 6.
London. 56. Anthony Becqu and J. Quarre, glass makers, to same. Request permission to cut wood, make charcoal, &c. in Windsor Great Park, and to convey it from thence. Fr.

Sept. 7.
London. 57. Fr. Walsyngham to same. Information of a Frenchman and an Italian secretly lodged in London. It is desired the Lord Mayor should give the assistance of his officers to search the house in which they reside. Suggests that all tavern keepers shall give information of foreigners residing with them.

Sept. 7.
Ivy Lane. 58. Peter Osborne to same. Has heard of the tenders to increase the Queen's customs and subsidies inwards, within the port of London. Shews how unpopular comptrollers appointed for such service are.

Sept. 7. 59. Marq. Winchester to same. Proceedings in the matter of the three merchants, Harry Ravenscroft, George Alkynton, and Robert Wiltshier. Is loth to meddle in the affair. Their indifferent characters. The Patent gives them authority to examine merchandize coming inwards. *Incloses,*

> 59. I. *Commission by the Queen appointing Henry Ravenscroft, George Alkynton, and Robert Wiltshier, Surveyors of Customs, on all goods brought into the port of London, by way merchandize, wines only excepted.*

Vol. XLVII.

1568.
Sept. 8.
Cobham.
60. Lord Cobham to Sir Wm. Cecill. Arrival of Cardinal Chastillon and others from France. *Incloses,*

    60. I. *Rowland Mekley to Cobham. Informs him of the arrival of Card. Chastillon, who had fled on account of the troubles in France. The French King is at Orleans, the Prince of Condé and the Admiral at Rochelle. Dover, 8th Sept.* 1568.

Sept. 8.
London.
61. Mr. Morley (Surveyor of Customs) to same. The Lord Treasurer has written letters to all the ports for the furthering of the Queen's service and for the aid of the Surveyors of Customs. They have now brought the affairs of the ports into good order.

Sept. 8.
Fulham.
62. Bishop Grindall to same. Sends him some grapes. Requests a caveat against presentation to the vicarage of Catterick, void by the death of Mr. Hutton. Has received a letter from Mr. Bullinger, in which are contained certain Latin lines, as quoted.

Sept. 9.
63. Lionel Duckett to same. Has had no advice of the release of the English ships stayed at Dantzic. The delay will occasion great loss.

Sept. 10.
Dartington.
64. Sir Arthur Champernowne to same. Intelligence that the Queen of Scots has given and surrendered to the Duke of Anjou, brother to the King of France, all the title and interest she has, or pretends to have, in the realms of England and Scotland.

Sept. 10.
Cobham Hall.
65. Lord Cobham to same. The Cardinal, accompanied by twenty-seven persons, is on his way to London, and purposes to apply for an interview with the Queen.

Sept. 11.
Canterbury.
66. Henry Kyngesmyll to Leicester and Cecill. Found the Cardinal Chastillon and thirty persons, at Canterbury, among whom was M. de Lygy. The Cardinal will proceed on the morrow to Gravesend and thence to London by water.

Sept. 11.
67. Sir Thos. Gresham to Cecill. The Bishop of London is unable to receive the Cardinal into his house at Fulham. Has therefore prepared his own house for him with such entertainment as lies in his power. *Incloses,*

    67. I. *Kyngesmyll to Gresham. Cardinal Chastillon will take his voyage on Sunday morning towards Gravesend, and next day to London. Canterbury, 11 Sept.* 1568.

Sept. 11.
London.
68. Rowland Hayward and John Tamworth to same. The ship Primrose, belonging to Thomas Grey, of Harwich, is fittest to be employed to carrry the Queen's letter to Muscovia.

Sept. 12.
Barbican.
69. Mr. Richard Bertie to same. Having to send to Lady Strange, it would seem strange if he did not thank him for courtesies received. Has hastened south on hearing of the dangerous illness of the Duchess [of Suffolk]: for the same reason Lord Monteagle's men hastened northward. She is however recovering.

VOL. XLVII.

1568.
Sept. 13.
London.

70. Sir Thos. Gresham to Sir Wm. Cecill. Received the Cardinal on his arrival at Tower Wharf. Desires to know when he is to take him to Osterley. 15,000 of slate and 3,000 foot of board, for Cecill, has arrived.

Sept. 15.
Hartley Row.

71. Marq. of Winchester to the Council. Has left order with Ric. Stonley and Thos. Lovell, for certain payments to be made for Berwick. Will return to London within twenty days.

Sept. 15.
London.

72. Fr. Walsyngham to Cecill. Orders given for all strangers in London to be certified weekly. The two suspected persons kept close because of being infected with loathsome diseases. Descriptions of secret agents of the Cardinal Lorraine, in London.

Sept. 15.
Fulham.

73. Bishop Grindall to same. Sends him enclosed the presentation for East Riding, for which he thinks Mr. Parkinson the fittest. Thanks him for disposing otherwise of Card. Chastillon, as he had no means of lodging him.

Sept. 15.
London.

74. Henry Kyngesmyll to same. The Cardinal has sent M. de Ligi to declare the occasion of his coming. The Card. has been well received and entertained by Gresham.

Sept. 19.
Canterbury.

75. Lord Cobham to same. Arrival of the Bishop of Rennes (Bernardin Bochetel). War has been proclaimed at Calais against the Prince of Condé and his adherents.

Sept. 19.

76. Note of the capture of a ship of 90 tons belonging to one John Mychell of Truro, by French pirates.

Sept. 19.
London.

77. John Mershe to Cecill. Gives particulars of the operations of the French army in the Netherlands. The Papists endeavour to procure Godfrey Mareschall, a notable perverse Papist, to be appointed foreign Post Master.

Sept. 22.
Lambeth.

78. Archbishop Parker to same. Will perform what he desires relative to Mr. Wells. After much toil the English Bible has been completed. Some ornaments thereof are still wanting. Requests him to be patient until it be fully ready.

Sept. 23.

79. Memorandum of certain commissions, warrants, and letters to be issued. Letter for preservation of the Queen's game in Essex.

Sept. 24.

80. Winchester to same. Has received the warrant for 300*l.* to be paid to the Treasurer of Berwick. Will further the Privy Seal for the 500*l.* for Mr. Vice-Chamberlain.

Sept. 25.
London.

81. Dr. Lewes to the Council. States his opinion relative to the last arrest of the ships and goods of the English merchants at Dantzic. Recommends a friendly communication to be made to the authorities of that city.

Sept. 26.

82. The Queen to Henry Smith and James Morley. Suspends the execution of their commission for the survey of the customs on wines.

VOL. XLVII.

1568.
Sept. 27. 83. Certain Italian Musicians of the Queen to Sir Wm. Cecill. Pray for remission of a debt arising from their having received a pension without sufficient warrant. Ital.

Sept. 29. Shene. 84. Henry Kyngesmyll to the Earl of Leicester and Sir Wm. Cecill. The house appropriated for the Card. Chastillon is too far out of repair for him to occupy. Requests some order may be taken for lodging the Cardinal and M. de Lyzy.

Sept 29. 85. Account of the impost on wines, from Michaelmas 1567 to Michaelmas 1568, by the farmers thereof.

Sept. 29. 86. Brief declaration of the revenue of Edward Earl of Oxford, from certain lands in Wilts, Devon, Cornwall, Bucks, and Cambridgeshire, of which he was joint purchaser with his late father.

Sept. 29. Shene. 87. Tho. Lord Buckhurst to the Council. Is distressed the Queen was displeased with him for not having in better sort entertained the Cardinal at Shene. Details very minutely the whole proceedings of his reception, and the preparations made for his accommodation.

Sept. 30. Keswick. 88. Substance of Mr. Nedham's letter from Keswick respecting various mining transactions at that place. Progress of making copper, &c.

Sept. 89. Names of Commissioners for visitation of the Cathedral Church of Norwich, and for appointing statutes for the same.

Sept. 90. Account of customs and subsidies for merchandize shipped in England for Portugal and Barbary.

Sept. 91. Letters of protection for Sir Edward Rousse of Dunwich, Suffolk, from arrest or seizure of his goods, for one year.

Sept. 92. Memoranda of public business, by Sir Wm. Cecill. To raise money by loans and gifts. Aid to those of Rochelle. Resignation by the Queen of Scots to the Duke of Anjou, of her title and right to England, &c.

VOL. XLVIII. OCTOBER—DECEMBER, 1568.

1568.
Oct. 1. Keswick. 1. Substance of Mr. Ulstetts letter from Keswick, concerning mining affairs, fuel for smelting, &c.

Oct. 2. Sheen. 2. H. Kyngesmyll to Sir Wm. Cecill. Arrival of two gentlemen sent from the Cardinal's brother. M. de Cavaignes is expected in London. The Cardinal will proceed to the Court on Wednesday by way of Hounslow.

Oct. 2. Cobham Hall. 3. Lord Cobham to same. Has received letters from Rye announcing the arrival of M. de Gamages and family, and other fugitives, out of France. The Prince is with some force at Rochelle, and the Count de Montgomery in Picardy with 1,500 horse and 5,000 foot. Desires to know the Queen's pleasure respecting Captain Souze.

1568.

VOL. XLVIII.

Oct. 3.
Windsor.
4. The Council to Lord   . Concerning the grant of unreasonable leases by the Dean and Chapter of Carlisle. Desire him to ascertain how the case stands at present.

Oct. 3.
Windsor.
5. Same to   '. Complaint of the unreasonable grants of leases by the Church of Carlisle. Directions to procure the opinion of the Judges thereon. The bearer, Mr. Scott, is one of the Prebendaries.

Oct. 5.
Lambeth.
6. Archbishop Parker to Sir Wm. Cecill. Has caused a copy of the new edition of the Bible to be bound, which he requests he will present to the Queen. If this edition alone should be licensed to be read in churches, it would conduce to uniformity. Begs that Jugge only should have the publication of it. *Incloses,*

> 6. I. *Same to the Queen. Requests she will accept favourably the new edition of the Bible. It does not vary much from that which was commonly used, except in places where the true meaning of the Hebrew or Greek required alteration. Beseeches it may have her gracious favour and protection. Has been bold " with fewe wordes to expresse the incomparable " valewe of the treasure." 5 Oct. 1568.*
>
> 6. II. *List of the translators of the Bible, with enumeration of the separate books assigned to each, and the rules observed by them in that undertaking.*

Oct. 5.
7. Notes relative to the translation of the Bible, founded on the above, in Sir Jos. Williamson's hand.

Oct. 5.
[3° Nonas Oct.]
Cambridge.
8. William Maister to Cecill. Returns him thanks for favours received. Lat.

Oct. 5.
London.
9. H. Kyngesmyll to same. The Cardinal has determined that none of the French gentlemen with him shall repair to the Court until the Queen's pleasure be known. Desires to know Cecill's pleasure as to taking the Cardinal to Windsor.

Oct. 7.
Exeter.
10. Sir Arthur Champernowne to same. Intelligence received from France. A skirmish has taken place near Angers, between Capt. Byrsew's and M. Martigne's troops.

Oct. 7.
Gloucester.
11. Richard Cheney, Bishop of Gloucester, to same. Has been at Bristol and preached three sermons. Erroneous doctrines preached by one Norbrook. Has been advised to prosecute him, but as he has never spent two pence in law, he will end as he has begun.

Oct. 9.
Keswick.
12. Tho. Thurland to same. Great charges which he has incurred by mining operations. Prays he may have licence to go abroad, or that he may have grant of such suits as he can devise for his relief.

Oct. 12.
13. Minutes of the matters treated on by Geo. Nedham with Mr. Curwen for a little piece of ground for a wharf. Difficulty of procuring coal. Lease of land at Keswick required. Mr. Lamplugh should be continued in his office.

Vol. XLVIII.

1568.
Oct. 13.
Keswick.
14. Geo. Nedham to Lionel Duckett. Desires to know the Queen's pleasure as to prosecuting the search for gold on Crawford Muir, in Scotland.

Oct. 15.
London.
15. H. Kyngesmyll to Sir Wm. Cecill. Has put the house at Shene in better order for the residence of the Cardinal. There had not been time to do so when Leicester and himself passed that way.

Oct. 15.
Gloucester.
16. Bishop Cheney, to same. Attempts of his adversaries to impugn his preaching. States his opinions on several points, especially that of Free Will. Conduct of Norbrook, the preacher, at Bristol. Is willing to grant the farm of Maismore to Mr. Cecill.

Oct. 15.
Roper Lane.
17. Sir Roger Martyn (Lord Mayor) to same. John Alday, the printer, committed to the Poultry Compter, and the two Dutchmen who caused a certain book to be printed. *Annexed.*

17. I. "*Copie des Pointz ou articles arrestes par le Duc d'Albe et son nouveau Conseil de douze, &c. Dou en est evidemment á cognoistre les horribles Tirannies cruautes et larrecins du Duc d'Alba, et son conseil, troupeau sanguinaire.*" 18 Sept. 1568

Oct. 17.
18. Note of matters to be remembered relative to the mines. Bargain with Mr. Curwen for the ground at Workington, &c.

Oct. 19.
19. Marq. of Winchester to Cecill. The vintage fleet being daily expected, the noblemen and others are desirous of warrants for their imposts on wines.

Oct. 19.
Lekinfield.
20. Earl of Northumberland to same. Requests a final answer whether he is to have a reasonable composition for the mines or not; otherwise he must assert his right and title therein.

Oct. 20.
21. Sir Roger Martyn to same. Restraint of resort of foreigners and strangers to London, on account of infection. Stay ought to be made at Gravesend of all foreigners coming by sea.

Oct. 20.
Bristol.
22. Citizens of Bristol to same. Complain of very strange, perilous, and corrupt doctrines, contrary to the Gospel, being publicly preached by the Bishop of Gloucester, in Bristol Cathedral. *Inclosing,*

22. I. *Articles of erroneous doctrines openly uttered and published in Bristol by the Bishop of Gloucester, in three several sermons delivered on the 22d and 29th Aug. and Sept 1st.*

Oct. 21.
London.
23. Francis Walsyngham to same. Intelligence of twelve galleys in readiness at Marseilles for transporting certain soldiers into the north, for the better execution of some conspiracy.

Oct. 23.
[10. Cal. Nov.]
Cambridge.
24. Henry Cheke to same. Returns thanks for the many and great favours received from him. The kindness of Mr. Clerk. Lat.

Oct. 25.
Cobham.
25. Lord Cobham to same. Proceedings of the Prince of Condé. The Duke will not fight. The King of Denmark is to marry the sister of the Prince of Orange.

Vol. XLVIII.

1568.

Oct. 25.
Paul's.

26. Bishop Grindall to Sir Wm. Cecill. Explains the occurrence at the house of the Portuguese Ambassador. Order to apprehend the English persons coming from mass there, but the constable indiscreetly entered the Ambassador's house. *Incloses,*

  26. I. *Deposition of Humfrey Perwiche, Constable, and Ralph Typpynge, as to what passed at the Portuguese Ambassador's house at Hoxton, on Sunday the 24th October.*

Oct. 26.
Lewisham.
[*Lewsam.*]

27. Thomas Keys to same. Begs him to intercede with the Queen. Had rather end his life in her service than remain as a banished man from Her Majesty's presence.

Oct. 26.
[7° Cal. Nov.]
Cambridge.

28. William Maister to same. Requests him to procure him an advowson in the Queen's gift, that being void to which he had been presented, owing to a former grant. Lat.

Oct. 27.
York.

29. Sir Henry Gate to same. Hears nothing of the survey which was directed to be made of the decays at Scarborough Castle. Begs that he may not be pricked for Sheriff for the county of York.

Oct. 30.

30. Isaac Barro, of Trinity College, Camb. to same. Solicits licence to travel abroad. Lat.

Oct. 31.
Westminster.

31. Sir Henry Percy to same. Begs him to further the suit of the bearer, Master Raphael, for the office of Post Master to the foreigners.

Oct. 31.

32. Petition of Raphael Van de Putte to same. Solicits to be appointed to the office of foreign Post Master.

Oct. 31.
Dartington.

33. Sir Arthur Champernowne to Lord Clynton. Doubtful nature of the times for persons engaged in merchandize. They are not disposed to venture their lives and goods at this season of the year in the accustomed voyage to Bordeaux.

[Nov. 1?]

34. Edmonde Holme to Mr. Glaseour and Mr. Hurleston, at Chester. Detailing the circumstances under which Sir Ric. Mollineux, his son John Mollineux, and his daughters Jane, Alice, and Anne Mollineux, and other persons, took an oath declaring the Pope to be the supreme head of the church. [*See ante,* 1566, *Nov.* 2.]

Nov. 1 (?)

35. Relation of the proceedings with respect to the Papists and Recusants of Lancaster, indorsed "This is a note made by Wm. Glaseour " of the doyng before the Bishop and Commissioners of Ecclesias. " causes, in the Lancaster men's matters." Factious course held by Mr. Gerrard, one of the Commissioners.

Nov. 1.
Chester.

36. Bishop Downman to Cecill. Reports proceedings with the gentlemen of Lancashire in ecclesiastical affairs. Their conformity.

x

1568.   Vol. XLVIII.

Good services done by the preaching of the Dean of St. Paul's. Has visited the whole of his diocese. Requests renewal of his commendam for two benefices. *Incloses*,

    36. I. *Decree of Edw. Earl of Derby, William Downman, Bp. of Chester, and others, Ecclesiastical Commissioners, in the cases of certain persons of Lancaster charged with Recusancy.* Lathom, 31 July 1568.

    36. II. *Answer of Francis Tunstall to the articles objected against him by the above Ecclesiastical Commissioners.*

    36. III. *Answer of John Talbot to similar articles.*

    36. IV. *Answer of John Westby to similar articles.*

    36. V. *Answer of John Rigmaiden to similar articles.*

    36. VI. *Answer of Edw. Osbaldeston to similar articles.*

    36. VII. *Answer of Matthew Treves to similar articles.*

    36. VIII. *Answer of John Townley to similar articles.*

    36. IX. *Answer of John Mollinex to similar articles.*

    36. X. *Articles preferred by the same Eccl. Commissioners against Sir John Southworth, for not repairing to church, nor receiving the Sacrament, and for speaking against the Book of Common Prayer.*

Nov. 2. Dartington. 37. Sir A. Champernowne to Lord Clynton. Reports that eight of the Bordeaux fleet have been driven by stress of weather into Conquet, where they are all detained.

Nov. 6. 38. J. Lennard to Sir Wm. Cecill. Requests him to prevent his being chosen to serve as Sheriff of Kent, his office of Custos Brevium occupies the whole of his time.

Nov. 7. Dartington. 39. Sir A. Champernowne to same. Confirmation of the intelligence of the detention of the Bordeaux fleet at Conquet. Has stayed five French ships lately put into Dartmouth by reason of foul weather.

Nov. 12. 40. Marq. Winchester to same. Application of the Spanish Ambassador to be allowed the impost on 25 tuns of wine. Has many applications from noblemen on the same subject.

Nov. 13. York. 41. Matthew Hutton, Dean of York, to same. A good Archbishop is required for the diocese of York. Describes the qualifications he ought to possess. Recommends the Bishop of London to be translated thither.

Nov. 15. Dover Castle. 42. Lord Cobham to the Mayor, &c. of Sandwich. Mandamus to summon a jury on Admiralty causes.

Nov. 27 43. Wm. Humfrey to Cecill. Reports particulars of the iron works at Tintern, and in the vicinity of Bristol.

Vol. XLVIII.

1568. Nov. 28.	44. Marq. of Winchester to Sir Wm. Cecill. Has received the book of the impost on wines. Requests him to ascertain the Queen's pleasure relative to that matter.
Nov.	45. W. Daye, Provost of Eton, to Mr. Alington. Concerning the allowance which has yearly been made him of the impost on three tuns of wine.
Nov. (?)	46. Grant by the Queen to Ric. Courteis, her Chaplain, of a prebend in Canterbury, vacant by the death of Arthur St. Leger.
Nov. (?)	47. Address to the Queen from the strangers of the French and Dutch Churches in London. With lists of their names, the quarters of the town in which they reside, their trades and occupations.
Nov.	48. Estimate for victualling the Queen's ships Antelope, Swallow Aid, and the Phœnix for sea, under charge of William Wynter, Esq.
Fowey.	49. Relation by a Spaniard of the course of Mr. John Hawkyns' voyage to the West Indies.
Dec. 3. Plymouth.	50. William Hawkyns to Cecill. Mr. Wynter has informed him of a report that John Hawkyns, his brother, and a great number of men, had landed and been put to the sword by the Spaniards. Suggests inquiries to be made, and that King Philip's treasure in England might be seized.
Dec. 3. London.	51. Estienne Perrot to same. Concerning the lottery. Fr. *Incloses*,
	51. I. *Propositions or heads for drawing the lottery, regulation of prizes, &c.*
Dec. 4.	52. William Parteriche to same. Offers for farming the custom and impost on beer.
Dec. 4. St. Laurence Lane.	53. Bishop Jewell to same. Has briefly examined, and gives his opinion on certain Greek books. Objects to their being divided among the Bishops, but recommends they should be purchased for some of the colleges in Oxford or Cambridge.
Dec. 5. Westminster.	54. Grant by the Queen to William Cruys, Anne his wife, and Gamaliel Cruys, of certain lands and tenements at Fotheringay, in the county of Northampton, late in the occupation of James Cruys.
Dec. 7. London.	55. Bishop Jewell to Cecill. There is no better mode of disposing of the Greek books than to purchase and deposit them in some of the colleges of Oxford or Cambridge.
Dec. 10. Broonsebithe. [*Brancepeth.*]	56. Christopher Nevyll to same. Thanks for the letter in his favour addressed to the Dean and Prebendaries of Durham. They have declined out of covetousness to give him the fee enjoyed by his late brother, Sir Tho. Nevyll.

Vol. XLVIII.

1568.
Dec. 12.
London.
57. Bishop Jewell to Sir Wm. Cecill. Has taken order with the poor Greeks for their books. One of them, Nicolas de la Turre, offers his service to the Queen, in copying out any Greek Antiquities.

Dec. 13.
Durham.
58. The Dean and Chapter of Durham to same. Have considered, but cannot comply with, his gentle letters in behalf of Mr. Christopher Nevill, uncle to the Earl of Westmoreland, respecting a grant of the leading of their tenantry, with a yearly fee.

Dec. 13.
Sandwich.
59. Mayor, &c. of Sandwich, to same. Have elected William Southwick to be their Mayor, but he refuses to take the office upon him, being customer of the port, without the Queen's special warrant.

Dec. 19.
Dartington.
60. Sir Arthur Champernowne to same. Measures taken by him to recover such treasure of the King of Spain's as is at present in the western ports. The whole is supposed to be of the value of 400,000*l.* sterling, "*and therefore moste fytt for Hyr Matie.*"

Dec. 20.
London.
61. Francis Walsyngham to same. Acquaints him with a design between France and Spain for altering the religion of England, and placing the Queen of Scots on the throne.

Dec. 20.
Hampton.
62. Edward Horsey to same. Relates his proceedings in procuring possession of 59 coffers of Spanish treasure on board a Spanish ship in the river of Hampton [Southampton].

Dec. 23.
63. Marq. of Winchester and Sir Walter Mildmay to same. Desiring a warrant to be signed for money for extraordinaries for the Navy.

Dec. 29.
Downham.
64. Bishop Cox to same. States the reasons which induced him to contract matrimony. Requests Cecill to be his advocate with the Queen. Lat.

Dec. 29.
65. Tho. Windebank to same. Proceedings of the Spanish Ambassador touching the Post Mastership for strangers. All the Italians were unwilling to give their voice to Raphael, but inclined to favour Godfrey.

Dec. 31.
Prid.Cal.Jan.]
66. Dr. Walter Haddon to same. Recommends Mr. Clerk of Cambridge, as a worthy successor of that excellent and learned man, Sir Roger Ascham. Lat.

1568 (?).
67. The Dean and Chapter of Christ Church, Oxford, to same. Concerning the admission of one Glasier to Holy Orders. Lat.

68. A catalogue of books recently published.

69. Form of subscription by Justices of the Peace declaring their obedience to the Act for Uniformity of Common Prayer and administration of the Sacraments.

70. A note of such papers as are to be found in the State Paper Office, relative to precautions for preventing and diminishing the plague in London.

Vol. XLVIII.

1568 (?).

71. The Queen to the Exchequer. Licence for the Aldermen and Society of the Stillyard to export cloths, to a number not exceeding 8,000 pieces.

72. Note of such parcels of land as Lord Monteagle has promised that Mr. Pelham should purchase of him.

73. A pedigree of the family of Fitzwalter, deduced from Anselm Lord Fitzwalter, temp. William 1st, to 1568.

74. Inventory of the goods of Anthony Herwegs, citizen of Cologne, taken by pirates.

75. Note of ports in the West of England and other parts, to which Customers are appointed.

76. Note of the demand of money claimed by the Genoese, Luccoys, and Spaniards, as it was laden in Spain.

77. Note of the light horse certified in South Wales and North Wales.

78. Accompt of pelts and skins carried out of the realm by Merchant Strangers of the Low Countries.

79. Extracts from the registers of the Archbishops of Canterbury, in proof that the see of Lincoln is not exempt from the jurisdiction of the Archbishop of Canterbury. Lat.

80. Petition of Tho. Barrington Esqr. and Dame Winefride his wife, cousin and coheir of Margaret Countess of Salisbury, to the Queen. For licence to exchange certain lands and manors, the fee simple of which pertain in reversion to Her Majesty.

81. Genealogical memoranda of the representatives and heirs in reversion to the manor of Ware, in Hertford, and other lands, granted by Queen Mary to the Earl of Huntingdon, with remainder to Lady Winefride, one of the heirs of the Countess of Salisbury, &c. [*Probably relating to the preceding.*]

82. Petition of Robert Nele, of the Inner Temple, to the Council. Complains of the oppressions of John Dyon of Grymsby for matters of religion in the reign of the late Queen. Prays to be protected.

83. Petition of the poor inhabitants of the coasts of Norfolk and Suffolk to the Council, praying for a renewal of their privilege under Stat. 5 Eliz., permitting them to export fish duty free.

Vol. XLIX. January—May, 1569.

1569.
Jan. 1.
Plymouth.
1. Sir Arthur Champernowne, John Kylligrew, Wm. Hawkyns, and others, to the Council. Have stayed and landed from certain vessels at Saltash and Foy the Spanish plate and treasure. It is said to have been gathered by order of the Pope to be employed against the Protestants.

Jan. 1.
Plymouth.
2. Sir Arthur Champernowne to Sir Wm Cecill. Has nothing more to communicate concerning the stay of the Spanish goods and treasure. Requests stay may be made of the proceedings instituted by the Spanish Ambassador against William Hawkyns.

Jan. 1.
Ampton.
[Southampton.]
3. Lope de la Sierra to Anthonio de Guaras. Proceedings relative to the Spanish treasure taken out of his ship and lodged with the Mayor of Southampton. Has been urged to take his ship higher up the river for fear of pirates, but he avoided so doing.

Jan. 3.
Canterbury.
4. Wm. Lord Cobham to Cecill. Transmission of letters to the Spanish Ambassador by extraordinary means. Sends a packet he has intercepted. Describes a Frenchman who passed through Canterbury eight days since.

Jan. 3.
Canterbury.
5. Same to same. Intelligence that the English merchants and their goods are stayed in Flanders. Desires to know if he shall stay the Flemings at Dover and Sandwich.

Jan. 4.
Sandwich.
6. Wm. Southaick, Mayor, to same. Intelligence that all the English at Dunkirk have been imprisoned and their vessels seized

Jan. 4.
London.
7. Lawrence Carwoode to Wm. Marsden. Sends a letter for John Benet, and a testimonial from Mr. Tho. Ley to his brother Mr. Bryatt, about some cloths.

Jan. 4.
Plymouth
8. Champernowne, Hawkyns, and others, to the Council. Have observed their directions concerning shipping in their custody. Will preserve and place in safe custody all shipping that shall arrive; until the dangers of the sea, by reason of the French, may be avoided.

Jan. 4.
9. Sir Thomas Rowe, Lord Mayor of London, to Cecill. Has received intelligence of the arrest of English merchants at Antwerp. Has thought fit to stay all the posts which were ready to be despatched.

Jan. 5.
10. Sir Nich. Bacon to same. Advises seizure to be made of the Flemings' goods, to the Queen's use. Thinks what has been done in Flanders may be without the King of Spain's commission.

Jan. 6.
11. Sir Tho. Rowe to the Council. Informs them of the seizures he has caused to be made of the bodies and goods of certain Merchant Strangers.

Jan. 7.
London.
12. Same to same. Intelligence that the Secretary of the Spanish Ambassador had landed at Dunkirk, and caused sixteen Englishmen to be committed to prison there, and all Englishmen and their ships to be arrested, particularly the four last ships of the Merchant Adventurers.

Vol. XLIX.

1569.
Jan. 7. London.
13. Sir Tho. Offley, Mayor of the Staple, to Sir Wm. Cecill. Information that the goods and merchandize of the Merchants of the Staple have been stayed in Flanders.

Jan. 7 (?)
14. Merchant Adventurers to the Council. Explain the circumstances under which they sent the four last ships to Flanders, which have been arrested. Express great regret in having given offence thereby.

Jan. 8.
15. Same to same. Soliciting that measures may be taken for procuring satisfaction for arrest of their goods in Flanders, by the seizure of the property of Spanish subjects in London.

Jan. 8.
Lease from the Dean and Chapter of St. Paul's to the Mayor, &c., of London, of three houses or tenements in Wood-street, in the City of London, in reversion for 99 years after the year 1602, at the rent of 8l. per annum. *Sealed with two impressions of the Common Seal of London, in fine preservation.* [*Case B. Eliz. No. 4.*]

Jan. 9. Westminster.
16. Lord Adm. Clynton to Cecill. Recommends the two large Venetian vessels from London and from Flanders, which must necessarily touch in Spain, should be stayed for a month.

Jan. 9.
17. Memorial of George Kyghtley to the Council. Prays for some compensation for the loss of his lands and goods at Barrow (Bergen-op-Zoom), in Brabant, which the Duke of Alva has wrongfully deprived him of.

Jan. 10. Southampton.
18. Mayor, &c., of Southampton to same. Have stayed some vessels belonging to the subjects of the King of Spain. Desire further instructions. *Inclosing,*

> 18. I. *Note of such goods, ships, and men belonging to the merchants of Southampton as are known to be under the dominion of the King of Spain, together with a note of other merchants' goods being in the said parts, who have requested they should be stayed.*

Jan. 11.
19. Merchants of the Staple to same. Soliciting recompence for their losses by arrest of their goods and property in Flanders, from the property of Spanish subjects seized in England.

Jan. 11. Canterbury.
20. Lord Cobham to Cecill. Purposes to give directions throughout all the ports that the French may pass. Has intercepted a packet of letters. It will be necessary to put the coasts of the kingdom into a better state of defence.

Jan. 12. Totness.
21. Sir A. Champernowne to the Council. Has stayed all the ships of the King of Spain's subjects in Dartmouth and Plymouth. The ships are very large, and one of them has sprung a leak.

Jan. 12.
22. Tho. Windebank to Cecill. Has been suffering from a severe fit of the ague. Gives particulars of transactions respecting certain letters.

Jan. 13. Canterbury.
23. Lord Cobham to same. Has dispatched M. de la Croce. Packet arrived from Calais for the French Ambassador. Caused it to be

1569.

opened and found among other letters one to the Bishop of Glasgow, which he transmits. Conversation with La Croce.

Jan. 14.
London.
24. Dr. Valentine Dale to Sir Wm. Cecill. The conduct of the Spanish Ambassador puts him in remembrance of what he has read in the treatise of Petrinus Bellus, (one of the King of Spain's own men,) "*De re militari.*" He writes plainly "Legatos non esse tutos qui hostilia moliuntur aut excedunt fines mandati."

Jan. 14.
25. Sir Thomas Rowe to same. Has collected the principal matters touching the Queen's commission for arrest of Spanish merchants. Details his proceeding therein.

Jan. 16.
London.
26. Drs. David Lewes, Val. Dale, and Wm. Aubrey, to same. State their opinion in the case of the spoil committed by the King of Portugal's armada in the river of Cesto, on the ship and goods of Mr. William and Mr. George Wynter. Recommend letters of Marque be granted to them.

[Jan. 16.]
27. Articles to be alleged in Mr. Wynter's cause, abating the estimation of his loss in the river of Cesto. (*Probably subsequent to the above*).

Jan. 17.
Bolton.
28. Sir Fr. Knollys to the Queen. On the audacious boldness of the late proceedings of the Duke of Alva, particularly in connection with the Q. of Scots. Gives advice for the management of her Council. Is himself unfitted for a courtier.

Jan. 17.
Cambridge.
29. John Yonge, Vice Chancellor of Cambridge, to Cecill. Objects to the Ecclesiastical Commissioners exercising any jurisdiction within the University. Controversies between the town of Cambridge and the University.

Jan. 19.
30. Proposition by the Merchant Adventurers for the exportation of cloths and other English goods to Hamburgh and Emden.

Jan. 20.
Fowey.
31. John Kylligrew and others to the Council. Concerning the goods and treasure of the Spaniards in the ships stayed in the ports of the west of England.

Jan. 20.
Rochester.
32. Tho. Tayllour to Lord Cobham. Reports his interview with Mons. D'Assonleville, the Flemish Ambassador, and stayed him till further orders. Symond Starkey, and others, are in his company.

Jan. 20.
Rochester.
33. Same to same. The Flemish Ambassador finds himself aggrieved at being stayed. Assured him that Lord Cobham would show him every courtesy in his power. He has sent up his Secretary.

Jan. 20.
34. Lord Cobham to Cecill. Has sent the bearer with the servants and Secretary of Mons. D'Assonleville, the Flemish Ambassador, who is annoyed at his detention.

Jan. 20.
Abergwyly.
35. Richard Davies, Bishop of St. David's, to same. Concerning the right of presentation to the church of Llanarth, whether belonging to the Bishoprick of St. David's or a prebend belonging to the church of Llandewybrevy, and therefore devolving to the Crown. *Incloses,*

DOMESTIC—ELIZABETH.   329

1569.
VOL. XLIX.

35. I. *Declaration of the matter of Llandewybrevy, with the names of the Parsonages supposed to make a College there, shewing Llanarth to belong to the Bishoprick of St. David's.*

Jan. 20.
Plymouth.
36. Wm. Hawkyns to Sir Wm. Cecill. A small bark of his brother's (John Hawkyns) fleet has arrived at Plymouth. Sends her captain, Francis Drake, who can inform him of all proceedings of the expedition. Requests to have a share of the Spanish goods and treasure stayed in England.

Jan. 22.
Plymouth.
37. Same to the Council. Arrival of one of the small barks belonging to his brother's fleet. The return of his brother doubtful. Solicits some relief for the port and town of Plymouth.

Jan. 23.
38. Sir Thomas Rowe, Lord Mayor, to Cecill. Has appointed Mr. John Gresham and Mr. Aldersey to accompany M. D'Assonleville from Gravesend to London, and that he shall be lodged in the custody of Mr. Alderman Bond.

Jan. 25.
39. Same to the Lord Keeper. Has signified to D'Assonleville the Queen's pleasure concerning audience to be given him by the Council. He takes it very ill, saying his message is to the Queen.

Jan. 25.
On board the Minion.
40. John Hawkyns to Cecill. Notifies his arrival at Mountsbay with the Minion, which alone is left of all their fleet. Their losses by the treason of the Spaniards. All their business hath had infelicity, misfortune, and an unhappy end. *Incloses,*

40. I. *A note or journal by John Hawkyns of the places arrived at and the times, in the voyage made with the Jesus and the Mynion.* 1567 *and* 1568.

Jan. 25.
41. Petition of merchants of London trading to Rouen to the Council. To licence one John White to go with his hoy to Rouen, to bring home certain merchandize there belonging to them.

Jan. 27.
Plymouth.
42. William Hawkyns to Cecill. His brothers's arrival with the Minion in Mountsbay. Has sent a bark to him with provisions. Sir A. Champernowne will leave Plymouth with the Spanish treasure for Exeter.

Jan. 28.
Norwich.
43. John Parkhurst, Bishop of Norwich, Sir Edmund Wyndham, and others, Ecclesiastical Commissioners, to same. Detail their proceedings in the survey of the Cathedral Church of Norwich, and its establishment.

Jan. 30.
Westminster.
44. Gabriel Goodman, Dean, and others, Prebendaries of Westminster, to same. Are desirous to preserve the herse of the Lady Knollys in their church, claimed by the heralds.

Jan. 31.
45. Dr. Lewes, Judge of the Admiralty, to same. Concerning the question propounded to him, "*An legatus possit designare alium legatum?*" or whether D'Assonleville sent to the Queen by the Duke of Alva is to be accepted as Ambassador from the King of Spain or the Duke?

[Jan.]
46. Memorandum of increase of allowances to Officers in the department of the Comptroller of the Customs.

Vol. XLIX.

1569.

Feb. 2. — 47. Lancelot Lysley to Sir Wm. Cecill. The Commissioners appointed to issue the Queen's injunctions at Gosforth, on the part of the Court of Wards, have proceeded accordingly, but Ralph Alaker's wife refuses to give them possession.

Feb. 14. — 48. Sir Tho. Rowe to same. Recommends the bakers of London should be reincorporated by Charter.

Feb. 14. — 49. Petition of the Bakers' Company to same. Praying to be reincorporated by Charter.

Feb. [14 ?] — 50. Abstract of articles proposed to be inserted in the Charter for the incorporation of the Bakers' Company, London.

Feb. 22. — 51. Archbishop Parker to Cecill. In favour of the bearer, "a poor player man," who has discovered a mode of making brimstone.

Feb. 24. — 52. Charles Yetsweirt to same. Requests to be admitted into his service. Lat.

Feb. 25.
[5° Cal.Martii]
Rome. — 53. Declaratory sentence of Pope Pius V. against Queen Elizabeth, denouncing her as pretended Queen of England, and as a heretic, and absolving all her subjects from their oaths of fealty and obedience. *Printed Copy.*

Feb. 26. — 54. Simon Musgrave to Cecill. Concerning a plot of ground belonging to Mr. Curwen, near Workington, which is required for mineral works. *Incloses,*

54. I. *A plan of the ground required, as above, and of the river and town adjacent.*

March 1.
London. — 55. Opinion of Dr. Lewes respecting the goods and merchandize stayed in Britanny belonging to William Lawallen and other merchants of Cork. *Incloses,*

Feb. — 55. I. *Petition of William Lawallen and others, merchants of Cork, to Sir Wm. Cecill, stating that being bound for Bordeaux with wines they were driven into a harbour in Britanny, where they were spoiled of their goods to the value of 1200l., for which they solicit redress.*

March 1. — 56. Orders devised for restraint of the carrying over cloths into the Low Countries, or bringing commodities thence.

March 6.
London. — 57. John Hawkyns to Cecill. Sends him the manner of the Indies fleet. Requests he will suspend his opinion of the voyage, although it has not had a prosperous end. Solicits his favor towards the suits from Plymouth.

March 8.
Canterbury. — 58. Lord Cobham to same. The servants of the French Ambassador and of Sir H. Norreys are gone to Dover on their way to Boulogne. D'Assonleville is waiting to receive news. Increase of prices round Calais and Boulogne. There French pinnaces are off the Foreland and have taken divers vessels laden with corn.

Vol. XLIX.

1569.

March 8.
Canterbury.
59. Lord Cobham to Sir Wm. Cecill. The Captain of Calais has stayed three passengers of Dover and other English vessels and merchants, on information that two French ships laden with wine had been captured by Courtenay.

March 8.
Canterbury.
60. Same to same. The bearer has brought a letter from M. D'Assonleville, who is doubtful about passing over.

March 8.
61. Note of things to be provided for fitting out the ships Lion, Philip and Mary, Bonaventure, Primrose, Jenett, and the bark Bullein.

March 11.
Canterbury.
62. Lord Cobham to Cecill. M. D'Assonleville has passed over. The servants of Sir Hen. Norreys and the French Ambassador have taken their passage in another boat

March 12.
Oxford.
63. Philip Sidnei to same. Thanks him for his many favours. His progress in his studies. Begs him to excuse his troubling him with his rude letter. Lat.

March 14.
64. Petition of Anthony Anderson, of Dunwich, to same. To forward his suit for recovery of his ship, the Jesus; and also the suits of Roger Copinger, John Portingale, Nich. Galwan and Ric. Breede, of Youghall, touching the goods taken from them by the French.

March 16.
65. Heads of directions as to the mode of taking Musters throughout the kingdom.

March 17
London.
66. Wm. Malim (Guglielmo Malimio) to Cecill. Thanks him for his influence with the Earl of Leicester in his behalf. Mr. Wolley is now well provided, having succeeded the late Mr. Ascham. Sends Cecill a copy of complimentary Latin verses. Ital.

March 18.
67. Wm. Wynter to same. Is loth to trouble him as he knows he is overwhelmed with business, but begs him to consider the bill for supply of the office of Ordnance.

March 21.
Canterbury.
68. Lord Cobham to same. The Captain of Calais has suffered one of the passengers to come home. Most of the mariners belonging to other ships are stayed.

March 23.
[10 Cal. Apr.]
Chichester.
69. William Overton to same. Represents the distressed condition of his brother, which he has no means of alleviating. Lat.

March 25.
The Savoy.
70. Earl of Bedford to same. His friend the bearer has been hardly used by the Governor of Berwick touching certain fishings there.

March 26.
71. The Queen to certain Gentlemen and the Sheriff in every Shire. Appointing them Commissioners for taking Musters of men, horses, armour, and weapons, within the jurisdiction of each county.

March 26.
72. John Thaccher and others to Lord Cobham? Transmit him the depositions of certain men at Pevensey. *Inclosing,*

> 72. I. *Commission from the Lord Warden to John Thaccher and others, Jurats of Pevensey, to inquire as to certain wrecks within the Cinque Ports. Dover, 14 March 1568.*

1569.

Vol. XLIX.

    72. II. *Interrogatories to certain persons at Pevensey relative to a ship and goods wrecked there.*

    72. III. *Answers by various persons of Pevensey to the above interrogatories.* [*Five sheets.*]

March 27. 73. Henry Cheke to Sir Wm. Cecill. Gratefully acknowledges favours conferred. Lat.

March 27. 74. Account of artillery and stores delivered to John Kylligrew, Esq., Captain of Falmouth alias Pendennis Castle, co. Cornwall.

March 29. 75. Roger Edwards to Cecill. Sends him a treatise to be presented
Watling Street. to the Queen, which is not so well written as the state of the Prince and matter requireth.

March 29. 76. K. Duchess of Suffolk to same. Reminds him of a suit made by a poor Dutchman who desires to go over to fetch his wife and goods. Misery of those who suffer abroad for conscience sake.

March. 77. Names of persons to whom letters were sent in several Shires for setting out lances and light horsemen.

April 12. 78. The Queen to the Lord Keeper. To make out new commissions, extending the number of Commissioners in certain counties for maintaining horses and weapons, and taking General Musters.

April 27. 79. Proclamation for repressing pirates and rovers, and for preservation of trade at sea.

April 30. 80. J. Aldaye to Cecill. Is a prisoner in the Counter for debt. Thought he should have been protected under the Proclamation for the Lottery, but it was made a jest of. A Spaniard named Farrandina de Jarula has been brought into the prison, who took the treasure to the Duke of Alva. Sends some letters obtained from him.

May 2. 81. Tho. Cecill to his father, Sir Wm. Cecill. Reports to him particu-
Burleigh. lars of the works carrying on at Stamford and Burleigh. Recommends the purchase of some land from the Master of the Rolls.

May 5. 82. Dr. Lewes to same. Has given notice to such as have been spoiled by the French, or have had their goods stayed in France, to appear before him.

May 5. 83. Copy of a new Statute, respecting the office of Steward or Bursar of a College. Lat.

May 6. 84. Examinations of John Abels, and others, of the ship Camel, of Amsterdam, taken before Sir Henry Clynton, and others, in the County of Lincoln, touching their proceedings against Spanish subjects by virtue of Letters of Marque granted by Grave Lodowick.

May 9. Certificate of General Musters of horses, armour, and weapons, for the Wapentake of Barsetlaw, Nottingham. Taken before Sir Jervis Clifton and Sir John Hercye, Commissioners. [*See Vol.* lxii., *Musters, No.* 3.]

Vol. XLIX.

1569.
[May 9.] Certificate by Thos. Cowper, Sheriff, and Sir Wm. Merynge, of the number of horses, and muster of armour, weapons, &c., for the Wapentake of Newark and Thurgarton, Nottingham. [*See Vol.* lxii., *Musters, No.* 4.]

[May 9] 85. Summary of the General Musters for the whole county of Nottingham.

May 14. Westminster. 86. Attested copy of the Act 8_o Eliz., confirming the grant by the Queen to the Mayor &c., of Gloucester and their successors, of the house or hospital of St. Bartholomew at Gloucester, for support of a priest, a physician or surgeon, and forty poor people there.

May 20. 87. Names of those persons to whom Privy Seals were directed within the City of London for loan of certain sums of money to the Queen. Signed by the Queen.

May 28. 88. Roger Edwards to Mr. Marshe. Sends him a book that has been well accepted by the Queen, and is worthy to be read over and over again, although somewhat crabbed.

May 30. 89. Robert Huic^9 [q. Hicks] to Sir Wm. Cecill. Thanks for his seasonable aid in difficulty. Prays him to intercede with the Queen in his cause about certain timber trees. Lat.

Vol. L.   May, 1569.

1569.
May. 1. Certificate of General Musters of able men, horses, armour and weapons, for the whole county of Surrey, taken before Tho. Browne, Wm. More, Wm. Gresham, and others, Commissioners; and certificate of horse and armour in the same county.

Vol. LI.   June, 1569.

1569.
June 1 (?) 1. Second order by the Queen for putting in execution her commission for taking Musters of horse, armour and weapons throughout the realm. Extending the time for return of certificate until the 12th of August next. [*Minute corrected by Cecill.*]

June 1 (?) 2. Fair copy of the above, with further corrections by Cecill.

June 1 (?) 3. List of names of Commissioners for putting in force the statutes for horses, armour, &c., and for taking General Musters of able men, &c., throughout England and Wales, showing certain additions.

June 1. 4. Fair copy of above list, incorporating the additions.

June 6. 5. Account of the clear yearly value of lands, tenements, &c., of Walter Strickland, Esq., deceased, within the North Riding of the county of York, taken by Tho. Williamson, feodary, there.

1569.
June 7.

6. A treatise headed "A necessary consideration of the perillous "state of this tyme, comprised in two propositions and their ex- "planations, with some provisions for the same conteyned in two "degrees;" setting forth the danger to England and all nations professing the Gospel, by the unceasing efforts of the Pope to bring all again under his rule. Proposing a general association in England for protection of the Queen and defence of the Protestant religion. [*With very numerous corrections by Sir Wm. Cecill.*]

June 7.

7. Copy of the above, indorsed by Sir Jos. Williamson, "Reviewed, "corrected throughout in many places by ye proper hand of Sir "W. Cecyll, if he were not ye first framer of it. J. W."

June 27.
Leicester.

8. Sir Thomas Nevell, and others, Commissioners of Musters in Leicestershire, to the Council. Report their proceedings on that service.

June 27.

9. Commissioners of Musters for the County of Warwick to same. Certify their doings in the Musters. *Inclosing,*

> 9. I. *Certificate of the Musters for the County of Warwick and City of Coventry; number of able men, furniture of armour, &c.*

June 27.
Westminster.

10. The Queen to Ric. Cheyney, Bishop of Gloucester. Presentation of Dr. Thomas Cooper to the Deanery of that Cathedral Church, vice, John Man, dec^d.

June 27.
Winwicke.

11 Thos. Andrewe to the Council. Explains the reason of the delay in making a return relative to vagabonds, unlawful beggars, rogues, and Egyptians. *Incloses,*

> 11. I. *List of names of such sturdy vagabonds as were taken at Higham Ferrers, co. Northampton, and there whipped. 26 March,* 1569.
>
> 11. II. *Names of all those idle persons who have been apprehended and whipped in the open market at Peterborough. 25 March* 1569.

June 27.
Lincoln.

12. Sir Henry Clynton and others to same. Certifying their proceedings in the Musters in Lowthe and Horncastle, Lindsey Division, co. Lincoln. *Inclosing,*

> 12. I. *Certificate of arms, armour and weapons for the Hundred of Lowthe-Eske, Lindsey Division.*
>
> 12. II. *Muster roll of able men within the Hundreds of Lowthe and Calceworth, and the Wapentake of Hill, Lindsey Division.*
>
> 12. III. *Certificate of armour, &c., of the Town and Soke of Horncastle, whose soldiers were furnished and went forth under Captain Carsey.*
>
> 12. IV. *Certificate of arms, armour, and weapons within the Hundred of Calceworth, Lindsey Division, co. Lincoln.*
>
> 12. V. *Similar certificate for the Wapentake of Hill.*

DOMESTIC—ELIZABETH. 335

Vol. LI.

1569.
June 27. 13. Wm. Lord Wyllughby and others to the Council. Certify their proceedings in the Musters within the Sessions of Caister and Spittell, Lindsey Division, co. Lincoln. Desire to be supplied with arms and armour for sale. *Inclosing,*

> 13. I. *Certificate of arms, armour and weapons in the Wapentake of Well.*
>
> *Certificate of horse, armour, weapons, &c., in the Caister and Spittell, and other Wapentakes in Lindsey Division.* [See Vol. lxii. *Musters, No.* 5.]
>
> *Certificate by the Mayor, &c., of the armed men, armour, &c., within the City of Lincoln.* 21 June 1569. [See Vol. lxii. No. 6.]

June 28.
Auckland. 14. Bishop of Durham, Ch., Earl of Westmoreland, and others, Commissioners for the County Palatine of Durham, to same. Certify their doings in the Musters. The lordships and towns of Harte and Hartlepool refuse to appear, alleging that they belong to the County of Northumberland. *Inclosing,*

> 14. I. *Certificate of the General Musters of all the inhabitants of the County Palatine of Durham, their arms and armour, viz., for Easington Ward, Stockton Ward, Chester Ward, and Darneton or Darlington Ward, and the Lordship of Brancepeth.*
>
> 14. II. *Certificate of the statute for armour, weapons, and other warlike furniture for Chester Ward, co. Durham.* 28 *April* 1569.
>
> *Certificate of Musters of armour, weapons, and other warlike furniture, for Stockton Ward, co. Durham, taken before the Bishop of Durham and others, Commrs.* 26 *April* 1569. [See vol. lxii. *Musters, No.* 1.]
>
> *General certificate and abstract by the same Commissioners of the whole Musters of horse, armour, and weapons for the County Palatine of Durham,* 28 *June* 1569. [See vol lxii. *Musters, No.* 7.]

June 28.
Sarum. 15. Henry Lord Herbert, Sir John Zouche, and others, Commissioners of Musters for the County of Wilts, to same. Certify their doings in the Musters. *Inclosing,*

> 15. I. *Certificate and abstract of General Musters of horse and foot within the County of Wilts.*
>
> 15. II. *Another certificate similar in substance, but not duplicate.*

June 29
York. 16. Earls of Sussex, Northumberland, and Westmoreland, and others, Commissioners of Musters for the county of York, to same. Certify their proceedings. Change in the description of arms to be furnished by certain places. Request a supply of arms and munition may be

1569.

VOL. LI.

sent to Hull. Willingness of the people to provide themselves with arms. *Inclosing,*

 Certificate by the Earls of Sussex and Northumberland, of Musters of horse, armour, &c., within the Wapentake of Clarow, and Liberties of the same. [See Vol. lxii. Musters, No. 8.]

 Certificate by the same, of Musters of horse, armour, &c., within the Wapentake of Howdenshire. [See Vol. lxii. Musters, No. 9.]

 Certificate by the same, of Musters of horse, armour, &c., within the Wapentake of Holderness. [See Vol. lxii. Musters, No. 10.]

 Certificate by the same, of Musters of horse and armour, within the Wapentake of Harthill. [See Vol. lxii. Musters, No. 11.]

 Certificate by Sir Tho. Gargrave and John Vaughan, of Musters of horse, armour, &c., in the Wapentakes of Straffurth, Osgoodcross, Staincross, Agbridge, Morley, Staynecliffe, Yowcrosse, and Skyracke. [See Vol. lxii. Musters, No. 12.]

 Certificate by Sir Nich. Fairfax and Sir Henry Gate, of armour, weapons, horses, &c. for the Wapentake of Birdforth, co. York. [See vol. lxii., Musters, No. 2.]

 Certificate by same, of Musters of horse, armour, &c. within the Wapentake of Buckross. [See Vol. lxiii. Musters, No. 1.]

 Certificate by the same, of Musters of horse, armour, &c., within the Wapentake of Dickering. [See Vol. lxiii. Musters, No. 2.]

 Certificate by the same, of Musters of horse, armour, &c., within the Wapentake and Liberties of Pickering-lythe. [See Vol. lxiii. Musters, No. 3.]

 Certificate by the same, of Musters of horse, armour, &c., for the Wapentake of Bulmer. [See Vol. lxiii. Musters, No. 4.]

 Certificate by same, of Musters of horse, armour, and weapons within the Wapentake of Ridalle, N. Riding, co. York. [See Vol. lxiii. Musters, No. 5.]

 Certificate by the Earl of Sussex and Sir Tho. Gargrave, of Musters of horse, armour, and weapons within the Wapentake of Barkestone. [See Vol. lxiii. Musters, No. 6.]

 Certificate by the Earl of Westmoreland, Sir George Bowes, and Sir Wm. Eure, of Musters of horse, armour, &c., within the Wapentake of Allertonshire and Langbarge. [See Vol. lxiii. Musters, No 7.]

 Certificate by the same, of Musters of horse, armour, &c. within the Wapentakes of Hangeast, Hangwest, Gillingwest, Gillingeast, and Hullykelde. [See Vol. lxiii. Musters, No. 8.]

VOL. LI.

1569.
June 29.
Ipswich.

17. Commissioners of Musters for the County of Suffolk to the Council. Certify their doings in the Musters. Desire further time to furnish a more particular Certificate. *Inclosing,*

> *Certificate of all able men, horses, armour and weapon within the whole County of Suffolk, taken by Sir Robt. Wyngfeld, Sir Owyn Hopton and others, Commrs. [See Vol. lxiii. Musters, No. 9.]*

June 29.

18. Discourse on the question whether it would be profitable for the Commonwealth of England, that the Staple for spices be kept in England, and how it might be effected?

June 29.

19. Reasons for establishing a direct trade between England and Portugal.

June 30.
Cowdry.

20. Anth. Visct. Montague, and others, Commissioners of Musters for the county of Sussex, to the Council. Certify their doings in the charge committed to them. Have made inquiry and found the statutes relating to the keeping of horses, armour, &c., duly observed. *Inclosing,*

> 20. I. *Certificate of the General Musters of all able men, horses, &c., for the County of Sussex, the Cinque Ports excepted.*

VOL. LII. JUNE, 1569.

1569.
June 30.

1. Certificate by the Earl of Bedford, Arthur Lord Grey, of Wilton, and others, Commissioners of Musters, of the able men, horse, armour, &c., for the whole county of Buckingham.

June 30.
Bodmin.

2. Commissioners of Musters for the County of Cornwall to the Council. Certify their doings in the Musters. Scarcity of arms and armour. The county has been greatly impoverished by a general loss of cattle, horses, and sheep. Desire a supply of arms and munition. *Inclosing,*

> *Certificates of the Musters for the several Divisions of the County of Cornwall. Names of the able men. Observance of the statutes touching the breed and keeping of horses. Furniture of armour, &c.*

VOL. LIII. JULY, 1569.

1569.
July 2.

Commission of Inquiry relative to the proceedings of John Hawkyns, in the voyage undertaken by him, with certain ships under his command, to the West Indies, and hostilities with the Spaniards there. Depositions of witnesses, &c., attested by Dr. Lewes, Judge of the Admiralty, and Roger Parker, Notary Public.

Vol. LIV. JULY, 1569.

1569.
July 2. 1. Warrant to levy 200 able men within the County of   for service in Ireland.

July 2. 2. Notes of number of men and arms to be raised in various counties; ports for embarkation, &c. *In Cecill's hand.*

July 2. 3. The Council to the Sheriffs and Commissioners of Musters in the Counties of Somerset, Gloucester, Devon, Cornwall, and Dorset; to levy certain soldiers in those counties for service in Ireland.

July 2.
Kyrthinge.
4. Lord North and others, Commissioners of Musters for the County of Cambridge, to the Council. Certifying their doings in the Musters. *Inclosing,*

> 4. I. *Certificate of the Musters for the County of Cambridge. Number of able men. Observance of the statutes relative to the breed and keeping of horses. Furniture of armour, &c.* [See Vol. lxiii., *Musters, No.* 10.]

July 3.
York.
5. The Dean of York (Hutton), Suffragan of Nottingham, and Dr. Rokeby, to Sir Wm. Cecill. Have taken Musters of armour, &c., of the clergy within the Diocese of York, and transmit a schedule of the same. Have signified the orders of Council to the Bishops of Durham, Carlisle, and Chester.

Certificate of the General Musters for the County of Worcester. Number of able men. Inquisition upon the statutes touching the breed and keeping of horses. Furniture of armour, &c. [See *Vol.* lxiii., *Musters, No.* 11.]

July 8.
Hereford.
6. Sir James Croft, Sir Jas. Baskerville, and others, Commissioners of Musters for the County of Hereford, to the Council. Certify their proceedings and specify the numbers mustered. Will make a further return.

July 10. 7. Grant by Ivan Vazilewich, Emperor and Great Duke of Russia, of certain privileges to the Merchant Adventurers at the solicitation of Tho. Randolph, the English Ambassador, at the Court of Russia.

July 10. Certificate by Sir Tho. Wrothe, Tho. Seckforde, Sir Francis Jobson, and others, of the Muster of horses and armour in the county of Middlesex. [See *Vol.* lxiv., *Musters, No.* 1.]

July 10. Certificate of the General Musters for the County of Middlesex. Names of the able men, with their furniture of armour, &c. [See *Vol.* lxiv., *Musters, No.* 2.]

July 12.
Boston.
8. Commissioners of Musters for the Holland Division of the County of Lincoln to the Council. Certify their doings in the Musters. *Inclosing,*

> *Certificate of the Inquisition upon the statutes for the maintenance and breed of horses, provisions of armour, &c. And of the General Musters for Holland.* [See *Vol.* lxiv., *Musters, No.* 3.]

1569.

Vol. LIV.

July 12.
Salop.
[Shrewsbury.]
9. Sir Andrew Corbett, Sir Ric. Newport, and others, Commissioners of Musters for Shropshire, to the Council. Certify their doings in the Musters. Their opinion respecting the keeping of the arms and exercising the soldiers. Propose that Her Majesty should keep an appointed number of soldiers always in readiness for service. *Incloseing,*

    9. I. *Certificate of the General Musters of all sorts of men, and of horses, armour, and weapons within the County of Salop.*

July 14. 10. Names of the Commissioners of Musters for the city of Bristol.

July 20.
Shere.
11. Commissioners of Musters for Surrey to the Council. Give their opinions and answers to the various articles sent to them from the Council, relative to the increase of harquebusiers within that county.

July 20. 12. Directions how the General Musters and training of the soldiers may be most effectually accomplished, including the above answer of the Commissioners of Musters for Surrey; together with a relation of the orders used by the Duke of Tuscany for the exercise of war and training of soldiers.

July 21. 13. Note of Spanish money and silver bullion brought into the Tower of London from Dartmouth by John Barn and others, and laid up into the vault under the Jewel House in the Tower; and note of the Spanish rials received from William Wynter, by John Asteley, Master of the Jewel House.

July 24. 14. Duplicate of part of the above.

July 22.
Gloucester.
15. Edmond Lord Chandos, Sir Nich. Arnold, and others, Commissioners of Musters for Gloucestershire, to the Council. Give a general statement of the numbers mustered, and request leave to send full certificate after the harvest. *Inclosing,*

    15. I. *Abstract of the Musters of arms and armour for the County of Gloucester.*

July 22. 16. Sir Ralph Sadlier, Sir Edw. Capell, and others, Commissioners of Musters for the County of Hertford, to same. Certify their doings in the Musters, and give answers to the articles respecting the increase of harquebuses within the county. *Inclosing,*

    16. I. *Certificate of the General Musters, number of able men, horses, furniture of armour, &c., within the County of Hertford.*

July 25. 17. Certificate of the General Musters for the Wapentakes of Broxstow, Bingham, and Rushcliff, within the county of Nottingham.

July 25.
Warwick.
18. Sir Wm. Wygston, Sir Tho. Lucy, and others, Commissioners of Musters for the County of Warwick, to the Council. Reply to their letters as to increase of harquebusiers in that county. Have appointed divers places for practice of shooting. General search and punishment of offenders.

Vol. LIV.

1569.
July 31.
Newbury.

19. Sir Edw. Unton, and others, Commissioners of Musters for the County of Berkshire, to the Council. Certify their doings in the Musters. *Inclosing,*

 Certificates of the General Musters of able men, horses, armour, &c., in the Hundreds of Reading and Cheale, and the Borough of Reading, co. Berks. [See Vol. lxiv., *Musters No. 4.*]

 Certificate of General Musters of able men, &c., for the Hundreds of Faircross, Kintbury Egle, and Compton, and the Towns of Newbury and Hungerford, co. Berks. [See vol. lxiv., *Musters No. 5.*]

 Certificate of General Musters of able men, horses, armour, &c., in the Hundreds of Wantinge, Ganfield, Shrevenham, Lamborne, and Faringdon, co. Berks. [See Vol. lxiv., *Musters No. 6.*]

 Certificate of General Musters of able men, &c., for the Hundreds of Hormer, Ocke, and Moreton, and the Towns of Abingdon, and Wallingford, co. Berks. [See vol. lxiv., *Musters No. 7.*]

 Certificate of General Musters of able men, &c., within the Hundreds of Cookham, Bray, Ripplesmere, Sunning, Chardon, Wargrave, and Beynhurst, with the Town of New Windsor, co. Berks. [See Vol. lxiv., *Musters No. 8.*]

July ?

20. Certificate of able men furnished, and not furnished, in various Wapentakes, within Lindsey and Holland Divisions, co. Lincoln.

July ?

21. Certificates of coat and conduct money, and return of armour and weapons, in various Wapentakes, co. Lincoln.

Vol. LV   July, 1569.

1569.
July.

Book of General Musters of able men, horses, armour, weapons, &c., for the whole County of Somerset, certified by Sir Hugh Poulet, Sir Maurice Berkeley, and others, Commissioners for that county.

Vol. LVI.   August, 1569.

1569.
August.

1. Certificate by Viscount Hereford, Sir Wm. Grisley, and others, of the able men, horses, armour, &c., for the City of Lichfield, and General Musters for the whole County of Stafford.

August.

2. Certificate by Tho. Visct. Byndon, Sir Wm. Poulet, and others, of General Musters of all able men, horses, armour, &c., for the whole County of Dorset.

DOMESTIC—ELIZABETH. 341

Vol. LVII. August, 1569.

1569.
(August.) 1. Sir John Seintleger, Sir Arthur Champernowne, and Piers Edgecumb, Commissioners of Musters for the County of Devon. Certificate of the General Musters of able men, the breed and keeping, and number of horses, furniture of armour, &c., for the whole county.

(August.) 2. Certificate by the same Commissioners, and the Mayor, &c., of the City of Exeter, of Musters of the able men, armour &c., within that city and county.

Vol. LVIII. August—September, 1569.

1569.
August 1. 1. Sir John Zouche, Sir John Thynne, and others, Commissioners of
Devizes. Musters for Wiltshire, to the Council. Have received their letters containing articles respecting the increase and furniture of harquebusiers. Report their opinions thereon.

August 3. 2. Commissioners of Musters for Berkshire to same. Report their
Aylesbury. opinions respecting the training of harquebusiers in that county.

August 3. 3. Proclamation against the maintenance and harbouring pirates.

August 3. 4. Certificate by Edw. Earl of Derby, and others, of the General Musters for the whole County of Lancaster. Muster of the able men, horses, armour, weapons, &c.

August 5. 5. Sir Richard Fenys, [Fynes] and George Danvars, Commissioners of Musters for the County of Oxford, to Sir Francis Knollys. Certify their doings in the Musters. Request they may defer making a full Certificate till after harvest. *Inclosing*,

> 5. I. *Certificate of the Musters of armour and weapons, chargeable by statute within the County of Oxford, and the numbers of footmen and light horsemen.*

August 5. 6. Oliver Lord St. John, of Bletso, Sir Lewes Mordaunt, and others, Commissioners of Musters for the County of Bedford, to the Council. Certify their doings in the Musters. *Inclosing*,

> *Certificate of the General Musters for the whole county of Bedford. Number of able men, horses, armour, &c.* [*See Vol.* lxv., *Musters No.* 1.]

August 5. 7. Earl of Shrewsbury, Sir John Zowche, and others, Commissioners of Musters for the County of Derby, to same. Certify their doings in the Musters. Desire to be supplied with some arms. Cannot inforce the orders touching the exercising of harquebusiers. *Inclosing*,

> 7. I. *Certificate of the Musters of able men, with the armour and weapons, for the County of Derby.*

August 7. 8. Sir John Seintleger, Sir John Moore, and others, Commissioners
Exeter. of Musters for the county of Devon, to Sir Wm. Cecill. State various

342   DOMESTIC—ELIZABETH.

Vol. LVIII.

1569.

impediments that have prevented them from making their certificate within the time appointed. Request instructions as to firing the beacons.

August 7. Paston.
9. Sir Chr. Heydon, Sir Wm. Buttes, and Wm. Paston, Commissioners of Musters for the County of Norfolk, to the Council. Certify their doings in the Musters. *Inclosing,*

> *Certificate of the Musters for the County of Norfolk, and City of Norwich. Number of able men, horses, armour, &c.*

August 8.
Certificate by Edw. Lord Stafford, and Simon Harcourt, of the Musters of harquebusiers, pikemen, archers, and billmen, and of horses, armour, &c., in the Hundred of Cuddleston, co. Stafford. [*See Vol.* lxv., *Musters No.* 2.]

August 8.
Similar Certificate by Edw. Lord Duddeley, and Simon Harcourt, for the Hundred of Seysdon, in the County of Stafford. [*See Vol.* lxv., *Musters No.* 3.]

August 9.
Certificate by Sir Gervais Clyfton, John Byron, and others, and John Brownlowe, Mayor, of the Musters for the Town and County of the Town of Nottingham. Names of able men, harquebusiers, furniture of armour, &c. [*See Vol.* lxv., *Musters No.* 4.]

August 10.
10. Certificate by Sir Robt. Tyrwhyt, Sir Henry Darcy, and others, of Musters of able men, horses, and furniture of armour, &c., for the County of Huntingdon.

August 10. Chelmsford.
11. Robert Lord Ryche, John Lord Darcy, of Chiche, and others, Commissioners of Musters for the County of Essex, to the Council. Certify their proceedings in the Musters. *Inclosing.*

> 11. I. *Certificate of Musters of able men, horses, armour, weapons, &c., for the whole County of Essex.*

August 14.
12. Tho. Visct. Howard, of Byndon, Sir Wm. Poulet, and others, Commissioners of Musters for the County of Dorset, to the Council. Certify their proceedings on the Council's articles, relative to the maintenance and increase of harquebusiers.

August 15.
13. Certificate of Musters by Sir Thomas Rowe, Lord Mayor, and others, Commissioners of Musters for the City and suburbs of London, of the number of able men, armour, and weapons, within the same.

August 15.
14. Commissioners of Musters for the City of London, to the Council. State their mode of proceeding in the Musters, and their humble requests and petitions concerning the same, together with certificates of the total number of persons chargeable for horses, armour, &c.; and of the number of all freemen from the age of 16 to 60 within the city.

August 15
15. Certificate of Musters by Sir James Harington, and others, Commissioners, of the numbers of able men, horses, armour, &c., in the County of Rutland.

August 15.
Certificate by Richard Bertie, Robt. Carre, and others, Commissioners, of the names of persons chargeable to find armour; and of

1569.
Vol. LVIII.

the numbers of able men, horses, armour, &c., in Kesteven Division, co. Lincoln. [*See Vol.* lxv., *Muster, No.* 5.]

August 18. Leicester.
16. Earl of Huntingdon, Sir Tho. Nevell, and others, Commissioners of Musters for the County of Leicester, to the Council. Certify their doings in the Musters. Desire longer time for exercising the men in the use of the caliver. *Inclosing,*

> *Certificate of the General Musters for the whole County of Leicester, of the able men, horses, armour, &c.* [*See Vol.* lxv., *Musters No.* 6.]

August 18.
17. Certificate by Sir Jas. Croft, Sir Ric. Baskerville, and others, Commrs. of Musters for the County of Hereford. Number of horses, furniture of armour, &c.

August 20.
18. Wm. Lord Vaux (signed Harrowden), Sir John Spencer, Sir Humfrey Stafford, and others, Commrs. for the County of Northampton. Certificate of General Musters, number of able men, horses, armour, &c. Proceedings as to increase of harquebusiers.

August 24.
19. Answers of Lord Ryche, John Lord Darcy, of Chiche and others, Commissioners of Musters for the County of Essex, to the articles sent to them, relative to the musters of harquebusiers, &c. *Inclosing,*

> 19. I. *Answer to the articles touching the new increase of armour, and other things, within the Hundred of Chelmsford.*

Sept. 3.
20. The Queen to Dr. Lewes, Judge of the Admiralty Court, and others. Commission to inquire into all cases of spoils piratically committed upon subjects of the French King.

Sept 3.
21. Copy of the above.

Sept. 4.
Certificate of General Musters for the whole County of Warwick and the City and County of Coventry, together with the horses and armour within the same; and also the names of every city, borough, and township mustered before Sir Robt. Throkmerton, Sir Wm. Wigston, Sir Tho. Lucy and others, Commissioners, and delivered to the Lords of the Council on the 4th of September. [*See Vol.* lxv. *Musters, No.* 7.]

Sept. 8. Apthorp.
22. Sir Walter Mildmay to Sir Wm. Cecill. Would have been glad to have seen him. The Queen's safety, and the preservation of the cause of religion, are the two pillars on which the security of the State is founded.

Sept. 8.
23. Sir Ric. Wenman, Sir Ric. Fenys, and others, Commissioners of Musters for the County of Oxford, to the Council. Report, at considerable length, their opinions as to training and increase of harquebusiers.

Sept. 8 ?
Certificate by the Commissioners of Musters for the County of Oxford of all the able men, horses, armour, &c., within that county. *Probably transmitted with the above.* [*See Vol.* lxv. *Musters, No.* 8.]

Sept. 20. Bury St. Edmunds.
24. Sir Ambrose Jermyn, Sir Robt. Wyngfeld, and others, Commissioners of Musters for the county, of Suffolk to the Council. Report

Vol. LVIII.

1569.

their proceedings on that service, and give their opinions as to increase of harquebusiers. *Inclosing,*

Sept. 24.
Kenninghall.

24. I. *Certificate of the Musters of the number of able men, horses, armour, &c. within the whole County of Suffolk.*

24. II. *Schedule of names of such towns in Suffolk as are best for furnishing harquebusiers, and the numbers likely to be raised.*

24. III. *Certificate of lancers and light horses out of the County of Suffolk.*

Duke of Norfolk to the Queen. Explains the motives which induced him suddenly to withdraw from the court and to retire to his own private house. Protests his unfailing loyalty, and that he has never in the Queen of Scots' cause dealt further than he has declared to Her Majesty. [*See Feb.* 1570.]

Sept. ?

Certificate of Edmund Lord Chandos, Sir Nich. Arnold, and others of the Musters for the whole County of Gloucester. Number of able men, horses, furniture of armour, &c. [*See Vol.* lxv. *Musters, No.* 9.]

Sept. ?

25. Certificate by Sir John Savage, Sir Hugh Cholmeley, and others, of the furniture of horses, armour and weapons, and of General Musters of the whole County of Chester.

Sept.

26. Account of woollen commodities exported and shipped from the port of London for one year, ending Michaelmas 1569.

Sept.

27. A note of such sums of money as have passed by writ of Privy Seal, from Oct. 1566 to Sept. 1569.

Vol. LIX. October—November, 1569.

1569.
Oct. 1.
Ashford.

1. Lord Cobham, Sir Thomas Kemp, and others, Commissioners of Musters for the County of Kent to the Council. Report their opinion touching the increase of harquebusiers in that county. *Inclosing,*

1. I. *Brief Certificate of all able men, armour, and weapons, within the Lathes of St. Augustine, Scray, and Shipway, and part of the Lathe of Aylesford.*

1. II. *Estimate of the expence of establishing certain places for the practice of harquebusiers in the County of Kent, and of rewards for those who shall be skilful in shooting with the harquebus.*

Oct. 4.
Burnham.

. Sir Henry Nevell to Sir Wm. Cecill. The Duke [Norfolk?] will appoint no other than his own man "at the fylling of his flagyns" [*flaggons?*]. The trial of the murder [*of Darnley?*] must needs be a safety unto the Queen.

DOMESTIC—ELIZABETH.

Vol. LIX.

1569.
Oct. 7.
Windsor.

3. Earl of Leicester and Sir Wm. Cecill to Fr. Walsyngham. Order has been given to arrest Roberto Ridolphi, who is to remain in Walsyngham's house. To inform Mr. Randolph of it, who is at John Duddeley's house.

Oct. 8.

4. The Queen to Sir Francis Knollys. Directions to repair to the Duke of Norfolk, and to conduct him to the Tower. Sir Henry Nevell is to assist and to have charge of him. The Duke is to have no conference with any person.

Oct. 8.]

5. List (in Cecill's hand) of "Persons charged at the time that the "D. of Norfolk was first apprehended for his intended marriage with " the Scots' Queen."

Oct. 8.
Bristol.

6. The Mayor and Commissioners of Musters for the City of Bristol to the Council. Certify their doings in the Musters. *Inclosing,*

> 6 I. *Certificate of the General Musters of able men, horses, and armour within the City of Bristol.*

Oct. 10.

7. Sir Henry Nevell to Cecill. The Duke (of Norfolk) desires permission to write to the Queen, or that she will send some person to confer with him.

Oct. 10.

8. Certificate by Sir Henry Seymour, Sir Adrian Ponynges, and others, Commissioners of Musters, of able men, horse, armour, and weapons, and General Musters of the whole County of Southampton.

Oct. 15.
Northampton.

9. Sir Humphrey Stafford, Sir John Spencer, and others, Commissioners of Musters for the County of Northampton, to the Council. Have sent a more particular certificate, containing the names of the gentlemen, &c. Cannot certify the names of all the able men without remustering. *Inclosing,*

> 9 I. *Certificate of the names of the gentlemen of Northampton, with the number of horses, furniture of armour, &c., to be supplied by them.*

Oct. 19.
Windsor.

10. Earl of Leicester and Sir Wm. Cecill to Fr. Walsyngham. The Queen approves of the proceedings in the examination of Mr Ridolphi, but finds that some of his answers are very different from the truth. Send articles on which he is to be further examined.

Oct. 23.
Windsor.

11. Same to Mr. Walsyngham and Peter Smith. Directions to interrogate Ridolphi about his transactions with the Queen of Scots. His papers to be searched.

Oct. 27.

12. Same to same. Have received Mr. Ridolphi's letter to the Queen. His servants or factors may be allowed to resort to him.

Oct. 29.

13. Petition of John Thomas to the Queen. Prays for compensation for loss of his ship and cargo, taken and plundered by Capt. Jones and his accomplices.

Oct.

14. List of names of Justices and others in various English counties. Indorsed by Cecill "October 1569."

346   DOMESTIC—ELIZABETH.

1569.   VOL. LIX.

Oct. ?   15. Lists of Councillors, Nobility, Clergy, and (apparently) Justices of Peace, in every county.

Oct. ?   16. List of nobility and of gentlemen (probably Justices of the Peace), alphabetically arranged.

Oct. ?   17. Bartholomew Clerke to Sir Wm. Cecill. Defends himself from certain charges brought against him, and hopes he shall still retain Cecill's good opinion. Lat. [*Much defaced: the date is wholly conjectural.*]

Nov. 5.   18. Thomas Bury to same. Reminds him of a former application
London.   for money due to him and others, by the deceased Bishop of Aquila. Gives list of the said Bishop's debts.

Nov. 11.   19. Earl of Leicester and Cecill to Fr. Walsyngham. The Queen
Windsor.   being disposed to act with clemency towards Ridolphi, will restore him to liberty under certain conditions.

Nov. 16.   20. Sheriff and Justices of Nottinghamshire to the Council. Re-
Mansfield. port of the Earls of Northumberland and Westmoreland having assembled in arms and caused mass to be said at Durham. Nottingham is quiet, and many have subscribed for observance of the statute of Uniformity, of which they will send a ertificate.

Nov. 18.   21. Bishop of London and others, Justices of Middlesex, to same. Have assembled for the purpose of subscribing to the provisions of the Act for Uniformity of public worship. *Inclosing*,

            21 I. *Declaration by the Bishop of London, the Sheriffs and Justices of Peace of Middlesex, of their bounden duty to observe the statute for Uniformity of Common Prayer, and administration of the Sacraments.* Nov. 14, 1569.

            21 II. *List of those now in commission of the peace in Middlesex, and of those not now in commission.*

Nov. 18.   22. Declaration by the Marq. of Northampton, Lord Vaux, of Harrowden, and others, Justices of Peace for the County of Northampton. Acknowledge it to be their bounden duty to conform to the Act of Parliament for Uniformity of public worship.

Nov. 19.   23. Notes, in Sir Wm. Cecill's hand, relative to measures to be taken in consequence of the insurrection by the Earls of Northumberland and Westmoreland.

Nov. 20.   24. Another paper of notes by Cecill, on the same business.

Nov. 22.   25. Sir Francis Leche, Sir John Zowche, and others, Justices of Peace of the County of Derby, to the Council. The county is in a state of tranquillity. *Inclosing*,

            25 I. *Declaration of the Justices, &c. of Derbyshire to observe the Act for Uniformity of Common Prayer.*

Nov. 22.   26. Lord Adm. Clynton to same. A supply of weapons and powder
Royston.   is necessary for Lincolnshire. Artillery, &c. to be provided.

DOMESTIC—ELIZABETH. 347

Vol. LIX.

1569.
Nov. 22. 27. Note of the remain of various arms and stores within the Office of Ordnance.

Nov. 24. 28. Edw. Earl of Derby to the Queen. Has received from the Earl
Lathom House. of Sussex information that the Earls of Northumberland and Westmoreland are in open rebellion. Will use all diligence to keep the county of Lancaster in obedience.

Nov. 24. 29. Same to Sir Wm. Cecill. Requests him to present his letters to
Latham. the Queen. *Incloses,*

    29 I. *Copy of his Letter to the Queen. Latham House, 24 Nov.*

Nov. 24? 30. The Queen to the Earl of Derby. Directions to raise the whole force of Lancashire and Cheshire, and with those of Nottingham and Derby under the Earl of Shrewsbury, to join with the Lord Adm. Clynton, and to proceed against the Earls of Northumberland and Westmoreland, now in rebellion.

Nov. 24 ? 31. Same to Lord Adm. Clynton. Directions to take the command of such levies as shall join him under the Earls of Derby and Shrewsbury, and to march at once against the rebels.

Nov. 24 ? 32. Memoranda for letters to be written into certain counties, for the levying of troops to serve in the army under the Earl of Warwick, &c.

Nov. 24 ? 33. Note of the shires and numbers of men appointed to be in readiness in each at an hour's warning.

Nov. 24 ? 34. Note of the numbers appointed to serve under the Earl of Warwick, and to assemble at Leicester.

Nov. 24. 35. Note of the numbers appointed to be commanded by the Earl of Warwick and the Lord Admiral, to assemble at Leicester on the 5th of December.

Nov. 25. 36. Sheriff and Justices of Peace of Berkshire to the Council.
Reading. Request their advice on certain points of their Lordships' letters respecting the uniformity of public worship.

[Nov. 26.] 37. Justices of Peace for the Lathe of Sutton-at-Hone, Kent, to the Council. Certify their proceedings relative to the Act for Uniformity of Common Prayer. *Inclosing,*

    37 I. *Declaration by the Justices of Peace of the Lathe of Sutton-at-Hone of their willingness to observe the Act for Uniformity of Common Prayer, &c.*

    37 II. *Bond of William Roper, of Eltham, Kent, to be of good behaviour, and to appear before the Council when summoned. 25 Nov. 1569.*

Nov. 26. 38. Declaration of Richard Bentoun, of Kingsnorton, in the County of Worcester, communicated by Lord Willoughby, touching the proceedings of the rebels in the North.

VOL. LIX.

1569.

Nov. 26. 39. Declaration by the Sheriff and Justices of Peace of Shropshire to the Council, of their obedience to the Act for Uniformity of public worship.

Nov. 26-27. 40. Form of proclaiming Thomas Percy, Earl of Northumberland, and Charles, Earl of Westmoreland, traitors, at the castle of Windsor, and of degrading the said Earl of Northumberland from his dignity as a Knight of the Garter.

Nov. 27.
Chartley. 41. Walter Viscount Hereford, to the Queen. Will repair will all the force he has to Leicester, and will faithfully serve her against the rebels.

Nov. 27. 42. Same to Sir Wm. Cecill. Has received the Queen's commands to repair to Leicester where he is to find the Earl of Warwick and the Lord Admiral.

Nov. 28. 43. Report by Henry Knolles and others, of the examination of Thomas Wood, the priest, in the Tower, being threatened with the rack, as to words uttered by him and one Wm. Fenner. Standen also examined.

Nov. 28. 44. Declaration by the Bishop of Bath and Wells, and others, Justices of Somerset, to the Council. Certify their obedience to the Act for Uniformity of public worship.

Nov. 28.
Dorking. 45. The Sheriff and Justices of Surrey to same. Certify their proceedings relative to the Act of Uniformity. *Inclosing,*

    45 I. *Declaration of Sir Henry Weston, Sheriff, and others, Justices of Surrey, of their obedience to the provisions of the Act for Uniformity of Common Prayer and observance of the Sacraments.* 17 *Nov.* 1569.

Nov. 28.
Winchester. 46. Justices of Peace of Hampshire to same. Certify their obedience to the Act for Uniformity of Common Prayer, &c. Lord Chidiock Poulet objects to part, and Anth. Cope, an excommunicated person, "refuseth to subscribe most obstinately." *Inclosing,*

    46 I. *Declaration of the Bishop of Winchester and others, Justices of Hampshire, of their readiness to observe the Act of Uniformity, observance of Sacraments, &c.* 14 *Nov.* 1569.

Nov. 29.
Cobham. 47. Lord Cobham to same. Transmits the letter and declaration of the Mayor, &c. of Canterbury.

Nov. 29.
Canterbury. 48. Mayor, &c. of Canterbury to same. Have, by advice of their counsel Serjeant Lovelace, assembled and voluntarily subscribed to an instrument certifying their obedience to the Act for Uniformity of Common Prayer and observance of the Sacraments. [*This letter is apparently dated* 1563, *and in the papers of that year it was found, from whence it has been removed, for there is no doubt it appertains to the year* 1569. *Mr. Lovelace, their Counsel, was not made Serjeant at-Law till Easter Term,* 9 *Eliz.* 1567.] *Inclosing,*

    48 I. *Declaration by the Mayor, Aldermen, Common Council, and others, of the City of Canterbury, of their willingness to observe the Act of Uniformity, &c.* 29 *Nov.* 1569.

DOMESTIC—ELIZABETH.

VOL. LIX.

1569.

Nov. 29.
Wickham.
49. Justices of Peace of Buckinghamshire to the Council. Certify their subscription to the letters which their Lordships have transmitted. *Inclosing,*

> 49 I. *Declaration by the Justices of Buckinghamshire of their determination to observe the Act for Uniformity of Common Prayer and administration of the Sacraments. Wendover, 17 Nov. 1569.*
>
> 49 II. *Similar declaration by Edmund Asshefyld and others, Justices of Buckingham, not at present within the shire.*

Nov. 29.
50. Declaration by the Earl of Pembroke, Bishop of Salisbury, Sir John Thynne, and others, Justices of Peace of the county of Wilts, of their willingness to observe the Acts for Uniformity of divine service, &c.

Nov. 29.
Leicester.
51. Earl of Warwick to the Council. Has arrived at Leicester where he awaits the coming of his companies. Has received intelligence from the Lord Admiral of the rebels' state and proceedings.

Nov. 29.
Leicester.
52. Same to same. The Lord Admiral having been appointed to march towards Doncaster for its better security, he has warned the levies of soldiers from Lancashire, Salop, and other counties, to proceed at once towards that town.

Nov. 29.
Lincoln.
53. Lord Adm. Clynton to Sir Wm. Cecill. Has received his joint commission with the Earl of Warwick, and purposes to be at Newark with his whole force on Thursday or Friday next. Has received the treasure.

Nov. 29.
Lincoln.
54. Same to the Council. Has received the Queen's command for him to join the Earl of Warwick at Leicester. Desires a supply of armour and weapons.

Nov. 29.
55. Memoranda, in the handwriting of Sir Wm. Cecill, relative to measures to be taken on the emergency of the rebellion in the North, with the relative situations of various towns from London to Brancepeth, northward.

Nov.
56. Account of emptions and charges of carriage of ordnance and munitions, from the Tower of London to Leicester and other towns.

Nov.
57. Names of the Lieutenants of Counties, with their styles and titles, as they were rehearsed in the Commissions issued at Windsor, all in Nov., 12 Eliz., except the two last.

Nov.
58. Another copy of the above list.

Nov.
59. Another list of names of Lieutenants of various counties.

No
60. List of names of Lieutenants in certain counties.

Nov
61. The names of the Deputy Lieutenants in certain counties and ports.

Nov. ?
62. Names of the counties not yet supplied with Lieutenants.

Vol. LIX.

1569
Nov. 63. Orders to be observed by Lieutenants of Counties throughout the realm.

Nov. ? 64. Estimate of the charges of two days' training, from the numbers of 500 to 5,000.

Nov. ? 65. Number of horsemen and footmen put in readiness from certain counties; part to form a guard for the Queen's person.

Nov. ? 66. Names of noblemen and others to take charge of the force for guard of the Queen's person.

Nov. ? 67. Declaration by the Justices of Nottingham of their readiness to observe the Act of Uniformity of Common Prayer and service in the Church.

Nov. 68. A brief of the number of captains, their officers, and soldiers, levied in the South, against the rebels in the North, specifying the names of all the officers; the whole army, as well horse as foot, amounting to 14,215 men.

Vol. LX. December, 1569.

1569.
Dec. 1. 1. Justices of Peace of Norfolk to the Council. Proceedings
Norwich. respecting uniformity of divine service. Have taken measures to repress vagrancy and sedition. *Inclosing,*

    1. I. *Declaration by the Bishop of Norwich and others, Justices of the Peace, of their obedience to the Act for Uniformity of public worship, and administration of the Sacraments.*

    1. II. *Declaration by John Jenney of his obedience to the Act for Uniformity public worship.*

Dec. 1. 2. Commrs. of Musters for Berks to the Earl of Leicester. Pray to
Illesly. have a warrant from him, as Lord Lieutenant, for levying fines in that county. Great deficiency of horses.

Dec. 1. 3. Account of the monthly charges which her Majesty is at, for forts and castles in the County of Kent.

Dec. [1?] 4. Notes in Cecill's hand of measures to be taken on the emergency of the rebellion in the North. A guard for the Queen's person. To stay all young men at Cambridge and Oxford, being sons or kinsfolk of any of the rebels, &c.

Dec. 1. 5. Earl of Warwick to the Council. Has thought it best to send
Leicester. the forces by the nearest route to Nottingham. Great diligence used by Visct. Hereford in assembling his force. Artillery and great ordnance much wanted.

    6. Same to Sir Wm. Cecill. Will march forward with all expedition.
Leicester. Has spoken to Visct. Hereford about the Marshalship; Mr. Highfield will be his Provost Marshal. Has appointed Mr. Spenser to be Master

1569.

	of the Ordnance. Mr. Darrell, Surveyor of the Victuals, has received 500l. of the 2000l. lately sent down.
Dec. 1. Lincoln.	7. Lord Adm. Clynton to Sir William Cecill. The bands under his charge are going to Newark, and had better remain there till the arrival of the Earl of Warwick. Letters received from Sir Ralph Sadlier.
Dec. 1. Lincoln.	1. Same to same. Has written to the Earl of Sussex, which will shew what he has done in consequence of the Queen's instructions. Shall be able to send him 700 men. *Incloses,*

        8. I. *Clynton to Sussex. Gives particulars of the supplies which will be furnished to him. Desires directions as to sending treasure to him. The Earl of Warwick is at Leicester. Braunceton, Dec.* 1.

Dec. 1. Lincoln.	9. Same to Sir Walter Mildmay. Commends Sir Walter's son who has arrived. The bands under his command are about to march for Newark. His horsemen and harquebusiers are in want of training, and there is a lack of arms and armour.
Dec. 1. Sandal Castle.	10. Sir Edw. Carey to Lord Clynton. Has been engaged in mustering the stewardship of Wakefield. Has received directions to join him, Lord Clynton. Is in want of armour and munition. Secure mode of sending it by the assistance of Lord Darcy.
Dec. 2. Leicester.	11. Warwick to the Council. Difficulty of sending supplies to Sussex, either by the Lord Admiral or by himself. Is very desirous to hasten forward.
Dec. 2. St. Alban's.	12. Sheriff and Justices of Hertfordshire to same. Have assembled at Ware and subscribed the articles for Uniformity of public worship. *Inclosing,*

        12. I. *Declaration by the Justices of Herts of their obedience to the Act for Uniformity of Common Prayer, &c.* 21 *Nov.* 1569.

Dec. 3. Blandford.	13. Justices of Peace for Dorsetshire to same. Declaration of their readiness to obey and observe the Act for Uniformity of public worship.
Dec. 3. Leicester.	14. Warwick to Cecill. Has written to the Queen concerning the 1,500 men required by the Earl of Sussex. Will soon be ready to march forward, and shall be unhappy if he is not in place to venture his life against those traitorous villains.
Dec. 3. Newark-upon-Trent.	15. Clynton to same. Has applied to Sussex to know to what place the money and armour shall be sent. Has come to Newark, and will march next day towards Doncaster. Thanks for the two pieces of ordnance sent from Cecill's house at Burleigh. Vessels should be stationed off the coast to intercept succours to the rebels from Flanders.
Dec. 3.	16. Marq. of Winchester to the Council. Forwards a letter, from Mr. Thomas Wentworth, of intelligence concerning the rebels. Will

Vol. LX.

write to Mr. Gargrave and the Receiver to call on the collector to bring the Queen's money into York with speed. *Incloses,*

 16. I. *Tho. Wentworth to the Marquis of Winchester. The rebels have been lying between York and Tadcaster for a week or upwards. A great company of gentlemen and soldiers are with the Lord President, at York. Lord Darcy at Doncaster. The country is sorely charged in making sundry kinds of musters and organized robberies under that name. Scroby, 30 Nov.* 1569.

Dec. 4.
Canterbury.

17. Justices of Peace for East Kent to the Council. Certify their subscription to the articles for Uniformity. *Inclosing,*

 17. I. *Declaration by the Justices of Peace of the Lathes of St. Augustine, Shepway, and Scray, declaring their readiness to obey the Act for Uniformity of public worship, observance of the Sacraments. &c. Canterbury, 26th November* 1569.

Dec. 4.
Lewes.

18. Sheriff and Justices of Sussex to same. Have assembled at Steyning and subscribed their Lordships' order (for uniformity of public worship). Willm. Shelley and Willm. Scott, Esquires, did not appear. William Dawtrey and James Page, Esquires, refuse to subscribe. *Inclosing,*

 18. I. *Declaration by the Justices of Sussex of their obedience to the Act for Uniformity of Common Prayer and service in the Church.*

Dec. 4.
Newark.

19. Lord Clynton to the Council. Arrival of Mr. Warcop and Mr. Edm. Hall from York, where the Earl of Sussex has appointed the armour and the treasure to be conveyed. Warwick has set forward to meet Lord Clynton at Doncaster. *Incloses,*

 19. I. *Sir Tho. Gargrave to Clynton. The Lord Darcy and himself have agreed to convey the treasure and munition from Doncaster to York. The two Earls are far off in the Bishopric of Durham, and purpose to attack Newcastle or Barnard Castle where Sir Geo. Bowes is. Pountefrett Castle, 3 Dec.* 1569.

Dec. 5.
Tuxford in the Clay

20. Clynton to Sir Wm. Cecill. The Earl of Warwick is going to Nottingham and from thence to Doncaster. The greatest part of the bands under Clynton's charge have marched to Bawtry. The 2,000*l.*, to be sent by Mr. Sadlier at York will be delivered there to-morrow by Lord Darcy and Sir Thomas Gargrave.

Dec. 6.
Worcester.

21. Bishop of Worcester and Justices of that county, to the Council. Have assembled and agreed obediently to subscribe for observance of the Act for Uniformity of Common Prayer. *Inclosing,*

 21. I. *Declaration by the Bishop and Justices of the County and also of the City of Worcester, of their obedience to the Act for Uniformity of Common Prayer and administration of Sacraments &c.*

Vol. LX.

1569. Dec. 6.	22. Justices of Peace of the County of Hereford to the Council. Proceedings in procuring subscriptions for observance of the Act for Uniformity. John Scudamore, of Kenchurch, Thomas Havard, and Henry Dudestone, have refused to subscribe. *Inclosing,*

    22. I. *Declaration by the Bishop and Justices of Peace of Herefordshire of their willingness to observe the Act of Uniformity and Common Prayer. 19th Nov.* 1569.

    22. II. *John Scudamore, of Kenchurch, to the Justices of Hereford. Declines to subscribe the articles for Uniformity of Public Worship on account of scruples of conscience. 19th Nov.* 1569.

Dec. 7. Nottingham.	23. Earl of Warwick to same. If the country had been in greater readiness he could have used more speed. Is now determined to advance forward with such companies as he has in readiness. Provision of carriages. Robt. Lockye, a servant of Westmoreland's, is coming up to London.
Dec. 7. Scroby.	24. Lord Clynton to same. The Earl of Sussex has requested him to hasten forward his men to march to Barnard Castle to the rescue of Sir George Bowes. *Incloses,*

    24. I. *Earl of Sussex to Clynton. Desires him to hasten his reinforcements, to go to the rescue of Sir Geo. Bowes at Barnard Castle. 6th Dec.* 1569.

    24. II. *Clynton to Sussex. Will use all diligence in sending his men towards Sir Geo. Bowes. They have been much wearied by marching with their armour in foul ways, and are unwilling to march above five or six miles a day. Scroby, 7th Dec.* 1569.

Dec. 7. Doncaster.	25. Same to Sir Wm. Cecill. Has arrived at Doncaster, and is putting his men in readiness to join the Earl of Sussex. Requests armour and weapons. Has arrested and examined a servant of the Earl of Northumberland's.
Dec. 9.	26. Account of charges of five hoys, with 60 men each, and of four ships of war, for the transportation of troops.
Dec. 10. Bodmin.	27. Justices, &c., of Cornwall to the Council. Delay in receipt of their letters for suppressing slanderous reports. Punishment of vagrants, &c. Certify their proceedings in subscribing to the Act for Uniformity of Religion; Sir John Arundell and Sir Wm. Godolphin only excepted. *Inclosing,*

    27. I. *Declaration by the Justices of Cornwall of their willingness to obey the Act for Uniformity of Common Prayer, &c.*

Dec. 10.	28. Account of the delivery of 16 bags of Spanish rials into the hands of Mr. Tho. Stanley, Treasurer of the Mint, with the daily receipt of the same from him.
Dec. 11.	29. Memorandum of sums paid to Sir Thos. Gresham by Mr. Tho. Stanley of the Mint, to the 11th of December.

1569.
Vol. LX.

Dec. 11. 30. Sir John Savage to the Council. The declaration has been zealously subscribed by the Justices of Chester, out of duty to the Queen, "by whom is opened to us the plain path of virtue to our eternal salvation." *Incloses*,

    30. I. *Declaration by the Justices of Chester of their submission to the Act of Parliament for Uniformity of Common Prayer.*

Dec. 12.
Tower. 31. Sir Wm. Pelham to Sir Wm. Cecill. Requests payment for certain munitions furnished for service in the North. *Incloses*,

    31. I. *Charges of 12 carts and other emptions for furnishing a quantity of warlike stores, as specified, to the Earl of Warwick at Leicester.*

Dec. 12.
Doncaster. 32. Lord Clynton to same. Is now about to set forward towards the Earl of Sussex. Will make all possible haste, but the bands of horse and harquebusiers came in but last night. Many gentlemen are in Barnard Castle with Sir Geo. Bowes.

Dec. 12.
Doncaster. 33. Same to same. The bearer, Chester Herald, has delivered his charge and received acquittance, but will not take anything for his expences.

Dec. 13.
Wetherby. 34. Warwick and Clynton to the Council. Proceedings to relieve Sir Geo. Bowes at Barnard Castle, but he had been compelled to evacuate it on account of the desertion of the garrison over the walls. They now await the arrival of soldiers under Lord Willoughby. Want money.

Dec. 14.
Wetherby. 35. Same to same. Have advertised of the departure of Sir Geo. Bowes from Barnard Castle. Schedule of officers' and soldiers' wages received. Conflicting position of officers of the same rank in the two armies. Money wanted. *Inclosing*,

    35. I. *Schedule of the various officers in the army under the command of the Lord Lieutenants General, Warwick and Clynton; with the rate of pay added to several, by Cecill.*

Dec. 14.
Wetherby. 36. Clynton to Cecill. Seven of the Queen's ships have been seen off Scarborough. He will march on the morrow with his force for Boroughbridge to act with Sussex against the rebels.

Dec. 15.
Wetherby. 37. Warwick and Clynton to the Council. Cannot appoint Mr. Jenison to the office of Muster Master: the place has long since been given to Leonard Earsbie.

Dec. 16.
Maidstone. 38. Justices of Kent of the Lathe of Aylesford to same. Have assembled and subscribed according to their bounden duty the declaration for Uniformity. *Inclosing*,

    38. I. *Declaration by the Justices of the Lathe of Aylesford, that it is their bounden duty to observe the contents of the Act of Parliament for Uniformity of Common Prayer, Church Service, and Administration of Sacraments.*

Dec. 16.
Exeter. 39. Justices of Peace for the County of Devon to same. Proceedings relative to subscribing the declaration of Uniformity: James Courteney, Esq., declines to subscribe. *Inclosing*,

    39. I. *Declaration by the Bishop of Exeter and Justices of Peace of Devonshire of their obedience to the Act of Uniformity of Common Prayer, Church Service, &c.* 24th Nov. 1569.

Vol. LX.

1569.

39. II. Declaration by Jas. Courteney, Esq., of his reasons for declining to subscribe to the Act for Uniformity of Common Prayer. Nevertheless he is ready to serve the Queen to the uttermost of his power. *7 Dec.* 1569.

Dec. 17.
Ripon.

40. Earl of Warwick and Lord Clynton to the Council. Have in the army with them a greater number of willing and active soldiers than they can supply with powder, and therefore request a supply.

Dec. 18.
Ripon.

41. Same to same. Intelligence that the rebels are dispersed and their horse fled from Durham to Hexham, and from thence, it is thought, to some part of Scotland. Intention to pursue them. Will not reduce their force until the Queen's pleasure be known.

Dec. 19.
Darnton.
(Darlington.)

42. Same to same. The rebels continue their flight and have passed the Tyne at Hexham. Purpose to follow them. Lord Willoughby and diverse gentlemen of note are left in the rear.

Dec. 21.
Durham.

43. Warwick, Clynton, and Hereford to same. Want of money, especially for pay of the army if disbanded, there not being more than 1,500*l.* in the hands of Mr. Carr, the Treasurer.

Dec. 22.
Durham.

44. Warwick to Sir Wm. Cecill. Recommends the bearer, Mack Williams, his servant, "a toward yonge gentleman." The rebels being fled, he wishes himself now out of that miserable country.

Dec. 22.
Durham.

45. Warwick and Clynton to the Council. Wrote from Ripon to know the Queen's pleasure as to discharge of part of the army. Have discharged and sent home 2,000, being chiefly Lancashire and Cheshire men. The country is still in some peril.

Dec. 22.
Durham.

46. Edw. Horsey to Cecill. Dispersion of the rebels, who, having began a lewd enterprise, beastly and cowardly performed the same. Hopes the Queen will punish them. If any part of the forces are retained, hopes that he and his soldiers may be none of them.

Dec. 22.
Aldermaston.

47. Sheriff and Justices of the Peace for Berkshire to the Council. Proceedings in procuring subscriptions for observance of uniformity of Divine Service, &c. Edmund Plowden declines to subscribe. *Inclosing,*

47. I. *Declaration by the Justices of Berkshire of their willingness to observe the Act of Uniformity, Administration of the Sacraments, &c.*

47. II. *Bond of Edmund Plowden, of Shiplake, to be of good behaviour for one year, and to appear before the Council upon summons.* 20 *Dec.* 1569.

Dec. 23.

48. Examinations of Tho. Lees and others taken, before Henry Beecher, Sheriff of London and Alderman of Southwark, and Robt. Draper, touching certain treasonable discourses held by Henry Shadwell and others, concerning the rebellion in the North.

Dec. 24.

49. Deposition of Henry Shadwell of London, Vintner, before Robert Draper, Steward of the Borough of Southwark, concerning a conversation which he had with one Harry White touching the rebellion in the North.

1569.

VOL. LX.

Dec. 24.
Darnton.
50. Lord Clynton to Sir Wm. Cecill. Measures taken for discharging certain of the soldiers. Many of the rebels taken. The Earls have fled into Scotland conducted by an outlaw of the Borders. Has written to the Earl of Derby to watch the coasts of Cheshire and Lancashire, to intercept them in case they should take shipping.

Dec. 25.
Durham.
51. George Freville to same. Report that the Earl of Northumberland has been taken " as he was wandering alone disguised in simple apparel."

Dec. 25.
Stony Stratford.
52. Edw. Aglionby to same. Has reached Stony Stratford with great difficulty, the frost being so severe. Will proceed to Northampton, Leicester, and Newark.

Dec. 25.
53. Sir Thomas Goldyng, Sheriff of Essex, and others, to the Council. Certify their proceedings relating to the Act for Uniformity of Common Prayer. *Inclosing,*

    53. I. *Declaration by Lord Rich, Lord Darcy, and others, Justices of Essex, of their submission to the Act for Uniformity of Common Prayer, &c. Chelmsford, 25 November* 1569.

    53. II. *Lord Rich, John Lord Darcy, of Chiche, and others, to the Council. State that Lord Morley demurred to subscribe the declaration, on the plea of being a nobleman. Chelmsford, 2 Dec.* [*erroneously, November*] 1569.

Dec. 27
54. Deposition of Ric. Whittacres, Waterman, touching a conversation which took place in his boat on St. Thomas's day between two persons, relative to the rebellion in the North.

Dec. 27.
Northallerton.
55. Clynton to Cecill. Recommends Mr. Robt. Constable to his favour, who has been diligent in the Queen's service, for a lease of the house and park of Kirby Moorside, which Christopher Nevell had.

Dec. 27.
Boroughbridge.
56. Warwick and Clynton to the Council. Have discharged 6,000 men, and on the morrow will discharge more. Have been obliged to borrow money to pay them. Report that Northumberland is taken by the Armstrongs.

Dec. 28.
Newark.
57. Edw. Aglionby to Cecill. Has arrived at Newark but cannot proceed further until he obtains sufficient convoy of horse from the Lord Lieutenants.

Dec. 28.
58. Account of the monthly charge of all her Majesty's forts and castles in Kent, from the 1st to the 28th of December.

Dec. 30.
Boroughbridge.
59. Warwick and Clynton to the Council. Proceedings in discharging the army. Have discharged 7,000, and await the arrival of the treasure to discharge the remainder.

Dec. 30.
Boroughbridge.
60. Same to Cecill. Particulars of the force which they purpose to retain. Warwick begins his journey homewards to-morrow. Two of the Nortons have surrendered themselves.

Dec. 30.
Boroughbridge.
61. Clynton to same. Gives his opinion as to the reduction of the army, and to leave only sufficient forces under Sussex for the execution of justice. Reserves 1,400 men till further orders.

DOMESTIC—ELIZABETH. 357

Vol. LX.

1569.
Dec. 30. 62. Justices of Suffolk to the Council. Proceedings in subscribing
Ipswich. the declaration of obedience to the Act of Uniformity. Have taken
bonds of those who have refused to subscribe. *Inclosing,*

    62. I. *Declaration by Tho. Lord Wentworth, Sir Wm. Cordell, and others, Justices of Suffolk, of their obedience to the Act of Parliament for Uniformity of Common Prayer, &c.*

    62. II. *Bond of Sir Henry Bedingfeld for his good behaviour towards the Queen, and for his appearance before the Privy Council upon being summoned.* 1 Dec. 1569.

    62. III. *Similar bond of Thos. Rous, Esq.* 1 Dec. 1569.

    62. IV. *List of persons formerly in the Commission of the Peace for Suffolk who have subscribed, and of such as have refused to subscribe.*

Dec. 63. Justices of Peace of the County of Leicester to same. Proceedings in subscribing to the Act of Uniformity. The County is in very good state and quietness. *Inclosing,*

    63. I. *Declaration by the Justices of the Peace of Leicestershire of their willingness to obey and observe the Act for Uniformity of Common Prayer, &c.*

Dec. 64. Estimate of the rate of entertainment for a band of demi-lances and a band of light horse, each to consist of the number of 100 men.

Dec. 65. A note of the numbers of the horsemen which served under Mr. Charles Howard, General of the Horse, of the army levied in the South.

1569. 66. List of the officers and servants of the Queen's Household who are fit for military service, specifying their names and the numbers they can furnish.

1569. 67. Brief statement of ordnance, artillery, munitions, and habiliments of war, sent northward against the rebels, and to Windsor Castle.

1569. 68. Estimate of the remain of ordnance, &c., in charge of James Spencer, Master of the Ordnance for the Queen's army levied in the South.

1569. 69. A perfect note of powder, as well corn as serpentine, received by James Spencer, and by him delivered to the captains of the army levied in the South.

1569. 70. Abstract of the examinations of such gentlemen of the Inns of Court as have lately been summoned before the Commissioners for Ecclesiastical Causes, together with their answers to the interrogatories put to them.

1569. 71. A minute and statistical account of the visitation of the Province of Canterbury, comprising the establishment of the Courts of Arches and Faculties, and particulars of the See of Chichester, *sede vacante*, and articles of disorders in that Diocese, contrary to the Queen's injunctions.

Vol. LX.

1569 (?) 72. Petition of Stephen Harrington, third son of James Harrington, to Sir Wm. Cecill. That he will procure of the Queen license for him to purchase the reversion of the manors of Farleton, Bryarleye and Hemmesworthe, or to have them otherwise assured to him.

73. Petition of Tho. Baker, of Brighthelmston, to same. Prays for restitution of his goods, of which he had been spoiled and wrongfully deprived by certain Frenchmen in Britanny.

74. Petition of Lady Talboys to the Council. Praying that execution of certain bonds might not be enforced in the absence of Sir Peter Carew, her husband.

75. Notes of public business, in Cecill's hand, to be considered. The troubles in France and Spain; the Bulls from Rome; rebellion in the North, &c.

76. Memorandum of the sum owing by the Earl of Oxford to the Queen, for the tenths of his lands and two subsidies.

77. Proposals submitted to Cecill for utterly abolishing usurious transactions within the realm.

78. Observations on maintaining the trade with Portugal.

79. John? Hastings to Cecill. Touching the preservation of amity and increase of trade with Portugal.

80. Arm. Waad. to same. In favour of Mr. Cockeram, and soliciting that time may be granted to him for the payment of his debt to the Queen, he having been deprived of his office in the customs, which he had purchased for a large sum. Evils of that system.

81. Note of certain articles of merchandize. *Fr.*

82. Note of certain documents to be prepared, and of arms and munition to be provided.

83. Lists of Justices of Peace for various counties in England, and for all the Welch counties, on eighteen separate leaves of paper.

84. Note of arrears due to the Crown by certain noblemen as specified.

85. Account of debts due to the Crown by certain noblemen, upon specialities.

Vol. LXI. 1569.

1569. Volume relating to the Musters and military force of the County of Warwick, containing the commission from the Queen; instructions to the Commissioners; their correspondence with the Government, Earl of Warwick, &c.; Letters of Deputation to Sir Fulke Greville and Sir Thos. Lucy: and copies of the Musters for the county, &c. [*A Certificate of Musters of later date (1605) for the Hundred of Barlichway is entered at the end of the volume, in which the name of William Shakespere occurs, as a trained soldier of the town of Rowington.*]

Vol. LXII. 1569.

1569. Case containing Certificates of Musters, previously described in their chronological order.

Vol. LXIII. 1569

1569. Similar case of Certificates of Musters.

Vol. LXIV. 1569.

1569. Similar case of Certificates of Musters.

Vol. LXV. 1569.

1569. Similar case of Certificates of Musters.

Vol. LXVI. January—February, 1570.

1570.
Jan. 1. Boroughbridge. 1. Lord Adm. Clynton to Sir Wm. Cecill. Arrival of Mr. Aglionby with the treasure. Sir Ralph Sadleir has requested that a large portion of it should be appropriated to payment of the bands under the Earl of Sussex.

Jan. 2. Boroughbridge. 2. Same to the Council. Transmits his opinion as to the reduction of the army, and of those which should be retained. *Incloses,*

2. I. *Names of the Captains serving in the army of the North.*

Jan. 2. Boroughbridge. 3. Same to same. Reports measures which he has taken for discharge of the army. Requests their Lordships to further his suit to Her Majesty for his recall.

Jan. 3. Boroughbridge. 4. Same to Sir Ralph Sadleir. Is sorry he cannot send him so much as 3,000*l.* for the purposes which he has stated. Has sent him 1,500*l.* by Mr. Parke.

Jan. 6. Wetherby. 5. Same to Cecill. Trusts he has seen his letters announcing the arrival of Mr. Aglionby with the treasure. All the army is discharged excepting 1,500 men.

Jan. 6. 6. The Queen to Sir Ralph Sadleir. Directions for the discharge of the armies under the Earl of Sussex, the Earl of Warwick, and Lord Clynton. Has written to Sussex on the subject, with whom he is to consult, and to report their opinion.

Jan. 6. 7. Same to Clynton. Desires his opinion as to the number of men necessary to be retained in garrison on the frontiers.

1570.

Vol. LXVI.

Jan. 6.
8. Note of the leases of lands and tenements held by the principal rebels within the County Palatine of Durham, forfeited by their taking part in the rebellion of the Earls of Northumberland and Westmoreland.

Jan. 7.
Hume Castle.
9. Duchess of Northumberland to Lord [Hunsdon]. Thanks for his comfortable letters; she thought that nothing but death could separate her from her husband. Requests him to make intercession with the Queen for her children and servants.

Jan. 8.
Wetherby.
10. Lord Adm. Clynton to Sir Wm. Cecill. Sends a note from Mr. Carr of money received. Has written to the Earl of Sussex and to the Lords of Council, as to reduction of the army.

Jan. 11.
Windsor.
11. The Queen to Justices of Peace, Mayors, &c. To assist Edward Carey, Esq., a Groom of the Privy Chamber, to seize and take into his possession the lands, goods, and chattels belonging to Sir John Neville, one of the rebels.

Jan. 11.
Gloucester.
12. Edmd. Lord Chandos and others, Justices of Gloucestershire, to the Council. Have assembled and subscribed the declaration for Uniformity of Common Prayer. Mention several persons who have not subscribed, and reasons for their refusal. *Inclosing,*

12. I. *Declaration by the Justices of Gloucestershire of their obedience to the Act of Parliament for Uniformity of Public Worship.*

Jan. 12.
Wetherby.
13. Clynton to Cecill. Has conferred with the Earl of Sussex, and agreed as to the number of soldiers to be retained in garrison in the North.

Jan. 15.
Doncaster.
14. Same to same. Has furnished and appointed 300 harquebusiers and 100 horse to continue on the Borders, according to the determination of Sussex and Sadleir. Is on his way to the Court.

Jan. 16.
Newark-on-Trent.
15. Same to same. Has received his letter of the 14th inst. Appropriation of the treasure sent for paying off the army.

Jan. 16.
16. The Queen to Clynton. Does not think there is sufficient occasion to retain the 300 footmen on the Borders; and therefore directs that they shall be discharged.

Jan. 16.
Windsor.
17. Same to the Officers of Customs in the Ports of London, &c. Commands them to give place to the farmers of the new impost, in all matters concerning wines.

Jan. 19.
Sempringham.
18. Clynton to Cecill. Measures taken for discharging the forces placed in garrison by the Earl of Sussex. Sends up a writing from William Norton. *Incloses,*

18. I. *Information by William Norton of the dealings of Thomas Bischop with the Earls, who were confident of aid of men, money, and munitions.*

VOL. LXVI.

1570?
Jan. 22.
Beaudley.

19. The Vice President and Council of Wales to the Council. Transmitting returns from the Justices, &c., of all the Counties in Wales, except Flint and Carnarvon, of the declaration to observe the Act of Uniformity, &c The country is quiet, and no false rumours spread abroad. *Inclosing,*

 19. I. *Declaration of Justices, &c., of Denbigh, to observe the Act of Uniformity and Administration of the Sacraments. Ruthyn, 19 Nov.* 1569.

 19. II. *Similar declaration by the Justices, &c., of Radnor. Nov?*

 19. III. *Similar declaration by the Justices, &c., of Cardigan.*

 19. IV. *Similar declaration by the Justices, &c. of Anglesey. Nov.?*

 19, V. *Similar declaration by the Justices, &c., of Carmarthen. Nov.?*

 19. VI. *Similar declaration by the Justices, &c., of Pembroke. 10 Dec.* 1569.

 19. VII. *Similar declaration by the Justices, &c., of Haverforwest. 10 Dec.* 1569.

 19. VIII. *Similar declaration by the Justices, &c., of Merioneth. Dolgelly, 10 Dec.* 1569.

 19. IX. *Similar declaration by the Justices, &c., of Montgomery. 10 Dec.* 1569.

 19. X. *Similar declaration by the Justices of Brecknock.*

 19. XI. *Similar declaration by the Justices of Glamorgan.*

 19. XII. *Certificate by the Justices of Glamorgan of the reasons alleged by Sir Thomas Stradling for refusing to subscribe the declaration for observance of the Act of Uniformity, &c.* 21 *December,* 1569.

 19. XIII. *Bond of Sir Thomas Stradling, of St. Donat's, Glamorgan, for his personal appearance when called on.*

Jan. 22.

20. The Queen to Marq. Winchester. To permit the farmers of the duties on wines to enjoy the benefit of their lease according to the intent and purpose of the same. *Draft.*

Jan. 22.

21. Fair copy of the above, with further corrections.

Jan. 23.
Hampton Court

22. Same to the Sheriff of Sussex. Directions to seize the castles, manors, &c., belonging to the Earl of Northumberland within the County of Sussex, and to deliver the same to Charles Howard, Esq.

Jan. 24.

23. Same to the Officers of the Navy. To get ready the ship Aid, to act as convoy to the great Venetian ship in the Downs.

Vol. LXVI.

1570.
Jan. 24.
Hampton Court.
24. The Queen to the Farmers of Customs. To permit the Vidame of Chartres to enjoy the privilege of receiving certain wines for his own use, duty free.

Jan. 24.
25. Fair copy of the above, with alteration.

Jan. 25.
Abergwylly.
26. Richard Davies, Bishop of St. David's, to the Council. In reply to the articles addressed to him by their letters of the 6th of Nov. Implores them to consider the spiritual sores and diseases of his diocese. *Incloses,*

> 26. I. *State of the diocese of St. Davids; of the ecclesiastical officers, decay of churches, names and benefices of prebends, impropriations, &c.; with suggestions for remedy of the same.* 25 *January,* 1570.

Jan. 26.
27. Accounts of Sir Ralph Sadleir and Robert Carr, Treasurers of the armies in the North, for suppression of the rebellion there.

Jan. 26.
Warwick.
28. Justices of Warwickshire to the Council. Have partly subscribed the certificate for Uniformity of Common Prayer, but the disturbances in the North have prevented its completion.

Jan. 26.
Matharne.
29. Hugh Jones, Bishop of Landaff, to same. State of religion in his diocese; names of his officers and of the prebendaries of Landaff, and their appointments.

Jan. 26.
30. Sir Wm. Cecill to Mr. Alderman Rowe and Mr. Francis Walsyngham. Discharge of the bond taken of Mr. Rudolphi for keeping his house and restraint of his liberty during the Queen's pleasure.

Jan. 29.
31. Jean de Ferriers, Vidame of Chartres, to Cecill. Has caused the Queen's letter in his favour to be presented to Gardiner, Farmer of the Customs. It has not been complied with conformably to the Queen's intentions. Fr.

Jan.
32. Statement of the request of the Company of Merchant Adventurers, touching restitution of their goods seized in the territories of King Philip.

Feb. 1.
Newark.
33. Wm. Herreson, Alderman, and others, of Newark-on-Trent, to Cecill. Refusal of messengers on special service, to the payment of twopence per mile to persons supplying them with post-horses.

Feb. 1.
34. Account of the supply, for present service of the navy, of brass and iron ordnance and other stores; with the prices of the same.

Feb. 5.
35. The Queen to Winchester. Concerning sundry irregularities committed against the farmers of the imposts on wines, contrary to their letters patent.

Feb. 13.
36. Estimates of certain proportions of victuals to be placed in staple for service by sea or land, at the ports specified.

Feb. 15.
The Tower.
37. True note of the journey of Thomas Blackwell, lately made by him into the North, and so back again to London, describing the occurrences which took place.

VOL. LXVI.

1570.

Feb. 15. 38. The Queen to the Lieutenants of Shires. To hold general musters of all persons chargeable with providing horses and geldings, to see them properly armed and furnished, and to make certificate of the same.

Feb. 6. Lease in reversion from the Dean and Chapter of St. Paul's to John Incent, Gentleman, Proctor of the Arches and Chapter Clerk, of certain tenements called St. Erhenwald's tenements, in Knight Rither Street, abutting upon the capital messuage sometime called Montjoye Place, and now being the Doctors' Commons of the Arches. [*Case B. Eliz. No. 5.*]

Feb. 18. 39. The Queen to the Earl of Derby. Desires that his daughter-in-law, Lady Margaret Strange, should continue in attendance on her. Is sorry to perceive how much she is grieved by the death of her father the Earl of Cumberland, and has licensed her to dispose of certain lands for payment of her debts.

Feb. 18. 40. Same to Henry Stanley Lord Strange. Wishes Lady Margaret Strange to continue her attendance on her. Has granted license to him and to Lady Strange to make sale of some convenient portion of certain lands in the tenure of the Duchess of Suffolk.

Feb. 18. 41. Memorandum of a letter to the Surveyor of Woods in Middlesex, concerning the enclosure of certain lands at Knightsbridge, for preservation of the game, according to the information of Francis Neville, Esq., of Hyde Park.

Feb 20. 42. Memorandum in Cecill's hand, touching various transactions and affairs relating to provision of arms, military stores, Parliament, and other points of public business.

Feb. 21. 43. Thomas Marshe to the Council. Has taken the examinations of Putenham and Hodges. *Incloses,*

    43. I. *Interrogatories to be administered to John Hodges on behalf of George Putenham, as to the design of killing Mr. Secretary, &c.* 19 *Feb.* 1570.

    43. II. *Answers of John Hodges, of Olton, in the County of Norfolk, to the above, touching certain felonious purposes of killing Mr. Secretary Cecill.* 19 *Feb.* 1570.

    43. III. *Interrogatories by John Hodges to be administered to George Putenham, Esq.* 20 *Feb.* 1570.

    43. IV. *Deposition of George Putenham, of co. of Southampton, Esq., upon certain interrogatories administered to him relative to the conduct of John Hodges. Opinions of various parties. Influence of the Earl of Leicester, who is described as "the chick that sytteth next the henne." Design to kill Sec. Cecill.* 20 *Feb.* 1570.

Feb. 20. 44. Note of the whole delivery, by Sir Tho. Gresham, of 62 bags of Spanish rials into the hands of Mr. Tho. Stanley, Treasurer of the Mint; with the redelivery of the same from the Mint in money.

VOL. LXVI.

1570.
Feb. 45. Note in Sir Wm. Cecill's hand, of the order in which the rebels, being taken, may be indicted and tried, and disposal of their lands.

Feb. 46. Declaration of abuses in the practice of the Canon Law.

Feb. 47. Statement of the case of the Earl of Oxford as to his claim to certain lands, not devised by the late Earl to the Countess his wife, since dead.

Feb. 48. Copy of part of the above.

Feb. 49. Rental of divers manors, &c., in the Counties of Essex, Cambridge, Chester, Northampton, and Warwick, the jointure of the late Countess of Oxford.

Feb. 50. Suit of Capt. Thomas Leighton to the Council, for allowance of conduct money and other charges for the officers and 500 common soldiers on a march from Wetherby to London.

Feb. 51. Note of the most necessary munitions to be provided at this present in the Office of Ordnance.

Feb. 52. Account of artillery, carriages, armour, and other Ordnance stores.

Feb.? 53. Articles disproving the suit of Ric. Putenham to the Queen, for restitution of 900*l*. paid into the Exchequer by Francis Morris, to the prejudice of George Putenham.

Feb. *prob.* 54. Declaration by Queen Elizabeth to all her loving subjects on the suppression of the rebellion in the North; setting forth the malicious libels, both from abroad and at home, which led to that rebellion; the principles on which her government had hitherto been conducted; the unexampled prosperity enjoyed by England since her accession; her determination to continue in support of the true Christian religion; to administer the laws with moderation, but at the same time with severity, against the disturbers of public tranquillity; and exhorting all classes to continue in loyalty and obedience to the Throne and the laws of the realm.

February. 55. An elaborate paper in Cecill's hand, headed, "Copy of a Letter from a Gentillman in England, to his Coosyn, a Student, in Paris," being in answer to a false and scandalous book lately published in France, under the title, "A Discourse of Trobles newly happened in England in Octobre, with a Declaration made by ye Erle of Northumberland and other Great Lordes of England." [*The publication of this scandalous book is noticed in the dispatches of the Ambassador in France. 25 and 27 February, 1570.*]

Vol. LXVII. MARCH—APRIL, 1570.

1570.
March 3.　　1. Edward Chester (son of Sir Robt. Chester) to Sir Wm. Cecill. Reporting the slanderous conversation of one John Handford, a prisoner, that Cecill and the Lord Keeper had consulted together to have the Duke of Norfolk, now prisoner in the Tower, secretly put to death.

March 4.　　2. Note by Sir Tho. Gresham, of two bonds for prolongation of the debt due to Ellias' wife.

March 4.　　3. Estimate of debts due to the officers and captains of the army, unpaid, being the declaration of Robt. Carr, Treasurer of the army of the South.

March 4.　　4. The Queen to Lord Trer. Winchester. The commissions issued for increasing the number of horsemen and footmen, properly equipped with armour and weapons, are to remain in force, and be duly put in execution.

March 7.　　5. Interrogatories ministered to Robt. Spencer, Edwd. Chester, and John Handford, with their respective answers, relative to the slanderous imputations against the Lord Keeper and Sir Wm. Cecill, of their design to have Norfolk put to death secretly.

March 7.　　6. James Paget to Cecill. Has received Privy Seals for a loan in Hampshire, and communicated thereon with Sir Henry Wallop. Others in the county are well able to contribute. *Incloses*,

　　　　6. I. *List of Persons in Hampshire to whom Privy Seals were addressed ; some of whom are dead, some decayed, and others well able to pay.*

　　　　6. II. *List of persons of ability in Hampshire to whom Privy Seals for a loan might be sent.*

March 8.　　7. The Queen to the Lord Mayor, &c., of London. Musters to be taken by Thomas Manners and Robert Constable, of 500 soldiers, harquebusiers, ordered to repair to York.

March 10.　　8. Note of demi-lances and light horsemen to be raised and furnished by the clergy in the several sees and archdeaconries ; and of the numbers to be raised in various shires. *Two lists.*

March 10.　　9. The Queen to Cecill. Authorizing him to affix her signature, by stamp, to the letters addressed to the knights, esquires, and others in diverse shires, to levy and furnish lances and light horsemen for service in the North.

March 10.　　10. Same to an Archbishop or Bishop. Directions to levy a certain number of horsemen to serve as lances or light horsemen, to be supplied by the clergy of their respective dioceses.

March 10.　　11. Same to the Lieutenants of Shires. Having occasion to send a number of horsemen towards the borders of Scotland ; they are to levy the number appointed for their respective counties. Description and quality of arms and armour to be furnished.

VOL. LXVII.

1570.
March 10. 12. The Queen to the Lieutenants of certain Shires, specified in the margin. Has found it expedient to cause certain soldiers to be levied in the South of her realm for service on the Borders. Directions to levy and see furnished the number assigned to them.

March 10.
HamptonCourt. 13. Same to an Esquire. Requiring him to provide one able man and horse, or able gelding, fully furnished with armour, weapon, &c., to serve in the wars as a demi-lance, to be at York by the 1st of April next. [*Signed by stamp.*]

March 10. 14. Same to a Knight or a Gentleman. To provide and furnish a lance or light horse.

March. 10. 15. List of gentry in the County of Buckingham to whom letters were to be sent to furnish demi-lances and light horsemen, with a special letter to Sir Wm. Dormer.

March 11.
HamptonCourt. 16. Note of letters sent to the Lieutenants of Shires and Bishops for levying demi-lances and light horse.

March 12. 17. Sir Wm. Cecill to Bishop Bullingham. Requests of him the advowson of a prebend called Faringdon, to be bestowed on one who is a good scholar in the University of Oxford.

March 12. 18. Estimate of charges of the Queen's ships Bonaventure and Antelope, to be employed in convoying the Hamburgh fleet.

March 14. 19. The Queen to the Earl of Derby. Approves of his allowing the Lady Margaret, his son's wife, to part with a portion of her land in payment of her debts. Gives him permission to be absent from St. George's Feast.

March 14. 20. Same to Lord Strange. Concerning the permission to him and his wife to sell a portion of land for payment of her debts. Censures his desire to appropriate any part to the payment of his own debts.

March 14.
Tower. 21. Sir Francis Jobson and Sir Henry Nevell to the Council. Have examined Thomas Bates on the interrogatories directed to them. *Inclosing,*

    21. I. *Examination of Thomas Bates as to transmission of money to the Earl and Countess of Northumberland, during or since the rebellion.*

March 15. 22. The Queen to Arthur Lord Grey (of Wilton). Sanctions the orders given by him for furnishing certain demi-lances and light horsemen in co. Bucks, though varying from her former directions.

March 17. 23. Certificate of muster of lances and light horsemen, with their furniture, within the County of Northampton, taken before Sir Rob. Lane and Sir Ric. Knyghtley.

March 18.
Warwick. 24. Justices of Warwickshire to the Council. Have assembled and all subscribed the articles for Uniformity of Common Prayer, except Sir Robt. Throkmorton, Thomas Throkmorton, and Robert Midlemore. *Inclosing,*

    24. I. *Certificate by the Justices of Warwickshire of their submission to the articles for Uniformity of Common Prayer and Service in the Church.*

Vol. LXVII.

1570.

March 19. 25. The Queen to the Sheriff and Justices of Wilts. To carry into effect the levy of 50 footmen and certain horsemen, notwithstanding the death of the Earl of Pembroke, the Lord Lieutenant.

March 20.
Strenisham.
26. Sir Thomas Russell to the Earl of Leicester. Touching the horse and foot sent out of Worcestershire into the North. *Incloses,*

    26. I. *List of names of soldiers discharged on plea of sickness by one William Price, Lieutenant of Thomas Maynard, Esq., with the sums of money exacted from each man.*

March 20.
Shelford.
27. Thomas Stanhope to Sir Wm. Cecill. Is an humble suitor for the wardship of his sister's child, eldest son of Thomas Cooper, of Thurgarton, Notts.

March 22. 28. The Queen to the Countess of Pembroke. Condoles with her on the death of the late Earl of Pembroke.

March 22. 29. Same to the Earl of Shrewsbury. Recommends the Lord Talbot, his son, to his especial protection; whose father-in-law, the Earl of Pembroke, has lately deceased.

March 24.
Sudeley.
30. Edm. Lord Chandos to the Council. Has caused 100 foot furnished, and 20 demi-lances, with eight light horsemen, of Gloucestershire, to set forward to the Earl of Sussex. Death of Wm. Reede. *Incloses,*

    30. I. *Names of gentlemen who have furnished demi-lances and light horse, to serve in the North.*

March 23.
Fakenham.
31. Sir Christopher Heydon and Sir William Buttes to same. Measures taken for levying horse and foot within the County of Norfolk. Names of those not furnishing any. Death of Sir Edward Wyndham. *Inclosing,*

    31. I. *List of gentlemen of the County of Norfolk furnishing demi-lances and light horses, with the names of those gentlemen omitted in the calendar for the same.*

March 23. 32. The Queen to the Lord Adm. Clynton. Directions to set forth the Bonaventure and the Philip and Mary, to convoy the vessels of the Merchant Adventurers bound for Hamburgh.

March 23. 33. Estimate of the profit arising to the Queen by the coinage of certain Spanish money.

March. 34. The Queen to George Throckmorton, Sergeant of her Hawks. To receive and withhold the rents of certain lands at Fulbrook and Marston, in the county of Bucks, the property of Ric. Norton, concerned in the rebellion in the North.

March 30. 35. Sir Ric. Fenys to the Council. Has, according to the Queen's instructions, levied 50 footmen in the county of Oxford, furnished with armour and weapons. *Incloses,*

    35. I. *List of gentlemen of Oxfordshire furnishing demi-lances and light horsemen.*

VOL. LXVII.

1570.

March 31. 36. Lord Chandos to the Council. Sends their Lordships the names of such gentlemen of best wealth in the county who may be charged with provision of lances and light horse.

March 31. 37. Account of debts due to divers persons for provisions brought in for supply of the Office of Ordnance, from the 1st of October, 1569, to 31st March following.

March 31. 38. Decree of the Ecclesiastical Commissioners for the diocese of Chester, shewing that Cuthbert Clifton, Esq., has appeared before them, and made submission to the articles objected against him; and that he is therefore required reverently to attend divine service and receive the Holy Communion.

March 31. 39. Certificate of the muster of horses and geldings in the County of Buckingham; with a note of the lances and light horse gone to the north parts.

April 2. York. 40. Jherom Bowes to Sir Wm. Cecill. Solicits postponement of the payment of a fine in the Court of Wards, due for the marriage of James Calthrop, the Queen's ward.

April 3. Stamford. 41. Jane Cecill (mother of Sir William) to her son. Requests that the wardship of William Croftes may be granted to John Croftes of Ketton, his uncle.

April 5. Hampton. Sir Henry Wallop and Sir Wm. Kyngesmyll to Cecill. Report particulars of their conference with the Captain of Portsmouth, touching the defence of that place, [*See 28 April.*]

April 6. 42. Note of the arraignment at Westminster of Thomas, William, Christopher, and Marmaduke Norton, Thomas Byshoppe, Tho. Hussy, Oswald Wilkinson, and Tho. Bates, concerned in the late rebellion.

April 6. 43. Request of Sir John Perrot that the wardship of William Warren may be granted to John Voell, Alderman of Haverfordwest.

April 7. 44. Sir Francis Leek to the Council. Various persons mentioned in the Privy Seals addressed to himself and others for loans to the Queen, are not, nor ever were, resident in Derbyshire. *Incloses,*

    44. I. *List of persons who may be assessed for loans to the Queen in the County of Derby.*

April 7. 45. W. Saunders to same. Reports proceedings of the Justices of Northampton in search for vagrants. *Incloses,*

    45. I. *Certificate of vagrants apprehended within the Hundred of Fawlesley.*

    45. II. *Certificate of vagrants apprehended within the Hundred of Cleyley.*

April 8. Shelford. 46. Tho. Stanhope to Cecill. Has received a number of Privy Seals for loans in Nottinghamshire. Mr. John Manners is unable to advance the sum required. Prays to be discharged from the task of collecting the loans. *Incloses,*

    46. I. *Lists of Privy Seals returned within the County of Nottingham, and names of persons omitted, but who are well able to contribute towards the loans.*

Vol. LXVII.

1570. April 8. Bradwall.	47. John Leyghe, "the Queenes Maties ward," to Sir Wm. Cecill. A commission has been issued from the Court for examination of waste, supposed to be committed by his uncle Sir Ralph Leicester. Prays that his uncle may be allowed to enjoy his lease to the end of the term.
April 8. Norwich.	48. Edward Clere to the Privy Council. Has amended the superscriptions of divers Privy Seals sent to him, addressed to parties in Norfolk. Has transmitted a list of persons who have been omitted.
	48. I. *List of persons to whom Privy Seals were sent in the County of Norfolk, with particulars of their respective cases, who are dead, &c.*
	48. II. *Names of sundry persons in Norfolk able to contribute.*
April 8. Lyndeleye.	49. Margaret Palmes to Lady Stafford. Prays for grant of the manor of Farneley, the property of one Henry Johnson, attainted.
April 9. Shelford.	50. John Manners to Cecill. Has received a Privy Seal for the loan of 100*l.* Prays to be discharged of such assessment, to which his estate is not adequate.
April 9.	51. John Villers to same. Is in great distress. Beseeches him to further, by his authority, the grant of Thurland's wardship, which has been bestowed on him; but there is some difficulty in passing it.
April 9. Newcastle.	52. Jherom Bowes to same. Prays for a further postponement of the fine on the marriage of James Calthorp, of Norfolk, the Queen's ward.
April 10. Stowey.	53. Humfrey Colles to the Council. Has delivered the Privy Seals for the county of Somerset, and received answers from various parties. *Incloses,*
	53. I. *List of persons assessed by Privy Seals within the County of Somerset, &c.*
April 10. Stowey.	54. Same to Cecill. Has returned the Privy Seals for the County of Somerset, addressed to persons who are now dead or abiding out of the county.
April 10. Paul's Belchamp.	55. Sir Tho. Goldyng, Sheriff of Essex, to same. Prays, on account of his great charges, that the Privy Seal addressed to him for loan of 50*l.* might be revoked.
April 10. Paul's Belchamp.	56. Same to the Council. Has found many persons who are competent to contribute to the loans, who had no Privy Seals addressed to them. *Incloses,*
	56. I. *List of persons who are of ability to contribute on letters of Privy Seal, within the County of Essex.*
April 10. Helston.	57. Justices of Cornwall to the same. Have required the subscription of Sir Willm. Godolphin and Sir John Arundel to the articles for Uniformity of Common Prayer. Godolphin has subscribed, but Arundel has declined. *Inclosing,*
	57. I. *Certificate, by Sir William Godolphin, of his obedience to the Act for Uniformity of Common Prayer.*
	57. II. *Recognizance of Sir John Arundell, of Lanherne, for his good behaviour and appearance before the Privy Council when required.*

Vol. LXVII.

1570.
April 11. Sutton.
58. Sir Francis Leek to the Council. Mentions the names of several parties who might be added to the contributors in Derbyshire.

April 12.
59. Notes, by Capt. Styrley, of persons confederate with the Duke of Norfolk in a plot for releasing the Queen of Scots. Particulars of the whole scheme, in which Chr. Norton was to carry off the Queen of Scots.

April 12.
60. Additional list of sundry persons in Norfolk assigned to make loans to the Queen, with particulars of their estates and ability.

April 15. Sutton.
61. Sir Francis Leek to Sir Wm. Cecill. Has received and delivered Privy Seals addressed to persons within the County of Derby.

April 17. Mount Edgcumbe.
62. P. Edgecumbe to same. Concerning the collection of the loans on Privy Seals within the County of Cornwall, giving information of parties able to subscribe.

April 17. Mount Edgcumbe.
63. Same to the Council. Has delivered the letters of Privy Seal to the persons to whom they were addressed, with the exception of Mr. Carnsewe, who had died.

April 18.
64. Order of proceeding at the funeral of the late Right Hon. William Earl of Pembroke in St. Paul's Cathedral.

April 18. Bugden.
65. Justices of Huntingdon to the Council. Proceedings in the Musters. Money expended for purchase of armour and warlike stores for the service in the North.

65. I. *Certificate of Sir Robert Tyrwhyt of the horsemen mustered in the County of Huntingdon.*

April 19. York.
66. Sir William Ingleby to same. Delivery of the Privy Seals directed to certain knights and gentlemen of the County of York. Some are dead and others are resident out of the county.

April 20.
67. Reginald Grey to same. Has been appointed collector of the money to be raised on Privy Seals in Bedfordshire. Returns one directed to Edmund Ashfold, Esq., he not being resident in the county.

April 21. Hemington.
68. Sir Edwd. Mountagu to Sir Walter Mildmay. Has delivered twenty Privy Seals within the County of Northampton. Particulars of various parties. *Incloses,*

68. I. *List of persons of good wealth and ability in the County of Northampton to whom Privy Seals might be addressed.*

68. II. III. *Two other lists of persons able to contribute in Northampton.*

69. Earl of Northampton to Cecill. Edward Watson, of Rockingham, has been required by Privy Seal for a loan of 100 marks; thinks that not more than 50*l.* should be required of him.

Vol. LXVII.

1570.
April 22.
Warblington.
70. George Cotton to Sir Wm. Cecill. Prays to be discharged of the loan now required of him by Privy Seal.

April 23.
Bedhampton.
71. Lady Jane Cotton to same. Prays to be discharged of the loan of 50*l.* required of her by Privy Seal.

April [26].
72. James Paget to the Council. Particulars of the collection of the loan on Privy Seals in the County of Hants. *Incloses,*

> 72. I. *List of persons to whom Privy Seals were addressed in the County of Southampton, with particulars of their various estates, the sums raised, &c.*

April 26.
73. Same to Cecill. Refers to the above letter, which he has sent unsealed for him to peruse. Speaks in favour of several persons in the county for remission of the sums required of them by Privy Seal.

April 28.
[4 Cal. Maii.]
St. John's Col.
74. The Master and Fellows of St. John's College, to same. Requesting his assistance in a suit between the College and one Snagg, a rich man. Lat.

April 28.
Oxford.
75. George Danvars to the Council. Concerning the delivery of Privy Seals in the County of Oxford, with a list of persons to whom addressed, and the sums required of each.

April 28.
Oxford.
76. Same to Cecill. Is troubled with the examination of certain massmongers. The Privy Seal addressed to Mr. Rookes, who resides in Buckinghamshire, has been sent to him.

April 28.
Hampton.
77. Sir Hen. Wallop and Sir Wm. Kyngesmyll to the Lord Treasurer. Refer to their letter of the 5th as to the musters, to which they desire answer. Have had a meeting on the Council's letters of the 10th of April.

April 28.
York.
78. Sir Henry Gate to Cecill. Reported death of the Bishop of Carlisle. Recommends that Richard Barnes, Bishop of Nottingham, should be promoted to that Bishoprick.

April 28.
Bodmin.
79. Declaration by R. Greynvill and Robert Hill of their submission to the Act for Uniformity of Common Prayer and Service in the Church; taken before the Justices of Cornwall.

[April 28.]
80. Similar declaration by Sir Basyl Fylding, Fulk Grevyle, Henry Knollys, and others.

April 29.
Stowey.
81. Humfrey Colles to Cecill. Sends further list of persons of ability, to whom letters of Privy Seal for loans, within the County of Somerset, might be addressed.

April 29.
Hertford.
82. Certificate by John Purevey and George Dacres of collections made and sums expended for provision of armour and arms within the Hundred of Hertford, Herts.

April 29.
St. Alban's.
83. Similar certificate by Sir John Butler and others for the Hundred of Dacorum, Herts.

1750.
April 29. 84. Similar certificate by Sir John Butler and others, for the Hundred of Caysho, Herts.

April 30.
York. 85. Antony Thorold to Sir Wm. Cecill. Solicits that the Privy Seal for the loan of 100 marks addressed to the Lady Constable, a poor aged gentlewoman, may be recalled. Solicits the office of Deputy Custos Rotulorum in Kesteven, for himself.

April.
Bradwall. 86. Sir William Sneyde to the Council. Has delivered all the Privy Seals for loans in the County of Stafford, except one to Sir Thos. Fitzherbert, who is a prisoner in the Fleet. Names of such persons who may best be excused, with a list of names of those who can well contribute.

April 30.
Bury. 87. Ambrose Jermyn, Wm. Waldegrave, and others to same. Certify the sums collected and expended for providing military equipments within the County of Suffolk. *Inclosing,*

    87. I. *Amount of money levied and expended for armour and shot within the several Hundreds of the County of Suffolk.*

    87. II. *Account of the charge of 50 footmen of the County of Suffolk, under command of Henry Mildmay, by order of Lord Wentworth, Lord Lieutenant of Suffolk and Norfolk.*

April.
Hooke. 88. Sir William Poulet to same. Has received the Privy Seals addressed to persons in the County of Dorset, and caused them to be delivered, and will remit the money when received. *Incloses,*

    88. I. *Names of persons in Dorsetshire to whom the Queen's letters of Privy Seal have been directed, who are dead, and of those who are able to contribute.*

April. 89. Account of money due to Mr. Edwd. Horsey for himself and his band serving in the North. Certified by Alex. Skynner.

April (?). 90. Certificate of Sir Morris Barkeley, Sir Ralph Hopton, and others, Commissioners of Musters for the County of Somerset, East of the Water of Perrot, of sums collected and expended for equipments of soldiers for Ireland within the said county.

April (?). 91. Certificate, by the same, of sums of money bestowed on the equipment of every soldier sent into Ireland; with the cost of every description of armour and weapons.

April (?). 92. Certificate by Sir Hugh Poulet and others, Commissioners for the County of Somerset, West of the Water of Perrot, of the sums levied and paid for equipment of soldiers, provision of armour, &c. and charge of the soldiers sent to Ireland.

April (?). 93. The names of such prisoners as are remaining within the Tower of London; including the Duke of Norfolk, William, Marmaduke, Thomas, and Christopher Norton. [*The two latter were executed on the 27th May.*]

VOL. LXVII.

1570.
April (?) — 94. Confession of Jenny, as to his connexion with the Earls of Northumberland and Westmoreland, and with Mr. Ratcliffe, the brother of the Earl of Sussex, and of the part he took in the late rebellion.

April. — 95. Note of points constituting the legal offence of High Treason; in the hand of Sir Gilbert Gerrard, Att. Gen.

VOL. LXVIII. MAY 1st—15th, 1570.

May 1. — 1. Certificate of Rowland Lytton, Geo. Horsey, and Tho. Docwra, for the Hundred of Broadwater and Half Hundred of Hitchen, Herts. Specifying sums raised and expended in furnishing the soldiers for the North.

May 2. Clifton. — 2. Sir Jervis Clyfton to Sir Wm. Cecill. On behalf of the Lady Constable, of Kynolton, Nottinghamshire, an aged widow, who desires to be exempt from a loan of 100 marks required of her.

May 2. Worcester. — 3. Sir Tho. Russell, Sir Fulk Greville, and Sir John Lyttleton to the Council. Have examined the persons complaining of exactions by Wm. Price. He confesses the charge respecting passports. *Inclosing,*

    3. I. *Examinations of sundry persons taken at Worcester before Sir Thomas Russell, and others, relative to exactions of Wm. Price, in taking money for passports for discharge of soldiers.* 1 *May* 1570.

    3. II. *Abstract of the examinations against Wm. Price and Mr. Manours, for exacting money of the soldiers for passports for their discharge.*

May 3. Hemington. — 4. Sir Edward Mountagu to same. Has received and delivered the Privy Seals; and sends account of those who have paid. *Incloses,*

    4. I. *Answers to the first Privy Seals within the County of Northampton, with particulars of various parties.*

May 3. — 5. Account of the charges of all manner of arms, armour, stores, &c., provided for the Wapentakes, Holland Division, in the co. of Lincoln.

May 4. — 6. Edw. Clere to Cecill. Returns the Privy Seal addressed to Clement Paston. Proceedings in urging loans by other parties in Norfolk.

May 4. Canterbury. — 7. Archbishop Parker to same. Prays that some lands belonging to Manchester College might be assigned over to St. John's College, where Cecill was first brought up.

May 5. — 8. Certificate by the Justices of Peace in the several Hundreds of Leicestershire, and of the town of Leicester, of collection and disbursements made for the equipment of soldiers.

374   DOMESTIC—ELIZABETH.

Vol. LXVIII.

1570.
May 5.   9. Inquisition, post mortem, taken at Stratford Langhorne, in Essex, by Richard Browne, Escheator, concerning the estate of Ralph Latham, deceased.

May 6.
Saxlingham.   10. Sir Christopher Heydon and Sir William Buttes to the Council. Soliciting the discharge of the Privy Seal addressed to Thomas Crofts for the loan of 100 marks.

May 10.   11. Bishop Scambler, Tho. Cecill, and other Justices of Northamptonshire, to the Marquis of Northampton. Certifying the sending of their certificate. *Inclosing,*

> 11. I. *Certificate or answer to certain articles sent by the Council, touching expenditure of money in the Hundred of Neasborough for furniture of armour, &c.*

May 10.   12. Certificate of Tho. Pygott and Geo. Fysshe, Esquires, of charges for furniture of armour, weapons, &c., within the three Hundreds of Byckelswade, Wixhamtry, and Clifton, in the County of Bedford.

May 10.   13. Certificate of Oliver Lord St. John, of Bletso, and others, of the charges for equipment of soldiers in the three Hundreds of Berford, Stoddon, and Wylly, and the Town of Bedford.

May 10.   14. Certificate of Sir Henry Cheyne and Ralph Astry, of the charges for armour, &c., for the Hundreds of Manshead, Flytt, and Redburn-Stoke, co. Bedford.

May 10.   15. Certificate by the same, of soldiers equipped and sent forth from certain places in Bedfordshire.

May 10.
Saxlingham.   16. Sir Christopher Heydon and Sir Wm. Buttes to the Council. Send a brief statement of the money raised and expended for armour, weapons, &c., within the County of Norfolk. Inquiry as to robberies and misorders in the county. Apologize for having solicited the remission of some Privy Seals.

May 10.
Hereford.   17. Sir Thomas Baskervyle, Sir James Baskervyle, and others, Justices of Hereford, to the same. Certify their proceedings in procuring returns of the sums collected and expended for armour and munitions within the said county. *Inclosing,*

> 17. I.–VIII. *Eight schedules of returns of money raised and expended in several Hundreds in Herefordshire for provision of armour, weapons, &c.*

May 10.   18. Certificate of collections and disbursements for armour, weapons, &c., within the Hundred of Odsey, co. Herts.

May 10.   19. Similar certificate for the Hundred of Edwinstree, in the same county.

May 10.   20. Similar certificate for the Hundred of Braugham, co. Herts.

May 10.   21. Certificate of the Musters of the County of Salop, as well as horsemen as footmen, with account of assessments and disbursements for their equipment, &c., by Sir Andrew Corbett and others; and for the Town of Shrewsbury.

Vol. LXVIII.

1570.
May 11. 22. Marquis of Winchester to Sir Hen. Wallop and Sir Wm. Kyngesmyll. In answer to their letters of 30 April about musters taken in the County of Southampton. Deficiency of provender for horses. Garrison of the Isle of Wight.

May 11. 23. Deposition of William Atkinson, relative to his correspondence and transactions with Leonard Dacre.

May 11.
Brigstock. 24. Lord Vaux of Harrowden, Sir Edmund Brudenell, and others, to the Earl of Northampton. Certificate of the money assessed and expended within the East part of the County of Northampton, for armour, horses, furnishing of soldiers, &c.

May 12.
Worcester. 25. Sir Tho. Russell, and others, Justices of Worcestershire, to the Council. In answer to the articles forwarded by their Lordships. Trust it will be perceived they have endeavoured to do their duty; and give a statement of armour and furniture provided by the county.

May 12.
Horncastle. 26. Certificate by the Justices of Lindsey Division, Lincolnshire, of arms, armour, weapons, &c., furnished by the inhabitants of the Soke of Bolingbroke.

May 13.
Sudeley Castle. 27. Lord Chandos to the Council. Proceedings of the Justices of Gloucestershire in making returns of the expenses sustained by the county for providing arms, armour, &c. *Incloses,*

27. I. *Certificate of the money raised and expended in the Hundred of Kisgate, and other Hundreds in the County of Gloucester, for provision of arms, armour, &c.*

27. II. *Similar certificate for the seven Hundreds of Cirencester, &c.*

27. III. *Similar certificate for the Division of Barckley, shewing the proportions sent into the North and to Ireland.*

27. IV. *Similar certificate for the City of Bristol.*

27. V. *Similar certificate for the City and County of the City of Gloucester.*

27. VI. *General certificate for the whole County of Gloucester, signed by Lord Chandos the Lord Lieutenant.*

May 13.
Nottingham 28. John Byron and others, Justices of Nottinghamshire, to the Council. Have made strict inquiry into the conduct of the Captains who had been remiss in returning their armour and weapons. *Inclosing,*

28. I. *Certificate of the raising of 700 armed footmen for service in the North, and of the armour and weapons furnished to them, and of the quantities returned, &c.*

May 14. 29. Certificate of the charges of all manner of armour, powder, shot, weapons, &c., in certain Wapentakes of Kesteven Division, co. Lincoln. within the allotment of Robert Carre and Ric. Diseney, Esquires.

Vol. LXVIII.

1570.
May 14.
London.
30. H. Paineter, Clerk of the Ordnance, to Sir Wm. Cecill. Has opened his letters in absence of the Lieutenant of the Ordnance, and has considered the proportion of military equipments to be sent to Ireland. *Incloses*,

    30. I. *Account of the quantities and charge of military stores to be sent by land to Westchester for Ireland.*

May 15.
Nottingham.
31. John Byron, Sheriff, and Justices of Nottingham, to the Council. In answer to articles of inquiry as to expense of furnishing armour, &c. *Inclosing*,

    31. I. *Account of money levied in the County of Nottingham for purchase of armour and weapons, supplied since the beginning of May* 1569.

May 15.
London.
32. Lionel Duckett to Cecill. Requests that the Queen would be pleased to appoint certain officers for superintendence of the copper works; recommends Mr. Ric. Dudley and Mr. Dalston. Desires a lease of some of the Earl of Northumberland's lands.

Vol. LXIX. May 15th—31st, 1570.

May 15.
Gorhambury.
1. Grant by the Queen to Edward Herbert, Esq., of the office of Keeper of the Castle of Lyons, commonly called Holt Castle, in the Marches of Wales; and of the manors of Holt, Bromefield, and Yale, parcel of the lands of the late Sir Wm. Stanley, attainted.

May 16.
Hemington.
2. Sir Edward Mountagu to the Marquis of Northampton. Has received his letters, with a bill of John Browne's allegations, which he has already answered.

May 17.
Elnesto.
[Elstow?]
3. Henry Cheke to Cecill. Thanks for his patronage bestowed on him, and requests continuation of his favours. *Lat.*

May 17.
Beconsfield.
4. Justices of Buckinghamshire to Lord Grey of Wilton, Lord Lieutenant of that county, in reply to articles forwarded by the Lords of the Council. Account of money raised and expended for armour and weapons within the three Hundreds of Chiltern.

May 18.
5. Certificate of Justices for the same county of the charges of equipping certain soldiers in the Hundreds of Newport, Assenden, Buckingham, Aylesbury, and Cotteslowe.

May 18.
Colcum.
6. Sir Peter Carew to Cecill. Has caused the hulk to be delivered to the Fleming, and has dealt with the mariners agreeably to his instructions. The sum of 200*l.* is required to pay all in full.

May 20.
Exeter.
7. Justices of Devon to the Council. Concerning the equipment of soldiers in that county, and of the charges of sending some into Ireland.

May 22.
8. Certificate by Sir Ric. Knyghtley, Sir John Spencer, and others, of the money assessed and expended within the Hundreds of Sutton, Warden, and other Hundreds of the County of Northampton, for armour, horses, furnishing of soldiers, &c.

1570. May 22.	9. Similar certificates by Sir Robt. Lane, Sir John Fermour, and others, for other Hundreds of the same county.
May 23.	10. Sir Robt. Lane and Sir Richd. Knyghtley to the Council. Certify that John Browne, of Helmedon, is not able to contribute the loan of 50l. on the Privy Seal directed to him.
May 23.	11. Sheriff and Justices of Wilts to same. Certify their reply to the articles relative to collections and disbursements for military equipments, within the Hundreds of Chippenham, Malmsbury, and other Hundreds of that county.
May 24. WoottonBasset.	12. Sir John Danvers and other Justices of Wilts, to same. Similar certificate for the Hundreds of Highworth, Kingsbridge, and other Hundreds in the same county.
May.	13. Similar certificate by the Earl of Pembroke, Sir George Penruddoke, and others, Justices of Wilts, for the Hundreds of Amesbury, Elstub, and other Hundreds in the same county.
May 24. Bangor.	14. Nicholas Robinson, Bp. of Bangor, to the Council. Particulars of the disorderly services performed in Beaumaris, at the interment of the corpse of one Lewis Roberts, out of mere ignorance and in compliance with a foolish custom. The parties have all done penance.
May 25. Bedwyn.	15. T. Blagrave to Sir Wm. Cecill. Has been required by Privy Seal for a loan of 50l., which he prays may be revoked.
May 25.	16. Sir Wm. Pykerynge, and others, Justices of Middlesex, to the Council. Certificate of collections and disbursements made for provision of armour and weapons in that county.
May 26.	17. Archbishop Parker to Cecill. Thomas Keys, late Serjeant Porter, has solicited redress at his hands in virtue of his pastoral office. A gentleman, named Culpeper, has married the sister of Leonard Dacre, and as he absents himself from the Communion he has cited him to appear. *Incloses,*
	17. I. *Thomas Keys to Archbp. Parker. Prays that he will be a mean to the Queen for mercy, and that, according to the laws of God, he may be permitted to live with his wife. Sandgate Castle, 7 May* 1570.
May 26. Chester.	18. Sir John Savage to Cecill. Has used all diligence in the collection of the loan on Privy Seals; and has commanded defaulters to appear before the Council.
May 26. Norwich.	19. Edward Clere to the Council. Has sent up the money collected on Privy Seals. The defaulters have been ordered to appear before their Lordships.
May 26. Ipswich.	20. Sir Robt. Wyngfeld, and others, Justices of Suffolk, to same. Transmit schedules of the sums collected and expended, and of the armour and weapons provided within their division of that county.
May 29. Stafford.	21. Justices of the Peace of Staffordshire to same. Send certificate of the expenses sustained by the county, and apologize for their delay. *Inclosing,*

Vol. LXIX.

1570.

21. I.–VI. *Six certificates of the money assessed on the several Divisions and Hundreds of the County of Stafford for armour, horses, furnishing of soldiers, &c.*

May 29.
Isle of Wight.
22. Edward Horsey to Sir Wm. Cecill. Certain men-of-war are cruizing off the Isle of Wight, under plea that they are authorized by the Queen of Navarre. Denies that they are succoured by any within the Isle.

May 29.
23. Same to same. Explains that he has written the preceding letter that it may be shewn to the Spanish Ambassador. French news.

May 30.
Wells.
24. Bishop Barckley to same. Requests him to obtain licence for him to assign certain lands belonging to the Lordship of Banwell, Somersetshire, for three lives or twenty-one years.

May.
Black Raven,
Old Bailey.
25. James Longworth, Feodary of Warwick, to Sir Anthony Cooke. An escheat has been issued against him and his sureties on account of his office of Feodary. Requests that he will befriend him in this extremity.

May.
26. Return of the quantity of armour brought in by certain gentlemen of the County of Buckingham, by order of Lord Grey, of Wilton; of those who have requested further time, and of those who have not brought in their armour.

May ?
27. Short arguments disclosed on the behalf of certain citizens of London, occupying the trade of vintners, not being free of that company.

May ?
28. Proclamation for repressing piracy and sea rovers, and to regulate the sale of goods reputed to be taken from pirates.

May ?
29. Names of gentlemen in Rutlandshire able to contribute to the loan.

May ?
30. Certificate by the Earl of Shrewsbury of the remain of armour and weapons, and of the sums expended for the same, within the County of Derby.

May ?
31. Several certificates of various dates by Sir Henry Wallop, Sir Wm. Kyngesmyll, and others, Justices of Peace of Hampshire, of the remain of armour, weapons, &c., and of the sums received and paid for the same within that county.

May ?
32. Offer of A. B. [Tho. Smythe ?] to advance yearly Her Majesty's custom and subsidy on all foreign wares and merchandize brought into the ports of London, Sandwich, and Chichester, wines only excepted.

DOMESTIC—ELIZABETH.

Vol. LXX. May, 1570.

1570.
May 27.
Chatsworth.
1. Earl of Shrewsbury to the Privy Council. Sends the book of certificates for the County of Nottingham of the sums raised and expended for provision of armour, &c. Thought fit to send the entire books rather than abstracts, as they elucidate the charges against Mr. Molyneux, Mr. Lassells, and other Captains who served against the rebels in the North. *Incloses,*

    1. I. *Justices of Nottinghamshire to Lord Shrewsbury. Send the books of Bassetlaw Wapentake, and explain the charges against Molyneux and Lassells.*

    1. II. *Certificate by Geo. Nevell, Esq., of the money raised and expended in the equipment of soldiers, and for armour, weapons, &c., for the Wapentake of Bassetlaw, co. Notts.*

    1. III. *Similar certificate by John Manners and Tho. Stanhope, Esqrs., for the Wapentake of Bingham.*

    1. IV. *Similar certificate by John Byron (Sheriff) and Francis Molyneux, Esqrs., for the Wapentake of Broxtow.*

    1. V *Similar certificate by Robert Markham for the Wapentake of Newark.*

    1. VI. *Similar certificate by the same for the Wapentake of Thurgarton, and by Wm. Hereson and others for the Borough of Newark-on-Trent.*

    1. VII. *Similar certificate by Sir Jervis Clyfton for the Wapentake of Rushcliffe.*

    1. VIII. *Similar certificate by Sir Jervis Clyfton and other Justices for the Town and County of the Town of Nottingham.*

May 28.
2. Certificate by Vincent Harris and Arthur Harris, Esqrs., of the sums collected and expended in equipment of soldiers, and provisions of armour, weapons, &c., within the Hundred of Rochford, co. Essex.

May 28.
3. Similar certificate by the same for the Hundred of Dengie, in the same county.

May.
4. Similar certificate by Tho. Lucas and Geo. Tuke, Esqrs., for the Half Hundred of Winstree in the same county.

May.
5. Similar certificate by the same for the Half Hundred of Thurstable, in the same county.

May.
6. Similar certificate by the same for the Hundred of Lexden, in the same county.

May.
7. Similar certificate by the same for the Hundred of Tendring, in the same county.

May.
8. Similar certificate by the same for the Town of Colchester, in the same County.

VOL. LXX.

1570.
May. 9. Similar certificate by Henry Fortescue and Francis Harvey, Esqrs., for the Half Hundred of Witham, in the County of Essex.

May. 10. Similar certificate by Sir Edward Ryche for the Hundred of Barstable, in the same county.

May. 11. Similar certificate by the same for the Hundred of Chafford, in the same County.

May. 12. Similar certificate by Thos. Barryngton, Mathy Bradbury, and Kellam Throkmorton, for the Hundred of Dunmow, in the same county.

May. 13. Similar certificate by Harry Lord Morley and Tho. Frank, of charges for the Hundred of Harlow, in the same county.

May. 14. Similar certificate by Sir Tho. Goldyng, Sheriff, and Francis Harvey, for the Hundred of Hinkford, in the same county.

May. 15. Similar certificate by Sir Tho. Smith and James Altham for the Hundreds of Ongar and Waltham, in the same county.

May. 16. Similar certificate by Sir Anthony Cooke for the Liberty of Havering-atte-Bower, in the same county.

May. 17. Similar certificate by the same for the Half Hundred of Becontree, in the same county.

May. 18. Similar certificate by the Bailiffs and Justices of the Borough of Maldon, in the same county.

VOL. LXXI. JUNE—JULY, 1570.

June 2.
Stoke Dry. 1. Kenelme Digby to Sir Wm. Cecill. In behalf of John Flower, Sheriff of Rutland, to be discharged of the Privy Seal for the loan of 50*l.*, addressed to him.

June 2.
Althorp. 2. Sir John Spenser and Thos. Lee to same. Measures taken by them for letting to the best advantage the manor of Hodnell, co. Warwick, part of the estate of Tho. Wilkes, deceased. *Inclosing,*

    2. I. *Account of pastures and meadows belonging to the manor of Hodnell, in the County of Warwick, demised by Sir John Spencer and Thos. Lee.*

June 5.
Newington Green. 3. Richd. Bertie to same. The bearer is one of the persons with whom he has negociated for bringing foreigners into Lincolnshire. Has informed the Earl of Leicester of the transactions in that matter.

June 7. 4. Thomas Stanhope to the Council. Recommends Mr. Edwd. Skipworth, of Nottingham, to be discharged of the Privy Seal for the loan of 50*l.*

VOL. LXXI.

1570.
June 7.
Bemyche Loge.
[Beamish?]
5. Sir Henry Percy to Sir Wm. Cecill. Desires to have his counsel as to the mode of proceeding with his brother, who he hears is very penitent, and his wife is in great distress. Hopes certain of his lands will not be granted away. *Incloses,*

> 5. I. *Sir Henry Percy to his brother the Earl of Northumberland. Reproaches him with his proceedings in the late rebellion. Urges him to seek the Queen's mercy, and to think on the misery and desolation he has occasioned.*

June 8.
Bruges.
6. Harry Lord Morley to the Queen. Beseeches her not to entertain any doubt of his loyalty on account of his leaving the kingdom. He knows the malice of the Lord Keeper and Mr. Secretary against him. Solicits permission for his wife and children to join him.

June [8].
Bruges.
7. Same to his wife Lady Morley. Has arrived in safety at Bruges. Has written a humble letter to the Queen, and solicited that she will allow her and his children to come over to him.

June 8.
8. Sir William Sneyde to the Council. Forwards a list of such persons in Staffordshire who have or have not paid the contributions required by letters of Privy Seal.

June 9.
9. Same to same. Has delivered the Privy Seal for loan of 50*l.* to John Bowes, who prays to be exempt therefrom.

June 10.
Gray's Inn.
10. Edward Stanhope to Cecill. Richd. Whitmore, who has attended the Council to shew his inability to contribute, desires to know when his further attendance may be required.

June 11.
Queen's College.
11. Wm. Chaderton to same. Requests that some effectual means may be taken for a reformation of the disorders in the University of Cambridge, encouraged by the evil doctrines and conduct of Mr. Cartwright, Mr. Chapman, and Mr. Some.

June 12.
Norwich.
12. Edward Clere to the Council. Is of opinion Mr. Wheteley may well be charged with the whole or part of the loan assessed on him by Privy Seal.

June 12.
13. Table of fees of the Secretary and Clerk of the Signet, for the Council in the Marches in Wales.

June ?
14. Fees and allowances to the Lord President and Council for the Marches in Wales.

June 15.
15. Surrender to the Queen by Francis Newdegate, Esq., and the Lady Ann, late Duchess of Somerset, of all their right and title to the manors of Mochelney, Drayton, Westover, and Fifehead, co. Somerset, and in the manors of Berwick, Bassett, and Kingston Deverell, co. Wilts. Attested by John Vaughan. Lat.

June 15.
16. Substance of the speech of the Lord Keeper in the Star Chamber upon the subject of some unfounded reports that had been circulated as to an inquisitorial power being exercised in matters of religion.

June 16.
17. Draft of the same. The whole in Cecill's handwriting.

Vol. LXXI.

1570.

June 16. 18. Alexander Nowell, Dean of St. Paul's, to Sir Wm. Cecill. The Latin catechism, which he wrote about seven years since, and dedicated to him, is now at length printed, by appointment of the Archbishops of Canterbury and York.

June 18. 19. Duke of Norfolk to the Queen. Had hoped that by her merciful goodness he might have been allowed to remain at his own house on account of his health. Beseeches her to remember what he declared in December last, that he never purposed to deal any further in the matter of the Queen of Scots.

June [20]. 20. Account of the Customs and Subsidies of London, Sandwich, and Chichester, for the eleven years of the Queen's reign; with estimates of amount of fine (5,000*l*.) to be paid by Mr. Tho. Smythe on the new rent.

June 20. 21. Articles for drawing a lease to pass from the Queen to Thomas Smythe of the customs and subsidies in the ports of London, Sandwich, and Chichester, wines only excepted.

June 22. 22. Certificate by Tho. Meade and others of the sums raised and expended for provision of armour, &c., for certain Hundreds in the County of Essex.

June 25.
St. Paul's. 23. Edmond Grindall, Archbishop of York, to Cecill. Complains of the unsound doctrines promulgated by Mr. Cartwright, Reader of the Lady Margaret Divinity Lecture in the University of Cambridge. Has been to see Cecill's children and buildings at Waltham. *Incloses,*

    23. I. *Positions written and delivered by Mr. Cartwright to the Vice-Chancellor of Cambridge.*

June 26.
Wyttenham. 24. William Dunche to same. Has received large sums under the letters of Privy Seal. Sends particulars of other persons in Berkshire able to contribute.

June 26.
Oatlands. 25. The Queen to the Marquis of Winchester. Warrant for the Merchants of the Stillyard to export 8,000 unwrought cloths.

June 27.
Dartington. 26. Sir Arthur Champernowne to Cecill. Arrival of Mons. de Brickevile. Details intelligence brought by him from France.

June 29. 27. The Vice-Chancellor (John Meye) and Heads of Houses in Cambridge, to Cecill. Favour shewn to Mr. Freake in his preferment: in the P. S. complain of the conduct and doctrines of Mr. Cartwright.

June 29. 28. Summary of the whole amount raised and expended for the equipment of soldiers, furniture of armour, weapons, &c., within the County of Essex.

June 29. 29. Account of sums of money received for the Queen's use by the collectors of loans on Privy Seals in various counties of the realm.

June. 30. Petition of the inhabitants of Cirencester, Gloucestershire, to the Council. Pray to be relieved from the tyranny of certain mischievous Papists.

VOL. LXXI.

1570.
June. 31. Willm. Thorneton to Sir Wm. Cecill. Details his forlorn and distressed condition. Prays him to stay any new Privy Seal.

June. 32. Dr. Martin a Rhurnbeck, Chief Physician to the Duke of Norfolk, to same. Is in attendance on the Duke, whose health is greatly disordered. He is likely to fall into a dropsy, &c.

June? 33. Tho. Aldrich, Alan Par, and fourteen others of Cambridge, to same. Have taken no part with Mr. Cartwright relative to the question of apparel; but have conducted themselves with due moderation and caution. Lat.

July 1. 34. Proclamation against bringing in seditious books and Popish Bulls.

July 3.
[5° Non. Julii.]
Cambridge. 35. Alan Par, Tho. Aldrich, and twenty-one other scholars of Cambridge, to Cecill. In favour of Mr. Cartwright, and replying to the calumnies which have been promulgated in the University against the doctrines he has preached. Lat.

July 4.
The Tower. 36. Duke of Norfolk to same. Represents the bad state of his health, and the sufferings he endures by his confinement in the noisome airs of the Tower.

July 4. 37. Sir William Sneyde to the Council. His collection comes in very slowly. Has sent precepts to all who have not paid in Staffordshire. *Incloses,*

37. 1. *Names of those persons who have paid and have not paid on the Privy Seals, with the amount of sums contributed.*

July 7.
Westminster. 38. Archbishop Grindall, Gabriel Goodman and Thomas Wattes, Visitors for the Savoy, to Cecill. Inquiring into the state of the Hospital of the Savoy. Spoil committed by Tho. Thurland, the Master there. If he continues in office the house cannot long stand. *Inclosing,*

38. I. *Brief note of the misdemeanors of the Master of the Savoy, partly confessed by him and partly proved by oath of the chaplains and others; together with an account of the sums of money which the Master has burthened that Hospital with.*

July 7.
Leominster. 39. James Warnecombe to same. Has collected near 1,000 marks on Privy Seals in Herefordshire. Has omitted Tho. Baskervile from his list, he being Sheriff.

July 9. 40. T. Cartwright to same. Hopes he shall retain his good opinion. Repels the calumnies against him, and justifies his conduct and teaching. Lat.

July 9.
Bruges. 41. Lord Morley to the Earl of Leicester. Sends him a copy of the letter he lately wrote to the Queen. [8 June.] Begs him to intercede with Her Majesty for his wife and some of his children to be allowed to come over to him.

VOL. LXXI.

1570.
July 9.
Mounthall.
42. Sir Tho. Smith to Sir Wm. Cecill. Proceeding in naming parties who might be assessed on the loans. The money comes in but slowly.

July 10.
Nottingham.
43. Ralph Barton to same. Prays to be exempt from contributing 50*l.* towards the loan, on account of inability.

July 11.
44. Confession of John Jernegan, touching his conference with one Broke and Mr. Helmes, relative to Mr. Redman and Mr. Appleyard. His second confession. [*Much obliterated by damp.*]

July 12.
Exeter.
45. Sir Arthur Champernowne to Cecill. Intelligence that the garrison of Rochelle has defeated the King's forces in their neighbourhood. Upon these news he will venture to set forth two ships.

July 13.
Ivington.
[Evington.]
46. James Warnecombe to same. Incloses a statement of the collection of the loan for the County of Hereford.

July 13.
Gorhambury.
47. Sir Nichs. Bacon, L.K., to same. Recommends the bearer, Mr. Cowte, to be exempt from a Privy Seal.

July 14.
48. Confession of John Jernegan, relative to the firing of the beacons, transactions with Broke, and conversation with Appleyard. His third answer.

July 15.
Canterbury.
49. Roger Manwood to Lord [Cobham?]. Has examined the Charter of the Cinque Ports, and finds they are exempt " *de prestacionibus,*" which he considers to mean " *of loans* " and from other aids, contributions, &c.

July 20.
50. Proclamation for making inventories of goods, ships, &c., taken from Spanish subjects, to be returned to the Court of Admiralty.

July 20.
51. Commission to John de Calvetta and others to survey the goods of the King of Spain's subjects which have been stayed and arrested in England.

July 20.
52. Indictment of John Marten and others, mariners, for robbing a Dutch ship of Embden, within the jurisdiction of the Cinque Ports.

July 21.
Farley.
53. Sir H. Wallop and Sir Wm. Kyngesmyll to Cecill. Measures which they have taken for furnishing the county with arms and armour. Many refuse to pay the reasonable sums assessed upon them for increase of armour.

July 23.
Isle of Wight.
54. Edward Horsey, Capt. of the Isle of Wight, to the Council. Certifies the number of ships and mariners stayed by him within the Island. Their willingness to serve. *Incloses,*

 54. I. *List of names of the mariners commanded by the Captain of the Isle not to depart from Mead-Hole, and list of shipping stayed there.*

DOMESTIC—ELIZABETH.

VOL. LXXI.

1570.

55. Archbishop Grindall to Sir Wm. Cecill. Interview with the Queen, and a sitting appointed on the business of the Savoy. Great sums of money converted by Thurland, the Master, to his own private purposes.

July 24.
Bindon.

56. Thomas Lord Howard, of Bindon, to the Council. Ships of the burthen of 30 tons and upwards which have been stayed by him pursuant to their Lordships' order. *Incloses,*

> 56. I. *Certificate of the names of all the ships of the burthen of 30 tons, of the masters and mariners in the ports and havens of Dorset, stayed by Lord Howard, Vice Admiral. 20 July, 1570.*

July 26.
Portsmouth.

57. Sir Adrian Ponynges to same. Forwards a certificate of ships stayed. *Incloses,*

> 57. I. *Certificate of all such ships, masters, sailors, and fishermen as are stayed within the County of Hampshire by Sir Adrian Ponynges, Vice Admiral of the said county. 24 July 1570.*

July 27.
Westminster.

58. Archbishop Grindall to Cecill. If the Master of the Savoy does not, from remorse of conscience, resign his office, the visitation must proceed. Intends to depart northward on Tuesday next. Prays for grace in his high function. Cambridge scholars. Cartwright has a busy head.

July 28.
5° Cal. Aug.]

59. Walter Haddon to same. He is suffering from the stone, and unable to ride on horseback. Requests him to send for his colleague out of Suffolk to supply his place. Lat.

July 28.

60. The Queen to the Lord Keeper. Directions to make out a Commission of Oyer and Terminer for the City of London, for trial of John Felton, prisoner in the Tower, charged with high treason; and another for the trial of seditious and rebellious persons in Norfolk and the City of Norwich. Names of Commissioners.

July 28 ?

61. Names of conspirators in Norfolk, of the charges against each, and of the witnesses to prove the same. Sent from Mr. Clere and Mr. Drury.

July 28 ?

62. The Queen to the Deputy Lieutenants of Norfolk. Directions to repress the conspiracy entered into at Norwich, and to take order for maintaining the peace of that city.

July 29.
London.

63. John Southcot and Tho. Stanley, of the Mint, to the Council. Have examined John Bulkeley, student of Oxford, and William Bedo, prisoners in the Tower, and forward their depositions. *Inclosing,*

> 63. I. *Examination of John Bulkeley, touching his communications with William Bedo as to casting a figure for recovery of lost money. 28 July 1570.*
>
> 63. II. *Examination of William Bedo, stationer, touching certain conferences which he had with John Bulkeley, who undertook to shew him various alchemical secrets and practices for diminishing and lessening the coin of the realm by sweating, &c.*

B B

VOL. LXXI.

1570.
July 29.
Stanway Hall.
64. Edmond Bokking to same. Stay made of ships according to instructions. There has been a great press for the purpose of supplying the Queen's ships with mariners. *Incloses,*

  64. I. *Certificate of vessels stayed at Harwich, Brightlingsey, East Mersey, and other ports in the County of Essex.*

July 29.
London.
65. Dr. Valentyne Dale to Sir Wm. Cecill. Transmits, by direction of Dr. Haddon and others, answers to the questions proposed. *Incloses,*

  65. I. *Questions moved relative to prizes taken by the subjects of the Queen of Navarre, within an English port, from the subjects of France and Spain; with answers thereto.*

July 29 ?
66. Articles against the Master of the Savoy, declaring the disorders committed by him in his government of that Hospital, by the misappropriation of its funds, &c.

July 29.
67. Note by Mr. Hillary, Auditor of the Savoy, of the sale of lands belonging to that Hospital, by Mr. Thurland, the Master.

July 30.
The Dean's House, St. Paul's.
68. Archbishop Grindall to Cecill. The Commissioners for visiting the Savoy, having found the Master unwilling to resign, have proceeded to pass sentence of deprivation. *Incloses,*

  68. I. *Decree of the Commissioners for visiting the Savoy, by which Thomas Thurland, Master of the said Hospital, is, for misgovernment and abuses, for ever deprived of that office. Read 29 July* 1570.

July 30.
PendenisCastle.
69. John Kylligrew to the Council. Has stayed several French vessels in the harbour of Falmouth; but has given them hopes of a quick discharge.

July 30.
70. The names of all the Queen's ships, barks, and galleys, with the amount of their tonnage and number of men.

July 30.
71. Justices of Staffordshire to the Council. In behalf of John Skeffinton, to be excused from the loan of 50*l.* required of him.

July 30.
Stamford.
72. Lady E. Cave and Mr. Roger Cave to Cecill. Her Ladyship's son-in-law, John Skevington, Esq., has received a Privy Seal for the loan of 50*l.*, which for divers causes he is unable to contribute. *Inclosing,*

  72. I. *Certificate by Sir William Sneyde to the Council, of the inability of John Skevington, of Fisherwick, to contribute the loan of* 50*l.* 24 *June* 1570.

July.
73. Lady Julyane Holcroft to same. Prays to be discharged from the Privy Seal for a loan, on account of her poor estate, and having daughters attending on the Queen.

July 30.
Bristol.
74. John Die, Deputy to Mr. William Wynter, Vice Admiral of Somerset, to the Council. Has stayed all the ships and mariners in the County of Somerset and City of Bristol. *Incloses,*

  74. I. *Certificate of ships and mariners stayed in the ports of Somerset and City of Bristol, for the service of the Queen.*

VOL. LXXI.

1570.
July. 75. Certificate of the number of all mariners within the County of Devon, and of the shipping within the ports of the same.

July. 76. Certificates of ships stayed within the County of Sussex of 30 tons burthen and upwards, and of all mariners within the said county.

uly. 77. Note of such sums of money as have been received to the Queen's use under Privy Seals within the County of Somerset.

July. Detailed account of public charges due and paid in several departments of the State: Ireland, the Borders, Ambassadors, Works, &c. [*Case* E. *Eliz. No.* 1.]

VOL. LXXII. JULY, 1570.

July. Certificates by Richard Markham, Ric. Diseney, Robert Carre, Antony Thorold, John Harrington, William Saville, and John Bussy, Esquires, of the sums raised and expended within the Lindsey Division of the County of Lincoln, for provision of armour and weapons, equipment of soldiers, and of the quantities of armour returned. Four schedules.

VOL. LXXIII. AUGUST—SEPTEMBER, 1570.

August 1. 1. The Queen to the Lord Adm. Clynton. Thanks for his diligence in putting the whole navy in readiness. Soldiers and mariners to be pressed to man the ships.

August 1.
Standon. 2. Sir Ralph Sadleir to Sir Wm. Cecill. Has no great desire to be a courtier, but prefers living quietly at home. If peace follow in France, he hopes those who profess God's true religion will be protected. If Scotland is sure, Spain and France can do us little harm.

August 2. 3. Account by William Fuller, Auditor, of the possessions of Edward late Duke of Somerset, in the Honour of Hampton Court and the Manors of Isleworth and Twickenham. *Indorsed* " for Sir Tho. Gresham."

August 3. 4. Cecill to the Vice Chancellor and Heads of Colleges in Cambridge. On the novel doctrines moved by Mr. Cartwright, as Reader of the Divinity in that University. Requests their advice and opinions.

August 3. 5. The Queen to the Lieutenant of the Tower and Sir Henry Nevell. To remove the Duke of Norfolk from the Tower to his own house at the Charterhouse, for fear of the infection of the plague.

August 5.
Howard House. 6. Duke of Norfolk to the Queen. Thanks for her clemency in having released him out of the infectious Tower. Assures her of his loyalty and attachment.

VOL. LXXIII.

1570.
August 8.
Bristol.
7. Earl of Bedford to Sir William Cecill. Has been requested by Sir Peter Carew and Sir John Perrot to recommend the bearer, Richard Doddridge, who cannot advance the loan required of him. The plague is very prevalent at Exeter. The letters respecting Covent Garden have been sent to him long since.

August 8.
8. William Lower, Vice Admiral of Cornwall, to the Council. On the stay of shipping in the ports of the above county. *Incloses*,

8. I. *Certificate of such ships and barks above the burthen of 30 tons, with the masters and mariners, stayed within the County of Cornwall.*

August 9.
Lanherne.
9. E. Arundel to Mr. Edgcumb, Sheriff of Cornwall. His brother, Sir John Arundel, has taken order for payment of 100*l*. by way of loan to the Queen.

August 10.
Mannington.
10. John Dodge to Cecill. Concerning certain recusants in Norfolk, particularly one Drythicke or Dirrich, a rank Papist, late chaplain to the Archbp. of Canterbury. Particulars of other Papists.

August 11.
Cambridge.
11. Dr. Edw. Hawford, Dr. John Whitgyfte, and Dr. Henry Harvy, to same. Have thought it expedient to stay Mr. Cartwright from reading, lest his being permitted to do so should give countenance to his new and dangerous doctrine.

August 11.
3o Id. Aug.
Cambridge.
12. Thomas Aldrich and twenty-one others of Cambridge to same. In favour of Mr. Cartwright. Lat.

August 12.
Leicester.
13. Earl of Huntingdon and Mr. Kenelme Digby to the Council. Certify that Anthony Colly, of Glaston, in co. Rutland, is unable to contribute the loan of 50*l*., demanded of him. *Inclosing*,

13. I. *Articles preferred by Anthony Colly, of Glaston, setting forth that he is unable to make personal appearance before the Council, or to contribute a loan of 50l., as required.*

August 12.
14. Certificate by Sir Henry Gate of ships and mariners stayed within the County of York.

August 13.
15. Sir Tho. Woodhowse and Henry Woodhowse, Esq., to Cecill. Report their proceedings in the stay of ships and mariners in Norfolk and Suffolk. *Inclosing*,

July 20?
15. I. *Book of the number of mariners and of all ships, &c., above 30 tons, in the Counties of Norfolk and Suffolk, taken by Sir Tho. Woodhowse and Henry Woodhowse, Vice Admirals there.*

August 13.
Gorhambury.
16. Sir Nich. Bacon to same. Returns the letters concerning Scottish affairs. The Queen's charges there will be trebled. The chief hope of comfort is the evil state of France, Spain, and Flanders.

August 14.
Cobham.
17. Lord Cobham to same. If peace, now concluded in France, breed not unquietness in us, it is well. Intelligence of the state of the navy in Flanders.

Vol. LXXIII.

1570.

August 15. 18. Dr. John Storye to Sir Wm. Cecill. Notifies his arrival at Yarmouth. If he is to be restored to his former keeper, hopes he shall not have more than one iron on his legs.

August 15. Boston. 19. Anthony Kyme to same. Inquiry as to prisoners in the gaol of Lincoln for debts due to the Court of Wards and Liveries. Report of their names. Has delivered the Privy Seal addressed to Mr. George Mounson.

August 17. 20. Mr. Lyndford, of Queen's College, Cambridge, to same. Touching a dispute between him, as Master of the Bedford Hospital, and the College, relative to the funds of the said Hospital. Prays the Chancellor's advice and interference therein. Lat.

August 18. St. Albans. 21. Wm. Parker to same. Desires an interview with him relative to Dr. Storye, whom he has brought from beyond sea and landed at Yarmouth.

August 18. Cobham. 22. Lord Cobham to the Council. It is necessary at the present time to increase the means of defence at Sandwich, at the three castles between that place and Dover, and Dover Castle itself. Has stayed all ships above 30 tons. *Incloses*,

22. I. *Estimate of the charges of a certain number of men to reinforce the garrisons of Sandwich, Dover, and other places on the Kentish coast.*

August 18. Cobham. 23. Same to Cecill. Has written to the Lords as to increased defence. Recommends some small boats should be licensed to export beer or other commodities to Flushing, as a means of gaining intelligence.

August 18. Cobham. 24. Same to same. Additional intelligence of the increase of the fleets in Flanders, Dr. Storye and Parker are conveyed out of Flanders: no common prison will suffice for Storye.

August 18. Cambridge. 25. Tho. Cartwright to Chancellor Cecill. Acknowledges letters some time since received from him: urges new arguments in support of his own doctrines. Lat.

August 19. 26. Dr. John Whitgyfte to same. Thinks he does not fully understand the opinions of Mr. Cartwright; enumerates some of them. Himself with others have almost finished the draft of new Statutes and Orders for the University.

August 21. Lease from John Searle to Robt. Came, of Thaxsted, of a certain barn and appurtenances, parcel of the Manor of Epping, co. Essex, and the Parsonage of Epping, with all the tithes of corn and grain to the same belonging. [*Case* B. *Eliz.* No. 6.]

August 24. Mons Ottery. 27. Earl of Bedford to Cecill. Has received a letter, unsigned, from Mr. Edgcombe, Receiver of the Loan for Cornwall. Sir Arthur Champernowne has written for release of some of the vessels stayed by him. The plague is hot at Exeter. *Incloses*,

27. I. *P. Edgcombe to the Earl of Bedford. Solicits that himself, Mr. Mylliton, Mr. Bevill, and Mr. Killygrew, may be excused from contributing to the loan. Has written to Sec. Cecill, and sent the names of six persons to whom Privy Seals might be addressed. Shelstone, 18 Aug. 1570.*

Vol. LXXIII.

1570.

August 24. Norwich. — 28. Clement Paston to Sir Wm. Cecill. Faithful execution of the Queen's commission in Norfolk and Norwich. The conspirators and abettors of the late horrible treason are now weeded out, and have received their just desert.

August 25. Lambeth. — 29. Archbishop Parker to same. Dr. Thirleby is desirous, at the time of this his great sickness, to remove from the Archbishop's house to some of his own friends. The Bishop of London's recovery is doubtful.

August 26. London. — 30. Thomas Wattes to same. Dr. Storye has been brought to his house from Yarmouth. The Lollards' Tower, of which the locks and bolts of the doors were broken off at the death of Queen Mary, and never since repaired, shall be got ready for his reception.

August 26. Cobham. — 31. Lord Cobham to same. Progress of the Spanish Queen in Flanders, accompanied by certain Walloon guards. Reinforcements from Spain expected in Flanders.

August 27. — 32. John Mershe to same. Transactions of Dr. Storye at Yarmouth, where he was tampered with by one Gosling, one of the Bailiffs. The Lollards' Tower is being prepared for him. Advises Parker should be present when Storye is examined.

August 27. — 33. The Queen to the Lieutenants of Suffolk, Essex, Kent, and Sussex. To levy certain mariners and soldiers, in their respective shires, for service in the navy.

August 29. — 34. George Danvers to Cecill. Has sent up the amount collected for the loan by letters of Privy Seal in the County of Oxford. Sends the names of persons who could afford to contribute.

August 29. Cawood. — 35. Archbishop Grindall to same. Has recovered from the ague. Has not been well received; the greater part of the gentlemen of the county being not well affected towards godly religion, and among the common people many superstitious practices remain.

August 29. — 36. The Queen to Lord Adm. Clynton. Has appointed her navy to put to sea under the charge of Charles Howard and William Wynter. Other persons enumerated are to be appointed by him to their respective ships.

August 29. — 37. Another copy of the above, with the names of the ships and their commanders filled in.

August 30. — 38. Estimate of the charge of pressing 400 mariners from divers places to man the Queen's ships.

August 30. — 39. Estimate for the wages of mariners and gunners serving in the Queen's ships.

Auus 30. — 40. Estimate for certain necessary stores for ten of the Queen's ships appointed for the seas.

August 31. Theobalds. — 41. Sir Nich. Bacon to Cecill. Concerning the execution of the counterpart of the lease granted by the Queen to Mr. Smythe, the Customer.

VOL. LXXIII.

1570.
August 31. Bruges.
42. Lord Morley to the Queen. Beseeches her to pardon his having departed the kingdom without licence. He was constrained to that step by a scruple of conscience. Lady Northumberland has landed at Sluys, with the object of appealing to the Queen of Spain.

August.
43. Names of gentlemen in the County of Hertford who have contributed loans to the Queen on letters of Privy Seal.

August.
44. Note of sums of money taken up in the City of London on the first of August, by Sir Thomas Gresham, for the Queen's service.

August.
45. Particular of the sum of 5,000*l.* taken up in London by the same.

August.
46. The Queen to the Treasurer of the Exchequer. To pay over the moiety of the fine of 5,000*l.*, payable by Thomas Smythe, Farmer of the Customs of the port of London, into the hands of Richard Stonley, Esq., one of the Tellers.

August.
47. Account of the charges and total expences of the Assizes holden at Kendall, in the time of Lancelot Pickering, Esq., Sheriff of Westmoreland.

August.
48. Certificate of all the shipping above 30 tons, and of the masters and mariners, taken upon the general stay made in the year 1570.

August. (?)
49. "An advertisement mete for all persons, that is, for good subjects to contynue in their dutyes, for waveryng subjects to becom constant in theirs, and for all unloyall subjectes to know ther errors and by repentance to recover mercy," &c., detailing the practices of the Papists in promulgating slanderous libels, the monstrous assumption of the Pope in issuing a Bull of Excommunication against Queen Elizabeth, &c. [*Entirely in Cecill's hand.*]

Sept. 1.
50. The Queen to the Earl of Bedford. Directions to assist ·Mr. Robert Colshill, a Gentleman Pensioner, in his claims against certain parties for depasturing cattle on the Forest of Exmoor.

Sept. 2. Barn Elms.
51. Thomas Smythe, Customer of the port of London, to Sir Wm. Cecill. Solicits him to expedite the sealing of his grant of the Customs.

Sept. 3.
52. The request and humble suit of Peter Blackborne, for a reformation of the great abuse of clothing within the realm; with a note from the Earl of Leicester to Cecill, calling his attention to the importance of the subject. As Leicester has been ill, and Cecill taken physic, he could not therefore call upon him.

Sept. 4.
53. Thos. Wattes to Cecill. Committal of Dr. Storye to the Lollards' Tower. Strict order is given that he shall be kept from conference with any person whatever. Request of the Archbishop of York for a license in mortmain for Pembroke Hall, Cambridge.

VOL. LXXIII.

1570.

Sept. 5. London. — 54. Tho. Heneage to Sir Wm. Cecill. The Queen has requested to know what money he has in hand remaining of the loan. Therefore subjoins an account of the whole receipt of the loan in various counties, and what remains in hand.

Sept. 6. — 55. Francis Harrington to same. Solicits the wardship of Roger Walpole's daughters, now left by the death of Mr. Robert Walpole, their grandfather.

Sept. 7. Bletso. — 56. Examinations taken before Oliver Lord St. John, of Bletso, and Ralph Astry, Esq., as to a rape committed by James Langrake on Emme Panton, of Turvey, in the County of Bedford.

Sept. 8. — 57. Tho. Heneage to Cecill. Regrets to hear of his indisposition. Sends an abstract of the particular payments on the loan in each county. *Incloses,*

    57. I. *Account of the receipts of the loan money, from the collectors in every county.*

Sept. 9. London. — 58. Thomas Staverton to same. Communicates a letter of intelligence from one in Spain, of a treasonable plot to deliver certain towns of Ireland into the hands of the King of Spain.

Sept. 10. Basing. — 59. Marquis of Winchester to same. Desires to continue in the guardianship of the three daughters of Mr. Andrews, of Fryvock, Hampshire, and that the wardship of young Lambert may not yet be disposed of.

Sept. 10 Sypton. — 60. Anthony Wyngfeld to same. Requests him to stand his friend for lease of certain lands fallen to a ward called Dero.

Sept. 10. Howard House. — 61. Duke of Norfolk to same. Thanks for his friendly letter. Hopes all promises will be duly kept by the French, to the preservation of God's true religion. Hopes to hear of his better health.

Sept. 11. — 62. John Mershe to Leicester and Cecill. In favour of the three young men who brought over Dr. Storye, and who now solicit payment of their charges.

Sept. 14. Tavistock. — 63. Earl of Bedford to Cecill. Forwards letters, by which he will perceive the intentions of the French towards Ireland. Desires to have the wardship of the son and heir of one Christopher Chudley, if he should die. *Incloses,*

    63. I. *Mayor, &c., of Plymouth to the Earl of Bedford. Intelligence from Conquet in Brittany, that certain French ships are there furnished with a great number of men for a descent on Ireland. Plymouth, 13 Sept. 1570.*

Sept. 14. — 64. John Mershe to Leicester and Cecill. Concerning the charges of the young men who brought Dr. Storye from Antwerp, which, though unreasonable, admit of consideration. Arrival of the Earl of Westmoreland at Antwerp. *Incloses,*

    64. I. *Statement of the charges incurred in bringing Dr. Storye from Antwerp.*

DOMESTIC—ELIZABETH.

Vol. LXXIII.

1570.
Sept. 19. — 65. Duke of Norfolk to Sir Wm. Cecill. Has omitted nothing that lay in his power to recover the Queen's favour; hopes therefore by his assistance to obtain it.

Sept. 20.
Gresham House. — 66. Sir Tho. Gresham to same. Desires the expedition of some merchants' bonds; and also for the passing of a grant made to him by the Queen. Requests to be released from the charge of Lady Mary Grey.

Sept. 24. — 67. John Mershe to Leicester and Cecill. Has not yet been able to proceed with the examination of Dr. Storye. Mercantile affairs. Discontent at the taking of a Spanish ship by young Wynter.

Sept. 25. — 68. The Queen to John Parkhurst, Bishop of Norwich. To inquire into certain innovations attempted by some prebendaries of that church, who have entered the choir of the church, broken down the organs, and committed other outrages.

Sept. 25.
Reading. — 69. The Council to the Judge of the Admiralty Court. On complaint of the losses sustained by Robt. Christmas, in Portugal, to give orders for the stay of the goods of Portuguese subjects in England, to the same amount.

Sept. 26.
Offington. — 70. William Lord Lawarre, Richard Covert, and Walter Waller to Cecill. Certify that Dame Margery Henly, widow, is wholly unable to contribute the loan of 50*l.*, required of her by Privy Seal.

Sept. 27.
Halswell. — 71. Susan Hallswell, widow, to same. Thanks for the wardship of her son. Begs he will continue to befriend her, and that she may have a lease of the Queen's thirds of her late husband's land.

Sept. ? — 72. The answers of Lawrence Nowell, Dean of Lichfield, charged by Peter Morwin with uttering seditious speeches against the Queen and the Earl of Leicester. Attested by Thos. Bentham, Bishop of Coventry and Lichfield.

Vol. LXXIV. October—December, 1570.

Oct. 1. — 1. Account of the remain of armour in divers of the Queen's armouries; with a rate by the month, and so by the year, for the charges of the said remain.

Oct. 1. — 2. Duplicate of the above, with slight addition at the end.

Oct. 1. — 3. Account of the charge of ordnance and munitions delivered to sundry places in the realm, to Ireland, the Navy, and otherwise by the Queen's warrants.

Oct. 1. — 4. Detailed account of debts due in the Office of Ordnance at Michaelmas last.

Oct. 1 — 5. Detailed account of debts due in the Office of the Armoury to the last of September.

Vol. LXXIV.

1570.

Oct. 2.
Windsor.
6. B. Hampton to Sir Wm. Cecill. Return of Mr. Walsyngham from the French Court. The King of Spain is in great danger from the Moors in Granada. Enumeration of their forces. The Queen of Spain is supposed to have passed the Narrow Seas.

Oct. 3.
Merton College.
7. Arthur Atee to same. Apologises for not having written since his return to Oxford from Spain. Lat.

Oct. 5.
8. Award between Sir Christopher Danby and Edward Earl of Derby, relative to the bounds of Kirkby and Masham, co. York.

Oct. 10.
Windsor.
9. Countess of Lennox to Cecill. Beseeches him to remember that innocent King (of Scotland), and hopes that he will not be the worse for any treaty.

Oct. 10.
Cobham.
10. Lord Cobham to same. Sends a packet from Mr. Fitzwillyams in which are letters from his brother Harry. Movements of the Duke of Alva.

Oct. 13.
11. Sir Tho. Gresham to same. Gives particulars of money taken up at Hamburgh. Cecill's pillars of marble have arrived in good order.

Oct. 22.
London.
12. Fr. Walsyngham to same. Hopes the Queen has made choice of some other than himself to succeed Sir Henry Norris in France. Conversation with Ridolphi about the differences between Flanders and England.

Oct. 22.
Wyttenham.
13. William Dunche to same. Touching the collection of the loan money in Berkshire. Sends names of those who have not paid.

Oct. 22.
London.
14. Sir Tho. Gresham to same. Further detail of money transactions with foreign merchants. Desires permission to go with his wife and family to his house at Maysfield, Sussex. Desires to know what he shall do with Lady Mary Grey.

Oct. 23.
London.
15. Same to same. Informs him the Merchant Adventurers are about to send a post on the morrow to Hamburgh, so that the bonds may be forwarded by that conveyance.

Oct. 23.
Newport.
16. Avery Phillips to same. Conspirators in the Isle of Wight in connexion with those in Ireland. Their intention to go into Spain, and from thence to return into Ireland.

Oct. 25.
PlymouthRoad.
17. John Corbyn to same. Arrival of a bark from Waterford at Plymouth, bringing intelligence that 30 sail of Spanish vessels had been seen on the west coast of Ireland.

Oct. 25.
Whaddon.
18. Arthur Lord Grey, of Wilton, to the Council. Great default of armour, weapons, and equipments found at the musters taken for the County of Wilts. The armour of the county is kept at Aylesbury.

Oct. 26.
London.
19. Sir Tho. Gresham to Cecill. Note of bonds received and despatched. Solicits the office of Feodary of Somerset for John Coles who married his niece, and the Stewardship of Wimbledon for Mr. Reve. Requests a special licence for a ship to go to Flanders with alabaster, as he had a special licence for transportation of his stones from Antwerp for his Burse.

VOL. LXXIV.

1570.
Oct. 26.
Yenwith.

20. Richard Dudley to Sir Wm. Cecill. Has received the Queen's order and 24 stamps for marking the copper made at the mines. Measures taken in pursuance thereof.

Oct. 27.
London.

21. Jehan Lover to same. Progress of mining operations. Wishes him to procure an extension of a former bargain for three or four thousand quintals of copper, to three or four hundred thousand quintals.

Oct. 27.
Carlisle.

22. Richard Barnes, Bishop of Carlisle, to same. Has entered into his charge, and hopes to work good in it. Finds the people of Cumberland and Westmoreland more conformable and tractable in matters of religion than those of Yorkshire. In Lancashire the people fall from religion, revolt to Popery, and refuse to come to church. *Incloses*,

  22. I. *List of Gentlemen of Cumberland and Westmoreland, with notes and observations on their principles and conduct.*

Oct. 30.

23. The Queen to Lord Morley. Order for him to return to England, and to repair to her presence without delay.

Oct. 30.

24. Brief note of all monies received by William Pelham, Esq., Lieutenant-General of the Ordnance, by Privy Seals between 1 Jan. and 30 Oct. 1570.

Oct.
Howard House.

25. Duke of Norfolk to Cecill. Is glad to hear of his safe return, and of his escape from sickness. Hopes now to obtain more grace by his means.

Oct.

26. Roger Ramsden, Martin Bragge, and Simon Jewkes, merchants, to same. Regret their account of charges in bringing Dr. Storye into England has not been satisfactory. Explain several items, and request his favour in the settlement of it.

Oct. ?

27. Petition of Anne Winchcombe, widow of Henry Winchcombe, of Newbury, to same. Prays he would take order with Mr. Rockhole for the transfer to herself of the wardship of her son, on the payment of a reasonable sum of money.

Nov. 2.
Lambeth.

28. Archbishop Parker to same. Sends a clause in the late Ecclesiastical Commission which has been accidentally omitted. Wishes Mr. Day, Provost of Eton, to be a Commissioner. *Incloses*,

  28. I. *Draft of a clause in the Ecclesiastical Commission, empowering the Commissioners to award punishment by fine and imprisonment to offenders, at their discretion.*

Nov. 7.
Cambridge.

29. John Whitgyfte, Vice Chancellor, and others of the University, to same. Thank him for procuring the new statutes for the University, and censuring the conduct of Mr. Cartwright, against whom they intend to proceed to deprivation.

  29. I. *Copy (in Whitgyfte's hand) of Mr. Cartwright's propositions of the doctrines taught by him relating to Episcopal Jurisdiction, the Functions of the Ministry, &c.*

1570.

Nov. ?   30. Twenty-six propositions relating to doctrines in the Church, &c., by Cartwright, including the foregoing six propositions. Indorsed by Cecill. "1570. *Articuli propositi et divulgati p Cartwrytū et alios.*"

Nov. 10.   31. Particulars of the case between the Earl of Arundel and Lord Lumley, for recovery of a considerable debt owing to King Henry VIII. by the Florentines.

Nov. 10.
Cawood.   32. Archbp. Grindall to Sir Wm. Cecill. Had given orders for searching the Countess of Northumberland's house, and for the mass priests that might be found therein to be sent to him. Three had been sent, one of whom was Henry Comberford. Has been obliged to resort to law for dilapidations. *Incloses,*

> 32. I. *Examination of Henry Comberford before the Ecclesiastical Commissioners for the County of York. He defends the service of the Mass, and supposes the Countess of Northumberland to have been possessed of evil spirits.* 8 *Nov.* 1570.

Nov. 14.   33. Proclamation against harbouring seditious persons and rebels, and from bringing in traitorous books and writings from abroad.

Nov. 15.   34. The Queen to the Lieutenants of Shires. The late unnatural rebellion in the North being suppressed, she has thought it expedient to revoke her Commissions of Lieutenancy. Returns her hearty thanks for their services.

Nov. 15.   35. Same to same and their Deputies. Discharging them from all duties under their Commissions of Lieutenancy, and directing them to exercise vigilant care as ordinary magistrates.

Nov. 15.   36. List of Lords Lieutenants and their Deputies to whom the above were addressed.

Nov. 16
St. Asaph.   37. Tho. Davies, Bishop of St. Asaph, to Cecill. Has reduced hi diocese to better order, but some disorderly persons still remain. He therefore prays that an Ecclesiastical Commission for his diocese may be issued.

Nov. 17.   38. Note by John Hamby, Auditor; of the rate of the charges of postage of the loan money, according to the distances of the shires from London. With warrant of the Council for payment of the same. *Annexed.*

> 38. I. *Copy of former warrant of Council for payment of charges for carriage of the loan money. Attested by John Hamby.*

Nov. 21.   39. The Queen to Lord Keeper Bacon. To issue Commissions for inquiry as to persons who have departed out of the realm without license, and what goods and lands they had at their departing.

Nov. 24   40. Sir Rowland Haywarde, Lord Mayor of London, to Cecill. Has made inquiry concerning the imprisonment of Mr. Tho. Lee, and sends certain depositions respecting the same.

VOL. LXXIV.

1570.
Nov. 26.
New Park.
41. Edw. Earl of Derby to Sir Wm. Cecill. Thanks for his friendly advice, and is glad to know the Queen is to be the judge of his conduct. Has sent up his two sons according to her commandment.

Nov. 27.
Cambridge.
42. William Fulk to same. Has been informed by the Archbp. of Armagh (Tho. Lancaster) of his good opinion towards him. Offers to clear himself of the charges objected against him. Desires to be restored to his former appointment. *Lat.*

Nov. 30.
43. George Nedham to same. Sends an account of their mining operations. Intelligence received of great damage done in the Netherlands by inundations.

Nov.
44. Names of the Justices in different Rapes of the County of Sussex, with note of the expediency of sending a Commission into that county for ecclesiastical causes.

Nov.
45. The Queen to the town of Colchester. To shew favour to Thos. Heneage, Esq., Treasurer of the Chamber, in the lease of certain grounds. Draft in Cecill's hand.

Dec. 4.
[Prid. Non. Dec.]
Cambridge.
46. Barthw. Clerke to Cecill. Desires his favour, and hopes that he will use his influence in advancing the interests of the University. *Lat.*

Dec. 13.
47. Jehan Lover to same. Report of the mining operations; particulars with respect to the production of copper. *Incloses,*

> 47. I. *Jehan Lover to the Queen. Solicits aid in support of the great charges sustained in prosecuting mining transactions.*

Dec. 14.
48. Indenture of lease by the Queen to Francis Godolphin, Esq., of the Scilly Islands, for the term of 38 years.

Dec. 15.
Valenciennes.
49. Lord Morley to Mr. Fitzwilliams. Professes his loyalty, and his friendship for Sir Wm. Cecill. Purposes to go to Aquisgrano [Aix] for the benefit of the waters.

Dec. 20.
Cambridge.
50. Henry Cheke to Cecill. Thanks him for his many favours, but feels the impossibility of his ever making any return. Compliments him on his fortune and power. *Lat.*

Dec. 23.
51. The Queen to Tho. Fanshawe, Remembrancer of the Exchequer. To permit Oliver Dawbeny to peruse certain accounts for the purpose of discovering frauds in the Customs.

Dec. 27.
Lambeth.
52. Archbp. Parker to the Queen. Urgently denies having shewn wilfulness or ingratitude. States particulars of his obtaining the farm and the house at Charing. The County of Kent is quiet, and in a state of obedience to the laws.

Dec. 29.
[4° Cal. Jan.]
Norwich Castle.
53. Thomas Cecill to Cecill. Acknowledges his liberality, and addresses certain Latin verses on the new year to him, and solicits him to get him out of prison. *Lat.*

DOMESTIC—ELIZABETH.

1570.

Vol. LXXIV.

Dec. 30. 54. The Queen to Sir Ralph Sadleir. Authorizes him to deliver to Sir Wm. Cecill certain oak timber trees, to be taken out of the Manor of Hartingfordbury and Enfield.

Dec. Hampton Court. 55. The Queen to the Vice-President of Wales. Warrant for levying certain foot soldiers in the Principality, to attend Sir John Perrot, who has been appointed President of Munster.

Dec. ? 56. Danl. [Hechstetter ?] to Sir Wm. Cecill. Desires his aid in furthering the mineral affairs by assisting Hans Lover in the management of them. Recommends the reports of the quantities received by Mr. Dudley for the Queen should be fully known. They suffer by the restraint on foreign trade.

Vol. LXXV. Undated, 1570.

1570 ? 1. Project by a person unknown, for raising the amount of Customs by increase of duties on certain articles specified.

2. Statement shewing the mode by which the revenue derived from the Customs and Subsidies of Tonnage and Poundage may be increased.

3. Instructions for obtaining a lease of the office of the Butlerage for a term of years for the Earl of Leicester, at such reasonable rent as by the Lord Treasurer shall be thought expedient.

4. Claim of the Lord Admiral to all leather seized and forfeited for illegal exportation.

5. Memorandum for a grant to John Smythe, the Queen's Surveyor in Oxfordshire, of the wardship of one Bosworth, co. Warwick.

6. Note of the purport of the petition of Lord Mountjoy to the Queen, for exchange of certain lands.

7. A brief declaration by John Johnson, of abuse in the size of wood for fuel, and how to remedy the same, and for regulating the woodmongers of London.

8. Wm. Humfrey to Cecill. The Governors of the Mineral and Battery Works have granted him a lease for procuring gold and silver from lead and stone. Discovery of calamine and copper in abundance. Solicits a lease of an old lead mine in the Manor of Calver, part of the inheritance of Anne Shakerley.

9. Estimate of a proportion of victuals for 100 men monthly, serving at sea.

10. Abstract of depositions against John Purdewe, of Winchester, charged with the death of one Gennynges.

11. Petition of Geo. Fenner, of Chichester, to the Council. Prays redress for great losses, by spoils and robberies committed on divers ships by the Spaniards in the Low Countries.

DOMESTIC—ELIZABETH.

1570 ?

Vol. LXXV.

12. Petition of John Marshal, Tho. Castlyn, and others, to the Council. Pray for redress of losses by means of spoil committed on them by the Flushingers.

13. Petition of the owners, masters and mariners belonging to the River Thames, to same Praying that letters missive may be sent to the merchants trading to Spain and Portugal, commanding that no ship carrying corn into those countries shall bring back any commodities from thence, salt only excepted.

14. Petition of George Barne, alderman, and 24 others, merchants of the City of London, to same. Solicit a grant of letters of assistance for the better execution of a commission for recovery of the ship Francis, taken by French pirates.

15. Petition of merchants and fishermen of Yarmouth to same. Complaining of injuries sustained by the town of Yarmouth and the coasts of Norfolk by pirates; and beg for protection of two of the Queen's ships.

16. Note of the great decay of the Navy, showing the necessity for the increase of seamen; recommending the trade in wines to be left open, and encouragement be given to the fisheries.

17. Mr. Owen to Sir Wm. Cecill. A complimentary epistle. Lat.

18. Note of services offered to the Queen by Emery Molyneux, of new inventions of shot and artillery, to be used principally in naval warfare; protection of ports and harbours; a new shot to discharge a thousand musket shot; with wild fire not to be quenched. Particulars of offensive and defensive inventions detailed.

19. Names of persons who bought goods taken out of the ship Jonas, of Queenborough, by Hicks the pirate.

20. Petition of Nicholas Masselin to the Council. Prays for redress for detention of his vessel and cargo by the Spaniards.

21. Suit of Sir William Fitzwilliams to the Queen. For grant of the arrears of concealed rents, fee farms, and mesne reservations upon patents made before the 27th Henry VIII.

22. Memorandum by the Marquess of Winchester of the yearly revenue of the Duchy of Cornwall.

23. Petition of Lawrence Cookson, Garbeller of the City of London, to Cecill. Complains of obstructions offered to him in execution of his office by the Lord Mayor and merchants of London, which office he held by legal conveyance from Anthony White.

24. Another petition from same to same. Further complaints of obstruction in execution of his office of Garbeller by the Lord Mayor, &c., of London. Prays for protection.

1570 ?

25. Another petition of Lawrence Cookson to the Council. Shews that great frauds are practised by adulterating drugs, spices, seeds, &c., brought from beyond sea. Prays for their Lordships' aid in the execution of his office of Garbeller.

26. Arguments to prove that the patronage of the office of Garbeller belongs to the City of London.

27. Copies of three letters, from whom does not appear. The first, thanks for examination of witnesses: the second, thanks for benevolence shown to a foreigner: the third, to the Lord Mayor, recommending the widow of Anthony W[hite], late Garbeller of London, for a compensation for the profits of that office. The latter dated "*From my House at St. Bartholomews.*"

28. The Queen to the Lord Treasurer, Sir Walter Mildmay, and others. Directions to determine the suit long dependent between the Earl of Hertford and the Lord Wentworth, for certain concealed lands.

29. Masters, &c., of the Trinity House of Newcastle-upon-Tyne, to the Council. Pray for preservation of their privilege of piloting all ships and vessels of strangers, in and out of that river.

30. Submission of certain tenants of the Earl of Shrewsbury, in his Manor of Glossopdale, acknowledging that they have unlawfully assembled to resist giving up their tenements, the leases of which had expired at Michaelmas last.

31. The humble suit of Richard Topclyffe to the Queen. For grant of the lands and possessions lately belonging to old Richard Norton, the rebel.

32. Memorandum of the value of the lands *per ann.* belonging to old Ric. Norton, for which Richard Topclyffe is a suitor.

33. Note of the parcels of such lands as were lately belonging to John Gower, of Richmond, one of the rebels, for which John Stanhope is a suitor.

34. Articles for a grant of certain liberties to be made to the inhabitants of the Isles of Sheppey and Harty.

35. Another draft of the above articles; some enlarged, others abbreviated.

36. Articles touching the better government and defence of the Island of Sheppey, by the encouragement of the manufacture of leather, wools, skins, &c., under superintendence of Andreas de Loo.

37. Device by Andreas de Loo for the bringing in, maintenance, training up, and continuance of 100 able men, with shot and other weapon, for defence of the Isle of Sheppey, by establishment of the manufacture of leather, &c.

38. Copy of the above.

1570?

Vol. LXXV.

39. The answer to the device of furnishing the Isle of Sheppey with 100 able shot, without charge to the realm, against the plan proposed by Andreas de Loo.

40. Remarks by Tho. Fludd, on the condition of the Isle of Sheppey, and of the reasons why it is not inhabited as in times past; in favour of the grant of certain liberties.

41. Regulations proposed for transporting of corn, fish, and other commodities from the Isle of Sheppey.

42. Inhabitants of the Isle of Sheppey and Harty to the Lord Treasurer. Disordered condition of the islands; regulations which are expedient to be adopted for their government.

43. Statement of causes why the Isle of Sheppey is not so well kept, maintained, and defended as it has been, principally by decay of the House of Shurland, maintained by Sir Tho. Cheyne, late Lord Warden.

44. Suit of Frances, wife of William Cheney, for renewal of the lease of her father's House of Shurland, in the Isle of Sheppey, for 21 years.

45. Articles agreed upon with Mr. Crispe and Mr. Taylor, for farm of the House of Shurland.

46. Certain offers made for a lease, to be granted to four gentlemen, of Shurland House, park, and demesnes, now in the occupation of Mr. Holstocke.

47. "The Plotte of Sherland Howse in Sheppie."

48. The Queen to the Marq. of Winchester, William Lord Howard, Lord Chamberlain, Sir Fr. Knolles, and Sir Walter Mildmay. Commission to survey the ordnance, munition, and armour within the Offices of Ordnance and Armoury, and for the government of the same.

49. Commission from the Queen to the Lord Treasurer, Lord Chamberlain, Mr. Comptroller, Mr. Vice-Chamberlain, and Mr. Mildmay. For surveying the Office of Ordnance and the Office of the Armoury, and for supplying the same with stores, &c.

50. A project or reasons set down, in which is manifested a mean whereby all strangers may be kept to make their due employments, to the advancement of Her Majesty's customs, and for retaining the coin and bullion within the realm; by Tho. Ferrers.

51. Petition of John Johnson to Sir Wm. Cecill. Requests that examination be made of a lease, by which one-half of the lordship of Beckenham, Kent, the property of one Tyrrell, a ward, is demised to Robert Ligh, by Humphrey Tyrrel and Jane his wife.

1570?

Vol. LXXV.

52. Proposed measures for providing against the infection of the plague in London. *In the Italian language.*

53. Treatise in the Italian language against excessive usury. In the same handwriting as the preceding, and indorsed "1570. *A Provision against Usurie. Calvacanti.*"

54. A device for the remedying of some part of the inconveniences which daily grow in the realm by usury and dry exchange. Proposing the establishment of the office of Royal Exchanger. Indorsed, "*Mr. Taverner.*" [*Probably the foundation of the subsequent Act,* 13 *Eliz., cap.* viii.]

55. Petition of Reginald Metcalf, Preacher, to the Council. Prays to enjoy the commodities and tithes belonging to his benefice of Stanton in Norfolk, against the riotous dealings of one Bartholomew Baxter.

56. List of military stores required for the Isle of Wight. Signed by the Marq. of Winchester.

57. Note of lands, &c., in the possession of Sir John Perrot, which he desires to exchange for other Crown lands. [*Much mutilated and decayed.*]

58. A treatise intituled "England Triumphant," addressed "To all Monarchs, Kings, and Princes Absolute of Christendom." Setting forth in a historical form the power, pre-eminence, and glory of Britain, and her independence of the Pope in spiritual matters, from the earliest ages. [*This curious paper is wholly in Cecill's hand, but apparently was left by him in an unfinished state.*]

59. Fair copy of the above, with many corrections and additions by Cecill.

60. Proposals of (N.) for grant in fee-farm of the salt marshes adjoining the Camber, he covenanting to keep in repair the decayed harbour of Rye, according to the device of Adryan Skedam.

61. Petition of Dorothy Keill, wife of Thos. Keill prisoner in the Marshalsea, to Sir Wm. Cecill, that the Queen would be pleased to set him at liberty.

62. Articles exhibited by John Adams against Tho. Hackluyt, for divers riotous proceedings in forcibly expelling him from the Stewardship of Leominster, and holding Courts there.

63. Robt. Walter, of All Soul's Coll., Oxford, to Cecill. Complains of the state of insubordination into which some members of that College have lapsed. Lat.

64. Petition of Robert Pinder to the Lord High Treasurer, for recovery of a debt of 300*l.*, due to him by Mr. Henry Howard.

65. Petition of Griffen Jones to the Council, for recovery of a debt of 33*l.* and 6*d.*, due to him by the same.

Vol. LXXV.

1570 ?

66. Note of the contents of the letter to Her Majesty written from Jo. Peterson, native of Lubeck. On the subject of alchemy: offering to her three wonderful alchemical glasses; and of the undertaking by Robert Smythe, on the peril of his head, to bring 40,000 dollars into the Queen's coffers by their means.

67. Genealogy of Alice Long, wife of John Archmore by whom she had 13 daughters, and aunt of William of Wickham, founder of New College, Oxford: with additions by Sir Wm. Cecill.

68. Genealogical note, showing the descent of John Winchester, an idiot, and the tenure of his land.

69. Warrant to pay the sum of 266*l*. 13*s*. 4*d*. to David Smyth, the Queen's embroiderer, for a side-saddle of black velvet, richly embroidered with gold and pearls, and the harness, &c., of silk and gold.

70. Statement why the town of Winchelsey is in its present poor and lamentable decay. Proposes the reconstitution of its haven.

71. Note of privileges and liberties granted to the Doctors of Physic; and their incorporation into a Company, with the title of President and College of Physicians. Questions touching the extent of their powers.

72. Account of the whole charge and receipt of the Honour of Beaulieu, alias New Hall cum Membris, with payments to Lord Wharton and others.

73. Sir Wm. Cecill to the Bishop of London. Sends the confession of Wm. Apleforth, who denies the slanderous words said to have been spoken by him against the Queen. Requests the Bishop to send for John Hill, and examine him thereon.

74. William Ryce, prisoner in the Tower, to the Queen. Laments his breach of the laws, and humbly implores her pardon.

75. Petition of Elizabeth Gaywood, prisoner in the Tower, wife of John Gaywood, to same. Laments her folly in committing a breach of the laws, by which herself and husband are brought into great trouble. • Solicits her gracious pardon.

76. Plan for uniting the Town and the University of Cambridge under one Corporation, by the title of "Chancellors, Governors, Scholars, and Burgesses of the University of Cambridge."

77. Extracts from ancient charters of the privileges granted to the Chancellor and other Officers of the University of Cambridge. [*Imperfect.*]

78. Account of "the summe that the Colledges in Cambridge did "spend of wheat for bread, and mault for drinke, in the space of one "whole year, 1570." Trinity College alone consumed 2250 barrels of beer, with wheat at 13*s*. 4*d*. per quarter.

Vol. LXXV.

1570 ?

79. Extract from the local statutes of Queen's College, Cam., showing that there is but one Fellow for all the Principality of Wales.

80. Note of such of the old articles as are thought necessary to be reformed in the Marches of Wales, together with new ones required.

81. Draft of an article for the better service of Her Majesty by her attorney (Tho. Atkyns) in the Marches of Wales. Atkyns to be also of the Council.

82. Draft of preamble to the orders set down by the Privy Council for direction and reformation of the Queen's Court in the Marches of Wales.

83. Mr. Townsend's notes touching sundry things to be reformed in Wales, and added to Her Majesty's instructions given to her Council there.

84. [   ] to Sir Wm. Cecill. Proposing the issue of a base coinage to defray the charges for the reparation of harbours, havens, and castles throughout the kingdom, and particularly for the repair of Dover Haven.

85. Fourteen depositions by Katharine Pycas and others, touching certain seditious words said to have been spoken by John Turner against the Queen, in taking forcible possession of Bramblety Chapel and lands; on the part of Lord of Buckhurst.

86. Statement of the proceedings of Hugh Trevanyon against Stephen Rithe, at the time when Rithe was to have possession of certain lands of the inheritance of the said Hugh Trevanyon.

87. Note of the Dean and Chapter of the Cathedral Church of Hereford, touching the rectory of Lugwardin, in that county; proposing to found a Divinity Lecture, or to erect a new Free Grammar School in Hereford, with the income of the rectory.

88. Statement of the income and value of the Archdeaconry of Surrey, by John Watson.

89. An estimate of the charge for two additional buildings in the garden side of the Earl of Derby's house, in Channel [Canon] Row.

90. Grant of a mortmain for St. John's College, Cambridge. Confirming the grants and privileges of the said College.

91. Inquisition, post mortem, of lands, &c., in the Manors of Chakenden and Kidlington, co. Oxford, parcel of the possessions of the late John Kete.

92. Notes on the degrees of Nobility, Hereditary Succession of Dignities, Places of Honor, &c.

93. Grant of letters of naturalization to Alexander Fidelis, a citizen of Venice. Lat.

1570 ?

VOL. LXXV.

94. Note of powder, armour, and other munitions, provided at Antwerp by Richard Clowgh, factor to Sir Ths. Gresham.

95. A note of the munition received by Humfrey Wyllson, Master of the Clement of London.

95. Suggestion that the Registrar of the High Commissioners for Ecclesiastical Causes should be sent for, to answer for setting certain Papists at liberty, without sufficient security.

97. Petition of Andrew Smythe, Clerk of the Woodyard, to Sir Wm. Cecill. For some allowance in consideration of the many years he has served Her Majesty.

98. John Gwyn to same. Compliments him on his learning and power. Solicits his assistance for the obtaining of a small rectory in the University of Oxford, in the gift of the Keeper of the Great Seal. Lat.

99. Summary of the Musters of able men, arms, armour, light horsemen, &c., for all the counties of England, amounting in the whole to 589,981 men.

100. Report by Dr. Lewes on the petition of Robert Saxie, Geo. Higgons, and others, merchants of Bristol, complaining of the detention of their ships in Spain, in consequence of the capture of a Spanish ship by Tho. Cobham ; recommending letters to be written to the King of Spain, demanding restitution.

101. The Queen to the Company of Merchant Adventurers. Desiring them to prohibit Tho. Clecher from intermeddling with the trade of merchandize in the Low Countries, contrary to their privileges, and not being free of their Company.

102. Answer of the Merchant Adventurers of England against the pretensions of the Merchant Staplers to export cloths to the Low Countries.

1570.

VOL. LXXVI. 1570.

Register Book of Grants of Dispensations for plurality of Benefices, from 1559 to 1570, specifying the names of the clergy to whom granted, and of the livings and other offices held by them.

Vol. LXXVII. January—April, 1571.

1571.
Jan. 8.
Marshalsea.
1. Wm. Herlle to the Lord Keeper. Complains of the contest which he has to maintain with ill fortune, not with justice. Has been committed to close prison, and is in want of money, credit, and apparel.

Jan. 10.
London.
2. Sir Tho. Gresham to Sir Wm. Cecill. Sends a letter from the four gentlemen of Cologne, by which he will perceive how the bargain for 100,000 dollars proceeds. Has sent Tho. Dutton to Hamburgh to take up money there.

Jan. 14.
Boynton.
3. Wm. Strickland to same. Reports the finding of certain coins of Vespasian and other Roman Emperors in the ruins of a house demolished by the sea, in the village of Awburn, on the coast near Holderness.

Jan. 14.
4. Account of moneys made within the office of Thomas Stanley, Under Treasurer of the Mint, from the first to the thirteenth year of the Queen's reign.

Jan. 18.
Ludlow.
5. The Queen and Council for the Marches of Wales. Warrant for Sir John Perrot, appointed President of the Council of Munster, to levy 34 men in Wales, to serve as footmen under him in Ireland.

Jan. 20.
6. Memorial of instructions by Cecill (and in his hand) to be observed by the Earl of Rutland in travelling abroad for his improvement. Rules for his conduct and guidance.

Jan. 21.
7. Archbishop Parker to Cecill. Concerning the question " An principibus sit potius resistendum quam obediendum in rebus adiaphoris?" Inconvenience will follow if this matter, thus begun, be slyly, with a flourish, passed over. Has written to Mr. Mullyns on the subject.

Jan. 27.
St. Asaph.
8. Tho. Davies, Bishop of St. Asaph, to same. Is a suitor to him in a godly and useful cause, which the bearer, Mr. Evans, will explain. Incloses,

    8. I. *List of Commissioners for Ecclesiastical Causes within the diocese of St. Asaph.*

Jan. 31.
9. Order in Council for discharge of the inhabitants of the Cinque Ports from the loan money assessed on them by letters of Privy Seal. [*No such order as the above is entered on the Council Register, but on the 21st of Dec. 1570, the inhabitants of the Cinque Ports, then in attendance on the Council, were ordered to pay in their money on the loan, or to return home and bring certificate from the Lord Warden of their inability so to do.*]

Jan. 31.
Grimsthorp.
10. Richard Bertie to Cecill. As the Queen is about to grant a lease of her customs, begs his friendly aid to prevent any prejudice thereby to the Duchess of Suffolk and himself, in their right to certain customs in the port of Boston.

Vol. LXXVII.

1571.

Jan. 31. Bisham.	11.	Lady Elizabeth Hoby to Sir Wm. Cecill. Requests to have certain timber out of Shrawnell Park for repair of a bridge and certain mills in Ewsham. Solicits his favour in behalf of one Edmond Rockery, of Cambridge, who is in trouble for certain words spoken by him.
Feb. 3.	12.	Declaration of the election of Thomas Cowper as Bishop of Lincoln, by the Sub-dean and Chapter of that See.
Feb. 4.	13.	Wm. Herlle to Cecill. Entreats his compassion for his afflicted condition. Lat.
Feb. 5. Serjeant's Inn.	14.	Wm. Lovelace, Roger Manwood, and John Jefferey, Serjeants-at-Law, to Mr. Hampton. State their opinion that the inhabitants of the Cinque Ports, by their charter, are exempt from payment of loans on letters of Privy Seal.
Feb. 12.	15.	Note of the money paid out of the Receipt, since 12 July, 1570, upon ordinary and extraordinary warrants.
Feb. 14.	16.	Wm. Norton to Cecill. Prays that he will show him some favour. Solicits pardon, and protests that he will in future continue loyal and obedient to his Sovereign.
Feb. 25. Westminster.	17.	Letters Patent of creation of Sir William Cecill as Baron Burghley.
Feb. 26.		Lease from the Dean and Chapter of St. Paul's to Thomas Mountayn, Parson, and the Churchwardens of the Parish of St. Faith, of a piece of void ground in the church-yard of St. Paul's [*Case B. Eliz. No.* 7.]
Feb. 28. Middle Temple.	18.	Ric. Hakluyt to Lord Burghley. Sends intelligence of Spanish preparations, but knows not against whom they are designed.
Feb.	19.	Memorandum by Burghley relative to the shipping of cloths and kerseys out of the realm without restraint or licence.
Feb.	20.	Charge of the Under Treasurer of the Mint according to the covenants of the indenture with the Queen.
Feb.	21.	Goldsmiths of London to Burghley and Sir Walter Mildmay, Commissioners for the Mint. Complain of the delay by the Treasurer of the Mint in issuing coin for the bullion brought into the Mint to be made into money.
Feb.	22.	Articles for grant of certain liberties to be made to the inhabitants of the Isle of Sheppey, addressed to the Attorney and Solicitor General; signed by Burghley and Mildmay.
Feb.	23.	Articles for a grant of certain liberties to the inhabitants of the Isles of Sheppey and Harty. Same as the above, with some additional articles.
Feb.	24.	The names of such rebels as be fled into the Low Countries and there remain. Indorsed by Lord Burghley, "*Mr. Fitzw^{ms} memoryalle of rebels in ye Low Contryes.*"

Vol. LXXVII.

1571.
March 1. 25. Paper indorsed by Lord Burghley, "Textus Jur. Civil. de actis. ab Incarcerato."

March 2.
Canterbury. 26. Henry Kyllygrew to Burghley. Has delivered the Queen's packet to Mrs. Walsyngham. Went to visit the Cardinal (Chastillon), who being ill, he could neither see him nor his wife. Mrs. Walsyngham has received a present of wine from the Cardinal's wife, by Dr. Pena.

March 6.
Cambridge. 27. The Master and Fellows of St. John's College to same, and others. With thanks for the administration of Sir Ambrose Cave's will. Lat.

March 7. 28. Sir Owyn Hopton to same. Particulars of the monthly charges of the diet of the Earl of Desmond and his brother, in the Tower.

March 7.
London. 29. Lionel Duckett to same. Divers of the Company for Mineral affairs have conferred with Mr. Lover and Hechstetter, touching the state thereof. Great want of money; requests him to appoint a place for a meeting of the Court. *Incloses*,

> 29. I. *Statement of Jehan Lover and Daniel Hechstetter to the Company for the Mines Royal; with list of names of proprietors to partake of the profits. 5 March.*

March 7.
London. 30. Sir Tho. Gresham to same. Offers of a loan of money from Hamburgh merchants. Trusts the four gentlemen of Cologne will do something. There is yet 25,000*l.* or 30,000*l.* in Spanish money in the Tower. Suggests its being recoined into English money.

March 13.
London. 31. Lord Cobham to William Cryspe, his Lieutenant at Dover Castle. Has been pressed by Card. Chastillon to stay the execution of certain prisoners condemned for murder and piracy.

March 23.
The Rolls. 32. Sir Willm. Cordell to Burghley. Sends precedents of certain writs as to election of Recorders. Mr. Pate, Recorder of Gloucester, has been unkindly used.

March 24. 33. The Company of the Mines Royal to the Earl of Leicester and Lord Burghley. Requests that the bargain for the copper be completed, and also the warrant for discharge of the impost on wines.

March 27. 34. State of the debt for which Mr. Cockeram stands bound. Indorsed by Burghley, "*Inter Wm. Wade et Cockeram.*"

March 28.
Bristol. 35. Mayor, &c., of Bristol, to Burghley. Complaining of the private statute procured in the last Parliament, for incorporating the Merchant Adventurers of Bristol. Great damage will thereby ensue to the commerce of Bristol. Pray it may be repealed.

March 28. 36. Instructions given to John Morgan, of Caermarthen, sent with two vessels to the seas for the service of the Queen's Majesty, to cruise off the coasts of Ireland and Spain, and to observe any preparations making in the Spanish ports.

Vol. LXXVII.

1571.
March 29.
37. Lionel Duckett to Lord Burghley. Was yesterday with Sir Walter Mildmay, touching the Privy Seal for money for the copper sold to the Queen. The proposed delay of payment will be very prejudicial.

March 30.
Canterbury.
38. Roger Manwood and Tho. Leighton to the Earl of Leicester and Lord Burghley. Detailed report on the death of Card. Chastillon; there appears to be no ground for the suspicion that he had been poisoned. Have however ordered six of his servants into custody.

March.
39. Abstract of numerous warrants issued for various items of public expenditure from Oct. 1569 to March 1571; amongst others a warrant (Feb. 1571) to deliver to the Lady Margaret Lennox 800*l.* of the Queen's Majesty's gift.

March.
40. Note of the restitution of temporalities to the several Bishops from 2° Eliz.

March.
41. Declaration of the Queen's supremacy and of homage, by William Bradbridge, B D., Bishop Elect of Exeter.

April 3.
42. Book of Articles propounded by Matthew Parker, Archbishop of Canterbury, and agreed to in the Synod at St. Paul's, on the 3rd of April, 1571.

April 5.
[Nonis Aprilis.]
43. Caspar Vosbergh to Burghley. Progress of the works at Stamford. Lat.

April 6.
44. Note of proceedings in the House of Commons as to Burgesses for certain places in reference to the return for the Borough of Minehead.

April [7].
45. Account of the sums of money due to Sir Owyn Hopton, Lieut., and other Officers of the Tower, for their fees and usages for the quarter ending Lady Day 1571.

April 7.
46. Account by Sir Owyn Hopton of the sums due to him for the diet and charges of prisoners in the Tower, from the 1st of Feb. to the 7th of April 1571, including the names of Tho. Hussye, William and Marmaduke Norton, Wm. Parker, Dr. Storye, &c.

April 9.
Hurst.
47. John Morgan to the Council. Reports that 300 sail of hulks, bound towards Spain, have appeared off the coast of the Isle of Wight.

April 10.
48. Heads of a Bill for the better impannelling of juries.

April 10.
49. Francis Harington to Burghley. Concerning the management of certain drains and sewers in the fens between Spalding and Pinchbeck, co. Lincoln.

April 11.
50. Note by Valentine Harries of an Act made for maintaining navigation, and Her Majesty's provision; and the abuses of such as should reform it, particularly in the fisheries and trade of fishmongers.

DOMESTIC—ELIZABETH.

Vol. LXXVII.

1571.
April 14.
51. Olyver Dawbeney to Lord Burghley. Requests he will pardon his slackness in not having acquainted him with his proceedings in trying the concealments of the Customs.

April 15.
Grimsthorpe.
52. K. Duchess of Suffolk to same. Concerning the petition of her son Mr. Grey to be restored to his rightful inheritance, the Earldom of Kent.

April 18.
53. Wm. Humfrey to same. Delay in executing the lease of the Manor of Calver. New establishment of the Mint contemplated; hopes no unfair practices will be attempted. Effect of the foreign exchange.

April 21.
54. State of various Bills in both Houses in the Sessions of 13° Eliz. to the 21 of April.

April 21.
55. Bill for the establishment of seven banks to be kept in the Cities of London, York, Norwich, Coventry, West Chester, Bristol, and Exeter, to be known by the name of "Banks for the Relief of Common Necessity," and to lend money on pledges or pawns at the rate of 6 per cent.

April 23.
56. Bishop Pilkington to Burghley. Intelligence brought by Wm. Lee, the chief man of the late Earl of Westmorcland, of the deaths of the Earl's eldest son, Lord Neville, and of Lady Mary Neville, the Earl's sister; the Lady Adeline only remaining. Old Salvin has also died and been buried "without priest or prayer." Particulars of many of the rebels.

April 25.
Howard House.
57. Duke of Norfolk to the Council. The bad state of his health and his private affairs oblige him to make suit to the Queen for greater freedom of his person. The physicians tell him that if he does not take exercise his body is not likely to endure.

April 25.
58. Book of Orders for the strangers of the City of Norwich, overseen, allowed, and ordered by the Right Hon. Sir Walter Mildmay, Sir Thomas Smythe, and Sir William Cordell; with copy of the letter from the Council to the Mayor, &c., of Norwich, establishing the same.

April 26.
59. Protestation willingly made by Christopher Goodman, preacher of God's word, concerning his dutiful obedience to the Queen's person and government: made at Lambeth before the Archbishop of Canterbury and other Bishops.

April 27.
60. Bill against "Disguised Priests," or Professors of the Romish religion, being found in England, disguised in the apparel of serving men, or mariners; and for the punishment of gypsies remaining in England. [*Imperfect.*]

April 28.
Gresham House
61. Sir Tho. Gresham to Burghley. Transmits letters received fron his agent at Antwerp concerning a loan to the Queen. Reque ts directions as to payments becoming due to the City of London.

April 30.
London.
62. Same to same. Particulars of sums borrowed at Antwerp for the Queen, for which he requests bonds to be issued. Solicits the removal of Lady Mary Grey.

Vol. LXXVII.

1571.
April. 63. Duchess of Suffolk to Lord Burghley. Thanks for his courteous enquiries after her health. Excuses herself for not having waited on the Queen.

April.
Middlesex. 64. Indictment of Richard Norton, late of Norton Conyers, co. York, Thomas Markenfield, Chr. Nevell, Francis Norton, and Tho. Jenney alias Jennynges, for treasonably conspiring against the Queen, together with Dr. John Storye, Wm. Parker, and John Prestall. Lat.

April. 65. Caspar Vosbergh to Burghley. Concerning the uses of woad in dyeing. Lat.

April. 66. List of dispensations to hold benefices, granted to scholars within collegiate age, from 27 January 1569 to 20 April 1571.

67. Aldermen and Merchants of the Stillyard to Burghley. Pray for a patent under the Great Seal authorizing them to export cloths.

68. Petition of the same to the Queen and both Houses of Parliament, that the Act restraining the exportation of cloths be repealed and annulled.

April (?) 69. Petition of the Freemen of the Company of Fishmongers to the Parliament. Complaining of the non-observance of Lent, whereby the sale of fish and encouragement to the fisheries were greatly injured; giving the names of the butchers who killed and sold flesh during Lent.

70. Note of objections against the Bill touching fraudulent accomptants.

71. Draft of a bill for relief of vicars and curates lacking needful sustentation in their cures, whereof the rectories are impropriate, &c.

72. A motion of succession in the Parliament a° xiii^{mo} Elizabeth R^{ne} &c. [*Two copies of this elaborate paper will be found in Vol.* xxvii., *Nos.* 33 *and* 34, *under the date of* 28 *January* 1563. *As the Journals, both of the Lords and Commons, in the Session of April and May* 1571, *are wholly silent on the subject of the succession, it may be presumed the above given date of* xiii°. *Eliz. is not the true one.*]

73. Copy of the Act of Parliament, whereby certain offences are made treason.

74. Extract from the Act of Parliament 13th of Eliz., touching reform of certain ministers of the Church.

75. An Act for the relief of the poor, and for reformation of idleness.

76. The brief of the Bill of Mortmain, with the opinion of Her Majesty's Attorney and Solicitor thereupon.

Vol. LXXVII.

1571.

77. Bill against such as depart or remain out of the realm without licence.

78. Articles devised for establishing a General Recorder for the Realm of England, who shall control and oversee every other Recorder under him, and ascertain that they execute justly and truly the charge committed to them. [*Imperfect; the first and second sheets wanting.*]

79. Act of Parliament for improving the navigation of the river Lee, otherwise called Ware River, between London and Ware.

Vol. LXXVIII. MAY—JUNE, 1571.

May 1. 1. Statement of the inconveniences which may arise by William Martin's letters of marque.

May 2. 2. Duchess of Suffolk to Burghley. Relies on his friendship to support and forward the cause of her son Grey.

May 2. Gedney. 3. Adlard Welby to same. Transactions at a Session for the Sewers in the fens in Lincolnshire.

May 3. Bishopsthorpe. 4. Archbishop Grindall to same. Ill treatment of John Frampton in the Inquisition in Spain; his suit to be remembered in the treaty of restitution between England and Spain.

May 4. 5. John Mershe and Tho. Aldarsey to same. Report their examination of the case of John Frampton, and the treatment he received in the Spanish Inquisition.

May 4. [4° Non. Maii] London. 6. Thomas Gardiner to same. Entreats pardon for his error, and solicits to be released from confinement. Lat.

May 7. 7. Names of the Lords' Committees on the bill for increase of tillage, and maintenance of the navy.

May 8. 8. A true certificate of all such strangers as are now resident and abiding within the town of Harwich.

May 11. Colchester. 9. Bailiffs of Colchester to the Council. Have caused a true and perfect note to be taken of all strangers resident within their town. *Inclosing,*

    9. I. *Certificate and particular description of all manner of strangers now remaining within the town of Colchester.* 11 *May,* 1571.

May 12. 10. Brief declaration and certificate of all strangers and aliens dwelling within the Borough and Liberty of Great Yarmouth, Norfolk.

1571.
May 14.

May 18.
Portsmouth.

May 20.
Lynn.

May 20.
Westminster.

May 21.
Portsmouth.

May 21.

May 21.

May 25.

May 25.

May 25.

May 25.

May 25.

May 25.

May 25.

Vol. LXXVIII.

11. List of Bills passed in the Lower House, and sent to the Lords, with list of Private Bills also passed, and those remaining in the Lower House.

12. Sir H. Wallop, Sir Wm. Kyngesmyll, and John Basyng, Commissioners for the survey of Portsmouth, to the Council. Have made survey of the town and fortifications, and of the stores remaining there, of which they send particular books.

    12. I. *Book declaring the view and survey of stores, &c., remaining in Portsmouth after the death of Sir Adrian Ponynges, delivered over to Sir Henry Radeclyff, now Captain there.* 16 *May*, 1571.

13. The Mayor and Corporation of Lynn to same. Have, according to their command, taken a note of all the foreigners residing within that town. *Inclosing*,

    13. I. *A true and perfect note of all the strangers abiding within the town of Lynn, Norfolk.* 18 *May*, 1571.

14. The Queen to the Lord Mayor and Sheriffs of London. Ordering them to forbear dealing in their Courts in any suits appertaining to the Admiralty Court.

15. Sir Henry Radeclyff to the Council. Reports proceedings of Wallop, Kyngesmyll, and Basyng, in surveying the Isle and town of Portsmouth. Several ships fitting out for service of the Prince of Orange.

16. Note of fees payable in the Mint to the officers and workmen there.

17. Schedule of Acts passed both Houses; of Bills passed in the Upper House and sent down, of those not sent down, and of those yet remaining there.

18. K. Duchess of Suffolk to Lord Burghley. Thanks for his courteous usage of her son Grey. Describes her former gracious reception by the Queen, but cannot now account for the alteration of Her Majesty towards her.

19. Certificate of the Flemings dwelling in the town of Dover.

20. Bill for incorporating the Universities of Oxford and Cambridge.

21. Another copy of the above.

22. Another Copy. [*Imperfect; the last sheet wanting.*]

23. Saving clause of the Act for incorporation of the Universities of Cambridge and Oxford.

24. Objections against the Bill for the Universites of Cambridge and Oxford, as to provision of grain and victuals.

DOMESTIC—ELIZABETH.

1571.
May 25.

Vol. LXXVIII.

25. Answers to the objections brought against the Bill for the reformation of the Liberty of five miles to both the Universities.

May 25. 26. Fair copy of the above.

27. The names of all the towns within five miles distance from the bounds and limits of the University of Cambridge.

28. Extract from Charter of Henry VIII., and from the Act 13 Eliz., relative to the Liberties of the University of Oxford.

May 27. 29. Certificate of the names of all strangers resident and abiding within the port and town of Sandwich, how many of them be denizens, and what nation they be of.

May 29. 30. Bond by John Tyrell, of Warley, co. Essex, for performance of the orders appointed by Lord Clynton and Lord Burghley, concerning the title of John Taylor to certain lands and hereditaments, mortgaged by Wm. Porter.

May 29. 31. Note of the dissolution of Parliament in the 5th and 13th of Elizabeth.

May 31.
Westminster.
32. The Queen to Sir Hugh Cholmeley, Vice-President, and the Council of Wales. Directions to inquire into the proceedings of Sir John Perrot, who has abused his license to levy certain soldiers among the tenants of the manors where he had rule.

May. 33. Account of the prisoners in the Tower, with demand for their diet for nine months.

May 34. MS. treatise in Italian touching criminal law.

May ? 35. Notes in Burghley's hand, touching subjects to be proposed in Parliament for encouragement of shooting with the harquebuss and hand-guns, fast days, corporation of gunners, &c.

May ? 36. List by the same, of the English counties, with numbers set against several, probably for levies.

May ? 37. [*Anonymous*] to Burghley. A long discourse, urging a unity in sound and true doctrine, *indorsed*, "toching ʊoming to yᵉ Chirch, and receaving yᵉ Sacrament."

June 5. 38. Orders and dealings in the Church of Northampton (for divine service), established and set up by consent of the Bishop of Peterborough, the Mayor and Brethren of the town there, and others; with a confession of faith subjoined.

June 10.
Tottenham.
39. Earl of Hertford to Burghley. His continued sorrow for want of the Queen's favour, and the endeavour to bring in question great part of the title of his lands.

June 12. 40. Thomas Wilbraham to same. Sends precedents from the law books of the order of battle or judicial combat. [*Inclosed is a note from W. Clederow to James Humfrey, but whether connected with the above, or not, is uncertain.*]

Vol. LXXVIII.

1571.

June 13.
[*Idibus Junii.*]
Wertheim.
41. Lodowick, Count of Stolberg, to the Duchess of Suffolk. Proffers of service. Lat.

June 16.
42. Duchess of Suffolk to Lord Burghley. Reports her conversation with the Queen, touching the claim of her son Grey to the Earldom of Kent.

June 20.
43. A valuation of certain coins of gold of the English Mint, and that of other countries which have been brought into the realm, as appears by certain proclamations; attested by Tho. Stanley, Treasurer of the Mint.

June 24.
44. Demands of Sir Owyn Hopton, Lieut. of the Tower of London, for diet and charges of certain prisoners therein remaining, as named.

June 24.
45. Account of sums due to the Lieutenant and other Officers of the Tower for their several fees and wages to Midsummer.

June 25.
46. Abstract of the clauses contained in the Queen's letters patent to Sir Humphrey Gilbert for executing the Statutes for maintenance of Artillery, and for having horse, armour, and weapons.

47. Lord Chief Justice Catelyn to Burghley. Transmits his opinion on the Commission of Oyer and Determiner, Anno Reg. Mariæ 1°, with respect to the attainder of Robert Duddeley, now Earl of Leicester.

June 30.
48. Copy of the above.

June.
Westminster.
49. Letters patent by the Queen for securing the repayment of certain sums of money to Sir Rowland Hayward and others, citizens of London, who have advanced the same to her by way of loan. Lat.

June.
50. Olyver Dawbeney to Burghley. Concerning the execution of Her Majesty's commission for concealment of Customs. *Incloses*,

    50. I. *Statement of the causes that have prevented the execution of the Patent for concealment of Customs.*

June.
51. Roger Ramsden to same. Details the circumstances of the entrapping and bringing over of Dr. Storye, for which he and his companions solicit recompence. Liberal course towards Parker, one of them.

June.
52. Roger Ramsden, Martin Bragge, and Symon Jewkes, to same. Have continually followed the Court for money owing to them. Desires his help in a certain suit for their relief. *Indorsed*, "*Ramsden, &c., that brought over Story.*"

June.
53. Lists of names of gentlemen in Derbyshire, Staffordshire, Leicestershire, and Nottinghamshire, with those "out of the Lone boke."

June.
54. Bill in Chancery by Francis Alford, of London, against Wm. Porter and Lodowick Greville, Esq., of the County of Warwick, to defraud Wm. Clopton Esq., by fraudulent conveyance of the Manor of Aston-sub-Edge, &c.

Vol. LXXVIII.

1571.
June.
55. The causes which moved Francis Alford to take the penalty of a bond of 300*l.* against Lodowick Greville, being bail for Porter ; whereas the said Alford was to pay but 150*l.* to the creditors to whom he stood for Porter.

Vol. LXXIX. June, 1571.

June.
A volume of depositions, ex parte Lodowick Greville, deft., versus Francis Alford, plt.. in the case charging Greville with acting in conjunction with Wm. Porter to defraud Wm. Clopton ; together with numerous letters, briefs, informations, answers, replications, &c., on both sides. [*Many papers relating to this confused and intricate suit are scattered throughout the correspondence of this reign.*]

Vol. LXXX. July—August, 1571.

July 4.
1. Note of the terms of a certain demise by way of lease at an annual rent of 20*l.* 10*s.* 8*d.* Lat. Indorsed, "*Mr. Hudson's suite.*"

July 5.
2. Justice Catelyn to Lord Burghley. Is grieved at the message he has received from the Queen by Mr. Hatton. Explains his opinion on the judgment given in favour of the Earl of Leicester. Dares not alter the ancient forms of Court.

July 11.
The Minories.
3. Lady Eleanor Pelham to Mr. John Lee. Is sorry to hear of his treatment by Lord   . Advises him to persevere in his present course.

July 12.
4. Tho. Stanley to Burghley. Begs that he may enjoy his office at the Mint, according to the covenants of his indenture, and that it be not infringed by the new orders. *Incloses,*

July 7.
4. I. *Note of money owing to divers persons payable from the revenue of the Mint.*

July 19.
Gresham House.
5. Sir Thomas Gresham to Burghley. Thanks for the removal of the Lady Mary (Grey). Statement of the several sources of her income.

July 20.
Cambridge.
6. The Master and Fellows of Queen's College to same. Requesting permission to search among the records formerly belonging to the Monastery of Crowland, for evidence in their favour in a suit in which they are engaged. Lat.

July 21.
7. William Burd to same. Complains of a letter respecting himself delivered by Mr. Ric. Carmarthen to Alderman Hawes. *Incloses,*

7. I. *W. Fleetwood and others, Commissioners of inquiry into the Customs, &c., to Alderman Hawes. Requiring him to certify what payments he has made to any of the Queen's officers by way of duty on wares shipped by him, in which Mr. Burd was implicated.*

DOMESTIC—ELIZABETH. 417

Vol. LXXX.

1571.
July 24.   8. Thomas Cobham [Brooke?] to Lord Cobham, his brother. Has made inquiries as to the commission granted to certain rovers by the Count Lodovick, and reports their proceedings.

July 26.
London.   9. Sir Rowland Haywarde, Lord Mayor, and Wm. Fletewoode, Recorder of London, to Lord Burghley. Touching certain slanderous speeches uttered against the Queen, Leicester, Bedford, Bacon, and others of the Court, by one Thomas Bales, a butcher.

July 30.
Ely House.   10. Henry Skypwith to same. Cannot on a sudden communicate the names of all (of Norfolk's household) who are in town, but there is Cuthbert Reade, his steward, and Dr. Wynnyat, who has read to the Queen of Scots; other persons enumerated.

July.   11. Declaration of Robert Earl of Leicester and William Lord Burghley, concerning the right of visitation delegated by Sir Thomas Whyte, founder of St. John's College, Oxford, to Sir Willm. Cordell and William Roper, Esqrs., during life, now claimed by Robert, Bishop of Winchester.

July ?   12. Legal arguments delivered by the Counsel of Sir Wm. Cordell, Master of the Rolls, justifying his right of visitation over St. John's College, Oxford, in pursuance of the will of Sir Thomas Whyte, the founder, against the claim of the Bishop of Winchester.

July ?   13. Paper of notes of legal points relative to the above.

August 1.
Gresham House.   14. Sir Tho. Gresham to Burghley. Requests him to remember his suit for the removal of the Lady Mary Grey.

August 1.   15. William Sharington to same. Reports the dissemination of libellous matters. Sends him copy of a bill which was affixed against a post in the city.

August 3.
Gorhambury.   16. Grant by the Queen to Sir Walter Mildmay of certain lands in the forest of Rockingham, co. Northampton.

August 6.   17. Notes in the handwriting of Lord Burghley, touching certain propositions for the Queen's marriage, headed by him, "*A short consideration of a long matter.*"

August 7.
London.   18. Declaration for calculating the profits arising on 130,000*l.* sterling by way of banking. Fr.

August 12.
London.   19. Dr. Val. Dale to Burghley. Has received his letter by Mr. Horsey's man. Does not find any particular complaint against Michael Coxe. Fiesco differs but in few points from the Spanish merchants.

August 13.
London.   20. Tho. Lord Buckhurst to same. Gives an account of his receiving the French Ambassador at the Blackfriars, where he landed. Wishes to know when he will have audience.

August 14.
London.   21. Same to same. Desires instructions how the French Ambassador, M. Foitz (Foix), should conduct himself, if he meets the Queen when she is hunting.

1571.

VOL. LXXX.

August 14. 22. Lord Buckhurst to Lord Burleigh. Mr. Foitz, the French Ambassador, is very desirous to have an interview with the Queen, and has proposed to come to the Court on the morrow.

August 20. 23. Note by Sir Tho. Gresham of the prolongation of the Queen's debts due the 20th Feb., and prolonged until the 20th of Aug. 1571.

August 20. 24. Certificate by Sir Tho. Mildmay and Jo. Pynchon, of the apprehending and punishment of rogues and vagabonds within the Hundred of Chelmsford, co. Essex.

August 20. 25. Similar certificate by Sir Anth. Cooke and others, taken within the Liberty of Havering, co. Essex.

August 20. 26. Similar certificate by the same, taken within the Hundred of Becontree, co. Essex.

August 20. 27. Certificate of all the vagabonds, rogues, and mighty valiant beggars (men and women) taken in the first watch at Southcley, in the Wapentake of Bassetlaw, co. Notts, before Nicholas Powtrell, and by him examined, whipped, stocked, and punished, according to law.

August 20. 28. Similar certificate from the same place, examined before Geo. Nevell, Esq., Sheriff of the County of Nottingham.

August 20. 29. Similar certificate by Sir Jervais Clyfton within the Hundred of Rushclyff, same county.

August 20. 30. Certificate of vagabonds and sturdy beggars apprehended and punished with stocking and whipping, within the Hundreds of Whitstone and Bysley, co. Gloucester.

August 21. 31. Capt. Edward Horsey to Burghley. Certain hulks have not
Isle of Wight. been stayed, for the wind being fair they had sailed to the westward. Has expedited the fitting out of the hulk for Martin Frobiser.

August 21. 32. Certificate by the constables of Chadlington of the rogues and vagabonds arrested, whipped, and passed, in the Hundred of Chadlington, and at Chipping Norton, co. Oxford.

August 21. 33. Similar certificate by the Justices of Peace for certain Hundreds in the County of Gloucester.

August 21. 34. Commission by the Queen to Ralph Lane to search certain ships of Brittany, reputed to be laden with unlawful goods, and to seize the same.

August 21. 35. Certificate by the constables of the Hundred of Ploughley, Oxford, that they have caused watch to be kept, and that no rogues or vagabonds have been found within that Hundred.

August 22. 36. Similar certificate by the Constables for the Hundred of Dorchester, co. Oxford.

August 22. 37. Certificate by the Constables of the Hundred of Binfield, Oxford, of the arrest and punishment of vagabonds and suspected persons within that Hundred.

1571.   VOL. LXXX.
August 22. 38. Certificate of George Tuke, Esq., Justice of Peace for the Half Hundreds of Wynstay and Thurstable, co. Essex, touching the search made for rogues and vagabonds therein.

August 22. 39. Similar certificate by Francis Harvye, Esq., for the Half Hundred of Witham, co. Essex.

August 23. 40. Justices of Gloucester to the Council. Watch and ward kept
Winchcomb. for apprehension of rogues and vagabonds in the division of Kistgate, co. Gloucester, have been duly observed.

August 24. 41. Thomas Gardiner to Lord Burghley. Takes the opportunity
[9° Cal. Sept.] of addressing him on their wine cause, by means of the bearer,
London. Robinson. Lat.

August 24. 42. Robert Strange to the Council. Watch duly kept in Ciren-
Cirencester. cester and the seven Hundreds adjacent, and no disorderly persons found.

August 24. 43. Certificate by Henry Cryspe and others, Justices of Kent, of
Canterbury. search and watch made for vagrant persons in the Lathe of St. Augustine.

August 24. 44. Sheriff and Justices of Surrey to the Council. Certify their
Dorking. proceedings in keeping watch and ward for, and apprehending of rogues and vagabonds. *Inclosing,*

July 30. 44. I. *Certificate of rogues and vagabonds apprehended, whipped, and punished within the Hundreds of Kingston, Emelynbridge, Copthorne, and Effingham.*

44. II. *Similar certificate for the Hundreds of Tandridge and Reigate.*

44. III. *Similar certificate for the Half Hundred of Wallington.*

44. IV. *Similar certificate for the Hundreds of Woking, Godley, Farnham, Godalming, Blackheath, and Wootton.*

44. V. *Similar certificate for the Hundreds of Brixton and Wallingford.*

August 25. 45. The High Constables of Ewelme to Sir Edmund Ashfield and others, Justices of Oxford. Make certificate of search for rogues and vagabonds in the Half Hundred of Ewelme.

August 25. 46. Similar certificate, addressed to Mr. Gybbons, Sheriff of Oxfordshire, from the Constables of the Hundred of Thame.

August 25. 47. Similar certificate by the Constables of the Hundred of Lewknor, co. Oxford.

August 26. 48. Duke of Norfolk to the Earl of Leicester and Lord Burghley. Laments the Queen's determination to visit his son's house, who is not of age to receive her. Protests that he has always advocated the marriage of the Queen.

1571.

August 26. 49. Certificate by the bailiffs of the Borough of Maldon, Essex, of vagabonds and idle persons apprehended within the jurisdiction of the same.

August 27. Cambridge. 50. John Whitgyfte and others, of the University of Cambridge, to Lord Burghley. Complain that George Adams, purveyor of conies for the University, is obstructed by the purveyors of conies for the Queen.

August 27. 51. The Constables of the Hundred of Wootton to Thomas Pennyston, Esq. Certify that they have caused privy watch and search to be made throughout the said Hundred, and specify the vagrants apprehended and punished.

August 27. Gloucester. 52. William Wynter and others, Justices of Gloucestershire, to the Council. Have made search in certain Hundreds for vagabonds, but have none but such poor beggarly persons as are not thought fit to trouble their Lordships with.

August 28. 53. Justices of Kent to same. Have made search in the Lathe of Aylesford, and apprehended thirteen men and women, stout and valiant vagabonds, all of whom have been stocked and whipped severely.

August 29. Portsmouth. 54. Sir Henry Radclyffe to Burghley. Has been prevented from writing by sudden sickness. Has examined, since his arrival, one Cranley concerning Stuckley. A number of mariners there in Frobiser's service. Shipping news. *Incloses,*

> 54. I. *Declarations of Richard Cranley and Tho. Hyat as to transactions with Hooper and Rigsby.* 23 *Aug.* 1571.
>
> 54. II. *Deposition of Rigsby as to Stuckley's slanderous conversation relative to the Queen.*
>
> 54. III. *Confession of James Rigsby, detailing the treasonable and railing conversations of his master, Tho. Stuckley, in Spain, relating to Q. Elizabeth; his design to land in Ireland with a large Spanish force, &c.*

August 30. Worcester. 55. Justices of Worcestershire to the Council. Certify their doings in searching for vagabonds throughout the county, and that very few have been found.

August 30. 56. Certificate by the constables of the Hundred of Bampton, co. Oxford. Watch and ward kept in every town and village. Particulars of vagrant persons who have been apprehended and punished.

August 31. 57. Similar certificate by the constables of the Hundred of Bloxham, in the same county.

58. Similar certificate for the Hundred of Banbury.

August 31. Clurewall. 59. Richard Bayneham, Sheriff of Gloucester, to the Council. Forwards certificates of several Justices within the said county, of the apprehension of rogues and vagabonds. *Incloses,*

> 59. I. *Certificate by Walter Compton, Esq., of the apprehension and punishment of vagabonds and sturdy beggars in the Hundreds of Teuxbury and Deerhurst, co Gloucester.*

DOMESTIC—ELIZABETH.

VOL. LXXX.

1571.
August.

60. Certificate of vagabonds and beggars arrested in certain Hundreds in co. Northampton: "all which were punyshed by stock-"inge, with sharpe and severe whippinge."

61. Thomas Constantine and others to Lord Burghley. Requesting him to procure a grant of Letters Patent to William Hunt, as Surveyor of Merchandize of the Merchant Strangers in the City of London.

62. Warrant to the Lord Keeper to prepare commissions for putting in execution the Act for maintenance of artillery and debarring unlawful games; and the Act for the having of horse armour and weapon.

63. Instructions by the Queen to the Commssioners in every county appointed for putting in force the Act for maintenance of artillery, and the Act for having horse armour and weapons, with powers to compound with the defaulters in the same. *Annexed*,

> 63. I. *Provisions of the Act for maintenance of artillery and suppressing unlawful games; and also of the Act for the having of horse armour and weapons, with the rates of composition for defaulters.*

August ?

64. Giles Lambarde, draper, to Burghley ?. Proposes a device for the manufacture of English oils for the use of the clothiers, and thereby to lessen the price of foreign oils, the farming of which he solicits.

VOL. LXXXI. SEPTEMBER—OCTOBER, 1571.

Sept. 2.
Tower.

1. Sir Thos. Smith and Dr. Tho. Wylson to Burghley. Higforth has deciphered the ticket he wrote by the Duke's commandment, and is at last willing to reveal anything. The Duke (Norfolk) being taken as it were ἐπ' αὐτοφώρῳ, it were fit he were more safely kept. Substance of the ticket. The Duke sends by the bearer, Mr. Browne, £600 in gold, sealed in a bag, to be conveyed to Lord Herries in Scotland, and by him to Lethington and Grange.

Sept. 2.

2. Lord Buckhurst to same. The French Ambassador has visited the Tower, and viewed the artillery, armoury, &c., and attended a banquet prepared for him. Discharge of ordnance on his departure.

Sept 3.

3. Same to same. Has sent for Partrich the goldsmith, and has stayed the delivery of the plate till the whole is supplied. The French will away with all speed.

Sept. 3.
Apthorp.

4. Sir Walter Mildmay to same. Thanks him for communications relative to Scottish affairs. Approves of the answer given to the French.

Sept. 4.
London.

5. Sir Tho. Gresham to same. Statement of the quantity of foreign coin brought into the Tower. Urges his suit for removal of Lady Mary Grey.

1571.

VOL. LXXXI.

Sept. 4.
London.
6. Lord Buckhurst to Lord Burghley. Departure of the French Ambassador toward Dover. M. Foitz has received thankfully Her Majesty's present. The plate was very fair, and of a thousand marks value. Expresses gratitude that the Queen approves of his own services. Hopes the Duke (Norfolk) will be able to clear himself.

Sept. 4.
Plymouth.
7. John Hawkyns to same. FitzWilliams is returned from Spain, where his message was well received. Spanish intrigues to invade the realm, and set up the Q. of Scots, to whom King Philip has sent a ruby of great price. Has received his pardon from the King of Spain.

Sept. 5.
Howard Place.
8. Sir Ralph Sadlier to same. Has received his letters by Baker of Waltham. The Duke has been examined upon interrogatories, and denies all with which he has been charged. He is now in close custody.

Sept. [6.]
9. The Queen to Sir Ralph Sadlier and Sir Tho. Smith. Warrant and directions to convey the Duke of Norfolk to the Tower, to be kept close prisoner there, under the personal attendance of Henry Skypwith.

Sept. 5.
Canterbury.
10. Lord Cobham to Burghley. Chanced to be at Canterbury when M. de Foix passed through; invited him to dine with him: their conversation. Death of Capt. Keys, the Serjeant Porter; recommends his younger brother Thomas (Brooke) to succeed him.

Sept. 6.
Dover.
11. Thos. Randolphe to same. Has accompanied M. de Foix to Dover, who was very honourably entertained at Canterbury, and was saluted on his departure from Dover by three or four shot from the Castle.

Sept. 8.
Gresham
House.
12. Sir Thos. Gresham to same. Has prolonged all the Queen's debts in Flanders for six months longer. Death of Mr. Keys, the Serjeant-Porter, which Lady Mary taketh grievously.

Sept. 10.
Much Bromley.
13. Wm. Cardynal to James Alltham, Esq. High Sheriff of Essex. Warrants were delivered to the High Constable of Tendring Hundred for the apprehension of vagabonds. Two have been arrested and whipped.

Sept. 12.
Lisle Cave to his father. Expressive of his dutiful affection. Has received his letter of the 13th Aug. Fr. [See France, Vol. li. 1571.]

Same to his brother. Assures him of his continued affection, tho' he does not write as often as he could wish. Fr. [See France, Vol. li., 1571.]

Sept. 13.
14. Certificate of Sir Edmund Brudenell and others, Justices of Northamptonshire, of the apprehension of rogues and vagabonds taken at the second watch, kept the 12th of September; five men and two women, and all were stocked, whipped, and sent to their places of abode.

Sept. 13.
15. Similar certificate by the constables of the Hundred of Chadlington, Oxford.

1571.
Sept. 13.
 16. Similar certificate by the constables of the Hundred of Ploughley, co. Oxford.

 17. Similar certificate by the constables of the Hundred of Bullington, same county.

Sept. 16.
Dorking.
 18. Justices of Surrey to the Council. Watch and search have been made throughout the county for apprehension of rogues and vagabonds. *Inclosing,*

 18 I. *Certificate by the constables of the Half Hundred of Brixton, Surrey, that at the privy search no rogues, vagabonds, nor masterless men were found.*

Sept. 12.
 18. II. *Certificate of the rogues and vagabonds found and punished within the Hundreds of Tandridge and Reigate.*

Sept. 13.
 18. III. *Similar certificate for the Hundreds of Kingston, Elmenbridge, Copthorne and Effingham.*

Sept. 12.
 18. IV. *Similar certificate for the Hundreds of Blackheath, Woking, Godley, Farnham, and Godalming.*

Sept. 17.
Wincheleomb.
 19. Sir. Tho. Chamberlayne and others to the Council. Have used all diligence in the search for masterless men and vagabonds in the County of Gloucester.

Sept. 18.
 20. Certificate by the constables of the Hundred of Bampton, co. Oxford, of search and watch for rogues and vagabonds, and particulars of those apprehended and punished.

Sept. 18.
Hereford.
 21. The Bishop and Justices of Hereford to the Council. Certify their proceedings in the search and watch kept for rogues and vagabonds within that county.

Sept. 20.
Huntley.
 22. Sir Nich. Arnold, Wm. Wynter, and others, Justices of Gloucestershire, to same. Certify their proceedings in the search and watch for rogues and vagabonds. *Inclosing,*

 22. I. *Confession of John Latymer, son of Sir John Latymer, on his apprehension by the watch, professing the utmost zeal for the service of the Queen of Scots. 14 Sept. 1571.*

Sept. 20.
 23. Certificate of the arrest and punishment of vagrants and beggars at various places in Nottinghamshire.

Sept. 21.
Leicester.
 24. Justices of Leicestershire to the Council. Have caused search and watch to be kept for rogues and vagabonds throughout the county. *Inclosing,*

 24. I. *Certificate of rogues and vagabonds apprehended within the Hundred of Sparkenhoe, co. Leicester.*

 24. II. *Similar certificate of persons apprehended by the watch for the Hundred of Gartrey, same county.*

 24. III. *Similar certificate for the Hundred of East Goscott, same county.*

 24. IV. *Similar certificate for the Hundred of Framland same, county.*

Vol. LXXXI.

1571.
Sept 22.
Tixall.
25. Sir Walter Ashton, Sheriff, to the Council. Arrest and punishment of rogues and vagabonds within the county of Stafford. *Incloses*,

    25. I. *Certificate of the watch and search for rogues and vagabonds at various places in the county of Stafford. Signed by Bishop Bentham.*

    25. II. *Similar certificate for other places in the same county.*

    25. III. *Similar certificate for Burton-on-Trent, same county.*

    25. IV. *Similar certificate for Colton, same county.*

    25. V. *Similar Certificate for the Hundred of Offlow, same county.*

    25. VI. *Similar certificate for other places in the Hundred of Offlow, same county.*

    25. VII. *Similar certificate for West Bromwich, in the same Hundred.*

    25. VIII. *Similar certificate for Trentham, same county.*

Sept. 24.
Keninghall.
26. Philip Earl of Surrey to Lord Burghley. Laments the unhappy position of the Duke his father. Hopes the Queen, by his means and of those of other friends, will mitigate her anger.

Sept. 24.
Cirencester.
27. Robt. Strange to the Council. Watch and ward had been made for rogues and vagabonds in Cirencester and the seven adjacent Hundreds, but no suspected persons found.

Sept. 30.
Baconsthorp?
28. Sir Christopher Heydon and others to same. Report their proceedings at Kenninghall and other of the Duke of Norfolk's houses in Norfolk, and made inventories at the same. *Inclosing,*

    28. I. *Inventory of the goods of the Duke of Norfolk, within the county of Norfolk, as taken by Sir Christopher Heydon, Sir Willm. Buttes, Edwd. Clere, and Thomas Sydney, Esqrs. and by them committed to the custody of certain persons within named.*

Sept. ?
29. Complaint of the citizens of London of their grievances, by the allowing of aliens to settle in the city and suburbs.

Oct. 1.
[Cal. Octob.]
Augsburg.
30. John Langnaver, Melchoir Link, and others, to the Queen. Request a confirmation of their privileges in the mines. Lat.

Oct. 1.
Augsburg.
31. Same to the Earl of Leicester. With memorial to the Queen on the above mentioned subject annexed.

Oct. 1.
Augsburg.
32. Same to Lord Burghley. On same subject, with copy of the same memorial to the Queen.

Oct. 1.
Indenture of assignment from Thomas Walsingham, of Chiselhurst, and William Crowmer to Thomas Randolph, Esq., of Letters Patents for the custody of the Manor and Hundred of Middleton and Merden, co. Kent, at the rent of one hundred pounds per annum, to be paid to Anne Walsingham, the intended wife of the said Tho. Randolph, during her life, from and after the day of his decease. [*Case B. Eliz. No. 8.*]

VOL. LXXXI.

1571.
Oct. 2.
Crosby Ravensworth.
33. Lancelot Pykerynge to Lord Burghley. Explains the book of charges for the diet of the Justices of Assize for the county of Westmoreland, made by him as Sheriff of the county.

Oct. 3.
Richmond.
34. Wm. Herlle to same. Applies to have a grant of the office of Surveyor of Foreigners, towards whom much vigilance is necessary.

Oct. 3
35. Same to the Queen. Solicits to be appointed Surveyor of Foreigners. Proposes that every stranger, on his entering or going out of the kingdom, should receive a ticket with a seal attached.

Oct. 5.
Gresham House.
36. Sir Tho. Gresham to Burghley. Sends the counterbond for the City, which must be signed and sealed. Reminds him of his suit for removing the Lady Mary Grey.

Oct. 7.
Osterley.
37. Lady Mary Keys (Grey) to same. Prays to be restored to the Queen's favour; God having now removed the occasion of Her Majesty's justly conceived displeasure towards her. [*It is remarkable that in all her previous letters Lady Mary signed her own name " Graye;" but the moment her husband died she signed herself by his name, " Keys."*]

Oct. 8.
38. Sir. Tho. Gresham to same. Has sent for the City counterbond, as the post departs that night.

Oct. 8 ?
Lisle Cave to his brother. Expressing his joy at receiving some letters from him by Philip. Fr. [*See France, Vol.* li., 1571.]

Oct. 11.
39. Extract from the examination of the Duke of Norfolk as to conveyance of letters to and from the Queen of Scots, by means of H. Goodere.

Oct. 12.
40. Certificate of the constables of Bullington Hundred, co. Oxford, of watch and search made for rogues and vagabonds in that Hundred, but none were found therein.

Oct. 12.
Baconsthorpe.
41. Sir Chr. Heydon and Sir William Buttes to the Council. Have taken order for establishing the ordinary household of the Earl of Surrey, and the rest of the Duke of Norfolk's children, at Walden in Essex. *Inclosing,*

41. I. *List of names of persons appointed to remove to Walden, and there to remain in ordinary, in number sixty-five.*

Oct. 12.
42. Certificate of watch and ward for vagrants kept in the Hundred of Dorchester, co. Oxford, "where all things be well, thanks be to God."

43. Similar certificate by the constables of the Hundred of Pirton, same county.

44. Certificate of vagabonds taken within the Hundred of Fawlesley, and whipped at Daventry, co. Northampton, according to the statute. [*Six out of the seven thus whipped being females.*]

45. Similar certificate for other Hundreds, in the same county.

Oct. 13.
46. Similar certificate for other Hundreds, in the same county.

VOL. LXXXI.

1571.
Oct. 14. Grant of Arms to Henry Draper, of Colbrook, Middlesex, by Robt. Cooke, Clarencieux. [*In Grant of Arms, No.* 10.]

47. Declaration made to Lord Burghley, by Lord Cobham, of the matter with which he has been charged, in which his ungracious brother, Thomas Cobham, was touched; as to letters brought secretly from Flanders for the Bishop of Ross, which, if known, would be the undoing of the D. of Norfolk.

Oct. 15. 48. Bishop Pilkington to Burghley. Particulars of the ill state of the country in the North, by means of the connexions of the persons engaged in the late rebellion.

Oct. 16.
Dorking. 49. Sir William More and others, Justices of Surrey, to the Council. Proceedings in the search for rogues and vagabonds in the county of Surrey. *Inclosing,*

    49. I. *Certificate of all such rogues and vagabonds as were taken within the Hundreds of Kingston and Elmynbridge, co. Surrey. Oct.* 12.

    49. II. *Similar certificate for the Hundred of Brixton, same county Oct.* 12.

Oct. 20.
Isle of Wight. 50. Edw. Horsey to Burghley. Disorderly proceedings of certain vessels on the high seas, under colour of the Prince of Orange's commission. Speaks in favour of one Mr. Younge.

Oct. 20.
Tower. 51. Henry Skypwith to same. Repeats the conversation he has lately had with the Duke of Norfolk, who is ready to answer to any articles that may be sent to him.

Oct. 23
Charlcote. 52. Thomas Asheton to same. Dissatisfaction among the people with regard to Norfolk's affair. The Papists find too much favour at Court. Recommends Sir Andrew Corbett, who is the only fit and trustworthy man to have charge in those parts.

Oct. 25.
London. 53. Sir Rowland Haywarde, Lord Mayor, to the Council. Has assembled the aldermen at the house of Mr. Alderman Allyn (Lord Mayor elect), and they have agreed to the orders inclosed. *Incloses,*

    53. I. *Regulations for examination of foreigners in all the ports and towns near London.*

Oct. 26.
Gresham
House. 54. Sir Tho. Gresham to Burghley. Has received the Queen's warrant for certain payments due in the City. The Lady Mary desires to be removed to her father-in-law's, Mr. Stokes.

Oct. 27 (?) 55. Notes of heads of examination to be administered to Henry Goodere. (*In Walsyngham's hand.*)

Oct. 27.
From Prison
in the Tower. 56. H. Goodere to Burghley. Confesses at length the particulars of his communications with the Queen of Scots, the Bishop of Ross, and the Duke of Norfolk. His correspondence with the latter in cypher. Protests his innocence of any treasonable designs.

Vol. LXXXI.

1571.
Oct. 30.   57. Examination of John Hamelin, servant to the Earl of Northumberland at the time of the rebellion in the North, as to a message brought to him and the Earl of Westmoreland, by Havers, the Duke of Norfolk's man.

Oct. 30.
Dunham.   58. William Bouthe, Sheriff of Cheshire, to the Council. Touching the apprehension and punishment of rogues, vagabonds, and sturdy beggars in that county.

Oct. 31.   59. Wm. Allyn, Lord Mayor, and Recorder Fletewoode to Lord [Burghley?]. Have examined John Hawes and his servant as to his correspondence with Spain. *Inclosing,*

    59. I. *Power of attorney from Morgan Robyns to Mr. Hawes, son of Alderman Hawes, to act for him in Spain; attested by Don Gerard Despes, the Spanish Ambassador, and the Bishop of Ross.*

    59. II. *Examination of John Hawes relative to his conveying a letter received of one Morgan, to the Duchess of Feria, in Spain, supposed to be from the Queen of Scots. 31 Oct. 1571.*

    59. III. *Dorothy Essex (the Duchess of Feria's woman) to Mr. Hawes. Her Grace has answered the Queen of Scots' letter. Particulars of Morgan's matter. The King of Spain has been gracious to him for the Queen of Scots' sake. From Squiriall [Escurial].*

Oct. 31.]   60. Intelligence by Rowland Brittan respecting the designs of the King of Spain on Ireland. Conveyance of letters from the Queen of Scots to King Phillip, by John Hawes.

Oct. 31.   61. Sir Henry Cryspe and others to the Council. Have been to Sandwich and Dover, and selected the best prisoners from the freebooters there, and the remainder are to be sent out of the realm. Particulars of the goods seized and now in safe custody.

Oct.   62. Note of repairs done within the Castle of Windsor, from June 6, 1570, to October 31, 1571, and of the repairs to be done in the following spring.

Vol. LXXXII.   November, 1571.

Nov   "The reporte of the searche of all the straungers wythin London "and Southwark, and the liberties thereof, made the x. day of No-"vember, 1571." By the Mayor and Aldermen of London. This return gives the names of all the foreigners in London, distinguishing their nations, the wards and parishes in which they dwelt, their trades and occupations, time of their abode in the realm, and the churches or congregations they frequent, amounting in the whole to 4631 persons.

VOL. LXXXIII. NOVEMBER—DECEMBER, 1571.

1571.
Nov. 1. 1. Certificate by the constables of the Hundred of Bullington, Oxford, of the apprehension of vagrants.

Nov. 1. 2. Similar certificate for the Hundred of Dorchester, same county.

Nov. 1. 3. Similar certificate for the Hundred of Ploughley, same county.

Nov. 1 4. William Allyn, Lord Mayor, to Lord Burghley. Requests that the penalties for making great and monstrous hose, usually worn by the common people, granted by the Queen to one Digby, might not be enforced.

Nov. 4. 5. Countess of Lennox to same. Expresses the anxiety and vex-
Islington. ations she sustains in bringing up her only son Charles. Solicits Burghley to receive him into his house, as a ward.

Nov. 6. 6. Wm. Herlle to same. Reports a conversation with one Horneby about Dawbeny and the payment of certain customs.

Nov. 7. 7. Richd. Hakluyt to same. Touching the conduct and practices of
Middle Temple. John Horneby, late clerk to Mr. Coleshill, in the service of the Customs, whose conduct has ruined an honest virtuous gentleman, Mr. Dawbeny.

Nov. 7. 8. Sir Walter Mildmay to same. Has ascertained the names of the gentlemen resident near Kimbolton, and indicates those most fit to be trusted. Solicits Burghley in favour of Walsyngham. *Incloses,*

    8. I. *List of gentlemen resident at various places in the vicinity of Kimbolton.*

Nov. 8. 9. William Booth to same. Expresses his gratitude towards him, and his wishes for his prosperity. Lat.

10. Declaration of persons examined by Wm. Williams and Robt. Hornby, touching matters between Gervis Basyl, a warder of the Tower, and Elizabeth Massy, wife of Roger Massy, parson of the said Tower.

Nov. 10. 11. The Duke of Norfolk's confession. " Being commanded by Her " Ma^{ty} to sett downe the trueth, he writeth as followeth: A breef " declaration of those things which I have omitted in my examinations " touching the whole proceedings with the Queene of Scotts, either by " myself or any other to my knowledg, before my first trouble or since. " 10 November, anno 1571."

Nov. 18. 12. Wiliam Herlle to Burghley. Long details of his conver-
London. sation with John Horneby, relative to his practices in the Customs. Recommends the suit of a walloon named Frances Franckard, who had two projects,—one for manufacturing salt of salt; the other for making salt of salt water. Also urges R. Smith's suit, who had purchased the office of Searcher in the Customs.

Nov. 19. 13. The offer and contract of Francis Franckard to the Lords of the Privilege of the Salt, to establish and perfect his invention of making salt from salt water, under certain conditions.

	Vol. LXXXIII.
1571.	
Nov. 20.	14. Brief statement of the Loan, from April to November, 1571.
Nov. 21.	15. Sir Walter Mildmay to Lord Burghley. The bearer, Mr. Robinson, brings with him the books touching the farm of the impost of wines, and also the warrant for allowance of the impost. The French Ambassador claims more than any Duke has.
Nov. 22. Westminster.	16. Peter Osborne to same. Tender made touching the erecting of certain salt-pans proposed by Francis Franckard, which he recommends.
Nov. 23.	17. Warrant by the Queen to the Exchequer, for repayment of the sums advanced to her by way of loan.
Nov. 25.	18. Lodowick Grevylle to Sir W. Cordell. Explains his transaction with William Porter as to the purchase of certain lands, and his suit with Clopton and Alford.
Nov. 26. Westminster.	19. Sir Walter Mildmay to Burghley. Information as to the value of some of Norfolk's lands, and concerning a certain payment to be made immediately to one Hayward. Has taken order in the Earl of Hertford's causes. *Incloses,*
	19. I. *Memorandum of the rent and value of the Lordship of Cloume, and of the offers made to the Duke for it.*
Nov. 26. London.	20. Sir Tho. Gresham to same. Has spoken to Sir Walter Mildmay touching Lord Thomas Hayward's matter. Money due to the merchants of London. Wishes the Lady Mary removed.
Nov. 29.	21. Further offer of Francis Franckard to the Lords of the Salt Works, for establishing works for manufacturing salt upon salt, under certain conditions.
Nov. 30. Ivy Lane.	22. Peter Osborne to Burghley. Further proceedings with Franckard in the business of the salt works.
Nov. 30.	23. Note by Sir Tho. Gresham of the prolongation of the Queen's debts, due May 1571, until the last of November.
Nov.	24. Heads of the principal matters wherewith the Duke of Norfolk is chargeable, partly by his own confession and otherwise. [*In Burghley's hand, and indorsed by him,* "1571. Octob. Novemb. " Substance of thynges wherewith the Q. Ma^{ty} did charge the D. of " Norfolk on Thursday."]
Nov. ?	25. Substance of various letters and correspondence between Norfolk and the Queen of Scots. [*Indorsed,* "Mr. Hexte, his note " drawen owt of certayne of the D. of Norfolkes letters found."]
Nov.	26. Observations on the question whether pirates ought to be allowed benefit of clergy.
Nov. ?	27. Petition of Thomas Duck, Yeoman of the Cellar, to Burghley. Solicits a lease of the farm called West Lavington, co. Wilts.

Vol. LXXXIII.

1571.
Nov. ?
28. Petition of William Whartone to the Queen. Prays for pardon as he has not been able fully to accomplish the service of revealing the Queen of Scots' secret practices, or of getting possession of the book of prophecies relating to Her Majesty.

29. Articles touching the bill for religion: "A recital of former statutes against such as reconcile or be reconciled to the obedience of Rome, against their due allegiance to Her Majesty."

Dec. 1.
30. Chief Justice Catelyn to Lord Burghley. Controversy between the Courts of King's Bench and Exchequer, as to their respective jurisdiction over the attendance of the Marshall.

Dec. 8.
London.
31. Tho. Brune to Mr. John Lee. Has written twice to him; wishes him to keep certain things till they meet. Dutch.

Dec. 8.
32. Translation of the above. Indorsed by Wm. Herlle, "*Thomas Brunes lře.*"

Dec. 12.
33. Oath of a Privy Councillor, as taken by the Earl of Shrewsbury on the 12th of December.

Dec. 17.
Windsor Castle.
34. Chapter of Windsor to Burghley. Claim by Mr. Middlemore to the lands given by the will of King Henry VIII., for maintenance of the Poor Knights of Windsor.

Dec. 20.
35. Note of cloths shipped and to be shipped on Sir Henry Nevill's licence.

Dec. 21.
36. An envelope addressed "The Certificate of the Rogues in Cambridge and Huntingdon shires." *Inclosing,*

    36. I. *Certificate of the rogues and vagabonds taken and punished in the Hundred of Laytanstone, Hunts.* 12 *Sept.*

    36. II. *Similar certificate for the Hundred of Hurstingston, same county.* 12 *Sept.*

    36. III. *Similar certificate for the Hundred of Normancross, same county.* 14 *Sept.*

    36. IV. *Similar certificate for the Hundreds of Radfield and Chevelye, Stane, Staplowe, and Flendyshe, co. Cambridge.* 12 *Sept.*

    36. V. *Similar certificate for the Hundreds of Wetherley and Tryplowe, Armyngford and Stowe, same county.* 12 *Sept.*

    36. VI. *Similar certificate for the Hundreds of Chesterton, Papworth, and Northstowe, same county.* 12 *Oct.*

    36. VII. *Similar certificate for the Isle of Ely, same county.* 12 *Sept.*

Dec. 29.
37. Declaration of certain merchants touching the trade with Portugal, and for opening the trade thither.

Dec.
38. Proclamation for execution of the laws made against unlawful retainers. [*This proclamation was made on the 3d of January following.*]

Vol. LXXXIII.

1571.
Dec.
39. Thomas Havers to Lord Burghley. Laments his hard estate and, petitions for liberty to remain at his own house in readiness to be called upon by the Lords.

Dec ?
40. Notes (in Gerrard's hand) from the examinations of Wm. Barker and the Bishop of Ross, implicating Sir Henry Percy in the design of the escape of the Queen of Scots.

Dec ?
41. Interrogatories to be propounded to Charles Arundel and Henry Howard at their examination, as to the combination made at the supper in Fish Street and at the Earl of Northumberland's. Speeches against Her Majesty, &c.

1571.
42. Order by the Lord Treasurer against the exportation of grain.

43. Certain articles touching the evil behaviour of Anne, wife of John Gaynesford, of Lingfield in the County of Surrey, particularly with regard to the death of her servant, Agnes Rayner.

44. Note of the office of cellarer appertaining to the Custom House, to be granted by the Queen's Majesty.

45. A brief note of such provisions of saltpetre and gunpowder allowed to divers persons by William Pelham, Esq., Lieut. of the Ordnance, during four years last past.

46. Particulars of the proposals of Richard Martin for undertaking the coinage at Her Majesty's Mint.

47. Another offer for farming the Mint.

48. Note of the revenue that may grow to the Queen upon the coinage of 350 lbs. of gold, and 32,000 lbs. of silver; giving such allowance as was made by indenture dated 6 April, 24th Henry VIII.

49. Note of points to be considered if the Queen let her Mint to farm.

50. The effect of the suit of the church of St. Paul's to the Queen's Majesty; and for founding a school at Middleton in Lancashire with the property of Robt. Nowell, brother of the Dean of St. Paul's.

51. Refutation of the atheistical opinion that men and women might beget themselves.

52. Lists of ships belonging to and remaining in the port of Bristol since the confirmation of certain Letters Patents.

53. Account of fees of the signet arising in the Hanaper and Petty Bag Offices from 1559 to 1571.

54. A diary of public and private transactions. In Lord Burghley's hand, and indorsed by him, " A sumarye frō 1558 & 1559, untill 1571, " Entred." [*This diary differs in several particulars from that published at the end of Murdin's State Papers, and contains many entries not there given. From the word* "ENTRED," *it may be inferred that this is one portion of a draft diary from which Burghley subsequently formed the more extended one published by Murdin.*

DOMESTIC—ELIZABETH.

Vol. LXXXIII.

1571 ?

55. The requests of Sir Henry Norris, desiring license to export 500 sacks of wool yearly for five years.

56. List of English Peers.

57. Note of what parcels of land the Lady Russell is to have for her daughters, of whom she has the wardship.

58. Randell Starkey and George Kightley, freemen of London, to Lord Burghley. Complain of stay made of their goods in the Low Countries by the Duke of Alva. Pray that he will procure redress for the injury they have sustained.

59. Marquis of Winchester to Robert Hare. Has discharged the Treasurer of the Mint from payment of the merchants.

60. Statement of the case of certain lands forfeited by the Earl of Arundel and Lord Lumley, for a debt due to Aldermen Jackman and Lambert.

61. Notes relative to money raised by subsidies and loans, by various monarchs of the realm, from Edward IV. to the 13th of Queen Elizabeth.

62. Form of oath to be administered to freemen of the fellowship of Merchant Adventurers for discovery of lands, &c.

63. List of names of certain rebels in the late Northern rebellion, and now remaining beyond sea, with marginal notes by Burghley,

64. Order that the men of Aldborough are to pay such fines as shall be imposed on them by Sir Robt. Wingfield and Mr. Jermye, for trafficking with pirates.

65. Forms of letters of safe conduct, to John de Rosse, servant to Mr. Fr. Walsyngham, for France ; to Alex. Stevenson, for Scotland ; to M. de Nivelt, and others, for Germany.

66. An elaborate table or description of the foundation of the University of Cambridge, and of the benefactors thereof, from the earliest period to the year 1571.

67. Short rules or maxims of law, indorsed by Burghley " D. of Norfolk," probably for use at the time of the Duke's trial.

68. Certain articles by the Merchants of the Stillyard, shewing the impossibility of bringing in of bow staves, according to the provisions of the Act of 13 Eliz.

Vol. LXXXIV. 1571.

1571.
Dec.

1, Certificate of the names and sirnames of all the strangers, as well denizens, as others, dwelling in St. Catherine's, Shoreditch, Finsbury, Grub-street, St. Giles's in the Fields, and other Hamlets near London, in the County of Middlesex, taken the 20th of December, Anno Reg. Eliz· 14° 1571.

1571.
Dec.

Vol. LXXXIV.

2. Certificate made by the Lord Mayor (?) to the Council, of all the strangers that are presently abiding in London, and the liberties and suburbs of the same, distinguishing the wards and parishes in which they reside, their trades, number in families, &c. [*Very similar but not identical with Vol. lxxxii.*]

Vol. LXXXV. January—March, 1572.

1572.

Jan. 7.
Gresham House.
1. Sir Tho. Gresham to Lord Burghley. Detention of some bonds and letters at the City of Arcke, in Flanders. Requests the removal of Lady Mary Grey, for the quietness of his poor wife.

Jan. 8.
Great St. Bartholomew.
2. Chief Justice Catelyn to same. Respecting the controversy between the jurisdictions of the Courts of King's Bench and Exchequer.

Jan. 8.
3. Copy of the above; with a state of the case of Calverley *v.* Clowtier in the King's Bench.

Jan. 12.
The Tower.
4. Sir Owyn Hopton to the Earl of Leicester and Lord Burghley. Particulars of the access of certain persons to the Duke of Norfolk in the Tower, and of the attempts to convey letters to him. Particulars of other prisoners.

Jan. 12.
5. Suggestions for a Commission, and opinions as to the mode of proceeding for the sale of Spanish goods and shipping arrested in England.

Jan. 15.
6. Interrogatories by Burghley for the examination of Wm. Barker's man as to his communications with the Duke of Norfolk.

[Jan. 15.]
7. Examination of William Davy, servant of Wm. Barker, in answer to the above.

Jan. 16.
Tarrowe near Norwich.
8. Raphe Shelton, Sheriff of Norfolk, to the Council. In answer to their letters of the 5th of January, touching certain condemned prisoners and the treatment they receive.

Jan. 16.
9. Minutes of evidence in the hand of the Attorney-General Gerrard, to be brought forward against the Duke of Norfolk at his trial, from various examinations.

Jan. 16.
10. Relation of the principal charges against the Duke of Norfolk as to his connexion with the Queen of Scots; his opinion with others of her intercourse and correspondence with Bothwell, as detailed in a letter from them to Queen Elizabeth, from York, 11 October 1568.

Jan. 17.
11. Relation, in Burghley's hand, of "The ordre in tyme how the " matters have proceded to come to the knolledg of the attemptes " wherewith the Duke of Norfolk hath bene charged, before he was " indyted of treason."

Jan. 17.
12. Relation of the arraignment and condemnation of the Duke of Norfolk, written the day after his trial.

Vol. LXXXV.

1572.
Jan. 17.
The Tower.
13. Harie Skypwith to Lord Burghley. Conveys to him the last request of the Duke of Norfolk, that he might be allowed to speak with Dix and Hassat, as to his debts; and also to be attended by Mr. Fox, his old schoolmaster.

Jan. 19.
The Tower.
14. Same to same. The Dean of St. Paul's (Nowell) and Mr. Fox have visited the Duke, who also requests that Mr. Dearing and Mr. Samson might come to him.

Jan. 19.
Great St. Bartholomew.
15. Chief Justice Catelyn to same. Further detail as to the jurisdiction of the King's Bench and the Exchequer. Disparaging speeches among the prisoners in the Bench against Leicester and Burghley since Norfolk's condemnation.

Jan. 19.
The Tower.
16. Sir Owyn Hopton to same. Notifies that the Duke is determined to speak very evil of the Bishop of Ross and Barker. Doubts if the ghostly counsel of the Dean of Paul's and Mr. Fox may win him from that uncharitable course.

Jan. 20.
The Tower.
17. Skypwith to same. Since the visit of Mr. Samson, the Duke has refused to be confronted with Mr. Barker. Requests to know if Dix and Hassat are to be admitted.

Jan. 20.
18. Confession of Geo. Fypson relative to Norfolk's accusation of Burghley, charging him with having sent 100,000*l.* to France without warrant; and scene between the Queen and Burghley in the Council Chamber.

Jan. 20.
19. Confession of John Guye to the same effect; with a further confession on the 28th of January.

Jan. 20.
20. Examination of Roger Water respecting the words spoken by George Fypson against Burghley and Leicester on the night that the Duke of Norfolk was condemned.

Jan. 22.
21. Examination of Tho. Stanbrydge relative to the accusation of Burghley by the Duke of Norfolk and the scene in the Council Chamber.

Jan. 22.
22. Examination of James Clunne, to the same effect.

Jan. 22.
Audley End.
23. Henry Phillips to Burghley. Has completed the inventory of all the Duke's goods at Audley End. Requests a supply of money for their expenses.

Jan. 22.
Portsmouth.
24. Edward Horsey to same. Reports to him the capture of a Spanish ship by Captain Skonewall. Has had an interview with the Master, and sends up the letters and books found in the said ship.

Jan. 23.
Tower.
25. Harie Skypwith to the Earl of Leicester and Lord Burghley. The Duke is greatly troubled with the speeches of Her Majesty, and is determined to write another letter to her. Asks permission to bring the said letter himself.

Jan. 23.
26. Examination of William Barker, taken by Sir Fr. Knollys, Sir Walter Mildmay, and Tho. Wylson, relative to transactions between the Bishop of Ross and the Duke of Norfolk.

DOMESTIC—ELIZABETH. 435

Vol. LXXXV.

1572.
Jan. 27.
Canterbury.
27. Richard Beseley to Lord Burghley. Notifies information by one Alexander, Curate of Chartham, that Dr. Gyfford had lately arrived from Rome, and reported that the plans of the Duke of Norfolk had long been known there. Advises Burghley not to take any physic of Dr. Gyfford lest he might be "*Italionated.*"

Jan. 29.
Cawood.
28. Archbishop Edmund Grindall to same. Gives his opinion as to the practice of advowsons, particularly in the case of Mr. Webster. Mr. Roo, his chaplain, had been presented and instituted to the prebend before Burghley's letter in favour of Webster arrived. Answer as to Broxbourne parsonage granted in reversion to Sir George Penruddock. Desires him to look to his own preservation against "*obdurate papistes and Italionate atheistes.*"

Jan.
29. Names of merchants and others proposed to be nominated in the Commission for sale of goods and merchandize arrested in England.

Jan. 31.
30. Commission to Sir Tho. Gresham, Sir Rowland Haywarde, and others, for the sale of goods and merchandize belonging to subjects of the King of Spain arrested in England. Lat.

Jan. ?
31. Instructions by the Queen to Lord Treasurer Winchester and others, a Committee of Privy Council, to superintend the execution of all affairs connected with the arrest of the Spanish subjects and goods in England, and for the prohibition of traffick with Spain.

Jan.
32. Names of certain Merchants Strangers "*that demaunded letters.*"

Jan.
33. Information by Mr. Rooksby as to the intercourse of the Earls of Northumberland and Westmoreland with the Duke of Norfolk. Particulars as to the lands of Leonard Dacre, and of property of the Duke, at Hinderskelf.

Feb. 2.
Cambridge.
34. Roger Kelk, Vice-Chancellor, and others, of Cambridge, to Burghley. Have examined John Bonyfelowe, a scholar of Cambridge. *Incloses,*

 34. I. *The Mayor, &c. of Norwich, to the Mayor and Justices of Cambridge, informing them of accusations made by one John Edeham against a scholar of Clare Hall. Norwich, 20 Jan.* 1572.

 34. II. *Examination of John Bonyfelowe, scholar of Cambridge, before the Chancellor and others, relative to slanderous words spoken of Leicester and Burghley; and that if the Duke were executed there would be a rising in Norfolk.*

Feb. [2.]
35. Commission for restoring to the subjects of the King of Spain and others, the goods and merchandize arrested in England, being their private property. Lat.

Feb. 3.
Tower.
36. Sir Owyn Hopton to the Earl of Leicester and Lord Burghley. The Duke earnestly desires that his mother, Lady Steynings, might be sent home before his execution, the sudden news of which might be the death of her.

E E 2

Vol. LXXXV.

1572.

Feb. 6.
The Tower.
37. Harie Skypwith to Lord Burghley. Sends the Duke of Norfolk's letters to Her Majesty, and he is very desirous to receive an answer before his execution. He also requests to see his lordship.

Feb 9.
38. R. Halton to same. Presentments against Wm. Birde for concealed Customs, whose practices have nearly ruined Mr. Dawbeney.

Feb. 9.
39. Oliver Dawbeney to same. Case against Mr. Birde for concealments of Customs. Informs him of his expenses. Recommends Rob. Gynes and Mr. Halton to confer with him.

Feb. 10.
40. Dawbeney, and others, to same. Detail their services, and request that he would take the case of Mr. Birde into his own hands.

Feb. 10.
41. Edmond Mathew and Richard Carmarden to same. On the same affair. Request the return of the books and minutes used on the trial.

Feb. 11.
42. Thomas Duke of Norfolk to his son Philip Howard. Takes his solemn farewell of him and the rest of his children, being written on the [presumed] morning of his execution :—" Your erthelye father " sume tyme Norfolke, now Tho. Howard." [*This pathetic letter has been written at Norfolk's dictation, and he has added in his own hand, " examynyd by my selfe." It is indorsed by Lord Burghley,* " 27 Feb. 1571, hora V^a mane. D. of Norfolk to his sõne."]

Feb. 11.
43. Copy of the above.

Feb. 15.
The Tower.
44. Harie Skypwith to Burghley. Has informed the Duke of the probability of his approaching execution. His resignation. Suggests that Mr. Dearing might be permitted to visit him.

Feb. 15.
45. Lady Kath. Mountjoy to same. Sir Humfrey Gilbert has offered to pay 500*l.* or 400*l.* a-year for her house, for the alum and copperas works.

Feb. 16.
46. Estimate of the stock remaining at the copper mines and the value thereof at Christmas last.

Feb. 17.
Dover.
47. Wm. Cryspe and Edw. Boys to the Council. Informing them that the two Boyers claimed by the Merchants of the Stillyard had received passports and everything requisite for their passage to London. A pack of canvass in the house of Mr. Rowland Myckley has been sold.

Feb. 20.
Tower.
48. Edmund Powell, prisoner in the Tower, [to Burghley ?]. Details the progress of the design made by him and Sir Henry Percy to effect the escape of the Queen of Scots. Requests to be liberated.

Feb. 20.
49. Wm. Dodington to Burghley. Respecting the Queen's right to Llandewybrevi College. Explanation as to Stanley's accompt, relative to the coinage in the Mint. Prays Burghley to assist him out of his troubles.

1572.   Vol. LXXXV.

Feb.
St. Paul's.
50. Edwyn Sandys, Bishop of London, to the Council. Has examined the foreigners taken in a search made by the Lord Mayor. Incloses,

    50. I. *Examination of several foreigners, the time of their abode in England, profession of faith, &c.*

Feb. 23.
The Tower.
51. Sir Henry Percy to the Earl of Leicester and Lord Burghley. Flies to them as his best refuge in his hard case. Declares that any fault on his part was through forgetfulness and not disloyalty. Submits himself to Her Majesty, and prays they will endeavour to obtain his liberty.

Feb. 24.
Dartmouth.
52. Sir Arthur Champernowne to Burghley. The peace in France is not likely to continue. Notifies to him that two ships were prepared off St. Malo to sail to Scotland. Events in France.

Feb. 27.
53. Oliver Dawbeney to same. Informs him of the contents of his last letters. Requests that he will signify to Mr. Fanshawe not to obstruct him in suing out a new Commission for the trial of Mr. Birde and others.

Feb. 28.
The Tower.
54. Harie Skypwith to same. The Duke of Norfolk desires permission to write to the Queen. Ill state of his health.

Feb. 28.
55. Deposition of Ro. Higford relative to certain letters Mr. Tho. Cobham had shown him in Lord Cobham's house at Black-Friars, of which he had abstracted two. Observation thereon by Francis Bertie.

Feb. 29.
Burghley House
56. Thomas Cecill to his father Lord Burghley. Informs him of the birth of his third son, on the 29th of Feb. He wishes the Earl of Rutland and the Bishop of Peterborough may be his godfathers.

Feb. 29.
57. Commission to George Wynter, John Hawkins, and others, for the clearing the British seas of pirates and freebooters.

Feb. 29.
58. List of names, probably of the Commissioners in the preceding.

Feb.
59. Letters of notification to all Vice Admirals, Justices of the Peace, &c., of the appointment of John Haydon, Geo. Saunders, and Geo. Southerton, as Deputy Commissioners, for the custody and sale of Spanish goods and merchandize in the Counties of Dorset, Devon, and Cornwall.

Feb.
60. Notes in Burghley's hand respecting the woollen trade and manufacture of England.

Feb.
The Tower.
61. Petition of Brian Lassells, attested by Sir Owyn Hopton, to Council. Prays for the Queen's mercy that he may be released from the Tower. Details his transactions in the affairs of the Queen of Scots and the Duke of Norfolk.

Mar. 1.
62. Deposition by Ro. Higford, relative to his communications with Tho. Cobham; and his conference with Lord Cobham to stand surety for him for a loan of 40*l.* negociated by Mr. Good.

1572.

Vol. LXXXV.

Mar. 1. 63. Johan Lover to Lord Burghley. Progress of the copper mines. Great delay caused by the contentious dealing of some of the Company. Is ready to submit his accounts to be examined when Burghley thinks fit.

Mar. 4. 64. Notes of evidence against Lord Montague, concerned in the intended marriage between the Duke of Norfolk and Queen of Scots.

Mar. 5.
Mayfield. 65. Sir Tho. Gresham to Burghley. Prays him to remember his request for removal of Lady Mary Grey. State of the Queen's debts in Flanders. Has sent home Derrick, the surgeon, who had brought his leg to some good pass.

Mar. 6. 66. Robert Hogan to same. Information of one Digby, Stukeley's man, who was most privy of his master's doings relative to Ireland. The Duke of Alva is preparing many ships in Flanders.

Mar. 11. 67. Christopher Baker to [the Council?]. Complains of the great waste of oak timber in the County of Sussex fit for the building of ships. List of the names of woodbrokers in Sussex.

Mar. 12. 68. Giles Lambarde to Burghley Proposals for farming all foreign oils and soap made or imported into England.

Mar. 12. 69. Comparative estimates of the expenses of six, four, or ten ships, and the three galleys.

Mar. 13.
York. 70. Tho. Fayrfax to Burghley. Explains the doings of his servants in removing the goods from Hinderskelf Castle; the surmises against them are utterly false. His proceedings in taking inventories there. *Incloses,*

> 70. I. *Inventory of all the goods and implements remaining in Hinderskelf Castle, belonging to the Duke of Norfolk, taken by Tho. Fayrfax, Sheriff of Yorkshire.* 27 *Jan.* 1572.
>
> 70. II. *John Blenerhayset to Tho. Fayrfax. Demanding that the goods taken from Hinderskelf Castle, during the absence of Richard Longley, keeper of the said Castle, should be immediately restored. London,* 22 *Feb.* 1572.

Mar. 15. 71. Account of the supply of ordnance, munition, and other necessaries for the full furniture of twenty-three ships and galleys appointed to the seas, with an estimate of what will remain after their equipment.

Mar. 16. 72. John Lonyson to Burghley. Desires he may enjoy the farming of the Mint according to his grant thereof. *Incloses,*

> 72. I. *Note of the last offer of Mr. Martin relative to the farming of the Mint.*

Mar. 20. 73. Alexander Nowell, Dean of St. Paul's, to same. The Duke of Norfolk is in want of certain necessary apparel. Ill state of the Duke's health, who now seems weary of his unhappy life.

Vol. LXXXV.

1572.

Mar. 23.
Dartington.
74. Sir Arthur Champernowne to Lord Burghley. Notifies many ships are preparing in Brest, St. Malo, and other ports on the French coast. The force he has is too small to encounter them.

Mar. 24.
75. Edward Dering to same. Requests that Thomas Cartwright might be permitted to return to England. Proposes that on the departure of [Anthony Rodolph] Cevallerius Cartwright should be appointed to fill his place as Hebrew Professor in the University of Cambridge. Lat.

Mar. 25.
76. Caspar Vosberghius to same. Urges him to solicit the Queen for a grant of certain privileges to the Church at Stamford. Lat.

Mar. 26.
Oxford.
77. George Lord Audley to same. Apologizes for not having hitherto written to him. Has feared to intrude on his important cares and occupations. Lat. [*This is clearly dated March* 26, 1571, *which, from the indorsement, appears to be an error for* 1572.].

Mar. 28.
78. Offer of John Lonyson to farm the working of the Mint, giving for every pound weight of gold, 2s. 6d., and 9d. for every pound weight of silver.

[Mar. 28.]
79. Note of what the Farmer of the Mint is to gain yearly paying the Queen 12d. on every pound weight of silver coined. [*Indorsed by Burghley,* "*First offer.*"]

[Mar. 28.]
80. Offer for farming the Mint, on the same principle as in the 32nd Henry VIII. [*Indorsed,* "*The offer of* 9d—*Lañison's last offer.*"]

[Mar. 28.]
81. Proposal that the Queen should for one or two years make trial of the offer for farming the Mint. [*Indorsed,* "*The laste offer—Lañyson,* 2s. *upon gold,* 9d. *uppon silver.*"]

Mar.
Grant to John Marquis of Winchester of the keeping of St. Andrew's Castle, upon the sea coast at Hamble, co. Southampton, for life, from the death of William the late Marquis. Lat. [*See Warrant Book*, I., p. 169.]

Vol. LXXXVI. April—May, 1572.

April 1.
1. William Herlle to Burghley. The examination of Mr. Chillester on the interrogatories. Chillester is a dangerous fellow, but from whom much information might be gained if skilfully handled.

April 4.
Tower.
2. Henry Wriothesley Earl of Southampton to same. Hopes that through his favour he may be able to obtain the Queen's good will. Denies the charges of misconduct during his imprisonment. Requests to be restored shortly to his liberty and Her Majesty's favour.

April 10.
3. Dean Alex. Nowell to same. Desires authority (to be antedated) for having administered the Communion to the Duke of Norfolk, at Easter last. Requests to know if to-morrow is appointed for his execution.

VOL. LXXXVI.

1572.
April 10.   4. John Welshe, "pauperrimus," to Lord Burghley. Prays for his interest to be admitted a scholar in Trinity College, Camb. Lat.

April 10.
[4° Id. Apr.]   5. Caspar Vosberghius to same. Articles for the regulation and endowment of the German Church at Stamford. Lat.

April 10.
Tower.   6. Harie Skypwith to same. Rumour of the Duke of Norfolk's sudden execution. Desires to know if he is to deliver up his charge without sufficient warrant.

April 10.
Dartmouth.   7. James Pilleton to same. Informs him of the proceedings of the Lord Fleming of Ireland, and of the preparations by him and others in the ports of France.

April 14.
Barbican.   8. Richard Bertie to same. Sends a collection of court-rolls and other papers relative to the Barony of Willoughby, which he claims in right of his wife.

April 15.
Reigate.   9. Henry Weston, and others, to the Council. Proceedings in the arrest and punishment of vagabonds. *Incloses*,

     9. I. *Certificate by Henry Weston and William More of the names of rogues and vagabonds stocked and whipped in several Hundreds in the County of Surrey.*

     9. II. *Similar certificates by J. Skynner for the Hundreds of Tandridge and Reigate, same county.*

April 15.   10. Dean A. Nowell to Burghley. The Duke desires that he might receive a previous warning of his execution. His ill state of health.

April 18.
The Tower.   11. Harie Skywith to same. Informs him of the fast declining state of the Duke of Norfolk's health occasioned by his close imprisonment and want of exercise.

April 18.   12. Justices of the Holland Division, co. Lincoln, to the Council. Have kept strict search for all rogues and vagabonds and such as eat meat on fast-days; and intend monthly to observe the same.

April 18.
[14 Cal. Maij.]
Cambridge.   13. Trinity College, Cambridge, to the Queen. Relative to the suit of Mr. John Manners for the parsonage of Barrington. Lat.

April 19.   14. William Meadley to Burghley. Detail of transactions between himself, Sir Tho. Smith, Sir Humfrey Gilbert, and Lady Mountjoy, relative to establishing copperas, copper, and alum works, and for transmuting iron into copper with vitriol.

April 19.   15. Indenture between Queen Elizabeth and John Lonyson on his appointment to the office of Master Worker of the Mint; with observations on the effect of the articles of the same.

April 19   16. Sir Richard Wenman to Sir Francis Knollys. Himself and the Justices of Oxfordshire have acted according to the directions they have received from the Privy Council. *Incloses*,

     16. I.—16. XV. *Fifteen Certificates from all the Hundreds in the County of Oxford, of the apprehension and punishment of rogues and vagabonds.*

Vol. LXXXVI.

1572.
April 20.
12 Cal. Maij.
Cambridge.
17. Dr. Whitgyfte, Master, and the Seniors of Trinity College, to Lord Burghley. Relative to Mr. Manners' suit about the Rectory of Barrington. Lat.

April 21.
Cockermouth.
18. George Lamplughe to the Earl of Leicester and Lord Burghley. Intelligence of a foreign ship seen off the coast, supposed to be a pirate, or a ship from France to give intelligence to the friends of the Earls of Northumberland and Westmoreland and the Dacres. Explains his taking an inventory of certain goods belonging to the Duke of Norfolk.

[April 22.
London.
19. Sir Gilb. Gerrard and Tho. Bromley, the Att. and Sol. General, to Burghley. Opinion of the Judges touching Mr. Bertie's claim to the Barony of Willoughby in right of his wife.

April 23.
20. Dr. Whitgyfte to same. Acquaints him that there is no statute directing the service to be sung in Trinity College, Cambridge. No one can prove any crime against him either in doctrine or conversation.

April 23.
21. Justices of Middlesex for the Hundred of Ossulton to the Council. Have appointed searchers to detect all persons eating or dressing flesh on fast-days, and have arrested and punished a number of rogues and vagabonds.

April 23.
Althorp.
22. John Spencer, Sheriff of Northampton, to same. Order taken by the Justices for the prevention of eating flesh at times forbidden. Search for vagabonds and rogues. *Incloses,*

    22. I. *Certificate by John Osberne of vagabonds, rogues, and sturdy beggars taken and punished within the Hundred of Rothwell, co. Northampton. 27 March.*

    22. II. *Similar certificate by Wm. Lord Vaux of Harrowden and Sir Edw. Mountagu for several Hundreds in the East part of the same county. 28 March.*

    22. III. *Similar certificate by Tho. Spencer for Hundreds in the West part of the same county. 28 March.*

April 24.
Gloucester.
23. Richard Pate to Burghley. Complains of sinister means used to prevent him in his election for Parliament, being Recorder of the City.

April 26.
Gresham House.
24. Sir Tho. Gresham to same. Requests Mr. Serjeant Manwood may not be appointed Judge, as there were others of more ancient standing. Urges the removal of Lady Mary Grey, seeing that Mr. Stokes is now married.

April 26.
Lambeth.
25. Lord Henry Howard to same. Laments the renewed strictness of his imprisonment. Prays Burghley to obtain permission from the Queen that he may be restored to liberty. Would rather have an open imprisonment in the Fleet than the close keeping in the Archbishop's Palace.

April 28.
Blanford Forum.
26. James Lord Mountjoy to Leicester and Burghley. Progress in the alum works. Wishes to know their pleasure as to the house his wife and children have an interest in.

1572.

VOL. LXXXVI.

April 28.
Aylesbury.
27. The Justices of Buckingham to the Council. Have strictly obeyed their orders for the observance of fast-days. *Inclosing,*

    27. I. *Certificate of rogues and vagabonds taken and punished within the three Hundreds of Cotteslowe, County of Buckingham.*

    27. II. *Similar certificate for the three Hundreds of Aylesbury, same county.*

April 30. 28. Justices of Middlesex to same. Have strictly enforced their orders against eating meat on fast-days, and have punished various rogues and vagabonds lately taken.

April 30.
Prid.Cal.Maias.
Cambridge.
29. The Vice-Chancellor and Senate of Cambridge to Lord Burghley. Praying his support and interference to prevent further encroachments on their privileges by the Town of Cambridge.

April. 30. Sir Thos. Stanley to same. Requests his influence with the Queen to mitigate the rigour of his imprisonment.

May 1.
The Tower.
31. Harie Skypwith to same. The Duke of Norfolk greatly laments his former doings, and is very desirous to manifest his love and regard to Her Majesty. His ill health.

May 2.
The Rolls.
32. Sir Wm. Cordell, Master of the Rolls, to same. Relative to precedents in creating a peer of the realm, and the calling of barons by writ.

May 2.
At Court.
33. Lady Mary Sydney to same. Requests him to use his endeavours that her husband may not be raised to the peerage, in consideration of their inability to maintain a higher title than they now possess.

May 3.
Westminster.
34. Sir Gilb. Gerrard to same. Sends the book for Bertie, who is to bear the title and name of Baron (of Willoughby) only during life. Sends also interrogatories for examination of the Bishop of Ross and others.

May 4.
Greenwich.
35. Creation of Walter Earl of Essex and Edward Earl of Lincoln. Description of the ceremony and expenses attendant on the same. [*Signed, Wm. Penson, Lancaster.*]

May 14. 36. Wm. Herlle to Burghley. Has fallen into a very distressed condition by his zeal in Her Majesty's service. Solicits some assistance in money matters.

May 16. 37. Richard Bertie to same. The Queen is pleased his cause shall be heard. Hopes he will be one of the Judges in his claim to the title of Willoughby.

May (17). 38. Bill for Assurance of Bargains, Sales, and Conveyances of Lands to be made without covin.

May 17. 39. Instructions touching the Bill of secret Conveyances, Bargains and Sales to be made without covin.

DOMESTIC—ELIZABETH. 443

1572.   Vol. LXXXVI.

May 17? 40. Bill for the making of oils in England. Confirming the Queen's letters patent granting certain privileges to the inventors of the making of oil out of seeds grown in England equal to the Spanish and foreign oils.

May 17? 41. Petition of Giles Lambarde to the Queen and Parliament, for a grant of certain imposts on every broad-cloth for the term of 30 years, on condition that the foreign oil shall be sold in London at a reduced price.

May 18. 42. Wm. Herlle to Sec. Lord Burghley. Complains of malice, continued ill usage, and injuries offered to him by John Smith, on account of his services to Her Majesty.

May 19. 43. Sir Richard Fenys to same. Relative to a bill proposed by him for the punishment of Robberies committed in Colleges. Explains the circumstances under which the bill was drawn.

May 19. 44. Wm. Meadley to same. Has long expected the ending of the copper matters, but has been encountered by Mr. Gilbert's malice and foul charges. Has at last found a favourable ground yielding plenty of ore. Now is the time for transmutation by the ripening of the earths. Desires his own name to be inserted in the patent.

May 20. 45. Bill for Rites and Ceremonies of the Church, authorizing Ministers to make Alterations in the Prayers and administration of Sacraments, consistent with the Doctrines of the Reformed Church. [*Indorsed* " *Vacat quia nova.*" *The Bill for Rites and Ceremonies was read a third time and committed 20 May.*]

46. Copy of the above.

May 20. 47. Robert Bell, Speaker, to Burghley. States the progress of the
Middle Temple. bill for giving power to Bishops to permit any authorized preacher to use Rites and Ceremonies in the Church, otherwise than as prescribed by the Book of Common Prayer.

May 21. 48. Bill (" Nova ") for permitting alterations in the Celebration of Divine Service, so far as the same are in accordance with the Act for Uniformity of Common Prayer. [" *The first readings.*"]

May 24. 49. Lady Mary Grey to Burghley. Deplores her miserable and
Gresham wretched case, destitute of means to support herself. Solicits him to
House. procure from the Queen some augmentation to her income.

May 25. 50. Dr. Stephen Nevison to Burghley. Advocates the policy of
London. not showing mercy to those who are disaffected towards Queen Elizabeth. Lat.

May 26. 51. Dr. Lawrence Humfrey to the Earl of Leicester and Lord Burghley. Measures necessary to be taken for preserving the ancient privileges of the Universities.

May 27. 52. Original report and resolution of the Committee of the House of Commons for hearing the Cause between Alford and Greville, as to the fraudulent conveyance made by Wm. Porter to Edm. Porter, of the Manor of Ashton Underedge, and sale of the same to Francis Alford.

DOMESTIC—ELIZABETH.

Vol. LXXXVI.

1572.

May 28. 53. Notes and observations by Dr. Humfrey on the bills in Parliament concerning the Universities.

May 29.
Dover.
54. Henry Middelmore to Lord Burghley. Requests him to take into consideration his claim to the lease of certain lands at Windsor granted to him by letters patent. The Prebends of Windsor now seek for a new grant in confirmation of the same lands to them.

May 31.
Tower.
55. Harie Skypwith to Burghley. Has warned the Duke of Norfolk to prepare for death. The Duke was very desirous to see the Dean of St. Paul's, that he might end his days with him.

May. 56. State, by Sir Tho. Gresham, of all the Queen's debts due in London and Flanders.

May. 57. The Regents and Non-Regents of Cambridge (167 signatures) to Burghley. Soliciting the exercise of his powerful influence for the continuance of their ancient statutes and privileges. Lat.

May. 58. Reasons for matters offered in Parliament as to safety of the realm, settlement of the succession, &c.

May? 59. Certain objections why George Gascoigne, (the poet), ought not to be admitted to be a burgess of the Parliament,—a common rhymer, a notorious ruffian, an atheist, and a godless person.

May. 60. Petition of the merchants, owners, and mariners of England to the House of Lords tendering objections to the bill against ingrossing of spices. *Incloses,*

    60. I. *Objections on the behalf of the merchants, &c., against the bill agreed upon in the Lower House, prohibiting the ingrossing of sugars, spices, fruit, oils, and other kinds of merchandise.*

May? 61. Instructions from the Committee of Council to the Commissioners for the sale of ships' goods arrested in England belonging to subjects of the King of Spain. General directions for their proceedings in the sale of the goods and distribution of the proceeds. Signed by Burghley, Lyncoln, Sussex, and Leycester.

May? 62. Contents of the bill exhibited for the maintenance of the Cob of Lyme Regis, with answer of the Merchants of the Country to the same.

Vol. LXXXVII. May, 1572.

[?] 1. Map of the Isle of Sheppey, containing a general view of the whole island, with a particular reference to Lord Cheyne's possessions.

May. 2. Survey of the manors, lordships, lands, tenements, advowsons, &c., belonging to Sir Henry Cheyne, Lord Cheyne of Tuddington, situate and being in the Isle of Sheppey, in the County of Kent; and of all manner of franchises, liberties, and royalties to the same belonging. 15 May 1572.

Vol. LXXXVII.

1572. 3. Survey of the Manors of Minster and Shurland, in the Isle of Sheppey, belonging to Henry Lord Cheyne of Todyngton, co. Kent, taken by virtue of a Commission under the Exchequer Seal, directed to Wm. Homberston and Thomas Fludd. Dated 27 Nov. 1573.

Vol. LXXXVIII. June—October, 1572.

June 1.
Lambeth.
1. Archbishop Parker to Lord Burghley. Returns the discourse of Cambridge, and thinks their demands have a captious spirit.

June [1.]
Westminster.
Commission appointing the Earl of Leicester to be Lieutenant for Her Majesty in her absence at St. George's Feast, to be solemnized at Windsor Castle, on the   of June. [See Warrant Book, No. 1., p. 5.]

June [1.]
Westminster.
Commission to the Earl of Leicester, directing him to accept and admit the "Duke of Memorancye," the Earl of Essex, Lord Burghley, Lord Grey of Wilton, and Lord Chandos, to be Knights of the Order of the Garter, to take their oaths, and to install them accordingly. [See ib., p. 6.]

June [1.]
Dispensation for the Earls of Arundel, Derby, and Lincoln, Lord Howard of Effingham, the Earl of Sussex, Viscount Montague, the Earls of Shrewsbury and Warwick, and Lord Hunsdon, to be absent from the Feast of the glorious Martyr St. George about to be holden at Windsor Castle. [See ib., p. 6.]

June 1.
2. Harie Skypwith to Burghley. Resigned state of the Duke of Norfolk's mind. The Dean of St. Paul's attended him last night, and the Lieutenant of the Tower has warned him to prepare for death on Monday.

June 2.
3. Sir Owyn Hopton to the Earl of Leicester and Lord Burghley. Desires directions as to the burial of the Duke, "*whose dead corse remayneth in the churche here unburyed.*"

June 2.
4. Dr. Christopher Langton to Burghley. Compliments him. His pension from Lord Monteagle. Lat.

June 2.
Westminster.
5. Archbishop Grindall to same. Has, with other Bishops, been with the Queen to move her that the Bill for coming to Divine Service might, by her assent, be propounded.

June 3.
6. Dr. Whitgyfte and others, Heads of Houses of Cambridge, to same. Requests that those who object to the Statutes given by Her Majesty to the University may be severely punished.

June 4.
7. Ralph Lane to same. Proposes a plan for keeping soldiers in readiness for an expedition to the East.

June 4.
[Prid. Non. Jun.]
Cambridge.
8. The Proctors, and others, of Cambridge, to same. Return thanks to him for his care and attention to their affairs. Lat.

1572.
June 5.

Vol. LXXXVIII.

9. Dr. Whitgyfte, Master of Trinity, to Lord Burghley.. In commendation of the Statutes given by Elizabeth to the University of Cambridge. Requests that he will not make any alterations in them; they have not been objected to by the Heads of Colleges. *Incloses,*

    9. I. *The Vice Chancellor and Heads of Houses to Whitgyfte, expressive of their approbation of the recent Statutes.* 3 *June* 1573.

June 5.
[Non. Jun.]
London.

10. Dr. William Maister, Chancellor of Norwich, to same. Requests the Queen's permission that he may be allowed to enjoy the living of some rectory or prebend for three or four years. Lat.

June 6.

11. Edmond Mathew to same. Requests to be authorized to put in force the Act 5 Eliz. cap. 4 & 5, for Regulation of Artificers, &c. *Incloses,*

    11. I. *The effect of certain branches of the Statute for Artificers and Labourers; and suit for a grant to Ric. Carmarden and Edm. Mathew to carry the same into effect.*

June 10.
Cambridge.

12. John Becon, Arthur Purefay, Proctors, and others, of the University, to same. Proposing a stay of the ordinary Election of Readers for the next year.

June 10.

13. Dr. Whitgyfte, and some of the Heads of Houses at Cambridge, to same. Complaining of the conduct of the Proctors.

June 11?

14. An Act to provide remedy against fraudulent means used to defeat Wardships, Liveries, and Premier Seizins.

June 11.

15. Another copy.

June 11.

16. The effect of the bill in Parliament for the Court of Wards touching Leases and Commissions. Leases above 99 years to be void against Her Majesty. Objections against the bill.

June 12.

17. Lawrence Johnson to Burghley. Requests payment of money due to him, and that he may be continued in the service of the Mint.

June 16.
Walden.

18. Philip Howard Earl of Surrey to same. Laments the death of his father (Duke of Norfolk). Requests Burghley will take him and the rest of the unfortunate Duke's family under his protection; and that he will solicit the Queen in their favour. Lat.

June 16.
[16° Cal. Quintil.]

19. Geo. Lawghton (preceptor of the late Duke of Norfolk's children,) to same. Informs him of the progress the children have made under his care. Lat.

June 17.

20. Description of the ceremony of the installation of Francis Duke of Montmorency, Walter Earl of Essex, William Lord Burghley, Arthur Lord Grey of Wilton, and Edmund Lord Chandos, as Knights of the Garter, at Windsor, June 17, with copy of the bill of expenses for hatchments and rewards. By Wm. Penson, Lancaster Herald.

June 21.

21. Thomas Lever to Burghley. Evils attendant on the present management of leases of impropriate benefices and hospitals. Proposed remedies for the same.

	VOL. LXXXVIII.
1572. June 20 ?	22. Tract intituled, "IPSWICH out of ENGLAND, or ANTWERP in "ENGLAND;" being an argument addressed to the Council, by John Johnson and Christopher Goodwyn proposing the establishment of a Mart Town in England, viz., Ipswich, in the County of Suffolk, and so to draw the whole trade there from Antwerp.
June 21. Westminster.	23. John Johnson to Lord Burghley. Mr. Marshe has not answered the device for the establishment of a Mart Town in England. Suggests the incorporation of a new Company of Merchants to enjoy such rights as are possessed by the Merchants Adventurers.
June 23. London.	24. The Wardens and Company of Dyers of London to same. Observations on Mr. Hastings' plan for the dyeing of all cloths and manufactures in England, with curious particulars of the art and mystery of dyeing.
June 24.	25. Schedule of Bills in various stages of progress in both Houses of Parliament.
June 25.	26. Schedules of Acts passed the Lower House and still remaining in the Upper House, and of Acts remaining in the Lower House.
June 25.	27. Schedule of Acts passed in both Houses to the 25th of June.
June 25. St. John's.	28. John Becon (*signed* Beacon), Proctor of Cambridge, to Burghley. In answer to his letters as to Lord North's son, and as to the stay of the election of Lecturers. Explains the usual course as to the latter.
June 26. Milk Street.	29. Robert Hogan to the Earl of Leicester. Is ready to perform any service that may be in his power. Treasonable dealings in Spain of Maurice, Archbishop of Cashel, now prisoner in Scotland. Spanish league with Denmark and Sweden. Solicits a lease of part of Sir Francis Englefyld's lands.
June 28. [4 Cal. Ju.] St. John's.	30. John Becon, Proctor, to Burghley. Desires his favourable acceptance of his communications about the Elections. Lord North's son has been made Senior Master of Arts. Lat.
June 29.	31. Bill for Assurance of Lands, &c., to certain hospitals in London.
June.	32. Minutes of information in the Court of King's Bench against Mr. Birde.
June.	33. Note of parcels of Customs contained in the information in the King's Bench, supposed to be concealed by Wm. Birde.
June.	34. Articles for an Act in Parliament, touching Impropriations, and for saving the Right of Patrons to Presentations.
June.	35. Act for revival of the Statute of 2 Ric. II., prohibiting retailing of linen cloth, &c., by strangers in London, or other cities and towns corporate.
June ?	36. An Act prohibiting strangers born to sell by way of retail foreign wares brought into the realm.
June ?	37. Proviso to be added to the "Act relating to the Succession of "the Crown."

VOL. LXXXVIII.

1572.
June ?   38. John Johnson and Chr. Goodwyn to Sir Tho. Smith, Secretary of State. In support of their device for erecting Ipswich into a Mart Town, which will be found necessary, profitable, and good for the whole state of the realm.

June ?   39. Observations by John Johnson, in reply to the doubts raised that the erection of a Mart Town would be the cause of rebellion in England.

June ?   40. Further reasons offered by Johnson to prove the commodity of erecting the Mart Town at Ipswich, which would not interfere with, but rather increase, the prosperity of London.

June ?   41. A discourse by John Johnson, touching losses sustained by English Merchants, of the contention with Strangers for privileges and liberties, and how both may be remedied; viz., by the establishment of Mart Towns in England.

June ?   42. Statement by the Merchants Adventurers of the advantages to England of adhering to the ancient Mart Towns abroad, and the danger that would result in straggling from them.

June ?   43. Description of necessary Magistrates to be appointed for the Mart Town to be established at Ipswich, for the government of the same; of which John Johnson solicits certain offices to be granted to himself.

June ?   44. Order for regulation of the merchants that shall trade to the Mart Town to be kept in England.

             45. Statement of advantages to be obtained by the establishment of a Mart Town in England. [*In the handwriting of Lawrence Tomson.*]

June ?   46. " A peece of a discourse for the establishing of a Mart in " England." [*In L. Tomson's hand. A fragment, giving a historical description of the Mart Towns in Flanders, and the benefit to arise by the establishment of the same in England.*]

June ?   47. Statement of Mr. Hoddosdon's reasons against Johnson's device for the erecting of a Mart in England; and suggesting that, if so erected, London would be preferable to Ipswich.

June ?   48. Proposition by John Johnson, for the appointment of an officer to prevent the exportation of all commodities prohibited by law.

June ?   49. Another proposition by John Johnson, for the appointment of an officer to inspect and survey all goods exported by licence.

July 2.   50. Earl of Leicester to Lord Burghley. He is told to hold out to the last, but must soon be in attendance for the Progress. They are altogether hunters, and do nothing but ride about from bush to bush, with a crossbow in their necks. Wishes to hear any news.

July 14.
Gorhambury   51. Grant by the Queen to Thomas West of the manors, lands, tenements, &c., in Wappingthorne, Tottington, Worwood, East Grinsted, West Grinsted, &c., in co. Sussex, late in the occupation of John Leedes, now a fugitive beyond sea.

DOMESTIC—ELIZABETH.

1572.

Vol. LXXXVIII.

July 27.
Andover.
52. John Jefferey to the Council. Death of Mr. Justice Weston. Has explained to the gentlemen of the country the true intention of the statute regulating the transportation of grain. *Incloses,*

    52. I.—IV. *Four certificates of the quantity and price of grain in the Counties of Dorset, Somerset, Devon, and Cornwall.*

July ?
53. Suit of the City of London for restraint of the exportation of grain, particularly from the Port of Lynn. [*A proclamation was issued on the 16th Sept.* 1572, *"for restraint of transportation of "grain beyond the seas."*]

Vol. LXXXIX. August—October, 1572.

August 1.
1. Chief Justice Catelyn and Sir G. Gerrard to the Council. Have conferred with the Justices of Norfolk and Suffolk as to the supply of grain in those counties. Recommend prohibition of exportation of grain. *Inclosing,*

    1. I. II. *Two certificates of the quantity and price of grain in the Counties of Norfolk and Suffolk.*

August 5.
Gorhambury.
2. Grant by the Queen to William Lord Howard of Effingham, of the office of Keeper of the Privy Seal. Lat.

August 10.
Edgcote.
3. Lord Burghley to the Earl of Leicester. Has returned to the Court, and found the French Ambassador there. Are drawing on towards Warwick and Kenilworth. News of the Court. Mr. Pyckman has been sent to confer with Sir H. Gilbert how the French might be prevented from taking Flushing. Foreign news. The Queen's intended gift to Sir H. Lee. Irish news. The Queen of Scots is very desirous to come to Kenilworth.

Sept. 1.
Saint Mary's College.
4. Thomas White and others of St. Mary's College, Winchester, to Lord Burghley. Refers to his decision the application of Humfrey Wickam, for admission of his son into that college, as of founder's kin. Controversy between Sir Ric. Fynes and the said Humfrey Wickam.

Sept. 1.
5. Reasons and proofs alledged by Humfrey Wickam before the apposers and electioners in the College of Winton, to confirm his alliance to William Wickham, founder of the said College.

Sept. 4.
6. Christopher Gregory's oration in Magdalen College, Oxford, on the arrival of the Earl of Leicester, Chancellor of the University, and Lord Treasurer Burghley. Lat.

Sept. 4.
Oxford.
7. Geo. Lord Audley to Burghley. Compliments him on his great abilities, and returns him thanks for his former kindness. Congratulatory verses on his visit to Oxford. Lat.

Sept. 13.
8. Estimate of the charges of the ships appointed to ride off Sheerness for protection of the ships in Gillingham Water.

Sept. 16.
Woodstock.
9. Proclamation for restraint of transportation of grain beyond the seas.

450   DOMESTIC—ELIZABETH.

VOL. LXXXIX.

1572.
Sept. 16. 10. Memorial of inquisitions and order committed to Sir Peter Carewe, Sir Thomas Wroth, Mr. Hen. Knolles, and the Recorder of London, for things to be done in the Tower of London.

Sept. 16. 11. Copy of the above.

Sept. 25.
Romford.
12. Certificate of the General Musters of able men, armour, and weapons within the Liberty of Havering atte Bower, co. Essex, returned by order of Council.

Sept. 25 ? 13. Similar certificate for the Hundred of Hinckford, in the same county.

Sept. 29. 14. Declaration by Chidiock Wardour to Lord Treasurer Burghley of the receipts in the Exchequer for one year ending Michaelmas, 14° Eliz., amounting to the sum of 284,806*l*. 9*s*. 7*d*. Lat.

Sept. 29 ? 15. Memorandum in Burghley's hand of things requisite to be done for putting the coasts and realm of England in readiness against any invasion.

Sept. 29. 16. Note of English rebels and papists in the Low Countries, and in what places they remained on the 29th of September.

Sept. 17. Certificate of able men, armour, weapons, and furniture for the wars, in various Hundreds in the Lathe of Aylesford in the County of Kent.

Sept. 18. Certificate of Musters of able men, armour, and weapons in the seven Hundreds of Cranbrook, Barkley, Blackburn, Marden, Selbrickenden, Rolvenden, and Great Barnfield, co. Kent.

Sept. 19. Certificate by the Justices of Peace of the Musters of able men, armour, and weapon, within the Lower Division of the Lathe of Sutton at Hone, co. Kent.

Sept. 20. Similar certificate for the Upper Division of the same Lathe.

Oct. 1. 21. Certificate of able men, armour, &c., in the Hundreds of Ayhorne and Maidstone in the Lathe of Aylesford, co. Kent.

Oct. 3. 22. Similar certificate of able men in the Hundred of Calehill, same county.

Oct. 3. 23. Certificate of able men and arms within the Hundred of Wye, in the Lathe of Scray, same county.

Oct. 3. 24. Certificates of the General Musters of able men, &c., within the Half Hundred of Witham, in the County of Essex.

Oct. 3. 25. Similar certificate for the Hundreds of Chelmsford, Rochford, and Dengy, same county.

Oct. 3.
Exeter.
26. Justices of Devon to the Council. Have sent up, by the Sheriff, certificate of Musters for the County of Devon. *Inclosing,*

  26. I. *Certificate of able men mustered within the County of Devon, with the names of the Captains appointed to command them.*

DOMESTIC—ELIZABETH. 451

VOL. LXXXIX.

1572.
Oct. 3. 27. Note of the dimensions of various fortifications in the Town of Portsmouth, taken by the Earl of Leicester and "Mr. Treasurer."

Oct. 4. 28. Raphe Shelton to the Council. Has carefully travelled with
Norwich. the Justices of Peace in promoting the Musters and appointment of Captains in the County of Norfolk. *Incloses,*

    28. I. *Certificate by the Justices of Peace of able men and arms in the County of Norfolk, with names of the Captains commanding them.*

Oct. 6. 29. Certificate of able men and arms within the Rape of Chichester, in the County of Sussex.

Oct. 6. 30. Thomas Visct. Bindon to the Council. Details his proceedings
Bindon. in putting the County of Dorset in a state of defence, and procuring Musters of the able men, surveys of the castles and garrisons, provisions of armour, &c. *Incloses,*

    30. I. *Certificate of all the able men, armour, weapons, &c., in the County of Dorset, amounting to 3,030 men, with names of the Captains appointed to command them.*

    30. II. *Certificate by John Rogers, Mayor of Poole, of the state of the castle of Brounkeshey, near Poole, and of the want of carriages for the ordnance there.* 28 Sept. 1572.

Oct. 9. 31. Certificate by Sir Walter Waller, and others, of able men, armour, and weapon, within the Rape of Pevensey, co. Sussex.

Oct. 10. 32. Certificate of Musters of able men, &c., within the Rape of Arundel, co. Sussex.

Oct. 10 ? 33. Similar certificate of Musters of able men, &c., in the Rape of Lewes, the same county.

Oct. 10. 34. Sir P. Edgecumb and Geo. Kekewiche to Wm. Mohun, Sheriff of
Mount Cornwall. Certify the number of able men within the Hundred
Edgecombe. of Easte, in the County of Cornwall, with the names of the Captains commanding them.

Oct. 12. 35. Justices of Kent to Walter Meynye, High Sheriff. Send him their certificate for the Lathe of St. Augustine's. *Inclosing,*

    35. I. *Certificate of Musters of able men within the Lathe of Saint Augustine's, co. Kent, and names of their Captains.*

Oct. 12 ? 36. Certificate by Sir Tho. Scott, Tho. Honywood, and Ralph Heyman, of able men and armour within certain Hundreds in the Lathe of Shepway, co. Kent.

Oct. 12 ? 37. Certificate by Tho. Coppinger of the number of able men, armour, and weapons, within several Hundreds in the Lathe of Aylesford, in the same county.

F F 2

Vol. LXXXIX.

1572.
Oct. 18. 38. Thomas Sturges, Under-Sheriff of Suffolk, to the Council. Transmits certificates of Musters taken in Suffolk. *Incloses,*

 38. I. *Certificate by the Justices of Peace of the Musters of able men, and the Captains commanding them within several Hundreds of the Franchise of Bury, co. Suffolk.* 29 *Sept.* 1572.

 38. II. *Similar certificate for the Hundred of Hartesmere, in the same county.* 3 *Oct.* 1572.

 38. III. *Similar certificate for the Hundreds of Mutford, Lovingland [Lothingland], Blything, and Wangford, in the same county.* 9 *Oct.* 1572.

 38. IV. *Similar certificate for the Hundred of Hoxone, in the same county.* 10 *Oct.* 1572.

 38. V. *Similar certificate for several Hundreds within the Franchise of St. Etheldred, in the same county.* 17 *Oct.* 1572.

 38. VI. *Similar certificate for the Hundreds of Bosmere and Cleydon, and Stowe, in the same county.*

 38. VII. *Similar certificate for the Hundred of Sampford, in the same county.*

Oct. 21. 39. The Queen to the Earl of Shrewsbury. Particulars of her late illness, supposed to be the small pox; thanks for his solicitude about it.

Oct. 22.
London. 40. Jo. Lloyd to Edmund Catesby. Informs him of the proceedings respecting the due execution of his father-in-law's will, opposed by one Holcome.

Oct. 26.
Penryn. 41. John Kyllygrew and Richard Trevanyon to the Sheriff of Cornwall. Certificate of Musters of able men within the Hundreds of Penwith and Kerr.

Oct. 28.
Ludlow Castle. 42. Sir Henry Sydney, Lord President of Wales, to the Council. Details his proceedings in taking the Musters, and sends certificates from some of the counties under his government. Much of the armour had become rusty and cankered from disuse. *Incloses,*

 42. I. *Certificate of Musters of able men, armour, and weapons in the Counties of Gloucester, Pembroke, Glamorgan, and Cardigan, with names of the Captains leading them.*

Oct. 28.
Bodmin. 43. Certificate of Musters of able men, &c., within the Hundreds of Stratton, Lasnewith, and Trigge, in the County of Cornwall.

Oct. 31.
Larrethow. 44. Similar certificate for the Hundred of West, in the same county.

Oct. 45. Similar certificate for the Hundreds of Powder and Pider, in the same county.

Oct. ? 46. Note of fines levied on various persons in Norfolk, Sussex, London, and Southwark, for illegally transporting grain.

VOL. LXXXIX.

1572.
Oct. 47. Chr. Hatton to ▲▲▲▲ [Queen Elizabeth]. Defends himself from the charges of unthankfulness, covetousness, and ambition, which had caused her displeasure towards him. Has most entirely loved her person and service, to the which he has everlastingly vowed his whole life, liberty, and fortune. Signs himself, "*Your dispayrynge* "*moste wretchyd bondman.* CHR. HATTON."

Oct. 48. Note of the most necessary places to be next repaired within the castle of Windsor.

Oct. ? 49. Petition of Thos. Canata, Venetian, to the Queen. Solicits licence to export 200 tons of beer, on condition of his making known to Her Majesty certain inventions useful for the defence of the realm.

Oct. ? 50. Petition of John Babbington to the Council. Desires that the suit commenced by him in the Sheriff's Court in London, against Walter Kyrbie, may not be stayed by their order, on pretence of service to the Earl of Leicester.

Oct. ? 51. Muster Roll of shot and pikemen in several Hundreds in the County of Somerset.

VOL. XC. NOVEMBER—DECEMBER, 1572.

Nov. 5. 1. John Paulet Marquis of Winchester to the Council. Prepara-
Winchester. tions for putting Portsmouth and the Isle of Wight in a good state of defence. *Incloses,*

1. I. *Order taken at Winchester by the Marquis of Winchester, for the better relief of Portsmouth and the Isle of Wight.*

1. II. *A certificate of the forces in various Hundreds appointed for the defence of the town and island of Portsmouth.*

1. III. *Similar certificate of forces appointed for relief of the Isle of Wight.*

1. IV. *Schedule of forces in various Hundreds appointed to guard the coasts of Hampshire.*

1. V. *Schedule of forces for defence of the body of the shire, to repair to places where attempts shall be offered.*

1. VI. *Schedule of boats appointed in several parts, for conveying men into the Isle of Wight, upon any attempt.*

Nov. 19. 2. Sir Henry Sydney to Lord Burghley. Thanks for his warrant for his entertainment in Ireland. Justifies the course he has pursued as to selection of Sheriffs for Wales; and enters into particulars relative to many of the gentlemen he has nominated.

454   DOMESTIC—ELIZABETH.

1572.   VOL. XC.

Nov. 20. 3. Sir Henry Sydney to the Council. Exonerates himself from the
Ludlow Castle. unjust imputations made on him, in his return of persons for Sheriffs
in Wales. *Incloses,*

   3. I. *Return of persons nominated for Sheriffs for Wales made to the Lord Keeper to be presented to Her Majesty.*

   3. II. *Roll by the Justices of Assize of persons returned for Sheriffs for Wales.*

Nov. 5. 4. Indenture of an agreement between Thomas Henneage of the Queen's Chamber and Peter Vavasour of the Middle Temple, for surrender of all Vavasour's estate and interests in Thornton, houses and other lands in Yorkshire, to the said Tho. Henneage.

Nov. 25. 5. Sir Richard Fenys to Lord Burghley. Complains of the wrong interpretation of Bishop Wyckham's statutes to the prejudice of New College, Oxford. Doubts the right of Edw. Wykeham to bear the arms of Bishop Wyckham. *Incloses,*

   5. I. *Articles relating to the breach of certain orders and statutes relative to the Elections of Scholars of Winchester College.*

   5. II. *Copy of part of Bishop Wykeham's statutes relating to the Election of Scholars. Lat.*

Nov. 29. 6. Same to same. Requests the appointment of two civil and two temporal lawyers, with two heralds, to hear the claim between himself and Mr. Wykham.

Nov. 7. Notes for the Solicitor-General of the case in Chancery between Mr. Alford, plaintiff, and Mr. Lodovike Grevell, defendant, and Mr. W. Porter, as to fraudulent conveyance of lands at Ashton, &c.

Dec. 2. 8. Walter Earl of Essex to Burghley. Exceptions to some appointed
Durham Place. to be Sheriffs in Wales. Hopes a good Sheriff will be appointed for Carmarthen. Condemns Sir Henry Jones and David Phillips, and recommends Roderick Gwyn and Tho. Williams.

Dec. 2. 9. The Queen to . Directions to discontinue
HamptonCourt. the watching of the beacons until further notice.

Dec. 8. 10. Abstract of charges against the Earl of Arundel, from examinations taken during the trial of the Duke of Norfolk. Arundel set at liberty.

Dec. 11. 11. Earl of Leicester to Burghley. The Queen is sorry for the mischance of Mons. le Duke, and desires him to delay the passage of M. Mauvissiere as long as possible. God grant the safe delivery of the poor gentleman.

Dec. 11. 12. T. Digges to same. Has waded as far as ancient grounds of astrology would bear him to sift out the unknown influence of this new star or comet. Sends notes of his observations and predictions.

Dec. 13. 13. Agreement between Lord Burghley and Thomas Smith for licence to export 4,000 tons of beer.

Dec. 21. 14. Short abstract of certain of Sir John Perrot's debts.

Vol. XC.

1572.
Dec. 22. 15. Wm. Fairfax, Sheriff of Yorkshire, and others, to Lord Burghley and Sir Walter Mildmay. Repairs requisite to be done in Her Majesty's castle of Sheriffhutton, with an estimate of the expenses.

Dec. 16. Order of the ceremonies at the funeral of Edward Earl of Derby ; and detail of the order and ceremonies to be observed at the funeral of a Countess.

1572. 17. Certificate of the state of Dover Castle and other forts and garrisons on the sea coasts of the County of Kent, with estimate of men and arms requisite for their defence.

18. Names of the noblemen, gentlemen, yeomen, and chief franklins within the County of Southampton, with note of every of their dispositions. A.D. 1572.

19. Estimate for certain new buildings to be erected and set up at Woolwich by Mr. Allen, the Queen's Majesty's merchant. 1572.

1572 ? 20. Tho. Castelyn to   . Recommending the case of some Merchant Adventurers whose cloths had been lost by shipwreck, and who now wished to export the same number free of duty.

21. Declaration of William Martens of his long and tedious suits in Dantzic, wherein he finds that justice has not been done him by the King of Poland.

22. Observations and objections to several provisions of the Act 5 Eliz. cap. 8. for tanners ; in recommendation of a grant to some person for carrying the said Act into execution.

23. Proposals for the making of white salt in England ; terms demanded by the inventor.

24. Notes of reasons and proofs for the maintenance of the wine measures, and of the inconvenience that will grow to the whole realm by the innovation now attempted by the Mayor of New Sarum, the wine measure of Salisbury being declared by him to be false.

25. Plan for the defence of the kingdom ; that every gentleman of 500l. a-year should keep in readiness for service one man-at-arms well appointed, and so on in like proportion.

26. Supplication of the bowyers, drawn into articles, praying Her Majesty not to dispense with the last statute made for the bringing in of bowstaves.

27. Statement of evils that will arise by interruption of commercial intercourse with Flanders. Suggestions for a Diet for settlement of affairs.

28. Minutes of the licence to be granted to Sir Peter Carew for the exportation of beer, on condition of importing certain quantities of foreign grain into England.

29. Examination of an Italian whether he was at the conference for the coining of money, or had been in conference with the Bishop of Ross.

Vol. XC.

1572?   30. Petition of Lewes Ap Owen Ap Mericke to the Council. Complains of having been fraudulently arrested, at the suit of one William Thomas while attending on the Council, on the complaint of certain abuses of bribery within the Counties of Anglesea and Carnarvon.

31. Statement of the evil dealings of Tho. Keppis, bailiff of *your Lordship's* manor of Wibosson, in the County of Bedford, in concealments and other practices.

32. Contents of the Patents made in 34 Hen. VIII. to the inhabitants of Beccles, now surrendered. Particulars of the new grant of incorporation now required.

33. Petition of William Newe, of Bridgenorth, to Lord Treasurer Burghley. Prays permission to pay by instalments the fine of 20l., levied on his wife Edyth.

34. Estimates for the construction of the bridge at the entrance of the town of Portsmouth, with the gate and drawbridge there, and for the bridge of the citadel, by Thomas Frymleye.

35. Duplicate of the above.

36. Grant by the Queen to Edw.   , Esq., of the sole privilege of enforcing the Acts 5th & 6th Edward VI. and 13th Eliz., against monopolists, forestallers, and engrossers of corn, and for granting licences to traffic in corn, cattle, and other articles.

37. Petition of the Company of Woolmen of London to the Lord Treasurer, requesting him to obtain the Queen's permission for taking off the restraint on the trade in wool, by an Act passed in the 5th & 6th years of King Edward VI.

38. Reasons to dispense, by some convenient licence, with the provisions of the Act of 5 Edw. VI. cap. 7, against buying and selling of wools.

39. Petition of Richard Southworth to Lord Burghley, requesting him to appoint Sir Edmund Trafford and Sir John Radcliffe to examine his father, Sir John Southworth, whether he had endeavoured to procure him to disinherit his elder brother, Thomas Southworth.

40. Another petition on the same subject, from the same to the same; nearly verbatim.

41. Effect of the decree made by Archbishop Warham, 17 Hen. VII. touching the right of the Lord of the Manor of Wimbledon to make seizure of copyhold lands, &c. of the manor, on account of waste committed by the tenant for life. [*Indorsed by Burghley* "*Mr. Wel.—Case.*"]

42. Petition of Jan de Beaulieu to the Queen. Complains of the award given in the Admiralty Court in favour of Benedict Spinola, who refuses to submit himself to the arbitration of those appointed by Her Majesty to hear and determine the suit.

Vol. XC.

1572?   43. Petition of Tho. Kelyng (Saymaster to the Goldsmiths' Hall in London) to the Queen. Has been deprived of his office of Assay Master to the Goldsmiths' Hall by the procurement of Alderman Martyn, for adhering to Her Majesty's standard for silver. Desires to be protected in the faithful discharge of his duty.

44. Petition of Anthony Gwerras to the Council. Prays for restoration of certain brass pieces cast away within the Liberties of the Earl of Huntingdon.

45. Information by the Warden and other Officers of the Mint to the Commissioners of the Mint against John Lonyson, Master Worker, who, by his fraudulent practices, had lowered the standard of the gold and silver coinage. [*Lonyson's appointment of Master Worker of the Mint is dated 29 April* 1572, *which see.*]

46. Geometrical analysis of a column of the composite order; a fragment, probably, from some work on architecture.

47. Extracts from the accompts of Sir Wm. Petre, (late Treasurer of First Fruits and Tenths), and others, relative to the fees received by the Chancellor and Treasurer of the Exchequer.

48. Petition of Humfrey Ap John and Rynallde Ap John to [Walsyngham?] against the vexatious suits of Tho. Arrowsmythe, praying for return of their evidences, and that the injunction against them may be dissolved.

[The Council ?] to the Company of the Royal Mines in Cumberland. That Daniel Hechstetter, Work Master of the Royal Mines, had made trial of a process newly invented by Henry Pope for the roasting of lead and copper ore, and recommends its adoption.   [*See Vol.* xlv., *p.* 76.]

Appointment of James Parkinson, to be Captain of Calshot Castle, co. Southampton, for life.   [*See Warrant Book,* I., *p.* 173.]

Commission to Dr. Lewes, Judge of the Admiralty, Valentine Dale, and others,to hear and determine all causes for the punishing of pirates. Lat.   [*See ib., p.* 14.]

Grant to Tho. Somerset and Tho. Seckford, junr., of the portership and keeping of the prisoners in the Marches of Wales. [*See ib., p.* 160.]

Grant by the Queen to William and John Watson of the keeping of the ordnance stores in the Tower of London. Lat. [*See ib., p.* 157.]

Grant to B. N. of the office of Clock Maker to the Queen, in reversion after the death or surrender of N. V.   [*See ib., p.* 120.]

Grant to Edward Yonge of the office of Master Mason at the Tower of London, and other royal residences, in place of H. L., lately defunct. Lat.   [*See ib., p.* 122.]

VOL. XC.

1572 ?   Grant to Tho. C. of the office of Keeper of the Ponds in the park at Westminster, and at Hampton Court, upon the resignation of Tho. B. [*See Warrant Book,* I., *p.* 115.]

Grant to Henry Guildeford of the office of Captain of the Green Bulwark of Arcliffe, and the Black Bulwark on the pier at Dover, in reversion after the death or surrender of John Barley. [*See ib., p.* 156.]

Grant to M. S. and R. B. of a gunner's room in the Tower of London. Lat. [*See ib., p.* 126.]

Grant to William B. of the office of Chief Gunner in Windsor Castle, in place of R. M., lately defunct. Lat. [*See ib., p.* 128.]

Grant to J. S. of a gunner's place, and of the office of Yeoman of the Ordnance in the Tower of London, in reversion after the death or surrender of Tho. S. Lat. [*See ib., p.* 129.]

Grant to Tho. F. of a waiter's room in the Port of London for life. [*See ib., p.* 115.]

VOL. XCI.   JANUARY—JUNE, 1573.

1573.
Jan. 2.   1. Memorandum of the appointment of George Earl of Shrewsbury, to the office of Earl Marshal of England, vacant by the attainder of Thomas Duke of Norfolk.

Jan.   2. Order for the ceremonies to be observed at the funeral of Reginald Grey Earl of Kent, by Glover, Somerset Herald.

Jan. 8.   3. Indenture of award by Raffe Sheldon and John Tracy, arbitrators in the matters between Edmund Catesby and Tristram Holcome, ot Aston-under-Edge, relative to a legacy left to Elizabeth Catesby by Anthony Porter, her father.

Feb. 13.   4–10. Seven receipts for money, from Feb. 1572, to 13 Feb. 1573, paid by Mr. John Purvey, for Lord Burghley, to various persons, viz.; four from Tho. Bellot, for wood sales; one from Tho. Bennett, for sale of a marsh called Curstmarsh, in the Honor of Hoddesdonbury; one from Wm. Fordham, for sale of a weir in Waltham parish; and the last from L. Bingham, due to the Queen for the Hundred of Hertford and Braughing, co. Hertford.

March 1.   Clause of a will bequeathing 2000*l.* to a daughter, to be paid to her on the day of her marriage; with legal opinions thereon. [*See Nov.* 14, 1578.]

March 4.   11. Harry Lord Morley to Lord Burghley. Requests that by his
Bridgis.   lordship's kindness he may obtain the Queen's favour. Thanks for
[Bruges.]   kindness shown to his wife and son during his exile.

DOMESTIC—ELIZABETH. 459

1573.   Vol. XCI.

March 12.   12. Bond of Sir Peter Carew, for the return or payment of ammunition received by him for the defence of certain port towns in Devon and Cornwall.

March 14.   Instructions for execution of the Commission directed to all the Justices of the Peace in every shire, for the General Musters and training of all manner of persons able for the war, to serve as well on horseback as on foot. [*See Vol.* xciii., *No.* 18.]

March 27.   13. Bond of Sir Peter Carew, for return or payment of ammunition and other things requisite for furnishing of Her Majesty's ship the Primrose, with schedule of materials consumed and spent in the voyage to Rochelle.

March ?   14. Notes relative to the Earl of Essex's debt to the Queen, and his proposal for settlement of the same.

March ?   The Queen to the Bishops. To furnish the number of horses and armour assessed upon them, and to urge the clergy within their dioceses willingly to do the same. [*See Warrant Book*, I., *p.* 15.]

March ?   15. Declaration of the money remaining in the hands of Humfrey Michell, Clerk of the Honor and Castle of Windsor, of the sums expended by him in the late repairs; and of repairs still remaining to be done.

March ?   Rate of assessment on land and goods for furnishing lances and light horses. [*See Vol.* xlv., *p.* 36.]

April 11.   16. Dr. Lewes to Lord Burghley. Has carefully considered the
London..   papers sent to him respecting the money covenanted by the Queen to be paid to the Luccans. His opinion thereon.

April 28.   17. Sir Chr. Heydon and Sir William Buttes to same. The City of
Baconsthorpe. Norwich request a separate commission for the return of Musters within their Liberties.

April 30.   18. Lord North to same. Sends all the information he could obtain
Kirtling.   of one Booth, formerly servant to the Earl of Oxford. Conversation between Booth and Mr. Bird of Bennet College. He is also known to one Thimbleby.

April   19. Lady Mary Sydney to same. Thanks him for his kindness in her suits, for which she was much indebted to her friend Lady Hoby. Excuses herself on account of her ill health, and begs him not to be offended at her boldness.

April.   20. Articles of complaint exhibited to the Privy Council, by Wm. Noble, of Oxford, against certain rude and unruly persons of the University. Particulars of many riots and misdemeanors and unlawful assemblies.

May 3.   21. Lord North, and others, to the Council. Report on the Musters
Drayton.   for the County of Cambridge, excepting the Isle of Ely. *Inclosing,*

    21. I. *Certificate of all the able men within the County of Cambridge.*

1573.   VOL. XCI.

May 4.
Audley End.
22. Philip Howard Earl of Surrey to Lord Burghley. Thanks him for his kindness to him and his family since his father's death.

May 5.
Bodmin.
23. Justices of the Peace of Cornwall to the Council. Proceedings in taking the Musters for the county. Will make a return of horses and geldings. *Inclosing,*

23. I. *Certificate of all the able men within the County of Cornwall, with the names of their Captains.*

May 6.
Wisbeach.
24. Lord North, the Bishop of Ely, and others, to same. Return of Musters taken within the Isle of Ely. *Inclosing,*

24. I. *Certificate of all the able men within the Isle of Ely.*

May 7.
London.
25. Dr. Lewes to Burghley. His opinion on the papers respecting the Luccans' money; being a copy of his former letter of 11 April, which could not then be found.

May 8.
Exeter.
26. Sir Gawen Carewe, and others, to the Council. Particulars of the Musters in Devon, where there were found to be 10,000 able men, of which 1,000 might be selected for training; but, on account of the falling off of their trade, they were not able to defray the expense of it.

May 10.
Worcester.
27. Sir Tho. Russell, and others, to same. Musters of the county. The Bailiffs of Worcester refuse to permit them to take the muster of men within the City; for which they recommend the issuing of a special Commission.

May 12.
28. John Cobham, and others, to same. Certificate of Musters taken within the Hundreds of Milton, Teneham, Feversham, and Boughton, in the Lathe of Scray, co. Kent.

May 12.
29. Similar certificate by T. Wotton and others, for the Hundreds of Ayhorne and Maidstone, in the Lathe of Aylesford, co. Kent. Request to know the number of men to be trained.

May 15.
The General Musters of the Borough Town of St. Albans, of all able men, armour, and weapons within the same, taken before John Snape, Mayor, Sir Richard Rede, and others, Commissioners. [*See Vol.* xciv. *Musters, No.* 1.]

May 19.
Chesterfield.
30. Earl of Shrewsbury, Sir John Zowche, and others, to the Council. Proceedings in taking the Musters in Derbyshire, there being found 4,000 able men within the county; the training of 500 of which will be as much as the county can bear.

May 24.
Cowdrey.
31. Anthony Viscount Mountague to Burghley. Price of grain and the amount exported within the County of Sussex. Complains of the officers of the Customs. Much grain has been exported from Chichester. Has caused a large quantity to be sold.

May 25.
32. Certificate by Sir Thomas Gresham, and Dr. Lewes, of the procurations from certain persons, for various sums of money underwritten to Mr. Benedict Spinola.

May 26.
33. Petition of Henry Osmonde to Burghley. Requests him to give order for the payment of 57*l.* lent by him to Mr. Henry Howard.

VOL. XCI.

1573.
May 28. 34. Certificate of able men, armour, and arms mustered by the Commissioners for the Seven Hundreds, and the Hundred of Little Barnfield, co. Kent.

May 31. 35. An Order concerning certain articles objected against Dr. Kelke, Master of Mag. Coll., Cambridge, and by certain of the Fellows of the said College.

May 31.
Gravesend. 36. William Fawnt and John Wotton to Lord Burghley. Have been assaulted between Gravesend and Rochester, and fired on by three of the Earl of Oxford's men, who escaped towards London. Desire some redress.

May. 37. Names of the Lathes, Hundreds, and Towns in the County of Kent.

May ? 38. Note of the lands demised by Her Majesty to the Countess of Northumberland, in the County of Pembroke.

June 1.
Lincoln. 39. Henry Lord Clynton, Charles Wyllughby, and others, to the Council. Proceedings in taking the General Musters of the County of Lincoln. *Inclosing,*

    39. I. *Certificate of Musters of able men and arms within the County of Lincoln, with the numbers selected to be trained.*

June 2.
Cowdrey. 40. Viscount Mountague, and others, to same. Musters for the County of Sussex. The expenses paid by this shire for the suppression of the late rebellion, and the decay of trade, made it difficult for them to defray the charges for training a number of men. *Inclosing,*

    40. I.—VII. *Seven certificates of Musters for the County of Sussex.*

June 3. 41. Certificate of Musters of able men and arms within the Upper Division of the Lathe of Sutton at Hone, co. Kent. Signed by Sir Wm. Damsell and others.

June 3. 42. Similar certificate of Musters for the Lower Division of the same Lathe. Signed by Sir Henry Sydney and others.

June 5.
Kirtling. 43. Lord North, and others, to the Council. Have taken the Musters for the town of Cambridge, as directed by their Lordships. *Inclosing,*

    43. I. *A certificate of Musters for the town of Cambridge.*

June 6. 44. Commission to the Earl of Warwick, Master of the Ordnance, and Wm. Pelham, Esq., Lieutenant of the Ordnance, for the making of saltpetre.

June [7.] 45. Chr. Hatton to ΔΔΔ [Queen Elizabeth.] Expressing the pleasure her gracious letters afforded to him. His love of Her Majesty, and his grief on account of absence, having been two days away from Her Majesty. He will wash away all faults with the tears that fall from her poor "Liddes." [*This letter has no date, but according to Hatton's own data, in his letter of the 17th, its date must have been on the 7th of June, and not on the 5th, as assigned by Sir H. Nicolas in his Memoirs of Hatton, p. 25.*]

1573.
June 8.
Salop.

46. Sir Henry Sydney, and others, Commissioners for Musters in the County of Salop, to the Council. Detail their proceedings and certify the numbers of able men within the county. Had not appointed Captains, the Lord President (of Wales) being then absent out of the country. [*But it is signed by him.*]

June 11.
Greenwich.

47. Proclamation of Queen Elizabeth, commanding the observance of Divine Service as set forth in the Book of Common Prayer, and for suppressing books entitled "*An Admonition to the Parliament.*"

June 15.

48. Brief declaration of the accounts of the Tellers of the Exchequer, showing the amount of their receipts and items of expenditure.

June 16.
Barmesey.

49. Sir Henry Radcliffe, Capt. of Portsmouth, to Lord Burghley. Requests a supply of ordnance for the fortifications at Portsmouth. A receipt for the same by Henry Stile.

June 16.

50. Duplicate of the above with note of certain process indorsed.

June 16.

51. Indenture between Sir H. Radcliffe and the Earl of Warwick, for the above ordnance received for the defence of Portsmouth.

June 17.
Antwerp.

52. Chr. Hatton to the Queen. Expresses his devotion to her. It is twelve days since he saw the brightness of that sun that giveth light to his soul. Has received great honour in Flanders for her sake. Beseeches her not to forget her "*Liddes*" that are so often bathed with tears for her sake. ["*Liddes*" or "*Lyddes*" *was the name of affection applied by Queen Elizabeth to Sir Chr. Hatton.*]

June 18.
Leicester.

53. Commissioners of Musters for the County of Leicester to the Council. Certify their doings in the Musters, and desire instructions respecting the appointing of Captains and training the soldiers. *Inclosing*,

53. I. *Certificate of the numbers of all persons able to serve, as well on horseback as on foot, &c. within the County of Leicester.*

June 20.

54. Indenture between John Asteley, Treasurer of the Queen's Jewels, and Robert Bestney, of Northaw, Herts, granting to the latter the Mastership of the Game in Enfield chase and park, and the office of Steward and Ranger of the Manor of Enfield.

June 22.

55. Sir Henry Cryspe, and others, to Council. Respecting the number of able men to be trained within the Lathe of St. Augustine, Kent. *Inclosing*,

55. I. *Certificate of Musters for the Lathe of St. Augustine, Kent.*

June 22.
Somerton.

56. Sir Hugh Poulet, and others, to the same. Have taken the Musters of co. Somerset, amounting to 6,000 able men. The charge for training a selected number would be a very heavy burthen on the country. Have not yet received a certificate of the breed of horses.

June 24.

57. Bond of Queen Elizabeth, countersigned by the Privy Council, for the payment of 11,000*l.* to Benedict Spinola, a merchant of Genoa. [*Cancelled and indorsed* "11,000*l.* all payd. W. Burghley."]

1573.   VOL. XCI.

June 25. Worcester.
58. Commissioners of Musters for the County of Worcester to the Council. Certify their doings in the Musters. Have delayed training the men till after the harvest. *Inclosing,*

    58. I. *Certificate of the Musters of all the able men within the County of Worcester.*

June 26. At the Court.
59. Earl of Leicester to Lord Burghley. Sends for his inspection a letter directed to "The Earl of Leicester and Lord Burghley," which he thinks right for him to see.

June 28. Norwich.
60. Commissioners of Musters for the County of Norfolk to same. Have taken General Musters of the county, but have not appointed Captains nor commenced training the soldiers till they receive further instructions. *Inclosing,*

    60. I. *Certificate of all the able men, as well as those selected and chosen, within the County of Norfolk.*

June 30. Hertford.
61. Sir Ralph Sadleir, and others, to the Council. Proceedings in the Musters for the County of Hertford. That they have met with much inconvenience for want of a sufficient number of gentlemen for Captains. Various impediments to the training of soldiers. *Incloses,*

    61. I. *Certificate of the General Musters for the County of Hertford.*

June. Chester.
62. Richard Dutton, Mayor, and others, Commissioners of Musters for the City of Chester, to same. Have taken the Musters within their city. *Inclosing,*

    62. I. *Muster Roll of the names of all the able men furnished with arms and armour within the City of Chester.*

June ?
Grant to Giles Baron Chandos of the office of Chief Steward of the Manor of Hailes, and of several Hundreds in co. Gloucester, and Keeper of Braidon Forest, co. Wilts, for life. Vacant by the death of the late Edmund Lord Chandos. Lat. [*See Warrant Book* I., *p.* 171.]

June ?
63. Abstract of all the certificates, as well of the number of able men as of unable men within the shires of England and Wales.

June ?
64. Petition of John Calvetto, John Baptista Sambitores, and Philip Asheliars, on behalf of the merchants of Spain and Flanders to the Queen. Praying for a commission of inquiry touching the goods embezzled or deceitfully sold belonging to the merchants of their nations.

June ? Hampton Court.
65. Commission from the Queen to Sir Peter Carew, Christopher Hatton, Esq., Captain of the Queen's Guard, and others, to make search for all goods and merchandise belonging to the subjects of the King of Spain, and other foreigners, which may by any means have been embezzled or concealed since the year 1568.

June ?
66. Note of inconveniences arising from the ingrossing of certain foreign commodities, and the statutes against the ingrossers; giving the current prices of various wines, spices, drugs, &c.

DOMESTIC—ELIZABETH.

1573.

June ?   67. Petition of John Barker and others to the Council. Complaining of the seizure of their ship the "Thomas" and her cargo, and praying compensation out of the goods of Spanish subjects seized in England.

June ?   68. Note of the value of Spanish property seized in England, with allowance out of it to British subjects for property arrested in Spain and Flanders.

VOL. XCII. JULY—NOVEMBER, 1573.

July 1.
Salisbury.
1. The Commissioners of Musters for Wiltshire to the Council. Certify their doings in the Musters. The county having been heavily taxed could not defray the expense of training. Desire further directions therein. *Inclosing*,

 1. I. *Certificate of General Musters of all able men, lances, and light horse, within the County of Wilts; taken before the Earl of Pembroke, Sir John Zowche, and others, Commissioners.* [*See Vol.* xciv. *Musters, No.* 2.]

July 2.
Salisbury.
2. Wm. Davy, Mayor, and others, Commissioners of Musters for the town of Salisbury, to same. Certify their doings, and promise to use all diligence in training a chosen number. *Inclosing*,

 2. I. *Certificate of General Musters for the town of New Sarum.*

July 2.
Winchester.
3. Commissioners of Musters for Hampshire to same. Promise to send the certificates of the General Musters as soon as possible, and explain the cause of their delay. Certain persons wilfully refuse to appear. Have made choice of 500 able men to be trained. *Inclosing*,

 3. I. *Names of such recusants as have refused or neglected to furnish themselves with horses and armour.*

July 6.
Westchester.
4. Thomas Might to Lord Burghley. Solicits a lease of a farm of the value of 50*l.* a year, in consideration of his great losses and services.

July 7.
Churcham.
5. Richard Arnold to Francis Walsyngham. Has been prevented by extreme sickness from sending the brace of greyhounds, which he now begs of him to accept.

July 8.
Oxford.
6. Commissioners of Musters for the County of Oxford to the Council. Proceeding in the Musters. Desire to know what numbers of them shall be trained and exercised. *Inclosing*,

 6. I. II. *Certificates of General Musters of able men, &c., for the whole County of Oxford.* [*See Vol.* xciv. *Musters, No.* 3.]

July 9.
Greenwich.
Grant by the Queen to John Easton of an almsroom in St. Stephen's Church, Westminster, for his services at Newhaven. [*See Warrant Book*, I., *p.* 2.]

[July 9 ?]   Grant by the Queen to Walter Tomas of the place of one of Her Majesty's falconers for life, the same as John Talbott of late had. [*See ib.*, *p.* 2.]

DOMESTIC—ELIZABETH. 465

1573. Vol. XCII.

July 13. 7. Copy of court-roll of the Manor of Hedingham, of the surrender of a cottage and garden, called Shedds, by John Woodd, in favor of Matthew Alystone.

July 14. Certificate by John Rogers, Mayor, Sir Henry Ashley, and others, of the Musters for the town and county of Poole, co. Dorset. [*See Vol.* xciv. *Musters, No.* 4.]

July 15. 8. Certificate of General Musters for the Borough of Boston, co. Lincoln, taken before the Deputies of William Lord Burghley, Recorder of the same, and others, Commissioners.

July 20.
Stafford.
9. Tho. Lord Paget, and others, to the Council. Return of Musters for the County of Stafford. From various causes specified, the country is too poor to support the expense of training a large number of men. Names of gentlemen appointed Captains.

July 22. 10. Certificate of the Musters of horsemen taken at St. Giles's Hill, for the County of Southampton.

July 22.
Dorchester.
11. Commissioners of Musters for the County of Dorset to the Council. Proceedings in the Musters. Difficulty of keeping their extended line of coast in a state of defence. Have selected 500 for training, but the inhabitants are unwilling to be burthened with the charges of it. *Inclosing,*

    11. I. *Certificate of Musters by Tho. Lord Howard of Bindon, and others, for the County of Dorset.*

July 24.
Guildford.
12. Commissioners of Musters for the County of Surrey to same. Detail their proceedings. Have selected 300 men for training, but the county is unable to bear the expense. *Inclosing,*

    12. I. *Certificate of Musters for the County of Surrey.*

July 27.
Aylesbury.
13. The Earl of Bedford, and others, to same. Relative to the Musters for the County of Buckingham. *Inclosing,*

    13. I. *Certificate of General Musters of able men, horses, armour, &c., for the County of Buckingham.*

July 31.
Oxford.
14. The Mayor, &c., of Oxford to same. Musters for the city, which, on account of having been visited by the plague, and other causes, could not defray any charges for the training a large number of men. *Inclosing,*

    14. I. *Certificate of the Musters for the City of Oxford and suburbs of the same.* [*See Vol.* xciv. *Musters, No.* 5.]

July ? 15. Warrant of the Queen to the Lord Treasurer to pay the sum of 300*l.* quarterly, to the Vidame of Chartres ; and to Captain Mazynes (Mascino del Bene ?) the sum of 40*l.*, and, hereafter, 15*l.* quarterly, during pleasure.

July ? Warrant by the Queen for a tenement belonging to the manor of Turloye, co. Cornwall, of the yearly value of 26*s.* 8*d.*, to be made over to a Yeoman of the Chamber by copy of court-roll. [*See Warrant Book, No.* I., *p.* 5.]

Q Q

VOL. XCII.

1573.
July ? 16. Chr. Hatton to ΔΔΔ♂ [Queen Elizabeth.] Has suffered greatly from his illness. His love of Her Majesty. Speaks allegorically of the sheep [himself] and the boar [Earl of Oxford]. Desires to know if the report of her illness were true.

July ? Grant to [   ] of certain lands at Wapping Thorne, Tottington, and other places in Sussex, lately belonging to R. W. of Wapping Thorne, forfeited by virtue of the statute against fugitives. Lat. [See *Warrant Book, No. I., p. 4.*]

August 3. London. 17. Francis Walsyngham to Lord Burghley. Sends a letter from an Italian relating to the doings of the Prince of Orange; and copy of advertisements lately received by M. de Plessis out of Germany. Attempt on the life of the Prince of Orange.

August 4. Dartington. 18. Sir Arthur Champernowne to same. Gives his opinion that much might be gained by taking advantage of the present state of France.

August 8. London. 19. John Southcot to same. Has taken care to examine the title deeds, and to do all things requisite for the secure purchase of lands in Lincoln, for Burghley, from the Earl of Pembroke.

August 10. 20. "Lyddes" [Chr. Hatton] to ΔΔΔ♂ [Queen Elizabeth]. His love and faith are infinitely enlarged. The letter by Mr. Henneage warms his heart's blood with joys above joys. Thanks her for her royal gifts, and on the knees of his heart commends his faithful love to her.

August 24. Warwick. 21. Sir Tho. Lucy, Sir Fowlke Grevyle, and others, to the Council. Excuse their long delay in forwarding the Musters. *Inclosing,*

21. I. *Certificates of General Musters of all able men, horses, &c., within the County of Warwick and the City of Coventry.*

August 26. Certificate by Sir Andrew Corbett, and others, of Musters and view of armour for the town of Ludlow, co. Salop. Received at Dover, 26th August. [See *Vol.* xciv., *No.* 6.]

August 27. Certificate of demi-lances, light horse, &c., within several Hundreds in the County of Berks, mustered at Abingdon on the 27th of Aug., 1573. [See *Vol.* xciv., *No.* 7.]

Aug. 20. Similar certificate for other Hundreds in the same County. [See *ib., No.* 8.]

Brief extract of all the demi-lances and light horse within the same County. [See *ib., No.* 9.]

Brief extract of the General Musters, as well of all the men, as also of all armour and furniture meet for footmen, within the said County. [See *ib., No* 10.]

1573.

VOL. XCII.

August 28. Bristol.
22. Mayor, &c. of Bristol, to the Council. Have executed the Commission for Musters, according to their duties. *Inclosing,*

22. I. Certificate of the Musters of able men from 16 to 60 years of age within the City of Bristol. [See Vol. xciv., No. 11.]

August.
23. Certificate of Musters for the Lathe of Shepway, and certain Hundreds in the Lathe of Scray, Kent. Lat.

August. St. John's College.
24. Appeal of Stephen Cardinall, Laurence Wasshington, and many others, fellows of St. John's College, Cambridge, to Lord Burghley, relative to the election of a Master of their College. Lat.

August.
25. Answers to certain articles of Mr. Lane's suit for the forfeitures of bonds, commonly called port bonds, taken for transporting goods to or from port to port within the realm.

Sept. 3.
Certificate of Musters for the town and liberties of Lynn-Regis in the County of Norfolk; taken the 3rd of September. [See Vol. xciv., No. 12.]

Sept. 17. Gorehambury.
26. Lord Keeper Bacon to Lord Burghley. Sees no cause for the meeting of Parliament unless there be great likelihood of proceeding in the marriage. Observations relative to the proclamation against seditious books and libels.

Sept. 21. Rochester.
27. Adrian de Gomiecourt to same. Solicits him to assist the Baron de Berlaymont in the recovery of a pair of bloodhounds. French.

Sept. 22. Chobham.
28. Nicholas Heyth (formerly Bp. of Worcester) to same. Thanks for his kind letter, and promises if he is examined relative to certain things, he will speak nothing but the truth. Is grateful for having lived many years in great quietness of mind.

Sept. 27. London.
29. Sir Henry Nevell to same. Had written to him as to the copyhold for Mrs. Seamer. Has often sent to Mrs. Barker for the court-rolls, but cannot get them. Details what he knew respecting the libels against his lordship by the late Duke of Norfolk.

Sept. 29.
30. Articles of a bill for the true dyeing of wools and cloths.

Sept.
31. Note of a bond between Lord Burghley and Richard Topcliff, for the payment of the sum of 50*l*.

Sept.
·32. The Vidame of Chartres to the Queen. Apologizes for having solicited her in favour of one Richard Eden, and requests that he may be admitted as one of the Poor Knights of Windsor. Fr. *Annexed,*

32. I.—III. Three papers of memoranda relating to Ric. Eden. Lat.

Oct. 5. Bishopsthorpe.
33. Archbp. Grindall to Burghley. Grieves at his being disquieted by these false slanderous printed libels, published by rank traitorous papists; by whose "libels Medcea is made an innocent, open rebellion is extenuated, and y⁰ late crocodile Duke justified."

Oct. 6.
34. Complaint by Mr. John Fortescue against Lord Grey and his men, for hunting within his manor of Salden, and of the uncivil language of Lord Grey to him in the Chamber of Presence.

1573.
Oct. 6.

35. Examination of Mr. Fortescue's men relative to the late affray between them and Lord Grey's men, for hunting within their master's manor of Salden.

Oct. 6.

36. Lord Grey's declaration to the Privy Council, relative to the dispute between him and Mr. Fortescue, respecting the right of hunting within the manor of Salden, adjoining Whaddon Chase.

Oct. 7.
outhampton.

37. Mayor, &c., of Southampton, to the Council. Relative to the return of Musters for that town. *Inclosing,*

 37. I. *Certificate of Musters of able men and armour for the town and county of the town of Southampton.*

Oct. 10.
Exeter.

38. Mayor, &c., of Exeter, to same. Specify the result of Musters for the county of the City of Exeter.

Oct. 12.

Certificate of all the able horse and geldings now ready furnished, with armour and shot, in the County of Surrey. [*See Vol.* xciv. *Musters, No.* 13.]

Oct. 14.

39. Extract of an Exchequer record relating to the manors of Clerkenwell, Newington Barrowe, Friern Barnet, and Hackney, formerly belonging to the Knights of St. John of Jerusalem.

Oct. 21.
Westminster.

40. Commission for restraint of transportation of corn and grain, and for bringing it into public market.

Oct. 21.

41. Copy of the above ; with the names of the Commissioners in certain counties for that purpose.

Oct. 27.
The Court.

42. Rafe Lane to Lord Burghley. Sends a letter of Capt. Byngham, but which had been misdirected to him. Begs Burghley to excuse the poor man's errors, and obtain a pension for him.

Oct. 28.
York.

43. Henry Earl of Huntingdon to Sec. Sir Tho. Smith. Notifies to him the sending of the Musters for the County of York. Respecting question as to the best mode of keeping the arms and armour of the county. *Incloses,*

 43. I. *Certificate of the General Musters of able men and their furniture for the County of York.*

Oct. 30.

44. Lionell Duckett, Alderman, to Burghley. Sends two letters received from Sweden. Suggests that a quick letter from the Queen to the King of Sweden, and a kind one to the Archduke Charles, would be of service in restoring the money and the liberation of old John Dymock.

Oct.

45. Petition of Acerbo Velutelli to the Council. Complains of the non-payment of certain insurances he effected on two ships which had been captured by the inhabitants of Flushing.

Oct.

46. Reasons why the English merchants trading with France do not desire to have any staple towns.

DOMESTIC—ELIZABETH. 469

Vol. XCII.

1573.
Nov. 2.
Northwich Castle.
47. Commissioners of Musters for the County of Chester to the Council. Certify their doings in taking the General Musters of all the men, horses, armour, &c. Provision for the defence of the shire. *Inclosing,*

    47. I. *Certificate of the number of common soldiers without armour in the County of Chester, amounting to 2,063 able men: and also, a muster book containing the names and number of all knights, esquires, gentlemen, and freeholders within the County of Chester, with the horses, armour, and other furniture; amounting to 937 men.* Nov. 2. [*See Vol.* xciv. *Musters, No.* 14.]

Nov. 3.
48. Note relative to a lease of the manor of Down Court, in Kent, belonging to St. John's College, Cambridge, demised to one Dr. Woodward.

Nov. 14.
Gresham House.
49. Sir Thomas Gresham to his servant Tho. Celye. Instructions for the direction of his private business and household affairs.

Nov. 17.
Hereford.
50. James Whytney, and others, to the Council. Have taken the General Musters of the County of Hereford, of which they send a "Summarie Booke." The county can hardly bear the charge for training soldiers. *Inclosing,*

    50. I. *"A Summarie Booke" of the General Musters for the County of Hereford, taken by virtue of Her Majesty's commission, dated* 14 *March, Anno Reg.* 15.

Nov. 17.
Hereford.
51. Gregory Prise, Mayor, and others, to the Council. Make a return of Musters for the City of Hereford. *Inclosing,*

    51. I. *Certificate of the Musters for the City of Hereford.*

Nov. 27.
Survey of the manors of Minster and Shurland in the Isle of Sheppey, belonging to Henry Lord Cheyne. [*See Vol.* lxxxvii., *No.* 3.]

Nov. ?
52. Petition of Roger Townesend and Wm. Dyx to the Council. That the possessions and revenues of the Earl of Arundel might be conveyed to Wm. Dyx, for payment of the debts and legacies of the late Duke, and the debts of the Earl and his brethren.

Nov.
Certificates of the General Musters for the whole County of Southampton. [*See Vol.* xciv. *Musters, No.* 15.]

Nov. ?
53. General return of Musters for all the counties in Wales, stating the number of able men, trained and selected, armour and munitions, &c.

Nov. ?
Certificate of the numbers of trained and untrained men in the County of Hertford, with the Captains, and of the arms and munitions in the county.

VOL. XCIII. DECEMBER, 1573.

1573.
Dec. 2.
1. John Fortescue to [the Council]. Complains that Lord Grey and John Zowche, with their men, laid wait for him and most unmercifully beat him in Chancery Lane. Solicits redress and personal security.

Dec. 5.
Blackmore Park.
2. Jo. Hornyolde to Lord Burghley. Stating his claim to right of commonage in Malvern Chase. *Incloses,*
2. I. *A note of spoils committed upon the woods in Malvern Chase, in Worcestershire.*

Dec. 6.
3. Certificate of the quantity of all sorts of grain laid up in the storehouses at Lynn Regis.

Dec. 11.
4. A large collection of copies of upwards of 45 letters and other papers, purporting to be a correspondence between Tho. Browne, Tho. Cartwright, and others: the first being a warrant dated 11 Dec. from the Ecclesiastical Commissioners, for the apprehension of Cartwright. The whole inclosed in a parchment cover indorsed by Lord Burghley thus:—

"1573. *A lewd practise of on*
"*Nedehā, under collor to appre-*
"*hend Mr. Cartwright he gat*
"*mõny of y^e Archbish. of Canter-*
"*bury.*"

"1573. *A lewd practise of on*
"*Nedehũ, y^t counterfetted all y^e*
"*l$\bar{r}$es included, to abuse D. Pker,*
"*Archb. of Cantyrbury, w^t opinion*
"*y^t Mr. Cartwrytt was in Eng-*
"*land.*"

Dec. 16.
5. Answer of E[dward] D[ering] to the four articles propounded to him by the Council, concerning the doctrine and government of the Church of England, with statement of his exceptions to the first, third, and fourth articles.

Dec. 20.
Grant to James Rushell, one of the Queen's running footmen, of a pension of 40*l.* a year for life. [*See Warrant Book,* I., *p.* 1.]

Warrant by the Queen appointing Francis Walsyngham, Esq., one of her principal Secretaries of State. [*See Warrant Book,* I., *p.* 3. *Walsyngham took the oaths before the Council on the 21st Dec.* 1573. *Co. Reg.*]

Dec. 22.
6. Lease from Tho. Henneage and Anne his wife, to Michael Henneage, his brother, of certain tenements and pastures in the manor of Fauxflete alias Thornton House, in the parish of Blacktofte, co. York, in reversion after the expiration of the term now held by Geo. Aske. [*Case B. Eliz. No.* 10.]

Dec. 24.
Westminster.
7. Warrant to the Treasurer and Chamberlains of the Exchequer to imprest 500*l.* to Lewis Stockett, Surveyor of the Works, to provide building materials, in addition to sums formerly paid for works and expenses of the Queen's palaces and gardens from Christmas 1572 to Michaelmas 1573.

Dec.
8. A paper headed "The distressed state of the Church of England by division." Describing the number of tenets and practices of various religious sects, particularly the Papists and Puritans, and the evil effects of all on true religion.

DOMESTIC—ELIZABETH. 471

VOL. XCIII.

1573.
9. Book containing lists of the Sheriffs in England and Wales; lists of the members of the Council of the North; and of the Justices of Assize and Justices of Peace in the several counties of England and Wales. [*Indorsed, Liber Pacis de Anno Regni Reginæ Elizabeth Sexto-Decimo.* 1573.]

10. Certificate of the names of the Dean and Prebendaries of Christ's Church, Canterbury, and of the servants and men belonging to them able to bear arms.

1573 ?
11 Grant to Edmund Powell of pardon and remission of the fine of 3,000 marks, on condition of paying the sum of 20*l.* a year for his life.

12. Petition for a grant to John Giles of pardon, and for his readmission into the Company of Merchant Adventurers of England, notwithstanding his having intermarried with Anne Hack, a native of Antwerp, in Brabant.

13. Note of goods lost by Thomas Castelyn, merchant of London, taken by the Flushingers. [*Indorsed* "*An ould matter dealt in* "*by Danyell Rogers at his late beynge in Flanders.*"]

14. Abstract of the whole number of able men in the several counties of England fit for Her Majesty's service; in all 202,004.

15. Declaration of certain English merchants trading to Antwerp, touching the violation of their ancient privileges.

16. Particulars of the lands belonging to Lord Cheyne in the Isle of Sheppey; and of the quantity and amount sold to the Queen and others.

17. State of the case touching the advowson of Sampford Peverel in Devonshire, within the diocese of Exeter, Sir Amias Poulet being the very patron. Also, state of the case of the parsonage of South Petherton.

18. Copies of instructions, commissions, letters, &c. for taking the General Musters of the realm, firing and defence of the beacons, &c. from 1544 to 1573. [*This appears to have been part of a book. The most important entry is that in* 1573, *which is probably the commission and instructions for the Musters of the* 14*th of March in that year, and is often referred to.*].

19. The Countess of Shrewsbury to   . That they were all in good health. Expresses her wishes for him to write a letter to her son, according to the purport she dictates.

20. Exposition of the tenets and opinions of Dr. Martin [Luther] and his followers.

21. Petition of William Aldwen to the Council. Acknowledges that he has offended God and the Queen's Majesty in matters of religion, for which he is heartily sorry, and prays for pardon.

Vol. XCIII.

1573 ?

22. Petition of the Mayor, &c. of Rye, to the Council. For aid in the repair of the puddle and creek of Rye, which will be done for the sum of 3,000*l*.

23. Petition of Thos. Manley, son and heir apparent of Wm. Manley, to hold the manor of Wettenhall, co. Chester, in farm, till livery of the same be legally sued, and that the intruders therein may be ordered to account for the same.

24. Petition of Wm. Hill, prisoner in the Fleet, to the Council. Complains of the obduracy of some of his creditors, who had kept him in prison for above eighteen months. Prays some course may be taken with them for his relief.

25. Things necessary to be resolved on by Council before the coinage can be proceeded in. Whether it shall be done by the Officers of the Mint, or by the Hayes, according to their offer.

26. Orders and regulations extracted from Stat. 5 Eliz. cap. 4., touching artificers, labourers, servants of husbandry, apprentices, &c., with notes and observations showing the evil effects of the non-observance of the said Act.

27. Note of the causes why both lawful and unlawful artificers desire to have the statute touching them to be put in execution and observed.

28. Note showing that many of the Queen's subjects are put to great trouble and charges in law for unlawfully exercising of occupations.

29. Note showing that very many and great commodities will arise by means of the suit touching artificers.

30. Note of the manner how artificers shall sue for their releases and licences; and how they may obtain the same under the Great Seal.

31. Note of the reasons why lawful artificers desire that unlawful artificers may be licensed to continue in their occupations.

32. Proposal that for the more plain understanding of the suit of artificers, the things desired by them are drawn into three several books.

33. A book touching a proclamation for the execution of the statute of artificers; with a draft of the proposed proclamation.

34. A book for erecting of an office and officer to register apprentices' indentures, and to make and keep such records as are necessary for the observation of the statute; with a note of the articles and branches of the Stat. 5 Eliz. cap. 4, touching artificers, whereupon the erecting of this office and officer is chiefly grounded.

35. A book touching a grant from the Queen, that for divers considerations certain artificers, who have unlawfully entered into occupations, &c., may be licensed to continue in the said occupations still; with draft of Letters Patent in conformity thereto.

Vol. XCIII.

1573 ?   36. Note showing that such of the three books touching artificers as shall in anything appear inconvenient, may either be reformed or wholly rejected, and the other proceed.

37. Account of the consumption of woods in the clothing parishes in Kent ; not accounting for the woods spent by Sir Ric. Barker in his iron works.

Opinion of Bartholomew Clerk, William Aubrey, and others, Doctors of Civil Law, on the right of a woman divorced from her husband for his offence, to retain possession of her lands and goods. [See Vol. xlv., p. 8.]

Observations on the duties of good magistrates. [See Warrant Book, I., p. vi.]

Form of a licence to buy and sell certain quantities of wool. [See Warrant Book, I., p. 3.]

[Walsyngham] to   . The Queen hesitates to sign the pardon granted to Mr. Tho. Hussey, at the request of the Earl of Bedford, until she may be assured it will not prejudice the bearer. [See Vol. xlv., p. 22.]

Vol. XCIV. 1573.

1573.   Case containing certificates of General Musters in the year 1573, described in their chronological order.

Vol. XCV. January—June, 1574.

1574.

Jan. 5.   1. Memoranda (in F. Walsyngham's hand,) of business transacted in Council. Principally for a supply of victuals and money for Ireland.

Jan. 7.   2. Note of letters, to be written to the Justices of the Peace in various shires for the levying of men to serve in Ireland.

Jan. 7.   3. Another paper of memoranda by Walsyngham, of business transacted in Council on various subjects. Review of Captain Morgan's men.   Mr. Hatton's request as to a ship in the Isle of Purbeck thought inconvenient.

Jan. 8.   Lease from Tho. Elliot to Francis Hunt, of a messuage or tenement in the parish of St. Lawrence, in the Old Jury, within the City of London, for 21 years.   [Case B. Eliz. No 11.]

Jan. 8.   4. Note of business in Council. The grant of 100 last of herrings for the Ambassador.   Hatton's request.   Order for money, and transportation of Captain Morgan's soldiers into Ireland ; and for money and men to be sent there, &c.

Jan. 8.   5. Another note of business in Council. Principally relating to Ireland.

1574.   Vol. XCV.

Jan. 9. 6. Another note of business in Council. Supplies for Ireland.

Jan. 10. 7. Another note of business in Council. Supply of men and money for Ireland.

Jan. 14. 8. Eight acquittances of Thos. Bellot, and Thos. Pudsey, for money received of Mr. John Purvey, for woodsales and rents, on behalf of Lord Burghley.

Jan. 15. 9. Note of business in Council. Irish affairs. Order on Blande's petitions, and for Tho. Hussey's delivery.

Jan. 21. The Court. 10. Lord Burghley to the President and Fellows of Gonvil and Caius College, Camb. Directs them to proceed in an orderly and proper manner to the election of a new Master of their College, in place of the late Master, Dr. Caius.

Jan. 22. 11. Certificate of the Commissioners for the restraint of the exportation and monopoly of grain within the County of Essex Names of the offenders in certain Hundreds.

Jan. 25. 12. The Queen to the (Justices?) of Berkshire, Oxfordshire, Lancashire, Cheshire, and Shropshire. Directions for the levying of a certain number of soldiers to serve in Ireland.

Jan. 25. 13. Same to the Lord President of Wales. Similar directions for levying of men to be sent to Ireland.

Jan. 25. 14. Same to the Justices of Stafford and Derby. Similar directions for the levying of men for Ireland.

Jan. 15. Note of all the furnaces which do daily cast guns and shot of iron; with the names of the various manufacturers.

Jan. 16. Petition of Ralph Hogge, the Queen's Gunstone maker and Gunfounder, to the Council. Complains of the infringement of his Patent for the sole exportation of iron ordnance.

Jan. 17. Note of all such persons as have made fines upon port-bonds, for the carrying of corn between port and port.

Feb. 1. 18. John Marq. of Winchester, Bishop Horn, and Wm. Lord Lawarre, to the Council. Transmit books of General Musters for the County of Southampton, and the Muster book of horse for the same. Request instructions as to training the selected number of soldiers.

Feb. 3. 19. Lionell Duckett to Lord Burghley. Requests the Queen's letter in his favour to the King of Sweden. Also for a warrant in behalf of the merchants of Russia for the passing of certain hides.

Feb. [15]. 20. Declaration of Christopher Baker touching iron furnaces, and of the great consumption of oak wood in Sussex, Surrey, and Kent by the iron mills and furnaces.

Feb. 15. 21. List of names of the owners of iron works and furnaces, and the places where they are planted, in Kent, Sussex, and Surrey, signed by Christopher Baker.

DOMESTIC—ELIZABETH.

1574.
Feb. 22. Hampton Court.
Feb. 26. Hampton Court.
Feb. 28. Hampton Court.
March 1. Hampton Court.
March 4. Greenwich.
March 5. Greenwich.
March 6. Greenwich.
March 7. Greenwich.
March 10. Greenwich.
March 16.
March 16.
March 21. Greenwich.
March 22.
March 22.
March 26 ?
March ?

VOL. XCV.

22. Bond of William Walpole, under the penalty of 2,000*l.*, not to found or sell iron ordnance without a licence from the Queen.

23-26. Similar bonds of John Thorpe, Robert Raynold, John Duffyld, and John Fawkener.

27–29. Similar bonds of John Lambard alias Gardiner, Tho. Gratwicke, and Robert Whytfyld.

30. Similar bond of Roger Gratwyk, of Sullington, co. Sussex.

31–40. Similar bonds of Geo. Bullen, Nich. Pope, Tho. Isted, Tho. Collen, Tho. Glydd, Alexr. Farmer, John Everysfylde, Nynyan Challoner, Stephen Collens, and Geo. Maye.

41–49. Similar bonds of Edw. Elryngton, Wm. Webb, Nich. Fowlle, John Baker, Robt. Hodgson, Tho. Dyke, Tho. Haye, Arthur Myddleton, and John Palar

50.–52. Similar bonds of Tho. Ellys, John Gardyner for Isabell Asheburnham, and the same John Gardyner for John Asheburnham.

53–56. Similar bonds of John Carpenter, Robert Woody, Wm. Relfe, and the same Wm Relfe for John Relfe.

57, 58. Similar bonds of Tho. May and Barth. Jeffery.

59, 60. Similar Bonds of John Stace and Sir Ric. Baker.

61. Names of noblemen and gentlemen summoned to appear before the Council; and list of the names of the furnaces and forges in Surrey, Sussex, and Kent, and in whose occupation they are.

62. Bond of Sir Thomas Gresham not to found or sell iron ordnance without licence.

63. Petition of divers gentlemen of the West parts of England to the Queen. Soliciting her to allow of an enterprise for discovery of "sundry ritche and unknowen landes." [*Indorsed*, "*Sir Humfrey* "*Gilbert, Sir Geo. Peckham, Mr. Carlile, and Sir Ric. Grenvile, and* "*others, voyages.*"]

64. Gentlemen of the West parts to the Lord High Admiral (Lincoln). Soliciting his goodwill and assistance in furtherance of their projected voyage. *Inclosing,*

    64. I. *Specification in detail of the advantages to be gained by their proposed voyage of discovery South of the equinoctial line.*

Grant to Sir Tho. Co   and to his son R. C   of the office of fitting out and convoying over the fleet of the Merchants of the Staple to Hamburgh. Lat. [*See Warrant Book,* I., *p.* 138, *and also p.* 7.]

Grant in reversion to R. Co   of the Comptrollership of the Customs in the Port of London, after the death or surrender of Tho. Co   . Lat. [*See Warrant Book,* I., *p.* 140.]

VOL. XCV.

1574.
March 26.
Greenwich.
65. Warrant to Dirick Anthonie, Graver of the Mint, for the making and engraving of two signets of gold with the royal arms and scriptures; one of which was to remain with Francis Walsyngham, Esq., Principal Secretary of State.

March 29.
66. Note of certain words reported by Margaret Taylor, wife of Tho. Taylor, in Flanders, relative to Sir John Nevel, and others. Also, copy of a letter from Tho. Tompson to Mr. Tomlingson, relating to the health and condition of his friends and connexions. [*Indorsed*, "*Copies of l'res from ye rebels in Flanders, surprized.*"]

March.
67. Commission for taking General Musters throughout the kingdom, according to the tenor of the Commission and instructions of the preceding year.

March?
68. Note of the number of men to be levied in Wales and several of the counties of England, with their arms, &c.

March?
69. Note that the number of pieces necessary to be cast for the furniture of the realm, are 600 tons; and the reasons for the same.

March?
70. Orders to be observed by the founders and buyers of ordnance, restricting the number of guns to be cast for the only use of the realm.

March?
Grant to William Walding of the sole privilege of writing and flourishing the Queen's name and title in all charters and books to pass the Great Seal. Half of the fines for infringement of the grant to be paid to the use of the poor children within the Hospital of the Grey Friars, London. [*See Warrant Book*, I., *p.* 9.]

March?
71. Grant of pardon to John Jones, for the murder of Morgan John Williams. Signed by Sir Henry Sydney and Sir John Throkmarton. Lat.

March?
Licence to William Heidon to export ten serplers of wool from any port in the county of Norfolk. [*See Warrant Book*, I., *p.* 8.]

April 3.
Greenwich.
Fr. Walsyngham to Lord Adm. Lincoln. Had immediately moved Her Majesty as to the benefice of Burton, but it had been disposed of. Advertisements of news from France and Spain. [*See Vol.* xlv., *p.* 29.]

April 3.
Fr. Walsyngham to Sir Walter Mildmay. Has shown his certificate to the Earl of Leicester, relative to the confirmation of the charters of the City of Chester. [*See ib., p.* 29.]

April 3.
London.
72. Fr. Walsyngham, Sir Walter Mildmay, and others, to the Council. Their proceedings in the examination and settlement of a controversy between the officers of the County Palatine and the corporation of Chester. Examination of the city charter. *Inclosing,*

> 72. I. *Certificate by the above of the order set down by them in the controversy between the Queen's Officers of the Exchequer of the Principality of Chester and the Mayor and Aldermen of the City of Chester.*

DOMESTIC—ELIZABETH. 477

1574.
Vol. XCV.

April 3? 73. Note of certain special points to be touched upon in the letter from the Council to the City of Chester on the conduct of Ric. Dutton, their Mayor, founded on a misconception of a clause of præterea in their late renewed Charter. [*Ric. Dutton, Mayor of Chester, was in London in attendance on the Council in March,* 1574. *Co. Reg.*]

April 4. 74-77. Bonds of Thomas Stolyon, John Frenche, Christopher Darell,
Greenwich. and Anthony Morley, not to found or sell ordnance without licence from the Queen.

April 4. 78. Note of business propounded in Council by Mr. Walsyngham, with orders thereon. Not convenient to have any plays, for fear of the plague.

April 4. 79. Names of owners and founders of iron ordnance, and of the places where the furnaces are situated.

April 5. 80. Note of business in Council. Principally relating to the affairs of Ireland.

April 20. 81. Estimate of the charges for the victualling of twenty-four of the Queen's ships, by Edward Baeshe.

April 25. 82. Richard Coortesse, Bishop of Chichester, to Lord Burghley. Certifies him of the prices of grain. Combination to rob the Frenchmen that make glass. Complains of pirates on the coast of Sussex.

April. 83. Lord Burghley's notes of public business and private affairs. Feb.—Apr. 1574.

May 1. 84. Note of corn powder bought of Henry Dale, haberdasher, with the prices of the same.

May 4. 85. Lord Burghley to Francis Walsyngham, Sec. of State. Intercession to be made for Thomas Bath *alias* Thomazo, arrested in Flanders for a spy, and in danger of death. Stay of mariners. The Earl of Bedford proposed to take charge of the Counties of Devon, Dorset, and Cornwall.

May 9. 86. Memorandum of business propounded in Council.

May 10. 87. Certificate by William Dodington and John Coniers of money and munition remaining unaccounted for by the Earl of Warwick; extracted from the accounts of Richard Dennys, cousin and heir to Sir Maurice Dennys, decd.

May 24. Note of the men, with their furniture and artillery, requisite for setting forth twenty-four of the Queen's ships to the seas. [*See Vol.* xcvi., *p.* 281. *and Vol.* cxv., *No.* 1.]

May 24. A note of powder for the callivers and great ordnance for the Queen's navy. [*See Vol.* xcvi., *p.* 288, *and Vol.* cxv., *No.* 1.]

May 24. 88. Remembrances delivered by Edward Baeshe, relative to the supplying of the navy with provisions for two months.

May 28. 89. Note of powder remaining in store and to be provided within fourteen days.

1574.
May.

Vol. XCV.

90. Note of the places in Barbary traded to by English merchants who are content not to trade beyond Cape Riol, which is to the South-west of the kingdom of Barbary.

May.

91. A survey of the chambers and societies of all the Inns of Court, together with certain devices for the government of the worthy and necessary sort, and for the exclusion of the unworthy and unnecessary number and sort thereof.

May?

92. Petition of a poor woman to the Queen. Details the hardships she suffers in consequence of discovering certain conspiracies; viz., practice of the Earl of Oxford to carry off the Duke of Norfolk; clipping the coin; release of Earl of Desmond, &c.; and praying for relief. [*Desmond was released in March 1573, and this petition is described as being a little more than a year after that event.*]

Vol. XCVI. May, 1574.

An ancient volume, originally bound in parchment, with the title, "*England. Matters of State and Force of the Kingdome.*" Containing entries of lists of Justices of Peace, General Musters, lists of ships, names of noblemen and gentlemen in service, church livings, &c.; of various dates from May, 1574. The following are the contents; the entries, having dates, being also inserted in their chronological order. Some of the entries are not very accurately made.

Pages 1 to 169. Returns of the names of the Hundreds and other divisions in the several counties of England and Wales, with the names of resident Justices of Peace and other officers.

P. 173. The names of the Vice-Admirals in England.

P. 175. The number of churches in every shire.

P. 179. Valuation of the several livings of all the Bishops in England.

P. 182. List of the Bishopricks throughout England, with their clear revenues.

P. 183. Valuation of the several livings of all the Deans in England.

P. 185. Note of such ecclesiastical persons as have more livings than one.

P. 191. The names of all the towns where the posts are, between Berwick and the Court.

P. 192. Names of the post towns coming out of Ireland to London, and from London to Dover.

P. 193. Orders appointed to be generally observed by the Queen's posts throughout the realm.

P. 199. Declaration of Christopher Barker [Baker] touching iron furnaces; names of places where iron works and furnaces are erected, &c.

Pp. 207 to 236. The taxation of the subsidies in divers cities, towns, and ports for the City of London and other counties and towns.

Vol. XCVI.

1574.   P. 237. Note of such towns and persons as are to contribute to the loan.

P. 238. Names of the Judges, Sergeants, and Pleaders.

P. 241. Names of the officers of the Queen's Courts of Record at Westminster, both English and Latin.

P. 247. Names of the Doctors of the Civil Law and the Ministers of the Ecclesiastical Courts.

P. 251. List of noblemen and gentlemen that have served and are fit to serve in foreign employments.

P. 253. Names of such noblemen and gentlemen as have served in war.

Pp. 254 and 255. Names of Captains at Berwick and in Ireland.

P. 256. Men of service, fit for charge, out of pay.

P. 257. Names of sundry gentlemen and Captains for the sea.

P. 259. Names of forts and castles along the sea coasts, with the Captains that have charge of them.

P. 262. Names of gunners in ordinary and in pension in the towns, castles, &c. in Kent, Sussex, Southampton, and Isle of Wight.

P. 265. The charge of Berwick and other holds in the East March.

Pp. 267 to 273. List of ships, &c. in various ports, and in the river Thames and its creeks, and the names of the masters that have taken charge in the Thames. 6 Feb. 1577.

P. 275. Names of Her Majesty's ships, number of men, &c. requisite for setting forth the same. 10 Aug. 1577.

P. 281. Note of the men, provision, &c. requisite for setting forth twenty-four of the Queen's ships. 24 May 1574.

P. 288. A note of powder for the callivers and great ordnance about Her Majesty's navy. 24 May 1574.

P. 292. Note of 1,000 soldiers, with their Captains, to be levied in Wales, and how they are to be furnished with weapons.

P. 293. Note of the Queen's ships now at sea under Henry Palmer; and estimate of the charges of 1,000 men to serve in six of the Queen's ships for six weeks. 17 July 1576.

P. 294. Survey of all the Queen's ships, boats, &c., with estimates of repairs, expenses in harbour, &c. 1 Feb. 1576.

P. 297. Proportion of powder and munitions for the full furniture of three of the Queen's ships appointed to the seas. Aug. 1576.

Pp. 300 to 303. Furniture, &c., for three other ships sent to the seas in May last past. Aug. 1576.

Vol. XCVI.

P. 304. Estimate of the charges of setting forth to the seas twenty of the Queen's ships, for one month. 1 Jan. 1578.

Note of mariners, gunners, &c., to be had out of certain shires. 1 Jan. 1578.

P. 308. Note of all cordage and sail canvass delivered out of the store at Deptford, as well for the ships at sea as for rigging two new ships for the year 1577. 1 Jan. 1578.

Pp. 308 to 315. Note of cordage, sails, and other stores furnished to several ships serving in various parts. Aug. 1577.

P. 316. Account of the full furniture of ordnance, brass and iron shot, and other munitions for twenty-four ships, now to be sent to sea. 1 June. 1574.

P. 323. Account of armour for the said twenty-four ships. 1 June.

Pp. 327 to 392. Abridgment of the general certificates of the Musters taken throughout the whole realm, divided into counties and towns. 1577.

P. 394. Certificate of Musters of the City of London. 15 Aug. 1569.

P. 405. Certificate of the inns and ale-houses in sundry shires. 1577.

P. 415. Names of all the ports, creeks, and landing-places in England and Wales.

Vol. XCVII. June—July, 1574.

1574.
June 1?   1. Instructions given by the Queen's Majesty to her right trusty and right well-beloved cousin and counsellor the Earl of Bedford, Lieutenant of her Counties of Devon and Cornwall and her City of Exeter. To take Musters and put in readiness the whole force of the country, furniture of horse, arms, armour, &c., and for general defence of the same.

June 1.   2. Further instructions to the Earl of Bedford for government of the same counties and city.

June 1.   Entries of the above. [*See Vol.* cxxxiv., *pp.* 698–704.]

June 1.   Instructions for the Lieutenants of Counties. Directions for General Musters and to provide for defence of their counties; of the same tenor as the preceding instructions to Bedford. [*See Vol.* cxxxiv., *p.* 705.]

June 1.   Special article in the above instructions for the Lieutenants of Norfolk and Lincoln. [*See ib., p.* 709.]

June 1.   3. Account of the full furniture of ordnance, brass and iron, shot, and all other munitions and habiliments of war for twenty-four ships now appointed to be sent to sea; together with the charge of the ordnance, &c., to be supplied.

June 1.   Entry of the above. [*See Vol.* xcvi., *p.* 316.]

Vol. XCVII.

1574.
June 1. 4. Account of armour and other things requisite for the furnishing of the said twenty-four ships, and for the repair and mending of the same.

June 1. Entry of the above. [*See Vol.* xcvi., *p.* 323.]

June 1 ? 5. Abstract drawn out of the above account of provisions for the navy within the Office of Ordnance, showing how much of the same might be spared.

June 6. 6. A paper of intelligence. Conditions whereupon Sir Bryan McPhelim's pledges are delivered to the Earl of Essex. News from Antwerp and Holland. Death of Charles IX., and events in France.

June 6.
Bindon.
7. Thomas Viscount Howard of Bindon, to Lord Admiral Lincoln. Sends a certificate of the state of the castles and forts in the County of Dorset. Complains of the number of pirates and sea-robbers frequenting the coast.

June 7.
Poole.
8. Viscount Bindon, Wm. Lord St. John, and others, to the Council. Report on the condition of the castles and forts in Dorsetshire. Directions given for the better keeping of them. Complaint of pirates on the coast. *Inclosing,*

8. I. *A certificate of the repairs and munition required for the defence of the castles in Dorsetshire.*

June 12.
Pendennis
Castle.
9. Sir John Arundel and Richard Chamond to same. Report on the castles and forts in the County of Cornwall. *Inclosing,*

9. I. *Certificate of munition and other things already provided for the defence of various castles in co. Cornwall.*

June 13. 10. Note of business propounded in Council.

June 14. 11. Lord Burghley to Francis Walsyngham. The stay of the Queen's fleet has excited alarm. Thinks it had better be ordered to sail to the mouth of the Thames, which is much haunted by pirates. Thanks for his favor to Geo. Blyth.

June 14. 12. Commission to the Earl of Bedford and the Lord President of Wales to raise 1,000 men for service in Ireland, to be furnished with armour and weapons.

June 14.
Greenwich.
13. Warrant to the Exchequer for the payment of 1,000*l.* to the Earl of Bedford, for the sending of certain men into Ireland.

June 14.
St. Osythes.
14. John Lord Darcy of Chiche, and others, to the Council. Report on the state of the forts in Essex.

June 18.
Winchester.
15. William Lord Sandys, and others, to same. Report on the state of the forts in the County of Southampton. *Inclosing,*

15. I. *Certificate of ordnance and munition in the castles and fort in Hampshire and the Isle of Wight.*

H H

1574.   Vol. XCVII.

June 19. 16. Note of business propounded in the Council. Touching the iron mills, &c.

June 19.
Greenwich. 17. Orders set down by the Council, concerning the casting of iron ordnance.

June 21. 18. Lord Burghley to Francis Walsyngham. Sends letters from Sir James Harington and Mr. Kenelme Digby, with the Council's letters. Requests for Musters in Rutland. Also that a warrant be sent for the payment of 11,000l. to Mr. Spinola. *Incloses*,

18. I. *Note of date of Mr. Spinola's bonds.*

June 21.
Baconsthorp. 19. Sir Chr. Heydon and Sir Wm. Buttes to the Council. Have not yet received one of the Queen's letters for the Musters. Will however take the Musters. Promise shortly to send the Musters for Norfolk, and forward the certificates. The City of Norwich requires a separate commission.

June 29. 20. Note of business propounded in Council, touching pirates, &c.

June. 21. Instruction by Queen Elizabeth to Sir Henry Sydney, Lord President of Her Majesty's Council within Her Dominion and Principality of Wales, and the Marches of the same; and to all mentioned and appointed to be of the said Council.

June. 22. The names of those that are appointed to be of the Queen's Majesty's Council in the Principality and Marches of Wales.

June ? 23. Petition of John Vaughan, of the Isle of Wight, to Walsyngham. Requesting that he may be freed from his imprisonment, having been confined for seventeen weeks.

June ? 24. Petition of the Mayor, &c., of Newcastle to the Queen. To have the castle of Tynemouth united to their Corporation, for which they would discharge Her Majesty of 400 marks yearly, payable by her for keeping the castle in repair.

June ? 25. Petition of John Langrake, Merchant, of Colchester, to the Council. Complaining that his ship the "Marygold," had been robbed and spoiled by certain Frenchmen from Dieppe; and soliciting the arrest of the first ship that may arrive from that port.

July 1. [Walsingham ?] to . To stay the indictment against Peter Evers, a young gentleman of Lincolnshire, who had been incited to counterfeit foreign coin; but having voluntarily acknowledged his offence had been discharged by the Council. [*See Vol.* xlv., *p.* 26. *In June* 1574, *Peter Evers was committed to the Marshalsea for coining Portuguese coin, and on the* 1st *of July was placed under the custody of Mr. Justice Mounson. Co. Reg.*]

July 2.
London. 26. Drs. Wm. Aubrey and Ro. Forthe to Walsyngham. Report on the case between Monsr. Calvart and the men of Sandwich; and also in the case of Wm. Crispe and Thomas Knolles.

Vol. XCVII.

1574.
July 5. 27. David Jones to Mr Mylls (Walsyngham's Secretary). Acknowledging that he had been confessed in the Marshalsea, and two other persons with him, Mr. Blewitt, of the Hanging Sword, in Fleet Street, and Mr. David Sadler. A mass was to be performed next Sunday at Bishop Heath's, late Archbp. of York.

July 6.
Ethrope.
28. Sir Wm. Dormer to the Council. Reasons for the neglect of sending certificate of Musters of horses for the County of Buckingham. A new commission requisite.

July 6.
Richmond.
29. The Council to the Vice-Admiral of Sussex. Order for the stay of shipping in all the ports of Sussex, except fishing boats, or those going from port to port.

July 6.
Rochford.
30. Commissioners of Musters for the County of Essex, to the Council. Proceedings in taking the Musters; and for putting the shire in a state of defence to resist a foreign enemy.

July 7. 31. Certificate by Lord Darcy of Chiche, and the Bailiffs, &c., of Colchester, of Musters of able men, &c., within that town.

July 8.
Winchester.
32. Lord Thomas Poulet, the Earl of Southampton, and others, to the Council. Return of Musters and survey of the County of Southampton. *Inclosing,*

 32. I. *Certificate of the dangerous places for the landing of an enemy on the coasts of Hampshire, from Bournemouth, in Westover Hundred, to the East Haven of Hayling Island. June 25.*

 32. II. *Certificate of the forces from various Hundreds appointed for the defence of the Isle of Wight, Portsmouth, and towns on the coast of Hampshire.*

 32. III. *Certificate of boats appointed for conveying men to the Isle of Wight, upon any attempt.*

 32. IV. *General certificate of the Musters for the whole County of Southampton. Number of horses, furniture of arms, &c.*

July 12. 33. Note of business propounded in the Council. Relating to Ireland.

July 12.
South
Bemflete.
34. Henry Appulton to Walsyngham. Apprehension of Davy Jones; has examined him but has not committed him yet to prison. Sends two letters written by him.

July 12.
Ruthin.
35. Commissioners of Musters for the County of Denbigh. Report their proceedings, and state of the Musters of the county.

July 13.
Windsor.
36. Richard Willes to Walsyngham. States his opinion on some doctrinal points, and his protestation against Popery.

July 18.
Kirtling.
37. Lord North, and Sir Giles Alyngton, to the Council. Proceedings in the Musters. Complain of opposition they met with from Mr. Edward Styward; "a blynde man, verie ryche, and the moste untractable man in Her Majesty's service." *Inclosing,*

 37. I. *Certificate of Musters of horses and geldings in the County of Cambridge, furnished with armour and weapon.*

Vol. XCVII.

1574.
July 19. Torperley.
38. The Sheriff and Justices of Chester to the Council. Report on the Musters and other defences of the County of Chester.

July 20.
39. David Jones to Mr. Mylls. Has given information that Napper was in Mr. Tyrrell's house. An old priest, named Latymer, is in the Clink, and a lot of outlandish men and Englishmen in the Marshalsea. Asks leave to go to Dr. Heath's house.

July 22. Flint.
40. Commissioners of Musters for Flintshire to the Council. Certify particulars of their doings in the Musters. The inhabitants of the county are very poor and but few in number. Names of the Captains, &c. *Inclosing,*

40. I. *Certificate of the names of the gentlemen appointed to furnish light horsemen; and the names of gentlemen who have furnished light horse, although not chargeable by law.*

40. II. *Muster Roll of five hundred footmen certified out of the County of Flint, furnished as required.*

July 30.
41. Lord Burghley to Walsyngham. Sends a letter from Sir Wm. Wynter and Mr. Pelham, that Queenborough was a place well suited to make a naval depôt. Stay of English ships and goods in Rouen. Supply of corn and grain in the City. Complaints by the Ambassador of Portugal against the Lord Admiral. Intends to prohibit unlawful gaming among the Guards.

July 30. Sarum.
42. Earl of Pembroke, and others, to the Council. Transmitting certificate of the Musters taken within the County of Wilts. *Inclosing,*

42. I. *Certificate of demi-lances and light horses for the County of Wilts. Devizes, 16 July.*

July ?
43. Answers to certain articles touching the charges of the several parishes in the Isle of Axholme, Lincoln, for the furnishing and training of soldiers, provision of armour, weapons, &c.

July ?
44. Similar return of answers to certain articles touching the charges of the several parishes in the Wapentake of Manley, co. Lincoln.

Vol. XCVIII. August—October, 1574.

August 1. Worcester.
1. Richard Ligon, High Sheriff, Sir John Lyttelton, and others, to the Council. Proceeding in taking General Musters in the County of Worcester, and preserving the peace of the same. *Inclosing,*

1. I. *Certificate of General Musters of all able men, horses, arms, &c., in the County of Worcester.*

August 1 ?
Walsyngham ? to [Burghley ?] He is not forgotten in his absence by his friends. The Earl of Oxford's return has very much qualified Her Majesty's displeasure, but she does not mean to wrap up his contempt without some kind of reprehension. *Copy.* [*See Vol.* xlv., *p.* 59.]

DOMESTIC—ELIZABETH. 485

Vol. XCVIII.
1574.

August 3.   2. Lord Burghley to Fr. Walsyngham. The Earl of Oxford will
Theobalds.   obey the Queen's commands to go to her in Gloucestershire. He is
fearful if he shall recover Her Majesty's favour. Burghley himself
cannot be present, but hopes Walsyngham and Hatton will continue
Oxford's friends.

August 3.   3. Earl of Shrewsbury to the Council. Musters of light horses in
Sheffield.   the County of Derby by the gentlemen. Requests to be informed if
the freeholders should be dealt with to furnish light horses. *Incloses,*

     3. I. *Muster Roll of light horses for the County of Derby, with the
names of the gentlemen furnishing them.* 20 *July.*

August 3.   4. Sir Henry Weston, and others, to same. Musters of able horses
and geldings in the County of Surrey. Complain of Thomas Wylford,
who refuses to appear. *Inclosing,*

     4. I. *Certificate of the Musters of able horses and geldings in the
County of Surrey.*

     4. II. *Note of such as made default to produce their horses at the
Musters. Signed by the Earl of Arundel.*

August 3.   5. Presentment by the churchwarden and other persons relative to
the church and parsonage of Middleton, Warwickshire.

August [7.]   [Walsyngham?] to [Burghley?]. Although his lordship seems
wholly dedicated to a private life, yet he sends him some news
from Court and from abroad. The Earl of Oxford is restored to
favour. Peremptory order taken for the submission of Desmond.
Foreign news. [*See Vol.* xlv., *p.* 60.]

August 7.   6. Brief declaration of the charges of the diets at the celebration of
the French King's obsequies at St. Paul's; stating the various kinds of
provisions and the prices charged.

August 7.   7. Bishop Cox to Sec. Sir Thomas Smith. Requests him to forward
Doddington.   the certificate of Musters for the Isle of Ely. *Incloses,*

     7. I. *Certificate by Bishop Cox and Lord North of Musters of light
horse within the Isle of Ely.* 19 *July.*

August 8.   8. Lord Henry Clynton and Charles Lord Willoughby to the
Lincoln.   Council. Have taken the Musters of lances and light horses. *Inclose,*

     8. I. *Certificate of the number of demi-lances and light horses fur-
nished within the County of Lincoln, chargeable by statute,
and encreased by the benevolence of the county.*

August 10.   9. Evidence given by Richard Gawyn respecting correspondence
with the English fugitives in Flanders, at the instigation of John
Chancellor; delivery of letters to Lady Morley, the Countess of Northumberland, &c.

1574.
VOL. XCVIII.

August 13. 10. David Jones to Mr. Mylls. Requests to know if he might attend the service at the Charter House, to which many papists resorted. Would have been in danger of starving, only for one Mrs. Cawkon, formerly Mrs. Terell. Information respecting other papists.

August 13. 11. Mayor and Aldermen of Chester to the Council. Request
Chester. repayment of 150*l.*, lent by them to Capt. Bryan Fitzwilliams for conveyance of soldiers to Ireland.

August 15. 12. Viscount Mountague, and others, to the Council. Musters of
Cowdry. the County of Sussex. Request to be informed if the watch is to be continued on the approach of winter. *Inclosing,*

   12. I. *Certificate of able men, horses, and arms within the County of Sussex, and of Captains appointed to the same.*

August 15. 13. Prayer by Queen Elizabeth on her arrival at Bristol, giving thanks for her preservation on that long and dangerous journey. [*See another copy, Vol.* cxiii., *No.* 13. *The date is taken from the contemporary copy in the Lansdowne Collection, Vol.* 115., *No.* 45.]

August 25. 14. Earl of Rutland to Walsyngham. Sends certificate of the Musters for Nottingham, and explains the cause of the smallness of the numbers. *Incloses,*

   14. I. *Certificate of Musters of the horses and geldings in the County of Nottingham chargeable by statute.*

August 27. 15. Sir William Wynter and Mr. Wm. Pelham to the Council.
London. Report their proceedings in putting the Isle of Sheppey and the Medway into a state of defence. Will report verbally as to Queenborough.

[August.] 16. Certificate by Sir Andrew Corbett, Sir Arthur Maynwaryng, and others, of the General Musters for the County of Salop, in anno. Eliz. 16°.

Sept. 1. 17. Thomas Prydeaux to his brother Richard Prydeaux. Has sent
Ghent. his wife and daughter to England to visit him, and greatly commends them The times are variable—dearth, desolation, and danger, both bodily and ghostly, occupy the world.

Sept. 1. 18. Justices of Merioneth to the Council. Report relative to the
Bala. Musters for the said shire. *Inclosing,*

   18. I. *Muster Roll and certificate of able men, horses, armour, and weapons within the County of Merioneth.*

Sept. 5. 19. Sheriff and Justices of Anglesey to same. Their observance of
Anglesey. the instructions relative to the Musters. State of the island, in which there are no horses fit for service. Danger of invasion. *Inclosing,*

   19. I. *Muster Roll of the names of the able men, furniture of armour, &c. in the Isle of Anglesey.*

Vol. XCVIII.

1574.
Sept. 9.
Raighlye Park.
20. Edward Bury to Robt. Lord Rich. Has apprehended, examined, and searched Anthony Tyrell, who had intended to cross over to Flanders, and transmits many papers seized on him. *Incloses,*

> 20. I.-XXIII. *A large collection of letters and papers found on Anthony Tyrell; principally drafts of letters to his relatives and friends, and copy of a holy and vertuous sermon on the miracle of the "Five barley loaves and two small fishes."*

Sept. 13. 21. David Jones to Mr. Mylls. Speaks of some who knew him in prison. Requests the loan of 2s., to be left for him at the George.

Sept. 18.
Stafford Castle.
22. Lord Stafford, Edw. Lord Duddeley, and Tho. Lord Paget, to the Council. Proceedings and certificate of the Musters of light horses and demi-lances in the County of Stafford.

Sept. 21. 23. Edward Mangell, and others, to same. Detail their proceedings in taking Musters of the able men, horses, and arms within the County of Glamorgan.

Sept. 27. 24. The Commissioners of Musters for the County of Montgomery to same. Certifying their doings in the Musters, and particulars of the state of the county. The beacons are duly watched and kept. *Inclosing,*

> 24. I. *Muster Roll of the names of the gentlemen charged with the keeping of demi-lances and light horse. Names of the able men, furniture of armour, &c.*

Sept. 30. 25. Certificate of the horses and geldings for the wars within the County of Middlesex. Mustered by Sir Edw. Harbert, Sir Tho. Gresham, and John Asteley, Esq.

Sept. ? 26. Suit of   Hennadge? for abatement on his licence for the exportation of 3,000 dikers of leather.

Oct. 6. 27. Certificate of defaults and wants of the castle of Portland. [*Indorsed,* "6 Octob frō Viscōt Byndon."]

Oct. 6. 28. Note of certain rebels and fugitives in Flanders, and return of John Hamond to England. Provisions exported from England to the Netherlands.

Oct. 7.
London.
29. William Holstok to Lord Burghley. Report on the state of Lord Cheyne's house at Shurland; only forty deer now in the park there. On next Saturday the house and park will be delivered up to him in the Queen's name.

Oct. 10. 30. Note of business to be propounded in Council.

Oct. 12. 31. Similar paper of business in Council. Requests of the French Ambassador.

Oct. 15. 32. Similar paper of business in Council.

Oct. 17. 33. Similar paper of business in Council.

1574.   VOL. XCVIII.

Oct. 18.   34. Grant of the office of Clerk of the Parliaments to Francis Spil-
HamptonCourt.   man and Anthony Mason alias Wyckes, in place of Sir John Mason, dec. and the said Francis Spilman.

Oct. 21.   35. State of the church of Bromyard, in the diocese of Hereford, and notice of the Bishop of Hereford's letters against the information for three prebends in that church.

Oct. ?   36. Note of certain objections to be made to the brewers, at the solicitation of Jeffrey Duppa, touching the quality of the beer brewed for Her Majesty's household.

37. An estimate of all manner of charges for the brewing of 13 tons of beer in London. [*Indorsed,* "*Mr. Crane's Bill for Brewing of Beer.*"]

38. Orders issued by the Privy Council to be observed in the City of London, for preventing the spreading of the plague; with answers as to what had already been done therein.

VOL. XCIX.   NOVEMBER—DECEMBER, 1574.

Nov. 4.   1. Account of Lord Lumley's debt, and how it grew to King Henry VIII.; and how much of the said debt hath been paid, and the sum that yet remains unpaid; with assurance of the Earl of Arundel and Lord Lumley for discharge thereof.

Nov. 6   2. Henry Earl of Derby, and others, to the Council. Report of
Lathom.   Musters for the County of Lancaster. Precautions for defence of the coasts, and for watching the beacons.

Nov. 15.   3. Mayor, &c. of Norwich to same. Relative to the Musters for the city. Cause of delay. *Inclosing,*

3. I. *Certificate of the number of persons between the ages of* 16 *and* 60 *that did appear for the City of Norwich,* 14 *July,* 1574, *amounting to* 2,120 *persons.*

Nov. 16.   4. Certificate of all the light horses and horses for demi-lances, with their furniture, charged by statute and improvement, within the County of Oxford.

Nov. 17.   5. Articles of agreement made by Sir Chr. Wraye, Lord Chief Justice, and others, between Mr. Francis Rollstone and his son George Rollstone.

Nov. 18,   6. Lord Morley to Lord Burghley. Has written several letters, but
Lisbon.   fears they have been intercepted. Hopes for the Queen's mercy, and to be restored to her favour. Explains his motives for leaving England. Is now going to Venice.

Nov. 22.   7. Warrant to the Lord Treasurer to pay the sum of 389*l.* 11*s.* 8*d.*
HamptonCourt.   to Lord Cobham for extraordinary charges for defence of various castles and forts in Kent.

Nov.   8. Requests by the merchants trading into Spain and Portugal for incorporation and confirmation of former privileges.

1574.
Nov.

Vol. XCIX.

9. Petition of Alderman Tho. Pullison, and many others, merchants trading to Spain and Portugal, to the Council. Praying to be admitted into any new company that may be incorporated for an exclusive trade into those countries.

Dec. 2.
The Arches.

10. Dr. Lewes to Lord Burghley. Requests him to consider the claim of the Chapter of Landaff for the custody of the temporalitie during the vacancy of that bishoprick. *Incloses,*

> 10. I. *Copy of the Letters Patent of King Edward II., granting to the Chapter of Landaff the custody of the temporalities of the bishoprick during the vacancy of that see.* 4 *March,* 1318.

Dec. 2.

11.   to same. Urging the petition of Mrs. Jone widow of the late Bishop of Landaff, to occupy the house of Matharne during the vacancy of the bishoprick.

Dec. 3.

12. Margaret Countess of Lennox to same. Laments the heavy burthen of the Queen's displeasure. Sends him the copy of a letter she has written to the Earl of Leicester. *Incloses,*

> 12. I. *Countess of Lennox to the Earl of Leicester. Explains her visit to the Countess of Suffolk at Rufford. Conversation with the Queen as to marriage of her son with the daughter of the Countess of Shrewsbury. Requests his kind influence in her favour.*

Dec. 10.
Hackney.

13. Same to same. Thanks him for presenting her excuse to the Queen. Excuses herself for visiting the Countess of Shrewsbury, and consenting to her son's marriage.

Dec. 17.
Dover Castle.

14. Writ from Wm. Lord Cobham, Lord Warden of the Cinque Ports, to the Bailiff, &c. of Hythe, to produce records in the case of William Dalmyngton *versus* William Amye, in the Admiralty Court of the Cinque Ports.

Dec. 22.

15. Walsyngham to the Earl of Huntingdon. Sends interrogatories for the examination of the Lady Lennox's secretary, upon matters connected with the marriage of Charles Lord Darnley with the daughter of the Countess of Shrewsbury. Anxiety of Guerras to know the movements of the Countess of Lennox.

Dec. 26.
Hampton Court.

The Council to the Dean and Chapter of Bath and Wells. Marvelling they have refused to confirm a lease of [the manor of Banwell?] granted by the Bishop of Bath, at the Queen's request, to Lord Henry Seymour. Desire them to confirm the said lease or to appear and show cause why they do not. [*See Vol.* xlv., *p.* 17.]

Dec. 28.
Hampton Court.

16. Burghley to Thomas Coppley. Has received his letter declaring the continuance of his duty of allegiance to the Queen. Answers at great length to that and former letters. Regrets that for religious scruples he has left his native land, and recommends him to consider the foundations of such a change. Requests him to give information respecting the authors of the libels of late published against him and the Lord Keeper.

1574.
Dec.

1574?

17. Arguments by Thomas Coppley, proving that the conveyances he had made of his lands, previous to his going abroad, were good and valid in law, and that it would be great injustice to defeat them on the ground of his quitting the kingdom without licence.

18. Table of the Hundreds appointed for the defence of Portsmouth, the Isle of Wight, and the sea coast of Hampshire, for the years 1571, 1572, 1573; with additions and alterations made in 1574.

19, 20. Two copies of the above.

21. Note of monies raised by loan from the Bishops in their several dioceses.

22. Statement of losses sustained by Thomas Pullysson, Alderman of London, and Humphry and Edmund Martine, from the Prince and States of Holland, by reason of the detention and confiscation of their ship at Flushing.

23. Petition of George Southaick, Merchant Adventurer, to Mr. Sec. Walsyngham. Solicits a commission concerning his suit to Her Majesty, and promises not to put the same in execution without his consent.

24. Answer of the Dean and Canons of Windsor to Messrs. Middlemore and Hatche's allegations respecting the enforcement of the feefarm of lands belonging to the Poor Knights of Windsor; with statement of income and expenditure of those lands.

25. List of names of Knights of the Garter.

26. Petition of William Symonds to the Council. Praying to be relieved from a false verdict given against him in an action brought against him by William Napper for usury.

27. Reasons offered to the Queen for the establishing of an exclusive trade with the Barbary States.

28. Reasons for a Charter of Incorporation of the Meer Merchants trading for wines and other commodities into France, to guard against the injuries done to the trade by the retailers encroaching upon the merchants.

29. Another copy of the above.

30. Fragment of part of the above; with apostils in the hand of Lawrence Thompson.

31. Fragment of another copy of the above.

32. A discourse of the advantages to be gained by establishing an office for the sealing of all cloths according to the laws of the realm.

33. Petition of Carlin Heraut, Captain of the gallion named the "Great Holy Ghost," of Marseilles, to the Council. Praying that his ship, now under arrest in the Thames, may be released, or that he may be paid for her freight.

Vol. XCIX.

1574?

34. Note of the sale of the manor of Romborough by the Earl of Arundel to Mr. Holland.

35. Grant of licence to John Wakeman of the Town of Gt. Yarmouth, and Katharine, his wife, to export 4,000 quarters of wheat and 4,000 quarters of barley and malt out of Norfolk and Suffolk, during the next five years.

36. A brief of the leases and estates of the Prebend of Buckingham, as it is related by Mr. Pagitt, with the answers of Robert Jhonsoun, declaring the true state of the cause, as it is in deed; attested by Lord Henry Seymour. [*Indorsed* "*Mr. Bretts' allegations with Jhonsoun's answers.*"]

37. " Rates for the customs of harness and munitions."

38. Particulars of the late dissolved monastery of Thorney Abbey, in the County of Cambridge, with a survey of the same. [*Indorsed by Cecill,* "*Thorney. Sir W. Russell.*"]

39. Note of the yearly value of the manors of Blecheley in Buckingham, and of Brampton in the County of Hereford. [*Indorsed,* "*Lord Grey's suit for the exchange of the Manor of Spaunton in Com. Ebor.*"]

40. E. Clerke to [.] Complains of Tho. Peniston, who unjustly impeached the marriage of his son with Anne Conysby, and desires that Peniston may be commanded to tell where she, Conysby, is hid.

41. Report to the Queen by an Italian, of his survey of the ports of Rye and Sandwich, touching the necessary repairs; requests some remuneration.

42. Petition of Zecheus Garratt to Sec. Walsyngham. Complains of being defrauded of the sum of 33*l.* by Stephen Stringer, servant to Sir Tho. Gawdie.

43. Petition of John Ducke and others, Moneyers of the Mint, to Lord Burghley and Sir Walter Mildmay. Claiming allowance for waste in the coinage of gold, and for the making of small money.

44. Petition of same to same. Soliciting payment of arrears due to them, or for some convenient sum of money to relieve their extreme necessity.

45. Petition of Tho. Husee to the Earls of Leicester and Bedford. Desires their letters to call Geo. Lamplughe before them, to compound with his daughter for such lands as he had received from Her Majesty.

46. Plan for the proposed new quay at Portsmouth, by Richard Popinjaye.

47. Accompt of money expended, by whom does not appear. Sums to Tho. Danett, Mrs. Jane Danett, and others.

48. Names of the overseers and assistants of the river Thames, from Isleworth to Greenwich.

1574?

Vol. XCIX.

49. Names of certain persons desired by Sir John Smyth to be permitted to have access to him, for the compounding of certain debts and suits in law.

50. List of the officers and servants of the armoury at Greenwich, with a note of their wages.

51. The Fellows, &c., of Magdalen College, Cambridge, to Lord Burghley, Sir Francis Knollys, and others. Complimentary, and expressing gratitude for benefits conferred on their College. Lat.

52. Petition of Richard Startute to the Earl of Lincoln, Lord Admiral. For letters of reprisal against the ships and goods of Brittany, to make satisfaction for loss of his ship and goods taken by the "Brave" of Conquet.

53. The reply of Thomas Browne and Geo. Tarperley unto the answers of Master Gerrard, relative to the seditious words of Richard Jones, whereupon the whole state of the case dependeth.

54. A brief note or device for the maintenance of tillage and husbandry, and for supplying the markets at a reasonable price, by establishing an officer for granting licences for the exportation of grain.

55. A small book containing a roll or register of the names of all the Catholics in England in 1574, and also a list of heretics.

56. Book containing entries of abstracts of the General Musters for the several counties, cities, and towns of England and Wales, in the years 1573 and 1574. [*This book originally had a parchment cover which is a fragment of an old Latin and English dictionary, extending from Exo. to Fa., which is preserved.*]

57. Petition of the parishioners of St. Buryan, co. Cornwall, to the Lord Treasurer, Sir Walter Mildmay, and Chief Baron Saunders. Asserting theirs to be a parish church and not a deanery or collegiate church, as untruly suggested.

58. Plan of the Parish of St. Buryan and the adjacent parishes, from Mounts Bay to Whitsand Bay and the Scilly Isles.

59. Detail of the ceremonies to be observed at the funeral of Lady Eleanor Neville, daughter of Henry Earl of Westmoreland, and late wife of William Pelham, Esq., of Brooklesby. [*Imperfect.*]

60. The names of the Commissioners for Causes Ecclesiastical within the Province of York.

61. Account of the expenditure of beer, ale, and wine in the Queen's Household, in anno 16° Eliz., amounting to 9,371*l.* 5*s.* 9¾*d.*

62. Petition of the merchants trading to France to the Council. Requesting payment for the wines supplied by them for the Household during the last fourteen months.

Grant to S.W of a yeoman waiter's place in the Tower of London, on the first vacancy, with a fee of 8*d.* per diem. [*See Warrant Book*, I., *p.* 127.]

1574.

VOL. C. 1574.

1. Book of the valuation of benefices in all the dioceses in England and Wales, with the tenths of the same.

2. "The valuation of the cathedral churches and the spiritual "promotions in the same, within the office of Mr. Conniers."

3. Similar valuation, within the office of Mr. Doddington.

VOL. CI. 1574.

Book containing the valuation of benefices and spiritual promotions in several counties and cities, with the tenths of the same.

VOL. CII. 1574.

Book of the valuation of benefices in various counties, from 15*l.* to 30*l.* per annum, with the tenths of the same.

VOL. CIII. JANUARY—JUNE, 1575.

1575.
Jan. 6.
London.

1. Dr. Wm. Chaderton to Lord Burghley. Reasons for the expulsion of Mr. Jones, late fellow and bursar of Queen's College, Cambridge. Complains of Mr. Rockrey. Desires a letter to Mr. Lewis Dive, touching Mr. Stokes, his brother.

Jan. 8.

2. Thomas Barbar to same. Desires reservation of the lease of the parsonage of St. Katharine Christchurch, in London, and the garden plot of seven acres there, given to Magdalen College, Cambridge, by the late Lord Audley.

Jan. 18.
Cambridge.

3. Dr. Andrew Perne to same. All the Colleges have resumed their accustomed exercises in learning, except St. John's. Precautions for abating the plague in Cambridge. Conveying water to Cambridge for scouring the King's Ditch. *Incloses*,

3. I. *Device and estimates for conveying water from Trumpington Ford unto the King's Ditch in Cambridge, by Richard Brown.*

3. II. *Device by John Bryant for the conveyance of water from the King's Mills to the head of the King's Ditch, against Pembroke Hall.*

Jan. 20

4. Table of allowances in the Queen's Household; with specification of the Bouge of Court, and the allowances to each individual. Lat.

Jan. 21.
London.

5. Thomas Wattes to Burghley. States the result of his inquiries respecting the parsonage and garden of St. Katharine, Christchurch, belonging to Magdalen College, and now let on lease to Mr. Benedict Spinola.

VOL. CIII.

1575.
Jan. 21.
Paris.
6. Lord Morley to Lord Burghley. Has been driven by imminent necessity to repair into those parts. Prays to be restored to the Queen's favour. His only fault was leaving England without permission.

Jan. 26.
Magdalen Coll.
7. Dr. Roger Kelk to same. The College have acted according to his request respecting Mr. Spinola. Recommends one Brommell to be selected for the vacant fellowship.

Jan. 31.
8. Rodolph Jones to same. Complains of the severity he met with in his expulsion from Queen's College. Endeavours to retain Burghley's good-will. Lat.

Jan.
9. Declaration of Tho. Thorney, of Portsmouth, of his being robbed of his ship and goods in the harbour of the Hogge, in Normandy.

Feb. 18.
10. Commissioners of Musters for Buckinghamshire to the Council. Certify their doings in the Musters, and apologise for their delay. *Inclosing,*

    10. I. *Certificate of the demi-lances and light horse furnished within the County of Buckingham.*

Feb. 19.
Queen's Coll.
11. Dr. Wm. Chaderton to Burghley and Sir Tho. Smith, Secretary of State. The expulsion of Mr. Jones was a matter of necessity, which makes it desirable that on no consideration he be again admitted into the College. *Incloses,*

    11. I. *Detail of circumstances and causes of proceeding against Mr. Jones, of Queen's Coll., who is of a factious mind and contentious nature. Signed by Dr. Chaderton and others. Jan. 26.*

Feb. 26.
Queen's Coll.
12. Robert Soome and Edmund Rockrey, Fellows of Queen's Coll., to Burghley. In favour of Mr. Jones who had been hardly treated. Lat. *Inclosing,*

    12. I. *Testimonial from certain of the Fellows of Queen's Coll., concerning Dr. Chaderton's proceedings in the expulsion of Mr. Jones. 29 Jan. Signed by Soome, Rockrey, and others.*

Feb.
13. Conditions of the obligation by which the Merchants Adventurers are permitted by the Spanish Governor-General of the Low Countries to trade to Antwerp by the river Scheldt.

Feb.
The Queen to Sir Hen. Sydney. Condoles with him on the death of his daughter Ambrozia Sydney. Offers to receive his surviving daughter (Mary) as a visitor. [*See Warrant Book,* I., *p.* 83. *Ambrozia died at Ludlow Castle, 2 Feb.* 1575.]

March 7.
Queen's Coll.
14. Robt. Garrett, and others, Fellows of Queen's College to Burghley and Sir Thomas Smith. State the real cause of the expulsion of Mr. Jones, was that of his not being able to clear his college accounts when called upon by the Master.

VOL. CIII.

1575.
March 9.
15. Earl of Leicester to Secretary Walsyngham. The Queen desires further examination to be made by Lord Burghley, Walsyngham, and Sir W. Mildmay in the affair mentioned. No determination has been come to respecting the Irish affairs.

March 10.
London.
16. Walsyngham to Leicester. Has received the Queen's directions that the parties accused by the stationer should be arrested and examined. Fears no good will come of that course. Laments there had been no determination respecting Ireland, and proposes the Earl of Essex to be recalled. Recommends that an ambassador be immediately sent to Scotland.

March 20.
London.
17. Same to same. Informs him of all that had taken place respecting the league with Denmark. Little good can be expected from sending an ambassador into Scotland, unless some concessions were made by Her Majesty.

March 25.
Cambridge.
18. Dr. Andrew Perne to Lord Burghley. Sends the evidence relative to Mr. Jones. Reminds him that the works on law and medicine, which he promised to send to the University library, have not been received. Enumerates many liberal gifts made to the library by the Archbp. of Canterbury and others. *Incloses*,

18. I. II. *Depositions of various Fellows of Queen's College, taken before Dr. Perne, Vice-Chancellor, respecting the expulsion of Mr. Jones, late Fellow and Bursar of the College; with copy of certain statutes of the College, relative to the case of Mr. Jones.*

March 28.
Pembroke.
19. John Vaughan to [Burghley?]. Reports the quantity of corn shipped for Ireland on the commissions of Edward Waterhouse and Tho. Sackford. Great frauds committed by variation in the quantity and contents of the bushel measure.

March 30.
Redcross Street.
20. Wm. Herlle to Burghley. Events in Germany and the Low Countries. Sends the licence for exportation of 2,000 cloths granted to Paul Buys and his colleagues.

March 31.
21. The Wardens of the Bakers to same. Certify that the foreign corn in the Bridgehouse was unsound and not fit for use.

March 31.
22. Jas. Hawys, Lord Mayor of London, to same. Requests licence for the transportation of 400 quarters of damaged wheat without duty now lodged in the Bridgehouse.

March?
23. Complaint against some person for serving writs upon scholars of Cambridge, and taking money not to prosecute them, and for contempt offered to the Vice-Chancellor.

April 2.
Grant of Arms to Henry Archer of Theydon Gernon, Essex, by Robt. Cooke, Clarencieux. [*See Grant of Arms, No.* 11.]

April 3.
Westminster.
24. Burghley to Wm. Herlle. Has written to Mr. Smith according to his request, and wishes to be informed of the effect. Is glad Paul Buys and his colleagues have departed. "The best trial of all men is "the touchstone of their honest lives, for it is impossible to gather figs "from thorns." Can do nothing for his brother, Laurence Johnson.

Vol. CIII.

1575.
April 8.   25. Confession of faith and appeal to the Queen's mercy, of five Dutchmen condemned for Anabaptism.

April 11.   26. Lord Burghley to Sec. Fr. Walsyngham. Thanks for his Italian
Westminster.   advices, " wherin a man may see that the world is made of a round " substance, that it cannot stand still." The Earl of Sussex is at Bermondsey taking physic. Favour of the Queen to the Earl of Essex. Has shown to the Queen the Scottish Regent's letter. His son (Cecill) intends to travel for a year.

April 11.   27. Walsyngham to Burghley. Has been informed by a Scottish gentleman that the Regent was inclined to favour the Hamiltons and the French interest. Discourses on the policy to be pursued towards Scotland.

April 12.   28. Walsyngham to the Queen. Has learned from a Scottish gentleman that the Regent was inclined to favour the French interest, and seeks to take the charge of the young King from Sir Alexander Erskin. Recommends that the breach with Scotland should not be suffered to increase.

April 13.   29. Henry Earl of Derby to Burghley. Offers to furnish timber
New Park.   from his park of Hawarden for Her Majesty's service in Ireland.

April 14.   30. Walsyngham to the Queen. States his opinion, as commanded, respecting the policy that should be observed with regard to Scotland.

April 19.   31. Burghley to Walsyngham. Returns his writings with many thanks and is glad he is at Court: would gladly help the plough with him either in the ridge or furrow. Is in doubt respecting the affairs of Scotland. Is better in health and can go softly with the help of one staff.

April 21.   32. Tho. Kendall to Tho. Windebank. Complimentary. Is richer
Norwich.   in years and diseases than in any other riches, and intends giving up his school. The city is filled with strangers.

April 25.   33. Agreement between the strangers of the Dutch congregation in the town of Colchester and the bailiffs and commonalty of the said town.

April 25?   34. Complaints of the burgesses of Colchester against the foreigners and strangers inhabiting their town.

April 28.   35. The Master and Fellows of Magdalen Coll., Cambridge, to
Magdalen   Burghley. State their reasons that Mr. Lucas Clason should not be
College.   restored to his Fellowship; they think themselves happy to be so rid of him. Burghley has been misinformed as to Henry Vause.

May 3.   36. Robert Cruse to same. Has all his life been loyal to his Queen, and had no evil intention in going to France. Had associated there with the disaffected Scots for the sake of gaining information, which he had now returned to disclose.

DOMESTIC—ELIZABETH. 497

1575. VOL. CIII.
May 3. 37. Robert Cruse to Lord Burghley. Sends information respecting the dealings of several Scots, refugees in France, and the plans of the rebels for liberating the Queen of Scots.

May 4. 38. Same to same. Answers to all the questions he has sent him respecting his dealings with the disaffected Scots, and long detail of all his proceedings in France.

May 4. 39. Note of matters to be propounded in Council.

May 6. 40. Robert Cruse to Burghley. Solicits pardon for his misdoings in talking with Scots : declares his loyalty.

May 6. 41. Burghley to Mr. Sec. Walsyngham. Returns the letter of
Westminster. M. Lanquett, and marvels he does not write more about the proceedings of the Duke of Saxe with his theologians. Recommends Henry Knolles and Norton to be made choice of in addition to Mr. Solicitor and Mr. Randolph, to examine a number of prisoners.

May 7. 42. Inconveniences that would happen within the Bishoprick of Durham on dissolution of the County Palatine there.

May 8. 43. Note of Minutes of Council, and of subjects to be considered.

May 8. 44. Ceremonies at the election and installation of Charles Lord Howard, of Effingham, as Knight of the Garter.

May 12. 45. Order in Council for the settlement of divers controversies, debates, and strifes between the University of Oxford on the one side, and the Mayor, &c. of the city on the other side, touching the use and exercise of sundry charters and privileges claimed by both of them. [*This controversy, as appears by sundry entries in the Council Register, was commenced in the month of Sept.* 1574, *and finally concluded on the* 12th *of May following.*]

May 12. 46. Request of the Judge of the Admiralty to the Lord Chief Justice of the Queen's Bench, with the answers to the same, as to writs of prohibition and practice of the Admiralty Court.

May 15. 47. Note of matters to be propounded in Council.

May 15. 48. Burghley to Walsyngham. Danger of the Archbishop of Canterbury. Recommends the Archbishop of York to be appointed his successor.

May 16. 49. Alex. Nowell, Dean of St. Paul's, to Burghley. Recommends the Archbp. of York to be appointed to succeed Archbishop Parker, if he should die.

May 17. 50. Reasons for granting the suit of William Gregorie, of Exeter, for protection for two years against his creditors.

May 28 51. Dean and Chapter of Worcester to Burghley. Request that
Worcester. their college may not be deprived of the farm of Dunhamsted on Mr. Ralph Holiwell's pretence of concealed lands.

I I

1575.

VOL. CIII.

May 28. 52. Sir Francis Englefyld to William Cotton at Antwerp. Congratulates him on the good success of his suits, and hopes the performance may be as good. Fears the news of their banishment may deter many from lending their assistance in the cause.

May 28. 53. Lord Henry Howard to Mr. Secretary Walsyngham. Regrets the loss of the Queen's favour, and requests him to pity his case, seeing he had no evil intention, and to speak in his behalf.

June 4. 54. Estimate of Works at Somerset House; and also a note of expenses in the Queen's palaces and household, the first item of which is,—for the "boylinge of the brawnes agaynst Christmas at Hampton "Court, 8*l*. 14*s*." Other items for the revels occur.

June 4 ? 55. Note of the conveyance of Somerset House, otherwise called Chester Place, to the late Duke of Somerset and the Lady Anne, Duchess of Somerset, his wife.

June 6.
Pembroke. 56. John Vaughan, Customer of Milford, to Lord Burghley. Sends the commissions of Tho. Sackford and Edward Waterhouse, and complains of illegal shipment of corn and malt by them, and of their smuggling a quantity of hops.

June 9.
Oxford. 57. Dr. Lau. Humfrey to same. The restoration of Noble has been earnestly urged in convocation, but he refuses to submit. His cause and that of the scholars are referred to Burghley's decision.

June 9. 58. Requests made unto the Queen by the inhabitants of the Isle of Sheppy for liberties, whereby the said isle may be better peopled, and of more force to withstand the enemy.

June 16.
Tuddington. 59. Earl of Leicester to Burghley. Sends the note the Queen talked to him of at Hatfield, respecting a new rate of poundage. Particulars relating to the wardship of young Varney, for whom a marriage has been proposed with one of Mr. Cave's daughters, Burghley's niece. The wardship at length transferred to Sir John Hibbott. *Incloses,*

  59. I. *Note of rates of poundage to be increased, with an estimate of one year's imports.*

June 17. 60. Petition of Stephen Lane, John Phillips, and others, of Oxford, to Burghley. Praying they might not be called to give evidence respecting the affray at the house of William Noble, in which Tho. Hickson and other students of Christ Church were implicated.

June 18.
Milford. 61. Robert Hickes to Brother Callys. Has heard from him by Mr. Ellys. All he possesses is at his service. Is now on board the "Neptune," at Millford, with a prize of corn.

June 22
London. 62. William Villers to Lau. Tomson. Complains of the obstacles offered by Alderman Pullison and the two Martins to his acting with Mr. Rogers as his associate in the Merchants' causes.

DOMESTIC—ELIZABETH.

VOL. CIII.

1575.
June 25. 63. Lord Burghley to Mr. Sec. Walsyngham. Understands from him
Westminster. the Queen's intention to leave Greenwich. Has been so occupied that he has not had any time to attend to his own private affairs, and has only spent two evenings with his wife and children at Theobalds since the Queen's departure from London.

June 25. 64. Sir John Perrot to same. Requests that his book on con-
Carew. cealed lands may be returned as soon as certified, and that he may have fresh letters from the Council to the Lord Deputy of Ireland, for restitution of certain of the goods of the Peter and Paul of Marseilles.

June 25. 65. Thomas Cole to Mr. Tomson. With a statement of the expulsion of himself and others from Magdalen College; solicits his advice as to obtaining redress.

June 26. 66. Same to Mr. Mills. On the same subject, and earnestly requesting him to obtain Sec. Walsyngham's letter in their behalf to the Bishop of Winchester.

June 26. 67. Nicolas Lombard to same. On the same subject. Impugns Dr. Humfrey's motives in the late expulsions from Magdalen College. Solicits his good aid in their behalf.

June 28. 68. Burghley to Walsyngham. Sends letters for the Earls of Sussex
Theobalds. and Leicester. Is glad that he need not be at the Court till the 5th of July. [*This letter is dated by Burghley July 28, which is evidently an error for June.*]

June 29. 69. Sir Ralph Sadleir to Burghley. Returns the letters of Sir W.
Standon. Mildmay, and others. Has sent to Cornbury for the young Baron of Dunsany, and will examine him according to his instructions.

June 29. 70. Nicolas Lombard to Mr. Mills and Mr. Tomson. Stating the inflexible enmity of Dr. Humfrey, their President, towards those who had been expelled. Nothing would content him but their utter ruin.

June (?) 71. Articles concerning Mr. Tho. Brigenton and Mr. Chr. Gregory, not conforming to the statute " De Socijs et Schol. beneficiatis."

72. Articles respecting Mr. Wade not conforming to the statute " De numero Scholarium," &c.

73. Queries upon the statute " De electione officiariorum," and state of the case of the Fellows expulsed from Mag. Coll., Oxford.

74. Dr. Humfrey of Mag. Coll., Oxford, to [Burghley?]. Proposes a way by which certain persons in the University might retain their places, by not too strictly construing certain statutes.

75. Note of the wages of the captains, gunners, &c., in various forts and garrisons in the Isle of Wight.

June. 76. Memoranda, in Burghley's hand, for victuals for Berwick, Ireland, &c. Accompt of money for the Queen of Scots' diet, &c.

77. Brief declaration by Edward Baeshe for the victualling of Her Majesty's ships.

Vol. CIV. June, 1575.

1575.
June.

Volume, bound in parchment, headed "The Report of the Allot-"ments of Justices of Peace, &c., with their severall divisions in divers "shires," distinguishing the divisions and limits of each shire, the names of resident Justices of Peace, and of the Coroners and Clerks of the Peace within the same.

Vol. CV. July—December, 1575.

July 1.
Easton.

1. L[aurence] T[omson] to Dr. Humfrey. A letter of very friendly advice. Deplores the state of parties at Magdalen College, and censures his proceeding to such a severe measure as expulsion of Fellows for such a matter.

July 2.

2. Nic. Lombard to Mr. Tomson. With observations upon certain statutes, and the present state of affairs in the college. Solicits his help and that of Mr. Mills.

July 3.
Ivy Lane.

3. Peter Osborne to Lord Burghley. Sends the prices of certain wares and the rates they be now at in the Custom House. Recommends that the merchants trading to Spain should be incorporated into a company.

July 3.

4. Nicolas Gybbarde to Laurence Tomson. Regrets the prevalence of popery in the University, which is felt not in Magdalen College only, but pervades the whole body.

July 4.
Wellington.

5. John Popham to Edward Dyer. Returns his papers relative to the privileges of the tanners, with all exceptional points provided for. Decay of the leather trade.

July 4.

6. Copy of the will of Sir Thomas Gresham, from the Register of the Prerogative Court of Canterbury.

July 4.

7. Declaration on Dr. Humfrey's behalf touching his expelling Mr. Cole, and five other preachers out of Magdalen College, Oxford; together with answers by Mr. Cole, Nicolas Lombard, and others.

July 5.
Hyndelipe.

8. John Abington to Bishop Scorey. On the request of Mr. Richard Meye, for his Lordship to forbear pressing the repayment of the 40l. due by Meye to him. Copy sent by the bishop to Sec. Walsyngham.

July 6

9. List of the English fugitives abroad receiving pensions from the King of Spain, with list of those gone to Spain to sue for pensions. [*Superscribed*—" *To the Duchesse of Ferya.*"]

July 6.

10. Note of sundry English rebels and fugitives abroad, especially in the Low Countries, with the stipends received by them from the King of Spain; and stating the death of Leonard Dacre, on the 12th Aug. 1573. Lord Morley is gone into Spain.

July 8.
Over against
Durham Place.

11. Thomas Windebank to Sec. Francis Walsyngham. Answers touching the matter between Captain Sebastian and his cousin, a wench whom Sebastian claimed in marriage, and who was a fitter wife for him than for an honester man.

	Vol. CV.
1575. July 10.	12. University of Oxford to the Earl of Leicester. In behalf of Mr. Cole, Mr. Powell, and Mr. Lombard, expelled from Magdalen College.
July 10 ?	13. Petition from the Fellows and Students of Magdalen College to the Council. Praying they would take into favourable consideration the rigorous sentence of expulsion passed by Dr. Humfrey on the six Masters of Arts, Thos. Cole, and others.
July 10 ?	14. Draft of the above.
July 10 ?	15. Statement of the cause why Powell, Cole, and Lombard were removed out of Mag. Coll., Oxford.
July 11.	16. Sec. Fr. Walsyngham to the Bishop of Winchester, as Visitor of Mag. Coll., Oxford. Advocating the cause of Cole, Lombard, and the other expulsed Fellows, and censuring the intemperate proceedings of Dr. Humfrey, the President.
July 12.	17. Grant of Arms to Richard Jessopp, of Broomehall, Yorkshire, by William Flower, Norroy King at Arms.
July 15. London.	18. William Bond, Alderman, and others, to Walsyngham. Requests letters from the Queen to the French king, for obtaining compensation for the piratical capture of their ship the " Pelican," by Captain Landreaw.
July 16. Losely.	19. Bishop Horn to Walsyngham. Will do all that lieth in him to quench the fiery coals kindled in the Society of Magdalen College. And, on the same paper, copy of letter to the President and Fellows of the College, condemning the present unseemly proceedings, and directing that no elections should be made to the places of Mr. Cole and the other expelled Fellows.
July.	20. Declaration of Mr. Thomas Cole, William Powell, Henry West, Nicolas Lombard, Walter Enderbie, and Ralph Smith, as to the reason of their not acceding to the election of a Dean in Magdalen College.
July ?	21. Notes upon the statutes of Mag. Coll., Oxford; being mostly a draft of the foregoing.
July 29 ? Lichfield.	[Walsyngham ?] to Lord Adm. Lincoln. The Council approve of his proceeding against Brooke and others for piracy. Directions to prevent English mariners engaging in the Spanish service. Sr. H. Sydney is going into Ireland, and is to be of the Council. Sir John Foster and others, of the Borders, set at liberty by the Scots. [See Vol. xlv., p. 31. Sir Henry Sydney was sworn of the Council on the 31st July 1575.]
July 29 ? Lichfield.	[Same ?] to the Earl of Pembroke. Is glad to hear of the benefit my lady and he are likely to receive from the mineral waters. The disorders on the Borders are like to be amicably arranged; of which Mr. St. Loe will give him fuller particulars. [See ib., p. 29.]
July 29 ? Lichfield.	[Same] to Mr. Herbert. Thanks for his news. Nothing is thought of at Court but banquetting and pastime; but it was somewhat interrupted by fear of a breach with Scotland. [See ib., p. 30.]

VOL. CV.

1575.
July 29 ?
Lichfield.
[Sec. Fr. Walsyngham?] to Sir H. Wallop. Is sorry to hear that he is suffering from ague. Cautions him against a spare diet or taking over much of the mineral waters. Mr. St. Loe could inform him of the events on the Borders. [See Vol. xlv., p. 30.]

July ?
22. A particular declaration of spoils committed by the Spaniards and Flushingers on the ships and goods of George Fenner and others.

August 1.
23. Note of bonds entered into by the Earl of Essex for payment of various sums of money into the Queen's Exchequer, from June 21, 1573, to Aug. 1, 1575.

August 7.
Buxton.
24. Lord Burghley to Sec. Walsyngham. Troubles in France. The Queen's progress. Is sorry he cannot wait on Her Majesty on her arrival at Dudley, as he wished to further the suits of the Lord and Lady Dudley.

August 9.
Buxton Well.
25. Same to same. Sends a letter to be delivered to Lord Dudley, excusing his absence on account of illness. Irish finances.

August 9.
St. John's.
26. Henry Sekeford to Burghley. Wants money for the two shiploads of herrings he has sent to supply the garrisons in Ireland. *Incloses,*

 26. I. *Wm. Loune to Henry Sekeford. Relative to the state of affairs in France. Rochelle, 26 July 1575.*

August 15.
Worcester.
27. Walsyngham to Burghley. A day has been appointed for hearing the dispute between the inhabitants of Peke Forest and the Earl of Shrewsbury. Instructions for sending money to Antwerp. They were expecting to hear from Mr. Killygrew, of the Regent's acceptation of the message. Affairs of the Borders. Is coming homewards.

August 18.
Odiham.
28. Same to Sir Tho. Smith. 15,000*l.* to be sent to Antwerp by exchange; Mr. Thomas Aldersey to be intrusted with the payment of it, and the Elector Palatine to be certified of its arrival. Very few of the Council know of the transaction.

August 21.
Evesham.
29. Sir T. Smith to Burghley. That Her Majesty was contented with the news brought home by Walter Williams, saving a passage in the Palgrave's obligation. The money is to be hastened over. Sends Walsyngham's letter. The Regent of Scotland is friendly disposed towards England.

August 24.
30. A discourse respecting the establishing a staple at Newcastle for coals, and for tin and lead in other places.

August 26.
Padstow.
31. Indictments at the Sessions held at Padstow in Cornwall, against certain mariners of a bark called "La Cressant de Rochell" for unlawfully attacking a vessel belonging to the Isle of Man. Lat.

August 31.
32. Sir Fr. Englefyld to Mr. Cotton. Recommends the bearer Tho. Evans, who desires to follow his company as a merchant. He may be trusted, "although he be a Welshman." Commends Cotton's proceedings.

Vol. CV.

1575.

August 31. Westminster.	33.	Robert Petre to Lord Burghley. Has desired Mr. Burde to make over 1,000l. more, who informed him that the exchange was at present very dead, but he will do his best, as will also Mr. Smyth, his principal factor. Rate of the exchange.
August 31. Ivy Lane.	34.	Peter Osborne to same. Respecting the making over of 1,000l. to Antwerp, and the price of exchange.
Sept. 2. Westminster.	35.	John Lord Russell to same. Amendment in the health of his wife Lady Russell; he hopes she will go her full time and have safe delivery.
Sept. 4. Woodstock.	36.	Earl of Leycester to the Queen. Thanks her for her great affection showed towards her absent ō ō by the testimony of her own sweet hand. Will hasten to her blessed presence. [*Leicester in his letters to the Queen used the symbol ō ō as expressive of affection, in the same manner as Hatton used the word "Lids" or "Lyddes."*]
Sept. 5. Westminster.	37.	Robert Petre to Burghley. Mr. Marten will in two or three days furnish 3,000l. in angels. Mr. Aldersey and Mr. Osborne have not yet returned to London. Recommends Mr. Smyth, the customer, to forward the money to Antwerp.
Sept. 6? Tuesday. [Woodstock.]	38.	Leycester to the Queen. His affection. Hopes speedily to return to her, "our heaven on earth." Beauty of the country, where he is, in his survey, to prepare for her coming. The very seasons are subservient to her and pray for her presence. [*Queen Elizabeth was at Woodstock on the 11th of September 1575.*]
Sept. 12. Wimbleton.	39.	Sir Tho. Cecill to Burghley. Recommends the suit of Sir Henry Darcy for an exchange of his Manor of Sawley, in Yorkshire, for one of equal value in the County of Huntingdon.
Sept. 12. Woodstock.	40.	Walsyngham to same. The Queen desires him to send the money to Antwerp with as much secrecy as possible. The French Ambassador has had an interview with the Queen, and has obtained permission for his nephew to visit the Queen of Scots, and to deal with the Earl of Shrewsbury touching the Queen's diets.
Sept. 15. London.	41.	Benjamin Gonson to same. Safe arrival of the Earl of Pembroke and his Lady at Queenborough, in the "Achates;" the said ship is to be made ready to carry over the Ambassador of the Low Countries.
Sept. 20.		Grant of Arms to Simon Heynes, of Mildenhall, Suffolk, by Robt. Cooke, Clarencieux. [*See Grant of Arms, No. 12.*]
Sept. 23. London.	42.	George Gilpin to Burghley. Informs him of the arrival of Lady Morley, with her daughter and youngest son, at Antwerp.
Sept. 28. Pyrford.	43.	Lord Adm. Lincoln to same. Respecting the detention of certain Frenchmen who had been imprisoned on the charge of piracy. Their case shall be examined into.
Sept. 29.	44.	Note of induct and educt (imports and exports) in the port of London by the Merchants Strangers, from Michaelmas 1574 to the same feast 1575.

1575.

Sept. 29. Declaration of the account of Andrew Gedney, Sheriff of Lincoln, for one whole year ending Michaelmas Anno R.R. Eliz. 17°. [*Case B. Eliz. No. 12.*]

Sept. 30.
Theobalds.
45. Lord Burghley to Mr. Sec. Walsyngham. Recommends the suit of the bearer. The money has passed Bruges in safety towards Antwerp. Has spoken with the French Ambassador for the restitution of two English ships plundered by Frenchmen. Interview with the Portuguese Ambassador at Spinola's house, in his garden at Shoreditch. Particulars of their conference. Fearful fiery meteor on Michaelmas eve.

Sept. ?
46. Memorandum, for an adventure into France for provision of wines for the Royal Household. Articles to be settled with the farmer of the impost on wines.

Sept. ?
47. Note of abuses committed by the importers of wines by reason of the prices being restrained to 10*l.* the ton; with remedies for redress of the same.

48. Reasons to prove that prisoners committed from the Council Board should be sent to the Marshalsea, and not to the Fleet or other prisons.

49. Copy of the above.

Oct. 6.
London.
50. Benedict Spinola to Burghley. Congratulates him on the safe arrival of the Conte [Earl of Oxford] at Venice from Milan. His brother, Pasqual Spinola, will shortly be at Venice, to pay his respects to him there. His brother, Jacob Spinola, has paid the 1,000*l.* to Mr. James Harvy, at Antwerp.

Oct. 6.
Rycot.
51. Walsyngham to same. Endeavour of the Queen Mother of France to entrap her son. Arrival of a Spanish fleet off the coast of Devon. The Admiral and Vice Admiral landed at Dartmouth, supposed to land some treasure.

Oct. 11.
52. Sir Francis Englefylde to Mr. Cotton. Regrets that his diligence has been ill received; but his services to Don John and the cardinals have been acknowledged. Desires that Tho. Evans or Wm. Gylbard may write to him.

Oct. 15.
London.
53. Dr. David Lewes to Walsyngham. Relative to the case of the Frenchmen condemned for piracy, some of whom must be executed.

Oct. 17.
54. Information as to words spoken by Ric. Morice relative to the coming over of one Parry, servant to Hugh Owen, and of his resort to the Earl of Arundel's house, and of the concealment of Owen by the Vicar of Oswestry.

55. Copy of the above.

Oct. 17.
56. Interrogatories for the examination of the Vicar of Oswestry. Respecting the intercourse he had had, or was aware of, with any of the English rebels in foreign parts, particularly as to Hugh Owen and one Parry.

VOL. CV.

1575.

Oct. 17.	57. Similar interrogatories for the examination of Richard Kinneston.
Oct. 17.	58. Similar interrogatories for the examination of Ric. Morice.
Oct. 17.	59. Similar interrogatories for the examination of Tho. Parry.
Oct. 17.	60. Similar interrogatories for the examination of one Parry, servant of Hugh Owen.
Oct. 20.	61. Officers of the Port of Lynn to Lord Burghley. Information of the quantities of butter, malt, and other provisions shipped for Ireland from their port by Henry Underwood, deputy to Henry Sekeford.
Oct. 22.	62. Device by Alderman Haywarde for bringing 100,000*l.* into the kingdom, from abroad, on the security of bonds of the City of London.
Oct. 22 ?	63. Note of the charges of 100,000*l.*, to be provided upon finance for six years, for Her Majesty ; and the profits to arise by again lending the same at a greater interest.
Oct. 22 ?	64. Device respecting the best way of bringing a sum of money into this realm from Germany.
Oct. 27.	65. Warrant by the Queen to Sir Gilb. Dethick, Garter, for additions to the insignia of Lady Frances, late Duchess of Suffolk, 3 Dec. 1559 ; together with details of the ceremonies at the christening of Elizabeth, the first daughter of John Lord Russell, son and heir to Francis Earl of Bedford.
Oct. 28. Leicester.	66. Thomas Sampson to Burghley. Requests the confirmation in perpetuity of a certain lease bequeathed to the hospital at Leicester by its founders.
Oct. ?	67. A project for the prevention of conveying coin and bullion out of the realm, with note of the laws and statutes respecting merchants strangers and denizens.
Nov. 1. Windsor.	68. Instructions to Wm. Holstock, comptroller of the ships appointed by the Queen to repair to the seas with two of the royal ships for the taking of pirates, regulating the traffic of merchants, &c.
Nov. 3. Windsor.	The Queen to Lord Adm. Lincoln. Directions to set forth the two ships "Dreadnought" and "Foresight," to repress the pirates and freebooters infesting the Narrow Seas, by whom the merchants are daily spoiled and robbed. [*See Vol.* xl., *p.* 31.]
Nov. 3. London.	69. Sir Thomas Gresham to Mr. Sec. Walsyngham. Sends a copy of his instructions to negotiate a foreign loan. Is unable himself now to travel in such weighty affairs, "being 62 yeres of ayge and blynde and lame." Recommends Edmund Hogan, one of his former servants, to be employed in that service. Offers to take up the sum of fifteen thousand pounds Flemish, at Antwerp, and be responsible for the same. *Incloses,*
	69. I. *Minute of the instructions for the deputies in Germany, for the negotiating a loan there.*

1575.

Vol. CV.

Nov. 3 ? — 70. Memoranda for the direction of the agents intrusted with the management of the loan to be taken up abroad at interest.

Nov. 5.
London. — 71. Richard Martyn to Mr. Sec. Walsyngham. Is ready to undertake the receipt of the foreign loan by 20,000*l.* at a time, so as to discharge the interest and keep it in readiness for Her Majesty's service. Recommends certain arrangements for its receipt.

Nov. 14.
London. — 72. Andrew Palmer to same. Recommends the loan out of Germany to be received only in dollars.

Nov. 14 ? — 73. Answer to certain articles respecting the best way of receiving the money to be sent from Germany, and of repaying the same.

Nov. 14 ? — 74. Order for disposing of the money to be paid to the Queen's Majesty on its arrival in England.

Nov. 15. — 75. Earl of Leicester and Walsyngham to the Earl of Shrewsbury. Requesting him not to appoint a successor to the office of the Marshal of the King's Bench, void by the death of Mr. Verney, the Queen having nominated one to that place.

Nov. 17. — 76. Note of the Warrants for the Great Wardrobe, from Nov. 17, 1574, to Nov. 17, 1575.

Nov. 25. — 77. The Queen to Shrewsbury. Has ascertained that the office of Marshal of the King's Bench was in the royal gift. She is therefore sure that he will be satisfied that she has bestowed it on W.K., her near kinsman, rather than on Sir Wm. Fytzwylliams.

Nov. 27. — 78. Orders appointed by the Earl of Leicester, Constable of Windsor Castle, touching the repairs of the castle: intrusting to Hum. Michell, Hen. Hawthorne, Tho. Hatche, and Walter Jennins, the direction of the works.

Nov. 27 ? — 79. Humfrey Michell, Clerk of the Works at Windsor Castle, to Lord Burghley. Gives an abstract of the expenses incurred at the castle for repairs, during the last six years, amounting to 6,600*l.* States his past services, and requests to resign his office.

Nov. 28. — 80. Petition of the parishioners of Bulley, co. Gloucester, to the Lord Treasurer. Praying for the stay of any warrant for defacing their parish church, till their title and evidence be fully examined before the Court of Exchequer.

Nov. — 81. Note of fines to the Crown for alienations without licence, and of fines for writs of covenant.

Nov. ? — 82. Note of the price of the several sorts of arms and apparel for soldiers.

Nov. ? — 83. Proclamation by the Queen, prohibiting any of Her subjects from engaging in the service in the Low Countries, or of any other foreign prince or state, as mariners or soldiers.

DOMESTIC—ELIZABETH. 507

1575.   Vol. CV.

Dec. 10.   84. Sir Francis Englefyld to Mr. Cotton. Desires him not to let
Liege.   the opposition he has met with put a stop to his endeavours. Has been obliged to change his residence on account of his health and safety. Requests him to write.

[Dec. 10 ?]   85. Bishop Cox to [Lord North]. Upbraids him with uncharitable and ungrateful usage. Enumerates the many favors he has bestowed on him and his family, and urges him to mend his life.

Dec. 11.   86. Roger Lord North, Lord High Steward of Ely, to the Bp. of Ely.
Kirtling.   Answer to the accusations made against him by the bishop. Appeals to the Queen and the Council to decide the matters in controversy between them.

Dec. 11 ?   87. "Certayne articles gathered out of the declarations of sondrie " persons, wherewithe the Bushoppe of Elye is to be charged."

Dec.   88. Articles of complaint by Chr. Balam, Geo. Haysyll, of Cambridge, and Lawrence Johnson, of divers enormities and wrongs committed by Dr. Cox, now Bp. of Ely, and his officers; delivered to Lord North, High Steward of the Liberties of the Isle of Ely, to be preferred by him to the Queen's Majesty.

Dec. 11 ?   89. Petition of Bishop Cox to the Council. Respecting the mode in which he desires to answer the articles against him. Requests that Lord North may not be permitted to prefer the charges of his accusers.

Dec. 11 ?   90. Answer of the Bishop of Ely to the complaints of George Haysyll, and others, preferred unto the Queen's Majesty by the Lord North.

Dec. 15.   91. Dr. Tho. Wylson to Lord Burghley. Requests payment for the horses he bought in Flanders, to enable him to repay Sir Tho. Gresham of whom he had borrowed 500l.

Dec. 27.   92. Note of matters to be propounded in Council.

Dec. 29.   93. A device how the statutes of the realm are to be ordered and printed, to be submitted to Her Majesty's consideration. Names of competent men fit to be entrusted with the overseeing of the same, presented by Lord Keeper Bacon.

Dec. 29.   94. The Council to the Commissioners for the restraint of the exportation of grain in Norfolk, Gloucester, and Somerset, to permit Mr. Geo. Higgens of Bristol, to export certain quantities of wheat and barley, in consideration of his losses in the Queen's service.

Dec. 29.   95. Grant of Letters Patent by the Queen to William Wylson, of Market Raison, co. Linc., of licence to buy and sell again 4,000 tods of English wool within the term of the next four years; with account of the number of tods of wool, bought and sold by virtue of the same.

Dec.   96. The Council (?) to Mr. Justice Southcote. In favour of Richard More, of Bristol, that he may obtain just judgment against John Roberts, who under colour of law had illegally dispossessed him of his house and lands.

DOMESTIC—ELIZABETH.

1575.
Dec. 97. The Council (?) to the Lords Chief Justices and Justices of both Benches. To consider the abuses committed in practice by one Alexander Wildgoose, a lawyer, and to punish him in such manner as they shall think fit.

Dec. ? 98. Articles against the Bp. of Chichester and Mr. Worley, for giving licence to James Hoare to transport grain contrary to the statute.

VOL. CVI. 1575. UNDATED.

1575 ? Note of privileges possessed by the Hanse Towns in their trade with England. [*See Vol.* xlv., *p.* 93.]

1. Petition of Luke Griston [or Grimston ?] to Lord Adm. Lincoln. Desiring not to be further troubled to answer for the landing and buying of certain soap, as he has already satisfied his lordship respecting the same.

1575. 2. Petition of Thomas Wolley to the Council. For a new proclamation, or else for an old proclamation to be revived, against engrossers and monopolists of grain.

1575 ? 3. Book of the Justices of the Peace for the counties of Wales. Lat.

4. Petition of the Merchants of the Stillyard to Lord Burghley. For licence to permit them to import certain wares direct from the Low Countries without passing through Hamburgh, on account of the stay of intercourse.

5. Statement of the injuries sustained by the City of London from the Merchants of the Stillyard, particularly in the use of the chief cloth market called Blackwell Hall ; and of preventing Richard Yonge from exercising the office of packer.

6. Comparative value of English coin, with reference to the coinage of other states of Europe ; with propositions for raising the foreign exchanges in favor of England. [*Imperfect, first leaf wanting.*]

7. Note of the yearly value of the Earl of Essex's lands in the counties of Buckingham, Essex, and Pembroke.

8. Note of armour which Captain Carsey hath not delivered according to his appointment, and of the sums of money he hath exacted upon the country and various townships, co. Lincoln, and given no account of.

9. Offer of Thomas Moryson to compound with the Officers of the Queen's Household, in lieu of the oxen and sheep to be furnished by Lindsey Division, co. Lincoln.

10. Petition of William Michelot, citizen of St. Malo, to the Council. Prays to be released, having been arrested by Capt. Courteney of Dover, and since by some men of Chester, on pretence of reprisals.

DOMESTIC—ELIZABETH.

1575 ?

Vol. CVI.

11. Petition of George Monoux to the Queen. Against G. Stodderde and thirteen other merchants of London, for non-payment of 300*l.* assured by them in his ship and goods since lost.

12. Mrs. Hampton's suit to Her Majesty. For a grant of all forfeited bonds taken for transportation of goods from port to port, in consideration of her late husband's services.

13. Petition of Sir Tho. Browne and Mr. Geo. Rotherham to the Council. That they may be put in possession of certain lands bought by them of Mr. Innocent Reade and Elizabeth his wife, who refused to convey the said lands to the petitioners.

14. Note for orders to be observed in the Office of Ordnance for receipt and payment of money, payment of artificers and officers, receipt and issue of stores, &c., and the practice of military exercise and drilling in the artillery garden.

1575.

15. Statement by Thomas Fermor, how he came to the possession of the lands in Eyton and Claudvilde, formerly possessed by Thomas Ricards *alias* Fermor, of Whitney, co. Oxford.

16. Notes upon certain passages of the Scriptures. [*Written on the blank spaces of a letter signed " Edmond Mathew."*]

1575 ?

17. Petition of the inhabitants of Guildford to the Council. Praying that Walter Baspole, and Robert Phillipps, executors of the will of John Parkhurst, Bp. of Norwich, may be ordered to pay the several legacies to their town, and to others, or to show cause to the contrary.

18. The Council to the Justices of Assize. Exhorting them to discourage the practice of the Sheriffs giving expensive entertainments to the Judges at the assizes.

19. Copy of the above.

20. Particulars respecting certain counterfeiters of coin to be apprehended at Dover and Canterbury.

21. Suit of Nicholas Proctor to Burghley (?). Desiring that Mr. Francis Hastings, Mr. Fr. Brown, and Tho. Wood might be joined in commission to examine witnesses as to the value of certain lands in Leicestershire held by Proctor of one Peche.

22. Note of certain letters, writings, and other things landed at Sandgate Castle, in Kent, by Harry Wotton, said to be a brother of Lord Dacre, captured at sea by the " Ayde." [*Imperfect.*]

23. Contents of the grant to Sir Humfrey Gilberte, of the office of General Surveyor of all horses, armour, weapons, munitions, and artillery throughout England, for seven years. Signed " W. Fletewoode."

24. Description of new invented furnaces for ale or beer brewers, &c, and pumps for raising water from mines, by Peter Jordayne and his coadjutors, with application for grant of the exclusive use of them in England, to George Cobham, for the term of twenty-five years.

1575 ?

Vol. CVI.

25. Notes by Mr. Mershe (?) of the number of cloths shipped by the Merchants Adventurers, and of duties payable on the same.

26. Licence by the Queen to George Zolcher, to export free certain quantities of western cloths at the request of John Duke Casimir, for the use of his household.

27. Answer of the objections against a proposed charter for the hostage of merchant strangers in London.

28. The effect of the charter granted to the City of London, concerning the hostage of merchant strangers, providing that all merchant strangers, aliens, &c., coming into England, shall sojourn at the tables of free hosts.

29. Notes in Lord Burghley's hand, relative to the foreign trade of England; duty on cloths; comparative value of foreign measures and money; merchandise received in exchange from the several countries, &c. [*Indorsed*, "*The Rates of Cloths.*"]

30. Notes for raising the Customs payable on raisins, figs, currants, prunes, and dates.

31. Note of the yearly fees received by Sir Richard Southwell, by virtue of his offices of Master of the Armoury and Master of the Ordnance.

32. Propositions for the government of the Mint, whereby Her Majesty will yearly gain 2,038*l.* 8*s.* 9*d.* With request for an additional allowance of 250*l.* a-year amongst the Officers of the Mint.

33. Matters propounded by the Warden of the Mint for the benefit of Her Majesty's service in that department.

34. Abstract of grant to   of the sole privilege of indorsing and returning original writs within the City of London, for the term of twenty-one years.

35. Names of the Officers of Arms receiving fees and wages of the princes of this realm since the time of King Edw. IV. With list of Kings of Arms, &c. that be now dead offices and not chargeable.

36. The names of all the Officers of Arms, with request to know which of them shall attend upon Her Highness in this progress.

37. Account of the annual fees belonging to the several Officers of Arms; with request for increase of their allowances in the Household, or else board-wages.

38. Pedigree of Gilbert Lord Talboys, descended from Raufe Fitz Oswey, who came to England with Will. I.

39. Grant to Wm. Turpyn, Esqr., of the manor of Geddington, in the County of Northampton. [*Imperfect.*]

40. Memorial to Lord Burghley in behalf of Wm. Maister, who had received grant of the Vicarage of Burford, Oxford, claimed by Sir Edward Unton in right of his wife the Lady Warwick.

Vol. CVI.

1575 ?
41. Note of the money that may be saved by the purchase of powder, saltpetre, and other ordnance stores abroad.

42. Estimate of the expense of victualling 1,000 men and 1,000 horses for one month; viz., the men accompted after twenty flesh days and eight fish days. Price of provisions.

43. Note of armour and munition remaining in divers and sundry places within the realm over and besides the armories preserved for the Queen's own person.

44. Reasons contained in the Lord Mayor's letter why the writer might not keep Her Majesty's records in the Lord Mayor's Court. With answers to the same. [*Indorsed*, "*Ferdinando Richardson.*"]

45. Names of the sureties of John Turnpenny and Wm. Killingworth, who were committed to ward for hunting in Her Majesty's chase of Enfield.

46. Names of recusants discovered by the confession of Barnard and Elizabeth Johnson.

47. Petition of the inhabitants of Coxhall [Coggeshall ?], and other poor clothiers, to the Council. Stating that now no opposition is made to Mr. John Hastings' patent for the making of freesadoes after the manner of Harlaem; but that they are most unjustly vexed by him to their utter undoing.

48. Certain reasons set down by the clothiers of Suffolk why they desire a reformation of the statute regulating the manufacture of cloths, particularly against searching cloths in London, instead of at the place of manufacture.

49. Memorial to Lord Cobham. Exhibiting the decay of the cloth trade in Kent, and desiring an emendation of the statute 8 Eliz. against the exportation of unwrought cloths.

50. Note of sundry subtle practices to defeat the true meaning and intent of the statute against usury.

51. Particulars of the Earl of Rutland's suit desiring to purchase of the Queen the manor of Newark, he not having any house within the County of Nottingham.

52. Note of such charges as have and do yearly issue out of the lands of Mr. John St. John, Her Majesty's ward, son of Sir John St. John.

53. Grant to John Bovyat of the exclusive privilege of manufacturing saltpetre and gunpowder of stone minerals for the term of twenty-one years.

54. Note of fees paid on the coinage of tin in the stannary of Cornwall.

55. Notes concerning the order of coinage of tin in the Counties of Cornwall and Devon.

Vol. CVI.

1575? 56. Note of rents of certain manors in Cornwall by Henry Cheverton, Chief Seneschal in the same. Lat.

57. Petition of [Ald.] Edw. Osborne, Richd. Staper, and others, to the Council. Complaining of the piracy committed on their ship the "James," by the pirates Hodges, Clarke, and Worald, by whom their factor and three sailors had been slain.

58. A table showing the proportions and rates of charges for ordnance carriages, &c. when supplied by contract, and when made out of the Government stores.

59. Statement of the causes of the decay of the trade and shipping of Kingston-upon-Hull.

60. Statement of the causes of the decay of the office of the Admiralty, and the diminution of the Judge's income of that court.

61. Certificate of the value of the commodities brought in by the merchants of Muscovy, under the hand of Thomas Smythe.

62. Petition of Peter Morrice to Mr. Sec. Walsyngham. Solicits a Patent for him for the sole right of making and employing certain hydraulic engines for the raising of water, draining marshes, &c.

63. Petition of Christopher Bowyer and Nicholas Danyell to the Queen. For a lease in reversion of Her Majesty's toll tin, in the County of Cornwall, as formerly granted to Wm. Hollocome and Tho. Jarrett, decd.

64. Petition of Barnaby Acton to Walsyngham (?). That he would take order with Mr. Wells for the payment of the 20*l.* he had promised on the surrender of the lease of the farm of Clewar, in Berkshire.

65. An estimate of the charge for making of 1,500 jacks, plated before, for the furniture of the Queen's ships.

66. Remembrances touching the Office of the Armory. Note of armour to be repaired, and warrant for 500*l.* for that purpose.

67. Mr. Mydlemore's suit to the Queen for the nominating and appointing sheriffs and county clerks. Advantages to be derived by the proposed grant.

68. Petition of Otto de Baehere to the Queen. For licence to transport 1,600 cloths, in consideration of his draft of the arms and genealogies of England, called "Le Thrésor de la Noblesse," dedicated to Her Majesty. French.

69. Memorial touching the grant of the lands belonging to Lord Dacre, and the agreement between him, Lord Norreis, and Leonard Dacre. The Earl of Leicester's suit for confirmation of the leases taken under such agreement.

70. Order by the Queen for the better observance of Lent, by abstaining from the eating of flesh during that season, and on the usual fasting days.

DOMESTIC—ELIZABETH. 513

VOL. CVI.

1575 ? 71. Note of the number of parish churches in the several dioceses of England and Wales. "Summa totalis of all the parish churches " within the realm, 8,911; besides chapels and the churches within the " dioceses of Oxford and Bristol not certified."

72. Copy of the above.

73. Articles and objections against Beakyn's pretended lease of the escheated lands and all other the demesnes of the Bishoprick of Ely.

74. Description of the operation and advantages of a certain newly invented engine of war, whereby twenty-four bullets can be discharged from one piece at a time.

75. Notes by the inventor touching the engine of war. Expense of making a few at a time. It would require above 100 engines to be employed at once. Desires a yearly pension in consideration of his invention.

76. A note of the effects already performed by the engine of war; of which there are 200 engines and 3,000 bullets already delivered into the Tower for service.

77. Relation of former attempts for discovering a passage through the Straights out of the North Sea into the South Sea.

Grant to Christopher Baker for life of the office of clerk and keeper of the stores and store-houses at Deptford Strond, Chatham, Portsmouth, and elsewhere, in reversion after the death or surrender of Henry Gilman. [See *Spain* 1573, *June* 8 ?].

Licence to Tho. Norman, of Barnstaple, merchant, to collect alms in churches and towns in consideration of his losses sustained at sea, and personal sickness. [See *Warrant Book*, I., p. 17.]

List of the names of all the ports, creeks, and landing-places in England and Wales. [See *Vol.* cxxxv., *fol.* 1.]

VOL. CVII. JANUARY—MARCH, 1576.

1576.'
Jan. 1. 1. Amount of debts owing by Her Majesty upon privy seals.

Jan. 3 ? 2. Observations on fines, expenses, &c., in the Council of the Marches of Wales. Abuses in levying certain fines.

Jan. 3 ? 3. Note of questions proposed to be put to a certain person relative to grievances in the law courts of Wales during his continuance in office. Fines received by Mr. Gerrard.

K K

DOMESTIC—ELIZABETH.

1576.
Jan. 3.
The Arches.

VOL. CVII.

4. Dr. David Lewes to Mr. Sec. Walsyngham. Has studied the causes of the disorders and abuses in Wales. A sharp disease requires a sharp medicine. Complains of the excessive number of retainers in Glamorganshire. *Incloses,*

    4. I. *Statement of the abuses and grievances in Wales; evils of "fosterage" and of the gatherings called "comorthas." With suggestions for reformation of the same.*

Jan. 3?   5. Considerations on matters necessary to be reformed in the Council for the Marches of Wales, constitutions of the Law Courts, &c.

Jan. 3?   6. Copy of the above, with heads of things to be reformed by Parliament.

Jan. 3?   7. A memorial (by Walsyngham) of things to be redressed in Wales.

Jan. 3?   8. Note (by the same) of things to be reformed in the instructions.

Jan. 3?   9. Note of certain points to be reformed in the Court of the Marches of Wales.

Jan. 3?   10. Relation of the constitution and state of the Council in Wales. Reasons of its former prosperity and present decay, and the means to restore it.

Jan. 3?   11. List of names of officers in the present Council and Courts of Wales; the periods of service and qualifications, and nature of the duties to be performed by them.

Jan. 3?   12. Observations on the articles delivered by Mr. Townshend. The choice of a good Vice-President is very desirable.

Jan. 3?   13. The names of certain learned men in the laws of the realm, whereof one may be chosen to be joined in commission with Mr. Fetiplace. It is convenient one of the Justices should understand Welch.

Jan. 3?   14. A device how, without increase of Justices in Wales, to have the circuits performed by an association of two Justices. Order to be observed in the circuits.

Jan. 3?   15. List of the Deputy-Lieutenants in the Welch Counties, and in the four March Shires of Monmouth, Shropshire, Hereford, and Worcester.

Jan. 5.   16. Petition of William Revet to the Council. Relative to certain lands in Rickmansworth and Chalfont, claimed by John Sex, but which of right pertained to him.

Jan. 12.   17. Note of subjects to be propounded in Council.

Jan. 12.   18. The Company of Goldsmiths in London to Lord Burghley. In favor of Mr. Stephen Rychman to be appointed Master of Magdalen College, Camb., vacant by the death of Dr. Kelke. Recommended also by Dean Alexander Nowell.

DOMESTIC—ELIZABETH. 515

1576. VOL. CVII.
Jan. 13.   19. The Council to all persons holding lands, houses, or tenements of the Hospital of the Savoy. To attend before Sir W. Mildmay and Thomas Bromley, the Queen's solicitor, to give evidence respecting the tenure of the same.

Jan. 18.   20. Same to the Justices of Assize, in the County of Somerset.
HamptonCourt. To hear certain controversies between Sir John Stowell and Sir Amias Poulet and other gentlemen of that county.

Jan. 20.   21. William Gerrard to Mr. Sec. Walsyngham. Stating that upon an interview with him he hopes to be able to suggest certain remedies for the abuses in the Marches of Wales. Has compiled a large volume on the subject. *Incloses*,

    21. I. *A discourse of the estate of the country and people of Wales in the time of King Edward the First, and from that time until the establishment of a Council in the Marches of Wales, with orders devised to avoid and remove the evil practices and abuses at this day used.*

    21. II. *Abstract of the above discourse.*

Jan. 20.   22. Dr. John Still, Master of St. John's Col., Cam., to Lord Burghley. The conduct of Mr. Cocke is still supported and maintained by many of the seniors. His proceedings against Mr. Cocke. *Incloses*,

    22. I. *Copy of the statute "De dissentionibus sedandis," with copy of the arbitrement agreed upon by Dr. Hawford, Dr. Whytgifte, and Roger Goade; and letter of Bishop Cox to the Master and Seniors of St. John's, on the interpretation of the above statute.*

Jan. 20?   23. Order by the Bishop of Ely for Mr. Cocke's retractation of a common-place, made to the offence of Dr. Still, Master of St. John's, which before he had neglected to comply with.

Jan. 21.   24. The Countess of Northumberland to William Cotton. Her
Liege.   sorrow that she is not able to assist him in his difficult enterprise. Recommends him not to hazard any desperate attempt, but to abide the time till a more fitting opportunity occurs.

Jan. 26.   25. Thomas Turswell to Burghley. Solicits to have the keeping
King's College, of the library in Cambridge. Lat.
Cambridge.

Jan. 26.   26. Anne Seres to same. Recommends Mr. Turswell for the above appointment.

Jan. 27.   27. Mr. Sec. Walsyngham to William Gerrard. Desires him to bring the orders devised by him for the government of Wales. The grievances complained of are very great.

Jan. 27.   28. Burghley to Walsyngham. Has got the gout and taken pills to
His house   cure it. Arrival of Mons. de Champyney, who requests an audience.
next the Savoy. Desires to know Her Majesty's pleasure thereon. Substance of an interview with M. La Mott.

K K 2

1576.

Vol. CVII.

Jan. 29.
Rochester.
29. The Mayor, &c., of Rochester, to Lord Burghley. Sending letters brought from beyond the sea by two Irishmen, and stolen from them by one Edw. Knighte.

Jan.
[The Council ?] to the Bishop of London. Signify the Queen's pleasure that Lady Kildare might have free access to the earl her husband; with permission for them "to lye together, a thinge usuall "in such cases." [*See Vol.* xlv., *p.* 15. *On the 13th February Lady Kildare had licence to return to Ireland to take charge of the Earl's lands in his absence. Co. Reg.*]

Feb. 1.
Survey of all the Queen's ships, boats, barks, &c., with estimates of repairs necessary, expenses in harbour, &c. [*See Vol.* xcvi., p. 294.]

Feb. 8 & 9.
30. Resolution of the House for the commitment of Mr. Peter Wentworth, burgess of the borough of Tregony, for unreverend and undutiful words uttered by him in the House of Commons, with proceedings thereon.

Feb 9.
31. Request of Lord Norreis to the Court of Parliament. To be restored in blood and honours.

Feb. 10.
32. Articles agreed upon by the Committees touching a subsidy and two fifteenths.

Feb. 11.
33. Countess of Northumberland to Wm. Cotton. Is desirous to know of his proceedings, and thanks him for his favor and affection to some other person. More is expected of her than she is able to perform. Will be glad to see him if he comes over into those parts. [*Partly in cypher*].

Feb. 19.
34. Petition of Richard Maie, clothier of Worcester, "who gave "unto your Majestie the finest clothe in the worlde," to the Queen. Desires restitution of 200 marks lent to the wife of the Bishop of Hereford, on the promise of repayment out of a benefice, which he has never received.

Feb. 19.
Westminster.
35. Grant of reprieve to John Ovare, found guilty and condemned to death for robbery.

Feb. 19.
Holborn.
36. Bishop Cox to Burghley. Proposes the issuing of a commission for the appeasing of the controversies yet remaining in St. John's College, Cambridge.

Feb. 20.
37. Articles by John Pryce, the Queen's attorney in the Marches of Wales, of the imperfections in the service there, to the Queen's prejudice.

Feb. 24.
38. Edmund Grindall, Archbishop of Canterbury, to the Queen. Notifies the grant of a subsidy from the clergy. Lat.

Feb. 27.
Preamble to the Bill of Subsidy, entitled "An Oration to the Queen about the Subsidy." [*See Vol.* xlv., p. 12.]

Feb.
39. Notes of the liberties of the town of Queenborough, extracted from the charter.

Feb. ?
40. Articles agreed upon by the whole clergy of the province of Canterbury in the Convocation held at Westminster, in the year 1575, touching the admission of apt and fit persons for the ministry, and the establishment of good order in the Church.

	VOL. CVII.
1576.	
Feb. ?	41. Answer to objections for the restitution of a portion of the temporalities of the See of Canterbury. [*Indorsed by Grindall* "*Answar of objections for my restitution.*"]
Feb. ?	42. A paper headed "Reformatyons proponed in Parliament by " the Queene's Majestie in favour of justice and of hir welbeloved " subjectes"—viz., digest of the common law, choice of juries, tythes, excommunications, Court of Almoners, &c.
Feb.	43. An act for the more equal and speedy rating and collecting of charges and contributions for services in the country.
Feb. ?	44. Extracts from the Patent Rolls, in proof of the authority possessed and exercised by the Bishops of Durham, in the County Palatine of Chester, &c.
Feb. ?	45. Heads of several bills in various stages in the Lower House.
Feb. ?	46. Note of bills in the Upper House of Parliament.
Feb.?	47. Device for a bill for granting duties for maintenance of the harbours at Rye and Winchelsea, and for repairing Dover haven.
March 1.	48. Request of the clothiers to a member of Parliament that he would support the bill preferred by Sir Henry Pool, for reforming the abuses and deceits used in wool and yarn.
March 3.	49. Mr. Simmes to Lord Burghley. Requests that the consideration of the bill for the explanation of the Stat. 31 Hen. VIII., concerning abbeys, monasteries, and colleges, might be committed to the decision of certain learned men. *Incloses*,
	49. I. *Answers to the suggestions of the inconveniences that would arise if it be enacted that the statute of 31 H. VIII. should not extend to any of the colleges, as a bill to that purpose had passed both Houses.*
March 4.	50. Petition of the bailiffs, &c. of Great Yarmouth, to the Council. Request licence to transport 30,000 quarters of grain, to assist them in defraying the expenses for the reparation of their haven.
March 5.	51. Lawrence Cockson to Burghley. Solicits his aid in his enterprise for the growth and increase of flax, hemp, and rape seed. Advantages of the same.
March 5. Westminster.	52. The Council to Lord Adm. Lincoln. Directions to stay all ships belonging to Flushing and Zealand for their spoils committed on English subjects.
March 5.	53. Address of the House of Commons to the Queen. Requesting prohibition against the exportation of hemp and flax, &c., and regulations for the cultivation and employment of the same.
March 5.	54. Petition of the Mayor, &c. of the borough of Gateshead, to Burghley. Against the suit of the Mayor, &c. of Newcastle, for the annexation of Gateshead to Newcastle, which would be to their utter undoing and overthrow.

1576.

March 6. 55. Differences between the statute of 5 Eliz. and the new bill concerning tanning and curing of leather.

March 7. 56. Advantages to be gained by the bill for the avoiding false and counterfeit colours, and for bringing in a true and perfect manner of dyeing into the realm. With answers to the same.

March 7. 57. Consideration of certain inconveniences that may arise by the uniting of the borough of Gateshead to the town of Newcastle.

March 7. 58. Note of the stages of bills in the House of Commons.

March 8. 59. Another note of the stages of bills in both Houses of Parliament.

March 8. 60. Bill for the restriction and regulation of licences granted by the Queen for the exportation of wares forbidden by statute.

March 8. 61. Articles for an Act of Parliament touching impropriations.

March 9 ? 62. Minute of an explanation prescribed by Lord Burghley, to be declared by Mr. Cocke, that he had no intention in his speech to offer any affront to the Master of St. John's College.

March 10. 63. State of private and public bills passed and proposed in both Houses of Parliament.

March 10 ? 64. Substance of bills to be proposed in Parliament, with names of those to whom they are entrusted, for the confirmation of bishops' lands, for the better execution of penal laws, benefit of clergy, reformation of sheriffs, &c.

March 10 ? 65. Act for the augmentation of cures of small livings where the parsonages are impropriate and of certain values. [*Imperfect, the first leaf wanting.*]

March 10 ? 66. Act for the relief of vicars and curates lacking needful sustentation for their cures, whereof the rectories are impropriated.

March 10. 67. Certificate of the increased number of ships and vessels in various seaport towns since the enacting of the statute for maintenance of the navy, and abstinence from flesh on Wednesdays.

March 10. 68. List of ships newly built since the year 1571, and the ports to which they belong.

March 11. 69. Bill for confirmation of the Act 5 Edw. VI. against engrossers, forestallers, and regrators, and prohibiting the monopoly of all foreign goods and provisions.

March 11. 70. Copy of the preceding. With a note of the increase of prices of wines, spices, &c. since the 6th year of Her Majesty's reign.

March 11. 71. Dr. John Still, Master of St. John's, to Burghley. The troubles in the college have not ceased. Mr. Cocke and Mr. Smith, since their return, are rather more unquiet than amended. Mr. Cocke read the speech prescribed by Burghley, but made matters worse by his observations.

DOMESTIC—ELIZABETH. 519

1576. VOL. CVII.

March 11. 72. Petition of Dierick Flockarson, of Embden, to the Council. Against Sir A. Champernowne, for refusing payment of the freight of his ship of salt brought into Dartmouth by Flushingers.

March 11. 73. Petition of John Foxall and Barnard Feilde to same. Complaining of stay of their goods by the Inquisitors of Spain, and soliciting that Spanish goods to the same amount may be stayed in England.

March 11. 74. Petition of certain obedient subjects to the House of Lords. Soliciting their order to the Speaker of the House of Commons to read in full the bill for the better cultivation of flax, hemp, and rape seed.

March 12. 75. Mr. Recorder Fletewoode to Lord Burghley. Thanks him for his favours to himself and for the Bishoprick of Durham. Beseeches him that the bill for annexing Gateshead to Newcastle may not be permitted to pass.

March 12. 76. Petition of the inhabitants of Gateshead to same. Urging objections against the bill for uniting them to the town of Newcastle.

March 12. 77. Note of acts that came from the Lower House, and of the acts of the Upper House, in various stages.

March 12. 78. Similar lists of the stages of bills in the Upper and Lower Houses.

March 12 ? 79. Note of public bills passed in the Lower House, and of bills sent down from the Lords.

March 12 ? 80. Note of acts passed in both Houses, and of those now remaining in the Upper House.

March 12. 81. Another copy.

March 12 ? 82. Proviso in the bill against fraudulent conveyance or assurance of lands. Probably to the Act of Dilapidations.

March 12 ? 83. Brief of the articles in favour of the bill for Chichester haven, and reasons by the mayor and citizens why the same should be enacted.

March 13. Rothwell Market. 84. Presentment of the three several juries of the Hundreds of Corby, Rothwell, and Orlynbury to — Androwes, Esq., High Sheriff of Northampton, of the quantities of grain in the said Hundreds that may be spared to supply the markets.

March 14. 85. Note of the prorogation of Parliament till two of the clock tomorrow, when it was further prorogued till the 5th of Nov.

March 14 ? 86. Certificate by the Clerk of the Parliament, of such bills as were read in the House, and of those which had passed.

March 15. 87. Note of acts passed both Houses.

	Vol. CVII.
1576.	
March 15.	88. A note of the acts passed in both Houses during the session. "Those that be crossed are such as Hir Matie is thought will not assent unto."
March 18.	89. The Council to Sir Thomas Lucy, Tho. Smith, and John Hyckford. Desiring them to hear the complaints of the tenants of Wellford, in Gloucestershire, against Lodowick Grevill.
March 18.	90. Same to the lords and owners of Romney Marsh. To signify their opinion respecting the suit of the town of Hythe, relative to the construction of certain sewers near their town.
March 21.	[Sec. Walsyngham?] to the Mayor and Searcher of Dover. To suffer Mr. Cavaulti [Cavalcanti?] to pass beyond sea. And as the seas were thought to be somewhat dangerous to furnish him with a swift sailing bark. [*See Vol.* xlv. *p.* 61.]
March 23.	91. Writ of assistance by Dr. Lewes, Judge of the Admiralty Court, for recovery of the goods of five British ships wrecked on the coast of Sussex, "richlye laden with merchandizes from the Sowthe partes," [? *The return voyage of Sir H. Gilbert, and others. See* 22 *March,* 1574.]
March 23.	92. The Council to Lord Darcy, and others. To examine John Chapman, and others, authors of certain lewd and slanderous libels against the preachers cast abroad in the town of Colchester.
March 30.	93. Petition of John Rooper to the Council. Solicits the cancelling of his bond for the good behaviour of one John Prestall, which he had entered into at the request of Mr. Ric. Verney.
March ?	94. Lord Burghley to Walsyngham. Sends copy of the Queen's warrant, dated 11 Dec. 1572, for 9,000*l*. for expenses of the navy, payable in three years, which have expired. A new warrant will be necessary for payment of the balance still due.
March ?	95. Names and preferments of non-residents in Oxford, within a little compass. [*Indorsed,* " *L. Norris.*"]
March.	96. Note of the temporalities belonging to the See of Worcester.
March 31. Whitehall.	97. The Council to Commissioners in every shire throughout the realm. Directions for the assessing, levying, gathering, and answering to the Queen's use, the first payment of the subsidy granted to Her Majesty in the last session of Parliament.
March.	98. Collections out of the book of Entries of the Parliament, from the 13th to the 18th Eliz., relating to matters of religion and the affairs of the Church.

Vol. CVIII. April—August, 1576.

April 9.	1. Answer of Dr. Roger Goade, Provost of King's College, Camb., to certain articles exhibited against him by four of the younger company of the college.

DOMESTIC—ELIZABETH. 521

VOL. CVIII.

1576.
April 12. 2. Petition of John Roynion to [Sec. Walsyngham?]. Solicits him to procure from the Queen a payment of 30l. per ann., in lieu of the parsonage of Martocke, co. Somerset, which had been previously granted to Mr. Ellis.

April 12.
The Court. 3. [Sec. Walsyngham?] to Lord Burghley. In favor of John Roynion's suit, his parsonage of Martocke having been previously granted in reversion to Mr. Ellis.

April 16.
Gorhambury. 4. Commission to Thomas, Bishop of London for the time being, with many others, for relief of poor prisoners confined for debt in the Queen's Bench. [*It is uncertain who is indicated by* "THOMAS, *Bishop of London for the time being.*"]

April 19.
Westminster. 5. The Council to Visct. Montague, the Bp. of Chichester, and others, Commissioners. To permit Michael Hoare to transport ninety quarters of wheat to Ireland.

April 22. 6. Account of Lord Treasurer Burghley, by Chidiock Wardour his clerk, of the receipts in the Treasury of the Exchequer, from Michaelmas 1575, to Easter 1576.

April 23.
Gorhambury. 7. Commission to Edmund Grindall, Archbishop of Canterbury, and to many other Bishops, Officers of State, and others, for exercising ecclesiastical jurisdiction throughout the realm. [*Signed by the Queen, but much mutilated and defaced.*]

April 23. 8. Copy of the above, made before the mutilations.

April 23. 9. Note of such as have been Lieutenants of the Company and Order of the Garter, from 1566 to 1576, with list of the present Knights.

April 29
Greenwich. 10. The Council to Sir Thos. Scott, Mr. Thos. Wotton, and others. Authorizing them to hear and determine all matters in controversy between Captain Wm. Hawkes of Walmer Castle, and Mr. Henry Isham.

April 29. 11. Note of matters to be propounded in Council.

April 29. 12. Note of common fines and fines pro brevibus, by Mr. Wm. Dodyngton, for various years.

May 4. 13. The Council to the Recorder of London, Mr. Lovell, and others. In behalf of Mr. Chr. Hodsdon, and the children of Miles Wilson, likely to be deprived of their property by the evil administration of one Dr. Akworth.

May 4.
Greenwich. 14. Same to Mr. Osborne of the Exchequer, the Sheriff of Middlesex, and Mr. Ric. Martyn. To take an inventory of all goods and lands belonging to Thos. Grene, goldsmith, who had been apprehended on suspicion of treason.

May 7. 15. Same to Sir Thos. Lucas and the Bailiffs of Colchester. To examine the charges alleged against Ric. Southwell by Mr. Dorell and Mr. Christmas; and also the complaint of Southwell against John Christmas.

VOL. CVIII.

1576?
May 8. 16. Statement by Mr. Locke, of Englishmen who are opposed to the trade of the Company of Muscovia with Russia, and have induced the King of Denmark to obstruct the same.

May 9.
Greenwich. 17. The Council to the Vice President and Council in the Marches of Wales. To take order for payment of the arrears due to Mr. William Gerrard, one of the Council there, and now appointed Lord Chancellor of Ireland.

May 9. 18. Same to the Justices of Assize in the County of Pembroke. To settle the controversies between Sir John Perrot and Thomas Wirriott.

May 10.
Dublin Castle. 19. Sir Henry Sydney (as Lord President of Wales) to Mr. Secretary Walsyngham. Desires that the offices of Clerk of the Fines and Auditor in the Marches, by right being at his disposal, may not be bestowed on any person but with his consent.

May 10.
London. The Lord Mayor and Aldermen of London to Mr. Chr. Hatton. Recommending the suit of William Tipper, for a grant of the hosting of merchant strangers in London, the same as formerly granted to Wm. Hunt. [See Vol. cxxx., No. 25, fol. 1.]

May 13. 20. Dr. Goade, Provost of King's Coll., to Lord Burghley. The complainants against him have sent up Mr. Stokes. Desires to meet them face to face. Sends a letter from Mr. Redman which shows how Dr. Goade has been abused by their slanders.

May 14.
London. 21. Archdeacon Tho. Wattes to same. Requests that Mr. Dunning might be sent for, to answer charges made against the Provost of King's Coll. The complainants will not substantiate the articles against the Provost.

May 19. 22. The Council to the Commissioners of Wines in certain counties. To ascertain the quantity of wines imported from France, and by whom, and sold at a higher rate than 10l. the ton, contrary to the Queen's proclamation.

May 19. 23. Instructions given by the Privy Council to Henry Palmer, Esq., appointed to be Captain of the Queen's ships set forth for the clearing of the seas of pirates, excepting all ships under the Prince of Orange's commission.

May 19. 24. Minute of the above.

May. Note of the furniture of the three ships sent to the seas under the charge of Henry Palmer. [See Vol. xcvi. pp. 300, 301.]

May 20. 25. Note of matters to be propounded in Council.

May 23. 26. The Council to the Chancellor of the Duchy of Lancaster. To examine the complaints of the tenants and inhabitants within the liberties of the forest of the High-Peak, exhibited against the Earl of Shrewsbury and others.

DOMESTIC—ELIZABETH. 523

1576.   VOL. CVIII.

May 23. 27. Answer of Richard Candeler to a bill of fees set down by certain aldermen and citizens, appointed by Sir Ambrose Nicholas Lord Mayor of London, respecting his office for the making and registering of assurances, &c.

May 24. London. 28. Commissioners for relief of poor prisoners to the Council. Their proceedings. Complain of the opposition offered to the commission by the Marshal and his deputies, to the great sorrow and grief of the said poor prisoners.

May 24 ? 29. Petition of the poor prisoners of Her Majesty's Bench to the same. That Her Majesty's commission in the behalf of poor debtors may be maintained, and not hindered by the artifices of lawyers or the opposition of the Marshal.

May 24 ? 30. Petition of the poor prisoners in the King's Bench to the same. Praying that the Marshal of their prison may not be permitted to oppose the execution of the Queen's gracious commission in their favour. And that the Commissioners might sit within the prison.

May 30. St. John's College. 31. John Cocke, Fellow of St. John's, to Lord Burghley. His purgation of the accusations made against him to his lordship. Lat.

May ? 32. Petition of Mrs. Christian Lawson, wife of Tho. Lawson, late Mayor of York, to the Queen. For a lease of the manor of Arkendale, co. York.

May ? 33. Memorial of Sr. Wm. Gerrard and the Company of Merchants trading to Russia. That having great store of wares lying at the Narve in great danger, they were forced to hire three Lubeckers' vessels to transport the same, and request licence to bring the same into the realm.

May ? [The Council ?] to Lord Cobham. Had given letters to one Sowyer of Rye intending that he should go to the coast of Spain to bring intelligence, but which he had abused by spoiling certain Frenchmen. Directions to secure him if he comes within the liberties of the Cinque Ports. [*See Vol.* xlv. *p.* 33.]

June 1. 34. Same to the Commissioners for Grain. Great scarcity and high prices of grain. Directions to use great diligence to restrain the exportation of grain in the maritime counties.

June 2. 35. Sir Francis Englefyld to William Cotton. Has taken all the means in his power to accomplish his desire. Sir Tho. [Stuckley] is gone to Loretto. Directions for his guidance in some secret transaction. The plot is new, rare, and without precedent.

June 3. Greenwich. 36. The Council to the Commissioners of Sewers in certain counties. To aid in levying a rate in adjacent counties to assist the inhabitants of the Isle of Ely in the cleansing, scouring, and embanking the river of Wisbeach.

June 3. 37. Same to Lord Norreis, and others, Justices of Oxfordshire and Berkshire. To consult for the execution of the late statute made for the repairing of the bridges and highways near Oxford.

Vol. CVIII.

1576.

June 8.
Dartington.
38. Sir Arthur Champernowne to Lord Burghley. Arrival of intelligence of great cruelties inflicted on the inhabitants of Marrena by the people of Rochelle. Much corn exported.

June 9.
39. The Countess of Northumberland to Mr. William Cotton. Affairs of the recusants. Sir Thomas Stuckley is gone to Loretto. Ill health of Sir F. Englefield. Fears that the letter to be conveyed to Lawrence Blacknoll, which contained affairs of great moment, has not been delivered. [*The names of persons in this letter are expressed in cyphers.*]

June 9.
Greenwich.
40. The Council to Sir H. Wallop, Sir Wm. Kyngesmyll, and others. To make search in the house of Alexander Dearing for vestments, books, and other massing tools. And all public records belonging to the shire to be restored to the Bishop's Court.

June 9.
London.
D. Poilly to Mr. Cave. Sends him two cheeses from Miss Hampden his cousin, who thanks him for his promise of a copy of the New Testament with Beza's notes, translated by Thompson. French. [*See France, Vol.* li., *p.* 109.]

June 9.
Greenwich.
41. The Queen to the Lord Treasurer and the Lord Chancellor. Directions to buy in her name bullion to the amount of 40,000*l* of the merchants and goldsmiths.

June 10.
Greenwich.
Same to the Treasurer and Chamberlains of the Exchequer. To pay to the Lord Treasurer and the Lord Chancellor the money for purchase of the said bullion. [*Written on the same paper as the preceding.*]

June 14.
King's Bench.
42. James Whitney, and others, poor prisoners for debt in the King's Bench, to Sec. Walsyngham. In favor of Mr. Webbe to be appointed to keep the register-book of the Commissioners in their behalf.

June 15.
Liege.
43. Countess of Northumberland to her servant Peter Kerke. Is sorry his proceedings and endeavours fall out so unluckily. Recommends him to desist and shortly return. Her commendations to Mr. Cotton, Mr. Carew, and others.

June 15.
Dublin Castle.
44. Sir Hen. Sydney to Walsyngham. In favour of Mr. Walter, a principal pleader in the Court of Wales, against whom some persons "have geven foorthe undecent and slanderous reportes."

June 15.
Grant to Rafe Lane, Esq., of all forfeitures for transportation of bullion and jewels contrary to the statute. [*Docquet.*]

June 17.
45. Account of the debts owing by the Bp. of Worcester (Bullingham) at his death, and of the charges of his funeral, and discharge of his household. With a supplication to the Queen to consider the lamentable estate of his poor wife and children.

June 17.
46. Note of the causes why the late Bp. of Worcester was so greatly indebted.

June 23.
Agreement made between Dr. Martin Culpeper and John Sledd, Esq., before Sec. Walsyngham, relative to certain lands, &c., at Milton, in Oxfordshire. [*See Dom.* 14 *Nov.* 1578.]

DOMESTIC—ELIZABETH. 525

1576.   Vol. CVIII.

June 26.   47. Countess of Northumberland to William Cotton. Advises him to continue his endeavors till the middle of August next, when he would see what was best to be done. Affairs of the recusants. The King of Spain has a good opinion of him. Offers from France. Prays him to be very cautious, and have nothing to do with Thomas Coppley.

June.   48. The Mayor, &c. of Dover to the Council. Praying that the penalties under the Act 23rd Hen. VIII. may be applied to the repairs of Dover haven.

June ?   49. Instructions given by the Queen to Sir Henry Sydney, Lord President, and the Council of Wales, with certain alterations and additions to the former instructions. Orders of Council for the direction and government of the same. Note of the differences of the old and new instructions.

June.   50. Note of important public business to be attended to. [*In Lord Burghley's hand.*]

July 2.   51. Tho. Page's narrative of the adventures of his journey on the Continent, having failed to induce Sir Edward Kelly to favour the attempt of a discovery of a north-west passage to China and Cathay. Honours conferred on Kelly by the Emperor; and practices used to deprive him of the philosopher's stone, which he possessed.

July 4.   52. Note of charges by Edward Baeshe for victualling three of the Queen's ships for one month, or longer.

July 11.   53. Report by the same, on the necessity of keeping in store casks and clapboards to the extent of 10,000 tons.

July 12.   54. The Council to Wm. Waldegrave, Esq. They approve of the
St. James's. settlement of the strangers of Colchester at Halstead in Essex, and request him to draw out the form of a grant for that purpose.

July 13.   55. Note by Mr. Baeshe of things necessary to be done with speed for Her Majesty's service for the sea causes, especially for a sufficient supply of casks.

July 14.   56. The Wardens of the Goldsmiths to Ch. Hatton, Esq. In favour of Robert Sharpe to receive a commission to travel and make known to the Goldsmiths his art of planishing silver.

July 14.   57. John Thaxter and others, Fellows of Corpus Christi College, Cambridge, to Burghley. Have used their best endeavours to elect Mr. Brabon to the vacant Fellowship, but Mr. Reade has been elected, as they thought, contrary to their statute.

July 15.   58. The Council to the Lord Mayor of London. Directing them to recal their proclamation fixing the retail prices of wines, until wines may be procured at a lower rate than 10*l.* the ton.

July 15.   59. Note by Mr. Baeshe of the causes that occasion the present want of casks for the navy.

1576.
July 17. Vol. CVIII.

Note of ships now at sea under Hen. Palmer, and estimate of the charges of 1,000 men to serve in six of the Queen's ships for six weeks. [*See Vol.* xcvi. *p.* 293.]

July 17. Estimate for victualling the Queen's ships. [*See ib. p.* 294.]

July 17.
Court at
St. James's
60. The Council to the Justices of Assize for the County of Lancaster. To hear the complaint of Ralph Jolly against Mr. Brodshawe, for certain odious outrages committed by his procurement.

July 20.
St. James's.
61. Sec. Walsyngham to Sir H. Sydney (as Lord President of Wales). In behalf of Mr. Wigmore (whom the Queen favoured) to be appointed Clerk of the Fines in the Marches of Wales.

July 26. 62. Complaint of John Broke against the Company of Merchants for the Discovery of New Trades, by whom he had been unjustly imprisoned; with their answer to the same.

July 26. 63. State of the account between John Broke and the Company of Merchants for the Discovery of New Trades.

July 27. 64. Estimate of repairs required at Her Majesty's seven alms houses within Bishopsgate, London, "made by the advice of a carpenter and a tyler;" and also of repairs at the Queen's seven alms houses at Brentford, co. Middlesex.

July 27.
Louvain.
65. George Tyrell to Lord Burghley. Thanks him for the kindness shown to his son. Refutes the accusations of treason that were circulated against him.

July ? 66. Memorial against the unrestricted liberty of retailing wines, and of the evils likely to ensue thereby.

July. Orders established by the Privy Council regulating the manufacture and sale of iron ordnance. [*See Vol.* xlv., *p.* 23.]

August 1. 67. Instructions to William Holstok, Esq., Comptroller of the Queen's ships, appointed by Her Highness to serve at the seas, to take under his command three ships to scour the Narrow Seas, and to detain all ships belonging to Flushing.

August 1. Entry of the above. [*See Vol.* cxxxiv. *p.* 396.]

August 1. A proportion of powder and munitions for the full furniture of three of the Queen's ships now presently appointed to the seas. [*See Vol.* xcvi., *p.* 297.]

August 1. Furniture, stores, &c., for three other ships sent to sea in May last, under Henry Palmer and Sir Wm. Wynter. [*See ib., p.* 300, 303.]

August 1.
Buxton.
68. Sir Tho. Cecill to Burghley. Great assembly of ladies and gentlemen at Buxton. Is not quite satisfied with the persons appointed to hear the case between him and Lord Clynton. Requests that Lord Willoughby and the Earl of Rutland may be added to them.

August 1. 69. Particulars of Viscount Bindon's lands in several counties, appointed to be sold.

August 5.
Portsmouth.
70. Thomas Thorney to Mr. Baeshe. Notifies the burning of Her Majesty's buildings and store-houses at Portsmouth on the day before.

DOMESTIC—ELIZABETH. 527

VOL. CVIII.
1576

August 6.   The Council to William Holstok. The Flushingers having com-
Dover.   mitted many depredations on English subjects. He is to arrest all
ships at sea belonging to Flushing. [*See Vol.* cxxxiv., *p.* 397.]

August 6.   71. John Lord Darcy to Lord Burghley. Thanks him for satisfying Her Majesty with respect to his attendance on her.

August 6.   72. Edward Baeshe to same. The burning of Her Majesty's store-
London.   houses at Portsmouth on the 4th. Trusts that his great losses therein
may be favourably considered.

August 6.   73. Wm. Crowmer to same. Report of the exportation and price
Tunstall.   of corn, grain, and other victuals in the County of Kent. Requests
to know if the exportation of beer is to be prohibited.

August 7.   74. Lady M. Sydney to same. Understands by Mr. Hatton that
Paul's Wharf.   Her Majesty has refused her suit. Requests him, if he knows of the
manner of the refusal, to advise her what is best to be done considering
her poor estate.

August 7.   75, 76. The Countess of Northumberland (?) to Wm. Cotton. Has
Liege.   received his letters containing the discourse concerning the Ferroe Isles,
near the Orcades. Recommends him to leave his affairs in as good
condition as possible, and to retire to the Continent for a month or two.
[*Mostly in cypher, with a decypher.*]

August 8.   77. Same to same. Has communicated his last letter to Sir F. Englefyld. Urges him to continue his endeavours, for, in a short time,
the new governor, Don John, was expected, and the mutiny of the
Spaniards would then soon be settled.

August 8.   78. Thomas Hopton to Burghley. Complains of Mr. Hare, who
Westminster.   has arrested him for debt. Requests Hare may be sent for, that
Burghley may understand his unjust dealings towards him.

August 9.   79. Lady Dorothee Stafford to same. Thanks for his kindness to
her brother : Sir John Thynne is chiefly to be dealt with. Her son,
Sir Wm. Drury, requests permission to buy the household stuff and
cattle of Mr. Byrd, if they are to be sold.

August 16.   80. The Countess of Northumberland to William Cotton. The
letters and other things recently sent have been taken by the Flushingers. The mutiny of the Spaniards is appeased. Reports of troubles
in England. Desires to know something of the Carewes.

August 24.   81. Robert Harecourt to Mr. Sec. Walsyngham (?). Solicits to be set
at liberty upon sureties until the next term.

August ?   82. A brief discourse laying forth the uncertainty of Her Majesty's
present peace and quietness : to consider the action with the Prince of
Orange, the present state of France, and the inward corruption
at home.

August ?   83. Grant of licence to A.B. to export 12,000 broad cloths within
the space of two years ending Michaelmas 1578.

VOL. CIX. SEPTEMBER—NOVEMBER, 1576.

1576.
Sept. 4.
Otterden.
1. Mr. Asteley to Peter Osborne. Approves of the drawing up of some legal document, and suggests alterations.

Sept. 6.
Ware.
2. Tho. Fanshawe to Lord Burghley. Sends a clause to be inserted in Mr. Smithe's grant, and a warrant for discharge of the King of Spain's subjects of the Low Countries. Requests order for the making of the Temple bridge to Mr. Barnerd.

Sept. 6.
Windsor.
3. The Council to the Captain of the Isle of Wight. To give licence to Henry Jolliffe to capture the ship of Captain Gyliam, a French pirate.

Sept. 9.
London.
4. Rafe Lane to Burghley. Requests that his case may be heard in London, considering the heavy charges for the expenses of the witnesses in the country. Prays that the offenders of Lyme, who beat the pursuivant and threw him overboard, may be punished.

Sept. 10.
Canterbury.
5. Ric. Barrey, Lieut. of Dover Castle, to Lord Cobham. That the Strangers' congregation of Sandwich were unwilling to enter into bond for the safe return of the ship and mariners appointed to carry the remainder of the prisoners to Flushing. *Incloses*,

    5. I. *Petition of the congregation of Sandwich against their becoming sureties for the return of the ship and mariners from Flushing. Sandwich,* 10 *Sept. Lat.*

Sept. 12.
Purford.
6. Sec. Walsyngham to Burghley. Affairs of Flushing and the Low Countries. The English merchants there are set at liberty. The Queen will not determine about the customs till she receive from Burghley a statement of the several rates offered. She is doubtful of going to Odiham, for fear of expense to Walsyngham. Is desirous of being quit of the place he serves in.

Sept. 17.
NorthForeland.
7. Nicholas Gorges to Walsyngham. Will be ready to attend at Dover or the Downs to convey the ambassador to France. Mr. Holstok had received orders not to detain any of the ships from Flushing. Pirates between Portland and the Wight; desires to know if he shall intercept them.

Sept. 17.
NorthForeland.
8. Same to Lord Adm. Lincoln. To the same effect as the preceding. Illness of Captain Beston.

Sept. 17.
9. Account of the materials and cost of the Countess of Huntingdon's hearse.

Sept. 20.
10. Survey of the manor of Colequit, parcel of the Viscount Bindon's possessions, made by Sir Arthur Bassett and others.

Sept. 20.
11. Offers of the tenants for the purchase of the same, and of the sum finally offered by Mr. Edgecombe.

Sept. 28.
12. Accounts, presentments, &c. of the losses sustained by the Queen and Mr. Baeshe in the fire of the storehouses at Portsmouth on the 4th of August.

DOMESTIC—ELIZABETH. 529

VOL. CIX.

1576.
(Sept. 28.) 13. Petition of Thomas Poyner, and others, of Portsmouth, to the Council. Praying for remuneration for their losses in the fire of the storehouses at Portsmouth; "amountinge unto soche greate somes " as they are not able of themselves to recover the same." *Annexing*,

13. I. *Note of goods and merchandise belonging to Ric. Jarvis, John Humfrey, and Tho. Poyner, consumed in the fire at Portsmouth.*

Sept. 28. 14. Estimate and survey by Ric. Popynjay and Robt. Welles, of the charges of rebuilding the two storehouses lately consumed by fire at Portsmouth.

Oct. (2.) 15. Report made by order of the Lord Treasurer, on the difference between cloths for length, breadth, and goodness before and after they are dressed.

Oct. 2. 16. W[illiam?] D[avison?] to T. C. In behalf of his cousin, the bearer, repairing to Court about his special affairs.

(Oct. 2.) 17. Same to Lord B. [Burghley?]. In favour of A. B. a gentleman of York, his cousin.

Oct. 5. 18. Sir Wm. Wynter and Wm. Holstok to the Council. Employ-
London. ment of the Bark of Boulogne to convey a boat to Harwich. Her desertion, by the instigation of merchants of Ipswich, to convoy two of their ships to Dunkirk, and capture of the whole by the Flushingers.

Oct. 20. 19. Orders and decrees made by Sir Rowland Haywarde, and others, Commissioners of Sewers. Concerning the navigation of the river Lea from Enfield to Lea-mouth.

Oct. 21 ? 20. The Mayor, Aldermen, &c., of Newcastle-on-Tyne, to the
Newcastle. Council. Complaining of their charter being infringed by the arrest of John Baxter, a burgess of their town, by a process issued out of the Admiralty, in London.

Oct. 26. 21. Injunctions given by Bishop Scambler to be observed in the
Peterborough. Cathedral Church of Peterborough.

Oct. 22. Ground plan of improvements and alterations to be made in Windsor Castle. [*By Henry Hawthorn ?*]

Oct. ? 23. Estimate of the expense of a wall 10 feet long, 20 feet high, and 6 feet thick, for the terrace at Windsor Castle.

Oct. ? 24. Petition of John Doughtye to the Earl of Leicester. Prays him to intercede with the Council for his release from prison. Has been six months in the common gaol, "a very noysom place, re-" plenished with misery."

Nov. (9.) 25. Mr. Holstok to the Council. That as Her Majesty had not received the whole of Lord Cheyne's lands in Sheppey, he could not train the 100 harquebuzers according to his offer. Requests a grant of liberties for Sheppey. *Annexing*,

25. I. *Request of the inhabitants of the Isle of Sheppey to the Queen, for a grant of certain liberties, whereby the said isle may be better peopled and of more force to withstand the enemy.*

L L

DOMESTIC—ELIZABETH.

1576.
Vol. CIX.

Nov. 9. 26. Another paper of requests for certain liberties to be granted to the inhabitants of the Isle of Sheppey.

Nov. 10. 27. Brief summary of all the proceedings touching the convent seal plucking off, and all the suits and controversies between Mounson and Ascoughe.

Nov. 10. London. 28. Mr. Justice Mounson to Mr. Sec. Walsyngham. Requests that he may not be delayed in the prosecution of his suit against Ascoughe. Has suffered discomfort and discredit by Her Majesty's displeasure.

Nov. 13. Isle of Wight. 29. Edward Horsey, and others, to the Council. Have surveyed the fort in the Isle of Wight, called the West Cowe, according to their directions. *Inclosing,*

    29. I. *Survey of the castle of West Cowe, and estimate of the charges for the reparation of the same. Oct. 10.*

    29. II. *Ground plan of the castle of West Cowe.*

Nov. 17. The Arches. 30. Dr. Lewes to same. Relative to the fine of 401*l.* 7*s.* 0*d.* awarded to James Dirickson against John Baxter, of Newcastle, and refusal of the mayor of Newcastle to enforce the same.

Nov. 21. Windsor. 31. Humfrey Michell to Lord Burghley. Reports the progress of the works under his direction at Windsor Castle during the year, and requests Her Majesty's further directions. Suggests that Henry Hawthorn should make perfect plans for the gallery and banquetting house. *Incloses,*

    31. I. *Report of the works done at the castle during the year. Materials remaining in store.*

Nov. 32. Ground plan of the banquetting house at Windsor Castle. [*Probably by Henry Hawthorn.*]

Nov. 26. 33. Estimate of the charges of the new lock to be made at Waltham, if it be all of timber.

Nov. 26. Cambridge. 34. Dr. Tho. Ithell to Burghley. States the result of a search for precedents, relating to a new grant of Sturbridge fair, with respect to the privileges of the University. *Incloses,*

    34. I. *Notes of certain special matters, to be reserved out of the Charter, to be granted by Her Majesty to the town of Cambridge for Sturbridge fair.*

Nov. 30. Cambridge. 35. Dr. Goade, Vice Chancellor, and Heads of Houses, to same. Desiring his help for preservation of their privileges in relation to the jurisdiction and interest in Sturbridge fair.

Nov. 30. 36. Articles by John Johnson on the advantages of Mart Towns to be kept in England, in addition to the Book of Marts.

Nov. ? 37. John Johnson to Mr. Sec. Walsyngham. Gives his advice for remedy of the disorders in the wool trade. *Incloses,*

    37. I. *Note of remembrance for improving the wool trade.*

    37. II. *Discourse how to remedy the existing disorders in the same trade.*

DOMESTIC—ELIZABETH. 531

VOL. CIX.

1576.
Nov. Genealogical epitaph of Walter Devereux Earl of Essex and Eue, Earl Marshal of Ireland, Viscount Hereford and Bowrchier, who died at Dublin 21st Sept., aged 36, and was buried at Carmarthen 26th Nov., 1576. [*See Ireland, 25th March,* 1602.]

38. Names of proctors and registrars in the Court of Arches, and dates of their admission; with their taxation for a loan.

39. Names and dates of admission of the doctors of the civil law and of the ecclesiastical courts; with their taxation for a loan.

40. Names of the doctors of physic, of the college of physicians, in London; with their taxation for a loan.

41. Names of the judges, serjeants, and pleaders; with their taxation for a loan.

42. Note of the towns and persons that are to contribute to the loan, with sums required from each; and notes of the manner to be observed in the delivery of the money to the agent of Holland.

Nov. ? 43. Account of the particular valuation of the citizens in London in every ward for the subsidy at 50*l.* and upwards.

44. Account of the assessment of the citizens in London for the subsidy at 50*l.* and above. [*A little more extended than the preceding.*]

45. Account of the taxation of certain citizens in London for the subsidy below 50*l.*

Nov. 46. Note of taxation of the subsidy in the wards of London, and in Westminster and Southwark.

47. Note of the taxation of the subsidy in divers cities, towns, and ports in England.

48. Account of the second payment of the subsidy from the laity in Essex; with the names of the gentlemen rated at 20 marks in lands and above.

49. Names of the gentlemen and citizens of Norwich, with their assessment for the first payment of the subsidy.

50. Names of the gentlemen and citizens assessed at 20*l.*' and upwards, in divers cities, towns, &c., throughout England.

Nov. ? The Queen to the President and Canons of Lichfield. In favor of Dr. Brute Babington to be elected dean of that Church. [*See Warrant Book,* I., *p.* 89.]

DOMESTIC—ELIZABETH.

Vol. CX. December, 1576.

1576
Dec. 3. 1. Proviso to be made for the University, in the grant of Sturbridge fair to the town of Cambridge.

Dec. 5.
HamptonCourt. The Council to the Lord Mayor of London. Desiring him to take order with the merchants, for the sale of wines at certain reasonable prices. [*See Vol.* xlv., *p.* 19.]

Dec. 6.
Newport. 2 Precept from John Croft to Wm. Morgan and Rowland Morgan, Justices of the Peace. To repair immediately to Newport for the apprehension of a ship taken by John Callis the pirate, now at Newport.

Dec. 8. 3. Report of Mr. John Croft's journey for the apprehension of John Callis and others for piracy. Intercourse of Sir Wm. Morgan's men with the pirates.

Dec. 8 ? 4. Notes touching the commissions; with the names of the purchasers of the goods and merchandize unlawfully taken by John Callis, the pirate.

Dec. 12. 5. Bond of Ric. Offley and Martin De La Falye, merchants, to Roger Grice and James Warte. That they shall not be interrupted in the prosecution of their suit at Dunkirk against M. Hondt and Martin de Pressoir.

Dec. 13.
HamptonCourt. 6. Earl of Leicester and Lord Burghley to the Vice Chancellor of Cambridge. Recommending a conference with the mayor and corporation of that town upon certain articles relative to Sturbridge fair.

Dec. 13 ? 7. Articles of instructions touching Sturbridge fair, granted to the town of Cambridge.

Dec. 14. 8. Sir Thomas Offley to Mr. Secretary Walsyngham. For order to be taken by the Council to redress the evils attending on the buying and selling of wool by virtue of licences. Great enormities in ingrossing wools.

Dec. 26. 9. Names of such Englishmen as are certified into the Exchequer to be fugitives over sea contrary to the Stat. Anno. xiii° Eliz.

Dec. 27. 10. Serjeant Nicholas Barham to Burghley. Effect of the Letters Patent granted by the Queen for licence to strangers to settle at Sandwich and Maidstone.

Dec. 11. The Council to the Vice President (Sir Andrew Corbett) and Council of Wales. Enjoining a strict compliance with the orders and instructions sent. [*This is a minute dated Dec.* 1576, *but it has this endorsement:* "*This lre was dated at Westm^r the 24th of March* 1576;" *and a notice of it is entered on the Council register, dated April* 2, 1577.]

Dec. ? 12. The names of the Commissioners in the Principality of the Marches of Wales.

1576 ? 13. List of such as wish to become justices in Wales, with remarks on their individual characters and qualifications.

DOMESTIC—ELIZABETH. 533

Vol. CX.

1576 ? 14. Opinion of Mr. Justice Throckmarton for the supply of justices, and for facilitating the administration of justice in the Marches of Wales, without farther expense to Her Majesty.

15. Objections against the ancient orders put in execution in the Marches in Wales.

Dec. 16. Certain articles taken out of Alderman Marten's information preferred before the Council against Mr. Lonison, as to his altering the Mint standard.

1576 ? 17. Answer to the demand of allowance, in the offer for the Mint.

1576. 18. Suit of Thomas Castelin, soliciting a licence to search for and work any coal mines beyond the Trent.

19. A description of the courts of justice in England by Alexander Fisher. Detailing their constitution, duties of their officers, mode of practice, &c.

20. Note of "the Officers of Her Majesty's Courts of Record at Westminster, both English and Latin." Also lists of the post-towns between Berwick and Windsor, from Ireland to London, and from London to Dover.

21. Heads of articles for a grant of incorporation from the Queen to the Company of Kathai, or Cathay. Michael Lok to be the first Governor, and Martin Furbisher to be High Admiral of all the new discovered lands.

22. Articles agreed upon by the Company of Cathay to form the their grant of incorporation.

23. Note of the clear annual value of the tenths due by the clergy in the province of Canterbury.

1576 ? 24. Remembrance for Lord Burghley from the mayor and burgesses of the City of Bath. To be permitted to finish building the fair church commenced by the late Prior there, and not fully finished at the time of the suppression, and so yet remaineth; Edw. Colthurst, the proprietor, being contented to grant the same to the corporation.

25. Advice of the justices for putting certain penal statutes in execution. *Annexed*,

25. I. *A schedule of the statutes intended.*

26. Remembrances by Sir John Fetyplace to Mr. Sec. Walsyngham. Relative to Lady Englefyld's lands.

27. Lord Stafford to the Queen. Has altered his former petition, and now requests the grant of a lease of 200*l.* rent out of the attainted lands of his grandfather, and of such knights' fees as were omitted by the malice of Cardinal Wolsey.

VOL. CX.

1576?

28. Petition of the poor tenants, servants, and others, of John, late Marquis of Winchester, to the Council. Reciting many gifts and legacies to Dame Winifred his wife, and others, in his last will, and complaining that Mr. Henry Ughtrede, one of the executors, had unjustly delayed settling their claims.

29. Henry Ughtrede to same. In answer to the complaints of the tenants and servants of the late Marquis of Winchester.

30. Statement of the griefs of William Marquis of Winchester, against Lady Winifred, his father's wife, and Henry Ughtrede his brother-in-law; their sinister influence with his late father, John Marq. of Winchester, and unjust conversion of the family property.

31. Note of inconveniences caused to William Marquis of Winchester, by the strict letter of the covenants and bonds concerning the jointure of the Lady Marchioness, whereof he requires such reasonable mitigation as may stand with the security of his estate.

32. Lucas Clayssone to Lord Burghley. Solicits to be nominated to a fellowship in Magdalen College, Camb., in the gift of the Queen. Lat.

33. The Queen to same. To license John Pompart to ship 500 quarters of wheat, 6,000 planks, and 16 pieces of ordnance, at the suit of Monsr. de Mauvissiere, the French Ambassador.

34. Reasons why the bishops and clergy should not be exempt from furnishing horses and armour for defence of the realm, and how the same may be effected.

35. The Earl of Shrewsbury's answer to certain claims for leases and tithes of some of his manors and lands.

36. Note of the difference of riding charges of messengers and grooms in the time of Sir John Masone's being Treasurer of the Chamber, and in the time of Sir Tho. Heneage.

37. Proposal by Ed. Baeshe to the Queen, to pay the sum of 1,500*l.*, being a part of his debt of 2,000*l.*, by instalments of 100*l.* yearly. States his losses, particularly by the fire at Portsmouth.

38. Suit of John Asteley, Master of the Jewel House, for grant of the manor of Osmyngton, in fee-farm, or a lease of the same for 60 years.

39. Letters Patent granting to Wm. Kendall, of Launceston, in Cornwall, the sole privilege of making alum for 20 years.

40. Indenture of covenants between the Queen's Majesty and Wm. Kendall for the manufacture of alum within the realm of England.

41. Articles given in charge to the Middlesex Jury. To make inquiry touching the unlawful catching of fish, taking of spawn, and for preservation of fish in the Thames.

1576 ?

42. The effect of Henry Rodrigue's request touching the brokerage of assurances; that he and his executors may be solely appointed to deal therein.

43. Note of the charge of maintaining four of Her Majesty's ships at sea for two months.

44. Petition of John Martyn, John Shaplye, and many other merchants of Totness and Staverton, in the County of Devon, to the Council. That their Lordships would be pleased to be a means for the release of their goods, which, by order from the French king, had been stayed at Rouen.

45. Opinion of Dr. Wm. Aubrey, Jo. Hammond, and W. Lewyn, in the case of Mr. Rockery. That a Fellow of Queen's College, Cambridge, may enjoy a prebend and still keep his fellowship.

46. A breviate of the state of the City of Chester, what once it was, and of the miserable estate in which it now is.

47. Mr. Ballard's survey of the manor of Northborne, in Kent, with a note of the particular rents thereof, and of the rents paid to the Queen.

48. Information against Henry Kanter, *alias* Kalice, Tho. Cole, and others, for robbing Robert Fletcher, at Helford haven.

49. Another information against the same for robbing and threatening to kill Robert Fletcher.

50. Note of the improvement of the rent of the manor of Kingsey, in the County of Bucks.

51. Device by Stephen Parrott for the abolition of usury, by the establishment of a fund under the control of the Government.

52. The names of such gentlemen of living as dwell in the Hundreds of Rochford and Dengy, or in the confines thereof; probably for the Musters. [*Indorsed*, " A Remembrance about my brother Harris."]

53. List of gentlemen in the County of Hertford who may contribute towards the loan of 2,000*l.*, if any of those before set down for that purpose shall be excused or misliked.

54. Proposal of John Heth and Henry Anderson for the grant of a licence for the exclusive importation of Scottish salt.

55. A brief abstract and report of the state of the Isle of Sheppey, containing six parishes; what houses and ground every parish containeth, and how the same land is divided. [*Addressed to the Lord Treasurer.*]

56. Duplicate of the above; with a request that no one should occupy more than 250 acres of up-land within the said isle.

57. Informations concerning fines for alienations and writs of covenants whereupon fines are levied. Proposing to increase the Queen's revenues by farming the same at a rent certain.

Vol. CX.

1576 ?

58. List of the Chancellors, Clerks, and Speakers of Parliament, with the time they held office. 5° Edward III. to 22° Edward IV.

59. Notes for Mr. Wm. Drury, Marshal of Berwick. For a grant of the manor of Hadeneham to be held in fee-farm.

The Council (?) to the Lord Admiral (?). To give order for release of a Spanish pinnace, detained by the officers of the ordnance because a piece of brass ordnance in her was stamped with the English arms. [*See Vol.* xlv., *p.* 32.]

Instructions for the better direction of such as shall have licence to pass the seas for the taking of pirates and sea rovers, to be annexed to their commissions. [*See Vol.* cxxxiv., *p.* 422.]

Grant to Henry Sekeford, Groom of the Privy Chamber, of the Office of Master of the Toils, for life. [*See Warrant Book* I., *p.* 144.]

Walsyngham to [the Governor of the Isle of Wight ?]. The Council has committed to him, and others, the decision of a matter in controversy between the town of Poole and Mr. Hatton, owner of Cork [Corfe ?] Castle, concerning the taking of a pirate. Names of the gentlemen attending the Lord Lieut. [*See Vol.* xlv., *p.* 64.]

[Same ?] to   . The Queen allows his non-residence till Easter, on condition that he appoints a sufficient deputy to be his under sheriff. Sees no difficulty why he should refuse to take the oath required of him. [*See ib., p.* 62.]

[Same?] to [Lord Burghley ?]. The Queen desires Mrs. Bainton not to depart with her interest in the manor of Marston Bygot to John Lord Stourton, which might greatly prejudice Mr. Hatton. [*See ib., p.* 35.]

[Same ?] to [the Lieut. of the Tower ?]. The note he sent of the prisoners is lost : begs him to send a new note. Among others the Queen is content that Bishop be set at liberty. [*See ib., p.* 62.]

Vol. CXI. January, 1577.

1577.
Jan. 12. 1. Note by the Judge of the Admiralty for the sending for such persons as are accused of giving assistance to Callis and other pirates in Wales.

Jan. 15.
Greenwich. 2. Memorandum subscribed by Lord Burghley of his conversation with Giovanni Battista da Trento, a gentleman of Vicenza, who offered to reveal many important secrets on certain conditions. 1tal.

Jan. 15. 3. Giovanni Battista to Burghley. Complains of the conduct of his servants towards him. Ital.

Jan. 16. 4. Names of certain inhabitants of the Isle of Sheppey.

DOMESTIC—ELIZABETH. 537

1577. VOL. CXI.

Jan. 18. 5. Brief of the requests of the inhabitants of the Isle of Sheppey, for a grant of incorporation for the town of Minster, including certain parishes within the isle.

Jan. 18. 6. Another brief of the liberties and privileges desired by the inhabitants of Sheppey in the grant of incorporation. [*Addressed to Lord Treasurer Burghley.*]

Jan. 21. 7. The Council to the Vice-President and Council in the Marches of
Hampton Court. Wales. Directing that the case of David Wiottye, a pirate, and others of the like nature, should be referred to the Court of Admiralty.

Jan. 21. 8. Dr. Roger Goade to Burghley. States what has been done
Cambridge. in the matter of Sturbridge fair. A friendly conference has been held with their opponents, and parties from both sides will wait upon him.

Jan. 22. 9. The Lord Chamberlain and the Earl of Leicester to Sir Mathew
Hampton Court. Arondell, and others. Concerning the lands of Viscount Howard, of Bindon, assigned by Act of Parliament to Mr. Henry Howard and his wife.

Jan. 22. 10. Petition of the Mayor and Burgesses of Kingston-upon-Hull to the Queen. Praying for some yearly allowance towards their expenses.

Jan. 24. 11. Dr. Goade, Vice Chancellor, to Burghley. States the reasons
Cambridge. why the Sturbridge fair business has been so long delayed.

Jan. 25. 12. The Vice Chancellor and Heads of Houses of Cambridge to
Cambridge. same. Request his special direction in matters relating to Sturbridge fair, and accrediting Dr. Ithell as their solicitor.

Jan. 25. 13. Thos. Browne to same. Injury done to his mill near Bowbridge by altering the course of the water in the river Lea. Solicits his intervention with the landlord, Mr. Nicholas Sturley, for an abatement of the rent.

Jan. 28. 14. Reasons why the Archbp. of York should not depart from the house called Bishopsthorpe, belonging to that see, which was required for the Lord President of the North.

Jan. 29. 15. The Mayor of Haverfordwest to Sir John Perrot. Had no
Haverfordwest. knowledge of Callice, the pirate, being in their town. Has suffered by pirates himself, and complains of their increase.

Jan. 29. 16. John Davids, Justice of Peace, to same. Excuses himself for
Haverfordwest. not apprehending Callice, the pirate. Cardiff is the general resort of pirates, where they are sheltered and protected.

Jan. 30. 17. Another brief of liberties desired by the inhabitants of Sheppey. [*Differing slightly from those of the 18th of January.*]

Jan. 30. 18. Petition of the inhabitants of the Isle of Sheppey to Burghley. For licence to compound with Thos. Randolphe for the suit and service owing by them to the Queen's manor of Middleton, occupied by him.

1577.
Jan.

VOL. CXI.

19. Note of services due by certain of the inhabitants of Sheppey to the Queen's manor and leet of Middleton, whereof Thomas Randolphe, Esq., is farmer.

20. Duplicate of the above ; with an additional article.

21. Answer of Thomas Randolphe to the petition of the inhabitants of the Isle of Sheppey.

Jan.

22. Lord Burghley to the Lord President of the North (?) The Queen has nominated Bishop Sandys to be Archbp. of York, and therefore requests his lordship's assistance in obtaining possession of the houses of Bishopsthorpe and Cawood for his use.

Jan.

23. The case of the College of Worcester. Cases submitted to the consideration of the Doctors of the Ecclesiastical Courts.

Jan.

24 to 26. Note of the spoils made by Dr. Sandys upon the Bishoprick of Worcester and the Cathedral College there, and charges against him as Bp. of London. [*Three copies.*]

Jan.

27. A view of the chief Readers, double and single, and of the chief barristers, for their practice in the four Inns of Court. [*The date of this paper is fixed by the mention of Edw. Flowerdewe, of the Inner Temple, and Tho. Calby, of Gray's Inn, "to be double readers this nexte Lente;" which occurred in Anno 19° Eliz.*]

Feb. 1.

28. Richard Vaughan to Sir John Perrot. That John Brown had half a ton of wine brought into Milford haven by the pirate Edwd. Harberd, and that it was stayed for the Lord Admiral's use.

Feb. 4.
Westminster.

29. Commission by the Queen to Dr. David Lewes. For the summary hearing of all matters between merchants, relating to freight, contracts, charter-parties, &c.

Feb. 6.

30. The names of the ships throughout the realm above 100 tons, and the number of topmen under 100 tons, through all the ports of England; with the names of the masters who have taken charge in the river Thames.

Feb. 6.

Entry of the above. [*See Vol.* xcvi., *pp.* 267-273.]

Feb. 14.

31. Indenture of settlement between Thomas Elliott and Thomas Wheler, citizens of London, on Elliott's intended marriage with Anne Underyll, of London, widow.

Feb. 14.

32. Bond of Thomas Elliott in 300*l.* to Thomas Wheler, for the faithful performance of the said indenture.

Feb. 14.

33. Statement of sundry and chargeable services done by John Hawkyns, without any recompense hitherto.

Feb. 17.

34. Petition of merchants of London trading to Barbary to the Lord Treasurer. Against certain irregularities committed by other merchants in wrongfully obtaining possession of some sugars.

Feb. 21.
Cardiff.

35. Sir Wm. Harbertt, and others, to the Council. Their proceedings for restoring certain goods taken from Tho. Brown and others, by pirates, and sold in Wales.

DOMESTIC—ELIZABETH. 539

1577.   VOL. CXI.

Feb.   36. Sir John Perrot to the Council. Has arrested six pirates of
Carewe.   Callice's company and sent them to Pembroke gaol. Complains of
Ric. Nash's nipping letter on his committing them. Offers to scour
the seas and clear them of pirates, and to gain 2,000l. yearly in
customs.

Feb ?   37. Certificate by Sir John Perrot, of the persons who bought the
wines, &c., lately brought into Milford haven by Edward Harberd,
the pirate ; or that aided him or John Callice during their abode there.

Feb.   38. Mr. Leake's discourse. Relative to the history of the cloth trade,
and the means for preventing the abuses of clothiers, aulnagers, &c.,
existing at present in that trade.

Feb.   39. Requests made by the inhabitants within the Isle of Sheppey
for certain liberties, whereby the isle may be better peopled, and of
more force to withstand the enemy ; with answers to each article
(being those of the 9th Nov., 1576). [*Indorsed*, "*Considered by
Mr. Fludd, Surveyor.*"]

Feb.   40. Extracts from charters granted to the City of London, from
King John to Feb. 19° Eliz., relating to brokers. Lat.

March 9.   41. Edwyn Sandys, Archbishop of York, to Lord Burghley. Prays
London.   that he may not be forced to make restitution to his successor of the
commodities of the see of London, which he has expended for the
benefit of his bishoprick.

March 11.   42. Note of the revenue of the Archbishop of York, usually due
between Michaelmas and the Purification of our Lady.

March 12.   43. Orders of the Commissioners of Sewers respecting the stopping
up of a bye stream falling into the river Lea, on the Essex side, in
the tenure of Mr. Hickes.

[March 21.]   44. Instructions by the Council to the Lord Mayor and Aldermen
of London, for the levying and training of 2,000 shot, appointed by
Her Majesty's special letters to be selected and trained in the said
city ; and to be furnished with calivers, flasks, touch-boxes, and
murrions.

March 24.   45. Bishop Coortesse to Mr. Sec. Walsyngham. Those that are
Aldingborne.   backward in religion grow worse and worse on the report of Don
John's coming to the Low Countries. Recommends the oath of supremacy to be administered at the next sessions. Names of those
examined, and articles of examination.

March 27.   46. Same to the Council. Certifies his dealing with James Hore, of
Aldingborne.   Waterford, for permission to transport certain grain out of the County
of Sussex, for service in Ireland.

March 27.   47. Lord North, and others, to same. Proceedings in the Musters
Lynton.   for Cambridgeshire. Deficiency of calivers. Request directions as to
training the men.

VOL. CXI.

1577.
March 30.
London.
48. Sir Wm. Wynter, Tho. Randolphe, and others, to the Council. Preparations for Furbisher's voyage to Cathay; charges for the fitting out of three ships for the voyage. Amount of money subscribed, &c. Inclosing,

  48. I. *Estimate of the charges for setting forth the three ships for the voyage.* 26 *Mar.* 1577.

  48. II. *Names of the adventurers in Furbisher's second voyage, and of the sums subscribed by each.*

March.
49. Note of the provision and furniture necessary for the second vcyage under Captain Furbisher for the discovery of Cathay; with request for a grant of incorporation.

March 31.
Ludlow Castle.
50. The Council of Wales to the Council. Have commissioned Fabian Phillips and others to search out the pirates. Their success. Arrival of a French ship, well manned, with letters of marque from the Prince of Condé.

March ?
51. Note of the most necessary things to be first considered upon to be repaired within Windsor Castle during the year 1577 by Her Majesty's direction. A new banquetting house, gallery, &c.

March ?
52. Supplication of Ralph Lever and Mr. Fawset against the Dean and Chapter of Durham, for granting leases of 21 years of the manors, &c., belonging to the prebends. Desire redress from Her Majesty by visitation, *sede vacante*.

March ?
53. Petition of Tho. Browne, Scotchman, to Lord Burghley. Soliciting a warrant for passing certain quantities of cloths, recovered from the pirates and shipped by him from Cardiff to Bristol.

March.
54. Grant to A. B. of licence to buy and export 12,000 broad cloths, as well white as coloured cloths and kerseys, under certain rates of custom.

VOL. CXII. APRIL, 1577.

April 2.
Norwich.
1. Commissioners of Musters for the County of Norfolk to the Council. Have appointed four days in Easter week for the training of 500 men. Estimate of the wages of the soldiers.

April 2.
Chelmsford.
2. Same for the County of Essex to same. Estimate of the charge for training of 400 men. Require an extension of time for training the men.

April 3.
Winchester.
3. Same for Hampshire to same. Request that the time for the first training the 300 men may be deferred till the 1st of May.

April 3.
Ely.
4. Same for the Isle of Ely to same. Have not been able to make up the number of calivers required. Have appointed Wm. Roberts to train the 50 men.

1577.
April 3.
Cardiff.

V̨ol. CXII.

5. Fabian Phillips and Thomas Lewys to the Council. Detail their proceedings in the examinations of upwards of sixty of the pirates and their maintainers at Cardiff. Sir John Perrot's absence. Difficulties of their service, the town's people being unwilling to give any information. *Inclosing,*

    5. I. *The names of the pirates gathered out of the examinations.*

    5. II. *Examination of Simon Ferdinando, a Portuguese, relative to the doings of John Callice and other pirates.* 17 *March.*

    5. III. *Examination of Flowre Johnes, wife of John Wastell, relative to quantities of salt bought of pirates in Cardiff.* 25 *March.*

    5. IV. *Examination of Wm. Chick, of Ipswich, as to his services and manner of living.* 26 *March.*

    5. V. *Second examination of Wm. Chick, as to his dealings with John Callice and other pirates of Cardiff.* 26 *March.*

    5. VI. *Further examination of Wm. Chick, on his connexion with the pirates.* 27 *March.*

April 4.
Dorchester.

6. Commissioners of Musters for Dorset to the Council. Beg that the day for training the levies might be postponed till after the Easter holidays.

April 4.

7. Same for Northamptonshire to same. Excuse themselves for the delay in their former Musters, being near harvest time. Such persons as are rated at 5*l.* in the subsidy may contribute towards the expense of training the 200 men. *Inclosing,*

    7. I. *Estimate of the charge for equipping and training of 200 calivers.*

April 6.
Salisbury.

8. Same for Wiltshire to same. Estimate of the wages of the soldiers. Think that three or four days in the year might serve to muster them in.

April 6.

9. Bishop Coortesse to same. Found in his late visitation that many were unsound in religion. His proceedings with them within the diocese of Chichester.

April 10.

10. Commissioners of Musters for Bedfordshire to same. Request, on account of the poorness of the county, that 50 of the number required may be abated, and that they may use their discretion in assessing. *Inclosing,*

    10. I. *Estimate of the charges for furnishing and training 150 men for the County of Bedford.*

April 11.
Lincoln.

11. Same for Lincolnshire to same. The charge for training the 400 men will amount to above 320*l.* Request that all persons rated in the subsidy at above 40*s.* in lands, or 60*s.* in goods, may be charged in due proportion.

April 12.
Wells.

12. Same for Somerset to same. Have agreed to have 300 men in readiness, furnished with shot; and have appointed several trainers, one to every 50 soldiers.

VOL. CXII.

1577.
April 13. 13. Sir Thomas Palmer, and others, to the Earl of Arundel. Complaining of the proceedings of Bp. Coortesse in citing all the justices of the peace and gentlemen of the county, publicly to appear and answer to certain articles in Chichester Cathedral. *Inclosing,*

    13. I. *List of the names of the gentlemen cited to appear before the Bishop at the consistory of Chichester; with remarks on the transaction.*

April 15.
Reygate. 14. Commissioners of Musters for Surrey to the Council. Desire to have the number of 150 men abated, considering the state of the shire, and the services it has to render to Her Majesty. *Inclosing,*

    14. I. *An estimate of the charges for furnishing arms and training of 150 men as calivers; and proposals for levying money for that purpose.*

April 15.
Hertford. 15. Same for Hertfordshire to same. Have appointed Whitsun week for the first training of the 100 men, with estimate for the same. Great burdens already sustained by the county.

April 16.
Newbury. 16. Same for Berkshire to same. Requesting that Mr. Stafford and Mr. Molins may be joined with them in the commission. Propose a method of training the men in their respective divisions. *Inclosing,*

    16. I. *Certificate of the charges for the Musters; and how the same hath been levied upon the inhabitants.*

April 16.
Stafford. 17. Same for Staffordshire to same. Want of armour. Will commence training the 200 men as soon as possible.

April 16.
Huntingdon. 18. Same for the County of Huntingdon to same. Desire that the number of 50 may be abated from the 150 men appointed to be trained, and that they may use their own discretion in levying the charges. *Inclosing,*

    18. I. *Estimate of the charges for the furniture and training of 150 calivers.*

April 16.
Winchester. 19. Same for Hampshire to same. Report on the order they had taken towards training the 300 men as appointed, and the charges of the same. The training to commence on May-day next. *Inclosing,*

    19. I. *Note of the Captains appointed for the training of the 300 men in Hampshire.*

April 17.
Aldingborne. 20. Bishop Coortesse to same. That he would appear before them according to their direction. Exportation of grain. What he has done in matters of religion, he has done plainly and uprightly.

April 18. 21. Report of the Goldfinders on the value of the ore or gold earth delivered to them. With estimate of the amount of profit on the working of it.

April 20.
Cornwall. 22. Commissioners of Musters for Cornwall to the Council. Request the time for the first training the 200 men may be deferred till St. George's Eve. Trainers appointed. The county is very much destitute of men of good service, and unprovided of furniture of shot for them.

DOMESTIC—ELIZABETH. 543

1577.
VOL. CXII.

April 21. 23. Commissioners of Musters for Devonshire to the Council. Have
Exeter. taken order for selecting 500 men to be trained. Request directions from the Council to the Lord Warden of the Stannaries as to the 50 men allotted for the tinners. Have not yet determined on the Captains for training them.

April 21. 24. Note of the receipt in the Exchequer, from Easter 1577 till the 21st of April next following.

April 22. 25. Mr. Michael Lok to the Queen. Details his proceedings and plan to fit out an expedition with John Baptista Agnello, for bringing of gold ore from the lands discovered by Furbisher. *Incloses,*

 25. I. *Various little notes from John Baptista Agnello above referred to. Ital.*

 25. II. *Agreement between M. Agnello and Michael Lok for a voyage to bring home gold ore. London, 19 March. Ital.*

 25. III. *John Baptista Agnello to Michael Lok, on the proposed expedition. 4 April 1577. Ital.*

April 23. 26. Commission from the Queen to the Bishop of London, the
Westminster. Bishop of Rochester, Sir Chr. Wray, Sir Robt. Bell, Sir William Cordell, Knt., Doctors Thos. Wilson, John Gibbons, and John Griffith, for a special visitation of the University of Oxford. Lat.

April 24. 27. Fabian Phillips and Tho. Lewys to the Council. Certify their
Cardiff. doings in the examination of matters relating to pirates in Wales. *Inclosing,*

 27 I. *Examination of Wm. Chick, of Ipswich. Details his own recent transactions and intercourse with pirates at Cardiff. Ludlow, 11 April, 1577.*

 27. II. *Brief collection of proofs gathered out of the examinations of divers persons against John Ap John, John Robert Ap Jenñ, William Hurbart, and David Roberts, Esqrs., for buying goods unlawfully from the Commissioners at Cardiff.*

April 26. 28. David Lewes, Judge of the Admiralty, to the Council. Pro-
The Arches. ceedings against Rowland and Wm. Morgan, justices of peace, for not aiding John Crofts in the capture of a pirate's ship. *Incloses,*

 28. I. *Articles to be administered to Rowland Morgan and Wm. Morgan, relative to the assistance required from them by Crofts. With their answers.*

April 26. 29. Petition of Sir Thomas Palmer, Richard Ernlie, and Tho. Lewkenor, to the Council. Desiring redress from the injuries done to them in their reputation and character by the defamatory proceedings of the Bp. of Chichester, against them and other justices of Sussex. *Annexing,*

 29 I. *Articles declaring the injuries and wrongs done by the Lord Bp. of Chichester to Sir Tho. Palmer, Ric. Ernlie, and Tho. Lewkenor, Esqrs. Consisting of twenty articles.*

VOL. CXII.

1577.

April 26? 30. Answer of Bishop Coortesse, unto certain articles supposing to declare wrongs done to Sir Tho. Palmer and Mr. Ric. Ernlie, &c.

April 26? 31. Articles (38 in number) exhibited to the Council by Palmer, Ernlie, and Lewkenor, against the doings of the Bp. of Chichester, whereby it may appear how and by what means the Queen's Majesty's service within the County of Sussex hath been hindered and letted. With proofs for verification of the same.

April 26? 32. A breviat of the articles exhibited against the Bp. of Chichester, by Sir Tho. Palmer.

April 26? 33. Answer of the Bp. of Chichester to the 38 articles exhibited against him by Sir Tho. Palmer and others.

April 26? 34. Replication of Palmer, Ernlie, and Lewkenor, to the answer of the Bp. of Chichester.

April 26? 35. Palmer, Ernlie, and Lewkenor, to the Council. In answer to the bill delivered in by the Bp. of Chichester to the Council, touching his proceedings in causes of religion.

April 26? 36. Articles exhibited against the Bp. of Chichester, for granting licences for the exportation of corn.

April 26? 37. The answer of the Bp. of Chichester and Dr. Henry Worley to the information of William Grover against the Bp. of Chichester, relative to the transportation of corn.

April 26? 38. Answer of the Bp. of Chichester to the complaint of Walter Coverley, relative to the office of bailiwick of the Manhood.

April 26? 39. Replication of Walter Coverley (or Cubberley) to the answer of the Bp. of Chichester, made to the complaint of the said Walter.

April 26? 40. Answer of the Bp. of Chichester to the complaint of William Faires, relative to the right of commonage in the Manhood.

April 26? 41. The Bp. of Chichester's answer to the complaint of Edward Amyers, relative to his claim to the office of register of the diocese of Chichester.

April 26? 42. The replication of Edwd. Amyers to the answer of Ric. Bp. of Chichester, as to the office of principal registrar.

April 26? 43. Abstract of the charges against the Bp. of Chichester. [Indorsed, " General directorie to the crimes wherewith the B. is " charged."]

April 26? 44. Similar abstract. [Indorsed, " Particuler directorie to certeine " of the crimes wherewith the B. is charged."]

DOMESTIC—ELIZABETH. 545

1577.	Vol. CXII.
April 30. Minories.	45. Edwyn Sandys, Archbp. of York, to Lord Burghley. The preparation of his farewell speech, to be delivered at St. Paul's Cross, had prevented his visiting him. The Bishop of London's note is very incorrect. Is sore dealt withal, and most shamefully wronged on every side. *Incloses*,
	45. I. *The Bp. of London's note of the commodities growing to the Archbishop of York presently at his entrance into that see. With the Archbishop's answers to the same.*
April.	46. Names and offences of the convicted prisoners that went with Mr. Furbisher.
April.	47. The number of those that are assessed for the first payment of the subsidy within certain Hundreds in Northamptonshire.
April ?	48. Egremonde Radclyff to the Council. Desires to be permitted to take exercise in the little garden before his prison, and to be allowed a servant to attend him. [*Attested* " *Perused by me*, OWYN HOPTON."]
April ?	49. The order thought meet by the Commissioners appointed to examine the Bp. of Chichester, and the conclusion of their conferences. Conditions prescribed for the bishop's observance.
April ?	50. Answer of the Bp. of Chichester to the above order set down for him.
April.	51. Statement of the many oppressions committed by Giles Lord Chandos, particularly against Tho. Bushell, in relation to a murder committed in the house of John Yate, servant of Lord Chandos; and also against Thomas Smith, a justice of peace, and others; with the insolent and contemptuous demeanour of Chandos towards the Council of the Marches of Wales.

	Vol. CXIII. MAY, 1577.
May 3.	1. John Lord Darcy to the Earl of Sussex. Requests that Sir Tho. Lucas, Edmund Pirton, and Thomas Taye may be joined with him in the Commission of Musters, as those in the former commission were all dead or gone.
May 6.	2. Tho. Randolphe to Burghley. Sends a note of the inhabitants of the Isle of Sheppey. They desire to be free from the purveyors. *Incloses*,
	2. I. *List of the names of the inhabitants within the Isle of Sheppey.*
May 9.	3. Petition of Richard Coxe to Burghley. Complains that for five years Mr. Henry Howard has been indebted to him to the amount of 67*l.* 11*s.* 4*d.*, which still remains unpaid.
May 10. Warwick.	4. Commissioners of Musters for the County of Warwick to the Council. Have trained 200 men at Warwick and Coventry. Names of the Captains appointed. *Inclosing*,
	4. I. *Note of charges for training 200 harquebusiers within the County of Warwick.*

M M

Vol. CXIII.

1577.
May 12.
Dorchester.
5. Commissioners of Musters for the County of Dorset to the Council. Preparations for training the number appointed. The arms and ammunition must be procured from London. A new warrant required for the Isle of Purbeck. The town of Poole refuse to bear their share in the charges. Names of the trainers and training places.

May 14.
Comforte.
6. Henry Lord Abergavenny and Sir Tho. Cotton to same. Have mustered 100 men to be trained with calivers in the Lathe of Aylesford, Rochester furnishing 10 of the number.

May 15.
7. Terrier or bounder of the lands, &c. of the Prebend of Browneswood, in the parish of Hornsey, Middlesex, belonging to the Cathedral Church of St. Paul's. Made by John Harington.

May 17.
Aylesbury.
8. Commissioners of Musters for the County of Buckingham to the Council. Have selected the 200 men appointed to be trained. Note of the charges for the same, proposed to be defrayed by a general rate on the county.

May 17.
9. Book of presentments of the juries sworn in Wareham and Melcombe Regis, by virtue of a commission from the Admiralty. Concerning inquiries to be made of pirates and spoils committed by them.

May 18.
Sutton.
10. Henry Cobham and Sir Tho. Walsyngham to same. Proceedings in selecting and training 500 shot for the County of Kent. Eighty men allotted to their Lathe of Sutton-at-Hone. Preparations for the training, &c. *Inclosing,*

    10. I. *Note of the charges for training 80 men.*

May 19.
Southwark.
11. Commissioners of Musters for the County of Surrey to the Council. That they had committed to Mr. Laurence Pecock the training of the 150 calivers appointed to that shire.

May 22.
12. Instructions given to Martin Furbisher, to be observed in the voyage now recommended to him for the North-west passage and Cathay, in the Ayde, the Gabriel, and the Michael.

May 22.
13. Draft of the above.

May 22.
Entry of the above. [*See Vol.* cxxxiv., *p.* 420..]

May 22.
14. Abstract of the above. [*On the other side of this leaf is a prayer by Queen Elizabeth, on her being at Bristol,* 15 *Aug.* 1574.]

May 23.
15. Lord Cobham, Lord Warden, to the Council. Depredations by pirates. Necessity for sending out ships for their suppression.

May 27
Leicester.
16. Commissioners of Musters for the County of Leicester to the Council. Their proceedings in training the 150 men according to their instructions. The poorness of the shire.

May 31.
The Court.
17. Sec. Walsyngham to Lord Burghley. The news of the revolt of D'Anvyle is true, and Her Majesty is much perplexed with it. Laments that the Queen still persists in the controversy with the Archbp. of Canterbury. Proceedings towards his deprivation.

DOMESTIC—ELIZABETH.

VOL. CXIII.

1577.	
May.	18. List of commissioners for the trial of pirates and piracies within the jurisdiction of the Cinque Ports. [*Signed by Wm. Lord Cobham.*]
May. Bruges.	19. Decree of the Company of the Merchants of the Staple enacted for the better regulation of the trade in wool.
May.	20. Extract from the account of John Genkins of sums received by him for her Majesty's use from the revenue of the archbishoprick of York during the vacation of the see, viz., from Feb. 15, 1576, till Michaelmas following.
May. Greenwich.	21. The Council to the Justices of Peace in various counties. For restraint of the licences granted by the Queen for buying and selling of wool; and to certify the names of all broggers and engrossers
May.	22. Another copy of the above.
May.	23. List of the names of pirates in the gaol of Weymouth. [*Mutilated.*]
May.	24. Note of the aiders and partners of Callice and other pirates, drawn from the depositions and presentments of various persons at Lulworth in the County of Dorset.
May ?	25. Notes from the depositions of various persons in Dorsetshire, relative to Callis and other pirates, their aiders, &c.
May.	26. Depositions of various persons relative to the resort of Court, Hickes, Callis, and other pirates in the County of Dorset, and the dealings of the inhabitants with them.
May.	27. Thomas Browne, a Scot, to Lord Burghley. Solicits that if it should please the Queen to grant a pardon to John Callice the pirate, the pardon may be given to him as part recompense for the goods taken from him by the said pirate.
May.	28. Interrogatories to be ministered to Charles Ratclif, touching certain libels against the Earl of Leicester and Burghley. His speech relative to the Catholics and the Queen of Scots, and as to Mounford, a Jesuit, Sir Tho. Cornwallis, and other Papists; consisting of forty-seven articles.
May ?	29. Answers by Ratclif to some of the preceding interrogatories. [*Imperfect.*]
May ?	30. Interrogatories to be ministered to John Bacon, of what he had heard from Chs. Ratclif and Robert Sutton, concerning the libels against Leicester and Burghley. Publication of the Rheims Testament, &c.
May ?	31. Petition of Nich. Taylior to the Council. Against John and Francis Pilkington, Prebendaries of Durham, who had turned him out of his tenement. Desires letters to Richard Bishop of Durham for his restitution.
May ?	32. Memoranda by Burghley, relative to the Musters. [*Indorsed: "A memorial for the continuance of the Commission for Musters."*]

1577.	Vol CXIV. June–July, 1577.
June 2. Exeter.	1. Commissioners of Musters for the County of Devon to the Council. Certify their proceedings for the training of the 500 men. The charges, and names of the Captains appointed for that purpose.
June 2.	2. Same for the County of Kent to same. Their proceedings for the Musters and training of the men appointed for the Division of the Lathe of St. Augustin.
June 3. Cambridge.	3. Dr. Ithell to Lord Burghley. On the choice of a new Master for St. John's College, now vacant by resignation of Dr. Stile. Dr. Perne, Mr. Ric. Howland, and others, are candidates. Their qualifications.
June 4. Stafford.	4. Commissioners of Musters for Staffordshire to the Council. Certify their proceedings for training 200 men. Roger Stamford and Francis Collyer appointed to train them.
June 4. Norwich.	5. Same for the County of Norfolk to same. Certify their proceedings; and request to use other days for the training of the men, as they were not able to accomplish it in the four days in Whitsun week.
June 4. Oxford.	6. Same for Oxfordshire to same. Certify their doings in mustering and training the 200 men appointed, and the assessment for their charges.
June 6.	7. Dr. Ric. Longworth to Burghley. Several candidates for the Mastership of St. John's. Would himself accept the office if that might be an occasion of peace and quietness.
June 7.	8. Testimonial under the hands and seals of divers gentlemen, witnessing that the Bp. of Chichester was not drunk at the dinner at Mr. John Sherewin's house, "as by some he was unjustly sclaundered."
June 9. Norwich.	9. Thomas Kendall to Tho. Windebank, one of the Clerks of the Privy Signet. His kind reception at Norwich. Requests to be remembered to his friends in town, and to be favoured with a letter. French.
June 9.	10. Petition of Tho. Taylor to Burghley. Solicits his aid for payment of the sum of 25l. 14s. 4d., due to him by Mr. Henry Howard, for ready money, meat, and drink.
June 10.	11. Henry Hawthorne to Burghley. Suggests an alteration to be made at the end of the terrace at Windsor Castle next the College; and that timber trees of young growth may not be felled without his consent. Request of the citizens of Reading for the stones of the abbey for their streets.
June 10 ?	12. Plan of the gallery and other alterations in Windsor Castle, by H. Hawthorne, surveyor of the works.
June 12.	13. Estimate of ordnance for the castle of St. Mawe's at Falmouth.

DOMESTIC—ELIZABETH.   549

VOL. CXIV.

1577.
June 13.
Huntingdon.
14. Commissioners of Musters for the County of Huntingdon to the Council. Proceedings for training the 150 men appointed. Names of the Captains. *Inclosing,*

14. I. *Estimate of charges for the training 150 men within the County of Huntingdon.*

June 15.
. Somerton.
15. Justices of Somersetshire to same. They have put the 300 men in readiness for Ireland. Complain of the burdens thrown on their county.

June 16.
Cambridge.
16. Dr. Roger Goade, Vice Chancellor, and Heads of Houses, to Burghley. Acquainting him that by the kind offices of Lord North, they have made a good agreement with the town in the matter of Sturbridge fair.

June 18.
17. Petition of George Dickens to the Council. For payment of the sum of 35*l.* 18*s.*, due to him by Mr. Henry Howard.

June 18
18. Petition of Thomas Taylor to same. For payment of 25*l.* 14*s.* 4*d.*, due to him by Mr. Henry Howard.

June 18.
19. Petition of James Taylor to same. Prays for the payment of 4*l.* 13*s.* 2*d.* owing to him by Mr. Henry Howard.

June 18.
20. Petition of Robert Pinder to the Lord High Treasurer. For recovery of a debt of 300*l.* due to him by Mr. Henry Howard.

June 18.
21. Petition of Griffen Jones to the Council. For recovery of a debt of 33*l.* and 6*d.*, due to him by the same.

June 21.
Fulham.
22. John Aylmer, Bp. of London, to Mr. Sec. Walsyngham. Requests his advice and the Queen's approbation of the plan proposed for proceeding against the Papists, who increase in number and obstinacy, by fines rather than by imprisonment, which, " by sparing their housekeeping, greatly enricheth them."

June 22.
23. Walsyngham (?) to the Attorney-General. To hasten his answer to the Council, touching the fittest means to punish the aiders of pirates about Cardiff.

June 26.
Indenture of sale and conveyance from Francis Alford to his brother Roger Alford, of the manor of Aston under Edge, co. Gloucester; late the property of William Porter, deceased. [*Case* B, *Eliz.* No. 13.]

June 26.
Lease from the Dean and Chapter of St. Paul's to Justinian Kydde, of the vaults under the quire of St. Paul's, and the sheds lately called " Jesus Crowdes" and other premises lately in the occupation of John Cawoode, stationer, deceased. [*Case* B, *Eliz.*, No. 14.]

June 27.
24. Petition of Gryffyn Jones to the Council. For payment of 33*l.* 0*s.* 6*d.* due to him by Mr. Henry Howard.

Vol. CXIV.

1577. June 27. Newbury.	25. The clothiers of the town of Newbury to the Council. Stating their opinion on the cause of the high price of wools, and how the same might be best remedied.
June 28. London.	26. Tho. Heton, Governor of the Company of Merchants Adventurers, to same. Report on the cause of the high price and dearth of wools.
June 28 ?	27. Certificate of the clothiers of Wiltshire to same. The high price of wool caused by greedy covetousness of the Merchant Staplers.
June 30.	28. Similar certificate by the clothiers of Worcester.
June.	29. A declaration to the Queen and Council of the causes of the decay of the Company of the Merchants of the Staple, and how the same may be remedied.
June.	30. Opinion of the Mayor of the Staple for reformation of disorders in the buying and retailing of wool.
June.	31. The Mayor of the Staple's collection of the names of the chief buyers and broggers of wool.
June.	32. Certificate and opinion of the clothiers of Gloucestershire, touching the scarcity and high price of wool.
June.	33. Answer of the clothiers of Suffolk to certain articles propounded by the Council, touching the cause of the scarcity and high price of wool, and the best remedy for the same.
June.	34. Abstract of the opinions of the clothiers of Wiltshire, Gloucestershire, Essex, and the staplers, of the cause of the scarcity and high price of wool.
June.	35. Collection of statutes touching the buying and selling of wool.
June.	36. Mr. Mershe's note of advice to the Council touching the buyers of wool.
June.	37, 38. Certain articles necessary to be considered of, touching licences of wool granted or hereafter to be granted. [*Two copies.*]
June.	39. Articles alleged by the Merchants of the Staple what are the causes of the dearth of wools, and the remedies how they are to be reformed ; with a breviate of the same.
June.	40. William and Thos. Freman to the Company of the Merchants Adventurers. Stating their opinion of the causes of the scarcity and high price of wool.
June.	41. to Mr. Symon Bowyer. Information respecting the licences granted to John Aldridge and others for the buying and selling of wool.
June.	42. Names of the deputies appointed by James Cottesford for the buying of wool, according to his licence.

1577.
June.

Vol. CXIV.

43. Articles collected out of the statutes of the realm, proving the antiquity of the Company of the Merchants of the Staple, and that they are good and profitable members of the commonwealth.

June. 44. Propositions by John Hawkyns (?) for a voyage to be made in the Swallow and the Pelican to Alexandria, Tripoli, Constantinople, &c.

June.
Greenwich.
[The Council?] to the Justices of Dorsetshire. Directions to levy and equip 100 men for the service in Ireland; to be sent to Bristol immediately on the receipt of a letter from the Lord Deputy. [*See Vol.* xlv., *p.* 76.]

June? [The Council?] to the keeper of Waltham forest. Advise in what manner he shall best permit the Portuguese Ambassador to hunt and kill deer in certain walks in that forest. [*See ib., p.* 36.]

July 1. 45. Schedule of such debts of Mr. Henry Howard as were discharged in part or whole by the Council's warrants to the Master of the Rolls.

July 1. 46. The names of such persons as are appointed Special Commissioners of Musters for every shire, for execution of such instructions as were annexed to the former General Commissions for Musters, in the 15th year of the Queen's reign.

July 1? Instructions given by the Privy Council to the late Commissioners appointed for the taking of the Musters, and for the present levying and training of certain numbers of soldiers, appointed by the Queen's letters tohe selected and trained. [*See Vol.* cxxxiv. *p.* 692.]

July 6. 47. Note of parcels of wool bought by the clothiers of Coggeshall, in Essex, of staplers and broggers since the 1st of Aug., 1576.

July 6.
The Arches.
Opinion of Drs. Lewes and Awbrey on the complaint of the Ambassador of Flanders relating to Wm. Tipper's hosting of merchant strangers. [*See Vol.* cxxx., *March* 1579, *No.* 25.]

July 7. 48. Gye Lyte to Lord Burghley. Solicits payment of the remainder of the debt owing to him by Mr. Henry Howard.

July 7. 49. Bond of Ralph and Thomas Ithell, for Mr. Ralph's appearance when cited by the Vice-Chancellor of the University of Cambridge.

July 7. 50. Answer of John Skerne to the complaint of the Lord Viscount Byndon. Denies that he was privy to any leases being made by Mr. Henry Howard.

July 9. 51. Presentments of the Jury at the Admiralty Court of the Cinque Ports. [*Nearly obliterated.*]

July 11. 52. Tho. Maston's accompt of ready money received for the impost of money delivered by exchange, from Sept. 27, 1576, to July 11, 1577.

July 15. 53. Note of yearly rents paid by Prebends of the Cathedral Church of Exeter, and misappropriated. [*Indorsed*, "*For Mr. Brōkard.*"]

VOL. CXIV.

1577.
July 17. 54. Orders set down by the Queen for the better direction and reformation of Her Highness's Court in the Marches of Wales; with additional orders as to appointment and attendance of councillors, &c.

July 17.
Greenwich. 55. Minute of the above additional orders.

July 17.
Yarmouth. 56. Certificate by the bailiffs of Great Yarmouth in behalf of four Scotchmen, part owners of the Scotch ship, the Fortune, of Aberdeen, taken by force in Laystoft Roads, by one Captain Phibson.

July 19. 57. Deposition of Herman Runge touching his ship, the "Jonas," taken by the pirate Robert Hickes, and afterwards pawned and sold to Sir John Perrot for 10*l*.

July 22. 58. John Johnson's discourse to the Queen and Council for the repairing of the decayed state of the Merchants of the Staple, and for the erection of certain new staples.

July 22.
Cambridge. 59. Dr. Andrew Perne to Lord Burghley. Proceedings in the election of Mr. Howland to the Mastership of St. John's College. Hopes soon to finish the new statutes for that college. Recommends Mr. Digory Nicholls to be Master of Magdalen College.

July. 60. Instructions by the Council to Mr. Geo. Winter to take command of the Lyon, the Foresight, and the Dreadnought, to cruise off the Irish coasts, and to watch La Roche, a Frenchman, who was fitting out certain ships, in conjunction with James Fitzmorris, an Irish rebel.

July. 61. Return of the stores, &c. on board the Lyon, the Dreadnought, and the Foresight, now presently appointed to the seas.

July ? 62, 63. Two petitions of Richard Lombard, of Bristol, to the Lord Treasurer. Solicits a licence to transport 600 quarters of wheat and malt to Ireland, duty free.

64. Note of the impost levied by the Venetians on the wines of Candia, laden in English bottoms.

65. Tabular account of the rise and progress of the trade in wines, and of the advantage of its being reserved to the Company of Regular Vintners.

66. Treatise concerning the origin and establishment of commerce and marts, and the wealth and power they afford to the State.

July ? 67. Mr. Highfeld's advice to Lord Burghley on the subject of military preparations. The necessity of having in readiness a sufficient number of "shot on horseback." Effectiveness of archery, and reasons why the same should not be discontinued in war.

July ? 68. Directions for the better and more speedy execution of the commission for the punishment of the aiders of pirates.

DOMESTIC—ELIZABETH. 553

1577. July ?	VOL. CXIV. Considerations " how such as are backward and corrupt in religion may be reduced to conformity, and others stayed from like corruption." Proceedings against Watson, Fecknam, and others. Removing corrupt schoolmasters. The orders for redress of Inns of Court to be executed. [*See Vol.* xlv., *p.* 10. *The order for government of the Inns of Court was passed in Council* 31 *May* 1574.]
July ?	[Walsyngham ?] to the Bishop of London. A consultation to be held to establish some general order for the stricter execution of the statutes against such as refuse to attend the Church. To consider what should be done with Watson, Fecknam, Harpsfield, and others, corrupt schoolmasters. [*See ib., p.* 21.]
[July ?]	69. The Council to certain Bishops. To take into their custody Drs. Feckenham, Watson, and others; with directions to the bishops as to the reception and entertainment of them in their houses, at table, &c.
July.	70. Form of admission and of the oath taken by the Master of St. John's College, Camb. Lat. [*Probably of Dr. Ric. Howland in July* 1577.]

VOL. CXV. AUGUST—SEPTEMBER, 1577.

August 10.	1. Lists of Her Majesty's ships, their names, burden, number of men, &c. Lists and estimates for setting forth 24 ships to the seas, 24th May, 1574, and for victualling the same, by Edw. Baeshe. [*See also Vol.* xcvi., *pp.* 275, 281.]
August 10 ?	Note of cordage, sails, and other stores furnished to several ships serving in various parts. [*See Vol.* xcvi., *pp.* 308, 315.]
August 14. The Court.	2. Mr. Sec. Walsyngham (?) to the Earl of Shrewsbury. The Queen desires Mr. Sacheverell might be re-admitted into the commission of the peace, unless there were any substantial reasons to the contrary.
August 14. The Court.	3. Same to the Earl of Bedford. Respecting Mr. Sacheverell's re-admittance into the commission of the peace.
August 17.	4. Note of the charges for re-victualling the Queen's Majesty's three ships, the Lyon, the Dreadnought, and the Foresight, now at sea, for one month longer.
August 18. Oatlands.	5. The Council to Sir Henry Radeclyff. To oversee the works at Portsmouth, under the charge of Ric. Popynjay, and the expenditure of the money for the repair of the forts.
August 19. London.	6. to Walsyngham (?). Origin of the claim to proxies by the bishops and archdeacons in respect of their visitations, &c.
August 19.	7. Walsyngham to Burghley. Has nominated Christopher Huddesdon to receive the 20,000*l.* appointed by Her Majesty for the purchase of gunpowder and saltpetre.
August 20.	8. Warrants for the payment and employment of the sum of 20,000*l.* to the person nominated by Mr. Walsyngham for the purchase of gunpowder and saltpetre. [*Three warrants on one paper.*]

1577.   VOL. CXV.

August 21.   9. Indenture of award by Peter Cox, Esq., Mayor of Poole, and others, between Mr. Henry Asheley and Charles le Berquier, relative to 140 quarters of salt lately landed at Poole.

August 28.   10. Certificate of the Musters for the town of Great Yarmouth, names of the able men between 60 and 16 years, furniture of armour, weapons, &c. [*Greatly injured by damp.*]

August 29. Oatlands.   11. Sec. Walsyngham to Lord Burghley. Advertisements from the continent. The Queen's design to secure Scotland by pension. The King of Portugal's preparations. *Incloses,*

               11. I. *Advertisements from Rochelle. Aug.* 19, 1577

August 30.   12. Report by Wm. Perrott on the ship discovered and captured by him off Great Grimsby by order of the Mayor and Aldermen of Kingston-on-Hull.

August. Richmond.   13. The Council to the Commissioners of Musters for the County of Essex. Thanks to those who had been diligent in performing their instructions. If any have been remiss it should immediately be reformed. Desire to be advertised of their proceedings in training the men appointed.

August.   14. Names of commissioners appointed in sundry shires to have the special oversight for the restraint of the unlawful buying and engrossing of wool.

August ?   15. The answer of Richard Bolde to certain articles touching an imposition to be levied in the County of Lancaster, for support of recusants in prison under Mr. Worseley's charge.

August ?   16. Interrogatories proposed for the examination of John Sharp, touching the shipping of certain packs of wool from Romney.

August ?   17, 18. Form of a recognizance for ale-house keepers. The party to be bound by recognizance in the sum of 20s., and two sufficient sureties in 10s. each. [*Two copies.*]

August ?   19. Proofs on behalf of the plaintiffs, touching the rights of the tenants of Bromham as to commonage in the forest of Melksham, against Sir Henry Baynton, defendant.

August?   20. Petition of Roger Poittow, merchant of Normandy, to the Council. Complains that his ship, named the "Pelican, of Kyllebeufe," laden with fish and oil, from Newfoundland, had been taken and plundered by John Granger, of Plymouth, and three of the mariners killed.

August ?   21. Estimate of the charge of two of Her Majesty's barks, viz., the Achates and the Merlin, to be set to the seas in warlike manner, for apprehending pirates in the mouth of the river Thames.

Sept. 13. Corpus Christi Coll.   22. Robert Norgate, Master of Corpus Christi College, Cambridge, to Burghley. In reply to his recommendation of one Booth for a fellowship in that college.

Vol. CXV.

1577.
Sept. 13.
23. Edmund Freke Bp. of Norwich, and others, Justices of the Peace of the County of Norfolk, to the Council. Report their proceedings for restraining the buyers and sellers of wool. *Inclosing,*

 23. I. Copy of the recognizance that certain men therein named be bound not to buy and sell wool unlawfully.

Sept. 15.
Gorhambury.
24. Lord Keeper Bacon to the Queen. Does that by letter which he would do in person but for an unable and unweildy body. Threatening aspect of affairs. Hostilities with Spain and France to be expected and provided against. Remedies to obviate the same.

Sept. 18.
25. Sec. Walsyngham to Tho. Randolphe. Excuses his delay in writing by reason of the urgency of public business, in which he will shortly be relieved by the appointment of Dr. Wylson, and thinks he has not been well used by Mr. Copinger. Mr. Manhod had failed in his suit. Affairs of Scotland.

Sept 19.
Launceston.
26. Commissioners of Musters for the County of Cornwall to the Council. Have been obliged to defer taking the Musters on account of the plague.

Sept. 23.
Chipping Wickham.
27. Justices of Buckinghamshire to same. Have taken a note of all the alehouses, inns, and taverns within the county. *Inclosing,*

 27. I. Certificate of the number and names of keepers of alehouses, inns, and taverns within the County of Buckingham.

Sept. 23.
Chipping Wickham.
28. Same to same. Certify their proceedings for the restraint of broggers and engrossers of wool.

Sept. 23.
Hertford.
29. Justices of Hertfordshire to same. Their proceedings for restraint and punishment of the broggers and engrossers of wool.

Sept. 23.
30. Certificate of General Musters for the County of Buckingham, taken the 23rd of September, 1577.

31. Particular of the rental of the manor of Abbot Isle, with the value of the same at 80 years purchase.

Sept. 23.
Indenture of sale from the trustees appointed by Act of Parliament to discharge the debts of the Visct. Howard of Byndon, to Edmond Gill, of one third part of the manor of Abbot's Isle, co. Somerset, parcel of the inheritance of the late John Lord Marney, deceased. [*Case* B. *Eliz.* No. 15.]

Sept. 26.
32. Names of commissioners specially appointed in divers shires upon the sea coasts to examine the favourers and aiders of pirates, and purchasers of pirates' goods.

Sept. 27.
Corpus Christi Coll.
33. Robert Norgate to Lord Burghley. Mr. Booth declines to pass an examination as to his proficiency in learning until a fellowship becomes vacant.

Sept. 28.
Worcester.
34. Commissioners of Musters for Worcestershire to the Council. Relative to their doings in the Musters of able men, horses, and armour. *Inclosing,*

 34. I. Certificate of the General Musters for the County of Worcester.

DOMESTIC—ELIZABETH.

1577. VOL. CXV.

Sept. 29. Account of Charles Boothe, Receiver General of Fines and Amerciaments in the Principality of Wales, under Sir Henry Sydney, Lord President, for one whole year ending Michaelmas Anno R.R. Eliz. 19°. [*Case C. Eliz. No. 1.*]

Sept. 35. Report to the Council of the arrival of Capt. Furbisher's ships, the Ayde and Gabriel, at Bristol, and the Michael in the Thames. Order must be taken for discharging the mariners and landing the ore. Proposes Michael Lok to be Treasurer. [*On the 28th Sept. the Council directed Furbisher to unload his ships at Bristol. Co. Reg.*]

Sept. ? Orders to be put in execution throughout the realm in towns and villages infected with the plague. [*Probably in September 1577. See Vol. xlv., p. 27.*]

36. Names of certain persons in various ports who have been dealers with pirates; and upon whom warrants have been served for their appearance.

37. An estimate of the price to be allowed to the brewers for ale and beer per ton.

38. Answer to certain articles propounded by [Lord Burghley] touching the advancement of Her Majesty's customs.

Sept. 39. Plan of Southsea Castle, showing the extent of wall not yet countermured.

40. Reasons advanced by Mr. Symon Bowier to the Merchants of the Staple in proof of the justness of his suit for regulating the trade in wools; with their answers to the same.

Sept. 41. Note of the inconveniences that may ensue to the Merchants of the Staple and the general trade of the realm by permitting strangers to transport wool out of England by special licence.

42. Note of the works finished and of such as remain to be done a Portsmouth, which were not included in the former estimates.

43. The names of some of those who come out of the Low Countries and from Rome into England as spies, and do stir up the people to sedition.

44. Petition of Nicholas Jarden, the Queen's pewterer, to the Queen. Solicits the exclusive right of making all measures used in selling wine, ale, and beer by retail.

45. Petition of John Mathew and Oliver Higgyns, (executors to Pawlyn Wythens, of East Smithfield, widow, deceased), to Burghley. For payment of 12*l.* 12*s.*, owing to her by Mr. H. Howard, for guns, &c., taken by him at divers times from her shop, and sold by him to supply his wants.

46. Petition of John Welde, of London, to Sec. Walsyngham. Solicits to be appointed officer and wool searcher, to detect and punish by law all frauds and deceits in the buying and selling of wool.

DOMESTIC—ELIZABETH. 557

1577. VOL. CXV.
Sept. ? 47. Petition of Peter Blackborough to the Council. For liberty to prosecute his suit in the Star Chamber against certain clothiers of Wiltshire and Somerset. [*On the 9th of Sept.* 1577, *Sir Harry Sherington, and others, were by order in Council directed to take into consideration the complaint of Peter Blackborough against the clothiers. Co. Reg.*]

48. Reasons why some sorts of cloths transported by the Merchants Adventurers ought not to be dressed on this side the sea.

Sept. ? 49. [Walsyngham?] to Sir Robert Wyngfeld and Mr. Jermye. To cess fines upon certain men of Aldborough, who had in their possession the goods taken from some Scotchmen by pirates. [*On the 4th of Aug.* 1577, *Sir R. Wyngfeld and others were directed to repair to Aldborough to examine such as had any goods of the subjects of Scotland. Co. Reg.*]

VOL. CXVI. 1577.

Oct. 1. 1. Account of salaries and allowances of the officers of works and artificers in ordinary employed at Windsor Castle.

Oct. 3. 2. Commissioners of Musters for Staffordshire to the Council. Their
Stafford. proceedings in the Musters. The alehouses and victualling houses within the shire amount to 105. *Inclosing,*

  2. I. *Certificate of the General Musters of able men, armour, weapons, &c., for the County of Stafford.*

Oct. 4. 3. Same for the County of Essex to same. Certify their doings for
Chelmsford. the return of the Musters. *Inclosing,*

  3. I. *Certificate of the General Musters for the County of Essex.*

Oct. 4. 4. Justices of the Peace for the County of Devon to same. Excuse
Exeter. themselves for not having as yet done anything relative to the matter of Musters and certificate of the number of alehouses, as required. Promise to send certificates after Christmas.

Oct. 6. 5. Commissioners of Musters for the town of Cambridge to same. Their execution of the Commission for Musters. *Inclosing,*

  5. I. *Certificate of Musters for the town of Cambridge.*

Oct. 7. 6. Indenture of articles agreed on between John Richardson, of Pershore, gentleman, and William Gaile, miller, for a lease of the mills called Piddle Mills; the miller, among other things, covenanting to keep the swans at the said mills.

Oct. 8. 7. Justices of Hertfordshire to the Council. Have inquired and
Hertford. taken account of the number of inns, taverns, and alehouses in the county. *Inclosing,*

  7. I. *Certificate of the number of inns, taverns, and alehouses within the shire, and the town of St. Albans.*

Oct. 11 8. Commissioners of Musters for Essex to the Council. Relative to
Colchester the training of the 100 men allotted to four Hundreds in the County of Essex. Disorderly behaviour of Edw. Dirowghe, one of the trainers. *Inclosing,*

  8. I. *Certificate of the charges expended for the training of the 100 shot in four Hundreds within the County of Essex.*

1577.
Oct. 11.
Ipswich.

9. Commissioners of Musters for the County of Suffolk to the Council. Excuse the loss of their former certificate. Their course in taking the present Musters, and training of the 300 men, and charges of the same. Names of the Captains appointed. *Inclosing*,

 9. I. *Certificate of the General Musters for the County of Suffolk.*

 9. II. *Certificate of the number of inns, taverns, and alehouses within the County of Suffolk.*

Oct. 11.
Norwich.

10. Same for the County of Norfolk to same. General Musters. Their doings for the training of the 500 selected men. The number of taverns, inns, and alehouses amount to 480; and the occupiers of them are the poorest class of people in the county. *Inclosing*,

 10. I. *Certificate of the General Musters for the County of Norfolk.*

Oct. 12.
Colchester.

11. Same for the town of Colchester to same. Certify their doings in the Musters. *Inclosing*,

 11. I. *Certificate of the Musters for the town of Colchester within the County of Essex.*

Oct. 12.
Colchester.

12. Justices of Essex to same. Certify the number of alehouses, &c., within the Hundreds of Tendering, Lexden, Winstree, Thurstable, Witham, and the town of Colchester.

Oct. ?

13. Certificate of the names and dwelling-places of such as have been and are licensed to be alehouse keepers within the County of Essex for eight previous years, ending at the Epiphany, 1577.

Oct. 13.

14. Note of money presently to be disbursed for mariners' wages of the three ships returned with Mr. Furbisher.

Oct. 14.

List of the Commissioners appointed in divers shires on the sea coasts to inquire of such as within five years past have set forth ships to the seas in warlike sort; and likewise to examine who have been favourers, abettors, and assisters of pirates. [*See Vol.* cxxxv., *end.*]

Oct. 15.

15. The Council to the Bishop in every diocese. To certify the names of all persons that refuse to attend church to hear divine service; with the value of all their lands and goods.

Oct. 15.
The Court.

16. Sec. Walsyngham to Justice Manwood. For detention of two persons in Canterbury till after the examination of Mr. Somersett.

Oct. 15.
Cambridge.

17. Commissioners of Musters for Cambridgeshire to the Council. Have taken the General Musters in their county, except for the town of Cambridge and the Isle of Ely. Small number of able men within the shire. *Inclosing*,

 17. I. *Certificate of the General Musters for the County of Cambridge, including the numbers of inns, taverns, and alehouses.* [*N.B. The return of inns, &c., has been cut off, and removed from that of the Musters.*]

 17. II. *Certificate of inns, taverns, &c., cut from the above.*

DOMESTIC—ELIZABETH. 559

1577.
Oct. 16.
Southampton.

Vol. CXVI.
18. The Mayor, &c., of Southampton to the Council. Certifying their proceedings in the Musters. *Inclosing,*
 18. I. *Certificate of General Musters for the town of Southampton.*

Oct. 16.
19. Commissioners of Musters for the County of Kent to same. Have taken Musters of the whole county, Canterbury and the Five Ports excepted ; and also of the number of alehouses. *Inclosing,*
 19. I. *Certificate of the General Musters for the County of Kent.*
 19. II. *Certificate of taverns, inns, and alehouses in Kent.*

Oct. 16 ?
20. Certificate of the number of alehouses, inns, and taverns within the liberties of the Cinque Ports in Aug. and Sep., 1577.

Oct. 16
Oxford.
21. Commissioners of Musters for Oxfordshire to the Council. Have finished the training of the 200 soldiers ; and taken the General Musters for that county. *Inclosing,*
 21. I. *Certificate of the General Musters for the County of Oxford.*

Oct. 16.
Cowdrey.
22. Viscount Mountague to Mr. Sec. Walsyngham. Sends the letter and certificate of Musters for the Council. Desires that the commission for restraint of the exportation of grain may be renewed. Prices of corn in Sussex.

Oct. 16.
Cowdrey.
23. Commissioners of Musters for Sussex to the Council. Have carefully executed the taking of the Musters. *Inclosing,*
 23. I. *Certificate of the General Musters for the County of Sussex.*

Oct. 16.
24. Order of Council for payment of 800*l.* by the adventurers in Mr. Furbisher's voyage to the North-west to Mr. Lok, the treasurer, for discharge of the mariners and soldiers.

Oct. 16.
Windsor.
25. The Council to the Warden and Workmaster of the Mint. Direct him to receive ore brought from the North-west parts by Mr. Furbisher ; and to place the same in the Tower under four several locks and keys.

Vol. CXVII. October 18th to 31st, 1577.

Oct. 18.
1. Accompt of the full furniture of Her Majesty's ships the Lion, the Dreadnought, and Foresight, sent to the seas on the 20th of July ; with the several wastes and remains of the said ships upon their return the 18th Oct. 1577.

Oct. 20.
2. Certificate by the Bp. of Rochester and others, of the Papists in the diocese of Rochester who do not come to church or receive the communion ; with the valuation of their lands and goods.

Oct. 20.
Warwick.
3. Commissioners of Musters for Warwickshire to the Council. Certifying their proceedings for the General Musters and in procuring returns of the number of alehouses ; and also for the encouragement of archery. *Inclosing,*
 3. I. *Certificate of the General Musters for the County of Warwick.*
 3. II. *Certificate of the number of alehouses, inns, &c., within the County of Warwick.*

VOL. CXVII.

1577.
Oct. 21.
Cobham.
4. Lord Cobham to the Council. Has quieted the disorderly conduct of the inhabitants at Dover at the late Musters. Has suffered the French mariners to depart from Rye on account of the plague there and at Dover. Sends certificate of the Musters. *Incloses,*

  4. I. *Certificate of the Musters of able men and horses within the liberties of the Cinque Ports, and their limbs [or members].*

Oct. 21
Ashford.
5. Justices of Kent to same. Have been directed by the Archbp. of Canterbury to make certificate of all such persons as refuse to attend church, which they have done accordingly. *Inclosing,*

  5. I. *Certificate of recusants in the County of Kent refusing to attend church. [Indorsed, " Certificat non-perfect."]*

Oct. 22.
Chesterfield.
6. Justices of Derbyshire to same. Report their proceedings for restraint of the unlawful buying and engrossing of wool.

Oct. 23.
7. Commissioners of Musters for Hertfordshire to same. Transmit certificate of the General Musters for the county. *Inclosing,*

  7. I. *Certificate of the General Musters for the County of Hertford.*

Oct. 23.
Bowghton.
8. Sir Edwd. Mountagu to Bishop Scambler. An unavoidable engagement will prevent him from attending his lordship till Tuesday next.

Oct. 24.
Lambeth.
9. Archbp. Grindall to the Council. Sends the certificate of Sir Tho. Scott and Mr. Tho. Wotton, relative to the recusants within his diocese. Desires their Lordships to be intercessors with Her Majesty to be restored to her favour and to his liberty.

Oct. 24.
Bishops Waltham.
10. Bishop Horn to same. Sends certificate of recusants in the County of Southampton, and promises the like for Surrey. *Incloses,*

  10. I. *Certificate of recusants in the County of Southampton, with the valuation of their lands and goods.*

Oct. 24.
Wells.
11. Gilbert Berkeley Bishop of Bath and Wells to same. Has not yet been able to make certificate of recusants within the County of Somerset. Dorset is not within his diocese. Suggests some other of the justices may be joined in the commission.

Oct. 24.
12. Bishop Cheney to same. Sends certificate of such as refuse to attend the church; but cannot yet learn the value of their lands and goods. Reasons of the Puritans for not attending church. *Incloses,*

  12. I. *Certificate of the names of certain persons who refuse to come to church within the diocese of Gloucester.*

Oct. 25
13. Tho. Cowper Bishop of Lincoln to same. Gives the names and particulars of various persons within his diocese not coming to church.

DOMESTIC—ELIZABETH. 561

VOL. CXVII.

1577.
Oct. 25.
Guildford.
14. Sir Wm. More and Sir Tho. Browne to the Council. Report relative to the recusants in the County of Surrey. *Inclosing,*

 14. I. *Certificate of all such persons as refuse to come to church, with the value of their lands and goods.*

 14. II. *Similar certificate, but differently arranged.*

Oct. 26.
Chesworth.
15. Bishop Coortesse to same. States the names of such as refuse to come to church to hear prayer within the diocese of Chichester, with the value of their lands and goods.

Oct. 26.
Peterborough.
16. Bishop Scambler to same. Certifies the number of recusants within his diocese, with the value of their lands and goods. Suggests more information would have been obtained by a return of those refusing to receive the communion.

Oct. 26.
College of Windsor.
17. John Piers Bishop of Rochester, and Sir Henry Nevell, to same. Send certificate of all persons of Berkshire who refuse to attend church to hear divine service. *Inclosing,*

 17. I. *Certificate of such disobedient persons that refuse to receive the holy communion, with the value of their lands and goods.*

Oct. 26.
Salop.
18. Commissioners of Musters for Shropshire to same. Certify their doings in the Musters. *Inclosing,*

 18. I. *Certificate of the General Musters for the County of Salop.*

Oct. 27.
Leicester.
19. Mr. Francis Hastings and Mr. Adrian Stockes to same. Require a longer time to make certificate of the recusants in Leicestershire.

Oct. 27.
York.
20. Earl of Huntingdon, and others, to Archbp. Sandys. Have done their best to discover the value of the lands and goods of such as refuse to come to church. The time appointed was too short.

Oct. 28.
Clifton.
21. Sir John Horsey and Geo. Trencharde to the Council. Difficulty of obtaining information respecting recusants within the County of Dorset, as it was uncertain in whose diocese the shire was.

Oct. 28.
Brocket Hall.
22. Sir John Brokett, and others, to same. Certify the names of several recusants in the County of Hertford, with the value of their lands and goods.

Oct. 28.
Bishopsthorp.
23. Archbishop Sandys to same. His doings in procuring returns of such as refuse to come to church within his diocese. Has not yet had time to visit his diocese : they are a stiff-necked, wilful, and obstinate people. *Incloses,*

 23. I. *Certificate of recusants refusing to attend the church within the diocese of York, with an estimate of the value of their lands and goods.*

 23. II. *Similar certificate of recusants in other bishopricks within the province of York.*

Oct. 28.
Sheffield.
24. Earl of Shrewsbury to Sec. Walsyngham. That he would be favourable to his servant Sutton in his suit against the Goldsmiths.

1577.
Oct. 28.
Newton Feres.

25. Wm. Bradbridge, Bishop of Exeter, to the Council. Relative to his efforts to procure returns of recusants in his diocese. *Incloses,*

 25. I. *Certificate of such persons as refuse to come to church in the County of Cornwall, with the value of their lands and goods.*

Oct. 28.
Wilton.

26. Henry Earl of Pembroke to same. Sends certificate of recusants in Wiltshire. *Incloses,*

 26. I. *Certificate of such in the County of Wilts as refuse to attend the church, with the value of their lands and goods.*

Oct. 29.
Norwich.

27. Bishop Freke to same. Sends certificate of recusants: many will probably conform. Lady Paulet has left the diocese, and Lady Jerningham, being often troubled with certain melancholy passions, has service in English said in her own house. *Incloses,*

 27. I. *Certificate of recusants in the County of Norfolk, with the value of their lands and goods.*

Oct. 30.
Ely.

28. Bishop Cox to same. Certifies the names of the recusants within his diocese. Has done all in his power to bring them to conformity. *Incloses,*

 28. I. *Certificate of recusants in the diocese of Ely.*

Oct. 30.

29. Certificate of the General Musters for the Isle of Ely.

Oct.
Guildford.

30. Justices of Surrey to the Council. Have taken account of the number of alehouses, &c., within their county; excepting only the borough of Southwark. *Inclosing,*

 30. I. *Certificate of the number of alehouses, inns, and taverns in the County of Surrey.*

Oct.

31. Certificate from the Commissioners for pirates in Essex, of the creeks and landing-places in several Hundreds in that county.

32. Certificate of the number of innholders, taverners, and alehouse keepers within the County of Southampton.

33. Certificate of the General Musters for the County of Southampton.

34. Certificate of the number of inns, taverns, and alehouses within the borough of Boston.

35. Names of the towns, hundreds, officers, and freeholders in Cheshire, in the time of John Warren, Esq., being Sheriff.

36. Certificate of Musters of horses, able men and arms, of the clergy of the diocese of Chester.

37. Certificate of the just number of all the inns, taverns, and alehouses within the Counties of York, Durham, Cumberland, and Westmoreland.

DOMESTIC—ELIZABETH. 563

1577. VOL. CXVII.

Oct. ? 38. Causes moving the poor inhabitants of Lancashire, Richmond, Westmoreland, Cumberland, and the bishoprick of Durham, to make petition to the Queen's Highness, to have licence and dispensation for the buying and selling of wools. [*Signed, John Byron, K.*]

39. Declaration of Christopher Baker of the names of the iron works and furnaces, and the places where they are planted, and names of the proprietors. Also lists of all the landing-places, ports, and creeks in England and Wales.

40, 41. The personal answers of John Vassall and Richard Stapers to the articles or positions ministered on the behalf of James Jellee and Martin Simondson, touching the detention of Captain Simondson's ship at Plymouth, and its subsequent wreck on the Goodwin Sands. [*Two papers.*]

42. Certificate of General Musters of able men, armour, weapons, wheelwrights, smiths, &c. for the whole County of Wilts.

43. Certificate of the Musters within the city of New Sarum. [*Probably transmitted with the above.*]

44. Similar certificate of General Musters for the County of Derby.

45. General certificate of Musters of able men, armour, weapons, horses, &c., for the whole County of Somerset; amounting to the number of 6,500 men.

46. Similar certificate of General Musters for Shropshire.

VOL. CXVIII. NOVEMBER, 1577.

Nov. 1. 1. Certificate by William Raynsford, Mayor, of the number of taverns, inns, and alehouses within the town of Northampton.

Nov. 1. 2. Archbp. Sandys to the Council. Sends certificate of recusants
Bishopsthorp. out of Nottinghamshire. Was in hopes none would have been found there. *Incloses,*

    2. I. *Sir John Byron and Robert Markham to Archbp. Sandys. Send certificate of recusants. Southwell, 30 Oct. Inclosing,*

    2. II. *Certificate of recusants in the County of Nottingham, and of the value of their property.*

Nov. 1. 3. Commissioners of Musters for Leicestershire to same. Pro-
Leicester. ceedings in taking the Musters. Reasons of the decrease in the number of horse. *Inclosing,*

    3. I. *Certificate of the General Musters for the County of Leicester.*

Vol. CXVIII.

1577.
Nov. 2.
Kettering.
4. Commissioners of Musters for Northamptonshire to the Council. Certify their doings for the Musters, and also the number of taverns, inns, and alehouses within the county. Names of certain persons who refuse to contribute. *Inclosing*,

  4. I. *Certificate of the General Musters for the County of Northampton.*

Nov. 2. 5. Certificate of all the alehouses or tippling houses in the County of Nottingham, and liberties of the same.

Nov 2. 6. Certificate of General Musters for the County of Nottingham.

Nov. 2. 7. Bishop Scorey to the Council. Certifies the number of recusants within the diocese of Hereford. *Incloses,*

  7. I. *Certificate of the recusants within the diocese of Hereford, with an estimate of the value of their lands and goods.*

Nov. 3.
Bangor.
8. Nicholas Robinson Bishop of Bangor to John Whitgyfte Bishop of Worcester. That there were within his diocese no recusants with the exception of one old priest, named Barker, a very poor man.

Nov. 3.
Whaddon.
9. Arthur Lord Grey, and others, to the Council. Certify that within the County of Buckingham there are none that refuse to come to the church.

Nov. 4.
St Asaph.
10. Wm. Hughes Bishop of St. Asaph to Bishop Whitgyfte. There are no persons within his diocese refusing or neglecting to come to church.

Nov. 5.
udlow Castle.
11. Bishop Whitgyfte to the Council. Certificates of proceedings respecting recusants in his diocese and in Wales. The Dean of Worcester and Mr. Harewell have not quite understood the Council's letters. He himself sends a list of recusants within his diocese, and prays for God's sake some discipline may be provided for them. *Incloses,*

  11. I. *Bishop Davies to Bishop Whitgyfte. Certifies there are no recusants within his diocese of St. David's. Abergwilly, 28th Oct., 1577.*

  11. II. *Wm. Blethym Bp. of Landaff to same. Sends certificate of the number of recusants in his diocese. Matharn, 25th Oct.*

  11. III. *Tho. Wilson, Dean of Worcester, and Edmund Harewell to same. Sends a note of persons detected in the late visitation; whereof some are drunkards, some excommunicated, and all either poor or very beggars. Inclosing,*

  11. IV. *Note of persons detected in the Bishop of Worcester's late visitation.*

  11. V. *Certificate of recusants within the County of Warwick, within the diocese of Worcester, presented in the visitation*

Nov. 5. List of Commissioners to inquire of pirates and their aiders and abettors within the limits of the Cinque Ports. [*See Vol.* cxxxv., *end.*]

DOMESTIC—ELIZABETH. 565

1577.
Nov. 6.

Vol. CXVIII.
12. "A discourse how Hir Majestie may annoy the King of Spayne;" proposing to fit out a fleet of ships of war, under pretence of a voyage of discovery, and so to fall upon the enemy's shipping and destroy his trade in Newfoundland and the West Indies, and to possess those countries. The projector offers to conduct the expedition and urges dispatch, " for the winges of man's life are plumed with the feathers of " death." [*This has been signed, but the signature has been obliterated with a pen. It is, however, conjectured to be* H. GYLBERTE. *In the following year Sir Humfrey Gylberte received a patent for the occupation and settlement of Newfoundland.*]

Nov. 6.
Madrid.

13. Dr. Sanders to Dr. Allen. Affairs of the Papists. Laments the ill success of their plans in England. No reliance is to be placed on the assistance of Spain, but the Pope offered 2,000 men for Ireland. The state of Christendom dependeth on the stout assailing of England.

Nov. 6.

14. Wm. Fletewoode, Recorder of London, to Mr. Sec. Walsyngham. Has examined Damian Dela, by whom it appears that John Baptista, a Spaniard, in London, gives great intelligence to Anthony Gwarras, and is so busy a spy that he may well be called " Polypragmos." *Incloses,*

14. I. *Examination of Damian Dela, relative to information furnished by John Baptista to Anth. Gwarras. Mass celebrated in the household of Señor Gerraldi.*

Nov. 7.
Leicester.

15. Justices of Leicestershire to the Council. Send certificate of the number of inns, &c. Most of the alehouse keepers are very poor, and of mean abilities. *Inclosing,*

15. I. *Certificate of the taverns, inns, and alehouses in the County of Leicester.*

Nov. 9.
Wells.

16. Bishop Berkeley to same. Further dealings as to the number of recusants within his diocese. *Incloses,*

16. I. *The names of such as do refuse to come to the church in the County of Somerset, with the value of their lands and goods.*

Nov. 10.
Eccleshall Castle.

17. Bishop Bentham to same. Proceedings as to recusants within his diocese. Understands there are none in Warwickshire. *Incloses,*

17. I. *Certificate of recusants within the Counties of Stafford, Derby, and Shropshire in the diocese of Coventry and Litchfield.*

Nov. 10.
Roke Savage.

18. Sir John Savage to the Earl of Leicester. Sends the certificate of Musters for Leicestershire.

Nov. 11.
Ipswich.

19. The Commissioners of Musters for the town of Ipswich to the Council. Certify their doings in the Musters, and taking account of alehouses, &c. *Inclosing,*

19. I. *Certificate of the General Musters for the town of Ipswich.*
19. II. *Certificate of the number of alehouses, inns, and taverns.*

VOL. CXVIII.

1577. Nov. 13.	20. Examination of John Laithwood, of Wigan, co. Lancaster, near Harrowden. Professes to be a Catholic, and refuses to take the oath of supremacy or to attend the church. [*Attested by Wm. Tate.*]
Nov. 14.	21. Further examination of John Laithwood. Particulars of his life. Will not resort to the church established by the laws of England.
Nov. 14. Arundel.	22. Commissioners for piracies in Surrey to the Council. Their proceedings. Have made choice of fit persons to act in the inquiry.
Nov. 14.	23. Bishop Scorey to the Lord Treasurer and Sir Walter Mildmay. Prays them to aid in the repairs of the chancel of Much-Wenlock, as Her Majesty receives the rents and tythes.
Nov. 15. Gloucester College.	24. Presentment, in the College of Gloucester, of Wm. Meredith, suspected to be "an horrible Papiste, and estemed to be worthe fiftie poundes."
Nov. 15. Sutton.	25. Sir Francis Leek to the Council. Sends the number and names of such as keep alehouses, inns, &c., in the county. *Incloses*,
	25. I. *Certificate of alehouses, inns, and taverns, and names of the occupiers, amounting to 750, in the whole County of Derby.*
Nov. 16. Windsor.	26. Extracts from the register of the Lords Commissioners for punishment of the aiders of pirates. Of proceedings against Sir Ric. Rogers, Francis Rogers, and others, for assisting and buying goods of Count Hekenberg, John Callis, and other pirates.
Nov. 18.	27. Judge Manwood to Sir Walter Mildmay. His opinion of the punishment to be awarded to the lewd fellow for persisting to speak ill of the Queen, after he had suffered the pillory and had his ears cut off. He may be either imprisoned for life or have part of his tongue cut off.
Nov. 18. Westminster.	28. Grant to Benjamin Gonson and John Hawkyns of the office of Treasurer of Marine Causes, for life.
Nov. 18. Peterborough.	29. Bishop Scambler to the Council. Information of other recusants in the Counties of Northampton, Huntingdon, and Rutland, not before certified.
Nov. 19.	30. Certificate of the General Musters for the County of Chester.
Nov. 20.	31. Certificate by the Mayor and Aldermen of Canterbury of the number of inns, taverns, and alehouses within the liberties of that city.
Nov. 20.	32. Bishop Cheney to the Council. Has inquired diligently of all such persons that refuse to come to church. *Incloses*,
	32. I. *Certificate of the recusants in the diocese of Gloucester, with the value of their lands and goods.*
Nov. 20.	List of Commissioners to inquire of pirates and their aiders and abettors in the Counties of Cardigan, Pembroke, Carmarthen, Monmouth, and Glamorgan. [*See Vol.* cxxxv., *end.*]

1577.		VOL. CXVIII.
Nov. 21.	33.	Petition of Richard Ellisworth, haberdasher, to Lord Burghley, for the payment of 14*l*. 5*s*. due to him by Mr. Henry Howard.
Nov. 21. Leicester.	34.	Mr. Francis Hastings and Adrian Stockes to the Council. Their endeavours to find out such as absent themselves from church. Mention the names of some they have recently discovered.
Nov. 22. Cambridge.	35.	Richard Howlande, Vice-Chancellor of Cambridge, to same. Certifies that he can hear of none in Cambridge who refuse to attend the church.
Nov. 23. London.	36.	Michael Lok to Mr. Sec. Walsyngham. Trial of the ore brought home by Mr. Furbisher ; the three workmasters are jealous of each other and as yet had not made a satisfactory report.
Nov. 24. Corpus Christi College.	37.	Dr. Wm. Cole, Vice-chancellor of Oxford, to the Council. Additional information as to recusants in the University and town of Oxford. *Incloses*,
	37. I.	*Certificate of the recusants within the University and town of Oxford.*
Nov. 24. Serjeants' Inn.	38.	Lord Chief Justice Chr. Wray to same. Inquiries in the Inns of Chancery as to recusants. *Incloses*,
	38. I.	*Certificate of such as refuse to attend church in the Inns of Chancery.*
Nov. 25. Tower Hill.	39.	Sir Wm. Wynter to Walsyngham. Reasons of the delay of Furbisher's coming to Bristol for the discharge of his ships. Impression of the richness of the gold ore brought home by him.
Nov. 25. Bristol.	40.	Edward Fenton to same. Delay in unloading the ore from the Aid and Gabriel. Commends Mr. Carew. Desires order may be given for discharging the mariners and unrigging the said ships. *Incloses*,
	40. I.	*Dr. Edwd. Dodding's report of the sickness and death at Bristol of the man brought home by Capt. Furbisher from the North-west. The woman was as yet alive. Lat.*
Nov. 25. East Smithfield.	41.	Jonas Schutz to same. Sickness has prevented him from making earlier trial of the ore brought by Captain Furbisher. Hopes to bring a sample to Court next Saturday.
Nov. 25 ?	42.	Jonas Schutz's estimate of the charges for melting down the gold ore and other charges.
Nov. 26.	43.	Burchard Raurych(?) [*indorsed Dr. Burcott*] to Sir Francis Walsyngham. Report on the amount of gold contained in one ton of the ore brought by Captain Furbisher. [*This is the first mention of Walsyngham, in this series, by his title of knight. But in the Irish Correspondence, in a letter from Sir Nicholas Bagenall to Walsyngham, dated Dublin, 15th Sept., he is addressed as* SIR *Francis.*]
Nov. 27.	44.	Certificate of the recusants in the archdeaconry of Colchester, with their several values.

1577.	Vol. CXVIII.
Nov. 28. Manchester.	45. Justices of Lancaster to the Council. Certifying the recusants in that county. *Inclosing,*
	45. I. *Certificate of recusants in the County of Lancaster, with an estimate of their lands and goods.*
Nov. 29	46. The examination of Cuthbert Mayne, priest, taken at Launceston not long before his execution.
Nov. [29.]	47. Names of Papists indicted or in prison concerned with Cuthbert Mayne in obtaining the instrument of absolution from the See of Rome, and for other papistical practices.
Nov. 29. Aldford.	48. G. Fyton to Sec. Walsyngham. Relative to the recusants in the County of Cheshire ; the chief of them are not touched who hear mass daily. *Incloses,*
	48. I. *Certificate of certain Papists refusing to attend the church, with the value of their lands and goods, in the County of Chester.*
Nov. [29.]	49. A copy of the certificate of recusants in the diocese of Chester which the late Bp. of Chester would have sent to the Council if he had not been prevented by death.
Nov. 29. Bremham.	50. Lewys Dyve to Walsyngham. Signifying the names of certain persons that refuse to attend church within the County of Bedford.
Nov. 29. Bury.	51. Justices of Suffolk to the Council. Send a certificate of the recusants in their county.
Nov. 30.	52. Certificate of the General Musters for the County of Lincoln.
Nov. 30.	53. Certificate of all the alehouses, inns, and taverns within the County of Lincoln.
Nov. 30. London.	54. Michael Lok to Walsyngham. Jonas Schutz is making trial of another way of melting the ore. Promises information as to Sir Lionel Ducket and Sir R. Heywood in the matter declared by Mr. Waterhouse. Richness of the ore brought home by Furbisher.
Nov.	55. Petition of Rowland Rayleton to the Council. For payment of 33*l.* due to him by Mr. Henry Howard, son of Lord Thomas Howard.
	56. Petition of Tho. Taylor to same. For payment the sum of 25*l.* 14*s.* 4*d.* due to him by the same.
	57. Petition of John Bowltinge to same. For payment of 15*l.* 4*s.* 4*d.* due to him by the same.
	58. Petition of Robert Motte to Lord Burghley. For payment of 10*l.* 10*s.* due to him by the same.
	59. Petition of Robert Moot (or Motte as above) to same. For payment of 5*l.* 5*s.* due to him by the same.
	60. Petition of Robert Pynder to same. For payment of 300*l.* due to him by same.

DOMESTIC—ELIZABETH. 569

1577.
Nov.

Nov. ?

Nov.

Nov. ?
HamptonCourt.

Nov.

Nov. ?

VOL. CXVIII.
61. Petition of Tho. Ayre to Lord Burghley. For payment of 182*l*. 13*s*. 4*d*. due to him by Mr. Henry Howard.

62. Petition of Griffen Jones to same. For payment of 16*l*. 10*s*. 3*d*., being a moiety of a debt of 33*l*. 0*s*. 6*d*. owing to him by the same.

63. Memorandum of the grant to Henry Mackwilliams and Robert Colshill of the Queen's moiety of the forfeitures for unlawful trans portation of corn.

64. Account of charges incurred for salaries and wages of the officers and artificers employed at the castle during the Queen's residence at Windsor.

65. Estimate of the expenses incurred for repairs done at Windsor Castle during the seven preceding years, amounting to 7,800*l*.

66. Warrant to the Treasurer and Chamberlains of the Exchequer for issuing money for the repair of Windsor Castle.

67. Plan of a proposed cut for bringing water from the Lea river to London, terminating at Moregate. [*Indorsed,* " *A trik of the plat* " *made in the Parliament tyme for the newe cut for bringing the* " *ryver of Lea to London.*"]

68. Certificate of recusants in the Middle Temple. Signed by the Recorder, Wm. Fletewoode, and John Popham.

69 Similar certificate for the Inner Temple.

70. Similar certificate of such as refuse to attend the church in Lincoln's Inn. [*Addressed to Sir Nicholas Bacon, Lord Keeper.*]

71. Similar certificate of such as refuse or neglect to attend church in Gray's Inn.

72. Certificate of certain recusants within the County of Somerset.

73. Certificate from Bishop Aylmer of such recusants, and others, as refuse to attend church within the diocese of London.

74. Petition of David Eudioche, merchant of Aberdeen, to Sir Francis Walsyngham. That he may receive restitution for three packs of skins, worth 63*l*., taken by English pirates, and now in the possession of John Fayreweather of Ipswich.

75. Petition of the creditors of Tho. Spearte, bankrupt (being poor clothiers of the North), to the Queen. Praying relief, as Spearte's lands and goods would not answer one third of his debts.

76. Information given by Laurence Dutton, Rafe Walton, and Wm. Gransom. Showing the unfair dealing of John Taylor, John Carpenter, and James Turner in usurping the riding journeys in the Chancery, under colour of their patents for the office of Messengers in the Exchequer.

77. Robert Markham, and others, of Nottinghamshire, to the Earl of Rutland. That they considered the rate of furniture and horses assigned to them above the due proportion.

DOMESTIC—ELIZABETH.

Vol. CXVIII.

1577.
Nov.
78. Certificate of the Musters for the City of Lichfield.
79. Certificate of the General Musters for the Isle of Anglesey.
80. Certificate of the General Musters for the County of Surrey.

Nov. ?
81. Certificate of the General Musters for the County of Radnor.
82. Baptista Agnello's request and proposal for trying the ore now in the mills at Dartford.

Vol. CXIX. December, 1577.

Dec. 1.
Uppingham.
1. Sir James Haryngton, and others, Justices of Rutland, to the Council. Certify the number of alehouses, inns, and taverns within that county ; for the most part very poor.

Dec. 1.
Substance of intelligence given by George Winter. How the goods (particularly elephants' teeth) taken by Robert Hickes and William Battes, notorious pirates, have been bestowed. [*See Vol.* cxxxv., *fol.* 15.]

Dec. 3.
2. Certificate of the number of wine taverns and alehouses within the Hundreds of Penwith and Kerryer in Cornwall.

Dec. 3.
3. Similar certificate for the Hundreds of Powder and Pyder in the same county.

Dec. 3.
London.
4. Justices of Middlesex to the Council. Certify the number of alehouses, inns, and taverns in that county.

Dec. 3.
5. Dr. H. Westfaling to Archbp. Grindal. Sends certificate of recusants within the diocese of Oxford. Reasons for its being imperfect in many respects. *Incloses,*

5. I. *Certificate of the names of those that refuse to attend the church within the diocese of Oxford, with the yearly value of their lands and goods.*

Dec. 3.
Lethringham.
6. Commissioners for piracy in Suffolk to the Council. Certify their doings in the matter of pirates, and their aiders, within the County of Suffolk. *Inclosing,*

6. I. *Certificate of creeks and havens in Suffolk, and of the names of pirates, and aiders of pirates, and the matters wherewith they are severally charged.*

Dec. 6.
7. Certificate of the number of innholders, taverners, and typlers within the Hundreds of Chelmsford, Rochford, Dengy, Barstaple, and Chafford, and the town of Maldon, in Essex.

Dec. 6.
London.
8. Sir Wm. Wynter and Michael Lok to Sir Fr. Walsyngham. Have been a long time about the second proof of the ore, the furnace not being powerful enough. Proposals of Jonas Schutz for melting the ore and erecting furnaces.

Dec. 6 ?
9. Four proofs of assays of the ore brought home by Capt. Furbisher. [*These proofs are curious, some of the gold still remaining attached to the paper by sealing wax.*]

DOMESTIC—ELIZABETH. 571

1577. Vol. CXIX.

Dec. 8 ?   10. Note of the charges for smelting one ton of the ore brought by Martin Furbisher, from the North-west voyage.

Dec. 10.   11. The names of such as were fined for dealing with pirates in the County of Monmouth.

Dec. 13.   12. Michael Lok to Sir Fr. Walsyngham. Have viewed various mills
London.   on the Thames, and find those at Dartford best suited for working the ore. The proposals of Dr. Burcot are out of reason, and inferior to those made by Jonas. Sebastian, the Dutch millwright and Hendrik, the mason, must be sent for. *Incloses,*

 12. I. *Note of conference with Dr. Burcot as to terms and conditions to be made with him for melting the ore.* •

 12. II. *Articles and conditions proposed by Dr. Burcot [Raurych], for smelting and refining the ore brought by Capt. Furbisher, or any other ore to be hereafter imported.* [*Dec.* 9 ?]

Dec. 13.   13. Mayor, &c. of Ipswich to the Council. Certifying their doings
Ipswich.   in the matter of pirates, and the aiders of pirates, within the town of Ipswich. *Inclosing,*

 13 I. *Certificate for the town of Ipswich, relative to matters of piracy.*

Dec. 20.   14. Claim of Wm. Vaughan for compensation for certain mills at Dartford, belonging to him, and now used for melting the ore brought home by Capt. Furbisher.

Dec. 20.   15. Giovanni Baptista Agnello to Walsyngham. His trial and
London.   report on the amount of gold contained in the ore brought by Furbisher. Ital.

Dec. 22.   16. Commissioners for piracy in the County of Gloucester to the Council. Their number are insufficient to proceed according to the instructions, for want of the assistance of the Mayor, &c. of Bristol. Some other gentlemen must therefore be named, and the commission extended to include Bristol and Gloucester.

Dec. 23.   17. Commissioners for piracy in the County of Norfolk to same.
Holt.   Their proceedings in the examination and punishment of the aiders of pirates. *Inclosing,*

 17. I. *Certificate of the offences and names of the pirates, and aiders of pirates, within the County of Norfolk.*

Dec. 27.   18. The Council to the Lord Pres. and Council of Wales. Com-
HamptonCourt. mittal of several persons of Carnarvon to prison in London, for factious complaints against the Queen's officers. Others to be examined in Wales relative to conventicles, and other unlawful assemblies.

Dec. 29.   19. Lord Thomas Howard and Sir Harry Asheley to the Council. The mayor, &c. of Poole refuse to act with them in the matters of piracy in the commission for Dorsetshire. They consider they are not authorized to examine any suspected person on oath.

VOL. CXIX.

1577.
Dec. 30.   20. A table showing the number of recusants in the several dioceses, counties, towns, and colleges, within England and Wales, with a note of their titles, rank, &c.

Dec.   21. General certificates of the number of taverns, inns, and alehouses, within the County of Berks., with the names of the owners, &c., in five separate returns.

22. Certificate of the General Musters for the County of Gloucester.

23. Depositions taken by commission out of the Admiralty for matters of piracy in Cornwall, particularly as to sale of goods taken out of the Flying Hart.

Abridgment of the general certificates of the Musters taken throughout the whole realm, divided into counties and cities. [See Vol. xcvi., pp. 327—392.]

Certificate of the inns and alehouses in sundry shires in England and Wales. [See Vol. xcvi., p. 405.]

Dec. ?   24. Abstract of the number of able men, trained and untrained, certified by the several counties of England and Wales.

25 Abstract of the number of horsemen, lances, light horse, carabines, and petronels, certified by the several counties of England and Wales.

26. A levy of lances and light horse upon sundry as well pluralists as recusants, as also of footmen in every shire; distinguishing the bishops, the pluralists, deans and chapters, and those who refuse to come to church.

27. Certificate of Musters for the County of Rutland.

28. Certificate of General Musters for the County of Denbigh, said to be in the 16th year of Eliz., but probably in the 19th, by the introduction of wheelwrights, smiths, &c.

[*Several papers relating to Capt. Furbisher's voyages, to which precise dates cannot be fixed, but all probably in the year* 1577, *as follows* :—]

1577?   29. Narrative of the doings of Michael Lok in the voyage to Kathai; describing the course of his life from 1552, following his vocation in the trade of merchandize; his zeal for the promotion of voyages of discovery, and development of the trade and commerce of England.

30. Mr. Lok's private memorial of expenses for the first and second voyages made by Captain Furbisher to Cathai and the North-west.

31. Martin Furbisher's requests to Her Majesty to be appointed High Admiral for life, and to his heirs, of all the countries already discovered, or hereafter to be discovered by him in the North parts; with other privileges.

DOMESTIC—ELIZABETH.

VOL. CXIX.

1577 ?

32. Brief note of all the charges of the Gabriel and Michael, and their pinnace, for the first voyage to Cathay, &c., sent with Martin Furbisher in June 1567. [*Sic,—but* 1576 ?].

33. Brief note of the cost and charges of the three ships for the second voyage for Cathai.

34. Brief note of the cost and charge of the three ships, the Ayde, the Gabriel, and the Michael, for the second voyage, sent with Martin Furbisher in May 1577. Names of the adventurers in both voyages; of those who have not paid, &c.

35. Names of the venturers of both the voyages made by Martin Furbisher to the North-west, 1576 and 1577.

36. Names of the venturers in Furbisher's voyages, distinguishing those of the first and second venture ; the Queen heading the list for 1,000*l.*

37. Names of the venturers in the first and second voyages for the North-west parts, under charge of Mr. Furbisher, 1577.

38. Another list of names of venturers in both voyages.

39. Another list of names of venturers in both voyages.

40. Names of the venturers in the second voyage for Cathai, besides their venture in the first voyage ; without the sums attached.

41. Similar list, with the sums attached.

42. Names of the venturers in the first and second voyage for Cathai, &c., which have paid.

43. Names of those who desire to be venturers now, which may be granted upon the whole venture, to supply money for wages.

44. Names of those who desire to be venturers in the goods now brought home.

45. Names of those who have subscribed, but not performed; and of those who were named but not subscribed.

46. Memoranda [*by Burghley*] of materials, workmen, and officers necessary for the North-west voyage.

47. Note of the cloths and other merchandize passed to Hamburg in one year, besides such as passed by the Merchants Adventurers.

48. Note of the matters objected against Steven de Brisa, *alias* Captain Nepyvila, a Frenchman, by Edward Chester, administrator of Dominick Chester, deceased.

49. Note of the clear yearly value of the bishoprics, deaneries, and archdeaconries, in the provinces of Canterbury and York.

1577 ? VOL. CXIX.

50. Particular of the licence granted to the mayor and burgesses of Hull for the transportation of 20,000 quarters of grain within the term of twenty years; with licence to Richard Edmonds to export 1,000 qrs. from the County of Norfolk.

VOL. CXX. 1577 ?

[*The papers in this volume are undated, but they are all probably in or about the year* 1577.]

1. Certificate of ships and vessels in the ports and towns of Essex, Suffolk, Norfolk, Kent, and Sussex.

2. William Garnett's request for delivery of a bond for certain money in the hands of the Earl of Essex's executors.

3. Henry Cobham to the Queen. Presents her with a book newly come forth, and desires to know if it should be suppressed. The French ambassador has sent two copies to France.

4. Notes in Burghley's hand of the money derived from the sale of the Lord Viscount (Bindon's) lands.

5. Petition of John Spencer, and others, merchants trading to Spain, to the Earl of Leicester and Lord Burghley. Have been with Signor Fiasco, as to restoration of their goods detained in Spain. Request that the Spanish goods at Plymouth and Dartmouth might be detained till they receive satisfaction.

6. Petition of John Foxall and Barnard Feld to Sir Fr. Walsyngham. That so much of the goods of Spanish subjects may be stayed as may suffice to recompense the spoil of their ship at Cadiz.

7. List of the President and Council for the Marches in Wales, as named in the instructions anno xix. Eliz. [*Signed by Sir Hen. Sydney.*]

[*The following papers seem alterations of former instructions for the Council of Wales,* (*see* Vols. xcvii., *No.* 21, cvii., 3-15, cviii., 49, *and* cx.. 11-15), *drafts of clauses, &c., probably in the year* 1577 :—]

8. Order by the Council in the Marches of Wales for regulation of the business in the law courts there, practice of attornies, fines, records, &c.

9. Observations on the preceding order, and the effect of its various articles, with the reasons for the same.

10. Notes by Mr. Grevil, for easing the Queen's charges in the Presidentship of Wales, without further burthen to the subject.

11. Draft and alterations in the 3rd and 4th articles of former instructions for Wales.

12. Fair copy of the above and other articles, with further corrections by Burghley, for reformation of former instructions.

DOMESTIC—ELIZABETH. 575

1577 ?

VOL. CXX.

13. Fair copies of various articles of former instructions, probably those of June 1576.

14. Notes of articles from the 19th to the 49th of former instructions, to be reformed and altered.

15. Petition of Roger Wyndham, of Norfolk, to the Council. Touching the wreck of a Scottish vessel at Runton. Desires that the cause touching their goods saved may be heard by impartial judges, as Sir Edw. Clere was partial and unjust, and his mortal enemy.

16. Petition of Edmund Windham to same. In behalf of his brother, touching the restoration of the goods belonging to the Scotch ship which was wrecked at Runton on the coast of Norfolk.

17. Petition of Richard Wilkinson to Lord Burghley. For payment of the sum of 275*l.* 13*s.*, for apparel sent by him into Ireland for the soldiers there, according to the direction of Sir H. Harrington, whereby he would be enabled to employ 100 poor people in Stamford.

18. M. Giovanni Jacopo Scaramuzza's proposal to the Queen of a new plan discovered by him for the discharge of Her Majesty's debts. Italian.

19. Effect of the same in English.

20. Petition of George Gilpin to Burghley. Requests him to present his suit to the Queen. *Incloses,*

20. I. *His suit to Her Majesty for the grant of the arrearages of certain concealed lands.*

21. Note of the imperfections of the present state of government in Lancashire.

22. Petition of the Dutch strangers inhabiting Halstead, in Essex, to Sir Francis Walsyngham. That forty families of strangers may be permitted to inhabit and dwell in Halstead, and quietly follow their trades.

23. Petition of John Errington and John Sedgwicke, merchants of Southampton, to same. For payment of the sum of 91*l.*, the residue due to them for hire of their ship in the Portugal voyage.

24. Mayor and Jurats of Dover to the Council. Soliciting funds for the repair of Dover harbour, moderate estimates for which had been given by Dutch engineers. *Inclosing,*

24. I. *Estimate of expenses for the repair of Dover harbour.*

24. II. *Plan of Dover harbour, by P. Symans, on a scale of " 20 rodes to one ynch."*

24. III. *Small sketch of Dover harbour.*

Vol. CXX.

1577?

25. List of ships, and estimate of the whole charge of the Vanguard and Rainbow.

26 Informations against Mrs. Awdley, widow, "a verie welthie and dangerous woman," bastard daughter of Sir Ric. Southwell, John Eve, Dr. Drewrie, and other papists, dwelling at Colchester and in other parts of Essex.

27. Copy of the preceding.

28. Notes touching the watercourse to be made from Mayton ferry, Kent, to the sea. [*Probably connected with the improvement of Rye harbour.*]

29. Memorandum of Edward Jukes, garnitor, of the quantities of wheat to be provided by Bennet Bysheley, Rice David, and Erasmus Skidmore, the Queen's purveyors for the several districts; with the capacity of the garners at Whitehall and at the Mews.

30. List of the messengers in ordinary and extraordinary of the Chamber and of the Receipt of the Exchequer.

31. The clause in the warrant for the allowance of the accompt of the Treasurer of the Chamber for such bills as he shall pay upon the Lord Chamberlain's, Mr. Vice Chamberlain's, or Mr. Secretary's hand.

32. Names of officers most meet to be placed at the Greencloth and in other offices of the household. [*Indorsed by Burghley "for placyng of officers in ye howshold."*]

33. Memorandum of the several times of the year for the delivery of oxen and sheep for the provision of the household by the purveyors of Northamptonshire and Lincolnshire.

34. Statement of duties to be performed by Robert Ardern as assistant to the Clerk of the Accatery.

35. An offer to serve the composition provisions for Her Majesty's household to the better contentment of the country, and the discharging Her Majesty of 205*l*. 6*s*. 8*d*. yearly, under certain conditions.

36. James Syde's note of the charges for certain service to be done with a ship of 100 tons, a bark of 30 tons, and a pinnace with 70 men, to be continued for two months.

37. Plan of the portion of Portsmouth adjoining to the Camber, with a view to the improvements to be undertaken there.

38. A copy of the statute of Trinity College, Cambridge, for letting leases, entitled, "Statutum de locationibus possessionum Collegii Sanctæ Trinitatis." Lat.

DOMESTIC—ELIZABETH.

VOL. CXX.

1577?

39. Extract from a statute of (Cambridge) University, touching the referring of disputes to the decision of the Chancellor. Lat.

40. Statement by Jacques Jellaie, of Roan, and Ric. Lee, merchant of London, touching a ship laden with wools purchased at Middleborough, which has been driven into Rye, and there detained by the Lord Warden.

41. Petition of George Thorneton to the Council. Great need of a harbour at Winchelsea. Requests that Tho. Diggs, Esq., and others, may be commissioned by their lordships to make a survey of the ground required for the construction of a new haven there.

42. Survey and report on the site for the new haven at Winchelsea.

43. Notes relative to the shipping of undressed cloths by the Merchants Adventurers. Suggestions for revoking their charter, and for giving them a new one. Propositions respecting the trade of the Merchants Adventurers.

44. Reasons showing that officers ought to be appointed for the reforming of such abuses as are used in measuring linen cloths.

45. Note of gentlemen residing within the County of Huntingdon, with the value of their lands and goods.

46. Petition of Wm. Spender, and others, owners of the John Baptist, the Elizabeth, and the Anne, to the Queen. Desiring satisfaction for injuries and losses; having been obliged by stress of weather to put into the port of New Croydon, in Brittany, were there attacked and spoiled of their goods.

47. The names of the proprietaries of the West Country and the several towns wherein they dwell.

48. Henry Hunte, John Beynham, and Wm. Cowell to Lord Burghley. Against the vexatious suits of Mr. Lane, clerk in the Exchequer, concerning the church of Bromyarde, under pretence that it was a college, he having now brought a new action against them in the Court of Exchequer.

49. Proofs against the declaration of Mr. John Lane, that the church of Bromyarde was called, taken, or reputed for a college.

50. A brief abstract of a discourse concerning an order to be put in practice within the city of London for the relief of their poor, so as they shall not need to range abroad in begging.

51. Petition of Robert Kitching, and others, Merchants of Bristol, to the Council. That they may be provided for in the same manner as the merchants of London, in consideration of the losses they have sustained by Spain.

52. Petition of Gabryell Cornewall to Sir Fr. Walsyngham. Complains of being molested in the living of Somerby, in Lincolnshire, by Tho. Beverley, the patron, and John Beverley, his father.

Vol. CXX.

1577 ?

53. Information against Silvester Bellowe and his sureties ; certain crosses brought over by Bellowe and given to his daughter.

54. Petition of Robert Tyndall, John Frampton, and Wm. Ellize, merchants, to Lord Burghley. Complain of being tormented by the inquisitors in Spain, and spoiled of their goods to the value of 2,228l. 10s. 6d. Desire that they may receive satisfaction out of the goods belonging to the subjects of the King of Spain, now under arrest in England.

55. Petition of Edw. Burnell to the Council. That by the means and devices of Walter Jones and Hen. Nedeham he had been dispossessed of his property by his younger brother William Burnell; prays to be restored to his rightful possessions.

56. Reasons which may move Her Majesty to like of Mr. Stanhope's suit, for the grant of a parcel of the Honor of Tudbery, of the yearly rent of 5l.

57. Petition of the bailiffs and inhabitants of Aldborough, Suffolk, to the Council. For licence to buy corn in Norfolk for the sustenance of their town.

58. Petition of Edw. Morris to Sir Fr. Walsyngham. That in consideration of his services in the late treaty with Spain it would please Her Majesty to grant him a lease of a house, fallen by attainder of the Duke of Norfolk.

59. "A note concerning Tho. Morris his cause." That having by licence transported certain corn to Spain, he was in danger of being imprisoned by the Company of Merchants trading to Spain, for breach of their privileges.

60. Extracts from the Rolls. "In Originalia," of 11 Edw. I., and 50 Edw. III., touching the King's supremacy. [*Indorsed by Burghley :* "*The Kinges Prerogatyve ageynst the Sea of Roome.*"]

61. Arguments and authorities in proof that the supremacy of the Pope cannot be maintained on the authority of the Scriptures ; in answer to the objections of the Papists. [*Indorsed by Lord Burghley :* "*Pro regia authorita.*"]

62. [Wm. Engelbert's?] estimate of charges for the making of engines and bullets and setting up forges. Desires that if his offers are not accepted he might be at liberty to make them to some foreign prince.

63. H. Maynard to   . That the estimate sent with his former letter was missing, and therefore desires him to send another.

64. Articles of accusation against Morrall, Catline, and Sharpe, for hearing of mass and keeping Popish books, and abuse of the orders for divine service.

65. Petition of Richard Cliborne, Prisoner in the Clink, to Walsyngham. For licence to spend six months at the Bath for the recovery of his health.

1577.

Vol. CXX.

66. Petition of Henry Yonges and Wm. Boale, of Norwich, to Sir Fr. Walsyngham. Pray to be released from the Marshalsea, where they had been sent for truly performing their duty as Wardens of the Cordwainers Company of Norwich.

67. The Gov. and Comp. of Merchant Adventurers to Lord Burghley. Complaining of the irregular trade carried on between the coasts of England and the revolted provinces of the Low Countries; and praying the same may be restrained by proclamation.

68. Memorial of Tho. Conyngesbye to Walsyngham. Exceptions against Wm. Rudhall, Esq; declaring that he cannot indifferently be chosen sheriff of the County of Hereford, as he has many suits depending in law against persons residing in that county.

69. Notes, taken out of the order, matter, and charge, whereby the sea-walls of Romney Marsh are made and preserved, to be followed as near as may be in the intended works at Dover harbour.

70.   to Burghley. Details the abuses in the offices of Alnage and Subsidy of Woollen Cloths, in the City of London, according to the acts in that case provided; and suggesting a plan for reformation of the same.

71. A list of the sureties of John Swynnerton the younger, with a brief note showing their sufficiency.

72. The clause in the statutes of "*Gunvile*" and Caius College, Cambridge, " De contentionibus evitandis." Lat.

73. Mrs. Pilkington's answer to the demands made by the Bp. of Durham, for dilapidations.

74. Information of the great negligence of the County of Berks, in training and exercising the militia. Deficiency of arms and furniture.

75. A note of certain disorders and evil dealings of Davy Atkinson, the pursuivant, for secretly procuring warrants under the Commissioners' hands for the arrest of certain persons on charges of piracy.

76. Note of certain things to be considered of, for the manner of proceeding in the punishment of the inferior sort of those who have been abettors of pirates.

77. Certificate from Pembroke, of the names of such persons as were known to have traded with Hicks the pirate, and to have had corn and salt from him.

78. Abridgment of such matters as are found against various persons concerning piracies within the County of Pembroke.

79. Names of divers persons certified by the Commissioners

Vol. CXX.

1577? 81. Note of fines received by virtue of the first Commission for Piracy; with the sums remaining in Mr. Henry Morgan's hands.

82. Names of the Deputies and Inquirers appointed to inquire into matters of piracy within certain Rapes in the County of Sussex.

83. The names of such persons as have been fined for matters of piracy, and the money from thence due to Her Majesty. For Mr. Sec. Walsyngham.

84. Edict in Latin and English for the restraint of piracies. [*The English portion wanting.*]

Vol. CXXI.

Manuscript book, entitled, "Liber Pacis de Anno XIX° Elizabeth, Reginæ." Containing: A list of the Council of the North; names of the Commissioners of Oyer and Terminer for causes in the North; names of the Council of the Marches of Wales, teste 24° Nov., XVII° Eliz.; names of the Justices of Assize; list of Sheriffs in England and Wales; names of the Justices of Peace in the several shires; and names of the Commissioners for Musters in the County of Lancaster.

Vol. CXXII. January—February, 1578.

1578.
Jan. 1. 1. Declaration of all such cordage and sail canvass as hath been delivered out of the great storehouse at Deptford Strond, as well for the ships serving at the seas as toward the rigging of the two new ships, the Revendge and the Skowte.

Copy of the above. [*See Vol.* xcvi., *p.* 308.]

Jan. 1. Estimate of the charges of setting forth to the seas twenty of the Queen's ships for one month. [*See ib., p.* 304.]

Note of mariners and gunners to be had out of certain counties, with their rate of wages, conduct money, &c. [*See ib. p.* 306.]

Jan. 2. 2. Confession of the men of Cardiff, relative to their traffic with pirates, with the fines assessed upon them.

Jan. 6. 3. Burchard Raurych [Dr. Burcott] to Sir Fr. Walsyngham. Report of the gold contained in the ore brought by Captain Furbisher. Does not find it of such goodness as he thought to have found it.

Jan. 7.
Millgate. 4. Tho. Fludd to Lord Burghley. Has surveyed the mills at Dartford. Conditions on which they may be procured for working of the ore.

DOMESTIC—ELIZABETH.   581

1578.   VOL. CXXII.
Jan. 11.   5. Commissioners of Musters for Devonshire to the Council.
Exeter.   Certify the Musters, number of inns, &c. within the county. *Inclosing,*

   5. I. *Certificate of the alehouses, inns, and taverns within the County of Devon.*

   5. II. *Certificate of the General Musters of able men, furniture of armour, weapon, &c. within the County of Devon.*

Jan. 11.   6. Commissioners for Piracy in Cornwall to same. Their pro-
Truro.   ceedings in the matters of piracy. *Inclosing,*

   6. I. *Certificate of the creeks and landing-places in the County of Cornwall, with the names of the deputies appointed for inquiry into matters of piracy.*

Jan. 12.   7. Commissioners of Musters for Bedfordshire to same. Their pro-
Bedford.   ceedings in the Musters. Reasons for not making an earlier return. *Inclosing,*

   7. I. *Certificate of the General Musters in the County of Bedford, with names of the Captains appointed to lead them.*

Jan. 15.   8. Offer by Tho. Howard Viscount Bindon for the purchase of the manor of Colquit. [*Indorsed*, "*Mr. Edgcomb's offers for ye maner of Colequit.*"]

Jan. 19.   9. Mr. Michael Lok to Sir Fr. Walsyngham. Estimates for erecting
London.   the mills at Dartford, furnaces, &c., for the working and melting of the ore brought by Capt. Furbisher.

Jan. 19.   10. The Council to Mr. Michael Lok. Directions to collect 900*l.* among the adventurers of the North-west voyage, for the erection of the mills and furnaces.

Jan. 20.   11. Commissioners of Musters for Dorsetshire to the Council. The
Dorchester. proceedings in taking the General Musters, with the exception of Poole and Purbeck. *Inclosing,*

   11. I. *Certificate of the General Musters for the County of Dorset.*

Jan. 20.   12. The Bailiff and Parishioners of Bishops-Castle, in Salop, to
Bishops-Castle. Lord Burghley. Solicit allowance towards repairing the chancel of their church, as the Queen received the rents of the parsonage.

Jan. 21.   13. Earl of Shrewsbury to the Council. Sends the certificate of
Sheffield. General Musters for the County of Derby.

Jan. 22.   14. Bishop Scorey to Burghley. Desires that order may be taken for reparation of the chancel of the church of Bishops-Castle.

Jan. 23.   15. Dr. Sec. Wylson to same. Audience of M. de Famar on the
HamptonCourt. affairs of Holland. The Queen desires Burghley's attendance at Court. Illness of Walsyngham. The Queen is much offended with the Archbishop, and wishes him to be deprived : suggests the milder course for him to resign. The Arch-Duke chosen Governor of the Low Countries. Mr. Sec. Walsyngham lieth sick upon his bed

	Vol. CXXII.
1578. Jan. 24. St. Donatt's.	16. Commissioners for Piracy in Glamorganshire to the Council. Have appointed deputies for certain ports and creeks within the same, for prevention of piracy. *Inclosing.*
	16. I. *List of ports and havens in Glamorgan, with names of deputies appointed to each.*
Jan. 24. London.	17. Geoffroy le Bramen to Sir Fr. Walsyngham. Report on trial of the gold ore brought by Captain Furbisher. The pure metal was with difficulty obtainable. Fr.
Jan. 24.	18. The Council to Commissioners for Piracy. To certify the true value of the lands and goods of the offenders.
Jan. 25. Hampton Court.	19. Articles set down by Lord Burghley, between Mr. Martin and Mr. Lonison, for regulating the rate of coinage at the Mint.
Jan 27. Horncastle.	20. Commissioners for Piracy in Lincolnshire to the Council. Explain that they have not sent any certificate relative to pirates but the one now sent. Insufficiency of power given to administer oaths by their deputies.
Jan. 27. Haverfordwest.	21. Commissioners for Piracy in Pembrokeshire to the Council. Have appointed and give a list of deputies they have named. *Inclosing,*
	21. I. *Presentment of the jury for the County of Pembroke for the suppression of piracy.*
Jan. 28. Wimborn.	22. Sir Harry Asheley to Walsyngham. Matters of piracy in Dorset. The powers given them by their commission are insufficient, being refused to sit at Poole. Sends certificate of the inns, &c. *Incloses,*
	22. I. *Certificate of the alehouses, inns, and taverns within the County of Dorset.*
Jan. 28.	23. Sir Fra. Godolphyn to Burghley. Touching Mr. Edward Barkley's claim to the Scilly Isles. Former state of the islands.
Jan. 31.	24. Commissioners for Piracy in the Cinque Ports to the Council. Their proceedings. Insufficiency of the powers given to them by their commission for examining suspected persons on oath. *Inclosing,*
	24. I. *Certificate of the names of the deputies appointed for matters of piracy, and the places assigned to them.*
Jan. 31. Wells.	25. Same for Somersetshire to same. Certify the names of the deputies appointed by them in every creek and landing-place within the county.
Jan.	26. Certificate of the General Musters for the County of Berks.
Jan.	27. The Queen to the Justices of the several shires. Orders to levy a certain number of soldiers and pioneers for immediate service.
Jan. ?	The Council to the Bishop of London. The Queen, in her late progress, having been informed that sundry persons in Commission of the Peace had of late years forborne to come to church : the Bishop is to make inquiry and certify the names of all such Justices within his diocese. [*See Vol.* xlv., *p.* 16.]

DOMESTIC—ELIZABETH.

1578.
Vol. CXXII.

Feb. 1.
Eccleshall Castle.
28. Bishop Bentham to the Council. Sends up a more perfect certificate of the recusants within his diocese. *Incloses,*

28. I. *Certificate of recusants within the diocese of Coventry and Litchfield, which come not to the church to hear divine service, with a valuation of their livings.*

Feb. 2.
Yarmouth.
29. Bailiffs of Yarmouth (Norf.) to Sir Fr. Walsyngham. Have apprehended the pirate named Tho. Hitchcok; and Scarborough the other pirate has been taken by Lord Clynton, in Lincolnshire.

Feb. 3.
30. Examination of John Penrose, of Bethick, in Cornwall, for matters of piracy, on board Hicks's ship.

Feb. 3.
Matharn.
31. Wm. Blethyn Bishop of Landaff to the Council. Sends certificate of the recusants within his diocese, with a note of the value of their lands and goods. Has been very ill and grievously tormented with sickness.

Feb. 4.
Exeter.
32. Earl of Bedford, and others, Commissioners for Piracy, to same. Their proceedings in matters of piracy, wherein they find no great matter of importance. Complaints against Gilbert Peppit, servant of the Lord High Admiral. *Inclosing,*

32. I. *Examinations relating to pirates, taken at Exeter on the 4th of January.*

32. II. *Another set of examinations taken 3 February.*

32. III. *Articles against Gilbert Peppit, Serjeant of the Admiralty, of dealings with various pirates in Devon.*

Feb. 7.
33. Petition of Walter Rypon, the Queen's coachmaker, to Lord Burghley. For payment of 43*l.* 6*s.* 8*d.*, due to him by Henry Howard, son and heir of Thomas Viscount Bindon.

Feb. 7.
London.
34. Justices of Kent to the Council. Find nothing of importance touching matters of piracy to certify to their Lordships.

Feb. 8.
Greenway.
35. Sir John Gilberte to the Earl of Bedford. Report of the attack and capture of a French ship by one Clarke, a pirate, in Dartmouth harbour; and plunder committed by other pirates.

Feb. 9.
36. Certificate of Musters for the borough of New Windsor.

Feb. 11.
Aukland.
37. Richard Barnes Bishop of Durham to the Council. That as he had not been appointed a commissioner in matters of piracy, he had forwarded their Lordships' letters to Sir George Bowes.

Feb. 13.
38. Petition of Robert Pynder, grocer, to Lord Burghley. Solicits payment of 200*l.*, remaining due to him by Mr. Henry Howard.

Feb. 13.
39. Duplicate of the above.

Feb. 16.
40. Petition of Jane Fiste, of Kingston-on-Thames, to same. For payment of 12*l.*, due to her late husband by Mr. H. Howard, for man's meat, horse meat, and lodging.

Feb. 18.
41. Sir Tho. Gresham to his servant Tho. Cely. Directions in various points of business. Alderman Dixe is content to remain bound to Mr. Cavendish. To borrow the sum of 500*l.* of Mr. Stoneley, of the Exchequer, for three days. Memoranda of Thos. Cely.

1578.

Feb. 18.	42. Articles for the examination of the pirate Hitchcok, of Great Yarmouth.
Feb. 18. Yarmouth.	43. Bailiffs of Yarmouth to Sir Fr. Walsyngham. Have examined the pirate Hitchcok on the interrogatories sent by Mr. [Adam] Fullerton. *Inclosing*,

      43 I. *Examination of the pirate Thomas Hitchcok as to his spoiling two Scottish ships; one in April,* 1574, *the other in August following. Feb.* 18.

Feb. 19.	44. Dr. Burchard Raurych to same. Has molten a portion of the ore, and desires his company at a public examination of it. Solicits, however, a private interview with him first at his own house.
Feb. 19. Northampton.	45. Mayor of Northampton to the Council. Himself and others have executed the commission for Musters. *Incloses*,

      45. I. *Certificate of General Musters for the town of Northampton.*

Feb. 20. Wells.	46. Commissioners for matters of Piracy in the County of Somerset to same. Send certificate concerning pirates and piracies. Excuse their delay by occasion of sickness.
Feb. 20.	47. Same in Sussex to same. Certify the value of the lands and goods of certain persons detected to have been dealers with pirates within the said county.
Feb. 20. Carmarthen.	48. Griffith Rise and William Davids, Commissioners of Piracy for Carmarthenshire, to same. Stating the cause of their not proceeding in the commission.
Feb. 21.	49. Commissioners for Piracy in Cornwall to same. Reasons offered in excuse for not having before certified their doings. The imperfection of the presentments from their deputies prevented them from making any earlier return. *Inclosing*,

      49. I. *Copy of the letter given by them to Sir John Killigrew, to be presented to their Lordships, dated Truro, Jan.* 10.

Feb. 21.	50. Petition of William Franccam to Lord Burghley. For payment of 3*l.* 17*s.* 8*d.*, due to him by Mr. Henry Howard.
Feb. 21.	51. Note by Edw. Baeshe, of the charges for victualling seven of Her Majesty's ships to be conveyed from Gillingham to Portsmouth.
Feb. 21.	52. Declaration of the quantity of gold and silver contained in two proofs of the ore brought by Captain Furbisher, according to Dr. Burchard's process.
Feb. 21.	53. Dr. Burchard Raurych to Sir Fr. Walsyngham. Sends the gold and silver obtained by him from 1 lb. and 1 cwt. of ore, and promises that from every ton he will obtain twenty times the amount.
Feb. 21.	54. Deposition of John Matthew, gunmaker, relative to the debt owing to him by Mr. Henry Howard.

VOL. CXXII.

1578.

Feb. 21. 55. Depositions of John Hawkyns, Benjamin Gonson, Wm. Pelham, Esqrs., and many others, creditors of Mr. Henry Howard, relative to the debts owing to them; taken before the Master of the Rolls.

Feb. 22. 56. Petition of Nicholas Webb to the Council. Complains that he has not received the overplus of the money levied upon the inhabitants of Gloucester and Tewkesbury for expenses of the bark Young. Can get no more than 40*l.* from Wm. Nichols.

Feb. 24. 57. Estimate of the charges for victualling and transporting seven of the Queen's ships from Chatham to Portsmouth, by John Hawkyns and Edw. Baeshe.

Feb. 26.
London. 58. Dr. Lewes to Sir Fr. Walsyngham. Has examined Gilbert Peppit, servant of the Lord Admiral, relative to pirates, according to the order prescribed. Is of opinion that Peppit was free from all suspicion of being an aider of pirates. *Incloses*,

58. I. *Articles for examination of Gilbert Peppit, as to his dealings with pirates and pirates' goods.*

58. II. *Answer of Gilbert Peppit, Serjeant of the Admiralty in Devon, to the articles of the presentments against him, touching his dealings with pirates.*

Feb. 26.
Norwich. 59. Commissioners for Piracy in the County of Norfolk to the Council. Have prosecuted with diligence their inquiries about pirates. Interpose in favour of Eustace Rolf, who had offended by compulsion. The prices of corn rather abate. *Inclosing*,

59. I. *Certificate of the true and just value of the lands and goods of certain persons detected in dealing with pirates.*

Feb. 26.
Winchester. 60. Commissioners for Piracy in Hampshire to same. Excuse the delay, and certify their proceedings in the matters of piracy.

Feb. 27. 61. Dr. Burchard Raurych (Dr. Burcott) to Walsyngham. Justifies the proof of the ore already made. Is indignant at the charge of incompetency raised against him by Jonas. Proposes to try on 2 cwt. more of the ore, and that two honest men should be appointed to see that it was roasted fairly.

Feb. 62. Details of the proceedings of Jonas Shutz and Dr. Burchard in the trial of the gold ore brought by Mr. Furbisher. Jonas accuses Burchard of evil manners and ignorance, and would have no dealings with him.

VOL. CXXIII. MARCH—APRIL, 1578.

1578.

March 2.
The Court.
1. The Council to Nich. Robinson Bishop of Bangor and Dr. Price. To examine certain persons who have been dealers with Hugh Owen, a rebel.

March 5.
Southampton.
2. Commissioners for Piracy in Hampshire to the Council. Have met about their commission for Piracy and make return of their doings. Inclosing,

    2. I. *Certificate of the names of such as be bound to appear for causes of piracy, with the amount of their bonds and sureties and value of their goods.*

March 6.
Wickham Market.
3. Commissioners for Piracy in Suffolk to the same. Certifying their doings in matters of piracy. Inclosing,

    3. I. *Certificate of the names, dwelling-places, and values of such persons as were presented for dealing with pirates, in the County of Suffolk.*

March 7.
Grove Place.
4. Sir Edward Hastings to Sir Francis Walsyngham. Communicates by the bearer account of their proceedings at Hampton, about a presentment from Christchurch, relative to piracies.

March 8.
5. Accompt taken at Muscovy House of 2 cwt. of the ore brought by Mr. Furbisher, molten and tried, made by Jonas Shultz, assisted by three Englishmen. Estimate of charges for another voyage by Capt. Furbisher.

March 10.
6. Notes in Lord Burghley's hand of transactions acted with foreign states, in the form of a diary.

March 11.
7. Walsyngham to the Lord Treasurer and the Lord Chamberlain. The Queen is desirous that a third voyage to the North-west parts should be made by Mr. Furbisher, and requests their opinions upon certain points relating to it.

March 12.
Haverfordwest.
8. Commissioners for Piracy in Pembrokeshire to the Council. Perceive that their former certificate has not come to hand. Send now a list of such offenders as are of ability in their county.

March 12.
9. The Queen to the Lord Mayor and Aldermen of London. Order to train and keep in readiness 2,000 soldiers, for service at a short warning.

March 13.
Hatfield.
10. Robert Abbott to Mr. Wylson. Good success of the new manufactory at Hatfield, for spinning yarn. Rate of wages paid to the spinsters.

March 19.
Certificate of fines levied on the aiders and abettors of pirates in the County of York. [*See Vol.* cxxxv., *fol.* 23.]

March 24.
Pwllely.
11. Bishop Robinson and Dr. Elis Price to the Council. Have searched for the persons supposed to have dealt with Hugh Owen, a

DOMESTIC—ELIZABETH.   587

VOL. CXXIII.

1578.

March 24. Lindhurst.
12. Commissioners for Piracy in Hampshire to the Council. Have taken examinations of several persons in the Isle of Wight, in answer to allegations against them. *Inclosing*,

12. I. *Certificate of the examinations of certain persons dwelling in the Isle of Wight, presented for dealing with pirates.*

March 27.
13. Commissioners for Piracy in Monmouthshire to same. State what they have done for the suppression of piracy. *Inclose,*

13. I. *Presentments of the deputies of the Commissioners for Monmouth, as to creeks and landing-places in that county, and dealings of various parties with pirates.*

March 28.
14. A Treatise or Concordance of all written Laws concerning Lords of Manors, their Free Tenants and Copyholders. By William Barlee. Addressed to the High Sheriff and Lieutenant of the County of Essex.

March 31.
15. Mr. John Hawkyns's additions to his own replies to the answers made by Horatio Palavicini to his demands, relative to the delay and consequent loss on lading a cargo of alum on board the "Lybanie" at Civita Vecchia.

March.
16. Letters Patents of Queen Elizabeth, granting licence for transportation of foreign wares and merchandise for which custom was paid at the first entry, and whereof no property is altered.

April 2.
17. A paper, indorsed "A Discourse touching the Kingdom's Perils, " with their Remedies, written by Secretary Wylson, and the copy all " of his hand wryting."

April 3. Rypley.
18. Sir Wm. Inglyby to Lord Burghley. Particulars of the rentals of certain lands in Aysemonderbye, lately belonging to Tho. Markynfeld, attainted of high treason.

April 8.
19. Details of the controversy between the Queen and the Merchants of the Stillyard. They demand a renewal of their ancient charters; and to prevent the free traffic for English merchandise at Hamburg.

April 9.
20. Considerations by Mr. Johnson of the advantage of establishing mart towns and staple for cloths in England by the Merchants Adventurers.

April 10. Whalley.
21. Edward Braddyll to Burghley and Sir Walter Mildmay. Has made a survey of Kendal Castle, which was rapidly diminishing in value, and in a short time would be a mass of ruin.

April 11. Truro.
22. Commissioners of Musters for Cornwall to the Council. Have proceeded to the execution of the commission for the General Musters, in which they had been delayed by the prevalence of the plague. *Incloses,*

22. I. *Certificate of the General Musters for the County of Cornwall.*

April 11.
23. Commissioners for Piracy for the Town of Ipswich to same.

DOMESTIC—ELIZABETH.

1578.   Vol. CXXII.

April 12. 24. Commissioners for Piracy in the County of Kent to the Council.
Canterbury. Certify that they had taken care to make diligent inquiry, and could
hear of no pirates, or dealers with pirates, except John Turnor of
Whitstable. That the most part of the harbours and ports were
within the liberties of the Cinque Ports.

April 12. 25. Commissioners for Piracy in the West part of Sussex to same.
Chichester. The jury have acquitted all persons charged with dealing with pirates
in those parts except Francis Cradle, who confesses receiving certain
salt and fish.

April 18. 26. Edward Rockrey to Lord Burghley. Desires to live quietly in
his fellowship, and not to be molested as he has been. Others have
held a prebend with the fellowship.

April 19. 27. The confession of Mercy Glowde, (indorsed, "*Gould, a lewd
woman about Cuckfield in Sussex*,") with the opinion of the jury
of matrons that there was no fault in her of her child's death.

April 21. 28. Evidences in support of the right of the Archbishop of York to
visit the province of Durham.

April 21. 29. The Vice-President and Council of Wales to the Council. Have
Worcester. caused Musters to be taken throughout the Principality of Wales.
Some of the counties have as yet made no return. *Inclose,*

29. I.—XVI. *Returns relating to General Musters from various
counties in the Marches of Wales, viz., Anglesey, Brecknock
(3 papers), Cardigan (4 papers), Carmarthen (2 papers),
Hereford, Montgomery, Pembroke (3 papers), and Radnor.*

April 21. 30. Abstract of the above. Certificates sent to the Lord President
and Council from the Commissioners of Musters.

April 22. 31. Minute of proceedings at St. George's Feast. Sir Fr. Walsyng-
ham chosen Chancellor of the Order of the Garter, in the room of
Sir Tho. Smith, deceased. Election of Henry, King of France,
Rodolph, Emperor of Germany, and Frederick, King of Denmark.
Lat.

April 24. 32. [Walsyngham?] to Burghley. In behalf of Mr. Wilmott's
The Court. suit for grant of a reversion of lands of 30*l.* a year.

April 24. 33. Deposition of Zacharias Jones as to his conversation with
Gifford about Sir Jo. Arundell, and others, being in prison. Implication
of Sir Christopher Hatton with the Papists.

April 27. 34. Inventory of goods taken from pirates by Captain Luke Warde,
and landed at Southampton.

April 28. 35. Certificate of the Earl of Arundel and other Justices of Sussex,
as to the quantity of wheat that might be spared for the provision of
London.

April.   36. [Walsyngham?] to Lord Chandos. The Council are disappointed
Greenwich. in not having received certificates of the aiders of pirates in the
County of Gloucester. Desires him to forward them without delay.

DOMESTIC—ELIZABETH. 589

1578. Vol. CXXIII.

April ? 37. Depositions of Hugh Randall respecting the piracy committed within the Straits of Malega by Philip Boyt, of late executed for the said piracy.

38. Note of the charges wherewith certain persons in Cornwall are charged as aiders and abettors of pirates.

39. Note of matters wherewith the persons of Cardiff are to be charged for piracy.

April. 40. Certificate from Adrian Gilberte, Deputy of the Port of Dartmouth, for matters of piracy. Charges against persons presented for dealings with pirates, particularly Robt. Plomley, Mayor of Dartmouth, with their answers to the same.

41. Note of the persons in Kent discovered by Jasper Swift to have bought goods of Captain Goore the pirate.

42. Names of the chief dealers with pirates in Dorsetshire.

43. Note of persons in Lincoln, with sums set against their names, probably fines for dealing with pirates.

44. Order by the Queen for the remedy of spoils and depredations committed by English pirates on the subjects of foreign princes in amity.

April ? 45. Orders to be observed on the election of foreign kings and princes as Knights of the Garter, as to notification and installation. [*In Walsyngham's hand, who became Chancellor of the Order in April, 1578, when two sovereigns were elected.*]

46. Oath of the Chancellor or Prelate of the Order of the Garter.

47. Notes relative to the office of Chancellor of the Order of the Garter.

48. Notes relative to the placing of the stalls of the Knights of the Garter, and the placing of foreign kings and princes elected.

49. List of Knights of the Garter.

Feb. ? 50. Names of such gentlemen and others as went the first and second voyages with Capt. Furbisher into the land now called " Meta Incognita ;" and now for their service desire to be received as adventurers gratis.

51. Note of the entertainment of the gentlemen and others in the voyage under Mr. Fenton to inhabit in the Newland "Meta Incognita."

Vol. CXXIV. May—June, 1578.

1578.

VOL. CXXIV.

May 3. 2. Account of the sums remaining unpaid by the Adventurers in Mr. Furbisher's voyage to' the North-west.

May 6. 3. Warrant to pay to Sir Hugh Paulett 100*l.* yearly, out of the casualties growing within the lordship of Taunton, until the sum of 300*l.* be paid, for the repair of the castle of Taunton.

May 8. 4. Edward Havard to his brother Mr. Nich. Havard. Solicits him to discharge his debts according to promise. Bewails his lost and ill spent time. Exhorts his brother to remember himself in time.

May 8. 5. Same (signed by reversion of the letters "Dravah") to Mr. Bagard. Returns thanks for his brotherly goodness and courtesy. Will always be grateful.

May 12. 6. Petition of the Mayor, &c. of St. Mary's in Hull, to Lord Treasurer Burghley. For augmentation of the stipend of the minister of that church.

May 13. 7. Petition of Richard Cox to same. Solicits payment of the moiety of 60*l.* 11*s.* 4*d.* yet owing to him by Mr. Henry Howard.

May 15. 8. Examination of Francis Lee, of Redreff, Gunpowder-maker to the Queen, relative to the debts owing to him by Mr. Henry Howard.

May 15. 9. Award given by Lord Burghley and Sir Fr. Walsyngham for the settlement of the dispute between Thomas Herell, Warden of Manchester College, and Alexander Nowell, Dean of St. Paul's; in behalf of the said college of Manchester.

May 18. 10. Names of such as were present at the felling of a tree and other unlawful acts committed in Horne Park, at Eltham in Kent.

May 20. Denbigh. 11. Commissioners for Ports and Havens in Denbigh to the Council. Certify there are no landing-places in that county.

May 21. 12. Articles of charges preferred by Richard Vaughan, Deputy Admiral in South Wales, against Sir John Perrot, of tyrannical conduct, trafficking with pirates, and subversion of justice. [*On the 21st of May, Vaughan's "booke of complaintes" against Sir John Perrot was referred by the Council to Dr. Dale and Dr. Lewes for examination and to make report thereon. Co. Reg.*]

May 30. 13. Petition of Tho. Clyffe to Lord Burghley. For payment of the sum of 77*l.* 8*s.* 4*d.* owing to him by Mr. H. Howard.

May. 14. Petition of William Francome to same. For payment of 3*l.* 17*s.* 8*d.* owing to him by Mr. Howard.

May ? 15. Instructions given by the Privy Council to certain persons in every county to take a view of the number of able men and armour certified by the Commissioners upon the late Musters taken.

16. A collection containing the names of such persons in the several counties mentioned, as have been the receivers, abettors or setters

DOMESTIC—ELIZABETH. 591

1578.   Vol. CXXIV.

June 1.   17. Maurice Wynne, Sheriff, and others, of Carnarvon, to the Lord
Carnarvon. President of Wales. Defend themselves from a charge of negligence
in making returns of Musters of their county. Detail their proceedings.

June 1.   18. Same to same. State of their county, and of the course
Carnarvon. pursued in taking Musters from the 16th of the Queen's reign.
Have selected 50 fit and able men to be trained as shot, under Capt.
Richard Gwyn.

June 1   19. List of the books possessed by Lady Mary Graye at the time of
her death, mostly of a religious character.

June 4.   Articles of agreement between Edward Sudley and John Rotheram,
for procuring a new patent of the office of Clerk of the Court of
Wards and Liveries to be made in their joint names, heretofore
granted to the said Edw. Sudley and John Dister, deceased. [*Case
C., Eliz. No. 2.*]

June 5.   20. Sir Rafe Bagenall to Lord Burghley. Requests restitution of the
London.   money wrongfully paid by him for several years to the curate of
Horton, and that order may be taken for the future.

June 5.   21. Dr. R. Goade to same. Relative to his proceedings in the
matter against Mr. Lake ; his doings wherein were necessary and just.

June 6.   22. Petition of Henry Osmond to same. For payment of 57*l*.
owing to him by Mr. H. Howard.

June 7.   23. Similar petition of Robert Moott (bell-founder). For the sum of
10*l*. 10*s*.

June 7.   24. Similar petition of Robert Pynder. For the sum of 200*l*. [*Two
copies.*]

June 7.   25. Similar petition of Rowland Rayleton. For the sum of 33*l*.

26. Another petition of Rowland Rayleton for the same.

June 7.   27. Similar petition of Henry Rollesley ; for the sum of 3*l*. 11*s*.
for hats.

June 7.   28. Articles for the examination of Richard Vaughan, Esq., on
behalf of Sir John Perrott, and his answers to them.

June 10. 29. Bishop Whytgifte, and others of the Council of Wales, to the
Worcester. Council. Are of opinion that 1,000 men would be in readiness and well
prepared for service in Ireland when needed. Send several certificates
of Musters.

June 12. 30. Petition of Tho. Starfforde and five others, inhabitants of
Hamme, to Burghley. For various sums owing to them by Mr.
Henry Howard.

June 14. 31. Depositions of certain witnesses on behalf of Richard Vaughan,
Esq., to the articles of examination, relative to the charges made by
him against Sir John Perrot.

1578. Vol. CXXIV.

June 15. 32. List of the creditors of Mr. H. Howard in the first schedule not yet paid any part, and in other schedules part paid.

33. Duplicate of the above.

June 15. 34. Similar list of creditors certified in the later schedule, and who have not yet been paid any part.

June 17. 35. Petition of Henry Hooper to Lord Burghley. For payment of 8*l*., owing to him by Mr. Howard.

June 17. 36. Similar petition of Gryffyn Jones. For the sum of 16*l*. 10*s*. 3*d*.

June 17. 37. Similar petition of John Crane. For the sum of 11*l*.

June 18. Exemplification under the Great Seal of grant to Tho. Randolphe of the Office of Keeper of the Manor and Hundred of Middleton and Merden, in the County of Kent. Lat. [*Case C. Eliz. No. 3.*]

June 18. 38. Petition of Dr. Lopes to Burghley. For payment of 20*l*. due to Mr. Spinola by Mr. Howard.

June 19. 39. Similar petition of Robert Pynder. For the sum of 200*l*.

40. Similar petition of Michael Blunte, Esq. For the sum of 57*l*.

June 20. 41. Similar petition of Thomas Ayere for payment of the sum of 91*l*. 6*s*. 8*d*. due to him by Henry Howard, Esq.

June 20. 42. List of the creditors of Mr. H. Howard who have received payment for part of their debts.

June 20. 43. Portion of the decree, enacted by the Confederate Cities of Germany, prohibiting English merchants from inhabiting and trading to Hamburgh until the charters of their ancient privileges be confirmed.

June 20. 44. Commissioners of Musters for Flintshire to the Council of Wales. Certify their proceedings in taking the General Musters of the county since the 16th of the Queen's reign. *Inclosing,*

44. I. *Certificate of the number of able men, horses, and arms within the County of Flint.*

June 21. 45. Petition of Tho. Andrews to Burghley. For payment of the sum of 15*l*. lent by him to Mr. H. Howard.

June 22. 46. Similar petition of Wm. Good. For the sum of 6*l*. 2*s*. 8*d*.

June 23. 47. Similar petition of Robert Pinder. For the sum of 200*l*.

June 23. 48. List of Mr. H. Howard's debts which have not yet been certified.

June 27. 49. Full account of all Mr. Howard's debts, unpaid and paid in part.

1578.
June 28. Brecknock.
51. Sheriff and Justices of Brecknock to the Council of Wales. That the 50 soldiers appointed for Ireland were trained, supplied with arms, and ready for service. Mr. Watkyn Phillips appointed Captain.

June 28. Brecknock.
52. Same to same. Have taken order for levying and employing the money in the Musters as directed by the Council.

June 28.
53. Examination of Henry Conway, relative to the sum of 10*l.* 9*s.* 11*d.*, owing to him by Mr. H. Howard.

June 29.
54. Brief note of Mr. Henry Howard's debts, with the sum total still remaining to be paid.

June 30. Aldford.
55. Mr. Fyton to Lord Burghley. Particulars of the claim made by Mr. Randle Maynwaringe, and Randle Brereton, Esqrs., to Rode Heath as a part of their manor of Eaton, it being part of the manor of North-Rode, within the County of Chester, and part of the possession of the Earl of Oxford.

June 30. Brecknock.
56. Sheriff and Justices of Brecknock to the Council of Wales. Certify the readiness of the 50 soldiers appointed to be trained for caliver shot.

June.
57. Mr. H. Howard's acknowledgment of the sum of 7*l.* 10*s.* due to Mr. Byrde, to be paid by Burghley.

58. Names of Thos. Starford and five others of Westham, in Essex, poor creditors of Mr. H. Howard, whom the Lord Chamberlain desires to have paid.

59. Petition of John Mathewe, gunmaker, to Burghley. For payment of 12*l.* 10*s.* 4*d.* owing to him by Mr. H. Howard.

60. Similar petition of Tho. Denman, mercer, to Burghley and others. For payment of 321*l.* 16*s.* 8*d.*, being part of the debt owing to him by Mr. Henry Howard.

61. Bill of parcels of Tho. Denman of the money due to him by Mr. H. Howard, being in all 355*l.*

62. Abstract of the above account.

63. Petition of William Good to Lord Burghley. For payment of 6*l.* 2*s.* 8*d.* due to him by Mr. H. Howard.

64. Similar petition of Henry Conway for the sum of 10*l.* 9*s.* 11*d.*

65. Similar petition of Rowland Rayleton, Robert Mootb, and Richard Mason to Burghley. For the sum of 47*l.* 8*s.* due to them.

66. Articles for the examination of certain witnesses on the behalf of Sir John Perrott against Richard Vaughan; with their answers to the same.

67. The answer of Sir John Perrott to the slanderous and most untrue articles exhibited against him by Richard Vaughan.

1578.

VOL. CXXV. JULY—SEPTEMBER, 1578.

July 1.
Bench Prison.
1. John Garland to Lord Burghley. Unjust dealing of some of the port of Lyme, by altering the custom books. Has received some satisfaction and reparation, as he supposes through his means, and returns him thanks for the same.

July 1.
Flint.
2. Commissioners of Musters for the County of Flint to the Council of Wales. Certify that the 50 able men appointed for the service in Ireland are trained and provided with arms and all things requisite.

July 1.
Llanristed.
3. Same for the County of Cardigan to same. Certify their doings in matters relating to the Musters. *Inclosing,*

    3. I. *Certificate of the General Musters, number of able men and arms within the County of Cardigan.*

    3. II. *Certificate of the Muster of the 50 men appointed to be trained with calivers.*

    3. III. *Certificate of the 50 soldiers appointed to be trained for Ireland.*

    3. IV. *Certificate of the Musters of 75 men to be trained and kept in readiness upon an hour's warning.*

July 1.
4. Petition of Griffyn Jones to Burghley. For payment of 16*l*. 10*s*. 3*d*. owing to him by Mr. H. Howard.

July 3.
5. Petition of Mary Harte, late wife of John Harte, alias Chester Herald, to same. For a warrant from his Lordship to Mr. Fanshawe, that she might obtain the new commission formerly granted to her.

July 3.
6. Petition of John Russell, in verse, to same. Requests an appointment in the Custom House at London.

July 3.
Fleet Prison.
7. George Felton, prisoner in the fleet, to the Council. Entreats their Lordships to be a means to obtain for him Her Majesty's pardon, having his poor wife and eleven children dependent on him.

July 5.
Putney.
8. John Byrche, Baron of the Exchequer, to Burghley. Has carefully revised and altered certain clauses in the Patent for farming the new draperies.

July 5.
Certificate of the General Musters for the County of Middlesex. [*See Vol.* xciv., *No.* 16.]

July 6.
9. Petition of Mary Harte to Burghley. Desires him to favour her former request.

July 6.
10. Petition of Ry. Weston to same. Applies to have the farming of the land and houses in the town of Hastings, parcel of the chantry lands there.

July 6.
11. 12. Petition of Rowland Rayleton to same. For payment of 33*l*. owing to him by Mr. H. Howard; for which he has been arrested. [*Two Copies.*]

July 6.
13. Similar petition of Robert Pynder, for the sum of 200*l*.

July 6.
14. Similar petition of Griffyn Jones, for the sum of 16*l*. 10*s*. 3*d*.

DOMESTIC—ELIZABETH.

1578.
VOL. CXXV.

July 7. 15. Account by Henry Killigrew, of money received by him for fines set on the dealers with pirates.

July 8.
Gravesend.
16. Information given by Michael Gilles, Captain of the Gift of God, relative to an Irish gentleman who desired to be carried over in his ship to France, being as supposed either a traitor or a priest.

July 9. 17. Petition of Arthur Michelson, mariner, to Lord Burghley. Desires that the money taken from him by the searchers at Lynn, may be restored.

July 10.
London.
18. Richard Clarcke to same. That he had restored to Mr. Michelson the sum of 40l., but retains 39l., as it was claimed by Mr. Lane on behalf of Her Majesty.

July 10. 19. Petition of Richard Hodges to same. Desires letters to the Lord President in the North, for his release, being committed upon suspicion of piracy.

July 12.
Bacon House.
20. Mr. Recorder Fletewoode to the Vice-Chamberlain. Description of Paris Garden, notorious for secret meetings of Foreign Ambassadors and their agents. Several examples mentioned. The French Ambassador discovered by the watch on the previous night, accompanied by Sir Warham St. Leger, and Sir Wm. Morgan. Resistance offered to the watch. The Ambassador "swore great othes "that he wold do many thinges," but the watch said unto him, "they "knew not his dignitie; and that they were night-walkers, contrarie "to the lawe."

July 12.
Bacon House.
21. Same to Burghley. He endeavoured to get into the house of St. Leger, at Chandos Place, and then went over to Paris Garden, where the place is so dark with trees that one man cannot see another, "except they have lynceos oculos or els cattes eys." Secret meeting there of Sir Warham St. Leger, Sir Wm. Morgan, and the French Ambassador. It is the very bower of conspiracy.

July 13.
Bacon House.
22. Same to same. Had been to the house of Sir Warham St. Leger, but could gain no entrance: found that he had departed by boat down the river into Kent.

July 14.
Havering.
23. Examinations taken by Burghley of Hugh Tailor and others, watermen, concerning the secret meeting of the French Ambassador with Sir Warham St. Leger and Sir Wm. Morgan, at Paris Garden.

July 14.
Leedes.
24. Sir Warham Sentleger to Burghley. Has received his summons to repair to the Court at Havering: will not sleep till he accomplishes it: but his horses are at pasture, unshod, and three miles off.

July 14.
Pirgo.
25. Sir James Croft, Comptroller of the Household, to same. Requests him to remember his suit to Her Majesty for a grant of lands of the value of 25l. yearly, during his life. His long services.

July 14. 26. David Yale to [Burghley?] That the free election of Master of Queen's College, Cambridge, may be permitted to the Fellows, if Dr. Chaderton, the present Master, is made Bishop of Chester. Lat.

P P 2

DOMESTIC—ELIZABETH.

Vol. CXXV.

1578.

July 15.
Brecknock.
27. Commissioners of Musters in the County of Brecknock to the Council in Wales. Their doings in the Musters. Have provided and keep a common armoury for the whole shire, as the people object to provide private armour. *Inclosing,*

    27. I. *Certificate of the General Musters for the County of Brecknock.*

    27. II. *Note of the arms and armour in the common armoury of the shire.*

July 16. 28. Petition of the Company of Painter Stainers of London to Lord Burghley. Stating they have, time out of mind, painted the royal castles, honours, manors, ships, funerals, tents, pavilions, and other regal exploits, but are now likely to be ruined by the heralds-at-arms, who for their own private gain prohibit them from "depicting "of any sortes of armes or purtrayctes aforesaide."

July 17.
Walden.
29. Anth. Crane, and others, to the Justices for the Division of Holland in Lincolnshire. The supplies for the household being deficient through their neglect, they have sent the bearer with authority to take up provisions within their liberties, wheresoever they may be found.

July 17. 30. Petition of John Bragge to Burghley. Desires protection for three months against his creditors, having left Portugal suddenly to give information of the plans of Stuckley.

July 18. 31. Petition of Ursula Morton to same. Solicits the liberation of her husband, Robert Morton, imprisoned in the Gatehouse at Westminster.

July 19.
Monmouth.
32. Commissioners of Musters for the County of Monmouth to the Council of Wales. Their former certificates having been lost by the negligence of the bearer, they now send a certificate of their doings. Have used their utmost endeavours to have everything duly performed. *Inclosing,*

    32. I. *Certificate of the General Musters for the County of Monmouth.*

July 19. Lease in reversion from Edwin Archbishop of York to the Queen, of the parsonage of Dancaster, the chapel of Loversall, and the manor of Cairehowse, and the tythes of corn and hay within the lordship of Warmesworth. [*Case C. Eliz., No.* 4.]

July 19. An inventory taken and made the 19th day of July, of all the goods wares and merchandize of pirates, found in Aldborough, co. Suffolk, by the bailiffs and officers there, remaining with Mr. Fullerton. [*See Vol.* cxxxv. p. 153.]

July 20.
Flint.
33. Sheriff and Justices of the County of Flint to the Council of Wales. Causes of their delay in certifying the Musters. The 50 soldiers appointed for Ireland were trained and well provided with arms. Desire to be discharged of the fines imposed on them for the delay.

DOMESTIC—ELIZABETH. 597

VOL. CXXV.

1578.
July 23.
Abergwilly.
Bishop Davies to Mr. Fabian Phillips. Exhorts him to have Rees Morgan and his sister examined before the Council of Wales, on the charges of incest and murder, as the mere rumour of such crimes was not sufficient to bring them into the Consistory Court of St. David's. [*See* 24 *July* 1579.]

July 23.
34. Commissioners of Musters for the County of Glamorgan to the Council in Wales. Certifying their proceedings in the General and Special Musters for the county. *Inclosing*,

34. I. *Certificate of the General Musters for Glamorganshire.*

July 24.
Carmarthen.
35. Same for the County of Carmarthen to same. Certifying the readiness of the soldiers appointed for various services. Their progress in Musters and training.

July 24.
Abergwilly.
36. Same to same. Certifying the readiness of the 50 soldiers appointed to be trained and provided with arms for service in Ireland. Harry Phillips appointed Captain.

July 24.
Carmarthen.
37. Same to same. Their doings in taking the General Musters and providing stores of armour and munition. *Inclosing*,

37. I. *Certificate of the General Musters and the Muster of 50 soldiers appointed to be trained with calivers for special service, within the County of Carmarthen.*

July 24.
Mag. Coll.
Oxford.
38. Richard Stanclyff to Mr. Tomson. Disorderly government and dealing in the University, where he finds injustice, colourable dealing, malicious seeking of advantage, and cruel subtlety. Many accuse Tomson of desiring the ruin of the colleges, and especially of Magdalen. They would talk as loud against Walsyngham if they durst. Desires that impartial judges may be appointed to decide the controversies respecting their statutes.

July 27.
39. Commissioners of Musters for Glamorgan to the Council of Wales. Complain that the sheriff of Glamorgan has imposed a fine on each of them for negligence in making certificate of Musters. Explain all their proceedings, and desire to be discharged of their fines.

July 30.
Stamford.
40. Richard Shute to Lord Burghley. Report on the progress of the works at Burghley-house. His old mistress is in good health. Has stayed the selling of timber by Mr. Vincent. Commissioners have been at his house about the return of the certiorari for Barhome matters.

July.
41. The Queen to the Marquis of Winchester. Desires a reconciliation between him and the Marchioness his wife; entreating him to receive her again into favour, who promises to love and obey him in all things.

July. Entry of the above. [*See Warrant Book, No* 1., *p.* 86.]

July.
42. Petition of John Hollingshed to Burghley. Complains that Tho. Gardyner had only obtained his letters for a pretended debt of 56*l.*, to delay his proceedings for the recovery of 72*l.* 18*s.* 11*d.*, justly due to him by Gardyner.

Vol. CXXV.

1578.
July. 43. Memoranda by Mr. Baeshe. Relative to victualling the Queen's ships; stay of all clap-board and cask; supply of timber, &c.

July. 44. Petition of Tho. Tylar, painter, to [Sr. F. Walsyngham?]. Solicits his influence with Sir Chr. Hatton, Vice-chamberlain, for a grant of one of the waiters' rooms at the water side, during the vintage time.

July? 45. Petition of Richard Matyson to Walsyngham. Desires order may be taken with one John Ashborneham for the payment of upwards of 40*l*., owing to him and his brothers for the space of twenty years, or that he may have leave to proceed against him at law.

July? 46. Sketch of the situation of the several houses named in Her Majesty's gestes, with plans of Lady Chester's house at Barkway, and Mr. Chester's house at Royston, being "a very unnecessary hows for "receipt of Her Majesty."

July? 47. Names of the Dutch ships that were stayed at Falmouth, the 25th of July, Anno   , by order of the Vice-Admiral.

July? 48. Account of expenditure for the Royal stables.

July? 49. Grant to John Medley of the sole right to an engine newly invented by him for draining mines, &c.

July? 50. Suit of Gherard Honricke, native of West Friesland, for letters patent to secure to him and his assigns, for the term of thirty years, the sole right to erect certain engines invented by him for the draining of mines.

July? 51. Same as the preceding; with corrections and additions in Lord Burghley's hand.

August 12. 52. John Aylmer, Bishop of London, to Burghley. In behalf of
Hornsey. S. Whythed, Nath. Traheron, and Wm. Trewlove, grandsons of Tho. Cawston, of Essex; to assist them in obtaining possession of the lands formerly belonging to their grandfather, of which they had been wrongfully dispossessed.

August 15 53. The Wardens of the Brown Bakers of London to same. Report
London. on the quality of certain quantities of grain stowed in the Bridgehouse; being damaged and unfit for use.

August 24. 54. Justices of the Holland Division of Lincolnshire to Anth. Crane,
Boston. and others, purveyors of the Household; stating that the neglect of furnishing provision for the Household rested with Tho. Whyte, their purveyor. Have removed him and put Benedict Anton in his place. Tho. Bryket, in their behalf, has taken up a larger proportion than he was warranted to do.

August? 55. Articles exhibited by Lawrence Dutton, and others, against Robert Gascoigne, ordinary messenger and post to Her Majesty, of fraud and ill-conduct in his office.

August. 56. Duplicate of the above.

DOMESTIC—ELIZABETH. 599

VOL. CXXV.

1578.
August ? 57. Answer of Robert Gascoigne to the articles exhibited against him by L. Dutton and others.

August ? 58. Articles objected against Robert Gascoigne by Mr. Randall [Randolph ?].

August ? 59. Robert Gascoigne's answer to the articles objected by Mr. Randall.
Daventry.

August ? 60. Certificate by Barth. Dodington of Mr. Gascoigne's bill for the charges of extraordinary posts in Her Majesty's progress, Anno 1574.

August ? 61. Supplication of Lawrence Dutton and Raffe Walton to the Council ? Proposing regulations to be observed by the Messengers of the Chamber, on pain of forfeiture of their places.

Sept. 7. 62. Act of Common Council and perpetual order hereafter for the election of the Mayor and certain officers of the town of Dover, and for the good government of the said town.

Sept. 10. 63. Richard Barrey to Lord Burghley. The Act of Council for
Dover Castle. election of officers at Dover was willingly accepted, and the old Mayor has been re-elected with the greatest quietness. No election for Mayor for the last twenty years has been "without blowes or " scratchinge."

Sept. 14. 64. John Sommers, bailiff of Hodsdon, to same. Information that
Hodsdon. the plague was in the house of John Squyer, keeper of the lodging-house called the " Bell," at Hodsdon, who refused to close his house and still received passengers coming to the Court.

Sept. 16. 65. Robert Beale to same. In behalf of the young Count of Schlicke
Odiham. (Gaspar Schlicke), who was in England for the purpose of visiting the Universities, and wished to be introduced to Her Majesty.

Sept. 19. 66. Examination of certain persons before Sir Edward Mansell, Sir Edward Stradlynge, and others, Commissioners for matters of piracy, for the County of Glamorgan ; charging them with dealings with Tho. Clarke, a pirate.

Sept. 20. 67. Lord Henry Seymour to Burghley. The Lord Chamberlain is
Bath. in good health and much visited. Some of the Lord Chamberlain's houses are much to be desired in that country.

Sept. 21. 68. Sir John Smythe to Sir Chr. Hatton. Proposes that Her Majesty would be graciously pleased to grant a release of the mortgage of his lands and take bonds from him for the payment of 2,000l. at Michaelmas, 1579. With a postscript by Hatton, signifying the Queen's pleasure to grant his request.

Sept. 21. 69. Sir Chr. Hatton to Burghley. The Queen is pleased to grant a
At the Court at release of the mortgage of Sir John Smyth's lands, on condition of his
Mr. Stoner's. paying 2,000l. at Michaelmas, 1579.

DOMESTIC—ELIZABETH.

1578.   VOL. CXXV.

Sept. 23.   70. Sir Humfrey Gylberte to Sir Fr. Walsyngham. Has sailed
Greenway.   from Dartmouth on the 23rd, with a fleet of 11 ships and 500 able
             men, for his intended voyage. Desires Walsyngham to keep him in
             Her Majesty's good favour and credit.

Sept. 26.   71. Henry, Earl of Derby, to Lord Burghley. In favour of Robert
Lathom House. Worseley. Desires Burghley not to believe the accusations against
             him.

Sept. 27.   72. Wm. Dyx, and Wm. Cantrell, to same. Their proceedings
Norwich.   relative to leases of the manor of Halvergate. Request him not to
             attend to the petition of some of the tenants, as all matters had been
             decided before Mr. Justice Gawdye.

Sept. 27.   73. Earl of Leicester to same. Considers himself slighted by him;
             especially in not being consulted in the matters relating to the mint and
             the new warrant. Refers to their long and zealous service together in
             the Queen's affairs, and laments his seeming coolness after a friendship
             of thirty years.

Sept. 28.   74. Dean Alex. Nowell to same. That the living of Wythingdon, in
             Gloucestershire, may be conferred on Mr. Wm. Whytaker, of Trinity
             College, Cambridge, in the event of Dr. Bullingham being preferred to
             the Bishoprick of Chester.

Sept. 29.   75. Declaration of the accounts of Sir Walter Mildmay, Chancellor
             and Under-Treasurer of the Exchequer, from Easter term, 1578, to
             Michaelmas following.

Sept. 29.   76. Note of the number of cloths exported, and of the customs paid
             by the merchants of the Stillyard, for two years ending Michaelmas,
             1578.

Sept. 29.   Account of Charles Boothe, Receiver-General of Fines and Amercia-
             ments in the Principality of Wales, for the year ending Michaelmas,
             Anno R.R. Eliz. 20°. [*Case C., Eliz., No. 5.*]

Sept. ?   77. List of the officers of the camp; with a note of their pay.

Sept. ?   78. Petition of Roger Nelson to Sir Fr. Walsyngham. Requests a
             letter to Captain Pearse for payment of 7*l.* 6*s.*, owing to him by Pearse
             Davis, his servant.

Sept. ?   Extension of licence to Tho. Bodley, M.A., to travel on the continent.
Greenwich.   [*See Warrant Book*, I., *p.* 16.]

Sept. ?   Warrant to the Lord Treasurer and Sir Walter Mildmay. To make
             a bargain with certain merchants for the purchase of some bullion to
             the amount of 20,000*l.* [*See Warrant Book*, I., *p.* 87.]

DOMESTIC—ELIZABETH. 601

1578.
VOL. CXXVI.

Oct. 1.
The Court.
1. Sec. Tho. Wylson to Lord Burghley. Has delivered his letter to the Earl of Leicester. Defeat and death of the King of Portugal. 8,000*l.* required by Mr. Davison for Duke Casimir, at which the Queen is marvellous angry.

Oct. 7.
2. A book containing the number and names of all the knights, esquires, gentlemen, and freeholders, within the County of Chester, together with their horses, armour and other furniture, of proportion.

Oct. 9.
3. The Council to Sir Phil. Parker, Sir Robt. Jermyn, Sir Tho. Gawdy, and others. Authorizing them to inquire into the matters in controversy between the Bishop of Norwich and Dr. Becon, his Chancellor, the circumstances being so rare and strange as to seem incredible; and, by their present authority, to restore Dr. Becon to his office.

Oct. 11.
Exeter.
4. Bridget Countess of Bedford to Burghley. Recommends that Mr. Woolton, a Canon of Exeter, may for his learning and ability be appointed Bishop of Exeter.

Oct. 12.
5. Burghley to Sir Fr. Walsyngham. Still continues in ill-health. The Queen's debts in Ireland are greater than he expected.

Oct. 12.
Ludham.
6. Edmund Freke Bishop of Norwich to the Council. Desires that Dr. Becon may not be re-admitted into the office of Chancellor, of which he had deprived him. Has dissolved his court of audience, and intends to exercise the whole jurisdiction himself.

Oct. 12.
Richmond.
7. The Council to Burghley. Desire that the letters and papers on which the indictment against John Prestall was framed several years past, might be sent to them.

Oct. 13.
Rochester.
8. Sir Wm. Wynter and Mr. Wm. Holstok to Walsyngham. Account of expenses of the Achates, Capt. Barnes, in attending Walsyngham and Lord Cobham in their late embassy to Holland.

Oct. 14.
Richmond.
9. Walsyngham to Burghley. The Queen does not think it needful he should attend the Court till the recovery of his health. The Sates are to have the 8,000*l.* Parliament prorogued to 22d January.

Oct. 17.
10. Earl of Leicester to Burghley. Extreme business has prevented him from answering his late friendly letter. The Queen has been marvellous ill many days with a pain in her cheek. Mr. Pack's suit to repair again to Court. The Queen intends to mediate in the affair between the Lord Chamberlain and Lord North. His endeavour to avoid disputes at Court.

Oct. 18.
11. Sec. Wylson to same. Advertisements out of the Low Countries. Death of Don John on the 2d of Sept. Civil disorders and military movements in Flanders. Sends an answer of one Lawrence Horseley, a seditious lewd fellow.

Oct. 21.
12. Sir Fr. Knollys to same. Desires to know when he may send for the bond of the Earl of Kildare. Sends a book on the sacrament to read during his illness. Death of the King of Portugal and Don John of Austria; and he heartily thanks God for it.

Vol. CXXVI.

1578.

Oct. 21.
Richmond.
13. Grant of licence to certain merchants to transport hides, goat skins not useful to be kept in store, on payment of the customs.

Oct. 24.
Norwich.
14. Bishop Freke to the Council. Protests against the commission for restoration of Dr. Becon. Is determined not to receive him back again as his Chancellor, and desires a commission to examine into his fraudulent dealings.

Oct. 25.
Theobalds.
15. Burghley to Walsyngham. Affairs of the Low Countries. Don John had received orders from the Emperor to retire his forces, but he fulfilled it by departing out of the world. Desires a warrant from the Queen for the grant of Chopwell to Sir Robert Constable.

[Oct. 25.]
16. Geo. Puttenham to the Council. Long detail of the causes preventing his personal appearance before them. The shameless conduct of Lady Windsor, his wife, and her children, and the outrageous violences of Lord Thomas Paulet, and others of that family, against him compel him to disobey the Council's letters. [*On 26 Oct. the Council granted letters of protection to Puttenham for twenty days, to make his appearance. Co. Reg.*]

[Oct. 25 ?]
17. Same to Sir John Throkmarton. Arguments and reasons against appearing before the Council or delivering himself into custody. Complains of ill-treatment and violence from all the Paulet family.

[Oct. 25 ?]
18. Another letter of exactly the same tenor, but differently arranged; with some concluding additions.

Oct. 29.
Norwich.
19. Bishop Freke to the Council. Finds himself grieved by the hard dealing of the Commissioners towards him. Desires to have a copy of all the examinations they may exhibit against him; and also a commission for discovery of the corrupt dealings of Dr. Becon.

Oct. 29.
20. The Council to Mr. Michael Lok. To collect 6,000*l.* from the adventurers to pay the crews of the ships returned with Captain Furbisher from the North-west voyage with a great quantity of ore.

Oct. 29.
21. Same to the Lord Mayor and Sir Wm. Cordell, to aid Mr. Lok in the above business.

Oct. 29.
22. Same to the Commissioners to procure and set down an account of Furbisher's voyage, and take charge of all charts, stores, &c.

Oct.
23. Articles wherein Edmund Bishop of Norwich desires the Council to take order for reformation of certain misdemeanors towards their Lordships and himself, by Dr. Becon. Feels assured he can answer anything he can be charged with by the commission.

Oct. ?
24. Observations on the privileges claimed by the Eastland merchants. [*Indorsed: " An indifferent plat for all parties interested, touching corporations for trades in foreign countries."*]

Oct. ?
25. Discourse respecting the liberties formerly granted to the English merchants trading to the Hanse towns, and their privileges in Hamburgh.

DOMESTIC—ELIZABETH. 603

1578.
Vol. CXXVI.

Oct. 26. Discourse of the trade of the Merchants Adventurers of the Dutch Guild called the Hanse. Their trade and privileges. Prices of foreign commodities imported by them. Decree of the Council, temp. Edw. VI., on the information exhibited against the Merchants of the Stillyard.

Oct. ? 27. Articles exhibited by the Merchants Adventurers respecting the trade of the merchants of the Hanse towns. That vent would be found elsewhere for English goods if prohibited by them.

Oct. 28. The effect of the privileges granted to the English merchants by the town of Hamburgh, above those enjoyed by other strangers.

Oct. 29. Orders to be observed in the establishing of marts within this realm.

Oct. 30. Consideration of the advantages that will encourage and draw the merchant strangers from the marts kept in the Low Countries unto marts and staples of cloth to be kept in England.

Oct. 31. Answer to certain doubts and objections urged against the establishment of marts and staples of cloth to be kept in England.

Oct. ? 32. Brief account of the expenses and of the sums paid for the second and third voyages of Capt. Furbisher.

[Oct.] 33. The humble suit of Tho. Bonham. For some allowance to be yielded him in consideration of his losses sustained in Captain Furbisher's voyage.

Oct. 34. Account of the stock of the adventurers in Captain Furbisher's voyages to the North-west; and of the amount invested by Mr. Lok and his family.

Oct. 35. Answer to Mr. Lok's request for 1200*l*., which he demands of the Company as due to him for his services for three years. Estimate of the amount to be allowed him.

Oct. 36. Names of certain of the adventurers in Captain Furbisher's voyages to the North-west.

Oct. 37. Petition of the Bakers of London to Lord Burghley. That the assize of bread had been appointed by the Lord Mayor and Aldermen of London to be kept at 28 ounces the penny wheaten loaf, which price, on account of the bad harvest, they could not keep, unless the exportation of corn was prohibited.

Oct. ? 38. Petition of Margaret Shawe to Walsyngham.(?) Solicits his interference for the deliverance of her poor husband, Randoll Shawe, detained prisoner in Spain.

Oct. ? 39. Petition of Henry Everard, prisoner at Bury in Suffolk, for religion, to the Council. Desiring to be set at liberty on account of the infection, and the illness of his wife, 24 miles off, who was not expected to live.

1578.
Nov. 5.
Abergwilly.
40. The Bp. of St. David's, and John Barlo, Esq. to Lord (Burghley.) Certify their proceedings in the detection and punishment of pirates, and the aiders of pirates in Wales. Have not been able to examine all persons suspected, as many of them were then absent at sea. *Inclosing,*

> 40. I. *The examinations and depositions of witnesses respecting matters of pirates taken at St. David's, Sept. 30. Names of the persons presented by the juries of every Hundred as dealers with pirates.*

Nov. 5.
Norwich.
41. Sir Philip Parker, and others, to the Council. Their proceedings in examining the controversy between the Bp. of Norwich and his Chancellor. The Bishop's disregard of the Council's letters, and his behaviour towards Dr. Becon in the consistory. Did not feel authorized to inquire who were the Bishop's advisers. *Inclosing,*

> 41. I. *Interrogatories to be ministered to certain deponents concerning the hard entreating of Dr. Becon, Chancellor of Norwich, and the breach of certain orders condescended unto by the Bishop of Norwich, before the Justices of the county: whereupon the deponents were examined by Sir Phil. Parker and others.*
>
> 41. II. *Depositions of the witnesses respecting the dealing of the Bp. of Norwich towards his Chancellor, taken before Sir. P. Parker and others Oct. 23, in answer to the above interrogatories.*
>
> 41. I II. *Extracts from the examinations in the matter between the Bishop and his Chancellor, showing the contempt of the Bishop towards the letters of the Council, and of his behaviour in the Consistory Court.*
>
> 41. IV. *Note of the extreme dealings of the Bishop of Norwich towards Doctor Becon, extracted out of the depositions.*

Nov 6?
42. Dr. Becon to the Council. Relative to the matters in dispute between him and the Bp. of Norwich. Is ready to be examined before a commission of lawyers appointed by the Council, and does not object to be examined by Commissioners to be nominated by the Bishop.

Nov. 6.
Richmond.
The Council to Sir John Throkmarton. Require him to appear before them to answer the complaints made by the Lady Windsor against his brother-in-law Mr. G. Putenham, and to stay in his hands all monies paid to the use of Mr. Putenham. [*See,* 21 *Nov.*]

Nov. 9.
Stoke.
43. Tho. Wyseman to the Earl of Leicester. Sends two devices for the Queen's service, one for reformation of the Household, the other for the increase of the revenue of the Exchequer.

DOMESTIC—ELIZABETH.

1578.

Vol. CXXVI.

[Nov. 12.] Sir Fr. Walsyngham to Lord Cobham. Desires him to deal with the widow, Mr. Sommer's neighbour, that she might be brought to give him satisfaction for her offence and unadvised behaviour. [*See, Vol.* xlv., *p.* 21.] [*On the 12th Nov. the Council directed Lord Cobham and Sir Chr. Allen to take order between Mr. Sommers and Mrs. Katherine Kelsam, relative to the fraudulent execution of a lease.*]

Nov. 12. 44. Sir H. Gylberte to Walsyngham. Complains of Mr. Knollys'
Plymouth. unkind and ill dealing towards him and other gentlemen in Devonshire, and of his separating company in the voyage. His fleet, however, of seven sail is sufficiently large to accomplish his business.

Nov. 14. 45. Portion of a MS. book, containing copies of various cases and awards, &c. Confession of John Fauke, soap maker, as to making soap with fish oils. Agreement between Dr. Martin Culpeper and Mr. John Sled. Submission of certain preachers, and form of licence to preach. Question of vacancy of livings on being elected to a bishoprick. Order between Alexander Irton and Tho. Hancock, Vicar of Amport, 14 Nov. 1578, and reply to the objections of the soap-makers as to the use of fish oils in the manufacture of soap.

Nov. 18. 46. Sir H. Gylberte to Walsyngham. Sends a certificate of the
Plymouth. causes of Mr. Knollys' departure from him, to be shown to the Queen and the Council. His cousin Denny accompanies Knollys in this breach. *Incloses*,

46. I. *The certificate of the causes why Mr. Henry Knollys quitted the company of Sir H. Gylberte as alleged before the Mayor of Plymouth and other gentlemen. Signed by Wm. Hawkyns, Walter Rauley, and others.*

Nov. 18. 47. Note by Mr. Palmer relative to the offer made at Muscovy House by Mr. Jonas Schutz, for smelting the ore brought by Captain Furbisher.

Nov. 18. 48. Dr. Degorye Nycoolls, Master of Mag. Coll., to Lord Burghley. Answers to the complaint of ingratitude alleged against him by Mr. Buckley. States the many services he has rendered to Buckley, and his unfitness for the office of proctor.

Nov. 49. The names of all the ships, officers, and gentlemen, with the
18 & 19. pieces of ordnance, &c., gone in the voyage with Sir Humfrey Gylberte, Capt. Walter Rauley, commanding the Falcon; also the names of the ships, officers, and gentlemen who went with Mr. Henry Knollys on the 18th Nov.

Nov. 21. 50. Sir John Gilberte to Walsyngham. Thanks for his favours
Greenway. shown to his brother Sir H. Gylberte, and his uncle Sir Arthur Champernowne. Is ready to perform any service in his power.

Nov. 21. 51. The Council to Sir J. Throkmarton. Send the articles
Richmond. objected against him by the Lady Windsor, and desire him immediately to attend the Council to answer them.

1578.   VOL. CXXVI.

Nov. 26. Arches at London.
52. Dr. Lewes, Judge of the Admiralty, to Sir Fr. Walsyngham. Transmits the certificates from the Bishop of St. David's, and others, of their proceedings against the aiders of pirates in Wales.

Nov. 28. Chepstow.
53. Commissioners for matters of piracy in Monmouthshire to the Council. Have obtained from juries presentments of the value of lands and goods of such persons as have been dealers with pirates in that county. *Inclosing,*

53. I. *Certificate of such as have been presented as abettors of pirates within the County of Monmouth.*

Nov. 28. Ipswich.
54. Bailiffs of Ipswich to Walsyngham. Have delayed to set at liberty Peter Falleis and John Martyn, committed on seven several actions, for want of sureties for their lawful discharge.

Nov. 29.
Grant of arms to Arthur Herrys, of Crixsey, Essex, by Wm. Flower, Norroy. [*See, Grant of Arms, No.* 13.]

Nov. [29.] Richmond.
55. The Council to the Judge of the Admiralty. To consider the claim of certain French merchants for restoration of goods belonging to them, detained in Guernsey.

Nov. 30.
56. Account of the monies not paid in by the adventurers in Mr. Furbisher's third voyage; and of the monies received and expended by Mr. Lok since his last account.

Nov. ?
57. Brief report of the account of Michael Lok, concerning the charges of three voyages into the North-west parts, under the conduct of Martin Furbisher, together with the charges of buildings at Dartford.

Nov.
58. Note of the money owing to the brewers and wine merchants for beer, ale, and wine for the Royal Household in the 20th year of the Queen's reign.

59. Note of the amount of fines and names of parties fined in the various counties of England and Wales detected to have been dealers with pirates, buyers, or conveyers of pirates goods, &c.

60. Dr. Becon's request; proposing that for the speedy determining the matters in controversy, two of the Council should be nominated for that purpose, and to have the opinion of Dr. Lewes as to revocation of the patent of Vicar-General.

Nov. ?
61. Petition of Henry Topcliff to Walsyngham. Solicits his letters to the Lord Chancellor to be released on bail, having been confined in the Bench for 16 months, at the suit of Tho. Brodewaie *alias* George.

Nov.
62. Petition of Edmond Mathewe to same. Solicits to be released from the Marshalsea, where he had been sent for permitting the escape of John Fanstone, who was now retaken.

Nov. ?
63. Consideration of the inconveniences that will arise by toleration of the soapmakers to use train oil and other corrupt oils in the making of soap.

DOMESTIC—ELIZABETH. 607

1578.

VOL. CXXVI.

64. Notes by Putenham addressed to Sir John Throkmarton on the state of his affairs and the controversy with Lady Windsor: with Throkmarton's opinion of him, that when once his turn was served " he was careless of all men, ungrateful in prosperity and unthankful " in adversity."

65. Notes by same for guidance of Throkmarton before the Council. Urges him not to yield to all that is demanded of him.

66. Other notes by same to same. Defies the Lords or any man living to give away any of his goods or livings but by order of law.

67. Extracts, in Geo. Putenham's handwriting, of passages from the life of Tiberius, showing excessive instances of tyranny and cruelties in various acts of Government.

VOL. CXXVII. DECEMBER, 1578.

Dec. 1 ? 1. Answer of the Bishop of Norwich to the articles exhibited against him, relative to the controversy with Dr. Becon, his Chancellor. Objects to the proceedings of Commissioners, and the partial mode in which the depositions were taken.

Dec. 1 ? 2. Dr. Becon to the Council. His chargeable attendance compels him to request a speedy resolution. Thinks it unjust the Bishop should have a copy of the commission merely for delays or malice. Is ready to have his own conduct subjected to a commission of inquiry, if necessary.

Dec. 2 ? 3. Proposals and terms submitted for settling the controversy between the Bishop and Dr. Becon.

Dec. 2 ? 4. Brief collection of the usage of the Bishop of Norwich towards the Lords of the Council in treating their letters with contempt, and otherwise, in the matter between him and Dr. Becon, and the final course of the affair. The Bishop's offer to compound with his Chancellor.

Dec. 2.
Guildhall. 5. Declaration made by the Mayor and Aldermen of London to the Alderman and Merchants of the Stillyard, and others of the Society of Merchants of the Hanse, resident in London. That if they desired the continuance of their ancient privileges and liberties within the City of London, similar immunities must be granted to their merchants trading to the Hanse Towns.

Dec. ? 6. Note of such horses as are accounted fit for war according to statute, and also articles how recusants, refusing to attend the church, might be lawfully punished and reduced to conformity.

1578.

Vol. CXXVII.

Dec. 3.
London.
7. Opinion of the Attorney-General relative to the power of the ecclesiastical law to punish and fine such as refuse to come to the church.

Dec. [7.]
8. The Council to the Earl of Pembroke and others; calling upon them to pay the amount of money due for their contributions in the adventure of Captain Furbisher's voyage to the North-west, and to pay the same into the hands of Mr. Tho. Allen, the Treasurer.

Dec. 7.
9. Fair copy of the above.

Dec. [7.]
10. General order, by command of the Queen, to the adventurers in Captain Furbisher's voyages, to pay in the whole amount of their proportions in the North-west voyage, otherwise called "Meta incognita."

Dec. 7.
11. Draft of the above, corrected by Lord Burghley.

Dec. 8.
London.
12. Tho. Allen to Sir Fr. Walsyngham. Clamour of the mariners returned with Captain Furbisher, for payment of their wages. Desires order may be taken for payment of the same by the adventurers. Only one ship paid, and that is Mr. Lok's.

Dec. 9 ?
Torrewood.
13. Tho. Ridgewaye to Sir John Gilberte. Confesses to the buying of a ton of wine from a pirate.

Dec. 11.
14. Note in Burghley's hand of the effect of the decree of the City of London, relative to the traffic of the English merchants trading to Hamburgh and the Hanse Towns.

Dec. 11.
Clyfte.
15. Francis Duke of Bedford to Walsyngham. Relative to certain persons fined for dealing with pirates. Mr. Ridgeway asks two or three days before he returns answer, and the Messrs. Plomelays desire their fines may be paid by instalments of 10*l.* yearly.

Dec. 11.
London.
16. Michael Lok to same. The adventurers have not paid in their shares. The great works at Dartford are at a stand, for want of additament from the north or west. Desires special letters to Mr. Edgecome to hasten the sending of a ton thereof.

Dec. 12.
17. William Bulkeley and others, of Magdalen Coll., Cambridge, to Burghley. With complaints against Dr. Degorye Nycoolls, the Master, who had expelled them from the college.

Dec. 12.
18. Charges of disorderly conduct alleged against Dr. Nycoolls; his enmity against all Welchmen; his kine milked at the College Hall door, and his wife such a scold as to be heard all over the college.

Dec. 12.
19. Dr. Degorye Nycoolls to Burghley. In answer to the complaint of certain of the fellows. Desires the case may be heard by some one appointed by his Lordship. Is going into Cornwall.

Dec. 15.
London.
20. Michael Lok to Walsyngham. There remains in his hands no money and goods belonging to the adventurers in Mr. Furbisher's voyage, as would plainly appear from his accounts.

DOMESTIC—ELIZABETH. 609

1578.   VOL. CXXVII.

Dec. 16.   21. Sir John Tracy, and others, Commissioners for piracy in Gloucestershire, to the Council. Their proceedings in the detection of dealers with pirates. Excuse their long delay. *Inclosing,*

21. I. *Certificate of the presentments made before them relative to the dealers with pirates within the County of Gloucester.*

Dec. 17 ?   22. Geo. Putenham to Sir John Throkmarton. Is ready to submit to imprisonment if his case demands it ; otherwise, for the stay of his own credit, would rather remain at liberty. Notes of his case indorsed.

Dec 18.
London.   23. Notarial instrument of the certificate of the bailiffs of Weymouth of the capture of the Flemish ship the Tennen, of Rotterdam, off Portland Road, by Capt. Denny.

Dec. 20.
Exeter.   24. Sir John Gilberte to Walsyngham. Thanks for his letter. The fleet under the command of Sir H. Gylberte was well provisioned, and victualled for a voyage of one year. One ship left behind because it leaked.

Dec. 20 ?   25. Sir John Throkmarton to same. Has caused Putenham to be arrested ; and promises to send 40*l.* for Lady Windsor's present relief.

Dec. 20 ?   26. Articles to be administered to George Putenham, Esq., relative to his transactions with Sir John Throkmarton.

Dec. 22.   27. Answer of George Putenham to the above interrogatories, relative to his dealings with Throkmarton.

Dec. 22 ?   28. Answer of Sir John Throkmarton to similar articles, *mutatis mutandis.*

Dec. 23.
St. Paul's.   29. Sir John Throkmarton to Walsyngham. Sends the 40*l.* for Lady Windsor, and desires the process in the Exchequer against him and Putenham may be stayed.

Dec. ?   30. Note of Mr. Geo. Putenham's dealings with his brother in the purchase of Sherfield, and making over his property to Sir John Throkmarton. [*With note on the back, probably by Throkmarton.*]

Dec. ?   31. Statement of the matters between Putenham and Throkmarton relative to the dispute with Lady Windsor, drawn out in the form of two tables.

Dec. ?   32. [Richard ?] Putenham to his brother Geo. Putenham. Complains of his ungrateful conduct towards some person to whom he is under the greatest obligations. His ill conduct has estranged him from all his friends and relations.

Dec. 25.   Lease for 21 years from the Dean and Chapter of St. Paul's to John Bradley, of a piece of void ground without the South door of the Cathedral Church of St. Paul's, on which a shop or shed is now builded. [*Case C., Eliz., No.* 6.]

Dec. 31.   33. Warrant to pay the sum of 5,714*l.* 2*s.* 2*d.* yearly to John Hawkyns, Treasurer of the Navy, in the room of Benjamin Gonson, deceased.

Q Q

1578.
Dec. 31.

VOL. CXXVII.

34. Sir Giles Pole to the Council. Excuses his neglect in making certificate in the matters of piracy. Sends now a certificate; which, however, he has not himself signed.

Dec. 31.
Llanbadarn Vawr.

35. Commissioners for piracy in Cardiganshire. Have employed themselves diligently in execution of their commission; appointed deputies, &c. *Inclosing,*

35. I. *List of creeks and landing-places within the County of Cardigan, with the deputies appointed thereto.*

Dec. ?

36. Complaint of Edw. Hurrocke, of Walverswike, co. Suffolk, against Richard Norrys, in the Admiralty Court of Dover, for the unlawful sale of a boat by him, which belonged to them jointly.

37. Proposition to enforce the acts for providing armour and horse, and for regulating apparel, and to apply the forfeitures towards the repair of Dover haven.

38. Account of the whole establishment and charges of the Queen's stables in the 20th year of her reign; giving the names of offices and officers, the salaries and wages, expenses of provisions, &c.

39. Remembrances concerning the reparations necessary in the Queen's Majesty's stables, and of works to be done upon the stables at Greenwich, Reading, St. Albans, Sheene, and Chertsey.

40. A declaration of the disorders and outrages committed by Tho. Chaderton and some of his relations, assaults upon Anne Thymblebie, Ambrose Hawkins, and others.

41. Note of the yearly value of the manor of Barn Elms, in Surrey, according to Mr. Ferrer's own note.

42. Information of masses said at Winchester, at the house used by "my Ladye West."

43. List of ships belonging to the ports of Lynn and Yarmouth. [*Indorsed,* "*Ships to be licensed for Norfolk and Suffolk.*"]

44. Extracts from the statutes of a certain college, "De Incremento " stipendij custodis," &c. Reasons why the Visitor's sentence concerning the increase of the Master's stipend and the 10l., is unjust and contrary to the statutes.

45. Composition of certain towns in Kent for the provisions to be supplied for the Royal Household.

46. Composition of various shires for provisions for the Household.

47. Note of deceits in the collection of fines and amerciaments in every county, due to Her Majesty, and the remedy thereof by a grant of the same in farm to some approved honest men.

VOL. CXXVII.

1578.
Dec. ?

48. Reasons for grant for 21 years of all the county clerks offices in England and Wales. Return of exigents, making indictments, &c.

49. Heads for a declaration respecting the dangers that threaten the kingdom. Justness of war with Spain. Reasons to induce Her Majesty to enter into action with the Low Countries against the King of Spain.

50. Edward Knyght to Lord Burghley. Solicits an appointment to a waiter's place in the customs in the port of London. States his services, and the causes which have reduced him to poverty.

51. Note of business to be performed.

52. Grant by the Queen, to Wm. le Grys of the office of Clerk of the Stable. Lat.

53. Anonymous petition. Desiring the furthering of certain suits to Her Majesty; one, the sole licence of importing paper.

54. Petition of John Calvetoe to Sir Fr. Walsyngham. Desires remuneration for loss of his goods taken in a Spanish ship by Capt. Denny in Sept. 1577; which matter had been submitted to the determination of Sir Edw. Horsey and Sir Wm. Wynter.

55. Petition of Henry Marr to same. To take order with Mr. Middleton for the execution of his agreement, or that he may have the forfeiture of Middleton's bond.

56. Petition of Barnard Grave, of St. Malos, to same. That his ship and goods having been taken by the English pirate Johnaman, and recaptured and brought to Plymouth by Mr. Wm. Hawkins, desires that he may be permitted to transport the same without paying custom.

57. Petition of Sir Tho. Golding to the Queen. For a patent for 21 years of the sole right to an invention designed by him for draining of marshes, supplying towns with water, and working of mills.

58. Petition of Richard Owen of Glasewryn, in Carnarvonshire, to the Council. Complains that William Apwilliam, late Deputy-Sheriff, Richd. Vaughan Aprice, and Gryffith Vaughan, his son, had unlawfully spoiled him of his lands and living; and prays that he may be permitted to prosecute his suit, *in formâ pauperis*, against them before the Council.

59. Petition of John Mynge to Walsyngham. Giving information that Robert Browne, the messenger, obtained 40s. from Tho. Etherick, Mayor of New Romney, by threatening him with a warrantto take him before the Council.

60. Petition of Roger Clark to same. To be admitted into the Company of Merchants trading to Spain and Portugal, having failed in his application to the President and Fellowship of the Company.

VOL. CXXVII.

1578 ?

61. Petition of John Hippesley and Chas. Dudley to the Council. To be restored to the possession of a lead mine at Mendippe, in Somersetshire, sequestered upon the complaint of John Brodrippe and his partners.

62. Petition to the Queen for a licence to restrain the exportation of certain kinds of fish taken on the coasts of Devon and Cornwall.

63. Petition of the master shipwrights of the Queen's ships and others to the Council. That a corporation may be granted to them within the liberty of the Thames and other places near adjoining.

64. Petition of Nicholas Petite to Sir Fr. Walsyngham. For his order to the bailiff of St. Katherine's to restore to him his bond for appearance on the suit of William de Molins, factor for Nicholas de la Hawe, who was now gone over to France.

65. Petition of the inhabitants of Grantham to the Council. Against the taking up of horses to ride post; the practice had so increased as to become intolerable.

66. Petition of Geo. Cottell to Walsyngham. His need and necessity compel him to sue for his assistance. Is known to him by having served Mr. Wilkes and Mr. Clarke in their offices.

67. Petition of the prisoners in the King's Bench to the Council. Praying for letters to the sheriffs in every shire to appoint bailiffs to collect subscriptions for their relief.

68. Petition of the Company of Brewers of London to same. Understand that Her Majesty findeth "hersealfe greatly greved and "anoyed with the taste and smoke of the sea cooles" used in their furnaces; offer to burn no more sea coal but wood only in those brewhouses nearest to the Palace of Westminster. [*On the 27th April, 1578, the Lord Mayor was desired to confer with the Brewers as to the device of two strangers for the sparing of wood. Co. Reg.*]

69. Petition of Wm. Souche (sub-almoner to the Queen) to same. Complains that Wm. Bradstock had sued out a writ of error, and Geo. Farewell had falsely altered the records of the parsonage of Spetsbury, in Dorsetshire. Desires protection and redress.

70. The suit of the town of Colchester in Essex to Walsyngham. For confirmation of grant of two little chantries within their town, given to them by King Henry VIII. towards the erection of a school.

71. Petition of Joseph Simonelli to same. Soliciting the Queen's order to restrain Tho. Briskett from vexatious proceedings at law against him.

72. The names of the eight hoys and their tonnage from several ports in Essex and Suffolk.

Vol. CXXVII.

1578 ?
73. List of the merchants trading to the East Countries, with their rate of taxation to each.

74. Robert Purtton (servant of Sir Tho. Lucy) to Sir Fr. Walsyngham. Solicits to be released out of prison, where he is not able to maintain himself for want of money and friends.

75. Note of divers sums of money imposed upon the officers of the ordnance by information.

76. "An abstract taken by John Edgar and Wm. Hoskins, Com-
" missioners for usury and concealments against the Queen's Majesty."
That certain of the Council may be appointed to hear and determine the offences already passed by jury.

77. Mr. Wiklif and Mr. Homfrey to Walsyngham (?). Objections that might be urged against the plan for coinage of small monies; with answers to the same.

78. A paper relative to the rate of coinage at the Mint. Difference of the monies coined in Lonyson's time and by Martin. Question as to responsibility in case of defalcation. [*Mr. Martin had a patent of the office of Warden of the Mint in July* 1578.]

79. "Reasons for the repeal of a branch of the statute of
" 1 Eliz., cap. 11., that no goods should be entered in the custom
" books, in any other names than the true owners, upon pain of for-
" feiture of the value of goods so entered."

80. Note of the rate of custom payable by the Merchants Strangers.

81. Note of matters wherewith the strangers of the Dutch and French congregations in the city of Norwich are charged.

82 " Remembrances of such debts and bonds as Sir James Croft
" and his friends jointly stand in danger of." Petitions to be made by the Lady Croft in the behalf of her husband to the Queen's Majesty. [*Indorsed, "S*ʳ *James Croft's Requests."*]

83. A proportion of victuals for 100 men for five months, containing 140 days, with an estimate of the charge thereof.

84. Note of pays allowed by the Earl of Sussex over and above the ordinary names of the prisoners in the pay books.

85. An anonymous letter. The writer's master and lady and all theirs are in good health. Was sorry for the sufferings he had experienced, and that he had not continued with them where he would have been welcome. [*Indorsed " Lettre unknowen ;" and then added in Lord Burghley's hand, " Qȝe—Who wrote this ?"*]

86. Observations in the cause in controversy between Bushie and Sir Edmund Brudnell; that the latter abused Sir Walter Mildmay, abused his wife, and abused Meers.

87. List of the ancient lords and nobility of England, with description of their arms.

Vol. CXXVII.

1578 ?   88. Causes which moved the Merchant Adventurers to obtain privileges at Embden and Hamburgh, and proofs that the passages from Embden into Germany and Italy are as commodious as those from Hamburgh : together with reasons to prove that the stay of the traffic to Hamburgh will not hinder the vent of commodities of this realm.

89. Names of the gentlemen possessing lands in the County of Chester, and who do not reside within the same. Names of Her Majesty's wards.

Vol. CXXVIII. 1578.

1578.   A thin MS. volume relating to the Cinque Ports, purporting to be written in the year 1578. Containing :—

1. "The copie of the Chartoure of the Five Portes, written in Anno " Domini MDLXXVIII." This is the inspeximus Charter of King Edward VI., dated the 20th November, 1548, reciting the Cinque Port Charters from the 6th of King Edward I., dated the 27th June, 1278.

2. Clause of "The Chartoure of the Five Portes to be free de tota " venditione suo Achato et Reachato et de toto mercato suo, graunted " to the Barons of the Portes, decimo septimo die Junij Anno " VII° Edwardi Primi, A Dñi, 1278."

"And after, that is to saie the firste yere of Richarde the Seconde, " A° Dñi 1377, the Citie of London had theire Chfe of foren " boughte and foren solde."

"So the Chartoure of the Portes is elder than the Chfe of London " XCIX yeres and more."

3. "Theise bin the usages of the cominaltie of the towne of Rie, " used the time oute of minde wch menns myndes cannot thincke " the contrarye." This is a long and curious collection of the bye-laws relating to the rights and privileges of the borough, and is termed "The CUSTUMALL of Rye."

4. The "peticions of the Barons of the Cinque Portes, holden at " Westminster in Easter terme the XXXI. yere of Kinge Edwarde the " Thirde." Containing the complaints of the Barons of the Cinque Ports against the factious dealing of the corporation of Yarmouth, a member of the Cinque Ports, inviolating the privileges of the ports, and resisting the authority of the Barons ; with the DITE or decree of the King upon each article of complaint.

5. "Here is thordinaunce of the Parliamente holden at Westm^r·, in " the terme of Easter, the yere of Kinge Edwarde the Thirde the " XXXVI." Regulating the herring fishery and vendition of herrings in the town and port of Yarmouth, and the privileges of the Barons of the Cinque Ports in the Fair of Yarmouth ; with copy of the King's grant for holding that fair.

VOL. CXXIX.   JANUARY—FEBRUARY, 1579.

1579.
Jan. 1.
1. William Cecill to his father. Promises to be diligent in his studies. Wishes his father a happy new year. Lat. [*Supposed to be Wm. Cecill, eldest son of Sir Thomas Cecill, second Lord Burghley and Earl of Exeter.*]

Jan. 2.
Mount Edgcombe.
2. Edw. Fenton to the Council. Reports his endeavours to obtain a supply of ore in the Western Counties to mix with the gold ore brought home by Furbisher. *Incloses,*

    2. I. *Calendar of several sorts of ores sent up in bags to London from Cornwall by Mr. Fenton.*

Jan. 7.
Carew.
3. Sir John Perrot, and other Commissioners for piracy in the County of Pembroke, to the Council. Report of their proceedings, with certain presentments and other matters touching piracies. *Inclosing,*

    3. I. *Presentments taken before Sir John Perrot, and others, concerning the persons accused of aiding and dealing with the pirates Hexte and Clarke, in co. Pembroke.* 12 Dec. 1578.

    3. II. *Note of the matters found and proved against the persons (named in a former schedule sent from the Council) as to the value of their lands and goods.*

[Jan. 13.]
Richmond.
4. The Council to the Earl of Pembroke and others. Requiring them forthwith to pay in the amount of their adventures in Capt. Furbisher's voyage. [*Headed, "The second minute for this purpose." In the Council Register a minute of this letter is entered on the 13th Jan., 1579, addressed to the Earl of Pembroke, Sir John Brockett, and others.*]

Jan. 13.
5. Matthew Fyeld to Sir Fr. Walsyngham. Has paid the 67*l.* 10*s.* due by him for Mr. Furbisher's voyage to Mr. Lok, before the receipt of his letter.

Jan. 13.
Exeter.
6. Edw. Fenton to the Council. Mr. Edgcombe has found the place of the ore delivered to Mr. Burcot, and offers to provide and deliver the ore at Dartford at his own charges.

Jan. 13.
Exeter.
7. Same to Walsyngham. His doings in Cornwall and the Western Counties to procure the ore. Wishes, if Mr. Edgcombe's offer is accepted, he might be employed in some service about the ore.

Jan. 13.
London.
8. Sir Lionel Duckett, and others, to same. That Sir Tho. Gresham had paid the 80*l.* required of him for his share in Furbisher's voyage.

Jan. 13.
London.
9. Tho. Allen to same. Slanderous accusations of him by Mr. Furbisher. Desires Furbisher's accounts should be audited and compared with those of Mr. Lok.

Jan. 13.
10. Declaration of the Bourgmasters and Council of the town of Hornes, relative to the Flemish merchant vessel taken by Capt. Denny off Portland Road. French.

Vol. CXXIX.

1579.
Jan. 14.
Limehouse.
11. Wm. Borowgh to Sir Fr. Walsyngham. Desires that his share of the charges in Mr. Furbisher's voyage may be subtracted from the money owing to him by Mr. Lok. Requests payment of the sum of 106*l.* still remaining due to him.

Jan. 14.
London.
12. Michael Lok to same. His adventure in Furbisher's last voyage amounted to 316*l.* 5*s.*, which he had already paid. Desires that the Earl of Oxford might be called upon for 450*l.* residue of the sum demanded.

Jan. 15.
Norwich.
13. Commissioners for piracy in the County of Norfolk to the Council. Their doings in levying the fines assessed on the dealers with and aiders of pirates. *Inclosing,*

13. I. *Certificate of the names of those that have paid their fines, of those that refuse, &c.*

Jan. 16.
Norwich.
14. Same to same. In behalf of John Parker, who it appears was ignorant of any illegality in the purchase of the fly-boat of Captain Bellingham.

Jan. 18.
15. Edmund Rockrey to Lord Burghley. Complains that the Master of Queen's Coll., Cam., molested him in his fellowship, because he also held a small prebend in the Cathedral of Rochester. *Incloses,*

15. I. *Certain articles respecting his right to retain the fellowship, extracted from the ancient statutes of the University.*

Jan. 20.
16. Edmund Coortesse, Vicar of Cuckfield, to the Lord Chief Justice, and rest of the Judges. Praying they would admit his complaint and answers to certain pretended articles exhibited against him by Edward Boyer and others. *Incloses,*

16. I. *Certificate of the parishioners of Cuckfield, co. Sussex, of the usefulness and pious labours of the Rev. Mr. Coortesse, Vicar of that parish. May* 24, 1576.

Jan. 22.
Truro.
17. Commissioners for piracy in the County of Cornwall to the Council. Certify their doings in levying the fines assessed on the dealers with and aiders of pirates. *Inclosing,*

17. I. *Certificate of the names of those that have paid their fines, for dealing with pirates, and of those that refuse.*

Jan. 22.
18. Same for the Liberties of the Cinque Ports to same. Appearance of various persons to answer for the fines levied on them for dealing with pirates. Some refuse and others are unable to pay.

Jan. 24.
London.
19. Sir Walter Mildmay to same. Necessity of a reformation in the weights for standard gold throughout the realm, and to prevent the clipping of the current coin. Proposed new management of the Mint.

Jan. 26.
Moscow.
Observations from Moscow respecting the voyage of Captain Furbisher to the North-west. The lands visited by him were under the dominion of Russia. Offence given by his taking away a man, woman, and child. [*See Russia, this date.*]

DOMESTIC—ELIZABETH. 617

VOL. CXXIX.

1579.
Jan. 26.
St. Bees.
20. James Gryndall to Francis Chaloner or Robt. Farnham. Urges them to protect the interest of his master in procuring due payment of the rent of the salt pans at St. Bees, farmed by Henry Was and Ric. Bowecocke. Suit against James Shelton for the tythes of Hensingham. Particulars of various rents and payments.

Jan. 27.
London.
21. Andrew Palmer to Lord Burghley and Sir Fr. Walsyngham. Cannot agree in opinion with Mr. Lonison respecting the weights for gold. Desires that the matter may be subject to a new inquiry.

Jan. 28.
Erwarton.
22. Sir Philip Parker to Walsyngham. Thanks him for his letter and his favourable opinion of him. Declares his innocency of the charge laid against him of dealing with pirates. *Incloses,*

22. I. *The presentment of the Commissioners in causes of piracy against Sir P. Parker, and his answer to the same.*

Jan. 30.
23. Dr. Wm. Chatterton to Burghley. Explains the circumstances of Mr. Rockrey resigning his fellowship at Queen's College. *Incloses,*

23. I. *Copy of the statute of Queen's College as to holding fellowships; with legal opinions thereon.*

Jan. 31.
Newton.
24. Commissioners for piracy in Carmarthenshire to the Council. Report their proceedings in execution of their commission. *Inclosing,*

24. I. *Presentments of the Jury on the articles given to the Commissioners for suppression of piracy in the County of Carmarthen.*

24. II. *Examination of John Lloyd, and others, before the Commissioners for suppression of piracy in Carmarthenshire.*

Jan.
25. Table of certain dispensations to be utterly abolished, as not agreeable to Christian religion, in the opinion of the Lords of the Council.

Jan.
26. Copy of preceding; together with a note of the order of proceeding from the Queen's Palace of Westminster to the Monastery there, at the time of Parliament.

Jan.
27. Petition of William Lytlestone to Burghley. For a grant of a lease of a certain value in reversion, or a licence for the transportation of calf skins, in consideration of his giving up his patent for the exportation of grain.

Jan. ?
28. Brief declaration of the total charges of Her Majesty's wardrobe due upon the accompt of John Fortescue, Esq., Master of the same, ended at Michaelmas last, and from Michaelmas to the Christmas following.

Jan.
29. Certificate of taking the oath of Thomas Markham, Sheriff of the County of Nottingham. Lat.

Feb. 3.
Matharn.
30. Wm. Blethyn Bishop of Landaff to Walsyngham. His endeavours to apprehend Popish and massing priests in Monmouth and Glamorgan. Roland Morgan, a determined Papist.

618 DOMESTIC—ELIZABETH.

1579. VOL. CXXIX.
Feb. 6. 31. Justices of Norfolk to the Council. Have examined Wm.
Baconsthorpe. Peirson as to his dealings with pirates. The country is quiet, and corn sold for a reasonable price. *Inclosing,*

  31. I. *Wm. Peirson's confession of his dealings with George Phipson the pirate. Feb. 2.*

Feb. 7. 32. Certificate by Henry Killigrew of the money remaining in his hands for fines upon persons for aiding pirates.

Feb. 8. 33. Commissioners for piracy in the County of Monmouth to the Council. Execution of their commission. Have appointed deputies in the various ports. *Inclosing,*

  33. I. *List of all the havens, creeks, and landing-places in the County of Monmouth, with the deputies appointed thereto.*

Feb. 9. 34. Indenture between Queen Elizabeth and Alexander Nowell, Dean, and the Chapter of St. Paul's. Grant of the manor of Barnes in Surrey, with its appurtenances in the parishes of Barnes, Putney, and Mortlake. Lat.

Feb. 9. 35. Note of the munition and other necessaries requisite for the furniture of Dover Castle, and of the ordnance, shot, and powder remaining in the castle.

Feb. 10. 36. Inventory of the furniture, munition, &c., belonging to the ship the Ayde, as she was bought of the Queen's Majesty in April 1577; and estimate of the value of the same by Sir Wm. Wynter and Wm. Holstok.

Feb. 10. 37. Inventory of the furniture, munition, &c. belonging to the Gabriel ; and the estimated value of the same.

Feb. 10. 38. Inventory of the furniture, munition, &c. belonging to the Judith ; and the estimated value of the same.

Feb. 10. 39. Inventory of the furniture, munition, &c. of the Michael ; and the estimated value of the same.

Feb. [13.] 40. Notes and points to prove the fraudulent and double dealings of Mr. Ste. Thimblebye, with Wm. Fearne, about the rectory of Belton.

Feb. 15 41. Minute of a conference had between certain of the University and the Mayor and others of the town of Cambridge, in presence of Lord Burghley, the Earl of Leicester, and Lord North, upon certain doubts on the several articles drawn up, in regard to Sturbridge Fair.

Feb. 17. 42. Commission of Oyer and Terminer for the Counties of Denbigh and Flint : addressed to the Bishops of Bangor and St. Asaph, Geo. Bromley, and others. Lat.

Feb. 17. 43. Amount of the gold, silver, &c. obtained from one ton of the ore brought by Capt. Furbisher, and melted at Dartford.

DOMESTIC—ELIZABETH. 619

1579.   VOL. CXXIX.

Feb. 18. 44. Michael Lok to Sir Fr. Walsyngham. Sends report of the
London. auditors on his accounts. Their hard dealing. Requests him to
examine his answer, and then to lay it before the Council. *Incloses,*

    44. I. *The answer of Michael Lok upon the second audit of his accounts by the Commissioners. Details at great length the history of the three voyages of Furbisher.* 20 Jan. 1579.

Feb. 21. 45. Certificate by Henry Killigrew of the money remaining in his hands for fines assessed on the aiders and dealers with pirates in Suffolk and Hampshire.

Feb. 24. Notes in the case *ex parte* Yarmouth *versus* Gorleston, and other towns in Lothingland, as to the exclusive privilege of unloading ships in harbour claimed by Yarmouth. [*See Dom. Eliz., Vol.* xlv., *p.* 7.]

Feb. 24. 46. Decree of the Privy Council upon a matter in controversy between the town of Great Yarmouth in Norfolk, and the towns of Gorleston and Little Yarmouth and other towns in Suffolk.

Feb. 28. 47. Proclamation by the Queen, declaring the renewal of the ancient
Westminster. free intercourse with the Low Countries, and prohibiting the pulling or clipping of wool or woolfels from Shrove Tuesday to the last day of June in every year.

Feb. ? 48. Petition of John Coysgarne to the Council. Against Chr. Jenye for cancelling a statute of 3,000*l.* and wrongfully detaining from him an indenture of covenants &c. Desires that Mr. Jenye may be called to answer.

    49. Names of such English merchants as trade into Normandy, in the dominions of the King of France.

Feb. 50. Relation of the abuses now existing in the trade of merchants into France ; with proposals for remedying the same, by the incorporation of a Company of the Mere Merchants.

    51. Petitions of the Mere Merchants trading to France. That they may be incorporated by the name of " Provost, Assistants and Fellow-" ship of English Merchants trading to France," with certain liberties and immunities.

Feb. 52. Substance of the matter in controversy between the merchants and the citizens of Chester trading to Spain and Portugal.

    53. Petition of the Mere Merchants of Chester to Walsyngham. That the retailers may be restrained from trading to Spain and Portugal as merchants; or else the Mere Merchants may be licensed to deal as retailers.

VOL. CXXX.   MARCH—APRIL, 1579.

1579.
March 6.   1. Sir Fr. Walsyngham to Bishop Coortesse. Desires him to deprive the Vicar of Cuckfield, in the diocese of Chichester, for his unworthiness; and to appoint Mr. Robinson, a man of very rare gifts, to succeed him in that vicarage.

March 6.   2. "Note of the lewd Vicar of Cuckfield in Sussex:" void of all learning and discretion, a scoffer at singing of psalms, a seeker to witches, a drunkard, infected with a loathsome disease, &c.

March 10.
London.   3. Anthony Gamage, and others, retailers of linen cloth in London, to Sec. Wylson. Against the granting of a corporation and exclusive privilege of a trade to France by the traders calling themselves " Mere Merchants." *Incloses*,

3. I. *Considerations whether it be advisable to grant the exclusive right of trade to France to the Company of Mere Merchants.*

March 12.
Whitehall.   The Council to the Justices of Assize. Requiring them to hear the complaint of Richard Knight against Thomas and John Blagrave, for carrying off their corn and fodder. [*See Vol.* xlv., *p.* 9.]

March 16.   4. Interrogatories to be ministered to Robert Harward, servant to Edmond Windham, as to the latter going armed with a dag to shoot at Lord Rich.

March 17.   5. Answer of Robert Harward to the above; and depositions of witnesses on the part of Lord Rich, relative to the affray with Edm. Windham.

March 17.   6. Articles to be objected on the part of Lord Rich against Mr. Windham. Desire of Lord Rich that they may be examined by the Council before Mr. Windham is liberated out of prison.

March (18.)   7. Declaration of Mr. Windham, under his own hand, of his affray with Lord Rich.

March 19.   8. Examination of Edw. Mordant and others, Lord Rich's servants, relative to the affray with Windham.

March 19.   9. Deposition of Henry Aldersey, witness on the part of Mr. Windham.

March 20.   10. Tho. Allen to Walsyngham. Sale of the ordnance and ship Gabriel. Many things yet remaining in Mr. Lok's hands might be sold.

March 21.   11. Deposition by Robert Harward, relative to the affray between his master and Lord Rich.

March 22.   12. Certificate by H. Killigrew of the money remaining in his hands for fines paid by the aiders of pirates.

March 23.   13. Petition of Henry Topclyff to the Council. Has been in prison nineteen months at the suit of Tho. Brodway *alias* George, for paying 35*l.* to Harman Van Oldensell. Desires that Brodway may not be discharged till he sets him at liberty.

March 24.   14. Declaration by Dr. Roger Goade, Provost of King's College, of the cause why Stephen Lake was deprived of his Fellowship in King's College, Cambridge.

DOMESTIC—ELIZABETH.

VOL. CXXX.

1579.
March 24. 15. Certificate by Jonas Schutz of the amount of gold and silver contained in two cwt. of ore brought home by Furbisher.

March [25.] 16. Note of the money paid to Mr. Lok, and remaining to be paid to Mr. Allen, by the Adventurers in Capt. Furbisher's three voyages; with the names of the Adventurers.

March [25.] 17. Relation of the abuses committed by Capt. Furbisher in the direction of the affairs committed to him by the Adventurers, for the bringing of ore and discovery of new lands; and the slanders by him against Mr. Lok.

March [25.] 18. Petition of Michael Lok to the Council. His exertions in promoting Furbisher's voyages. Prays that 1,200*l.* may be allowed on his accounts for the expenses incurred; having nothing in the world else to support himself, his wife, and fifteen children.

March [25.] 19. Statement of M. Lok's account of the money invested and expended by him in behalf of the Company of Adventurers in Capt. Furbisher's voyages.

March [25.] 20. Brief of the grant of incorporation and liberties by the Queen to Adrian Gilbert and others, to trade with the newly discovered lands in the North-west, and the discovery of a North-west passage.

March 28. 21. Sir Tho. Gresham, and others, to the Council. Order taken for
London. payment of the mariners. Desire that the Adventurers who have not yet paid, should be admonished to deliver in their contributions without delay. Offers of Mr. John Barton to make proof of the ore at Dartford. [*Signed by Sir Thomas Gresham, Dr. Dee the mathematician, Martin Frobisher, and others of celebrity.*]

March 30. 22. Bishop Coortesse to Sir Fr. Walsyngham. Prays to be relieved
Cherisworth. from the task of displacing the Vicar of Cuckfield, and that the whole case may be referred to the decision of Dr. Becon.

March. 23. Articles of objections against William Whittingham, Dean of Durham, as to the insufficiency of his ordination according to the practice of the Genevan church: with his answers.

March ? 24. Note of confessions and proofs against Mr. William Whittingham, Dean of Durham, in the Queen's Majesty's visitation of the Church of Durham.

March. 25. A MS. book of 39 folios with the title "The Prosecution of " William Tipper's suit to the Lord Mayor and Aldermen of London " for the hostage of merchants strangers," containing the history of his grant; objections to it; opinion of the Judges; correspondence with Flanders, and other papers relating to the same.

March ? 26. Estimate of expenses for provision of timber for the works to be carried on at Dover.

April 3. 27. Mr. Francis Godolphyn to Walsyngham. Desires that the
Launceston. difference between him and Mr. Edwd. Barkley, relative to the Scilly Isles, may be referred to his arbitration and Lord Burghley's.

1579.   Vol. CXXX.

April 3. 28. Dr. Goade to Lord Burghley. Mr. Stephen Lake, expelled from
King's College, King's College, has repaired to the Court to petition against him.
Cambridge. Desires that the hearing of the cause may be undertaken by his
Lordship. Expulsion of Mr. Harrison.

April 3. 29. Note of money received by Mr. Sommer and Mr. Windebank at
the Hanaper, for bills passed immediately, from the 19th of Feb. to the
3rd of Apr. 1579.

April 4. 30. Precedent of a warrant for calling a Parliament, in the vacancy
of the Lord Keeper, in 1° Eliz., and the same to Lord Burghley and
Earl of Leicester, 4 Apl. 1579.

April 5. 31. Note of cast iron ordnance sold under the licence of Mr. Wm.
Pistor, for exportation.

April 5. 32. Dr. Richard Howlande to Burghley. States the inconveniences
St. John's likely to result from establishing two fellowships for the law in St.
Coll. John's College, Cambridge.

April 7. 33. Answer given by the Council to the Deputies and Company of
Merchants Adventurers, touching their suit to restrain all persons
trading from England to any place between Embden and the Skawe.

April 8. 34. Bond of Robert Jones and John Roffe for Phillip Conway to
keep the peace towards William Gransham, a messenger of the
Chamber.

April 8. 35. Dr. Howlande to Burghley. Informs him of the particulars of
St. John's two elections to fellowships in their college.
Coll.

April 9. 36. Orders of Council respecting the passing of such things to Hamburgh as were intended to be transported before the restraint.

April 14. 37. Sir Richard Pype, Lord Mayor of London, to Burghley.
Requests licence to transport 500 quarters of damaged wheat, belonging to the city of London.

April 14. 38. Licence from James Cardinal Sabellus, the Pope's Vicar, to
Edward Reshton, authorizing him to say mass in England. Lat.

April 20. 39. Archbishop Sandys to Sir Fr. Walsyngham. Intention of Aylmer
Bishopsthorpe. Bishop of London to sue out a commission against him for dilapidations. His expenditure while Bishop of London, and many favors
and benefits conferred by him on Aylmer. Aylmer's ingratitude.

April 23. 40. Names of those Lords who have held the office of Lieutenants
on St. George's day in the Queen's absence at the Court, from the 12th
to the 21st year of her reign.

April 23. 41. Commissioners for piracy in Monmouthshire to the Council.
Usk. Have received and transmitted to Mr. Killegrew the sums for fines
for piracy. Names of such as are absent, or not to be found.

April 25. 42. Note of the sums remaining unpaid by the Adventurers in
Capt. Furbisher's voyages at the 25th of April; and of the balances due
from Mr. Lok.

DOMESTIC—ELIZABETH. 623

1579.   Vol. CXXX.

April 29.   43. Lists of prisoners committed for disobedience in matters of religion and discharged, from Apr. 30, 1577, to Apr. 29, 1579, and of those still remaining in the Fleet.

April 30.
Truro.   44. Commissioners for piracy in Cornwall to the Council. Have taken examinations and made inquiries concerning the complaints exhibited by John Thompson and Henry Dromont against one Grainger and Capt. Maris, pirates. *Inclosing,*

             44. I. *Examinations concerning pirates' goods landed at Helford and Falmouth by Marice and Grainger.*

             44. II. *Presentments of James Trypconye and others, deputies for the haven of Hayleford or Helford, touching piracies.*

             44. III. *Certificates by the Commissioners of proceedings in matters of piracy, and the value of pirates' estates.*

April 30.   45. Testimonial of Bishop Freke, the Mayor of Norwich, and others, declaring the great losses sustained by John Wakeman, merchant of Great Yarmouth, on the seas.

April.   46. The Council to the Adventurers in Furbisher's last voyage to the North-west, requiring those who have not yet paid up their shares to sign their names to a bill as security for the payment of their adventure

     47. Another copy.

April?   48. State of Mr. Hasting's suit for assurance in establishing the manufacture of frizados at Christ's Church in Hampshire, which he had introduced out of Holland.

     49. Proposed plan for the increase of Her Majesty's revenue, by the grant of parsonages impropriate, in fee-farm, at double rents.

     50. Petition of the Masters, Pilots, and Seamen of the Trinity House of Newcastle-upon-Tyne, to the Earl of Lincoln, Lord High Admiral. That the controversy between them and the Mayor, &c. of the said town, relative to their charter, may be heard at the next Star Chamber day.

     51. The Chancellor of Cambridge to the Vice-Chancellor. Directs him to take measures for enforcing the more punctual payment of commons by the pensioners and students.

April.   52. Certificate of examination of Mary (or Mercy) Gould, relative to concealment of the birth of her bastard child; imputing to the wife of Henry Boyer the administering drinks to procure abortion.

DOMESTIC—ELIZABETH.

VOL. CXXXI. MAY—AUGUST, 1579.

1579.
May 2.   1. Recognizance of John Christmas, of Colchester, for his appearance before the Council; taken before John Lord Darcy of Chiche, and others.

May 2.
Lewes.   2. Justices of Sussex to the Council. Contemptuous speeches against Her Majesty, supposed to have been spoken by John Turner in taking possession of the chapel and lands of Bramblety House for Lord Buckhurst. *Inclosing,*

> 2. I–XIII. *Thirteen depositions by Katharine Pycas, and others, touching certain seditious words said to have been spoken by John Turner against the Queen, in taking forcible possession of Bramblety Chapel and lands.*

May 7.   3. Grant of arms to Richard Johnson, Esq., of Gainsbrowe, in Lincolnshire, by William Flower, Norroy King-at-Arms.

May 7.
Cambridge.   4. Dr. Tho. Byng to Lord Burghley. Proceedings with the corporation of Cambridge, relative to enclosing Jesus Green. The corporation claim to be chief lords of the soil.

May 10.   5. Petition of Wm. Knight and Peter Hall, merchants of the Stillyard, to the Council. Desire that some order may be taken to indemnify them for their losses sustained by pirates, and for restitution of cloths concealed in Mr. Debdin's house, at Somerton, in Norfolk. *Inclosing,*

> 5. I. II. *Examinations of John Barle and William Ellis, about landing goods from a ship at Winterton, and conveying the same to Debdin's house.*

May 10.   6. Tho. Oglethorpe to his father Henry Oglethorpe. Has left Douay and entered the English seminary at Rheims. Tho. Wright has become a Jesuit at Rome. *Incloses,*

> 6. I. "*An Exhortation to his well beloved uncle Mr. Wm. Ogle-*
> "*thorpe, parson of Killington; advising him to consider*
> "*his woeful and damnable case, to leave vice & follow virtue*
> "*and honestness, whereby he may come to the eternal and*
> "*everlasting kingdom of Heaven.*"

May 11.   7. Wm. Lowre to the Council. Has taken order for the payment of the fines imposed upon Peter Killigrew, Oliver Carmynowe, Tho. Lowre, and Tho. Davy, for dealing with pirates.

May 15.
Westminster.   Lisle Cave to Robert Smythe. Professions of friendship by the bearer, to whom he refers him for intelligences. [*See France, Vol.* li., *p.* 108.]

May 16.
Blackfriars.   8. Lord Cobham to Sir Fr. Walsyngham. Against Francis Bolton, who has hitherto escaped payment of his fine by making a false declaration. *Incloses,*

> 8. I. *Note of the quantity of herrings bought by Francis Bolton, and of the fine set upon him for the same.*
>
> 8. II. III. *Depositions of Peter Nevoe and Nowel du Pont, as to sale of certain herrings to Francis Bolton.*

VOL. CXXXI.

1579.
May 17.
9. Petition of Mr. Edward Barkley to the Council. Touching his claim to a portion of the Isles of Scilly. Solicits a grant of the farm of the whole Isles. *Incloses,*

  9. I. *A note proving the title of the co-heirs of Tho. Whittington to the castle and Isles of Scilly.*

May 19.
10. Orders agreed on between Sir Fr. Walsyngham, Tho. Wylson, Sec. of State, and Tho. Randolphe, Master of the Posts, relative to the conveyance of letters or packets into France and Flanders.

May 19?
11. The order taken with Wm. Meo, post at Chester, for the posting and bringing to the Court such letters as shall arrive or be brought from Ireland directed for Her Majesty's affairs.

May 21.
Cambridge.
12. Dr. Thomas Byng to Lord Burghley. Further particulars about the common of Jesus Green at Cambridge, the fences for inclosure of which have been removed.

May 24.
Warham.
13. Mr. Henry Howard to same. Stay of the sale of the manor of Colequit by his father, to which he was no party.

May 27.
14. Bishop Aylmer to Walsyngham. Desires a commission for his cause of dilapidations against the Archbishop of York, late Bp. of London.

May 29.
15. Certain questions resolved for the Archbp. of Canterbury; being legal opinions respecting the dilapidations of a bishoprick. Lat.

May 29.
16. Copy of the above.

May 29.
17. Complaint of John Le Syra in the name of Eustace Travache, and others, in the Admiralty Court against Tho. Bicketon. Lat.

May 31.
Cuckfield.
18. Edmund Coortesse, Vicar of Cuckfield, to Walsyngham. Complains of the evil informations against him by such as were at enmity with him for punishing their evil doings. Desires a commission to inquire into his behaviour. Cannot surrender up his cure, as suggested by Lord Buckhurst, without committing simony.

May.
19. Drs. Tho. Byng and Andrew Perne to Burghley. Recommend Doctor Legg to be his commissary at Cambridge, in place of Dr. Ithell, deceased.

May.
20. Circumstantial account of the three voyages of Capt. Furbisher; of the ill success attending them by his mismanagement; of the proceedings in melting and assaying the ore brought home, ill usage of Mr. Lok and others; charges against him of arrogance, obstinacy in his government at sea, and unbearable insolence in all his doings.

June 3.
Bishopsthorpe.
21. Archbishop Sandys to Walsyngham. Desires him to move Her Majesty for the stay of the course which the Bishop of London intends against him for dilapidations. Solicits him to arbitrate in the matter.

R R

1579.

June 3? 22. Extract of the several papers concerning the case of dilapidations in controversy between the Archbp. of York and the Bp. of London.

June 12. 23. John Darell (son-in-law to the late Bp. of Winchester) to Lord Burghley. Desires that the process for recovery of the late Bishop's debts may be stayed, and that some convenient time should be appointed for payment of the same. [*Le Neve's Fasti, on the authority of the epitaph printed by Godwin, states Bishop Horn to have died on the 1st of June* 1580.]

June 14. 24. The Council to a Messenger of the Chamber. Warrant to bring up in custody all such as refuse to conform to the orders established for regulation of the company of merchants trading to Spain and Portugal.

June 15. 25. Examination of Tho. Asheleye, taken before Eustace Clovill, Esq., Justice of the Peace in Essex, touching certain evidences conveyed away by Mrs. Field from Dr. Atslowe's house, after his apprehension.

June 15. 26. Henry Bowyer to his brother Simon Bowyer. Has been unjustly charged by Coortesse, vicar of Cuckfield, in the case of Mercy Gold. The matter touching his wife is untrue and odious. Particulars of the whole case. *Incloses*,

26. I. *Copy of the certificate returned by the jury of women who examined Mercy Gold, for concealing the birth of a bastard child.*

June 21. 27. Tho. Might to the Earl of Sussex, Lord Chamberlain. Beseeches him for the love of God to speak to Walsyngham to move Her Majesty for an end to his long suit.

June 22. 28. Consideration of the second and third articles of the decree of Council respecting the trade of the Merchants of the Stillyard, and of the Merchants Adventurers, during the suspension of commercial intercourse with Hamburgh.

June 23. Exemplification of a decree of court revoking the grant of a market and fair for the town of Sittingbourne, being prejudicial to the market and fair held in the town and hundred of Middleton alias Milton, co. Kent. [*Case* C., *Eliz.* No. 7.]

June 26. 29. The Wardens, &c. of the Bakers' Comp. of London to Burghley. Certify that 80 quarters of wheat belonging to Mr. John Byrde were unfit to be uttered within the City.

June ? 30. Points for the consideration of Sir John Throkmarton on behalf of Geo. Putenham, with a view to a final settlement of the controversy with Lady Windsor; with Throkmarton's answers and observations in the margin.

June ? 31. Further note of petitions to be urged by Throkmarton on Putenham's behalf, when all the former points have been urged. [*The final agreement of both parties was made and signed on the* 13*th July* 1579, *and is entered in the Council Register of that date.*]

DOMESTIC—ELIZABETH. 627

VOL. CXXXI.

1579.
June ? 32. Points drawn up by Geo. Putenham for the private consideration and guidance of Sir John Throkmarton, in his appearance before the Council, for the settlement of the disputes between Putenham and Lady Windsor, his wife.

June. 33. Vehement presumptions, taken out of the examinations, concerning the murdering of Richard Mellershe and his son Tho. Mellershe. [*New examinations of persons suspected of murdering the Mellershes were ordered to be taken* 11 *June* 1579. *Co. Reg.*]

June ? 34. Petition of Katherine Hopkinson to Sir Fr. Walsyngham. Praying for licence for return of her husband, John Hopkinson, a reader of the Hebrew, Chaldee, Syriac, and Greek languages, who had been induced by papists and seminaries to go abroad without licence. *Annexed,*

July 1. 34. I. *Certificate, signed by Lancelot Andrewes and several others, in favour of Hopkinson, who had dwelled in Grub Street, St. Giles's, quietly and civilly.*

July 1.
The Bench. 35. Augustino Dinale to the Council. Prays to be relieved, being a poor debtor imprisoned at the suit of one Innocent Comy.

July 13. 36. Deposition of Anthony Style before Sir Fr. Walsyngham, touching certain presentments taken by the commission for matters of piracy in Norfolk, remaining in the keeping of William Heydon. Bonds of the pirates Ellis and Dibden.

July [15 ?] 37. Petition of Jaspar Waryne to the Council. Prays to be released from the Fleet, being committed for certain matters objected against him by Lord North [*Jaspar Waryne or Warren was committed to close custody in the Fleet* 22 *June* 1579. *Co. Reg.*]

July 19. 38. Inventory of the goods and merchandize found in certain houses in the town of Aldborough, Suffolk.

July 20. [The Council ?] to the Treasurer of the Navy. To take up materials and impress artificers for erecting a fort at Sheerness, for defence of the navy lying at Gillingham. [*See Vol.* xlv., *p.* 15.]

July 23. 39. Offers made by Wm. Awcher, Anthony Seyntleger, and others, for lease of Shurland House, and the lands formerly belonging to Lord Cheyne, within the isle of Sheppey.

July 23. 40. Another copy.

July 23 ? 41. Certain offers to be made to Her Majesty's Council, concerning the isles of Sheppey. Conditions of a lease to be made of Shurland House, and the lands formerly belonging to Lord Cheyne.

July 24.
Abergwilly. 42. Bishop Davies to Lord Burghley. Answers to the articles exhibited against him by Mr. Fabian Phillips. Ill conduct of Phillips in all public places. *Incloses,*

42. I. *Articles exhibited by Mr. Fabian Phillips against the Bishop of St. David's, with the Bishop's answer to the same, and copy of letter to Phillips, dated* 23 *July* 1578.

R

VOL. CXXXI.

1579.
July 25. The Council to Wm. Heydon and Nathaniel Bacon. To take order
Greenwich. between Reginald Metcalf of Thetford and Bartholomew Baxter, concerning the tythes of the benefice of Santon. [*See* 31*st May*, 1580.]

July 25. 43. Henry Blower, prisoner in the Marshalsea (who accused Hardyng), to Mr. Sec. Wylson. Desires to be liberated on account of his distressed condition. [*On* 25*th July* 1579, *a warrant was directed to the Knight Marshal to release H. Blower out of prison. Co. Reg.*]

July 26. 44. Petition of Tho. Standley to the Council. Desiring letters to assist him in the recovery of certain goods stolen from him when the ship called The Symond of Colborough, in Pomerland, was wrecked off the coast of Norfolk.

July 26. 45. Orders thought meet to be put in execution for the avoiding of such depredations as are committed by such as go to the seas under pretence to discover new trades.

July 27. 46. Doctor John Still to Lord Burghley. Solicits his advice as to
Trinity College. the election of a Divinity Lecturer in place of Dr. Chaderton. The most eligible candidates are Dr. Fulke and Dr. Barowe, the Frenchman. Thinks it might be some disgrace to the University to elect a stranger.

July 28. 47. Estimate of the charges for the equipment of 4 of Her Majesty's ships to be employed on the seas for two months.

July. 48. Mr. Carleton's memorial to the Council, for letters to be sent to the Bp. of Ely, John Payton, and others, for the scouring and banking of the river of Wisbeach. Removal of Dr. Feckenham.

July. 49. Account of the loans lately made by Her Majesty out of the Exchequer, as well to foreign states as to her own subjects.

July. 50. Petition of Annies Actton, widow, to the Council. For release of her son, Barnaby Actton, a prisoner in the Marshalsea, for being in company with Tho. Appletree, when he shot off the piece upon the water, to the danger of the Queen. [*This occurrence happened on the* 17*th July* 1579.]

July. 51. Tho. Appletree's petition to the Earl of Leicester. That he may be freed from his imprisonment in the Marshalsea, to which he had been committed for shooting unadvisedly, to the danger of the Queen, but for which he had received Her Majesty's pardon.

July ? 52. Lord Burghley (?) to   . To restrain the shipment of any kind of merchandize from that or any other port to Hamburgh, by reason of the suspension of all traffic with that city, in consequence of their ill usage of the Merchant Adventurers.

August 6. 53. Bassyngborne Gaudy to Leicester. Desires him to procure the
Westharling. enlargement of his brother-in-law, Henry Everard. The sickness continues in Bury where he is imprisoned.

DOMESTIC—ELIZABETH.

1579.   VOL. CXXXI.

August 6. Greenwich.   54. Sir Fr. Walsyngham to Lord Burghley. News from Ireland. A sea force will be the most effective against the rebels as the Earl of Desmond remains faithful. Arrival of Du Simiers from the Low Countries. Desperate state of things there. The Queen's contemplated marriage.

August 7. The Tower.   55. Geffrey Turvyle and H. Paineter to Walsyngham. Have taken up eleven wains for the carriage of the munition to Bristol for Ireland.

August 8. Greenwich.   56. Walsyngham to Burghley. An expedition by sea determined on as being most effective for Ireland. Preparations for the reception of Monsieur from Holland. Murray has returned to Scotland. The calm with the Low Countries cannot long endure.

August 9.   57. Estimate of the charges for the equipment of the Achates and other ships to be set forth and provisioned for two months, under the command of Sir John Perrot.

August 9. Cambridge.   58. Dr. Tho. Byng, Vice-Chancellor of Cambridge, to Burghley. Stating that Mr. Benett and Mr. Chaderton have been selected to preach before him and the Sheriff at the Northampton assizes.

August 10.   59. Account of the remain of all sorts of powder within Her Majesty's stores.

August 10. Greenwich.   Walsyngham to the Mayor of Bristol and Mr. Thomas Chester. Orders to provide victuals and shipping for 600 men, to be levied in South Wales and sent into Ireland by way of Bristol. [*See Vol.* xlv., *p.* 20.]

August 11. Bristol.   60. Mayor, &c. of Bristol to Walsyngham. Have, in conjunction with John Bland, procured provision for 600 men, and will speedily make provision for 600 more.

August 11.   61. Petition of Olyf Burr, of Southwark, coppersmith, to the Council. Desires that, in consideration of certain losses, his shipping may be employed by the Company of Merchants trading to Spain, in preference to any other.

August 12. Chester.   62. William Glaseor to Walsyngham. Stay of shipping at Liverpool and Chester. Provision of victuals for the 400 men to be sent to Ireland. Holyhead is preferable for the shipment of them.

August 12. Tavistock.   63. Fr. Earl of Bedford to same. The soldiers for Ireland will shortly be ready for embarkation. Report that a confederate of the traitor Fitzmorris was last year in Cornwall. Places requiring to be fortified in that county to resist the Spaniards.

August 12.   64. Estimate of the charges for fitting out four of the Queen's ships to the Indies, with five merchant ships and eleven pinnaces to be joined with them. [*Drawn by Mr. Hawkyns.*]

VOL. CXXXI.

1579.

August 12. Tavistock.
65. Earl of Bedford to the Council. The men appointed for the service in Ireland are ready for embarkation at Barnstaple. Rumours of Fitzmorris's rebellion and of foreign aid coming to his assistance.

August 13. Bristol.
66. Mayor, &c. of Bristol to same. Will give directions to the captains of the ships to disembark the soldiers at Waterford, if they could not be conveniently landed at Cork.

August 13. Chester.
67. William Glaseor to Sir Fr. Walsyngham. Receipt of letters as to shipping off 400 men out of North Wales. No mention of cheese in the order for the supply of provisions for them. The other provisions would be accordingly furnished.

August 16.
68. Rafe Lane to Lord Burghley. His plan to encounter the Spaniards in Ireland, for which he offers his service ; or else to have the Queen's letters in his particular favour to the Kings of Fez and Algiers.

August 16.
69. Laurens Nycholson to same. Relative to a certain release requested by Foxehole and Gwyne, in the hands of William Frankelen. Information of a good bargain of house and lands in Middlesex and Hertfordshire.

August 17. Westminster.
70. Charter of Incorporation of the Governor, Assistants, and Fellowship of the Merchants trading into the East Parts; Alderman Tho. Pullison to be the first and present Governor of the same.

August 17.
[Walsyngham] to Bedford. Is pleased at the order taken for resisting any foreign attempts. It is thought the Spanish navy will not stir this year. The Prince of Condé's preparations. Reception of the French King at Venice. [*See Vol.* xlv., *p.* 33.]

August 18. London.
71. Sir Henry Wallop to Walsyngham. Returns his notes relating to Irish affairs. Requests that no information may be received against George Clarke, Guardian of the House of Correction in Winchester, for employing the prisoners in the making of cloth and felt hats.

August 18. Dover.
72. Lord Cobham, Sir Tho. Scott, and others, Commissioners for repair of Dover haven, to the Council. Have surveyed the harbour and consulted Mr. Borrowes and Mr. Pett on the proposed works. Send a plan of the same "handsomlie sett owte." Estimate the charges at 21,000*l.* Propose the immediate erection of three 'groynes" to protect the haven. *Annexing,*

72. I. *Declaration by Mr. Burrowes of the advantages of making a good haven at Dover, according to the platt now generally agreed upon.*

72. II. *Survey of Dover harbour, showing the expenses and estimates of charges for putting it into a proper state of repair, by Matthew Rickwarth, Sluice Master of Dunkirk.*

August 19. Chester.
73. Wm. Glaseor to Burghley. Has taken order for the providing supplies for Ireland and lodging the soldiers till their embarkation. Desires letters may be sent to the bailiffs of Conway for the purchase of butter at the fair there.

VOL. CXXXI.

1579.

August 19. 74. Instructions given by the Privy Council to Sir John Perrot appointed Admiral of the Queen's Majesty's ships, presently sent to the seas, to cruize off the Western coast of Ireland to intercept and destroy the ships there on the landing of James Fitzmorris with foreign forces, &c. To act against pirates off Scilly, &c. [*These were issued by the Council on the 16th of August. Co. Reg.*]

August 19. List of gunners in ordinary serving in various towns, castles, bulwarks, &c. in the maritime counties. [*On the same paper as the preceding.*]

August 21. 75. Estimate of the charges for the furnishing and victualling the Scout, appointed to serve at sea for one month.

August 22. 76. Edmund Tremayne to Lord Burghley. Everything is ready
Collocumb. for the embarkation of the soldiers for Ireland. Is of opinion that the troubles in Ireland will soon be appeased. Betrayal of a confidential passage in Burghley's letter to the Earl of Bedford.

August 22. 77. Mr. Wm. Glaseor to same. Has received his letters to the
Chester. bailiffs of Conway for provision of victuals. Shipping for 200 horse and 400 footmen is also ready. Only 100 horse can be shipped at Liverpool. Price of munition.

August 22. 78. Wardens, &c. of the Company of White Bakers, to same. Certify that 800 quarters of wheat, remaining in the Bridge-house, are unwholesome and not fit for use within the city.

August 24. 79. Demand made by Edw. Baeshe for re-victualling the Queen's ships Revenge, Dreadnought, Swiftsure, Foresight, and the Achates for one month, serving under Sir John Perrot.

August 25. 80. Writ of summons by the Bp. of London for Richard Reynoldes, Rector of Stapleford Abbots, to appear and answer to certain allegations in St. Paul's Cathedral. [*Signed, W. Blakwell.*]

August 25. 81. The last will and testament of Wm. Norreys, Esq., son and heir apparent to the Lord Norreys of Ricot.

August 26. 82. Allowances demanded by Lord Cobham for certain posting about Her Majesty's special affairs.

Aug. [27]. 83. John Colles to Sir Fr. Walsyngham. The 300 soldiers appointed
Barton. to serve in Ireland are at Bristol, and waiting for a wind there.

August 28. 84. Petition of John Mellowe of London to the Council. For their Lordships' letters to the Lord Mayor, &c. in his favour, for payment of certain sums of money, rents, &c., due to him in right of his wife, an orphan of the city.

August 29. 85. Sir John Perrot to same. Reports his proceedings in search of
On board the pirates. His mariners very ill chosen. Report of a fleet preparing in
Revenge. Spain. Sundry merchants of Weymouth robbed by French pirates.

August. 86. Note of the cures effected by the healing properties of the new bath near Coventry.

August. 87. Petition of certain merchants trading to Spain, to the Council. For permission to sell, by retail, some Spanish wines which remain upon their hands.

VOL. CXXXI.

1579.
August ?

88. Petition of Simon Androwes to the Council. Touching the affray between Jenkins the pursuivant and one John Appleton, at Lachlard [Lechlade] in Gloucestershire. Desires to be released from his imprisonment in the Marshalsea for maiming the said Jenkins.

VOL. CXXXII. SEPTEMBER—NOVEMBER, 1579.

Sept. 4.

1. Sir Fr. Walsyngham to the Earl of Southampton and others, Commissioners for piracy within the County of Southampton. The absence of the Vice-Admiral of the county was not sufficient cause to prevent them from proceeding in the matters of piracy. The mayor of Southampton and other officers in privileged places have no right to oppose them.

Sept. 12.
Aldborough.

2. Sir Robert Wyngfeld to the Council. Sends up the persons charged with having received the goods taken by pirates from John Atchinson, merchant of Edinburgh. Others are at sea, and cannot yet be come by. *Incloses,*

2 I. *Schedule of such persons of Aldborough as were found to have in their houses the goods of John Atchinson, and the amount of fines set upon each.*

Sept. 12.
Aldborough.

3. Same to Walsyngham. Has sent up the persons accused of receiving the goods of John Atchinson. *Incloses,*

3. I. *Examination of certain persons suspected of receiving pirates' goods. Taken before Sir Robt. Wyngfeld and Robert Jermy at Aldborough, the 27th Aug.* 1577.

Sept. 13.
Aldborough.

4. Bailiffs of Aldborough to Walsyngham. Their proceedings in the controversy between Anthony Styles and Wm. Smith, the bearer ; the latter had behaved well throughout the whole business.

Sept. 13.
Havering.

Walsyngham? to the Attorney General. Requests another copy of the commission to the Earls of Leicester, Lincoln, and others, for taking general Musters of all the horsemen within the realm, as the copy formerly sent could not be found. [*See Vol.* xlv., *p.* 73.]

Sept. 14.
Collocumb.

5. Edmd. Tremayne to Lord Burghley. Account of his doings in the provision and setting forth of the 600 soldiers for Ireland. The letters for staying them arrived after their departure.

Sept. 15.
Tavistock.

6. Earl of Bedford to Walsyngham. Is sorry to find so many Spaniards landed in Ireland. Desires to be informed what he shall do with the persons stayed in the river of Falmouth on suspicion of travelling without licence, Defence of St. Michael's Mount. Earl of Ormond's departure for Ireland.

Sept. 16 ?

7. Articles of accusation by John Atchinson. Against the parties at Aldborough, for purchasing their goods from pirates.

Sept. 16.

8. Bond of Ric. Evans, Parson of Hoseley, co. Suffolk. To appear before the Council for dealings with pirates at Aldborough.

DOMESTIC—ELIZABETH. 633

1579. VOL. CXXXII.
[Sept. 18.] 9. Lord Cobham to Sir Fr. Walsyngham. Transmits a letter from the Justices of Kent relative to a contribution for the repairs of Dover haven, and thinks it strange it has been so long before delivery. *Incloses,*
    9. I. *Justices of Kent to Cobham. Proposing one uniform rate of assessment towards the works and repairs of Dover haven. Maidstone, 24th July 1579.*

Sept. 21.   10. Geo. Williams, a priest, to Mr. Shelton at Rouen. Desires him
Yew.   to send him word, in haste, if there were any ships there or at Newhaven, to convey him and some others to Ireland or Scotland. Mr. Griffith remaineth at Padua.

Sept. 27.   11. Proclamation by the Queen for the calling in of "a lewde sedi-
Giddie Hall.   tious booke" [The Gaping Gulfe] published against the Duke of Anjou and Her Majesty's intended marriage.

Sept. 29.   12. View of the accompts of the Great Wardrobe from Michaelmas 20 Eliz. to Michaelmas 21 Eliz. Lat.

Sept. 29.   13. Account of the expenses of the Great Wardrobe for the year ending Michaelmas 21 Eliz. Lat.

Sept. 30.   14. Wm. Glaseor to Lord Burghley. Receipt and delivery of letters;
Chester.   account of expenses of victualling and furnishing the soldiers for Ireland. Suggests regulations for the payment of soldiers' diets in future.

Sept.   15. The answer of the Merchant Adventurers to the articles lately presented by Tho. Lowe and Henry Parvish in defence of the trade used by them into Germany : with replication by Lowe and Parvish to the Merchants' objections.

Sept.   16. Brief declaration of the Merchant Adventurers to the articles exhibited by Lowe and Parvish.

Sept.   17. A treatise on the intentions of Spain, and how the plans of the Kings of Spain and France may be frustrated by forming a league with the King of Barbary. [*Indorsed "Discours of meanes to divert y* K. of Sp. intentions of imployment of forces in these partes."*]

Sept. ?   18. Articles to be considered concerning the Musters of the Queen's subjects and their furniture of armour.

Sept. ?   19. Precedents relating to pirates and the authority of the Lord Admiral in matters of piracy.

Sept. ?   20. Note of the timber and of the timber trees felled in Dean Forest.

Sept. ?   21. Petition on the behalf of the clothiers of Suffolk and Essex to Walsyngham. For a toleration of the statute regulating the making of cloths.

Sept. ?   22. Answer of the clothiers to the objections of the Lord Mayor. Desire that the merchants may not be permitted to buy any cloths which are not of the quality required by statute.

Sept. ?   23. Petition of Arnold Maignewe, merchant, to the Council. Solicits order may be taken with Innocent Lucatelli for the payment of 155l. 11s. 4d. owing to him, but which he cannot recover at law.

1579.
Oct. 4.
Trin. Coll.
Camb.

24. Dr. John Still to Lord Burghley. Election of Sir Tyrer and Sir Jones to Fellowships: contest for the Divinity Lectureship; Mr. Whitaker is the only remaining candidate. Increase of allowance to Dr. Barowe, who will continue to read the Lady Margaret's Divinity Lecture.

Oct. 5.
Greenwich.

25. Sir Fr. Walsyngham to Sir Humfrey Gylberte. His ship is no longer required for service in Ireland.

Oct. (5.)
Greenwich.

26–36. Circular from the Council to the Bishops. To give notice to the clergy and others that the seditious suggestions set forth in the book called "The Gaping Gulf" were without foundation; and that special noted preachers should declare the same to the people. *Eleven copies.* [*By an entry in the Council Register, dated Greenwich, 5 October 1579, it appears that letters relative to the book " The Gaping Gulf" were directed to eleven of the Bishops, "the minute of which remains in the Council Chest." As there are eleven copies here unfinished, some signed, others not fully signed, and some not signed at all, it is probable that none were sent, and that the matter dropped.*]

Oct. 8.
Whaddon.

37. Arthur Lord Grey of Wilton to the Council. Had at the last Quarter Sessions received the oaths of such of the Justices of Peace as had not been sworn at the Assizes. Names of those not sworn from various causes.

Oct. 8 ?

38. Names of the Justices of the Peace dwelling within the County of Flint: sworn.

Oct. 8 ?

39. Names of the Justices of the Peace dwelling within the County of Denbigh: sworn.

Oct. 8 ?

40. Names of the Justices of the Peace in Montgomeryshire: sworn.

Oct. 10.
Greenwich.

41. Articles of agreement between Her Majesty and John Hawkyns, Esq., Treasurer of the Navy, for the keeping afloat in harbour certain of Her Majesty's ships, well provided and furnished at his own costs and charges, under certain conditions.

Oct. 10.
Greenwich.

42. Articles of agreement between the Queen and Peter Pett and Matthew Baker, two of Her Highness' shipwrights, for works of carpentry for maintaining and repairing Her Majesty's ships in harbour, at their own costs and charges.

Oct. 10.
Sittingbourne.

43. Wm Crowmer to Walsyngham. His doings in the matter between Mr. Flete and Mr. Thwayts. Sends divers papers relative to the same. *Incloses,*

43. I. *Deposition of William Flete relative to his dealing with Edward Thwayts, concerning the sealing of a conveyance of the manor of Easture, in Sturmouth. Sept.* 19.

43. II. *Articles objected against William Flete by Edward Thwayts, relative to the manor of Easture, in Sturmouth, and the cancelling of a bond for* 2,000*l.*

43. III. *Wm. Flete's answer to the articles objected against him by Ed. Thwayts.*

43. IV. *Copy of the first part of the preceding paper.*

43. V. *Reply of E. Thwayts to the answer of Wm Flete.*

DOMESTIC—ELIZABETH. 635

Vol. CXXXII.

1579.
Oct. 16.
Westminster.
44. Grant to James Morrice of the office of Attorney of the Court of Wards and Liveries for life, with all fees, &c., the same as Richard Kyngesmylle, Thomas Wilbraham, Ric. Onslowe, Robert Nowell, Sir Nicholas Bacon, or Richard Goodriche have held the same. Lat.

Oct. 18
London.
45. Sir Owyn Hopton, Lieut. of the Tower, and Mr. Recorder Fletewoode, to Sir Fr. Knollys and Sir Fr. Walsyngham. Have examined the persons touching the sale of counterfeit and false wax. *Inclosing,*

45. I. *Interrogatories to be ministered to Tho. Bully, relative to the sale of certain false or mixed wax by Richard Laycolt to Tho. Nicholas. Sept. 20.*

45 II. *The depositions of Tho. Bully, relative to the sale of certain wax by Richard Laycolt to Tho. Nicholas. Taken, Sept. 23.*

45 III. *Depositions of Richard Laycolt on the same affair. Taken, Oct. 8.*

Oct 19.
46. Dr. Thomas Byng and Mr. Tho. Legge to Lord Burghley. Resignation of Richard Robinson, Under Bedel of the University of Cambridge; solicit that office for the bearer, John Standyshe.

Oct. 20.
Louvain.
47. Gilbert Burnford to Tho. Hale, or to Wm. Fortescue. God has hitherto delivered him from the plague and the sword. The dearth of all things is extreme, and therefore he desires assistance from all his friends. Sends letters. *Incloses,*

47. I. *G. Burnford [signed Bromisgrove] to Dr. Fecknam. Solicits his good offices to persuade Mr. Wilson to grant him a pension. His sufferings and diligence. Louvain, 19 Oct.*

47. II. *Same to Mr. Wilson. Has supported himself for ten years. Scarcity and plague. Solicits pecuniary assistance. Louvain, 18 Oct.*

47. III. *Same to Mrs. Mary Owen. Has escaped the plague and the sword, yet twice spoiled of soldiers. Desires her to procure him some pecuniary assistance. Louvain, 18 Oct.*

47. IV. *Same to Mr. Robert Chamberlaine. Great distress caused by war and famine. Half the people are dead, and the churchyards not able to receive them. Is in distress, and desires assistance. Louvain, 18 Oct.*

Oct. 21.
48. Samuel Norton to the Council. Complains of the servants of Hugh Smythe, one of whom had been slain by Tho. Pheere, warren keeper to Sir Geo. Norton, on whose lands they were poaching.

Oct. 23.
Chester.
49. William Glaseor to Burghley. Stay of embarkation and discharge of 300 soldiers out of Shropshire. Capt. Norris and 60 men embarked. Supply of victuals at Liverpool. The Lord Chancellor Gerrarde has arrived from Ireland.

Oct. 27.
Ludlow Castle.
50. Sir H. Sydney, President, and the Council of Wales, to Burghley. Submit a list of such gentlemen as are thought meet to be preferred for election as escheators within the twelve shires in Wales.

	VOL. CXXXII.
1579.	
Oct. 28. Dedford.	51. John Hawkyns to Lord Burghley. Sends a note of shipping set forth. Answers the complaints of Sir John Perrot. Proceedings in finishing the storehouse. Has a matter of importance to impart touching the sea service. *Incloses*,
	51. I. *Note of munition and naval stores returned in the ships under the command of Sir J. Perrot.*
Oct. 31.	52. Request of the farmers and tenants of the Isle of Sheppey for a lease of Shurland House and the lands there belonging to Her Majesty. Their offers.
Oct. 31 ?	53. Note of Mr. Awcher's and Mr. Cripse's offers for the same.
Oct.	54. Petition of John Price, prisoner in the Fleet, to the Council. Acknowledges his former misconduct with Vaughan and Torlles, who made him believe he could apprehend one Parsons, a Jesuit. He had apprehended two seminary priests and one massing priest, who were hidden in caves under ground. Offers to repay the money he had unlawfully obtained, and desires to be released from prison, having suffered the shameful punishment of the pillory. [*On the 6th Nov. 1579, he was released from the Fleet, giving bond for his re-appearance. Co. Reg.*]
Oct.	55. Note of the price of grain at Chichester, increased by reason of the great purchases made by one Bates and his factors, for supply of the markets at London and Rye.
Oct. ?	Licence to Sheriff of Oxfordshire to forbear his residence in that county for nine months; his usual dwelling and abode being in Buckinghamshire. [*See Warrant Book*, i., *p.* 88.]
Oct. ?	The Queen to the Lord Mayor, to provide that Henry Campion, the Queen's beer brewer, should not be elected Sheriff of London for the ensuing year. [*See ib., p.* 88.]
Nov. 7.	56. Dr. John Hatcher to Burghley. Notifies his election, on the 5th of Nov., to the office of Vice Chancellor of Cambridge. The University is quiet. Mr. Stringer, Bedel, will inform him of Dr. Byng's troubles with those of St. John's College.
Nov. 9. St. John's Coll.	57. Dr. Ric. Howlande to same. Desires his confirmation of the election of Wm. Billinglie to a scholarship, in which some irregularity had occurred. Recommends Mr. Newill of Pembroke Hall. Finds they possess a licence to purchase in mortmain, 60*l.* per annum.
Nov. 9. Chester.	58. Wm. Glaseor to same. The embarkation of soldiers at Liverpool had been prevented by contrary winds. Hay and oats could not be procured there. Sends his accounts for the office of customer. *Incloses*,
	58. I. *Mayor of Liverpool to Mr. Glaseor. For order to be taken for providing fodder for the soldiers' horses, all the hay and oats in Liverpool being spent. Liverpool, 5 Nov.* 1579.
	58. II. *Mr. Glascor's list of the names of the* 100 *soldiers sent by him into Ireland from Chester, selected from the* 400 *men raised in the Welch counties.*

DOMESTIC—ELIZABETH.

1579.
VOL. CXXXII.

Nov. 10. 59, 60. Accounts of the money due in surplusage to Her Majesty's brewers, for beer and ale from Nov. 1577 to Nov. 1579. Two papers.

Nov. [16.] 61. Petition of Sir Henry Radeclyff to the Council. For satisfaction for a ship and goods spoiled by Phillip van Asshelers, a pirate, off Flushing. And also that Mr. Heale and Mr. Hawkyns may be sent for to give an account of the stay of his ship called the Hand and Dragon. [*On the* 16 *Nov.* 1579, *Drs. Dale and Lewes were ordered by the Council to determine the latter affair. Co. Reg.*]

Nov. 18. Sir Fr. Walsyngham (?) to Archbishop Grindal. The Council desire
Hampton Court. that he would confer with those who had been long imprisoned for religion, particularly with Mr. Norton, late a student in Gray's Inn. [*See Vol.*xlv., *p.* 32.]

Nov. 19. 62. Sir Nicholas Woodrof, Lord Mayor of London, to Lord Burghley.
London. Report of the bakers concerning the wheat belonging to a Portuguese merchant at Ratclif, which is found unmeet to make bread of for the Queen's subjects.

Nov. 19. 63. Dr. Edw. Hawford, Master, and the Seniors of Christ's College,
Christ's Coll. Cambridge, to Burghley. Are of opinion Mr. Broughton cannot continue his fellowship there, being chosen to the Prebend of Durham. *Incloses,*

    63. I. *Copy of the statutes of Christ's College, relating to the above.*

Nov. 21. 64. Sir Nich. Arnold and W. Oldisworthe to Wm. Ayloffe and
Gloucester. Francis Wyndham, Esqrs. Certify that John Higford and George Huntley had taken the oaths prescribed for Justices of the Peace.

Nov. 23. 65. Memorandum of the appointment of Sir Wm. Gerrard to be one of the Masters of Her Majesty's Court of Requests; signified by letter of Mr. Sec. Wylson to the Masters of Requests.

Nov. 30. 66. Wm. Glaseor to Burghley. Has received divers sums of money
Inner Temple. for the service of the soldiers to be sent to Ireland by Sir Wm. Pelham and others. Will return his full accompt of expenses at Hilary term next. The whole charge will be nearly 1,400*l.*

Nov. 30. 67. Note of the charges of all posts extraordinary for Her Majesty's service in Ireland from Aug. 1 to Nov. 30, 1579.

Nov. 68. Sir Owyn Hopton to the Council. That he may be permitted to retain a boat found within the liberties of his manor of Walverswike till claimed by the owners.

Nov. 69. Petition of the tenants of Patterdale, co. Westmoreland to Burghley. Against the proceedings of Edward Lancaster and George Hudson. Pray that their parsonage of Patterdale may not be annexed to the rectory of Barton.

Nov. ? 70. Stephen Brinckley, prisoner in the Tower, to Walsyngham. Desires his favour for the orderly prosecuting by law of his title to certain lands detained from him.

DOMESTIC—ELIZABETH.

1579.
Nov. 71. Note of the quantities of corn shipped at various ports for exportation.

Nov. 72. Names of the Justices of the Peace for the Counties of Surrey, Sussex, Kent, Essex, and Hertford, who were sworn before the Justices of Assize, and of those who were absent, and therefore not sworn.

Vol. CXXXII.

Vol. CXXXIII. December, 1579.

Dec. 9. 1. Dr. John Hatcher, Vice-Chancellor, to Lord Burghley. Controversy between Mr. Drywood, of Trinity, and one Punter, a student of St. John's, Cambridge. Misconduct of the latter at the stage plays at Caius College and Trinity, and other unseemly behaviour.

Dec. 11.
Exeter.
2. Edmond Tremayne to same. Expenses in setting forth the soldiers for Ireland. Report of great preparations by sea making in Spain, to which country much ordnance had been imported from England. Thanks him for his kindness to Humphrey Michell. *Incloses,*

  2. I. *Accompt by Leonard Yeo, deputy of Mr. Tremayne, of the money expended for the setting forth the* 600 *soldiers for Ireland.*

Dec. 14.
Aukland.
3. Richard Barnes Bishop of Durham, and others, to same. Request permission for one Mr. Hugh Broughton, a learned and godly preacher, to read the Divinity Lecture there, and at the same time to retain his fellowship in Christ's College, Cambridge.

Dec. 17.
Christ's Coll.
Camb.
4. Dr. Edw. Hawford to same. Desires leave to proceed to an election for a fellow of Christ's College in place of Mr. Broughton, now chosen Divinity Reader in Durham.

Dec. 18 5. Particular of articles and agreements to be inserted in the lease granted to the farmers and tenants of Her Majesty, of the house of Shurland and other lands in the isle of Sheppey.

Dec. 20. 6. Note of such wood, by estimate, as doth remain in store, provided for the Queen's Majesty's expenses in the office of the Woodyard.

Dec. 24. 7. John Hawkyns to Burghley. Sends a note of the provisions remaining in store at Deptford, and in the ships at Chatham. Estimate of additional stores required.

Dec. 26.
Remsbury.
8. Earl of Pembroke and Sir Henry Sidney to Sir Edward Mawnsell [Mansfield ?]. Relative to building a bridge at Cardiff.

Dec. 29.
London.
9. John Hawkyns to Sir Fr. Walsyngham. On the supply of provisions and double furniture for Her Majesty's navy. Sends copies of papers delivered to the Lord Treasurer and Sir Walter Mildmay.

Dec. ? 10. Certificate of Lord Ch. Justice Dyer and Tho. Meade, of the names of Justices of the Peace for the Counties of Northampton, Warwick, Leicester, Derby, Nottingham, Lincoln, and Rutland, that received the oath of supremacy at the last assizes.

DOMESTIC—ELIZABETH. 639

VOL. CXXXIII.

1579
Dec.

11. Certificate by William Ayloffe and Francis Wyndham of the names of Justices of the Peace for Berkshire, Oxfordshire, Gloucestershire, Monmouthshire, Salop, Staffordshire, Herefordshire, and Worcestershire, that received the oath of supremacy.

12. Similar certificate by Sir Roger Manwood and Ed. Anderson for the Counties of Southampton, Wilts, Dorset, Somerset, Devon, and Cornwall.

13. Certificate of the names of Justices of the Peace in several counties who were warned to appear at the next assizes, having been absent during the former, signed by Sir Chr. Wray and Sir Gilbert Gerrard.

14. Book containing the names of the special Commissioners of Musters for the several counties for the year 1579.

15. Account of sums due for the provision of hay, oats, &c. for the Royal stable ; with a solicitation for present payment of the same.

16. Note of charges for the various forts and garrisons in the Isle of Wight.

17. Notes relating to Lady Gresham's lands. [*Indorsed by Burghley, " Lady Greshā landes in ye Bishopryck of Durhā." Sir Tho. Gresham died 21 Nov. 1579.*]

The Queen to Lady Norris. Condoles with her on the loss of her son. [*Probably William, Marshal of Berwick, whose will is entered 25 Aug., and who died 25 Dec. 1579. See Vol. xlv., p. 40.*]

1579 ?

18. Matters for consideration by the Privy Council, relative to the Lieutenancies of the Earl of Pembroke, in the Marches of Wales.

19. Names of the Deputy Lieutenants for all the counties in the Marches in Wales and the four Marcher shires.

20. Another copy of the above.

21. Estimate of the advantages to Her Majesty by establishing a pre-emption in tin. Plan for perfecting the same.

22. Note of the losses sustained by the merchants of Chester from shipwreck, and from depredations committed by the French since the year 1570.

23. Notes in Sir Fr. Walsyngham's hand, being considerations on the state of affairs in England. [*Probably about the time of the projected marriage with the Duke of Anjou.*]

24. Advice for the better establishment of the English trade at St. Jean de Luz and Bayonne.

25. Considerations touching the title of Henry, late Earl of Arundel, to certain lands made over by him for the payment of the Florentine debt to Her Majesty, and of the conveyance of the manor and castle o f Arundel to (Philip) the now Earl of Arundel.

Vol. CXXXIII.

1579 ? 26. State of the Earl of Arundel's lands at the time of his death, and the requests made by Lord Lumley to Her Majesty respecting the same.

27. Account of gunners in ordinary and pension, serving, in towns, castles, bulwarks, &c., within the Counties of Kent, Sussex, Southampton, and the Isle of Wight, with the names of commanders of the respective forts, &c.

28. Device for levying a toll of the merchants of the Hanse Towns on passing the Narrow Seas, entitled "*A brydell for the Hanse Townes if they bend themselves rather to will then reason.*"

29. Petition of George Eyre to Sir Fr. Walsyngham. For renewal and extension of his lease of the herbage of Crokehill, within the lordship of High Peak, co. Derby.

30. Petition of six poor men of the Queen's kitchen to same. Requesting him to consult with Dr. Dale as to their former suit to Her Majesty.

31. A note of certain statutes against false suggestors.

32. Names of recusants in certain Hundreds in Essex.

33. Directions for search and examination of certain Romish priests, particularly as to Thomas Owen and one Killingbeck. [*Indorsed*, "*A note of certain names and places.*"]

34. Note of the charges for certain naval and ordnance stores for Portsmouth.

35. Note of the rate of custom and duties payable by English ships passing the Sound.

36. List of the gentlemen in the County of Warwick charged with furnishing of demi-lances and light horse.

37. Names of Captains. [*Probably for foreign service.*]

38. A proportion of victuals for 4,000 men at sea for six weeks.

39. Petition of John Craven, butler of the Star Chamber, to Walsyngham. Solicits him to take order with Mr. William Dodington, for the payment of 40*l.* remaining due to him by Mr. Dodington, on his surrender of a parcel of the manor of Sturminster, co. Dorset.

40. Petition of John Pelham, ancient tenant of the lands of Sawcemers and Pomfrets, co. Essex, to the Council. Prays for protection against Nicholas and John Thurgood, who lawlessly and by force endeavour to expel him and his family from their house and lands.

41. Petition of Toby Colcloughe to Walsyngham. Complains of his long and unjust imprisonment by the Lady Harper, whose son he had taught and brought up.

DOMESTIC—ELIZABETH. 641.

VOL. CXXXIII.

1759? 42. Petition of Peter Tunell, ordinary post for France, to Sir Fr. Walsyngham. Against his unjust imprisonment by Martin Corbet, on account of the dispute with John le Roy at Paris. Desires that order may be taken with M. Corbet.

43. Petition of John Osbaston and Tho. Predy to the Council. Complain of the extreme dealing of George Whitton, of Woodstock, in taking unfair advantage of their bonds for money borrowed of him. Articles of their suit against Mr. Whitton.

44. Petition of Ric. Renoldes, parson of Stapelford, Essex, and Francis Bushe, constable, to same. Desire to be released from the Marshalsea, having been committed for the hurt done to one Morrice, sent to serve process upon Mr. Renoldes.

45. Notes by Walsyngham on "The order of proceeding to be held for the answering the Jesuits' and other Popish books."

46. Copy of the above.

47. An estimate of the charges of setting forth four ships of 200 tons each.

48. Note of the conveyance of the manor of Send to Sir Wm. Sherington; the subsequent sale of the manor, and claim made to it by Henry Sherington. [*Indorsed*, "*Arth. Halles.*"]

49. Petition of the inhabitants of Low Furnes, Lancashire, to Walsyngham. To be a means to Her Majesty to have a grammar school founded at Urswicke in Furnes.

50. Petition of Jehan Hacoul, factor for Jehan Pepin, of St. Malo, to the Queen and Council. Touching a ship named Le Volant, of St. Malo, laden with salt, and which was stayed at Bristol. French.

51. Petition of John Ball and others, of Bristol, to the Council. Pray they may not be compelled to redeliver the ship Le Volant, of St. Malo, nor to make restitution of her cargo of salt; and that the French should pay for the repairs. *Inclosing*,

51. I. *A bill of the charges disbursed upon the ship Le Volant.*

52. Memoranda in Lord Burghley's hand, of rates for footmen and horsemen, wages, victuals, &c.

53. Information against certain Papists in Shropshire and Hertfordshire.

54. Petition of the Mayor, Jurats, and whole Commonalty of the town and port of Dover, to the Council. Setting forth the great ruin and decay of their harbour, and soliciting an aid to their funds by a grant of the rates set upon alehouses and taverns, and also for a licence to fetch from the Newfoundland 200 or 300 tons of the ore discovered in the voyages of Capt. Furbisher,

Vol. CXXXIII.

1579 ?   55. Confession of Leonard Romsye, having been some time under the tuition of John Borne, glover, member of the family of Love: delivered to Thomas Barwicke, minister.

56. The answers of the clothworkers of London and Ipswich to such reasons as are preferred by the Merchants Adventurers, for repeal of certain branches of the statute of 8° Eliz. touching clothworkers.

Grant to Lancelot Bowstock of the office of Constable of Holt Castle, in the Marches of Wales. Lat. [*See Warrant Book*, I., p. 161.]

The Queen to the Lord Mayor, &c. of London. On behalf of George Bargeman, who had married Katherine W., an orphan, without licence of the city: his meaning was not to break the laws, but only to have an honest woman to his wife. [*See ib.*, p. 88.]

[Walsyngham?] to Mrs. Snowe. Desires to purchase her title to the lease in reversion of certain grounds about Wandsworth, now in the occupation of one Mr. Boyer. [*See Vol.* xlv., p. 73.]

[Walsyngham?] to ____ . Secretly advises him not to prosecute by way of indictment, those lately presented for refusing to attend the church, such severe proceedings not being advisable at present. [*See ib.*, p. 27.]

The Council to the Bishop of Norwich and the Justices of Norfolk. Commend their exertions in the erecting of a "fourme for the punish-"ment of loyterers, stubborne servantes, and the setting of vaga-"bondes, roagues, and other idle people to work, after the manner of "Bridewell." [*See ib.*, p. 32.]

Sir William Cavendish to the Queen. Requests that the pensions of 400*l.* a year bestowed upon his daughter the Countess of Lennox, and 200*l.* on her daughter the Lady Arbell (Arabella Stuart) may be continued so long as the lands appertaining to the Countess of Lennox remain in Her Majesty's hands. [*See ib., p.* 52.]

Vol. CXXXIV. 1579.

1579.   A volume of entries of instructions relating to Ambassadors, Admirals, Ireland, Borders, Scotland, Musters, &c., from Henry VIII. to the close of the year 1579,—the remnant of a larger volume formerly containing some originals and detached pieces, all of which have been taken out and placed in their proper series, leaving only those that could not be separated. The original indexes to the whole are retained.

Vol. CXXXV. 1579.

1579.   A volume, in its original binding, relating to pirates and piracies; abstracts of proceedings against the receivers and aiders of pirates, in all the maritime shires of England and Wales; list of ports, creeks, and havens; names of commissioners in the various counties for trial of piracies, &c., during the years 1577, 1578, and 1579.

DOMESTIC—ELIZABETH. 643

VOL. CXXXVI. JANUARY—MARCH, 1580.

1580.
Jan. 2. 1. Sir Roger Manwood to Mr. Boswell. To stay process of writs sent into Norfolk and other counties, relative to the lands of the late Sir Tho. Gresham, as Lady Gresham and Sir Henry Nevell would take the necessary steps next week in the county of Middlesex. With a note signed " Ann Greasham."

Jan. 10.
Stansted. 2. Edward Baeshe to Lord Burghley. Presents him with a nag and a gelding. Money owing to John Bland for victualling at Bristol.

Jan. 10.
Bedford. 3. Sir Ric. Greynvile to Viscount Howard, of Bindon. He and other trustees have endeavoured to effect a sale of the manor of Colquit in Cornwall, but failed, as the land was so strictly assured to Mr. Thomas Howard and his wife. 1,500l. only offered for it.

Jan. 18. 4. Note of matters to be contained in the Commission for the Musters, and for execution of the Statute for the breed of horses, mustering of horsemen, &c.: in the hand of the Earl of Sussex.

Jan. 18. 5. Copy of the above, with an additional article.

Jan. 18. 6. The Master and Fellows of Queen's College, Cambridge, to Burghley. Express their regret that his directions were not received in sufficient time to prevent the felling of part of their timber. The sale was made to raise a stock for the erection of a brewhouse.

Jan. 22.
Winchester. 7. Justices of Hampshire to the Council. Appointment of forces for the relief of Portsmouth and the Isle of Wight. Have not been able to dispose of the 300 shot exactly according to their Lordships' directions. *Inclosing,*

7. I. *Selections from the several Hundreds of Hampshire, of the number of men, arms, armour, boats, &c., appointed for the defence of the Isle of Wight, Portsmouth, and the adjacent coast.*

Jan. 22.
London. 8. William Chaderton, Bishop of Chester, to Burghley. Regrets the reckless felling of the woods belonging to Queen's College, Cambridge: but " a longe row of verey fayre ashes yet remain."

Jan. 23.
London. 9. Same to same. Laments the sale of the trees at Queen's; "the ornament, bewty, and defence of that Colledge." Hopes he will preserve "the longe row of goodly ashes."

Jan. 10. Memoranda by Burghley of business to be considered.

Jan.
Whitehall. 11. The Council to the Justices of Suffolk. To view and put in good order certain pieces of ordnance at Aldborough, Dunwich, Southwold, and Laistoft. Robert Day to have a reasonable stipend for his service therein.

Jan. 12. List of the Deputies appointed by Sir Robt. Wyngfeld and others, Commissioners for matters of piracy at Ipswich. Presentments made by them at their second sessions against various parties.

s s 2

VOL. CXXXVI.

1580.
Jan. 13 Conditions of the bonds taken of all owners and masters of ships in Norfolk, in which every one is severally bound in 100 marks to Her Majesty.

Jan. ? 14. Reasons why a Catholic cannot attend the Protestant Church, and that he cannot be required by law to do so.

Jan. 15. A brief advertisement to the recusants how to answer to the statute for not coming to the church: addressed to Sir Fr. Walsyngham.

16. Copy of the preceding.

Jan. 17. Orders touching recusants, with respect to the statute inflicting a penalty of 20*l.* per month for not attending church.

Jan. 18. Ralph Lever to Lord Burghley. States some objections to the appointment of Secretary Dr. Wylson as Dean of Durham; but is content to act as his Vice-Dean under certain conditions.

Feb. 1. 19. Estimate of the charges for 20 of Her Majesty's ships for 3 months: to be in readiness for all attempts of any foreign power.

Feb. 3. 20. The names of captains for sea service; showing the principal naval commanders of Elizabeth's reign.

Feb. 3.
St. John's Coll. 21. Dr. Richard Howlande to Burghley. States the number of scholars in St. John's College, Cambridge, limited by the statutes on Lady Margaret's foundation, to be twenty-four.

Feb. 3.
Cambridge. 22. Dr. John Hatcher, Vice-Chancellor, to same. Reports on the felling and sale of trees belonging to Queen's College; which was done upon great deliberation, and not in respect of any private gain or advantage. *Incloses,*

22. I. *The answer of all the Fellows of Queen's College as to the sale of the trees of their College, with note of those appointed to be felled.*

Feb. 5.
London. 23. Sir Nicholas Woodrofe, Lord Mayor, to same. Recommends the petition of the Bakers, for permission to export 400 quarters of damaged wheat.

Feb. 5. 24. Petition of the Master and Wardens of the White Bakers of London to same. That John Watson may be permitted to export 400 quarters of damaged wheat, not fit to be uttered in the city.

Feb. 11. 25. John Androwes and Bartyllme Cook, Officers of the port of Bristol, to [same ?] Reasons for authority to be given them to search all ships before their departure to the seas.

Feb. 13. 26. The Fellows of Queen's College, Camb., to same. State their reasons for the fall and sale of their woods, and the purposes to which the same was to be applied.

Feb. 15. 27. Note of the clear yearly rent of the manor and lordship of Colquit, made by Sir Arthur Basset and others; with the offers of Dr. John Hone for the purchase of the same.

DOMESTIC—ELIZABETH.   ·645

1580.   VOL. CXXXVI.

Feb. 20
Inner Temple.
28. Ran. Hurleston to Mr. Herlle.   In behalf of the bearer, Mr. Cowell, whom he has known for six or seven years.

Feb. 20.   29. Commission to Sir Roger Manwood, Dr. Val. Dale, and others, for restitution of all goods and merchandise which had been arrested in England, belonging to the subjects of the King of Spain.

Feb. 20.
Christ's Coll.
30. The Fellows of Christ's College, Camb., to Lord Burghley. Solicits the continuance of Mr. Broughton in their College.   Lat.

Feb. 24.
Royston.
31. Earl of Huntingdon to same.   Commends the bearer, Mr. Broughton, of Christ's College, Camb.   The want of maintenance in the University has made him desirous to accept of the prebend in Durham.   With a postscript in his favour, by Robt. Earl of Essex.

Feb. 24.
Leatherhead.
32. Justices of Surrey to the Council.   Certifying their doings in putting in readiness the 3,000 men required of them for the defence of landing places in Kent, Sussex, and Southampton; but the number of able men in the county amount only to 2,005, as appears by their last certificate.

Feb. 27?   33. Bishop Young to the Queen.   Has not felled any timber trees within the Bishoprick of Rochester, otherwise than for the reparation of his mansion house at Bromley.   There had been great waste of timber by his predecessors.

Feb. 27.   34. Estimate of the charges for six of Her Majesty's ships to be stationed off the Isle of Wight, for any service needful.

Feb.   35. Brief note or extract from the register of the High Court of Admiralty, of all such persons as have entered into bond for the tonnage of their ships, from Feb. 1, 1572, to Feb. 13, 1580.

March 2.   36. Estimate of the charges for the furnishing of the Revenge, the Swallow, and the Foresight, to serve at sea for three months.

March 4.   37. Estimate of the charges for ordnance, munition, and other things necessary for the furnishing of the above-named ships.

March 4.
Westminster.
38. Commission by the Queen, appointing Special Commissioners for enforcing the laws respecting the breed and furnishing of horses and geldings for service.

March 4.   39. Draft of the above.

March 4.   40. Remembrance for the Commissioners, probably for the breed of horses, &c.; days for meeting, dispatch of letters to Sheriffs, books of names of freeholders, &c. to be prepared.

March [4?]   41. Commission nominating Deputies in the several counties, to inquire into the number and breed of horses, the keeping of horses and geldings for service, &c., in virtue of the Commission of the 4th of March.

March [4.]   42. Instructions given to the Deputies of the Commissioners for the muster of horsemen, and increase and breed of horses.

1580

Vol. CXXXVI.

March 4 ?   43. List of certain shires, and the names of the Earls of Warwick and Leicester, and Sir Christopher Hatton; probably as Commissioners for the breed of horses.

March 7.   44. Petition of Mrs. Cheyney to the Council. Praying they would have some consideration for the many public services of Wm. Cheyney, her husband, and that he may be recompensed for his house let to Mrs. Weston.

March 11.   45. Certificate by John Piers, Bishop of Salisbury, of the wood sold since his coming to that Bishoprick. Desires that his bargain with Wm. Coothe may be completed.

March 15.   46. Notes of suits in the Court of Wards, and of the grants made to the Earl of Leicester.

March 15.   47. Account of the Loans lately made by the Queen out of the Receipt of the Exchequer, as well to divers Noblemen of the realm as to others; viz., to Sir John Smyth, the Earl of Leicester, Sir Henry Lee, Sir James Croft, Lord Stafford, Sir Rowland Haywarde, and Edw. Dyer.

March 15.   48. Examination of William Sobar, as to bringing money to Richard Creaghe from Kenrick, for whom also he had conveyed letters.

March 16.   49. Warrant to the Lord Chancellor to make out commissions for general musters throughout England; with form of the commission annexed.

March 16.   50. Copy of the above warrant and commission.

March 16.   51. Copy of the above commission only.

March 16.   52. Commission for general musters, with the names of the Special
Westminster. Commissioners in the shires throughout England, and for the cities, boroughs, &c. Instructions for the Commissioners. Articles for the furniture of horsemen, &c.

March 16.   53. Similar commission for the general musters in the county of
Westminster. Durham.

March 16.   54. Articles ministered to Richard Creaghe, prisoner in the Tower, relative to his dealings with Papists, and correspondence abroad with John Castell and others.

March 16.   55. Answers of Richard Creaghe (titular Archbishop of Armagh) to the above interrogatories.

March 16.   56. Articles drawn out of the two letters sent by Dr. Watson and Ric. Creaghe, one to the King of Portugal, the other to his Confessor.

March 16.   57. Articles for the examination of Dr. Watson, as to correspondence with John Castell in Portugal.

March 16.   58. Examinations of Hugh Kenrick, Protonotary in the Sheriff's Court of London, as to his knowledge of the doings of Ric. Creaghe and Dr. Watson. Correspondence with parties in foreign parts.

	VOL. CXXXVI.
1580.	
March 17.	59. Confession of Mrs. Elizabeth Kenrick, touching her knowledge of the cause of her husband's apprehension. His dealings with Watson and Creaghe.
March 17.	60. Examination of John Cowledge relative to the proceedings of Richard Creaghe while in his keeping three years. With postscript by Sir Owyn Hopton, that Creaghe had been in custody five years for papistry only.
March 17.	61. Interrogatories ministered to William Whitine relative to his knowledge of Antonio Fogaça, a Portuguese, and the Catholic prisoners about London, particularly Dr. Watson.
March 17.	62. Answer of Wm. Whitine, servant to Dr. Watson. His acquaintance with A. Fogaça, and delivery of two letters to Kenrick.
March 17.	63. The sayings of Wm. Whitine concerning A. Fogaça, set down under his own hand. Delivery of the two letters to him.
March 17.	64. Extracts out of divers letters of Antonio Fogaça, to the Duke of Alva, Secy. Sayas, the King of Portugal, the Duke of Guise, Friar Chaves, and Ruy Gomez de Sylva, from 1572 to 1577.
March 17.	65. Certificate by Bishop Whytgifte of such timber trees as he had by any means caused to be felled upon the lands of any of his houses of residence within the Bishoprick of Worcester.
March 17.	Instructions by the Council to Sir Wm. Wynter, appointed to go to the seas with three of the Queen's ships, and the two barks called the Achates and the Handmaid, to cruize off the Irish coast, to intercept any succours that might be sent by the King of Spain to aid the rebels in Ireland. To arrest all pirates that he may fall in with. [See Vol. cxxxiv, p. 628.]
March 18. Christ's Coll.	66. Dr. Edw. Hawford to Lord Burghley. Attempts in Christ's College to evade the Statutes of their Foundress. Mr. Broughton's fellowship was of King Edward VIth's foundation; which, however, is subject to the Statutes of the Foundress.
March 19.	67. Testimonial under the hand of George Kevall, notary public, that the Merchants of the Stillyard were not suffered by the officers of the Customs to export cloths, unless they paid strangers' custom.
March 20.	68. Answers of Antonio Fogaça to certain articles propounded. The term of his residence in England. Never had any acquaintance with Watson and Creaghe, nor sent any other letters than the two to the King and his Confessor.
March 22.	69. Articles to be ministered to Anthony Fogaça relative to his letters to the Duke of Alva, about the Earl of Westmoreland, &c.
March 22.	70. The same in Spanish.
March 22. Lambeth.	71. Archbp. Grindall to the Queen. Certificate of the timber trees felled on the lands belonging to the see of Canterbury, since his first entry therein.

1580.   Vol. CXXXVI.

March [25 ?]   72. Note of the armour and stores to be sent with the eleven ships, with necessaries for the dressing and well keeping of the same on shipboard during the voyage.

March 25.   73. Ric. Byngham to Sir Fr. Walsyngham. Their proceedings at
Queenborough. sea. They had gone as far as the Nore, but returned to Queenborough. Delay occasioned for want of provisions.

March 25.   74. Philip Sidnei to Arthur Atey, [Principal of Alban Hall,
Wilton. Oxford]. Thanks him as much as his love and his own gratefulness require. No news, but that all be well.

March 25.   75. Bishop Barnes to the Queen. Has felled no timber trees during his incumbency either of Carlisle or Durham.

March 28.   76. Dr. Tobie Matthew, Vice-Chancellor, to Arthur Atey. Missed
Christ's Church, him in the morning, having lain overlong in bed. Begs him to
Oxford. persuade Corranus to repair to Oxford as soon after the holidays as he could. Has visited Atey's Hall. Desires news on certain points, as briefly and as darkly as he can.

March 28.   77. Answer to certain points moved by the Bp. of Worcester upon Her Majesty's letters for restraint of the felling of timber.

March 28.   78. Tho. Clarke to John Talbot. Informs him that Robert Wotton
Hampton. had escaped, although confined in a chamber in his father's house, "having a horse locke on his lege," and all his clothes, to his shirt, taken away.

March.   79. Bishop Cowper to the Queen. His answer or certificate touching the timber trees felled by him within his diocese of Lincoln. Lat.

March.   80. Note of horse and armour to be furnished by gentlemen, according to the rate of their lands and goods.

March ?   81. Note of the number of lances and light horse to be levied on pluralists, distinguishing the pluralists by name in each diocese.

March.   82. Note of persons (principally transgressors of certain laws, pluralists, &c.,) meet to contribute towards the training of soldiers, without offence to the state and good liking of the people.

March ?   83. Remembrances for works to be done in and about the Castle of Windsor. "*The Maides of Honour desire to have their chamber ceiled, and the partition that is of boardes ther, to be made higher, for that their servauntes looke over.*"

March ?   84. Sir Henry Darcy, Sir Henry Cromwell, and Rob. Bevill, Commissioners of Musters for Huntingdonshire, to the Earl of Sussex. Have equally rated the whole county for furnishing light horsemen; but all show their disability for observance of the same. Names of persons who are either dead or have left the county. *Annexed,*

> 84. I. *List sent from the Council, of gentlemen in Huntingdonshire thought meet to be charged with the keeping of demilances and light horse in that county.*

DOMESTIC—ELIZABETH.

1580.
March ?
VOL. CXXXVI.

85. The Council to the Justices in every shire, to raise a fund for repair of Dover Haven, by levying a fine of 2s. 6d. upon every new licence for keeping alehouses; and all licences heretofore granted to be void from the last of May next, except such as shall pay the above fine.

VOL. CXXXVII. APRIL, 1580.

April 1.
Stansted.
1. Edward Baeshe to Lord Burghley. Detail of the expenditure of 4,000l. in Her Majesty's service. The estimate in setting forth Sir Wm. Wynter's ships. Desires instructions as to sale of the provisions that remained.

April 1.
2. William Holt to Thos. Philipson, Principal of St. Mary's Hall, Oxford. Desires him to give up a feather bed and certain books to Mr. Edw. Risheton. Writes in favour of the Catholic religion. Lat.

April 1.
Dorchester.
3. The Marquis of Winchester and others, Commissioners of Musters for Dorset, to the Council. Have caused the 4,000 men appointed for defence of the sea coast to be put in readiness, and have nominated captains to command them. Their opinions respecting the defence of the shire.

April 3.
4. Articles to be ministered to Antonio Fogaça, taken out of the matters extracted from his own letters.

April 3.
5. The answer of Antonio Fogaça to the articles propounded. States that he, as of himself, wrote that he wished Don John to be possessed of this crown, and matched with the Queen of Scots, his intent being only to procure the advancement of the Romish religion.

April [3.]
6 The answer of Antonio Fogaça to certain interrogatories That he himself indicted the two letters in Spanish. Gave money to Dr. Watson's servant to obtain his master's hand to the letters The sentence of excommunication copied out by the Fleming.

[April 3.]
7. Note of matters to be considered of by Mr. Secretary. To examine Lucius, the Dutchman, who translated Fogaça's letters from Spanish into Latin. Kenrick and Wm. Whitine to discover Paul Core the priest, and Nicholas Roscaroc.

April 3.
Stebunhuth.
[Stepney.]
8. Tho. Lord Wentworth to the Council. Has received their letters for taking general musters in Middlesex. The commission remains in the keeping of the Clerk of the Peace.

April 3.
9. Bishop Aylmer's certificate to Her Majesty of the number of timber trees felled and sold by him since his coming to the see of London.

April 3 ?
10. 11. Account of woods sold by the Bishop of London in anno 19 Eliz., out of the great park of Hornsey; together with the wood sold in Michaelmas last in Finchley Wood, Southwood, the great park and little park near Highgate. Two copies.

1580.	Vol. CXXXVII.
April 3 ?	12. Declaration of such woods and timber felled and sold by the Bishop of London within sundry places of his bishoprick, since Lady-day last was two years, amounting in the whole to the sum of 1,466*l*. 0*s*. 4*d*.
April 3.	13. Declaration made to Sir Walter Mildmay, Chancellor and Under Treasurer of the Exchequer, of the receipts in the Exchequer, from Sept. 29, 1579, to Easter, 1580.
April 4. Falmouth.	14. Ric. Byngham to Sir Fr. Walsyngham. Journal of their proceedings at sea after leaving Queenborough, and from thence to Falmouth. Advertisements received from a certain Irishman from Cork.
April 6.	15. Orders taken at Dorchester, the 6th of April, for the levying of 4,000 men for the defence of the shire.
April 6.	16. Arthur Fawnte to his brother Anthony Fawnte. In commendation of the great virtue and goodness of the bearer, who will speak with him on various points. Prays his brother to take care of his soul and the faith they had been brought up in.
April 7. The Court.	17. The Commissioners for enforcing the statutes respecting the breed and keeping of horses, to the Sub-commissioners for the county of Leicester. Directions for proceeding diligently under their commission. [*Indorsed. Sent with the first commissions.*]
April 7.	18. Same to the same, for the county of Kent.
April 7.	19. Same to same, for the county of Norfolk.
April 7. Newark.	20. The Earl of Rutland, Sir Jervis Clyfton, and others, to the Council. Desire that Sir Robert Constable, Sir Wm. Hollis, George Chowoorth, and Geo. Nevill, Esqrs., may be added to the other Special Commissioners for Musters in Nottinghamshire.
April 8. Cobham.	21. Lord Cobham to Sir Fr. Walsyngham. Requests a separate commission for musters for the Cinque Ports, as their charters exempted them from the rest of the shire.
April 9. Wells.	22. Bishop Berkeley and others, Justices of Somersetshire, to same. Request that Mr. John Syddenham might be joined in special commission with them for the musters. The bearer, Mr. Arthur Hopton, will give more information.
April 12. Venice.	23. Christopher Hodgson, "otherwise called Christophersonne," to his father, Christopher Hodgson. Professes his duty and affection. Commends the learning of the bearer, his special friend. Sends remembrances to all members of his family.
April 12.	24. John Boul to his sister Ellen. Thanks for various things she has sent him. Rejoices she is now a servant of God, and not of this world. Religious reflections. Delivery of some tokens. Desires her to persevere in the Romish religion.

DOMESTIC—ELIZABETH. 651

VOL. CXXXVII.

1580.
April 12.
London.
25. The Justices of Middlesex to the Council. Respecting the right of the Lieutenant of the Tower to take the muster of the Tower Hamlets. In all preceding musters they have been charged with the rest of the county. The Hamlets never belonged to the Abbey of Westminster.

April 14.
26. Faculty granted by Pope Gregory XIII. to Robert Parsons and Edmund Campion, moderating and explaining the Bull declaratory of Pope Pius V., against Queen Elizabeth and her adherents. Lat. [*Much decayed and mutilated.*]

April 14.
27. 28. Two copies; made before the mutilations.

April 14.
29. Proclamation for putting in execution the Statutes for the increase of horsemen and breed of horses for service.

30. Fair copy of the above, with further corrections.

April 15.
Chichester.
31. Wm. Overton to Mrs. Becon. Promises that if he should be appointed to a Bishoprick through the influence of her husband, Dr. Becon, he hoped they would come and live with him, and all that he had should be theirs. [*A copy in Dr. Becon's hand, with this note, "a true copy of the Lorde B. letters, written w*^{h}* his owne hand." Overton was elected Bishop of Coventry and Lichfield on the 10th of September following.*]

April 16.
Hereford.
32. Wm. Cicill, Sheriff, and others, Justices of Herefordshire, to the Council. Cannot execute their commission for the general musters, owing to the absence of Sir Henry Sydney and other Commissioners; and suggesting the names of other gentlemen to be joined in the commission.

April 16.
Wells.
33. Bishop Berkeley to the Queen. Certifies the number of timber trees felled by him since his coming to the Bishoprick of Bath and Wells.

April 16.
Rome.
34. Licence from Rome, for the safe passage of Mr. Edward Riston.

April 17.
35. George Digby to Arthur Atye. Desires the speedy dispatch of his footman, and the continuance of his friendship. Commendations to Mr. Sidney, if he be at Court, and to Mr. Cressy.

April 17.
Gloucester.
36. The Mayor, &c., of Gloucester, to the Council. Request to have a separate commission appointed to take the musters of their city. Sir Nich. Arnold and Thos. Purie, named in the late commission, are dead. Names of other gentlemen fit to be inserted.

April 18.
37. Richard Sugeham to Wm. Birde. Thanks for his courtesies. Sends one of his very dear friends to him, who will shew him many things he will like to know.

April 18.
Rome.
38. Robert Owen to Dr. Humphry Ely at Rheims. Sends his commendations. Departure of my Lord of St. Asaph and Mr. D. Morton for Venice. This day many of his countrymen depart from Rome, and withal good Father Campion. Is finely lodged in Rome, for which he pays but 26 Julies a month.

1580.
VOL. CXXXVII.

April 18. 39. Reasons for the Bp. of London why he desires that the matter of dilapidations may be determined by the Council.

April 19. 40. Receipt by the Bishop of Ely, and others, of letters from the Council for the musters in Ely and Cambridge.

April 21. 41. The Justices and Commissioners for the musters in Norfolk
East Dereham. to the Council. Desire a longer time to be given for certifying of the general musters ; having been delayed by the plague and other occasions.

April 22. 42. Edw. Lord Stafford, and others, to same. Request to know if
Stafford. they should muster the town of Stafford with the rest of the shire, as in the time of the late Earl of Essex. There are above fifty lusty young fellows in the town who have neither wife nor charge.

April 22. 43. Sir Henry Lee and others, Justices of Oxfordshire, to same.
New Wood- That the borough of New Woodstock claim the privilege of a
stock. separate commission for musters, the same as New Windsor.

April 23. 44. Commissioners of Musters for the county of Suffolk to same.
Ipswich. Their proceedings in taking the musters, for the whole county, with the exception of Ipswich. Greater quantity of arms and armour furnished than heretofore. State of defence of the county. Increase of the number of horses. *Inclosing,*

    44. I. *General certificate of the musters for the county of Suffolk, amounting to* 10,749 *able men, with the names of the captains and leaders appointed to command them.*

    44. II. *Particular certificate of musters in Suffolk, amounting to* 3,894 *able men.* [*Note : these certificates are made on printed forms, and are the first so executed.*]

April 23. 45. The names of such as have been the Sovereign's Lieutenants on St. George's day, since 16th year of the Queen's reign.

April 25. 46. John Cupper, Steward of New Woodstock, to Secretary Wilson. In favour of the privilege of a separate commission for the musters, the same as granted to the borough of Old Windsor.

April 26. 47. William Gifford, Fellow of the English College at Rome, to Wm. Middelmore. Desires to be informed of the state of their affairs in England. Sends four pair of hallowed beads and other Popish tokens. Had hoped to have seen one of his brothers at Rome.

April 27. 48. Commissioners of Musters for Lindsey Division, co. Lincoln, to
Lincoln. the Council. Certify their doings in the musters : the numbers being less than in the last certificate by omission of the musters for the city of Lincoln. *Inclosing,*

    48. I. *Certificate of the musters for the Division of Lindsey in the county of Lincoln.*

1580.	Vol. CXXXVII.
April 30. Hawkeslow.	49. John Middelmore to his son William, at Paris. Has received his letters. Desires him to continue firm in the Romish religion, and apply himself to his studies. Before he returns, to call on Mr. Talbot's son at Rouen, and to bring any letters he may wish to send.
April.	50–53. Abstracts and notes of Orders in Council, respecting the breed and keeping of horses; keeping musters; appointment of deputies, &c. *Four papers.*
April?	54. Brief of the Archbishop of Canterbury's defence and answer to the articles of dilapidations presented against him by the Bp. of London.
April?	55. Reply of the Bp. of London to the answer of the Archbishops of Canterbury and York in certain points of law, relating to the matter of dilapidations. Lat.
April. Norwich.	56. Mayor and Aldermen of Norwich to the Council. Desire a separate commission for musters within their city, according to their ancient privileges. *Inclosing,*
	56. I. *The names of such of the city of Norwich as the Mayor and Aldermen desire to be put into the commission for musters.*
April.	57. The Queen to the Commissioners and Justices of the Peace in the several counties. For the levying of horsemen and armour, for present service in Ireland.
April. Thornage.	58. Commissioners of Musters for the county of Norfolk to the Council. Certifying their doings in the musters. Deficiency of arms and armour. Have appointed the muster of horses for the 1st of June. Desire that the proportion of armour may be qualified.
April.	59. Certificate of musters of able men and horsemen for the county of Cambridge, with the names of the captains commanding them.
April.	60–65. Certificates of general musters of able men and armour in the divisions of Alton, Portsdown, Andover, Fawley, Redbridge, and Basingstoke, in the county of Southampton. Six returns.
April?	66. General certificate of musters of the whole county of Southampton, of able men furnished, complete and not complete.
April?	67. Certificate of the musters of footmen and horsemen within the city of Winchester.
[April.]	68. "A booke of the Names of ye Gentlmen and freholders in. "ye county of Warwicke;" placed under their respective hundreds [*In the hundred of Barlichway occur, among the freeholders, the names of* John Shakespeare *the father of* William Shakespeare, *and* Thomas Shakspere *of Rowington.*]

VOL. CXXXVII.

1580.
[April.] 69. Another book, similar to the above, with the title "A Booke of "the names and dwellinge places of yᵉ Gentlmen and freeholders "in yᵉ Countye of Warwicke;" divided in the same manner under hundreds, and subdivided into towns and villages, shewing the residences of each person. Thus John Shakespeare, under the contraction of "Shaxp," occurs at Stratford upon Avon; and Thomas Shakspere, under that of "Shaxpe," at Rowington. [*The same lists also contain the names of William Clopton, Adrian Quinie, John Coomes, John Sadler, and several other persons connected with the biography of Shakespeare.*]

April ? 70. Note or suggestions touching the provision of armes and furniture most apt and fit for light horsemen.

April ? 71. Certificate of the Musters for the City of Lincoln. Signed, among others, by the mark of Richard Hawkes, Mayor.

April. 72. Bishop Scorey to the Queen. Certifies his doings touching the felling of timber trees within his see of Hereford. Hopes to be allowed to have enough for necessary fuel for his household.

April. 73. Articles objected against the Bishop of London for the sale of timber trees within his see; with his answers to the same.

April. 74. Note of such liberties as the inhabitants within the precincts of the late dissolved houses of the Black and White Friars claim to have exempt from the city of London; shewing the Queen's interest therein, and the names of the honourable and worshipful persons now inhabiting the same. [*An Order in Council was passed on the 15th May 1580, deferring the final hearing of this controversy till the following Michaelmas. Co. Reg.*]

April. 75. Note of letters sent by the Commissioners for the increase and breed of horses, into various shires.

April. 76. W. B., preacher, Parson of Haddon, to the Archbishop of Canterbury, relative to the state of his suit against T. L., depending in the Consistory Court at St. Pauls, as appears by the reports of Dr. Walker and Mr. Archdeacon Mullens. Discouragement of the afflicted ministers by the course of proceeding in this suit.

VOL. CXXXVIII. MAY, 1580.

May 1. 1. Justices of Berkshire to the Council. Proceedings in taking
Farrington. the musters. Reasons why the numbers are less now than in the 15th year of Her Majesty's reign.

May 2. 2. Book of the names of the inhabitants within the Isle of Ely, charged by the Bishop to keep horses and geldings and furniture for service; signed by Bishop Cox.

May 2. 3. General certificate of Musters of able men, as well footmen as horsemen, for the county of Surrey, amounting to 7,384 men.

DOMESTIC—ELIZABETH. 655

1580.
Vol. CXXXVIII.

May 2. 4. Particular certificate of Musters of horsemen and footmen for the county of Surrey; the total being 2,120 able men complete.

May 3. 5. General certificate of Musters of footmen and horsemen, for the county of Cornwall.

May 3. 6. Particular certificate of Musters for the same county, amounting to 4,000 able men, with the names of the captains to command them.

May 5. 7. Comparative rates of various articles of munitions, naval and ordnance stores, for ready money, shewing the price paid by Government and the common price.

May 5.
Tattersall.
8. Commissioners of Musters for the Holland Division, co. Lincoln, to the Council. Send certificate of the Musters; the diminution from the 11th year of the Queen's reign being occasioned by the great deluge in the 12th year, and the want of resident gentlemen. *Inclosing,*

8. I. *Certificate of the general Musters for the parts of Holland in the county of Lincoln.*

8. II. *General certificate of Musters for the Holland Division.*

May 7. 9. Declaration by Thomas Hancocke, preacher, of the blasphemous speeches uttered by one Sherwood, a prisoner in the King's Bench, and his refusing to hear divine service.

May 8. 10. [Edward Havard] to Arden Waferer. Earnestly desires him to let him receive some money by the bearer; with a postcript by Fr. Waferer to his brother Arden, desiring him to grant Mr. Havard's request.

May 8. 11. Edward Havard [Dravah] to brother Gregory. Is in a very poor state. Hopes he has received money for him from Creswell. His next half year's annuity and all other money may be sent by the bearer. Thanks him for his gentle remembrance of his two pair of shoes.

May 8. 12. Same to his "alied brother," Mr. Thomas Hanbie. Thanks him for his kindness, and desires to be recommended to his good sister, Hanbie's wife. Has received the 40s. and returns his hearty thanks for the same.

May 9.
Ancaster.
13. Commissioners of Musters for Kesteven Division, co. Lincoln, to the Council. Send true and perfect certificates, and detail their doings in the musters. Causes of delay. *Inclosing,*

13. I. *Certificate of the Musters for the Division of Kesteven in the county of Lincoln.*

May 9.
Leicester.
14. Same for the county of Leicester to same. Desire a longer time for the viewing of the horsemen, on account of the leanness of their horses and geldings, owing to a deficiency of hay.

May 9.
Downham.
15. Bishop Cox to Sir Fr. Walsyngham. In favour of Sir Fr. Hinde's plan for uniting the livings of the two churches in the parish of Histon, co. Cambridge. Dr. Dale has stated a manifest untruth as to an annuity of 40*l.* a year.

1580.   Vol. CXXXVIII.

May 11. 16. Marquis of Winchester, and others, Commissioners for piracy,
Dorchester. co. Dorset, to the Council. Arrest and examination of Phillip Boyte, and others, for the spoiling of a Spanish ship. *Inclosing,*

    16. I. *Examination of Phillip Boyte before Ric. Pitt, Mayor of Weymouth, as to his capture of a Spanish ship, under the impression that war was declared between England and Spain.*

May 13. 17. Rich. Barrey, Lieutenant of Dover Castle, to Walsyngham.
London. Dr. Dale will not join with him in taxing the bill of Baron Manwood's two servants, for saving the merchants' goods, unless he sees the Order in Council for that purpose. The merchants desire an end of the matter.

May 16. 18. Sir Edm. Trafforde to the Earl of Leicester. State of the
Trafford. county of Lancaster, which is lamentable to behold, considering the great disorders thereof in matters of religion. Masses are said in several places. Desires that the offenders may be rigorously dealt with.

May 18. 19. Report of the charges of the Achates, discharged 18th May 1580; certified by John Hawkyns and Willm. Holstok.

May 19. 20. Justices of Somersetshire to the Council. Detail their proceedings in mustering the 4,000 able men selected for the defence of the sea coasts. The statute for the breed of horses is duly observed. *Inclosing,*

    20. I. *General certificate of Musters of able men, footmen and horsemen, of the whole county of Somerset.*

    20. II. *Particular certificate of Musters of the 4,000 men of the same county, selected for defence of the coasts, &c.*

May 20. 21. Certificate of Musters for the town and manor of Bradninch, in the county of Devon.

May 20. Commission by Sir Rowland Haward and George Barnes, Governors of the Company of English Merchants for discovery of New Trades, to Arthur Pet and Charles Jackman, for a voyage by them to be made for discovery of Cathay. [*See Dom.* 1586, (*Trade*), *fol.* 123.]

May 20. Instructions given by Richard Hakluyt to Arthur Pet and Charles Jackman, for prosecution of their voyage of discovery of the Northeast Streights; "not altogether unfit for some other enterprises of "discovery hereafter to be taken in hand." [*See ib., fol.* 159.]

May 22. 22. Declaration respecting the division of certain lands in Keythorpe and Gowdbie between Everard Digby and Henry Hall. Encroachments of Mr. Digby. Hall's desire that the bounds of their respective lands may be better defined.

DOMESTIC—ELIZABETH. 657

1580.   VOL. CXXXVIII.

May 25.   23. Dr. Edw. Hawford to Lord Burghley. Has received his letter
Christ's Coll. in favour of Hamond, with which they cannot comply, as the
Cambridge.   fellowship had been promised to several others before. Mr. Broughton still retains his fellowship.

May 25.   24. Commissioners of Musters in the county of Warwick to the
Warwick.   Council. Have viewed and mustered men and arms of the selected number within the shire. Delay by the sickness of Sir Fulke Greville. The commission for Coventry has not yet been received. *Inclosing,*

    24. I. *Certificate of Musters of able men of the county of Warwick.*

May 26.   25. Edward Bowghton to the Earl of Leicester. Proceedings in
Cawston.   the musters of Warwickshire. *Incloses,*

    25. I. *Certificate of Musters, same as in the preceding letter.*

May 27.   26. Walsyngham to Burghley. Laments his Lordship has so just
Barn Elms. cause of increase of grief, and that the matter should be made publick. Wishes Her Majesty were not so easily drawn to be an instrument to execute the passions of others. Has laboured to remove her displeasure.

May 31.   27. Particulars of the matter in controversy between Reginald
Stifkey.   Metcalf, preacher, of Thetford, and Bartholomew Baxter, a priest, relative to the tythes of the benefice of Santon ; with copy of letter from the Council to the Justices of Thetford ; viz., the Mayor, Mr. Wm. Heydon and Mr. Nathaniel Bacon, desiring them to hear the case, dated 25th July, 1579.

May 31.   28. Commissioners of Musters for Rutlandshire to the Council.
Uppingham. Certify the number of horses furnished, and send certificate of musters. *Inclosing,*

    28. I. *General certificate of Musters for the county of Rutland.*

May 31.   29. Same for the town of Boston to the Council. Certify their
Boston.   doings in the musters. *Inclosing,*

    29. I. *Certificate of the general Musters for the borough of Boston.*

May.   30. Report of the Customers of the port of London to Lord Burghley, of the Customs paid for goods and merchandise entered outwards, from Sept. 29, 1579, to Easter, 1580, and of the number of cloths passed upon the Lord Chamberlain's licence.

May.   31. Examination of John Errington, son to Lancelot Errington, dwelling at Denton, within three miles of Newcastle, touching his going into France.

May.   32. Note of letters taken with Harrington or Errington.

T T

1580.
May. VOL. CXXXVIII.
33. Notes relative to the musters. Points required in the Council's letters touching the musters, and notes of letters and certificates from various shires.

May? 34. Petition of Richard James, of London, brewer, to the Council. To be permitted to build on certain waste land in the precincts of St. Katharine's near the Tower; with certificate by Rauf Rokeby, the master, and Edw. Grafton, steward of St. Katharine's, that the suit was reasonable and necessary.

May? 35. Certificate of the persons charged for harness and light horses in the county of Suffolk, stating the number furnished and the residences of the parties: first certificate.

May? 36. General certificate of all the able men within the four jurisdictions of the Stannaries in the county of Devon, viewed and mustered by Sir Arthur Basset, deputy to the Earl of Bedford, Lord Warden of those jurisdictions.

May? 37. The Queen to the principal gentlemen in certain shires. Urges them to contribute liberally, and to raise a collection towards the relief of those of the religion in the town of Montpellier. "God's "merciful warning by the late earthquake being an extraordinary "admonition" to England to act with true Christian compassion towards the calamity of the afflicted. [*The earthquake, felt throughout England and France, happened on the 6th of April,* 1580.]

VOL. CXXXIX. JUNE, 1580.

June 1. 1. Sir Edward Horsey to Burghley. Intelligence of great preparations being made in Spain, probably for a descent on Ireland. "Cornelis is nowe boyling of his earth" to make saltpetre.
Isle of Wight.

June 1. 2. Commissioners of Musters for the county of Gloucester to the Council. Desire a longer time to certify the musters, and refer to the report of the bearer, Mr. Throckmerton.
Wootton under Edge.

June 1. 3. Sir Fr. Knollys to the Earl of Leicester. Thanks for his letters to so poor an object as he is. States his objections to the Queen's marriage with a French Prince. Her inevitable danger of the French bondage, are agreed upon by that holy father the Pope, and plotted out by the serpentine subtlety of the Queen mother's head. Prays the Queen may be blessed with a faithful husband.
Greys.

June 2. Indenture of agreement between Sir Wm. Catesby and Sir Robert Throkmerton, of Caughton, for the settlement of divers manors, &c., in the counties of Warwick and Gloucester, by way of jointure for Dame Anne, now wife of the said Sir William Catesby. [*Case C. Eliz.,* No. 8.]

June. 3. 4. Stephen Garnett to Lawrence Johnson. Begs to hear from him of his mother's infirmity. Is in health, but had been ill in Rogation week, with a trick in the head. Has to make an exposition of David's Psalms. On the same paper is a letter to his mother, relative to her health and his own.

DOMESTIC—ELIZABETH. 659

1580.
June 3.
The Arches.

Vol. CXXXIX.
5. Dr. Lewes to the Council. Desires instructions relative to the Portuguese merchandise brought into the realm by John Wynter, being taken by Drake and his company; the restitution of which is desired by the Ambassador of Portugal.

June 4. 6. Commissioners of Musters for Norfolk to the Council. Have mustered the demi-lances and light horse, which are in every way complete. Send certificates. Sir Wm. Paston has been appointed General of the horse, with meet officers under him. Defences of the county. *Inclosing,*

6. I. *General certificate of the musters for the county of Norfolk, as well horse as foot, amounting to 9,260 men, with names of the captains appointed to command them.*

6. II. *Names of all such persons within the county of Norfolk as be appointed to keep horses or geldings for service; with the numbers rated on each person.*

6. III. *Another list of persons, apparently draft of the above.*

6. IV. *Names of all such persons, knights, gentlemen, and freeholders of Norfolk, appointed to keep horses and geldings for service; specifying their places of residence throughout the county, and the numbers rated to each.*

6. V. *Similar list, but with a different arrangement of towns and villages.*

6. VI. *Another list of names of gentlemen in Norfolk charged with the keeping of demi-lances and light horse.*

June 6.
Paris.
7. Oswald Chamber to his father, Leonard Chamber. Not to expect his return at present. Desires him to remember his request.

June 6.
Paris.
8. Same to John Hemsworth, His continuance at Paris desired by his master. Requests him to take charge of his affairs at home. Mr. Hollinges suit.

June 7. 9. Grant to Robert Woodroffe the younger, second son of Sir Nicholas Woodroffe, Lord Mayor, of the office of Packership of London, in reversion after the death or surrender of Richard Young, with confirmation of the same, and names of the Aldermen then present.

June 8.
Paris.
10. Jo. Amyas ("for so ame I named at Parise") to John Talbot. That he would send him every information relative to his friend's estate. The matter stands doubtful between the people of Portugal and King Philip, whether they will accept him for their King, or not.

June 8.
Paris.
11. Same to Mrs. Anne Southworth. Thanks for her gentleness and courtesy. Sends her a piece of English money as a token. Desires to be commended to my lady her mother.

June 9.
Paris.
12. W. L. to Marmaduke Langdale. Touching Father Thomas, confessor to the Duke of Terra Nova. Probable appointment of the Duke to be Lieutenant of the King of Spain, in Milan. The Irish boy is at Rheims in good health.

T T 2

DOMESTIC—ELIZABETH.

VOL. CXXXIX.

1580.
June 9.
Cambridge.
13. The Mayor, &c. of Cambridge to the Council. Have mustered and viewed all the able men and armour within the town. Inclosing,

13. I. *Certificate of the Musters for the town of Cambridge.*

June 10.
Ivy Bridge.
14. Earl of Rutland to Sir Fr. Walsyngham. Sends the certificate of the horses for the county of Nottingham. The general certificate will shortly follow. Has received his letter desiring him to attend on the Lord Chancellor.

June 10.
15. Andrew Perne to Lord Burghley. Thanks for his favours to the University. The application of Lord North and the Mayor of Cambridge, in favour of some person, was to sustain certain pretended grievances supposed to be offered by the University to the Townsmen.

June 10.
Paris.
16. H. Sand to Tho. Harrington. Marvels that he has not received any letter from his wife. His great losses. Commends the bearer, Humphrey Havard, and desires to be informed if his parents would consent to his returning home. Note of all letters sent and received.

June 13.
17. Wm. Herlle to Burghley. Advertisements received from Holland of the intentions of Spain. Intimation of a proposed marriage between the Duke of Anjou and the daughter of the King of Spain. The county of Avignon to be erected into a kingdom, and the 17 Belgian provinces, &c. to be also erected into a kingdom for him. His opinion on the effects to be expected from the completion of such a scheme. Fate of the Protestant cause in Europe. Information by John Stamp of disaffection in Berkshire.

June 14.
Bromley
Pagetts.
18. Commissioners of Musters for the county of Stafford to the Council. Their doings in the musters. Reason why the numbers certified in their last certificate were less than in the 15th year of Queen Elizabeth. Sir Ralph Bagnall dead, and several of the Commissioners not resident in the county. Inclosing,

18. I. *General certificate of Musters for the county of Stafford.*

June 14.
Cambridge.
19. Dr. John Hatcher, Vice-Chancellor, and Dr. Thomas Byng to Burghley. Answer to the complaint made by the Townsmen, who, they solicit, ought to be compelled to specify the intolerable vexations and injuries they suffer from the University.

June 15.
20. Heads of Colleges to same. Appeal to him to resist the strange attempts against their statutes. Intrusion of two doctors of the town, at the pricking of two Regents to the four Lectures, viz. Philosophy, Rhetoric, Logic, and Mathematics. Two graces surreptitiously passed.

June 16.
St. Albans.
21. Commissioners of Musters for St. Albans to the Council. Have taken the general musters of all the able men, armour, and weapon in their poor town. Inclosing,

21. I. *Certificate of the general Musters for the town of St. Albans.*

DOMESTIC—ELIZABETH. 661

1580.   Vol. CXXXIX.

June 17. Norwich.   22. Commissioners of Musters for the city of Norwich to the Council. Have mustered all the able men between the ages of 16 and 60, particulars of which are stated.

June 17.   23. Same for the county of Chester to same. Detail their doings in the musters, which they have described in a "pye of squares." *Inclosing,*

     23. I. *Certificate of the general Musters for the county of Chester, furnished and unfurnished with armour, weapons, &c.*

June 17.   24. Commission out of the Court of Admiralty granted to Don Antonio de Castiglio for the recovery of the ship and goods taken at sea by Francis Drake and his company. *Annexed,*

     24. I. *Declaration by John Winter relative to the ship taken by Francis Drake, captain and general of five ships and barks bound for the parts of America for discovery and trade of merchandise.*

June 21.   25. The Council to the Lord President and Council of Wales. Directions to levy 800 men for the service of Ireland.

June 21. Cambridge.   26. Dr. John Hatcher to Lord Burghley. Reasons why the Heads of the University object to the Earl of Oxford's players shewing "their cunninge in certayne playes already practysed by them before "the Q. Matie;" the like haying been denyed to the Earl of Leicester's servants.

June 26.   27. The Fellows of Christ's College, Cambridge, to same? In behalf of Edward Negus, who had been refused admission to his fellowship by the negative voice of the Master.

June 27.   28. Richard Stonley to same. Declaration of the state of his accounts since Easter last. States the losses and hindrances he has sustained in the time of his 27 years' service.

June 27. Chester.   29. Wm. Glaseor to same. In the absence of Wm. Goodman, the Mayor, has taken order with Mr. Hardware his deputy, for the furnishing ships and provisions for transporting the 300 soldiers from Wales into Ireland. Note of prices, &c.

June 28.   30. Certificate of the Musters in the city of Lichfield, taken by Thomas Lord Paget, of Beaudesert, the bailiffs and sheriff of the city, and others.

June 28. London.   31. Sir Nicholas Woodrofe, Lord Mayor, to Sir Fr. Walsyngham. Musters in the city. Reasons why they had not made certificate earlier. Desires that the Lord Chancellor might be authorized to hasten the new commission.

June 28. Aylesbury.   32. Commissioners of Musters for the county of Buckingham to the Council. Excuse their delay in making certificate, and the reasons for the numbers being much fewer in the 20th than in the 15th year of Her Majesty's reign. *Inclosing,*

     32. I. *Certificate of the general Musters for the county of Buckingham.*

VOL. CXXXIX.

1580.
June 28.
Aylesbury.
33. Commissioners of Musters for the county of Buckingham to the Council. Certify their doings for the mustering of horsemen, which they have reduced into the form of a book, and send to their Lordships.

June 30.
Hertford.
34. Same for Hertfordshire to same. Their doings in taking the musters, and increase of the number of horses. Have refrained from appointing captains, as they have but few expert enough for that office. *Inclosing,*

  34. I. *Certificate of the general Musters for the county of Hertford.*

  34. II. *The number of demi-lances and light horse furnished complete, charged within the county of Hertford.*

  34. III. *Similar list of demi-lances and light horses for the county of Hertford, shewing the increase.*

June 30.
Worcester.
35. Same for the city of Worcester to same. Have taken the musters, and included therein all the pioneers and smiths in the city. *Inclosing,*

  35. I. *Certificate of the Musters for the city of Worcester.*

June 30.
Stamford.
36. Same for the town of Stamford to same. Particulars of the musters taken by them in the borough of Stamford.

June 30.
Beare.
37. Sir Henry Radeclyff to Lord Burghley. Transmits intelligence from Spain. Requests Mr. Sec. Walsyngham may be put in remembrance for a supply of munition for Portsmouth.

June.
Westminster.
38. The Queen to the Lord Chancellor. Forbids the passing of any grant under the Great Seal by immediate warrant. Signed in June, but dated the 22d of April before.

June.
39. Report of a difference between one Threddar, a townsman of Cambridge, and Mr. Whittnell, a Fellow of Trinity College. Threddar appears on summons, and produces a supersedeas from the Mayor, which Dr. Byng refuses to receive.

June ?
40. 41. Sir Ric. Norton to Sir F. Walsyngham. Two certificates of lands belonging to the Bishops of Winchester, at Farnham Castle in Surrey, Waltham in Hants, and Wolvesey House at Winchester.

June ?
42. General certificate of the musters of footmen and horsemen in the whole county of Oxford, amounting to 5,000 men, with names of the captains commanding them.

June ?
43. General certificate of musters of all the footmen in the county of Kent, except the cities of Canterbury and Rochester, and the Five Ports, by Thomas Fane, Esq., High Sheriff of the said county, amounting in the whole to 12,131 men, consisting of pikemen, gunners, archers, billmen, pioneers, carpenters, smiths, masons, and wheelwrights.

June ?
44. Names of the gentlemen appointed to furnish lances and light horses for the whole county of Kent, shewing the increase since the last certificate.

Vol. CXXXIX.

1580.
June ?   45. Names of the gentlemen within the Lathe of Sutton at Hone, co. Kent, thought meet to be charged with demi-lances and light horses.

June.   46. General certificate, by Lord Cobham and others, of musters within the Cinque Ports, and their members.

June.   47. Certificate of musters for the county of Derby. The number of footmen furnished and complete being 600, and the number of horsemen 40.

June ?   48. The names of all persons rated for finding demi-lances and light horses furnished, within the county of Essex.

June ?   49. Certificate of the names of gentlemen furnishing light horses and demi-lances in the county of Somerset.

June ?   50. 51. The names of the Lords of the Parliament, with the number of demi-lances and light horses appointed to be kept by them severally. Two copies.

June ?   52. The Council to the Commissioners of Musters in several counties. Thanks for their diligence, but suggesting that many parties might be rated to furnish a higher number of horses.

June ?   53. The Commissioners for Horses to the Sub-Commissioners in the shires which had neglected to return certificates. Expressing Her Majesty's displeasure, and commanding them to proceed in the musters without delay.

June ?   54. Petition of Wm. Van Dueton, Herman Elmanhurst, and others, Merchants of Hamburgh and Lubeck, to the Council. Praying for satisfaction for goods and merchandise taken from them by a ship belonging to Henry Sackford, Esq., and by another ship of Thomas Clerk's, a notorious pirate.

Vol. CXL. July, 1580.

July 1.   1. Sir Fr. Knollys to Sir Fr. Walsyngham. Condoles with him on the death of his daughter. Desires letters from the Council to repress the unruly dealings of Tho. and Edward Wyngfylde at Kymbolton. Lord Garret's sudden and untimely death has disordered all his household.

July 5.   2. The Officers of the Ordnance to Walsyngham. That the bows,
The Tower.   arrows, bills, and skulls, desired by the inhabitants of Pembroke, could be spared out of the stores in the Tower, at prices stated.

July 5.   3. The Mayor, &c. of Oxford to the Council. Have taken the
Oxford.   musters within the city and suburbs of Oxford; except the University. Difficulties that may arise from the increasing number of privileged persons. *Inclosing,*

3. I. *Certificate of the Musters for the city and suburbs of Oxford.*

1580.
July 5.
Brereton.

4. Wm. Brereton to the Earl of Leicester. Has sent a separate certificate of the number of persons chargeable with the keeping of horses in the county of Chester, and the number of horses rated.

July 6.
Newbury.

5. Commissioners of Musters for Berkshire to the Council. Certifying their diligence in taking the musters. *Inclosing,*

    5. I. *Certificate of the general Musters in the county of Berks, with the number of demi-lances and light horse.*

    5. II. *Particular certificate of the number of able men furnished in the same county.*

July 7.
Grays.

6. Sir Fr. Knollys to Walsyngham. Sends the correspondence between himself and Tho. Wyngfylde and his son Edward, relative to their destruction of woods and spoil of the estate at Kymbolton. Intention of Edward the son, to go to law for the lands. Himself and the Chancellor of the Exchequer have already raised above 600*l.* towards the marriage portions of Mr. Wyngfylde's three daughters. *Incloses,*

    6. I. *Information given by Mr. Treasurer's [Sir Fr. Knollys] two servants, Mowsdale and Knott, sent to Kymbolton to give warning to the purchasers of any trees offered for sale by Edw. Wyngfylde. Proceedings of Robert Dorrington and others, who bought trees after notice.*

    6. II. *Knollys to Tho. Wyngfylde. Informs him that the keeping of his lands and woods had been intrusted to him and the Chancellor of the Exchequer, and therefore advises him not to interfere in order to satisfy the prodigal lust of his lawless youthful son, Edw. Wyngfylde. Grays, 30 June 1580.*

    6. III. *Same to Edward Wyngfylde. Commanding him not insolently and unlawfully to intermeddle with the orders given by the Chancellor and himself relative to the lands at Kymbolton. Grays, 30 June.*

    6. IV. *Edw. Wyngfylde to Sir F. Knollys. In answer to his letter, has never objected to the orders given by his directions. Desires that he may enjoy the lands given to him by his father, the title to which he intends to try by law. Kymbolton, 4 July.*

July 8.
Oxford.

7. Commissioners of Musters for the county of Oxford to the Council. Refusal of Tho. Wennman, of Wytney Park, to furnish one light horse for Her Majesty's service, he being of ability and living meet for the same.

July 8.
Southwell.

8. Same for the county of Nottingham to same. Certify their doings in the musters which their poor small country is not able further to answer. *Inclosing,*

    8. I. *General certificate of the able men, furnished and unfurnished, in the county of Nottingham, amounting in the whole to 2,000 men.*

DOMESTIC—ELIZABETH. 665

1580.   VOL. CXL.

July 9.
Cobham.
9. Lord Cobham to Richard Barrey, Lieut. of Dover Castle. Sends the letter of Mr. Hawkyns and Mr. Holstok, for the levying of 160 sailors and mariners in Kent and Sussex. Carelessness of the Mayor of Sandwich.

July 10.
Portsmouth.
10. Sir Henry Radeclyff to Lord Burghley. His man has lately returned from Spain, and gives intelligence of the great preparations there: advises the bark should return and gain further intelligence secretly. The county is not in forwardness as to the musters, and not well organized in case of any alarm.

July 11.
Folk.
11. Thos. Chafin, Sheriff of Dorset, to Viscount Bindon. Complains of the misbehaviour of his son, Mr. Henry Howard, and of the outrageous treatment and abuse he has received from him. [*For this gross act Mr. Henry Howard was committed to the Marshalsea on the 31st of October following, where he remained till the 22nd of December, and was then discharged on acknowledging his fault. Co. Reg.*]

July 11.   12. Certificate of the general and special musters of able men, furnished and unfurnished, of the borough of Ipswich, in the county of Suffolk.

July 12.
Sarum.
13. The Mayor, &c. of the city of New Sarum to the Council. Have viewed all the able men meet to bear armour within their city. *Inclosing,*

13. I. *Certificate of the musters for the city of New Sarum.*

July 12.   14. William Parker to Burghley. Lord Morley's ill-will to his Lordship. Speech of certain of the servants of Lord Howard and the Earl of Arundel, charging Burghley and Leicester with being the cause of the Duke of Norfolk's death.

July 12.   15. Account of the charges of Tho. Randolphe, sent from Her Majesty to receive and entertain the Prince of Condé, during his sojourn in England.

July 13.
Norwich.
16. William Heydon and Nathaniel Bacon to the Council. That Bartholomew Baxter had broken the peace, and hazarded the forfeiture of his bond, by forcibly taking the tythes of lambs and wool of the benefice of Santon, against the claim of Reginald Metcalf, of Thetford.

July 13.   17. Certificate by Robert Petre of sums paid by him out of the Receipt, since the 5th of July last.

July 15.   18. Proclamation against spreading seditious rumours of the approach of a Spanish fleet, and a projected invasion of England by the Pope, the King of Spain, and other Princes. [*A draft wholly in Burghley's hand. This is the original of the printed proclamation, 15 July, 1580, from which however it varies in many particulars.*]

July 15.   19. Fair copy of the above; with considerable alterations by Burghley.

1580.
July 13.
20. Lord Burghley to the Justices of Gloucestershire. To permit Nicholas Wise Fitzjohn to buy 100 qrs. of wheat, and 250 qrs. of malt, within that county, for this year, and the same quantity next year, and to export the same to the city of Waterford.

July 20.
Launceston.
21. Commissioners for Musters in Cornwall to the Council. Have set forth 100 soldiers, furnished with armour and weapons, for Ireland. Their great expense in complying with the former order for 200 men for Ireland, whereby their little shire hath been greatly charged.

July 20 ?
22. Note of " the charge that the county of Cornwall hath been at since the first instructions for training of men, and how much the country shall be eased of that charge, which they most gratefully embrace."

July 20.
Kenilworth.
23. Earl of Leicester to Burghley. Explains the causes of his recent unkindness. Of late he has found less of Her Majesty's wonted favour. Particular of his suits to Her for some lands, which had been stayed, and the Queen fell into very hard terms, as well for the land as against the messenger. Desires a continuance of his friendship. The Castle of Banbury in good repair.

July 20.
Somerton.
24. Commissioners of Musters in Somersetshire to the Council. Have put in readiness 200 choice soldiers, and appointed George Popham to be their captain.

July 20.
25. Degory Nycoolls, Master of Magdalen College, Cambridge, to Lord Burghley. Sets forth the favorable intentions of the Lord Chief Justice towards that College. Their poverty, having but one scholarship.

July 20.
Paris.
26. T. Copley (Baron Copley) to same. Thanks him for his favorable mind towards him, but argues against the injustice of withholding from him his title, because conferred upon him by a foreign Prince. Instances many cases of titles of honour being conferred upon foreigners in England. Desires the restoration of Her Majesty's favor, and declares his zeal and fervent loyalty to her person and realm.

July 21.
Paris.
27. Same to same. Desires to offer him some present, and as he could not give him any massive thing, or of great value, he sends him a pedigree of Lady Burghley's family on the side of Belknape.

July 21.
Beare.
28. Sir Henry Radeclyff to the Council. Requests that artificers may be sent down for the scouring and trimming the armour, &c. under his charge at Portsmouth.

July 22.
Oatlands.
29. Sir Chr. Hatton to Burghley. Desires him to favour a renewal of his lease of the impost on wines. Acknowledges the recovery of his poor estate to have grown out of his great goodness and favour.

DOMESTIC—ELIZABETH. 667

1580. VOL. CXL.

July 22. 30. Commissioners of Musters in Staffordshire to the Council.
Wolverhampton. Have put in readiness 100 soldiers to be sent into Ireland, and appointed Mr. Timothy Egerton to be their captain.

July 25. 31. Sir Fr. Knollys to Walsyngham. Edw. Wyngfylde and his father persist in the spoil of the woods at Kymbolton. Desires a letter from the Council to restrain the sale of any timber there till after Christmas, and to warn Sir Harry Darcy and other purchasers.

July 27. 32. Commissioners for Musters in Leicestershire to the Council.
Leicester. Considerable time occupied in returning an extended certificate. Send that of their horsemen and particular persons charged.

July 27. 33. Knollys to Walsyngham. Is rejoiced the Council desires to see a true account of the revenues and profits of Thos. Wyngfylde's lands, as it will prove the falsehood of Edw. Wyngfylde's assertions. Sends two accounts by Mr. Marten, steward to his daughter the Countess. Desires another auditor might be appointed. *Incloses,*

33. I. *Note of the obligations made to Sir Walter Mildmay and Sir Francis Knollys of the sums placed out at interest by them, to sundry merchants, at the rate of 6 in 100, in trust for the use of the three daughters of Tho. Wyngfylde.*

July 30. 34. Mr. Watson's offers to be admitted into the offices of the Receipt and Star Chamber. Has an interest in the lease of Dr. Huyck's house.

July 30. 35. Commissioners for Musters in the county of Bedford to the Bedford. Council. Have used great care and diligence in taking the musters. Report on the amount of armour, and explain their certificate. *Inclosing,*

35. I. *General certificate of the Musters for the county of Bedford, of able men furnished and complete, and of horsemen, as well demi-lances as light horsemen, with the captains commanding them.*

July 30. 36. Certificate by Morris Pyckering, keeper of the Gatehouse, of the prisoners committed to his charge since 1577, and of those prisoners now remaining in his keeping.

July 31. 37. Certificate of prisoners committed to the Poultry Compter, principally for matters of religion, from the 29th of July 1577 to the 31st July 1580, stating the days on which they were actually committed, and under what authority.

July 31. 38. Similar certificate of the prisoners in the King's Bench committed within the last three years.

July 31. 39. Similar certificate by Tho. Lewys, keeper of the White Lion,
White Lion. Southwark, of the prisoners that are now or have been lately in his custody for matters of religion.

1580.
VOL. CXL.

July. 40. Similar certificate of all the prisoners remaining in the Marshalsea, for papistry.

July? 41. Resolutions upon the view of the certificates of the Lords Lieutenants of the several shires.

July? 42. Names of gentlemen appointed to furnish lances and light horse in the county of Cambridge.

July? 43. Articles to be alleged against certain persons for matters of religion.

July. 44. Examination of Mr. Abyngton's book of rates for the victualling of 3,500 soldiers, with the note of the prices to be allowed for provisions.

July? 45. List of counties which have certified their proceedings in the musters, and of those which have not yet returned certificates.

July? 46. The Council to Lord Cobham. Directs him to consult Sir Tho. Scott, Sir James Hales, and other competent persons, on the plans suggested for repair of Dover Haven, and to employ either Burrows, Eaton, Pett, Baker, or the Sluice Master of Dunkirk, to make surveys, and to give his opinion if the work could be successfully prosecuted.

VOL. CXLI. AUGUST, 1580.

Aug. 1. London.
1. Wm. Blunte, keeper of Wood Street Compter, to Sir Fr. Walsyngham. Certifies the names of the prisoners committed to the Compter for matters of religion.

Aug. 1. 2. Commissioners for Musters in the county of Essex to the Council. Their proceedings in the musters. Comparison between the number of able men furnished, now certified, and the returns of former musters. Have not appointed captains. Defences of the shire. *Inclosing,*

    2. I. II. *General certificates of musters of the whole county of Essex, amounting to 13,062 footmen and 300 horsemen, of whom 3,856 footmen were furnished complete. Two returns.*

    2. III. *Particular certificate of musters of the same county, with the numbers of captains, pioneers, and carriages.*

Aug. 2. 3. The form and effect of the proceedings of the Commissioners for causes Ecclesiastical, at Richmond in Yorkshire, at a meeting on the 2nd of August, summoned by their private letters. Presentment of various parties for ecclesiastical offences. Many refuse to appear, are either obstinate and rebellious, or else sick, or else they flee away. [*This private meeting is not detailed in the report of their public proceedings. See post.,* 16 *Aug.*]

DOMESTIC—ELIZABETH. 669

1580.

VOL. CXLI.

Aug. 3.
Wood Street
Compter.
4. Wm. Trewlock to Burghley and Walsyngham. Has come from the Low Countries to give information against Wm. Piper, who was treasonably dealing with the English rebels and the Spaniards there, by the influence of the Earl of Westmoreland. Has been arrested by Piper in an action for 500*l*.

Aug. 3.
Styfkie.
.5. Wm. Heydon and Nathaniel Bacon to the Council. Detail their proceedings in the controversy between Metcalf and Baxter for the benefice of Santon. Proposed that Baxter should restore the lambs he had wrongfully taken, but he obstinately refuses. They have therefore bound him over to appear before the Council on the 9th inst.

Aug. 4.
Paris.
6. T. Copley to Burghley. Takes advantage of Mr. Parry coming to England to renew his suit. Professes his zeal and loyalty to Her Majesty, and as an evidence of his fidelity, intends shortly to send home his wife, and hopes she will be well received.

Aug. 4.
Chester.
7. Wm. Goodman, Mayor of Chester, to the Council. Account of the charges for the victualling and transporting of 300 soldiers to Ireland. Desires payment of 155*l*. 5*s*. 6*d*. already expended, and to know how he should obtain money for the transporting of 500 more.

Aug. 5.
8. Sir Fr. Knollys to Walsyngham. Robert Doryngton boasts of the favour he has at Court; but he will say, unsay, or deny anything to suit his purpose. Sir Harry Darcy has received a letter from Edward Wyngfylde. Disclaims ever having received one penny profit from Mr. Wyngfylde's lands. *Incloses,*

> 8. I. *Edward Wyngfylde to Sir Henry Darcy. Solicits present payment for certain timber sold to him. The Council admits the justness of his suit, and the matter is to be heard again on Sunday next.*

Aug. 5.
Queen's Bench.
9. Representation by Tho. Hancocke, preacher, and others, to the Bishop of London, of the blasphemous speech of one Sherwood, prisoner in the King's Bench, who contemptuously refused to join in the Divine service.

Aug. 5.
Paris.
10. — G[ifford] to John Gifford, Esq., his father. Complains of hard usage, in forbidding his brother Edward to speak to him, and turning them both out into the world in a state of poverty.

Aug. 6.
Sudley.
11. Commissioners for Musters in Gloucestershire to the Council. Have taken the general musters of the county. *Inclosing,*

> 11. I. *General certificate of the musters for the county of Gloucester, as well footmen as demi-lances and light horse.*

1580.　　　　　　　　　Vol. CXLI.

Aug. 6.　　12. Effect of the licence granted to the town of Dover, to export
Oatlands.　certain quantities of beer and grain without custom.

Aug. 6.　　13. Licence by the Queen to Tho. Allyn, now Mayor, and to the
　　　　　　Jurats of the town and port of Dover, to export 4,000 tuns of beer,
　　　　　　30,000 qrs. of wheat, and 10,000 qrs. of barley or malt, custom free,
　　　　　　towards the repair of the haven of Dover.

Aug. 6.　　14. Fair copy of the above.

Aug. 7.　　15. Wm. Glaseor to Lord Burghley. The Irish troops embarked
Chester.　on the 1st instant driven back by stress of weather. Desires the
　　　　　　same allowance may be granted for coat and conduct money for the
　　　　　　500 soldiers now to be sent to Ireland, as was granted to the 300
　　　　　　last sent.

Aug. 8.　　16. Estimate of the cost for keeping Her Highness' whole navy,
　　　　　　being 14 sail of ships, ready for service upon 20 days' warning.

Aug. 8.　　17. Henry Earl of Kent to Sir Fr. Walsyngham. Transmits the
Waeste.　certificates of musters for Bedfordshire, which he desires to be for-
　　　　　　warded to the Council.

Aug. 10.　18. The Council to Wm. Heydon and Nathaniel Bacon. In answer
Oatlands.　to their letter of the 3rd instant, communicate the substance of
　　　　　　the order they have made in the controversy between Metcalf and
　　　　　　Baxter relative to the benefice of Santon. Metcalf is to enjoy quiet
　　　　　　possession of the same, and to receive from Baxter the tythes wrong-
　　　　　　fully taken by him.

Aug. 10.　19. Wm. Glaseor to Lord Burghley. Proceedings of Sir Hugh
Chester.　Cholmley and Mr. Hughes, the Receiver, with respect to the sale of
　　　　　　the Shire-hall to Mr. Bostock, which had been previously assigned
　　　　　　to himself. Bostock's contemptuous dealing and ill-will towards
　　　　　　him.

Aug. 10.　20. Same to same. The Lord Deputy of Ireland is still detained
Chester.　in Anglesey by contrary winds. Measures for the accommodation of
　　　　　　the 500 soldiers. Mr. Gascoigne, the new post-master, has arrived.

Aug. 10.　21. Same to Walsyngham. Has victuals in readiness to be sent
Chester.　to Ireland. The Lord Deputy still detained at Beaumaris.

Aug. 11.　22. Sir Edw. Horsey to the Earl of Leicester. Has delayed
Isle of Wight. coming to the Court, hearing he was at Kenilworth. Mr. Cornelis
　　　　　　desires longer time for the perfecting of his works. Sends a letter
　　　　　　from him making certain offers.

Aug. 11.　23. Benj. Titcheborne to Viscount Bindon and Lord Stourton.
Titchburn.　States the ill conduct of Mr. Henry Howard, towards the High
　　　　　　Sheriff of Dorset,his behaviour to himself, being a gentleman and
　　　　　　a stranger, was shameful.

DOMESTIC—ELIZABETH. 671

1580.   VOL. CXLI.

Aug. 12.
Lathom.
24. Earl of Derby to Leicester. Was delighted to see his hand to the comfortable letter that came from the Council, and at the same time he had received a most gracious letter from Her Majesty, which has encouraged him to prosecute those causes in matters of religion. Thanks Leicester for his kind advice given to him in the Queen's gallery, at Westminster.

Aug. 14 ?
25. Memoranda for a Commission for repair of Dover Haven. Names of Commissioners. Thos. Randolph and Thos. Smyth, the Customer, to be Treasurers. Suggestions for raising funds. The Bishops and Clergy to contribute, &c.

Aug. 15 ?
26. Heads of a Commission for the repair of Dover Haven, and of general directions for their proceeding in the execution of that work. [*On the 15th Aug., the Council addressed a letter to Lord Cobham, Sir Tho. Scott, Sir James Hales, Tho. Wotton, Edw. Boys, Richard Barrey, Wm. Partrych, and Henry Palmer, naming them Commissioners, with directions to consider of the plans for repair of the Haven. Co. Reg.*]

Aug. 15 ?
27. Instructions to the Commissioners for Dover Haven. To appoint a Treasurer, to aid Mr. Trewe in commencing the works, and to make estimates for two rods of the pier to be first erected, and overseers of the works to be appointed.

Aug. 16.
28. Notarial instrument of the declaration of the proceedings of the Commissioners for Ecclesiastical causes within the diocese and province of York; stating the number and places of their sittings, the juries impannelled, names of prisoners, recusants, &c., examined, and orders to be observed by the Mayor of Hull and keepers of the Castle and blockhouses there. [*This does not include the proceedings of the private meeting at Richmond, on the 2d of August. See that date.*]

Aug. 17.
Lawford.
29. John Talbott to the Earl of Leicester. Has been summoned to appear before the Council, to answer touching matters of religion. Desires an opportunity to consult some persons to satisfy his conscience. Protests his loyalty and obedience.

Aug. 17.
30. Petition of the Fellows of Corpus Christi College, Cambridge, to Lord Burghley, for redress of grievances. Complaining of the Master of the same (Robt. Norgate), who hath, in many points, infringed the good and wholesome statutes of the College. *Annexing*,

30. I. *Articles, whereupon the Fellows of Corpus Christi College have just occasion to complain against the Master of that College.*

Aug. 20.
Hereford.
31. Wm. Cicill, Sheriff, and others, Commissioners for Musters in the county of Hereford, to the Council. Have taken order to have the 200 soldiers in readiness for service in Ireland, and appointed Ric. Gwyn to be their Captain.

1580.
Aug. 20.
Dover.
32. Thomas Allyn, Mayor of Dover, and Thomas Andrewe, to Sir Fr. Walsyngham. Request to have a letter from the Council, directed to Sandwich and other ports in Kent, for leave to ship 2,400 quarters of wheat on their licence, to enable them to commence the works at Dover Haven.

Aug. 22.
Oatlands.
33. Dr. Richard Master to Lord Burghley. Describes the causes producing looseness of the teeth, from which his Lordship was suffering; prescribes for him, as counselled by Galen.

Aug. 22.
Bishopsthorpe.
34. Archbishop Sandys to John Wickliffe, keeper of his house at Battersey. Directs him to deliver up that house to the Lords of the Council, to be a prison for obstinate Papists.

Aug. 23.
Hertford.
35. Wm. Tooke, the younger, to Burghley. Sickness has prevented him from satisfactorily executing his place of Attorneyship. Desires leave to assign it over to John Hare of the Temple, who has married his near kinswoman.

Aug. 24.
Canterbury.
36. Sir Tho. Scott, Sir James Hales, and others, Commissioners for Dover Haven, to the Council. Have met upon their commission, and appointed a rate of wages for John Trewe while constructing the two rods of the pier. Desire a commission for Trewe to take up workmen. They estimate 20,000 qrs. of wheat might at once be spared for exportation.

Aug. 24?
37. Estimate of the sums to be raised throughout England by a tax on Victuallers for the works at Dover Haven.

Aug. 24.
The Court.
38. Sir Fr. Walsyngham to Burghley. Sends advertisements, shewing the uncertainty of the issue of the treaty of peace in France. Soldiers being raised in Switzerland. The Queen agrees that 500*l.* may be paid to the party for the secret cause that only himself and Burghley are aware of. She is uncertain what to do in that affair. Sends him a letter in Italian by an English Jesuit. To-morrow the Queen dines with the Duchess of Somerset.

Aug. 25.
Theobalds.
39. Burghley to Leicester. Thanks for his letter about the Queen's health, which is the only thread whereby his poor heart is tied to life. Commends the excellent qualities of the hound given to him by Leicester, "for she maketh my huntyng very certen; she hath " never fayled me; and this last weke she brought me to a stagg " wch myself had strycken with my bow, being forced to ye soyle, " wher w^t help of a gretar water spannyell y^t forced hym out of y^e " water, your good brache helped to pluck hym down." Commends Mr. North.

Aug. 25.
Blandford.
40. Commissioners for Musters in Dorsetshire to the Council. Have put 4,000 men in readiness for defence of the sea coasts, and selected 3,000 for the aid of Devon; but they cannot send their certificate until the end of September. State the causes of the delay.

1580.

Aug. 26.
Blandford.
41. Commissioners for Musters in Dorsetshire to the Council. Have appointed a new captain for the service in Ireland, in the room of Mr. George Turbervile, who was a great spurner of their authority.

Aug. 26.
London.
42. Sir Owyn Hopton and others to Burghley, Leicester, Sir Chr. Hatton, and the rest of the Commissioners for the office of the Armoury. Have made a survey of all the armour remaining in the Tower. Send an estimate of the charges for making rooms within the great White Tower for hanging up all the armour.

Aug. 28.
Barn Elms.
43. Robert Beale to Leicester. Has, with Mr. Alderman Martin, searched Mr. Stanihurst's house, but found no letters or papers as suspected: certain papers were found proving him to have been connected with mineral matters, but he denies ever meddling with coining or forgery.

Aug. 30.
Chester.
44. Hugh Rogerson, Mayor of Chester, to the Council. Relative to the lodging, victualling, and transportation of the troops for Ireland. Solicits payment of 259l. 19s. 5d. remaining due to him for the same. Was elected Mayor on the 19th Aug., Mr. Wm. Goodman, his predecessor, having died on the 13th.

Aug. 31.
45. Act of the Company of Merchants trading to Spain and Portugal, restraining the importation of any articles in exchange for corn sent thither, except bullion, salt, and oranges.

Aug.
46. Opinion of the Commissioners how a convenient sum of money might be levied for the making of Dover Haven. The points to be considered of: by licences for grain; by impositions on alehouses and on shipping; by benevolence, the Bishops to be written to; contributions from the City Companies, &c.

Aug.
47. An estimate, by Walsyngham, of the sums that might be raised by the licences for grain, by contributions, and by way of tax, for repair of Dover Haven.

Aug.
48. Ways to levy a convenient sum of money for the repair of Dover Haven; licences, taxation, the clergy, &c.; the sums remaining blank.

Aug.
49. Copy of the above, by Walsyngham, with the sums filled up, and the amounts likely to be produced.

Aug.?
50. Notes of fines for various offences; probably for raising money for Dover Haven.

Aug.?
51. Statement of the number of parishes in England and Wales, with the amount of fees to be charged upon the admission of every victualler, towards the repair of Dover Haven.

1580.

Vol. CXLI.

Aug. ?	52. Statement of the number of shires in England and Wales, their division into bishopricks and parishes, with the number of victuallers in the whole, for raising a fund for Dover Haven.
Aug. ?	53. Estimate for a contribution for the new building of the harbour of Dover; dividing England into shires, bishopricks, and parishes; the inns and taverns, Inns of Court, &c.
Aug. ?	54. The Council to the Justices of Peace in certain shires. Directions to levy at once the fines upon such alehouses as have not yet paid, and to transmit the same to Mr. Randolph, Treasurer for the works at Dover.
Aug. ?	55. Note of the counties that have not yet made any return of innholders, taverns, and alehouses.
Aug. ?	56. The Council to the Bishops. To urge the wealthy clergy to contribute liberally, at least to the extent of one tenth of their incomes for three years, towards the repair of Dover Haven, and pay over the sums collected to Tho. Smith and Tho. Randolphe, the Treasurers for that work.
Aug. ?	57. Memorandum of the rate of contribution to be taxed upon the clergy, and upon inns and victualling houses, for Dover Haven.
Aug. ?	58. An estimate of charges to be incurred for the repair of Dover Harbour.

Vol. CXLII. September, 1580.

Sept. 1. Cobham.	1. Lord Cobham to Sir Fr. Walsyngham. Sends a certificate from the Commissioners for the Pier, and requests the use of a house upon the Pier for Mr. Trewe; and that he might be furnished with commission to take up masons, &c. for the works at Dover. Other requests of Trewe's.
Sept. 1.	2. Sundry points, for the consideration of the Council, about the Haven and Pier at Dover; being the effect of Trewe's requests, mentioned in the above letter.
Sept. 1.	3. Requests of Mr. Trewe, to have the use of the house on the Pier; a commission to take up masons and workmen; leave to erect 100 foot of work, which would be a better proportion than two rods; to be continued in the work till its completion, and to appoint the clerks and overseers.
Sept. 1.	4. Requests of the town of Dover, touching their Haven. To compound with persons for exporting grain under their licence. Quantities in one year. That the City of London and resident gentry might be asked to contribute by way of loan, and a Treasurer to be appointed for sale of grain.

DOMESTIC—ELIZABETH. 675

1580. VOL. CXLII.
Sept. 2. 5. William St. Barbe to Sir Fr. Walsyngham. Complimentary.
Christ Church, Thanks him for his favours towards him. Lat.
Oxford.

Sept. 6. 6. Lord North and others, Commissioners for Musters in Cam-
Kirtling. bridgeshire, to the Special Commissioners for the Musters of Horses.
Are sorry their doings in the musters have not given satisfaction.
They now send certificates, and state the difficulty of rating men
to the true value of their livings. *Inclosing,*

    6. I. *Certificate of all persons rated to find horses and geldings
within the county of Cambridge, either by law or persuasion, with the number of the same. Sept.* 6.

Sept. 6. 7. Bishop Cox to same. Excuses his neglect, on account of his
Downham. age and infirmities, in not certifying the names of the persons rated
to keep horses. Desires to know if he should rate himself after the
same proportion as the laity. *Incloses,*

    7. I. *Certificate of the persons rated to keep horses and geldings,
as well those in the county of Cambridge, as those in
the Isle of Ely. Sept.* 6.

Sept. 7. 8. Sir Christopher Hatton to the Queen. △△△ Thanks
Bedford. for her exceeding and infinite parts of unspeakable goodness. " He
" should sin against a holy ghost most damnably, if towards Her
" Highness he should be found unthankful." The poor wretch his
sick servant receives his life again through her most princely love of
his poor master. Will live and die in pure and unspotted faith
towards her, for EveR.

Sept. 9. 9. Sir Henry Lee to Mr. Atey, Secretary to the Earl of Liecester.
Woodstock. Thanks for his information of news at Court. Wishes success to
Antonio, the new King of Portugal, and to our Irish causes.

Sept. 9. 10. Sir John Huband to Arthur Atey. Has made the Lord
Denbigh. President acquainted with his discourses. Great overthrow sustained
by the English in Ireland. Desires to know if Sir Fulke Greville is
to have the Mastership of the Game.

Sept. 9. 11. Commissioners for Musters in Essex to the Council, and to
Chelmsford. the Commissioners for Horses. Send certificates, and hope it will
be found they have rated themselves high enough. Their doings in
the commission. Excuse their delay in certifying the persons rated
for that service. *Inclosing,*

    11. I. *Certificate of the names of all persons rated or to be rated
for the finding of demi-lances and light horses furnished
for Her Majesty's service within the county of Essex.*

    11. II. *Fair copy of the above.*

DOMESTIC—ELIZABETH.

VOL. CXLII.

1580.
Sept. 10.
Theobalds.
12. Lord Burghley to the Officers of Ports. Not to permit the entry of any goods or merchandize from Paris, on account of the plague raging there.

Sept. 10.
Coleshull.
13. Commissioners for Muster of Horses in Warwickshire to the Council. Certify their doings in the musters, and commission for increase of horses. Request order for restraint of certain persons who refuse voluntarily to provide the horses and furniture rated by them. *Inclosing,*

13. I. *Certificate of the names of all gentlemen and others appointed to find lances or light horses within the counties of Warwick and the city of Coventry.*

Sept. 11. 14. Commission to John Trewe to provide and take up all manner of masons, carpenters, and labourers, and also ships, hoys, carts, horses, wains, waggons, all manner of iron mines, furnaces, and forges, shipwrights, smiths, timber, stone, &c., for carrying on the works at Dover Haven.

Sept. 11. 15. Copy of the above, with the clause relating to iron mines, furnaces, forges, &c. struck out.

Sept. 11. 16. The Queen to all Justices of Peace, &c. Notifies the granting of a commission to John Trewe, Surveyor of the works at Dover, to take up masons, carpenters, materials, &c., for the reparation of Dover Haven.

Sept. 12.
Theobalds.
17. Lord Burghley to Sir Jas. Hales, Ric. Barrey, Tho. Wilford, and Tho. Fludd, Surveyor of the county of Kent. To take a survey of Shurland House, and to report if any unlawful spoil had been committed there by Mr. Holstok.

Sept. 14.
Stafford.
18. Commissioners for the Muster of Horses in Staffordshire to the Council. Have amended their former certificate, and annexed the names of all persons chargeable with the providing of horses.

Sept. 15.
Ricot.
19. Same for Oxfordshire to same. Have inserted the parks where mares for breeding ought to be kept, but cannot discover any other defect in their former certificate.

Sept. 18. 20. A paper containing a series of letters and writings of various dates, from the 7th to the 18th Sept. 1580, from Thomas Poundes a Jesuit, addressed to Mr. Tripp, to the Privy Council in the name of all the Catholics in England, and to Sir Chr. Hatton, with a declaration in nine points or articles, opening the full enterprise and purpose of his coming into England. Indorsed, " *Certain Papistical* " *reasons set down for the withdrawing of men to come to the church,* " *sent from the Sheriff of Wiltshire.*"

Sept. 9.
Reading.
21. Commissioners for Muster of Horses in Berkshire to the Council. Send certificate of the whole number of persons chargeable with the keeping of horses, and the names and sirnames of every one charged either by statute or voluntary increase.

DOMESTIC—ELIZABETH. 677

1580. VOL. CXLII.

Sept. 19. Sir Chr. Hatton to the Queen. △△△♃ Has received her most gracious letters on his knees, with such reverence as becometh her most obliged bondsman, and offers himself, his life, and all that is him, to do her service. The cunning of her style of writing exceedeth all the eloquence of the world. Prays for her success in all her kingly affairs, and that they may EveR succeed. Against love and ambition she hath holden a long war, but now it is more than time to yield.

Sept. 21. 23. George Gifford to his brother Giles Gifford, student in New Inn. Thanks him for his letter, which brings him, as it were, home to behold the state of his father's house. All study has ceased at Paris by reason of the plague. Desires his uncle Robert may not come to Paris.

Sept. 22. Paris. 24. Same to his father John Gifford. Has joyfully received his letters. The great mortality in Paris obliges them to travel farther into France to a city called Muscyponte, in Lorraine. Wants money. Mr. Bayley, his tutor, has lent him 12 crowns.

Sept. 22. Rothwell. 25. Commissioners for Musters in Northamptonshire to the Council. Certify their doings in the musters, and excuse their delay. *Inclosing,*

25. I. *Certificate of the general musters of footmen and horsemen in the county of Northampton.*

Sept. 23. Padua. 26. Wm. Grene to Mr. Atey. Solicits him to write to inform him of health of his friends, and the state of the realm. Defeat and supposed death of Antonio ; the capitulation of Lisbon and conquest of all Portugal followed. The common speech is that the next voyage shall be to Ireland.

Sept. 23. Willoughby House. 27. Peregrine Bertie to Sir Fr. Walsyngham. Asserts his title to the baronies of Willoughby and Ersby, in right of his mother, the Duchess of Suffolk, lately deceased. Solicits his favour with Her Majesty, that he may be permitted to prove his claim by law.

Sept. 26. 28. Note of charges for extraordinary posts laid and prepared betwixt the Court at Richmond and Bristol, by Robert Gascoigne.

Sept. 27. Chatham. 29. John Hawkyns to Walsyngham. Reports the state of the naval preparations. Six ships would be ready by the next Saturday. Unwillingness of the mariners to serve.

Sept. 28. 30. [Anonymous] to same. Reports of the landing of some Spaniards and Italians in Ireland. Regrets that more credit has not been given to his information of the evil intentions of foreign Princes. Requests money and the return of his letters and informations.

Sept. 29. The Queen to the Bishops, &c. To incite the clergy to furnish light horses for service in Ireland, to resist the descent of certain foreign forces sent there by the Pope and his adherents. [*See Warrant Book,* I., *p.* 83. *These letters were ordered on the 29th of September. Co. Reg.*]

1580

Vol. CXLII.

Sept. 30. Rouen.
31. Wm. Clederow to Thos. Warcop, Gentleman Pensioner. Will proceed in his business as soon as he can, unless he hears to the contrary.

Sept.
32. Lists of the names of all the ecclesiastical persons within all the dioceses of the provinces of Canterbury and York, charged with the furnishing and keeping of demi-lances and light horse for Her Majesty's service.

Sept. ?
33. List of recusants within the diocese of Canterbury, stating their names, their property in lands and goods, and the assessment on them for lances and light horse. Indorsed by Walsyngham, "*The " pertyculer booke of recusantes, agreable with the scedules to be " sent with Her Ma^{ts} letters.*"

Sept. ?
34. Certificate of the general musters of all persons, furnished and unfurnished, within the several wards of Darlington, Stockden, Chester, and Easington, in the county palatine of Durham.

Sept. ?
35. General certificate of musters of foot and horse, furnished and unfurnished, for the county of Dorset, amounting to 6,000 able men.

Sept. ?
36. Particular certificate of musters for the county of Dorset, amounting to 3,000 furnished complete.

Sept.
37. Certificate of the county of Dorset of all the demi-lances and light horse, with the names of the noblemen and gentlemen, and the numbers furnished by each.

Sept. ?
38. Necessary points to be resolved of, by my Lords of the Council, relative to the defences for the county of Dorset.

Sept. ?
39. The names of such persons in the county of Essex as are severally rated by the Council's books for the finding of horses and geldings for Her Majesty's service, set down in such sort as they are there named ; together with the refusal or exception of such of them as find themselves grieved therewith. Noted by Burghley, "Y^e " second certificat from ye country."

40. Names of gentlemen residing in the several hundreds of Essex rated for the furnishing of lances and light horse.

41. Another list of names of gentlemen residing in certain hundreds of Essex, but for what particular service is not specified.

Sept. ?
42. Remembrances for the Clerks of the Signet, as to the fees and duties of their office.

Sept. ?
43. A note of the names of such as were committed for Papistry in the counties of Norfolk, Suffolk, and Cambridge.

Sept. ?
44. Commission to Wm. Hawkyns, to have charge of a fleet of ships to be employed on a voyage of discovery on the coasts of Africa and America. Authority to assist Don Antonio, King of Portugal, against any of his enemies.

DOMESTIC—ELIZABETH. 679

1580.
Sept. 45. Particular certificate of the musters of footmen and horsemen furnished complete in the county of Middlesex.

Sept. ? 46. Names of such persons as do find horses and geldings for the wars in the county of Middlesex, and the names of such as were charged to find horses and geldings and have not agreed thereto.

Sept. ? 47. Note of the charges for several forts and garrisons in the Isle of Wight.

Sept. ? 48. Account of the yearly charges of the Isle of Wight according to the new arrangement.

VOL. CXLIII.   OCTOBER, 1580.

Oct. 1. 1. Wm. Brereton to the Earl of Leicester. Explains the reasons
Chester. why last certificate had only his signature to it. The difference in the numbers certified must be attributed to "the Armytrition," who in his unskilfulness set down "his figure of 1 in shewe lyke to the "figure of 2." Sends a book of their horsemen by the bearer. Thinks the number of brood mares might be increased. *Incloses,*

    1. I. *Certificate of the number of footmen, able men, furnished and unfurnished, within the county of Chester. The total of able men furnished, 1,000, has evidently been altered by erasure.*

    1. II. *Certificate of the number of demi-lances and light horses furnished by the gentlemen of Cheshire, with the number of mares for breed in the county.*

Oct. 1. 2. Commissioners for Musters in Cheshire to the Council. Excuse
Chester. their former neglect, and certify the names of gentlemen chargeable with the keeping of horses and demi-lances. *Inclosing,*

    2. I. *Certificate of the number of horsemen furnished in the county of Chester, and of the gentlemen keeping mares for breeding.*

Oct. 3. 3. Same for the city of Gloucester to same. Their doings in the
Gloucester. musters. They had forborne the training and assembling of men for fear of infection of the plague, which continued from Easter till Michaelmas. *Inclosing,*

    3. I. *General certificate of Musters of footmen and horsemen for the city of Gloucester, with the captains commanding them.*

Oct. 4. 4. Justices of Dorsetshire to the same. Report of Mr. Henry
Bridport. Howard's undutiful speeches to his father, Viscount Bindon, when warned by him in Court to appear before the Council.

Oct. 4. 5. Rowland Stanley to his mother Mrs. Eliz. Stanley. His father is fully determined to leave the wars and retire to some private part of the country. Desires that the hawks and a greyhound may be sent with Tom; with a postscript to his sister.

1580.
VOL. CXLIII.

Oct. 4.
Gloucester.
6. Thos. Lane, Mayor, and the Aldermen of Gloucester, to Lord Burghley. Have received Her Majesty's grant of a custom house at Gloucester, and thank his Lordship for his kindness therein, and send him his patent and his fee to Christmas next.

Oct. 4.
Prescot.
7. Bishop Chaderton to Sir Fr. Walsyngham. Would do his diligence for the furnishing of light horsemen for Ireland. Many of the gentlemen of the county neglected to perform their parts, expecting some great change would shortly take place. Commends the Earl of Derby. Requests the release of his first fruits.

Oct. 5.
8. Probate of the will of Thos. Ellyott, citizen and pewterer of London, bequeathing, among other things, to Bartholomew Kirbye, parson of Harteshorne, his "nighte gowne furred with lambe and "faced with foynes."

Oct 7.
Rotta.
9. Licence granted by Robert Hanley to Philip Beste and others, to lade on board the Margrette Bonadventure, their several complements of Rotta, Sherris, and Chepiona fruits, by virtue of an Act made by the Company of Merchants trading to Spain and Portugal.

Oct. 8.
10. Sir Robert Wyngfeld and others, Commissioners for Musters in the county of Suffolk, to the Council. Cause of their not having before certified the names of the gentlemen charged with the keeping of horses. *Inclosing,*

    10. I. *Certificate of persons charged with lances and light horses; similar to the first certificate (May), but with more names inserted.*

Oct. 8.
Manchester.
11. Bishop Chaderton to Lord Burghley and Sir Fr. Walsyngham. Proceedings of the Earl of Derby and others in the affairs of Christ's College, Manchester. Motions that the College might be discharged of Mr. Herlle's pension. Sends the names of all such as were indicted at the last sessions for matters of religion; many of all sorts being reclaimed. Desires remembrance of his former suit for his fruits.

Oct. 10.
East Lulworth.
12. Mrs. Frances Howard (wife of Henry Howard) to Sir Fr. Walsyngham. Has of late written to him of her woeful estate. Her husband refused to bring her with him, and left her without either horses or money. Is in danger of her life.

Oct. 10.
Wareham.
13. Thos. Viscount Howard of Bindon, to the Council. Details the undutiful and irreverent conduct of his son Henry Howard towards him in open sessions, when commanded to appear before their Lordships. Desires his son's poor wife may be protected from the practices of him and of the quean he keeps, she having been already beaten most pitifully, and many ways else misused.

Oct. 10.
Wareham.
14. Same to Walsyngham. Has written to the Council on the ill conduct of his son H. Howard. Desires him to be a means that some good order may be taken for the safety of his wife.

DOMESTIC—ELIZABETH. 681

1580.   Vol. CXLIII.

Oct. 16.   15. Number of men rated by the Council to be trained and furnished in each of the counties where no training hath been.

Oct. 16.   16. Duplicate of the above.

Oct. 16.   17. George Carleton and Humfrey Michell to the Council. Reasons
Wisbeach   why they could not thoroughly acquaint their Lordships of the state
Castle.   of the recusants in Wisbeach Castle. The prisoners are eight in number, Watson, Fecknam, Younge, Windham, Oxenbridge, Mettam, Wood, and Bluet. Desire to know if their servants are to have free access to them, and whether they should have their meals together.

Oct. 18.   18. Notes of business to be performed relative to the musters.

            19. Fair copy of the above.

Oct. 18.   20. List of the names of all Her Majesty's ships, their tonnage, number of mariners, gunners, and soldiers; the charge for setting them forth to sea; together with the names of 22 merchant ships fit to join with the Queen's ships if needed.

Oct. 18.   21. Note of taxation set on the clergy of the province of Canterbury, for the charges of Mr. Daniel Rogers, sent into Germany.

Oct. 18.   22. Copy of the above.

Oct. 18.   23. Matters to be considered for the execution of the commission for the breeding of horses; a general order to be given for the keeping of mares and good stallions in all parks, pastures, and commons, in such sort as by the statute is appointed.

Oct. 18.   24. Another copy.

Oct. 18.   25. Another copy.

Oct. 18 ?   26. The distribution of the several counties for the Commissioners of Horses; a certain number of counties being assigned to particular Commissioners.

Oct. 19.   27. The information given by Christopher Bancroft against Arthur Blyncowe and others for matters of religion. Assault on Bancroft by one Goodridge.

Oct. 20.   28. Note of the cost of ale and beer brewed for Her Majesty's household, 21° and 22° Eliz., amounting to 4,690 tuns, 3 hogsheads, and 22 gallons, in the two years.

Oct. 22.   29. The Commissioners for Musters in the county of Hereford to
Wellington. the Council. Have mustered the whole forces of the county, being greatly hindered and very much letted therein, by means of the great infection of the plague. *Inclosing,*

            29. I. *Particular certificate of Musters for the whole county of Hereford, amounting to 6,102 men exclusive of the city of Hereford.*

1580.

VOL. CXLIII.

Oct. 24.
Richmond.
30. The Queen to Edmund Tremayne. To assist Francis Drake in sending up certain bullion brought into the realm by him, but to leave so much of it in Drake's hands as shall amount to the sum of 10,000*l.*, the leaving of which sum in his hands is to be kept most secret to himself alone.

Oct. 24.
Wareham.
31. Viscount Bindon to Sir Fr. Walsyngham. Desires him to favour his poor daughter-in-law, on her coming to London. Calls his attention to two statutes executed by his son Henry Howard, one to Mr. Andrew Dyer, the other to Robert Aden of Horsington, the husband of the naughty quean his son had taken into keeping.

Oct. 24.
Wareham.
32. Same to the Council. Had been induced to permit his daughter-in-law to repair to their Lordships, contrary to the orders sent to him, by her pitiful moan to him, she being in fear of her life by her husband's ill treatment.

Oct. 24.
Dover Castle:
33. Ric. Barrey to Lord Cobham. Has stayed Wm. Hyldesley at Dover, on his landing from abroad, with William Middlemore (nephew of Mr. Middlemore, of the Privy Chamber) in his company, who were bearers of letters from many young Papists and others abroad to their friends in England, together with two books, some crucifixes, a picture of "Marye Mawdlyn holowed, and certen other "tryffles." *Incloses,*

33. I. *Thos. Crofte to Mr. Geo. Mydelmore, his brother-in-law, "at the signe of the Bushope in Fleate Streate." Their safe arrival, but not without danger from the plague. Letters to be delivered to the carrier of Ludlow. Will write to his brother Alex. Crofte, to send Mydelmore some money. Poissy,* 3 *Oct.,* 1580.

33. II. *Tho. Bayly to Wm. Barnes. Desires repayment of money which he had lent to his brother Tho. Barnes.* 9 *Oct.* 1580.

33. III. *Same to Mr. Giles Gifford. Has lent money to George Gifford on his departure to Pontemuson, of which he requests repayment. George Gifford will soon want more money; he is a good youth, but somewhat sickly.* 9 *Oct.,* 1580.

33. IV. *Same to Wm. Hodges. Acquaints him with the sickness of his son William Hodges, and the idle and unruly conduct of his other son Master R., whose money in a short time would all be spent.* 9 *Oct.,* 1580.

33. V. *Edward Stransam to Mr. Middlemore, of Hawxley. Cause of sending home his son William Middlemore, who found the study of Latin very difficult. Commends his general conduct. Progress of Robert Middlemore in his studies.* 9 *Oct.,* 1580.

33. VI. *Same to Mr. Crocford. In commendation of his brother William Crocford, who cannot continue his studies on account of ill health, which has greatly increased his expenses.* 9 *Oct.,* 1580.

DOMESTIC—ELIZABETH. 683

1580.

VOL. CXLIII.

33. VII. *Christopher Turner to Mr. Hawverly. To send him a young youth, about the age of 12 or 13 years, that can handle his needle well. Poissy, 10 Oct.*, 1580.

33. VIII. *Richard Gī to Tho. Cornwell. Desires him to inform Mr. D. F. that he had only once heard from him, and desires to have no more to do for him at Paris.* 10 Oct.

33. IX. *Wm. Harrison to his father. Harrie Morgan is in good health. Has often written, but fears his letters have not all arrived safe.* 12 Oct.

33. X. *Owen Lloyd to Wm. Pryse. Desires him to send 16 pair of Oxford gloves, of the finest, of 5 or 6 groats a pair, of double chevrell, 6 for women, 6 for men, and 4 for very ancient and grave men, spiritual.* 13 Oct.

33. XI. *Richard Gifford to George Gifford. Marvels he has not heard from him for a long time. Desires him to continue his love and favour, and trusts he will keep his promise. Amiens, 12 Oct.*, 1580.

33. XII. *Tho. Crofte to his brother Alexander Crofte. The success of his journey has hitherto been very unfortunate, by reason of the wars, and the universal plague in France. Wants money. Poissy, 13 Oct.*, 1580.

33. XIII. *Peter Coppley to his father Tho. Coppley, at Bredon. Difficulties of his hard and perilous journey into France. His brother has resumed his studies. Requests money may be sent to him without delay. Poissy, 13 Oct.*

Oct. 24.
Colocumb.

34. Edmund Tremayne to Sir Fr. Walsyngham. His kind dealings towards Lord Grey gives great satisfaction to his friends, and especially the Earl of Bedford. Sends 15l. the half year's annuity due to Mr. Ric. Byngham. Is in grief for the death of his son who only lived 20 days. His increasing age and weakness prevents him from satisfactorily performing the duties of his office.

Oct. 24.

35. William Holstok's answer to Mr. Gorge's bill of complaints against him, for dilapidations at Shurland House; certified by Mr. Fludd.

Oct. 24.

36. Articles exhibited against the Master of Corpus Christi College, by Mr. Philip Nicols, Fellow of the same.

Oct. 24.

37. Protest of Dr. Robert Norgate, Master of Corpus Christi College, Cambridge, made before Doctor Hatcher Vice-Chancellor, and Doctor Byng, thinking it not lawful or reasonable for a Master to be called to account on the complaint of a single Fellow only. *Annexed,*

37. I. *Answer of Dr. Norgate to the complaints exhibited against him by Philip Nicols.*

1580.
Vol. CXLIII.

Oct. 24. 38. Mr. Philip Nichols' reply to the Master's first answer, which he made and delivered to Dr. Hatcher and Dr. Byng.

Oct. 25.
Bangor.
39. Bishop Robinson to the Council. Himself and the Dean of Bangor have sent three light horsemen to Chester. The Chapter are mostly non-resident, far apart, and could not be warned in time.

Oct. 26.
Corpus Christi College.
40. Dr. Norgate, the Master of Bennet (Corpus Christi) College, to Lord Burghley. Sends by Mr. Chevers, a Senior Fellow, his rejoinder to the reply of Mr. Nicols, whereby it may appear how unjustly he has been charged. *Incloses*,

    40. I. *Rejoinder by the Master of Corpus Christi College, to Mr. Nicols' reply; exhibited under his former protestation.*

Oct. 26. 41. Report by Sir James Hales and Tho. Fludd, of the survey made by them of Shurland House, on the alleged dilapidations there by Mr. Holstok. The house, in many places of the same, is much decayed.

Oct. 28.
Red Cross Street.
42. Wm. Herlle to Sec. Wylson. Sues for the release of R. Yorck, who had been unjustly committed on the charges of one Elkes, a man very infamous, a detractor, indicted of felony, and outlawed upon the same; of whom he sends some particulars.

Oct. 28.
Tatersall.
43. Henry Lord Clynton and others, Justices of Lincolnshire, to Lord Burghley. Causes of the breach of the composition in the parts of Lindsey, for the provision of Her Majesty's household. The Purveyor has taken the full number of sheep due, which was but twenty score.

Oct. 29. 44. Minute of the case between Mr. Cressey, Sir John Danvers, and Mr. R. Huddelston. Debt owing by Danvers to Mr. Wenman at the death of Mr. William Norrys.

Oct. ? 45. Orders to be observed by the several captains in the maritime counties, for the continuance of the training.

[Oct.] 46. The names of the martial men dispersed in certain counties within the realm.

[Oct.?] 47. Note of pikes and harquebuses wanting in the several shires, and desired to be supplied out of the Queen's stores in the office of the Ordnance.

Oct. ? 48. Petition of Michael Owen, Clerk in the Remembrancer's office in the Exchequer, to Walsyngham. Desires protection against his creditors for one year, so that he might be able to prove Her Majesty's title to certain escheated lands.

DOMESTIC—ELIZABETH.

VOL. CXLIV. NOVEMBER, 1580.

1580.
Nov. 1.
Red Cross Street.
1. Wm. Herlle to the Earl of Leicester. Begs him to recollect his advertisement about the Isles of Scilly. Reports his visit to the French Ambassador, and conversation with him on the affairs of England and Spain. Insidious designs of Spain. The French Ambassador declares he has too much honor, as a Frenchman, to be Hispaniolated: he sware a great oath he was offered 50,000 crowns as a bribe to become Spanish and to break off the match. The Spanish Amb. furious against Drake. Wonders at so vain and distempered a fellow as Daniel Rogers being sent on such weighty affairs. *Incloses,*

1. I. *Schedule of the names of the practisers and spies of the Spanish Ambassador.*

Nov. 1.
Corpus Christi Col., Oxon.
2. John Rainoldes to Sir Fr. Walsyngham. Thanks him for his interference as mediator in the differences between him and the Earl of Warwick. Lat.

Nov. 1.
Corp. Ch. Coll.
3. Same to Mr. Arthur Atey (Sec. to Leicester). Thanks him for his kindness in their affairs, he having been sent by the Bp. of Winchester to Walsyngham to get access to the Earl of Warwick to purge himself of certain crimes wherewith he had been unjustly charged. Hopes that a good President may be appointed for their College.

Nov. 2.
King's Coll. Camb.
4. John Harington to Walsyngham. Thanks for his patronage, and acquaints him that he has entered on the study of the Civil Law. Lat.

Nov. 3.
5. Justices of Staffordshire to the Council. State their opinion that John Archepole (or Archebold) had been very properly deprived of his office of Clerk of the Peace by Thos. Trentham, Esq., Custos Rotulorum, and Mr. Barroll appointed in his place.

Nov. 4.
Vere House.
6. Warrant of the Earl of Oxford to Edward Hubbert, his Receiver General, to pay 200*l.* yearly to Lady Oxford out of the rents of Lavenham Park.

Nov. 5.
7. Deposition of Harry Smyth, of Exeter, relative to the information given by Mrs. Weston, respecting one Clinton Atkinson, for whom Symon Knight, then Mayor of Exeter, endeavoured to procure a pardon.

Nov. 5.
Dover Castle.
8. John Garrett, Mayor, and others, Commissioners for Dover Haven, to Walsyngham. Have devised three ways for levying money for carrying on the works. The late restraint of transportation of grain will act injuriously. John Trewe is an able man.

Nov. 6.
9. Commission of Deputation from Edward Earl of Lincoln, Lord Admiral, Thomas Earl of Sussex Lord Chamberlain, Henry Earl of Huntingdon Lord President of the North, Ambrose Earl of Warwick Master of the Ordnance, Francis Earl of Bedford, Robert Earl of Leicester Master of the Horse, Sir Henry Sydney Lord President of Wales, and Sir Christopher Hatton Vice Chamberlain, Lords Commissioners for the increase and breed of Horses and for the keeping of horses and geldings for service, to Henry Lord Burgavenny, William Lord Cobham Lord Warden of the Cinque Ports, Sir Thomas Scott, Sir Thomas Walsingham, Sir Thomas Fane, and Thomas Wotton, Esq., appointing them Deputy Commissioners within the county of Kent, for the purposes of the above commission.

1580. VOL. CXLIV.

Nov. 6.   10. Similar commission by the above, to Edward Lord Morley, Robert Lord Riche, John Lord Darcy of Chiche, Sir Thomas Mildmay, Sir Thomas Barryngton, and Sir John Peter, for the county of Essex. [*This Commission is addressed to Thomas Lord Morley, but as no such name is to be found in the Peerages, it is presumed the party meant was Edward Lord Morley.*]

Nov. 6.   11. Copy of the above.

Nov. 6.   12. Draft of the above Commission of Deputation, addressed to certain noblemen and gentlemen in every county.

Nov. 6.   13. Instructions by the above Lords Commissioners for the increase and breed of Horses, and for the keeping of horses and geldings for service, to their Deputy Commissioners in every county, for the better carrying into effect the purposes of their commission. The Earl of Sussex to take special care to see the commission executed in Essex, Suffolk, Norfolk, Cambridge, and Kent.

Nov. 6.   14. Names of the Sub-commissioners for the breed and increase of Horses in the counties of Cambridge and Isle of Ely, Essex, Kent, Norfolk, and Suffolk.

Nov. 7.   15. Wm. Herlle to Leicester. Desires him to remember the suit
Redcross Street. of Sir E. Herbert. Recommends Griffith Lloyd to be appointed Sheriff of Montgomery, and not John Vaughan. News from Portugal. Sends a letter from Rouen touching the coming over of one Marshal, with seditious books from the Bishop of Ross and letters from the Earl of Westmoreland. Requests the reversion of the office of Searcher of London.

Nov. 7.   16. Same to Sir Edward Herbert. Has spoken with the Earl of
Redcross Street. Leicester for the choice of G. Lloyd to be Sheriff of Montgomery. The Earl has promised to assist Sir Edward in the ending of his accompts for the mint, and to favour his proceedings for Powys.

Nov. 8.   17. Edmund Tremayne to Walsyngham. His great satisfaction
Colocumb. in having Mr. Christopher Harris associated with him, in charge of the treasure brought home by Francis Drake. Harris he has long treated as a son, and Mr. Drake is also become of the same parentage. Has administered interrogatories to the gentlemen and others of Drake's company as to the value of his captures, reputed to the amount of one million and a half. Has left the amount of 10,000*l.* in Drake's hands, selected by himself. *Incloses,*

17. I. *The register of such treasure as is delivered unto Chr. Harris, Esq., to be safely conducted and delivered into the Tower, with the number of pieces in every pack, and what they contain in weight, at 5 score and 12 lbs. every hundred.* Signed E. TREMAYNE, FRAUNCIS DRAKE, and CHRI. HARRIS.

17. II. *The answer of Lawrence Elyot, John Chester, and others, the gentlemen, and nearly 50 others of Drake's company, to the interrogatories relative to the value of his prize, conduct during the voyage, and treatment of the Spaniards.*

VOL. CXLIV.

1580.
Nov. 8.
Colchester.
18. Nicholas Chalyner and Robert Lewis, preachers, and others, of Colchester, to Walsyngham. Desiring that their Christian brethren, the strangers of the Dutch Church and congregation, may not be expelled from the town of Colchester; their demeanor has been civil, honest, and godly. Advantages to the town by their employment.

Nov. 9.
Danbury.
19. Dr. George Wither to same. In favour of the strangers of the Dutch Church in Colchester. Advantages of their residence in that town.

Nov. 10.
London.
20. Wm. Herlle to Sir Edward Horsey. His friendship towards him. Intends to make a start to visit him. Vice-Admiral Byngham separated from the rest of the fleet, and driven to Smerwick, where the foreign aids do fortify. State of affairs in Ireland, Spain, Portugal, and France. *Incloses,*

20. I. *Advertisements and intelligence relating to France, Spain, Portugal, and Ireland.*

Nov. 11.
London.
21. Richard Bertie to the Earl of Leicester. Urges his son's title to the Baronies of Willoughby and Ersby. Begs that if the report on their suit is not to Her Majesty's satisfaction, it may be referred to the Martial Court of England. Precedents in support of his son's title.

Nov. 13.
22. Attestation of Thos. Wilford, President of the Company of Spanish Merchants. The Spanish merchants named were contented that Clinton Atkinson, condemned for piracy, should be pardoned at Her Majesty's pleasure.

Nov. 14.
Isle of Wight.
23. Sir Edward Horsey to Leicester. His entertainment of the Portuguese Ambassador, although he had forty of his household servants down in one night with the disease. The Ambassador's high commendations of Her Majesty and Leicester, and his and Mr. Younge's sudden sickness.

Nov. 14.
Arches.
24. Dr. Lewes to Walsyngham. States particulars how far Clinton Atkinson was concerned in the piracy committed on a Spanish ship.

Nov. 14?
25. Information of the escape of Clinton Atkinson the pirate, out of Exeter gaol, not without the consent or great negligence of the Mayor and gaoler, the Mayor having given him two very favourable testimonials. [*On the 24th of November, the Justices of Assize in Devon were directed to inquire into the particulars of Atkinson's escape from Exeter gaol. Co. Reg.*]

Nov. 14.
Smithfield.
26. Bishop Cowper to Walsyngham. Mr. Prise, of Washingley, being committed to the Fleet for non-conformity, suggests that Mrs. Prise should be sent for and examined, she being more obstinate and wilful than her husband. Requests that John Wharffe and John Moreley may be discharged, who are now both willing to conform.

DOMESTIC—ELIZABETH.

1580.   VOL. CXLIV.

Nov. 16. 27. Thos. Fane, jun., Sheriff of Kent, to the Council. Cause of the delay in certifying the number of horses. *Incloses,*

27. I. *Certificate of the number of horses mustered for service in the county of Kent, except the cities of Canterbury and Rochester, and the Cinque Ports.*

Nov. 17. 28. Wm. Herlle to the Earl of Leicester. Must proceed forthwith into Wales. Sir Edw. Herbert's thanks to his Lordship for procuring an impartial Sheriff in Montgomeryshire, for which office Griffith Lloyd is much to be preferred.

Nov. 17. *Windsor.* 29. Thomas Lord Paget to the Council. Having been fourteen weeks restrained of his liberty, he offers to have service in his house, and to be present at the same.

Nov. 18. *Petworth.* 30. Earl of Northumberland and Viscount Mountague to the Earl of Sussex. Have received directions as to the breed of horses, viewing of parks, &c., and will not fail, by God's grace, to follow the same. Themselves are the only two Commissioners, which are too few for so large a county as Sussex. Desire therefore that other gentlemen may be joined in commission with them.

Nov. 18. *St. Cross.* 31. John Watson, Bishop of Winchester, Sir Henry Radeclyff, and others, to the Council. Have apprehended and examined Elizabeth Saunders, sister of Dr. Saunders, with whom they found certain lewd and forbidden books, and a protestation or challenge of the Jesuits. Wm. Hoord, who first dispersed the said challenge, will not declare of whom he received the same.

Nov. 19. *Aldermanbury.* 32. Wm. Patten to Sir Fr. Walsyngham. Information respecting the farming of the Mines Royal; with particulars of the grants to Thomas Thurland and Daniel Hechstetter, and to William Humfrey and Christopher Schutz.

Nov. 19. 33. Note of the shareholders in the Mines Royal, shewing their separate interests, and the number of parts or shares held by each; Burghley and Leicester holding two parts each.

Nov. 21. *London.* 34. Thos. Randolphe to the Earl of Leicester. Desires that Mr. Chr. Goodman may be permitted to visit Scotland, where he hath left great testimony of his true service in Christ's church, and wishes to confirm the same with a few sermons before God takes him out of this world.

Nov. 21. *St. John's College.* 35. Dr. Richard Howlande to Lord Burghley. Enters into particulars of the controversy between the College and Mr. Ventris. If the sentence against him should be reversed, it would be a great hindrance to the College and to the privileges of the University.

Nov. 22. *St. Cross.* 36. Bishop Watson to Walsyngham. Is not at present able to send a perfect certificate of the recusants in his diocese of Winchester, but hopes shortly so to do. Has dealt with the husbands of recusants, who thought it something strange to be punished for their wives' faults. Desires to know how to proceed against widows.

VOL. CXLIV.

1580. Nov. 22. Richmond.		Sir Fr. Walsyngham to Lord Chancellor Bromley. Requests his opinion on the matter in dispute between Mr. Tho. Markham and the Earl of Rutland, concerning some walks in the forest of Sherwood. [*See Vol.* xlv., *p.* 70.]
Nov. 24.	37.	Certificate given by John Lychpoole to Sir John Fetiplace, of the conversation he had had with one William Pitts, a papist, who shewed him a writing by Mr. Campion, which he had from one Mr. Saunders.
Nov. 26. London.	38.	Robert Beale to the Earl of Leicester. Has examined Stanyhurst, who refers himself to Mr. Edw. Fitzgerald, Lieutenant of the Gentlemen Pensioners. *Incloses*,
	38. I.	*Examination of Richard Stanyhurst touching the conveying of the late Lord Garret [Gerald Fitzgerald, Lord Offaley,] into Spain, at the instigation of Tho. Fleming, a priest.*
Nov. 26. London.	39.	Jacomo Mannucci to Walsyngham. Forwards a letter from Captain Sassetti. Report of the death of the Queen of Spain. Affairs of Don Antonio. The Marshal de Retz and Mons. de Chaors exercise much influence over the new Duke of Savoy. Return of the Spanish forces from Flanders. Ital.
Nov. 28. Court at Richmond.	40.	W[illiam] H[erlle] to Mrs. Roper. Complains of her unkind dealing towards himself and his brother, with railing and scolding before strangers. His brother will not quit her house till the time appointed by law. Cautions her as to those about her, parasites that gape daily for her death.
Nov. 29. Blickling.	41.	Sir Edward Clere to the Council. Many persons, committed for disobeying the Acts of Uniformity of Common Prayer, remain in improper custody. Proposes to keep them at his several houses.
Nov. 30. Richmond.		Walsyngham (?) to the Recorder of London. Directions for the reprieve of one Browinger and his man, condemned for a robbery, until further investigation be made. [*See Vol.* xlv. *p.* 71.]
Nov.	42.	Instructions by the Lords of the Council to certain persons appointed by order from Her Majesty to repair into certain counties, to view the number of men and armour certified by the Commissioners upon the late Musters taken ; with a view to the increase of men and armour.
Nov.	43.	Instructions, a portion of the above, for the maritime counties, for defence against any attempt of invasion.
Nov. ?	44.	Project, in Walsyngham's hand, for establishing a company of such as shall trade beyond the equinoctial line: and, in consideration of the late notable discoveries made by Francis Drake, he to be appointed Governor of the same for life.
Dec. 2.	45, 46.	Articles exhibited to the Council against Edmond Plowden, Esq., of the Middle Temple, for matters of religion. [*Two copies.*]
Dec. 3. The Court.	47.	The Council to the Commissioners for Musters in Hampshire. Thanks for their diligence in Her Majesty's service.

1580.   VOL. CXLIV.

Dec. 12.   48. Declaration of John Parker, of Hagworthingam, Lincoln. How he was drawn from the service of God and became a Papist.

Dec. 13.   49. William Herlle to Sir Edw. Horsey. Is glad of his recovery,
London.   and will visit him shortly. Sends two papers of advertisements, one of peace in France with the Protestants. Queen Elizabeth is sharply set against the Papists. Success of the Spaniards in Portugal. With a P.S., that the cause of Don Antonio was flourishing, although the King of Spain had caused his second son to be crowned in Lisbon.

Dec. 14.   50. Same to Edw. Cornwall, (indorsed on the preceding letter "*Baron of Burford.*") Expresses his friendship towards him. Intends to visit him and to talk with him of "Drake's circuityon of the world."

Dec. 16.   51. "Declaration made by the Merchants Adventurers, of the continuance of them and their trade, with their petition for maintenance of their privileges according to their charters," &c.

Dec. 19.   52. Roger Lord North, and others, to the Earl of Sussex. Im-
Cambridge. perfections in the instructions sent to them from the Council as special Commissioners for Musters of horses in Cambridge. Desire to know if they shall use their own discretions in the service. *Inclosing,*

   52. I. *Certificate of the imperfections of their instructions from the Council.*

Dec. 20.   53. Henry Lord Norreys to the Council. Desires that deputies
Wytham.   may be appointed to assist him in the commission for the Muster of horses in Oxfordshire, Sir Edw. Umpton [Unton], Sir Henry Lee, and other Commissioners being unable to attend.

Dec. 20.   54. Opinion of the Earl of Sussex, Lord Chamberlain, on the reception to be given to the Ambassador from Savoy, to return the Garter from the late Duke. Recommends the Queen to be at the expense of his entertainment.

Dec. 20.   55. Amount of daily wages of the stonemasons and labourers now working at Folkstone, in preparing stone for the pier of Dover, and of the money received to the 20th of December.

Dec. 20.   56. Petition of Morris Pyckering [or Pickringe] to Lord Burghley. Being in trouble for distributing the money given to him by Sir George Peckham, for relief of poor prisoners confined in the Gatehouse for religion. Has always prayed for the Queen who hath defended us from the tyranny of the Devil, the Pope, and all his ravening wolves.

Dec. 20.   57. Certificate by Morris Pyckering of his interview with Sir George Peckham on the 18th of December, being at dinner at my Lord of Rochester's, in the close at Westminster, at a marriage.

Dec. 21.   58. Examination of Morris Pyckering by the Lord Chancellor and Lord Hunsdon, touching the money given to him by Sir George Peckham for the poor prisoners in the Gatehouse for religion.

1580.   VOL. CXLIV.

Dec. 23.   59. Barnard Mawde to Sir Robert Stapleton. His mother and
York.   children are well. Supposes that Wm. Beckwith can perform
nothing. W. S. and the Bishop have abused him about the 200*l.*
Private affairs. The Earl of Huntingdon is with the Earl of
Cumberland at Ripon.

Dec. 24.   60. Detailed account by Alderman Richard Martyn, Francis
Drake, and Christopher Harris, of the amount of gold and silver
bullion in ingots, brought from Sion, and laid up in a vault under
the Jewel House; the silver bullion weighing 22,899lbs. 5oz., the
coarse silver 512lbs. 6 oz., and the gold bullion 101lbs. 10 oz.
[*Indorsed by Burghley*, " *The quantite of bullion brought into y
Tower by Fr. Drake.*"]

Dec.   61. Nicolas Clarke to Sir Fr. Walsyngham. Desires that the
men serving in the bulwark of West Tilbury may receive their
wages quarterly, that their wages due from Lady-day last might
be paid this Christmas, and that he might have an annual allowance
himself.

Dec. 26.   62. Examination of John Taylor, taken before George Carey,
relative to his conversation with Roger Yardley, servant of
Mr. Gilbert (?).

Dec. 28.   63. Albericus Gentilis, " *Italus*," to the Earl of Leicester. Has
(5 Kal. Jan.)   sent letters to the illustrious Earl by Baptista Castellioni. His
Oxford.   hope of success in the University. Lat.

Dec. 31.   64. Extract from the examination of John Hart relative to the
Bull of Pope Pius V. for the excommunication of Queen Elizabeth;
and the Faculties granted to Robert Persons and Edmund Campion
by Pope Gregory XIII. relative to the interpretation of that Bull.

Dec. 31.   65. Copy of the above.

Dec.   66. Answer of Sir Henry Lee to certain allegations of George
Whitton, relative to a transaction about some venison and deer
stealing sixteen years since. Prays to be protected from Whitton's
slanderous clamours, and to be released from imprisonment.

67. Answers by Lawrence Argoll to such objections as may be
urged against his suit for registration of wills, by the Proctors of the
Arches and others.

68. Statement of the number of wills proved in the Prerogative
Court, communibus annis, from January 1575, to the last of December 1580, in support of Argoll's suit.

69. A discourse delivered to Mr. Sheldon, to persuade him to
conform. Arguments to prove it lawful for a Roman Catholic to
attend the Protestant service.

70. A consideration of the advantages to be gained by opening
a direct trade with Turkey, by Sir Fr. Walsyngham.

1580.

Vol. CXLIV.

71. A brief declaration of the profit, honor, and fame, that the Queen's most excellent Majesty and the whole Commons of the realm are to have by marts, to be kept in England; also an answer to certain doubts touching the same: by John Johnson.

72. Grant to William Herlle of the office of the Queen's Constable Ragler or Kilghmargh, in the County of Cardigan, for life.

73. Account of the establishment of the Tower "Anno regni Regis Ricardi Secundi quarto," stating the fees pertaining to the Constable of the Tower and other officers, its jurisdiction, and boundaries of the franchise on the water side from London Bridge to the Abbot of Tower Hill's Mill. [*Copy: made probably in the year* 1580.]

74. Grievances of the citizens of London who deal in soapmaking. Patent for soapmaking granted by Her Majesty. Unfair dealings of Lawrence Coxson and Lawrence Mellowe, in the sale of impure oils to the soapmakers, at exorbitant prices. [*An order was taken with Lawrence Mellowe as to sale of his oils on the 8th Feb.* 1580, *Co. Reg., to which this seems to be subsequent.*]

Grant to Ralph Brookes of the office of Rougecroix, Pursuivant at Arms, for life, in place of Tho. Dawes, lately defunct. Lat. [*Warrant Book*, I., p. 17.]

Vol. CXLV. 1580.

A book, of the class called "Liber Pacis," containing the names of the Council in the North, and of the Commissioners of Oyer and Terminer there; of the Council in the Principality of Wales; of the Judges on the Circuits; and of the Justices of Peace in all the counties in England and Wales.

Vol. CXLVI. 1580? Undated.

[All the papers in this volume are undated, but are presumed to be of the year 1580.]

1580?

1. Lord Henry Howard (son of Henry Earl of Surrey) to Queen Elizabeth. Having been for more than twelve years sequestered from the comfort of her cheerful looks, he (at very great length) dedicates and sends to her a translation from the Spanish of a brief treatise, which came to his hands by chance, of the letter of instructions given by the Emperor Charles V., on his renunciation of all his sovereignties to his son King Philip the Second of Spain, which, because it toucheth principles and points of policy most suitable to the present time, Lord Howard thinketh it not unworth Her Majesty's profound consideration. [*The translation of the Emperor's letter is annexed.*]

1580 ?

VOL. CXLVI.

2. Estimate of the charges for the wages and entertainment of 600 foot and 100 horse for four months.

3. Note of the number of men, pikes, bills, and bows, to be levied in several counties.

4. Note of persons who have neglected to furnish the prescribed number of lances and light horse; being Sir Jervis Clyfton and Sir Anthony Strelly.

5. Note of five lances and light horse furnished in Cambridgeshire.

6. Abstract of the abuses committed by the Captains in the County of Essex, in illegally discharging their men. Loss of arms, clothing, &c.

7. Names of the Captains and old soldiers who served at Newhaven and are still living.

8. Brief of Mr. Ric. Arnold's proofs that there was an entail of the lands of his brother Sir Nich. Arnold: with Mr. Lucy's answers to the same.

9. Tables showing how all degrees of persons in England, from the King to the yeoman, ought to proportion their expenditure. Lat.

10. Presumptions of the unsoundness of many in Balliol College in matters of religion. Such persons as Brian, Parsons, Turner, Bagshaw, Staverton, and one Pilcher being grievously suspected of Papistry.

11. Proclamation for preserving peace and amity with foreign states by repressing the unbridled and licentious outrageousness of pirates and sea rovers, which at this day commit more spoils and robberies on all sides than hath been heard of in former times.

12. Considerations touching the right of the King of Spain to prohibit the trade of English merchants to the Indies. [*Probably with reference to Drake's operations against the Spaniards in South America.*]

13. Declaration of the foreign wares and commodities most in demand for England.

14. Deposition of Richard Ward, giving information as to certain words spoken by Mr. Cator against the Lord Steward at a dinner at Twyford in Berkshire.

15. Maliverey Catilyn to Sir Fr. Walsyngham. Deplores the swift passage of time, which unawares hath stolen away his sweetest years. Fears Walsyngham has forgotten him, and prays to be restored to his most desired favour.

1580 ?

Vol. CXLVI.

16. Particular of the tenure and yearly value of the manor of Godalming, co. Surrey, whereof Sir Wm. More desireth the fee farm.

17. Petition of Wm. Tirwhitt to the Council. Prays for liberty to go into Lincolnshire for three months for recovery of his health, and for settlement of the estate of his brother Marmaduke Tirwhitt, lately deceased.

18. Names of certain English fugitives pensioned by the King of Spain, Thos. Goldwell Bishop of St. Asaph, Dr. Morton, and others.

19. Statement of the suit against Dr. Powell by Mr. Sheppard Subdean of Gloucester, before the Bishop of London, and others, in commission; during the vacancy of the see of Gloucester.

20. Notes out of Harrison's Book, headed " A Treatise stirring up "unto carefull desiringe and dutifull laboringe for true Churche "Government. To all his Christian brethren in England which "wayte for the Kingdom of Christe."

21. Petition of the Merchants of the Staple to the Council. Object to remove their Staple to the Brill in Holland, and pray that no licences may be granted for ten or twelve years after the expiration of their present grant.

22. Edmund Coortesse to Sir Fr. Walsyngham. Desires redress of certain wrongs sustained at his adversaries' hands. The return of his money had never been offered. Solicits letters to Dr. Moorley to reinstate him in his prebend, and that he may be put in quiet possession of the vicarage of Cuckfield. [*On the 5th of Feb.* 1581, *the Bishop of London was directed to proceed to the deprivation of Coortesse from his vicarage of Cuckfield, and from all other ecclesiastical functions. Co. Reg.*]

23. The humble requests of the merchants trading to Spain and Portugal for licence to freight ships to Spain, and for sequestration of certain Portuguese property in England.

24. Muster roll of the town of Grantham cum Soca, specifying the names of the freeholders, the Queen's Majesty being "Chiefe Ladye and Mistress " in each of the towns and villages enumerated.

25. Names of the chief lords and freeholders in the hundreds of Nesse, Beltisloe, and Aveland, in Kesteven division, co. Lincoln.

26. Names of the ports and creeks where Custom-house officers are resident.

27. Order from the Queen to the officers of the Mint, limiting the coinage of certain coins of gold and silver.

28. Answer of Alexander de Cone, merchant, to the articles ministered to him upon his oath, relative to his attendance at church, the sending of money out of the realm, receiving Popish books, &c.

1580?

Vol. CXLVI.

29. Petition of Christopher Dethick to the Council against John Chetham, who had deprived him of his inheritance, and otherwise defrauded him. Desires that bonds may be taken of Mr. Chetham, and a committee appointed to inquire into his case.

30. Evidence relating to the suit between Lady Croker and Sir Henry Lee. Assurance of the leases of Hooknorton to Lady Croker.

31. Depositions of John Brayne and Robert Milles, touching the offers made to Amy Wilborne, now the wife of one Blackman, on the behalf of Mr. Ashburnham, for his debt of 50l.

32. Substance of the suit in controversy between John Sutton, plaintiff, and John Erington, defendant, touching the payment of 190l. to Wm. Gelborne in Sutton's name.

33. Note of extremities surmised to have been offered by Erington to Sutton, and of those offered by Sutton to Erington. Breaking into the house of one Merrivall, a bankrupt.

34. Alderman Tho. Pullyson to the Council. Answers to the unjust complaint of Tho. Gylbert, touching the lease of Guerras' house, which he, Pullyson, held direct by lease from the Drapers' Company.

35. A note of the matter in controversy between Sir Tho. Hennage, Nicholas Seintleger, and the Lady Finche his wife, touching the possession of certain lands in reversion after the death of Dame Katharine Moyle, her mother. Assurance of lands to her son Moyle Finche.

36. Note of the benefits that Mr. Moyle Fynche received, besides the assurance of the land promised; the manor of Wyllmyngton, &c.

37. Memorials to be "inferred" to the Lord Treasurer and Mr. Secretary, touching the fortifications of Milford Haven, wherein three forts must be made. Authority to Sir John Perrot to cut down wood for timber, to impress workmen, &c.

38. Petition of the tenants and inhabitants of Cowpon, in the County Palatine of Durham, to Mr. Tho. Wylson, Sec. of State and Dean of Durham, against the sale of salt, at Yarom, in Yorkshire, by the Scots, who pay no duty nor other custom for unloading the same.

39. Petition of Tho. Wynington, to Sir Fr. Walsyngham. That having come from Moscow to London, about certain disorders there committed by one Northen, a merchant, he had been imprisoned at the instance of the Master and Governors of the Company of Moscovia. Desires that he will proceed to the hearing of the matter.

40. Articles of petition by Sir Tho. Gerrard and Sir Geo. Peckham to Walsyngham. Sir Humfrey Gylberte having assigned to them his patent for the discovery and conquest of certain heathen lands, they request licence for certain persons to quit England under their authority for that purpose.

1580?

Vol. CXLVI.

41. Petition of Wm. Sherington to the Council. His suit with Wm. Fulwood for wrongfully withholding a statute staple of 300*l*. Desires that their Lordships would determine his suit with Mr. Fulwood according to equity and conscience, and that the award against him in the Court of Common Pleas may be stayed.

42. Petition of Tho. Greye, of Langley, to Sir Fr. Walsyngham. Relative to his suit with Michael Haselrige. Desires him to signify to the Court of the Duchy of Lancaster, his satisfaction with their award.

43. Report on the suit between Haselrige and Greye : their petitions to Walsyngham.

44. Petition of Tho. Clyffe, hosier. Desiring the enlargement of Anthony Cooke, his apprentice, and Wm. Foster, who had been committed to the Marshalsea for abusing one of the Queen's messengers.

45. John the Almain to Walsyngham. Recommends one of his countrymen, who had invented an harquebuse " that shall containe " ten balls or pelletes of lead, all the which shall goe off, one after " another, having once given fire, so that with one harquebuse " one may kill ten theeves or other enemies without recharging."

46. Petition of Henry Jolif, of Newport, to the Council. Seeking redress against the subjects of the French king, having been six several times spoiled by them at sea.

47. Answer of Mr. Cressye to Sir John Daver's complaint as to the sale of the manor of Eaton, and the receipt of monies on behalf of the late Mr. [Wm.?] Norris, the executorship to whose estate Mr. Cressye had relinquished.

48. Petition of —— Lambart to Walsyngham. In behalf of his father John Lambart, of Calton, in Yorkshire. Desires that in consideration of the losses and injuries sustained in the late rebellion, the fee-farm of certain lands in Craven might be granted to him.

49. Answer to the questions in debate between Mr. Yorke and Mr. Allen ; with reasons to prove the same, whereby it will appear that Allen, for upwards of 30 years, has lived by way of trade and selling merchantable wares. Mr. Plowden's reasons thereon.

50. Note of the geldings Martin Mondet, a Frenchman, has transported out of the realm during the four years last past.

51. Petition of the Company of the Eastland Merchants to Walsyngham. Complain that their residence at Elbing has not been successful, by reason of Merchant Strangers shipping their goods at other ports.

52. Petition of the same to the Council. To the same effect.

DOMESTIC—ELIZABETH. 697

1580 ?

VOL. CXLVI.

53. Certain reasons shewing what commodities would ensue, if strangers were bound to ship to and from the East parts, as the English merchants are bound.

54. The answer of Martin de la Fallia to the articles exhibited against him by John Leake, informer, for dealings in wools, by virtue of the licence of Sir Francis Walsyngham.

55. Petition of Venetian merchants residing in London to the Council. Praying licence to unlade three ships lately arrived with currants, wines, &c., without paying the new imposts upon the same.

56. Petition of Tho. Milwarde, of Dover, to Sir Fr. Walsyngham. To be permitted to go on with the erection of the water mill in the stream near Dover prison.

57. Petition of Tho. Egerton to Walsyngham. Prays to enter into a composition for his lands extended for debt to Her Majesty, which was, in Queen Mary's days, very hardly adjudged against him; and according to the said extent can not be wholly paid in a great number of years.

58. Wm. Greves to same. Desires that the hearing of his case may be postponed, and that he may not be condemned on the evidence of Tho. Greves. Ill conduct of the said Tho. Greves and Tho. Griffith.

59. Requests to the Lord Treasurer as to purveyance of wood for Her Majesty's household.

60. D. Hector's request to Lady [Walsyngham?] to intercede with her husband for the reversion of Andreas de Loo's licence, to be granted to him for 10 or 12 years.

61. Purport of the suit of Wm. Harbrowne, of Yarmouth, for a licence to himself and his son for 21 years, for the making of salt upon salt, i.e., white salt out of brown, to be limited to the town of Yarmouth and its members.

62. A paper, probably relating to an improvement in the quadrant or sextant. [*Indorsed:* "*The proposition of an instrument for navigation, whereby at all hours of the day and night, seeing the sun or stars, one may know by land or sea, as well the longitude as the latitude, whereof the use is never known or found before*"]

63. Supplication of the town of Halsted, Essex, to Walsyngham. That 20 families or more of the Dutchmen now removed to Colchester might be commanded to return to Halsted, there to continue their trade of bay-making as heretofore; their departure from thence having much impoverished the neighbourhood. *Annexing,*

63. I.–VIII. *Eight petitions from various towns adjoining Halsted, in favour of the preceding petition, viz., Pedmersh, Little Maplestead, Yeldham, Colne Engayne, Great Maplestead, Gosfeld, Hedingham Sybell, and Castle Hedingham.* [*All these petitions, and the one from the town of Halsted, are numerously signed.*]

1580?

VOL. CXLVI.

64. Proposition for the confirmation and better ordering of lands held by Deans and Chapters.

65. Articles objected before the Council against Edw. Bowghton, of Cawston, in the County of Warwick, a favourer of notorious Papists, as Nicholas Greenhill, Barnard Field, and others; a packer of juries, an oppressor of the people of Rugby, having displaced one Richard Seele from the school there; incontinent in his living, and an obstinate Puritan.

66. Petition of Mons. Coedor to Sir Fr. Walsyngham. Losses sustained by him from English pirates. Desires that the licence granted to him by Her Majesty may be exchanged for some other.

67. List of eight ships and two barks half manned; and estimate of the charges for victuals and wages.

68. Similar estimate for seven of the above ships and the two barks.

69. Estimate of several rates for victualling for 6,000, 8,000, or 10,000 men for 14 days.

70. Names of Captains to serve on the seas.

71. Articles concerning Her Majesty's imposts and customs. Offer addressed to the Queen to undertake the monthly revision of the customers' accompts, and detail of the advantages to be gained thereby.

72. Project for improving the customs and preventing the deceits of officers, by establishing warehouses for the reception of merchants' goods previous to loading on board ship.

73. Declaration of certain merchants who have traded to Portugal, of their opinion touching the trade of Portugal, with their humble petition for re-opening the trade thither, suspended in consequence of the irregular trade of some Englishmen to the Indies.

74. Answer of the merchants trading to Amsterdam in Holland, to the allegations made by the Merchant Adventurers, accusing them of irregular trading.

75. Petition of the Aldermen and Company of Merchants of the Stillyard to Lord Burghley. Praying to be relieved from the payment of the new imposts on certain Spanish and sweet wines brought by them into England.

76. Reasons by the Company of Merchant Adventurers against admission of any Merchant of the Staple into their fellowship.

77. Reasons delivered by Mr. Simon Bowyer to the Merchants of the Staple, as to frauds and irregular dealings by broggers and others in the wool trade, with the answers of the Staplers to the same.

78. Answer of Drs. William Fulke and John Still to certain propositions of one Shales, on the authority of the Fathers, in support of the Scriptures, and the spiritual gifts of the Saviour; as lately renewed in the writings of the Jesuits Campion, Dureas, and others.

1580 ?

Vol. CXLVI.

79. Orders for the better increase of learning in the inferior ministers, and for more diligent preaching and catechising. Every unlicensed minister to provide himself with a Bible and Bullinger's Decades; and every licensed preacher to preach yearly, in propriâ personâ, at least twelve sermons.

80. Memorandum of the numbers of men had out of certain shires to sundry places at several times.

81. Signor Pompeo Loiani to Lord Burghley. Advocates the expediency of establishing a Bank of Augmentation. *Incloses,*

81. I. *Propositions for establishing a Bank of Augmentation with a capital of 50,000 marks, to pay 12 per cent. per ann. Form of patent, regulations, &c.*

82. "A Brieffe Table faithfullie gathered out of the great bookes of depositions against Dr. Tho. Powell," of adultery, drunkenness, and many other crimes committed by him in Gloucestershire; with names of deponents, &c.

83. Request of the Merchant Adventurers that no unfair advantage shall be taken of them by the clothworkers, in the shipment of their cloths. Are willing to export one dressed with nine undressed cloths.

84. Declaration of William Gowltye, Mayor, and others, of Orford, with respect to the charges against Mr. Agas their minister. They had sufficiently proved the articles against him before the Ecclesiastical Commission, and now refer their case to be heard before the Council. [*Indorsed,* " *The Mayor of Orford's answer to Sir Phil. Parker touching Agas.*"]

85. Deposition by James Coo concerning the demand of Mr. Agas for tythes, which Coo and others do not deny.

86. Reasons why there should be no malt carried in boats or barges to London by the river Lea.

87. [   ] to Secretary Wylson. In favour of certain Merchants of the Stillyard, who had been robbed of a quantity of cloths by Walter Dabernal and his accomplices, near Margate.

88. Note of the supply of ordnance for the town of Aldborough, in the County of Suffolk. [*Signed by* [*Sir*] *William Pelham.*]

89. Particular, signed by Wm. Pelham and Anthony Smyth, relative to the tenure of the lands and tenements held by the tenants of the Manor of Barrowe. 300*l.* is required for repair of the jetties and waterworks to resist the violence of the Humber.

90. Particular of the Manor of Hazelber Bryan, in the County of Dorset, containing an abstract of the tenure and liberties of the manor, with a list of the freeholders and tenants.

1580 ?

Vol. CXLVI.

91. A note of the lands belonging to John Sacheverell, Esq., in the County of Derby ; the Manor of Buxstone, &c. Lat.

92. Notes and directions relating to the Mint, and the Standard of Coinage. [*Indorsed*, "*Gold and silver reckoned by pound weights.*"]

London.
93. Warrant addressed to Abraham Jacob. Remitting the impost on certain wines for private use of some person of quality.

94. Orders by the Queen's Highness, specially to be observed for better service in the Office of Ordnance. [*Indorsed*, "*For Her Majesty's Service, submitted to your Honor's private consideration.*"]

95. Letters of denization for Peter Beard, born in the Low Countries.

96. " The just and true considerations why and wherefore John " Campynet, deceased, did reserve to him and his heirs the Lordship " of Tekencote, which was the inheritance of Margaret, his late wife, " and now wife unto Paule Gresham." Lease of Tekencote to Wm. Campynet.

97. Propositions by Gawen Smith, for the erection of a beacon on the Goodwin Sands, twenty or thirty feet above high water mark, and able to receive and preserve 30 or 40 persons at least.

98. Comparative statement of the values of gold and silver and foreign coin ; proposing the Queen should raise her coinage by a penny in the shilling and twelvepence in the angel, in order to meet the course of exchange in France.

99. A memorial [by whom does not appear] for Mr. Eely, a licenciate, to tell Hughe Lygon that his brother Rafe had received one letter from him since his departure, and liked well of his doings in his affairs.

100. Tho. Heath to his father Mr. Tho. Heath, dwelling in the Parsonage of Fulham. Commends the bearer. Has been a whole year and received neither money nor letters, and has been maintained by his tutor. Desires to be placed with another tutor.

101. " Articles against the servant of Mr. Greene, that went " away when he should have come to his examination before Dr. " Hamon ;" delivered by John Young. Robert Greene disowns him as his servant.

102. Information by Anthony Gibon of two Englishmen from Boulogne, landed at Purfleet above Gravesend, having certain jewels and a cross of gold with them.

103. Depositions by John Treman, Parson of Binfeld. Touching certain libellous speeches uttered by Mr. Drewe's servant.

104. Information given by the constables of Malden against Richard Woodhouse, Edw. Wells, and John Cannonden. For opposing the constables in execution of the warrant for arrest of Woodhouse for his misdemeanor with the wife of one John Clark, quarrelling with the watch, and breaking the peace by Wells and Cannonden.

1580 ?

Vol. CXLVI.

105. Answer to the preceding articles objected against Cannonden and Woodhouse.

106. Petition of Wm. Copland and Anthony Greene (orphan of Tho. Greene, who died in Muscovia,) to the Queen. Against the injurious dealings of Alderman Branche, of London, and Mr. Stonley of the Exchequer, and corrupt dealing of the Master of Requests. Solicit the determination of their suit may be referred to the Lord Chancellor, the Earl of Leicester, and Mr. Secretary.

107. Petition of John Blagrave to Sir. Fr. Walsyngham. For letters patent for 21 years for certain improvements in the construction of kilns and furnaces, and a new crushing mill.

108. Petition of Wm. Charnell, of Snarestone, in Leicestershire, to same. Desires to be heard or released upon bail for his personal appearance; and that the horses remaining at his charges at the Blue Bell in Holborn may be discharged.

109. Petition of Thos. Wilford to Lord Burghley. Solicits leave to inclose a small piece of common named West's moore, in the parish of Yateley, Berks; and to have timber allowed him for building a small cottage.

110. Petition of Stephen Davys, of Crambrok, Kent, to the Council. Desires recompense for repeated losses sustained by him in Dieppe and at sea, by the depredations of the French, to the amount of above 500*l*.

111. Note to some Lord. Reminding him that he had divers times been at the writer's house in Covent Garden, where he came to speak with Mr. Roloc. [*Apparently a postscript to some letter.*]

112. Brute Babington, of Cambridge, to Burghley. Complains of being disturbed in possession of the living of Thurcaston, Leicester, by the farmer of the late incumbent. Prays for warrant of sequestration until his pretended title is tried at law.

113. Petition of Richard Casye to same. Had been committed to Newgate upon the unjust complaint of Mr. Benedict Spinola, relative to a lease of certain lands and tenements in London. Desires to be discharged from prison, and to have the Queen's pardon.

114. Supplication to all charitable and well disposed Catholics in behalf of the religious Virgins and Brethren of Syon in England, of the order of St. Saviour, commonly called the order of St. Byrgitt, dissolved by King Henry VIII., when Katherine Palmer with other her sisters withdrew into Flanders, but are now residing in great distress at Rouen in Normandy.

115. Petition of John Benbrick, of Rye, prisoner in the Marshalsea, to same. Requests him to prefer his suit to the Council, being a very poor man and having no friends.

1580 ?

VOL. CXLVI.

116. Petition of Philip Jones to Lord Burghley. That on liberty be granted to the Flemings to transport pelts out of England, until the imposition on hops and alum in Flanders should be taken off.

117. Suit of Francis Fortescue, son of Henry Fortescue, for a licence of alienation and sale of the Manor of Moore Hall, Essex, the Manor of Ayworthe in Bedfordshire, and the third part of the Manor of Trumpington, granted by King Henry VIII. to the said Henry Fortescue, and the heirs male of his body.

118. Petition of John Rothermaker, factor for Giles Hosteman, to the Council. Desires a warrant from the Admiralty for restitution of all goods unlawfully sold or saved in December last, from the wreck of the boat named the Angel Gabriel, of Antwerp.

119. Petition of John Bradford, of Exeter, to the Queen. Against Andrew Hill, who, having been condemned to death for highway robbery, had received Her Majesty's warrant of protection, which he fraudulently used against his creditors.

120. Petition of Richard Lowther, Gerard Lowther the elder, and Gerard Lowther the younger. For the lease of certain lands in Westmoreland, promised to them by the Earl of Leicester for their services.

121. Grant of licence by the Queen to Wm. Sanderson, minister of King's Lynn, and vicar of Terrington, of non-residence from his said vicarage for life.

122. Petition of Anne Alen to the Queen, praying for a free pardon for her husband, Marten Alen, who had been sentenced to death, but now living in exile at Caen in Normandy.

123. Suggestion that one Tho. Wallker, a merchant, who had obtained a safe conduct from the French King to trade into any parts of France, should have a similar licence of Her Majesty, and so to open a secret communication with Rouen, by means of a merchant named George Glover dwelling there. Unlawful trade carried on with France by way of Jersey and Guernsey.

124. Reasons to prove that the grant of the suit for the return of original writs will not be prejudicial to the subject.

125. Opinion on the right of strangers to partake of bankrupts' goods rateably with English creditors.

126. Opinions of certain Doctors of the Civil Law upon a case testamentary, for legacies and the custody and education of the legatees in their non-age.

127. Calculations of the difference between wine and ale measures.

128. Reasons to move Her Majesty for the confirmation of the Cathedral Churches erected by Hen. VIII., called into question for want of the records of that time, and the lands of most of them being purchased covertly at a small rate, as concealed.

1580 ?

Vol. CXLVI.

129. Names of Papists, informed of by Alex. Stringer, who are about to return into England from France.

130. A note of persons suspected in religion in the North parts, Sir Thomas Graye, Ralph Graye, the old Lady Ratcliffe, Francis her son, and others.

131. Certain inconveniences likely to ensue if commission shall be granted from the Queen for exercise of the Archbishop of Canterbury's jurisdiction in Courts of Audience.

132. Petition of Jane Gouldwyar, "a pore afflyctted creator," to Sir Fr. Walsyngham. Has been a prisoner in the Clink for twelve months for conscience sake. Having five small children destitute and wandering about, prays to be released.

133. Orders agreed on between Walsyngham, Tho. Wylson, and Tho. Randolphe, Master of the Posts, for conveyance of packets and letters into France or Flanders.

134. Resolutions by the parishioners of Christ's Church, London. For the due ministration of divine service in their church, the daily lectures to be maintained, the penny and penny loaf to be weekly given away to the poor, and the poor singing men to be continued in the Quyer, "in respect they have bene trayned in the scyence of musick all theyr life."

135. Plan for the improvement of part of Cambridge, in the High Street, opposite St. Mary's Church.

136. Order that the Master and Fellows of Christ's College, Cambridge, shall maintain one Fellow and three Scholars beyond the number specified by the foundation.

137. The names of certain persons having their sons beyond sea, brought up in foreign seminaries; also of such as are receivers of Papists, and the shires and places of their dwelling.

Warrant to pay the yearly fee of 20l. to Anne Vavassor, Gentlewoman of the Bed Chamber. [*See Warrant Book,* I., *p.* 86.]

Grant to Ro. H., of the office of Clerk of the Mint, in the Tower, and Surveyor of the Melting-houses, and to Paul Swallow, the office of Clerk of the Irons. Lat. [*See ib., p.* 112.]

Grant to M. F. [Martin Furbisher?] of the office of Clerk of Her Majesty's Ships, in reversion after the death or surrender of G. W., a former grant in reversion to John Hawkyns having been surrendered by him. [*See ib., p.* 118.]

Grant to Henry Lord Norris, of Rycott, of the office of Porter of the Outer Gate of Windsor Castle, and Keeper of the Armoury and Ordnance in the castle, vacant by the death of Ric. Ward, Esq., Cofferer of the Household. Lat. [*See Warrant Book,* I., *p.* 126.]

1580?

Vol. CXLVI.

Grant to R. W., of the office of Receiver of the Royal Revenue in the Duchy of Lancaster, and of lands of the late monastery of Furness. [*See ib., p.* 135.]

Sir Fr. Walsyngham (?) to [   ]. Understands that Mr. Thomas Gawdie has had great losses by law suits. Requests he will sell a quantity of alum to Gawdie on favourable terms. [*See Vol.* xlv., *p.* 74.]

GENERAL INDEX.

A.

A........., Henry, 24.
Abbeylands, 164.
Abbott's Isle, Manor of, 555.
Abbott, Robert, 586.
Abbott, William, 170
Abduction, 219.
Abels, John, 332.
Aberdeen, 552, 569.
Abergavenny, Lord, *see* Nevill.
Abergwilly, 268, 328, 362, 564, 597, 604, 627.
Abingdon, 153, 156, 340, 466.
Abington, John, 118, 209, 210, 224, 228, 500, 668.
Abortion, Crime of, 623.
Abraham, John, 80, 84, 85, 87–89.
Absolution, Instrument of, 568.
Acanthinus, 33.
Accatery, Clerk of the, 576.
Accession of Edw. VI., 1; of Mary, 54; of Elizabeth, 115, 116, 143, 154.
Achates, The, 503, 554, 601, 629, 631, 647, 656.
Achurch, *see* Thorpe Achurch.
Acliff, William, 257.
Acontio, Giacopo, 243.
Acton, Barnaby, 512.
Acton Trussel, Manor of, 249.
Actton, Annies, 628.
Actton, Barnaby, 628.
Adams, ..., 201.
Adams, George, 420.
Adams, John, 402.
Adams, Nicholas, 51.
Aden, Robert, 682.
Administration, 521, 696. *See* Wills.
Admiral, Lord High, *see* Seymour. Howard. Clinton.
Admirals, *see* Vice-Admirals.
Admiralty, the Fleet, Navy, &c., 2, 3, 5, 7, 11, 15, 44, 55, 61, 62, 72, 87, 90–94, 96–98, 100–106, 109, 112, 119, 121, 126, 131, 132, 144, 146, 148, 152–156, 158, 165, 172, 180, 192, 200, 203, 205, 208, 211, 212, 214, 216, 219–222, 227, 242, 244, 249, 254, 259, 260, 264, 268, 277, 287, 297, 305, 310, 322–324, 329, 331, 351, 353, 354, 361, 362, 366, 367, 378, 386, 387, 390, 393, 398, 408, 409, 413, 437–439, 459, 477, 479–481, 499, 505, 512, 516, 520, 522, 525–527, 535, 536, 546, 552, 553, 566, 576, 580, 584, 585, 598, 612, 613, 627–629, 631, 634, 636, 633, 640–542, 644, 645, 647, 649, 655, 670, 677, 678, 681, 698, 702.

Admiralty, Authority of the Lord Admiral' 633.
Admiralty Court, 10, 21, 22, 164, 175, 235, 246, 258, 277, 282, 329, 330, 332, 343, 384, 393, 413, 456, 489, 497, 512, 520, 529, 536–538, 543, 551, 572, 606, 625, 645, 661.
Admiralty Court, *see* Lewes.
Adventurers, *see* Furbisher, Merchant Adventurers.
"Advertisements, the," Treatise of, 272.
Africa, 178, 183, 215, 260, 678.
Agard, Thomas, 10.
Agas, Mr. 699.
Agbridge, Wapentake of, 336.
Aglionby, Edward, 356, 359.
Agmondesham, John, 21.
Agnello, Giovanni (or John) Baptista, 543, 570, 571.
Aid or Ayde, The ship, 96, 213, 228, 244, 254, 323, 361, 509, 546, 556, 567, 573, 618.
Aids, *see* Revenue.
Aix, or Aix la Chapelle (Aquisgraine), 67, 307.
Akworth, Dr., 521.
Alaker, Ralph, 330.
Alan, Richard, 35.
Alba, Duke of, *see* Alva.
Alban Hall (Oxford), 166, 648.
Alborne Hall, *see* Alban.
Alborough, *see* Aldborough.
Alchemy, 77, 243, 269, 273, 275–277, 289, 385, 493.
Aldarsey (or Aldersey), Thomas, 65, 73, 239, 412, 502, 503. *See* Aldersey.
Alday, John, 320, 332.
Aldaye, James, 84, 132.
Aldborough, 93, 432, 596, 627, 632, 643.
Aldborough, Bailiffs, &c., 578, 632.
Aldborough, Fines on inhabitants of, for piracy, 557.
Aldborough, Ordnance for, 699.
Aldermanbury, 688.
Aldermaston, 355.
Alderney, 15.
Aldersey, Henry, 620.
Aldersey, Mr., 329.
Aldersey, Wm., 279.
Aldersey, *see* Aldarsey,
Aldford, 568, 593.
Aldgate, 195, 230.
Aldingborne, 19, 539, 542.
Aldrich, Thomas, 190, 383, 388.
Aldridge, John, 550.

Y Y

706 GENERAL INDEX.

Aldwen, Wm., 471.
Alehouse keepers, Recognizance of, 554, 555.
Alehouses, Inns, Taverns, &c., 185, 315, 480, 557, 558, 562–566, 568, 570, 572, 581, 641, 649.
Alehouses, Fines on, for repair of Dover haven, 673, 674.
Alen, ..., 307.
Alen, Anne, 702.
Alen, Francis, 223, 313.
Alen, Marten, 702.
Alexander, ... 434.
Alexander, Nicholas, 104.
Alexandria, 551.
Alford, ..., 154, 155.
Alford, Francis, 415, 416, 429, 443, 454, 549.
Alford, Lancelot, 119.
Alford, Roger, 549.
Algiers, 295, 630.
Alienations, 506, 702. Fines on, 535.
Aliens, 36–38, 47, 99, 109, 179, 190, 205, 210, 211, 213, 216, 231, 285, 295–297, 380, 404, 410, 412–414, 424–427, 432, 447, 496, 505, 647.
Alington, H., 194, 208, 213.
Alington, Mr., 323.
Alisholte, Forest of, 113.
Alkynton, George, 314, 315.
Allatt, Mr., 304.
Allegiance. *See* Oaths.
Allen, Sir Christopher, 258, 605.
Allen, Dr., 565.
Allen, John, 45.
Allen, Mr., 106, 455, 696.
Allen, or Alleyn, Thomas, 150, 151, 608, 615, 620, 621.
Allerton, *see* Northallerton.
Allertonshire, Wapentake of, 336.
Alley, William, Bishop of Exeter, 354.
Allington Castle, 60, 144.
Allington, Ric., 111, 197.
All Soul's College (Oxford), 402.
Allyn, Thomas, 670, 672.
Allyn, William, 267, 426–428.
Almain, John, the, 696.
Almain Armourers, *see* Armourers.
Almain Refiners, *see* Refiners.
Almains, *see* Germany.
Almayne, Martain, 207.
Almoner, Royal, 56, 96, 612.
Almoners, Court of, 517.
Alms, Licence to collect, 513.
Almshouses, The Queen's, 526.
Almsmen, 27, 186, 208.
Alnage, *see* Aulnage.
Alnetanus, or Alneto [Lannoy], Cornelius, *see* Lannoy.
Alsop, John, 120.
Altham, James, 380, 422.
Althorpe, 295–297, 330, 331.
Alton, Division of, 653.

Alum, Alum Mines, &c., 253, 272, 288, 436, 440, 443, 534, 587, 702, 704. *See* Mines.
Alva, or Alba, Duke of, 42, 65, 299, 320, 327–329, 332, 394, 432, 438, 647.
Alvecote, 285.
Alveley, Prebend of, 110.
Alyff, ..., 131.
Alyn, Hugh, 303.
Alyngton, Sir Giles, 483.
Alystone, Matthew, 465.
Ambassadors, 8, 26, 33, 38, 48, 54, 57, 58, 69, 71, 80, 84, 87, 108, 128, 129, 135, 136, 138, 175, 186, 211, 221, 240, 241, 243, 244, 247, 273, 308, 309, 312–316, 321, 322, 324, 326–331, 338, 364, 378, 387, 394, 417, 418, 421, 422, 427, 429, 449, 454, 473, 484, 487, 495, 503, 504, 515, 528, 534, 551, 574, 581, 601, 642, 659, 681, 685, 687, 690.
Ambassadors, Secret meetings of, in Paris Garden, 595.
America, 260, 661, 678.
America, South, 693.
Amesbury, Hundred of, 377.
Amiens, 683.
Amondesham, William, 201.
Amport, Vicar of, 605.
Ampton, *see* Southampton.
Amsterdam, 258, 332, 698.
Amyas, Jo., 659.
Amyce, Roger, 295.
Amye, William, 489.
Amyers, Edward, 544.
Anabaptists, 46, 158, 496.
Ancaster, 655.
Anderson, Anthony, 331.
Anderson, Edward, 639.
Anderson, Henry, 535.
Andover, 24, 44, 57, 178, 449, 653.
Andrew, Thomas, 334, 592, 672.
Andrewes, Lancelot, 627.
Andrewes, Stephen, 11.
Andrews, Mr., 392.
Androwes, ..., Sheriff of Northampton, 519.
Androwes, John, 644.
Androwes, Simon, 632.
Angel Gabriel, The, 702.
Angers, 319.
Anglesey, Isle of, 194, 268, 301, 361, 456, 486, 570, 588, 670.
Anglesey, Sheriff of, 486.
Angus, Earl of, *see* Douglas.
Anjou, Duke of, 316, 318, 320, 454, 629, 633, 639, 660. *See* Elizabeth.
Anne of Cleves, *see* Cleves.
Anne, The, 203, 577.
Annot, Thomas, 176.
Anonymous, 613.
Antelope, The, 323, 366.
Anthonie, Dirick, 476.
Anthony, Anthony, 226.
Antiquaries, Society of, 26, 54, 114.

GENERAL INDEX. 707

Antiquities, Roman, 406.
Antiquity, Monuments of, 158, 159.
Anton, Benedict, 598.
Antonio, King of Portugal, 675, 677, 678, 689, 690.
Antonio, Marco, 172.
Antwerp, 42, 69, 72, 74, 86, 87, 89, 90, 103, 118, 136, 164, 187, 188, 195, 202, 204, 205, 211, 217, 219, 238, 239, 247, 255, 267, 268, 285, 326, 392, 394, 405, 410, 447, 462, 471, 481, 494, 498, 502–505, 702.
Ap John, *see* John.
Ap John, Walter, 10.
Apleforth, John, 192.
Apleforth, William, 403.
Apologia Ecclesiæ Anglicanæ, 192.
Apparel, 62, 68, 107, 141, 169, 199, 200, 262, 263, 267, 269, 272, 273, 282, 290, 680.
Apple trees, 97.
Appleton, John, 632.
Appletree, Hundred of, 124.
Appletree, Thomas, 628.
Appleyard, John, 171.
Appleyarde, Mr., 240, 384.
Applierd, ..., 291.
Apprentices, Act of, 286, 472, 473.
Apprentices' indentures, Registry of, 472, 473.
Appulton, Henry, 483.
Aprice, Gryffith Vaughan, 611.
Aprice, Richard Vaughan, 611.
Ap Richard, *see* Richard.
Apthorp, 232, 343, 421.
Apthorpe, Manor of, 13, 14.
Apwilliam, William, 611.
Aquila, Bishop of, 346.
Aquisgraine, *see* Aix.
Arabella, (or Arbella,) Lady, *see* Stuart.
Archbishop, Consecration of, 135, 138, 143, 144.
Archbishopricks, 138.
Archduke, The, 302, 581.
Archepole (or Archebold), John, 685.
Archer, Henry, 495.
Archery, 185, 552, 559.
Arches, The, 489, 514, 530, 543, 551, 606, 659, 687.
Arches, Court of, 21, 32, 131, 240, 246, 258, 279, 281, 282, 357, 363, 531.
Arches, Proctors of the, 531, 691.
Architecture. *See* Buildings.
Archmore, John, 403.
Arcke, City of, 433.
Arcliffe bulwark, 458.
Arden, Mr., 183.
Ardern, Robert, 576.
Argoll, Lawrence, 691.
Arkendale, Manor of, 523.
Armagh, Archbishop of, *see* Lancaster.
Armagh, Primate of, 302.
Armagh, Titular Archbishop of, *see* Creaghe.
Armeley, Manor of, 170.

Armour, Naval, 480, 481.
Armour, Repairing of, 666.
Armour, &c., Surveyor of, 509.
Armourers, Almain, 133, 145.
Armoury, The, 114, 117, 118, 130, 133, 139, 144, 154, 173, 187, 192, 199, 205, 242, 246, 249, 300, 393, 401, 492. *See* Windsor Castle.
Armoury, Commissioners for survey of the 673.
Armoury, County, 596, 667.
Armoury, Master of the, 510.
Armoury, Office of, 512.
Arms and Armour, 101, 108, 118, 124, 140, 142, 144, 145, 148, 153–156, 170, 173, 178, 179, 200, 205, 207, 208, 210, 211, 214, 218, 225–227, 230, 242, 246, 247, 249, 254, 266, 269, 276, 290, 345, 363–366, 370, 373–378, 382, 384, 387, 393, 394, 415, 455, 486, 491, 506, 508, 511, 542, 610, 648, 653, 693. *See* Musters. Ordnance.
Arms, College of, *see* Heralds.
Arms, Grant of, 4, 27, 92, 131, 149, 214, 247, 249, 426, 495, 501, 503, 606, 624. *See* Heralds' College.
Arms, Kings of, 510.
Arms, Officers and Office of, *see* Heralds' College.
Arms, Royal, and Arms of England, *see* Royal Arms.
Armstrong, Francis, 44, 69.
Armstrong, Mr , 30.
Armstrong, Thomas, 62, 63.
Armstrongs, The, 356.
Army, 44, 65, 67, 92–99, 103, 105, 110, 116, 127, 138, 139, 145, 147–149, 155, 156, 158, 166, 169, 175, 203–207, 210, 214–222, 224–228, 232, 234, 275, 288, 291, 292, 294, 310, 347, 350, 353–357, 359, 360, 364–367, 370, 373, 375, 387, 402, 445, 474, 479, 481, 486, 511, 552, 600, 641, 693, 699.
Army, *see* Coat and Conduct, Foreign Service, Levies, Musters.
Armyngford, Hundred of, 6, 430.
Arnold, ..., 72.
Arnold, Sir Nicholas, 60, 72, 77, 78, 82, 339, 344, 423, 637, 651, 693.
Arnold, Richard, 464, 693.
Arondell (or Arundell), Sir Humfrey, 21, 22.
Arondell, Sir Matthew, 537.
Arran, Earl of, 150.
Arres, Elizabeth, 186.
Arres, John, 186.
Arrest, 456, 477.
Arrest for debt, 527.
Arrest of merchants, shipping, &c. abroad, 326, 327, 432, 484.
Arrest of shipping or goods, 239, 326–328, 362, 384, 391, 393, 427, 432, 433, 435, 444, 463, 464, 482, 506, 519.
Arrest of shipping in England, 490, 598, 645, 694.
Arrest of Spanish goods, 574, 578.

Y Y 2

GENERAL INDEX.

Arreton, Centon of, 143.
Arrows, *see* Armour, Bows.
Arrowsmith, Thos., 457.
Art, Works of, 288.
Artificers, Regulation of, 446, 472, 473.
Artillery, 170, 399. *See* Ordnance.
Artillery, Maintenance of, 415, 421.
Artleborough, 206.
Arundel, 153, 224.
Arundel, ..., 81, 566.
Arundel Castle, 639.
Arundel, Charles, 431.
Arundel, E........., 388.
Arundel, Earl of, *see* Fitzalan, Howard.
Arundel, Sir John, 481.
Arundel, Lady, 50, 146.
Arundel, of Lanherne, Sir John, 146, 177, 353, 369, 388.
Arundel, of Trerice, Sir John, 41, 56, 94, 177, 179.
Arundel Place, 123.
Arundel, Rape of, 139, 264, 267, 451.
Arundel, Sir Thomas, 50.
Arundel, Sir Jo., 588.
Arundell, *see* Arondell.
Ascham, Roger, 261; Sir Roger, 324, 331.
Ascoughe, ..., 530.
Ashburnham, Mr., 695.
Ashby de la Zouche, 149.
Asheburnham, Isabell, 475.
Asheburnham, (or Ashborneham), John, 475, 598.
Asheley, Sir Harry, 465, 571, 582.
Asheley, Henry, 554.
Asheleye, Thomas, 626.
Asheliars, Philip, a pirate, 463, 637.
Asheton, Thomas, 426.
Ashfield, (or Asshefield), Edmund, 301, 349; Sir Edmund, 419.
Ashfold, Edmund, 370.
Ashford, 344, 560.
Ashley, Mrs., 82.
Ashley, (or Aschyly), Mrs. Katherine, 13, 14.
Ashridge, 23, 29, 45, 60, 154.
Ashton, (or Assheton) Christopher, 73, 76, 78–84, 86.
Ashton, Sir Walter, 424.
Ashton, *see* Aston.
Aske, George, 470.
Aslaby, *see* Assulby.
Assart lands, 188, 283.
Assaults, 64, 470, 620.
Assays of money, *see* Mint. Pyx.
Assemblies, Unlawful, *see* Unlawful assemblies.
Assenden, Hundred of, 376.
Asshefyld, *see* Ashfield.
Assheton, *see* Ashton.
Assize, Justices of, *see* Justices.
Assize of bread, in London, 603.
Assizes, 122, 178, 391.
Association for protection of the Queen, 334.

Assonleville, Mons. d' 328, 329–331.
Assulby or Aslaby, Manor of, 119.
Assurance on ships, 509.
Assurances, 535.
Assurances, Register of, 523.
Asteley, John, 276, 339 462, 487, 534.
Asteley, Mr., 528.
Astley, College of, 296.
Aston, 186.
Aston, or Ashton-under-Edge, 237, 261, 309, 415, 443, 454, 458, 549.
Aston, d', *see* Daston.
Astrology, 67, 219, 309, 312, 454.
Astronomy, 292, 454.
Astry, Ralph, 374, 392.
Aswardhurn, Wapentake of, 135.
Atchinson, John, 632.
Atey, (Atee, Atye), Arthur, 394, 648, 651, 675, 677, 685.
Atheism, 431.
Atkinson, Clinton, a pirate, 685, 687.
Atkinson, Davy, 579.
Atkinson, William, 375.
Atkyns, Thomas, 404.
Atkynson, Edmund, 88.
Atslowe, Dr., 626.
Attainder, 119.
Attorney General, 105, 249, 549, 608.
Atye, *see* Atey.
Aubrey, or Awbrey, Dr. William, 114, 169, 328, 473, 482, 535, 551.
Auchar, Sir Anthony, 22, 33.
Auckland, 105, 335, 583, 638.
Audeley, Robert, 175, 270.
Audience, Courts of, 703.
Audley End, 434, 460.
Audley, Joan Lady, 166.
Audley, Lord, *see* Touchet.
Audley, Manor of, 165.
Audley, *see* Awdley.
Augmentation, Bank of, 699.
Augmentation of livings, 220, 518.
Augmentations, Chancellor of, *see* North, Sakevyle.
Augmentations, Court of, 9, 10, 51, 52, 55, 147, 271.
Augsburg, (Augusta), 74, 130, 270, 274, 424.
Augustine Friars, The, 150.
Aulnage, 539. Abuses in, 579.
Austen, John, 64.
Austria, Don John, of, 504, 527, 539, 601, 602, 649.
Aveland, Wapentake of, 135, 694.
Averly, ..., 200.
Avignon, 660.
Awbrey, *see* Aubrey.
Awburn, 406.
Awcher, Mr. 636.
Awcher, William, 627.
Awdley, Mrs., 576.
Awger, John, 233.

Axholme, Isle of, 484.
Ayde, *see* Aid.
Ayere, *see* Ayre.
Ayhorne, *see* Eyhorne.
Aylesbury, 341, 394, 442, 465, 546, 661, 662.
Aylesbury, Hundred of, 6, 376, 442.
Aylesford, Lathe of, 344, 354, 420, 450, 451, 460, 546.
Aylestone, William, 258.
Ayleworth, John, 195.
Aylmer, John, Bishop of London, 543, 545, 549, 552, 569, 582, 598, 622, 625, 626, 631, 649, 650, 652–654, 669, 694.
Aylmer, William, 40.
Ayloffe, William, 637, 639.
Aymour, 125, 126.
Ayre, (or Ayere,) Thomas, 569, 592.
Ayscough, Sir Francis, 34, 50, 118, 123.
Aysemonderbye, 587.
Aysshe, Thomas, 80.
Ayworthe, Manor of, 702.

B.

B........., A., 527, 540.
B........., A., of York, 529.
B........., R., 458.
B........., Thomas, 458.
B........., W., 654.
B........., William, 458.
Babbington, John, 453.
Babham, John, 6.
Babington, Dr. Brute, 531, 701.
Back, Peter, 293.
Bacon House, 595.
Bacon, John, 547.
Bacon, Nathaniel, 628, 657, 665, 669, 670.
Bacon, Sir Nicholas, (Lord Keeper), 132, 135, 143, 158, 162, 165, 171, 207, 230, 235, 237, 268, 287, 308, 326, 329, 332, 365, 381, 384, 385, 388, 390, 396, 406, 417, 454, 467, 489, 507, 555, 569, 635.
........., his speech, 302.
Bacon, Mr., 118.
Bacon, Thomas, 116.
Baconsthorpe, 185, 261, 262, 424, 425, 459, 482, 618.
Baddilsmere, 63.
Baden, Christopher, Marquis of, 257, 270.
Baehere, Otto de, 512.
Baeshe, (Basshe or Bashe), Edw., 105, 148, 205, 209–211, 250, 268, 287, 477, 499, 525–528, 534, 553, 584, 585, 598, 631, 643, 649.
Bagard, Mr., 590.
Bagat, Stephen, 249.
Bagenall, Sir Nicholas, 367.
Bagenall, *see* Bagnal.
Bagendon, 61.
Bagnal, (or Bagnold,) Sir Ralph, 41, 80, 82, 591, 660.

Bagshaw, ..., 693.
Bagshot, 229.
Bainton, Mrs., 536.
Baker, ..., 422, 668.
Baker, Christopher, 438, 474, 478, 513, 563.
Baker, John, 475.
Baker, Sir John, 91, 118.
Baker, Matthew, 634.
Baker, Richard, 174, 258.
Baker, Sir Richard, 475.
Baker, Thomas, 357.
Baker. *See* Barker.
Bakers Company, The, 330, 495, 598, 603, 626, 631, 637, 644. *See* London. White Bakers.
Bala, 264, 486.
Balam, Christopher, 507.
Balborowe, Jerome, 224, 230.
Baldes, Anthony, 64.
Baldwyn, Dr. Francis, 183.
Bales, Thomas, 417.
Ball, John, 641.
Ballard, Mr., 535.
Ballerd, ..., 33.
Balliol College, 693.
Baltonsborough, (or Balstonbury,) Manor of, 41, 42.
Bampton, Hundred of, 420, 423.
Banbury, 28.
Banbury Castle, 666.
Banbury, Hundred of, 420.
Bancroft, Christopher, 681.
Bangor, 301, 377, 564, 684.
Bangor, Bishop of. *See* Robynson.
Bangor, Dean and Chapter of, 684.
Bangor, Diocese of, 564.
Bank of Augmentation, Establishment of, 699.
Bankrupts, Bankruptcy, 92, 94, 569, 695, 702.
Banks, Banking, 410, 417.
Bannister, Hugh, 193.
Banwell, Lordship of, 378.
Banwell, Manor of, 489.
Baptist, ..., 84.
Baptista, John, 565.
Barbar, Thomas, 493.
Barbaro, Ludovico, 270.
Barbary, (or Barbary States,) 183, 265, 288, 290, 303, 318, 478, 490, 568, 633.
Barber surgeons, 150.
Barbican, The, 316, 440.
Barckley, Division of, 375.
Barckley, Gilbert, Bishop of Bath and Wells, 172, 348, 378, 489, 560, 564, 650, 651.
Bardfield, Manor of, 28.
Bargeman, George, 642.
Barges, Master of the, 107.
Barham, Nicholas, 295, 532.
Barholm, or Bereholm, 38, 47, 89, 597.
Bark of Boulogne, The, 529.
Barkeley, Sir Morris, 139, 340, 372.
Barker, ..., 564.

GENERAL INDEX.

Barker, Christopher, 167.
Barker, John, 158, 464.
Barker, Mrs., 467.
Barker, Sir Richard, 473.
Barker, William, 152, 153, 431, 433, 434.
Barkestone, Wapentake of, 336.
Barking Marsh, 113.
Barkley, Edward, 582, 621, 625.
Barkley, Hundred of, 450.
Barkley, (Berkeley,) Lady, 66, 73, 74.
Barkway, 598.
Barle, John, 624.
Barlee, William, 587.
Barley, John, 458.
Barley, *see* Corn.
Barlichway, Hundred of, 358, 653.
Barlo, John, 604.
Barlow, William, Bishop of Bath, 28, 32, 37, 47; Bishop of Chichester, 141, 150, 221, 252, 314.
Barmesey, 462.
Barnard Castle, 352–354.
Barn Elms, or Barnes, Manor of, 391, 610, 618, 657, 673.
Barn, John, 339.
Barne, George, 399.
Barne, Sir George, 232.
Barnes, Capt., 601.
Barnes, Emme, 174.
Barnes, George, 656.
Barnes, Richard, Bishop of Carlisle, 371, 395; Bishop of Durham, 547, 579, 583, 638, 648.
Barnes parish, 618. *See* Barn Elms.
Barnes, Thomas, 167, 682.
Barnes, William, 682.
Barnesley, 61.
Barnet, 8, 108.
Barnet, *see* Friern Barnet.
Barnerd, Mr., 528.
Barnfield Little, Hundred of, 461.
Barnstaple, 513, 630.
Barnstaple, Manor of, 113.
Baron, John, 238.
Barowe, Dr., *see* Barro.
Barrey, Richard, 528, 599, 656, 665, 671, 676, 682.
Barrington, Dame Winefride, 325.
Barrington, Parsonage of, 440, 441.
Barrington, Thomas, 325.
Barro, or Barowe, Dr. Isaac, 321, 628, 634.
Barroll, Mr., 685.
Barrough, Mr., 252.
Barrow, *see* Berghem or Bergen-op-Zoom.
Barrowdon, Manor of, 36, 38, 201.
Barrowe, Manor of, 699.
Barrowe, Stephen, 266.
Barryngtom, Thomas, 380; Sir Thomas, 686.
Barsetlaw, Wapentake of, 332, 379, 418.
Barstable, Hundred of, 380, 570.
Barthlett, ..., 271.

Barton, 631.
Barton, John, 621.
Barton, Ralph, 384.
Barton, Rectory of, 637.
Barton on Humber, Parsonage of, 294.
Barton Yerles, 31.
Barty, *see* Bertie.
Barwicke, Thomas, 642.
Barwyke, Mr., 28.
Basil, the Great, 49.
Basing, 62, 392.
Basing, Mr., 203.
Basing, Lord St. John of, *see* Paulet.
Basingstoke, 272, 653.
Baskerville, Sir James, 338, 343, 374.
Baskervyle, Sir Thomas, 374, 383.
Baspole, Walter, 509.
Bassett, Sir Arthur, 528, 644, 658.
Basset, James, 65–73.
Basset, Manor of, 381.
Basset, William, 105.
Baston, 28, 45, 194.
Baston Dyke, 46,
Basyl, Gervis, 428.
Basyng, John, 120, 413.
Basyng, Roger, 34.
Batehall (?), 149.
Bates, ..., 636.
Bates, Leonard, 286.
Bates, Thomas, 366, 368.
Bath, 43, 578, 599.
Bath, Bishop of, *see* Barlow, Bourn, Barckley.
Bath, Countess of, 157.
Bath, Earl of, *see* Bourchier.
Bath, Knights of the, 55.
Bath, Mayor, &c., of, 533.
Bath, Thomas, alias Thomazo, 477.
Bath and Wells, Bishoprick of, 560, 565, 651.
Bath and Wells, Dean and Chapter of, 489.
Battersey, 672. *See* Papists.
Battery Works, *see* Mines.
Battes, William, a pirate, 570.
Battista, Giovanni, 536.
Bawcriff, ..., 78.
Bawdwen, Agatha, 198.
Bawdwen, John, 198.
Bawtry, 352.
Baxter, Bartholomew, 402, 628, 657, 665, 669, 670.
Baxter, Edward, 217.
Baxter, John, 529, 530.
Baxter, Matthew, 171.
Bayley, Mr., 677.
Bayley, Nicholas, 32.
Bayly, Thomas, 682.
Bayne, Ralph, Bishop of Lichfield, 127.
Bayneham, Richard, 420.
Baynes, William, 110.
Baynton, Sir Henry, 554.
Bayonne, 639.

GENERAL INDEX. 711

Beacon, *see* Becon.
Beacon on the Goodwin Sands, 700.
Beacons, The, 7, 8, 91, 100, 153–155, 303, 342, 384, 454, 471, 487, 488.
Beakyn, ..., 513.
Beale, Robert, 599, 673, 689.
Beamish, 381.
Beamont, John, 30.
Beard, Peter, 700.
Beare, 662, 666.
Beare, Richard, 203.
Beaudesert, 661.
Beaudley, 163, 361.
Beaulieu, 5, 31, 48, 180, 403.
Beaulieu, Jan (or John,) de, 294, 456.
Beaumaris, Borough of, 194, 195, 377 670.
Beaumont, John (Master of the Rolls), 39.
Beaumont, Dr. Robert, 186, 191, 252, 253, 262, 267, 282.
Beaupre, Edmund, 262.
Beccles, 456.
Beckenham, Lordship of, 401.
Beckensall, Awdrey, 109.
Becku, (alias Dolin), Anthony, 297, 315.
Beckwith, William, 691.
Becon, Dr., 601, 602, 604, 606, 607, 651.
Becon, Mrs., 651.
Becon, (Beacon,) John, 446, 447.
Becon, *see* Beakyn.
Beconsfield, 376.
Becontree, Half Hundred of, 380, 418.
Bedell, Bessy, 78, 80.
Bedell, (Bedyll, Bethell), John, 73, 76–80, 93.
Bedford, 374, 392, 581, 643, 667, 675.
Bedford, Bridget Countess of, 601.
Bedford, Earl of, *see* Russell.
Bedford Hospital, Master of the, 389.
Bedfordshire, 21, 158, 166, 175, 341, 370, 374, 456, 541, 568, 581, 667, 670, 702.
Bedhampton, 371.
Bedingfield, Sir Henry, 357.
Bedo, William, 385.
Bedwin, 377.
Beecher, Henry, 355.
Beer, 119, 164, 212, 227, 268, 307, 309, 310, 323, 389, 453–455, 488, 509, 527, 702. *See* Brewers.
Beer, Price and sale of, 556.
Beer and ale in the Queen's Household, 492.
Beer Brewer, the Queen's, 636, 637.
Beer Haven, 251.
Beggars, 334, 577. *See* Vagrants.
Bekesbourn, 244.
Belgium, 660.
Belknape, Family of, 666.
Bell, Robert, Speaker, 443.
Bell, Sir Robert, 543.
Bell, Roger, 174.
Bellachio, (or Bellachy), Vincent, 5, 17.
Bellarmin, 285.
Bellasis, (or Bellowsesse), Dr. 23, 40.

Bellfounder, *see* Moott.
Bellingham, Capt., 616.
Bellot, Thomas, 458 474.
Bellowe, Silvester, 578.
Bells, 158.
Belsyse, 170, 171, 256, 275.
Belteslow, Wapentake of, 124, 694.
Belthorp, Lands of, 197.
Belton, 36.
Belton, Rectory of, 618.
Belvoir, 156, 158.
Bemyche Lodge, 381.
Benbow, John, 77.
Benbrick, John, 701.
Benefices, Valuation of, 493.
Benefit of Clergy, 429, 518.
Benet, John, 326.
Benet, Mr., 629.
Benevolence, The, 314.
Benger, Sir Thos., 195, 205, 212, 233.
Benlowes, Mr., 65!
Bennet College, *see* Corpus Christi.
Bennet, Thomas, 458.
Bent, ..., 312.
Bentham, Thomas, Bishop of Lichfield and Coventry, 251, 393, 424, 565, 583.
Bentoun, Richard, 347.
Bereholm, *see* Barholm.
Berford, Hundred of, 374.
Berghem (or Bergen), op Zoom (or Barrow), 238, 327.
Berkeley, *see* Barckley, Barkley, Barkeley.
Berkeley, Henry Lord, 110.
Berkeley, William Viscount, 244.
Berkeswell, Manor of, 113.
Berkhamstead, 100, 169, 195.
Berkshire, 2, 20, 70, 78, 148, 152–156, 208, 225, 227, 241, 246, 287, 290, 340, 341, 347, 350, 355, 382, 394, 466, 474, 512, 523, 542, 561, 579, 582, 660, 664, 693, 701.
Berkshire, Alehouses in, 572.
Berkshire, Justices of, 639, 654.
Berkshire, Surveyor of. 295.
Berlaymont, Baron de, 467.
Bermondsey, 496.
Bermondsey, *see* Barmesey.
Berquier, Charles le., 554.
Bersona, John de, 289.
Bertie, Francis, 123, 238, 251, 255, 268, 274, 437.
Bertie, Peregrine, 135, 677, 687.
Bertie, Richard, 41, 135, 177, 292, 297, 316, 342, 380, 406, 440, 441, 687; claims the title of Willoughby, 442.
Berwick. 48, 120, 131, 139, 144, 145, 149, 153, 155, 161, 163, 164, 170, 225, 250, 275, 276, 278, 283, 286, 317, 331, 478, 499, 533.
Berwick, Edmund, 16.
Berwick, Governor of, 331.
Berwick, Marshal of, 536, 639.

712 GENERAL INDEX.

Berwick, Manor of, 191, 381.
Berwicke, Cuthbert, 219.
Berye, G., 254.
Beseley, Richard, 287, 435.
Best, John, Bishop of Carlisle, 180, 192, 281, 298, 338, 371.
Best, Thomas, 40.
Beste, Philip, 680.
Bestney, Robert, 462.
Beston, Capt. George, 203, 528.
Bethick, 583.
Bevell, Margaret, 60.
Bevell Robert, 60.
Bevell, William, 60.
Beverley, 171.
Beverley, John, 577.
Beverley, Thomas, 577.
Bevill. Mr., 389.
Bevill, Robert, 648.
Bewdley, 13.
Beybush, 166.
Beynham, John, 577.
Beynhurst, Hundred of, 310.
Beza, Theodore, 257, 524.
Bible, The, 158, 166, 187, 192, 218, 239, 283, 317, 319, 699.
Bicketon, Tho., 625.
Biggleswade, (Byckelswade), Hundred of, 374.
Bill, Dr., 11, 56.
Bille, Mr., 304.
Billingiie, William, 636.
Billingsgate, 150.
Bindon, 385, 451. *See* Byndon.
Binfeld, Parson of, 700.
Binfeld, Hundred of, 418.
Bing, *see* Byng.
Bingham, L., 458.
Bingham, Wapentake of, 339, 379.
Bird, or Birde, *see* Burd. Byrde.
Bird, John, Bishop of Chester, 6.
Bird, Mr., 459.
Birdforth, Wapentake of, 336.
Birkhed, Thomas, 29.
Birkman, Andrew, 239.
Birth, Concealment of, 626.
Biscay, 311.
Bischop, (or Byshoppe,) Thomas, 197, 199, 200, 360, 368.
Bisham, 44, 47, 95, 301, 407.
Bishop, ..., a prisoner, 536.
Bishopricks, 127, 130, 138, 141, 148, 371, 489.
Bishopricks, List of, 478.
Bishopricks, Vacancy of, 547, 605.
Bishopricks, Values of, 573.
Bishops, The, 2, 7, 21, 27, 28, 33, 35, 51, 52, 54, 95, 127, 135, 136, 141, 143, 147–150, 152, 154, 161, 163, 171, 179, 183, 190, 201, 203, 218, 239, 241, 251, 253, 272, 273, 281, 284, 409, 443, 445, 459, 478, 490, 521, 534, 552, 558, 582, 634, 674, 677.
Bishops' books, The, 136.

Bishops Burton, 50.
Bishopscastle, 581.
Bishopscastle, Bailiffs, &c., 581.
Bishopsgate, 526.
Bishopsgate Street, 268.
Bishops Lands, 138, 518.
Bishops, Proxies of, 553.
Bishopsthorpe, 412, 467, 537, **538**, **561–563**, 622, 625, 672.
Bishops Waltham, 560.
Blackborne, Peter, 391.
Blackborough, Peter, 557.
Blackbourn, Vicar of, 307.
Blackbourne, Margaret, 128.
Blackburn, Hundred of, 450.
Blackfriars, 81, 95, 253, 417, 437, 624.
Blackfriars, Liberties in the Precincts of, 654.
Blackheath, Hundred of, 135, 419, 423.
Blacklock, Mr.
Blackman, (now Wilborne), **Amy**, 695.
Blackmore Park, 470.
Blacknoll, Lawrence, 524.
Blacktoft, Parish of, 470.
Blackwell, Thomas, 362.
Blackwell, W., 631.
Blackwell Hall, 508.
Blagge, Sir George, 13.
Blagrave, John, 620, 701.
Blagrave, T., 377.
Blagrave, Thomas, 620.
Blakman, Andrew, 21.
Bland, ..., 476.
Bland, John, 287, 629, 643.
Bland, Simon, 274.
Blandford, 351, 672, 673.
Blandford Forum, 441.
Blankeney, 32.
Blasphemy, 655, 669.
Blaxton, Mr., 183.
Blecheley, Manor of, 491.
Blenerhayset, John, 438.
Blethyn, William, Bishop of Llandaff, **564**, 583, 617.
Bletshee, (or Bletso), 148, 392.
Blewet, Sir Roger, 59.
Blewitt, Mr., 483.
Blickling, 184, 185, 689.
Blockhouses, *see* Forts.
Blonequet, Christopher, 72.
Bloodhounds, 467.
Blount, James, Lord Mountjoy, 135, **137**, **139**, 141, 182, 272, 277, 288, 398, 441.
Blount, John, 66, 74.
Blount, Sir Richard, 237, 243.
Blower, Henry, 628.
Bloxham, Hundred of, 420.
Blue Bell, in Holborn, The, 701.
Bluet, ..., 681.
Blunt, Thomas, 186.
Blunte, Michael, 592.
Blunte, William, 668.

Blyncowe, Arthur, 681.
Blyth, Geo., 481.
Blythe, 282.
Blything, Hundred of, 452.
Boale, William, 579.
Bochetel, Bernardin, 317.
Bocholt, *see* Buckholt.
Bocton, (or Boughton,) Malherbe, 201.
Bodleigh, John, 166.
Bodley, Thomas, 600.
Bodmin, 252, 337, 353, 371, 452, 460.
Bodmin, Mayor of, 21.
Bohemia, King of, 67, 77.
Bohun, Mr., 261, 263.
Bokking, Edmond, 386.
Bolde, Richard, 554.
Boleyn, Sir James, 184, 185.
Bolingbroke Castle, 263.
Bolingbroke, Soke of, 292, 375.
Bollyngton, Hundred of, 138.
Bolmer, Manor of, 112.
Bolton, 328.
Bolton, Francis, 624.
Bolton, Parsonage of, 223.
Boltons, 10.
Bomelius, Dr. Eliseus, 295, 305, 308.
Bonar, ..., 171.
Bonaventure, The, 331, 366, 367.
Bond, Alderman, 308, 329.
Bond, William, 246, 501.
Bonde, George, 127.
Bonds, 475, 477, 532, 641, 644, 645.
Bonds, by Merchants, 90, 91.
Bonds, Cancelled, 520.
Bond, forfeited, Grant of, 509.
Boner, (alias Savage,) Edmund, Bishop of London, 21, 22, 120, 125, 148, 203, 239, 307.
Bonham, 34.
Bonham, Thomas, 603.
Bonvise, Mr. 67, 68.
Bonyfelowe, John, 435.
Boocher, ..., 87, 89.
Books, 113, 187–189, 192, 196, 219, 221, 239, 268, 275, 282, 283, 324, 364, 383, 462, 467, 495, 512, 574.
Books, *see* Sedition.
Books, The Bishops', 136.
Boolles, Mr., 123.
Booth, ..., 459, 554, 555.
Booth, William, 428.
Boothby Graffo, Wapentake of, 135.
Boothe, Charles, 556, 600.
Bordeaux, 321, 322, 330.
Borders, The (towards Scotland), 8, 37, 39, 44, 48, 61, 74, 93, 114, 153, 161, 166, 229, 278, 313, 356, 359, 360, 365, 366, 387, 501, 502, 642.
Boreham, 152.
Borne, John, 642.
Borough, Thomas, 206.

Boroughbridge, 354, 356, 359.
Borowgh, William, 616.
Borroghe, *see* Burgh.
Borrowdale, (or Boroughdale,) 255, 300.
Borrowes, Mr., 630.
Borton, Francis, 98, 99.
Bosmer and Cleydon, Hundred of, 7, 452.
Bossevyle, (or Bosvyle,) Ralph, 107, 186.
Bostock, Mr., 670.
Boston, 30, 31, 47, 150, 166, 198, 297, 338, 389, 406, 465, 598, 657.
Boston, Alehouses, &c., in, 562.
Boston, Mayor, &c., of, 31, 47, 198.
Boston, Recorder of, 32.
Boswell, Mr., 643.
Bosworth, ..., 398.
Bothwell, Earl of, 291, 293, 433.
Bouche of Court, 493.
Bouchier, Mr., 75.
Bouger, Thomas, 84.
Boughton, Hundred of, 460.
Boughton, *see* Bocton.
Boul, Ellen, 650.
Boul, John, 650.
Boulogne, 10, 23, 26, 27, 29, 44, 92, 149, 312, 330, 529, 700.
Bourchier, John, Earl of Bath, 85, 104, 110.
Bourchier, Lady Anne, Marchioness of Northampton, 5.
Bourn, (or Borne,) Gilbert, Bishop of Bath, 108, 123, 172.
Bourne, 33.
Bourne, Sir John, Secretary of State, 61, 76, 91, 92, 149, 223.
Bournemouth, 483.
Bouthe, William, 427.
Bovyat, John, 511.
Bow Bridge, 166, 537.
Bowecocke, Richard, 617.
Bower, Walter, 32.
Bowes, ..., 77, 114.
Bowes, Sir George, 336, 352—354, 583.
Bowes, Jherom, 368, 369.
Bowes, Sir John, 51.
Bowes, John, 381.
Bowes, Mr., 10.
Bowes, Sir Martin, 276.
Bowes, Sir Robert, Master of the Rolls, 40.
Bowghton, 560.
Bowghton, Edward, 657, 698.
Bowier, Francis, 303.
Bowier, *see* Bowyer.
Bowltinge, John, 568.
Bows and arrows, 663. *See* Crossbows.
Bowstaves, 143, 172, 432, 455.
Bowstock, Lancelot, 642.
Bowthe, Mr., 110.
Bowyer, Christopher, 512.
Bowyer, Henry, 623, 626.
Bowyer, John, 60, 103.
Bowyer, Mrs., 626.

GENERAL INDEX.

Bowyer, Simon, 550, 556, 626, 698.
Bowyer, William, 181, 233, 234, 290–293, 298.
Bowyers, 455.
Boxall, (or Boxoll,) Dr. John, Sec. of State, 102, 112, 115, 117, 201.
Boxgrave, Manor of, 52.
Boyer, Edward, 616.
Boyer, Mr., 642.
Boyer. *See* Bowyer.
Boyers, ..., 436.
Boynton, 406.
Boys, Edward, 436, 671.
Boyt, Philip, 589, 656.
Boyton, Manor of, 58.
Brabant, 188, 327, 471.
Brabon, Mr., 525.
Brabrame, 21.
Bracton, Henry, de, 174.
Bradbridge, William, Bishop of Exeter, 409, 562.
Bradbury, John, 251.
Bradbury, Mathy, 380.
Braddyll, Edward, 587.
Bradford, John, 702.
Bradford, Walter, 270.
Bradley, John, 609.
Bradninch, Manor of, 656.
Bradridge, Barton of, 58.
Bradstock, William, 612.
Bradwall, 369, 371.
Bragge, John, 596.
Bragge, Martin, 392, 395, 415.
Braidley, 53.
Braidon Forest, Keeper of, 463.
Braifelde, Rectory of, 31.
Braintree, 256.
Bramber, Rape of, 7, 136, 139, 264, 267.
Bramblety House and Chapel, 404, 624.
Brameley, Manor of, 170.
Bramen, Geoffroy le, 582.
Bramfeld, William, 166.
Bramley, Richard, 270.
Brampton, Chantry, of, 191.
Brampton, Manor of, 491.
Brancepeth, 185, 322, 335, 349, 351.
Branche, Alderman, 701.
Brandling, Sir Robert, 33, 147, 219.
Brandon, Charles, Duke of Suffolk, 142.
Brandon, Lady Frances. *See* Dorset.
Brandon, Robert, 161.
Brandon, *see* Suffolk, Duchess of.
Brantar, John, 303.
Brasborough, Manor of, 193.
Brass Ordnance, 480.
Brathmere, Fishing of, 111, 113.
Braughing, (Braugham,) Hundred of, 374, 458.
Braunceton, 351.
Brave, The ship, 492.
Brawn, boiling of, 498.
Bray, Hundred of, 156, 340.

Braye, John Lord 84.
Brayne, John, 695.
Bread, Assize of, 603.
Bread Street. 177.
Brecknock, 588, 593, 596.
Brecknockshire, 295, 361, 596.
Brecknockshire, Sheriff of, 593.
Brecon, *see* Brecknock.
Bredon, 683.
Breede, Richard, 331.
Bremen, 292.
Bremham, 568.
Brentford, 526.
Brentwood, 22, 157, 176.
Brereton, 664.
Brereton, Lady, 199.
Brereton, Randle, 593.
Brereton, Thomas, 286.
Brereton, William, 664, 679.
Brereton, Sir William, 6, 107.
Brest, 162, 439.
Bretagne, *see* Brittany.
Bretons, The, 203, 215, 216.
Brett, Mr., 491.
Brewers, Brewing, Breweries, 5, 148, 164, 187, 227, 251, 265, 488, 509, 556, 606, 612, 658.
Brewers, Company of, 612.
Brewers, *see* Beer.
Brian, ..., 693.
Bribery, 456.
Brickett, ..., 63.
Brickvile, Mons. de, 382.
Bridewell, 183; Treatment of vagabonds in, 642.
Bridgehouse, London, The, 495, 631; Grain stowed in, 598.
Bridgenorth, 177, 456.
Bridgewater, 169.
Bridlington, 211.
Bridport, 679.
Briet, Pierre, 297.
Brigandine, The, 219.
Brigenton, Thomas, 499.
Brigham, Nicholas. 77, 101, 102.
Brighthelmston, 358.
Brightlingsey, 386.
Brigstock, 375.
Brill, The, 694.
Brimicham, Manor of, 113.
Brimstone, 172, 330.
Brinckley, Stephen, 637.
Brisa, Steven de, alias Capt. Nepyvila, 573.
Briskett, Thomas, 612.
Bristol, 16, 17, 159, 160, 170, 196, 266, 275, 287, 319–322, 339, 345, 375, 384, 386, 388, 410, 431, 467, 486, 507, 540, 546, 551, 552, 556, 567, 571, 577, 592, 629–631, 641, 643, 677.
Bristol, Bishoprick of, 196, 513.
Bristol Castle, 275, 278.

GENERAL INDEX. 715

Bristol, Mayor, &c. of, 170, 175, 196, 345, 408, 467, 571, 629, 630.
Bristol, Merchant Adventurers of, 408.
Bristol, Mint at, 3, 4, 7. 8, 18, 170.
Bristol, Port of, 431, 644.
Brittan, Rowland, 427.
Brittany, 10, 11, 92, 162, 202, 203, 205, 215, 303, 330, 358, 392, 418, 492, 577.
Brivarri, Peter Ortiz de, 102.
Brixton, Hundred of, 135, 423, 426.
Broad Cloths, *see* Cloths.
Broadwater, Hundred of, 373.
Brocke, Mr., 133.
Brocket Hall, 561.
Brockett, *see* Brokett.
Brockhusen, ..., 87.
Brodewaie, Thomas, 606.
Brodgate, 11; House of, 399.
Brodrippe, John, 612.
Brodshawe, Mr., 526.
Brodway, alias George, Thomas, 620.
Broggers, *see* Wool.
Broke, ..., 384.
Broke, John, 526.
Broke, Robert, 21.
Brokehowse, ..., 62.
Brokers, 539.
Brokett, (or Brockett,) Sir John, 561, 615.
Brome, 142, 149, 157.
Bromefield, Manor of, 376.
Bromfield, (or Bromefeld,) William, 121, 164, 172, 206, 232.
Bromham, 12; Tenants of, 554.
Bromhill, 168.
Bromisgrove, *see* Burnford.
Bromley, (Kent), 4; The Bishop's House at, 645.
Bromley, *see* Much Bromley.
Bromley, George, 618.
Bromley Pagetts, 660.
Bromley, Thomas, Solicitor General, 441, 515; Lord Chancellor, 689, 690, 701.
Bromme, John, 272.
Brommell, ..., 494.
Bromyard, Church of, 488, 577.
Bronkard, Mr., 551.
Brookdorp, Pawell, 231.
Brooke, 74, 97.
Brooke, ..., a pirate, 501.
Brooke, Elizabeth, Marchioness of Northampton, 239, 250, 253, 259.
Brooke, George, Lord Cobham, 39, 43, 57, 58, 62, 68, 115, 511, 523, 528, 546, 547, 560, 605, 624.
Brooke, Henry, 394.
Brooke, Thomas, 422.
Brooke, William, 62; Lord Cobham, and Lord Warden of the Cinque Ports, 128, 129, 135, 138, 141, 145, 162, 174, 198, 206, 224, 239, 253, 257, 258, 260, 275, 284, 287, 289, 292, 308–310, 312–318, 320, 322, 326–328, 330, 331, 344, 348, 384,

Brooke, William, Lord Cobham—*continued.*
388, 390, 394, 408, 417, 422, 426, 437, 488, 489, 577, 601, 630, 631, 633, 650, 663, 665, 668, 671, 674, 682, 685. *See* Cobham.
Brookes, Ralph, (Rougecroix,) 692.
Broomehall, 501.
Broonsebithe, *see* Brancepeth.
Brough, 177.
Broughton, 30, 303.
Broughton, Hugh, 637, 638, 645, 647, 657.
Brounkeshey Castle, 451.
Browinger, ..., 689.
Brown, Fr., 509.
Brown, John, 47, 538.
Brown, Leonard, 88.
Brown, Mr., 27, 155.
Brown, Mr. Justice, 249.
Brown, Richard, 493.
Browne........8, 205.
Browne, Alys, 22
Browne, Sir Anthony, Master of the Horse, 1, 3, 4; Viscount Montague, 63, 70, 75, 102, 106, 108, 112, 129, 162, 171, 298, 337, 438, 445, 460, 461, 486, 521, 559. 688.
Browne, Charles, 162.
Browne, Edward, 270.
Browne, Elizabeth, Lady, 4.
Browne, John, 22, 40, 158, 162, 191, 376, 377.
Browne, Martha, 158.
Browne, Mr., 38, 136, 421.
Browne, Richard, 374.
Browne, Robert, 611.
Browne, Roger, 263.
Browne, Thomas, 68, 179, 233, 235, 333, 470, 492, 532, 538, 540, 547.
Browne, Sir Thomas, 509, 561.
Browne, Valentine, 97, 99.
Browneswood, Prebend of, 546.
Brownlowe, Thomas, 342.
Broxash, Hundred of, 123.
Broxbourne, Parsonage of, 435.
Broxton, Hundred of, 122.
Broxtow, Wapentake of, 339, 379.
Brudenell, Sir Edmund, 375, 422, 613.
Bruerne, Mr., 234.
Bruges, 161, 273, 381, 383, 391, 458, 504, 546.
Bruges, *see* Brydges.
Brune, John, 47.
Brune, Thomas, 430.
Bruno, Hans, 48
Brunswick, Duke of, 313.
Bruschetto, Antonio, 274.
Brussells, (Bruxelles,) 66–72, 74–77, 80, 82, 83, 85, 86, 88, 101–103, 175, 204, 299.
Bryant, John, 493.
Bryarlye, Manor of, 358.
Bryatt, Mr., 326.
Bryckhowse, George, 3.
Bryde (?), Sylvester, 314.
Brydeman, Mrs., 96.

Brydges, (or Bruges,) Edmund, Lord Chandos, 161, 339, 344, 360, 367, 368, 375, 445, 446, 463.
Brydges, Giles, Lord Chandos, 463, 545, 588.
Brydigonne, Sebastian, 251.
Bryket, Thomas, 598.
Brytton.........174.
Bucer, Martin, 19, 27, 32.
Bucer, Mrs., 32.
Buckholt, (or Bocholt,) Godfrey de., 87, 95.
Buckholt, Mrs., 251, 296.
Buckhurst, Lord, see Sackville.
Buckhurst, alias Monkhill, 4.
Buckingham, Duke of, see Stafford.
Buckingham, Hundred of, 376.
Buckingham, N., 17.
Buckingham, Prebend of, 491.
Buckinghamshire, 6, 20, 100, 125, 148, 154, 185, 209, 232, 269, 301, 318, 337, 339, 366–368, 371, 376, 378, 442, 465, 483, 491, 494, 508, 535, 546, 555, 564, 636, 661.
Buckinghamshire, Alehouses, &c., in, 555.
Buckinghamshire, Lord Lieutenant of, 376.
Buckinghamshire, Sheriff of, 301.
Buckley, Mr., 605.
Buckross, Wapentake of, 336.
Bucks, see Deer.
Bucler, Sir Walter, 45.
Buclowe, Hundred of, 122.
Buelth, Stewardship of, 111.
Bugden, 370.
Buildings, 53, 84, 85, 104, 105, 187, 190, 191, 198, 199, 200, 202, 211, 243, 317, 394, 404, 409, 455, 456, 457, 459, 597.
Buildings, see Windsor.
Bulkeley, John, 385.
Bulkley, William, 608.
Bull, John, 232, 260.
Bull of Excommunication, 391, 691.
Bullein, The bark, 331.
Bullen, Geo., 475.
Buller, John, 116.
Bulley, Parishioners of, 506.
Bulleyn, Sir James, 266.
Bullinger, Henry, 316 ; his Decades, 669.
Bullingham, Dr., 600.
Bullingham, Nicholas, 118 ; Bishop of Lincoln, 267, 307, 366 ; Bishop of Worcester, 524.
Bullington, Hundred of, 423, 425, 428.
Bullion, 18, 140, 159,–161, 164, 204, 232, 253, 297, 505, 524, 600, 682, 691. See Mint, Coin.
Bullock, Geo., 127.
Bulls Papal, 330, 358, 383, 391, 691.
Bully, Thomas, 635.
Bullyn, William, 171.
Bulmer, Wapentake of, 336.
Bulwarks, see Forts.
Bumpstede, Christopher, 190.
Buntingford, 174.

Burcot, see Raurych.
Burd, see Bird.
Burd, (or Birde,) William, 416, 436, 437, 651.
Burde, Mr., 503.
Burfield, Manor of, 230.
Burford, Baron of, see Cornwall.
Burford, Vicarage of, 510.
Burgavenny, (Abergavenny,) see Nevill.
Burgh, (or Burge, Borroghe,) John, 44, 47.
Burgh, William, Lord Burgh, 257.
Burghley-house. See Burleigh.
Burghley, Lord and Lady, see Cecill.
Burglary, 100.
Burgundians, 102.
Burials, see Funerals.
Burlace, John, 301.
Burleigh, and Burleigh house, 46, 84, 85, 97, 187–191, 193, 194, 198–200, 211–213, 216, 219, 243, 280, 332, 351, 437, 597.
Burley, (Essex), 173.
Burman, Thomas, 176.
Burne, 194.
Burne, Mr., 297.
Burnell, Edward, 578.
Burnell, William, 578.
Burnet, Bishop, 12.
Burnford, (or Bromisgrove,) Gilbert, 635.
Burnham, 185, 343.
Burr, Olyf, 629.
Burrell, William, 144.
Burrows, 668.
Bursar, Office of, 332.
Burse, (Gresham's,) 394.
Bursted, see Little Bursted.
Burthropp, Rectory of, 5.
Burton, Anthony, 200, 201.
Burton, Benefice of, 476.
Burton, John, 46, 272.
Burton-on-Trent, 424.
Bury or Bury St. Edmonds, 343, 372, 568, 603, 628.
Bury, Edward, 487.
Bury, Franchise of, 452.
Bury, Thomas, 346.
Bury, William, 79, 81.
Busbredge, Thomas, 159.
Bushe, Francis, 641.
Bushell, Thomas, 545.
Bushie, ..., 613.
Busshe, ..., 8.
Bussy, John, 387.
Butcher, Dr., 186.
Butcher, John, 75.
Butchers, 411.
Butler, ..., 67.
Butler, Sir John, 371, 372.
Butler, Lady, 81, 82.
Butler, Thomas, Earl of Ormond and Ossory, 314, 632.
Butlerage of England, 278; office of, 398.

GENERAL INDEX. 717

Butteler, Catharine, alias Throgmorton, 76.
Butter, 505, 630.
Buttes, Sir William, 342, 367, 374, 424, 425, 429, 482.
Buttisbury, 217.
Buxton, 502, 525.
Buxton (or Buxstone), Manor of, 700.
Buxton Wells, 502.
Buys, Paul, 495.
Byckelswade, *see* Biggleswade.
Bygott, William, 75, 81, 83.
Byland, 45.
Byndon or Bindon, Viscount of, *see* Howard.
Byng, Mr., 183.
Byng, Thomas, 280. Dr. Thomas, 624, 625, 629, 635, 636, 660, 662, 683, 684.
Byngham, Capt. Richard, 468, 648, 650, 683, Vice Admiral, 687.
Byrche, John, 21, 594.
Byrd, Mr., 527.
Byrde, John, 626.
Byrde, Mr., 593.
Byron, John, 342, 375, 376, 379, 563.
Byrsew, Capt., 319.
Bysheley, Bennet, 576.
Byshoppe, *see* Bischop.
Bysley, Hundred of, 418.

C.

C........., T., 529.
C........., Thomas, 458.
Cabbages imported, 147.
Cabot, Sebastian, 65.
Cade, William, 110.
Cadiz, 574.
Caen, 220, 702.
Cairehouse, Manor of, 596.
Caister, Wapentake of, 335.
Caius, Dr., 264, 267, 474.
Caius College, Stage plays at, 638. *See* Gonville.
Calais, 4, 30, 32, 42–45, 61, 65–67, 85, 88, 92, 93, 96-99, 104, 114, 159, 162, 168, 209, 258, 269, 307, 308, 310, 312, 317, 327, 330, 331.
Calais, Lord Deputy of, 37.
Calamine, 305. *See* Mines.
Calby, Thomas, 538.
Calceworth, Hundred of, 334.
Calehill, Hundred of, 450.
Calfhill, James, 175, 243, 278.
Calf skins, 617.
Calivers, 477, 479, 542, 546.
Calivers, training of, 539–541.
Callis, (or Callice, Callys), John, a pirate, 498, 532, 536, 537, 539, 541, 547, 566.
Calshot Castle, 298, 457.
Calthrop (or Calthorp), James, 368, 369.
Calton, 696.
Calvacanti, ..., 402

Calvart, Monsr., 482.
Calver, Manor of, 398, 410.
Calverley, ..., 433.
Calvetta or Calvetoe, John de, 384, 463, 611.
Calvin, John, 11, 183, 221.
Calvinists, 291.
Camber, or Camber Castle, 16, 119, 226, 402, 576.
Camberton, Rectory of, 223.
Cambridge, 5, 15–18, 32, 36, 121, 124, 125, 132, 138, 184, 186, 187, 202, 211, 242, 244, 245, 250, 252, 253, 267, 269, 271, 278, 280, 287, 291, 293, 298, 301, 302, 305, 319-321, 328, 383, 385, 389, 395, 397, 403, 407, 408, 416, 420, 435, 440, 441, 442, 445, 446, 461, 467, 493, 507, 532, 548, 549, 552, 557, 558, 567, 618, 624, 625, 629, 652, 660–662, 690, 701.
Cambridge, Conveyance of water to, 493.
Cambridge, Improvements in the High Street, 703.
Cambridge, Mayor, &c. of, 36, 125, 242, 278, 660, 662.
Cambridgeshire, 6, 21, 109, 111, 124, 148, 215, 255, 318, 338, 364, 430, 459, 483, 491, 539, 558, 653, 655, 668, 675, 678, 686, 690, 693.
Cambridgeshire, Alehouses, &c. in, 558.
Cambridge University, 5, 11, 14, 15, 17, 18, 33, 36, 54, 55, 64, 101, 121, 123, 126, 127, 130-132, 134, 137, 138, 145, 165, 175, 176, 182, 184, 186, 187, 190, 209, 211, 234, 242–244, 248, 252, 253, 257, 261-263, 267, 268, 271, 273, 274, 282, 292, 302, 304, 305, 323, 328, 350, 371, 381, 382, 387–389, 391, 395, 397, 403, 404, 413, 414, 420, 432, 435, 439, 440– 447, 461, 467, 469, 474, 492, 493, 495, 496, 516, 520, 530, 532, 534, 535, 537, 549, 553, 554, 577, 579, 595, 600, 616, 618, 622, 623, 625, 635, 636, 638, 644, 645, 660, 661, 688.
Cambridge University, Chancellor of, 121, 132, 137, 182, 190, 389, 623. *See* Cecill.
Cambridge University, Consumption of Beer in the Colleges, 403.
Cambridge University, Divinity Lecture, 628, 634.
Cambridge University, Hebrew Professor, 439.
Cambridge University Library, 495-515.
Cambridge, Proctors of, 445–447.
Cambridge University, Stage plays at, 638, 661.
Cambridge University, Vice-Chancellor of, 127, 130–132, 145, 175, 184, 211, 244, 261-263, 282, 302, 305, 328, 382, 387, 395, 435, 442, 446, 495, 530, 532, 537, 549, 551, 567, 623, 629, 636, 638, 644, 660, 683.
Came, Robert, 389.
Camel, The, 332.
Camerhurst, Joachim, 18.
Campanet, *see* Campynet.
Campden, 186.
Campion, Edmund, the Jesuit, 651, 689, 691, 698.
Campion, Henry, 636.

Campynet, John, 700.
Campynet (now Gresham), Margaret, 700.
Campynet (or Campanet), William, 43, 63, 700.
Canata, Thomas, 453.
Candeler, 523.
Candeler, Richard, 156, 232.
Candia, Wines of, 552.
Canford, 69, 70.
Cannock, Forest of, 165, 180.
Cannonden, John, 700, 701.
Canonbury, 3, 8.
Canon Row, 29, 117, 200, 404.
Canterbury, 9, 18, 52, 55, 59, 93, 98, 99, 101, 128, 207, 238, 240, 258, 308, 316, 317, 326, 327, 329, 331, 348 ,352, 373, 384, 408, 409, 419, 422, 435, 509, 528, 558, 559, 588,.662, 672, 688.
Canterbury, Alehouses, &c. in, 566.
Canterbury, Archbishop of, *see* Warham, Cranmer, Pole, Parker, Grindall.
Canterbury, Archbishoprick of, Recusants in, 678.
Canterbury Cathedral, 297, 471.
Canterbury, Dean and Chapter of, 119, 287, 471.
Canterbury, Diocese of, 647.
Canterbury, Jurisdiction of the Archbishop of, 703.
Canterbury, Mayor, &c. of, 348, 566.
Canterbury Park, 115, 116, 136.
Canterbury, Prebends of, 119, 273, 471.
Canterbury, Prerogative Court of, 500, 691.
Canterbury, Province of, 108, 135, 138, 143, 145, 179, 218, 300, 325, 357, 516, 535, 573, 678.
Canterbury, Temporalities of, 517.
Cantrell, William, 600.
Canvass, 436, 580. *See* Cloths.
Cape Riol, 478.
Capels, Family of, 256.
Capon, *see* Salcot.
Captains, Names of, 698.
Captives, *see* Slavery.
Carden, *see* Cawarden.
Cardiff, 537, 538, 540, 541, 543, 549, 580, 589, 638.
Cardigan, 267.
Cardigan Castle, 170.
Cardiganshire, 267, 273, 361, 452, 566, 588, 594, 610, 692.
Cardinall, Stephen, 467.
Cardmaker, Mr., 33.
Cards, *see* Playing Cards.
Cardynall, William, 422.
Carew, George, 234.
Carew, John, 58.
Carew, Lord, 152.
Carew, Lordship and Castle of, 63.
Carew, Mr., 197, 524.
Carew, Sir Peter, 10, 56, 57–59, 72, 75, 127, 162, 244–246, 251, 261, 313, 358, 376, 388, 450, 455, 459, 463.

Carewe, 539, 567, 615.
Carewe, Sir Gawen, 56–59, 73, 115, **313, 460.**
Carewes, The, 527.
Carey, Edward, 360.
Carey, Sir Edward, 351.
Carey, George, 691.
Carey, Henry, Lord Hunsdon, 360, **445, 690.**
Carfoxe, 28.
Carisbrooke Castle, 149.
Carlby, Manor of, 193.
Carleton, George, 628, 681.
Carlile, Mr., 475.
Carlisle, 37, 42, 225, 242, 278, 299, **395.**
Carlisle, Archdeacon of, 117.
Carlisle, Bishop of, *see* Oglethorpe. Best. Barnes.
Carlisle, Bishoprick of, 112, 148, 180, 395, 648.
Carlisle Cathedral, 40, 298, 299, 319.
Carlisle, College of, 281.
Carlisle, Deanery of, 158, 162, 319.
Carlisle, Prebendaries of, 281, 319.
Carmarden (or Carmarthen), Richard, 416, 436, 446.
Carmarthen, 531, 408, 584, 588, 597.
Carmarthenshire, 41, 124, 268, 361, **454, 566,** 584, 597, 617.
Carmynowe, Oliver, 624.
Carnarvon, 571, 591.
Carnarvonshire, 268, 301, 361, **456, 591, 611.**
Carnarvonshire, Sheriff of, 591.
Carnsewe, Mr., 370.
Carpenter, John, 475, 569.
Carr, John, 132.
Carr, Robert, 42, 355, 360, 362, 365.
Carr, William, 170.
Carré (or Quarre), Jean, 297, 315.
Carre, Robert, 342, 375, 387.
Carre, William, 248.
Carrow, John, 65.
Carsey, Captain, 334, 508.
Cartar (or Carter), Roger, 79, 84.
Carter Lane, 301.
Cartwright, Thomas, 381–383, 385, **387–389,** 395, 396, 439, 470.
Carvill, Mr., 149.
Carwoode, Lawrence, 326.
Cary, ..., 67.
Cashel, Maurice Archbishop of, 447.
Casimer, John Duke, 510, 601.
Casks for the Navy, 525.
Casselin, Mr., 216.
Castelin, Thomas, 533.
Castell, ..., 22, 78.
Castell, John, 646.
Castellioni, Baptista, 691.
Castelyn, Edward, 142, 143.
Casterton, Manor of, 38, 198.
Castiglio, Don Antonio de, 661
Castle Hedingham, 697.
Castle-mead, 233.

Castles, see Forts.
Castleton, 194.
Castlyn, Thomas, 399, 471, 455.
Castro, Duchess de, 88.
Casye, Richard, 701.
Catechism, The, 44, 51, 382, 699.
Catelyn (or Catlen), Sir Robert, 107. Lord Chief Justice, 174, 200, 215, 416, 430, 433, 434, 449.
Catesby, Dame Anne, 658.
Catesby, Edmund, 452, 458.
Catesby, Elizabeth, 458.
Catesby, Sir William, 658.
Cathaia, see Cathay.
Catharine of Arragon, Queen, 55.
Cathay, 281, 287, 288, 525, 540, 546, 572, 573, 656.
Cathay (or Kathai), Company of, 533.
Cathedral Churches, Confirmation of, 702.
Catholics, List of, in England, 492.
Catholics, see Church Affairs, Papists, Roman Catholics.
Cathrop, Lordship of, 35.
Catilyn Maliverey, 693.
Catline, ..., 578.
Cator, Mr., 693.
Catterick, Vicarage of, 316.
Cattle, 5.
Caughton, 658.
Cavaignes, Mons. de, 318.
Cavalcante, Guido, 213, 269.
Cavalcante, Stiatta, 90, 91.
Cavalcanti, (or Cavaulti), Mr., 520.
Cave, Sir Ambrose, 95, 117, 129, 139, 148, 249, 304, 309, 408.
Cave, Lady E., 386.
Cave, Lisle, 422, 425, 624.
Cave, Mr., 498, 524.
Cave, Mrs. Margaret, 188, 189, 191.
Cave, Richard, 295.
Cave, Roger, 188, 189, 191, 386.
Cavendish, Mr., 583.
Cavendish, Sir William, 642.
Cawarden, (or Carden), Sir Thomas, 12, 77–79, 116.
Cawdwell, Geoffrey, 256.
Cawkon, Mrs., 486.
Cawood, 182, 188, 193, 390, 396, 435, 538.
Cawood, John, 116, 235, 268, 549.
Cawston, 657, 698.
Cawston, Thomas, 108, 598.
Cayewood, Richard, 89.
Caytho, Hundred of, 372.
Caythropp Park, 32.
Cayworth, William, 86, 89, 90, 92, 198, 283.
Cecilia, Lady, Marchioness of Baden, 257, 258, 261, 267, 269–271.
Cecill, Mrs. Jane, (Burghley's mother), 191, 219, 368, 597.
Cecill, Lady, 79, 95, 216, 311. Pedigree of Lady Burghley's family, 666.
Cecill, Margaret, 43, 188. See Cave.

Cecill, Mr., 320.
Cecill, (or Cecyll), Robert, 39, 41, 47, 51.
Cecill, (Little Tannikyn), 95.
Cecill, Thomas, (a prisoner), 397.
Cecill, Thomas, 43, 86, 176–205 208, 209, 211–214, 216, 217, 332, 373, 437; Sir Thomas, 503, 526, 615.
Cecill, William, (son of the above ?), 615.
Cecill, William, 3, 7, 12, 15, 21, 23; Secretary of State, 29, 32; Sir William, 35, 49, 41–43, 49, 50, 54, 55, 64, 80, 84, 86, 88, 89, 96, 100, 105, 115, 120, 121, 127, 130, 135, 151-153, 158, 160, 163, 164, 167, 168, 170, 171, 176–178, 180–182, 185, 187–189, 194, 195–197, 202, 205, 214, 215, 219, 220, 222, 224, 233, 236, 244, 248, 249, 257, 261, 267, 277, 278, 281, 282, 285, 286, 288, 290, 303, 304, 313, 334, 338, 343, 346, 350, 358, 363, 364. 368, 397, 398, 402; Lord Burghley, 407, 408, 414, 417, 431–435, 445, 450, 465, 467, 474, 477, 481, 482, 484, 485, 489, 491, 492, 495, 496, 498, 508, 510, 514, 518, 525, 533, 535, 536, 547, 552, 556, 573, 574, 576, 578, 579, 582, 586, 590, 598, 600, 608, 613, 618, 621, 622, 638, 639, 641, 665, 676, 678, 691, 695, 697.
........., his buildings, gardens, rents, and property, 15, 19, 30, 32, 38, 44–47, 49, 51, 55, 62–64, 69, 80, 84–90, 92, 96, 97, 100, 133, 171, 180, 182, 187, 188, 190, 191, 194, 195, 198–202, 211–213, 216, 219, 235, 239, 283, 288, 398, 456, 458, 474, 503, 630, 688.
........., Secretary of State, 29.
........., knighted, 35.
........., Chancellor of Cambridge, 121.
........., elected Member for Lincolnshire, 215.
........., his instructions for the young Earl of Oxford, 215; and for the Earl of Rutland, 406.
........., created Lord Burghley, 407, and Knight of the Garter, 445, 446.
........., his illnesses, 515, 601. Suffers from his teeth, 672.
........., libels of him, 547, 665.
........., desired to attend at Court, 581.
........., presents to him, 643.
........., quarrel with Leicester, 600, 666.
........., his letters :—
........., To the University and Colleges of Cambridge, 121, 125, 126, 130, 132, 263, 267, 282, 387, 474, 532.
........., to the Earl of Warwick, 160.
........., to Thomas Windebank, 183, 187–189, 192, 197, 200, 208, 211, 213.
........., to his son Thomas, 184, 187, 189, 197.
........., to Sir Wm. Petre, 230.
........., to the Lord Treasurer Winchester, 239.
........., to Sir Roger Ascham, 261.
........., to Sir Ralph Sadleyr, 308, 309.
........., to Walsyngham, 345, 362, 481, 482, 484, 485, 494, 496, 497, 499, 502, 504, 515, 520, 601, 602.

GENERAL INDEX.

Cecill, William, *his letters*—cont. :—
........., to Leicester, 449, 499, 672.
........., to Thomas Copley, 489.
........., to the Earl of Sussex, 499.
........., to various other persons, 94, 207, 208, 215, 222, 230, 231, 237, 241, 288, 289, 345, 362, 366, 403, 495, 628, 666.
........., *letters to him* :—
..........., From Queen Elizabeth, 130, 168, 182, 312, 365; and her displeasure, 657.
........., from his son Thomas, 526.
........., from Walsyngham, 528, 629.
........., from the University of Cambridge, 629, 666, 671.
........., from various other persons, 2, 3, 6, 9, 14–16, 18–22, 27–51, 63, 64, 84, 88, 94, 95, 115–119, 121, 123–134, 136, 137, 139–145, 148–151, 153–164, 167, 169–188, 191, 192, 194–198, 202–222, 226–229, 234–238, 240–244, 247–264, 266–324, 326–333, 338, 343, 345, 346, 349–356, 358–360, 365, 367–373, 376–378, 380–399, 401, 402, 404, 406–422, 424–447, 449, 453–456, 458, 459, 463, 464, 467, 468, 470, 474, 484, 485, 487, 489, 492–500, 502–507, 509, 515–517, 519, 521, 524–530, 532, 534, 537–540, 545, 547, 548, 551–559, 575, 577–583, 587, 588, 590–592, 594–601, 604, 605, 611, 616, 617, 622, 624–628, 630–638, 643–645, 647, 649, 657, 658, 660–662, 665, 666, 669, 670, 672, 673, 680, 684, 688, 690, 698, 701, 702.
........., has the settlement of Henry Howard's debts. *See* Howard.
Cecill, William, *see* Mines.
Cecill, *see* Cicill.
Cecyll, *see* Cecill.
Celye, Thomas, 469, 583.
Cesto, River of, 328.
Cevallerius, Anthony Rodolph, 439.
Chaderton, Mr., 629.
Chaderton, Thomas, 610.
Chaderton, Dr. William, 381, 493, 494, 595, 617, 628. Bishop of Chester, 643, 680.
Chadlington, Hundred of, 418, 423.
Chafford, Hundred of, 380, 570.
Chafin, Thomas (Sheriff of Dorset), 665, 670.
Chakendon, Manor of, 241, 404.
Chalenors, The, 28, 196.
Chalfont, 514.
Challenges, *see* Duels.
Challenor, John, 354.
Challiner, Nynyan, 475.
Chaloner, Francis, 255, 617.
Chaloner (or Challenor), Sir Thomas, 12, 97, 186, 188, 191, 195–197, 254, 255.
Chalyner, Nicholas, 687.
Chamber, Groom of the, 536.
Chamber, Messengers of the, 599, 622, 626.
Chamber, Treasurer of, 576. *See* Masone, Sir John.
Chamber, Yeoman of the, 465.

Chamber, Henry, 41.
Chamber, Leonard, 659.
Chamber, Oswald, 659.
Chamberlain, Sir Leonard, 93, 125.
Chamberlain, Sir Ralph, 104.
Chamberlaine, Robert, 635.
Chamberlaine, Sir Thomas, 72, 73, 423.
Chamberlayn, Thomas, 17.
Chambers, Dr. Richard, 177, 186.
Chambrelayne, George, 163.
Chamond, Richard, 481.
Champernowne, Sir Arthur, 57, 59, 226, 316, 319, 321, 322, 324, 326, 327, 329, 341, 382, 384, 389, 437, 439, 466, 519, 524, 605.
Champneys, ..., 132.
Champneys, Thomas, 281.
Champyney, Mons. de, 515.
Chanata, Tomazo, 119.
Chancellor, John, 485.
Chancery, Court of, 63, 84, 164, 165, 306.
Chancery, Inns of, 567.
Chancery, Messengers of, 569.
Chancery, Records of, 290, 292.
Chancery Lane, 14, 273, 470.
Chandos, *see* Brydges.
Chandos, Lady Elizabeth, 137.
Chandos Place, 595.
Chanon or Channel Row, *see* Canon Row.
Chantries, 12, 51, 61.
Chaors, Mons. de, 689.
Chapel Royal, 77.
Chapman, John, 520.
Chapman, Mr., 381.
Chardon, Hundred of, 340.
Charing, 397.
Charing Cross, 121.
Charities, Public, 509.
Charlcote, 426.
Charles, Archduke, 468.
Charles V., the Emperor, 692.
Charles IX., King of France, 316, 481.
Charlotte, The ship, 211.
Charnell, William, 701.
Charter House, The, 142, 387, 486.
Chartham, Curate of, 435.
Chartley, 348.
Chartres, 214.
Chartres, Vidame de, 208, 211, 212, 297, 362, 465, 467.
Chastillon, Cardinal, 220, 316–320, 408, 409.
Chatham, 297, 585, 638, 677.
Chatham (Cheatham), Manor of, 27, 191.
Chatham Yard, 513.
Chatsworth, 185, 379.
Chaves, ..., Friar, 647.
Chenle, Hundred of, 340.
Checkers, The, 73. *See* Chekers.
Chedsey, Dr., 127.
Cheese, Present of, 524.
Cheke, Henry, 269, 320, 332, 376, 397.

GENERAL INDEX. 721

Cheke, John, 8, 11, 14, 33 ; Sir John, 35, 43.
Cheke, Mr., 86.
Cheke, Thomas, 143.
Chekers, The, 260, 263, 271, 278, 290.
Chelmsford, 59, 65, 137, 342, 356, 540, 557, 675.
Chelmsford, Hundred of, 343, 418, 450, 570.
Chelsea, 3, 38, 48, 50, 271, 296.
Chelsea, Parson of, 271.
Chelveley, 294.
Cheney, Francis, 401.
Cheney (or Cheyney), Richard, Bishop of Gloucester, 199, 284, 319, 320, 324, 560, 566.
Cheney, William, 401.
Chepiona fruits, 680.
Chepstow, 606.
Chepynge Campden, 186.
Cherburg, 45, 76.
Cherisworth, 621.
Chertsey, 610.
Chertsey Abbey, 4.
Chese lands, 136.
Cheseworth, Manor of, 12, 166.
Chesham, 100.
Cheshire, see Chester, County of.
Cheshunt, 11.
Chestelet Valley, 201.
Chester, 122, 288, 291, 292, 294, 303, 321, 377, 410, 463, 464, 476, 477, 486, 508, 535, 625, 629-631, 633, 635, 636, 661, 669, 670, 673, 679, 684.
Chester, Bishop of, see Bird, Scot, Downman, Chaderton.
Chester, Bishoprick of, 6, 148, 203, 368, 562, 568, 600.
Chester, Charters of, 476, 477 ; and Clause of Præterea in, 476, 477.
Chester, Sale of the Shire Hall, 670.
Chester, County of, 6, 84, 107, 122, 147, 149, 215, 266, 286, 291, 344, 347, 354-356, 364, 469, 472, 474, 484, 562, 566, 568, 593, 601, 614, 661, 664, 679.
Chester, County Palatine of, 476, 517.
Chester, Dominick, 573.
Chester,'Edward, 365, 573.
Chester, John, 686.
Chester, Lady, 598.
Chester, Mayor, &c., of, 175, 288, 477, 486, 661, 669, 673.
Chester, Mere Merchants of, 619, 639.
Chester, Mr., 598.
Chester Place, see Somerset House.
Chester, Sir Robert, 109, 111, 119, 365.
Chester, Sheriff of, 427, 484, 562.
Chester, Thomas, 629.
Chester, Sir William, 174, 178, 181-183, 236.
Chester Herald, see Hart.
Chester Ward, 335, 678.
Chester West, 232, 285, 376.
Chesterfield, 460, 560.

Chesterton, 255.
Chesterton, Hundred of, 430.
Cheston, 5.
Chesworth, 561.
Chetham, John, 695.
Chetwood, Mr., 128.
Cheveley, Hundred of, 6, 430.
Chevers, Mr., 684.
Cheverton, Henry, 512.
Cheyne, Sir Henry, Lord Cheyne, 268, 374 444, 445, 469, 471, 487, 529, 627.
Cheyne, Sir Thomas, Lord Warden of the Cinque Ports, 5, 26, 33, 45, 58, 59, 88, 95, 97-99, 103, 104, 121, 401.
Cheyney, Mrs., 646.
Cheyney, William, 646.
Cheynis, 127.
Chichester, 19, 251, 305, 314, 331, 398, 460, 588, 636, 651.
Chichester, Bishop of, see Sampson, Day, Scorey, Barlow, Coortesse.
Chichester Cathedral, 542.
Chichester, Deanery of, 49, 283, 305.
Chichester, Diocese of, 40, 111, 314, 357, 541, 561, 620.
Chichester, haven or port of, 252, 378, 382, 519.
Chichester, Sir John, 136, 140, 313.
Chichester, John, 279.
Chichester, Mayor, &c., of, 252, 519.
Chichester, Prebendaries of, 35, 150.
Chichester, Rape of, 7, 136, 139, 264, 267, 451.
Chichester, Register of, 544.
Chiche, Lord Darcy of, see Darcy.
Chick, William, 541, 543.
Chidle, see Chudleigh.
Chidley, John, 232.
Chigwell, Parish and manor of, 4, 28.
Child murder, 588.
Children, William, 311.
Chilford, Hundred of, 6.
Chillester, Mr., 439.
Chillinge, 76.
Chiltern Hundreds, The, 376.
China, 525.
Chippenham, Hundred of, 377.
Chipping Norton, 418.
Chipping Wickham, 555.
Chiselhurst, 424.
Chittewood, ..., 41.
Chobham, 467.
Cholmeley, Sir Roger, 88.
Cholmondeley (or Cholmley, Chumley), Sir Hugh, 288, 291, 292, 294, 344, 414, 670.
Chomelly, Bennet, 286.
Chopwell, 602.
Choristers, see Music.
Chovoorth, George, 650.
Christchurch, Canterbury, 471.
Christchurch, Dean of, 9, 307, 324.

Z Z

Christchurch (Hants), 623.
Christ Church (London), 703.
Christ Church (Oxford), 27, 63, 85, 192, 193, 195, 208, 233, 307, 324, 498, 586, 648, 675.
Christ Church, Vicar of, 29.
Christ's College (Cambridge), 16, 125, 132, 637, 638, 645, 647, 657, 661, 703.
Christ's College, Manchester, 680
Christenings, 247, 276, 505¹
Christen Malford, Manor of, 224, 230, 235.
Christmas, John, 521, 624.
Christmas, Robert, 393.
Christmas, Observance of, 143, 264, 498.
Christopherson, John, 64.
Christophersonne, *see* Hodgson.
Chrysostom, 292.
Chudleigh (or Chidle, Chudley), Christopher, 77, 79, 392.
Church Affairs (Edward VI.), 5, 7, 8, 11, 14, 15, 17–19, 21, 22, 27, 28, 30, 31, 33–35, 39–41, 44–46, 48–53.
.... (Queen Mary), 54, 56, 63, 74–77, 79, 83, 87–89, 96, 102, 103, 108–112, 114.
.... (Queen Elizabeth), 119, 120, 123, 125, 127, 129, 130, 132–138, 143, 145, 147–150, 158, 163, 165, 170, 173, 174, 177, 180, 183, 184, 186, 187, 192, 201, 203, 204, 208, 215, 218, 220, 221, 223, 229, 232–235, 241, 243, 248, 250, 251, 253, 254, 262, 267, 271–273, 281, 283–285, 287, 290, 291, 293, 297, 299, 300, 301, 303–308, 310, 312, 319, 320–322, 324, 328, 334, 362, 368, 371, 377, 381–383, 387–390, 392, 393, 395–397, 402, 405, 409–411, 414, 426, 430, 435, 444, 445, 446, 462, 470, 471, 483–486, 493, 496, 516, 520, 539, 541, 542, 544, 549, 552, 558, 560–562, 565–570, 572, 578, 582, 583, 586, 601–604, 607, 608, 616, 617, 620, 621, 623, 637, 642, 644, 654, 656, 658, 660, 668, 671, 678, 681, 687–690, 693, 694, 698, 699, 703. *See* Conventicles.
Church Government, Treatise on, 694.
Churcham, 464.
Churches, Numbers of, 170, 478.
Churches, *see* Parish Churches.
Chute forest, 178.
Chynery, Allen, 179.
Cicill, William, 279, 651; Sheriff of Hereford, 671.
Cinque Ports, 26, 33, 44, 45, 58, 59, 73, 88, 95, 98, 103, 121, 128, 135, 138, 162, 165, 174, 206, 208, 220, 224, 246, 277, 284, 310, 331, 337, 384, 401, 406, 407, 489, 523, 546, 547, 559, 560, 564, 582, 588, 616, 650, 656, 662, 663, 688.
Cinque Ports, Admiralty Court of, 551.
Cinque Ports, Alehouses in, 559.
Cinque Ports, Charters of, 614.
Cinque Ports, Lord Warden of, *see* Cheyne. Brooke.
Circuits, Judges on the, 692.
Cirencester, 382, 419, 424.

Cirencester, Hundred of, 375, 419.
Civil Law, College of, 17.
Civil Law, Doctors of the, 479, 531.
Civita Vecchia, 587.
Clafton, Little and Great, 48.
Claims, Court of, *see* Court.
Clap-boards, 525, 598.
Clapham, Mr., 21.
Clarcke, Richard, 595.
Clare Hall, (Camb.,) 15–18, 435.
Clarencieux, *see* Hawley, Le Neve, Harvey, Tonge, Cooke.
Clarentieux [Tonge], Mrs. Susan, 110.
Clark, John, 700.
Clark, Mrs., 700.
Clark, Roger, 611.
Clarke, ..., 264.
Clarke, Francis, 214–218.
Clarke, George, 630.
Clarke, Mr., 612.
Clarke, Nicolas, 691.
Clarke, Thomas, a pirate, 512, 583, 599, 615 648, 663.
Clarow, Wapentake of, 336.
Clarvys, Harbert, 44.
Clason, *see* Clayssone
Claudvilde, 509.
Clavering Lucas Pitchards, Manor of, 66.
Clavering, Thomas, 164, 175.
Clayssone (or Clason), Lucas, 496, 534.
Clayton, Mr. 212.
Clayton, Thomas, 86.
Clecher, Thomas, 405.
Clederow, William, 414, 678.
Clement, D., 44.
Clement, John, 283.
Cleobury Mortimer, Manor of, 286.
Clercke (or Clerke), Bartholomew, 257, 260, 291, 346, 397, 473.
Clere, Edward, 369, 373, 377, 381, 385, 424 ; Sir Edward, 575, 689.
Clere, Sir John, 94, 158.
Clergy, Benefit of, 429, 518.
Clergy, Exemption from Musters, 534.
Clergy, Subsidies of, 516.
Clergy, The, to furnish horsemen, &c., 365, 366, 677, 678, 680. *See* Musters.
Clergy, Taxation of the, for charges of an Ambassador, 681.
Clergy, *see* Church Affairs, Subsidy, Marriage.
Clerk, D., 114.
Clerk, Mr., 320, 324.
Clerk of the Market, 245.
Clerk of the Stable, 611.
Clerke, E., 491.
Clerke, Edmund, 110.
Clerke, George, 57, 61.
Clerkenwell, Manor of, 468.
Clerks of the Council, *see* Privy Council.
Clerks of the Peace, *see* Peace.

Cleveland, 107.
Cleves, Lady Anne of, 43, 63, 87.
Clewar, Farm of, 512.
Cleyley, Hundred of, 368.
Cliborne, Richard, 578.
Clifford, George, Earl of Cumberland, 691.
Clifford, Henry, Earl of Cumberland, 167, 363.
Clifford, Sir Ingram, 37.
Clifton, 373, 561.
Clifton, Cuthbert, 368.
Clifton, Hundred of, 374.
Clifton, *see* Clyfton.
Clink, The, 484, 578, 703.
Clippers of coin, 237.
Clipping, *see* Coinage.
Clockmaker, The Queen's, 457.
Clopton, William, 235, 309, 415, 416, 429, 654.
Cloth of Gold, 2.
Cloth Trade, History of, 539.
Clothiers, 169, 243, 270, 421, 511, 516, 517, 550, 551, 569, 557, 633.
Cloths, 44, 68, 89–91, 119, 126, 128, 137, 139, 143, 161, 169, 171, 176, 178–180, 182, 188–190, 193, 198, 222, 224, 226, 231, 235–237, 239–247, 267, 269, 274, 277, 284, 285, 288, 299, 304, 305, 307–309, 311, 315, 325, 326, 328, 330, 382, 391, 407, 411, 421, 430, 443, 447, 455, 467, 494, 508, 510–512, 516, 529, 540, 557, 573, 577, 587, 600, 603, 623, 633, 647, 698, 699.
Cloths, Licence to export, 527, 657.
Cloths, Linen, 620.
Cloths, Sealing of, 490.
Cloths, Woollen, 579.
Cloths, *see* New Draperies.
Clothworkers of London and Ipswich, 284, 6 4
Cloume, Lordship of, 429.
Cloutier, ..., 433.
Clough, Richard, 405.
Cloville, Eustace, 626.
Clunne, James, 434.
Clurewall, 420.
Clybburne, ..., 127.
Clyff, 64.
Clyff, John, 90.
Clyff Park, 89, 194, 283.
Clyffe, Thomas, 590, 696.
Clyfte, 608.
Clyfton, Sir Jervis, 332, 342, 373, 379, 418, 650, 693.
Clynton, Edward Lord, Lord High Admiral, 7, 13, 32–34, 41, 64, 101–106, 108, 113, 148, 153, 154, 156, 164, 166, 172, 173, 177, 202, 203, 205, 215, 216, 225, 227–229, 233, 257, 278, 305, 321, 322, 327, 346, 349, 351–356, 359, 360, 387, 390, 398, 414; Earl of Lincoln, 442, 444, 445, 475, 476, 481, 484, 492, 501, 503, 505, 508, 517, 526, 528, 538, 583, 585, 623, 632, 685.
Clynton, Sir Henry, 332, 334; Lord Clynton, 461, 485, 583, 584.
Clypsham, 84.

Co, ..., R., 475.
Co, ..., Sir Thomas, 475.
Coachmaker, The Queen's, 583.
Coals, 275, 282, 319, 502, 533, 612.
Coat and Conduct Money, 110, 164, 166, 174, 205, 206, 229, 231.
Coberley, 79.
Cobham, Cobham Hall, 43, 129, 196, 260, 275, 292, 309, 310, 312–317, 320, 348, 387, 389, 390, 394, 560, 650, 665, 674.
Cobham, Elizabeth, 100.
Cobham, George, 119, 509.
Cobham, Henry, 129, 546, 574.
Cobham, John, 460.
Cobham, Lady, 258.
Cobham, Lord, *see* Brooke.
Cobham, Thomas, 405, 417, 426, 437.
Coboz, Lazarus, 170.
Cock, John, 129.
Cock, Robert, 40.
Cocke, John, 515, 518, 523.
Cockeram (or Cockerham), Philip, 119, 315, 358, 408.
Cockerell, Robert, 98, 99.
Cockermouth, 441.
Cockson (or Coxsoon, Cookson), Lawrence, 237, 399, 400, 517, 692.
Coddenham, Mr., 311.
Coedor, Mons. 698.
Cogan Pill, 105.
Coggeshall, 511, 551.
Coin, coinage, 10, 11, 18, 19, 30, 32–35, 46, 97, 149, 155, 156, 158, 159–162, 164, 165, 168, 170, 175, 182, 190, 192–194, 197, 204, 232, 237, 240, 242, 252, 253, 260, 265, 269, 288, 291, 306, 309, 385, 404, 408, 415, 421, 431, 439, 471, 491, 505, 508, 582, 613, 616, 617, 694, 700. *See* Mint.
Coin, Foreign, 700.
Coinage, Standard of, 700.
Coiners, Coining, 177, 309, 455, 478, 482, 509.
Coins, Roman, 406.
Coke, ... 298.
Coke, John, 30.
Cokerell, Thomas, 132.
Colas, Hierom, 35.
Colborough, 628.
Colbrook, 426.
Colby, Mr., 310.
Colchester, 18, 109, 140, 237, 379, 397, 412, 482, 496, 557, 558, 576, 624, 687, 697.
Colchester, Alehouses, &c., in 558.
Colchester, Archdeaconry of, 567.
Colchester, Bailiffs, &c., of, 483, 496, 521.
Colchester, Dutch Church in, 687.
Colchester, Preachers in 520.
Colchester, Strangers at, 525.
Colchester School, 612.
Colcloughe, Toby, 640.
Colcum, 376.
Cole, ..., a pirate, 17.

724　GENERAL INDEX.

Cole, Arthur, 105, 110
Cole, Edward, 109.
Cole, Henry, Provost of Eton, Dean of St. Paul's, 116, 127, 144.
Cole, Humfrey, 258.
Cole, Thomas (of Oxford), 499, 501.
Cole, Thomas, 535.
Cole, Dr. William, 567.
Colebrooke, Manor of, 224, 230.
Coles, John, 394.
Coleshill, Mr., 428.
Coleshull, 676.
Collections, 204, 239, 295, 301, 307, 658. *See* St. Paul's.
Colleges, Act concerning, 517.
Colleges, Recusants in, 572.
Colleges, Robberies in, 443.
Colleges, Statutes of, 610, *see* Cambridge, Oxford.
Collen, Thomas, 475.
Collens, Stephen, 475.
Colles, Humfrey, 369, 371.
Colles, John, 631.
Colleweston, Manor of, 13, 14, 277.
Collsonsack, Richard, 169.
Colly, Anthony, 388.
Collyer, Francis, 548.
Colne Engayne, Town of, 697.
Colne House, 226, 231.
Colocumb, 631, 632, 683, 686.
Cologne, 73, 239, 254, 325, 406, 408.
Cologne, Archbishop of, 68, 119.
Colonna, M. Antony de, 88.
Colquit, or Colequit, Manor of, 528, 581, 625, 643, 644.
Colsell, Mr., 106.
Colshill, Robert, 391, 569
Colte, Roger, 169.
Coltehirste, Mathew, 126.
Colthurst, Edward, 533.
Colton, 424.
Colville, Mr. 141, 291.
Combe, 60, 282.
Combe Nevell, or Combe Park, 40.
Comberford, Henry, 396.
Comet, A wonderful, 454. *See* Meteor.
Comforte, 546.
Common Law, Reform in, 517.
Common Pleas, Court of, 107, 125, 189, 285, 508, 696.
Common Prayer, 17, 18, 22, 33, 45, 132, 134. 136, 143, 170, 203, 235, 322, 462, 689, *See* Religion.
Common, Right of, 554.
Commons, The Speaker, 519.
Commons, House of, 409, 443, 517 ; Expulsion of a Member, 516. *See* Parliament.
Commonwealths-men, 22.
Communicants, 234.
Communion, *see* Sacrament.
Como, Jasper, 16.

Comorthas, Practice of, in Wales, 514.
Compter Prison, The, 273.
Compter Prisons, *see* White Lion. Wood Street.
Compton, ..., 233.
Compton, Hundred of, 340.
Compton, Walter, 420.
Comy, Innocent, 627.
Concealed lands, Concealments, 155, 290, 399, 400, 410, 415, 436, 456, 499, 586, 613, 702 ; Grants of, 575.
Condé, Prince of, 198, 214, 314, 316–318, 320, 540, 630, 665.
Cone, Alexander, de, 694.
Coneynger, Great, 36.
Conference, Religious, 127.
Confession, Catholic, 483.
Coniers, John, 477, 493.
Conies, 420.
Conjurations, *see* Witchcraft.
Conquet, 106, 202, 322, 392, 492.
Consecrations, *see* Archbishops, Bishops.
Consistory Courts, 597.
Conspiracy, 478. *See* Treason.
Constable, Sir John, 12.
Constable, Lady, 372, 373.
Constable, M., 148.
Constable, Robert, 301, 356, 365, 602.
Constable, Sir Robert, 650.
Constable Ragler, Office of, 691.
Constantine, Thomas, 421.
Constantinople, 73, 551.
Conventicles, 308, 571.
Conveyances, Fraudulent, 519.
Conveyances of land, Bill of, 442.
Convicts, Transported, 545.
Convocation, 143, 218, 516.
Convoy, 102, 144, 227, 529.
Conway, Bailiffs of, 630, 631.
Conway, John, 111.
Conway, Henry, 593.
Conway, Philip, 622.
Conyers, Sir George, 122.
Conyers, James, 304.
Conyers, John, 304. *See* Coniers.
Conyers, John Lord, 37, 39, 92.
Conyngesbye, Thomas, 579.
Conysby, Anne, 491.
Coo, James, 699.
Cook, Bartyllme, 644.
Cook, William, 177, 208, 241, 254, 279.
Cooke, Sir Anthony, 41, 43, 44, 208, 257, 378, 380, 418.
Cooke, Anthony, (an apprentice), 696.
Cooke, Richard, 23, 505, 106.
Cooke, Robert, (Clarencieux), 426, 503, 495.
Cookham, Hundred of, 156, 340.
Cookson, *see* Cockson.

GENERAL INDEX.   725

Coomes, John, 654.
Cooper, Dr. John, 334.
Cooper, Thomas, 89, 367.
Coortesse, Edmund, 616, 620, 621, 625, 626, 694.
Coortesse (or Courtes, Curtis, Cortesse), Richard, 262-264, 268, 283; Bishop of Chichester, 314, 323, 477, 508, 521, 539, 541-545, 548, 620, 621.
Coothe, William, 646.
Cope, Anthony, 348.
Copinger, Mr., 555.
Copinger, Roger, 331.
Copland, William, 701.
Copley, Mrs., 669.
Copley (or Coppley), Peter, 683.
Copley, Thomas, 489, 490, 525, 666, 669, 683.
Copper, Copper Mines, *see* Mines.
Coppinger, Thomas, 451.
Coppley, *see* Copley.
Copthall, 34, 131, 243.
Copthorne, Hundred of, 135, 419, 423.
Copwold, Sir John, 41.
Copyholders, 266.
Corbet, ..., a pirate, 238, 251, 298.
Corbet, Sir Andrew, 164, 339, 374, 426, 466, 486, 532.
Corbet, Martin, 641.
Corby, Hundred of, 519.
Corby, Parsonage of, 36.
Corbyn, John, 394.
Cordage, 580.
Cordell, William, 65, 66, 68, 80; Sir William, and Master of the Rolls, 111, 157, 171, 173, 280, 357, 408, 410, 417, 429, 442, 543, 602.
Cordwainers, Wardens of the, 579.
Core, Paul, 649.
Corfe, alias Cork Castle, 536.
Cork Castle, *see* Corfe.
Cork City, 330, 650.
Cork Haven, 251.
Corn, 26, 29-31, 104, 185, 222, 227, 250, 252, 253, 255, 258,-260, 262-265, 267-269, 283, 286, 299, 399, 431, 456, 468, 470, 484, 507, 576, 578. *See* Regrators.
Corn, Damaged, 626, 631.
Corn, Exportation of, 491, 492, 495, 498, 569, 578, 603, 638, 644, 666, 672.
Corn, Price of, 559, 585, 618.
Corn, Toll for grinding, 4.
Cornbury, 499.
Cornelis, Mr., 658, 670.
Cornelisson, Adrian, 95.
Cornelius, Dr., 27, 49.
Cornelius, Mr., *see* Vos.
Cornewaleys, Sir Thomas, 60, 107, 115, 131, 142, 149, 157, 293, 547.
Cornewall, Gabriell, 577.
Cornewayle, ..., 80, 81.
Cornish (or Cornysshe), Henry, 39, 45, 47.

Cornwall, 10, 19, 20, 51, 56, 58, 62, 94, 100, 101, 121, 146, 157, 179, 202, 217, 233, 235, 244, 252, 307, 309, 318, 332, 337, 338, 353, 369-371, 388, 389, 437, 449, 451, 459, 460, 465, 477, 480, 481, 492, 502, 511, 512, 534, 542, 555, 562, 572, 581, 583, 584, 587, 589, 612, 615, 616, 623, 629, 643, 655, 666.
Cornwall, Alehouses in, 570.
Cornwall, Duchy of, 52, 55, 304, 399.
Cornwall, Sheriff of, 388, 451, 452.
Cornwall, Vice Admiral of, 388.
Cornwall, Edward, (Baron of Burford), 690.
Cornwall, Robert, 59.
Cornwallis, *see* Cornewaleys.
Cornwallys, Sir John, 56.
Cornwell, Thomas, 683.
Cornysshe, *see* Cornish.
Coronation of Edw. VI., 1, 2; of Queen Mary, 55; of Queen Elizabeth, 117, 118, 120, 125, 128, 176, 264.
Coroners, 500.
Corpus Christi (or Bennet) College, (Camb.), 127, 190, 459, 525, 545, 555, 671, 683-685.
Corpus Christi Col. (Oxford), 186, 312, 567.
Corranus, ..., 648.
Corringham, Prebend of, 40.
Corringham, Wapentake of, 108.
Corsica, 243.
Corso, San Pietro, 243.
Coryat, George, 277.
Coseworth (or Cosowarthe), John, 55, 308.
Cosham, Manor of, 248.
Cotman, William, 56.
Cottell, George, 612.
Cottesford, James, 550.
Cotteslowe, Hundred of, 376, 442.
Cotton, George, 62, 371.
Cotton, Lady Jane, 371.
Cotton, Mr., 502, 504, 507.
Cotton, Sir Richard, 13.
Cotton, Robert, 110.
Cotton, William, 498, 515, 516, 523-525, 527.
Cotton, Thomas, 15.
Cotton, Sir Thomas, 546.
Cottswolds, The, 168, 169.
Coulynge, William, 76.
Council, The, *see* Privy Council.
Council of State, 222.
Councils, General, 131, 158, 165, 173, 175.
Count Palatine, *see* Palatine.
Counterfeiting the coin, 10, 11, 78, 309.
County clerks, 512.
County clerk's Office, Grant of, 611.
Court, ..., a pirate, 547.
Court, The, 123, 156, 157, 225, 229, 231, 236, 237, 240, 250, 286, 299, 318, 319, 360, 418, 426, 442, 449, 463, 468, 474, 478, 485, 496, 499, 501, 521, 546, 552, 558, 581, 586, 588, 595, 599, 601, 650, 670, 672, 677, 689.
Court, Bouge (or Bouche) of, 493.
Court of Claims, 1, 118.

GENERAL INDEX.

Court, Inns of, *see* Inns.
Courtelease, 144.
Courtenay, ..., 331.
Courtenay, Edward, Earl of Devonshire, 65–77, 80, 82–86.
Courtenay, Peter, 19.
Courteney, Capt., 508.
Courteney, James, 354, 355.
Courteney, John, 125.
Courteney, Sir William, 84.
Courtezans, 80.
Courts, Ecclesiastical, 479.
Cousen, Jean, 312.
Cousin, Mons', 257.
Covenants, Writs of, 535, 506.
Coveney, Thomas, 105, 186.
Covent Garden, 388, 701.
Coventry, 60, 308, 309, 334, 343, 410, 466, 545, 657, 676.
Coventry, Mayor, &c., 308.
Coventry, New baths at, 631.
Coventry, Bishop of, *see* Lichfield.
Coverley, Walter, 544.
Covert, Richard, 57, 393.
Cowbridge, 176.
Cowdrey, 162, 171, 337, 460, 461, 486, 559.
Cowell, Mr., 645.
Cowell, William, 577.
Cowes, West (Isle of Wight), 530.
Cowledge, John, 647.
Cowling Castle, 57, 58.
Cowlyn, John, 56.
Cownsell, Hugh, 220, 223, 228, 285.
Cowper, Thomas, Bishop of Lincoln, 333, 407, 560, 648, 687.
Cowpon, Tenants of, 695.
Cowte, Mr., 384.
Cox, Peter, 554.
Cox, Richard, Bishop of Ely, 135, 141, 158, 187, 188, 192, 239, 262, 263, 267, 324, 460, 485, 507, 515, 516, 562, 628, 652, 654, 655, 675.
Cox, Richard, 590.
Coxe, ..., 298.
Coxe, Dr., 5.
Coxe, alias Devon, John, 173, 174.
Coxe, Michael, 417.
Coxe, Mr., 194.
Coxe, Richard, 545.
Coxhall, *see* Coggeshall.
Coxson, *see* Cockson.
Coysgarne, John, 619.
Cradle, Francis, 588.
Crambrok (Kent), 701.
Cranbourne Chace, 112.
Cranbrook, Hundred of, 450.
Crane, ..., 36.
Crane, Anthony, 596, 598.
Crane, John, 592.
Crane, Mr., 488.
Cranley, Richard, 420.

Cranmer, Thomas, Archbishop of Canterbury, 20, 22, 24–26, 32, 45, 46, 54, 77, 106, 222.
Cranmore, 45, 89.
Cranwell, Mr., 75.
Craven, John, 640.
Craven, Lands in, 696.
Crawford Muir, 279, 283, 320.
Creaghe, Richard, (Titular Archbishop of Armagh), 646, 647.
Creations, 35, 55, 63, 407, 442.
Crediton, 8.
Crediton, Deanery of, 8.
Creditors, 702. *See* Debtors. Protection.
Cressy (Cressey, Cressye), Mr., 651, 684, 696.
Creswell, ..., 655.
Crewkerne (or Crockhorne), Manor of, 72.
Cripplegate, 271.
Cripse, Mr., 636. *See* Cryspe.
Crispe, Mr., 401.
Crispe, William, 482.
Crixsey, 606.
Croce, M. de la, 327, 328.
Crocford, Mr., 682.
Crocford, William, 682.
Croft, Sir James, 60, 61, 258, 259, 338, 343, 595, 613, 646.
Croft, Lady, 613.
Crofte, Alexander, 682, 683.
Crofte, Thomas, 682, 683.
Croftes, John, 368, 532, 543.
Croftes, William, 368.
Crofts, Thomas, 374.
Crokehill, Herbage of, 640.
Croker, Lady, 695.
Cromplysts, *see* Cloths.
Cromwell, Sir Henry, 648. *See* Crumwell.
Cross, Mr., 15.
Crossbows, 167.
Crossed Friars, 148.
Crossen, 120, 123.
Crouch, William, 37.
Crowe, William, 83.
Crowland, *see* Croyland.
Crowley, Mr., 271.
Crowmer, William, 424, 527, 634.
Crown, The Royal, 6, 83.
Crown debts, 575. *See* Public Expenditure.
Crown jewels, 6, 14, 26, 129, 146, 147, 161.
Crown lands, 5, 51, 53, 55, 61, 70, 74, 91, 100, 102, 106, 108, 110–112, 119, 134–136, 155, 162, 163, 166, 167, 169, 181, 188, 191, 197, 204, 211, 225, 230, 237, 241, 245, 246, 248, 273, 285, 287, 290, 292, 399, 402, 461, 533.
Crown revenues, 4, 5, 18, 70, 74, 91, 112, 118, 123, 130, 135, 136, 146, 166, 208, 358, 418.
Croyland, or Crowland, 84, 88.
Croyland Monastery, 31, 416.
Croydon, 87, 91, 138, 179, 273, 276, 310–312.
Crumwell, Lady Elizabeth, 46.
Cruse, Robert, 496, 497.

GENERAL INDEX. 727

Crushing mill, Invention of, 701.
Cruys, Anne, 323.
Cruys, Gamaliel, 323.
Cruys, James, 323.
Cruys, William, 323.
Cryspe (or Crypse, Crisp), Sir Henry, 101, 124, 132, 258, 310, 419, 427, 463.
Cryspe, William, 121, 241, 310, 408, 436.
Cryston, Manor of, 55.
Cubberley, *see* Coberley.
Cuckfield, 588, 625.
Cuckfield, Parishioners of, 616.
Cuckfield, Vicar of, 616, 620, 621, 625, 694. *See* Coortesse.
Cuddleston, Hundred of, 342.
Culpeper, ..., 377.
Culpeper, Dr., Martin, 524, 605.
Culpeper, Thomas, 8, 60, 61, 88.
Culstocke, 55.
Cumberland, 179, 191, 252, 266, 280, 288, 291, 292, 303, 395, 457, 563.
Cumberland, Alehouses, &c., in, 562.
Cumberland, Earl of, *see* Clifford.
Cunstable, Martin, 114.
Cupper, John, 241, 652.
Curates, *see* Vicars.
Currants, 510.
Curriers Company, 282.
Curstmarsh, 458.
Curwen, Hugh, Archbishop of Dublin, 298; Bishop of Oxford, 298, 307.
Curwen, Mr., 315, 319, 320, 330.
Custom House, 105.
Custom House officers, 694.
Customs, The, 45, 70, 89, 91, 105, 109, 116, 117, 119, 159, 166, 167, 182, 186, 187, 193, 223, 230, 231, 238, 245, 247, 261, 264, 267, 268, 277, 278, 289, 298–300, 310, 314-318, 323-325, 329, 358, 360–362, 378, 382, 390, 391, 397, 398, 401, 406, 410, 415, 416, 418, 428, 431, 436, 437, 460, 500, 503, 539, 540, 556, 587, 594, 595, 598, 602, 611, 613, 640, 644, 647, 657, 680, 695.
Customs, Comptroller of, 329, 475.
Customs, Proposals for improving the, 698.
Cutlerd, John, 191, 252, 267.
Cypræus, Paul, 170.

D.

Dabeney (or Dawbeny), William, 68, 72.
Dabernal, Walter, 699.
Dacorum, Hundred of, 371.
Dacre, Alice, 5.
Dacre, Edward, 223.
Dacre, George Lord, 280, 286.
Dacre, Lady, 289.
Dacre, Leonard, 119, 375, 377, 435, 500, 512.
Dacre, Lord, 509, 512.
Dacre, Sir Thomas, 41.
Dacre, William, Lord, 92, 119, 280, 286.
Dacre, *see* Fynes.
Dacres, George, 371.
Dacres, The, 441.
Dado, Carlo, 17.
Dale, Henry, 477.
Dale, Dr. Valentine, 244, 298, 314, 328, 386, 417, 457, 590, 637, 640, 645, 655, 656.
Dale, Rectory of, 28.
Dallison, William, 61.
Dalmyngton, William, 489.
Dalston, Mr., 376.
Dalton, James, 283.
Dalton, Ralph, 122, 149.
Dalyson, George, 19.
Dalyson, William, 19, 105.
Dammart, 201.
Damsell, Mr., 42.
Damsell, Sir William, 211, 461.
Danbury, 687.
Danby, Sir Christopher, 394.
Dancaster, Parsonage of, 596.
Danet, or Dannet, Mr., 189, 273.
Danett, Mrs. Jane, 491.
Danett, Thomas, 491.
Dantzic, 237, 313, 314, 316, 317, 455.
Danvars (or Danvers), George, 341, 371, 390.
Danvers, or Davers, Sir John, 377, 684.
D'Anvyle, Revolt of, 546.
Danyell, John, 16, 79, 80, 81, 83, 84.
Danyell, Nicholas, 512.
Danyell, Thomas, 59.
Darby, Walter, 273.
Darcy, Sir Arthur, 29, 69.
Darcy, Sir Harry, or Henry, 342, 503, 648, 667, 669.
Darcy of Chiche, John Lord, 268, 342, 343, 351, 352, 356, 481, 483, 520, 527, 545, 624, 686.
Darcy, Mr., 131.
Darcy, Sir Thomas, 3, 8, 20, 24; Lord Darcy of Chiche, Lord Chamberlain, 39, 49, 50, 106, 108, 110.
Dare, Martin, 78.
Darell, Christopher, 477.
Darell, Edward, 210, 224, 225.
Darell, John, 626.
Darell, Thomas, 230, 231.
Darkenall, ..., 198.
Darlington, 51, 316, 321, 322, 324, 382, 439, 466, 355, 356, 524.
Darlington Ward, 335, 678.
Darneton, *see* Darlington.
Darnley, Lord, *see* Stuart.
Darrel, Hugh, 22, 173, 174.
Darrell, Mr., 351.
Dartford, 5", 59.
Dartford, Smelting mills at, 570, 571, 580, 581, 606, 608, 615, 618, 621.

Dartmoor, 180.
Dartmouth, 59, 261, 322, 327, 339, 437, 440, 504, 519, 574, 583, 589, 600.
Dartmouth, Mayor of, 589.
Dassonleville, *see* Assonleville.
Daston, Anne, 261.
Daston, Anthony, 261.
Dattylo, Cecase, 18.
Daventry, 425, 599.
Davers, *see* Danvers.
David, Rice, 576.
Davids, John, 537.
Davids, William, 584.
Davies, John, 60.
Davies, Richard, Bishop of St. David's, 328, 362, 604, 606, 627.
Davies, Thomas, Bishop of St. Asaph, 396, 406, 564, 597.
Davis, Pearse, 600.
Davison, William, 529, 601.
Davy, ..., 75.
Davy, Thomas, 624.
Davy, William, 433, 464.
Davys, Stephen, 701.
Dawbeney, Olyver, 16, 309, 310, 397, 410, 415, 428, 436, 437.
Dawbeny, *see* Dabeney.
Dawe, John, 224, 234.
Dawes, Thomas, 692.
Dawtrey, Sir Francis, 23, 76.
Dawtrey, William, 352.
Day, George, Bishop of Chichester, 19, 35.
Day, John, 177.
Day, Robert, 643.
Day, William, Provost of Eton, 314, 323, 395.
Daye, Mr., 186.
Deal, 101.
Dean forest, 275, 633.
Deaneries, 12.
Deans and Chapters, Lands held by, 698.
Dearing, Alexander, 524.
Dearing, Mr., 434, 436.
Dearth, 12.
Debtors, Relief of, 521, 523, 612.
Debts, Debtors, 131, 266, 389, 454, 460, 472, 492, 497, 524, 527, 545, 548, 549, 551, 567–569, 583, 590–594, 596–598, 600, 606, 620, 624, 627, 633, 695, 702.
Debts of the Crown, *see* Public Expenditure.
Debts, *see* Howard, Henry.
Declarations, 364.
Dedford (Deptford?) 636.
Dedycke, William, 84.
Dee, Dr. John, 67, 219, 621.
Deeping, 45, 47, 63, 89.
Deeping, East, 29.
Deer, (Buck, Does,) 41, 64, 67, 68, 105, 118, 165, 181, 191, 198, 211, 219, 267, 273, 315, 487, 551.
Deer stealing, 691.

Deerhurst, Hundred of, 420.
Defence of the Realm. *See* Musters. Nation. Realm.
Dela, Damian, 565.
De la Garde, Baron, 39.
De la Prey, Monastery of, 31.
De la Warr, Lord, *see* West.
Delecrest, Monastery of, 41.
Delves, George, 175.
Demilances, *see* Musters.
Denbigh, 590, 675.
Denbighshire, 107, 361, 483, 572, 618, 634.
Dengie, or Dengy, Hundred of, 379, 450, 535, 570.
Denization, Letters of, 700.
Denizens, *see* Aliens.
Denman, Dr. John, 38.
Denman, Thomas, 593.
Denmark, 103, 303, 447, 495, 588.
Denmark, King of, *see* Frederick II.
Denney, Mr., 3.
Denny, Captain, 605, 609, 611, 615.
Denny, Manor of, 111.
Dennys, Richard, 477.
Dennys, *see* Denys.
Denton, 35, 47, 63, 657.
Denton, Mr., 289.
Denys, Sir Maurys, 206–210, 212, 227, 477.
Denys, Sir Thomas, 10, 19, 56, 57, 59.
Deprivation, 546; of an archbishop, 581; of a clergyman, 620, 621, 694.
Deptford, 210, 480, 636, 638.
Deptford Strond, 213, 513, 580.
Derby, 124.
Derby, Countess of, 303.
Derby, Earl of, *see* Stanley.
Derby Place, 15.
Derbyshire, 120, 124, 148, 183, 185, 188, 341, 346, 347, 368, 370, 378, 415, 460, 474, 485, 560, 563, 565, 581, 640, 663, 700.
Derbyshire, Alehouses, &c., in, 566.
Derbyshire, Justices of, 638.
Dereham, East, 652.
Dering, Edward, 439, 470.
Dero, ..., 392.
Derrick, ..., a surgeon, 438.
Deryng, ..., 22.
Desmond, Earl of, 408, 478, 485, 629.
Despes, Don Gerreau, 313, 315, 427.
Dethick, Christopher, 695.
Dethicke, ..., 264.
Dethicke, Sir Gilbert, Garter, 2, 27, 143, 149, 505.
Dethicke, John, 77, 79, 80, 83, 84, 249, 295.
Devereux, Robert, Earl of Essex, 645.
Devereux, Walter, Viscount Hereford, 111, 181, 340, 348, 350, 355; Earl of Essex, 442, 445, 446, 454, 459, 481, 495, 502, 508, 531, 574, 652.
Devizes, 341, 484.

GENERAL INDEX. 729

Devon, 8, 10, 18-20, 44, 51, 56-59, 62, 67, 71, 100, 101, 125, 157, 224, 232, 244, 252, 261, 275, 309, 318, 338, 341, 354, 376, 387, 437, 449, 450, 459, 460, 471, 477, 480, 504, 511, 535, 543, 548, 557, 581, 583, 605, 612, 656, 658, 672, 687.
Devon, Admiralty in, 583, 585.
Devon, Alehouses, &c. in, 557, 581.
Devon, Justices of, 639.
Devon, Vice Admiral of, 226.
Devon, John, *see* Coxe.
Devonshire, Earl of, *see* Courteney.
Dewy, Thomas, 172.
Diaceto, Florence de, 64.
Diary, Lord Burghley's, 431.
Dibden, ..., a pirate, 627.
Dickens, George, 549.
Dickering, Wapentake of, 336.
Diconson, Cuthbert, 163.
Dictionary, Latin, 492.
Die, John, 386.
Dieppe, 8, 177, 201, 203, 205, 207-211, 213-215, 219, 315, 482, 701.
Digby, ..., 428, 438.
Digby, Anthony, 156.
Digby, Everard, 656.
Digby, George, 651.
Digby, Harry, 29.
Digby, Jasper, 29.
Digby, John, 95.
Digby, Kenelme, 380, 388, 482.
Digby, Mr., 45.
Digges, T., 454.
Diggs, Thomas, 577.
Dilapidations, 134, 396, 538, 539, 579, 622, 625, 626, 652, 653.
Dilapidations, Act of, 519.
Dinale, Augustino, 627.
Dioceses, The, 493.
Dirichson, James, 530.
Dirowghe, Edward, 557.
Dirrich, *see* Drythicke.
Discovery, *see* Voyages.
Diseney, Richard, 375, 387.
Dispensations, 135, 190, 405, 411.
Dispensations abolished, 617.
Dispensations, Office of, 218.
Dister, John, 591.
Dive (or Dyve), Lewis, 493, 568.
Divine Service, Celebration of, 443, 445, 462, 655, 669, 703. *See* Church.
Divorce, 5, 238, 473.
Dix, ..., 434. *See* Dyx.
Dixe, Alderman, 583.
Dobson, Mr., 15.
Doctors' Commons, 363. *See* Arches.
Docwra, Thomas, 373.
Docwray, Anthony, 126.
Dodding, Edward, 567.
Doddington, 485.
Doddridge, Richard, 388.

Dodge, John, 58, 388.
Dodinghurst, Manor of, 65.
Dodington, Bartholomew, 187, 248, 292, 599.
Dodington, William, 436, 477, 493, 521, 640.
Does, *see* Deer.
Dogs, 672, 679. *See* Bloodhounds. Greyhounds. Lion. Spaniels.
Dolin, *see* Becku.
Dolls imported, 147.
Domestic Economy, 693.
Dominick, ..., 75.
Donat, Anthony, 90.
Doncaster, 349, 351-354, 360.
Donhedmary, Parson of, 103.
Don John, *see* Austria.
Donne Ralph, 84.
Donnynge, John, 264.
Dorchester, 138, 465, 541, 546, 581, 649, 650, 656.
Dorchester, Hundred of, 138, 418, 425, 428.
Dorell, Mr., 521.
Dorking, 348, 419, 423, 426.
Dormer, Jane, *see* Feria.
Dormer, Lady, 163.
Dormer, William, 6.
Dormer, Sir William, 366, 483.
Dorothy, Mrs., 3.
Dorrell, Mr., 302.
Dorrington (or Doryngton), Robert, 664, 669.
Dorset, Frances Brandon, Marchioness of, 11 ; Duchess of Suffolk, 11, 64, 128, 142, 143, 217, 294, 505.
Dorset, Marquis of, *see* Grey.
Dorset, 19, 67, 91, 100, 101, 131, 141, 146, 148, 157, 262, 272, 338, 340, 342, 351, 372, 385, 437, 449, 451, 465, 477, 481, 541, 546, 547, 551, 561, 571, 581, 582, 589, 612, 640, 649, 656, 672, 673, 678, 679, 699.
Dorset, Alehouses in, 582.
Dorset, Defences of the county, 678.
Dorset, Justices of, 639.
Dorset, Sheriff of, 665, 670.
Doryngton, *see* Dorrington.
Donay, 624.
Doughtye, John, 529.
Douglas, Archibald, Earl of Angus, 221.
Douglas, Lady Margaret, Countess of Lennox, 38, 49, 164, 197, 199-205, 209, 211, 212, 216, 218, 221, 257, 259, 272, 289, 295, 296, 301, 305, 394, 409, 428, 489.
Douglas, George, 221.
Dounapney, 60.
Dover, 44, 59, 95-99, 102, 106, 113, 145, 171, 188, 189, 225, 227, 240, 241, 253, 257, 258, 271, 286, 307, 310, 313, 315, 316, 330, 331, 389, 413, 422, 427, 436, 444, 466, 478, 508, 509, 527, 533, 560, 630, 672, 682, 697.
Dover, Admiralty Court of, 95, 610.
Dover Castle, 88, 98, 99, 113, 121, 174, 240, 277, 284, 322, 369, 408, 422, 455, 489, 528, 599, 618, 656, 665, 682, 685.

GENERAL INDEX.

Dover Castle, Constable of, 26, 88, 174, 284.
Dover, Common Council of, 599.
Dover Downs, 52.
Dover, Elections at, 599.
Dover haven or harbour, Commissioners for repair of, 670–674 : licence to export beer and grain, 670 : their instructions, 671, 672 : power to impress workmen, &c., 676 : the repairs, works, &c., 404, 517, 525, 575, 579, 610, 621, 630, 633, 641, 649, 668, 670–674, 685, 690.
Dover harbour, Plans of, 575.
Dover, Mayor, &c., 520, 525, 575, 599, 641, 670, 672.
Dover Pier, 117, 253, 458.
Dover, Passage at, 520.
Dover, Searcher at, 520.
Dover, Watermill at, 697.
Dowe, Anne, 157.
Dower, 147.
Down Court, 469.
Downham, 192, 324.
Downham (in the Isle of Ely), 655, 675.
Downman (or Downham), William, Bishop of Chester, 203, 305, 307, 321, 322, 338, 568.
Downs, The, 52, 102, 228, 361, 528.
Downynge, Edmond, 58.
Draining, 512, 598, 611.
Draining, Pumps for, 509.
Drake, Francis, 329, 659, 661, 682, 685, 686, 689–691, 693.
Drama, The (Plays, Masks, Revels), 1, 40, 46, 82, 143, 250, 330, 498.
Drama, Players, and Stage Plays at Cambridge, 638, 661.
Draper, Sir Christopher, 285.
Draper, Henry, 426.
Draper, Robert, 355.
Draper, William, 75.
Draperies, *see* Cloths, New Draperies.
Drapers, 169.
Drapers' Company, The, 695.
Dravah, *see* Havard.
Draycot, Dr. Anthony, 173.
Drayton, 291.
Drayton, Manor of, 381.
Dreadnought, The, 505, 552, 553, 559, 631.
Drew, Martin, 61.
Drewe, Mr., 700.
Drewe, Richard, 107.
Drewrie, Dr., 576.
Droits, *see* Admiralty.
Dromont, Henry, 623.
Drunkenness, 564.
Dru Dru, 170.
Drury, Mr., 385.
Drury, Sir William, 12, 527.
Drury, William, 536.
Drury, Thomas, 22.
Drythicke (or Dirrich), ..., 388.
Dryver, E., 225.
Drywood, Mr., 638.

Dublin, Archbishop of, 9. *See* Curwen.
Dublin Castle, 522, 524.
Duchy Lands, 123.
Duck, Thomas, 429.
Ducke, John, 491.
Duckett, Lionell, Alderman, 251, 255, 270, 271, 279, 291, 294, 300, 301, 316, 320, 376, 408, 409, 414, 468. Sir Lionell, 568, 615.
Duddeley, Lord Ambrose, 39, 50, 160 ; Earl of Warwick, 203, 206, 207, 209, 218, 226–229, 236, 237, 285, 298, 304, 347–356, 358, 359, 445, 461, 462, 477, 646, 685.
Duddeley, Andrew, 2. Sir Andrew, 37, 39, 46, 49.
Duddeley, Arthur, 48.
Duddeley, Edward Lord, 342, 487.
Duddeley, Lord Guildford, 57.
Duddeley, John, 209, 345.
Duddeley, John, Earl of Warwick, 3, 6–9, 13–15, 18, 21, 22, 26, 27, 29, 32 ; Duke of Northumberland, 35–42, 44–51, 54, 64, 74.
Duddeley, Lord Robert, 52. **Master of the Horse,** 129, 139, 142, 151, 155, 171, 199, 207, 233, 240, 243 ; Earl of Leicester, 244, 251, 280, 288, 304, 308, 309, 312, 313, 316, 320, 331, 345, 346, 363, 380, 391, 398, 415–417, 434, 451, 453, 476, 489, 491, 495, 499, 501, 506, 512, 537, 565, 574, 601, 618, 622, 628, 632, 646, 656–658, 664, 665, 670, 671, 701, 702.
........., his correspondence with Francis Yaxley, 138, 194.
........., letters to Burghley, 154, 209, 269, 293, 296, 302, 448, 454, 463, 498, 601 ; and quarrels with him, 600, 666.
........., report that the Queen was with child by him, 157.
........., Constable of Windsor Castle, 200.
........., correspondence with the Queen, and interest in her affairs, visits, &c., 229, 246, 269, 273, 278, 291, 293, 363, 448, 449, 498, 503.
........., his connexion with trade and with voyages of discovery, 220, 236, 260, 265, 288, 314, 380, 391 ;
........., and with mining operations, 254, 255, 270, 275–277, 288–300, 302, 398, 408, 424, 688.
........., created Earl of Leicester, 244.
........., letters from various persons to him, 202, 221, 225, 229, 235, 236, 251, 270, 272, 275, 276, 291, 318, 350, 367, 383, 392, 393, 419, 433–435, 437, 441, 443, 445, 447, 449, 489, 529, 673, 675, 679, 685–689, 691.
........., correspondence with the Earl of Hertford, 236, 237, 238, 240, 310.
........., letters to other persons, 253, 345, 346, 495, 532.
........., his lands and other property, 245, 246, 258, 286, 304, 398.

Duddeley, Earl of Leicester, visits Oxford, 277, 278.
........., Lieutenant at St. George's Feast, 445.
........., libels against him, 547.
........., his players at Cambridge, 661.
Duddeley (or Dudley), Lord, see Sutton.
Dudestone, Henry, 353.
Dudley, 502.
Dudley, Charles, 612.
Dudley, Henry, 73, 76, 78–84, 86, 88.
Dudley, Lady, 77, 502.
Dudley, Mr., 19.
Dudley, Richard, 376, 395, 398.
Dudley, Thomas, 84, 88, 89.
Dudley, see Duddeley.
Duels, (Challenges, Duelling,) 152.
Dueton, William Van, 663.
Duffyld, John, 475.
Dugdale, James, 188.
Dumbritton, 6.
Dunche, William, 382, 394.
Dundee, 235.
Dunham, 427.
Dunham, Parson of, 148.
Dunhamsted, Farm of, 497.
Dunkirk, 97, 99, 102–104, 326, 529, 532.
Dunkirk, Sluice Master of, see Rickwarth.
Dunmow, Hundred of, 380.
Dunn, Thomas, 192.
Dunning, John, 247.
Dunning, Mr., 522.
Dunsany, Baron of, 499.
Dunstable, 158.
Dunwich, 318, 331, 643.
Duppa, Jeffrey, 488.
Duræus, ..., a Jesuit, 698.
Durant, Edward, 198.
Durham, Archdeacon of, 233.
Durham, Bishop of, see Tunstall, Pilkington, Barnes.
Durham, Bishops of, their jurisdiction in Chester, 517.
Durham, Bishoprick of, 47, 48, 50, 105, 122, 137, 146, 148, 161, 175, 176, 187, 188, 352, 497, 519, 563, 639, 648.
Durham, City of, 149, 163, 324, 346, 355, 356.
Durham, County of, 122, 335, 646.
Durham County, Alehouses in, 562.
Durham, Dean and Chapter of, 33, 46, 48–50, 91, 104, 149, 161, 323, 324, 540.
Durham, Dean of, 621, 644.
Durham, Divinity Lecture at, 638.
Durham, Palatinate of, 38, 335, 352, 360, 497, 678, 695.
Durham Place, 2, 50, 150, 273, 454, 500.
Durham, Prebends and Prebendaries of, 149, 163, 323, 540, 547, 637, 645.
Durham, Visitation of, 588, 621.
Durrant, Robert, 189.
Du Simiers, see Simiers.

Dutch Church or Congregation, 28, 177, 205, 221, 323, 496, 613. See Colchester.
Dutch artisans in Colchester and Halsted, 697.
Dutch engineers, 575.
Dutch strangers, 575.
Dutch, The. See Holland.
Dutton, Laurence, 569, 598, 599.
Dutton, Richard, 463, 477.
Dutton, Thomas, 406.
Dyeing, 293, 411, 447, 467, 518.
Dyer, Andrew, 682.
Dyer, Edward, 500, 646.
Dyer, Eleanor, 110.
Dyer, Sir James, 125 ; Lord Chief Justice, 638.
Dyer, Joan, 110.
Dyer, Katherine, 110.
Dyer, Simon, 110.
Dyer, Sir Thomas, 37.
Dyers' Company, The, 447.
Dyke, Thomas, 475.
Dylay Wood, 51.
Dylett, George, 309.
Dymocke, John, 311, 468.
Dymok, ..., 16.
Dymoke, Sir Edward, 34, 98, 264.
Dyon, John, 34, 325.
Dyrrick, ..., 45.
Dyson, Humphrey, 114, 232.
Dyve, see Dive.
Dyx, William, 277, 434, 469, 600.

E.

Earl Marshal, The, 291, 458.
Earsbie, Leonard, 354.
Earthquake in England and France, 658.
Easington Ward, 335, 678.
Eason, John, 28.
East Deeping, see Deeping.
East Dereham, see Dereham.
East Friesland, see Friesland.
East Goscote, see Goscote.
East Grinsted, see Grinsted.
East Hampstead, see Hampstead.
East Harptre, see Harptre.
East Haven, 483.
East Lulworth, see Lulworth.
East Marches, see Marches.
East Mersey, see Mersey.
East Parts, Incorporation of merchants trading to the, 630, 696, 697.
East Riding, see York.
East Smithfield, see Smithfield.
East Tanfield, see Tanfield.
East Thorndon, see Thorndon.
Easte, Hundred of, 451.

GENERAL INDEX.

Easter, 79.
Easterlings, The, 64, 158, 236, 288.
Eastland Merchants, 602, 613. *See* East Parts.
Easton, 500.
Easton, John, 464.
Easture, Manor of, 634.
Eaton, ..., 668.
Eaton, Manor of, 598, 696.
Ebden, Mr., 149.
Eccles, John, 150.
Eccleshall Castle, 565, 583.
Ecclesiastical Affairs, *see* Church.
Ecclesiastical Courts, 538.
Ecclesiastical Jurisdiction and Commissions, 2, 203, 215, 232, 247, 357, 368, 395, 397, 405, 470, 492, 521, 668, 671, 699.
Ecclesiastical Law, 608.
Eddesbury, Hundred of, 84, 122.
Edeham, John, 435.
Eden, Richard, 467.
Edgar, John, 613.
Edgcomb, Sir Richard, 94.
Edgcote, 449.
Edgecombe, Mr., 528, 581, 608, 615.
Edgecumb, Piers, 252, 341, 370, 388, 389; Sir Piers, 451.
Edinburgh, 632.
Edmonds, Richard, 574.
Edmonton, Hundred of, 122.
Edmunds, Thomas, 186.
Edward VI., King of England, 1-4, 7-9, 11-14, 18-20, 22-27, 31-42, 44-55, 85, 119, 121, 135, 142-144, 167, 276, 456, 603, 614, 647.
Edward's College (Cambridge), 17.
Edwards, Roger, 332, 333.
Edwinstree, Hundred of, 374.
Eely, Mr., 700.
Effingham, Hundred of, 135, 419, 423.
Effingham, *see* Howard.
Egerton, Thomas, 697.
Egerton, Timothy, 667.
Egmont, Count D', 58, 62.
Egyptians, *see* Gypsies.
Elbing, 696.
Elections, 212, 213, 215-217, 278.
Elector Palatine, The, 502.
Elephants' teeth, 570.
Elizabeth, Princess, 23, 25, 29, 45, 50, 54, 57, 60, 61, 67, 82, 83, 86, 101.
........., Queen of England, 115, 116, 118, 120, 122, 123, 129, 130, 131, 133, 134, 137, 141, 143, 144, 147-155, 161, 167-169, 174-176, 180, 186, 201, 202, 204, 209, 211, 216-218, 222, 231, 234, 236, 238, 240, 243, 249, 250, 257, 265, 268, 269, 271, 273, 274, 276, 277, 283, 286, 288-291, 293, 295, 296, 301, 302, 304, 310, 314, 318-321, 330, 334, 343, 346, 348-351, 354, 360, 364, 376, 385, 392, 399, 408, 409, 413, 415, 418-421, 424, 425, 428, 434, 436, 439, 442, 443, 446, 449, 454, 458, 462, 470, 473, 475, 478, 480, 482, 484, 485, 488, 489, 493, 495, 498,

Elizabeth, Queen of England—*continued.*
499, 501, 503, 505-507, 510, 512, 513, 516, 521, 523, 524, 527, 530, 534, 546, 549, 550, 552-554, 560, 563, 566, 569, 575, 578, 580-582, 589, 595, 599, 605, 606, 611, 613, 618, 619, 622, 624-626, 631, 633, 634, 640, 641, 646, 654, 658, 661, 662, 665, 671, 672, 676, 687, 689, 690, 694, 700, 702.
........., implicated with Lord Seymour, 13, 14.
........., her lands and property, 14, 36, 45, 50, 51, 166, 167, 190, 191, 192, 237, 245-248, 259, 266, 294, 296, 317, 323, 358, 367, 381, 448, 498, 506, 511, 519, 628, 636, 638, 646, 666, 697.
........., her journeys and progresses, 28, 136, 137, 279, 289, 419, 486, 498, 499, 501-503, 510, 528, 582, 598, 599, 601.
........., proposals and addresses for marriage, 42, 101, 121, 217, 218, 280-283, 417, 517, 629, 633, 639, 658, 672, 685.
........., reputed to be with child by Leicester, 157; is unkind to him, 666.
........., her coronation, 176.
........., dealings with Lady Margaret Lennox, 197, 199-202.
........., proclamation against painting her picture, 232.
........., her favour to Hatton, and his letters to her, 242; 416, 453, 461-463, 466, 503, 676, 677.
........., the Pope's bulls against her, 330, 350, 651, 691.
........., a guard for her personal protection, 350, 511.
........., her debts, and expenditure of beer in her household, 492, 601, 637, 681.
........., her favour to Essex, 496.
........., her almshouses, 526.
........., subscribes to Furbisher's voyages, 573, 586, 608.
........., interposes between the Marquis of Winchester and his wife, 597.
........., her displeasure and kindness to Burghley, 601, 657.
........., her illnesses, 601.
........., policy towards Holland, 611.
........., is annoyed with the smoke of breweries, 612.
........., shot at on the Thames, 628.
........., loans by her to noblemen and others, 628, 646.
........., *her letters* :—
.... To the Queen Dowager, 5.
........., to the Protector Somerset, 11, 23, 28.
........., to Queen Mary, 62.
........., to Cecill, 130, 365, 534.
........., to Leicester, 498.
........., her letters of condolence, 363, 367, 494, 495, 639.
........., her letters to various other parties, 117, 119, 126, 129, 133-138, 140, 141, 143, 144, 150-161, 165, 170-172, 175, 178, 183-185, 187, 189, 195, 197, 203-207, 210, 214, 224, 226, 229-231, 239-

GENERAL INDEX. 733

Elizabeth, Queen, *her letters—continued.*
247, 253, 255, 257, 259, 267, 269, 280, 287–289, 298, 300, 305, 306, 309, 317, 328, 345, 359–363, 366, 367, 385, 387, 390, 391. 393, 395, 397, 398, 401, 413, 422, 429, 430, 452, 459, 505, 506, 636, 642, 653, 677, 682.
........., *letters to her* :—
........., From the Duchess of Suffolk, 120.
........., from Leicester, 229, 291, 503.
........., from Lord Keeper Bacon, 555.
........., from Lord Henry Howard, 692.
........., from various persons, 115, 134, 144, 165, 166, 219, 221, 229, 249, 253, 256, 279, 284, 288, 291, 299, 300, 344, 347, 381–383, 387, 391, 397, 403, 425, 429, 433, 440, 443, 467, 482, 496, 509, 533, 537, 574, 596, 642, 645, 648, 651.
Elizabeth Jonas, The, 154.
Elizabeth, The, 203, 577.
Elken, Richard, 27.
Elkes, ..., 584.
Elkington, Manor of, 167.
Ellerton, Manor of, 119.
Ellias' wife, 365.
Elliot, Thomas, 473, 538.
Ellis, ..., a pirate, 627.
Ellis, Mr., 521.
Ellis, Richard, 238.
Ellis, William, 624.
Ellison, Matthew, 219.
Ellisworth, Richard, 567.
Ellize, William, 578.
Ellyott, John, 268.
Ellyott, Thomas, 150, 680.
Ellys, Hugh, 41.
Ellys, Mr., 498.
Ellys, Thomas, 475.
Elmanhurst, Herman, 663.
Elmbridge (or Elmynbridge), *see* Emelynbridge.
Elnesto (or Elstow), 376.
Elryngton, Edw., 475.
Elstub, Hundred of, 377.
Eltham, 106, 190, 347, 590.
Elthorne, Hundred of, 123.
Elviston, 166.
Ely, 188, 562, 652.
Ely, Bishop of, *see* Goodrich, Thirlby, Cox.
Ely, Bishoprick of, 135, 513, 562.
Ely House, 417.
Ely, Isle of, 6, 262, 430, 459, 460, 485, 507, 523, 540, 558, 562, 654, 675, 684, 686.
Ely, Lord High Steward of, 507.
Ely Place, 6, 8, 14, 22, 29, 37.
Ely, Dr. Humphrey, 651.
Elyot, Lawrence, 686.
Elyot, Robert, 264.
Embargo on Shipping. *See* Shipping.
Embden, 237, 239, 241, 248, 258, 328, 384, 519, 614, 622.

Embden, John, Count of, 237, 242.
Embroiderers' Hall, Office of Arms at, 214.
Emelynbridge, Hundred of, 135, 419, 423, 426.
Emly (or Emlin), ..., 87, 89.
Emperor of Germany, The, 26, 49, 55, 65–68, 70–72, 87, 90, 114, 117, 118, 243, 245, 271, 277, 291, 295, 588, 602. *See* Charles V. Ferdinand. Maximilian.
Emperors, The Twelve, 182.
Enbroke, Manor of, 295.
Enchantments, *see* Witchcraft.
Enchuysen, 87.
Enclosures, *see* Inclosures.
Enderbie, Walter, 501.
Enfield, 1, 58, 185, 398, 462, 529.
Enfield Chace, 511.
Enfield, Manor of, 462.
Engelbert, William, 578.
Engine of War, Invention of, 513.
Engines, Engineers, 119, 254, 509.
Engines, Hydraulic, 512.
England, Projected invasion by Spain, 665.
England, Arms of, *see* Royal Arms.
England, Triumphant, 402.
Englefyld, Sir Francis, 65–73, 91, 106, 116, 203, 227, 238, 246, 447, 498, 502, 504, 507, 523, 524, 527.
Englefyld, Dame Katharine, 227, 238, 533.
English Fugitives, *see* Fugitives.
Engrossers, or Ingrossers, &c., 463 ; Bill against, 518. *See* Grain, Wool.
Entercourse, Treaty of, 244, 266.
Entwyssell, Wilfrid, 209.
Epping, Manor of, 389.
Epping, Parsonage of, 389.
Eresbye, Lawrence, 45.
Eresby, Mr., 194.
Eric, King Elect, Prince and Duke of Sweden, 101, 140, 144, 157, 158, 257, 261, 275.
Ernewood, Manor of, 248.
Ernlie, Richard, 543, 544.
Errant, Thomas, 244.
Errington, or Harrington, John, 575, 657, 695.
Errington, Lancelot, 657.
Error, Writ of, 612.
Ersby, Barony of, 677, 687.
Ersbye, 28, 29.
Erskin, Sir Alexander, 496.
Erwarton, 617.
Escheators, 61, 107, 374, 378.
Escrick, Manor of, 167.
Escrope, Manor of, 169.
Escurial, The, 427.
Espes, *see* Despes.
Essenden, Living of, 97.
Essex, ..., 22.

Essex, County of, 2, 4, 28, 34, 44, 55, 58, 61, 62, 65, 98, 99, 104, 107, 109, 113, 116, 127, 128, 139, 149, 152, 157, 173, 174, 176, 210, 215, 217, 218, 225, 230, 239, 243, 247, 256, 257, 259, 268, 270, 293, 317, 342, 343, 356, 364, 369, 374, 379, 380, 382, 384, 386, 388, 390, 414, 418, 420, 422, 425, 450, 474, 481, 483, 495, 508, 525, 531, 539, 540, 554, 557, 558, 562, 574, 576, 598, 606, 612, 626, 640, 641, 663, 668, 675, 678, 693, 701.
Essex, Alehouses in, 558, 570.
Essex, Clothiers of, 550, 633, 697.
Essex, Deaneries in, 12.
Essex, Deputy Commissioners for Horses in, 686.
Essex, Dorothy, 427.
Essex, Earl of, see Devereux.
Essex, Escheator of, 374.
Essex, Justices of, 638.
Essex, Lady, 205.
Essex, Sheriff of, 422, 587. See Goldyng.
Estanfelde, Manor of, 191.
Estcourt Lands, 43.
Estimates, see Admiralty.
Estofte, Mr., 136.
Eston, 52, 236.
Etherick, Thomas, 611.
Ethiopia, 215.
Ethridge, ..., 171.
Ethrope, 483.
Eton (Berks), 9, 20.
Eton (Chester), 149.
Eton College, 11, 15, 183, 184.
Eton, Francis, 170.
Eton, Provost of, 144, 184, 194. See Day.
Eton, Robert, 29.
Eudioche, David, 569.
Eunapius, publication of his works, 311.
Eure, William, Lord, 48.
Eure, Sir William, 336.
Evans, Mr., 406.
Evans, Richard, 632.
Evans, Thomas, 502, 504.
Eve, John, 576.
Everard, Henry, 603, 628.
Evercriche, Manor of, 40, 128.
Evers, Peter, 482.
Everysfylde, John, 475.
Evesham, 502.
Evington, 384.
Ewelme, Half Hundred of, 419.
Ewithington, Prebend, 272.
Ewrby, 35.
Ewsham, 407.
Ewyaslacy, Hundred of, 123.
Exchange, 510.
Exchange, Foreign, 32, 51, 136, 161, 170, 180, 307, 402, 410, 503, 508, 551, 700.
Exchange of Lands, see Crown Lands.
Exchanger, Royal, 402.

Exchequer, The, 3, 42, 52, 59, 61, 62, 76–78, 90, 96, 106, 107, 109, 112, 135, 151, 152, 159, 165, 170, 176, 190, 191, 194, 195, 198, 222, 232, 235, 249, 262, 268, 271, 285, 289, 294, 303, 306, 308, 312, 391, 407, 429, 431, 450, 457, 462, 470, 481, 502, 521, 524, 532, 543, 577, 600, 604, 646, 650, 684.
Exchequer, Chamberlain of, 43.
Exchequer, Chancellor of the, 91, 118, 457.
Exchequer, Court of, 430, 433, 434, 506, 577, 594.
Exchequer, Messengers of, 569, 576.
Exchequer, Remembrancer of, 106, 303, 397.
Excommunication, 348, 517, 649.
Excommunication, Bull of. See Bull.
Executions, 408, 435, 436, 439, 445, 504, 587, 589.
Exeter, 56–59, 100, 101, 116, 125, 162, 183, 205, 217, 232, 234, 261, 313, 319, 329, 341, 354, 376, 384, 388, 389, 410, 450, 460, 468, 480, 497, 543, 548, 557, 581, 583, 601, 609, 615, 638, 685, 702.
Exeter, Bishop of, see Voysey, Alley, Bradbridge.
Exeter, Bishoprick of, 409, 471, 562, 601.
Exeter, Earl of, see Cecill.
Exeter, Gertrude, Marchioness of, 65–72, 74.
Exeter, Mayor, &c. of, 116, 128, 205, 341, 468, 687.
Exeter, Prebends of, 551.
Exeter Gaol, Escape from, 687.
Exmoor forest, 391.
Expenditure, see Public Expenditure.
Expulsions from College, 493–495, 498–501. See King's College, Cambridge.
Eyer, John, 116.
Eyhorne (or Ayhorne), Hundred of, 450, 460.
Eyre, George, 640.
Eyre, Justices in, 104, 237, 249.
Eytou, 509.

F.

F ...., Mr. D., 683.
F ...., Thomas, 458.
Faculties, Court of, 190, 218, 357.
Faircross, Hundred of, 340.
Faires, William, 544.
Fairfax, Guy, 183.
Fairfax, Sir Nicholas, 336.
Fairfax, Thomas, 193.
Fairfax, Sir William, 6.
Fairfax, William, 455.
Fairs, Grants of, 626. See Sturbridge.
Fakenham, 367.
Falcon, The, 228, 605.
Falcon Grey, The, 93.
Falconry (falcons, goshawks, hawks, hawking), 44, 136, 144, 464, 679.

GENERAL INDEX. 735

Falleis, Peter, 606.
Fallia, Martin De la, 532, 697.
Falmouth, 92, 146, 214, 332, 386, 548, 598, 623, 632, 650.
False suggestors, 640.
Famar, M. de, 581.
Famine, *see* Dearth.
Fane, Sir Ralph, 36.
Fane, Sir Thomas, 685.
Fane, Thomas, jun., Sheriff of Kent, 662, 688.
Fane, *see* Vane.
Fanshaw, Henry, 397.
Fanshaw, Mr., 269, 437, 594.
Fanshawe, Thomas, 528.
Fanstone, John, 606.
Fareham, Hundred of, 7.
Farewell, George, 612.
Faringdon, Prebend, 366.
Farleton, Manor of, 358.
Farley, 384.
Farmer, Alexander, 475.
Farmer, Sir William, 15.
Farneley, Manor of, 369.
Farnham, 250, 294, 662.
Farnham, ..., widow, 196.
Farnham Castle, 251.
Farnham, Hundred of, 135, 419, 423.
Farnham, Robert, 617.
Farrington, 654.
Farrington, Hundred of, 156, 340.
Farsett, Manor of, 214.
Fast days, 221, 229, 233, 512; Eating flesh on, 440-442.
Fast days on Wednesdays, 518.
Fasts, Popish, 183.
Fauke, John, 605.
Faulsete, Richard, 167.
Fauntleroy, Mr., 34.
Fauxflete, Manor of, 470.
Fawkener, Henry, 158.
Fawkener, John, 475.
Fawkener, Martha, 158.
Fawlesley, Hundred of, 368, 425.
Fawley, Division of, 653.
Fawnt, William, 461.
Fawnte, Anthony, 650.
Fawnte, Arthur, 650.
Fawset, Mr., 540.
Faye, 11.
Fayre, William, 268.
Fayreweather, John, 569.
Fayrfax, Thomas, 438.
Fearne, William, 618.
Feecamp, 248.
Fecknam, or Feckenham, Dr., 552, 628, 635, 681.
Fecknam, John, 201, 203, 250, 251.
Fees, 3, 52, 105, 381, 431, 678.
Feilde, *see* Field.
Felonies, Commission for, 249.
Felton, George, 594.

Felton, John, 385.[1]
Feltwell, 263.
Fenner, George, 279, 280, 398, 502.
Fenner, William, 348.
Fens, The, 272, 278, 409, 412, 628. *See* Sewers.
Fens, Draining of, 611.
Fenton, Edward, 567, 589, 615.
Fenton, Mr., 63.
Fenys, *see* Fynes.
Feodaries, 241, 296, 333, 378, 394.
Ferdinand, Emperor of Germany, 243, 245.
Ferdinando, Simon, 541.
Feria, Count De, 102, 106.
Feria, Jane Dormer, Countess de, 146, 147, 163; Duchess, 427, 500.
Fermor, Thomas, 509.
Fermor, *see* Ricards.
Fermour, Sir John, 377.
Fernam, John, 201.
Ferrabosco, Alfonso, 299.
Ferrara, 76, 77, 152.
Ferrara, Duke of, 42, 77, 152.
Ferrer, Mr., 610.
Ferres, Mr., 255, 401.
Ferriers, Jean De, *see* Chartres.
Ferroe Isles, 527.
Ferrybridge, 149.
Ferrys, Lord, 124.
Ferys, ..., 67.
Fetiplace, Mr., 514.
Fetyplace, Sir John, 533, 689.
Feversham, Hundred of, 460.
Fez, King of, 630.
Fezard, John, 103.
Fiasco (or Fiesco), Signor, 417, 574.
Fidelis, Alexander, 404.
Field (or Feilde), Barnard, 303, 519, 574, 698.
Field, Mrs., 626.
Fielding, *see* Fylding.
Fiesco, *see* Fiasco.
Fifehead, Manor of, 381.
Fifield, 78.
Figs, 510.
Figueroa, John De, 74-76, 80, 81, 88.
Finances, *see* Revenues.
Finch, Henry, 175.
Finch (or Finche), Lady, 258, 695.
Finch (or Fynche), Moyle, 695.
Finch, Sir Thomas, 116.
Finchingfield, 247.
Finchley, 217.
Finchley Wood, 649.
Fines, 474, 506, 521, 530, 580, 597, 610, 618-620, 622, 624.
Fines, Clerk of the, 522.
Fines on pirates, 580. *See* Pirates.
Finsbury, 432.
Finsbury Fields, 83.
Fire, *see* Portsmouth Yard.

Fire-arms, new invention, to fire ten times, 696.
Firrar, William, 103.
First Fruits, Court of, 52, 55, 126, 267, 457.
First Fruits and Tenths, 49, 63, 120, 126, 141, 273, 285, 457, 680.
Fish, Fisheries, 147, 176, 206, 220, 247, 325, 399, 409, 411, 473, 483, 534, 554, 614.
Fish days, 32, 220-222, 233.
Fish, Exportation of, 612.
Fish extraordinary, 292.
Fish Street, 431.
Fisher, ..., 279.
Fisher, Alexander, 533.
Fisher, John, 39, 95, 208.
Fisher, Mr., 266.
Fisher, Thomas, 9, 28.
Fisherwick, 386.
Fishmongers' Company, 167, 409, 411.
Fisshe, Thomas, 86, 150.
Fiste, Jane, 583.
Fiste, Mr., 583.
Fitzalan, Henry, Earl of Arundel, 19, 27, 36, 48, 56, 57, 93, 102, 108, 123, 135, 136, 140, 152, 153, 155, 163, 206, 245, 252, 289, 298, 396, 432, 445, 454, 469, 485, 488, 491, 504, 542, 588, 639, 640.
Fitzgarret, Sir James, 41.
Fitzgerald, Edward, 689.
Fitzgerald Gerald, Earl of Kildare, 6.
Fitzgerald Gerald, Lord Offaley, 663, 689.
Fitzherbert, Sir Thomas, 255, 372.
Fitz Jeffrey, Alexander, 250.
Fitzjohn, Nicholas Wise, 666.
Fitzmorris, James, 552, 629-631.
Fitz Oswey, see Oswey.
Fitzwalter, Anselm, Lord, 325.
Fitzwalter, Family of, 325.
Fitzwalter, Lord, see Ratcliffe.
Fitzwilliam, Hugh, 273, 278.
Fitzwilliam, Thomas, 273.
Fitzwilliams, Capt. Bryan, 486.
Fitzwilliams, John, 198.
Fitzwilliams, Mr., 4, 397, 407, 422, 397.
Fitzwilliams, Sir William, 399, 506.
Fitzwilliams, see Fytzwilliams.
Five Ports, The, see Cinque Ports.
Flamock, William, 41.
Flanders, (Flemings, Low Countries), 42, 44, 47, 65, 69, 70, 74, 87, 90, 102, 104, 162, 171, 182, 235-239, 243, 246, 249, 258, 260, 265, 266, 269, 285, 292, 294, 296, 297, 300, 307, 313, 314, 317, 325-328, 330, 332, 351, 384, 388-390, 394, 397, 398, 405, 407, 413, 422, 426, 432, 433, 438, 444, 448, 450, 455, 463, 471, 476, 477, 485, 487, 494, 495, 500, 503, 505-508, 528, 539, 551, 556, 579, 581, 601-603, 611, 619, 621, 625, 629, 660, 669, 689, 700-702.
Flatcher, Hugh, 60.
Flatcher, John, 60.
Flax, 517, 519.
Flaxwell, Wapentake of, 135.

Flecchar, George, 22.
Fleet of 20 ships, 580. *See* Admiralty.
Fleet Bridge, 77.
Fleet Prison, 103, 125, 173-175, 179, **274-276, 284**, 235, 372, 441, 504, **594, 623, 627,** 636, 687.
Fleet Street, 14, 483, 682.
Fleetwood, Mr., 164, 187.
Fleming, Lord, 440.
Fleming, Thomas, 689.
Flemish Weavers, *see* Weavers.
Flendyche, Hundred of, 6, 430.
Flesh, Licence to eat, 32, 43. *See* **Fast days.**
Fletcher, Robert, 535.
Flete, William, 634.
Fletewood, William, (Recorder,) 416, **417, 427,** 447, 509, 519, 521, 565, 569, **595, 635,** 689.
Flint, 484, 594, 596.
Flintshire, 269, 361, 484, 592, **594, 596,** 634.
Flockarson, Dierich, 519.
Floods, *see* Inundations.
Florence, Duke of, 118, 131.
Florence and Florentines, 90, 131, 396 ; Debt of, 639.
Flourishing, *see* Writing.
Flower de Luce, The, 219.
Flower, John, 380.
Flower, William, (Norroy,) 41, 247, 501 ; 606, 624.
Flowerdewe, Edward, 538.
Flud, Richard, 75.
Fludd, Mr., 539.
Fludd, Thomas, 401, 445, 580, 676, 683, 684.
Flushing, Flushingers, 389, 399, 449, **468, 471,** 490, 502, 517, 519, 526-529, **637.**
Flying Hart, The, 572.
Flytt, Hundred of, 374.
Fogaça, Antonio, 647, 649.
Fogg, Sir John, 57.
Foies, M. De, 315.
Foix, Mons. De, 417, 418, 422.
Folk, 665.
Folkestone, 277, 284, 690.
Folkestone, Mayor, &c. of, 284.
Fonthill Gyfford, 139.
Forbes, William, 200.
Force (or Fors), M. De, 210.
Force of the realm, 303. *See* **Nation.**
Forcet, ..., 252.
Ford, 115.
Ford, ..., 46.
Fordham, William, 458.
Foreign Coin, *see* Coin.
Foreign Exchange, *see* Exchange.
Foreign Loans, *see* Loans.
Foreign Posts, *see* Posts.
Foreign Service, 501, 506.
Foreign States, Amity with, 693.
Foreign Wares, Exportation of, 587, 693.

Foreigners, Surveyor of, 425, 426.
Foreigners, *see* Aliens, Southampton, Strangers.
Foreland, The, *see* North Foreland.
Foresight, The, 505, 552, 553, 559, 631, 645.
Forestallers and Regrators, *see* Regrators.
Forests, 237.
Forests, *see* Eyre. Woods.
Foret, M. de la, 273.
Forfeitures, 13, 524.
Forgeries, 46, 233, 235.
Forges, *see* Furnaces.
Forrest, Gyles, 40.
Forster, ..., 171.
Forster, Sir John, 229, 501.
Fortescue, Francis, 702.
Fortescue, Henry, 380, 702.
Fortescue, John, 467, 468, 470, 617.
Fortescue (Foteskew), Mabell, 152, 164, 171, 177.
Fortescue, William, 635.
Forth, Firth of, 7.
Forthe, Dr. Robert, 482.
Forts (Blockhouses, Bulwarks, Garrisons, &c.), 2, 44, 96, 101, 105, 106, 110, 116, 118, 127, 138, 149, 163, 172, 202, 204, 213, 246, 310, 350, 356, 375, 404, 413, 451, 455, 458, 462, 479, 481, 488, 499, 639, 679, 695.
Fortune, The, 552.
Foster Lane, 172.
Foster, John, 124.
Foster William, 227, 696.
Fosterage, Practice of, in Wales, 514.
Fotheringay, 323.
Foudre, Pile of, 292.
Founder's Kin, 449.
Fowey (or Foy), 179, 186, 323, 326, 328.
Fowler, John, 9, 13.
Fowler, Mr., 71, 203.
Fowler, Thomas, 61.
Fowlle, Nicholas, 475.
Fox, John, 93.
Fox, Mr., 434.
Foxall, John, 246, 519, 574.
Foxehole, ..., 630.
Foy, *see* Fowey.
Framland, Hundred of, 423.
Frampton, John, 412, 578.
Franccam (or Francomb), William, 584.
France, the French, 3, 7, 8, 10, 11, 15, 21, 23, 30, 33, 38, 39, 42, 44–49, 54, 64, 67–69, 75, 76, 78–80, 82, 84–88, 91-95, 97, 101, 102, 104, 106, 119, 128, 129, 134–138, 144, 145, 151–155, 162, 177, 183, 196, 198, 200, 202, 203, 209–211, 213, 215, 216, 219, 224, 228, 229, 234, 235, 238–244, 247, 250, 265, 273, 276, 287, 292, 295, 297, 300, 302, 307–309, 314–320, 324, 326, 327, 331, 332, 343, 358, 364, 378, 382, 384, 386–388, 392, 394, 417, 418, 421, 422, 432, 437, 439–441, 449,

France, the French—*continued*.
466, 476, 481, 487, 496, 501–504, 517, 522, 523, 525, 527, 528, 535, 552, 555, 574, 588, 595, 619, 620, 625, 641, 657, 658, 672, 677, 682, 683, 685, 687, 690, 696, 700-703. *See* Ambassadors.
France, Admiral of, 220, 314, 316.
France, Constable of, 48, 88.
France, King of, *see* Francis I., Henry II. Francis II., Charles IX.
France, Merchants trading to, 490, 492, 619.
France, Queen of, 68.
France, the Queen Mother, 504.
Francis I., King of France, 3, 114.
Francis II., King of France, 144, 151, 210, 211.
Francis, John, 23.
Francis, The, 399.
Francis, Dr. Thomas, 175, 292, 304.
Franckard, Francis, 428, 429.
Franckleyne, Nicholas, 191.
Francklyn, Dr., 233.
Frank, Thomas, 380.
Frankelye, 164.
Frankelyn, William, 630.
Frankford, 209, 211, 239.
Freake, Mr., 382.
Frederick II., King of Denmark, 157, 248, 275, 303, 320, 522, 588.
Freeman, Morrys, 167, 295,
Freer, Dr., 174.
Freke, Edmund, Bishop of Norwich, 555, 562, 601, 602, 604, 607, 623, 642.
Freman, Thomas, 550.
Freman, William, 550.
French Congregation, or Church, the, 205, 257, 323, 613.
French, Mariners, 560.
French Queen, the, *see* Mary.
Frenche, John, 477.
Fresneda, Bernard de, 66, 67.
Freville, George, 356.
Friern Barnet, Manor of, 468.
Friesland, John, Count of, *see* Embden.
Friesland, East, 238.
Friesland, West, 598.
Frizados, Manufacture of, 623.
Frize, Menard, 275.
Frobiser, *see* Furbisher.
Frodsham, Edward 84.
Frokmarten, *see* Throkmerton.
Frost, Humfrey, 144.
Frosts, great, 356.
Frymley, Thomas, 456.
Fryvock, 392.
Fuggar, John, 279.
Fugitives, 466, 485, 487, 498, 500, 504, 532, *see* Aliens.
Fugitives, English, pensioned by Spain, 694.
Fulbrook, 367.
Fulham, 34, 183, 185, 205, 277, 295, 296, 314 317, 549.

3 A

GENERAL INDEX.

Fulham, Parsonage of, 700.
Fulke, William, 261, 262, 271, 397, Dr., 628, 698.
Fulkers, the, 155.
Fuller, ..., 16.
Fuller, William, 387.
Fullerton, Adam, 584, 596.
Fulmerston, ..., 27, 28, 30.
Fulmerston, Richard, 99.
Fulstow, Mr., 177.
Fulwell, Stephen, 315.
Fulwood, William, 696.
Funerals:
  Of King Henry VIII., 2.
  Of Mary, the French Queen, (sister of Henry VIII.,) the Empress Isabella, and Francis I., 3.
  Of King Edw. VI., 54.
  Of the Queen of Spain. 67.
  Of Queen Mary, 117.
  Of the Emperor, 117, 118.
  Of Henry II. of France, 136, 138.
  Of Frances Duchess of Suffolk, 143, 505.
  Of Margaret Duchess of Norfolk, 234.
  Of the Emperor Ferdinand, 245.
  Of the Marchioness of Northampton, 250, 253.
  Of Lady Catharine Grey, 306, 308.
  Of Lady Knollys, 329.
  Of William Earl of Pembroke, 370.
  Of Edward Earl of Derby, 455.
  Of Reginald Earl of Kent, 458.
  Of Charles IX., King of France, 485.
  Of Lady Eleanor Neville, wife of Wm. Pelham, 492.
  Of the Countess of Huntingdon, 528.
  Of Bishop Bullingham 524.
  Of Walter Devereux, Earl of Essex, 531.
  Superstitions at, 377.
Furbisher (or Frobiser, Frobisher), Captain Martin, 273, 274, 418, 420, 533, 540, 543, 545, 546, 556, 558, 559, 567, 568, 570-573, 580-582, 584-586; his third voyage, 589, 590, 602, 603, 605, 606, 608, 615, 616, 618, 619, 621-623, 625, 641, 703.
Furnaces, 251, 274, 475, 477, 478, 509, 570, 578, 581, 701.
Furnes, Monastery of, 641, 704.
Fyeld, Matthew, 615.
Fylding, Sir Basyl, 371.
Fynche, Mr., 101.
Fynche, see Finch.
Fynes, Gregory, Lord Dacre of the South, 142.
Fynes (Fenys), Sir Richard, 341, 343, 367, 443, 449, 454.
Fynesbury, see Finsbury.
Fypson, George, 434.
Fyshe, see Fisshe.
Fysshe, George. 374.
Fytiplace, ... a pirate, 267.
Fytleforde, 131

Fyton, G., 568.
Fyton, Mr., 593.
Fytzwilliam, William, 16.
Fytzwilliams, Lady Anne, 126.

G.

Gabriel, The, 546, 556, 567, 573, 618, 620.
Gage, James, 102.
Gage, Sir John, 110, 113.
Gaile, William, 557.
Gainsborough, 624.
Gale, John, 10.
Gallowe Clowe, The, 296.
Galtres Forest, 92.
Galvanus, Gabriel, 90.
Galwan, Nicholas, 331.
Gamage, Anthony, 620.
Gamages, M. de, 318.
Game, 40, 157, 317, 363, 462, see Deer.
Game, Mastership of the, 675.
Gaming, 192, 484.
Gammage, John, 177.
Ganfilde, Hundred of, 156, 340.
Ganthorn, G., 53.
Gaping Gulfe, The, 633, 634.
Garde, see De la Garde.
Gardenar, Thomas, 305, 306.
Gardening, Gardens, &c., 171, 184, 185, 188, 189, 194, 197, 198, 212, 219, 271, 277.
Gardiner, Thomas (of the Receipt), 196, 412.
Gardiner, Thomas (Farmer of Wine Duties), 362, 419.
Gardiner, see Lambard.
Gardyner, John, 475.
Gardyner, Stephen, Bishop of Winchester, 1, 2, 8, 27, 28, 32, 54, 57-63, 65-67, 69, 70, 72, 123.
Gardyner, Thomas, 597.
Gargrave, Sir Thomas, 129, 149, 206, 258, 336, 352.
Garland, John, 594.
Garnett, Stephen, 658.
Garnett, William, 574.
Garnham, John, 21.
Garrard, Sir William, 83, 182, 183, 251, 284, 287, 312.
Garrard, see Gerrard.
Garratt, Zecheus, 491.
Garrerde, Robert, 217.
Garret, Lord, see Fitzgerald.
Garret, Sir William, 175, 178.
Garrett, John, 685.
Garrett, Robert, 494.
Garrisons, see Forts.
Garter, the Order, Knights, Installations, &c., 50, 51, 102, 133, 134, 141, 237, 239, 271, 348, 445, 446, 490, 497, 521, 588, 589, 622,
Garter, Return of, from Savoy, 690.
Garter, Chancellor of the, 588, 589.

GENERAL INDEX. 739

Garter, King-at-Arms, 264. *See* Dethicke. St. George's Feast.
Gartrey, Hundred of, 423.
Gascoigne, Adam, 191.
Gascoigne, George, 444.
Gascoigne, Mr., 9, 20, 194, 670.
Gascoigne, Robert, 598, 599, 677.
Gaskin, Mons., 213.
Gate, Sir Henry, 321, 336, 371, 388.
Gatehouse Prison, 175, 596, 690; List of Prisoners in, 667.
Gates, Sir John, 20, 39, 51, 106, 123.
Gateshead, 517–519.
Gattys, George, 69.
Gaudie, or Gawdy, Sir Thomas, 491, 600, 601.
Gaudy, Bassingborne, 628.
Gawdie, Thomas, 704.
Gawyn, Richard, 485.
Gayle, Francis, 192.
Gayle, Robert, 192.
Gaynesford, Anne, 431.
Gaynesford, John, 431.
Gaywood, Elizabeth, 403.
Gaywood, John, 179, 403.
Geddington, Manor of, 510.
Gedney, 46, 84, 150, 263, 412.
Gedney, Andrew, 504.
Gelborne, William, 695.
Geldings, *see* Horses, Musters.
Gellye, Edward, 276.
Genealogies, 256, 510, 512.
Geneva, 11, 211.
General Pardon, 1, 21. *See* Pardons.
General Councils, *see* Councils.
Genevan Church, The, 621.
Genkins, John, 547.
Gennet, The, *see* Jennet.
Gennynges, ..., 398.
Genoa, 243, 325, 462.
Genoia, *see* Guinea.
Gent, William, 101.
Gentilis, Albericus, 691.
Gentlemen Pensioners, 151, 213, 391, 678, 689.
Geography, 496.
George, *see* Broadway.
George, The, 233.
Gerard, William, 200.
German Church, 177, 203.
Germany, (Germans, Almains,) 18, 19, 31, 42, 61, 71, 103, 177, 204, 211, 213, 214, 217, 243, 270, 274, 275, 277, 279, 280, 432, 466, 495, 505, 506, 588, 614, 681, *See* Emperor.
Germany, Confederate Cities of, 592.
Gerraldi, Senor, 565.
Gerrard, G., 308.
Gerrard, Sir Gilbert, (Attorney General,) 166, 190, 225, 233, 249, 273, 431, 433, 441, 442, 449, 639.
Gerrard, Master, 492.
Gerrard, Mr., 321.

Gerrard, Richard, 84.
Gerrard, Sir Thomas, 695.
Gerrard, William, 177, 513, 515, 522; Sir William, Lord Chancellor of Ireland, 522, 635, 637.
Gerrard, Sir William, merchant, 523.
Gervase, Dr., 166.
Gest (or Gheast), Edmund, 137; Bishop of Rochester, 284.
Gestes, Royal, *see* Progresses.
Gibbes, Richard, 272.
Gibbons, Dr., John, 543. *See* Gybbons.
Gibbs, Mr., 207.
Gibbs, William, 59.
Gibon, Anthony, 700.
Giddy (or Giddie) Hall, 43, 633.
Gifford, ..., 588, 669.
Gifford, Edward, 669.
Gifford, George, 677, 682, 683.
Gifford, Giles, 677, 682.
Gifford, John, 669, 677.
Gifford, Richard, 683.
Gifford, Robert, 677.
Gifford, William, 652.
Gift of God, The, 595.
Gheast, *see* Gest.
Ghent, 87, 88 204, 486.
Gilbert, Mr., 691.
Gilberte, Adrian, 589, 621.
Gilberte, Sir John, 583, 605, 608, 609.
Gilberte, Sir Humphrey, *see* Gylberte.
Giles, John, 471.
Giles, Robert, 276.
Gill, Edmond, 555.
Gilles, Michael, 595.
Gillingeast and Gillingwest, Wapentakes of 336.
Gillingham, 584.
Gillingham Water, 172, 189, 213, 449, 627.
Gilman, Henry, 513.
Gilpin, ..., 19.
Gilpin, George, 251, 503, 575.
Ginger, 239.
Gipsies, *see* Gypsies.
Gisburgh, 191.
Glamorgan, 617.
Glamorganshire, 7, 176. 361, 452, 487, 514, 566, 582, 592, 597, 599.
Glamorganshire, Sheriff of, 105, 597.
Glascock, John, 231.
Glaseor (or Glaseour), William, 52, 321, 629–631, 633, 635–637, 661, 670.
Glasewryn, 611.
Glasgow, Bishop of, 328.
Glasier, ..., 324.
Glasier, Hugh, 119.
Glass, and Glassworks, 62, 256, 297, 315, 477.
Glassyor, John, 89.
Glaston, 388.
Glastonbury 36–39, 47.
Glossopdale, Manor of, 400.

Gloucester, 32, 122, 160, 186, 319, 320, 329, 360, 375, 420, 441, 452, 571, 585, 637, 651, 679, 680.
Gloucester, St. Bartholomew's Hospital in, 333.
Gloucester, Bishop of, *see* Hoper. Cheney.
Gloucester, Bishoprick of, 39, 186, 190, 199, 560, 566, 694.
Gloucester College, 566.
Gloucester, Custom House at, 680.
Gloucester, Deanery of, 334.
Gloucester, Mayor, &c., of, 242, 333, 651, 680.
Gloucester, Musters of the City, 651.
Gloucester, Recorder of, 408, 441.
Gloucester. Subdean of, 694.
Gloucestershire, 8, 32, 40, 60, 61, 120, 141, 160, 161, 186, 226, 237, 275, 294, 309, 338, 344, 360, 367, 368, 375, 382, 418–420, 423, 463, 485, 506, 507, 520, 549, 571, 572, 588, 600, 609, 632, 658, 666, 669, 699.
Gloucestershire, Clothiers of, 550.
Gloucestershire, Justices of, 639.
Gloucestershire, Lord Lieutenant of, 375.
Gloucestershire, Sheriff of, 25, 275, 420.
Glover, George, 143, 702.
Glover, Robert (Somerset Herald), 458.
Gloves, 17, 171, 221 ; from Oxford, 683.
Glowde, *see* Gould.
Glydd, Thomas, 475.
Glynn, Dr., 21.
Glynne, John, 233.
Goade, Dr., Roger, 515, 520, 522, 530, 537, 549, 591, 620, 622.
Goche (or Gouch, Gough), R., 7, 63, 83.
Godalming, Hundred of, 135, 419, 423.
Godalming, Manor of, 694.
Goddard, Robert, 206.
Goddeshalffe, Edward, 150.
Godley, Hundred of, 135, 419, 423.
Godolphin, Francis, 397, 582, 621.
Godolphyn, Sir William, Captain of the Isles of Scilly, 10, 26, 113, 125, 353, 369.
Godsalve, Sir John, 43.
Gold, Smelting of, *see* Ore.
Gold and Silver Ore, 584.
Gold Coinage, 694, 700, *see* Coin.
Gold, *see* Gould.
Gold Mines, *see* Crawford Muir. Mines.
Goldfinders, 542.
Golding, ..., 23.
Goldney, ..., 171.
Goldsmiths, 170, 172, 257, 267, 270, 305, 306, 308, 521, 524, 561.
Goldsmiths' Company, 160, 290, 291, 306, 407, 457, 514, 525, 561.
Goldwell, 132.
Goldwell, Mrs. Francis, 256, 257.
Goldwell, John, 132.
Goldwell, Stephen, 132.
Goldwell, Thomas, Bishop of St. Asaph, nominated to Oxford, 111, 118, 132, 651, 694.
Goldwyn, William, 15.
Goldyng, Arthur, 224, 225.

Goldyng, Sir Thomas, 356, 369, 380, 611.
Gomez, Ruiz, 75, 90.
Gomiecourt, Adrian de, 467.
Gonnor, M. de 240, 241.
Gonson, Benjamin, 15, 90, 92, 104, 109, 112, 138, 144, 189, 192, 260, 268, 505, 566, 585, 609.
Gonville Hall, 264.
Gonville and Caius College, 267, 474, 579.
Gonzaga, Don Cæsar de, 87.
Good, Mr., 437.
Good, William, 592, 593.
Goodacre, Anne, 238.
Gooddinge, Edward, 293.
Goodere, Henry, 425, 426.
Goodlad, John, 87.
Goodram Toft, 272.
Goodman, Christopher, 688.
Goodman, Gabriel, Dean of Westminster, 293, 304, 329, 383, 410.
Goodman, John, Dean of Wells, 28, 32, 33.
Goodman, William, 661, 669, 673.
Goodrich, Thomas, Bishop of Ely, 11, 16 ; Lord Chancellor, 39, 44, 54.
Goodriche, Richard, 635.
Goodrick, Richard, 21, 29, 30, 34, 35, 43, 44.
Goodridge, ..., 681.
Goodwin Sands, 73, 287, 289, 309, 563 ; Beacon on the, 700.
Goodwyn, Christopher, 447, 448.
Googe, Mr., 230, 231.
Goore, Captain, 589.
Gore, Hundred of, 122.
Gorge, Mr., 683.
Gorges, Nicholas, 528.
Gorhambury, 299, 312, 376, 384, 388, 417, 448, 449, 467, 521, 555.
Goring, Sir William, 12, 19.
Gorleston, 619.
Gosberkyrke, Manor of, 30, 32.
Goscote, East, Hundred of, 423.
Gosfeld, 697.
Gosfield Hall, 300.
Gosforth, 330.
Goshawks, *see* Falconry.
Gosling, ..., 390.
Gosnall, Mr., 8.
Gottzo, Nicholas de, 90.
Gough, *see* Goche.
Goughe, Joyne, 10.
Gould (or Gold, Glowde). Mercy or Mary, 588, 623, 626.
Gouldwyar, Jane, 703.
Gouxland, 46.
Gowdbie, Lands in, 656.
Gower, John, 400.
Gowltye, William, 699.
Grafton, 101, 112.
Grafton, Edward, 658.
Grafton Pastures, 126.
Grafton, Richard, 20, 54.
Graham, Archibald, 164.

GENERAL INDEX.   741

Graham, Prebend of, 112.
Grain, 508, 519, 523. *See* Bridgehouse. Corn. Engrossers.
Grain, Commissioners of, 523.
Grain, Exportation of, 449, 452, 456, 460, 468, 474, 507, 508, 517, 521, 524, 527, 534, 539, 542, 544, 552, 559, 574, 617, 685.
Grain, Importation of, 455.
Grain, Prices of, 477, 527, 636.
Granada, 394.
Grange, ..., 421.
Granger, John, a Pirate, 554, 623.
Gransham, or Gransom, William, 569, 622.
Grant of Arms, *see* Arms.
Grantham, 30, 45, 46, 63, 278, 612.
Grantham cum Soca, 694.
Grantham, Vicarage of, 30.
Grapes, 277, 316.
Gratwicke, Thomas, 475.
Gratwyk, Roger, 475.
Grave, Barnard, 611.
Gravesend, 57, 132, 174, 188, 316, 320, 329, 461, 595, 700.
Gray and Graye, *see* Greye.
Graye, Lady Mary, *see* Grey.
Graye, Ralph, 703.
Graye, Thomas, 48.
Graye, Sir Thomas, 703.
Graynfyld, John, 10, 11, 59.
Grays (or Greys), 658, 664.
Grays Inn, 19, 202, 282, 381, 538, 569, 637.
Great Barnfield, Hundred of, 150.
Great Holy Ghost, The ship, 490.
Great Maplestead, *see* Maplestead.
Great Seal, The, 476, 662.
Great Wardrobe, *see* Wardrobe.
Great Yarmouth, *see* Yarmouth.
Greatford, *see* Gretford.
Greek Manuscripts, 292, 323, 324.
Green Cloth, Board of, 576.
Green, John, 196.
Green, Michel, 196.
Green, Thomas, 266.
Greene, Anthony, 701.
Greene, Mr. 700.
Greene, Robert, 700.
Greene, Thomas, 701.
Greenhill, Nicholas, 698.
Greenway, 583, 600, 605.
Greenwich, 15–17, 40, 51, 69, 75, 77, 79, 90, 95, 100–102, 127, 130, 145, 154, 155, 171, 175–177, 179, 190–192, 202–206, 221, 225–227, 240, 242, 249, 254, 269, 297, 309, 442, 462, 464, 475–477, 482, 491, 492, 499, 521, 522, 524, 536, 546, 551, 552, 588, 600, 610, 628, 629, 634.
Gregorie, William, 497.
Gregory XIII., Pope, 651, 691.
Gregory, Christopher, 449, 499.
Gregory, Mr., 183.
Grene, Mr. Roke, 300.

Grene, Thomas, 521.
Grene, William, 677.
Greneway, Richard, 6.
Grenfelde, *see* Graynfyld.
Grenfelde or Grenvile, Sir Richard, *see* Greynvile.
Gresham, John, 329.
Gresham, Sir John, 13, 51.
Gresham, Lady, 433, 639, 643.
Gresham, Margaret, 700.
Gresham, Paul, 700.
Gresham, Thomas, 44, 51, 66, 68, 69, 100, 102, 103, 115, 121. Sir Thomas, 128, 141, 153–155, 160, 170, 173, 180, 182, 189, 195, 198, 204, 205, 211, 227, 232, 255, 257, 266, 268, 279, 316, 317, 353, 363, 365, 387, 391, 393, 394, 405, 406, 408, 410, 416–418, 421, 422, 425, 426, 429, 433, 435, 438, 441, 444, 460, 469, 475, 487, 500, 505, 507, 583, 615, 621, 639, 643.
Gresham, William, 333.
Gresham House, 393, 410, 416, 417, 425, 426, 433, 441, 443, 469.
Gresley (or Grisley), Sir William, 193, 340.
Gretford (or Greatford), 124, 243.
Greves, Thomas, 697.
Greves, William, 697.
Grevil, Mr., 574.
Greville, Sir Edward, 95.
Greville (or Grevyle), Sir Fulk, 95, 358, 371, 373, 466, 657, 675.
Greville, Lodowick, 235, 237, 415, 416, 429, 443, 454, 520.
Grey, *see* Gray.
Grey, Lady Catharine, Lady Hertford, 64, 184, 194, 195, 206, 230, 235, 240, 272, 286, 294, 300, 301, 304–306, 308.
Grey, Lady Frances, *see* Dorset.
Grey Friars, London Hospital of, 476.
Grey, Henry, Marquis of Dorset, 13, 18, 21, 33. Duke of Suffolk, 35, 42, 43, 47, 56–60, 64, 103, 128, 293.
Grey, Henry, Earl of Kent, 670.
Grey (Gray), Lady Jane, 11, 13, 49. Queen, 54, 57.
Grey, Sir John, 230.
Grey, Lord John, 21, 52, 57, 58, 60, 127, 128, 151, 195, 235, 240.
Grey, Lord, 36, 491, 683.
Grey (or Graye), Lady Mary (wife of Thomas Keys), 64, 256, 257, 260, 263, 271, 277, 278, 283, 290, 294, 297, 377, 393, 394, 410, 416, 417, 421, 422, 425, 426, 429, 433, 438, 441, 443, 591.
Grey, Mr., 29, 30.
Grey, Reginald, 370, 410, 412, 413, 415. Earl of Kent, 458.
Grey, Thomas, 316.
Grey, Lord Thomas, 21, 58, 60.
Grey of Wilton, Arthur Lord, 248, 337, 366, 376, 378, 394, 445–448, 470, 564, 634.
Grey of Wilton, William Lord, 20, 22, 101, 159, 169, 248.

GENERAL INDEX.

Greye, Thomas, 696.
Greyhounds, 464, 672, 679.
Greyme, Justice, 107.
Greymes, The, 39.
Greynvile, Sir Richard, 10, 475, 643.
Greynvill, R., 371.
Greys, *see* Grays.
Greysley, Hundred of, 124.
Greytree, Hundred of, 123.
Grice, Roger, 532.
Griffith, Dr. John, 543.
Griffith, Mr., 633.
Griffith, Thomas, 697.
Grimsby, Great, 554.
Grimsthorpe, 21, 29, 35, 39, 41, 64, 100, 406, 410.
Grimston (or Griston), Luke, 508.
Grimsworth, Hundred of, 124.
Grindall, Edmund, 5. Bishop of London, 134 141, 150, 173, 179, 183–185, 192, 194, 196, 201, 204, 205, 209, 221, 235, 237, 239, 246, 255, 260, 268, 271–273, 277, 292, 295, 296, 298, 300–302, 308, 314, 316, 317, 321, 322, 346. Archbishop of York, 382, 383, 385, 386, 390, 391, 396, 412, 435, 445, 467, 495, 497; recommended for Canterbury, *ib.*; Archbishop of Canterbury, 516, 517, 521, 560, 570, 577, 581, 625, 637, 647, 653, 654.
Grinsted, East, 448.
Grinsted, West, 43, 448.
Grisley, *see* Gresley.
Griston, *see* Grimston.
Groby, House of, 299.
Grove Place, 586.
Grover, William, 544.
Grub Street, 432, 627.
Gruffyth, Rice, 111.
Gryffyn, Edward, 105.
Grymeston, Edward, 104.
Gryndall, James, 617.
Grys, William le, 611.
Guards, The, *see* Queen's Guards.
Guarras, (Gwarras, Gwerras,) Anthony, 73, 326, 457, 489, 565, 695.
Guernsey, 93, 112, 310, 606, 702.
Guichardin, Vincent, 90.
Guidodi, Signor, 131.
Guildeford, Henry, 458.
Guildford, 19, 35, 62, 465, 561, 562.
Guildford, Inhabitants of, 509.
Guildford Park, 311.
Guildhall, 135, 607.
Guineas, (or Genoia,) 215, 247, 273, 281, 294, 299.
Guise, Duke, and House of, 101, 151, 210, 211, 217, 647.
Guisnes, 39, 42, 88, 98, 113, 138.
Gunfounder, Office of, 474.
Gunfounding, 476.
Gunfoundries, *see* Iron Ordnance.

Gunners, 2, 146. 166, 225, 230, 247, 276, **479**, 480, 499; Lists of, 631, 640.
Gunners, Corporation of, 414.
Gunpowder, 42, 43, 113, 117, 140, 146, **153**, 160, 195, 237, 357, 431, 477, 511, **526**, 618, 629.
Gunpowder, Purchase of, 553.
Gunpowder Maker, the Queen's, 590.
Gunvile, *see* Gonville.
Gunwynne, John, 33.
Guye, John, 434.
Gwerras, *see* Guarras.
Gwyn, John, 405.
Gwyn, Richard, 591, 671.
Gwyn, Roderick, 454.
Gwyne, ..., 630.
Gwynne, John, 181.
Gybbarde, Nicolas, 500.
Gybbons, Mr., 419.
Gyffard, William, 13, 14.
Gyfford, Dr., 435.
Gylbard, William, 504.
Gylbarte, *see* Gilbert.
Gylbert, Thomas, 695.
Gylberte, (or Gilbert,) Humfrey, 287, 288; Sir Humfrey, 415, 436, 440, 443, **449**, 475, 509, 520, 565, 600, 605, 634, 695.
Gylberte, Sir John, *see* Gilberte.
Gyle, John, 21.
Gyle, Richard, 21.
Gyliam, Captain, 528.
Gynes, Robert, 436.
Gypsies, 137–139, 141, 334, 410.
Gyre, Robert, 76.

H.

H., ..?......, Ro., 703.
Hack, Anne, 471.
Hackluyt, Thomas, 402.
Hackney, 489.
Hackney, Manor of, 11, 468.
Hackneymen, *see* Posts.
Hacoul, Jehan, 641.
Hadenebam, Manor of, 536.
Haddington, 10.
Haddon, Parson of, 654.
Haddon, Dr., Walter, 43, 196, 202, 273, **312**, 324, 385, 386.
Haddon, William, 89.
Hadlow, 60.
Hadnall, Manor of, 171.
Hadnoll, Stephen, 55, 61, 62, 66.
Hadrianus, Junius, 309, 311.

GENERAL INDEX. 743

Hagworthingam, 690.
Haidon, *see* Haydon.
Hailes, Manor of, 463.
Hailow, Hundred of, 380.
Hainault Walk, 123.
Hakluyt, Richard, 407, 428, 656.
Hale, Thomas, 635.
Hales, Sir James, 668, 671, 672, 676, 684.
Hales, John, 9, 125, 126, 306.
Halfnaked, Lands in, 52.
Halingbury Morley, 184.
Hall, Arthur, 46, 51, 120, 641.
Hall, Christopher, 295.
Hall, Edmund, 36, 124, 243, 352.
Hall, Francis, 42, 43, 45, 151.
Hall, Henry, 656.
Hall, John, 46.
Hall, Peter, 624.
Halle, Elizeus, 201.
Halliday, (or Halydaye,) Adam, 163, 196.
Hallrennys, 279.
Hallswell, Susan, 393.
Hallye, Lucas de, 309.
Hallykelde, Wapentake of, 336.
Halstead or Halsted, 525; Strangers in, 575, 697.
Halsted, Manor of, 55, 259.
Halswell, 393.
Halton, R., 436.
Halvergate, Manor of, 600.
Hamble, 439.
Hamburgh, 238, 328, 366, 367, 394, 406, 408, 475, 508, 573, 587, 592, 602, 608, 614, 622, 626, 628, 663.
Hamby, John, 396.
Hamelin, John, 427.
Hamelsett, Manor of, 191.
Hamiltons, The, 496.
Hamme, *see* Westham.
Hammes or Hampnes, 88.
Hammond, Jo., 535.
Hammond, Mr., 304.
Hamon, Dr., 700.
Hamond, ..., 657.
Hamond, John, 487.
Hampden, Miss, 524.
Hampshire (Southampton), 7, 51, 75, 76, 86, 110, 113, 148, 153, 162, 163, 177, 184, 206, 217, 227, 263, 264, 287, 298, 345, 348, 363, 365, 371, 375, 378, 385, 392, 439, 453, 455, 457, 464, 465, 469, 474, 479, 481, 483, 490, 540, 542, 560, 562, 585–587, 619, 623, 632, 640, 643, 653, 689,
Hampshire, Alehouses, &c. in, 562.
Hampshire, Justices of, 639, 643.
Hampshire, Landing-places in, 645.
Hampshire, Vice Admiral of, 632.
Hampstead, East, 155.
Hampton, 586, 648. *See* Southampton.
Hampton, Bernard, 155, 394, 407.
Hampton, Mrs., 509.

Hampton-in-Arden, Manor of, 266.
Hampton Court, 4, 5, 9, 10, 23, 33–35, 44, 63, 67, 68, 131, 136–138, 162, 171, 179, 189, 190, 207, 208, 240, 244, 249, 260, 271, 290. 360, 362, 366, 387, 398, 454, 458, 463, 475, 488, 489, 515, 532, 537, 569, 571. 581, 582, 637.
Hamsted, Hadrian, 203.
Hamyldon, Hundred of, 7.
Hanaper, Clerk of the, 125.
Hanaper, Office of, 431, 622.
Hanbie, John, 36.
Hanbie, Mrs., 655.
Hanbie, Thomas, 655.
Hancocke, Thomas, 605, 655, 669.
Hand and Dragon, The, 637.
Handford, John, 365.
Handguns, 167.
Handmaid, The, 647.
Hanesworth, 129.
Hangeast and Hangwest, Wapentakes of, 331, 336.
Hanging Sword, The, 483.
Hanington, William, 113.
Hanley, Robert, 680.
Hans, Ludwig, 258.
Hanse Towns, (or Hanzes,) 39, 65, 101, 508, 602, 603, 607, 608, 640. *See* Hamburgh. Stillyard.
Hansel, Christopher, 163.
Hanworth, 221, 236, 238, 240.
Harbart, William, 543.
Harberd, Edward, 538, 539.
Harbert, ..., 44.
Harbert, Sir Edmund, 487.
Harbertt, Sir William, 538.
Harbottle Castle, 241.
Harbrowne, William, 697.
Harcourt, Elizabeth, 188.
Harcourt, Mr., 126, 188, 189.
Harcourt, Simon, 342.
Harding, Dr. Thomas, 102, 103, 248, 281, 300.
Hardware, Mr., 661.
Hardy, Thomas, 127.
Hardyman, John, 172.
Hardyng, ..., 628.
Hare, John, 672.
Hare, Mr., 527.
Hare, Robert, 147, 432.
Hare, The, 205, 209.
Hareby, Manor of, 151.
Harecourt, Robert, 527.
Harewell, Edmund, 564.
Harford, John, 39.
Harfurd, 53.
Hargrave, ..., 307.
Harilsey, West, Manor of, 119.
Harington, Francis, 392, 409.
Harington, Sir James, 342, 482, 570.
Harington, John, 546, 685.
Harington, *see* Harrington, Harryngton, Haryngton.

GENERAL INDEX.

Harleston, John, 104.
Harley, John, 32, 48; Bishop of Hereford, 49, 50.
Harman, James, 110.
Harper, Sir George, 57, 61, 88.
Harper, Lady, 640.
Harper, Richard, 138.
Harpsfeld, Dr., 127, 293.
Harpsfield, ..., 552.
Harptree, *see* Parsonage of, 29.
Harquebus, 684 ; new invented one, 696.
Harquebusiers, 276, 301, 303, 339, 341–344, 351, 354, 360, 365, 414, 545.
Harries, Valentine, 409.
Harrington, Sir H., 575.
Harrington, James, 358.
Harrington, John, 387.
Harrington, Sir John, 36, 57, 63.
Harrington, Stephen, 68, 358.
Harrington, Thomas, 660.
Harrington, *see* Errington.
Harris, ..., 553.
Harris, Arthur, 379.
Harris, Christopher, 686, 691.
Harris, Vincent, 379.
Harrison, ..., 694.
Harrison, Mr., 622, 694.
Harrison, William, 683.
Harroppe, Ralph, 96.
Harrowden, 566.
Harrowden, *see* Vaux.
Harryngton, James, 105.
Harryngton, Lady Lucy, 280.
Hart, John, 691.
Hart, John, *see* Harte.
Hart, Lady, 258.
Hart, Mr., 169.
Hart, Manor of, 167.
Hart, The, 205.
Harte, 335.
Harte, John, Chester Herald, 354, 594.
Harte, Mary, 594.
Harteshorne, Parson of, 680.
Hartesmere, Hundred of, 452.
Hartgill, William, 34.
Harthill, Wapentake of, 336.
Hartingfordbury, Manor of, 398.
Hartlebury, 94.
Hartlepool, 157, 167, 335.
Hartley Row, 317.
Hartwell, 101.
Harty, Isle of, 400, 401, 407.
Harvey, Edmund, 166.
Harvey, Francis, 380, 419.
Harvey, Dr. Henry, 132, 148, 388.
Harvey, Thomas, 69, 71.
Harvey, Thomas, (Knight Marshal,) 100, 101.
Harvey, William, (Clarencieux,) 131, 143, 249.
Harvy, Anthony, 19.
Harvy, James, 504.
Harvye, Mr., 110.

Harward, Robert, 620.
Harwich, 2, 144, 225, 316, 386, 529.
Harwich, Strangers in, 412.
Haryngton, John, 212.
Haryngton, Mrs., 212.
Haryngton Robert, 63.
Haselborough, 101.
Haseley, 100.
Haselrige, Michael, 696.
Hassat, ..., 434.
Hastings, 198.
Hastings, Chantry Lands, 594.
Hastings, Rape of, 264.
Hastings, Sir Edward, 50, 60, 80, 91 ; Lord Hastings of Loughborough, 115, 119, 138, 176, 179, 180, 308, 309, 586.
Hastings, Francis, Earl of Huntingdon, 18, 38, 39, 75, 102, 106, 149, 325.
Hastings, Francis, 509, 561, 567.
Hastings, Henry Lord, 39, 73, 74 ; Earl of Huntingdon, 164, 170, 304, 343, 388, 457, 468, 489, 561, 645, 685, 691.
Hastings, John, 358, 511.
Hastings, Mr., 447, 623.
Hatche, Thomas, 490, 506.
Hatcher, Dr. John, 636, 638, 644, 660, 661, 683, 684.
Hatcher, Thomas, 282.
Hatchett, William, 111.
Hatfield, 13, 23, 28, 101, 183, 313, 498, 586.
Hatfield, Bailiff of, 111, 113.
Hatfield Park, 111, 113.
Hatley, Edm., 18.
Hatley, William, 167.
Hats, 630.
Hatton, Christopher ("Lyddes"), 242, 416, 453, 461–463, 466, 473, 485, 503, 522, 525, 527, 536; Sir Christopher, 588, 599, 646, 666, 673, 675–677, 685.
Hatton, Mr., 536.
Havant, Town of, 7.
Havard (alias Dravah), Edward, 590, 655.
Havard, Gregory, 655.
Havard, Humphrey, 660.
Havard, Mr., 183.
Havard, Nicholas, 590.
Havard, Thomas, 353.
Havens, *see* Ports.
Haverfordwest, 361, 368, 537, 582, 586.
Haverfordwest, Mayor of, 537.
Havering atte Bower, 123, 257, 380, 418, 450, 595, 632.
Havers, Thomas, 427, 431.
Havershow, 53.
Haward, Sir George, 141.
Hawarden Park, 496.
Hawe, Nicholas de la, 612.
Hawes, Alderman, 416, 427.
Hawes, John, 427.
Hawford, Dr. Edward, 132, 244, 245, 388, 515, 637, 638, 647, 657.
Hawfry, Michael, 295.

GENERAL INDEX. 745

Hawghton, Manor of, 167.
Hawkes, Richard, 654.
Hawkeslow, 653.
Hawkins, ..., 46.
Hawkins, Ambrose, 610.
Hawks, Hawking, *see* Falconry.
Hawks, Serjeant of the, 367.
Hawkyns, John, 279-281, 294, 299, 300, 323, 329, 330, 337, 422, 437, 538, 551, 556, 585, 587, 609, 629, 634, 636-638, 656, 665, 677, 703.
Hawkyns, William, 323, 326, 329, 521, 605, 611, 678.
Hawlden, 3.
Hawldendye, Francis, 296.
Hawley, Thomas, (Clarencieux,) 4, 92.
Hawthorne, Henry, 506, 529, 530, 548.
Hawtrey, Mr., 16, 257.
Hawverly, 683.
Hawxley, 682.
Hawys, James, 275, 495.
Hayberne, Thomas, 11.
Haydon, (or Haidon,) John, 67, 73, 437.
Haye, Mons. de la, 209.
Haye, Thomas 475.
Hayes, ..., 472.
Hayleford, *see* Helford.
Hayling Island, 483.
Haynes, William, 247.
Haysyll, George, 507.
Hayward, ..., 429.
Hayward, Lord Thomas, 429.
Hayward, *see* Howard.
Haywarde (or Haiwarde), Rowland, 275, 287, 316; Sir Rowland, 396, 415, 417, 426, 435, 505, 529, 568, 646, 656.
Haywarde, Thomas, 309.
Hayworthe, William, 167.
Hazelber Bryan, Manor of, 699.
Heale, Mr., 637.
Hearle, Mr., 125.
Heath, Nicholas, Bishop of Worcester, 6, 35; Archbishop of York, 75, 76, 85, 92, 109, 203, 467, 483, 484.
Heath, Thomas, 700.
eath, Thomas, jun., 700.
Hebborne, Richard, 122.
Hebrew Professor in Cambridge, 439.
Hechstetter, Daniel, 244, 245, 251-255, 258, 261, 270, 274, 279, 287-289, 300, 302, 310, 318, 398, 408, 457, 688.
Hector, D., 697.
Hedingham Castle, 3, 154, 173, 226.
Hedingham, Manor of, 465, 697.
Hedworth, Sir Ralph, 122.
Heidelberg, 205, 213.
Heidon, *see* Heydon.
Hekenberg, Count, 566.
Helford or Hayleford, 623.
Helford Haven, 535.
Hellard, William, 42.
Helmedon, 377.

Helmes, Mr., 384.
Helston, 309, 369.
Hemingford Abbots, 17.
Hemingham, 183.
Hemington, 370, 373, 376.
Hemmesworth, Manor of, 357.
Hemmyngford Graye, Bailiwick of, 108.
Hemp, 178, 180, 517, 519.
Hemsworth, John, 659.
Hendrick, ..., 571.
Hendy, Dr. Thomas, 11.
Heneage, (or Heuneage,) Ann, 243, 470.
Heneage, (or Hennage, Henneage,) Thomas, 238, 243, 268, 392, 397, 454, 470.
Heneage, Sir Thomas, 534, 695.
Henham, Vicar of, 217.
Henlowe, Alice, 61.
Henly, Dame Margery, 393.
Hennadge, ..., 487.
Henneage, Michael, 470.
Henneage, Mr., 466.
Henold, *see* Hainault.
Henry II., King of France, 39, 49, 62, 67, 77, 79, 81, 97, 134, 136.
Henry III., King of France, 588, 630, 633.
Henry VIII., King of England, 1, 2, 12, 44, 55, 64, 87, 114, 115, 119, 121, 133, 134, 142, 148, 165, 197, 199, 221, 223, 278, 287, 296, 396, 430, 488, 612, 701, 702.
Henshaw, Capt., 228.
Hensingham, 617.
Henson, Agnes, 214.
Henson, Richard, 214.
Henson, Rose, 214.
Heralds (Heralds College, Heraldry), 2, 3, 27, 41, 92, 214, 247, 264, 291, 295, 306, 329, 404, 442, 510, 594, 596, 613. *See* Arms, grants of, Clarencieux, Embroiderers' Hall.
Heraut, Carlin, 490.
Herbert, Edward, 376.
Herbert, Sir Edw., 686, 688.
Herbert, Henry, Lord Herbert, 62, 335. Earl of Pembroke, 377, 464, 466, 484, 501, 503, 562, 608, 615, 638, 639.
Herbert, Mr., 501.
Herbert, William, 105, 170.
Herbert, Sir William, 20, 22-25, 27, 32. Earl of Pembroke, 35, 43, 44, 47, 48, 54, 58, 62, 75, 83, 88, 93, 97, 99, 106, 108, 168, 220, 235, 260, 272, 278, 288-290, 296, 300, 302, 303, 314, 349, 367, 370.
Hercye, Sir John, 332.
Herd, Mr., 222.
Herefeld, 232.
Hereford, 123, 128, 196, 338, 373, 404, 423, 469, 651, 671.
Hereford, Bishop of, *see* Harley, Warton, Scorey.
Hereford, Bishopric of, 109, 134, 177, 196, 488, 564, 654.
Hereford, Dean and Chapter of, 134, 196, 404.

Hereford, Free Grammar School, 404.
Hereford, Viscount, *see* Devereux.
Herefordshire, 120, 123, 124, 148, 266, 275, 338, 343, 353, 374, 383, 384, 404, 469, 491, 514, 588, 671, 681.
Herefordshire, Justices of, 639, 651.
Herefordshire, Sheriff of, 579.
Herell, Thomas, Warden of Manchester College, 590.
Heresies, *see* Church Affairs.
Herlle, William, 244, 256, 406, 407, 425, 428, 430, 439, 442, 443, 495, 645, 660, 680, 684–690, 692.
Heron, George, 132.
Heron, Giles, 132.
Heron, John, 47.
Herreson, William, 362, 379.
Herries, Lord, 421.
Herrings and Herring Fishery, 473, 502, 614, 624.
Herrys, Arthur, 606.
Hertford, 1, 235, 371, 463, 542, 555, 557, 662, 672.
Hertford Castle, 166, 237.
Hertford, Earl of, *see* Seymour.
Hertford, Hundred of, 371, 458.
Hertford, Lady, *see* Grey.
Hertfordshire, 10, 60, 98, 100, 153, 154, 218, 224, 266, 325, 339, 351, 371–374, 391, 423, 458, 462, 463, 469, 535, 542, 555, 557, 560, 561, 630, 641, 662.
Hertfordshire, Alehouses, &c. in, 557.
Hertfordshire, Deaneries in, 12, 148.
Hertfordshire, Justices of, 638.
Hertfordshire, Sheriff of, 671.
Herwegs, Anthony, 325.
Hesse, Duke Augustus of, 209.
Hesse, Duke Frederick of, 209.
Hesse, Landgrave of, 209.
Heston, 201.
Heth. *see* Heath.
Heth, John, 535.
Hethcote, ..., 89.
Heton, Thomas, 550.
Heveningham Castle, 258.
Hever, 63.
Hever-Cobham, Manor of, 113.
Hewet, Sir William, 160.
Hexham, 355.
Hexte, a Pirate, *see* Hickes.
Hexte, Mr., 429.
Heydon, Sir Christopher, 185, 261, 262, 267, 342, 367, 374, 424, 425, 459, 482.
Heydon, William, 476, 627, 628, 657, 665, 669, 670.
Heylond, Robert, 5.
Heyman Ralph, 451.
Heynes, Simon, 503.
Heysell, 59.
Heyton, Manor of, 119.
Heyward, Thomas, 171.
Heywood, John, 112.

Hibbott, Sir John, 498.
Hickes, Mr., 539.
Hickes, or Hexte, Robert, a Pirate, 333, 399, 498, 547, 552, 570, 579, 583, 615.
Hickman, Anthony, 142, 143.
Hickson, Thomas, 498.
Hides, 474 ; Exportation of, 602.
Higford, or Hyckford, John, 520, 637.
Higford, or Higforth, Robert, 421, 437.
Higgens, or Higgons, George, 405, 507.
Higgyns, Oliver, 556.
Higham, Arthur, 225.
Higham, Sir Clement, 104.
Higham Ferrers, 334.
Higham, Manor of, 128.
Higham Park, 46.
Highfield, Mr., 350, 552.
Highgate Parks, 649.
High Peak, Forest of, 522.
High Peak, Lordship of, 640.
High Peak, Hundred of, 124.
Highway Robbery, 105, 189, 702.
Highways, Repair of, 523.
Highworth, Hundred of, 377.
Highworth, Parish of, 169.
Hill, Andrew, 702.
Hill, John, 192.
Hill, Robert, 371.
Hill, Wapentake of, 334.
Hill, William, 472.
Hillary, Mr., 386.
Hille, John, 192, 403.
Hilton, Sir Thomas, 122.
Hinde, Sir Francis, 655.
Hinderskelf Castle, 435, 438.
Hinkford, Hundred of, 380, 450.
Hinnes, (Henewes, Hennes, Hunnys,) William, 77, 82, 83.
Hippesley, John, 612.
Histon, Parish of, 655.
Hitchcock, Thomas, a Pirate, 583, 584.
Hitchen, Half Hundred of, 373.
Hoare, James, 508.
Hoare, Michael, 521.
Hoby, Lady Elizabeth, 301, 407, 459.
Hoby, Sir Philip, 26, 42–44, 47, 74, 95.
Hoby, Sir Thomas, 273.
Hockington, Manor of, 165.
Hockley, John, 140.
Hockley, Manor of, 104.
Hoddesdon, Mr., 448.
Hoddesdonbury, Manor of, 458.
Hodges, John, 363.
Hodges, Richard, a Pirate, 512, 595.
Hodges, Master R., 682.
Hodges, William, 682.
Hodges, William, jun., 682.
Hodgson, sen., Christopher, 650.
Hodgson, (alias Christophersonne,) Christopher, 650.

Hodgson, Robert, 475.
Hodnell, Manor of, 380.
Hodsdon, 599.
Hodsdon, Bailiff of, 599.
Hodsdon, Christopher, 521.
Hodsham Richard, 202.
Hogan, Edmund, 505.
Hogan, Robert, 438, 447.
Hogge, Bryan, 195.
Hogge, Ralph, 474.
Hogge, The, (La Hogue,) 494.
Hoke, Manor of, 110.
Holbeach, Henry, Bishop of Lincoln, 17.
Holborn, 182, 516, 701.
Holcam, Mrs., Gryzegon, 186.
Holcam, (or Holcome,) Trystram, 186, 452, 458.
Holcroft, Lady Julyane, 386.
Holderness, 406.
Holderness, Wapentake of, 336.
Holeycastle, Manor of, 165.
Holgate, Robert, Archbishop of York, 18, 74.
Holingworth, Reginald, 113.
Holinshed, Mr., 17.
Holiwell, Ralph, 497.
Holland, the Dutch, 64, 290, 292, 481, 490, 531, 581, 601, 611, 623, 629, 660, 694, 698. *See* Flanders.
Holland, Loan to the States, 502-504, 601.
Holland Division, *see* Lincolnshire.
Holland, Edward, Sheriff of Lancaster, 305, 307.
Holland, Mr., 491.
Holland, Seth, 137.
Holland, Thomas, 154.
Hollinge, Mr., 659.
Hollingshed, John, 597.
Hollis, Sir William, 650.
Hollocome, William, 512.
Holme, Edward, 321.
Holme, Gilbert, 191.
Holme, Manor of, 147.
Holstein, Duke of, 231.
Holstok, William, 110, 113, 205, 401, 487, 505, 526, 528, 529, 601, 608, 656, 665, 676, 683, 684.
Holt, 571.
Holt Castle, 376, 642.
Holt, Manor of, 376.
Holt, William, 649.
Holte, Humfrey, 110.
Holte, John, 42.
Holyhead, 629.
Holy Island, 144.
Homage, 266, 272.
Homberston, William, 445.
Homfrey, Mr., 613.
Hondt, Mr., 532.
Hone, Dr. John, 644.
Honnyng, William, 90.
Honour, Titles of, *see* Titles.

Honrick, Gerard, 172, 598.
Honywood, Thomas, 451.
Hoo, Vicar of, 136.
Hooge, Cornelius de, 309.
Hook, 262, 372.
Hooknorton, 695.
Hooper, ..., 420.
Hooper, Henry, 592.
Hoord, William, 688.
Hope, The, 205.
Hoper, (or Hooper,) John, Bishop of Gloucester, 31–33, 39. Bishop of Worcester, 39.
Hopkin, William, 60.
Hopkinson, John, 627.
Hopkinson, Katherine, 627.
Hops, 211, 498, 702.
Hopton, John, Bishop of Norwich, 110.
Hopton, Arthur, 650.
Hopton, Sir Owyn, 217, 261, 268, 300, 301 304–306, 308, 337, 408, 409, 415, 433–435, 437, 445, 545, 635, 637, 647, 673,
Hopton, Sir Ralph, 58, 372.
Hopton, Robert, 189.
Hopton, Thomas, 527.
Horden, Alexander, 160.
Hore, James, 539.
Hormer, Hundred of, 340.
Horn, (or Horne,) Robert, Dean of Durham, 46, 48, 50, 149, 163. Bishop of Winchester, 163, 177, 184, 186, 192, 208, 250, 251, 287, 294, 299, 312, 348, 417, 474, 499, 501, 560, 626.
Horncastle, 334, 375, 582.
Hornchurch, Parish of, 44.
Horne Park, 590.
Horneby, John, 428.
Horneby, Robert, 428.
Hornes, Bourgmasters, &c. of, 615.
Hornsey, 546, 598.
Hornsey Park, 649.
Hornyolde, Jo., 470.
Horse, Master of the, *see* Master.
Horseley, ..., 47.
Horseley, Lawrence, 601.
Horseman, Elizabeth, 50.
Horses and Geldings, 5, 68, 75, 115, 137, 150, 158, 193, 207, 214, 218, 233, 254, 299, 337, 484, 485, 507, 607, 643, 693, 696.
Horses, Commissioners for Increase and Breed of, 643-645, 650, 681, 685; their Instructions, 686; their Proceedings, Returns, &c., 643, 651, 653, 654, 656, 662-664, 675, 676, 678–680, 688, 690. *See* Musters.
Horses, Deputy Commissioners for Kent, 685; for Essex, 686; and for other Counties, *ib.*
Horses, Musters of, 3, 4, 12, 99, 101, 218, 254 255, 337, 350, 363, 365, 375, 421, 459 460, 474. *See* Musters.
Horsey, Edward, 78-81, 86, 264, 324, 355, 372, 378, 384, 418, 426, 434, 528, 530; Sir Edward, 611, 658, 670, 687, 690.

GENERAL INDEX.

Horsey, Francis, 78-81, 86.
Horsey, George, 373.
Horsey, Sir John, 58, 561.
Horsey, Mr., 417.
Horsington, 682.
Horsley, 4.
Horticulture, *see* Gardening, Trees.
Horton, 33.
Horton, Curate of, 591.
Horton, Mr., 149.
Horton, Roger, 79.
Horton, Lord Parr of, *see* Parr.
Horwood (or Whorwood), ..., 39.
Hose, Manufacture of, 428.
Hoseley, Parson of, 632.
Hosier, *see* Ozier.
Hosiers, 200, 428.
Hoskins, William, 613.
Hospitals, 446, 447.
Hosskyns, Dr., 103.
Hosteman, Giles, 702.
Hosting Strangers, Grant of, 510, 522, 551, 621.
Hothome, Manor of, 9.
Hounds, *see* Greyhounds. Bloodhounds.
Hounslow, 318.
House of Commons, *see* Parliament.
House of Correction in Winchester, 630.
House of Lords, *see* Parliament.
Household, The, 17, 31, 40, 42, 52, 62, 64, 91, 106, 107, 109, 112, 119, 133, 136, 146, 160, 184, 190, 193, 231, 232, 250, 256, 257, 269, 488, 493, 498, 504, 508, 510, 556, 604, 606, 610, 611, 617, 640, 703. *See* Game. Purveyors.
Household, Officers of the, 576.
Household, Cofferer of the, 41, 42, 109, 130, 131, 133, 146, 155, 160, 192, 703.
Household, Comptroller of, 91, 110, 112, 128, 154, 219, 223, 257.
Household, Lord Steward of, 93, 152, 155.
Household, Treasurer of, 152, 154.
Household, Vice Chamberlain of, 226, 257.
Household, Wines, Beer, and Ale, for the, 492, 681.
How, Thomas, 174.
Howard, Charles, 357, 361, 390.
Howard, Mrs. Frances, 537, 680, 682.
Howard, Sir George, 155, 165, 200, 207, 242.
Howard, Henry, 431.
Howard, Henry, (son of Viscount Bindon,) his debts and ill conduct, 243, 460, 537, 545, 548, 549, 551, 567-569, 583-585, 590-594, 625, 665, 670, 679, 680, 682.
Howard, Henry Earl of Surrey, 41, 692.
Howard, Lord, 665.
Howard, Lord Henry, 441, 498, 692.
Howard, Philip Earl of Surrey, 424, 425, 436, 446, 460; Earl of Arundel, 469, 639, 665.
Howard, Thomas, 643.
Howard, Thomas, Third Duke of Norfolk, 8, 57, 58.

Howard, Thomas, Fourth Duke of Norfolk, 98, 99, 106, 108, 115, 137, 142, 149, 153, 166, 173, 204, 231, 249, 252, 259, 280, 302, 344, 345, 365, 370, 372,-382, 383, 385, 387, 392, 393, 395, 410, 417, 419, 421, 422, 424-429, 432-442, 444, 446, 454, 458, 460, 467, 469, 478, 578, 665.
Howard of Bindon, Thomas Viscount, 340, 342, 451, 465, 481, 487, 526, 528, 537, 551, 555, 568, 571, 574, 581, 583, 625, 643, 665, 670, 679, 680, 682.
Howard of Effingham, Charles Lord, 497.
Howard of Effingham, William Lord, Lord Admiral, 60, 62, 91-94, 98, 100, 221, 256, 257, 304, 385, 401, 445, 449.
Howard House, or Place, 387, 392, 395, 410, 422.
Howdenshire, Wapentake of, 336.
Howland, Dr. Richard, (Master of St. John's College, Cambridge,) 548, 552, 553, 567, 622, 636, 644, 688.
Howlet, ..., 97.
Howseman, John, 119.
Howton, Manor of, 285.
Hoxone, Hundred of, 452.
Hoxton, 321.
Huband, Sir John, 675.
Hubbert, Edward, 685.
Hubblethorne, Lady, 176.
Huddelston, R., 684.
Huddesdon, Christopher, 553.
Hudson, George, 637.
Hudson, Mr., 416.
Hudson, William, 280.
Hugget, Alice, 587.
Huggon, William, 240, 290.
Hughes, Edward, 145.
Hughes, Mr., 670.
Hughes, William, 299; Dr. William, 301; Bishop of St. Asaph, 564, 618.
Huick, or Huyck, Dr., 195, 667.
Hull, *see* Kingston.
Hull, Mayor, &c., *see* Kingston.
Hulle, Matthew, 10.
Humber, The, 263, 296, 699.
Hume Castle, 360.
Humflete, 220.
Humfrey, James, 414.
Humfrey, John, 529.
Humfrey, Dr., Lawrence, 186, 192, 193, 253, 271, 443, 444, 498-501.
Humfrey, William, 192, 252, 254, 256-261 270, 274, 275, 278, 282-284, 287, 288 291, 296, 302, 305, 307, 311, 322, 398 410, 688.
Hummerston, Mr., 70, 72.
Hungatt, (or Hungate,) Mr., 102, 107
Hungerford, 340.
Hungerford, Sir Anthony, 60.
Hunnys, *see* Hinnes.
Hunsdon, Lord, *see* Carey.
Hunt, Mr., 49.
Hunt, Thomas, 473.

GENERAL INDEX. 749

Hunt, William, 421, 522.
Hunte, Henry, 577.
Hunter, Thomas, 63.
Hunting, 210, 417, 448, 467, 468, 511, 551, 672.
Huntingdon, 134, 542, 549.
Huntingdon, ..., 15.
Huntingdon, Countess of, 528.
Huntingdon, Earl of, *see* Hastings.
Huntingdonshire, 21, 134, 148, 165, 214, 227, 229, 231, 342, 370, 430, 503, 542, 549, 566, 577, 648.
Huntley, 423.
Huntley, Earl of, 208.
Huntley, George, 637.
Huntyngton, Hundred of, 124.
Hurleston, Ran., 645.
Hurleston, Richard, 303, 321.
Hurrocke, Edward, 610.
Hurst, 41, 409.
Hurst, James, 97.
Hurst, John, 217.
Hurstingston, Hundred of, 430.
Husbandry, *see* Tillage.
Husee, Thomas, 491.
Husey, Thomas, 32.
Hussey, ..., 10.
Hussey, Anthony, 87.
Hussey, Sir Harry, 23.
Hussey, Lord, 36.
Hussey, or Hussy, Thomas, 368, 409, 473.
Hussey, Sir William, 63.
Husseye, Thomas, 108.
Hutchenson, John, 111.
Hutton, Matthew, 186; Dr., 262, 295, 316; Dean of York, 322, 338.
Huyck, Dr., *see* Huick.
Hyat, Thomas, 420.
Hyckford, *see* Higford.
Hyde Park, 363.
Hyldesley, William, 682.
Hyll, Robert, 110.
Hynde, John, 194.
Hyndelipe, 503.
Hythe, 520.
Hythe, Bailiffs, &c. of, 489.

I.

Iceland, 248.
Iceland Fleet, The, 94.
Idiots, Idiotcy, 403.
Ightham, 56.
Ilford, 104.
Illesley, 350.
Imperfect Papers, 1, 55, 77, 94, 101, 114, 194, 287, 403, 413, 508-510, 518.
Imposts, the New, 697, 698.

Impressment of Carts, Horses, Waggons, Wains, &c. 65, 629.
Impressment of Seamen, &c., 390, 665. *See* Admiralty.
Impressment of Workmen for Building Ships, &c., 627, 672. *See* Workmen.
Impropriations, 127, 218, 411, 446, 447, 518, 623.
Incent, John, 147, 363.
Incest, Crime of, 597.
Inchkeith, 7.
Inclosures, 16, 18, 20, 74, 269.
India, the Indies, 173, 280, 281, 330, 629, 693, 698.
Indies, West, *see* West Indies.
Ingatestone, 32, 35, 173, 272.
Ingleby, (or Inglyby,) Sir William, 370, 587.
Ingoldmelles, 177.
Ingoldsby, Rectory of, 266.
Ingrossers, *see* Engrossers.
Injunctions, 22, 53, 54, 182, 183, 187, 330, 357.
Inner Temple, 538, 569, 637, 645.
Inns of Court, 357, 478, 552, 567, 674. Readers in, 538.
Inns and Alehouses, *see* Alehouses.
Inquisition, *see* Spain.
Inquisitions post mortem, 162, 374, 404.
Inquisitor of Flanders, 87.
Installations of Knights, 446,
Instructions, 480, 482, 522, 525, 526, 536, 539, 546, 551, 552, 590, 631, 642, 645-647, 656, 671, 686, 689, 690.
Insurance on Shipping, 468.
Insurrections, *see* Rebellions.
Intercourse, stay of, 508, *see* Entercourse.
Interludes, *see* Drama.
Interments, *see* Funerals.
Inundations, 397.
Invasion, 137, 303.
Inventions, 399, 512, 513, 578, 598, 611, 627, 696, 701.
Inventories, 12, 14, 59, 66, 115, 424, 434, 438, 441, 521, 596.
Inventories of Ships, 618.
Ippesley, 118.
Ipswich, 182, 183, 194, 227, 293, 337, 357, 377, 447, 448, 529, 541, 543, 558, 565, 569, 571, 587, 606, 643, 652, 665. *See* Clothworkers.
Ipswich, Alehouses in, 565.
Ipswich, Bailiff of, 606.
Ipswich, Mayor, &c., 571.
Ireland, ..., 237.
Ireland, the Irish, 6, 16-18, 35, 41, 46, 61, 87, 110, 131, 152, 154, 164, 165, 175, 203, 251, 254, 258, 259, 262, 269, 271, 275, 276, 287-289, 291, 292, 294-296, 298, 302, 311, 338, 372, 375, 376, 387, 392-394, 406, 408, 420, 427, 438, 447, 449, 453, 473, 474, 476-479, 481, 483, 486, 495, 496, 499, 501, 502, 516, 521, 531, 533, 539, 549, 551, 552, 575, 591-597, 601, 625, 629-631, 633, 634, 638, 642, 647, 653, 666, 675, 680.
Ireland, Lord Chancellor of, 522.

GENERAL INDEX.

Ireland, Lord Deputies of, 87, 104, 152, 499, 670.
Ireland, Designs of Spain on, and landing of Spaniards, 565, 632, 647, 677, 687.
Ireland, Levies of Men and Embarkation of Troops for, 629, 632, 633, 635–638, 661, 667, 669, 670, 671, 673.
Ireland, Rebellion of James Fitzmorris, 629–631.
Iron and Iron Works, 147, 274, 275, 473–475, 563.
Iron Furnaces, 474, 475, 478.
Iron Mills, 482.
Iron Ordnance, 476, 477, 480, 482, 526, 622. *See* Ordnance.
Irons, Clerk of the, 703.
Irthingborough, 206.
Irton, Alexander, 605.
Isabella, the Empress, 3.
Iseham, Robert, 111.
Isham, Giles, 101.
Isham, Henry, 521.
Isleworth, (or Istelworth,) 40, 123, 201, 387, 491.
Isley, Sir Harry, 56, 58, 60, 61.
Isley, William, 56, 58.
Islington, 428.
Isted, Thomas, 475.
Italian Church, The, 312.
Italy and Italians, 16–18, 66, 67, 69, 71, 73, 75, 77, 88, 147, 158, 187, 188, 198, 208, 211, 213, 239, 324, 466, 491, 496, 614, 691.
Ithell, Ralph, 551.
Ithell, Dr. Thomas, 530, 537, 548, 551, 625.
Ivan Vazilewich, Emperor of Russia, 338.
Ivington, *see* Evington.
Ivy Bridge, 660.
Ivy Lane, 195, 315, 429, 500, 503.

J.

Jackman, Alderman, 432.
Jackman, Charles, 656.
Jackman, Edward, 303.
Jacks (armour,) making of, 512.
Jackson, Ralph, 85.
Jackson, S., 56.
Jacob, Abraham, 700.
James VI., Prince, and King of Scotland, 276, 283, 293, 394, 496.
James, The, 512.
James, Richard, 658.
Jarden, Nicholas, 556.
Jarrett, Thomas, 512.
Jarula, Farrandina de, 332.
Jarvis, Richard, 529.
Jaye, Robert, 17.
Jefferey, John, 409, 449

Jeffery, Bartholomew, 475.
Jellee (or Jellaie), James, Jacques, 563, 577.
Jenkins, ..., a pursuivant, 632.
Jenkins? *see* Jenn.
Jenkinson, (or Jenckynson,) Anthony, 253, 281.
Jenison, Mr., 354.
Jenn, John Robert Ap, 543.
Jennet, The, 331.
Jenney, Edmund, 114.
Jenney, John, 350.
Jenney, alias Jennynges, Thomas, 411.
Jennins, Walter, 506.
Jenny, ..., 373.
Jennynges, *see* Jenney.
Jenye, Christopher, 619.
Jenyns, Sir John, 52.
Jerlitus, Hieronymus, 312, 313.
Jermy, Robert, 632.
Jermye, Mr., 432, 557.
Jermyn, Sir Ambrose, 157, 343, 372.
Jermyn, Sir Robert, 601.
Jernegan, Sir Henry, 57, 101, 106, 108, 121.
Jernegan, John, 384.
Jerningham, Lady, 562.
Jersey, 29, 93, 132, 310, 702.
Jesop, Richard, 501.
Jesuits, 624, 636, 641, 672, 676, 688.
Jesus, The, 220, 260, 329, 331.
Jesus College (Cambridge), 186.
Jesus-green (Cambridge), 624, 625.
Jewell, John, Bishop of Salisbury, 248, 300, 323, 324, 349.
Jewel House, The, 6, 14, 194, 339, 691.
Jewel House, Officers of the, 96, 104, 113, 161, 276, 462.
Jewel House, Master of the, 534.
Jewels, 172, 253, 267, 270, 271, 308, 422, 700. *See* Crown Jewels.
Jewkes, Simon, 392, 395, 415.
Jhonsoun, Robert, 491.
Jobson, Sir Francis, 188, 243, 255, 277, 338, 366.
John III., King of Sweden, 468, 474.
John, the Almain, 696.
John, Don, *see* Austria.
John, Humfrey Ap, 457.
John, John Ap, 543.
John Rynallde Ap, 457.
John Baptist, The, 577.
Johnaman, ..., a Pirate, 611.
Johnes, Mrs. Flowre, 541.
Johnson, Barnard, 511.
Johnson, Elizabeth, 511.
Johnson, George, 41.
Johnson, Henry, 369.
Johnson, John, 92, 94, 398, 401, 447, 448, 530, 552, 587, 692.
Johnson, Lawrence, 103, 446, 495, 507, 658.
Johnson, Richard, 92, 94, 624.
Jointures, 291, 364, 658.
Joliffe, or Joliff, Henry, 528, 696.

GENERAL INDEX.

Kesteven, 47, 135, 343, 372, 655.
Kesteven Division, see Lincolnshire.
Keswick, 250, 258, 372, 374, 376, 379, 287, 289, 291, 292, 294, 298, 300, 310, 315, 317-320.
Kete, John, 404.
Kettering, 564.
Ketton. 64, 368.
Kevall, George, 647.
Kew, 18, 66, 68, 109.
Keyle, Mr., 314.
Keyllwey (or Kalawaye, Kayleway, Kelleway, Kelway,) Robert, 4, 16, 47, 118, 138. 225, 243, 286.
Keyllwey, William, 124; Sir William, 207-222.
Keys, Thomas, Serjeant Porter, 96, 256, 257, 274-277, 284. 295, 321, 377, 422. *See* Grey, Lady Mary.
Keythorpe, Lands in, 656.
Kidderminster, Parsonage of, 48.
Kidlington. Manor of. 404.
Kightley, George, 432.
Kildare, Bishoprick of, 22.
Kildare, Earl of, 516, 601. *See* Fitzgerald.
Kildare, Lady, 516.
Killigrew, Henry, *see* Kyllygrew.
Killigrew, Sir John, 584.
Killigrew, Mr., 389.
Killigrew, Peter, 86, 87, 306, 308, 624.
Killigrew, *see* Kyllygrew.
Killingbeck, ..., 640.
Killington, Parson of, 624.
Killingworth Castle, *see* Kenilworth.
Killingworth, William, 511.
Killygrew, Mr., 502.
Kilmington, Manor of, 96.
Kilwick, Lands of, 197.
Kimbolton, 231, 276, 428, 663, 664, 667.
Kimbolton, *see* Woods.
King, Dr., 15.
King's Bench, Court of. 84, 107, 108, 125, 179, 285, 430, 433, 434, 447, 497, 508.
King's Bench, Marshal of, 506, 523.
King's Bench Prison, 174, 309, 521, 523, 524, 594, 606, 612, 627, 655, 669.
King's Bench, prisoners in, 667.
King's College, Cambridge, 186, 209, 260, 267, 301, 305, 515, 520, 522, 620, 622.
King's Ditch, Cambridge, 493.
King's Lynn, *see* Lynn Regis.
King's Printer, *see* Queen's Printer.
Kingsbridge, Hundred of, 377.
Kingsey, Manor of, 535.
Kingsland, Manor of, 266.
Kingsmell, Mr., 178.
Kingsnorton, Manor of, 266, 347.
Kingston (Surrey , 27, 59. 583.
Kingston, Sir Anthony, 73, 76, 78, 79, 82.
Kingston Deverell, Manor of. 381.
Kingston, Hundred of, 135, 419, 423, 426.
Kingston-on-Hull, 121, 193, 296, 336, 512.

Kingston-on-Hull, Mayor, &c. of, 537, 554, 574, 590.
Kinneston, Richard, 505.
Kintbury Egle, Hundred of, 340.
Kirby, 170.
Kirbye, Bartholomew, 680.
Kirkbride, Barnaby, 162.
Kirkby or Kirby Moorside. 155, 356, 394.
Kirkstall, Monastery of, 170.
Kirtling, (or Kyrtlinge,) 338, 459, 461, 483, 507, 675.
Kisgate, Hundred of, 375.
Kistgate Division, 419.
Kitchen, Anthony, Bishop of Llandaff, 143.
Kitching, Robert, 577.
Knappe, Manor of, 43.
Knevet, *see* Knyvett.
Knevit, Sir Henry, 167.
Knight, John, 43.
Knight Marshal, The, 127, 628.
Knight, Richard, 620.
Knight Ryder Street, 274, 363.
Knight, William, 186, 624.
Knighte, Edward, 516.
Knighthood, 5, 35, 85.
Knight's fee, Tenure of, 215, 243, 533.
Knights, *see* Garter, Windsor.
Knigts of St. John, *see* St. John.
Knightsbridge, 363.
Kniveton, Matthew, 111.
Knoll, 44.
Knolles, (or Knollys,) Henry, 144, 204, 205, 209, 213, 348, 371, 450, 497, 605.
Knolles, Thomas, 482.
Knollys, ..., 256.
Knollys, Lady Catharine, 146, 159, 241. 329.
Knollys, (Knolles, Knowlles,) Sir Francis, 2 ; Vice Chamberlain, 112, 156, 159, 181, 203, 226-229, 241, 249, 257, 328, 341, 345, 401, 434, 440, 601, 658, 663-665, 667, 669.
Knollys, Letitia, *see* Leicester.
Knollys, Robert, 159.
Knott, ..., 664.
Knoxe, John, 5, 46, 48, 50, 142, 238.
Knyght, Edward, 611.
Knyght, Robert, 4.
Knyght, Simon, 217.
Knyghtley, Richard, 109 ; Sir Richard, 304 366, 376, 377.
Knyvett, ..., 58.
Knyvett, Anthony, 58.
Kreek, Mr., 48.
Krigdote, Mr., 169.
Krugh, Benedict, 367.
Kydde, Justinian, 549.
Kyghtley, George, 327.
Kyllygrew, Henry, 202, 209, 210, 278, 408, 595, 618-620, 622.
Kyllygrew, John, 34, 326, 328, 332, 386, 452.
Kyllygrew, *see* Killigrew.
Kymball, Mr., 36, 305.

GENERAL INDEX. 751

Jolly, Ralph, 526.
Jonas, The, 399, 552.
Jones, ..., 302, 313, 634.
Jones, Alexander, 169.
Jones, Captain, 345.
Jones, David, 483, 484, 486, 487.
Jones, George, 141.
Jones, Griffen (or Gryffyn), 549, 569, 592, 594.
Jones, Sir Henry, 454.
Jones, Hugh, Bishop of Llandaff, 272, 362, 489.
Jones, John, 476.
Jones, Mrs., 489.
Jones, Philip, 702.
Jones, Richard, 492.
Jones, Robert, 622.
Jones, Rodolph, 493-495.
Jones, Walter, 295, 578.
Jones, Zacharias, 583.
Jopson, *see* Jobson.
Jordayne, Peter, 509.
Josephe, Joseph, 301.
Jourdain, Je., 315.
Jourdain, Nicolas, 315.
Judges, The Book of, 158.
Judges, The, 107, 108, 151, 285, 441, 479, 531, 616. *See* Circuits.
Judges opinions, 441, 621.
Judicial Combat, 414. *See* Wager.
Judith, The, 618.
Jugge, Richard, 173, 235, 268, 319.
Jukes, Edward, 576.
Julio, Dr., 272.
Junius Hadrianus, 309, 311.
Juries, 277, 409, 517, 519, 534, 546, 582, 588, 604, 606.
Jury of Matrons, 588, 626.
Justice, Administration of, 31.
Justice, Courts of, 533.
Justices of Assize, 248, 425, 454, 471, 515, 522, 526, 580, 620, 687, 638.
Justices of Peace, 7, 8, 18, 19, 21, 23-27, 30, 31, 35, 47, 56, 58, 65, 101, 120, 122, 137, 178, 181, 183, 209, 227, 250, 275, 280, 312, 324, 345-355, 357, 358, 360, 362, 366-368, 370, 371, 373, 374, 376, 377, 379, 386, 397, 419, 420, 423, 426, 427, 437, 440-442, 449, 451, 452, 459, 471, 473, 474, 478, 486, 500, 509, 532, 537, 543, 547, 553, 580, 582, 583, 598, 618, 624, 649, 653, 674, 676, 685, 692.
Justices of Peace, Oaths taken by, 634, 637-639.
Justices of Peace, or Liber Pacis, Books of, 508.
Justyce, Hugh, 28.

K.

K........., W., 506.
Kalice, *see* Kanter.
Kalowaye, *see* Keyllwey.

Kanter, alias Kalice, Henry, 535.
Kaylewey, *see* Keyllwey.
Keill, Dorothy, 402.
Keill, Thomas, 402.
Kekewiche, George, 451.
Kelk, Dr. Roger, 142, 188, 435, 461, 494, 514.
Kelke, Mr., 311.
Kell, Mr., 275.
Kellegrew, ..., 188.
Kelleway, or Kellwaye, Mr., *see* Keyllwey.
Kelly, Sir Edward, 525.
Kelsam, Mrs. Catherine, 605.
Kelsay, 50.
Kelwey, *see* Keyllwey.
Kelyng, Thomas, 457.
Kemp, Anthony, 75, 85.
Kemp, Lady, 222.
Kemp, Peter, 187-189, 191, 193-195, 198-201, 211-213, 216, 219, 243.
Kemp, Sir Thomas, 258, 344.
Kempe, Bartholomew, 190.
Kempe, Mr., 101, 109.
Kemys, Thomas, 207.
Kemys, Sir Thomas, 71.
Kenchurch, 353.
Kendal Castle, 587.
Kendall, 391.
Kendall, Thomas, 183, 185, 187, 188, 496, 548.
Kendall, William, 534.
Kenilworth (or Killingworth), 40, 60, 278, 449, 666, 670.
Kenninghall, 137, 344, 424.
Kenrick, Elizabeth, 647.
Kenrick, Hugh, 646, 647, 649.
Kent, County of, 4, 22, 27, 33, 42, 46, 52, 56-61, 63, 88, 95, 98, 99, 101, 127, 128, 136, 138, 141, 144, 157, 159, 162, 165, 168, 173, 174, 191, 207, 224, 240, 241, 254, 260, 271, 272, 284, 301, 315. 344, 347, 350, 352, 354, 356, 389, 390, 397, 419, 420, 424, 444, 445, 450, 451, 455, 460, 461, 462, 467, 469, 474, 475, 488, 509, 527, 535, 546, 548, 559, 560, 576, 583, 588-590, 592, 595, 610, 626, 640, 650, 662, 663, 665, 672, 688, 701.
Kent, Alehouses, &c. in, 559.
Kent, cloth trade in, 511.
Kent, Dep. Commissioners for Horses in, 685.
Kent, Earl and Earldom of, 410. *See* Grey.
Kent, Justices of, 633, 638.
Kent, Landing-places in, 645.
Kent, Mr., 192.
Kent, Sheriff of, 240, 241, 322, 451, 662, 688.
Kent, Simon, 17.
Kent, Surveyor of, 676.
Kentish Town, 242.
Keppis, Thomas, 456.
Kerke, Peter, 524.
Kerr, William, 175.
Kerr, Hundred of, 452.
Kerryer, Hundred of, 570.
Kerseys, *see* Cloth.

GENERAL INDEX. 753

Kymbolton, *see* Kimbolton.
Kyme, Anthony, 177, 389.
Kyngesmyll, Henry, 316–320.
Kyngesmyll, Sir Henry, 524.
Kyngesmyll, Richard, 118, 635.
Kyngesmyll, Sir William, 368, 371, 375, 378, 384, 413.
Kyngysmyll, John, 30.
Kynolton, 373.
Kynsland, Parsonage of, 258.
Kyrbie, Walter, 453.
Kyrkeland, Rectory of, 223.
Kyrlington, Mr., 194.
Kyrton, James, 286.
Kyrton, Margery, 286.
Kytchen, Christopher, 109.

L.

L.........., H., 457.
L.........., T., 654.
Labourers, 155. *See* Artificers. Impressment.
Lachlard, [Lechlade?], 632.
Lacock, 10.
Lacy, Henry, 63, 96.
Ladweke, John, 6.
Ladybrigg Close, 51.
La Hogue, *see* Hogge.
Laistoff, *see* Lowestoft.
Laithwood, John, 566.
Lake, Stephen, 591, 620, 622.
Lalam, 195.
Lallart, Arthur, 201, 203.
Lambard, John, alias Gardiner, 475.
Lambarde, Giles, 421, 438, 443.
Lambart, ..., 696.
Lambart, Francis, 132.
Lambart, John, 696.
Lambay, Island of, 254.
Lambe, Alan, 217.
Lambe, James, 217.
Lambe, William, 217.
Lambert, ..., 392.
Lambert, Alderman, 432.
Lambeth, 45, 106, 115, 116, 161, 183, 184, 196, 213, 235, 314, 317, 319, 390, 395, 397, 410, 441, 445, 560, 647.
Lamborne, Hundred of, 156, 340.
Lamot, *see* Mott.
Lamplugh, Mr., 242, 319.
Lamplughe, George, 260, 302, 303, 310, 441, 491.
Lancaster, County of, 148, 149, 191, 197, 266, 288, 292, 203, 321, 322, 341, 347, 349, 355, 356, 395, 431, 474, 488, 526, 554, 563, 566, 568, 575, 580, 641, 656.
Lancaster, Chancellor of the Duchy, 522.
Lancaster Deaneries, 234.
Lancaster, Duchy of, 46, 52, 61, 110, 113, 117, 129, 146, 215, 243, 281, 292, 309, 696, 704.

Lancaster, Edward, 637.
Lancaster Herald, *see* Penson.
Lancaster, Sheriff of, 305, 307.
Lancaster, Thomas, Archbishop of Armagh 397.
Lancaster, Vicarage of, 110.
Lanceknights, 16, 17.
Lances and Lighthorse, Certificates of, *see* Musters.
Landaff, *see* Llandaff.
Landgrave, The, 313.
Landing Places, *see* Ports.
Landreau, Captain, 501.
Lands, *see* Crown Lands.
Lands, Assurance of, 442, 447.
Land's End, The, 276.
Lane, John, 467, 577, 595.
Lane, Ralph, or Rafe, 418, 445, 468, 524, 528, 630.
Lane, Sir Robert, 366, 377.
Lane, Stephen, 498.
Lane, Thomas, 680.
Lane, William, 32.
Lanercost Priory, 41.
Langbarge, Wapentake of, 336.
Langdale, Dr., 102, 127.
Langdale, Marmaduke, 659.
L[angdale?], W., 659.
Langdon, Thomas, 96.
Langley, 696.
Langnaver, John, 424.
Langoo, Wapentake of, 135.
Langothbye, Parsonage of, 223.
Langrake, James, 392.
Langrake, John, 482.
Langton, Dr. Christopher, 445.
Languages, 627.
Lanherne, 146, 177, 388,
Lannison. *See* Lonison.
Lannoy (or Alneto), Cornelius de, 249, 256, 273, 275–277, 289, 292.
Lanquett, M., 497.
Lansdale, Roger, 21.
Lantrissent, Hundred of, 7.
Lanway, William, 4.
Lanyson, *see* Lonyson.
La Planché, ..., 310.
Lardge, Thomas, 152.
La Roche, ..., 552.
Larrethow, 452.
Lascelles, Christopher, 275, 283.
Lasco, John à, 144.
Lasnewith, Hundred of, 452.
Lassells, Brian, 437.
Lassells, Mr., 379.
Latham, Ralph, 374.
Lathom, 488, 671.
Lathom House, 149, 347, 600.
Latimer, Hugh, 5, 9, 16, 41, 106.
Latimer, Lady, 92, 93.
Latimer, Lord, *see* Nevill.

3 B

Latin Dictionary, 492.
Latin Secretary, 261.
Latten Manufacture, *see* Mines.
Latymer, ..., a priest, 484.
Latymer, John, 423.
Latymer, Sir John, 423.
Launceston, 534, 555, 568, 621, 666.
Launde, 46.
Laughton, Harry, 36.
Lavenham Park, 685.
Lavington, West, 429.
Law, Abuses in, 364.
Law, Treatise on, 414.
Law Courts, 53, 125, 533.
Lawallen, William, 330.
Lawarre, Lord, *see* West.
Lawford, 671.
Lawghton, George, 446.
Lawlye, Fr., 125, 126.
Lawson, Mrs. Christian, 523.
Lawson, Thomas, 523.
Laybourne, Mr., 208.
Laycolt, Richard, 635.
Layton, 280.
Laytonstone, Hundred of, 430.
Laystoft, *see* Lowestoft.
Lea or Lee River (or Ware River), 166, 412, 529, 537, 539, 569, 699.
Lead, 46, 49, 264.
Leake, Mr., 539.
Leases, *see* Crown Lands.
Leather, 264, 279, 282, 286, 311, 398, 400, 500, 518, 602, 617.
Leather, Exportation of, 487.
Leatherhead, 645.
Leaving the Realm. *See* Quitting.
Leche, ..., 10.
Leder, Olyver, 18.
Ledes (or Leedes) Castle and Park (in Kent), 22, 42, 595.
Lee, 28.
Lee, Sir Anthony, 6, 9.
Lee, Francis, 590.
Lee, Francis à, 195.
Lee, Sir Harry (or Henry), 269, 449, 646, 652, 675, 690, 691, 695, 697.
Lee, John, 416, 430.
Lee, Lawrence, 13, 14.
Lee, Richard, 577.
Lee, Sir Richard, 12, 222, 280.
Lee, Thomas, 230, 380, 396.
Lee, William, 410.
Lee River, *see* Lea.
Leeche, Mrs. Elizabeth, 158.
Leedes, *see* Ledes.
Leedes, Edward, 126.
Leedes, John, 448.
Leek, Sir Francis, 346, 368, 370, 566.
Lees, *see* Leighs.
Lees, Roger, 36.
Lees, Thomas, 355.

Leffnam, *see* Luffenham.
Legacies to Minors, 702.
Legge, Dr. Thomas, 625, 635.
Legh, Dr., 23.
Legh, Mr. Sheriff, 83.
Leicester, 122, 334, 343, 347–351, **354**, **356**, 387, 423, 462, 505, 546, 561, **563**, **565**, 567, 650, 655, 667.
Leicester, College of, 266.
Leicester, Dean of, 148.
Leicester, Honor of, 215.
Leicester Hospital, 505.
Leicester or Leycester, Earl of, *see* Duddeley.
Leicester, Letitia (daughter of Sir F. Knollys), Countess of, 667.
Leicester, Sir Ralph, 369.
Leicestershire, 21, 52. 58, 122, 148, 149, **164**, 232, 334, 343, 357, 373, 415, 423, 462, 509, 546, 561, 563, 565, 655, 667, 701.
Leicestershire, Alehouses in, 565.
Leicestershire, Justices of, 638.
Leigh, Sir Thomas, 135.
Leighs (or Lees, Lyes, co. Essex), 22, 28, 33, 56, 58, 256, 270.
Leighton, 134, 259.
Leighton, Capt. Thomas, 364, 409.
Leistoff, *see* Lowestoft.
Lekinfield, 320.
Lemborch alias Oste, Nicholas de, 240, 242.
Lemon trees, 198.
Lenard, Mr., 230.
Le Neve, William, Clarencieux, 118.
Le Nevé's Fasti, 626.
Lennard, J., 322.
Lennox, Earl of, *see* Stuart.
Lennox, Countess of, *see* Douglas.
Lent, 80, 248, 411, 512.
Lenwich, 33.
Leominster, 383, 402.
Lerpool, *see* Liverpool.
Lestrange, Sir Nicholas, 22, 41.
Lestwithiel, *see* Lostwithiel.
Le Syra, John, 625.
Letheringham, 570.
Lethington, ..., 421.
Letley, 106.
Letters, *see* Post Office.
Lever, Ralph, 540, 644.
Lever, Thomas, 446.
Leveson, Edward, 171.
Leveson, Thomas, 120.
Levies of men, 2, 53, 98, 99, 120, 224, 225, 227, 275, 288, 398, 414, 479, 481, 539, 582. *See* Army. Musters.
Levies of horse and foot for Ireland, 653. *See* Ireland.
Levizam, Margaret, 86, 151.
Levizam, Thomas, 150, 151.
Le Volant, The ship, 641.
Lewes, 352, 624.
Lewes, Barony of, 159.

GENERAL INDEX

Lewes, Rape of, 139, 267, 451.
Lewes, Dr. David, 131, 164, 235, 240, 246, 249, 258, 273, 274, 279-282, 294, 317, 328-330, 332, 337, 343, 393, 405, 457, 459, 460, 489, 504, 514, 520, 530, 538, 543, 551, 585, 590, 606, 637, 659, 687.
Lewes, John Ap Thomas, 10.
Lewes, Richard, 109.
Leweston, John, 276.
Lewin, William, 291, 302.
Lewis, The, 5.
Lewis, Signor Don, 92.
Lewis, Edward, 176.
Lewis, Robert, 687.
Lewisham, 141, 321.
Lewkenor, Thomas, 543.
Lewknor, ..., 81.
Lewknor, Hundred of, 419.
Lewson, John, 91.
Lewyn, W., 535.
Lewys, Thomas, 541, 543, 667.
Lexden, Hundred of, 379, 558.
Ley, Thomas, 326.
Leyghe, John, 369.
Leyghtone, 15.
Leyson, Dr., 41.
Leyton, Captain, 210.
Libels, 417, 467, 520, 547, 700.
Liber Pacis, xix° Eliz., 580, 692. *See* Justices of Peace.
Licences to travel, 321, 600.
Lichfield, 340, 501, 502, 570, 661.
Lichfield, Bailiffs, &c., of, 661.
Lichfield, Dean of, 531.
Lichfield, President and Canons of, 531.
Lichfield and Coventry, Bishop of, *see* Bayne, Bentham. Overton.
Lichfield and Coventry, Diocese of, 110, 251, 310, 565, 583.
Liege, 507, 515, 524, 527.
Lieutenants, *see* Lord Lieutenants.
Ligh, Robert, 401.
Light Horse and Horsemen, Arms for, 654, 693. *See* Musters.
Ligi, *see* Lygy.
Ligon, Richard, 484.
Limehouse, 616.
Lincoln, 34, 88, 108, 118, 123, 334, 335, 339, 351, 389, 461, 485, 652, 654.
Lincoln, Archdeacon of, 105, 118, 188.
Lincoln, Bishop of, *see* Holbeach, Tailour, Watson, Bullingham, Cowper.
Lincoln, Bishoprick of, 9, 41, 109, 111, 307, 325, 407, 648.
Lincoln Cathedral, 40.
Lincoln College, 278.
Lincoln, Deanery of, 40.
Lincoln, Earl of, *see* Clynton.
Lincoln, Lady, 183.
Lincoln, Mayor, &c., 654.
Lincoln, Recorder of, 465.
Lincolnshire (including Holland, Kesteven, and Lindsey Divisions), 5, 19, 28, 34, 36, 46,

Lincolnshire—*continued.*
47, 53, 89, 108, 124, 135, 151, 160, 166, 194, 214, 215, 257, 263, 364, 266, 272, 292, 293, 332, 334, 335, 338, 340, 343, 346, 372, 373, 375, 380, 387, 412, 440, 461, 465, 466, 480, 482, 484, 485, 507, 508, 541, 568, 576, 577, 582, 589, 596, 598, 624, 652, 655, 684, 690, 694.
Lincolnshire, Alehouses in, 568.
Lincolnshire, Deluge in, 655.
Lincolnshire, Justices of, 638.
Lincolnshire, Sheriff of, 504.
Lincoln's Inn, 67.
Lindhurst, 587.
Lindsey Division, *see* Lincolnshire.
Linen Cloths, 579.
Lingfield, 431.
Link, Melchior, 424.
Lion or Lyon, The, 104, 205, 331, 552, 553, 559.
Lion and Dog fight, 181.
Lisbon, 488, 677, 690.
Liskeard, Town of, 309.
Lister, Mr., 193.
Lister, Sir Richard, 41.
Lister, Richard, 41.
Litany, The, 119.
Literhows, Henry, 256.
Litster, ..., 46.
Littlar, Robert, 84.
Little Bursted, Parson of, 154.
Little Maplestead, *see* Maplestead.
Little Thornham, *see* Thornham.
Liveries, *see* Wards.
Liverpool, 279, 287, 629, 631, 635, 636.
Liverpool, Mayor, &c. of, 279, 636.
Livings, Augmentation of. *See* Augmentation.
Livings, Valuation of, 478, 493, 573.
Lixalde, Francis de, 299.
Llanarth, Church of, 328, 329.
Llanbadarn Vawr, 610.
Llandaff, Bishop of, *see* Kitchen, Jones, Blethyn.
Llandaff, Bishoprick of, 143, 272, 362, 564, 583.
Llandaff, Chapter of, 489.
Llandaff, Prebendaries of, 362.
Llandewybrevi College, 436.
Llandewybrevy, 328, 329.
Llandona, Parsonage of, 294.
Llanristed, 594.
Lloyd, Griffith, 686, 688.
Lloyd, John, 452, 617.
Lloyd, Oliver, 273.
Lloyd, Owen, 683.
Lloyde, John, 107.
Loans, 7, 16, 94-96, 98-102, 104, 111, 117, 161, 182, 185, 208, 219, 235, 285, 318, 333, 365, 368-374, 377, 378, 380-384, 388, 389, 391-396, 406, 408, 410, 415, 418, 422, 425, 426, 429, 432, 433, 462, 479, 490, 505, 513, 531, 535, 628, 648. *See* Privy Seals.

3 B 2

GENERAL INDEX.

Loans, Foreign, 503, 505, 506, 531.
Loans to Holland. *See* Holland.
Lock, Humphrey, 202.
Locke, Mr., 522.
Lockye, Robert, 353.
Locton, Mr., 83.
Loder, Manor of, 272.
Lodge, Alderman Thomas, 105, 164, 183, 215.
Lodging-houses, 599.
Lodowick, Grave, 332.
Loiani, Signor Pompeo, 699.
Lok, Mr., 27.
Lok, Michael, 147, 533, 543, 556, 559, 567, 568, 570-572, 581, 602, 603, 606, 608, 615, 616, 619-622, 625.
Lollards Tower, The, 390, 391.
Lombard, Nicholas, 499-501.
Lombard, Richard, 552.
London, 2, 7, 9, 11-13, 15, 18, 20, 21, 23-29, 31, 32, 34, 35, 41, 43, 47, 51, 54, 55, 58, 65-67, 70, 74, 75, 85, 91, 96, 98, 100-102, 104, 105, 108, 111, 113, 115, 116, 126, 133, 139, 154, 159, 161, 162, 165, 169, 172, 173, 177, 178, 181, 182, 185, 186, 188-191, 195, 197, 203, 206, 215, 216, 219, 221, 224, 231, 232, 234-236, 250, 255, 268, 269, 273, 275, 279, 282, 283, 285, 286, 290, 301, 312-315, 317, 320, 323, 324, 327, 330, 333, 342, 344, 360, 378, 382, 385, 391, 398, 399, 402, 410, 415, 424-426, 429, 432, 433, 447-449, 452, 473, 476, 484, 488, 493, 505, 508, 510, 511, 526, 539, 577, 588, 594, 596, 603, 607, 608, 612, 620, 622, 626, 636, 637, 661, 674, 692. *See* Bridge-House, Strangers, Woolmen.
London, Aldermen of, 659.
London, Assessment for a Loan, 531.
London, Bakers and Bakers Company of, 626, 644.
London, Bishop of, *see* Boner, Ridley, Grindall, Sandys, Aylmer, and Bishop Thomas, 521.
London, Bishoprick of, 9, 12, 34, 112, 185, 539, 569, 649, 650, 654.
London Bridge, 74, 692.
London, Garbeller of, 399, 400.
London, Lord Mayor, &c. of, 83, 99-101, 104, 105, 108, 111, 135, 160, 174, 178, 181, 182, 214, 215, 224, 231, 232, 250, 251, 255, 268, 285, 286, 312, 313, 315, 320, 326-329, 342, 365, 396, 398, 413, 417, 426-428, 433, 437, 495, 511, 522, 523, 525, 532, 539, 586, 602, 607, 621, 622, 631, 633, 636, 637, 642, 644, 659, 661.
London, Merchants of, 538.
London, Musters of, 480.
London, Orphans of, 631, 642.
London, Packership of, 659.
London, Port of, 458, 475, 478, 611, 657.
London, Recorder of, *see* Fletewood.
London, Seal of, 327.
London, Searcher of, 686.
London, Sheriffs and Sheriffs Court of, 206, 308, 355, 453, 636, 646.
London, Strangers in, 421, 432, 433, 437, 447.

London Stone, 116.
Long, Alice, 403.
Long, Mr., 3.
Long Melford, *see* Melford.
Longeworth, Dr. Richard, 261-264, 268, 273, 274, 304, 305, 548.
Longley, Richard, 438.
Longstable-mead, 233.
Longwel, Abraham, 40.
Longworth, James, 378.
Lonison, (or Lanison, Lonyson,) John, 265, 438-440, 457, 533, 582, 615, 617.
Loo, Andreas de, 400, 401, 697.
Lopes, Dr., 592.
Lord Admiral, *see* Seymour. Howard. Clynton.
Lord Admiral, Authority of the, 633.
Lord Chamberlain, 221, 537, 576, 599, *see* Darcy.
Lord Chancellor, *see* Ryche, Goodrich, Heath.
Lord Keeper, Office of, 116.
Lord Keeper, *see* Bacon.
Lord Marshal, 103.
Lord Mayor, *see* London.
Lord Protector, *see* Seymour.
Lord Privy Seal, *see* Russell, Paget.
Lord Steward, The, 693.
Lord Treasurer, *see* Paulet, Cecill.
Lord Warden of the Cinque Ports, *see* Cheyne, Brooke.
Lords, House of, 14, 50, 431, 517, *see* Parliament.
Lords Lieutenants, 26, 30, 31, 33, 57, 97-100, 102, 108, 129, 136, 140, 141, 152, 153, 158, 181, 225, 297, 349, 350, 356, 363, 365-367, 372, 375, 376, 385, 390, 396, 536, 668.
Lords Lieutenants, Instructions to, 480.
Loretto, 523, 524.
Lorraine, 67, 297, 677.
Lorraine, Cardinal of, 317.
Lorraine, Duchess of, 68.
Loseley, 311, 501.
Losse, Robert, 177.
Lostwithiel, 121, 309.
Lothingland, 147, 619, *see* Lovingland.
Lotteries, 312, 314, 323, 332.
Loudonthorpe, Manor of, 151.
Loughborough, Lord, *see* Hastings.
Loughter, Robert, 207.
Loune, William, 502.
Louvaine, 71-73, 310, 525, 635.
Love, Family of, 642.
Lovelace, William, 348, 407.
Lovell, Mr., 521.
Lovell, Thomas, 258, 259, 317.
Lover, (or Louver,) Hans, or Johan, 257, 258 261, 270, 274, 279, 300, 302, 395, 397 398, 408, 438.
Loversall, Chapel of, 596.
Lovingland, (or Lothingland,) Hundred of, 452
Low Countries, *see* Flanders.
Lowe, ..., 633.

Lowe, Simon, 104.
Lower, Philip, 17.
Lower, *see* Lowre.
Lowestoft, (Laystoft, Leistoft,) 147, 176, 235, 643.
Lowestoft Roads, 552.
Lowre, Thomas, 202, 624.
Lowre, William, 388, 624.
Lowth, 45, 334.
Lowthe-Eske, Hundred of, 334.
Lowther, 122.
Lowther, Gerard, 702.
Lowther, Gerard, junr., 702.
Lowther, Richard, 702.
Lubeck, 220, 314, 403, 523, 663.
Lubsthorpe, 164.
Lucas, Thomas, 379; Sir Thomas, 521, 545.
Lucatelli, Innocent, 633.
Lucca, the Luccans, 90, 325, 459, 460.
Lucius, the Dutchman, 649.
Lucy, Mr., 693.
Lucy, Thomas, 149; Sir Thomas, 304, 339, 343, 358, 466, 520, 613.
Luddington, 276.
Ludham, 601.
Ludham, John, 244.
Ludloe, Edward, 212.
Ludloe, Matilda, 212.
Ludloe, Robert, 212.
Ludlow, 60, 406, 466, 543.
Ludlow, the Carrier of, 682.
Ludlow Castle, 452, 454, 540, 564, 635.
Luffenham, Parsonage of, 200, 201.
Lugwardin, Rectory of, 404.
Lulworth, 547, 680.
Lumley, John Lord, 396, 432, 488, 640.
Lunatics, 116, 165, 183.
Lundy, George, 231.
Luther, Dr. Martin, 471.
Lutherans, 291.
Lybanie, The, 587.
Lychpoole, John, 689.
Lydd, (in Kent,) 168.
"Lyddes," *see* Hatton.
Lydford, Parish of, 180.
Lydney, Manor of, 32.
Lyell, Richard, 35.
Lyes, *see* Leighs.
Lyggons, Mr., 107.
Lygon, Hugh, 700.
Lygon, Rafe, 700.
Lygons, (or Lygyns,) Ferdinando, 79-81.
Lygy, (or Lyzy,) Mons. de, 316-318.
Lyme Regis, 444, 528, 594.
Lyndeleye, 369.
Lyndford, Mr., 389.
Lynerols, M. de, 229.
Lynn Regis, 22, 171, 253, 255, 413, 449, 467, 470, 505, 595, 610.
Lynn Regis, Minister of, 702.
Lynne, Randoll, 28.

Lynton, 539.
Lyon, The, *see* Lion.
Lyon, Alice, 4.
Lyon, John, 4.
Lyons, Castle of, 376.
Lysley, Lancelot, 330.
Lyster, *see* Lister.
Lysyngham, ..., a Pirate, 251.
Lyte, George, 551.
Lytlestone, William, 617.
Lyttelton, John, 164; Sir John, 373, 484.
Lyttleton, Sir Edward, 165, 180, 181.
Lytton, Rowland, 373.
Lyvesey, Robert, 105.

M.

M.........., R., 458.
Macclesfield, Hundred of, 122.
MacPhelim, Sir Bryan, 481.
Mackwilliams, Henry, 569.
Macwilliams, Mr., 355.
Madder, 293.
Madeira, Island of, 287.
Madrid, 565.
Mafio, Balthasar de, 90.
Magdalen College, (Camb.,) 142, 188, 461, 492, 493, 496, 514, 534, 552, 605, 608, 666.
Magdalen College, (Oxford,) 11, 29, 31, 43, 105, 186, 192, 193, 253, 449, 499, 500, 597.
Magdalen College, (Oxford,) Dean of, 501.
Magic, *see* Witchcraft.
Magistrates, good, 473.
Magnus, Thomas, 29.
Maids of Honour, The, 648.
Maidstone, 58, 60, 294, 295, 354, 450, 633.
Maidstone, Hundred of, 460.
Maidstone, Strangers at, 532.
Maie, Richard, 516.
Maignewe, Arnold, 633.
Maismore, Farm of, 320.
Maister, William, 510.
Maister, Dr. William, 319, 321, 446.
Makerel, Harry, 14.
Malby, Nicholas, 206.
Malden, Constables of, 700.
Maldon, 420, 570.
Maldon, Bailiffs, &c. of, 380.
Malega, Straits of, 589.
Malim, (Malimio,) William, 331.
Malines, 69.
Mallett, Dr. Francis, 145, 150.

Malling, 57.
Mallory, Robert, 111.
Mallwycke Park, 107.
Malmsbury, 43.
Malmsbury, Hundred of, 377.
Malorye, Sir Richard, 250, 251.
Malsanger, 66, 67, 69, 71.
Malt, 498, 505, 552, 699, *see* Brewers.
Malta, 256, 260.
Malvern Chace, 470.
Malyn, John, 105, 106, 112.
Mameranus, ..., 113.
Man, Isle of, 502.
Man, John, 334.
Manchester 568, 680.
Manchester College, 94, 373, 590.
Manchester, Warden of, 307.
Maneby, William, 53.
Manerbery, Farm of, 41.
Maners, Roger, 294.
Mangell, Edward, 487.
Manhod, Mr., 555.
Manhood, Bailifwick of, 544.
Manley, Thomas, 472.
Manley, William, 471.
Manley, Wapentake of, 484.
Manne, John, 263.
Manners, Edward, Earl of Rutland, 406, 437, 486, 511, 526, 569, 650, 660, 689.
Manners, Henry, Earl of Rutland, 13, 97–99, 106, 115, 156, 158, 230, 303.
Manners, John, 368, 369, 379, 440, 441.
Mannet Thomas, 365.
Mannington, 388.
Mannucci, Jacomo, 689.
Manors, Lords of, 587.
Manours, Mr., 373.
Mansell, or Mawnsell, Sir Edward, 599, 638.
Mansfield in Sherwood, 122, 346.
Manshead, Hundred of, 374.
Manslaughter, 169.
Manthorp, 47.
Mantua, 67, 75, 76.
Mantua, Duke of, 88.
Mantua, Matthew de, 17.
Manufactures, *see* Cloths.
Manuscripts, 222, 292, 323, 324.
Manwood, Roger, 307, 384, 407, 409, 441; Justice, 558, 566; Sir Roger, 639, 643, 645, 656.
Manxwell, Anthony, 111.
Maperley, Matthew, 278.
Mapledurham, 237.
Maplestead, Great and Little, 697.
Marare, Albert de, 90.
Marble Pillars, imported, 394.
Marbury, Humfrey, 250.
Marburye James, 190.
March, Earl of, *see* Plantagenet.
Marcham, Anthony, 278.
Marches, The East, 479.

Marches, The, *see* Borders, Wales.
Marden, Hundred of, 450.
Marden, Manor of, 266, 301.
Mareschall, *see* Marshall.
Margaret, Queen of Scotland, 221.
Margaret, Lady, Foundation and Divinity Lecture, at Cambridge, 634, 644.
Margate, 699.
Margrette Bonadventure, the, 680.
Mariano, Angelo, 87.
Maris, or Marice, Capt., a pirate, 623.
Markenfield, or Markynfeld, Thomas, 411, 587.
Market, Clerk of, *see* Clerk.
Market Raison, 507.
Mark-hall, 25.
Markham, Ellis, 188.
Markham, John.
Markham, Richard, 387.
Markham, Robert, 379, 563, 569.
Markham, Thomas, 617, 689.
Marney, John Lord, 555.
Marotzo, Francis, 90, 91.
Marque and Reprizal, Letters of, 19, 93, 224, 275, 313, 328, 332, 412, 492, 508, 540.
Marr, Henry, 611.
Marrena, 524.
Marriage of the Clergy, 324.
Marriages, 74, 131, 155, 175, 183–185, 187, 188, 195, 196, 199, 200, 205, 207, 211, 221, 230, 231, 241, 256, 257, 273, 277, 280, 291, 368, 369, 458, 471, 489, 491, 498, 500, 538, 690.
Marriages Royal, 4, 42, 55, 56, 58, 65, 101, 175, 195, 199, 217, 253, 269, 280–282, 291, 345, 417, 419, 467, 629. *See* Elizabeth.
Marsden, William, 326.
Marseilles, 320, 490, 499.
Marsh, Edward, 36.
Marshal, ..., 686.
Marshal, John, 399.
Marshal, Office of, 350.
Marshal, William, 166.
Marshall, ..., 307.
Marshall, Godfrey, 313, 317, 324.
Marshall, Mr., 110.
Marshall, Thomas, 105.
Marshalsea Prison, 136, 168, 174, 175, 179, 240, 402, 406, 482–484, 504, 579, 605, 628, 632, 641, 645, 696.
Marshalsea, Prisoners in, 668.
Marshe, Mr., 333, 447.
Marshe, Thomas, 363.
Marshfoot, 44.
Marsshe, John, 107.
Marston, 367.
Marston Bygot, Manor of, 536.
Mart Towns, 447, 448, 552, 587, 603. In England, 530, 692. Origin of, 552.
Marten, Edward, 295.
Marten, John, 384.
Marten, Mr., 667.

GENERAL INDEX.   759

Marten, Martens. *See* Martin. Martyn.
Martial Law, 98.
Martial Men, Names of, 684.
Martigne, M., 319.
Martin à Rhurnbeck, Dr., 383.
Martin, Dr., 471.
Martin, Thomas, 305.
Martin, William, 305, 412, 455.
Martine, Edmund, 490, 498.
Martine, Humphry, 490, 498.
Martinengo, The Abbot, 175.
Martocke, Parsonage of, 521.
Martyn, John, 306, 535, 606.
Martyn, (Marten, Martin), Richard, 306, 431; Alderman, 457, 503, 506, 521, 533, 582; Warden of the Mint, 613, 673, 691.
Martyn, Roger, Alderman, 111; Sir Roger 313, 320.
Martyn, Thomas, 65-67; Dr. 68, 87, 174.
Martyr, Peter, 158, 183.
Martyrs, *see* Church Affairs.
Marwood, John, 159.
Mary (the French Queen), sister of Henry VIII., 3, 217, 286.
Mary, Princess of England, 3, 5, 13, 20-22, 25, 31, 34, 42, 48, Queen, 54-72, 74, 75, 77, 78, 80, 82, 85-88, 90-107, 111-115, 117, 119, 121, 123, 124, 128, 133, 134, 137, 140, 141, 143, 146, 158, 197, 223, 325, 390, 697.
Mary, Queen of Scotland, 4, 6, 11, 87, 88, 144, 151, 152, 162, 175, 179, 195, 199, 202, 208, 217, 253, 256, 279. 286, 291, 293, 297, 309, 311, 316, 318, 324, 328, 344, 345, 370, 382, 417, 422, 423, 425-431, 433, 436-438, 449, 497, 499, 503, 547, 649.
Mary Bowes, The, 114.
Mary Fortune, The, 93.
Marygold, The, 482.
Masks, *see* Drama.
Masham, 394.
Mason, *alias* Wyckes, Anthony, 482.
Mason, Richard, 593.
Masone, Sir John, 56, 66, 69, 72-76, 80, 82, 84-86, 109, 115, 129, 130, 134, 136, 143, 146, 151, 180, 183, 249, 258, 271, 275, 488, 534.
Masone, Lady, 86, 274.
Mass, service of, 34, 96, 152, 173, 174, 179, 321, 346, 371, 396, 483, 565, 568, 578, 610, 617, 622, 656.
Mass Books, &c., 524.
Masselin, Nicholas, 399.
Massy, Elizabeth, 428.
Massy, Roger, 428.
Master, Dr. Richard, 672.
Master of the Barges, *see* Barges.
Master Gunner, The, 276.
Master of the Horse, 84, 91, 106, 155. *See* Browne. Duddeley.
Master of Requests, *see* Requests.
Master of the Rolls, *see* Beaumont, Bowes, Cordell.

Maston, Thomas, 551.
Matharn, 362, 489, 564, 583, 617.
Mathew, Edmond, 310, 436, 446, 509, 606.
Mathew, George, 7.
Matrons, Jury of, 588, 626.
Matson, Thomas, 15.
Matthew, Dr. Tobie, 648.
Matthew, John, 556, 593, 584.
Matthewe, Henry, 136.
Matthewe, Thomas, 104.
Matyson, Richard, 598.
Maunder, ..., 21.
Maundy, The, 236.
Maunsell, Richard, 9.
Mauvissiere, Mons., 454, 534.
Mawde, Barnard, 691.
Mawnsell, *see* Mansell.
Maximilian, Emperor of Germany, 243, 271.
May, Thomas, 475.
Maydewell, Lawrence, 232.
Maye, Geo., 475.
Maye, *see* Mey.
Mayfield, 394, 438.
Maynard, H., 578.
Maynard, Thomas, 367.
Mayne, Cuthbert, 568.
Mayneman, Thomas, 40.
Maynwaringe, Randle, 593.
Maynwaryng, Sir Arthur, 486.
Mayton ferry, 576.
Mazines, Capt., (Mascino del Bene ?), 211, 465.
Mead-hole, 384.
Meade, Thomas, 382, 638.
Mendley, William, 440, 443.
Measures, 455, 495, 556. Of wine and ale, 702.
Meath, Bishop of, 9.
Meden, 246.
Medicine, (Medical receipts, &c.,) 51, 239, 252, 502.
Medina, Dukes of, 217.
Medine, (now Newport,) *see* Newport.
Medley, George, 195.
Medley, John, 598.
Medlow, 198.
Medway, The, 486.
Meers, ..., 613.
Meffyn, Lord, 309.
Meidlar, Thomas, 276.
Mekley, Rowland, 316.
Melburneholme, Hundred of, 124.
Melcombe Regis, 546.
Melford, Long, 157.
Melford Hall, 157.
Melksham, Forest of, 554.
Mellershe, Richard, 627.
Mellershe, Thomas, 627.
Melles, Rectory of, 142.
Mellowe, John, 631.
Mellowe, Lawrence, 692.
Melton, 217.

Melton Fauconbridge, Manor of, 113.
Melurine, Signior, 226.
Melvyn, Mr., 283.
Members of Parliament, 96.
Memorancye, *see* Montmorency.
Mendippe, 612.
Menvile, Ninian, 29.
Menye, Walter, 451.
Meo, William, 625.
Merchant Adventurers, 45, 65, 87, 101, 116, 128, 139, 161, 164, 182, 198, 208, 215, 217, 231, 236-238, 241-244, 246, 247, 267, 280, 284, 285, 287, 314, 326-328, 338, 362, 367, 394, 405, 408, 432, 447, 448, 455, 471, 490, 494, 510, 550, 557, 573, 577, 579, 587, 603, 614, 622, 626, 628, 633, 642, 690, 698, 699. *See* Bristol.
Merchant Adventurers, Charter of, 577.
Merchant Staplers, *see* Staplers.
Merchants of the Stillyard, *see* Stillyard.
Merchant Strangers, 182, 219, 223, 247, 257, 259, 292, 294, 299, 313, 324-326, 421, 435, 503, 510, 603, 613, 696. *See* London. Strangers.
Merchant Strangers, Hosting of, 621.
Merchants, Bonds of, 90, 91, 182, 185.
Merchants, *see* Spain.
Merden, Manor of, 272, 424, 592.
Mere Merchants, Company of, 619, 620.
Meredith, William, 566.
Mereworth, 56, 58, 59, 61.
Mericke, Lewis Ap Owen Ap, 456.
Merioneth, 264, 301, 361.
Merionethshire, 486.
Merley, Nicholas, 149.
Merlin, The, 554.
Merrivall, ..., a Bankrupt, 695.
Mersey, East, 116, 386.
Mershe, John, 101, 235-238, 241, 285, 308, 317, 390, 392, 393, 412, 510, 550.
Merton College, (Oxford,) 166, 177, 195, 201, 394.
Mervyn, Sir John, 139.
Merynge, Sir William, 333.
Message, *see* Parliament.
Messengers, 362, 569, 576, 598, 599, 611, 622, 626, 698.
Messengers, Charges of, 534.
Meta Incognita, Land, 589, 608.
Metcalf, Reginald, 402, 628, 657, 665, 669, 670.
Meteor, a fearful one, 504. *See* Comet.
Mettam, ..., 681.
Meux, Monastery of, 119.
Mews, The, 48, 576.
Mey, (or May, Maye,) Dr. William, 11, 143; proposed for York, 154.
Meye, John, 382.
Meye, Richard, 500.
Meynell, Robert, 122, 188.
Michael, The, 546, 556, 573, 618.
Michelgrove, 276.

Michell, Humfrey, 85, 459, 506, 530, 638, 681.
Michelot, William, 508.
Michelson, Arthur, 595.
Middelmore, (or Middlemore,) Henry, 430, 444, 490, 682.
Middelmore, John, 653.
Middelmore, Robert, 682.
Middelmore, William, 652, 653, 682.
Middelmore, *see* Mydlemore.
Middle Temple, The, 407, 428, 443, 454, 569.
Middleburgh, 258, 289, 577.
Middleham, Stewardship of, 92.
Middlemore, *see* Middelmore, Midlemore, Mydlemore.
Middlesex, 40, 98, 119, 122, 129, 148, 230, 255, 338, 346, 363, 377, 411, 426, 432, 441, 442, 487, 526, 534, 546, 594, 630, 643, 649, 679.
Middlesex, Alehouses in, 570.
Middlesex, Clerk of the Peace of, 649.
Middlesex, Justices of, 651.
Middlesex, Receiver of, 119.
Middlesex, Sheriffs of, 346, 521.
Middleton, or Milton, (Kent,) Manor of, 272, 303, 424, 537, 538, 592, 626. *See* Milton.
Middleton, Parsonage of, 485.
Middleton, School at, 431.
Middleton, Mr., 611.
Middleton, William, 47.
Middleton Cheney, Rectory of, 171.
Midlemore, Robert, 366.
Might, Thomas, 464, 626.
Milan, 66, 504, 659.
Milcote, 237.
Mildenhall, Manor of, 142, 503.
Mildmay, Henry, 372.
Mildmay, Mr., 95, 351.
Mildmay, Thomas, 157.
Mildmay, Sir Thomas, 418, 686.
Mildmay, Sir Walter, 4, 26, 97, 99, 118, 138, 162, 164, 170, 177, 198, 225, 232, 248, 250, 254, 273, 283, 289, 290, 295-297, 306, 309, 310, 324, 343, 351, 370, 400, 401, 407, 409, 410, 417, 421, 428, 429, 434, 455, 476, 491, 492, 495, 499, 515, 566, 587, 600, 613, 616, 638, 650, 667.
Milford, 498.
Milford Haven, 267, 538, 539, 695.
Military, *see* Army, Ordnance, Musters.
Military service, 479.
Militia, The, 579. *See* Musters.
Milk Street, 447.
Mill Park, 63.
Milles, Robert, 695.
Millgate, 580.
Milling, Rowland, 87.
Mills, (or Mylls), Francis, 483, 484, 486, 487, 499, 500.
Milner, John, 89.
Milton, (Oxfordsh.,) 524.
Milton in Cleveland, Manor of, 107.

Milton, (or Mylton, Middleton in Kent). 136, 144, 159, 171, 309. *See* Middleton.
Milton, Hundred of, 460.
Milwarde, Thomas, 697.
Mina, Journey of, 74.
Minehead, 409.
Mines—Alum, Mineral, and Battery works, &c. 180, 244, 245, 250-261, 266, 270, 272, 274-280, 282-284, 287-292, 294, 298, 300-303, 305, 307, 310-312, 315, 317-320, 322, 330, 376, 395, 397, 398, 408, 409, 424, 436, 438, 440, 443, 457, 542, 612, 673, 676, 688.
Mines, Draining of, 509, 598.
Mines Royal, Farming of, 688.
Minion, The, 215, 247, 329.
Ministers, Increase of Learning in, 699.
Minories, The, 169, 195, 196, 230, 297, 416, 545.
Minors, *see* Legacies.
Minster in Sheppey, Manor of, 445, 469, 537.
Mint Affairs, (Bullion, Coinage, &c.,) 3, 4, 7, 19, 30, 52, 59, 60, 77, 97, 110, 114, 119, 156, 159-166, 170, 176, 177, 182, 197, 204, 232, 256, 259, 260, 265, 288-291, 305, 306, 339, 363, 367, 385, 406, 407, 410, 413, 415, 416, 431, 432, 436, 438-440, 457, 491, 510, 533, 582, 613, 616, 686, 700. *See* Bristol. Coin.
Mint, Clerk of the, 703.
Mint, Graver of the, 476.
Mint, Officers of the, 114, 232, 290, 291, 407, 413, 416, 431, 432, 438, 440, 446, 457, 472, 510, 694.
Mint, Moneyers of the, 491.
Mint, Treasurer and Comptroller of, 97, 133, 232, 353, 432, *see* Pekham.
Mint, Warden of the, 52, 510, 559, 613.
Mitchell, Humphrey, 72, 73.
Mizes, Collector of, 384.
Mochelney, Manor of, 381.
Modbury, 180.
Mohun, William, 451.
Molins, Mr., 542.
Molins, William de, 612.
Mollineux, *see* Molyneux.
Molyneux, Alice, 321.
Molyneux, Anne, 321.
Molyneux, Edmond, 195.
Molyneux, Emery, 399.
Molyneux, Francis, 379.
Molyneux, Jane, 321.
Molyneux, John, 321, 322.
Molyneux, Mr., 379.
Molyneux, Sir Richard, 279, 281, 321.
Mompesson, Christopher, 58.
Monasteries, Act concerning, 517.
Monbary, Robert, 231.
Mondet, Martin, 696.
Money, Foreign, 140.
Money, Foreign Loans of, *see* Loans.
Money, *see* Coin, Mint, Pyx.
Monkhill, *see* Buckhurst.

Monmouth, 596, 617.
Monmouthshire, 148, 275, 514, 566, 571, 587, 596, 606, 618, 622.
Monmouthshire, Justices of, 639.
Monoux, George, 508.
Monse Awtrey, (or Mohuns Ottery,) 56, 59, 251, 389.
Monson, ..., 39.
Mont, Dr., 205.
Montague, Viscount, *see* Browne.
Monteagle, Lord, *see* Stanley.
Montgomeri, Mons., 214.
Montgomery, Count de, 318.
Montgomeryshire, 361, 487, 588, 634.
Montgomeryshire, Sheriffs of, 686, 688.
Monthall, *see* Mounthall.
Montjoye Place, 363.
Montluc, Mons., 287, 310.
Montmorency, Francis, Duke of, 445, 446.
Montmorency, Mons., 210
Montpellier, Collections for relief of those of the religion, 658.
Monuments, 158, 159.
Moore Hall, Manor of, 702.
Moore, Sir John, 341.
Moorley, Dr., 694.
Moors, The, in Spain, 394.
Moot, (or Motte) Robert, (bell-founder,) 568, 591, 593.
Morchard Episcopi, Manor of, 8.
Mordaunt, Edward, 620.
Mordaunt, John Lord, 225.
Mordaunt, Sir Lewis, 341.
More, Sir Christopher, 21.
More, Gabriel, 266.
More, Mr., 194.
More, Nicholas, 22.
More, Richard, 266, 507.
More, William, 21, 311, 333; Sir William, 426, 440, 561, 694.
Moregate, 569.
Moreley, John, 687.
Moreton, William, 6.
Morgan, Capt., 473.
Morgan, Harrie, 683.
Morgan, Henry, 110, 580.
Morgan, John, 408, 409.
Morgan, Rees, 597.
Morgan, Rice A., 17.
Morgan, Rowland, 532, 543, 617.
Morgan, Walter, 266, 280.
Morgan, William, 532, 543.
Morgan, Sir William, 532, 595.
Morice, Richard, 504, 505.
Morlaix, 140, 205, 215.
Morleston, Hundred of, 124.
Morlewood Park, 40.
Morley, Anthony, 477.
Morley, Edward, 23.
Morley, James, 278, 298, 299, 316, 317.

762 GENERAL INDEX.

Morley, John, 310.
Morley, Lady, 381, 383, 458, 485, 503.
Morley, Lord, see Parker.
Morley, Thomas, 207.
Morley, Wapentake of, 336.
Morrall, ..., 578.
Morren, (or Murren, or Murrey,) John, 125, 307.
Morrice, ..., 641.
Morrice, James, 635.
Morrice, Peter, 512.
Morris, Edward, 578.
Morris, Francis, 364.
Morris, Thomas, 578.
Morrisyn, Mr., 34, 45.
Morrys, William, 174.
Mors, John, 169.
Mortgage, 599.
Mortlake, 15, 315, 618.
Mortmain, Bill of, 411; Purchases in, 636.
Morton, Dr., 651, 694.
Morton, Hundred of, 156, 340.
Morton, Robert, 596.
Morton, Ursula, 596.
Morwin, Peter, 393.
Morys, William, 86.
Moryson, Thomas, 508.
Moscow, Moscovia, see Muscovy.
Motston, Centon of, 143.
Mott, M. la, 515.
Motte, see Moott.
Moulton, Robert, 106.
Moundeford, Osbert, 263.
Mounford, ..., a Jesuit, 547.
Mounson, George, 389.
Mounson, Mr. Justice, 482, 530.
Mount, The, (Cornwall,) 3.
Mount Edgecomb, 370, 451, 615.
Mount, John, 274, 282.
Mount, William, 294, 301.
Mountagu, Sir Edward, 370, 373, 376, 441, 560.
Mountain, Thomas, 407.
Mounte, John, 190.
Mounthall, 162, 203, 299, 384.
Mountjoy, Lady Kath., 436, 440.
Mountjoy, Lord, see Blount.
Mountsbay, 125, 329, 492.
Mountstevynge, John, 199, 206.
Mowsdale, ..., 664.
Moyle, Dame Katharine, 695.
Moyle, Sir Thomas, 59.
Much Bromley, 422.
Much Wenlock, 566.
Muchland, Manor of, 266.
Mug, Mr., 183.
Mullens, Archdeacon, 654.
Muller, Conrad, 239.
Mullyns, Mr., 406.
Munitions, 118, 155, 156, 158. See Arms. Ordnance Stores.
Munster, President of, 398, 406.

Murder, 125, 136, 175, 279, 280, 295, 363, 408, 476, 545, 588, 597, 627.
Murray, ..., 307.
Murray, Earl of, Regent of Scotland, 296, 629.
Murrey, Murren, see Morren.
Muscovy, 178, 179, 243, 616, 695, 701, see Russia.
Muscovy House, 586, 605.
Muscovy, Trade to, 512, 522, 695.
Muscyponte, see Pontemuson.
Musgrave, Cuthbert, 9.
Musgrave, Simon, 330.
Music, Musicians. 68, 146, 179, 270, 318.
Music, Maintenance of Choristers, 703.
Muskets, see Arms.
Musters, Training Soldiers, &c., 3, 4, 6, 7, 12, 53, 93, 94, 97–101, 108, 120–125, 128, 133–136, 138–141, 145, 148, 149, 152–158, 160, 163, 206, 207, 212, 218, 219, 254, 255, 257, 297, 298, 301, 303, 313, 325, 331–345, 349, 350, 352, 357–359, 363, 365–368, 370–380, 390, 405, 450–452, 459–469, 471, 473, 474, 476, 478–480, 482–488, 492, 494, 534, 535, 540–543, 545–549, 554, 555, 557–565, 568–570, 572, 581, 582, 584, 586, 587, 591, 592, 594, 596, 597, 633, 642, 643, 645, 648–666, 668, 673, 675, 678–681, 684, 689, 693. See Harquebusiers.
Musters, Commissioners for, 476, 551, 580, 632, 639, 643, 646, 663.
Musters, Instructions for, 331, 371, 476, 539, 590, 689, 690.
Mutford, Hundred of, 452.
Muye, Madame de, 314.
Mychell, John, 317.
Myckley, Rowland, 436.
Myddleton, Arthur, 475.
Myddleton, see Milton.
Mydelmore, George, 682.
Mydlemore, Mr., 512.
Mydwinter, John, 217.
Mylle, George, 264.
Mylliton, Mr., 389.
Mylls, see Mills.
Mylton, see Milton.
Mymms, Parish of, 10.
Mynde, John à, 61.
Mynge, John, 611.
Myrtle trees, 198.

N.

N......, B., 457.
N......, John, 173.
N......, Nicholas, 173.
N......, V., 457.
Namptwich, Hundred of, 122.
Namur, 67.

GENERAL INDEX. 763

Naples, 66, 172, 281.
Napper, ..., 484.
Napper, William, 490.
Narrow Seas, The, 15, 92–94, 96, 97, 102, 104–106, 112, 203, 205, 298, 394, 505, 526, 640.
Narve, The, 237, 246, 523.
Nash, Richard, 539.
Nassau, Count Lewis (or Lodowick) of, Prince of Orange, 313, 320, 413, 417, 426, 466, 522, 527.
Nation, State of the, 334, 358, 363, 364, 387, 388, 391, 402, 444, 450, 478, 496, 527, 555, 587, 611, 665. *See* Defence.
Naturalization, Letters of, 135.
Naval Stores, 480, 636, 640, 655.
Navarre, King of, 179, 209, 211.
Navarre, Queen of, 378, 386.
Naves, Marquis de les, 62.
Navigation, Maintenance of, 409, 412, 567, 697.
Navy, Naval Affairs, &c., *see* Admiralty.
Navy, Clerk of the, 703.
Navy, Comptroller of the, 526.
Navy, Expenses of the whole Navy, 670.
Navy, Maintenance of, 518.
Navy, Treasurer of the, 566, 627, 634.
Nawnton, (or Naunton,) ......, 27–31.
Neale, Mr., 269.
Neasborough, Hundred of, 250, 374.
Nedeham, ..., 470.
Nedeham, Henry, 578.
Nedeham, George, 258, 289–292, 294, 298, 300, 315, 317, 319, 320, 397.
Negroes, 299.
Negus, Edward, 661.
Nele, Robert, 325.
Nelson, Roger, 600.
Neptune, The, 498.
Nepyvila, *see* Brisa.
Nesbet, ..., 150.
Nesle, Marquis de, 135, 136, 248.
Ness, Wapentake of, 124, 694.
Netherlands, Netherlanders, *see* Flanders.
Nettlested, Manor of, 165.
Nevel, Sir John, 476.
Nevell, or Nevill, George, 379, 418, 650.
Nevell, (or Nevill,) Sir Henry, 35, 152–157, 243, 344, 345, 366, 387, 430, 467, 561, 643.
Nevell, Sir Thomas, 334, 343.
Nevell, *see* Nevyll.
Nevill, ..., 48.
Nevill, (or Nevyle,) Catharine, 92, 93.
Nevill, Charles, Earl of Westmoreland, 261, 324, 335, 336, 346–348, 352, 353, 356, 360, 373, 392, 410, 427, 435, 441, 647, 669, 686.
Nevill, ..., Lord, (son of the above,) 410.
Nevill, Henry, Lord Abergavenny, 57–59, 61, 67, 98, 240, 241, 257, 271, 546, 685.
Nevill, Henry, Earl of Westmoreland, 44, 45, 92, 106, 117, 155, 183, 185, 187, 188, 190, 197, 492.
Nevill, John, Lord Latimer, 92, 93, 193.

Nevill, *see* Nevell.
Neville, Lady Adeline, 410.
Neville, Lady Eleanor, 416, 492. *See* Funerals. Pelham.
Neville, Francis, 363.
Neville, George, 117.
Neville, Sir John, 360.
Neville, Lady Mary, 410.
Neville, Richard, Earl of Warwick, 70.
Nevison, Dr. Stephen, 443.
Nevoe, Peter, 624.
Nevyll, Christopher, 323, 324, 356, 411.
Nevyll, Sir Thomas, 323.
New Bark, the, 205.
New College, 186, 403, 454.
New Croydon, (in Brittany,) 577.
New Draperies, Patent for, 594.
New Hall, cum membris, 403.
New Inn, 677.
New Park, 397, 496.
New Romney, 174, 254, 611. *See* Romney.
New Sarum, 121, 455, 665. *See* Salisbury.
New Testament, The, 31, 524; the Rheims, 547.
New Trades, Company for Discovery of, 526, 628, 656.
New Windsor, *see* Windsor.
New Woodstock, 652.
New Year's Gifts, 96, 120, 178.
Newark, Manor of, 511.
Newark on Trent, 31, 63, 349, 351, 352, 356, 360, 362, 379, 650.
Newark, Wapentake of, 333, 379.
Newbury, 153, 243, 248, 340, 395, 542, 550.
Newcastle, 4, 5, 7, 104, 120, 148, 149, 157, 158, 202, 282, 313, 352, 369, 400, 502, 517–519, 529, 530.
Newcastle, Charter of, 623.
Newcastle, Mayor, &c. of, 157, 482, 517, 518, 529, 530, 623.
Newdegate, Francis, 241, 381.
Newdegate, John, 232.
Newdegate, Robert, 232.
Newdigate, John, 226.
Newdigate, Mr., 233.
Newe, Edyth, 456.
Newe, William, 456.
Newenden, 202.
Newfoundland, 554, 565, 641.
Newgate Prison, 179, 224, 701.
Newhall, 171, 173, 174, 179.
Newhaven, (in France,) 21, 29, 76, 77, 79, 106, 203, 205–220, 223–230, 247, 295, 464, 633, 693.
Newill, Mr., 636.
Newington, 192.
Newington Barrow, Manor of, 468.
Newington Green, 380.
Newlande, James, 309.
Newlands, 276, 288–290, 298.
Newport, 209, 532, 696.
Newport, (Flanders,) 239.

GENERAL INDEX.

Newport, Hundred of, 376.
Newport, (Medine. I. of Wight) 144, 394.
Newport, Richard, 95.
Newport, Sir Richard, 339.
Newton, 617.
Newton Feres, 562.
Newton, Mr., 186.
Nicholas, Sir Ambrose, 523.
Nicholas, Thomas, 635.
Nicholls, see Nycoolls.
Nichols, William, 585.
Nicholson, Edmund, 145.
Nicholson, Otho, 28.
Nicolas, Sir Harris, 461.
Nicols, Philip, 683, 684.
Nivelt, M. de, 432.
Nobility, Lists of, 613.
Noble, William, 459, 498.
Noblemen attainted, 119.
Nonconformity, 285, 293, 687.
Nonnius, Lodovicus, 115.
Non-residence, Licence for, 702.
Nonsuch, 136, 252, 289.
Norborough, 22.
Norbrook, ..., 319, 320.
Nore, The, 648.
Norfolk, 21, 22, 85, 98, 99. 111, 120, 122, 141, 148, 184, 214, 225, 227–229, 261–263, 283, 299, 325, 342, 350, 363, 367, 369, 370, 372–374, 385, 388, 390, 399, 402, 413– 415, 449, 451, 452, 463, 467, 476, 480, 482, 491, 507, 540, 548, 555, 558, 562, 571, 574, 575, 578, 585, 610, 616, 618, 619, 624, 627, 628, 643, 644, 650, 653, 659, 678, 686.
Norfolk, Alehouses, &c. in, 558.
Norfolk, Duchess of, 234, 299.
Norfolk, Duke of, see Howard.
Norfolk, Justices of, 642, 652.
Norfolk, names of Freeholders and Gentlemen, 659.
Norfolk, Sheriff of, 433.
Norfolk, Vice-Admiral of, 22, 388.
Norgate, Dr. Robert, 554, 555, 671, 683, 684.
Norham Castle, 176, 241.
Norman Cross, Hundred of, 430.
Norman, Thomas, 513.
Normandy, 76, 210, 212, 276, 494, 554, 619, 701, 702.
Normanton, 274.
Normanton, ..., 43.
Norreys, ..., 307.
Norreys, Henry, 207.
Norreys, (or Norreis, Norris,) Sir Henry 280, 300, 330, 331, 394; Lord Norreys, 512, 516, 523, 631, 690, 703.
Norris, ..., 243.
Norris, Capt., 635.
Norris, John, 208.
Norris, Sir John, 432.
Norris, Lady, 639.
Norris, Lord, 520.
Norris, Mrs., 146.

Norris, (or Norrys,) William, 639 684, 696.
Norroy King at Arms, see Flower.
Norryce, John, 110.
Norrys, Mr., 107.
Norrys, Richard. 610.
North, ..., 314.
North, The, see Borders, Rebellion.
North East, Voyage of Discovery, 656.
North, Sir Edward, 4, 9, 26, 29.
North Foreland, 254, 330, 528.
North, George, 270, 271.
North, Sir John, 447.
North, Lord President and Council of the, 131, 193, 471, 537, 538, 580, 595, 692.
North, Mr. 672.
North Marches, see Borders.
North Rode, Manor of, 593.
North, Sir Roger, 127; Lord North, 270, 338, 447, 459-461, 483, 485, 507, 539, 549, 600, 601, 618, 627, 675, 690.
North Seas, The, 2, 112, 253, 513.
North-west passage, or Voyage of, 546, 559, 567, 571–573, 581, 586, 590, 602, 603, 606, 608, 616, 621, 623.
North-west Passage, see Furbisher. Voyages.
Northallerton, 656.
Northampton, Borough of, 36, 122, 250, 345, 356, 414, 584.
Northampton, Alehouses, &c., 563.
Northampton, Assizes, 629.
Northampton, Church of, 414.
Northampton, Marchioness of, 62, 239, 250, 253, 259.
Northampton, Marquis of, see Bourchier, Parr.
Northampton, Mayor of, 584.
Northamptonshire, 21, 31, 36, 51, 52, 89, 101, 122, 154, 157, 162, 171, 215, 231, 250, 273, 323, 334, 343, 345, 346, 364, 366, 368, 370, 373–377, 417, 421, 422, 425, 510, 541, 545, 564, 566, 576, 677.
Northamptonshire, Alehouses in, 564.
Northamptonshire, Justices of, 638.
Northamptonshire, Sheriff of, 441, 519.
Northaw, 462.
Northborne, Manor of, 535.
Northborowe, Manor of, 162.
Northchurch, Parsonage of, 169, 233.
Northen, ..., 695.
Northstowe, Hundred of, 430.
Northumberland, 171, 222, 252, 282, 335.
Northumberland, Countess of, 360, 366, 381, 391, 396, 461, 485, 515, 516, 524, 525, 527.
Northumberland, Duke of, see Duddeley.
Northumberland, Earl of, see Percy.
Northwich, 122.
Northwich, Hundred of, 6, 122.
Norton, ..., 497.
Norton, Sir Anthony, 60.
Norton, Christopher, 368, 370, 372.
Norton Conyers, 411.
Norton, Edward, 144.
Norton, Eleanor, 136.

Norton, Francis, 411.
Norton, Sir George, 635.
Norton, Lady, 258.
Norton, Mr., 637.
Norton, Marmaduke, 368, 372, 409.
Norton Park, 101.
Norton, Richard, 367, 400, 411; Sir Richard, 662.
Norton, Samuel, 635.
Norton, Thomas, 136, 144, 159, 171, 272, 368, 372.
Norton, William, 360, 368, 372, 407, 409.
Nortons, The, 356, 372.
Norton Ferris, Manor of, 96.
Norwich, 15, 22, 157, 159, 171, 190, 231, 234, 267, 291, 302, 318, 329, 342, 350, 369, 377, 381, 385, 390, 410, 433, 435, 451, 459, 463, 482, 488, 496, 531, 540, 548, 558, 562, 579, 585, 600, 602, 604, 613, 616, 653, 661, 665.
Norwich, Bishop of, *see* Hopton, Parkhurst. Freke.
Norwich, Bishoprick of, 329, 562.
Norwich Castle, 397, 469.
Norwich, Chancellor of, 446, 601, 602, 604, 606, 607.
Norwich, Cordwainers Company in, 579.
Norwich, Dean and Chapter of, 303.
Norwich, Mayor, &c., 488, 623, 653.
Norwich, Prebendaries of, 393.
Norwich, Strangers in, 410.
Norwood, (in Kent,) 272.
Norwood, Richard, 44.
Nottingham, 342, 346, 350, 352, 353, 375, 376, 379, 380, 384.
Nottingham, Bishop of, 371.
Nottingham, Sheriff of, 418.
Nottingham, Suffragan of, 338.
Nottinghamshire, 111, 120, 140, 148, 202, 332, 333, 339, 346, 347, 350, 367, 368, 373, 375, 376, 379, 415, 418, 423, 511, 563, 569, 650, 660, 664.
Nottinghamshire, Alehouses in, 564.
Nottinghamshire, Justices of, 638.
Nottinghamshire, Sheriff of, 617.
Nowell, Alexander, Dean of St. Pauls, 185, 245, 274, 382, 434, 438–440, 444, 445, 497, 514, 590, 600, 618.
Nowell, Lawrence, Dean of Lichfied, 393.
Nowell, Mr., 211, 213.
Nowell, Robert, 431, 635.
Nun-Apleton, Manor of, 193.
Nuncio, *see* Rome.
Nunnyngton, Manor of, 191.
Nuns, House of, in Stamford, 89.
Nutt, ..., 81.
Nycholson, Laurens, 630.
Nycoolls, Dr. Degory, 552, 605, 606, 608.
Nycoolls, Mrs., a scolding wife, 608.

O.

Oatlands, 10, 30, 35, 382, 552, 554, 666, 672.

Oaths, (Allegiance, Supremacy, &c.,) 33, 115, 119, 137, 150, 167, 180, 239, 281, 303, 321, 430, 489, 536, 539, 566, 571, 582, 617. *See* Justices of Peace.
Obbe River, 253.
Obbyns, ..., 63.
Obits, 134.
Obsequies of the French King, *See* Funerals.
Ocke, Hundred of, 156, 340.
O'Connor, Owen, 314.
Odell, Ann, 128.
Odiham, 502, 599.
Odsey, Hundred of, 374.
Offaley, Lord, *see* Fitzgerald.
Offices, Sale of, 38.
Offington, 4, 31, 124, 393.
Offley, Richard, 532.
Offley, Sir Thomas, 241, 258, 312, 327, 532.
Offlow, Hundred of, 424.
Oglander, George, 144.
Ogle, Richard, 19, 30, 32, 42, 46, 47.
Ogle, Robert Lord, 108.
Ogle, Thomas, 84, 150, 272.
Oglethorpe, Henry, 624.
Oglethorpe, Dr. Owen, 29, 43; Bishop of Carlisle, 127.
Oglethorpe, Thomas, 624.
Oglethorpe, William, 624.
Oils, Manufacture of, 421, 438, 443, 444, 605, 606, 692.
Oking, Dr., 27.
Olain, John, 248.
Old Bailey, The, 88, 126, 378.
Old Jewry, The, 473.
Oldenburgh, Christopher, Count of, 204
Oldensell, Harman Van, 620.
Oldisworthe, W., 637.
Oldkirk, Parsonage of, 32.
Olton, 363.
Olyfe, William, 248.
O'Neil, ..., 269.
Ongar, Hundred of, 380.
Onley, Mrs., 269.
Onslow, Richard, 255, 635.
Onslowe, Fulke, 165.
Orange, Prince of, *see* Nassau.
Oranges, 216, 673.
Orbea, Dominico d', 65.
Orcades, The, 527.
Orders, Book of, 310.
Ordnance, Offices and Officers of, 42, 43, 61, 93, 97, 113, 118, 119, 121, 126, 130, 131, 134, 140, 146, 150, 154, 160, 164, 169, 192, 195, 196, 230, 232, 237, 239, 245, 249, 265, 285, 298, 315, 331, 347, 349, 350, 357, 364, 368, 376, 393, 395, 401, 431, 458, 461, 474, 476, 477, 481, 509, 512, 536, 613, 643, 663, 700.
Ordnance, Clerk of the, 276.
Ordnance, Export of, 534; to Spain, 638.
Ordnance, Iron, Sale of, *see* Iron Ordnance.
Ordnance, Lieutenant-General of, 275, 276, 298, 376, 431, 461.

Ordnance, Master of the, 510, 685.
Ordnance, Manufacture and Sale of, 146, 245.
Ordnance Stores, Munitions, &c., 113, 117, 118, 126, 138, 140–143, 145, 146, 150, 154, 160, 190, 206, 210, 214, 218, 227, 228, 237, 239, 249, 250, 265, 288, 294, 298, 332, 350, 354, 355, 357, 358, 362, 364, 368, 401, 405, 438, 451, 456, 457, 459, 462, 477, 479, 481, 511, 526, 618, 655, 684. *See* Armour. Brass Ordnance.
Ore, brought home by Furbisher, smelting of, 567, 568, 570, 571, 580, 581, 582, 585, 586, 602, 605, 608, 615, 618, 621, 625, 641. *See* Furbisher.
Orford, Mayor of, 699.
Organ makers, 174.
Oriel College, 31.
Original Writs, return of, 510, 702.
Oritz, Peter, 102.
Orleans, 204, 316.
Orleans, Bishop of, 66.
Orlynbury, Hundred of, 519.
Ormesby, Edward, 206.
Ormond and Ossory, Earl of, *see* Butler.
Orphans, *see* London.
Orwell (or Worrall) Park, 37, 47.
Osbaldeston, Edward, 322.
Osbaston, John, 641.
Osberne, John, 441.
Osborne, Edward, 512.
Osborne, Peter, 136, 164, 180, 195, 315, 429, 500, 503, 521, 528.
Osgoodcross, Wapentake of, 336.
Osland, John, 125, 126.
Osmonde, Henry, 460, 591.
Osmyngton, Manor of, 534.
Ossulston, Hundred of, 122, 441.
Oste, *see* Lemborch.
Osterley, 317, 425.
Osterwyck, 84.
O'Sullivan Beer, 251.
Oswestry, Vicar of, 504.
Oswey, Ralph Fitz, 510.
Otford, 39, 40.
Otterden, 528.
Ottery, *see* Monse Ottery.
Ottomanus, Otto Franciscus, 216.
Oulveston, Monastery of, 36.
Ovare, John, 516.
Overton, 118.
Overton, Richard, 219, 220.
Overton, Dr. William, 297, 305, 314, 331, 651; Bishop of Lichfield and Coventry, 651.
Owen, Dr., 113.
Owen, Hugh, 504, 505, 586.
Owen, Mr., 399.
Owen, Mary, 635.
Owen, Michael, 684.
Owen, Richard, 611.
Owen, Robert, 651.
Owen, Thomas, 586, 640.
Oxenbridge, ..., 681.
Oxenbridge, Sir Robert, 102, 117, 287.

Oxenden, William, 99.
Oxford, 11, 27, 28, 62, 177, 186, 187, 192, 193, 195, 237, 331, 371, 394, 449, 459, 464, 465, 498, 548, 559, 567, 648, 663, 664, 691.
Oxford, Bishop of, *see* Goldwell, Curwen.
Oxford, Bishoprick of, 111, 298, 307, 513, 570.
Oxford, Chancellor of, 449. *See* Cecill.
Oxford, Countess of, 50, 252, 364, 685.
Oxford, Earl of, *see* Vere.
Oxford gloves, 683.
Oxford, Mayor, &c. of, 186, 465, 497, 663.
Oxford, Prebends of, 158, 177, 192, 193, 195.
Oxford University, 11, 15, 29, 31–33, 36, 43, 53, 54, 62, 63, 130, 166, 175, 177, 183, 186, 188, 192, 195, 208, 233, 253, 277, 278, 284, 285, 307, 312, 323, 324, 350, 366, 385, 402, 403, 405, 413, 414, 443, 444, 449, 454, 459, 497, 499, 500, 501, 520, 543, 567, 597, 648, 663, 691.
Oxford University, Visitation of, 543.
Oxford, Vice-Chancellor of, 188, 567, 648.
Oxfordshire, 20, 138, 155, 157, 241, 341, 343, 367, 371, 390, 404, 418–420, 422, 423, 425, 428, 439, 440, 464, 474, 488, 509, 510, 523, 548, 559, 662, 664, 676, 690.
Oxfordshire, Feudary of, 241.
Oxfordshire, Justices of, 639, 652.
Oxfordshire, Sheriff of, 419, 636.
Oxfordshire, Surveyor of, 398.
Oyer and Terminer, Commission of, 385, 580, 618.
Ozier, (or Hosier,) Sir Richard, 11.

P.

Pack, Mr., 601.
Packer of Cloths, Office of, 508, 659.
Packets, *see* Post.
Padstow, 502.
Padua, 74, 77, 85, 86, 633, 677.
Page, James, 352.
Page, Thomas, 525.
Paget, Sir Henry, 109; Lord Paget, 291.
Paget, James, 365, 371.
Paget, Thomas Lord, 465, 487, 661, 688.
Paget, Sir William, Secretary of State, 1–3, 11, 15, 19, 24–26; Lord Paget, 27, 29, 30, 39, 47–49, 69, 72; Lord Privy Seal, 74–76, 100, 109, 110, 123, 126, 151, 167.
Pagitt, Mr., 491.
Paineter, H., 376, 629.
Painter, William, 276.
Painter Stainers Company, 596.
Pala Bartholomew, 182.
Palaces, Royal, 131, 136, 143, 189, 244, 262, 470, 498, 610. *See* Windsor.
Palar, John, 475.
Palatine, Count, 205, 213.
Palavicini, Horatio, 587.
Pallady, Anne, 174.

GENERAL INDEX. 767

Palmer, Andrew, 506, 617.
Palmer, Henry, 479, 522, 525, 671.
Palmer, Sir Henry, 105.
Palmer, John, 84.
Palmer, Katherine, Abbess of Sion, 701.
Palmer, Mr., 10, 605.
Palmer, Sir Thomas, 542-544.
Palmes, Margaret, 369.
Palsgrave, The, 502, 505.
Panswyke, 294.
Panton, Emme, 392,
Papal Bulls, *see* Bulls.
Paper, Importation of, 611.
Papists, Roman Catholics, 31, 74, 96, 127, 163, 173, 174, 183, 201, 281, 317, 321, 382, 388, 391, 395, 396, 405, 410, 426, 450, 467, 470, 486, 492, 547, 549, 559, 565, 566, 568, 576, 588, 627, 640, 641, 644, 646, 647, 649, 667, 668, 676, 678, 682, 689, 690, 691, 693, 696, 701. *See* Roman Catholics.
Papists, a Prison for, at Battersey, 672.
Papists, Receivers of, 703.
Papists, Return of, into England, 703.
Papworth, Hundred of, 430.
Par, Alan, 383.
Pardon Churchyard, 39.
Pardons, 2, 471, 473, 476, 496, 594, 702. *See* General Pardon.
Parham, *see* Willoughby.
Paris, 173, 178, 179, 181-185, 187-189, 193-196, 198-201, 211, 240, 364, 494, 641, 653, 659, 660, 666, 669, 676, 677, 683.
Paris, Provost of, 237.
Paris Garden, 595.
Parish Churches, Number of, 513.
Parkar, Dr., 126.
Parkar, Thomas, 171.
Parke, Mr., 359.
Parker, ..., 60.
Parker, Edward, Lord Morley, 665, 686.
Parker, Harry, Lord Morley, 25, 153, 356, 380, 381, 383, 391, 395, 397, 458, 488, 494, 500.
Parker, John, 616, 690.
Parker, Matthew, 5, 40, 123, 126 ; Archbishop of Canterbury, 134, 135, 138, 141-144, 150, 161, 170, 178, 179, 183, 184, 194, 195, 209, 229, 238, 240, 241, 260, 264, 273, 276, 283, 284, 297, 300, 310-312, 314, 317, 319, 497.
Parker, Sir Philip, 601, 604, 617, 699.
Parker, Roger, 337.
Parker, Thomas, Lord Morley, 686.
Parker, William, 389, 409, 411, 415, 665.
Parkers, Manor of, 41.
Parkhurst, John, Bishop of Norwich, 329, 350, 393, 509.
Parkinson, ..., 250.
Parkinson, James, 457.
Parkinson, Mr., 317.

Parliament, 12, 14, 31, 37, 38, 49-51, 65, 69, 70, 96, 98-100, 107, 108, 110, 116-118, 120, 121, 127, 129, 142, 143, 212, 213, 215-218, 220, 222, 278, 280-284, 286, 298, 363, 409-414, 441-444, 447, 462, 467, 514, 516, 519, 520, 536, 601, 617, 622. *See* Lords, House of. Peerage.
Parliament, Clerks of, 119, 488, 519.
Parliament, Peers of, 663.
Parliament, Records of, 290, 292.
Parliament, Reformations in, 517.
Parliament, State of Bills in, 517-520.
Parmenter, Robert, 310.
Parr, Catharine, Queen Dowager, 3, 5, 8, 9, 11, 13, 21.
Parr, William, Marquis of Northampton, 5, 13, 21, 36, 41, 66, 100, 121, 141, 154, 168, 239, 346, 370, 375, 376.
Parr, William, Lord Parr of Horton, 31, 52.
Parratt, *see* Perrot.
Parris, Humphrey, 140.
Parrott, Stephen, 535.
Parry, Mr., 669.
Parry, Mrs. Blanch, 146.
Parry, Lady, 294.
Parry, Thomas, 13, 14, 23, 28, 29, 45, 116; Sir Thomas, 128, 137, 152-157, 161 162, 173.
Parry, Thomas, (son of the above,) 173.
Parry, Thomas, 504, 505.
Parsonages, impropriate, 623.
Parsons, (or Persous,) Robert, the Jesuit, 636, 651, 691, 693.
Parteriche, William, 323.
Partrich, ..., the Goldsmith, 421.
Partridge, Affabell, 161.
Partridge, Edward, 276.
Partridges, 142, 149.
Partrych, William, 671.
Parvish, ..., 633.
Passage at the Ports, 115, 327, 331, 520. *See* Dover.
Passports, 146, 308, 373.
Pastimes, *see* Drama, Masks.
Paston, 342.
Paston, Clement, 373, 390.
Paston, William, 342 ; Sir William, 659.
Pate, Richard, Bishop of Worcester, 94, 101.
Pate, Richard, (Recorder of Gloucester,) 408, 441.
Patrons, Right of, 447.
Patten, William, 688.
Patteson, Mr., 300.
Patterdale, Parsonage of, 637.
Paulet Family, The, 602.
Paulet, Lord Chidiock, 101, 105, 117, 127, 207, 287, 348.
Paulet, John, Lord Saint John, 91, 99, 103, 106, 108, 113, 153, 163, 206, 227; Second Marquis of Winchester, 439, 453, 474, 534.
Paulet, Lady, 562.
Paulet, Marchioness of, 597.

GENERAL INDEX.

Paulet, Thomes Lord, 483, 602.
Paulet, William, Lord St. John of Basing, 4, 11, 24; Earl of Wiltshire and Lord Treasurer, 33; First Marquis of Winchester, 35, 48, 51, 54, 58, 65, 90, 92, 93, 102, 104, 105, 108, 113, 117, 118, 131–133, 135–141, 145, 147–150, 153, 154, 159, 161–164, 170, 171, 174, 175, 178, 180–182, 187, 189, 193–198, 205–208, 211, 212, 219, 222, 224, 225, 227, 230, 231, 234, 237, 239–245, 247, 248, 252, 254, 257, 258, 260, 261, 264, 269, 271–273, 276–279, 283, 289, 290, 296–300, 306, 307, 309, 311, 312, 314, 315, 317, 320, 322–324, 351, 352, 361, 362, 365, 371, 375, 382, 392, 399, 400–402, 431, 432, 435, 439.
Paulet, William, Third Marquis of Winchester, 534, 597, 649, 656.
Paulet, Dame Winifred, 534.
Paulett, see Poulet, Powlett.
Pauls Belchamp, 369.
Paulscray, 124.
Paul's Wharf, 527.
Pauncy, The, 2, 93.
Pavillions, see Tents.
Pawlett, (or Poulet,) Sir Hugh, 12, 37, 85, 91, 93, 123, 132, 140, 213, 310, 340, 372, 462, 590.
Pawnbrokers. Plan for establishing, 410.
Paycok, Robert, 6.
Payne, John, 41, 55, 203.
Payton, John, 628.
Peace, 115, 239, 242, 309, 387, 388, 437.
Peace, Clerks of the, 500, 685.
Peace, Justices of, see Justices.
Pear Trees, 97.
Pearne, see Perne.
Pearse, Captain, 600.
Pecke, ..., 39, 509.
Peckham, Sir George, 475, 690, 695.
Pecock, Laurence, 546.
Pecocke, Thomas, 125.
Pedmersh, 697.
Peerage, Claims of, 677, 687.
Peerage, The, 202, 410, 432, 440–442.
Peers, Lists of, 50, 303.
Peerse, John, 76, 79.
Peirson, William, 618.
Peke Forest, 502.
Pekham, Sir Edmund, Treasurer of the Mints, 8, 16, 18, 19, 30, 35, 51, 60, 161.
Pekham, Henry, 64, 78, 81–84.
Pekham, Sir Robert, 82.
Pelham, Lady Eleanor, see Neville.
Pelham, John, 640.
Pelham, Mr., 325, 484.
Pelham, William, 298, 303, 354, 395, 431, 461, 486, 492, 585; Sir William, 637, 699.
Pelham, William, 699.
Pelican, The, 501, 551, 554.
Pellowe, John, 180.
Pelts, see Skins.

Pembroke, 495, 498, 539, 663.
Pembroke, Countess of, 367, 501, 503.
Pembroke, Earl of, see Herbert.
Pembroke Hall (Cambridge), 17, 186, 298, 391, 493, 636.
Pembrokeshire, 41, 361, 452, 461, 508, 522, 566, 579, 582, 586, 588, 615.
Pemered (or Pennard) West, Manor of, 41.
Pena, Dr., 408.
Penal Laws, Execution of, 38, 518.
Penance, 377.
Pendennis Castle, 146, 332, 386.
Peniston, Thomas, 491.
Penley, 9.
Penn, ..., 45.
Pennard, see Pemered.
Penne, Thomas, 33.
Pennyston, Thomas, 420.
Penrith, Manor of, 266.
Penrose, John, 583.
Penruddock, George, 140; Sir George, 377, 435.
Penryn, 452.
Pensance, 6.
Penshurst, 3.
Pensions, Pensioners, 56, 104, 468, 470.
Penson, William, Lancaster Herald, 442, 446.
Penwith, Hundred of, 452, 570.
Penye, Paul, 125.
Pepin, Jehan, 641.
Peppit, Gilbert, 583, 585.
Percy, Sir Henry, 193, 321, 381, 431, 436, 437; Earl of Northumberland, 688.
Percy, Thomas, Earl of Northumberland, 147, 288–292, 295, 298, 300, 320, 335, 336, 346–348, 352, 353, 356, 360, 361, 364, 366, 373, 376, 381, 427, 431, 435, 441.
Perne, (or Pearne,) Dr. Andrew, 145, 245, 298, 493, 495, 548, 552, 625, 660.
Perroni, Captain Tiberio, 274.
Perrot, Estienne, 323.
Perrot, (Parratt, Parrot, Perot,) Sir John, 11, 63, 266, 368, 388, 398, 402, 406, 414, 454, 499, 522, 537–539, 541, 552, 590, 591, 593, 615, 629, 631, 636, 695.
Perrot, Water of, 372.
Perrott, William, 554.
Pershore, 557.
Persia, 246.
Persons, see Parsons.
Perwicke, Humfrey, 321.
Pet, Arthur, 656.
Peter, ..., a Trumpeter, 310.
Peter, John, 217, 686.
Peterborough, 118, 162, 164, 206, 334, 529, 561, 566.
Peterborough, Bishop of, see Pole, Scambler.
Peterborough, Bishoprick of, 118, 164.
Peterborough Cathedral, 529.
Peterborough, Deanery of, 9.
Peterborough, Dean and Chapter of, 164.
Peter and Paul, The, 499.

GENERAL INDEX. 769

Peterson, John, 251, 403.
Peterson, William, 303.
Petite, Nicholas, 612.
Peto, Mr., 72.
Petre, Robert, 503, 665.
Petre, Sir William, Secretary of State, 2, 4, 15, 19, 24, 25, 32-35, 37, 38, 49, 51, 54, 56-61, 65, 66, 68-72, 74, 81, 123, 154, 160, 168, 173, 212, 225, 230, 254, 273, 306, 457.
Pett, Mr., 630, 668.
Pett, Peter, 634.
Petty Bag, Clerks and Office of, 165, 431.
Petworth, 68.
Pevensey, 331, 332.
Pevensey Castle, 8.
Pevensey, Rape of, 264, 451.
Peveraro, Geronimo, 76.
Pewsham Forest, 62.
Pewterer, The Queen's, 556.
Pexall, Richard, 86.
Peyto, Francis, 87.
Pheere, Thomas, 635.
Phelips, Fr., 266.
Phibson, Captain, see Phipson.
Philip II., Prince, and King of Spain, 55-60, 62-67, 69-78, 80, 82-85, 87, 88, 90-94, 96, 98,-106, 108, 113, 134, 135, 297-299, 303, 323, 324, 326, 329, 362, 392, 394, 405, 422, 427, 435, 444, 500, 525, 565, 578, 611, 633, 647, 659, 665, 690, 692-694.
Philip and Mary, The, 331, 367.
Philipson, William, 649.
Phillipps, Robert, 110, 509.
Phillips, Avery, 394.
Phillips, David, 454.
Phillips, Fabian, 540, 543, 597, 627.
Phillips, Harry, 597.
Phillips, Henry, 434.
Phillips, John, 168, 498.
Phillips, Watkyn, 593.
Philoponus, see Windebank.
Philosopher's Stone, The, 525.
Philpot, Mr., 271.
Phipson, George, a pirate, 552, 618.
Phoenix, The, 96, 210, 213, 228, 323.
Physic, Doctors of, 531.
Physicians, College of, 304, 403, 531.
Picardy, 318.
Pickering, Launcelot, 391.
Pickering, Mr., 42, 48.
Pickering, Richard, 301.
Pickering, Sir William, see Pykerynge.
Pickering Lythe, Wapentake of, 336.
Pickringe, see Pyckering.
Pickworth, 63, 191, 198. See Pyckeworth.
Piddle Mills, 557.
Pider, Hundred of, 452.
Piers, John, Bishop of Rochester, 543, 559, 561, 646, 690.
Piers, Captain William, 303.

Pigeon, John, 108.
Pigna, John Battista, 152.
Pilcher, ..., 693.
Pilkington, Francis, 547.
Pilkington, James, 5 ; Bishop of Winchester, 147, 149; Bishop of Durham, 163, 175, 176, 187, 188, 241, 272, 273, 335, 338, 410, 426.
Pilkington, John, 547.
Pilkington, Leonard, 186.
Pilkington, Mrs., 579.
Pillafowdre Haven, 292.
Pilleton, James, 440.
Pillory, The, 35, 47, 98, 99, 566, 636, 669.
Pilotage, 400.
Pinchbeck, Mr., 297.
Pinchebeck, Lordship of, 19, 29, 30, 32, 42, 46, 47, 409.
Pinder, see Pynder.
Piper, Herman, 103.
Piper, William, 669.
Pipers. See Drama.
Pirates. Piracy, 7, 10, 16, 17, 44, 85, 86, 136, 164, 169, 176, 203, 219, 226, 236, 242, 244-246, 251, 254, 259, 267, 274, 276, 317, 324, 326, 331, 332, 341, 343, 378, 384, 399, 408, 417, 427, 429, 432, 437, 441, 457, 477, 481, 482, 494, 498, 501-505, 512, 517, 522, 528, 529, 532, 536-541, 543, 546, 547, 549, 552, 554, 556-558, 562, 569-572, 577, 579-590, 595, 596, 599, 604, 606, 608-611, 615-620, 622-624, 627, 628, 631-633, 642, 647, 656, 685, 687, 693, 696, 698, 701.
Pirates, Commissioners of, 555, 564, 566, 642, 643, 656.
Pirates, Lists of Aiders and Abettors in various Counties, 579, 590.
Pirgo, 151, 235, 240, 595.
Pirgo, Lands of, 128.
Pirry, Martin, 51.
Pirton, Edmund, 545.
Pirton, Hundred of, 425.
Pistolets (Money), 159.
Pistor, William, 586.
Pitt, Richard, 656.
Pitts, William, 689.
Pius V., Pope, 330, 651, 691.
Pix, see Pyx.
Plague, The, 31, 33, 39, 85, 86, 106, 122, 183, 226, 227, 229, 231, 233-236, 320, 324, 387-389, 402, 465, 477, 488, 493, 556, 560, 587, 599, 603, 628, 652, 676, 677, 679, 681-683.
Planché, La, 310.
Planishing, Art of, 525.
Plantagenet, Edward, Earl of March, 286.
Plantagenet, Richard, Duke of York, 256.
Playing Cards, 147, 192.
Plays, Players, see Drama.
Plessis, M. de, 466.
Plomclays, Messrs., 608.
Plumley, Robert, 589.
Ploughley, Hundred of, 418, 423, 428.

3 c

GENERAL INDEX.

Plowden, Edmund, 355, 689.
Plowden, Mr., 696.
Ployden, Mr., 307.
Plumbe, Robert, 112.
Plumpton, Parsonage of, 223.
Pluralists, 648.
Pluralities, 32, 282, 405.
Plymouth, 62, 90, 166, 186, 265, 276, 279, 281, 299, 300, 323, 326, 327, 329, 330, 394, 422, 554, 563, 574, 605, 611.
Plymouth, Mayor, &c. of, 14, 392, 605.
Plymouth Road, 394.
Poachers, Poaching, 511, 635.
Pocklington, Manor of, 197.
Poilly, D., 524.
Poisoning, 409, 435.
Poissy, 183, 682, 683.
Poittow, Roger, 554.
Poland, 243, 305, 455.
Poland, Queen of, 77, 82.
Pole, (or Poole,) David, Bishop of Peterborough, 92, 118, 164.
Pole, Sir Giles, 610.
Pole, Reginald, Cardinal, 11, 14, 17, 65-67, 69, 71, 74, 75; Archbishop of Canterbury, 76, 77, 90, 91, 94, 95, 101, 105, 106, 108, 115, 116, 119, 145.
Pollan, Valerand, 36, 37.
Pollard, Sir Hugh, 56.
Pollard, Sir John, 84.
Polsted, Henry, 21.
Polypragmos, 565.
Pomeraye, Andrew, 78.
Pomerland, 628.
Pomery, Sir Thomas, 21, 22.
Pomfret, 104.
Pomfret Castle, see Pontefract.
Pomfrets, Lands of, 640.
Pompart, John, 534.
Ponds, Keeper of the, 458.
Pont, Nowell du, 624.
Pontefract Castle, 352.
Pontemuson, (Muscyponte,) 677, 682.
Ponynges, (or Poynings,) Sir Adrian, 142, 163, 206-208, 212, 218, 221, 225-227, 235, 272, 345, 385, 413.
Pool, Sir Henry, 517.
Poole, 91, 272, 451, 465, 536, 546, 554, 581, 582.
Poole, Arthur, 145.
Poole, Sir Giles, 110.
Poole, Mayor of, 554, 571.
Poole, see Pole.
Pooley, ..., 20.
Poolye, Mr., 587.
Poor, Relief of the, 411, 577
Poor Knights, see Windsor.
Poor Prisoners, see Debtors.
Pope, The, 53, 66, 88, 175, 243, 281, 298, 321, 326, 330, 334, 391, 565, 578, 622, 658, 665, 677, 690. See Pius V. Gregory XIII.
Pope, Anthony, 165.

Pope, Francis, 270.
Pope, Henry, 457.
Pope, John, 103.
Pope, Mr., 30.
Pope, Nicholas, 475.
Pope, Sir Thomas, 101.
Popery, 119, 173, 174, 192, 203, 251, 253, 281, 293, 483, 500, 566, 678; see Church Affairs.
Popham, Alexander, 37.
Popham, George, 666.
Popham, John, 500, 569.
Popish Books, 578, 641, 688, 694.
Popish Priests, 617.
Popish Relics, 524, 578, 652, 682, 700.
Popynjay, Richard, 311, 491, 529, 553.
Porry, Henry, 5.
Port Bonds, 467, 474.
Portenary, ..., 170.
Porter, Anthony, 458.
Porter, Edm., 443.
Porter, William, 235, 237, 309, 414-416, 429, 443, 454, 549.
Portingale, John, 331.
Portington, John, 59.
Portland, Captain of, 91.
Portland, Isle of, 91, 276, 528.
Portland Castle, 487.
Portland Road, 609, 615.
Portrait of Queen Elizabeth, 232.
Ports, Creeks, Havens, and Landing Places, 247, 252, 259-264, 267-269, 282, 480, 513, 562, 563, 570, 574, 581, 582, 587, 588, 590, 610, 618, 642, 694.
Ports, Lists of, and names of Landing Places, 518, 563.
Ports, see Passage.
Portsdown, 154.
Portsdown, Hundred of, 7, 653.
Portsmouth, 1-3, 76, 82, 83, 87, 92, 100-102, 105, 106, 110, 113, 117, 120, 124, 127, 139, 140, 142, 148, 155, 156, 162, 163, 170, 203, 205-222, 224-231, 235, 242, 247, 265, 266, 272, 282, 297, 298, 307, 311, 315, 368, 385, 413, 420, 434, 451, 453, 456, 462, 483, 490, 491, 494, 525, 584, 585, 640, 643, 662, 665, 666.
Portsmouth, God's House at, 242.
Portsmouth, Mayor of, 1.
Portsmouth, Plan of, 576.
Portsmouth Yard, 513, 553, 556. Great fire at, 526-529, 534.
Portugal and Portuguese, 108, 183, 260, 299, 318, 321, 337, 358, 393, 430, 484, 488, 489, 504, 551, 575, 596, 601, 647, 659, 675, 677, 678, 686, 687, 690, 694, 698. See Spain.
Portugal, Ambassador from, 687.
Portugal, King of, 554, 601, 646, 647. See Antonio. Sebastian.
Portugal, Princess of, 260.
Porye, Dr. John, 126, 127, 130, 132.
Post-horses, 96, 362, 612.
Post towns, 478.; List of, 533.

GENERAL INDEX.

Post Office, *see* Posts.
Posts, Post Office, Packets, &c., 85, 86, 113, 214, 216, 286, 306, 326, 327, 478, 641.
Posts, charges of, in Progresses, &c., 599, 631, 637, 677.
Posts, foreign, 625, 703.
Posts, Masters of the, 109, 275, 306, 310, 312–314, 317, 321, 324, 625, 670, 703.
Poterelles, 10.
Potterspury, 101.
Pottery, Manufacture of, 256.
Pottyn, James, 103.
Poulet, Sir Amias, 471, 515.
Poulett, Sir William, 262, 340, 342, 372.
Poulett, *see* Paulet, Pawlet.
Poultry Compter, The, 320; Prisoners in, 667.
Poundage, Rate of, 498, *see* Tonnage.
Poundes, Thomas, 676.
Pountefrett, *see* Pontefract.
Powder, Hundred of, 452, 570.
Powder, *see* Gunpowder.
Powell, Captain, 79.
Powell, Edmund, 436, 471.
Powell, John, 107, 189, 309.
Powell, Dr. Thomas, 694, 699.
Powell, William, 501.
Power, Mr., 293.
Power, Richard, 179.
Powle, Michael, 100.
Powtrell, Nicholas, 122, 418.
Powys, 686.
Poyner, Thomas, 529.
Poynet, John, Bishop of Rochester; Bishop of Winchester, 32, 44.
Poynings, *see* Ponynges.
Præterea, Clause of, *see* Chester.
Prayers, 4, 119, 136, 276, 277, 280, 443, 486. *See* Church Affairs, Common Prayer, Elizabeth.
Preachers, Preaching, 125, 209, 248, 262, 293, 299, 319–322, 605, 687, 699. *See* Colchester.
Preaching Licences, 5, 15, 21, 22, 40, 41, 102.
Prebends, 488, 491, 588.
Precedence for the Lord Protector, 5.
Precedents, 53, 442.
Predy, Thomas, 641.
Predyaux (or Prideaux), John, 57, 105, 106.
Prerogative Court, *see* Canterbury.
Prescot, 680.
Prescott, ..., 272.
Presentations, 447.
Presentments, 519.
Presents, *see* Ambassadors, Christenings, New Years' Gifts.
Pressoir, Martin de, 532.
Prestall, John, 231, 411, 520, 601.
Prestall, Mr., 79.
Prestoll, Mr., 256.
Prestwood, Richard, 140.
Price, Dr. Elis, 586.
Price, John, 636.

Price, William, 367, 373.
Prideaux, *see* Predyaux, Pryceaux.
Priests, disguised, 410.
Primrose, The, 215, 247, 316, 331, 459.
Printers, *see* Queen's Printer.
Printing, 166, 167, 219, 320.
Prise, Gregory, 469.
Prise, Mr., 687.
Prise, Mrs., 687.
Prisoners, 106, 504. *See* the various Prisons.
Prisoners, Employment of, 630.
Prisoners, Lists of, 179, 224, 667, 668.
Prisoners in the Tower, 8, 11, 12, 26, 36, 60, 62, 75, 82, 174–176, 178–180, 188, 200, 201, 206, 230, 235, 241, 257, 259, 272, 275, 372, 385, 387, 408, 408, 409, 414, 415, 422, 433, 435–437, 536, 545, 637, 646.
Prisoners of War, 2, 101, 105, 240, 241, 244, 248.
Prisons, *see* Clink, Compter, Fleet, Gatehouse, Marshalsea, Newgate, Poultry Compter, Tower.
Priuli, Aloisius, 115, 116, 136.
Privateers, 426. *See* Marque.
Privilege, *see* Parliament.
Privy Chamber, 52, 69, 77, 78, 109, 110.
Privy Council, The, 1, 2, 7, 8, 10, 14, 15, 17, 19–27, 30–39, 41, 43–49, 51, 54, 55, 57–62, 65, 70, 72, 73, 75–76, 80, 82, 83, 85, 87, 88, 91, 93, 98, 99–101, 103, 105, 106, 108, 114, 115, 120, 127, 137, 141, 144, 149, 151, 152, 162, 173, 178, 182, 198, 212, 223, 224, 231, 235, 238, 240, 242, 243, 253, 270, 277, 280, 298, 311, 328, 406, 456, 470, 473–477, 481–483, 497, 502, 504, 507, 508, 514, 515, 517, 520–522, 524, 528, 532, 536, 539, 549, 551, 559, 561, 581, 582, 586, 590, 601, 602, 604–608, 615, 617, 619, 622, 626, 631, 634, 639, 643, 646, 649, 657, 661, 665, 668, 674, 676, 678, 681, 689.
Privy Council, Clerks of the, 106.
Privy Councillor, Oath of, 430.
Privy Seal, Keeper of the, 449. *See* Russell, Paget.
Privy Seals, 86, 94, 95, 116, 118, 223, 224, 234, 235, 254, 333, 344, 365, 368–374, 377, 380–383, 386, 387, 389–391, 393, 395, 406, 407, 409, 513.
Privy Signet, clerks of, 548.
Prizes, Prize Goods, &c., 100, 105, 153, 214, 216–218, 386, 434.
Proclamations, 1, 16, 18, 20, 23–26, 29–31, 33, 34, 38, 54, 59, 61, 93, 114, 115, 125, 128, 141, 158, 159, 161, 162, 179, 185, 188, 194, 197, 219, 229, 232, 234, 236, 239, 250, 253, 254, 268, 269, 287, 314, 332, 341, 378, 383, 384, 396, 430, 449, 461, 467, 472, 506, 508, 522, 619, 633, 651, 665, 693.
Procter, Richard, 294.
Proctor, Nicholas, 509.
Proctor, Office of, 605.
Proctors, *See* Arches.

3 c 2

Progresses, 43, 131, 137, 208, 266, 273, 276, 278, 290, 448, 449, 582, 598, 599.
Promoters, 114.
Promotions to Dignities, 1.
Prophecies, Book of, 430.
Protections for Debt, &c., 311, 319, 497, 684, 702.
Protector, The, *see* Seymour.
Protestant Church, 644.
Protestants, 130, 201, 300, 314, 326, 334, 690, 691. *See* Church Affairs.
Provisions, Price of, 511.
Provost, Mr., 293.
Proxies, 553.
Prune, Walter, 68, 74, 75, 86.
Pryce, John, 516.
Prydeaux, Richard, 486.
Prydeaux, Thomas, 486.
Psalms of David, Exposition of, 658.
Psalter, The, *see* St. Austin.
Public expenditure, 44–46, 49, 50, 55, 61, 62, 64, 74, 123, 130-133, 135, 136, 138, 139, 141, 147, 153, 155, 174, 178, 182, 192, 198, 204, 208, 218, 227, 244, 249, 252, 257, 266, 278, 287, 387, 409, 418, 438, 444.
Pudsey, Thomas, 474.
Puitz, *see* Putte.
Pullain, Gillot, 270.
Pullison, Alderman Thomas, 489, 490, 498, 630, 695.
Punter, ..., 638.
Purbeck, Isle of, 473, 546, 581.
Purdewe, John, 398.
Purefay, Arthur, 446.
Purfleet 700.
Purford, 528.
Purgatory, Book of, 307.
Purie, Thomas, 651.
Puritans, The, 470, 560, 698.
Purtton, Robert, 613.
Purvey, John, 224, 371, 458, 474.
Purveyors for the Household, Purveyance, 12, 231, 232, 247, 250, 257, 268, 420, 508, 545, 576, 596, 598, 610, 684, 697.
Putenham, George, 363, 364, 602, 604, 607, 609, 626, 627.
Putenham, Richard, 175, 364, 609.
Putney, 34, 44, 594, 618.
Putte, (or Puitz,) Raphael Vanden, 312-314, 321, 324.
Pwllely, 586.
Pycas, Catherine, 624.
Pyckering, (or Pickringe,) Morris, 667, 690.
Pyckeworth, 36.
Pyckman, Mr., 449.
Pyckrell, John, 125.
Pyder, Hundred of, 570.
Pye, The, in Smithfield, 5.
Pygott, Thomas, 374.
Pykerynge, Lancelot, 425.
Pykerynge, Sir William, 100, 103, 377.
Pynchebek, Geoffrey, 141.

Pynchin, Jo., 418.
Pynder, (or Pinder,) Robert, 402, 549, 568, 583, 591, 592, 594.
Pynynges, Henry, 95.
Pype, Sir Richard, 622.
Pyrford, 503.
Pyrrie, ..., 40.
Pyrryncle Mill, 309.
Pyx, The, 288, 291.

Q.

Quadrant, Improvement in the, 697.
Quarré, *see* Carré.
Queen, *see* Mary, Elizabeth.
Queen of Scots, *see* Mary.
Queen Dowager, *see* Parr.
Queenborough, 99, 118, 301, 399, 484, 486, 503, 516, 648, 650.
Queen's Bench. *see* King's Bench.
Queen's College (Cambridge), 125, 126, 165, 302, 381, 389, 404, 416, 493–495, 535, 595, 616, 617, 643, 644.
Queen's College (Oxford), 175, 177.
Queen's Guards, the, 107, 350, 484.
Queen's Printer, 54, 167, 235, 268.
Questor, Matthew de, 312.
Quinie, Adrian, 654.
Quitting the Realm, 396, 412, 490, 494, 496.

R.

Raby, 92.
Rack, The, *see* Torture.
Radbourne. Manor of, 171.
Radcliffe, Lady, 310.
Radcliffe, Sir John, 456.
Radcliffe, *see* Ratcliffe.
Radclyff, Egremonde, 545.
Radeclyff, Sir Henry, 413, 420, 462, 553, 637, 662, 665, 666, 688.
Radfield, Hundred of, 6, 430.
Radlowe, Hundred of, 123.
Radnor, 195, 570.
Radnor, Forest of, 170.
Radnorshire, 267, 361, 588.
Ragason, James, 90, 91.
Ragler, *see* Constable Ragler.
Ragusa, 90.
Raighlye Park, 487.
Raileton, *see* Rayleton.
Rainbow, The, 576.
Rainolds, John, 685.
Rainsford, Lady, 165.
Raisins, 510.
Ralegh, Walter, 59, 605.
Rampton, Thomas, 60.
Ramridge, Dr. John, 171, 173.
Ramsden, Roger, 392, 393, 415.

Randall, Hugh, 589.
Randall (Randolphe ?), Mr., 599.
Randall, Robert, 169.
Randolph, (or Randoll,) Edward, 63, 65, 224, 228, 237, 243, 245, 255, 275, 276, 625.
Randolph, Mr., 497.
Randolphe, Mrs. Anne, 424.
Randolphe, Thomas, 286, 301, 306, 310, 338, 345, 422, 424, 537, 538, 540, 545, 555, 592, 665, 671, 674, 688, 703.
Randolphe, *see* Randall.
Ransom, 159.
Ranzew, Mouritz, 231.
Rape, Crime of, 175, 177, 392.
Raskell, Lordship of, 190.
Rastall or Rastell, William, 107, 122.
Ratclif, Charles, 547.
Ratcliff, 32, 637.
Ratcliff, Roger, 189.
Ratcliffe, Francis, 703.
Ratcliffe, Henry, Earl of Sussex, 85.
Ratcliffe, Sir Humphrey, 166.
Ratcliffe, Lady, 166, 196, 279.
Ratcliffe, the old Lady, 703.
Ratcliffe, Mr., 373.
Ratcliffe, Thomas, Viscount Fitzwalter, 87; Earl of Sussex, 104, 120, 151, 152, 163, 176, 200, 247, 249, 253, 273, 291, 295, 302, 303, 308, 333, 347, 351–354, 356, 359, 360, 367, 373, 444, 445, 496, 499, 545, 613, 626, 643, 685, 686, 688, 690.
Rauley, *see* Ralegh.
Raurych ? Burchard, alias Dr. Burcott, 567, 571, 580, 584, 585, 615.
Ravenscroft, Henry, 314, 315.
Ravensworth, 425.
Ravile, J., 201.
Rawson, William, 107.
Rayleton, Edward, 568.
Rayleton, Rowland, 591, 593, 594.
Raylton, Gregory, 42, 43, 64.
Rayner, Agnes, 431.
Raynes, Robert, 111.
Raynestrop, Balthazar, 231.
Raynolds Mr., 109.
Raynolds, Robert, 136, 475.
Raynsford, William, 563.
Reade, Captain, 206.
Reade, Cuthbert, 417.
Reade, Mrs. Elizabeth, 509.
Reade, Innocent, 509.
Reade, Mr., 525.
Reade, or Rede, Sir Richard, 33, 35, 103, 460.
Readers, *see* Inns of Court.
Reading, 28, 29, 107, 109, 153, 241, 243, 340, 347, 393, 548, 610, 676.
Reading Abbey, 548.
Reading, Hundred of, 156, 340.
Reall, Tythes of, 97.
Realm, Defence of the, 327, 453, 455, 478, 488, 534, 633, 645, 649, 650, 672, 699. *See* Nation.

Realm, leaving the, 396, 412. *See* Parker.
Rebellion, (Insurrection, Rebels, Sedition, Treason,) 16, 18–26, 35, 36, 44, 48, 56–63, 73, 76–86, 118, 130, 346–356, 358–362, 364, 366–368, 373, 381, 385, 396, 426, 427, 432, 461, 696. *See* Treason.
Rebels, 396, 400, 407, 410, 411, 432, 476, 487. *See* Rebellion.
Rebels Abroad, 450, 669.
Record, Courts of, 250, 479, 533.
Recorder, The, *see* Fletewood.
Recorder, General Office of, 412.
Recorders, 408, 412.
Records, 111, 234, 290, 292, 293, 312, 468, 511, 524.
Recusants, 321, 322, 388, 464, 511, 524, 525, 554, 560–570, 572, 583, 607, 640, 644, 678, 680, 681, 698.
Recusants' Wives, 688.
Redbridge, 653.
Redburn-stoke, Hundred of, 374.
Redcross Street, 495, 684–686.
Rede, Mr. 94.
Rede, William, 30.
Rede, *see* Reade.
Redman, Dr., 17.
Redman, John, 248.
Redman, Mr., 384, 522.
Redreff (Rotherhithe), 590.
Reede, William, 367.
Refiners, 163, 164, 170, 542, 543. *See* Ore.
Refiners, Almain, 164, 170, 197, 252.
Reformation, *see* Religion.
Regency, 65.
Registry, *see* Strangers.
Regrators and Forestallers, 26, 34, 185, 26
Reigate, 256, 440, 542.
Reigate, Hundred of, 135, 419, 423, 440.
Relfe, John, 475.
Relfe, William, 475.
Relics, Popish, *see* Popish relics.
Religion, 520, 539, 552, 637, 693. *See* Church Affairs.
Religion, Articles of, 33, 46, 51, 127, 192, 218, 284, 381, 409.
Religion, Prisoners for, 667, 668, 690, 703.
Religion, Reformation of, 11, 114, 144.
Religion, Uniformity in, 46, 54, 134, 192, 193, 203, 218, 284, 293, 307, 308, 324, 346–357, 360–362, 366, 369, 371, 430, 689.
Religious Houses, 119, 287.
Remsbury, 638.
Rennes, Bishop of, 317.
Reprieve, 516.
Reprisals, *see* Marque.
Repyngton, Hundred of, 124.
Requests Court of, 637.
Requests, Masters of, 51, 103, 248, 701.
Reshton, Edward, 622.
Rest, John de, 99.
Restell, Mr., 33.
Restitution of Temporalities, *see* Temporalities

GENERAL INDEX.

Retainers, 168, 178, 430.
Retz, Marshal de, 689.
Reulx, Pieter de, 227.
Reve, Anthony, 190.
Reve, Mr., 394.
Reve, Thomas, 62.
Revelay, George, 5.
Revell, Nicholas, 200.
Revels and Tents, Office of, 131, 193, 251, 290. *See* Drama.
Revenge, the, 631, 645.
Revenue, 123, 129, 130, 135, 195, 279, 280, 303, 358, 398, 505, 517, 535, 580, 604, 623. *See* Crown, Customs, Loans, Revenues.
Revenue and Finances, Commissioners of, 100, 129.
Revet, William, 514.
Reygate, *see* Reigate.
Reynoldes, Richard, 631, 641.
Rheims, 547, 651, 659. English Seminary at, 624.
Rhine, The, 73.
Rhinehouse, or Rynehousen, 73, 213.
Rhingrave, The, 210.
Rhurnbeck. *See* Martin.
Ricards, alias Fermor, Thomas, 509.
Ricarvile, Mons., 213.
Rich, *see* Ryche.
Richard, John Ap Thomas Ap, 295.
Richards, John, 30.
Richardson, Ferdinand, 511.
Richardson, John, 557.
Richmond, Mary Duchess of, 15.
Richmond. Thomas, 248.
Richmond (Surrey), 18-20, 30, 43, 54, 93, 94, 105, 171, 190, 240, 242, 250, 255, 257, 293, 295, 425, 483, 554, 601, 602, 604-606, 615, 677, 682, 689.
Richmond (York), 44, 295, 400, 563, 668, 671.
Richmondshire, Stewardship of, 92.
Rickmansworth, 514.
Rickthorne, William, 186.
Rickwarth, Matthew, (Sluice Master of Dunkirk,) 630, 668.
Ricot, 504, 631, 676.
Ridalle, Wapentake of, 336.
Ridgewaye, John, 57.
Ridgewaye, Thomas, 608.
Ridley, Nicholas, Bishop of Rochester, 9, 11, 16-18, 22; Bishop of London, 34, 51.
Ridolphi, Roberto, 345, 346, 362, 394.
Rigges, *see* Rygges.
Rigmaiden, John, 322.
Rigsby, James, 420.
Rike, Stephen, 76.
Ringe, Herman, 73.
Riol, Cape, 478.
Riots, 402, 459.
Ripon, 355, 691.
Ripplesmere, Hundred of, 340.
Rise, Griffith, 584.

Rise, Mr., 71.
Risheton, or Riston, Edward, 649, 651.
Rites and Ceremonies, Bill for, 443.
Rithe, Stephen, 404.
Roan, *see* Rouen.
Robbery, 374, 443, 516, 535, 689, 702.
Roberts, David, 543.
Roberts, John, 266, 507.
Roberts, Lewis, 377.
Roberts, William, 540.
Robin Hood's Bay, 211.
Robinson, Mr., (a Clergyman,) 186, 620.
Robinson, Mr., (of the Wine Duties), 419, 429.
Robinson, Richard, 635.
Robinson, Dr. Thomas, 104.
Robinson, Thomas, 285.
Robinson, William, 285.
Robyns, Morgan, 427.
Robynson, Mr., 111.
Robynson, Dr. Nicholas, Bishop of Bangor, 281, 301, 377, 564, 586, 618, 684.
Rochelle, 209, 210, 310, 316, 318, 384, 459, 502, 524, 554.
Rochester, 57, 59, 184, 328, 461, 467, 516, 546, 601, 662, 688.
Rochester, Bishop of, *see* Ridley. Poynet. Scorey. Gest. Piers. Yonge.
Rochester, Bishoprick of, 46, 161, 559, 645.
Rochester Bridge, 184.
Rochester Castle, 202.
Rochester Cathedral, 47, 616.
Rochester, Mayor of, 270, 516.
Rochester, Robert, 48; Sir Robert, 68, 72, 91, 111, 112.
Rochester School, 184.
Rochford, 104, 270, 483.
Rochford, Hundred of, 379, 450, 535, 570.
Rockborne, (or Rokeburne,) 124, 207.
Rockhole, Mr., 395.
Rockingham, (or Rolingham,) 52, 370, 417.
Rockrey, Edmund, 407, 493, 494, 535, 588, 616, 617.
Rode, *see* North Rode.
Rode Heath, 593.
Rodolph, Emperor of Germany, 588.
Rodolphi, *see* Ridolphi.
Rodrigues, Henry, 535.
Roffe, John, 622.
Rogers, ..., 195.
Rogers, Daniel, 471, 681, 685.
Rogers, Sir Edward, 155, 219, 223, 257, 260.
Rogers, Francis, 566.
Rogers, John, 451, 465.
Rogers, Sir John, 58.
Rogers, Mr., 498.
Rogers, Richard, 290.
Rogers, Sir Richard, 566.
Rogers, William, 15-18, 240.
Rogerson, Hugh, 673.
Rogues, *see* Vagabonds.
Rokeburne, *see* Rockborne.

GENERAL INDEX.

Rokeby, Dr., 338.
Rokeby, John, 42.
Rokeby, Rauf, Master of St. Katherine's, 658.
Roke-Savage, 565.
Rolf, Eustace, 585.
Rolfe, William, 108.
Rolingham, *see* Rockingham.
Rolles, Robert, 208.
Rollesley, Henry, 591.
Rolls, The, 14, 111, 173, 292, 408, 442, 578.
Rolls, Master of the, 292, 293, 332, 551, 585. *See* Beaumont. Bowes. Cordell.
Rollstone, Francis, 488.
Rollstone, George, 488.
Roloc, Mr., 701.
Rolvenden, Hundred of, 450.
Romalde, Church, 298.
Roman Catholics, list of, in England, 492. *See* Papists.
Roman coins, 406.
Romans, King of the, 67.
Romborough, Manor of, 490.
Rome, 14, 17, 80, 94, 330, 435, 556, 568, 578, 624, 651, 652.
Rome, Church of, 17, 89, 119, 281, 293, 358, 430, 649, 650, 653.
Rome, English College at, 652.
Rome, Nuncio from, 154, 175.
Romford, 430.
Romney, 554. *See* New Romney.
Romney Marsh, 520, 579.
Romsye, Leonard, 642.
Rone, Anthony, 109.
Ronyon, *see* Roynion.
Roo, Mr., 435.
Rookes, Mr., 371.
Rooksby, Mr., 435.
Rooper, John, 520.
Roper-Lane, 320.
Roper, Mrs., 689.
Roper, William, 311, 347, 417.
Roscaroc, Nicholas, 649.
Rose Castle, 180, 192, 278.
Roses, Sugar of, 313.
Rosewell, William, (Solicitor General,) 190, 233.
Rosey, William, 77, 78, 80, 81, 83, 84.
Ross, Bishop of, 426, 427, 431, 434, 442, 455, 686.
Rosse, John de, 432.
Rotheram, John, 591.
Rotherham, George, 509.
Rotherhithe, *see* Redreff.
Rothermaker, John, 702.
Rothwell, 677.
Rothwell, Hundred of, 441, 519.
Rothwell Market, 519.
Rotta. 680.
Rotterdam, 609.
Rouen (Roan), 209-211, 213, 219, 329, 484, 535, 577, 635, 653, 678, 686, 701, 702.

Rouge Croix, *see* Brookes.
Rous, Thomas, 357.
Rouse Edward 13.
Rousse, Sir Edward, 318.
Rowe, Sir Thomas, 326, 328-330, 342, 362.
Rowington, 266, 358, 653, 654.
Rownore, 47.
Roy, John le, 641.
Royal Arms, The, 131, 143, 144, 476.
Royal Exchange. *See* Burse.
Royal Navy. *See* Admiralty, Shipping.
Royal Palaces. *See* Palaces.
Royal Stables. *See* Stables.
Royal Title, The, 74, 75, 82, 83, 144, 283, 318.
Roynion, (Ronyon, Roynon,) John, 29, 118, 521
Royston, 9, 41, 92, 346, 598, 645.
Rudhall, William, 579.
Rudolphi. *See* Ridolphi.
Rufford, 489.
Rugby, 698.
Rugby School, 698.
Rughfourthe, 151.
Runge Herman, 552.
Runton, 575.
Ruse, Peter de, 234.
Rushcliffe, Wapentake of, 339, 379, 418.
Rushe, Mr., 273.
Rushell, James, 470.
Russell, Elizabeth, 505.
Russell, Francis, Earl of Bedford, 73, 94, 100, 101, 108, 115, 127, 135, 136, 159, 162, 186, 241, 252, 331, 337, 388, 389, 391, 392, 417, 465, 473, 477, 480, 481, 491, 505, 553, 583, 608, 629-632, 658, 683, 685.
Russell, John, 594.
Russell, John Lord, 10, 13, 19, 21-25. Earl of Bedford, Lord Privy Seal, 41, 62, 74.
Russell, Lord John, 503, 505.
Russell, Lady, 432, 503.
Russell, Mr., 182, 222.
Russell, Sir Thomas, 367, 373, 375, 460.
Russell, Sir William, 491.
Russia, 178, 179, 280, 299, 300, 316, 338, 474, 522, 616, 695, 701. *See* Ivan. Muscovy.
Russia, Trade to, 523.
Ruthin, or Ruthyn, 361, 483.
Rutland, 21, 36, 89, 140, 156, 342, 378, 388, 482, 566, 572, 657.
Rutland, Alehouses in, 570.
Rutland, Countess of, 230.
Rutland, Earl of. *See* Manners.
Rutland, Justices of, 638.
Rutland, Sheriff of, 380.
Rybande, Mr., 210.
Ryce, William, 180, 403.
Ryche, Sir Edward, 380.
Ryche (or Rich), Richard Lord, (Lord Chancellor,) 22, 29, 33-36, 56, 57, 59, 99, 104, 157, 211, 225, 256, 270.
Ryche, Robert Lord, 342, 343, 356, 487, 620, 686.
Rychman, Stephen, 514.

GENERAL INDEX.

Rycot, *see* Ricot.
Rye, 16, 93, 95, 103, 201, 202, 205–209, 211–214, 219, 220, 226, 264, 314, 318, 523, 560, 577, 636, 701.
Rye, Custumall of, 614.
Rye Harbour, 119, 202, 402, 472, 491, 517, 576.
Rye, Mayor, &c. of, 16, 93, 103, 206, 207, 209, 210, 314, 472.
Rygges (or Rigges), William, 31, 35.
Rynehousen. *See* Rhinehouse.
Rypley, 587.
Rypon, Walter, 583.
Ryther, John, (Cofferer of the Household,) 41, 42.
Ryvet, Mr., 169.
Ryvett, Andrew, 75.

S.

S........., J., 458.
S........., M., 458.
S........., Thomas, 458.
S........., W. 691.
Sabellus, James, Cardinal, 622.
Sacheverell, John, 700.
Sacheverell, Mr., 553.
Sackford (or Sackforthe), Henry, 279, 663. *See* Seckford.
Sackford (or Seckford), Thomas, 279, 248, 495, 498.
Sackvile, Lady, 289.
Sackville, Mr., 179.
Sackville, Thomas, Lord Buckhurst, 318, 417, 418, 421, 422, 624, 625.
Sackville Place, 218.
Sackville, *see* Sakevyle.
Sacrament, The, 7, 11, 19, 21, 31, 45, 75, 79, 88, 93, 96, 174, 234, 243, 263, 284, 303, 322, 324, 346, 368, 377, 414, 439, 443, 445, 561, 601.
Sadberge, County of, 122.
Saddle, the Queen's, 403.
Sadler, David, 483.
Sadler, John, 654.
Sadlier, Sir Ralph, 308, 309, 351, 352, 359, 360, 362, 387, 398, 422, 463, 499.
St. Alban's, 107, 128, 132, 266, 280, 308, 313, 351, 371, 389, 460, 557, 610, 660.
St. Andrew's Castle (Hants), 264.
St. Andrew's, Monastery of, 31.
St. Asaph, 396, 406, 564.
St. Asaph, Bishop of. *See* Wood, Goldwell, Davies (Tho.), Hughes.
St. Asaph, Bishoprick of, 109, 132, 396, 406, 564.
St. Augustine, Lathe of, 344, 352, 419, 451, 462, 548.
St. Augustine's Park. *See* Canterbury.

St. Austin's Psalter, 96
St. Barbe, William, 675.
St. Bartholomew's, 299, 400.
St. Bartholomew the Great, 433, 434.
St. Bartholomew's (Gloucester), 242.
St. Bee's, 179, 191, 617.
St. Bridget, Order of, 701.
St. Buryan, Parishioners of, 492.
St. Catherine's, 313, 432.
St. Cross (Winchester), 688.
St. Crosse, Master of, 133.
St. David's, 604.
St. David's, Bishop of. *See* Young. Davies (Ric.)
St. David's, Bishoprick of, 328, 329, 362, 564.
St. David's Consistory Court, 597.
St. Donat's, 176, 361, 582.
St. Dunstan's, 14.
St. Dunstan in the Wolds, 52.
St. Edmundsbury, *see* Bury.
St. Elmo, 256.
St. Elyn's, *see* St. Helen's.
St. Englebert, alias Sandingfeld, 85, 88.
St. Erkenwald's Tenements, 363.
St. Ethelred, franchise of, 452.
St. Faith's, 38, 171, 407.
St. George's Feast, 51, 237, 239, 295, 366, 445, 588.
St. George's Feast, the Sovereign's Lieutenants at, 622, 652.
St. Germains, Borough of, 217.
St. Giles's, Cripplegate, 271.
St. Giles's in the Fields, 432, 627.
St. Giles's Hill, 465.
St. Helen's (Isle of Wight), 144, 217.
St. Ives, 17.
St. James's, 3, 9, 38, 45, 46, 56, 71–73, 85, 88, 96, 102–104, 106–113, 115, 187, 188, 246, 274, 525, 526.
St. James's Park, 458.
St. Jean de Lux, 639.
St. John, John, 511.
St. John, John Lord, 263.
St. John, Sir John, 511.
St. John, Lady, 276.
St. John, William Lord, 481.
St. John of Basing, *see* Paulet.
St. John of Bletshoe, Oliver Lord, 148, 158, 341, 374, 392.
St. John of Jerusalem, Knights of, 468.
St. John of Jerusalem, Prior of, 100, 101, 299.
St. John's, 3, 502.
St. John's College (Cambridge), 127, 176, 186, 187, 261–264, 268, 273, 274, 371, 373, 404, 408, 447, 467, 469, 493, 516, 518, 523, 548, 552, 553, 622, 636, 638, 644, 688.
St. John's College (Cambridge), Master of, 515.
St. John's College (Oxford), 417.
St. Katherine's, Christ Church, 493.
St. Katherine's, 612, 658.

GENERAL INDEX.

St. Katherine's Hospital, and Master of, 145, 150, 286.
St. Lawrence Lane, 323.
St. Lawrence, Old Jewry, 473.
St. Leger, Sir Anthony, 9, 22. 42, 98.
St. Leger, Arthur, 323.
St. Leger, see Seintleger, Sentleger, Seyntleger.
St. Leonards, 38, 80, 172.
St. Leonards, Forest of, 166.
St. Loe, Mr., 501, 502.
St. Loo, William, 61.
St. Malo's, 437, 439, 508, 611, 641.
St. Margaret's, Westminster, 204.
St. Marie, Mons., 211.
St. Martin's in the Fields, 308.
St. Martin's le Grand, 172, 181, 200.
St. Martin's, Rochelle, 209.
St. Martin's, Stamford, 87, 96.
St. Mary at Hill, 11, 86, 150.
St. Mary Overys, 75.
St. Mary's (Cambridge), 703.
St. Mary's Hall (Oxford), 649.
St. Mary's College (Winchester), 449.
St. Mary's, Guild of, 14.
St. Mary's in Hull, 590.
St. Mawes Castle, 548.
St. Mawes, Borough of, 217.
St. Michael's, 280.
St. Michael's (Stamford), 83.
St. Michael's Mount, 632.
St. Nicholas Island, 14.
St. Olave's, Silver Street, 192.
St. Olyve's, Winchester, 110.
St. Oswald's, Monastery of, 285.
St. Osyth, Manor of, 48.
St. Pancras, Prebendary of, 242.
St. Paul's, 485, 609.
St. Paul's Cathedral and Churchyard, 21, 22, 27, 38, 39, 67, 88, 116, 117, 177–179, 184–187, 199, 209, 239, 260, 268, 271, 273, 274, 301, 321, 370, 382, 386, 407, 431, 437, 546. 609, 631.
St. Paul's, Consistory Court of, 654.
St. Paul's Cross, 545.
St. Paul's, Dean of, see Nowell.
St. Paul's, Dean and Chapter, 2, 7, 27, 38, 39, 80, 116, 173, 185, 245, 272, 274, 301, 322, 327, 363, 382, 407, 549, 590, 609, 618.
St. Paul's, Synod at, 409.
St. Paul's Vaults, 549.
St. Peter's Grange, 280.
St. Peter's, Westminster, 147.
St. Quentin's, 94.
St. Saviour, Order of, 701.
St. Stephen's, Stamford, 83.
St. Stephen's, Westminster, 464.
St. Tron, 73.
St. Winnowe, 202.
Saker, The, 205, 209, 259.
Sakevyle, Mr., 252, 258.

Sakevyle, Sir Richard, Chancellor of the Augmentations, 10, 43, 118, 123, 128 132, 136, 138, 142, 151, 155, 160–164 170, 181, 182, 184, 198, 201, 219, 248 254, 266, 271.
Salcot (or Capon), John, Bishop of Salisbury, 27, 56.
Salden, Manor of, 467, 468.
Sale, Mr., 251.
Sales, Commissioners of, 91, 108. See Crown Lands.
Salisbury (Sarum, New Sarum), 27, 43, 44, 248, 335, 455, 464, 484, 541, 563, 665 See New Sarum.
Salisbury, Bishop of, see Jewell, Gest.
Salisbury, Diocese of, 102, 103, 646.
Salisbury, Sir John, 152.
Salisbury, Margaret, Countess of, 325.
Salkeld, Launcelot, 158.
Salmon, 176.
Salop, see Shrewsbury, Shropshire.
Salt, Salt Works, 168, 171, 214, 220, 232, 234, 238, 251, 255, 268, 274, 282, 293, 296, 399, 428, 429, 455, 519, 535, 541, 554, 641, 673, 695, 697.
Salt upon Salt, Manufacture of, 697.
Salt Marshes, 402.
Salt Pans, 617.
Saltash, 273, 326.
Saltpetre, 117, 172, 431, 461, 511, 658.
Saltpetre, Purchase of, 553.
Salute, Abbate de, 154.
Salvin, ..., 410.
Salwayn, Gerard, 122.
Sambitores, John Baptista, 463.
Samford, John, 32.
Sampford, Hundred of, 452.
Sampford Peverel, 471.
Sampson, Richard, Bishop of Chichester, 14.
Sampson, Thomas, 505.
Samson, Mr., 434.
Samson, Thomas, 49.
Samways, Geoffrey, 146.
Sanctuary, 266.
Sand, H., 660.
Sandal Castle, 351.
Sanders, Dr, 281, 565. See Saunders.
Sanders, Sir Thomas, 94.
Sanderson, ..., 163.
Sanderson, William, 702.
Sandford Courtenay, 20.
Sandgate Castle, 377, 509.
Sandingfeld, see St. Englebert.
Sandon, William, 110.
Sandown Castle (Isle of Wight), 105, 106.
Sandown Castle (Kent), 101.
Sandwich, 45, 141, 171, 179, 201, 253, 295, 310, 322, 324, 326, 378, 382, 389, 414, 427, 482, 528, 672.
Sandwich, Mayor of, 665.
Sandwich, Strangers at, 528, 532.
Sandwich, Survey of the Port of, 491.

778 GENERAL INDEX.

Sandys (or Sandes), Edwyn, 5, 132, 148; Bishop of Worcester, 223, 352; Bishop of London, 390, 403, 437, 516; Archbishop of York, 538, 539, 545, 546, 561, 563, 596, 622, 625, 626, 653, 672.
Sandys, William Lord, 481.
Santon, Tythes of, 628, 657, 665, 669, 670.
Sarum, *see* New Sarum, Salisbury.
Sassetti, Captain, 689.
Saterburn-mouth, 175.
Satin, 2, 110.
Saul, Mons., 183.
Saunders, Ambrose, 92, 94.
Saunders, Capt., 226.
Saunders, Dr., 688.
Saunders, Edward, 61.
Saunders, Sir Edward, 95, 125, 126, 492.
Saunders, Elizabeth, 688.
Saunders, Francis, 196, 206.
Saunders, George, 437.
Saunders, Mr., 689.
Saunders, W., 368.
Savage, *alias* Boner, *see* Boner.
Savage, Francis, 261.
Savage, George, 148.
Savage, Sir John, 148, 199, 288, 292, 294, 344, 354, 377, 565.
Saville, Edward, 129, 151, 206, 207.
Saville, Henry, 129, 151.
Saville, Sir Henry, 129.
Saville, Robert, 129, 207.
Saville, William, 387.
Savior, Davy, 230, 247.
Savoy, Duke of, 97, 98, 689, 690; Entertainment of Ambassadors from, 690.
Savoy, The, 85, 211, 246, 331, 383, 385, 386, 515, 690.
Savoy, Auditor of the, 386.
Savoy, Master of the, 34, 85, 180, 383, 385, 386. *See* Thurland.
Sawcemers, Lands of. 640.
Sawley, Manor of, 503.
Sawtrey, T., 83.
Saxe, Duke of, 497.
Saxie, Robert, 405.
Saxlingham, 374.
Sayas, ..., Secretary, 647.
Sayntmond, Sir Anthony, 9.
Saywell, Gilbert, 217.
Scambler (or Schambler), Edmund, Bishop of Peterborough, 164, 374, 414, 437, 529, 560, 561, 566.
Scape, Lewis, 238.
Scaramuzza, Giovanni Jacopo, 184, 573.
Scarborough, 7, 265, 321, 354.
Scarborough, ..., a pirate, 583.
Scare or Scarre, Andrew, 87, 89, 133.
Scavage, 285.
Scheldt, The, 494.
Schets, Balthazar, 48.
Schliche, Gaspar, Count, 599.
Schoolmasters, Corrupt, 552.

Schult, Jacob, 16.
Schutz (or Schulz), Jonas, 567, 568, 570, 571, 585, 586, 605, 621.
Schutz, *see* Shutz.
Scilly Isles, 3, 26, 34, 113, 125, 397, 492, 582, 621, 625, 631, 685.
Scorey, John, Bishop of Rochester, 33; Bishop of Chichester, 40; Bishop of Hereford, 134, 141, 161, 177, 183, 272, 353, 423, 488, 500, 516, 564, 566, 581, 654.
Scorey, Mrs., 516.
Scot, Cuthbert, Bishop of Chester, 127.
Scotch Salt, 535.
Scotland, the Scots, 2, 4–7, 10, 15, 42, 44, 48, 74, 87, 93, 95, 101, 134, 138, 142, 144, 150, 151, 153, 154, 162, 192, 197, 199, 209, 221, 229, 231, 235, 238, 252, 269, 273, 276, 278, 279, 283, 286, 291, 293, 295–297, 309, 311, 313–316, 320, 356, 387, 388, 421, 432, 437, 447, 495–497, 501, 552, 554, 555, 557, 575, 584, 629, 642, 633, 688, 695.
Scotland, King of, *see* James VI.
Scotland, Queens of, *see* Margaret, Mary.
Scotland, Regent of, 502.
Scott, Dr. Cuthbert, 174, 247.
Scott, Gregory, 299, 319.
Scott, Thomas, 258.
Scott, Sir Thomas, 451, 521, 560, 630, 668, 671, 672, 685.
Scott, William, 352.
Scout, (or Skowte), The, 580, 631.
Scray, Lathe of, 344, 352, 450, 460, 467.
Scriptures, The, 158, 251, 509, 698. *See* New Testament.
Scroby, 352, 353.
Scrope, Henry Lord, 229, 280.
Scudamore, John, 183, 353.
Sculpture, *see* Statuary.
Seals, 476.
Seamen, 608. *See* Admiralty, Shipping.
Seamer, Mrs., 467.
Search for Popish books, vestments, &c., 524.
Searle, John, 389.
Sebastian, ..., 571.
Sebastian, Captain, 500.
Sebastian, King of Portugal, 173, 287, 328.
Seckford, Thomas, 338.
Seckford, Thomas, jun., 457.
Secret Intelligence, Channel of, 702.
Secret Service, 672.
Secretary of State, 91, 476. *See* Paget, Petre, Smith, Cecill, Bourne, Boxall, Walsyngham, Wylson.
Sedgeley Park, 64.
Sedgwick, John, 575.
Sedition, Seditious Words, Seditious Books, &c., 98, 127, 154, 157, 167, 217, 268, 302, 383, 393, 396, 467, 492, 633, 634. *See* Rebellion.
Seele, Richard, 698.
Seeler, Jasper, (or Seler, Gaspar,) 164, 234.
Segwyck, 166.
Seintleger, Sir John, 57–59, 341.

GENERAL INDEX.

Seintleger, Nicholas, 695.
Sekeford, Henry, 502, 505, 536. *See* Sackford.
Sekes, William, 295.
Selbrickenden, Hundred of, 450.
Seminaries, Foreign, 703. *See* Rheims.
Seminary Priests, 636.
Sempringham, 33, 34, 41, 47, 278, 360.
Sempringham Priory, 5.
Send, Manor of, 641.
Sentleger, Warham, 258; Sir Warham, 595.
Seres, Anne, 515.
Seres, William, 235.
Serjeant Porter, *see* Keys.
Serjeants' Inn, 407, 567.
Serjeants-at-Law, 106, 107, 407, 441.
Serle, Henry, 244, 245, 278.
Sermons, 487.
Settrington, 150, 152, 164, 171, 257.
Sewell, ..., 162.
Sewer of England, Office of, 120, 176.
Sewers, and Commissioners of, 42, 46, 201, 202, 272, 278, 292, 296, 297, 409, 412, 523, 529, 539. *See* Fens.
Sex, John, 514.
Sextant, Improvement in the, 697.
Sexto, Augustine de, 90.
Seyman, Richard, 42.
Seymaur, Lord Edward, 250, 301.
Seymour, Edward, 238.
Seymour, Edward, Earl of Hertford, Duke of Somerset, Lord Protector, 1-30, 36-38, 40, 46, 48, 49, 51, 74, 125, 291, 303, 387, 498.
Seymour, ..., (daughters of Somerset,) 46.
Seymour, Sir Edward, 23; Earl of Hertford, 174, 178, 182-185, 194, 195, 206, 221, 230, 236-238, 240, 241, 274, 310, 400, 414, 429.
Seymour, Sir Henry, 23, 345.
Seymour, Henry, 240, 274.
Seymour, Lord Henry, 489, 491, 599.
Seymour, Mr., 124.
Seymour, Thomas, Lord Seymour, Lord High Admiral, 2, 3, 7-15, 62, 169.
Seyntleger, Anthony, 627.
Seyntlo, Lady Elizabeth, 183, 185.
Seyntlo, Mr., 183.
Seyntlo, Sir William, 127, 185.
Seyntlow, Sir John, 37, 84.
Seysdon, Hundred of, 342.
Shadwell, Henry, 355.
Shakespeare, John, 653, 654.
Shakespeare, William, 358, 653, 654.
Shakespere, Roger, 40.
Shakespere, Thomas, 653, 654.
Shales, ..., 698.
Shaplye, John, 535.
Shard, Gregory, 37.
Sharington, Mr., 43.
Sharington, Sir William, 3, 4, 7, 8, 13, 14.
Sharington, William, 417.
Sharington, *see* Sherington.

Sharp, John, 554.
Sharpe, ..., 578.
Sharpe, Robert, 525.
Shawe, Margaret, 603.
Shawe, Randall, 603
Shearmen, Company of, 275.
Sheep, 239.
Sheerness, 118, 449, 627.
Sheffield, 12, 92, 485, 561, 581.
Sheldon, *see* Shelton.
Sheldon, Raffe, 458.
Sheldon, William, 116.
Shelford, 367-369.
Shelley, lands of, 166.
Shelley, Edward 31.
Shelley, Sir James, 276.
Shelley, William, 352.
Shelstone, 389.
Shelton, ..., 198.
Shelton, Elizabeth, 266.
Shelton, James, 617.
Shelton, (or Sheldon,) Mr., 633, 691.
Shelton, Raphe, 433, 451.
Shene, (or Sheen,) 10, 26, 47, 107, 200-205 209, 211, 212, 215, 318, 320, 610.
Shene, Prior of, 203.
Sheppard, Mr., 694.
Sheppy, Isle of, 59, 99, 118, 400, 401, 407, 444, 445, 469, 471, 486, 498, 529, 530, 535-539, 545, 627, 636, 638.
Shepway, Lathe of, 344, 352, 451, 467.
Sherborne, or Sherburn, 19, 58, 129.
Sherburn House, 23.
Sherburn, Vicar of, 129.
Shere, 339.
Sherewin, John, 548.
Sherfield, 609.
Sheriff Hutton, 190, 455.
Sheriffs, 7, 23-25, 31, 33, 34, 56, 60, 72, 86, 88, 95, 104, 105, 112, 120, 128. 181, 197, 206, 210, 214, 216, 222, 223. 226, 232, 240, 241, 257, 273, 275, 288, 297, 305, 307, 321, 322, 331, 333, 338. 346-348, 351, 355, 356, 361, 367, 369, 376, 379, 380, 388, 391, 418, 422, 424, 427, 433, 441, 453-455, 470, 484, 504, 512, 519, 536, 579, 580, 597, 611, 612, 629, 636, 645, 662, 665, 686, 688.
Sheriffs Court, The, 453.
Sheriffs, Entertainments, 509.
Sheriffs, Reformation of, 518.
Sherington, Sir Harry, 557.
Sherington, Henry, 641.
Sherington, William, 696.
Sherington, Sir William, 641.
Sherland, or Shirland, *see* Shurland.
Sherley, Francis, 43.
Sherlonde, Richard, 234.
Sherman, ..., 286.
Sherman, Ralph, 31.
Sherry, *see* Wines.
Shers, John, 243, 251, 256, 276, 277.
Sherwood and Sherwood Forest, 669, 689.

GENERAL INDEX.

Sherwood, ..., 655.
Sherwood, Mr., 124.
Shetlington, 175, 187.
Shields, 5.
Ship-building, 107, 131, 141, 210, 438, 518.
Shiplake, 355.
Shipman, Thomas, 3.
Shipping, 7, 10, 30, 39, 64, 73, 77, 87, 88, 90, 92, 93, 97, 103, 125, 126, 128, 131, 133, 150, 164, 165, 172, 178, 189, 203, 205, 208–210, 213, 215, 218–220, 223, 225, 226, 237, 239, 258, 261, 273, 305, 313, 314, 316, 317, 322, 326, 327, 329–331, 345, 376, 384–391, 393, 398, 399, 405, 407, 409, 418, 431, 437, 439, 464, 482, 490, 509, 512, 523, 528, 535, 536, 552, 554, 559, 567, 575, 577, 585, 587, 600, 606, 611, 615, 621, 629, 637, 641, 644, 645, 656, 680, 687, 697.
Shipping, Arrest of, in England, 517, 598.
Shipping, Embargo on, 128, 133, 483.
Shipping, *see* Arrests, Insurance, Ports, Voyages.
Ships, Lists of, 479, 518, 538, 553, 574, 576, 610, 612, 681, 698. *See* Admiralty.
Ships, Survey of 516.
Shipwreck, 509, 520, 563, 575, 639, 702. *See* Wrecks.
Shipwrights, 612.
Shipwrights, The Queen's, 634.
Shoreditch, 432, 504.
Shorers, The 74.
Shotsham, Thomas, 150.
Shrawnell Park, 407.
Shrewsbury, 121, 132, 162, 275, 285, 339, 374, 462, 561.
Shrewsbury, Countess of, 471, 489.
Shrewsbury, Earl of, *see* Talbot.
Shrivenham, Hundred of, 156, 340.
Shropshire, 13, 121, 139, 148, 248, 286, 339, 348, 349, 374, 462, 466, 474, 486, 514, 561, 563, 565, 581, 586, 635, 641.
Shropshire, Justices of, 639.
Shurland, (or Sherland,) House, 58, 59, 401, 445, 487, 627, 636, 638, 676, 683, 684.
Shurland, Manor of, 469.
Shustoke, 41.
Shute, Captain John, 224.
Shute, Richard, 597.
Shutz, (or Schutz,) Christopher, 256, 258, 259, 274, 688.
Sidney, (or Sidnei,) Philip, 331, 648, 651, 678.
Sidney, *see* Sydney.
Sierra, Lope de la, 326.
Signet, Clerks and Office of the, 52, 64, 90, 381.
Silks, Manufacture of, 147, 190, 314.
Silles, Mary, 152, 164, 171.
Silver Mines, *see* Mines.
Simiers, Du, 629.
Simmes, Mr., 517.
Simondson, Martin, 563.
Simonelli, Joseph, 612.
Simony, 625.

Sion, (Sion House or Monastery of,) 10, 11, 14, 18–20, 26, 40, 203, 272, 691.
Sion, Abbess of, 701.
Sion, Religious Virgins and Brethren of, 701.
Sittingbourne, 59, 136, 626, 634.
Six Clerks, The, 165.
Skarresdale, Hundred of, 124.
Skawe, The, 622.
Skedam, Adryan, 402.
Skeffington, *see* Skevington.
Skerne, John, 551.
Skevington, Christopher, 107.
Skevington, (or Skeffington,) John, 171, 386
Skidmore, Erasmus, 576.
Skins and Pelts, 325, 702.
Skipwith, Sir William, 292.
Skipworth, Edward, 380.
Sklater, *alias* Tomson, Thomas, 63.
Skonewall, Captain, 434.
Skowte, The, *see* Scout.
Skynner, Alderman, 372.
Skynner, J., 440.
Skynner, Mr., 18.
Skynner, Ralph, 161.
Skypwith, Henry, (or Harrie,) 417, 422, 426, 434, 436, 437, 440, 442, 444, 445.
Skyracke, Wapentake of, 336.
Slander, 217, 403, 420, 435, 548.
Slave Trade, The, 299, 300.
Slavery, 295.
Sleape, William, 280.
Slebidge, Commandery of, 266.
Sledd, John, 524, 605.
Siegge, Roger, 36, 244, 245, 278, 305
Sluice Master, The, *see* Rickwarth.
Sluys, 274, 391.
Slythehurst, Thomas, 105.
Smalford, 280.
Smallwell, John, 41.
Smart, ..., Parson, 140.
Smelting, *see* Ore.
Smerwick, 687.
Smetheley, Anthony, 296.
Smith, Dr., 48.
Smith, Gawen, 700.
Smith, Henry, 166, 278, 298, 299, 317.
Smith, Hugh, 310.
Smith, John, 443.
Smith, Sir Lawrence, 288, 291, 292, 294.
Smith, Mr., 190, 261, 263, 518.
Smith, Peter, 186, 345.
Smith, R., 428, 495.
Smith, Ralph, 501.
Smith, S., 16.
Smith, Thomas, 520, 545, 674.
Smith, Thomas, Secretary of State, 9, 11 ; Sir Thomas, 14–21, 23, 25, 68, 139, 158, 162, 203, 241, 299, 304, 380, 384, 410, 421, 422, 440, 448, 468, 485, 494, 502 ; Deceased, 588.
Smith, William, 235, 632.
Smith, *see* Smithe, Smyth, Smythe.

GENERAL INDEX. 781

Smithe, Mr., 528.
Smithfield, 5, 687.
Smithfield, East, Manor of, 150, 556, 567.
Smyth, ..., 294.
Smyth, Anthony, 699.
Smyth, David, 403.
Smyth, Harry, 685.
Smyth, Sir John, 492, 646.
Smyth, Mr., 503.
Smyth, Nicholas, 64.
Smyth, Thomas, 258, 259, 261, 454, 671.
Smythe, Andrew, 405.
Smythe, Augustine, 42.
Smythe, Elizabeth, 40.
Smythe, Hugh, 635.
Smythe, John, 398.
Smythe, Sir John, 599.
Smythe, Robert, 403, 624.
Smythe, Thomas, 378, 382, 390, 391, 512.
Smythe, *see* Smith.
Snagg, William, 175.
Snagge, Thomas, 187, 371.
Snape, 93.
Snape, John, 460.
Snarestone, 701.
Sneyde, William, 120 ; Sir William, 372, 381, 383, 386.
Snowden, Forest of, 586.
Snowe, Mrs., 642.
Soap and Soapmakers, 438, 508, 605, 606, 692.
Sobar, William, 646.
Soldiers, Training of, 648. *See* Musters.
Solicitor General, 105, 247.
Some, *see* Soome.
Somer, John, 105.
Somerby, Living of, 577.
Somers, Mr., 234.
Somerset, 16, 19, 27, 29, 36, 38, 40–42, 44, 55, 67, 72, 96, 104, 128, 139, 148, 155, 159, 160, 227, 275, 338, 340, 348, 369, 371, 372, 378, 381, 386, 387, 394, 449, 453, 462, 507, 515, 541, 549, 555, 560, 563, 565, 569, 582, 584, 612, 663, 666.
Somerset, Clothiers of, 557.
Somerset, Feodary of, 394.
Somerset, Justices of, 650, 656.
Somerset House, 289, 292.
Somerset House, *alias* Chester Place, 498.
Somerset Place, 32, 189, 269.
Somerset, Vice-Admiral of, 386.
Somerset, Duchess of, 3, 5, 9, 14, 29, 30, 147, 174, 184, 236, 291, 310, 381, 498, 672.
Somerset, Duke of, *see* Seymour.
Somerset Herald, *see* Glover.
Somerset, Mr., 558.
Somerset, Thomas, 457.
Somerset, William, Earl of Worcester, 41, 69, 231, 284.
Somerton, 462. 549, 624, 666.
Sommer, Mr. 196, 605, 622.
Sommers, John, 599.
Soome, Robert, 381, 494.

Sorcery, *see* Witchcraft.
Sotham, Thomas, 150.
Souche, William, 612.
Souger, Jerome, 84.
Sound Dues, The, 640.
South America, 693.
South Bemflete, 483.
South Sea, The, 513.
South Waltham, *see* Waltham.
Southack, George, 490.
Southaick, William, 324.
Southampton, 559, 575, 586, 588.
Southampton, Earl of, *see* Wriothesley.
Southampton Mayor, &c. of, 463, 559, 632.
Southampton, *see* Hampshire.
Southcote, Mr. Justice, 507.
Southsea Castle, 556.
Southwark, 1, 2, 9, 30, 57, 531, 546, 562, 629, 667.
Southwell, 664.
Southwell, Fr., 109.
Southwell, Richard, 521.
Southwell, Sir Richard, 26, 74, 108, 117, 118, 121, 130, 134, 171, 510, 576.
Southwell, Sir Robert, 56, 57, 59–61, 88.
Southwold, 653.
Southwood, 649.
Southworth, Anne, 659.
Sowyer, ..., 523.
Spa, The, 311.
Spain, Spaniards, 48, 55, 56, 58, 61, 62, 64, 69, 76, 77, 83, 90, 114, 115, 154, 162, 175, 176, 186, 191, 214, 217, 219, 234, 236, 238, 239, 246, 260, 279–281, 292, 297, 298, 300, 303, 306, 308, 311–314, 323–329, 332, 337, 339, 353, 358, 362, 363, 368, 378, 384, 386–388, 390, 392–394, 398, 399, 405, 407–409, 412, 417, 420, 422, 427, 433–435, 437, 447, 463, 476, 488, 489, 500–502, 504, 523, 525, 527, 528, 555, 565, 574, 603, 611, 629, 645, 656, 660, 662, 665, 669, 685, 686, 689, 690, 692, 693.
Spain, Attempts and Designs on England, 629, 630, 633, 660 665.
Spain, Attempts and Designs on Ireland, 629, 630, 632, 647, 658, 687.
Spain, King of, *see* Philip II.
Spain, Inquisition in, 217, 412, 519, 578.
Spain, Prince of, 690.
Spain, Queen of, 67, 390, 391, 394, 689.
Spain, Proposition to invade Spain, 565.
Spain, Treaty with, 578.
Spain and Portugal, Merchants trading to, 488, 489, 578, 611, 619, 626, 629, 631, 673, 680, 687, 694.
Spalding, 19, 46, 150, 409.
Spaldingmore, 147.
Spaniels, 672.
Spanish Fleet and Navy, 92, 630, 631, 628.
Spanish Goods, Arrest and Sale of, 435, 437, 463, 464, 574, 578, 645.
Spanish Money, 408.
Spanish Wines, 631. *See* Wines.

Spaunton, Manor of, 491.
Speaker, The, *see* Bell. Commons. Williams.
Spearte, John, 569.
Spelthorne, Hundred of, 123.
Spence, Henry, 242.
Spencer, ..., 272.
Spencer, Charles, 169.
Spencer, James, 350, 357.
Spencer, John, 304, 441, 574.
Spencer, Sir John, 310, 343, 345, 376, 380.
Spencer, Robert, 267, 365.
Spencer, Thomas, 441.
Spencer's Lands, 70.
Spendelo, Mr., 254.
Spender, William, 577.
Spes, *see* Despes.
Spetsbury, Parsonage of, 612.
Spices, Bill against engrossing, 444.
Spices, Prices of, 518.
Spices, Staple of, 337, 400, 463.
Spies, 82, 477, 565, 685.
Spies, Foreign, 556.
Spilman, Francis, 488.
Spilsby, Chantry, 27, 30.
Spilsby, Manor of, 292.
Spinning, *see* Yarn.
Spinola, Baptist, 253, 307.
Spinola, Benedict, 128, 456, 460, 462, 493, 494, 504, 701.
Spinola, Capt., 18.
Spinola, Jacob, 504.
Spinola, Mr., 482, 592.
Spinola, Pasquil, 253, 504.
Spinsters, Rate of Wages, 586.
Spires, 73, 205, 213.
Spiritual Court, The, 185.
Spittel, 335.
Springfield, 107.
Springham, Richard, 147.
Spydell, Sebastian, 244.
Squyer, John, 559.
Stable, Clerk of the, 611. *See* Household.
Stables, Royal, The, 132, 598, 610, 611, 639.
Stace, John, 475.
Stafferton, Mr., 230.
Stafford, 122, 181, 377, 465, 542, 548, 557, 652, 676.
Stafford Castle, 180, 234, 487.
Stafford, Lady Dorothee, 527.
Stafford, Edward, Duke of Buckingham, 55.
Stafford, Edward Lord, 342, 646, 652.
Stafford, Henry, Lord Stafford, 55, 110, 139, 165, 180, 181.
Stafford, Henry, Duke of Buckingham, 131.
Stafford, Sir Humfrey, 343, 345.
Stafford, Lady, 369.
Stafford, Lord, 487, 533.
Stafford, Mr., 238, 542.
Stafford, Robert, 270.
Stafford, Sir Robert, 28, 80, 82, 121, 124.

Staffordshire, 36, 41, 64, 120, 122, 139, 165, 180, 217, 249, 340, 342, 372, 377, 378, 381, 383, 386, 415, 424, 465, 474, 487, 542, 548, 557, 565, 652, 660, 667, 676, 685.
Staffordshire, Alehouses in, 557.
Staffordshire, Clerk of the Peace of, 685.
Staffordshire, Sheriff of, 424.
Stainbarge, *see* Steynberg.
Staincross, Wapentake of, 336.
Staines, 19.
Stambridge, Mr., 143.
Stamford, 9, 28, 30, 31, 34, 45, 47, 49, 63, 64, 80, 83, 87–89, 96, 133, 180, 191, 193, 198, 201, 212, 213, 293, 332, 368, 386, 409, 439, 575, 597, 662.
Stamford, Aldermen, &c. of, 45, 47, 49, 63, 64, 96, 180.
Stamford, German Church at, 439, 440.
Stamford-cum-Cranmore, 89.
Stamford, Roger, 548.
Stamp, John, 660.
Stamp, Signings by, 4, 23, 365, 366.
Stanbrydge, Thomas, 434.
Stanclyff, Richard, 597.
Standen, ..., 348.
Standley, Thomas, 628.
Standon, 387.
Standyshe, John, 635.
Stane, Hundred of, 6, 430.
Stangrave, Manor of, 191.
Stanhope, Edward, 381.
Stanhope, John, 379, 400.
Stanhope, Sir Michael, 9.
Stanhope, Mr., 578.
Stanhope, Thomas, 367, 368, 380.
Stanley, Edward, Earl of Derby, 94, 106, 149, 197, 203, 288, 303, 305, 322, 341, 347, 356, 366, 394, 397, 445, 455.
Stanley, Elizabeth, 679.
Stanley, Sir George, 303.
Stanley, Henry, Lord Strange, 167, 295, 363, 366; Earl of Derby, 488, 496, 600, 671, 680.
Stanley, Rowland, 679.
Stanley, Thomas, 132, 160, 164, 176, 177, 204, 259, 260, 287, 290, 291, 305, 306, 353, 363, 385, 406, 415, 4 6, 436.
Stanley, Sir Thomas, 442.
Stanley, Sir William, 52, 376.
Stanley, William, Lord Monteagle, 316, 325, 445.
Stannaries, the, 252, 307–309, 511, 512, 658. *See* Tin.
Stannaries, Lord Warden of the, 308, 309, 543, 658.
Stanstead, Manor of, 55, 62, 149, 259, 643, 649.
Stanton, 402.
Stanton, William, 78–81, 83.
Stanway Hall, 386.
Stanyhurst, Richard, 673, 689.
Staper, or Stapers, Richard, 512, 563.

GENERAL INDEX. 783

Staple, The, 502.
Staple of Cloth in England, 603.
Staple, Mayor of the, 550.
Staple, Merchants of the, 4, 37, 48, 105, 139, 161, 168, 169, 174, 241, 243, 258, 269, 275, 276, 305, 307, 308, 327, 405, 475, 547, 550, 552, 556, 694, 698.
Staple Towns, 468, *see* Mart Towns.
Stapleford Abbots, Rector of, 631, 641.
Staplehoo (or Staplowe), Hundred of, 430.
Stapleton, Ro., 296.
Stapleton, Sir Robert, 6, 691.
Stapleton, Thomas, 150.
Star, remarkable, *see* Comet.
Star Chamber, The, 98, 288, 298, 302, 381, 557, 640, 667.
Starfforde, Thomas, 591, 593.
Starkey, Randell, 432.
Starkey, Symond, 328.
Startute, Richard, 492.
State, Council of, 222.
State Paper Office, 63, 178, 324.
Stationers' Company, 167.
Statuary, 182, 189, 288.
Statute Laws, 5.
Statutes Penal, Execution of, 533.
Statutes, Printing of, 507.
Staunford, Manor of, 111.
Staverton, 535.
Staverton, ..., 693.
Staverton, Thomas, 392.
Stay of Goods, *see* Arrest.
Staynecliffe, Wapentake of, 336.
Stebunhuth, *see* Stepney.
Stenographia, The Book of, 219.
Stephenson, H., 89.
Stepney (Stebunhuth), 15, 649.
Steppin, William, 107.
Stere, Nicholas, 302, 313.
Stevenson, Alexander, 432.
Steward, John, 41.
Stewart, Mr., 314.
Steynbergh, John, 180, 279.
Steyning, 352.
Steynings, Lady, 435.
Stile, Henry, 462.
Stifkey, 657, 669.
Still, Dr. John, 515, 518, 548, 628, 634, 698.
Stillyard (or Hanse), Merchants of the, 38, 51, 65, 101, 137, 161, 171, 174, 181, 189, 193, 224, 226, 231, 240, 241, 244, 246, 247, 274, 288, 311, 325, 382, 411, 432, 436, 508, 587, 600, 603, 607, 624, 626, 647, 698, 699.
Stilton, 259.
Stockbridge, 217.
Stockes, (or Stokes), Adrian, 164, 426, 441, 561, 567.
Stockett, Lewis, 470.
Stockett, T., 311.
Stockholm, 275.
Stockton (or Stockden) Ward, 335, 678.

Stodderde, George, 509.
Stoddon, Hundred of, 374.
Stoke, 604.
Stoke Denys, Manor of, 128.
Stoke Dry, 380.
Stoke-gursey, Lordship of, 66.
Stoke Park, 101.
Stoke and Bradley, Manor of, 58.
Stokes, Dr. John, 262, 271.
Stokes, Mr., *see* Stockes.
Stokes, Mr. (of King's College), 493, 522.
Stolberg, Lodowick, Count of, 415.
Stolyon, Thomas, 477.
Stonecote, 272.
Stonemasons, Wages of, 690.
Stoner, Mr., 599.
Stonley, Richard, 59, 146, 158, 317, 391, 583, 661, 701.
Stony Stratford, 356.
Stooker, Lancelot, 82.
Stores, Keeper of the, 513.
Storie, John, 75.
Storye, Dr. John, 27, 389–393, 395, 409, 411, 415.
Storms, 176, 177, 190, 219, 225, 226, 228.
Stortford, Vicar of, 154.
Storthes, Gervays, 42.
Stoughton, Anthony, 110.
Stoughton, Thomas, 153.
Stoultz, Leonard, 279.
Stourton, Manor of, 34.
Stourton, Charles Lord, 29, 54, 96.
Stourton, John Lord, 536, 670.
Stowe, 45, 89.
Stowe, Hundred of, 6, 430, 452.
Stowe, Rectory of, 5.
Stowell, Sir John, 515.
Stowey, 369, 371.
Stoyte, John, 124.
Stradlyng, Sir Thomas, 176, 361.
Stradlynge, Sir Edward, 599.
Straffurth, Wapentake of, 336.
Strand, The, 211, 246.
Strange, Le, *see* Lestrange.
Strange, Lord, *see* Stanley.
Strange, Lady Margaret, 167, 295, 303, 316, 363, 366.
Strange, Robert, 419, 424.
Strangers, 505, 575.
Strangers' Church, 528.
Strangers' Church in London, 144, 150, 299.
Strangers in London, 317, 320, 321, 323, 324, 401, 427, 432, 433, 522, 551.
Strangers in Norwich, 496.
Strangers' Duties, 647.
Strangers, *see* Aliens, Colchester, Hastings, London, Maidstone, Merchant Strangers, Norwich, Sandwich.
Strangeways, James, 119.
Strangwishe, George, 91.
Strangwyshe, Henry, 132, 136, 164.
Stransam, Edward, 682.

784 GENERAL INDEX.

Strasburg, 202, 205, 213.
Stratford on Avon, 654.
Stratford, Stony, 356.
Stratford Langthorne, or Langhorne, 4, 374.
Stratton, Hundred of, 452.
Strelley, Philip, 225.
Strelley, Sir Anthony, 693.
Strenisham, 367.
Stretford, Hundred of, 124.
Strickland, Walter, 333.
Strickland, William, 188, 252, 406.
Strille, Angier de la, 241, 244.
Stringer, Alexander, 703.
Stringer, Mr., 636.
Stringer, Stephen, 491.
Strond, 213.
Strowel, John, 67.
Stuard, Dr., 136.
Stuart, Lady Arbella, 642.
Stuart, Charles. 257, 428 ; Lord Darnly, 489.
Stuart, Henry, Lord Darnley, 195, 199, 201, 253, 256, 344.
Stuart, Matthew, Earl of Lennox, 49, 104, 150, 197, 199–206, 209, 211, 212, 216, 218, 257, 258, 261, 269, 293, 295, 296, 301.
Stubbes, Christopher, 173, 174.
Stubbes, Mrs., 174.
Stucley, Thomas, 153, 155.
Stuckley, ..., ..., 596.
Stuckley, Thomas, 420.
Stuckley, Sir Thomas, 523, 524.
Studley, John, 248.
Stukeley, ..., a Pirate, 251.
Stukely, Thomas, 106, 310, 438.
Stukley, ..., 44, 46, 51, 106.
Stumpe, James, 43.
Stumpe, John, 82.
Sturbridge Fair, 6, 530, 532, 537, 549, 618.
Sturges, Thomas, 452.
Sturley, Nicholas, 537.
Sturminster, Manor of, 640.
Sturmouth, 634.
Sturtenn, John, 270.
Style, Anthony, 627, 632.
Style, The, 312.
Styntor, Ruben, 110,
Styrley, Capt., 370.
Styward, Austen, 125.
Styward, Edward, 483.
Subbarton, 35.
Subsidies, 4, 37, 54, 74, 94–96, 98, 100, 101, 105, 107, 111, 114, 117, 129, 136, 143, 145, 148, 186, 222, 230, 231, 275, 277–280, 283, 285, 290, 294–296, 301, 382, 398, 432, 478, 516, 520, 531, 545.
Succession, The, 175, 217, 218, 222, 256, 280–283, 286, 411, 444, 447.
Sudeley, 161, 367, 669.
Sudeley Castle, 8, 10, 375.
Sudley, Edward, 591.

Suffolk, 5, 20, 98, 99, 111, 142, 147, 148, 155, 160, 225, 257, 261, 268, 288, 293, 299, 310, 318, 325, 337, 343, 344, 347, 372, 377, 385, 388, 390, 447, 449, 452, 491, 503, 538, 568, 570, 578, 586, 603, 610, 612, 619, 627, 632, 643, 658, 665, 678, 680, 686, 699.
Suffolk, Alehouses, &c. in, 558.
Suffolk, Clothiers of, 511, 550, 633.
Suffolk, Justices of, 643, 652.
Suffolk, Sheriff of, 452.
Suffolk, Vice Admiral of, 22, 388.
Suffolk, Countess of, 489.
Suffolk, Duchess of, 363.
Suffolk, Duke of, *see* Brandon, Grey.
Suffolk, Frances Duchess of, *see* Dorset.
Suffolk, Katharine Duchess of, 3, 21–32, 35, 39, 41, 120, 123, 177, 297. 316, 332, 407, 410–413, 415, 440, 441, 677.
Sugars, 444, 538.
Sugeham, Richard, 651.
Suggestors, *see* False Suggestors.
Sullington, 475.
Sulphur, 160.
Sulyarde, Sir John, 104.
Sumptuary, Laws, *see* Apparel.
Sunning, Hundred of, 340.
Sunninghill, 153–157.
Superstitious Uses, 233, 285.
Supremacy, The, 250, 281, 321, 409, 578.
Supremacy, Oath of, *see* Justices of Peace. Church Affairs. Oaths.
Surback, Symonde, 248.
Surgery, Surgeons, 9, 81, 239, 438, 672.
Surplice, The. *See* Apparel, Church Affairs.
Surrey, 2, 7, 21, 40, 89, 98, 102, 109, 129, 135, 139, 148, 152, 155, 177, 290, 333, 339, 348, 419, 423, 426, 431, 465, 468, 474, 475, 485, 542, 546, 560, 561, 566, 570, 610, 618, 654, 655, 662, 694.
Surrey, Alehouses in, 562.
Surrey, Archdeaconry of, 404.
Surrey, Justices of, 638, 645.
Surrey, Earl of, *see* Howard.
Sussex, County of, 3, 7, 12, 41, 102, 123, 136, 139, 140, 148, 152, 155, 159, 168, 206, 207, 227, 264, 267, 271, 276, 337, 352, 361, 387, 394, 397, 438, 448, 451, 452, 460, 461, 466, 474, 477, 479, 486, 520, 539, 543, 544, 559, 580, 584, 588, 616, 620, 624, 640, 645, 665, 688.
Sussex, Countess of, 39, 131.
Sussex, Earl of, *see* Ratcliffe.
Sussex, Justices of, 638.
Sussex, Vice Admiral of, 483.
Sutton, 370, 546, 566.
Sutton, Hundred of, 376.
Sutton, Lordship of, 46.
Sutton at Hone, Lathe of, 347, 450, 461, 546, 663.
Sutton, ..., 561.
Sutton, Edward, Lord Duddeley (or Dudley), 62, 110, 502.

GENERAL INDEX.

Sutton, John, 695.
Sutton, Robert, 547.
Sutton, alias Dudley, Robert, Earl of Leicester, *see* Duddeley.
Swafield, Parsonage of, 36.
Swale, Mr., 304.
Swallow, The, 205, 244, 281, 323, 551, 645.
Swallow, Paul, 703.
Swanmote, Court of, 84.
Swans, 84, 557.
Swaton, 47.
Sweden and Swedes, 138, 140, 157, 158, 243, 267, 269, 275, 313, 447, 468.
Sweden, Duke of, *see* Eric.
Sweden, King of, *see* Eric; John II.
Sweet, Richard, 140.
Swift, Jasper, 589.
Switzerland, 211; Soldiers raised in, 672.
Swynnerton, John, 579.
Sybell, 697.
Syddenham, John, 650.
Syde, James, 576.
Sydmanton, 30.
Sydney, Ambrozia, 494.'
Sydney, Sir Henry (Lord President of Wales), 35, 39, 49, 67, 152, 163, 175, 177, 200, 225, 442, 452-454, 461, 462, 476, 482, 494, 501, 522, 524-526, 556, 574, 635, 638, 651, 685. *See* Wales.
Sydney, Lady Mary, 442, 459, 494, 527.
Sydney, Thomas, 424.
Sydney, *see* Sidney.
Sylva, Ruy Gomez de, 647.
Sylver, Richard, 21.
Sylvius, Abel, 285, 303.
Sylyard, Margaret, 131.
Symans, P., 575.
Symond, The, 628.
Symonds, Dr., 304.
Symonds, William, 490.
Sympson, Thomas, 270.
Synod, 409.
Syon, *see* Sion.
Sypton, 392.
Syra, John le, 625.

T.

Tadcaster, 352.
Tailer, William, 125, 132.
Tailor, Hugh, 595. *See* Taylor.
Tailors, 200, 282.
Tailour, John, Bishop of Lincoln, 41.
Tailour, Thomas, 151.
Taithwell, Vicar of, 34.
Talbot, Francis, Earl of Shrewsbury, 49, 83, 92, 106, 132, 149.
Talbot, George Lord, 104, 129, 151; Earl of Shrewsbury, 183, 191, 193, 206, 207, 237, 288, 341, 347, 367, 378, 379, 400, 430, 445, 458, 460, 485, 502, 503, 506, 522, 534, 561, 581.

Talbot, Gilbert Lord, 367.
Talbot, John, 322, 648, 653, 659, 671.
Talbot, Mr., 230.
Talbott, John, 464.
Talboys, Gilbert Lord, 510.
Talboys, Lady, 338.
Talgarth, 295.
Tampion, Henry, 201.
Tamworth, Borough of, 217.
Tamworth, John, 316.
Tamworth, Mr., 214, 255.
Tandridge, Hundred of, 135, 419, 423, 440.
Tanfield, East, 259.
Tanfield, West, 259.
Tankersley, 129.
Tanners, Tanning, 455, 500, 518.
Tannikyn, *see* Cecill.
Tarlink, M. G., 269.
Tarperley, George, 492.
Tarrowe, 433.
Tate, William, 566.
Tattersall, 655, 684.
Tattershall Castle, 29, 30.
Taundene, *see* Taunton.
Taunton Castle, 590.
Taunton, Lordship and Manor of, 159, 241, 590.
Taverner, Mr., 402.
Taverner, Robert, 58.
Taverner, Roger, 58, 248.
Taverns, *see* Alehouses, Inns, &c.
Tavistock, 392, 629, 630, 632.
Tawley, Abbey of, 266.
Tawney, William, 61.
Taye, Thomas, 545.
Taylior, Nicholas, 547.
Tayllour, Thomas, 328.
Taylor, James, 549.
Taylor John, 414, 569, 691.
Taylor, Margaret, 476.
Taylor, Mr., 401.
Taylor, Thomas, 476, 548, 549, 568.
Tedder, Lewes, 22.
Teddesley, Manor of, 165, 180.
Tekencote, Lordship of, 700.
Tempest, Robert, 122.
Tempests, *see* Storms.
Temple, The, 286, 325, 428, 443. *See* Inner Temple. Middle Temple.
Temple Bar, 73.
Temple Bridge, 528.
Temporalities, Restitution of, 409, 517, 520.
Tendring, Hundred of, 379, 422, 558.
Tennen, The, 609.
Tennis Balls, imported, 147.
Tenths of the Clergy, 533.
Tents, *see* Revels.
Tents and Pavilions, Office of, 193.
Tenures, 169.
Terell, Mrs., 486.
Terra Nova, Duke of, 659.

3 D

786 GENERAL INDEX.

Terrington, Vicar of, 702.
Testament, *see* New Testament.
Testons, 160-162, 164.
Teuxbury, Hundred of, 420.
Tewkesbury, 585.
Teynham, Hundred of, 460.
Thame, Hundred of, 138, 419.
Thames, The, 59, 156, 164, 282, 292, 399, 479, 481, 490, 491, 538, 554, 556, 571, 612.
Thames, Fishing in the, 534.
Thanksgiving, 235, 260.
Thaxstead, 389.
Thaxter, John, 525.
Thaydon, *see* Theydon.
Theaker, *see* Thetcher.
Theale, Hundred of, 156.
Theobalds, 310, 390, 485, 499, 504, 602, 672, 676.
Theophilus, *see* Cecill, Thomas.
Thetcher, (Thaccer, Theaker,) John, 102, 264, 331.
Thetford, 657, 665.
Thetford Hall, 194.
Thetford, Mayor, &c., 657.
Theydon, Gernon, 495.
Theydon, Mount, 158.
Thimbleby, ..., 459.
Thimblebye, Stephen, 618.
Thirlby, Bishop of Ely, 75, 76, 100, 135, 188, 203, 239, 390.
Thomas, Father, 659.
Thomas, John, 345.
Thomas, Robert, 195.
Thomas, William, 43, 44, 59, 61, 456.
Thomas of Woodstock, 131.
Thomazo, *see* Bath, 477.
Thompson, ..., 524.
Thompson, ..., Auditor, 271.
Thompson, John, 623.
Thomson, Richard, 164.
Thomson, *see* Tomson.
Thornage, 653.
Thorncombe, Manor of, 230, 232.
Thorndon, East, 33.
Thorne, Nicholas, 3.
Thorneton (or Thorne), Bailiff of, 111, 113.
Thorneton, George, 577.
Thorneton, William, 383.
Thorney Abbey, 491.
Thorney, Thomas, 494, 526.
Thornham Little, Rectory of, 142.
Thornton, 454.
Thornton House, 470.
Thorold, ..., 32.
Thorold, Anthony, 372, 387.
Thorpe, John, 475.
Thorpe and Thorpe-Achurche, 36, 84, 88, 89, 213.
Thorpewaterfelde, Manor of, 36.
Threddar, ..., 662.
Thrésor de la Noblesse. Book of, 512.

Throckmarton, Mr. Justice, 532.
Throckmerton, Mr., 658.
Throckmorton, George, 367.
Throckmorton, Mr., 11, 266.
Throgmorton, Anthony, 76.
Throgmorton, Clement, 304.
Throgmorton, Lady Frances, 137, **142**.
Throgmorton, George, 137, **142**.
Throgmorton, *see* Butteler.
Throkemorton, Robert, 149.
Throkmarton, John, 103, 118.
Throkmarton, Sir John, 476, **602**, **604**, **605**, 607, 609, 626, 627.
Throkmarton, Michael, 67, 75, 76.
Throkmerton, Clement, 95.
Throkmerton, Esq., John, 79.
Throkmerton (or Throgmerton), **John**, 76, 78-83.
Throkmerton, Sir Robert, 95, 343, **366**, 658.
Throkmerton, Sir Thomas, 78.
Throkmerton, Kellam, 380.
Throkmerton, Sir Nicholas, 78, 115, 118, **121**, 128,181, 184,185, 187,197,200, 204,218, 220, 291, 295, 297, 300, 304, **314**, **315**.
Throkmorton, Thomas, 366.
Throp Mountvell, 14.
Thurcaston, Living of, 701.
Thurgarton, 367.
Thurgarton, Wapentake of, 333, 379.
Thurgood, John, 640.
Thurgood, Nicholas, 640.
Thurland, ..., 369.
Thurland, Thomas, (Master of the Savoy), 180, 244-246, 250-255, 257, **272**, **274**, 276, 278, 279, 283, 287-289, 300, **302**, 303, 312, 319, 383, 384, 386, **688**.
Thurstable, Half Hundred of, 379, **419**, **558**.
Thurston, William, 150.
Thwayts, Edward, 634.
Thymblebie, Anne, 610.
Thymblebie, Dionysius, 105.
Thynne, Sir John, 27, 29, 341, **349**, 527.
Tiger, The, 238.
Tikinhill, House of, 163.
Tilbury, West, 45, 691.
Tildesley, William, 201.
Tillage, 5, 222, 412, 492.
Tilts, *see* Tournaments.
Timber, 496. *See* Woods.
Timber for the Navy, 598.
Timber Trees, felling of, in Bishopricks, 643-651, 654.
Tin, Tinners, 62, 252, 308, 309, 502, 512, 543. *See* Stannaries.
Tin, Coinage of, 511.
Tin, Pre-emption of, 639.
Tintern and Tintern Abbey, 278, **322**.
Tipper, William, 522, 551, 621.
Tirrell, Edmund, 104.
Tirrell, William, 26, 90.
Tirrell, *see* Tyrell.
Tirwhitt, Marmaduke, 694.

GENERAL INDEX. 787

Tirwhitt, William, 694.
Titchburn, 670.
Titcheborne, Benjamin, 670.
Titenhanger, 310.
Titles, *see* Royal Titles.
Titles of Honour, conferred by Foreign Princes, 660.
Tiverton, 56, 59.
Tixall, 424.
Todyngton, *see* Tuddington.
Toft, Manor of, 30, 32.
Toils, Master of the, 536.
Tolls, *see* Corn.
Tolson, 131.
Tomas, Walter, 464.
Tomewe, Mr., 113.
Tomlingson, Mr., 476.
Tomlyn's Wood, 13.
Tompson, Thomas, 476.
Tomson, Lawrence, 448, 490, 498-500, 597.
Tomson, *see* Sklater.
Tomworth, Stewardship of, 111.
Tomyow, Richard, 198.
Tonbridge, *see* Tunbridge.
Tonge, Mrs., (Clarentieux,) 110.
Tonnage and Poundage, 186.
Tooke, William, 672.
Topcliff, 290.
Topcliff (or Topclyff), Henry, 606, 620.
Topcliff (or Topclyffe), Richard, 400, 467.
Topper, Nicholas, 36.
Torlles, ..., 636.
Torperley, 484.
Torr, 57.
Torrewood, 608.
Torture, 81, 348.
Torvor, Manor of, 266.
Totness, 327, 535.
Totness, Archdeacons of, 207.
Tottenham, 414.
Tottenham Court (or Tottenhall), 27, 155.
Tottington, 448, 466.
Toucher, Lazarus, 7.
Touchet, George, Lord Audley, 439, 449.
Touchet, Henry, Lord Audley, 165, 493.
Touchet, James, Lord Audley, 166.
Touchet, John, Lord Audley, 51.
Tournaments, 202, 264.
Towcester, 314.
Tower, The, 1, 8, 11, 12, 24, 26, 36, 42, 43, 54, 55, 60-62, 70, 75, 82, 83, 96, 102, 116-118, 127, 131, 133, 138, 140, 142, 144-146, 148, 150, 151, 154, 156, 160, 161, 164, 166, 169, 170, 174-176, 178-180, 188, 189, 192, 194-197, 200-202, 204, 206, 230, 232, 234, 235, 237, 239, 241, 243, 247, 249, 250, 257, 259, 260, 265, 266, 272, 275-277, 290, 312, 339, 345, 348, 349, 354, 362, 365, 366, 372, 383, 385, 387, 403, 408, 409, 414, 415, 421, 422, 426, 428, 433-437, 439, 440, 442, 444, 445, 450, 457, 458, 492, 513, 559, 629, 658, 663, 686, 691, 703.

Tower, The, establishments of, 692.
Tower Hamlets, 133, 651.
Tower Hill, 567, 692.
Tower, Lieutenant of the, 536, 651.
Tower, Master Mason of the, 457.
Tower, Officers of, 11, 26, 70, 96, 102, 131, 133, 139, 176, 178, 189, 197, 201, 206, 230, 241, 243, 261, 276, 387, 409, 415.
Tower, Parson of the, 428.
Tower, Precincts of, 651.
Tower, Survey of Armour in, 673.
Tower Wharf, 317.
Tower, *see* Mint, Prisoners, Records.
Townesend, Roger, 469.
Townley, John, 322.
Townshend, Mr., 8, 404, 514.
Towthorpe, Manor of, 151.
Toynton, 177.
Tracy, Elizabeth, 37.
Tracy, John, 458.
Tracy, Sir John, 609.
Tracy, Richard, 251.
Trade, 37, 38, 44, 51, 64, 65, 68, 74, 90, 91, 108, 123, 126, 128, 129, 147, 158, 162, 167, 168, 173, 180, 183, 191, 198, 201, 215, 217, 218, 231, 235-238, 240, 241, 243-249, 260, 265, 266, 269, 276, 279-281, 284, 285, 288, 290, 296, 300, 303, 313, 314, 318, 321, 326, 329, 330, 332, 337, 344, 358, 398, 405, 408, 430, 435, 437, 444, 447, 448, 455, 463, 467, 468, 471, 472, 475, 478, 488-490, 494, 498, 500, 503, 508, 510, 512, 518, 522, 523, 527, 528, 530, 533, 538, 552, 557, 574, 575, 577, 579, 587, 592, 600, 602, 603, 607, 608, 611, 613, 614, 619, 620, 622, 626, 628, 629, 639, 640, 673, 680, 687, 690, 691, 693, 696-699, 702. *See* New Trades, Voyages.
Trade, Company for, 689.
Trafford, 656.
Trafforde, Sir Edmund, 456, 656.
Traheron, Bartholomew, 35, 49.
Traheron, Nath., 598.
Trained Bands, Training, *see* Musters.
Traitors, *see* Treason.
Translation, *see* Bible.
Transmutation of Metals, *see* Alchymy.
Transportation, 427.
Trappes, Anthony, 88.
Travache, John, 625.
Travacie, Eustace, 265.
Travel, Foreign, Cecil's Instructions for, 406.
Travel, Licence to, *see* Licences.
Travers, Mr., 19.
Travers, William, 168.
Treason, 167, 272, 344, 345, 348, 355, 373, 385, 390, 392, 394, 411, 426, 433, 521, 526, 587. *See* Rebellion.
Treasure, 324, 326, 328, 329, 332, 339, 349, 351-353, 359, 360, 363, 408, 682.
Treasure, Spanish, 504.
Treasure brought home by Drake, 686, 691.

3 D 2

GENERAL INDEX.

Treasurer of the Chamber, 109, 115, 139, 143, 275.
Treasury, The, 309.
Treaties, 123, 244, 412.
Trees, 85, 112, 197, 198, 212, 219, 333, 398, 407. *See* Timber trees.
Tregony, Borough of, 217, 516.
Trelawny, John, 71.
Treman, John, 700.
Tremayne, ..., 78, 81–83, 86.
Tremayne Captain, 212, 213, 215, 225.
Tremayne, Edward, 631, 632, 638, 682, 683, 686.
Tremayne, John, 307.
Tremayne, Nicholas, 248.
Tremayne, Richard, 72, 78, 82, 86.
Trencharde, George, 561.
Trendell, ..., 291.
Trent, The, 104, 237, 533.
Trent, Council of, 243.
Trentham, 424.
Trentham, Thomas, 685.
Trento, Giovanni Battista da, 536.
Trere, *see* Van Trere.
Trerice, 177, 179.
Tresham, Dr., 62.
Tresham, Sir Thomas, Prior, of St. John's, 68, 69, 71, 100, 101.
Trester, John, 202.
Trevanyon, Sir Hugh, 10, 404.
Trevanyon, Richard, 452.
Treves, Matthew, 322.
Trewe, John, 671, 672, 674, 676, 685.
Trewlock, William, 669.
Trewlove, William, 598.
Trigge, Hundred of, 452.
Trinity College (Cambridge), 64, 186, 191, 204, 250, 293, 321, 403, 440, 441, 446, 576, 600, 628, 634, 662; Stage Plays at, 638.
Trinity College (Oxford), 105.
Trinity Hall (Cambridge), 15–18.
Trinity House, The, 399. *See* Deptford Strond.
Trinity House, Newcastle, 623.
Triplow, Hundred of, 6, 430.
Tripoli, 551.
Tripp, Mr., 676.
Tritemius, Johannes, 219.
Trocheley, 60,
Troisrieux, Dominicque, 288.
Trollope, Thomas, 178, 180.
Troops, Shipment of, for Ireland, 629–631. *See* Ireland.
Troughton, ..., 7, 63.
Troughton, Thomas, 35.
Troutbeck, Manor of, 191.
Trumpington, 493, 702.
Truro, 309, 317, 581, 584, 587, 616, 623.
Trypoonye, James, 623.
Tucker, Stephen, 192.
Tudbery, Honor of, 578.

Tuddington, or Todyngton, 444, 445, 498.
Tuke, George, 379, 419.
Tunbridge, 3, 61.
Tunell, Peter, 641.
Tunstall, 527.
Tunstall, Cuthbert, Bishop of Durham, 29, 33, 34, 42, 47, 105, 117, 137, 138, 142.
Tunstall, Francis, 322.
Turbervile, George 673.
Turkey, the Turks, 277, 691.
Turloye, Manor of, 465.
Turner, ..., 693.
Turner, Christopher, 683.
Turner, Edward, 80, 81.
Turner, James, 569.
Turner, John, 624.
Turner, William, 18, 29, 31, 32; Dean Wells, 33.
Turnips, imported, 147.
Turnor, John, 588.
Turnour, Edward, 116, 117, 120, 124.
Turnpenny, John, 511.
Turpin, ..., 14.
Turpyn, William, 510.
Turre, Nicholas de la, 324.
Turswell, Thomas, 515.
Turvey, 392.
Turvyle, Geffrey, 629.
Tuscany, Duke of, 339.
Tutchet, *see* Touchet.
Tutting, John, 149.
Tuxford in the Clay, 352.
Tuydall, Mr., 194.
Twickenham, Manor of, 387.
Twyford, 693.
Twysden, William, 191.
Tyburn, 189.
Tychefeld, Hundred of, 7.
Tykyncote, 28.
Tylar, Thomas, 598.
Tyldsley, William, 185.
Tymwell, Serjeant, 69.
Tymyng, William, 87, 88.
Tyndall, Robert, 578.
Tyne, The, 355.
Tynemouth, 144, 147.
Tynemouth Castle, 193, 482.
Tynker, Philip, 177.
Tynne, James, 308.
Typpynge, Ralph, 321.
Tyrell, Anthony, 487.
Tyrell, Charles, 56, 59.
Tyrell, George, 526.
Tyrell, Sir Henry, 56.
Tyrell, John, 414.
Tyrer, ..., 634.
Tyrrel, Humphrey, 401.
Tyrrel, Jane, 401.
Tyrrell, ..., 401.
Tyrrell, Sir John, 142, 235.
Tyrrell, Mr., 484.

U.

Tyrrell, *see* Tirrell.
Tyrwhitt, Sir Robert, 13, 15, 46, 53, 134, 259, 342, 370.
Tythes, 36, 97, 147, 280, 284, 294, 493, 517, 596, 617, 699. *See* Santon.

U.

Ughtred, Henry, 534.
Ulstatt, *see* Hechstetter.
Ulterfines, *see* Cloths.
Umpton, *see* Unton.
Underwood, Henry, 505.
Underyll, Anne, 538.
Uniformity, *see* Church Affairs ; Religion.
Universities, *see* Cambridge, Oxford.
Unlawful Assemblies, 126, 571.
Unlawful Games, 421.
Unton, (or Umpton,) Sir Edward, 156, 340, 510, 690.
Unton, Lady, 510.
Uphill, 55.
Upnor Castle, 172, 202, 204, 213.
Uppingham, 570, 657.
Upsall, Manor of, 104.
Upton, John, 114.
Urswicke, Grammar School at, 641.
Ushant, 87.
Usury, 100, 182, 358, 402, 490, 511, 535, 613.
Utenhovius, Carolus, 254.
Utenhovius, Johannes, 144, 177, 204, 237, 242.
Uvedall, *see* Vuedall.
Uxbridge, 24.

V.

Vagabonds, Vagrants, Beggars, 23, 286, 334, 350, 353, 368, 418-427, 430, 440-442, 642. *See* Gypsies.
Vagatts, Island of, 253.
Vagrants, *see* Vagabonds.
Valenciennes, 397.
Valuation of Livings, *see* Livings.
Van Brunswick, Owter, 16.
Van Dueton, *see* Dneton.
Van Trere, John, 296.
Vane, Sir Ralph, 4.
Vane, *see* Fane.
Vanden Putte, Raphael, 312, 313, 324.
Vanguard, The, 576.
Vannes, Peter, 42, 74, 86, 87.
Varney, *see* Verney.
Vassall, John, 563.
Vaughan, ..., 636.
Vaughan, Cuthbert, 198, 228.
Vaughan, Edward, 1, 2.
Vaughan, Lady Eleanor, 295.

Vaughan, Geoffrey, 215, 258.
Vaughan, John, 21, 83, 103, 218, 249, 257, 336, 381, 482, 495, 498, 686.
Vaughan, Mr., 119, 171.
Vaughan, Richard, 538, 590, 591, 593.
Vaughan, Sir Roger, 176, 295.
Vaughan, William, 200, 571.
Vause, Henry, 496.
Vause, Lawrence, 281, 307.
Vaux of Harrowden, William Lord, 343, 346 375, 441.
Vavasour, Peter, 454.
Vavassor, Anne, 703.
Velles, M. de, *see* Veulles.
Velsius Justus, 221.
Velutelli, Acerbo, 468.
Velvet, 2, 107, 110, 118, 176.
Venables, Sir Thomas, 6.
Venetian Merchants, 697.
Venetian Ship, The great, 361.
Venice, Venetians, 23, 28, 42, 43, 64, 74-76, 80, 82, 84-87, 90, 91, 96, 182, 239, 243, 256, 276, 279, 304, 327, 404, 453, 488, 504, 522, 630, 650, 651.
Venice Glass, 297.
Venison, 105, 155, 247, 312, 691. *See* Deer.
Ventris, Mr., 688.
Venturini, Burgatio, 208.
Vere, Edward, Earl of Oxford, 215, 224-226 230-233, 235, 236, 241, 246, 249, 252, 254, 261, 290, 300, 318, 358, 364, 459, 461, 466, 478, 484, 485, 504, 593, 616, 661, 685.
Vere, John de, Earl of Oxford, 3, 23, 58, 98, 108, 116, 137, 140, 144, 154, 158, 173, 176, 184, 215, 224, 230, 233, 303, 318, 364.
Vere House, 685.
Vere, Lady Mary, 225.
Verney, ..., 498.
Verney, Edmund, 84.
Verney, Francis, 84.
Verney, Mr., 506.
Verney, Richard, 520.
Verses, 120, 202, 248, 277, 278, 309, 313, 331, 397, 449, 594.
Veulles (or Velles), M. de, 177, 210.
Vicars, Old, 14.
Vicars and Curates, Relief of, 411, 518.
Vice-Admirals, 180, 385-388, 478, 632.
Vicenza, 536.
Victuallers, Tax on, for Repair of Dover Haven, 672. *See* Dover.
Victualling the Forces, 169, 362, 511, 643. *See* Admiralty, Army.
Victualling, Rate and Prices for, 668, 698.
Victualling Houses, 250.
Victuals, *see* Corn.
Victuals, Surveyor of, *see* Baeshe, Darrell.
Vienna, 277.
Viglius, Mons., 66.
Villers, John, 369.
Villers, William, 498.

Vincent, David, 260.
Vincent, Mr., 597.
Vintners, 378.
Vintners' Company, 283, 378, 552.
Visitations, 11, 14–18, 34, 36, 130–132, 134, 136, 137, 141, 142, 145, 148, 177, 184, 188, 251, 267, 281, 312, 318, 329, 357, 383, 385, 386, 417, 540, 541, 543, 544, 553, 564, 588, 621. *See* Oxford.
Vitriol Works, 440.
Vivian, Michael, 179.
Voel, John, 368.
Vos, Cornelius de, 253, 254.
Vosbergh, Caspar, 409, 411, 439, 440.
Voyages of discovery, trade, &c., 74, 178, 183, 215, 220, 247, 253, 260, 273, 281, 287, 288, 299, 300, 316, 323, 330, 337, 475, 513, 520, 525, 533, 540, 543, 546, 551, 557–559, 565, 570–573, 581, 586, 589, 590, 600–602, 605, 608, 609, 615, 616, 619, 621, 622, 625, 641, 648, 656, 661, 678, 689, 690, 695.
Voyages, *see* Drake, Furbisher, Gilberte, Hawkyns.
Voysey, John, Bishop of Exeter, 8, 56.
Vuedall (or Uvedall), Richard, 75, 76, 78, 80.
Vyllars, Mr., 154.
Vyllers, Geoffrey, 83.

W

W........., G., 703.
W........., Katherine, 642.
W........., R., 466, 704.
W........., S., 492.
Waad (or Wade), Armigill, 119, 170, 171, 202, 206–209, 212, 225, 269, 275–277, 292, 315, 358.
Waad (or Wade), William, 315, 408, 499.
Wadley, 156.
Waeste, 670.
Waferer, Arden, 655.
Waferer, Fr., 655.
Wager of battle, (or judicial combat,) 414.
Wages, 185; of labourers, 690. *See* Spinsters.
Waggons or Wains, *see* Impressment.
Wainfleet Haven, 292.
Wait, Thomas, 103.
Wakefield, 351.
Wakefield, Thomas, 255.
Wakeman, John, 491, 623.
Waldegrave, ... (son of Sir Edward,) 182.
Waldegrave (or Walgrave), Sir Edward, 55, 68, 71, 91, 100, 104, 107, 108, 110, 113, 117, 118, 123, 171, 173, 174, 176, 179, 182, 184.
Waldegrave, Lady 174, 176, 184.
Waldegrave, William, 372, 525.
Walden, 425, 446, 596.
Walding, William, 476

Wales, 59, 65, 94, 95, 106, 108, 123, 124, 140, 143, 152, 163, 170, 175, 244, 259, 264, 266, 301, 325, 333, 358, 362, 398, 404, 406, 452, 457, 463, 469, 471, 476, 478, 479, 502, 513–515, 532, 533, 536, 538, 543, 563, 564, 571, 572, 580 588, 593, 604, 606, 634, 636, 639, 642, 661, 673–675, 688, 692.
Wales, Admiralty in, 590.
Wales, Clerk of the Fines in, 522, 526.
Wales, Court of, 524.
Wales, Deputy Lieutenants in, 639.
Wales, Escheators in, 635.
Wales, the Four Marcher Shires of, 514.
Wales, Instructions for, 525, 574, 575.
Wales, Judges in, to understand Welsh, 514.
Wales, Law Courts in, 513, 514, 515.
Wales, Lord President, Vice President, and Council of, 56, 94, 106, 108, 109, 123, 124, 126, 132, 140, 152, 163, 175, 193, 200, 268, 284, 285, 361, 381, 398, 404, 406, 414, 452, 474, 481, 482, 513, 514, 516, 522, 525, 526, 532, 537, 540, 545, 552, 556, 571, 574, 575, 580, 588, 591–594, 596, 597, 635, 661, 675, 692.
Wales, North, 630; South, 629.
Wales, Receiver of Fines and Amerciaments, 556. 600.
Wales, Reformation of the Courts in, 552.
Wales, Sheriffs in, 453, 454, 471.
Walgrave, J., 47.
Walgrave, Mr., 208.
Walker, Dr., 654.
Walker, John, 67, 68, 72, 80 82, 84.
Walkerne, Parsonage of, 109.
Waller, George, 142.
Waller, Walter, 393; Sir Walter, 451.
Wallerthum, Sir William, 85, 103.
Wallingford, 153, 156, 340, 419.
Wallingford Castle, 112.
Wallington, Hundred of, 135, 419.
Wallis, Ralph, 86.
Wallker, Thomas, 702.
Walloons, The, 310, 390.
Wallop, Sir Henry, 365, 368, 371, 375, 378, 384, 413, 502, 524, 630.
Wallop, Sir Oliver, 104.
Walmer, 101. *See* Wolmer.
Walmer Castle, 521.
Walpole, Robert, 392.
Walpole, Roger, 392.
Walpole, William, 475.
Walpull, ..., 82.
Walsham, Manor of, 111.
Walshe, Edward, 18.
Walsingham, Anne, 424.
Walsingham, Thomas, 258, 424; Sir Thomas, 685.
Walsyngham, ..., (a daughter of Sir Francis Walsyngham,) 663.
Walsyngham, Francis, 278, 314, 315, 317, 321, 324, 345, 346, 362, 394, 428, 432, 457, 464, 466; Secretary of State, 470, 473, 476, 477, 481, 486, 489–491, 495–506,

Walsyngham, Francis—*continued.*
    512, 514, 515, 520–522, 524, 526–528, 530, 532, 533, 536, 539, 546, 549, 552–559, 561; Sir Francis, 567–571, 574, 575, 577–586, 588, 590, 597, 598, 600, 601, 603, 605, 606, 608, 609, 611–613, 615–617, 619–622, 624–627, 629–635, 637–642, 644, 648–650, 655–657, 660, 662–664, 667–670, 672–674, 677, 678, 680, 682–689, 691, 693, 698, 701, 703, 704.
........., his Illness, 581.
........., Chancellor of the Garter, 588, 589.
Walsyngham, Lady, 697.
Walsyngham, Mrs., 408.
Walter, Mr., 524.
Walter, Robert, 502.
Waltham, 9, 184, 382, 422, 458, 530.
Waltham Forest, 104, 116, 123, 249, 551.
Waltham, Hundred of, 380.
Waltham (in Hants), 662.
Waltham, South, 192, 208.
Waltham Tower, 3.
Walton, Rafe, 569, 599.
Walverswike, Manor of, 610, 637.
Wandisford, Mich., 122.
Wandsworth, 642.
Wangford, Hundred of, 452.
Wansted, 31.
Wantinge, Hundred of, 156, 340.
Wappingthorne, 448, 466.
War, 94, 95, 97, 103.
War, Declaration of, 91.
War, Engine of, 399, 513.
War, Prisoners of, *see* Prisoners.
Warblington, 371.
Warcop, Mr., 352.
Warcope, Thomas, 279, 678.
Ward, Richard, 133, 693, 703.
Warde, ..., 257.
Warde, Capt. Luke, 588.
Warde, Richard, 41.
Warde, Roger, 84.
Warde, Thomas, 152, 153.
Wardelham, Manor of, 113.
Warden, Hundred of, 376.
Wardour, Chidiock, 450, 521.
Wardrobe, the Great, 40, 91, 114, 117–119, 130, 132, 137, 186, 245, 260, 269, 506, 617, 633.
Wards and Liveries, Court of, 52, 89, 91, 107, 109, 113, 118, 128, 130, 142, 146, 165, 166, 211, 214, 235, 283, 286, 294, 301, 303, 330, 367–369, 389, 446, 472, 591, 635, 646.
Wards, Master of the Court of, 91, 106, 128.
Wards, Wardships, 19, 41–43, 46, 51, 60, 65, 106, 110, 111, 128, 177, 182, 186, 198, 200, 206, 207, 212, 215, 225, 252, 296, 303, 367–369, 392, 393, 395, 398, 401, 428, 432, 498, 511, 614.
Ware, 27, 325, 351, 412, 528.
Ware River, *see* Lea River.

Wareham, 546, 625, 680, 682.
Wargrave, Hundred of, 340.
Warham, Mr., 69.
Warham, William, Archbishop of Canterbury, 456.
Wark Castle, 241.
Warley, 414.
Warlike Engines, *see* War.
Warmesworth, Lordship of, 596.
Warmyngton, Robert, 120.
Warnecombe, James, 383, 384.
Warner, Sir Edward, 100, 117, 133, 150, 175, 176, 184, 189, 197, 206, 258, 261.
Warner, Sir John, 142.
Warner, Mr., 49.
Warner, Stephen, 267.
Warr, Lord De la, *see* West.
Warrants, Regulation for the passing of, 662.
Warren, John, 562.
Warren, William, 368.
Warren, *see* Waryne.
Warte, James, 532.
Warton, Robert, Bishop of Hereford, 134.
Warton, *see* Wharton.
Wars, Treasurer of the, 97.
Warwick, Borough of, 21, 149, 339, 362, 366, 449, 466, 545, 559, 657.
Warwick Castle, 3, 60.
Warwick, Countess of, 9.
Warwick, Earl of, *see* Duddeley, Nevill.
Warwick, Feodary of, 378.
Warwick, Incorporation of Preachers in, 304.
Warwick, Lady, 510.
Warwick Lane, 21.
Warwick Park, 3.
Warwick's Lands, 70.
Warwickshire, 40, 41, 95, 129, 139, 148, 171, 215, 237, 266, 285, 294, 334, 339, 343, 358, 362, 364, 366, 380, 398, 415, 466, 545, 559, 564, 565, 640, 657, 658, 676, 698.
Warwickshire, Alehouses, &c. in, 559.
Warwickshire, Justices of, 638.
Warwickshire, Names of Freeholders in the County, 653, 654.
Waryne, (or Warren,) Jasper, 627.
Washingley, 687.
Was, Henry, 617.
Wasse, Henry, 80, 82.
Wasshington, Laurence, 467.
Wastell, John, 541.
Watch, The, 486, 595; Quarrel with the, 700.
Watch and Ward. 276, 419, 420, 422–425, 440.
Water, Roger, 434.
Waterford, 394, 539, 630, 666.
Waterhouse, Edward, 495, 498.
Waterhouse, Mr., 568.
Waterworks, 28, 255, 493, 569, 611
Watling Street, 332.
Watson, ..., 553. 681.
Watson, Dr., 646, 647, 649.

GENERAL INDEX.

Watson, Edward, 52, 370.
Watson, John, 404, 457, 644.
Watson, John, Bishop of Winchester, 685, 988.
Watson, Mr., 135, 136.
Watson, Dr. Thomas, Bishop Elect of Lincoln, 91.
Watson, William, 457.
Wattes, Thomas, 383, 390, 391, 493, 522.
Watts, Richard, 204.
Wattz, Thomas, 155.
Waughendoorpe, Adam, 274.
Wax Counterfeit, 635.
Waxham, 22.
Wayneham, Mr., 45.
Weavers (Flemish), 36–38, 47, 293.
Webb, Nicholas, 585.
Webb, Richard, 276.
Webb, William, 475.
Webbe, Mr., 174, 524.
Webster, Mr., 435.
Webtree, Hundred of, 123.
Weder, James, 96.
Weke-Fitzpayne, Manor of, 66.
Welbury, Manor of, 286.
Welby, Adlard, 46, 263, 412.
Weld, John, (of Eton,) 149.
Weld, John, (of London,) 149.
Welde, John, 556.
Welden, Edward, 41.
Welden, Thomas, 41.
Weldon, Thomas (Cofferer), 131, 133, 146, 155, 169, 192.
Well, Wapentake of, 335.
Welles, John, 267, 274, 287.
Welles, Robert, 265, 529.
Wellford, Tenant of, 520.
Wellington, 500, 681.
Wells, 28, 33, 306, 378, 541, 560, 565, 582, 584, 650, 651.
Wells, Dean and Deanery of, 28, 32, 33, 306.
Wells, Edward, 700.
Wells, Lordship of, 28.
Wells, Prebendaries of, 306.
Wells, Mr., 317, 512.
Wells, Robert, 170.
Welshcrofte, 52.
Welsh Lake, 269.
Welshe, John, 440.
Wendover, 295, 349.
Wenlingburghe, Rectory of, 31.
Wenman, Sir Richard, 343, 440.
Wenman, Thomas, 664, 684.
Wentworth, Mrs. Barbara, 74.
Wentworth, Sir John, 272, 300.
Wentworth, Michael, 42.
Wentworth, Mr., 126.
Wentworth, Peter, 516.
Wentworth, Thomas, 145, 351, 352.
Wentworth, Thomas, first Lord Wentworth, 3.

Wentworth, Thomas, second Lord Wentworth, 104, 158, 214, 255, 357, 372, 400, 649.
Werdon, Thomas, 6.
Werrall, Hundred of, 122.
Wertheim, 415.
West Bromwich, 424.
West Chester, see Chester.
West Country, The, 577.
West Cowe, see Cowes.
West Friesland, see Friesland.
West Grinsted, see Grinsted.
West Harilsey, see Harilsey.
West, Henry, 501.
West, Hundred of, 452.
West Indies, 299, 323, 337, 565.
West, John, 100.
West, Lady, 610.
West Lavington, see Lavington.
West Parts, Gentlemen of, 475.
West Pemered (or Pennard), see Pemered.
West Tanfield, see Tanfield.
West Tilbury, see Tilbury.
West, Thomas, 448.
West, Thomas, Lord Lawarre, 3, 4, 9, 30, 31, 43.
West, William, Lord Lawarre, 126, 393, 474.
Westby, John, 322.
Westcote, 64.
Western Counties, 615.
Western Ports, 325, 328.
Westialing, Dr. Herbert, 192, 195, 570.
Westham (or Hamme), 591, 593.
Westharling, 628.
Westhatche, Manor of, 28.
Westminster, 1, 2, 4, 5, 8, 11, 12, 14, 15, 25–27, 29–33, 36, 37, 46, 47, 52, 55, 56, 60–63, 65, 66, 70, 74, 91, 93, 100, 103, 106, 117, 127, 173, 174, 179, 181, 189, 195, 200, 216, 237, 245, 249, 333, 464, 479, 531.
Westminster Abbey, 651.
Westminster, Archdeacons of, 172.
Westminster, Bailiwick of, 233.
Westminster Close, 690.
Westminster, Convocation at, 516.
Westminster, Dean of, see Goodman.
Westminster, Dean and Chapter of, 147, 187, 293, 329.
Westminster, Diocese of, 9, 187.
Westminster, High Steward of, 181.
Westminster, Palace of, 612, 617.
Westminster, Prebends of, 187, 295, 329.
Westminster, Provost of, 293.
Westminster, Sanctuary at, 266.
Westminster School or College, 208, 293.
Westmonege, Island of, 248.
Westmoreland, 122, 191, 280, 395, 425, 563, 637, 702.
Westmoreland, Alehouses, &c. in, 562.
Westmoreland, Sheriff of, 391, 425.
Westmoreland, Earl of, see Nevill.
Weston, Bailiffwick of, 7.

Weston, Henry, 440.
Weston, Sir Henry, 348, 485.
Weston, Hugh, 80.
Weston, Mr. Justice, 449.
Weston, Mrs., 646, 685.
Weston, Richard, 105, 138.
Weston, Dr. Robert, 246.
Weston, Ry., 50.
Westover, Manor of, 381.
Westover, Hundred of, 483.
Westwood (Kent), 141.
Wetherby, 354, 359, 360, 364.
Wetherley, Hundred of, 6, 430.
Wettenhal, Manor of, 472.
Wexford, 276.
Weymouth, 59, 91, 547, 631.
Weymouth, Bailiff of, 609.
Weymouth, Mayor of, 656.
Whaddon, 248, 394, 564, 634.
Whaddon Chace, 468.
Whalley, 587.
Whalley, Richard, 15, 27–29.
Wharffe, John, 687.
Wharton, Lady, 174, 176.
Wharton, Lord, 403.
Wharton, Thomas, Lord Wharton, 50.
Wharton, Sir Thomas, 110, 113, 152, 171, 173, 174, 176, 179, 180.
Whartone, William, 430.
Whawton, Manor of, 119.
Wheat, damaged, to be exported, 622, 637.
Wheat, Supply of, 588. *See* Corn.
Wheler, Thomas, 538.
Wheteley, Mr., 381.
Whetle, George, 273.
Whetnal, manor of, 286.
Wheyton, Thomas, 64.
Whiddon, Sir John, 126.
Whipping, *see* Vagabonds, Vagrants.
Whitaker, Mr., 634.
Whitborne (or Whiteburne), 177, 183, 272.
Whitby, Town of, 7.
White, Mr. Alderman, 78.
White, Anthony, 399, 400.
White Bakers, Company of, 644.
White, Dr., 287.
White, Harry, 355.
White, John (Alderman of London), 111.
White, John (of Flushing), 329.
White, John, Bishop of Winchester, 124, 127.
White Lion Prison, and Prisoners in, 667.
White, Thomas (a conspirator), 77, 78, 80, 81, 83, 84.
White, Thomas (of Winchester), 449.
White Friars, 116; Liberties in the Precincts of, 654.
Whitehall, 143, 195, 520, 643.
Whitehall, Garners at, 576.
Whitford, Manor of, 71.
Whitgyfte, John, 262, 287, 293, 388, 389, 395, 420, 441, 445, 446, 515; Bishop of Worcester, 564, 591, 647, 648.
Whithel, David, 185.

Whitine, William, 647, 649.
Whitmore, Richard, 381.
Whitney, 509.
Whitney, James, 524.
Whitsand Bay, 492.
Whitstable, 588.
Whitstone, Hundred of, 418.
Whittacres, Richard, 356.
Whittingham, William, 621.
Whittington, Thomas, 625.
Whittnell, Mr., 662.
Whitton, George, 641, 691.
Whorwelle, 272.
Whorwood (or Horwood), Margaret, 41. *See* Horwood.
Whytaker, William, 600.
Whyte, John (Sheriff of Hampshire), 86, 229, 263.
Whyte, Sir Thomas, 103, 111, 417.
Whyte, Thomas (of Dorset), 131.
Whyte. Thomas (a purveyor), 598.
Whytfyld, Robt., 475.
Whythed, H., 55.
Whythed, S., 598.
Whytney, James, 469.
Wiat, Sir Thomas, 56–62, 64, 88, 118, 130.
Wiat, *see* Wyatt.
Wibosson, Manor of, 456.
Wickham, 349.
Wickham, *see* Chipping Wickham.
Wickham, Humfrey, 449.
Wickham Market, 586.
Wickham, William of, 403, 449, 454.
Wickham, *see* Wykeham.
Wickliffe, John, 672.
Wigan, 566.
Wight, Isle of, 2, 76, 79, 82, 83, 91, 99–101 103–106, 131, 139, 140, 143, 144, 148, 149, 153, 154, 162, 163, 177, 218, 227, 253, 263, 264, 375, 378, 384, 394, 402, 409, 417, 425, 453, 479, 481–483, 490, 499, 528, 530, 536, 587, 639, 640, 643, 645, 658, 670, 679, 687.
Wight, Captain of the, *see* Horsey.
Wightman, William, 15, 152.
Wigmore, Mr., 526.
Wigmore, Roger, 3.
Wigston, Sir William, *see* Wygston.
Wikes, ..., 72.
Wiklif, Mr., 613.
Wilborne, Amy, 695.
Wilbraham (or Wilbram), Richard, 95, 96, 104, 117.
Wilbraham, Thomas, 414, 635.
Wilcocks, Henry, 175.
Wildgoose, Alexander, 508.
Wilford, Thomas, 676, 687, 701.
Wilkes, Joan, 266.
Wilkes, Mr., 612.
Wilkes, Thomas, 171, 226, 380.
Wilkes, William, 226.
Wilkinson, Oswald, 314, 368.

Wilkinson, Richard, 575.
Will, of King Henry VIII., 1, 2, 64, 133, 134.
Willeigh, Manor of, 48.
Willes, Richard, 483.
William, William ap, 611.
William of Wickham, *see* Wickham.
Williams, Edward, 188.
Williams, George, 35, 36, 38, 45-47, 62-64, 69, 633.
Williams, Henry, 245.
Williams of Thame, John Lord, 112, 123, 124, 126, 128, 132, 139, 147.
Williams, Sir John, 16, 41, 48, 55.
Williams, Mr., 73.
Williams, Mr. Mack, 355.
Williams, Morgan John, 476.
Williams, Thomas, 162; (Feodary of Devon), 232.
Williams, Thomas (Speaker), 217, 382.
Williams, Thomas (of Carmarthen), 454.
Williams, Walter, 502.
Williams, William, 258, 259, 428.
Williamson, Sir Joseph, 319, 334.
Williamson, Nicholas, 211.
Williamson Park, 63.
Williamson, Thomas, 333.
Willoughby, Baron, *see* Bertie.
Willoughby, Barony of, 440, 441, 677, 687.
Willoughby of Parham, Charles Lord, 485.
Willoughby of Parham, William Lord, 45, 108, 292, 335, 347, 354, 355.
Willoughby, Lord, 526.
Willoughby House, 677.
Wills, 126, 184, 198, 217, 255, 266, 269, 408, 458, 500, 509, 534, 680, 691, 702.
Willson, Dr., 286.
Willughby, *see* Willoughby, Wyllughby.
Wilmot, Mr., 588.
Wilson, Miles, 521.
Wilson, Mr., 635.
Wilson, Thomas, 100, 203, 251.
Wilson, Thomas (Dean of Worcester), 564.
Wilson, Sir Thomas, 178.
Wilson, *see* Wylson.
Wilton, 25, 43, 44, 47, 48, 62, 106, 562, 648.
Wilton, Lord Grey of, *see* Grey.
Wiltshier, Robert, 314, 315.
Wiltshire, 2, 12, 34, 41, 62, 70, 123, 139, 140, 148, 153, 169, 208, 226, 227, 230, 246, 318, 335, 341, 349, 367, 377, 381, 394, 429, 463, 464, 484, 541, 562, 563.
Wiltshire, Clothiers of, 550, 557.
Wiltshire, Earl of, *see* Paulet.
Wiltshire, Justices of, 639.
Wiltshire, Sheriff of, 676.
Wimbledon, 15, 43, 44, 46, 55, 79, 89, 94, 394, 456, 503.
Wimborn, 582.
Winchelcomb. *see* Winchcomb.
Winchelsea, 403.
Winchelsea Harbour, 517, 577.
Winchester, 18, 21, 117, 133, 153, 192, 297, 298, 348, 398, 449, 453, 464, 483, 540, 542, 585, 610, 643, 653, 662, 688.

Winchester, Bishop of, *see* Gardyner, Poynet, White, Pilkington, Horn, Watson.
Winchester, Bishoprick of, 28, 110, 112, 133, 147, 149, 159, 168, 662, 668.
Winchester Castle, 117.
Winchester College, 15, 133, 449, 454.
Winchester, Dean and Chapter of, 102, 133, 163.
Winchester, House of Correction in, 630.
Winchester, John, 403.
Winchester, Marquis of, *see* Paulet.
Winchester Palace, 57, 60.
Winchcomb (or Winchelcomb), 419, 423.
Winchcombe, Anne, 395.
Winchcombe, Henry, 395.
Windebank, Mr., 622.
Windebank, Thomas, (called Philoponus,) 176 185, 187-189, 192-202, 204, 205, 208, 209, 211-214, 216, 324, 327, 496, 500, 548.
Windham, ..., 681.
Windham, Edmund, 575, 620.
Windsor, 2, 9, 16, 19, 24-26, 29, 42, 44, 153, 156, 158, 229, 233, 236-239, 244, 258, 293, 297, 300, 319, 340, 345, 346, 349, 357, 360, 394, 483, 505, 528, 530, 533, 559, 566, 583, 652, 688.
Windsor Castle, 24, 25, 68, 104, 112, 131, 133 137, 166, 189, 200, 236, 250, 296, 298, 348, 357, 427, 430, 445, 453, 459, 506, 569.
Windsor Castle, Chief Gunner in, 458.
Windsor Castle, Constable of, 506.
Windsor Castle, Keeper of the Armory in, 506.
Windsor Castle, Repairs and Works at, 529, 530, 540, 548, 557, 569, 648.
Windsor Castle, Porter of the Outer Gate of, 703.
Windsor, Chapel of, 15, 42, 134, 296.
Windsor College, 42, 130, 133, 134, 137, 141, 234, 561.
Windsor, Dean and Chapter of, 133, 141, 430, 490.
Windsor Forest, 112, 188, 247, 249, 315.
Windsor, Mayor, &c., of, 153.
Windsor Park, 157.
Windsor, Poor Knights of, 3, 42, 130, 133, 134, 137, 141, 430, 444, 467, 490.
Windsor, Prebendaries of, 42, 105, 110, 111, 444.
Windsor, Edward Lord, 157, 278, 310, 311.
Windsor, Sir Edward, 225.
Windsor, Lady, 157, 225, 602-604, 605, 607, 609, 626, 627.
Windsor, William Lord, 9.
Wine Measures, 702.
Wines, 23, 64, 105, 109, 118, 119, 163, 164, 171, 182, 185, 187, 189, 204, 210, 211, 214-216, 219, 222, 230, 231, 234, 235, 241, 242, 247, 261, 269, 277-279, 283, 285, 298, 299, 315, 317, 318, 320, 322, 323, 330, 331, 360, 361, 362, 382, 408, 419, 429, 455, 453, 492, 504, 538, 539, 552, 606, 608, 631, 666, 680, 698.
Wines, Commissioners of, 522.
Wines, Importation of, 522; Impost on, 700.

Wines, Prices and Sale of, 504, 518, 522, 525, 526, 532, 556.
Winfield, 193.
Wingate, Mr., 193.
Wingfield, *see* Wyngfeld.
Wingham, Michel, 196.
Winstree, Half-hundred of, 379, 558.
Winter, *see* Wynter.
Winters, *see* Frosts.
Winterton, 624.
Winwicke, 334.
Wiottye, David, 537.
Wireworks, 296. *See* Mines.
Wirksworth, Hundred of, 124.
Wirriott, Thomas, 522.
Wisbeach, 460, 681.
Wisbeach River, 523, 628.
Wiscote, Manor of, 294.
Wiseman, *see* Wyseman.
Witchcraft (Sorcery, Magic, &c.), 142, 173, 174.
Witham or Wytham, 38, 63, 280, 690.
Witham, Half-hundred of, 380, 419, 450, 558.
Witham, South, Bailiff of, 63.
Wither, Dr. George, 687.
Wittlesford, Hundred of, 6.
Wixhamtry, Hundred of, 374.
Woad, 227, 241, 242, 411.
Woburne, 186.
Woking, Hundred of, 135, 419, 423.
Wolfe, George, 212.
Wolfe, John, 167.
Wolffe, Peter, 61.
Wolley, Ambrose, 15.
Wolley, Mr., 331.
Wolley, Thomas, 508.
Wolman, Ch., 43.
Wolmer, Forest of, 113.
Wolsey, Hundred of, 124.
Wolsey, Thomas, Cardinal, 55, 533.
Wolverhampton, 667.
Wolvesey House, 662.
Wood, ..., 681.
Wood, John, 235, 306, 465.
Wood, Mr., (nominated Bishop of St. Asaph,) 109.
Wood, Purveyance of, 697.
Wood, Richard, 3.
Wood, Thomas, 174, 182, 229, 348, 509.
Wood-beam, The, 132.
Woodbridge, 235.
Woodbridge Priory, 5.
Woodd, John, 465.
Woodford, Parish of, 4.
Woodhouse, Richard, 700, 701.
Woodhouse, Sir Thomas, 22, 141.
Woodhows, Sir William, 22, 94, 97, 203.
Woodhowse, Henry, 388.
Woodhowse, Sir Thomas, 388.
Woodlock, Sir Thomas, 16.
Woodmongers of London, 398.

Woodrofe, Sir Nicholas, 637, 644, 659, 661.
Woodrofe, Robert, 659.
Wood's Grove, 41.
Woods and Forests (Wood Sales, &c.), 34, 35, 40, 64, 70, 80, 113, 140, 141, 165, 180, 182, 185, 237, 247, 249, 253, 260, 286, 438, 473, 474, 633. *See* Timber. Trees.
Woods, Felling of, in Dean Forest, 633 ; and at Kimbolton, 664, 667.
Woods, Surveyor of, 363.
Woodstock, 277, 449, 503, 641, 671. *See* New Woodstock.
Woodstock, Thomas of, 131.
Wood Street Compter, 292, 668, 669.
Woodward, Dr., 469.
Woodward, Richard, 112.
Woody, Robert, 475.
Wood-yard, Clerk of the, 405, 638.
Wool, Woolfells, &c., 4, 5, 37, 105, 114, 161, 168, 169, 199, 214, 222, 230, 245, 264, 270, 275-277, 298, 299, 344, 400, 432, 437, 456, 467, 473, 476, 507, 517, 532, 547, 550, 551, 556, 560, 563, 577, 619 697.
Wool, Commissioners for regulating Sale of, 554.
Wool, Dearth of, 550.
Wool Trade, The, 698.
Woolaston, 31.
Woolmen, Company of, 456.
Woolton, Mr., 601.
Woolwich, 131, 455.
Wootton Basset, 377.
Wootton, Mr., 162.
Wootton, Hundred of, 135, 419, 420.
Wootton-under-Edge, 658.
Worald, ..., a Pirate, 512.
Worcester, 101, 116, 132, 352, 373, 375, 420, 460, 463, 484, 498, 502, 555, 588, 591, 662.
Worcester, Bailiffs of, 460.
Worcester, Bishop of, *see* Heath, Hoper, Pate, Sandys, Bullingham, Whitgyfte.
Worcester, Bishoprick of, 48, 112, 223, 538, 564, 647, 648.
Worcester, Clothiers of, 516, 550.
Worcester, College of, 538.
Worcester, Countess of, 231.
Worcester, Dean of, 38, 137, 564.
Worcester, Dean and Chapter of, 45, 223, 497.
Worcester, Earl of, *see* Somerset.
Worcester, Prebends of, 48, 50.
Worcester, Temporalities of, 520.
Worcestershire, 58, 116, 120, 125, 126, 148, 160, 266, 286, 338, 347, 352, 367, 375, 420, 463, 470, 484, 514, 555.
Worcestershire, Justices of, 639.
Worcestershire, Sheriff of, 484.
Worell, 55.
Workhouses, 642.
Workington, 315, 320, 330.

GENERAL INDEX.

Workmen, Labourers, &c., Impressment of, 627, 672, 674, 695. *See* Impressment.
Works, Office and Officers of, 165, 166, 189, 192, 201, 262, 287, 387.
Works, Surveyor of the, 470.
Worley, Dr. Henry, 508, 544.
Wormslow, Hundred of, 123.
Worrall (or Orwell) Park, 37, 47.
Worselcy, Mr., 554.
Worseley, Robert, 600.
Worsley, John, 264.
Worsley, Richard, 120, 153.
Worth, ..., 86.
Wortham, 142.
Worthe, Forest of, 12.
Worthington, Mr., 302.
Worthorp, 200.
Worthy-Mortimer, Manor of, 110.
Worwood, 448.
Wotton, Sir Edward, 22.
Wotton, Harry, 509.
Wotton, John, 461.
Wotton, Dr. Nicholas, 26, 87, 88, 136, 155, 180, 287, 297.
Wotton, Robert, 648.
Wotton, Thomas, 124, 128, 201, 258, 260, 295, 460, 521, 560, 671, 685.
Wotton-under-Wyver, Manor of, 36, 80.
Wray, Serjeant, 307; Lord Chief Justice Sir Christopher, 488, 543, 567, 639.
Wrecks, 174, 287, 289, 309, 331, 332, 455, 628. *See* Shipwreck.
Wrench, ..., 298.
Wrenthorp, Manor of, 12.
Wridefyn, Manor of, 113.
Wright, Thomas, 624.
Wriothesley, Henry, Earl of Southampton, 439, 483, 632.
Wriothesley, Thomas, Earl of Southampton, 13, 24, 297, 303.
Writing, 476.
Writs. *See* Original Writs.
Wroth, ..., 57.
Wrotham, 58.
Wrothe, Sir Thomas, 28, 40, 338, 450.
Wroughton, Sir William, 123.
Wrytza, Bastian, 90, 91.
Wulvesey, 177.
Wy, Robert, 16.
Wyat, Little, "a Bastard," 60.
Wyat, *see* Wiat.
Wybarne, Thomas, 164.
Wyckes, *see* Mason.
Wye, Hundred of, 450.
Wygges, Robert, 305, 306.
Wygmor, Hundred of, 124.
Wygston, Sir William, 95, 339, 343.
Wykeham, Edward, 454.
Wylford, Thomas, 485.
Wyllmyngton, Manor of, 695.
Wyllson, Humfrey, 405.
Wyllughby, Charles, 461.

Wylly, Hundred of, 574.
Wylson, Thomas, 312, 313; Dr. Thomas, 421, 434, 507, 543; Secretary of State, 586, 587, 601, 620, 625, 628, 637, 644, 652, 684; Dean of Durham, 695, 703.
Wymberley, Thomas, 63.
Wynbeshe, Mr., 32, 33.
Wyndebanck, Richard, 207. *See* Windebank.
Wyndeyatt, Manor of, 66.
Wyndham, Sir Edmund, 329, 367.
Wyndham, Francis, 637, 639.
Wyndham, Roger, 575.
Wyndham, Thomas, 7.
Wyngfeld, Mr. Anthony, 392.
Wyngfeld, Sir Anthony, 26, 34.
Wyngfeld, Dorothy, 5.
Wyngfeld, Mr. Robert, 212, 308.
Wyngfeld, Sir Robert, 337, 343, 377, 432, 557, 632, 643, 680.
Wyngfylde, Edward, 663, 664, 667, 669.
Wyngfylde, Thomas, 663, 664, 667; his three Daughters, 664, 667.
Wynington, Thomas, 695.
Wynne, Maurice, 591.
Wynnington, John, 266.
Wynnyat, Dr., 417.
Wynser, Mrs., 280.
Wynstay, Half-hundred of, 419.
Wynter, ..., jun., 393.
Wynter, George, 39, 328, 437, 552, 570.
Wynter, John, 659, 661.
Wynter, Mr., 298.
Wynter, William, 39, 93, 102, 106, 126, 131, 140, 144, 156, 189, 203, 208, 225, 228, 229, 260, 287, 323, 328, 331, 339, 386, 390, 420, 423; Sir William, 484, 486, 529, 540, 567, 570, 601, 611, 618, 647, 649.
Wyntney, 258.
Wyre, Forest of, 126, 182.
Wyse, Andrew, 131.
Wyseman, Thomas, 246, 604.
Wytham, *see* Witham.
Wythens, Pawlyn (widow), 556.
Wythers, George, 127.
Wythingdon, Living of, 600.
Wytney Park, 664.
Wyttenham, 382, 394.
Wytton, Thomas, 268, 269.

Y.

Yale, David, 595.
Yale, Manor of, 376.
Yanworth, Manor of, 8.
Yarborough, 53.
Yardley, Roger, 691.
Yarmouth (or Great Yarmouth, Norfolk), 111, 141, 147, 169, 173, 291, 389, 390, 399, 412, 491, 517, 552, 554, 583, 584, 610, 614, 619, 623, 697.
Yarmouth, Bailiff of, 583, 584.

GENERAL INDEX.   797

Yarmouth Fair, 614.
Yarmouth Haven, (Norfolk,) Repair of, 517.
Yarmouth, Little, (Suffolk,) 619.
Yarmouth, (Isle of Wight,) 76, 143.
Yarn, new manufactory for spinning, 586.
Yarom, 695.
Yate, Mr., 238.
Yate, John, 545.
Yateley, 701.
Yaxlee, Margaret, 142, 177.
Yaxley, ..., 28.
Yaxley, Francis, 90, 131, 138, 142, 149, 152, 157, 158, 160, 164, 170, 171, 177, 183, 185, 194, 195, 201.
Yaxley, Vicar of, 149.
Yeldham, 697.
Yendall, Parson, 140.
Yenwith, 395.
Yeo, Leonard, 638.
Yeoman Waiter, Office of, 492.
Yernley, John, 12.
Yetsweirt, Charles, 330.
Yetsweirt, Nicasius, 90.
Yew, 633.
Yollyston, 136.
Yonge, Edward, 457.
Yonge, John, 11, 159.
Yonge, Dr. John, 298, 328; Bishop of Rochester, 645.
Yonge, *see* Young.
Yonger, Thomas, 274.
Yonges, Henry, 579.
Yorck, R., 684.
York, 6, 18, 46, 182, 192, 202, 289, 321, 322, 335, 338, 352, 365, 366, 368, 370-372, 410, 438, 468, 529, 561, 691.
York, Archbishop of, 109, 112, 154, 161, 322, 537, 588. *See* Holgate, Heath, Mey, Young, Grindall, Sandys.
York, Archbishoprick and Diocese of, 9, 109, 112, 148, 182, 311, 322, 338, 539, 547, 561.
York, Archdeaconry of the East Riding, 29.
York, Council at, 299, 352.
York, Dean of, *see* Hutton.
York, Duke of, *see* Plantagenet.

York, Ecclesiastical Commission for, 132, 141, 145, 148, 668, 671.
York, Mayor of, 523.
York, Mr., 46.
York, Province of, 132, 141, 145, 148, 218, 492, 573, 668, 671, 678.
York, Sheriff of, 321.
Yorke, Sir John, 30, 161.
Yorke, Mr., 696.
Yorkshire, 9, 12, 18, 111, 112, 119, 122, 136, 145, 170, 190, 191, 197, 211, 252, 259, 274, 285, 286, 296, 317, 321, 333, 335, 370, 388, 394-396, 411, 454, 468, 470, 491, 501, 523, 561, 668, 695, 696.
Yorkshire, Alehouses, &c., in, 562.
Yorkshire, Feodary of, 333.
Yorkshire, Receiver of, 39.
Yorkshire, Sheriff of, 438, 455.
Youghall, 331.
Young, the Bark, 585.
Young, John, 209-211, 213, 214, 219, 220, 700.
Young, Mr., 39.
Young, Richard, 508, 659.
Young, Thomas, Bishop of St. David's, 151, 161; Archbishop of York, 182, 183, 185, 188, 193, 229, 261.
Young, *see* Yonge.
Younge, ..., 681.
Younge, Mr., 426, 687.
Yowcrosse, Wapentake of, 336.

Z.

Zanzy, Capt. Petro, 15.
Zealand, 517.
Zibrandson, Agas, 258.
Zolcher, George, 510.
Zouch, George Lord, 231.
Zouche (of Wilts), Sir John, 335, 341.
Zowche, John, 470.
Zowche (of Derby), Sir John, 341, 346, 460.
Zowche (of Wilts), Sir John, 464.
Zurich, 158.

ERRATA.

Page 24, Art. 22, *for* Lord Paget, *read* Sir William.
,, 28, Art. 12, *for* Sir Thomas, *dele* Sir.
,, 42, Art. 55, *for* 8th Aug., *read* 7th Aug.
,, 59, running date, *for* 1553, *read* 1554.
,, 60, Art. 12, *for* Sir Thomas Culpeper, *dele* Sir.
,, 63, Art. 24, *for* Gaddilsmere, *read* Baddilsmere.
,, 110, Art. 4, *for* [Harvey ?], *read* [Tonge].
,, 123, Art. 47, *for* Elthorpe, *read* Elthorne.
,, 147, Art. 33, *for* 1599, *read* 1559.
,, 177, Art. 21, *for* Camb., *read* Oxford.
,, ,, Art. 26, *for* John, *read* Sir John.
,, ,, Art. 32, *for* Seory, *read* Scorey.
,, 204, first date, *for* 1652, *read* 1562.
,, 240, Art. 9, *for* Earl of, *read* Lord.
,, 245, Art. 10, *for* Hamford, *read* Hawford.
,, 250, Art. 35, *for* date April 15, *read* April 13.
,, 251, Art. 41, *for* Lincoln, *read* Lichfield.
,, 254, Art. 75, *for* Cocke, *read* Cooke.
,, 255, Art. 2, *dele* from water.
,, 288, Art. 17, *for* Shropshire, *read* Shrewsbury.
,, 290, Art. 51, *for* William, *read* Thomas.
,, 298, Art. 60, *for* Pembroke College, *read* Hall.
,, 324, Art. 59, *for* Southwick, *read* Southaick.
,, 338, Art. 4, *for* Kyrthinge, *read* Kyrtlinge.
,, 340, Vol. LV., *for* Maurice Berkeley, *read* Morris Barkeley.
,, 343, Art. 17, *for* Sir Ric., *read* Sir James.
,, 346, Art. 25, *for* Leche, *read* Leeke.
,, 360, Art. 9, *for* Duchess, *read* Countess.
,, 367, Art. 31, *for* Edward, *read* Edmund.
,, 370, Art. 69, *for* Earl, *read* Marquis.
,, 372, running date, *for* 1750, *read* 1570.
,, ,, Art. 87, *for* Ambrose, *read* Sir Ambrose.
,, 375, Art. 24, *for* Earl, *read* Marquis.
,, 394, Art. 14, *for* Maysfield, *read* Mayfield.
,, 418, Art. 29, *for* Hundred, *read* Wapentake.
,, 419, Art. 43, *for* Henry, *read* Sir Henry.
,, 490, Art. 30, *for* Thompson, *read* Tomson.
,, 503, Art. 35, *for* John Lord Russell, *read* Lord John.
,, 505, Art. 65, same, same.
,, 548, Art. 3, *for* Stile, *read* Still.
,, 582, Art. 23, *for* Sir Fra, *dele* Sir.
,, 588, *for* Vol. cxxii., *read* cxxiii.
,, ,, Art. 26, *for* Edward, *read* Edmund.
,, 617, Art. 23, *for* Chatterton, *read* Chaderton.

IN THE PRESS.

CALENDAR OF STATE PAPERS, DOMESTIC SERIES, JAMES I., 1603–1625. Edited by Mrs. Mary Ann Everett Green, Author of the Lives of the Princesses of England.

LONDON:
Printed by GEORGE EDWARD EYRE and WILLIAM SPOTTISWOODE,
Printers to the Queen's most Excellent Majesty. 1856.

www.ingramcontent.com/pod-product-compliance
Ingram Content Group UK Ltd.
Pitfield, Milton Keynes, MK11 3LW, UK
UKHW020629301225
9774UKWH00082B/1004